$$\text{Debt Ratio} = \frac{\text{Total Liabilities}}{\text{Total Assets}}$$

$$\text{Debt/Equity Ratio} = \frac{\text{Total Liabilities}}{\text{Shareholders' Equity}}$$

$$\text{Debt to Tangible Net Worth Ratio} = \frac{\text{Total Liabilities}}{\text{Shareholders' Equity} - \text{Intangible Assets}}$$

$$\text{Operating Cash Flow/Total Debt} = \frac{\text{Operating Cash Flow}}{\text{Total Debt}}$$

Profitability

$$\text{Net Profit Margin} = \frac{\text{Net Income Before Noncontrolling Interest, Equity Income, and Nonrecurring Items}}{\text{Net Sales}}$$

$$\text{Total Asset Turnover} = \frac{\text{Net Sales}}{\text{Average Total Assets}}$$

$$\text{Return on Assets} = \frac{\text{Net Income Before Noncontrolling Interest and Nonrecurring Items}}{\text{Average Total Assets}}$$

$$\text{Operating Income Margin} = \frac{\text{Operating Income}}{\text{Net Sales}}$$

$$\text{Operating Asset Turnover} = \frac{\text{Net Sales}}{\text{Average Operating Assets}}$$

$$\text{Return on Operating Assets} = \frac{\text{Operating Income}}{\text{Average Operating Assets}}$$

$$\text{DuPont Return on Operating Assets} = \frac{\text{Operating Income}}{\text{Margin}} \times \frac{\text{Operating Asset}}{\text{Turnover}}$$

$$\text{Sales to Fixed Assets} = \frac{\text{Net Sales}}{\text{Average Net Fixed Assets}} \text{(Exclude Construction in Progress)}$$

$$\text{Return on Investment} = \frac{\text{Net Income Before Noncontrolling Interest and Nonrecurring Items} + [(\text{Interest Expense}) \times (1 - \text{Tax Rate})]}{\text{Average (Long-Term Liabilities} + \text{Equity})}$$

$$\text{Return on Total Equity} = \frac{\text{Net Income Before Nonrecurring Items} - \text{Dividends on Redeemable Preferred Stock}}{\text{Average Total Equity}}$$

$$\text{Return on Common Equity} = \frac{\text{Net Income Before Nonrecurring Items} - \text{Preferred Dividends}}{\text{Average Common Equity}}$$

$$\text{Gross Profit Margin} = \frac{\text{Gross Profit}}{\text{Net Sales}}$$

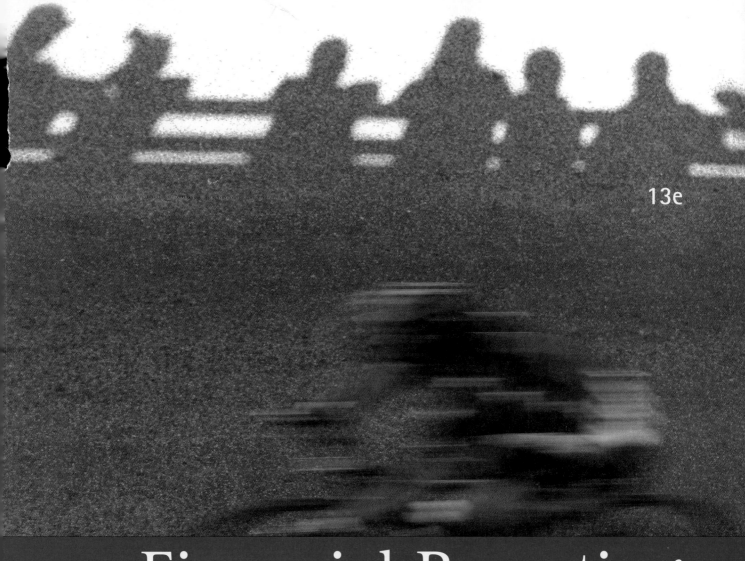

13e

Financial Reporting
& Analysis

Using Financial Accounting Information

CHARLES H. GIBSON
The University of Toledo, Emeritus

SOUTH-WESTERN
CENGAGE Learning·

Australia • Brazil • Japan • Korea • Mexico • Singapore • Spain • United Kingdom • United States

Financial Reporting & Analysis,
Thirteenth Edition

Charles H. Gibson

Vice President of Editorial, Business: Jack W. Calhoun

Editor-in-Chief: Rob Dewey

Sr Acquisitions Editor: Matt Filimonov

Associate Development Editor: Julie Warwick

Editorial Assistant: Ann Loch

Director, Marketing: Lysa Lysne

Associate Marketing Manager: Heather Mooney

Content Project Manager: Emily Nesheim

Media Editor: Jessica Robbe

Manufacturing Planner: Doug Wilke

Sr Marketing Communications Manager: Libby Shipp

Production Service: Cenveo Publisher Services

Sr Art Director: Stacy Shirley

Internal Designer: PreMediaGlobal

Cover Designer: KeDesign, Mason, OH

Cover Image: R Sherwood Veith/iStockphoto.com

Director, Rights Acquisition: Audrey Pettengill

For product information and technology assistance, contact us at
Cengage Learning Customer & Sales Support, 1-800-354-9706

For permission to use material from this text or product, submit all requests online at **www.cengage.com/permissions**
Further permissions questions can be emailed to
permissionrequest@cengage.com

Library of Congress Control Number: 2012930416

Student Edition ISBN 13: 978-1-133-18876-6
Student Edition ISBN 10: 1-133-18876-1
Student Edition package ISBN-13: 978-1-133-18879-7
Student Edition package ISBN-10: 1-133-18879-6

South-Western Cengage Learning
5191 Natorp Boulevard
Mason, OH 45040
USA

Cengage Learning products are represented in Canada by Nelson Education, Ltd.

For your course and learning solutions, visit **www.cengage.com**

Purchase any of our products at your local college store or at our preferred online store **www.cengagebrain.com**

Printed in the United States of America
2 3 4 5 6 7 15 14 13

Dedication

This book is dedicated to my wife, Patricia, and daughters Anne Elizabeth and Laura.

Special Dedication

To hardworking students mastering financial reporting and analysis.

Charles Gibson is a certified public accountant who practiced with a Big Four accounting firm for four years and has had more than 30 years of teaching experience. His teaching experience encompasses a variety of accounting courses, including financial, managerial, tax, cost, and financial analysis.

Professor Gibson has taught seminars on financial analysis to financial executives, bank commercial loan officers, lawyers, and others. He has also taught financial reporting seminars for CPAs and review courses for both CPAs and CMAs. He has authored several problems used on the CMA exam.

Charles Gibson has written more than 60 articles in such journals as the *Journal of Accountancy, Accounting Horizons, Journal of Commercial Bank Lending, CPA Journal, Ohio CPA, Management Accounting, Risk Management, Taxation for Accountants, Advanced Management Journal, Taxation for Lawyers, California Management Review,* and *Journal of Small Business Management.* He is a co-author of the Financial Executives Research Foundation Study entitled, "Discounting in Financial Accounting and Reporting."

Dr. Gibson co-authored *Cases in Financial Reporting* (PWS-KENT Publishing Company). He has also co-authored two continuing education courses consisting of books and cassette tapes, published by the American Institute of Certified Public Accountants. These courses are entitled "Funds Flow Evaluation" and "Profitability and the Quality of Earnings."

Professor Gibson is a member of the American Accounting Association, American Institute of Certified Public Accountants, Ohio Society of Certified Public Accountants, and Financial Executives Institute. In the past, he has been particularly active in the American Accounting Association and the Ohio Society of Certified Public Accountants.

Dr. Gibson received the 1989 Outstanding Ohio Accounting Educator Award jointly presented by the Ohio Society of Certified Public Accountants and the Ohio Regional American Accounting Association. In 1993, he received the College of Business Research Award at the University of Toledo. In 1996, Dr. Gibson was honored as an "Accomplished Graduate" of the College of Business at Bowling Green State University. In 1999, he was honored by the Gamma Epsilon Chapter of Beta Alpha Psi of the University of Toledo.

Brief Contents

Contents

Chapter 2   Introduction to Financial Statements and Other Financial Reporting Topics   54

FORMS OF BUSINESS ENTITIES   54

THE FINANCIAL STATEMENTS   55

Balance Sheet (Statement of Financial Position) • Statement of Stockholders' Equity (Reconciliation of Stockholders' Equity Accounts) • Income Statement (Statement of Earnings) • Statement of Cash Flows (Statement of Inflows and Outflows of Cash) • Notes

THE ACCOUNTING CYCLE   58

Recording Transactions • Recording Adjusting Entries • Preparing the Financial Statements • Treadway Commission

AUDITOR'S OPINION   60

Auditor's Report on the Firm's Internal Controls • Report of Management on Internal Control over Financial Reporting

MANAGEMENT'S RESPONSIBILITY FOR FINANCIAL STATEMENTS   65

THE SEC's INTEGRATED DISCLOSURE SYSTEM   66

PROXY   68

SUMMARY ANNUAL REPORT   69

THE EFFICIENT MARKET HYPOTHESIS   69

ETHICS   69

SEC Requirements—Code of Ethics

CONSOLIDATED STATEMENTS   72

ACCOUNTING FOR BUSINESS COMBINATIONS   73

SEC – PAPER FILINGS – EDGAR – XBRL   73

SUMMARY 73 / QUESTIONS 74 / PROBLEMS 75 / CASES 80

Chapter 9   For the Investor   365

Chapter 10   Statement of Cash Flows   393

Summary Analysis Nike, Inc. (Includes 2011 Financial Statements of Form 10-K)   438

NIKE–BACKGROUND INFORMATION   438

Management's Discussion and Analysis of Financial Condition and Results of Operations (See 10-K, Item 7, In Part) • Vertical Common-Size Statement of Income (Exhibit 1) • Horizontal Common-Size Statement of Income (Exhibit 2) • Three-Year Ratio Comparison (Exhibit 3) • Ratio Comparison with Selected Competitor (Exhibit 4) • Selected Competitor • Ratio Comparison with Industry (Exhibit 5) • Summary • Nike 2011 (Exhibit 12-1)

Chapter 11   Expanded Analysis   482

FINANCIAL RATIOS AS PERCEIVED BY COMMERCIAL LOAN DEPARTMENTS   482

Most Significant Ratios and Their Primary Measure • Ratios Appearing Most Frequently in Loan Agreements

FINANCIAL RATIOS AS PERCEIVED BY CORPORATE CONTROLLERS   484

Most Significant Ratios and Their Primary Measure • Key Financial Ratios Included as Corporate Objectives

FINANCIAL RATIOS AS PERCEIVED BY CERTIFIED PUBLIC ACCOUNTANTS   486

FINANCIAL RATIOS AS PERCEIVED BY CHARTERED FINANCIAL ANALYSTS   486

FINANCIAL RATIOS USED IN ANNUAL REPORTS   487

DEGREE OF CONSERVATISM AND QUALITY OF EARNINGS   488

Inventory • Fixed Assets • Intangible Assets • Pensions

FORECASTING FINANCIAL FAILURE   489

Univariate Model • Multivariate Model • Nike Z Score

ANALYTICAL REVIEW PROCEDURES   492

MANAGEMENT'S USE OF ANALYSIS   492

USE OF LIFO RESERVES   493

Note 4—Inventories

GRAPHING FINANCIAL INFORMATION   494

MANAGEMENT OF EARNINGS   496

THE HOUSING BUST   499

VALUATION   500

Multiples • Multiperiod Discounted Valuation Models • What They Use • International Aspects • Valuation as Seen by Management Consultants • From Page V • Dot.coms

SUMMARY 504 / QUESTIONS 505 / PROBLEMS 506 / CASES 522

Chapter **12**   Special Industries: Banks, Utilities, Oil and Gas, Transportation, Insurance, and Real Estate Companies   540

BANKS   540

Balance Sheet • Liabilities • Shareholders' Equity •
Income Statement • Ratios for Banks

REGULATED UTILITIES   551

Financial Statements • Ratios for Regulated Utilities

OIL AND GAS   558

Successful-Efforts versus Full-Costing Methods • Supplementary Information
on Oil and Gas Exploration, Development, and Production Activities • Cash Flow

TRANSPORTATION   560

Financial Statements • Ratios

INSURANCE   564

Balance Sheet Under GAAP • Assets • Assets—Other than Investments •
Income Statement Under GAAP • Ratios

REAL ESTATE COMPANIES   570

SUMMARY 570 / QUESTIONS 571 / PROBLEMS 572 / CASES 577

Chapter **13**   Personal Financial Statements and Accounting for Governments and Not-for-Profit Organizations   588

PERSONAL FINANCIAL STATEMENTS   588

Form of the Statements • Suggestions for Reviewing the Statement of Financial
Condition • Suggestions for Reviewing the Statement of Changes in Net Worth •
Illustration of Preparation of the Statement of Financial Condition • Illustration of
Preparation of the Statement of Changes in Net Worth

ACCOUNTING FOR GOVERNMENTS   592

ACCOUNTING FOR NOT-FOR-PROFIT ORGANIZATIONS OTHER THAN
GOVERNMENTS   597

1. SFAS No. 93, "Recognition of Depreciation By Not-for-Profit Organizations" • 2. SFAS
No. 116, "Accounting for Contributions Received and Contributions Made" • 3. SFAS
No. 117, "Financial Statements of Not-for-Profit Organizations" • 4. SFAS No. 124,
"Accounting for Certain Investments Held By Not-for-Profit Organizations" • Applicability of
GAAP to Not-for-Profit Organizations • Budgeting by Objectives and/or Measures of
Productivity

Appendix   **Thomson ONE Basics and Tutorial   615**

Preface

This book teaches financial accounting from both the user's and the preparer's perspectives. It includes the language and the preparation of financial statements. Reliance is placed on actual annual reports, 10-Ks, and proxy statements. Sufficient background material is included, facilitating its use for students who do not have prior courses in accounting or finance.

Tell me, I'll forget.
Show me, I may remember.
Involve me, I'll understand.

This proverb describes the approach of this book—involving students in actual financial statements and their analysis and interpretation. Its premise is that students are better prepared to understand and analyze real financial reports when learning is not based on over-simplified financial statements.

From this basic premise come the many changes to this edition. Those changes, supported by our technology tools, focus on the goal of this text, which is to involve students in actively learning how to read, understand, and analyze the financial statements of actual companies. These changes are discussed in this preface.

Significant Items

The following notable items are available in this edition to increase its relevance to students and its flexibility for instructors:

1. Coverage of ethics has been expanded.
2. International accounting has been updated to reflect the substantial changes that have taken place. This includes model financial statements.
3. Internet exercises have been updated and new exercises added.
4. Questions have been updated and new questions added.
5. Problems have been updated and new problems added.
6. Where appropriate, cases have been updated and new cases added. This includes more than 70 revised and new cases.
7. Exhibits and cases are extensively based on real companies to which students would relate.

- Access to Thomson ONE—Business School Edition™ This high-tech feature is available with every new book. This access to a version of the professional research tool allows students to become familiar with the software that is used in practice. Chapter cases on the text Web site, for every chapter with the exception of Chapter 13, walk users step-by-step through those databases as they learn how to access financial information covered in the text. Thomson ONE—Business School Edition provides information on 500 companies, combining a full range of fundamental financials, earnings estimates, market data, and source documents with powerful functionality.

  Market index information is available for a variety of indexes. The database gives you the ability to compare firms against their peers in a portfolio context. There are detailed historical and current financial statements from several different sources. Also available as summary information is financial ratio analysis. Historical stock price information and analysis, along with earnings estimates, is presented. Both fundamental and technical financial analysis is provided. Recent news reports are available. Filings the company has made with the SEC, such as 10-K and 10-Q, are also available.

  The Thomson ONE—Business School Edition provides information on market indexes such as the Dow Jones Industrial Average and the Standard and Poor's 500.

  It also provides a powerful and customizable report-writing function that enables you to develop custom financial reports for the firm.

- FinSAS Financial Statement Analysis Spreadsheets (by Donald V. Saftner, University of Toledo) allow students to perform analysis on any set of financial statements using the ratios covered in the text. Users enter income statement, balance sheet, and other data for two to five years. The result is a 2- to 5-year ratio comparison by liquidity, long-term debt-paying ability, profitability, and investor analysis. The result also includes common-size analysis of the income statement (horizontal and vertical) and common-size analysis of the balance sheet (horizontal and vertical). Downloadable in Excel® from the product Web site through CengageBrain.com, *FinSAS* can save users hours of number crunching, allowing them to concentrate on analysis and interpretation.

- Flexible (by Donald V. Saftner, University of Toledo) is designed to accompany and complement FinSAS. *Flexible* allows for common-size analysis (horizontal and vertical) of any financial schedule as well as statements. *Flexible* can be used to analyze financial statements (common-size) in a different format (user-defined) from the format of *FinSAS*. Downloadable in Excel® from the product Web site through CengageBrain.com, like FinSAS, *Flexible* can save users hours of number crunching, allowing them to concentrate on analysis and interpretation.

Actual Companies

The text explains financial reporting differences among industries, including manufacturing, retailing, service firms, and regulated and nonregulated industries. The text also covers personal financial reports and financial reporting for governments and other not-for-profit institutions.

Statements of actual companies are used in illustrations, cases, and "To the Net" cases. The actual financial statements highlight current financial reporting problems, including guidelines for consolidated statements, stock-based compensation, postretirement benefits, and the harmonization of international accounting standards.

Extensive Use of One Firm

An important feature of this text is the extensive use of one firm, Nike, Inc., as an illustration. By using Nike's 2011 financial report and industry data, readers become familiar with a typical competitive market and a meaningful example for reviewing financial statement analysis as a whole. (See Chapters 6 through 10 and Summary Analysis—Nike, Inc.)

Flexible Organization

This text is used in a variety of courses with a variety of approaches. It provides the flexibility necessary to meet the needs of accounting and finance courses varying in content and length. Sufficient text, questions, "To the Net" Web site cases, problem materials and cases are presented to allow the instructor latitude in the depth of coverage. Access to Thomson ONE—Business School Edition™ is also included with every new book. Accounting principles are the basis for all discussion so that students can understand the methods used as well as the implication for analysis. The following is an outline of our chapter coverage:

Chapter 1 develops the basic principles of accounting on which financial reports are based. A review of the evolution of GAAP and the traditional assumptions of the accounting model helps the reader understand the statement and thus allows for a better analysis. An extensive review of harmonization of international accounting standards in included. Also included is financial reporting for small and medium sized entities (SMEs).

Chapter 2 describes the forms of business entities and introduces financial reports. This chapter also reviews the sequence of accounting procedures completed during each accounting period. It includes other financial reporting topics that contribute to the understanding of financial reporting, such as the auditor's report, management's discussion, management's responsibility for financial statements, and summary annual report. The efficient market hypotheses, ethics, consolidated statements, accounting for business combinations, and the SEC-paper filings-Edgar-XBRL are also covered.

Chapter 3 presents an in-depth review of the balance sheet, statement of stockholders' equity, and problems in balance sheet presentation. This chapter gives special emphasis to inventories and tangible assets. A model IFRS balance sheet has been included. Also included are subsequent events.

Chapter 4 presents an in-depth review of the income statement, including special income statement items. Other topics included are earnings per share, retained earnings, dividends and stock splits, legality of distribution to stockholders, and comprehensive income. A model IFRS balance sheet has been included.

Chapter 5 is an introduction to analysis and comparative statistics. Techniques include ratio analysis, common-size analysis, year-to-year change analysis, financial statement variations by type of industry, review of descriptive information, comparisons including Standard Industrial Classification (SIC) Manual, and North American Industry Classification System (NAICS), relative size of firm, and many library sources of industry data.

Chapter 6 covers short-term liquidity. This chapter includes suggested procedures for analyzing short-term assets and the short-term debt-paying ability for an entity. This chapter discusses, in detail, four very important assets: cash, marketable securities, accounts receivable, and inventory. It is the first to extensively use Nike as an illustration.

Chapter 7 covers long-term debt-paying ability. This includes the income statement consideration and the balance sheet consideration. Topics include long-term leasing, pension plans, joint ventures, contingences, financial instruments with off-balance sheet risk, financial instruments with concentrations of credit risk, and disclosures about fair value of financial instruments.

Chapter 8 covers the analysis of profitability, which is a vital concern to stockholders, creditors, and management. Besides profitability ratios, this chapter covers trends in profitability, segment reporting, gains and losses from prior period adjustments, comprehensive income, pro forma financial information, and interim reports.

Chapter 9, though not intended as a comprehensive guide to investment analysis, introduces analyses useful to investors. Besides ratios, this chapter covers leverage and its effect on earnings, earnings per share, stock-based compensations, and stock appreciation rights.

Chapter 10 reviews the statement of cash flows, including ratios that relate to this statement. This chapter also covers procedures for developing the statement of cash flows.

A summary analysis of Nike is presented after Chapter 10, along with the Nike 2011 financial statements. The summary analysis includes Nike background information.

Chapter 11 covers an expanded utility of financial ratios. This includes the perception of financial ratios, the degree of conservatism and quality of earnings, forecasting financial failure, and analytical review procedures, management's use of analysis, use of LIFO reserves, graphing financial information, management of earnings, and valuation.

Chapter 12 covers problems in analyzing six specialized industries: banks, utilities, oil and gas, transportation, insurance, and real estate. The chapter notes the differences in statements and suggests changes or additions to their analysis.

Chapter 13 covers personal financial statements and financial reporting for governments and other not-for-profit institutions.

A very extensive glossary defines terms explained in the text and terms frequently found in annual reports and the financial literature. The text also includes a bibliography of references that can be used in exploring further topics in the text.

Student Resources via CengageBrain.com

Students and instructors have immediate access to financial statement analysis and classroom tools needed for the course at **CengageBrain.com**. Through this Web site, you will find the following supplementary materials available to both instructors and students:

- *FinSAS*—financial statement analysis spreadsheets (both blank and sample Nike versions) designed to perform analysis using ratios covered in the text.
- *Flexible*—allows for common-size analysis (horizontal and vertical) of any financial schedule as well as statements.
- Thomson ONE—Business School Edition™—provides online cases tied to the book's chapter content for users of new books, utilizing its powerful suite of research tools for 500 companies.
- Study Tools—such as an interactive quiz, flashcards and crossword puzzle.

Instructor Resources via http://login.cengage.com

Instructors should login through **http://login.cengage.com** to access the following, password-protected resources:

- Solutions Manual—prepared by the author and includes a suggested solution for each question, problem, case.
- PowerPoint® Slides—available to enrich classroom teaching of concepts and practice.
- Test Bank—prepared by the author and includes problems, multiple-choice, true/false, and other objective material for each chapter. The Test Bank is available in Microsoft® Word. All Test Bank questions are now tagged by level of difficulty, topic, Bloom's Taxonomy, AICPA, ACBSP and other business program standards to allow greater guidance in developing assessments and evaluating student progress.
- Thomson ONE—Business School Edition™—suggested solutions to the online cases.
- Instructor's Resource CD-ROM—The IRCD includes the entire instructor resource package on one convenient disc. Included are the Solutions Manual (including the To The Net case solutions as well as solutions to the Thomson ONE online cases), the PowerPoint® Slides, ExamView® testing software, a computerized version of the Test Bank, as well as the Test Bank in Microsoft® Word files. FinSAS and Flexible will also accompany the IRCD.

Acknowledgments

I am grateful to many people for their help and encouragement during the writing of this book. I want to extend my appreciation to the numerous firms and organizations that granted permission to reproduce their material. Special thanks go to the American Institute of Certified Public Accountants, the Institute of Certified Management Accountants, and the Financial Accounting Standards Board. Permission has been received from the Institute of Management Accountants to use questions and/or unofficial answers from past CMA examinations.

I am grateful to the following individuals for their useful and perceptive comments during the making of the thirteenth edition:

- Pamela Benner, *Stark State College*
- Charles Pendola, *St. Joseph's College*
- Michael Flores, *Wichita State University*
- Timothy Dimond, *Northern Illinois University*
- William Mesa, *Colorado Christian University*
- Lawrence Gamble, *Mountainstate University*
- Frank DeGeorge, *West Virginia University*
- Deborah Leitsch, *Goldey-Beacom College*
- William Hahn, *Southeastern University*
- Antoinette Clegg, *Northwood University and Delta College*
- Hongxia Wang, *Ashland University*
- Richard Dumont, *Post University*
- Maryln Fisher, *Regis University*

I am very grateful to Donald Safner (University of Toledo) for his careful, timely, and effective revision of the *FinSAS* spreadsheet tool and *Flexible* for this edition, and to Timothy Dimond (Northern Illinois University) for his careful textbook review.

Charles H. Gibson

Actual Companies and Organizations

Real-world business examples are used extensively in the text, illustrations, and cases.

AAII

Abbott Laboratories

Abercrombie & Fitch Co.

Advanced Micro Devices, Inc.

Air Products and Chemicals, Inc.

AK Steel Holding Corporation

Alexander & Baldwin, Inc.

Alliant Energy Corp.

Amazon.com, Inc.

American Accounting Association

American Greetings

American Institute of Certified Public Accountants (AICPA)

Ann Taylor Stores Corp.

Apple, Inc.

Arden Group, Inc.

AT&T, Inc.

BancFirst Corporation

Belden

Best Buy, Inc.

Boeing

Borders Group

Boston Celtics

Briggs & Stratton

Bristol-Myers Squibb Company

CA, Inc., and Subsidiaries

Camden National Corporation

Carlisle Companies Incorporated

CenturyLink, Inc.

China Unicome (Hong Kong) Limited

Chubb Corporation

Citigroup, Inc.

City of Toledo, Ohio

Columbia Bancorp

Conoro Phillips

Convergys Corporation

Cooper Tire & Rubber Company

Costco Wholesale Corporation

Crane Co.

Cummins, Inc.

Dell, Inc.

Deloitte Touche Tohmatsu Limited

D.R. Horton

Dynatronics

Eastman Kodak Company

Emerging Issues Task Force (EITF)

Exxon Mobil

FASB Accounting Standards Codification™ (Codification)

FedEx Corporation

Financial Accounting Foundation (FAF)

Financial Accounting Standards Advisory Council (FASAC)

Financial Accounting Standards Board (FASB)

Flowers Food Inc.

Freeport-McMoran Cooper & Gold, Inc.

Frisch's Restaurants, Inc.

Ford Motor Co.

Gap, Inc.

Gentex Corporation

Global Diversified Financial Services

Google, Inc.

Government Accounting Standards Board (GASB)

Hasbro, Inc. and Subsidiaries

Hershey Foods Corporation

Hess Corporation

Hewlett-Packard Company

Honeywell International Inc.

Independent Bank Corporation

Indestructible 1, Inc.

Intel Corporation

International Accounting Standards Board

International Accounting Standards Committee

Johnson & Johnson

KB Home

Kellogg Company

Kelly Services, Inc.

Kimberly-Clark Company

Kroger Co.

Lennar Corporation

Limited Brands, Inc.

Lucas County, Ohio

McDonalds

3M Company

Merck & Co.

Molson Coors Brewing Company

Motorola Mobility

Motorola Solutions, Inc.

Nike

Nordson Corporation

Northrop Grumman Corp.

Occidental Petroleum Corporation

Omnova Solutions

Owens Corning Fiberglass Corporation

Owens-Illinois

Panera Bread

Perry Ellis International

PG&E Corporation

Phoenix Footwear Group, Inc.

Priceline.com

Public Company Accounting Oversight Board (PCAOB)

Quaker Chemical Corporation

Reliance Steel & Aluminum Co.

Reynolds American Inc.

Ryder System

Safeway Inc.

Sanmina-Sci Corporation

Santander Holdings U.S.A., Inc.

Securities and Exchange Commission (SEC)

Sherwin-Williams Company

Simpson Manufacturing Co., Inc.

Skechers U.S.A., Inc.

Southwest Airlines Co.

Sovereign Bank

Starbucks Corporation

Target Corporation

Taser International

Tech Data Corporation

Terra Industries

The Chubb Corporation

The Dow Chemical Company

The GEO Group, Inc.

The Gorman-Rupp Company

The Ohio Society of Certified Public Accountants

The Procter & Gamble Company

The Sara Lee Corporation

The Shaw Group, Inc.

The Standard Rubber Company

Toledo Mud Hens Baseball Club, Inc.

Transact Technologies

T. Rowe Price Group, Inc.

United Airlines

Vulcan Materials Company

Wal-Mart Stores, Inc.

Walt Disney

Weyerhaeuser Company

Whole Foods Market, Inc.

Wisconsin Energy Corporation

World Wide Entertainment

Yahoo! Inc.

Yum! Brands, Inc.

Zebra Technologies Corporation

R. Sherwood Veith/iStockphoto.com

Chapter

1

Introduction to Financial Reporting

Users of financial statements include a company's managers, stockholders, bondholders, security analysts, suppliers, lending institutions, employees, labor unions, regulatory authorities, and the general public. These are internal and external stakeholder groups. They use the financial reports to make decisions. For example, potential investors use the financial reports as an aid in deciding whether to buy the stock. Suppliers use the financial reports to decide whether to sell merchandise to a company on credit. Labor unions use the financial reports to help determine their demands when they negotiate for employees. Management could use the financial reports to determine the company's profitability.

Demand for financial reports exists because users believe that the reports help them in decision making. In addition to the financial reports, users often consult competing information sources, such as new wage contracts and economy-oriented releases.

This book concentrates on using financial accounting information properly. It introduces a basic understanding of generally accepted accounting principles and traditional assumptions of the accounting model. This aids the user in recognizing the limits of financial reports.

The ideas that underlie financial reports have developed over several hundred years. This development continues today to meet the needs of a changing society. A review of the evolution of generally accepted accounting principles and the traditional assumptions of the accounting model should help the reader understand financial reports and thus analyze them better.

Development of Generally Accepted Accounting Principles (GAAP) in the United States

Generally accepted accounting principles are accounting principles that have substantial authoritative support. The formal process of developing the accounting principles that exist today in the United States began with the Securities Acts of 1933 and 1934. Prior to these laws, the New York Stock Exchange (NYSE), which was established in 1792, was the primary mechanism for establishing specific requirements for the disclosure of financial information. These requirements could be described as minimal and only applied to corporations whose shares were listed on the NYSE. The prevailing view of management was that financial information was for management's use.

The stock market crash of 1929 provoked widespread concern about external financial disclosure. Some alleged that the stock market crash was substantially influenced by the lack of adequate financial reporting requirements to investors and creditors. The Securities Act of 1933 was designed to protect investors from abuses in financial reporting that developed in the United States. This Act was intended to regulate the initial offering and sale of securities in interstate commerce.

In general, the Securities Exchange Act of 1934 was intended to regulate securities trading on the national exchanges, and it was under this authority that the **Securities and Exchange Commission (SEC)** was created. In effect, the SEC has the authority to determine GAAP and to regulate the accounting profession. The SEC has elected to leave much of the determination of GAAP and the regulation of the accounting profession to the private sector. At times, the SEC will issue its own standards.

Currently, the SEC issues Regulation S-X, which describes the primary formal financial disclosure requirements for companies. The SEC also issues Financial Reporting Releases (FRRs) that pertain to financial reporting requirements. Regulation S-X and FRRs are part of GAAP and are used to give the SEC's official position on matters relating to financial statements. The formal process that exists today is a blend of the private and public sectors.

A number of parties in the private sector have played a role in the development of GAAP. The American Institute of Certified Public Accountants (AICPA) and the Financial Accounting Standards Board (FASB) have had the most influence.

American Institute of Certified Public Accountants

The **AICPA** is a professional accounting organization whose members are certified public accountants (CPAs). During the 1930s, the AICPA had a special committee working with the New York Stock Exchange on matters of common interest. An outgrowth of this special committee was the establishment in 1939 of two standing committees, the **Committee on Accounting Procedures** and the **Committee on Accounting Terminology**. These committees were active from 1939 to 1959 and issued 51 Accounting Research Bulletins (ARBs). These committees took a problem-by-problem approach because they tended to review an issue only when there was a problem related to that issue. This method became known as the brush fire approach. The committees were only partially successful in developing a well-structured body of accounting principles. ARBs are part of GAAP unless they have been superseded.

In 1959, the AICPA replaced the two committees with the **Accounting Principles Board (APB)** and the **Accounting Research Division**. The Accounting Research Division provided research to aid the APB in making decisions regarding accounting principles. Basic postulates would be developed that would aid in the development of accounting principles, and the entire process was intended to be based on research prior to an APB decision. However, the APB and the Accounting Research Division were not successful in formulating broad principles.

The combination of the APB and the Accounting Research Division lasted from 1959 to 1973. During this time, the Accounting Research Division issued 14 Accounting Research Studies. The APB issued 31 Opinions (APBOs) and 4 Statements (APBSs). The Opinions represented official positions of the Board, whereas the Statements represented the views of the Board but not the official opinions. APBOs are part of GAAP unless they have been superseded.

Various sources, including the public, generated pressure to find another way of developing GAAP. In 1972, a special study group of the AICPA recommended another approach—the establishment of the **Financial Accounting Standards Board (FASB)**. The AICPA adopted these recommendations in 1973.

Financial Accounting Standards Board

The structure of the FASB is as follows: A panel of electors is selected from nine organizations. They are the AICPA, the Financial Executives Institute, the Institute of Management Accountants, the Financial Analysts Federation, the American Accounting Association, the Security Industry Association, and three not-for-profit organizations. The electors appoint the board of trustees that governs the **Financial Accounting Foundation (FAF)**. There are 16 trustees.

The FAF appoints the **Financial Accounting Standards Advisory Council (FASAC)** and the FASB.

The FASAC has approximately 30 members. This relatively large number is designed to obtain representation from a wide group of interested parties. The FASAC is responsible for advising the FASB. There are seven members of the FASB. Exhibit 1-1 illustrates the structure of the FASB.

The FASB issues four types of pronouncements:

1. STATEMENTS OF FINANCIAL ACCOUNTING STANDARDS (SFAS). These Statements establish GAAP for specific accounting issues. SFASs are part of GAAP unless they have been superseded.
2. INTERPRETATIONS. These pronouncements provide clarifications to previously issued standards, including SFASs, APB Opinions, and Accounting Research Bulletins. The interpretations have the same authority and require the same majority votes for passage as standards (a supermajority of five or more of the seven members). Interpretations are part of GAAP unless they have been superseded.
3. TECHNICAL BULLETINS. These bulletins provide timely guidance on financial accounting and reporting problems. They may be used when the effect will not cause a major change in accounting practice for a number of companies and when they do not conflict with any broad fundamental accounting principle. Technical bulletins are part of GAAP unless they have been superseded.
4. STATEMENTS OF FINANCIAL ACCOUNTING CONCEPTS (SFACs). These Statements provide a theoretical foundation on which to base GAAP. They are the output of the FASB's Conceptual Framework project, but they are not part of GAAP.

Operating Procedure for Statements of Financial Accounting Standards

The process of considering an SFAS begins when the Board elects to add a topic to its technical agenda. The Board receives suggestions and advice on topics from many sources, including the FASAC, the SEC, the AICPA, and industry organizations.

For its technical agenda, the Board considers only "broken" items. In other words, the Board must be convinced that a major issue needs to be addressed in a new area or an old issue needs to be reexamined.

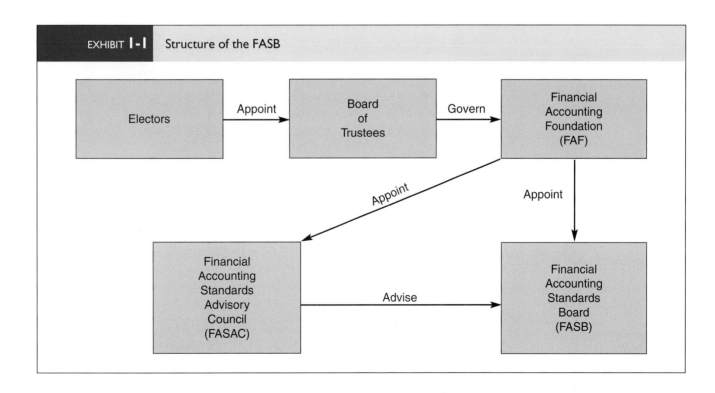

| EXHIBIT 1-1 | Structure of the FASB |

The Board must rely on staff members for the day-to-day work on projects. A project is assigned a staff project manager, and informal discussions frequently take place among Board members, the staff project manager, and staff. In this way, Board members gain an understanding of the accounting issues and the economic relationships that underlie those issues.

On projects with a broad impact, a **Discussion Memorandum (DM)** or an **Invitation to Comment** is issued. A Discussion Memorandum presents all known facts and points of view on a topic. An Invitation to Comment sets forth the Board's tentative conclusions on some issues related to the topic or represents the views of others.

The Discussion Memorandum or Invitation to Comment is distributed as a basis for public comment. There is usually a 60-day period for written comments, followed by a public hearing. A transcript of the public hearing and the written comments become part of the public record. Then the Board begins deliberations on an **Exposure Draft (ED)** of a proposed Statement of Financial Accounting Standards. When completed, the Exposure Draft is issued for public comment. The Board may call for written comments only, or it may announce another public hearing. After considering the written comments and the public hearing comments, the Board resumes deliberations in one or more public Board meetings. The final Statement must receive affirmative votes from five of the seven members of the Board. The Rules of Procedure require dissenting Board members to set forth their reasons in the Statement. Developing a Statement on a major project generally takes at least two years, and sometimes much longer. Some people believe that the time should be shortened to permit faster decision making.

The FASB standard-setting process includes aspects of accounting theory and political aspects. Many organizations, companies, and individuals have input into the process. Some input is directed toward achieving a standard less than desirable in terms of a strict accounting perspective. Often, the result is a standard that is not the best representation of economic reality.

FASB Conceptual Framework

The Conceptual Framework for Accounting and Reporting was on the agenda of the FASB from its inception in 1973. The Framework is intended to set forth a system of interrelated objectives and underlying concepts that will serve as the basis for evaluating existing standards of financial accounting and reporting.

Under this project, the FASB has established a series of pronouncements, SFACs, that are intended to provide the Board with a common foundation and the basic reasons for considering the merits of various alternative accounting principles. SFACs do *not* establish GAAP; rather, the FASB eventually intends to evaluate current principles in terms of the concepts established.

To date, the Framework project has issued seven Concepts Statements:

1. *STATEMENT OF FINANCIAL ACCOUNTING CONCEPTS NO. 1*, "Objectives of Financial Reporting by Business Enterprises"
2. *STATEMENT OF FINANCIAL ACCOUNTING CONCEPTS NO. 2*, "Qualitative Characteristics of Accounting Information"
3. *STATEMENT OF FINANCIAL ACCOUNTING CONCEPTS NO. 3*, "Elements of Financial Statements of Business Enterprises"
4. *STATEMENT OF FINANCIAL ACCOUNTING CONCEPTS NO. 4*, "Objectives of Financial Reporting by Nonbusiness Organizations"
5. *STATEMENT OF FINANCIAL ACCOUNTING CONCEPTS NO. 5*, "Recognition and Measurement in Financial Statements of Business Enterprises"
6. *STATEMENT OF FINANCIAL ACCOUNTING CONCEPTS NO. 6*, "Elements of Financial Statements" (a replacement of No. 3)
7. *STATEMENT OF FINANCIAL ACCOUNTING CONCEPTS NO. 7*, "Using Cash Flow Information and Present Value in Accounting Measurements"

Concepts Statement No. 1, issued in 1978, deals with identifying the objectives of financial reporting for business entities and establishes the focus for subsequent concept projects for business entities. Concepts Statement No. 1 pertains to general-purpose external financial reporting and is not restricted to financial statements. The following is a summary of the highlights of Concepts Statement No. 1.[1]

1. Financial reporting is intended to provide information useful in making business and economic decisions.
2. The information should be comprehensible to those having a reasonable understanding of business and economic activities. These individuals should be willing to study the information with reasonable diligence.
3. Financial reporting should be helpful to users in assessing the amounts, timing, and uncertainty of future cash flows.
4. The primary focus is on information about earnings and its components.
5. Information should be provided about the economic resources of an enterprise and the claims against those resources.

Issued in May 1980, "Qualitative Characteristics of Accounting Information" (SFAC No. 2) examines the characteristics that make accounting information useful for investment, credit, and similar decisions. Those characteristics of information that make it a desirable commodity can be viewed as a hierarchy of qualities, with *understandability* and *usefulness for decision making* of most importance (see Exhibit 1-2).

Relevance and reliability, the two primary qualities, make accounting information useful for decision making. To be relevant, the information needs to have *predictive* and feedback value and must be *timely*. To be reliable, the information must be *verifiable*, subject to representational faithfulness, and *neutral*. Comparability, which includes consistency, interacts with relevance and reliability to contribute to the usefulness of information.

The hierarchy includes *two constraints*. First, to be useful and worth providing, the information should have *benefits that exceed its cost*. Second, all of the qualities of information shown are *subject to a materiality threshold*.

SFAC No. 6, "Elements of Financial Statements," which replaced SFAC No. 3 in 1985, defines 10 interrelated elements directly related to measuring the performance and financial status of an enterprise. The 10 elements are defined as follows:[2]

1. ASSETS. Assets are probable future economic benefits obtained or controlled by a particular entity as a result of past transactions or events.
2. LIABILITIES. Liabilities are probable future sacrifices of economic benefits arising from present obligations of a particular entity to transfer assets or provide services to other entities in the future as a result of past transactions or events.
3. EQUITY. Equity is the residual interest in the assets of an entity that remains after deducting its liabilities:

$$\text{Equity} = \text{Assets} - \text{Liabilities}$$

4. INVESTMENTS BY OWNERS. Investments by owners are increases in the equity of a particular business enterprise resulting from transfers to the enterprise from other entities of something of value to obtain or increase ownership interests (or equity) in it. Assets, most commonly received as investments by owners, may also include services or satisfaction or conversion of liabilities of the enterprise.
5. DISTRIBUTION TO OWNERS. Distribution to owners is a decrease in equity of a particular business enterprise resulting from transferring assets, rendering services, or incurring liabilities by the enterprise to owners. Distributions to owners decrease ownership interest (or equity) in an enterprise.
6. COMPREHENSIVE INCOME. Comprehensive income is the change in equity (net assets) of a business enterprise during a period from transactions and other events and circumstances from nonowner sources. It includes all changes in equity during a period except those resulting from investments by owners and distributions to owners.
7. REVENUES. Revenues are inflows or other enhancements of assets of an entity or settlements of its liabilities (or a combination of both) from delivering or producing goods, rendering services, or carrying out other activities that constitute the entity's ongoing major or central operations.

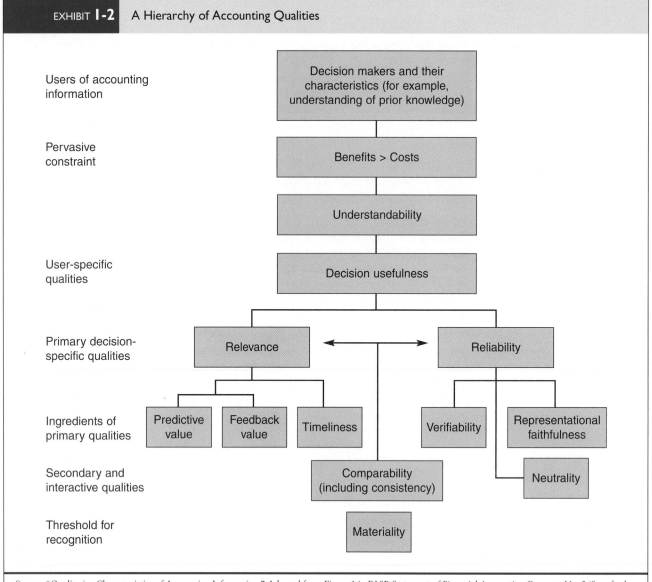

EXHIBIT **1-2**   A Hierarchy of Accounting Qualities

Source: "Qualitative Characteristics of Accounting Information." Adapted from Figure 1 in FASB *Statement of Financial Accounting Concepts No. 2* (Stamford, CT: Financial Accounting Standards Board, 1980).

8. EXPENSES. Expenses are outflows or other consumption or using up of assets or incurrences of liabilities (or a combination of both) from delivering or producing goods, rendering services, or carrying out other activities that constitute the entity's ongoing major or central operations.

9. GAINS. Gains are increases in equity (net assets) from peripheral or incidental transactions of an entity and from all other transactions and other events and circumstances affecting the entity during a period except those that result from revenues or investments by owners.

10. LOSSES. Losses are decreases in equity (net assets) from peripheral or incidental transactions of an entity and from all other transactions and other events and circumstances affecting the entity during a period except those that result from expenses or distributions to owners.

"Objectives of Financial Reporting by Nonbusiness Organizations" (SFAC No. 4) was completed in 1980. Organizations that fall within the focus of this statement include churches, foundations, and human-service organizations. Performance indicators for nonbusiness organizations include formal budgets and donor restrictions. These types of indicators are not ordinarily related to competition in markets.

Issued in 1984, "Recognition and Measurement in Financial Statements of Business Enterprises" (SFAC No. 5) indicates that in order to be recognized an item should meet four criteria, subject to the cost-benefit constraint and materiality threshold:[3]

1. DEFINITION. The item fits one of the definitions of the elements.
2. MEASURABILITY. The item has a relevant attribute measurable with sufficient reliability.
3. RELEVANCE. The information related to the item is relevant.
4. RELIABILITY. The information related to the item is reliable.

This concepts statement identifies *five* different *measurement attributes* currently used in practice and recommends the composition of a full set of financial statements for a period. The following are five different measurement attributes currently used in practice:[4]

1. Historical cost (historical proceeds)
2. Current cost
3. Current market value
4. Net realizable (settlement) value
5. Present (or discounted) value of future cash flows

This concepts statement probably accomplished little relating to measurement attributes because a firm, consistent position on recognition and measurement could not be agreed upon. It states: "Rather than attempt to select a single attribute and force changes in practice so that all classes of assets and liabilities use that attribute, this concepts statement suggests that use of different attributes will continue."[5]

SFAC No. 5 recommended that a full set of financial statements for a period should show the following:[6]

1. Financial position at the end of the period
2. Earnings (net income)
3. Comprehensive income (total nonowner change in equity)
4. Cash flows during the period
5. Investments by and distributions to owners during the period

At the time SFAC No. 5 was issued, financial position at the end of the period and earnings (net income) were financial statements being presented. Comprehensive income, cash flows during the period, and investments by and distributions to owners during the period are financial statements (disclosures) that have been subsequently developed. All of these financial statements (disclosures) will be covered extensively in this book.

SFAC No. 7, issued in February 2000, provides general principles for using present values for accounting measurements. It describes techniques for estimating cash flows and interest rates and applying present value in measuring liabilities.

The FASB Conceptual Framework for Accounting and Reporting project represents the most extensive effort undertaken to provide a conceptual framework for financial accounting. Potentially, the project can have a significant influence on financial accounting.

Additional Input—American Institute of Certified Public Accountants (AICPA)

As indicated earlier, the AICPA played the primary role in the private sector in establishing GAAP prior to 1973. It continues to play a part, primarily through its Accounting Standards Division. The Accounting Standards Executive Committee (AcSEC) serves as the official voice of the AICPA in matters relating to financial accounting and reporting standards.

The Accounting Standards Division has published numerous documents considered as sources of GAAP. These include Industry Audit Guides, Industry Accounting Guides, and Statements of Position (SOPs).

Industry Audit Guides and Industry Accounting Guides are designed to assist auditors in examining and reporting on financial statements of companies in specialized industries, such as insurance. SOPs were issued to influence the development of accounting standards. Some SOPs were revisions or clarifications of recommendations on accounting standards contained in Industry Audit Guides and Industry Accounting Guides.

Industry Audit Guides, Industry Accounting Guides, and SOPs were once considered a lower level of authority than FASB Statements of Financial Accounting Standards, FASB Interpretations, APB Opinions, and Accounting Research Bulletins. However, since the Industry Audit Guides, Industry Accounting Guides, and SOPs deal with material not covered in the primary sources, they, in effect, have become the guide to standards for the areas they cover. They are part of GAAP unless they have been superseded.

Emerging Issues Task Force (EITF)

The FASB established the EITF in July 1984 to help identify emerging issues affecting reporting and problems in implementing authoritative pronouncements. The Task Force has 15 members—senior technical partners of major national CPA firms and representatives of major associations of preparers of financial statements. The FASB's Director of Research and Technical Activities serves as Task Force chairperson. The SEC's Chief Accountant and the chairperson of the AICPA's Accounting Standards Executive Committee participate in EITF meetings as observers.

The SEC's Chief Accountant has stated that any accounting that conflicts with the position of a consensus of the Task Force would be challenged. Agreement of the Task Force is recognized as a consensus if no more than two members disagree with a position.

Task Force meetings are held about once every six weeks. Issues come to the Task Force from a variety of sources, including EITF members, the SEC, and other federal agencies. The FASB also brings issues to the EITF in response to issues submitted by auditors and preparers of financial statements.

The EITF statements have become a very important source of GAAP. The Task Force has the capability to review a number of issues within a relatively short time, in contrast to the lengthy deliberations that go into an SFAS.

EITF statements are considered to be less authoritative than the sources previously discussed in this chapter. However, since the EITF addresses issues not covered by the other sources, its statements become important guidelines to standards for the areas they cover.

A New Reality

In November 2001, Enron, one of the largest companies in the United States, recognized in a federal filing that it had overstated earnings by nearly $600 million since 1997. Within a month, Enron declared bankruptcy. The Enron bankruptcy probably received more publicity than any prior bankruptcy in U.S. history. This attention was influenced by the size of Enron, the role of the auditors, the financial loss of investors, and the losses sustained by Enron employees. Many Enron employees lost their jobs and their pensions as well. There were approximately two dozen guilty pleas or convictions in the Enron case including Ken Lay, former Enron chair. Ken Lay died before he was sentenced; therefore, Judge Sim Lake erased his convictions.

In June 2002, WorldCom announced that it had inflated profits by $3.8 billion over the previous five quarters. This represented the largest financial fraud in corporate history. Soon after the WorldCom fraud announcement, WorldCom declared bankruptcy. (In November 2002, a special bankruptcy court examiner indicated that the restatement would likely exceed $7.2 billion.) On July 13, 2005, Bernard J. Ebbers, founder and former chief executive officer (CEO) of WorldCom, was sentenced to 25 years in prison for orchestrating the biggest corporate accounting fraud in U.S. history.

The WorldCom fraud compelled Congress and President George W. Bush to take action. Congress, with the support of President Bush, acted swiftly to pass legislation now known as the Sarbanes-Oxley Act of 2002.

The Sarbanes-Oxley Act has many provisions and clearly has far-reaching consequences for financial reporting and the CPA profession. While it is not practical to review the Act in detail, because of its importance to financial reporting, some additional comments are in order.

Sarbanes-Oxley Section 404 requires companies to document adequate internal controls and procedures for financial reporting. They must be able to assess the effectiveness of the internal controls and financial reporting.

Companies have found it difficult to comply with Section 404 for many reasons. Internal auditing departments have been reduced or eliminated at many companies. Some companies do not have the personnel to confront complex accounting issues. This lack of adequate competent personnel to confront complex accounting issues in itself represents an internal control weakness.

Sarbanes-Oxley makes it an administrative responsibility to have adequate internal controls and procedures in place. Management must acknowledge its responsibility and assert the effectiveness of internal controls and procedures in writing.

The SEC requires companies to file an annual report on their internal control systems. The report should contain the following:[7]

1. A statement of management's responsibilities for establishing and maintaining an adequate system
2. Identification of the framework used to evaluate the internal controls
3. A statement as to whether or not the internal control system is effective as of year-end
4. The disclosure of any material weaknesses in the system
5. A statement that the company's auditors have issued an audit report on management's assessment

The financial statements auditor must report on management's assertion as to the effectiveness of the internal controls and procedures as of the company's year-end. Sarbanes-Oxley has changed the relationship between the company and the external auditor. Prior to Sarbanes-Oxley, some companies relied on the external auditor to determine the accounting for complex accounting issues. This was a form of conflict of interest, as the auditor surrendered independence in assessing the company's controls, procedures, and reporting.

Not only have some companies found that they do not have adequately trained personnel to confront complex accounting issues, but external auditors have also been pressed to provide trained accounting personnel. This has led some auditing firms to reduce the number and type of companies they will audit.

The spring of 2005 represented the first reporting season under Sarbanes-Oxley. Hundreds of companies acknowledged that they had "material weaknesses" in their controls and processes. In some cases, this led to financial statements being restated.

Implementing Sarbanes-Oxley has resulted in several benefits. Companies have improved their internal controls, procedures, and financial reporting. Many companies have also improved their fraud prevention procedures. Systems put in place to review budgets will enable companies to be more proactive in preventing potential problems. Users of financial statements benefit from an improved financial product that they review and analyze to make investment decisions.

Unfortunately, implementing Sarbanes-Oxley has been quite costly. Some firms question the cost-benefit of compliance with Sarbanes-Oxley. In time, we will know how much of the cost was represented by start-up cost and how much was annual recurring costs. The substantial cost of implementing Sarbanes-Oxley will likely result in future changes to this law.

Publicly held companies are required to report under Sarbanes-Oxley, whereas private companies are not. Many state-level legislators have proposed extending certain provisions of Sarbanes-Oxley to private companies. Such proposals are controversial because of the cost. Some private companies support these proposals.

Most of the publicity relating to Sarbanes-Oxley has been related to Section 404, but the Act includes many other sections. This book will revisit Sarbanes-Oxley when covering other areas, such as ethics, in Chapter 2.

Sarbanes-Oxley created a five-person oversight board, the Public Company Accounting Oversight Board (PCAOB). The PCAOB consists of five members appointed by the SEC. Two must be CPAs, but the others cannot be CPAs.

Among the many responsibilities of the PCAOB is to adopt auditing standards. This will materially decrease or eliminate the role of the AICPA in setting auditing standards.

The PCAOB sets an annual accounting support fee for the standard-setting body (FASB). The PCAOB also establishes an annual accounting support fee for the PCAOB. These fees are assessed against each issuer.

The CEO and the chief financial officer (CFO) of each issuer must prepare a statement to accompany the audit report to certify that disclosures fairly present, in all material respects, the operations and financial condition of the issuer.

In addition to appointing the five members of the PCAOB, the SEC is responsible for oversight and enforcement authority over the Board. In effect, the PCAOB is an arm of the SEC.

As described in this chapter, the setting of accounting standards has been divided among the SEC, FASB, EITF, and AcSEC. By law, the setting of accounting standards is the responsibility of the SEC. The SEC elected to have most of the accounting standards developed in the private sector with the oversight of the SEC. This substantially meant that the SEC allowed the FASB to determine accounting standards. The FASB allowed some of the standards to be determined by the EITF and the AcSEC of the AICPA.

The FASB has announced that it is streamlining the accounting rule-making process by taking back powers it had vested to AcSEC (an arm of the AICPA). The AcSEC will be allowed to continue with industry-specific accounting and audit guides (A&A guides). The AICPA is to stop issuing general-purpose accounting SOPs.

The FASB has also streamlined the accounting rule-making process by taking back powers it had vested to the EITF (an arm of the FASB). Two FASB members will be involved in the agenda-setting process of the EITF. Statements of the EITF will go to the FASB before release.

FASB Accounting Standards Codification™ (Codification)

As indicated in this chapter, there have been many sources of authoritative U.S. GAAP. This has resulted in thousands of pages addressing U.S. GAAP and some confusion as to the level of authoritative GAAP.

To provide a single source of authoritative U.S. GAAP, the FASB released a Codification of U.S. GAAP in 2009. With the Codification, all other literature is considered nonauthoritative. The Codification excludes governmental accounting standards.

The Codification substantially improves the ease of researching U.S. GAAP. Preparers and auditors of financial statements need to reference the Codification when dealing with GAAP. The Codification does not change GAAP.

The Codification arranges U.S. GAAP into approximately 90 accounting topics. A separate section on the Codification includes relevant SEC guidance using the same topical structure.

> The Codification is organized in a tiered structure. Information is organized into eight areas ranging from industry-specific to general financial statement matters. Within each area are topics, subtopics, sections, subsections, and paragraphs, where details of the technical content reside.[8]

The Codification provides electronic real-time updates as new standards are released. The Codification is a fee-based service. A no-frills version is free.

Traditional Assumptions of the Accounting Model

The FASB's Conceptual Framework was influenced by several underlying assumptions. Some of these assumptions were addressed in the Conceptual Framework, and others are implicit in the Framework. These assumptions, along with the Conceptual Framework, are considered when a GAAP is established. Accountants, when confronted with a situation lacking an explicit standard, should resolve the situation by considering the Conceptual Framework and the traditional assumptions of the accounting model.

In all cases, the reports are to be a "fair representation." Even when there is an explicit GAAP, following the GAAP is not appropriate unless the result is a "fair representation." Following GAAP is not an appropriate legal defense unless the statements represent a "fair representation."

Business Entity

The concept of separate **entity** means that the business or entity for which the financial statements are prepared is separate and distinct from the owners of the entity. In other words, the entity is viewed as an economic unit that stands on its own.

For example, an individual may own a grocery store, a farm, and numerous personal assets. To determine the economic success of the grocery store, we would view it separately from the other resources owned by the individual. The grocery store would be treated as a separate entity.

A corporation such as Ford Motor Company has many owners (stockholders). The entity concept enables us to account for the Ford Motor Company entity separately from the transactions of the owners of Ford Motor Company.

Going Concern or Continuity

The **going-concern assumption**, that the entity in question will remain in business for an indefinite period, provides perspective on the future of the entity. The going-concern assumption deliberately disregards the possibility that the entity will go bankrupt or be liquidated. If a particular entity is in fact threatened with bankruptcy or liquidation, then the going-concern assumption should be dropped. In such a case, the reader of the financial statements is interested in the liquidation values, not the values that can be used when making the assumption that the business will continue indefinitely. If the going-concern assumption has not been used for a particular set of financial statements, because of the threat of liquidation or bankruptcy, the financial statements must clearly disclose that the statements were prepared with the view that the entity will be liquidated or that it is a failing concern. In this case, conventional financial report analysis would not apply.

Many of our present financial statement figures would be misleading if it were not for the going-concern assumption. For instance, under the going-concern assumption, the value of prepaid insurance is computed by spreading the cost of the insurance over the period of the policy. If the entity were liquidated, then only the cancellation value of the policy would be meaningful. Inventories are basically carried at their accumulated cost. If the entity were liquidated, then the amount realized from the sale of the inventory, in a manner other than through the usual channels, usually would be substantially less than the cost. Therefore, to carry the inventory at cost would fail to recognize the loss that is represented by the difference between the liquidation value and the cost.

The going-concern assumption also influences liabilities. If the entity were liquidating, some liabilities would have to be stated at amounts in excess of those stated on the conventional statement. Also, the amounts provided for warranties and guarantees would not be realistic if the entity were liquidating.

The going-concern assumption also influences the classification of assets and liabilities. Without the going-concern assumption, all assets and liabilities would be current, with the expectation that the assets would be liquidated and the liabilities paid in the near future.

The audit opinion for a particular firm may indicate that the auditors have reservations as to the going-concern status of the firm. This puts the reader on guard that the statements are misleading if the firm does not continue as a going concern. For example, the annual report of Phoenix Footwear Group, Inc. indicated an uncertainty about the company's ability to continue as a going concern.

The Phoenix Footwear Group, Inc. annual report included the following comments in Note 2 and the auditor's report.

PHOENIX FOOTWEAR GROUP, INC.
NOTES TO CONSOLIDATED FINANCIAL STATEMENTS—Note 2
January 3, 2009

2. GOING CONCERN

The consolidated financial statements have been prepared assuming that the Company will continue as a going concern. The Company has incurred net losses for the last two fiscal years and has been in continuing default on its existing credit facility. As of December 29, 2007, the Company was not in compliance with the financial covenants under its credit facility. The Company did not request a waiver for the respective defaults as it was in the process of replacing the existing facility with a new lender. In June 2008, the Company entered into a Credit and Security Agreement with Wells Fargo Bank, N.A. ("Wells Fargo") for a three-year revolving line of credit and letters of credit collateralized by all of the Company's assets and those of its subsidiaries. Under the facility, the Company can borrow up to $17.0 million (subject to a borrowing base which includes eligible receivables and eligible inventory), which, subject to the satisfaction of certain conditions, may be increased to $20.0 million. The credit facility also includes a $7.5 million letter of credit sub facility. The Company has been in continuing default under the Wells Fargo credit facility since September 27, 2008 by failing to meet the financial covenant for income before income taxes. Additionally, the Company expects that it will not meet this financial covenant as of the end of the first quarter of fiscal 2009 or thereafter unless this financial covenant is amended. Because of the Company's current defaults, its current lender can demand immediate repayment of all debt and the bank can foreclose on the Company's assets. The Company presently has insufficient cash to pay its bank debt in full. The Company has been in continuing discussions with Wells Fargo regarding its restructuring activities in an effort to obtain a waiver of the past financial covenant default and amend future financial covenants. The bank is continuing to evaluate the Company's restructuring activities and has provided no assurance that it will provide a waiver or amend the Company's agreement. Accordingly, there can be no assurance when, or if, an amendment or waiver will be provided. This raises substantial doubt about the Company's ability to continue as a going concern. The accompanying financial statements do not include any adjustments relating to the recoverability and classification of asset carrying amounts or the amount and classification of liabilities that might result should the Company be unable to continue as a going concern.

Source: Phoenix Footwear Group, Inc., 2009 10-K

REPORT OF INDEPENDENT REGISTERED PUBLIC ACCOUNTING FIRM
(In Part)

To the Board of Directors and Stockholders of Phoenix Footwear Group, Inc.
Carlsbad, California

The accompanying financial statements have been prepared assuming that the Company will continue as a going concern. As discussed in Note 2 to the financial statements, the Company incurred a net loss of $19,460,000 for the year ended January 3, 2009 and the Company is not in compliance with financial covenants under its current credit agreement as of January 3, 2009. These factors, among others, as discussed in Note 2 to the financial statements, raise substantial doubt about the Company's ability to continue as a going concern. Management's plans in regard to these matters are described in Note 2 to the financial statements. The financial statements do not include any adjustments that might result from the outcome of this uncertainty.

/s/ Mayer Hoffman McCann P.C.
San Diego, California
April 20, 2009

Source: Phoenix Footwear Group, Inc., 2009 10-K

Time Period

The only accurate way to account for the success or failure of an entity is to accumulate all transactions from the opening of business until the business eventually liquidates. Many years ago, this time period for reporting was acceptable because it would be feasible to account for and divide up what remained at the completion of the venture. Today, the typical business has a relatively long duration, so it is not feasible to wait until the business liquidates before accounting for its success or failure.

This presents a problem: Accounting for the success or failure of the business in midstream involves inaccuracies. Many transactions and commitments are incomplete at any particular time between the opening and the closing of business. An attempt is made to eliminate the inaccuracies when statements are prepared for a period of time short of an entity's life span, but the inaccuracies cannot be eliminated completely. For example, the entity typically carries accounts receivable at the amount expected to be collected. Only when the receivables are collected can the entity account for them accurately. Until receivables are collected, there exists the possibility that collection cannot be made. The entity will have outstanding obligations at any time, and these obligations cannot be accurately accounted for until they are met. An example would be a warranty on products sold. An entity may also have a considerable investment in the production of inventories. Usually, until the inventory is sold in the normal course of business, the entity cannot accurately account for the investment in inventory.

With the time period assumption, we accept some inaccuracies of accounting for the entity short of its complete life span. We assume that the entity can be accounted for with reasonable accuracy for a particular period of time. In other words, the decision is made to accept some inaccuracy, because of incomplete information about the future, in exchange for more timely reporting.

Some businesses select an accounting period, known as a **natural business year**, that ends when operations are at a low ebb in order to facilitate a better measurement of income and financial position. In many instances, the natural business year of a company ends on December 31. Other businesses use the **calendar year** and thus end the accounting period on December 31. Thus, for many companies that use December 31, we cannot tell if December 31 was selected because it represents a natural business year or if it was selected to represent a calendar year. Some select a 12-month accounting period, known as a **fiscal year**, which closes at the end of a month other than December. The accounting period may be shorter than a year, such as a month. The shorter the period of time, the more inaccuracies we typically expect in the reporting.

At times, this text will refer to *Accounting Trends & Techniques,* a book compiled annually by the American Institute of Certified Public Accountants, Inc. *Accounting Trends & Techniques* "is a compilation of reporting and disclosure data obtained from a survey of the annual reports to stockholders of 600 publicly traded companies. This AICPA publication is produced for the purpose of providing accounting professionals with an invaluable resource for incorporating new and existing accounting and reporting guidance into financial statements using presentation techniques adopted by some of the most recognized companies headquartered in the United States. The annual reports surveyed were those of selected industrial, merchandising, technology, and service companies for fiscal periods ending between February and January 2008."[9]

Exhibit 1-3 summarizes month of fiscal year-end from a financial statement compilation in *Accounting Trends & Techniques.*

In Exhibit 1-3 for 2009, 141 survey companies were on a 52- to 53-week fiscal year.[10]

Monetary Unit

Accountants need some standard of measure to bring financial transactions together in a meaningful way. Without some standard of measure, accountants would be forced to report in such terms as 5 cars, 1 factory, and 100 acres. This type of reporting would not be very meaningful.

EXHIBIT **1-3**	Month of Fiscal Year-End*			
	2009	2008	2007	2006
January	26	27	28	27
February	7	8	8	8
March	17	17	17	17
April	8	9	9	9
May	16	15	19	17
June	33	33	40	42
July	8	8	9	10
August	14	13	14	14
September	37	31	43	47
October	14	14	17	16
November	10	9	13	12
Subtotal	190	184	217	219
December	310	316	383	381
Total Entities	500	500	600	600

*2008–2009 based on 500 entities surveyed; 2006–2007 based on 600 entities surveyed
Source: Accounting Trends & Techniques. Copyright © 2010 by American Institute of Certified Public Accountants, Inc. P 39. Reprinted with permission.

There are a number of standards of measure, such as a yard, a gallon, and money. Of the possible standards of measure, accountants have concluded that money is the best for the purpose of measuring financial transactions.

Different countries call their monetary units by different names. For example, Japan uses the yen. Different countries also attach different values to their money—1 dollar is not equal to 1 yen. Thus, financial transactions may be measured in terms of money in each country, but the statements from various countries cannot be compared directly or added together until they are converted to a common monetary unit, such as the U.S. dollar.

In various countries, the stability of the monetary unit has been a problem. The loss in value of money is called **inflation**. In some countries, inflation has been more than 300 percent per year. In countries where inflation has been significant, financial statements are adjusted by an inflation factor that restores the significance of money as a measuring unit. However, a completely acceptable restoration of money as a measuring unit cannot be made in such cases because of the problems involved in determining an accurate index. To indicate one such problem, consider the price of a car in 2001 and in 2011. The price of the car in 2011 would be higher, but the explanation would not be simply that the general price level has increased. Part of the reason for the price increase would be that the type and quality of the equipment changed between 2001 and 2011. Thus, an index that relates the 2011 price to the 2001 price is a mixture of inflation, technological advancement, and quality changes.

The rate of inflation in the United States prior to the 1970s was relatively low. Therefore, an adjustment of money as a measuring unit was thought to be inappropriate because the added expense and inaccuracies of adjusting for inflation were greater than the benefits. During the 1970s, however, the United States experienced double-digit inflation. This made it increasingly desirable to implement some formal recognition of inflation.

In September 1979, the FASB issued *Statement of Financial Accounting Standards No. 33,* "Financial Reporting and Changing Prices," which required that certain large, publicly held companies disclose certain supplementary information concerning the impact of changing prices in their annual reports for fiscal years ending on or after December 25, 1979. This disclosure later became optional in 1986. Currently, no U.S. company provides this supplementary information.

Historical Cost

SFAC No. 5 identified five different measurement attributes currently used in practice: historical cost, current cost, current market value, net realizable value, and present value.

Often, historical cost is used in practice because it is objective and determinable. A deviation from historical cost is accepted when it becomes apparent that the historical cost cannot be recovered. This deviation is justified by the conservatism concept. A deviation from historical cost is also found in practice where specific standards call for another measurement attribute such as current market value, net realizable value, or present value.

Conservatism

The accountant is often faced with a choice of different measurements of a situation, with each measurement having reasonable support. According to the concept of **conservatism**, the accountant must select the measurement with the least favorable effect on net income and financial position in the current period.

To apply the concept of conservatism to any given situation, there must be alternative measurements, each of which must have reasonable support. The accountant cannot use the conservatism concept to justify arbitrarily low figures. For example, writing inventory down to an arbitrarily low figure in order to recognize any possible loss from selling the inventory constitutes inaccurate accounting and cannot be justified under the concept of conservatism. An acceptable use of conservatism would be to value inventory at the lower of historical cost or market value.

The conservatism concept is used in many other situations, such as writing down or writing off obsolete inventory prior to sale, recognizing a loss on a long-term construction contract when it can be reasonably anticipated, and taking a conservative approach toward determining the application of overhead to inventory. Conservatism requires that the estimate of warranty expense reflects the least favorable effect on net income and the financial position of the current period.

Realization

Accountants face a problem of when to recognize revenue. All parts of an entity contribute to revenue, including the janitor, the receiving department, and the production employees. The problem becomes how to determine objectively the contribution of each segment to revenue. Since this is not practical, accountants must determine *when* it is practical to recognize revenue.

In practice, revenue recognition has been the subject of much debate, which has resulted in fairly wide interpretations. The issue of revenue recognition has represented the basis of many SEC enforcement actions. In general, the point of recognition of revenue should be the point in time when revenue can be reasonably and objectively determined. It is essential that there be some uniformity regarding when revenue is recognized, so as to make financial statements meaningful and comparable.

Point of Sale

Revenue is usually recognized at the point of sale. At this time, the earning process is virtually complete, and the exchange value can be determined.

There are times when use of the point-of-sale approach does not give a fair result. An example would be the sale of land on credit to a buyer who does not have a reasonable ability to pay. If revenue were recognized at the point of sale, there would be a reasonable chance that sales had been overstated because of the material risk of default. Many other acceptable methods of recognizing revenue should be considered, such as the following:

1. End of production
2. Receipt of cash
3. During production
4. Cost recovery

End of Production

The recognition of revenue at the completion of the production process is acceptable when the price of the item is known and there is a ready market. The mining of gold or silver is an example, and the harvesting of some farm products would also fit these criteria. If corn is harvested in the fall and held over the winter in order to obtain a higher price in the spring, the realization of revenue from the growing of corn should be recognized in the fall, at the point of harvest. The gain or loss from holding the corn represents a separate consideration from the growing of the corn.

Receipt of Cash

The receipt of cash is another basis for revenue recognition. This method should be used when collection is not capable of reasonable estimation at the time of sale. The land sales business, where the purchaser makes only a nominal down payment, is one type of business where the collection of the full amount is especially doubtful. Experience has shown that many purchasers default on the contract.

During Production

Some long-term construction projects recognize revenue as the construction progresses. This exception tends to give a fairer picture of the results for a given period of time. For example, in the building of a utility plant, which may take several years, recognizing revenue as work progresses gives a fairer picture of the results than does having the entire revenue recognized in the period when the plant is completed.

Cost Recovery

The cost recovery approach is acceptable for highly speculative transactions. For example, an entity may invest in a venture search for gold, the outcome of which is completely unpredictable. In this case, the first revenue can be handled as a return of the investment. If more is received than has been invested, the excess would be considered revenue.

In addition to the methods of recognizing revenue described in this chapter, there are many other methods that are usually industry-specific. Being aware of the method(s) used by a specific firm can be important to your understanding of the financial reports.

The FASB and the International Accounting Standards Board (IASB) have been working on a new standard to make revenue recognition more consistent in practice (the IASB is introduced later in this chapter). It appears that a new SFAS will be approved in 2012 with an effective date in a subsequent year.

Matching

The revenue realization concept involves when to recognize revenue. Accountants need a related concept that addresses when to recognize the costs associated with the recognized revenue: the **matching concept**. The basic intent is to determine the revenue first and then match the appropriate costs against this revenue.

Some costs, such as the cost of inventory, can be easily matched with revenue. When we sell the inventory and recognize the revenue, the cost of the inventory can be matched against the revenue. Other costs have no direct connection with revenue, so some systematic policy must be adopted in order to allocate these costs reasonably against revenues. Examples are research and development costs and public relations costs, both of which are charged off in the period incurred. This is inconsistent with the matching concept because the cost would benefit beyond the current period, but it is in accordance with the concept of conservatism.

Consistency

The **consistency concept** requires the entity to give the same treatment to comparable transactions from period to period. This adds to the usefulness of the reports, since the reports from one period are comparable to the reports from another period. It also facilitates the detection of trends.

Many accounting methods could be used for any single item, such as inventory. If inventory were determined in one period on one basis and in the next period on a different basis, the resulting inventory and profits would not be comparable from period to period.

Entities sometimes need to change particular accounting methods in order to adapt to changing environments. If the entity can justify the use of an alternative accounting method, the change can be made. The entity must be ready to defend the change—a responsibility that should not be taken lightly in view of the liability for misleading financial statements. Sometimes the change will be based on a new accounting pronouncement. When an entity makes a change in accounting methods, the justification for the change must be disclosed, along with an explanation of the effect on the statements.

Full Disclosure

The accounting reports must disclose all facts that may influence the judgment of an informed reader. If the entity uses an accounting method that represents a departure from the official position of the FASB, disclosure of the departure must be made, along with the justification for it.

Several methods of disclosure exist, such as parenthetical explanations, supporting schedules, cross-references, and notes. Often, the additional disclosures must be made by a note in order to explain the situation properly. For example, details of a pension plan, long-term leases, and provisions of a bond issue are often disclosed in notes.

The financial statements are expected to summarize significant financial information. If all the financial information is presented in detail, it could be misleading. Excessive disclosure could violate the concept of full disclosure. Therefore, a reasonable summarization of financial information is required.

Because of the complexity of many businesses and the increased expectations of the public, full disclosure has become one of the most difficult concepts for the accountant to apply. Lawsuits frequently charge accountants with failure to make proper disclosure. Since disclosure is often a judgment decision, it is not surprising that others (especially those who have suffered losses) would disagree with the adequacy of the disclosure.

Materiality

The accountant must consider many concepts and principles when determining how to handle a particular item. The proper use of the various concepts and principles may be costly and time-consuming. The materiality concept involves the relative size and importance of an item to a firm. An item that is material to one entity may not be material to another. For example, an item that costs $100 might be expensed by General Electric, but the same item might be carried as an asset by a small entity.

It is essential that material items be properly handled on the financial statements. Immaterial items are not subject to the concepts and principles that bind the accountant. They may be handled in the most economical and expedient manner possible. However, the accountant faces a judgment situation when determining materiality. It is better to err in favor of an item being material than the other way around.

A basic question when determining whether an item is material is: "Would this item influence an informed reader of the financial statements?" In answering this question, the accountant should consider the statements as a whole.

The Sarbanes-Oxley Act has materiality implications. "The Sarbanes-Oxley Act of 2002 has put demands on management to detect and prevent material control weaknesses in a timely manner. To help management fulfill this responsibility, CPAs are creating monthly key control processes to assess and report on risk. When management finds a key control that does not meet the required minimum quality standard, it must classify the result as a key control exception."[11]

Industry Practices

Some industry practices lead to accounting reports that do not conform to the general theory that underlies accounting. Some of these practices are the result of government regulation. For example, some differences can be found in highly regulated industries, such as insurance, railroad, and utilities.

In the utility industry, an allowance for funds used during the construction period of a new plant is treated as part of the cost of the plant. The offsetting amount is reflected as other income. This amount is based on the utility's hypothetical cost of funds, including funds from debt and stock. This type of accounting is found only in the utility industry.

In some industries, it is very difficult to determine the cost of the inventory. Examples include the meat-packing industry, the flower industry, and farming. In these areas, it may be necessary to determine the inventory value by working backward from the anticipated selling price and subtracting the estimated cost to complete and dispose of the inventory. The inventory would thus be valued at a net realizable value, which would depart from the cost concept and the usual interpretation of the revenue realization concept. If inventory is valued at net realizable value, then the profit has already been recognized and is part of the inventory amount.

The accounting profession is making an effort to reduce or eliminate specific industry practices. However, industry practices that depart from typical accounting procedures will probably never be eliminated completely. Some industries have legitimate peculiarities that call for accounting procedures other than the customary ones.

Transaction Approach

The accountant records only events that affect the financial position of the entity and, at the same time, can be reasonably determined in monetary terms. For example, if the entity purchases merchandise on account (on credit), the financial position of the entity changes. This change can be determined in monetary terms as the inventory asset is obtained and the liability, accounts payable, is incurred.

Many important events that influence the prospects for the entity are not recorded and, therefore, are not reflected in the financial statements because they fall outside the **transaction approach.** The death of a top executive could have a material influence on future prospects, especially for a small company. One of the company's major suppliers could go bankrupt at a time when the entity does not have an alternative source. The entity may have experienced a long strike by its employees or have a history of labor problems. A major competitor may go out of business. All these events may be significant to the entity. They are not recorded because they are not transactions. When projecting the future prospects of an entity, it is necessary to go beyond current financial reports.

Some of the items not recorded will be disclosed. This is done under the full disclosure assumption.

Cash Basis

The **cash basis** recognizes revenue when cash is received and recognizes expenses when cash is paid. The cash basis usually does *not* provide reasonable information about the earning capability of the entity in the short run. Therefore, the cash basis is usually *not* acceptable.

Accrual Basis

The **accrual basis** of accounting recognizes revenue when realized (realization concept) and expenses when incurred (matching concept). If the difference between the accrual basis and the cash basis is not material, the entity may use the cash basis as an alternative to the accrual basis for income determination. Usually, the difference between the accrual basis and the cash basis is material.

A modified cash basis is sometimes used by professional practices and service organizations. The modified cash basis adjusts for such items as buildings and equipment.

The accrual basis requires numerous adjustments at the end of the accounting period. For example, if insurance has been paid for in advance, the accountant must determine the amounts that belong in prepaid insurance and insurance expense. If employees have not been paid all of their wages, the unpaid wages must be determined and recorded as an expense and as a liability. If revenue has been collected in advance, such as rent received in advance, this revenue relates to future periods and must, therefore, be deferred to those periods. At the end of the accounting period, the unearned rent would be considered a liability.

The use of the accrual basis complicates the accounting process, but the end result is more representative of an entity's financial condition than the cash basis. Without the accrual basis, accountants would not usually be able to make the time period assumption— that the entity can be accounted for with reasonable accuracy for a particular period of time.

The illustration on the following page indicates why the accrual basis is generally regarded as a better measure of a firm's performance than the cash basis.

Assumptions:

1. Sold merchandise (inventory) for $25,000 on credit this year. The merchandise cost $12,500 when purchased in the prior year.
2. Purchased merchandise this year in the amount of $30,000 on credit.
3. Paid suppliers of merchandise $18,000 this year.
4. Collected $15,000 from sales.

Accrual Basis		Cash Basis	
Sales	$ 25,000	Receipts	$ 15,000
Cost of sales (expenses)	(12,500)	Expenditures	(18,000)
Income	$ 12,500	Loss	$ (3,000)

The accrual basis indicates a profitable business, whereas the cash basis indicates a loss. The cash basis does not reasonably indicate when the revenue was earned or when to recognize the cost that relates to the earned revenue. The cash basis does indicate when the receipts and payments (disbursements) occurred. The points in time when cash is received and paid do not usually constitute a good gauge of profitability. However, knowing the points in time is important; the flow of cash will be presented in a separate financial statement (statement of cash flows).

In practice, the accrual basis is modified. Immaterial items are frequently handled on a cash basis, and some specific standards have allowed the cash basis.

Harmonization of International Accounting Standards

The impetus for changes in accounting practice has come from the needs of the business community and governments. With the expansion of international business and global capital markets, the business community and governments have shown an increased interest in the harmonization of international accounting standards.

Suggested problems caused by the lack of harmonization of international accounting standards include the following:

1. A need for employment of key personnel in multinational companies to bridge the "gap" in accounting requirements between countries.
2. Difficulties in reconciling local standards for access to other capital markets.
3. Difficulties in accessing capital markets for companies from less developed countries.[12]
4. Negative effect on the international trade of accounting practice and services.[13]

Domestic accounting standards have developed to meet the needs of domestic environments. A few of the factors that influence accounting standards locally are as follows:

1. A litigious environment in the United States that has led to a demand for more detailed standards in many cases.
2. High rates of inflation in some countries that have resulted in periodic revaluation of fixed assets and other price-level adjustments or disclosures.
3. More emphasis on financial reporting/income tax conformity in certain countries (for example, Japan and Germany) that no doubt greatly influences domestic financial reporting.
4. Reliance on open markets as the principal means of intermediating capital flows that has increased the demand for information to be included in financial reports in the United States and some other developed countries.[14]

The following have been observed to have an impact on a country's financial accounting operation:

1. Who the investors and creditors – the information users – are (individuals, banks, the government).
2. How many investors and creditors there are.

3. How close the relationship is between businesses and the investor/creditor group.

4. How developed the stock exchanges and bond markets are.

5. The extent of use of international financial markets.[15]

With this backdrop of fragmentation, it has been difficult, if not impossible, in the short run to bring all national standards into agreement with a meaningful body of international standards. But many see benefits to harmonization of international accounting standards and feel that accounting must move in that direction.

The United Nations (UN) has shown a substantial interest in the harmonization of the international accounting standards. The UN appointed a group to study harmonization of the international accounting standards in 1973. This has evolved into an ad hoc working group. Members of the working group represent governments and not the private sector. The working group does not issue standards but rather facilitates their development. The UN's concern is with how multinational corporations affect the developing countries.[16]

Many other organizations, in addition to the UN, have played a role in the harmonization of international accounting standards. Some of these organizations include the Financial Accounting Standards Board (FASB), the European Economic Community (EEC), the Organization for Economic Cooperation and Development (OECD), and the International Federation of Accountants (IFAC).

In 1973, nine countries, including the United States, formed the International Accounting Standards Committee (IASC). The IASC included approximately 100 member nations and well over 100 professional accounting bodies. The IASC was the only private-sector body involved in setting international accounting standards. International Accounting Standards (IAS) were issued by the IASC from 1973 to 2000.

The IASC's objectives included the following:

1. Developing international accounting standards and disclosure to meet the needs of international capital markets and the international business community.

2. Developing accounting standards to meet the needs of developing and newly industrialized countries.

3. Working toward increased comparability between national and international accounting standards.[17]

The International Accounting Standards Board (IASB) was established in January 2001 to replace the IASC. The IASB arose from a review of the structure of the IASC. The new structure has characteristics similar to those of the FASB. The IASB basically continues the objectives of the IASC.

The IASB does not have authority to enforce its standards, but these standards have been adopted in whole or in part by approximately 100 countries. Some see the lack of enforcement authority as a positive factor because it enables the passing of standards that would not have had the necessary votes if they could be enforced. This allows standards to be more ideal than they would otherwise be if they were enforceable. The IASB issues International Financial Reporting Standards (IFRSs). The term *IFRSs* now refers to the entire body of international standards. The IASB lacks an independent and assured source of funding. The FASB has a dependent and assured source of funding by way of an issuer accounting support fee.

The IASB follows a due-process procedure similar to that of the FASB. This includes Exposure Drafts and a comment period. All proposed standards and guidelines are exposed for comment for about six months.

The Financial Accounting Standards Board and the International Accounting Standards Board met jointly in Norwalk, Connecticut, on September 18, 2002. They acknowledged their commitment to the development of high-quality, compatible accounting standards that could be used for both domestic and cross-border financial reporting. (This is known as the Norwalk Agreement.)

Since the Norwalk Agreement, the FASB and IASB have made significant progress. In joint meetings in April and October 2005, the FASB and the IASB reaffirmed their commitment to the convergence of U.S. GAAP and International Financial Reporting Standards. In a joint meeting held on February 27, 2006, they agreed on a road map for convergence between U.S. GAAP and IFRS. The road map has resulted in many standards being issued where the U.S. and international standards are similar.

In 2007, President Bush signed an agreement between the United States and the European Union that sets the stage to allow many public companies to drop U.S. GAAP in favor of more flexible international rules. Also in 2007, the SEC announced that it would accept financial statements from private issuers without reconciliation to U.S. GAAP if they are prepared using IFRSs as issued by the International Accounting Standards Board.

The American Accounting Association has a Financial Reporting Policy Committee that is charged with responding to Discussion Memoranda and Exposure Drafts on financial accounting and reporting issues. In responding to the SEC release, this committee stated that, "Based on our review of the literature, the committee concluded that eliminating the reconciliation requirement was premature."[18] They offered points in support of their conclusion. Several of these points follow:[19]

1. Material reconciling items exist between U.S. GAAP and IFRS, and the reconciliation currently reflects information that participants in U.S. stock markets appear to impound to stock prices.

2. Cross-country institutional differences will likely result in differences in the implementation of any single set of standards. Thus, IFRS may be a high-quality set of reporting standards (pre-implementation), but the resulting published financial statement information could be of low quality, given inconsistent cross-border implementation practices.

3. Legal and institutional obstacles inhibit private litigation against foreign firms in the United States, and the SEC rarely undertakes enforcement actions against cross-listed firms. In the absence of a reliable enforcement mechanism, even high-quality accounting standards can yield low-quality financial reporting.

4. Differential implementation of standards across countries and differential enforcement efforts directed toward domestic and cross-listed firms create differences in financial reporting even with converged standards. Whether the required reconciliation mitigates differences in implementation or improves compliance is an open issue. However, the SEC should understand the role of the reconciliation in mitigating differences in implementation and compliance before it is eliminated.

5. Harmonization of accounting standards could be beneficial to U.S. investors if it yields greater comparability and if IFRS provides information U.S. investors prefer for their investment decisions. Harmonization appears to be occurring via the joint standard-setting activities of the FASB and the IASB; thus, special, statutory intervention by the SEC appears to be unnecessary.

Ray Ball, a professor of accounting at the University of Chicago, noted a number of problems with implementing IFRS. Several of his comments follow:

1. "On the con side, a deep concern is that the differences in financial reporting quality that are inevitable among countries have been pushed down to the level of implementation, and now will be concealed by a veneer of uniformity."[20]

2. "Despite increased globalization, most political and economic influences on financial reporting practice remain local. It is reinforced by a brief review of the comparatively toothless body of international enforcement agencies currently in place."[21]

3. "The fundamental reason for being skeptical about uniformity of implementation in practice is that the incentives of preparers (managers) and enforcers (auditors, courts, regulators, boards, block shareholders, politicians, analysts, rating agencies, the press) remain primarily local."[22]

4. "Under its constitution, the IASB is a standard setter and does not have an enforcement mechanism for its standards."[23]

5. "Over time the IASB risks becoming a politicized, polarized, bureaucratic, UN-style body."[24]

In 2009, the SEC released for public comment a proposed road map for adoption of IFRS by public companies in the United States. "While many expressed support for the goal of high-quality globally accepted accounting standards, the request for comments produced numerous critics of the SEC's proposed road map. Commentators have serious concerns about the cost of adoption, the benefits of adoption, compared to convergence, and whether IFRSs were in fact as good as or better than U.S. GAAP.[25]

On the cost of adoption there are a number of issues, notably the upfront tax issues, the cost to implement, and additional taxes from increased reported income. These costs likely exceed hundreds of billions of dollars. There are also likely substantial legal costs from the United States changing from a rules-based standard to a principles-based approach.[26] The IFRS principles-based approach allows more latitude in using and applying professional judgment.

The FASB and the IASB had been using a convergence approach to international accounting, especially since 2002. This approach had widespread support in the United States. When the SEC proposed a road map that would require U.S. companies to adopt IASB standards, substantial opposition arose. It appears that the United States will be moving toward using some form of international standards. It is not certain how that will be achieved. In 2011, the SEC presented the ideas that a 'condorsement' approach may be the way for the U.S. to move to IFRS. As of early 2012, the SEC had not made a decision on this issue, and if adopted, the details of implementation.

It was envisioned that the 'condorsement' approach would take five to seven years to implement, with the IFRS as the reference point.

Under the 'condorsement' approach, the FASB and the IASB would continue to work on the memorandum of understanding projects. The FASB would not likely undertake new projects.

The FASB would evaluate the differences between U.S. GAAP and IFRS, and determine whether IFRS standards are suitable for U.S GAAP, considering U.S. capital markets.

The FASB would participate in the process for developing IFRS, but U.S. GAAP would continue to be controlled by U.S. regulation.

Financial Reporting Standards for Small and Medium-Sized Entities (SMEs)

In the United States the issue of financial reporting standards for small and medium-sized entities has been debated for many years. These debates did not result in separate standards for SMEs.

International separate standards for SMEs was an issue going back to the IASC. The IASB carried this project forward when it replaced the IASC. After a 5-year study of the topic, the IASB published an IFRS for SMEs in 2009.

Many jurisdictions under the IFRS have adopted or plan to adopt IFRS for SMEs.

The issue of SMEs is not part of the road map of convergence between IFRS and U.S. GAAP.

In the United States there have been numerous studies and reports on GAAP for private companies. These studies and reports go back approximately 40 years. This issue has again become a major issue for U.S. GAAP.

In 2010 a Blue Ribbon Panel on Private Company Financial Reporting was appointed. This panel represented a cross-section of financial reporting constituencies.

In January, 2011 this panel submitted a report on the future of standard setting for private companies to the Financial Accounting Foundation (FAF). The FAF oversees the Financial Accounting Standards Board.

The two most significant blue ribbon panel recommendations are that:[27]

- A new, separate board with standard setting authority be established under the oversight of the FAF. The board would coordinate activities with the FASB but not be subject to FASB approval.
- Changes and modifications be made to existing and future GAAP that recognize the unique needs of users of private company financial statements. All such changes would reside in the FASB Accounting Standards Codification®.

The FAF trustees formed a Trustee Working Group in March, 2011 to address accounting standard setting for nonpublic entities.

Using the Internet

The Internet is a global collection of computer networks linked together and available for your use. Information passes easily among these networks because all connected networks use a common communication protocol. The Internet includes local, regional, national, and international backbone networks.

There are many reasons for using the Internet. Some of these reasons include (1) retrieving information, (2) finding information, (3) sending and receiving electronic mail, (4) conducting research, and (5) accessing information databases.

Companies' Internet Web Sites

The majority of publicly held companies in the United States have established a Web site on the Internet. The contents of these Web sites vary. A few companies only provide advertisements and product information. In these cases, a phone number may be given to ask for more information. Other companies provide limited financial information, such as total revenues, net income, and earnings per share. These companies may also provide advertisements and a phone number for more information. Many companies provide comprehensive financial information and possibly advertisements. The comprehensive financial information may include the annual report and quarterly reports. It may also include the current stock price and the history of the stock price.

Helpful Web Sites

A number of Web sites can be very useful when performing analysis. Many of these Web sites have highlighted text or graphics that can be clicked to go to another related site. Several excellent Web sites follow:

1. SEC EDGAR DATABASE: www.sec.gov. The Securities and Exchange Commission provides a Web site that includes its Edgar Database. This site allows users to download publicly available electronic filings submitted to the SEC from 1994 to the present. By citing the company name or ticker symbol, you can select from a menu of recent filings. This will include the 10-K report and the 10-Q.
2. FASB: www.fasb.org. Many useful items can be found here, including publications, technical projects, and international activities.
3. FEDERAL CITIZEN INFORMATION CENTER: www.info.gov. This site serves as an entry point to find state, federal, and foreign government information.
4. U.S. GOVERNMENT ACCOUNTABILITY OFFICE (GAO): www.gao.gov/. This is an independent, nonpartisan agency that works for Congress. The GAO issues more than 1,000 reports each year.
5. VIRTUAL FINANCE LIBRARY: http://fisher.osu.edu/fin/overview.htm. This site contains substantial financial information.
6. FINANCIAL MARKETS/STOCK EXCHANGES
   a. NYSE EURONEXT: www.nyse.com
   b. CME GROUP: www.cmegroup.com
   c. NASDAQ STOCK MARKET: www.nasdaq.com
   d. NYSE: www.nyse.com
   e. CHICAGO BOARD OF TRADE: www.cbot.com. The contents of the financial markets/stock exchange sites vary and are expanding.
7. NEWSPAPERS
   a. *THE WALL STREET JOURNAL:* www.wsj.com
   b. *THE NEW YORK TIMES:* www.nytimes.com
   c. *FINANCIAL TIMES:* http://news.ft.com
   d. *INVESTOR'S BUSINESS DAILY:* www.investors.com
      These sites contain substantial financial information, including information on the economy, specific companies, and industries.

8. AICPA: www.aicpa.org. The AICPA is the national organization for U.S. certified public accountants. This site contains substantial information relating to the accounting profession.
9. INTERNATIONAL ACCOUNTING STANDARDS BOARD (IASB): www.iasb.org. The IASB sets global financial accounting and reporting standards. This site helps accountants keep abreast of financial accounting and reporting standards worldwide.
10. PCAOB: www.pcaobus.org. The PCAOB is the private-sector corporation created by the Sarbanes-Oxley Act of 2002. This Board is responsible for overseeing the audits of public companies and has broad authority over public accounting firms and auditors. Its actions are subject to the approval of the Securities and Exchange Commission.
11. FINANCIAL PORTALS
    a. THE STREET.COM: www.thestreet.com
    b. SMART MONEY'S MAP OF THE MARKET: www.smartmoney.com
    c. YAHOO! FINANCE: http://finance.yahoo.com
    d. MORNINGSTAR.COM: www.morningstar.com
    e. MSN MONEY: http://moneycentral.msn.com
    f. MARKETWATCH.COM: www.marketwatch.com
    g. BRIEFING.COM: www.briefing.com
    h. ZACKS INVESTMENT RESEARCH: www.zacks.com
    i. BIGCHARTS: www.bigcharts.com
    j. DOW JONES INDEXES: www.djindexes.com
    k. RUSSELL INVESTMENTS: www.russell.com
    l. STANDARD & POOR'S: www.standardandpoors.com
    m. WILSHIRE ASSOCIATES: www.wilshire.com
    n. BLOOMBERG.COM: www.bloomberg.com

    These financial portals provide information on stock quotes, individual companies, industries, and much more.

Summary

This chapter has reviewed the development of U.S. generally accepted accounting principles and the traditional assumptions of the accounting model. You need a broad understanding of GAAP and the traditional assumptions to reasonably understand financial reports. The financial reports can be no better than the accounting principles and the assumptions of the accounting model that are the basis for preparation.

This chapter introduced "Harmonization of International Accounting Standards" and Financial Reporting Standards for Small and Medium-Sized Entities (SMEs). It also introduced helpful Web sites that can be very useful when performing analysis.

Questions

Q 1-1 Discuss the role of each of the following in the formulation of accounting principles:

a. American Institute of Certified Public Accountants
b. Financial Accounting Standards Board
c. Securities and Exchange Commission

Q 1-2 How does the concept of consistency aid in the analysis of financial statements? What type of accounting disclosure is required if this concept is not applied?

Q 1-3 The president of your firm, Lesky and Lesky, has little background in accounting. Today, he walked into your office and said, "A year ago we bought a piece of land for $100,000. This year, inflation has driven prices up by 6%, and an appraiser just told us we could easily resell the land for $115,000. Yet our balance sheet still shows it at $100,000. It should be valued at $115,000. That's what it's worth. Or, at a minimum, at $106,000." Respond to this statement with specific reference to the accounting principles applicable in this situation.

Q 1-4 Identify the accounting principle(s) applicable to each of the following situations:

a. Tim Roberts owns a bar and a rental apartment and operates a consulting service. He has separate financial statements for each.

b. An advance collection for magazine subscriptions is reported as a liability titled Unearned Subscriptions.

c. Purchases for office or store equipment for less than $25 are entered in Miscellaneous Expense.

d. A company uses the lower of cost or market for valuation of its inventory.

e. Partially completed television sets are carried at the sum of the cost incurred to date.

f. Land purchased 15 years ago for $40,500 is now worth $346,000. It is still carried on the books at $40,500.

g. Zero Corporation is being sued for $1 million for breach of contract. Its lawyers believe that the damages will be minimal. Zero reports the possible loss in a note.

Q 1-5 A corporation like General Electric has many owners (stockholders). Which concept enables the accountant to account for transactions of General Electric separate and distinct from the personal transactions of the owners of General Electric?

Q 1-6 Zebra Company has incurred substantial financial losses in recent years. Because of its financial condition, the ability of the company to keep operating is in question. Management prepares a set of financial statements that conform to generally accepted accounting principles. Comment on the use of GAAP under these conditions.

Q 1-7 Because of assumptions and estimates that go into the preparation of financial statements, the statements are inaccurate and are, therefore, not a very meaningful tool to determine the profits or losses of an entity or the financial position of an entity. Comment.

Q 1-8 The only accurate way to account for the success or failure of an entity is to accumulate all transactions from the opening of business until the business eventually liquidates. Comment on whether this is true. Discuss the necessity of having completely accurate statements.

Q 1-9 Describe the following terms, which indicate the period of time included in the financial statements:

a. Natural business year

b. Calendar year

c. Fiscal year

Q 1-10 Which standard of measure is the best for measuring financial transactions?

Q 1-11 Countries have had problems with the stability of their money. Briefly describe the problem caused for financial statements when money does not hold a stable value.

Q 1-12 In some countries where inflation has been material, an effort has been made to retain the significance of money as a measuring unit by adjusting the financial statements by an inflation factor. Can an accurate adjustment for inflation be made to the statements? Can a reasonable adjustment to the statements be made? Discuss.

Q 1-13 An arbitrary write-off of inventory can be justified under the conservatism concept. Is this statement true or false? Discuss.

Q 1-14 Inventory that has a market value below the historical cost should be written down in order to recognize a loss. Comment.

Q 1-15 There are other acceptable methods of recognizing revenue when the point of sale is not acceptable. List and discuss the other methods reviewed in this chapter, and indicate when they can be used.

Q 1-16 The matching concept involves the determination of when to recognize the costs associated with the revenue that is being recognized. For some costs, such as administrative costs, the matching concept is difficult to apply. Comment on when it is difficult to apply the matching concept. What do accountants often do under these circumstances?

Q 1-17 The consistency concept requires the entity to give the same treatment to comparable transactions from period to period. Under what circumstances can an entity change its accounting methods, provided it makes full disclosure?

Q 1-18 Discuss why the concept of full disclosure is difficult to apply.

Q 1-19 No estimate or subjectivity is allowed in the preparation of financial statements. Discuss.

Q 1-20 It is proper to handle immaterial items in the most economical, expedient manner possible. In other words, generally accepted accounting principles do not apply. Comment, including a concept that justifies your answer.

Q 1-21 The same generally accepted accounting principles apply to all companies. Comment.

Q 1-22 Many important events that influence the prospects for the entity are not recorded in the financial records. Comment and give an example.

Q 1-23 Some industry practices lead to accounting reports that do not conform to the general theory that underlies accounting. Comment.

Q 1-24 An entity may choose between the use of the accrual basis of accounting and the cash basis. Comment.

Q 1-25 Why did the FASB commence the Accounting Standards Codification™ project?

Q 1-26 Would an accountant record the personal assets and liabilities of the owners in the accounts of the business? Explain.

Q 1-27 At which point is revenue from sales on account (credit sales) commonly recognized?

Q 1-28 Elliott Company constructed a building at a cost of $50,000. A local contractor had submitted a bid to construct it for $60,000.

a. At what amount should the building be recorded?

b. Should revenue be recorded for the savings between the cost of $50,000 and the bid of $60,000?

Q 1-29 Dexter Company charges to expense all equipment that costs $25 or less. What concept supports this policy?

Q 1-30 Which U.S. government body has the legal power to determine generally accepted accounting principles?

Q 1-31 What is the basic problem with the monetary assumption when there has been significant inflation?

Q 1-32 Explain the matching principle. How is the matching principle related to the realization concept?

Q 1-33 Briefly explain the term *generally accepted accounting principles*.

Q 1-34 Briefly describe the operating procedure for Statements of Financial Accounting Standards.

Q 1-35 What is the FASB Conceptual Framework for Accounting and Reporting intended to provide?

Q 1-36 Briefly describe the following:

a. Committee on Accounting Procedures
b. Committee on Accounting Terminology
c. Accounting Principles Board
d. Financial Accounting Standards Board

Q 1-37 The objectives of general-purpose external financial reporting are primarily to serve the needs of management. Comment.

Q 1-38 Financial accounting is designed to measure directly the value of a business enterprise. Comment.

Q 1-39 According to SFAC No. 2, relevance and reliability are the two primary qualities that make accounting information useful for decision making. Comment on what is meant by relevance and reliability.

Q 1-40 SFAC No. 5 indicates that, to be recognized, an item should meet four criteria, subject to the cost-benefit constraint and materiality threshold. List these criteria.

Q 1-41 There are five different measurement attributes currently used in practice. List these measurement attributes.

Q 1-42 Briefly explain the difference between an accrual basis income statement and a cash basis income statement.

Q 1-43 The cash basis does not reasonably indicate when the revenue was earned and when the cost should be recognized. Comment.

Q 1-44 It is not important to know when cash is received and when payment is made. Comment.

Q 1-45 Comment on what Section 404 of the Sarbanes-Oxley Act requires of companies.

Q 1-46 Under the Sarbanes-Oxley Act, what must the financial statement auditor do in relation to the company's internal control?

Q 1-47 Comment on perceived benefits from Section 404 of the Sarbanes-Oxley Act.

Q 1-48 Comment on the responsibility of private companies under the Sarbanes-Oxley Act.

Q 1-49 If its accounting period ends December 31, would a company be using a natural business year or a fiscal year?

Q 1-50 Describe the book *Accounting Trends & Techniques*.

Q 1-51 Comment on the materiality implications of the Sarbanes-Oxley Act.

Q 1-52 Briefly describe the PCAOB.

Q 1-53 The SEC released for public comment a proposed road map for adoption of IFRS by public companies in the United States. What were the serious concerns?

Q 1-54 Describe the Norwalk Agreement.

Q 1-55 The SEC announced that it would accept financial statements from private issuers without reconciliation to U.S. GAAP if they are prepared using IFRS, as issued by the International Accounting Standards Board. Comment on possible problems with this position.

Q 1-56 Professor Ball noted a number of problems with implementing IFRS. What were the problems noted by Professor Ball?

Q 1-57 In what year did the IASB publish an IFRS for SMEs? How did this impact the road map of convergence between IFRSs and U.S. GAAP?

Problems

P 1-1 FASB Statement of Financial Accounting Concepts No. 2 indicates several qualitative characteristics of useful accounting information. Following is a list of some of these qualities, as well as a list of statements and phrases describing the qualities.

a. Benefits > costs
b. Decision usefulness
c. Relevance
d. Reliability
e. Predictive value, feedback value, timeliness

f. Verifiability, neutrality, representational faithfulness
g. Comparability
h. Materiality
i. Relevance, reliability

_____ 1. Without usefulness, there would be no benefits from information to set against its cost.

_____ 2. Pervasive constraint imposed on financial accounting information.

_____ 3. Constraint that guides the threshold for recognition.

_____ 4. A quality requiring that the information be timely and that it also have predictive value, feedback value, or both.

_____ 5. A quality requiring that the information have representational faithfulness and that it be verifiable and neutral.

_____ 6. These are the two primary qualities that make accounting information useful for decision making.

_____ 7. These are the ingredients needed to ensure that the information is relevant.

_____ 8. These are the ingredients needed to ensure that the information is reliable.

_____ 9. Includes consistency and interacts with relevance and reliability to contribute to the usefulness of information.

Required Place the appropriate letter identifying each quality on the line in front of the statement or phrase describing the quality.

P 1-2 Certain underlying considerations have had an important impact on the development of generally accepted accounting principles. Following is a list of these underlying considerations, as well as a list of statements describing them.

a. Going concern or continuity
b. Monetary unit
c. Conservatism
d. Matching
e. Full disclosure
f. Materiality
g. Transaction approach
h. Accrual basis
i. Industry practices
j. Verifiability
k. Consistency
l. Realization
m. Historical cost
n. Time period
o. Business entity

_____ 1. The business for which the financial statements are prepared is separate and distinct from the owners.

_____ 2. The assumption is made that the entity will remain in business for an indefinite period of time.

_____ 3. Accountants need some standard of measure to bring financial transactions together in a meaningful way.

_____ 4. Revenue should be recognized when the earning process is virtually complete and the exchange value can be objectively determined.

_____ 5. This concept deals with when to recognize the costs that are associated with the recognized revenue.

_____ 6. Accounting reports must disclose all facts that may influence the judgment of an informed reader.

_____ 7. This concept involves the relative size and importance of an item to a firm.

_____ 8. The accountant is required to adhere as closely as possible to verifiable data.

_____ 9. Some companies use accounting reports that do not conform to the general theory that underlies accounting.

_____ 10. The accountant records only events that affect the financial position of the entity and, at the same time, can be reasonably determined in monetary terms.

_____ 11. Revenue must be recognized when it is realized (realization concept), and expenses are recognized when incurred (matching concept).

_____ 12. The entity must give the same treatment to comparable transactions from period to period.

_____ 13. The measurement with the least favorable effect on net income and financial position in the current period must be selected.

(continued)

(P 1-2 CONTINUED**)**

_____ 14. Of the various values that could be used, this value has been selected because it is objective and determinable.

_____ 15. With this assumption, inaccuracies of accounting for the entity short of its complete life span are accepted.

Required Place the appropriate letter identifying each quality on the line in front of the statement describing the quality.

P 1-3

Required Answer the following multiple-choice questions:

a. Which of the following is a characteristic of information provided by external financial reports?

1. The information is exact and not subject to change.
2. The information is frequently the result of reasonable estimates.
3. The information pertains to the economy as a whole.
4. The information is provided at the least possible cost.
5. None of the above.

b. Which of the following is _not_ an objective of financial reporting?

1. Financial reporting should provide information that is useful to present and potential investors and creditors and other users in making rational investment, credit, and similar decisions.
2. Financial reporting should provide information to help present and potential investors and creditors and other users in assessing the amounts, timing, and uncertainty of prospective cash receipts from dividends or interest and the proceeds from the sale, redemption, or maturity of securities or loans.
3. Financial reporting should provide information about the economic resources of an enterprise, the claims against those resources, and the effects of transactions, events, and circumstances that change the resources and claims against those resources.
4. Financial accounting is designed to measure directly the value of a business enterprise.
5. None of the above.

c. According to FASB Statement of Financial Accounting Concepts No. 2, which of the following is an ingredient of the quality of relevance?

1. Verifiability
2. Representational faithfulness
3. Neutrality
4. Timeliness
5. None of the above.

d. The primary current source of generally accepted accounting principles for nongovernment operations is the

1. New York Stock Exchange
2. Financial Accounting Standards Board
3. Securities and Exchange Commission
4. American Institute of Certified Public Accountants
5. None of the above.

e. What is the underlying concept that supports the immediate recognition of a loss?

1. Matching
2. Consistency
3. Judgment
4. Conservatism
5. Going concern

f. Which statement is *not* true?

1. The Securities and Exchange Commission is a source of some generally accepted accounting principles.
2. The American Institute of Certified Public Accountants is a source of some generally accepted accounting principles.
3. The Internal Revenue Service is a source of some generally accepted accounting principles.
4. The Financial Accounting Standards Board is a source of some generally accepted accounting principles.
5. Numbers 1, 2, and 4 are correct.

g. Which pronouncements are *not* issued by the Financial Accounting Standards Board?

1. Statements of Financial Accounting Standards
2. Statements of Financial Accounting Concepts
3. Technical bulletins
4. Interpretations
5. Opinions

P 1-4

Required Answer the following multiple-choice questions:

a. Which of the following does the Financial Accounting Standards Board *not* issue?

1. SOPs
2. SFASs
3. Interpretations
4. Technical bulletins
5. SFACs

b. According to SFAC No. 6, assets can be defined by which of the following?

1. Probable future sacrifices of economic benefits arising from present obligations of a particular entity to transfer assets or provide services to other entities in the future as a result of past transactions or events
2. Probable future economic benefits obtained or controlled by a particular entity as a result of past transactions or events
3. Residual interest on the assets of an entity that remains after deducting its liabilities
4. Increases in equity of a particular business enterprise resulting from transfers to the enterprise from other entities of something of value to obtain or increase ownership interests (or equity) in it
5. Decrease in equity of a particular business enterprise resulting from transferring assets, rendering services, or incurring liabilities by the enterprise

c. According to SFAC No. 6, expenses can be defined by which of the following?

1. Inflows or other enhancements of assets of an entity or settlements of its liabilities (or a combination of both) from delivering or producing goods, rendering services, or other activities that constitute the entity's ongoing major or central operations
2. Outflows or other consumption or using up of assets or incurrences of liabilities (or a combination of both) from delivering or producing goods, rendering services, or carrying out other activities that constitute the entity's ongoing major or central operations
3. Increases in equity (net assets) from peripheral or incidental transactions of an entity and from all other transactions and other events and circumstances affecting the entity during a period, except those that result from revenues or investments
4. Decreases in equity (net assets) from peripheral or incidental transactions of an entity and from all other transactions and other events and circumstances affecting the entity during a period, except those that result from expenses or distributions to owners
5. Probable future economic benefits obtained or controlled by a particular entity as a result of past transactions or events.

(*continued*)

(P 1-4 CONTINUED**)**

   d. SFAC No. 5 indicates that an item, to be recognized, should meet four criteria, subject to the cost-benefit constraint and the materiality threshold. Which of the following is *not* one of the four criteria?

     1. The item fits one of the definitions of the elements.
     2. The item has a relevant attribute measurable with sufficient reliability.
     3. The information related to the item is relevant.
     4. The information related to the item is reliable.
     5. The item has comparability, including consistency.

   e. SFAC No. 5 identifies five different measurement attributes currently used in practice. Which of the following is *not* one of the measurement attributes currently used in practice?

     1. Historical cost
     2. Future cost
     3. Current market value
     4. Net realizable value
     5. Present, or discounted, value of future cash flows

   f. Which of the following indicates how revenue is usually recognized?

     1. Point of sale
     2. End of production
     3. Receipt of cash
     4. During production
     5. Cost recovery

   g. *Statement of Financial Accounting Concepts No. 1,* "Objectives of Financial Reporting by Business Enterprises," includes all of the following objectives, except one. Which objective does it *not* include?

     1. Financial accounting is designed to measure directly the value of a business enterprise.
     2. Investors, creditors, and others may use reported earnings and information about the elements of financial statements in various ways to assess the prospects for cash flows.
     3. The primary focus of financial reporting is information about earnings and its components.
     4. Financial reporting should provide information that is useful to present and potential investors and creditors and other users in making rational investment, credit, and similar decisions.
     5. The objectives are those of general-purpose external financial reporting by business enterprises.

P 1-5 The following data relate to Jones Company for the year ended December 31, 2011:

Sales on credit	$80,000
Cost of inventory sold on credit	65,000
Collections from customers	60,000
Purchase of inventory on credit	50,000
Payment for purchases	55,000
Cash collections for common stock	30,000
Dividends paid	10,000
Payment to salesclerk	10,000

Required
   a. Determine income on an accrual basis.
   b. Determine income on a cash basis.

P 1-6 Matching Acronyms
Required Listed on the following page are phrases with the appropriate acronym. Match the letter that goes with each definition.

a. Generally accepted accounting principles (GAAP)
b. Securities and Exchange Commission (SEC)
c. Financial Reporting Releases (FRRs)
d. American Institute of Certified Public Accountants (AICPA)
e. Certified public accountants (CPAs)
f. Accounting Principles Board (APB)
g. Accounting Principles Board Opinions (APBOs)
h. Accounting Principles Board Statements (APBSs)
i. Financial Accounting Standards Board (FASB)
j. Financial Accounting Foundation (FAF)
k. Financial Accounting Standards Advisory Council (FASAC)
l. Statements of Financial Accounting Standards (SFASs)
m. Statements of Financial Accounting Concepts (SFACs)
n. Discussion Memorandum (DM)
o. Exposure Draft (ED)
p. Accounting Standards Executive Committee (AcSEC)
q. Statements of Position (SOP)
r. Emerging Issues Task Force (EITF)
s. Public Company Accounting Oversight Board (PCAOB)

_____ 1. Accounting principles that have substantial authoritative support

_____ 2. A task force of representatives from the accounting profession created by the FASB to deal with emerging issues of financial reporting

_____ 3. A proposed Statement of Financial Accounting Standards

_____ 4. Issued by the Accounting Standards Division of the AICPA to influence the development of accounting standards

_____ 5. Created by the Securities Exchange Act of 1934

_____ 6. A professional accounting organization whose members are certified public accountants

_____ 7. Issued official opinions on accounting standards between 1959 and 1973

_____ 8. Represent views of the Accounting Principles Board but not the official opinions

_____ 9. This Board issues four types of pronouncements: (1) Statements of Financial Accounting Standards, (2) Interpretations, (3) Technical bulletins, and (4) Statements of Financial Accounting Concepts

_____ 10. Governs the Financial Accounting Standards Board

_____ 11. These statements are issued by the Financial Accounting Standards Board and establish GAAP for specific accounting issues

_____ 12. Statements issued by the Financial Accounting Standards Board to provide a theoretical foundation on which to base GAAP; they are not part of GAAP

_____ 13. Serves as the official voice of the AICPA in matters relating to financial accounting and reporting standards

_____ 14. Presents all known facts and points of view on a topic; issued by the FASB

_____ 15. Responsible for advising the FASB

_____ 16. Represented official positions of the APB

_____ 17. An accountant who has received a certificate stating that he or she has met the requirements of state law

_____ 18. Issued by the SEC and give the SEC's official position on matters relating to financial statements

_____ 19. Adopts auditing standards

Cases

Case 1-1 STANDARD SETTING: "A POLITICAL ASPECT"

This case consists of a letter from Dennis R. Beresford, chairperson of the Financial Accounting Standards Board, to Senator Joseph I. Lieberman. The specific issue was proposed legislation relating to the accounting for employee stock options.

Permission to reprint the following letter was obtained from the Financial Accounting Standards Board.

August 3, 1993

Senator Joseph I. Lieberman
United States Senate
Hart Senate Office Building
Room 316
Washington, DC 20510

Dear Senator Lieberman:

Members of the Financial Accounting Standards Board (the FASB or the Board) and its staff routinely consult with members of Congress, their staffs, and other government officials on matters involving financial accounting. For example, FASB members and staff met with Senator Levin both before and after the introduction of his proposed legislation, Senate Bill 259, which also addresses accounting for employee stock options.

The attachment to this letter discusses the accounting issues (we have not addressed the tax issues) raised in your proposed legislation, Senate Bill 1175, and issues raised in remarks introduced in the *Congressional Record*. My comments in this letter address an issue that is more important than any particular legislation or any particular accounting issue: why we have a defined process for setting financial reporting standards and why it is harmful to the public interest to distort accounting reports in an attempt to attain other worthwhile goals.

Financial Reporting

Markets are enormously efficient information processors—when they have the information and that information faithfully portrays economic events. Financial statements are one of the basic tools for communicating that information. The U.S. capital market system is well-developed and efficient because of users' confidence that the financial information they receive is reliable. Common accounting standards for the preparation of financial reports contribute to their credibility. The mission of the FASB, an organization designed to be independent of all other business and professional organizations, is to establish and improve financial accounting and reporting standards in the United States.

Investors, creditors, regulators, and other users of financial reports make business and economic decisions based on information in financial statements. Credibility is critical whether the user is an individual contemplating a stock investment, a bank making lending decisions, or a regulatory agency reviewing solvency. Users count on financial reports that are evenhanded, neutral, and unbiased.

An efficiently functioning economy requires credible financial information as a basis for decisions about allocation of resources. If financial statements are to be useful, they must report economic activity without coloring the message to influence behavior in a particular direction. They must not intentionally favor one party over another. Financial statements must provide a neutral scorecard of the effects of transactions.

Economic Consequences of Accounting Standards

The Board often hears that we should take a broader view, that we must consider the economic consequences of a new accounting standard. The FASB should not act,

Source: Financial Accounting Standards Board. Used with permission.

critics maintain, if a new accounting standard would have undesirable economic consequences. We have been told that the effects of accounting standards could cause lasting damage to American companies and their employees. Some have suggested, for example, that recording the liability for retiree health care or the costs for stock-based compensation will place U.S. companies at a competitive disadvantage. These critics suggest that because of accounting standards, companies may reduce benefits or move operations overseas to areas where workers do not demand the same benefits. These assertions are usually combined with statements about desirable goals, like providing retiree health care or creating employee incentives.

There is a common element in those assertions. The goals are desirable, but the means require that the Board abandon neutrality and establish reporting standards that conceal the financial impact of certain transactions from those who use financial statements. Costs of transactions exist whether or not the FASB mandates their recognition in financial statements. For example, not requiring the recognition of the cost of stock options or ignoring the liabilities for retiree health benefits does not alter the economics of the transactions. It only withholds information from investors, creditors, policy makers, and others who need to make informed decisions and, eventually, impairs the credibility of financial reports.

One need only look to the collapse of the thrift industry to demonstrate the consequences of abandoning neutrality. During the 1970s and 1980s, regulatory accounting principles (RAP) were altered to obscure problems in troubled institutions. Preserving the industry was considered a "greater good." Many observers believe that the effect was to delay action and hide the true dimensions of the problem. The public interest is best served by neutral accounting standards that inform policy rather than promote it. Stated simply, truth in accounting is always good policy.

Neutrality does not mean that accounting should not influence human behavior. We expect that changes in financial reporting will have economic consequences, just as economic consequences are inherent in existing financial reporting practices. Changes in behavior naturally flow from more complete and representationally faithful financial statements. The fundamental question, however, is whether those who measure and report on economic events should somehow screen the information before reporting it to achieve some objective. In FASB Concepts Statement No. 2, "Qualitative Characteristics of Accounting Information" (paragraph 102), the Board observed:

> Indeed, most people are repelled by the notion that some "big brother," whether government or private, would tamper with scales or speedometers surreptitiously to induce people to lose weight or obey speed limits or would slant the scoring of athletic events or examinations to enhance or decrease someone's chances of winning or graduating. There is no more reason to abandon neutrality in accounting measurement.

The Board continues to hold that view. The Board does not set out to achieve particular economic results through accounting pronouncements. We could not if we tried. Beyond that, it is seldom clear which result we should seek because our constituents often have opposing viewpoints. Governments, and the policy goals they adopt, frequently change.

Standard Setting in the Private Sector

While the SEC and congressional committees maintain active oversight of the FASB to ensure that the public interest is served, throughout its history the SEC has relied on the Board and its predecessors in the private sector to establish and improve financial accounting and reporting standards. In fulfilling the Board's mission of improving financial reporting, accounting standards are established through a system of due process and open deliberation. On all of our major projects, this involves open Board meetings, proposals published for comment, "field testing" of proposals, public hearings, and redeliberation of the issues in light of comments.

Our due process has allowed us to deal with complex and highly controversial accounting issues, ranging from pensions and retiree health care to abandonment of

(*continued*)

(**CASE I-I** CONTINUED)

nuclear power plants. This open, orderly process for standard setting precludes placing any particular special interest above the interests of the many who rely on financial information. The Board believes that the public interest is best served by developing neutral accounting standards that result in accounting for similar transactions similarly and different transactions differently. The resulting financial statements provide as complete and faithful a picture of an entity as possible.

Corporations, accounting firms, users of financial statements, and most other interested parties have long supported the process of establishing accounting standards in the private sector without intervention by Congress or other branches of government. Despite numerous individual issues on which the FASB and many of its constituents have disagreed, that support has continued. The resulting system of accounting standards and financial reporting, while not perfect, is the best in the world.

Conclusion

We understand that there are a number of people who believe that their particular short-term interests are more important than an effectively functioning financial reporting system. We sincerely hope, however, that you and others in the Congress will review the reasons that have led generations of lawmakers and regulators to conclude that neutral financial reporting is critical to the functioning of our economic system and that the best way to achieve that end is to allow the existing private sector process to proceed. We respectfully submit that the public interest will be best served by that course. As former SEC Chairman Richard Breeden said in testimony to the Senate Banking Committee in 1990:

> The purpose of accounting standards is to assure that financial information is presented in a way that enables decision-makers to make informed judgments. To the extent that accounting standards are subverted to achieve objectives unrelated to a fair and accurate presentation, they fail in their purpose.

The attachment to this letter discusses your proposed legislation. It also describes some aspects of our project on stock compensation and the steps in our due process procedures that remain before the project will be completed. In your remarks in the *Congressional Record*, you said that you will address future issues, including an examination of the current treatment of employee stock options, over the next weeks and months. We would be pleased to meet with you or your staff to discuss these topics and the details of our project. I will phone your appointments person in the next two weeks to see if it is convenient for you to meet with me.

Sincerely,

Dennis R. Beresford
Dennis R. Beresford

Enclosure

cc: The Honorable Connie Mack
 The Honorable Dianne Feinstein
 The Honorable Barbara Boxer
 The Honorable Carl S. Levin
 The Honorable Christopher J. Dodd
 The Honorable Arthur J. Levitt

Required

a. "Financial statements must provide a neutral scorecard of the effects of transactions." Comment.

b. "Costs of transactions exist whether or not the FASB mandates their recognition in financial statements." Comment.

c. In the United States, standard setting is in the private sector. Comment.

d. Few, if any, accounting standards are without some economic impact. Comment.

CASE 1-2 POLITICIZATION OF ACCOUNTING STANDARDS—A NECESSARY ACT?

On October 3, 2008, Congress passed the Emergency Economic Stabilization Act of 2008. This Act mandated that the SEC conduct a study on mark-to-market accounting standards. The SEC had a 90-day period in which to conduct the study.

On December 30, 2008, the SEC released the "Report and Recommendations Pursuant to Section 133 of the Emergency Economic Stabilization Act of 2008: Study on Mark-to-Market Accounting."

The Executive Summary of the SEC report included these comments:

> The events leading up to the Congressional call for this study illustrated the need for identifying and understanding the linkages that exist between fair value accounting standards and the usefulness of information provided by financial institutions. In the months preceding passage of the Act, some asserted that fair value accounting, along with the accompanying guidance on measuring fair value under SFAS No. 157, contributed to instability in our financial markets. According to these critics, fair value accounting did so by requiring what some believed were potentially inappropriate write-downs in the value of investments held by financial institutions, most notably due to concerns that such write-downs were the result of inactive, illiquid, or irrational markets that resulted in values that did not reflect the underlying economics of the securities. These voices pointed out the correlation between U.S. GAAP reporting and the regulatory capital requirements of financial institutions, highlighting that this correlation could lead to the failure of long-standing financial institutions if sufficient additional capital is unavailable to offset investment write-downs. Further, they believed the need to raise additional capital, the effect of failures, and the reporting of large write-downs would have broader negative impact on markets and prices, leading to further write-downs and financial instability.

> Just as vocal were other market participants, particularly investors, who stated that fair value accounting serves to enhance the transparency of financial information provided to the public. These participants indicated that fair value information is vital in times of stress, and a suspension of this information would weaken investor confidence and result in further instability in the markets. These participants pointed to what they believe are the root causes of the crisis, namely poor lending decisions and inadequate risk management, combined with shortcomings in the current approach to supervision and regulation, rather than accounting. Suspending the use of fair value accounting, these participants warned, would be akin to "shooting the messenger" and hiding from capital providers the true economic condition of a financial institution.

The recommendations and related key findings of the SEC report were the following:

1. Recommendation—SFAS No. 157 Should Be Improved, but Not Suspended
2. Recommendation—Existing Fair Value and Mark-to-Market Requirements Should Not Be Suspended
3. Recommendation—Additional Measures Should Be Taken to Improve the Application of Existing Fair Value Requirements
4. Recommendation—The Accounting for Financial Asset Impairments Should Be Readdressed
5. Recommendation—Implement Further Guidance to Foster the Use of Sound Judgment
6. Recommendation—Accounting Standards Should Continue to Be Established to Meet the Needs of Investors
7. Recommendation—Additional Formal Measures to Address the Operation of Existing Accounting Standards in Practice Should Be Established
8. Recommendation—Address the Need to Simplify the Accounting for Investments in Financial Assets

In April 2009, the FASB issued three staff positions intended to provide additional application guidance and enhance disclosures regarding fair value measurement and impairments of securities.

The new rules made it easier for banks to limit losses. The FASB in effect ratified proposals it had put out for comment two weeks earlier.

Source: Financial Accounting Standards Board   *(continued)*

(**CASE 1-2** CONTINUED)

The FASB was criticized for politicization of accounting standards. Some saw it as an erosion of the independence of the accounting standard-setting process.

Required

a. The Emergency Economic Stabilization Act of 2008 was passed during a time of substantial stock market declines in the United States and the world. In your opinion, was Congress correct in directing a review of an accounting standard? Discuss.

b. Did the SEC play a proper role in addressing the standards that governed mark-to-market accounting? Discuss.

c. Did the SEC have the authority to change mark-to-market accounting for U.S. GAAP? Discuss.

d. Did the FASB follow its usual procedures in addressing the mark-to-market issue? Discuss.

e. Is politicization of accounting standards justified under material economic turmoil? Comment.

CASE 1-3 INDEPENDENCE OF ACCOUNTING STANDARD SETTERS

Speech by SEC Chairman:
Remarks before the AICPA National Conference on Current SEC and PCAOB Developments

by

Chairman Christopher Cox
U.S. Securities and Exchange Commission
Washington, DC
December 8, 2008

Note: Selected comments from Chairman Christopher Cox's speech are the basis for this case.

Good morning to all of you, and let me add my welcome to the AICPA's National Conference on Current SEC and PCAOB Developments. It is a pleasure to join you at this Conference once again. And while the Conference topics this year are focused as always on the cutting-edge issues that concern you in your practice, more than ever before the subjects that you'll cover this week are of great importance to our nation and the economy as a whole.

From issues such as fair value measurement, to the future of international accounting and reporting, to corporate governance and MD&A and the SEC's coming interactive data revolution, the Conference agenda is truly cutting edge and consequential. As leaders in your profession, I am especially grateful that you have taken the time to be here, in order to carry forward this important work and to help confront these challenges that concern not only our nation's economy but the world's.

I want you to know that the Securities and Exchange Commission is a strong supporter of your efforts, and that's why not only I, but also a range of top staff from the SEC, including our Chief Accountant, Conrad Hewitt; John White, the Director of the Division of Corporation Finance; Linda Thomsen, Director of the Division of Enforcement; and Jim Kroeker and Paul Beswick, our Deputy Chief Accountants, will be participating with you in this event.

The timing for the presentations you will hear could not be more critical. And since the issues you are addressing in your daily work go far beyond the normal conference agenda, to the very core of the financial turmoil in our financial system, it's fitting that the people who will be speaking are leading the efforts to help investors and markets manage through that turmoil with sound and consistent accounting standards.

The AICPA's 121-year history, dating back to 1887, makes this one of the oldest professional organizations in the country. From the founding of the American Association of Public Accountants, as it was then called, with a membership of only a few hundred to your more than a third of a million members today, the accounting profession has been vital to our nation's economic health and prosperity. Americans have always entrusted you with great responsibility, both individually and as a profession. And through thick and thin you have maintained their confidence.

Source: U.S. Securities and Exchange

Even in the post–Sarbanes Oxley, post–Enron environment, accountants have continued to enjoy a solid reputation among the public, and among business decision makers. That's a testament to your integrity and professional competence. Business executives—your clients—give you a favorability rating of 95%. At the SEC, where we're focused on investor protection, we're most impressed that investors give you a favorability rating of 97%. That's as close to perfect as you're likely to get in this life. None of this means that anyone in this room can afford to be complacent. You have a reputation, and a future, to protect. Together, we've all got to remain vigilant.

The role of the accounting profession, at its core, is parallel to that of the SEC. We both have the goal of ensuring full and accurate financial information is reported by companies. And in fact, given that the AICPA's history dates back even further than the SEC's, it was left for accountants to handle the Panic of 1884 on their own when this market crash hit the country.

Like the current global financial turmoil, America's Panic of 1884 was also precipitated by a credit crisis. When New York's national banks refused to lend any additional money and began calling in their loans from borrowers in the West and South, at a time when the nation didn't have the central bank policy levers that are used today, it caused a dramatic spike in interest rates. One contemporary commentator noted that loans at the time "commanded three percent interest and commission per day on call"—or a staggering annualized compound interest rate of several hundred thousand percent. Although the aftermath of the panic was less serious than some other economic shocks, nearly 11,000 businesses failed in 1884 alone.

In those the early days of organized accounting in America, the profession was small. A quarter-century before, city directories listed just 14 accountants offering services to the public in New York City, four in Philadelphia, and one in Chicago—a far cry from AICPA's 350,000 members today.

As one who formerly taught federal income tax, I'm obliged to point out that what really sparked the growth of the accounting profession in the early 20th century was the ratification of the 16th Amendment to the Constitution in 1913. The adoption of a federal income tax suddenly gave rise to the new field of tax preparation. Accountants quickly asserted their authority in this new field—in competition with law firms, of course, which also touted their expertise.

But the defining moment for the nascent field of modern accounting came in the aftermath of the Great Depression. As some of the largest and most profitable companies in the world fell victim to the crushing financial impact, much of the blame was directed at members of the accounting profession, who were accused in court and in the press of negligence, incompetence, and fraud.

In hindsight, we know that the fault did not lie so much with the practitioners of accounting, but with the lack of objective and widely accepted accounting standards. In the absence of industry-wide standards, accountants were forced to make ad hoc determinations across a range of business situations. Ten companies in the same industry could, and often did, use ten different standards. Clearly something had to change, and AICPA led the charge.

This history is directly relevant to us today, when accounting standard setting is at the center of the debate over how banks and financial firms got into—and how they can get out of—the current financial turmoil. It was to solve the problem of accounting improvisation that in 1939, AICPA created its own rule-making body, the Committee on Accounting Procedure, to help set industry-wide standards on contentious issues. The industry also accepted government licensing for CPAs, who were made responsible—and personally liable—for the auditing of publicly-traded companies.

The Committee on Accounting Procedure was a huge improvement on the lack of process and procedure that had existed before. But because it dealt with standards on an issue-by-issue basis as they arose, rather than offering a comprehensive framework for all accounting standards, there was still more work to be done. To address those concerns the AICPA replaced the Committee on Accounting Procedure, 20 years after it was formed, with the Accounting Principles Board, and gave it a broader mandate. It is from the opinions of the Accounting Principles Board between 1959 and 1973 that much of U.S. GAAP has evolved.

(continued)

The Accounting Principles Board, in turn, was succeeded by a fully independent Financial Accounting Standards Board in 1973, under the oversight of the SEC.

The reasons for creating a non governmental body are completely familiar to us today—to be fair and objective, based on expert analysis and judgment, and free of both political and business influence so that accounting standards could be applied consistently across all situations in thousands of different companies. Those reasons for independent private sector standard setting are as relevant and important today as they ever were.

Since then, Congress has consistently restated its purpose in providing the SEC with oversight responsibility for the FASB's independent standard-setting activities. In the Sarbanes-Oxley Act of 2002, the Congress recognized the importance of having an independent standard-setting process in order to facilitate accurate and effective financial reporting, and to protect investors. In the Emergency Economic Stabilization Act of 2008, the Congress described the SEC's role as ensuring that accounting standards work in the public interest and are consistent with the protection of investors.

In creating the first body to set such standards, AICPA and the accounting profession helped America emerge from its darkest economic hour, and you and your peers set down a structural foundation for the economic growth and success of the past 70 years. Now we find ourselves in another economic crisis, and once again the role of accounting standards and the accounting profession is being challenged. As we respond to these new challenges, we must continue to protect the independence of the standard-setting process.

If we learned one painful lesson from the events of the 1930s, and from the more recent scandals of the S&L crisis in the 1980s and Enron, WorldCom, and the rest in the 1990s and the first part of this decade, it is how vitally important it is to protect the independence of accounting standard setters and ensure that their work remains free of distortions from self-serving influences.

That priority must also be reflected in any regulatory reform undertaken by the next Congress and the new administration. Accounting standards-setting should remain an independent function, and regulatory oversight of the independent private-sector standard setter should not become entangled with the competing priorities of evaluating and addressing systemic risk. Accounting standards should not be viewed as a fiscal policy tool to stimulate or moderate economic growth, but rather as a means of producing neutral and objective measurements of the financial performance of public companies.

Accounting standards aren't just another financial rudder to be pulled when the economic ship drifts in the wrong direction. Instead they are the rivets in the hull, and you risk the integrity of the entire economy by removing them.

There are those who say that independent standard setting is important, and who will agree that private-sector standard setting is preferable to ensure that the process is not detached from reality—but who nonetheless say that while these things are true in ordinary times, these are not ordinary times. Therefore, they argue for setting aside the normal approach to standard setting, which identifies issues for consideration, gives the public exposure documents, includes outreach efforts, and then solicits comments on the exposure documents, and finally considers all of the resulting comments in finalizing and issuing new accounting standards. All of that, they say, should be set aside and replaced with a quick fix, whether the standard setters agree or not.

This view gives short shrift not only to the principle of independence, but also to the credibility of the standard-setting process and investor confidence in it.

The truth is that the value of independent standard setting is greatest when the going gets tough. The more serious the stresses on the market, the more important it is to maintain investor confidence.

A few years ago, during the consideration of a particularly contentious and important accounting rule, the then-Comptroller General, David Walker, wrote a letter on this very point to the Chairman and Ranking Member of the Senate Banking Committee, who were then Richard Shelby and Paul Sarbanes. "[T]he principle of independence," he said, "both in fact and in appearance, is essential to the credibility of and confidence in any authoritative standard-setting processes."

And about the FASB's role as the SEC's designated independent private-sector standard-setting body, the GAO had this to say:

This time-tested and proven deliberative process has served to strengthen financial reporting and ensure general acceptance of the nation's accounting standards. This process is especially important given the complexity and controversial nature of some accounting standards.

The established process that the GAO was referring to includes important safeguards for all users of financial statements, including obtaining feedback from groups such as financial statement preparers, auditors, individual investors, institutional investors, lenders, creditors, professional analysts, and various other parties. These processes are designed to ensure that the competing interests and demands of the various groups are carefully and independently balanced. And that, in turn, is absolutely essential to ensuring that accounting standards promote transparent, credible, and comparable financial information.

None of this is to say that standard setters can or should turn a blind eye to the events in the world around us; or ignore the valid criticism and input of leaders in business, politics, and academia; or endlessly debate and deliberate instead of act when action is required. To the contrary, that is what the transparent process is for. It is meant to achieve results, and to keep standards current.

Standards must keep pace with the real world to stay relevant, and they must be refined over time to better address weaknesses, as we have recently seen with the problems in valuing assets in illiquid markets. I believe it is critical that FASB complete its analysis of the SEC's request for expeditious improvement in the impairment model in FAS 115, made formally last October, in accordance with its established independent standard-setting process.

As we have learned, illiquid markets bring new challenges to the measurement of fair value that could not have been fully appreciated in past years. These challenges have brought into focus the need for further work on improving the tools that companies have at their disposal to achieve transparent, decision-useful financial reporting.

Transparency is the cornerstone of world-class financial reporting. Transparent and unbiased financial reporting allows investors to make informed decisions based on a company's financial performance and disclosures. A clear, concise, and balanced view into the companies that participate in our capital markets is fundamentally important to those who choose to invest in our markets. Informed decision making results in efficient capital allocation.

Required

a. "Accounting standards should not be viewed as a fiscal policy tool to stimulate or moderate economic growth, but rather as a means of providing neutral and objective measurements of the financial performance of public companies." Comment.

b. Letter of David Walker, then-Comptroller General (in Part).
"This time-tested and proven deliberate process has served to strengthen this financial reporting and ensure general acceptance of the nation's accounting standards. This process is especially important given the complexity and controversial nature of some accounting standards." Comment.

CASE 1-4 LOOKING OUT FOR INVESTORS

Speech by SEC Chairman:
Address to the Council of Institutional Investors

by

Chairman Mary L. Schapiro
U.S. Securities and Exchange Commission
Council of Institutional Investors—Spring 2009 Meeting
Washington, DC
April 6, 2009

Note: Selected comments from Chairman Mary L. Schapiro's speech are the basis of this case.

Thank you, Joe, for that lovely introduction, and I want to thank you and Ann for inviting me to join you today. It's really an honor to be here.

Source: U.S. Securities and Exchange

(*continued*)

(**CASE 1-4** CONTINUED)

When I first arrived at the SEC two months ago, I noticed a very large, framed quote prominently displayed outside the Chairman's Office. It's a quote from former Chairman (and later Supreme Court Justice) William O. Douglas. And, it says, "We are the investor's advocate."

Usually, that's the only part of his quote we ever hear. But the full statement is more enlightening. It reads:

We have got brokers' advocates; we have got Exchange advocates; we have got investment banker advocates; and WE are the investors' advocate.

The date of that quote is 1937. Seventy-two years later, there are even more advocates for all of the various participants in our markets, but the SEC remains the only federal agency dedicated to looking out for investors. And surely there has been no time in history that investors have been more in need of an advocate than today.

You—the trillions of dollars that are represented in this room—need an advocate that is strong and effective. In our time together this morning, I'd like to share with you my plans for ensuring both.

The Role of Regulation in Our Markets

Now over the past many months, there's been much talk in Washington and around the globe, about the need to rethink our regulatory system. It is a discussion that has been given urgency by the financial crisis we face—and the quest for solutions.

But as we consider how to address this crisis, I think it is useful to remember that there are myriad reasons for how we got here. The ink on the Sarbanes-Oxley Act of 2002 was hardly dry before we began to hear concerns from some quarters about the costs of "over-regulation," the stifling of innovation, and the superior ability of markets to protect themselves from excesses.

Over the last 15 years, regulations that had once walled off the less risky from more risky parts of our financial system were incrementally weakened. Competition for market-based financing among banks, securities firms and finance companies resulted in a dramatic increase in leverage and risk for both corporate and consumer borrowers.

Standards deteriorated and financial activity moved away from regulated and transparent markets and institutions, into "shadow markets." Regulatory and enforcement resources, most notably at the SEC, declined.

Regulatory reform will seek to address these and the many other causes of the weaknesses in our system and the broader economy.

The SEC's Role

But, fixing all of these problems—whether it's the state of our automobile industry, the soundness of our banking system, or the integrity of our credit or derivatives markets—will take time and involve many moving parts. I'd like to outline how I see the SEC's role and, as I mentioned, my plans for ensuring that the SEC is a strong and effective advocate for investors.

Investor protection starts with fair and efficient capital markets. The SEC's job is to ensure that these markets are:

- First, structured effectively. This means that customer orders are priced, processed, and cleared in an orderly and fair way.
- Second, that they're fed by timely and reliable information. This is imperative whether that information is provided through words or numbers.
- Third, that they're well served by financial intermediaries and other market professionals. These professionals must be competent, financially capable, and honest.
- And fourth, that they're supported by a strong and focused enforcement arm. Returning to former Chairman Douglas' words, we need to have the "shotgun-behind-the-door … loaded, well-oiled, cleaned, ready for use, but with the hope that it will never have to be used."

In each of the following four areas, the SEC has recently experienced both successes and challenges.

Required
a. Comment on the costs of overregulation.
b. Comment on the costs of underregulation.
c. In your opinion, will the SEC now move toward overregulation or underregulation?

Case 1-5 FLYING HIGH*

Note 1
Summary of Significant Accounting Policies (in Part)

Contract accounting—Contract accounting is used for development and production activities predominately by the Aircraft and Weapons Systems (A&WS), Network Systems, Support Systems, and Launch and Orbital Systems (L&OS) segments within Integrated Defense Systems (IDS). These activities include the following products and systems: military aircraft, helicopters, missiles, space systems, missile defense systems, satellites, rocket engines, and information and battle management systems. The majority of business conducted in these segments is performed under contracts with the U.S. government and foreign governments that extend over a number of years. Contract accounting involves a judgmental process of estimating the total sales and costs for each contract, which results in the development of estimated cost of sales percentages. For each sale contract, the amount reported as cost of sales is determined by applying the estimated cost of sales percentage to the amount of revenue recognized.

Sales related to contracts with fixed prices are recognized as deliveries are made, except for certain fixed-price contracts that require substantial performance over an extended period before deliveries begin, for which sales are recorded based on the attainment of performance milestones. Sales related to contracts in which we are reimbursed for costs incurred plus an agreed upon profit are recorded as costs are incurred. The majority of these contracts are with the U.S. government. The Federal Acquisition regulations provide guidance on the types of cost that will be reimbursed in establishing contract price. Contracts may contain provisions to earn incentive and award fees if targets are achieved. Incentive and award fees that can be reasonably estimated are recorded over the performance period of the contract. Incentive and award fees that cannot be reasonably estimated are recorded when awarded.

Program accounting—We use program accounting to account for sales and cost of sales related to all our commercial airplane programs by the Commercial Airplanes segment. Program accounting is a method of accounting applicable to products manufactured for delivery under production-type contracts where profitability is realized over multiple contracts and years. Under program accounting, inventoriable production costs, program tooling costs, and warranty costs are accumulated and charged as cost of sales by program instead of by individual units or contracts. A program consists of the estimated number of units (accounting quantity) of a product to be produced in a continuing, long-term production effort for delivery under existing and anticipated contracts. To establish the relationship of sales to cost of sales, program accounting requires estimates of (a) the number of units to be produced and sold in a program, (b) the period over which the units can reasonably be expected to be produced, and (c) the units' expected sales prices, production costs, program tooling, and warranty costs for the total program.

We recognize sales for commercial airplane deliveries as each unit is completed and accepted by the customer. Sales recognized represent the price negotiated with the customer, adjusted by an escalation formula. The amount reported as cost of sales is determined by applying the estimated cost of sales percentage for the total remaining program to the amount of sales recognized for airplanes delivered and accepted by the customer.

Service revenue—Service revenue is recognized when the service is performed. This method is predominately used by our Support Systems, L&OS, and Commercial Airplanes segments.

(continued)

---

*"The Boeing Company, together with its subsidiaries … is one of the world's major aerospace firms." 10-K

(CASE 1-5 CONTINUED)

Service activities include the following: Delta launches, ongoing maintenance of International Space Station, Space Shuttle and explosive detection systems, support agreements associated with military aircraft and helicopter contracts, and technical and flight operation services for commercial aircraft. BCC lease and financing revenue is also included in "Service revenue" on the Consolidated Statements of Operations. See the "Lease and financing arrangements" section below for a discussion of BCC's revenue recognition policies.

Notes receivable—At commencement of a note receivable issued for the purchase of aircraft or equipment, we record the note and any unamortized discounts. Interest income and amortization of any discounts are recorded ratably over the related term of the note.

Required

a. **Contract Accounting (in Part)**
"Contracts may contain provisions to earn incentive and award fees if targets are achieved. Incentive and award fees that can be reasonably estimated are recorded over the performance period of the contract. Incentive and award fees that cannot be reasonably estimated are recorded when awarded."
Comment on the difficulty in determining which incentive and award fees can be reasonably estimated.

b. **Program Accounting (in Part)**
"We recognize sales for commercial airplane deliveries as each unit is completed and accepted by the customer. Sales recognized represent the price negotiated with the customer, adjusted by an escalation formula."
Comment on the difficulty in determining the sales amount.
"The amount reported as cost of sales is determined by applying the estimated cost of sales percentage for the total remaining program to the amount of sales recognized for airplanes delivered and accepted by the customer."
Does it appear more difficult to determine the sales or cost of sales? Comment.

c. **Service Revenue (in Part)**
"Service revenue is recognized when the service is performed."
Is it difficult to determine service revenue? Comment.

d. **Notes Receivable**
"At commencement of a note receivable issued for the purchase of aircraft or equipment, we record the note and any unamortized discounts. Interest income and amortization of any discounts are recorded ratably over the related term of the note."
Is it difficult to determine revenue from notes receivable? Comment.

CASE 1-6 CENTERED IN HAWAII

Alexander and Baldwin, Inc.*

Notes to Consolidated Financial Statements (In Part)
Summary of Significant Accounting Policies (In Part)
December 31, 2010

Revenue Recognition: The Company has a wide variety of revenue sources, including shipping revenue, logistics services revenue, property sales, rental income, and sales of raw sugar, molasses and coffee. Before recognizing revenue, the Company assesses the underlying terms of the transaction to ensure that recognition meets the requirements of relevant accounting standards. In general, the Company recognizes revenue when persuasive evidence of an arrangement exists, delivery of the service or product has occurred, the sales price is fixed or determinable, and collectibility is reasonably assured.

*"Alexander & Baldwin, Inc. ("A&B") is a multi-industry corporation with its primary operations centered in Hawaii. It was founded in 1870 and incorporated in 1900. Ocean transportation operations, related shoreside operations in Hawaii, and intermodal, truck brokerage and logistics services are conducted by a wholly-owned subsidiary, Matson Navigation Company, Inc. ("Matson"), and two Matson subsidiaries. Property development and agribusiness operations are conducted by A&B and certain other subsidiaries of A&B." 10-K
Source: Alexander and Baldwin, Inc. 2010, 10-K

Voyage Revenue Recognition: Voyage revenue is recognized ratably over the duration of a voyage based on the relative transit time in each reporting period, commonly referred to as the percentage-of-completion method. Voyage expenses are recognized as incurred.

Logistics Services Revenue Recognition: The revenue for logistics services includes the total amount billed to customers for transportation services. The primary costs include purchased transportation services. Revenue and the related purchased transportation costs are recognized based on relative transit time, commonly referred to as the percentage-of-completion method. The Company reports revenue on a gross basis. The Company serves as principal in transactions because it is responsible for the contractual relationship with the customer, has latitude in establishing prices, has discretion in supplier selection, and retains credit risk.

Real Estate Sales Revenue Recognition: Sales are recorded when the risks and rewards of ownership have passed to the buyers (generally on closing dates), adequate initial and continuing investments have been received, and collection of remaining balances, if any, is reasonably assured. For certain development projects that have material continuing post-closing involvement and for which total revenue and capital costs are reasonably estimable, the Company uses the percentage-of-completion method for revenue recognition. Under this method, the amount of revenue recognized is based on development costs that have been incurred through the reporting period as a percentage of total expected development cost associated with the development project. This generally results in a stabilized gross margin percentage, but requires significant judgment and estimates.

Real Estate Leasing Revenue Recognition: Real estate leasing revenue is recognized on a straight-line basis over the terms of the related leases, including periods for which no rent is due (typically referred to as "rent holidays"). Differences between revenues recognized and amounts due under respective lease agreements are recorded as increases or decreases, as applicable, to deferred rent receivable. Also included in rental revenue are certain tenant reimbursements and percentage rents determined in accordance with the terms of the leases. Income arising from tenant rents that are contingent upon the sales of the tenant exceeding a defined threshold are recognized only after the contingency has been resolved (e.g., sales thresholds have been achieved).

Required

a. In general, what is the policy of Alexander & Baldwin for recognizing revenue?
b. Voyage Revenue Recognition: Revenue recognition – "commonly referred to as the percentage-of-completion method." "Voyage expenses are recognized as incurred." Could this represent a challenge when matching cost with revenue?
c. Logistics Services Revenue Recognition: "Revenue and the related purchased transportation are recognized based on relative transit time, commonly referred to as the percentage-of-completion method." Does this appear to be reasonable?
d. Real Estate Sales Revenue Recognition: There appear to be two methods used for revenue recognition for real estate sales. Describe these methods.
e. Real Estate Leasing Revenue Recognition: Describe this method.

CASE 1-7 CONTINUE AS A GOING CONCERN

Report of Independent Registered Public Accounting Firm
To the Board of Director and shareholders

We have audited the accompanying balance sheet of Indestructible I, Inc. as of December 31, 2009 and 2008 and the related statement of operations, stockholders' equity, and cash flows for the twelve months ended December 31, 2009 and 2008 and from inception (September 19, 2003) through the year then ended December 31, 2009. These financial statements are the responsibility of company's management. Our responsibility is to express an opinion on these financial statements based on our audit.

Source: Independent Registered Public Accounting Firm

(continued)

(**CASE 1-7** CONTINUED)

We conducted our audits in accordance with standards of The Public Company Accounting Oversight Board (United States). Those standards require that we plan and perform the audit to obtain reasonable assurance about whether the financial statements are free of material misstatement. An audit includes examining, on a test basis, evidence supporting the amounts and disclosures in the financial statements. An audit also includes assessing the accounting principles used and significant estimates made by management, as well as evaluating the overall financial statements presentation. We believe that our audits provide a reasonable basis for our opinion.

In our opinion, the financial statements referred to above present fairly, in all material respects, the financial position of Indestructible I, Inc. at December 31, 2009 and 2008 and the results of its operations and its cash flows for the twelve months ended December 31, 2009 and 2008 and from inception (September 19, 2003) through December 31, 2009 in conformity with U.S. Generally Accepted Accounting Principles.

The accompanying financial statements have been prepared assuming that the Company will continue as a going concern. The Company has suffered losses from operations and has a net capital deficiency that raises substantial doubt about its ability to continue as a going concern. The financial statements do not include any adjustments that might result from the outcome of this uncertainty.

Gately & Associates, L.L.C.
Lake Mary, FL
February 2, 2010

Required

a. What is the going-concern assumption?
b. Have the financial statements used the going-concern assumption?
c. What is the significance of the disclosure that this company may not be able to continue as a going concern?

CASE 1-8 ECONOMICS AND ACCOUNTING: THE UNCONGENIAL TWINS*

"Economics and accountancy are two disciplines which draw their raw material from much the same mines. From these raw materials, however, they seem to fashion remarkably different products. They both study the operations of firms; they both are concerned with such concepts as income, expenditure, profits, capital, value, and prices. In spite of an apparently common subject-matter, however, they often seem to inhabit totally different worlds, between which there is remarkably little communication."

"It is not surprising that the economist regards much accounting procedure as in the nature of ritual. To call these procedures ritualistic is in no way to deny or decry their validity. Ritual is always the proper response when a man has to give an answer to a question, the answer to which he cannot really know. Ritual under these circumstances has two functions. It is comforting (and in the face of the great uncertainties of the future, comfort is not to be despised), and it is also an answer sufficient for action. It is the sufficient answer rather than the right answer which the accountant really seeks. Under these circumstances, however, it is important that we should know what the accountant's answer means, which means that we should know what procedure he has employed. The wise businessman will not believe his accountant although he takes what his accountant tells him as important evidence. The quality of that evidence, however, depends in considerable degree on the simplicity of the procedures and the awareness which we have of them. What the accountant tells us may not be true, but, if we know what he has done, we have a fair idea of what it means. For this reason, I am somewhat suspicious of many current efforts to reform accounting in the direction of making it more 'accurate.'"

Source: Quotes from the article "Economics and Accounting: The Uncongenial Twins," in *Accounting Theory*, edited by W. T. Baxter and Sidney Davidson (Homewood, IL: R. D. Irwin, 1962), pp. 44–55.

"If accounts are bound to be untruths anyhow, as I have argued, there is much to be said for the simple untruth as against a complicated untruth, for if the untruth is simple, it seems to me that we have a fair chance of knowing what kind of an untruth it is. A known untruth is much better than a lie, and provided that the accounting rituals are well known and understood, accounting may be untrue but it is not lies; it does not deceive because we know that it does not tell the truth, and we are able to make our own adjustment in each individual case, using the results of the accountant as evidence rather than as definitive information."

Required

a. Assume that accounting procedures are in the form of ritual. Does this imply that the accountant's product does not serve a useful function? Discuss.
b. Does it appear that Kenneth Boulding, the author of this article, would support complicated procedures and a complicated end product for the accountant? Discuss.
c. Accounting reports must be accurate in order to serve a useful function. Discuss.

CASE 1-9 I OFTEN PAINT FAKES*

An art dealer bought a canvas signed "Picasso" and traveled all the way to Cannes to discover whether it was genuine. Picasso was working in his studio. He cast a single look at the canvas and said, "It's a fake."

A few months later, the dealer bought another canvas signed "Picasso." Again he traveled to Cannes, and again Picasso, after a single glance, grunted: "It's a fake."

"But cher maitre," expostulated the dealer, "it so happens that I saw you with my own eyes working on this very picture several years ago."

Picasso shrugged: "I often paint fakes."

Required

a. Assume that the accounting report was prepared using generally accepted accounting principles. Does this imply that the report is exactly accurate? Discuss.
b. In your opinion, do accountants paint fakes? Discuss.

*This case consists of a quote from Arthur Koestler, *The Act of Creation* (New York: Macmillan, 1964), p. 82.
Source: Arthur Koestler, The Act of Creation (New York: Macmillan, 1964), p. 82.

CASE 1-10 OVERSIGHT

Selected sections of the Sarbanes-Oxley Act follow:

Public Law 107-204—July 30, 2002
Section 1. Short title. This Act may be cited as the "Sarbanes-Oxley Act of 2002"

TITLE I—Public Company Accounting Oversight Board

Sec. 101. Establishment; Administrative Provisions

(a) Establishment of Board—There is established the Public Company Accounting Oversight Board, to oversee the audit of public companies that are subject to the securities laws, and related matters, in order to protect the interests of investors and further the public interest in the preparation of informative, accurate, and independent audit reports for companies the securities of which are sold to, and held by and for, public investors. The Board shall be a body corporate, operate as a nonprofit corporation, and have succession until dissolved by an Act of Congress.

(b) Duties of the Board—The Board shall, subject to action by the Commission under section 107, and once a determination is made by the Commission under subsection (d) of this section—

(1) register public accounting firms that prepare audit reports for issuers, in accordance with section 102;
(2) establish or adopt, or both, by rule, auditing, quality control, ethics, independence, and other standards relating to the preparation of audit reports for issuers, in accordance with section 103;

Source: U.S. Securities and Exchange

(*continued*)

(**Case 1-10** continued)

(3) conduct inspections of registered public accounting firms, in accordance with section 104 and the rules of the Board;

(4) conduct investigations and disciplinary proceedings concerning, and impose appropriate sanctions where justified upon, registered public accounting firms and associated persons of such firms, in accordance with section 105;

(5) perform such other duties or functions as the Board (or the Commission, by rule or order) determines are necessary or appropriate to promote high professional standards among, and improve the quality of audit services offered by, registered public accounting firms and associated persons thereof, or otherwise to carry out this Act, in order to protect investors, or to further the public interest;

(6) enforce compliance with this Act, the rules of the Board, professional standards, and the securities laws relating to the preparation and issuance of audit reports and the obligations and liabilities of accountants with respect thereto, by registered public accounting firms and associated persons thereof; and

(7) set the budget and manage the operations of the Board and the staff of the Board.

Sec. 102. Registration with the Board

(a) Mandatory Registration—Beginning 180 days after the date of the determination of the Commission under section 101(d), it shall be unlawful for any person that is not a registered public accounting firm to prepare or issue, or to participate in the preparation or issuance of, any audit report with respect to any issuer.

Sec. 103. Auditing, Quality Control, and Independence Standards and Rules

(a) Auditing, quality control, and ethics standards

(1) In General—The Board shall, by rule, establish, including, to the extent it determines appropriate, through adoption of standards proposed by 1 or more professional groups of accountants designated pursuant to paragraph (3)(A) or advisory groups convened pursuant to paragraph (4), and amend or otherwise modify or alter, such auditing and related attestation standards, such quality control standards, and such ethics standards to be used by registered public accounting firms in the preparation and issuance of audit reports, as required by this Act or the rules of the Commission, or as may be necessary or appropriate in the public interest or for the protection of investors.

Sec. 104. Inspections of Registered Public Accounting Firms

(a) In General—The Board shall conduct a continuing program of inspections to assess the degree of compliance of each registered public accounting firm and associated persons of that firm with this Act, the rules of the Board, the rules of the Commission, or professional standards, in connection with its performance of audits, issuance of audit reports, and related matters involving issuers.

Sec. 105. Investigations and Disciplinary Proceedings

(a) In General—The Board shall establish, by rule, subject to the requirements of this section, fair procedures for the investigation and disciplining of registered public accounting firms and associated persons of such firms.

(3) Noncooperation with Investigations

(A) In General—If a registered public accounting firm or any associated person thereof refuses to testify, produce documents, or otherwise cooperate with the Board in connection with an investigation under this section, the Board may—

(i) suspend or bar such person from being associated with a registered public accounting firm, or require the registered public accounting firm to end such association;

(ii) suspend or revoke the registration of the public accounting firm; and

(iii) invoke such other lesser sanctions as the Board considers appropriate, and as specified by rule of the Board.

Sec. 106. Foreign Public Accounting Firms

(a) Applicability to Certain Foreign Firms

    (1) In General—Any foreign public accounting firm that prepares or furnishes an audit report with respect to any issuer, shall be subject to this Act and the rules of the Board and the Commission issued under this Act, in the same manner and to the same extent as a public accounting firm that is organized and operates under the laws of the United States or any State, except that registration pursuant to section 102 shall not by itself provide a basis for subjecting such a foreign public accounting firm to the jurisdiction of the Federal or State courts, other than with respect to controversies between such firms and the Board.

Sec. 107. Commission Oversight of the Board

(a) General Oversight Responsibility—The Commission shall have oversight and enforcement authority over the Board, as provided in this Act.

Sec. 108. Accounting Standards

(a) Amendment to Securities Act of 1933—Section 19 of the Securities Act of 1933 (15 U.S.C. 77s) is amended

(b) Recognition of Accounting Standards

    (1) In General—In carrying out its authority under subsection (a) and under section 13(b) of the Securities Exchange Act of 1934, the Commission may recognize, as "generally accepted" for purposes of the securities laws, any accounting principles established by a standard setting body—

        (A) that—

            (i) is organized as a private entity;

            (ii) has, for administrative and operational purposes, a board of trustees (or equivalent body) serving in the public interest, the majority of whom are not, concurrent with their service on such board, and have not been during the 2-year period preceding such service, associated persons of any registered public accounting firm;

            (iii) is funded as provided in section 109 of the Sarbanes-Oxley Act of 2002;

            (iv) has adopted procedures to ensure prompt consideration, by majority vote of its members, of changes to accounting principles necessary to reflect emerging accounting issues and changing business practices; and

            (v) considers, in adopting accounting principles, the need to keep standards current in order to reflect changes in the business environment, the extent to which international convergence on high quality accounting standards is necessary or appropriate in the public interest and for the protection of investors; and

        (B) that the Commission determines has the capacity to assist the Commission in fulfilling the requirements of subsection (a) and section 13(b) of the Securities Exchange Act of 1934, because, at a minimum, the standard setting body is capable of improving the accuracy and effectiveness of financial reporting and the protection of investors under the securities laws.

Sec. 109. Funding

(a) In General—The Board, and the standard setting body designated pursuant to section 19(b) of the Securities Act of 1933, as amended by section 108, shall be funded as provided in this section.

(d) Annual Accounting Support Fee for the Board

    (1) Establishment of Fee—The Board shall establish, with the approval of the Commission, a reasonable annual accounting support fee (or a formula for the computation thereof), as may be necessary or appropriate to establish and maintain the Board. Such fee may also cover costs incurred in the Board's first fiscal year (which may be a short fiscal year), or may be levied separately with respect to such short fiscal year.

(continued)

(**CASE 1-10** CONTINUED)

(2) Assessments—The rules of the Board under paragraph (1) shall provide for the equitable allocation, assessment, and collection by the Board (or an agent appointed by the Board) of the fee established under paragraph (1), among issuers, in accordance with subsection (g), allowing for differentiation among classes of issuers, as appropriate.

(e) Annual Accounting Support Fee for Standard Setting Body—The annual accounting support fee for the standard setting body referred to in subsection (a)—

(1) shall be allocated in accordance with subsection (g), and assessed and collected against each issuer, on behalf of the standard setting body, by 1 or more appropriate designated collection agents, as may be necessary or appropriate to pay for the budget and provide for the expenses of that standard setting body, and to provide for an independent, stable source of funding for such body, subject to review by the Commission; and

(2) may differentiate among different classes of issuers.

TITLE II—Auditor Independence

Sec. 201. Services Outside the Scope of Practice of Auditors

(a) Prohibited Activities—Section 10A of the Securities Exchange Act of 1934 (15 U.S.C. 78j–1) is amended by adding at the end the following:

(g) Prohibited Activities—Except as provided in subsection (h), it shall be unlawful for a registered public accounting firm (and any associated person of that firm, to the extent determined appropriate by the Commission) that performs for any issuer any audit required by this title or the rules of the Commission under this title or, beginning 180 days after the date of commencement of the operations of the Public Company Accounting Oversight Board established under section 101 of the Sarbanes-Oxley Act of 2002 (in this section referred to as the "Board"), the rules of the Board, to provide to that issuer, contemporaneously with the audit, any non-audit service, including—

(1) bookkeeping or other services related to the accounting records or financial statements of the audit client;

(2) financial information systems design and implementation;

(3) appraisal or valuation services, fairness opinions, or contribution-in-kind reports;

(4) actuarial services;

(5) internal audit outsourcing services;

(6) management functions or human resources;

(7) broker or dealer, investment adviser, or investment banking services;

(8) legal services and expert services unrelated to the audit; and

(9) any other service that the Board determines, by regulation, is impermissible.

(h) Preapproval Required for Non-Audit Services—A registered public accounting firm may engage in any non-audit service, including tax services, that is not described in any of paragraphs (1) through (9) of subsection (g) for an audit client, only if the activity is approved in advance by the audit committee of the issuer, in accordance with subsection (i).

TITLE IV—Enhanced Financial Disclosures

Sec. 404. Management Assessment of Internal Controls

(a) RULES REQUIRED—The Commission shall prescribe rules requiring each annual report required by section 13(a) or 15(d) of the Securities Exchange Act of 1934 [15 U.S.C. 78m or 78o(d)] to contain an internal control report, which shall—

(1) state the responsibility of management for establishing and maintaining an adequate internal control structure and procedures for financial reporting; and

(2) contain an assessment, as of the end of the most recent fiscal year of the issuer, of the effectiveness of the internal control structure and procedures of the issuer for financial reporting.

(b) INTERNAL CONTROL EVALUATION AND REPORTING—With respect to the internal control assessment required by subsection (a), each registered public accounting firm that prepares or issues the audit report for the issuer shall attest to, and report on, the assessment made by the management of the issuer. An attestation made under this subsection shall be made in accordance with standards for attestation engagements issued or adopted by the Board. Any such attestation shall not be the subject of a separate engagement.

Required

a. The Sarbanes-Oxley Act refers to "the Commission" in several sections. To what Commission is the Sarbanes-Oxley Act referring?

b. Describe the responsibility of the Commission in relation to the "Board."

c. Describe the Board.

d. Describe the duties of the Board.

e. Who must register with the Board?

f. Describe the Board's responsibility as to the inspection of those registered with the Board.

g. Describe the responsibilities of the Board in relation to auditing standards.

h. Contrast the applicability of the Sarbanes-Oxley Act to domestic public accounting firms versus foreign public accounting firms.

i. Describe the recognition of accounting standards by the Commission as provided.

j. Comment on the funding for the:
   1. Board.
   2. Financial Accounting Standards Board.

k. Describe prohibited activities of the independent auditor. Can the independent auditor perform tax services for an audit client?

l. Describe management's responsibility in relation to internal controls.

m. Speculate on why Title IV, Section 404, "Management Assessment of Internal Controls," has received substantial criticism.

CASE 1-11 REGULATION OF SMALLER PUBLIC COMPANIES

The U.S. Securities and Exchange Commission (SEC) chartered the Advisory Committee on Smaller Public Companies on March 23, 2005. The charter provided an objective of assessing the regulatory system for smaller companies under the securities laws of the United States and makes recommendations for changes.

The SEC Advisory Committee gave its final recommendations to the SEC in April 2006. These recommendations included several primary recommendations, such as establish a scaled or proportional securities regulation for smaller public companies based on a stratification of smaller public companies into two groups; micro cap companies and small cap companies.*

The report indicates that a scales or proportional securities regulation for smaller public companies assures the full benefits and protection of federal securities regulation for investors in large companies that make up 94% of the total public U.S. equity capital markets....[†]

The committee acknowledges the relative risk to investors and the capital markets as it's currently used by professional investors when using proportional securities regulations.

Required It is perceived that the risk is greater when investing in smaller public companies with proportional securities regulations than in larger companies. Speculate on why the committee considers this risk worth taking.

---

*Final Report of the Advisory Committee on Smaller Public Companies to the U.S. Securities and Exchange Commission (April 23, 2006), p. 4.
[†]Ibid., p. 16.

CASE 1-12 STABLE FUNDING

Speech by SEC Chairman: (In Part)
Remarks Before the Financial Accounting Foundation's 2011 Annual Board of Trustees Dinner

by

Chairman Mary L. Shapiro
U.S. Securities and Exchange Commission
Washington, D.C.
May 24, 2011

"Funding for the GASB and IASB
In addition to the quality of its board and staff, one reason the FASB is able to maintain its position as a world leader is the independent and stable funding it has received, through the issuer accounting support fee, since enactment of Sarbanes-Oxley.

And this brings me to a third area in which I believe change would benefit investors: stable funding for other standard-setting boards.

The Governmental Accounting Standards Board establishes standards that state and local governments may elect to use when raising funds through issuance of municipal securities. And it is a leader in studying how well those standards work. Just last week, the FAF announced that GASB has commissioned an independent study on the purposes of financial accounting and reporting by state and local governments.

Designed to examine how GASB guidelines and standards help investors assess the accountability of local governments and their offerings, it is a timely reminder of the important and unique role that GASB fills.

I am pleased that the Dodd-Frank Act recognized the importance of sufficient and stable resources by authorizing the Commission to require a national securities association to fund the GASB by establishing an annual fee. The Commission recently directed FINRA to establish this fee which will strengthen the independence of the GASB as the Trustees will no longer need to solicit contributions from the very people who must apply the standards that the GASB develops.

Yet another important standard-setter, the IASB, lacks an independent and assured source of funding, as the IFRS Foundation has no authority to impose funding requirements. The threats of interference during the financial crisis serve as a continued reminder of the importance of financial independence for the IFRS Foundation and the IASB.

I know from my role as a member of the Monitoring Board that the trustees of the IFRS Foundation are working closely with regulatory and other public authorities and key stakeholder groups to explore more stable funding mechanisms. Until then, however, funding for the IASB will remain a challenge. And so the SEC's staff continues to evaluate short-and long-term options for assisting the IFRS Foundation. I would like to thank the FAF and its leadership for their continued input and support on this important issue."

Note: GASB is a branch of the Financial Accounting Foundation. The GASB is covered in Chapter 13 Personal Financial Statements and Accounting for Governments and Not-for-Profit Organizations.

Required
  a. How is the FASB funded?
  b. How is the GASB funded?
  c. How is the IASB funded?

Source: U.S. Securities and Exchange

CASE 1-13 RULES OR FEEL?

The FASB and the IASB have made progress toward convergence. The IFRS standards are considered to be more principles based than the U.S. rules-based GAAP. As of 2007, the IFRSs filled approximately 2,000 pages of accounting regulations.* When an IFRS or interpretation does not exist, then judgment must be used when applying an accounting policy.

*Lawrence M. Gill, "IFRS: Coming to America," Journal of Accounting (June 2007), p. 71

As of 2007, U.S. GAAP comprised over 2,000 separate pronouncements.** Many of the U.S. pronouncements were dozens of pages issued by numerous bodies.***

**Ibid.
***Ibid.

Required

a. "The IFRS standards are considered to be more principles based than the U.S. rules-based GAAP." Comment on the implications of this statement, including the legal implications.

b. U.S. GAAP has been considered by many to be the best GAAP in the world. Should the United States give up its GAAP?

Case 1-14 PCAOB ENFORCEMENT – IFRS STANDARDS

"The PCAOB has authority to investigate and discipline registered public accounting firms and persons associated with those firms for noncompliance with the Sarbanes-Oxley Act of 2002, the rules of the PCAOB and the Securities and Exchange Commission, and other laws, rules, and professional standards governing the audits of public companies, brokers, and dealers. When violations are found, the PCAOB can impose appropriate sanctions." (http://pcaobus.org/enforcement)

The IFRS standards are considered to be more principles based than the U.S. rules-based GAAP. The IASB does not have authority to enforce its standards.

Required

a. In your opinion, will it be more difficult for the PCAOB to enforce standards under an IFRS environment? Comment.

b. To the extent that the PCAOB attempts enforcement in an IFRS environment, will companies in the United States be at a disadvantage? Comment.

Source: U.S. Securities and Exchange

Web Case THOMSON ONE *Business School Edition*

Please complete the Web case that covers material discussed in this chapter at www.cengagebrain .com. You'll be using Thomson ONE Business School Edition, a powerful tool that combines a full range of fundamental financial information, earnings estimates, market data, and source documents for 500 publicly traded companies.

To the Net Case

1. Go to the FASB site (www.fasb.org).
   a. Click on "About FASB." Click on "Facts About FASB." Be prepared to discuss the mission of the Financial Accounting Standards Board.
   b. Under the "About FASB" tab, click on "FASAC." Read "An Overview." Be prepared to discuss.
2. Go to the SEC site (www.sec.gov).
   a. Under "Filings & Forms (Edgar)," click on "Search for Company Filings."
   b. Click on "Company or fund, etc."
   c. Enter the name of a company of your choice. Use this site to obtain the address of the company. Contact the company requesting a copy of its annual report, 10-K, and proxy. Compare the annual report with the 10-K.
3. Go to the IASB site (www.ifrs.org).
   a. Click on "About Us." Click on "About the Organisation." Be prepared to discuss.
   b. Click on "Standards Development." Click on "Standard-Setting Process." Be prepared to discuss.

(continued)

(**To The Net** CONTINUED)

4. Go to the PCAOB site (www.pcaobus.org).
   a. Comment on the PCAOB OVERSEES.
   b. Click on "About the PCAOB." Comment.

5. Go to the AICPA site (www.aicpa.org).
   a. Click on "Career." Click on "Career Paths." Comment on "Common Career Paths."
   b. Click on "Career." Click on "Diversity Initiatives." Comment on "Diversity Initiatives."

6. Go to the Yahoo! Finance site (http://finance.yahoo.com).
   a. Enter the name of a company in the "Get Quotes" box. Click on "Get Quotes." Comment on what you found.

Endnotes

1. *Statement of Financial Accounting Concepts No. 1*, "Objectives of Financial Reporting by Business Enterprises" (Stamford, CT: Financial Accounting Standards Board, 1978).

2. *Statement of Financial Accounting Concepts No. 6*, "Elements of Financial Statements" (Stamford, CT: Financial Accounting Standards Board, 1985).

3. *Statement of Financial Accounting Concepts No. 5*, "Recognition and Measurement in Financial Statements of Business Enterprises" (Stamford, CT: Financial Accounting Standards Board, 1984), par. 63.

4. *Statement of Financial Accounting Concepts No. 5*, par. 67.

5. *Statement of Financial Accounting Concepts No. 5*, par. 70.

6. *Statement of Financial Accounting Concepts No. 5*, par. 13.

7. Release No. 33-8238, February 24, 2004, Securities and Exchange Commission, Final Rule: "Management's Reports on Internal Control over Financial Reporting and Certification of Disclosure in Exchange Act Periodic Reports," www.sec.gov.

8. Caroline O. Ford and C. William Thomas, "Test-Driving the Codification," *Journal of Accounting* (December 2008), p. 62.

9. *Accounting Trends & Techniques* (New York: American Institute of Certified Public Accountants, 2008), preface.

10. Ibid., p. 39.

11. James Brady Vorhies, "The New Importance of Materiality," *Journal of Accounting* (May 2005), pp. 53–59.

12. Dennis E. Peavey and Stuart K. Webster, "Is GAAP the Gap to International Markets?" *Management Accounting* (August 1990), pp. 31–32.

13. John Hagarty, "Why We Can't Let GATT Die," *Journal of Accountancy* (April 1991), p. 74.

14. Dennis Beresford, "Internationalization of Accounting Standards," *Accounting Horizons* (March 1990), p. 10.

15. Gerhard G. Mueller, Helen German, and Gary Meek, *Accounting: An International Perspective*, 2nd ed. (Homewood, IL: Richard D. Irwin, 1991), pp. 11–12.

16. Ibid., pp. 45–46.

17. Peavey and Webster, "Is GAAP the GAP to International Markets?" p. 34.

18. "Response to the SEC Releases," Acceptance from Foreign Private Issuers of Financial Statements Prepared in Accordance with International Financial Reporting Standards Without Reconciliation to U.S. GAAP File No. 57-13-07, *Accounting Horizons* (June 2008), p. 225.

19. Ibid., 225.

20. Ray Ball, "International Financial Reporting Standards (IFRS): Pros and Cons for Investors," *Accounting and Business Research, International Accounting Policy Forum* (2006), pp. 5–6.

21. Ibid., 15.

22. Ibid.

23. Ibid., 17.

24. Ibid., 22.

25. "Where will the SEC take the IFRS Roadmap? An AICPA Analysis of Comment Letters on the SEC's Proposal." *American Institute of Certified Public Accountants* (April 27, 2009), www.ifrs.com/updates/aicpa/IFRS_SEC.html.

26. Ellen M. Heffes, "Legal Considerations in the Proposed Transition to International Financial Reporting Standards." *Financial Executive* (May 2009), pp. 14–15.

27. "Private Company Financial Reporting" *Journal of Accounting* (July 2011), AICPA Advocacy, pp. 84.

Introduction to Financial Statements and Other Financial Reporting Topics

This chapter introduces financial statements. Subsequent chapters present a detailed review of the principal financial statements. Chapter 3 covers the balance sheet, Chapter 4 the income statement, and Chapter 10 the statement of cash flows.

This chapter also reviews the forms of business entities and the sequence of accounting procedures (called the accounting cycle). Other financial reporting topics included in this chapter that contribute to the understanding of financial reporting are: Treadway Commission, auditor's opinion, auditor's report on the firm's internal controls, Report of Management on Internal Control over Financial Reporting, management's responsibility for financial statements, the SEC's integrated disclosure system, proxy, the summary annual report, the efficient market hypothesis, ethics, harmonization of international accounting standards, consolidated statements, and accounting for business combinations.

Forms of Business Entities

A business entity may be a sole proprietorship, a partnership, or a corporation. A sole proprietorship, a business owned by one person, is not a legal entity separate from its owner, but the accountant treats the business as a separate accounting entity. The profit or loss of the proprietorship goes on the income tax return of the owner. The owner is responsible for the debts of the sole proprietorship.

In the United States, a sole proprietorship may qualify to be treated as a limited liability company (LLC). As an LLC, the owner may limit the liability of the sole proprietor, but may increase the tax exposure of the proprietorship.

A partnership is a business owned by two or more individuals. Each owner, called a partner, is personally responsible for the debts of the partnership. The accountant treats the partners and the business as separate accounting entities. The profit or loss of the partnership goes on the individual income tax return of the partners. Like a proprietorship, a partnership may qualify to be treated as an LLC. As an LLC, the owners may limit the liability of the partners, but may increase the tax exposure of the partnership.

In the United States, a business **corporation** is a legal entity incorporated in a particular state. Ownership is evidenced by shares of stock. A corporation is considered to be separate and distinct from the stockholders. The stockholders risk only their investment; they are not responsible for the debts of the corporation.

Since a corporation is a legal entity, the profits or losses are treated as a separate entity on an income tax return. The owners are not taxed until profits are distributed to the owners (dividends). In the United States, some corporations qualify to be treated as a subchapter S corporation. These corporations do not pay a corporate income tax. The profits or losses go directly on the income tax returns of the owners.

In the United States, most businesses operate as proprietorships, but corporations perform the bulk of business activity. Because most business activity is carried on in corporations and because much of financial accounting is concerned with reporting to the public, this book focuses on the corporate form of business.

Accounting for corporations, sole proprietorships, and partnerships is the same, except for the owners' equity section of the balance sheet. The owners' equity section for a sole proprietorship consists of the owners' capital account, whereas the owners' equity section for a partnership has a capital account for each partner. The more complicated owners' equity section for a corporation will be described in detail in this book.

The Financial Statements

The principal financial statements of a corporation are the balance sheet, income statement, and statement of cash flows. Notes accompany these financial statements. To evaluate the financial condition, the profitability, and cash flows of an entity, the user needs to understand the statements and related notes.

Exhibit 2-1 illustrates the interrelationship of the balance sheet, income statement, and statement of cash flows. The most basic statement is the balance sheet; the other statements explain the changes between two balance sheet dates.

Balance Sheet (Statement of Financial Position)

A balance sheet shows the financial condition of an accounting entity as of a particular date. The balance sheet consists of three major sections: assets, the resources of the firm; liabilities, the debts of the firm; and stockholders' equity, the owners' interest in the firm.

At any point in time, the total assets amount must equal the total amount of the contributions of the creditors and owners. This is expressed in the accounting equation:

$$\text{Assets} = \text{Liabilities} + \text{Stockholders' Equity}$$

In simplistic form, the stockholders' equity of a corporation appears as follows:

Stockholders' Equity	
Common stock	$200,000
Retained earnings	50,000
	$250,000

This indicates that stockholders contributed (invested) $200,000, and prior earnings less prior dividends have been retained in the entity in the net amount of $50,000 (retained earnings).

Statement of Stockholders' Equity (Reconciliation of Stockholders' Equity Accounts)

Firms are required to present reconciliations of the beginning and ending balances of their stockholders' equity accounts. This is accomplished by presenting a "statement of stockholders' equity." Retained earnings is one of the accounts in stockholders' equity.

Retained earnings links the balance sheet to the income statement. Retained earnings is increased by net income and decreased by net losses and dividends paid to stockholders. There are some other possible increases or decreases to retained earnings besides income (losses) and dividends. For the purposes of this chapter, retained earnings will be described as prior earnings less prior dividends.

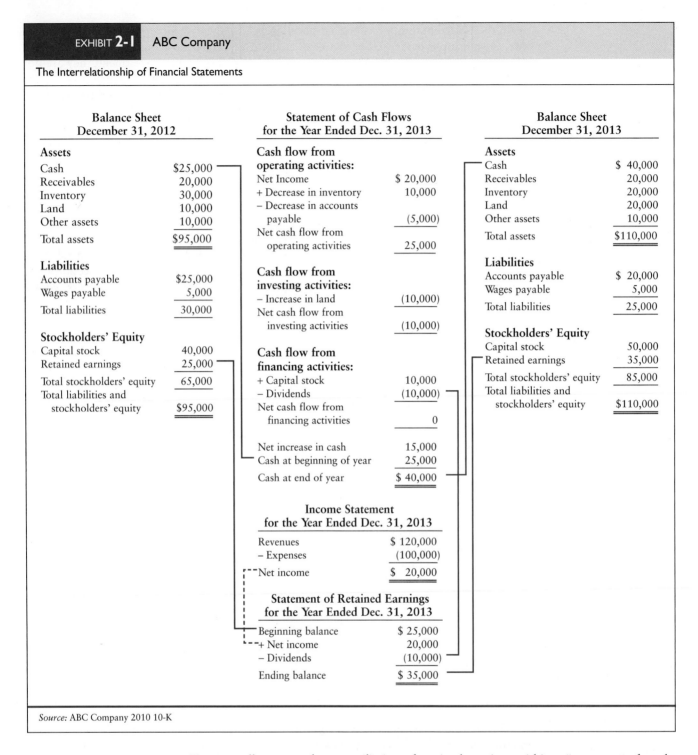

EXHIBIT **2-1**   ABC Company

The Interrelationship of Financial Statements

Balance Sheet
December 31, 2012

Assets

Cash	$25,000
Receivables	20,000
Inventory	30,000
Land	10,000
Other assets	10,000
Total assets	$95,000

Liabilities

Accounts payable	$25,000
Wages payable	5,000
Total liabilities	30,000

Stockholders' Equity

Capital stock	40,000
Retained earnings	25,000
Total stockholders' equity	65,000
Total liabilities and stockholders' equity	$95,000

Statement of Cash Flows
for the Year Ended Dec. 31, 2013

Cash flow from operating activities:

Net Income	$ 20,000
+ Decrease in inventory	10,000
– Decrease in accounts payable	(5,000)
Net cash flow from operating activities	25,000

Cash flow from investing activities:

– Increase in land	(10,000)
Net cash flow from investing activities	(10,000)

Cash flow from financing activities:

+ Capital stock	10,000
– Dividends	(10,000)
Net cash flow from financing activities	0
Net increase in cash	15,000
Cash at beginning of year	25,000
Cash at end of year	$ 40,000

Income Statement
for the Year Ended Dec. 31, 2013

Revenues	$ 120,000
– Expenses	(100,000)
Net income	$ 20,000

Statement of Retained Earnings
for the Year Ended Dec. 31, 2013

Beginning balance	$ 25,000
+ Net income	20,000
– Dividends	(10,000)
Ending balance	$ 35,000

Balance Sheet
December 31, 2013

Assets

Cash	$ 40,000
Receivables	20,000
Inventory	20,000
Land	20,000
Other assets	10,000
Total assets	$110,000

Liabilities

Accounts payable	$ 20,000
Wages payable	5,000
Total liabilities	25,000

Stockholders' Equity

Capital stock	50,000
Retained earnings	35,000
Total stockholders' equity	85,000
Total liabilities and stockholders' equity	$110,000

Source: ABC Company 2010 10-K

Firms usually present the reconciliation of retained earnings within a "statement of stockholders' equity." Some firms present the reconciliation of retained earnings at the bottom of the income statement (combined income statement and retained earnings). In this case, the other stockholders' equity accounts may be reconciled in a statement that excludes retained earnings. An additional review of the statement of stockholders' equity is in Chapter 3.

Income Statement (Statement of Earnings)

The **income statement** summarizes revenues and expenses and gains and losses, ending with net income. It summarizes the results of operations for a particular period of time. Net income is included in retained earnings in the stockholders' equity section of the balance sheet. (This is necessary for the balance sheet to balance.)

Statement of Cash Flows (Statement of Inflows and Outflows of Cash)

The statement of cash flows details the inflows and outflows of cash during a specified period of time—the same period that is used for the income statement. The statement of cash flows consists of three sections: cash flows from operating activities, cash flows from investing activities, and cash flows from financing activities.

Notes

The notes to the financial statements are used to present additional information about items included in the financial statements and to present additional financial information. Notes are an integral part of financial statements. A detailed review of notes is essential to understanding the financial statements.

Certain information must be presented in notes. Accounting policies are to be disclosed as the first note or in a separate summary of significant accounting policies (preceding the first note). Accounting policies include such items as the method of inventory valuation and depreciation policies. Other information specifically requiring note disclosure is the existence of contingent liabilities and some subsequent events.

Contingent liabilities are dependent on the occurrence or nonoccurrence of one or more future events to confirm the liability. The settlement of litigation or the ruling of a tax court would be examples of the confirmation of a contingent liability. Signing as guarantor on a loan creates another type of contingent liability.

An estimated loss from a contingent liability should be charged to income and be established as a liability only if the loss is considered probable and the amount is reasonably determinable. A contingent liability that is recorded is also frequently described in a note. A loss contingency that is reasonably possible, but not probable, must be disclosed even if the loss is not reasonably estimable. (This loss contingency is not charged to income or established as a liability.) A loss contingency that is less than reasonably possible does not need to be disclosed, but disclosure may be desirable if there is an unusually large potential loss.

Exhibit 2-2 illustrates a contingent liability note for FedEx Corporation whose fiscal year ended May 31, 2010. This contingency related to legal proceedings.

On May 13, 2009, the European Commission levied its largest ever anticompetitive fine against Intel Corporation. The European Commission fine was for $1.45 billion.

Subsequent events occur after the balance sheet date, but before the statements are issued. Two varieties of subsequent events are as follows. The first type consists of events related to conditions that existed at the balance sheet date, affect the estimates in the statements, and require adjustment of the statements before issuance. For example, if additional information is obtained indicating that a major customer's account receivable is not collectible, an adjustment will be made. The second type consists of events that provide evidence about conditions that did not exist at the balance sheet date and do not require adjustment of the statements. If failure to disclose these events would be misleading, disclosure should take the form of notes or supplementary schedules. Examples of the second type of such

---

EXHIBIT **2-2**	FedEx Corporation*

For the Fiscal Year Ended May 31, 2010
Contingencies (In Part)

Notes to Consolidated Financial Statements (In Part)

NOTE 16: CONTINGENCIES (In Part)

Wage-and-Hour. We are a defendant in a number of lawsuits containing various class-action allegations of wage-and-hour violations. The plaintiffs in these lawsuits allege, among other things, that they were forced to work "off the clock," were not paid overtime or were not provided work breaks or other benefits. The complaints generally seek unspecified monetary damages, injunctive relief, or both. The following describes the wage-and-hour matters that have been certified as class actions.

*"FedEx Corporation ("FedEx") provides a broad portfolio of transportation, e-commerce and business services through companies competing collectively, operating independently and managed collaboratively, under the respected FedEx brand." 10-K
Source: Fedex Corporation 2010 10-K

events include the sale of securities, the settlement of litigation, or casualty loss. Other examples of subsequent events might be debt incurred, reduced, or refinanced; business combinations pending or effected; discontinued operations; employee benefit plans; and capital stock issued or purchased. Exhibit 2-3 describes a subsequent event for Yum! Brands, Inc. and subsidiaries for the fiscal year ended December 25, 2010.

EXHIBIT **2-3**	Yum! Brands, Inc. And Subsidiaries*

For the Fiscal Year Ended December 25, 2010
Subsequent Event

Note 21 – Subsequent Event

Subsequent to the end of our fourth quarter, we decided to place our Long John Silver's and A&W All-American Food Restaurants brands for sale and began the process to identify a buyer. In the first quarter of 2011, we anticipate that we will recognize a non-cash pre-tax impairment loss in Special Items as a result of our decision to sell. The amount of the expected pre-tax loss as well as the related tax impact will be dependent upon indications we receive as to potential sales prices and structures. We do not expect the eventual sale to have a material impact to our ongoing earnings or cash flows.

*"YUM is the world's largest quick service restaurant ("QSR") company based on number of system units, with more than 37,000 units in more than 100 countries and territories. Through the five concepts of KFC, Pizza Hut, Taco Bell, LJS and A&W (the "Concepts"), the Company develops, operates, franchises and licenses a worldwide system of restaurants which prepare, package and sell a menu of competitively priced food items." 10-K
Source: Yum! Brands, Inc. and Subsidiaries 2010 10-K

The Accounting Cycle

The sequence of accounting procedures completed during each accounting period is called the accounting cycle. A broad summary of the steps of the accounting cycle includes:

1. Recording transactions
2. Recording adjusting entries
3. Preparing the financial statements

Recording Transactions

A **transaction** is an event that causes a change in a company's assets, liabilities, or stockholders' equity, thus changing the company's financial position. Transactions may be external or internal to the company. External transactions involve outside parties, while internal transactions are confined within the company. For example, sales is an external transaction, whereas the use of equipment is internal.

Transactions must be recorded in a **journal** (book of original entry). All transactions could be recorded in the general journal. However, companies use a number of special journals to record most transactions. The special journals are designed to improve record-keeping efficiency that could not be obtained by using only the general journal. The general journal is then used only to record transactions for which the company does not have a special journal. A transaction recorded in a journal is referred to as a **journal entry**.

All transactions are recorded in a journal (journal entry) and are later posted from the journals to a **general ledger** (group of accounts for a company). After posting, the general ledger accounts contain the same information as the journals, but the information has been summarized by account.

Accounts store the monetary information from the recording of transactions. Examples of accounts include Cash, Land, and Buildings. An accounting system can be computerized or manual. A manual system using T-accounts is usually used for textbook explanations because a T-account is a logical format.

T-accounts have a left (debit) side and a right (credit) side. An example T-account follows:

Cash

Debit	Credit

A double-entry system has been devised to handle the recording of transactions. In a double-entry system, each transaction is recorded, with the total dollar amount of the debits equal to the total dollar amount of the credits. The scheme of the double-entry system revolves around the **accounting equation:**

$$\text{Assets} = \text{Liabilities} + \text{Stockholders' Equity}$$

With the double-entry system, *debit* merely means the left side of an account, while *credit* means the right side. Each transaction recorded must have an equal number of dollars on the left side as it does on the right side. Several accounts could be involved in a single transaction, but the debits and credits must still be equal.

The debit and credit technique has gained acceptance over a long period of time. This book will not make you competent in the use of the double-entry (debit and credit) technique. Rather, it will enhance your understanding of the end result of the accounting process and enable you to use the financial accounting information in a meaningful way.

Asset, liability, and stockholders' equity accounts are referred to as **permanent accounts** because the balances in these accounts carry forward to the next accounting period. Balances in revenue, expense, gain, loss, and dividend accounts, described as **temporary accounts**, are closed to retained earnings and not carried into the next period.

Exhibit 2-4 illustrates the double-entry system. Notice that the permanent accounts are represented by the accounting equation: assets = liabilities + stockholders' equity. The temporary accounts are represented by revenue, expense, and dividends. (Gains and losses would be treated like revenue and expense, respectively.) The balance sheet will not balance until the temporary accounts are closed to retained earnings.

EXHIBIT **2-4**	Double-Entry System

Illustrating Relationship between Permanent and Temporary Accounts

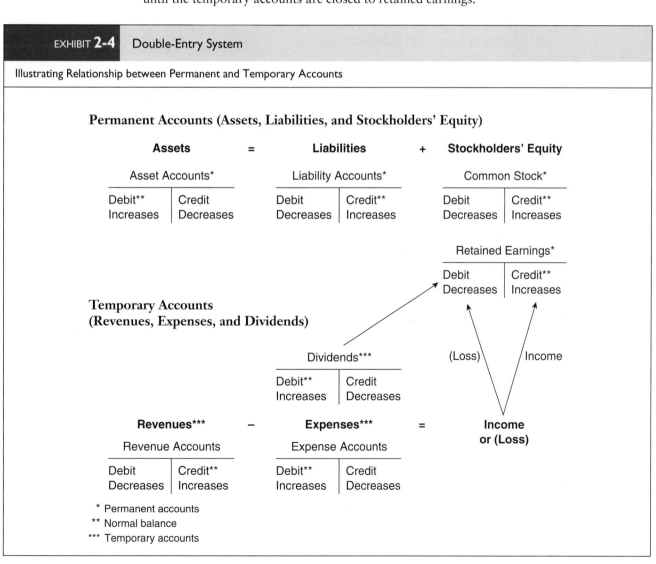

Recording Adjusting Entries

Earlier, a distinction was made between the accrual basis of accounting and the cash basis. It was indicated that the accrual basis requires that revenue be recognized when realized (realization concept) and expenses recognized when incurred (matching concept). The point of cash receipt for revenue and cash disbursement for expenses is not important under the accrual basis when determining income. Usually, a company must use the accrual basis to achieve a reasonable result for the balance sheet and the income statement.

The accrual basis needs numerous adjustments to account balances at the end of the accounting period. For example, $1,000 paid for insurance on October 1 for a one-year period (October 1–September 30) could have been recorded as a debit to Insurance Expense ($1,000) and a credit to Cash ($1,000). If this company prepares financial statements on December 31, it would be necessary to adjust Insurance Expense because not all of the insurance expense should be recognized in the three-month period October 1–December 31. The adjustment would debit Prepaid Insurance, an asset account, for $750 and credit Insurance Expense for $750. Thus, insurance expense would be presented on the income statement for this period as $250, and an asset, prepaid insurance, would be presented on the balance sheet as $750.

Adjusting entries are recorded in the general journal and then posted to the general ledger. Once the accounts are adjusted to the accrual basis, the financial statements can be prepared.

Preparing the Financial Statements

The accountant uses the accounts after the adjustments have been made to prepare the financial statements. These statements represent the output of the accounting system. Two of the principal financial statements, the income statement and the balance sheet, can be prepared directly from the adjusted accounts. Preparation of the statement of cash flows requires further analysis of the accounts.

Treadway Commission

Treadway Commission is the popular name for the National Commission on Fraudulent Reporting named after its first chairman, former SEC Commissioner James C. Treadway. The Commission has issued a number of recommendations for the prevention of fraud in financial reports, ethics, and effective internal controls. The Treadway Commission is a voluntary private-sector organization formed in 1985.[1]

The Committee of Sponsoring Organizations of the Treadway Commission (COSO) has released reports detailing internal control systems. These reports represent the standard for evaluating the effectiveness of internal control systems.

Section 404 of the Sarbanes-Oxley Act emphasizes the importance of internal control and makes management responsible for internal controls. The independent public accounting firm is required to give an opinion as to management's assessment of internal control and the effectiveness of internal control over financial reporting as of the balance sheet date.

The Management's Report on Internal Control over Financial Reporting and the independent public accounting firm report to the shareholders, and the board of directors often refers to the criteria established on internal control by COSO.

Auditor's Opinion

An auditor (certified public accountant) conducts an independent examination of the accounting information presented by the business and issues a report thereon. An auditor's report is the formal statement of the auditor's opinion of the financial statements after conducting an audit. Audit opinions are classified as follows:

1. UNQUALIFIED OPINION. This opinion states that the financial statements present fairly, in all material respects, the financial position, results of operations, and cash flows of the entity, in conformity with generally accepted accounting principles.
2. QUALIFIED OPINION. A qualified opinion states that, except for the effects of the matter(s) to which the qualification relates, the financial statements present fairly, in all material respects, the financial position, results of operations, and cash flows of the entity, in conformity with generally accepted accounting principles.

3. ADVERSE OPINION. This opinion states that the financial statements do *not* present fairly the financial position, results of operations, and cash flows of the entity, in conformity with generally accepted accounting principles.

4. DISCLAIMER OF OPINION. A disclaimer of opinion states that the auditor does not express an opinion on the financial statements. A disclaimer of opinion is rendered when the auditor has not performed an audit sufficient in scope to form an opinion.

Since the passage of Sarbanes-Oxley, the form of the audit opinion can vary substantially. Private companies are not under Sarbanes-Oxley, but an increasing number of private companies are complying with parts of the law. Some of the reasons for private companies to follow the law are the following:

1. Owners hope to sell the company or take it public.
2. Directors who sit on public company boards see the law's benefits.
3. Executives believe strong internal controls will improve efficiency.
4. Customers require strong internal controls.
5. Lenders are more likely to approve loans.[2]

The typical unqualified (or clean) opinion for private companies has three paragraphs. The first paragraph indicates that the financial statements have been audited and are the responsibility of the company's management. This paragraph states that the auditors have the responsibility to either express an opinion on these statements based on the audit or to disclaim an opinion.

The second paragraph indicates that the audit has been conducted in accordance with generally accepted auditing standards. This will typically be expressed in terms of standards of the Public Company Accounting Oversight Board (United States). These standards require the auditor to plan and perform the audit to obtain reasonable assurance about whether the financial statements are free of material misstatement. This paragraph also confirms that the audit provided a reasonable basis for an opinion.

The third paragraph gives an opinion on the statements—that they are in conformity with GAAP. In certain circumstances, an unqualified opinion on the financial statements may require that the auditor add an explanatory paragraph after the opinion paragraph. In this paragraph, the auditor may express agreement with a departure from a designated principle, describe a material uncertainty, detail a change in accounting principle, or express doubt as to the ability of the entity to continue as a going concern. An explanatory paragraph may also be added to emphasize a particular matter.

The audit opinion of a public company is similar to an opinion for a private company except that the public company comments will be added as to the effectiveness of internal control over financial reporting. An opinion is expressed as to management's assessment of, and the effective operation of, internal control over financial reporting.

When examining financial statements, review the independent auditor's report. It can be important to your analysis. From the point of view of analysis, financial statements accompanied by an unqualified opinion without an explanatory paragraph or explanatory language carry the highest degree of reliability. This type of report indicates that the financial statements do not contain a material departure from GAAP and that the audit was not limited as to scope.

When an unqualified opinion contains an explanatory paragraph or explanatory language, try to decide how seriously to regard the departure from a straight unqualified opinion. For example, an explanatory paragraph because of a change in accounting principle would not usually be regarded as serious, although it would be important to your analysis. An explanatory paragraph because of a material uncertainty would often be regarded as a serious matter.

You are likely to regard a qualified opinion or an adverse opinion as casting serious doubts on the reliability of the financial statements. In each case, you must read the auditor's report carefully to form your opinion.

A disclaimer of opinion indicates that you should not look to the auditor's report as an indication of the reliability of the statements. When rendering this type of report, the auditor has not performed an audit sufficient in scope to form an opinion, or the auditor is not independent.

In some cases, outside accountants are associated with financial statements when they have performed less than an audit. The accountant's report then indicates that the financial statements have been reviewed or compiled.

A **review** consists principally of inquiries made to company personnel and analytical procedures applied to financial data. It has substantially less scope than an examination in accordance with generally accepted auditing standards, the objective of which is the expression of an opinion regarding the financial statements taken as a whole. Accordingly, the accountant does not express an opinion. The accountant's report will indicate that the accountants are not aware of any material modifications that should be made to the financial statements in order for them to be in conformity with GAAP; or the report will indicate departures from GAAP. A departure from GAAP may result from using one or more accounting principles without reasonable justification, the omission of necessary note disclosures, or the omission of the statement of cash flows.

In general, the reliance that can be placed on financial statements accompanied by an accountant's review report is substantially less than those accompanied by an audit report. Remember that the accountant's report does not express an opinion on reviewed financial statements.

When the outside accountant presents only financial information as provided by management, he or she is said to have **compiled** the financial statements. The compilation report states that the accountant has not audited or reviewed the financial statements. Therefore, the accountant does not express an opinion or any other form of assurance about them. If an accountant performs a compilation and becomes aware of deficiencies in the statements, then the accountant's report characterizes the deficiencies as follows:

- Omission of substantially all disclosures
- Omission of statement of cash flows
- Accounting principles not generally accepted

Sometimes financial statements are presented without an accompanying accountant's report. This means that the statements have not been audited, reviewed, or compiled. Such statements are solely the representation of management.

Auditor's Report on the Firm's Internal Controls

For public companies reporting under Sarbanes-Oxley, a report on the firm's internal controls is required in addition to the audit report. The internal control report is usually much longer than the audit report. For some firms, the audit opinion and the report on the firm's internal controls have been combined. This results in one audit report that can be very long.

Exhibit 2-5 presents the audit report for T. Rowe Price Group, Inc. It is an unqualified opinion. T. Rowe Price Group, Inc., is a public company reporting under Sarbanes-Oxley. Exhibit 2-6 presents the auditor's report on T. Rowe Price Group, Inc.'s internal controls.

EXHIBIT **2-5**	T. Rowe Price Group, Inc.*

Audit Opinion – Unqualified Opinion – 2010 Annual Report

Report of Independent Registered Public Accounting Firm

The Board of Directors and Stockholders
   T. Rowe Price Group, Inc.:
   We have audited the accompanying consolidated balance sheets of T. Rowe Price Group, Inc. and subsidiaries ("the Company") as of December 31, 2010 and 2009, and the related consolidated statements of income, stockholders' equity, and cash flows for each of the years in the three-year period ended December 31, 2010. These consolidated financial statements are the responsibility of the Company's management. Our responsibility is to express an opinion on these consolidated financial statements based on our audits.

*"T. Rowe Price Group is a financial services holding company that derives its consolidated revenues and net income primarily from investment advisory services that its subsidiaries provide to individual and institutional investors in the sponsored T. Rowe Price mutual funds and other investment portfolios." 10-K
Source: T.Rowe Price Group, Inc, 2010 10-K

EXHIBIT **2-5**	T. Rowe Price Group, Inc. *(continued)*

We conducted our audits in accordance with the standards of the Public Company Accounting Oversight Board (United States). Those standards require that we plan and perform the audit to obtain reasonable assurance about whether the financial statements are free of material misstatement. An audit includes examining, on a test basis, evidence supporting the amounts and disclosures in the financial statements. An audit also includes assessing the accounting principles used and significant estimates made by management, as well as evaluating the overall financial statement presentation. We believe that our audits provide a reasonable basis for our opinion.

In our opinion, the consolidated financial statements referred to above present fairly, in all material respects, the financial position of T. Rowe Price Group, Inc. and subsidiaries as of December 31, 2010 and 2009, and the results of their operations and their cash flows for each of the years in the three-year period ended December 31, 2010, in conformity with U.S. generally accepted accounting principles.

We also have audited, in accordance with the standards of the Public Company Accounting Oversight Board (United States), the Company's internal control over financial reporting as of December 31, 2010, based on criteria established in Internal Control – Integrated Framework issued by the Committee of Sponsoring Organizations of the Treadway Commission (COSO), and our report dated February 8, 2011, expressed an unqualified opinion on the effectiveness of the Company's internal control over financial reporting.

/s/ KPMG LLP

Baltimore, Maryland
February 8, 2011

EXHIBIT **2-6**	T. Rowe Price Group, Inc.*

Auditors Report on the Firm's Internal Controls – 2010 Annual Report

Report of Independent Registered Public Accounting Firm

The Board of Directors and Stockholders
T. Rowe Price Group, Inc.:

We have audited T. Rowe Price Group, Inc. and subsidiaries' ("the Company") internal control over financial reporting as of December 31, 2010, based on criteria established in Internal Control – Integrated Framework issued by the Committee of Sponsoring Organizations of the Treadway Commission (COSO). The Company's management is responsible for maintaining effective internal control over financial reporting and for its assessment of the effectiveness of internal control over financial reporting, included in the accompanying Report of Management on Internal Control Over Financial Reporting. Our responsibility is to express an opinion on the Company's internal control over financial reporting based on our audit.

We conducted our audit in accordance with the standards of the Public Company Accounting Oversight Board (United States). Those standards require that we plan and perform the audit to obtain reasonable assurance about whether effective internal control over financial reporting was maintained in all material respects. Our audit included obtaining an understanding of internal control over financial reporting, assessing the risk that a material weakness exists, and testing and evaluating the design and operating effectiveness of internal control based on the assessed risk. Our audit also included performing such other procedures as we considered necessary in the circumstances. We believe that our audit provides a reasonable basis for our opinion.

A company's internal control over financial reporting is a process designed to provide reasonable assurance regarding the reliability of financial reporting and the preparation of financial

* "T. Rowe Price Group is a financial services holding company that derives its consolidated revenues and net income primarily from investment advisory services that its subsidiaries provide to individual and institutional investors in the sponsored T. Rowe Price mutual funds and other investment portfolios." 10-K
Source: T.Rowe Price Group, Inc, 2010 10-K

(continued)

EXHIBIT **2-6**	T. Rowe Price Group, Inc. (*continued*)

statements for external purposes in accordance with generally accepted accounting principles. A company's internal control over financial reporting includes those policies and procedures that (1) pertain to the maintenance of records that, in reasonable detail, accurately and fairly reflect the transactions and dispositions of the assets of the company; (2) provide reasonable assurance that transactions are recorded as necessary to permit preparation of financial statements in accordance with generally accepted accounting principles, and that receipts and expenditures of the company are being made only in accordance with authorizations of management and directors of the company; and (3) provide reasonable assurance regarding prevention or timely detection of unauthorized acquisition, use, or disposition of the company's assets that could have a material effect on the financial statements.

Because of its inherent limitations, internal control over financial reporting may not prevent or detect misstatements. Also, projections of any evaluation of effectiveness to future periods are subject to the risk that controls may become inadequate because of changes in conditions, or that the degree of compliance with the policies or procedures may deteriorate.

In our opinion, T. Rowe Price Group, Inc. and subsidiaries maintained, in all material respects, effective internal control over financial reporting as of December 31, 2010, based on criteria established in Internal Control – Integrated Framework issued by the Committee of Sponsoring Organizations of the Treadway Commission.

We also have audited, in accordance with the standards of the Public Company Accounting Oversight Board (United States), the consolidated balance sheets of T. Rowe Price Group, Inc. and subsidiaries as of December 31, 2010 and 2009, and the related consolidated statements of income, stockholders' equity, and cash flows for each of the years in the three-year period ended December 31, 2010, and our report dated February 8, 2011, expressed an unqualified opinion on those consolidated financial statements.

/s/ KPMG LLP

Baltimore, Maryland
February 8, 2011

Report of Management on Internal Control over Financial Reporting

Under Sarbanes-Oxley, management of public companies must present a Report of Management on Internal Control over Financial Reporting. Exhibit 2-7 presents the internal control report of management for T. Rowe Price Group, Inc., that was presented with its 2010 annual report.

EXHIBIT **2-7**	T. Rowe Price Group, Inc.*

2010 Annual Report

Report of Management on Internal Control Over Financial Reporting

To the Stockholders of T. Rowe Price Group, Inc.:

We, together with other members of management of T. Rowe Price Group, are responsible for establishing and maintaining adequate internal control over the company's financial reporting. Internal control over financial reporting is the process designed under our supervision, and effected by the company's board of directors, management, and other personnel, to provide reasonable assurance regarding the reliability of financial reporting and the preparation of the company's financial statements for external purposes in accordance with accounting principles generally accepted in the United States of America.

*"T. Rowe Price Group is a financial services holding company that derives its consolidated revenues and net income primarily from investment advisory services that its subsidiaries provide to individual and institutional investors in the sponsored T. Rowe Price mutual funds and other investment portfolios." 10-K

Source: T.Rowe Price Group, Inc, 2010 10-K

| EXHIBIT **2-7** | T. Rowe Price Group, Inc. (*continued*) |

There are inherent limitations in the effectiveness of internal control over financial reporting, including the possibility that misstatements may not be prevented or detected. Accordingly, even effective internal controls over financial reporting can provide only reasonable assurance with respect to financial statement preparation. Furthermore, the effectiveness of internal controls can change with circumstances.

Management has evaluated the effectiveness of internal control over financial reporting as of December 31, 2010, in relation to criteria described in Internal Control – Integrated Framework issued by the Committee of Sponsoring Organizations of the Treadway Commission (COSO). Based on management's assessment, we believe that the company's internal control over financial reporting was effective as of December 31, 2010.

KPMG LLP, an independent registered public accounting firm, has audited our financial statements that are included in this annual report and expressed an unqualified opinion thereon. KPMG has also expressed an unqualified opinion on the effective operation of our internal control over financial reporting as of December 31, 2010.

February 8, 2011

/s/ James A.C. Kennedy
Chief Executive Officer and President

/s/ Kenneth V. Moreland
Vice President and Chief Financial Officer

Management's Responsibility for Financial Statements

The responsibility for the preparation and for the integrity of financial statements rests with management. The auditor is responsible for conducting an independent examination of the statements and expressing an opinion on the financial statements based on the audit. To make financial statement users aware of management's responsibility, some companies have presented management statements to shareholders as part of the annual report. Exhibit 2-8 shows an example of a report of management's responsibility for financial statements as presented by Kellogg Company in its 2010 annual report.

| EXHIBIT **2-8** | Kellogg Company* |

Management's Responsibility for Financial Statements – 2010 Annual Report

Management is responsible for the preparation of the Company's consolidated financial statements and related notes. We believe that the consolidated financial statements present the Company's financial position and results of operations in conformity with accounting principles that are generally accepted in the United States, using our best estimates and judgments as required.

The independent registered public accounting firm audits the Company's consolidated financial statements in accordance with the standards of the Public Company Accounting Oversight Board and provides an objective, independent review of the fairness of reported operating results and financial position.

The board of directors of the Company has an Audit Committee composed of five non-management Directors. The Committee meets regularly with management, internal auditors, and the independent registered public accounting firm to review accounting, internal control, auditing and financial reporting matters.

Formal policies and procedures, including an active Ethics and Business Conduct program, support the internal controls and are designed to ensure employees adhere to the highest standards of personal and professional integrity. We have a rigorous internal audit program that independently evaluates the adequacy and effectiveness of these internal controls.

*"Kellogg Company, founded in 1906 and incorporated in Delaware in 1922, and its subsidiaries are engaged in the manufacture and marketing of ready-to-eat cereal and convenience foods." 10-K
Source: Kellogg Company 2010 10-K

The SEC's Integrated Disclosure System

In general, in the United States, the SEC has the authority to prescribe external financial reporting requirements for companies with securities sold to the general public. Under this jurisdiction, the SEC requires that certain financial statement information be included in the annual report to shareholders. This annual report, along with certain supplementary information, must then be included, or incorporated by reference, in the annual filing to the SEC, known as the 10-K report or Form 10-K. The Form 10-K is due 60 days, 75 days, or 90 days following the end of the company's fiscal year, depending on the market value of the common stock (see Exhibit 2-9). The annual report and the Form 10-K include audited financial statements.

EXHIBIT **2-9**	Form 10-K and 10-Q Deadline		
Category of Filer		Form 10-K Deadline	Form 10-Q Deadline
Large accelerated filer ($700 million or more market value*)		60 days	40 days
Accelerated filer ($75 million or more and less than $700 million market value*)		75 days	40 days
Nonaccelerated filer (less than $75 million market value*)		90 days	45 days

*Market value is the worldwide market value of outstanding voting and nonvoting common equity held by nonaffiliates.
Source: Adapted from Securities and Exchange Commission Release No. 33-8644, Revisions to Accelerated Filer Definition and Accelerated Deadlines for Filing Periodic Reports, December 21, 2005

The SEC promotes an integrated disclosure system between the annual report and the Form 10-K. The goals are to improve the quality of disclosure, lighten the disclosure load, standardize information requirements, and achieve uniformity of annual reports and Form 10-K filings.

In addition to the company's primary financial statements, the Form 10-K must include the following:

1. Information on the market for holders of common stock and related securities, including high and low sales price, frequency and amount of dividends, and number of shares.
2. Five-year summary of selected financial data, including net sales or operating revenues, income from continuing operations, total assets, long-term obligations, redeemable preferred stock, and cash dividends per share. (Some companies elect to present data for more than five years and/or expand the disclosure.) Trend analysis is emphasized.
3. Management's discussion and analysis (MDA) of financial condition and results of operations. Specifically required is discussion of liquidity, capital resources, and results of operations.
4. Two years of audited balance sheets and three years of audited income statements and statements of cash flow.
5. Disclosure of the domestic and foreign components of pretax income, unless foreign components are considered to be immaterial.

SEC requirements force management to focus on the financial statements as a whole, rather than on just the income statement and operations. Where trend information is relevant, discussion should center on the five-year summary. Emphasis should be on favorable or unfavorable trends and on identification of significant events or uncertainties. This discussion should provide the analyst with a reasonable summary of the position of the firm.

Exhibit 2-10 presents a summary of the major parts of the Form 10-K. In practice, some of the required information in the Form 10-K is incorporated by reference. Incorporated by reference means that the information is presented outside the Form 10-K, and a reference in the Form 10-K indicates where the information can be found.

A review of a company's Form 10-K can reveal information that is not available in the annual report. For example, Item 2 of the Form 10-K reveals a detailed listing of properties and indicates if the property is leased or owned.

EXHIBIT **2-10**	General Summary of Form 10-K

Part I

Item 1.	Business.
Item 1A.	Risk Factors.
Item 1B.	Unresolved Staff Comments.
Item 2.	Properties.
Item 3.	Legal Proceedings.
Item 4.	Submission of Matters to a Vote of Security Holders.

Part II

Item 5.	Market for Registrant's Common Equity, Related Stockholder Matters, and Issuer Purchases of Equity Securities.
Item 6.	Selected Financial Data.
Item 7.	Management's Discussion and Analysis of Financial Condition and Results of Operations.
Item 7A.	Qualitative and Quantitative Disclosures about Market Risk.
Item 8.	Financial Statements and Supplementary Data.
Item 9.	Changes in and Disagreements with Accountants on Accounting and Financial Disclosure.
Item 9A.	Controls and Procedures.
Item 9B.	Other Information.

Part III

Item 10.	Directors, Executive Officers, and Corporate Governance.
Item 11.	Executive Compensation.
Item 12.	Security Ownership of Certain Beneficial Owners and Management and Related Stockholders' Matters.
Item 13.	Certain Relationships and Related Transactions, and Director Independence.
Item 14.	Principal Accountant Fees and Services.

Part IV

Item 15.	Exhibits and Financial Statement Schedules.

Signatures

Exhibit	Index

The SEC requires that a quarterly report (Form 10-Q), containing financial statements and a management discussion and analysis, be submitted within either 40 or 45 days following the end of the quarter, depending on the market value of the common stock (see Exhibit 2-9). (The Form 10-Q is not required for the fourth quarter of the fiscal year.) Most companies also issue a quarterly report to stockholders. The Form 10-Q and quarterly reports are unaudited.

Exhibit 2-11 presents a summary of the major parts of the Form 10-Q. As with the 10-K, in practice some of the required information is incorporated by reference.

EXHIBIT **2-11**	General Summary of Form 10-Q

Filed for each of the first three fiscal quarters of the company's fiscal year

Part I Financial Information
    Item 1 Financial Statements
        Unaudited Condensed Consolidated Balance Sheets
        Unaudited Condensed Consolidated Statements of Income
        Unaudited Condensed Consolidated Statements of Cash Flows
        Notes to the Unaudited Condensed Consolidated Financial Statements
    Item 2 Management's Discussion and Analysis of Financial Condition and Results of Operations
    Item 3 Quantitative and Qualitative Disclosures about Market Risk
    Item 4 Controls and Procedures

(continued)

EXHIBIT **2-11**	General Summary of Form 10-Q (*continued*)

Part II Other Information
    Item 1   Financial Statements
    Item 1A Risk Factors
    Item 2   Unregistered Sales of Equity Securities and Use of Proceeds
    Item 3   Defaults Upon Senior Securities
    Item 4   (Removed and Reserved)
    Item 5   Other Information
    Item 6   Exhibits

In addition to the Form 10-K and Form 10-Q, a Form 8-K must be submitted to the SEC to report special events. Some events required to be reported are changes in principal stockholders, changes in auditors, acquisitions and divestitures, bankruptcy, and resignation of directors. The Form 8-K is due 15 days following the event.

The Forms 10-K, 10-Q, and 8-K filings are available to the public. Many companies are reluctant to send these reports to nonstockholders. In public companies, these reports can be found at www.sec.gov.

Proxy

The **proxy**, the solicitation sent to stockholders for the election of directors and for the approval of other corporation actions, represents the shareholder authorization regarding the casting of that shareholder's vote. The proxy contains notice of the annual meeting, beneficial ownership (name, address, and share ownership data of shareholders holding more than 5% of outstanding shares), board of directors, standing committees, compensation of directors, compensation of executive officers, employee benefit plans, certain transactions with officers and directors, relationship with independent accountants, and other business.

The proxy rules provided under the 1934 Securities Exchange Act are applicable to all securities registered under Section 12 of the Act. The SEC gains its influence over the annual report through provisions of the Act that cover proxy statements.

The SEC's proxy rules of particular interest to investors involve executive compensation disclosure, performance graph, and retirement plans for executive officers. These rules are designed to improve shareholders' understanding of the compensation paid to senior executives and directors, the criteria used in reaching compensation decisions, and the relationship between compensation and corporate performance.

Among other matters, the executive compensation rules call for four highly formatted disclosure tables and the disclosure of the compensation committee's basis for compensation decisions.

The four tables disclosing executive compensation are as follows:

- A summary executive compensation table covering compensation for the company's chief executive officer and its four other most highly compensated executives for the last three years.
- Two tables detailing options and stock appreciation rights.
- A long-term incentive plan award table.

The performance graph is a line graph comparing the cumulative total shareholder return with performance indicators of the overall stock market and either the published industry index or the registrant-determined peer comparison. This performance graph must be presented for a five-year period.

The pension plan table for executive officers discloses the estimated annual benefits payable upon retirement for any defined benefit or actuarial plan under which benefits are determined primarily by final compensation (or average final compensation) and years of service. Immediately following the table, additional disclosure is required. This disclosure includes items such as the relationship of the covered compensation to the compensation reported in the summary compensation table and the estimated credited years of service for each of the named executive officers.

For public companies, the proxy can be found at www.sec.gov.

Summary Annual Report

A reporting option available to public companies is to issue a **summary annual report.** A summary annual report, a condensed report, omits much of the financial information typically included in an annual report. A typical full annual report has more financial pages than nonfinancial pages. A summary annual report generally has more nonfinancial pages.[3] When a company issues a summary annual report, the proxy materials it sends to shareholders must include a set of fully audited statements and other required financial disclosures.

A summary annual report is *not* adequate for reasonable analysis. For companies that issue a summary annual report, request a copy of their proxy and the Form 10-K. Even for companies that issue a full annual report, it is also good to obtain a copy of the proxy materials and the Form 10-K. Some companies issue a joint annual report and Form 10-K, while other companies issue a joint annual report and proxy. A few companies issue a joint annual report, Form 10-K, and proxy. These joint reports are usually labeled as the annual report.

The Efficient Market Hypothesis

The **efficient market hypothesis (EMH)** relates to the ability of capital markets to generate prices for securities that reflect worth. The EMH implies that publicly available information is fully reflected in share prices. The market will not be efficient if the market does not have access to relevant information or if fraudulent information is provided.

There seems to be little doubt that the FASB and the SEC assess the impact of their actions on security prices. The SEC has been particularly sensitive to insider trading because abnormal returns could be achieved by the use of insider information.

If the market is efficient, investors may be harmed when firms do not follow a full disclosure policy. In an efficient market, the method of disclosure is not as important as whether the item is disclosed. It should not matter whether an item is disclosed in the body of the financial statements or in the notes. It is the disclosure rather than how to disclose that is the substantive issue.

Usually, there is a cost to disclose. An attempt should be made to determine the value of additional disclosure in relation to the additional cost. Disclosure should be made when the perceived benefits exceed the additional cost to provide the disclosure.

It is generally recognized that the market is more efficient when dealing with large firms trading on large organized stock markets than it is for small firms that are not trading on large organized stock markets.

Although the research evidence regarding the EMH is conflicting, this hypothesis has taken on an important role in financial reporting in the United States.

Ethics

"Ethics and morals are synonymous. While *ethics* is derived from Greek, *morals* is derived from Latin. They are interchangeable terms referring to ideals of character and conduct. These ideals, in the form of codes of conduct, furnish criteria for distinguishing between right and wrong."[4] Ethics has been a subject of investigation for hundreds of years. Individuals in financial positions must be able to recognize ethical issues and resolve them in an appropriate manner.

Source: Mary E. Guy, Ethical Decision Making in Everyday Work Situations (New York: Quorum Books, 1990), p. 5

Ethics affect all individuals—from the financial clerk to the high-level financial executive. Individuals make daily decisions based on their individual values. Some companies and professional organizations have formulated a code of ethics as a statement of aspirations and a standard of integrity beyond that required by law (which can be viewed as the minimum standard of ethics).

Ten essential values can be considered central to relations between people.[5]

1. Caring
2. Honesty
3. Accountability
4. Promise keeping
5. Pursuit of excellence
6. Loyalty
7. Fairness
8. Integrity
9. Respect for others
10. Responsible citizenship

Ethics can be a particular problem with financial reports. Accepted accounting principles leave ample room for arriving at different results in the short run. Highly subjective estimates can substantially influence earnings. What provision should be made for warranty costs? What should be the loan loss reserve? What should be the allowance for doubtful accounts?

In 1988 the American Accounting Association initiated a project on professionalism and ethics. One of the goals of this project was to provide students with a framework for evaluating their courses of action when encountering ethical dilemmas. The American Accounting Association developed a decision model for focusing on ethical issues.[6]

1. Determine the facts—what, who, where, when, how.
2. Define the ethical issues (includes identifying the identifiable parties affected by the decision made or action taken).
3. Identify major principles, rules, and values.
4. Specify the alternatives.
5. Compare norms, principles, and values with alternatives to see if a clear decision can be reached.
6. Assess the consequences.
7. Make your decision.

EXAMPLE 1: QUESTIONABLE ETHICS IN SAVINGS AND LOANS

In connection with the savings and loan (S&L) scandal, it was revealed that several auditors of thrift institutions borrowed substantial amounts from the S&L that their firm was auditing. It was charged that some of the loans involved special consideration.[7] In one case, dozens of partners of a major accounting firm borrowed money for commercial real estate loans, and some of the partners defaulted on their loans when the real estate market collapsed.[8] It was not clear whether these particular loans violated professional ethics standards. The AICPA subsequently changed its ethics standards to ban all such loans.

In another case, an accounting firm paid $1.5 million to settle charges by the California State Board of Accountancy that the accounting firm was grossly negligent in its audit of Lincoln Savings & Loan. The accounting board charged that the firm had agreed to the improper recognition of approximately $62 million in profits.[9]

EXAMPLE 2: QUESTIONABLE ETHICS IN THE MOTION PICTURE INDUSTRY

Hollywood's accounting practices have often been labeled "mysterious."[10] A case in point is Art Buchwald's lawsuit against Paramount Pictures for breach of contract regarding the film *Coming to America*. Paramount took an option on Buchwald's story "King for a Day" in 1983 and promised Buchwald 1.5% of the net profits of the film. Buchwald's attorney, Pierce O'Donnell, accused Paramount Studios of "fatal subtraction" in determining the amount of profit. Although the film grossed $350 million worldwide, Paramount claimed an $18 million net loss. As a result of the studio's accounting practices, Buchwald was to get 1.5% of nothing.[11] Buchwald was eventually awarded $150,000 in a 1992 court decision.[12]

Many Hollywood celebrities, in addition to Art Buchwald, have sued over Hollywood-style accounting. These include Winston Groom over the movie rights to *Forrest Gump,* Jane Fonda over a larger share of profits relating to *On Golden Pond*, and James Garner over his share of profits from *The Rockford Files* (a television program). Some of Hollywood's best creative work is in accounting.

EXAMPLE 3: QUESTIONABLE ETHICS IN THE INVESTMENT COMMUNITY

In recent years, the SEC has charged numerous individuals with operating a Ponzi scheme. The largest of these schemes in history came to light in 2008 when Bernard Madoff was charged with operating a giant Ponzi scheme of over $50 billion. Ponzi schemes are a type of pyramid scheme. They are named after Charles Ponzi, who duped investors into a postage stamp speculation back in the 1920s. None of the money, or only a small amount of the money, is invested. The party running the Ponzi scheme spends the money and uses proceeds to pay off investors who want their money back.

SEC Requirements—Code of Ethics

In January 2003, the SEC voted to require disclosure in a company's annual report as to whether it has a code of ethics that applies to the company's principal executive officer, principal financial officer, principal accounting officer or controller, or persons performing similar functions. The rules will define a code of ethics as written standards that are reasonably necessary to deter wrongdoing and to promote:

1. Honest and ethical conduct, including the ethical handling of actual or apparent conflicts of interest between personal and professional relationships.
2. Full, fair, accurate, timely, and understandable disclosure in reports and documents that a company files with, or submits to, the Commission and in other public communications made by the company.
3. Compliance with applicable governmental laws, rules, and regulations.
4. The prompt internal reporting of code violations to an appropriate person or persons identified in the code.
5. Accountability for adherence to the code.[13]

The SEC requires that a copy of the company's code of ethics be made available by filing an exhibit with its annual report (10-K) or by providing it on the company's Web site.

The SEC requirements were an outcome of the Sarbanes-Oxley Act. Exhibit 2-12 presents NIKE's code of ethics.

EXHIBIT **2-12**	The NIKE Code of Ethics*

Defining the NIKE Playing Field and the Rules of the Game

Do the Right Thing

A Message from Phil

At NIKE, we are on the offense, always. We play hard, we play to win, but we play by the rules of the game.

This Code of Ethics is vitally important. It contains the rules of the game for NIKE, the rules we live by and what we stand for. Please read it, and if you've read it before, read it again.

Then take some time to think about what it says and make a commitment to play by it. Defining the NIKE playing field ensures no matter how dynamic and challenging NIKE may be, our actions and decisions fit with our shared values.

Thank you for your commitment.

*Our principal business activity is the design, development and worldwide marketing of high-quality footwear, apparel, equipment, and accessory products." 10-K

(continued)

| EXHIBIT **2-12** | The NIKE Code of Ethics (*continued*) |

Philip H. Knight

Note: Philip H. Knight is the Chairman of the Board of Directors of NIKE.

The NIKE Code of Ethics is backed by a 28 page "Defining the NIKE Playing Field and the Rules of the Game."

The NIKE Code of Ethics can be found at www.nikebiz.com. Click on "Investors," click on "Corporate Governance," click on "Code of Ethics," and click on "Code of Business Conduct & Ethics." The Board of Directors of Nike, Inc., approved amendments to update the company's Code of Ethics, which became effective on March 30, 2009.

Consolidated Statements

Financial statements of legally separate entities may be issued to show financial position, income, and cash flow as they would appear if the companies were a single entity (consolidated). Such statements reflect an economic, rather than a legal, concept of the entity. For consolidated statements, all transactions between the entities being consolidated—intercompany transactions—must be eliminated.

When a subsidiary is less than 100% owned and its statements are consolidated, minority shareholders must be recognized in the consolidated financial statements by showing the noncontrolling interest under stockholders' equity on the balance sheet and the noncontrolling interest in income on the income statement. Noncontrolling accounts are discussed in detail in Chapter 3.

Consolidated statements are financial statements that a parent company produces when its financial statements and those of a subsidiary are added together. This portrays the resulting financial statements as a single company. The parent company concept emphasizes the interests of the controlling shareholders (the parent's shareholders). A subsidiary is a company controlled by another company. An unconsolidated subsidiary is accounted for as an investment on the parent's balance sheet.

Two reporting approaches can be used to present consolidated statements. In one approach, the subsidiary's accounts are shown separately from the parent's. This format is logical when the parent has a subsidiary in a different line of business. Ford Motor Company consolidates presenting the automotive and financial services category separately.

Most companies consolidate the parents and subsidiary accounts summed. The Dow Chemical Company consolidates summing the accounts.

The parent company can have legal control with ownership of a majority of the subsidiary's outstanding voting shares. The parent company can have effective control when a majority of the subsidiary board of directors can be elected by means other than by having legal control.

A company could have ownership of the majority voting shares and not have control. Such a situation would be a subsidiary that has filed for bankruptcy protection. In the bankruptcy situation, the judge in the bankruptcy court has assumed control.

Control can be gained by means other than obtaining majority stock ownership. The FASB recognizes a risks, rewards, decision-making ability and the primary beneficiary. Thus, consolidation would be required when a firm bears the majority (over 50%) of the risks and/or rewards of ownership. Examples of consolidating because of risks, rewards, and decision-making ability would be a contractual situation to accept substantial production or a loan situation which grants substantial control.

The consolidation of financial statements has been a practice in the United States for years; however, this has not been the case for many other nations. Some countries do not consolidate. Other countries use consolidation with different rules.

The IASC passed a standard that requires that all controlled subsidiaries be consolidated. Although IASC standards cannot be enforced, this standard will likely increase the acceptance of consolidation.

Accounting for Business Combinations

The combination of business entities by merger or acquisition is very frequent. There are many possible reasons for this external business expansion, including achieving economies of scale and savings of time in entering a new market. The combination must be accounted for using the **purchase method.**

The purchase method views the business combination as the acquisition of one entity by another. The firm doing the acquiring records the identifiable assets and liabilities at fair value at the date of acquisition. The difference between the fair value of the identifiable assets and liabilities and the amount paid is recorded as goodwill (an asset).

With a purchase, the acquiring firm picks up the income of the acquired firm from the date of acquisition. Retained earnings of the acquired firm do not continue.

SEC – Paper Filings – EDGAR – XBRL

In Chapter One it was reported that the Securities Act of 1933 was designed to protect investors from abuses in financial reporting in the United States. This act was intended to regulate the initial offering and sale of securities in interstate commerce. Also in Chapter One, it was reported that, in general, the Securities Exchange Act of 1934 was intended to regulate securities trading on the national exchanges, and it was under this authority that the Securities and Exchange Commission (SEC) was created.

The SEC requires companies with securities sold to the general public to submit various reports. Among these reports are the Form 10-K (annual report) and from 10-Q (quarterly report).

The SEC required these reports to be filed using paper documents. By 1996, the SEC installed its electronic disclosure system, EDGAR. The SEC made the EDGAR filings available on the internet. Not all reports to the SEC are made available on EDGAR.

In 2004 the SEC began investigating the possibility of having documents submitted in a tagged format (XBRL). XBRL stands for Extensible Business Reporting Language. The XBRL approach does not eliminate the existing filing requirements. The XBRL approach is not unique with the SEC as it is used for many products and many countries; for example, the bar code for items in a grocery store. Many countries have started to use bar codes (interactive data) in their financial disclosure statements.

With XBRL and the proper software, data users such as analysts and investors can extract financial data. This is much more efficient than sorting through many pages of data.

A firm submits the data to the SEC in EDGAR form and XBRL form at the same time. When using the internet and searching for the 10-K, the EDGAR form is indicated as "Documents" and the XBRL form is indicated as "Interactive Data."

The EDGAR form of the 10-K will have all parts of the 10-K (Exhibit 2-10), while the XBRL form will only have Item 8 Financial Statements and Supplementary Data. The XBRL presents a summary of the statements, notes, etc., while the EDGAR form presents the statements and then the notes. This comparison only applies to Item 8 in the 10-K.

There is a similar situation with the 10-Q. In this case, the entire quarterly report has 10 items (Exhibit 2-11). All are included with the EDGAR version. Only Item 1 is presented with the XBRL version.

In the section "To the Net" at the back of chapters in this book, there are many exercises where the SEC website, www.sec.gov, is used. These exercises usually only reference the financial statements and notes. These exercises can be worked using either the EDGAR form "Documents" or the XBRL from "Interactive Data." As indicated previously, a more meaningful use of the XBRL "Interactive Data" will require proper software.

Source: U.S Securities and Exchange

Summary

This chapter includes an introduction to the basic financial statements. Later chapters will cover these statements in detail.

An understanding of the sequence of accounting procedures completed during each accounting period, called the accounting cycle, will help in understanding the end result—financial statements.

This chapter describes the forms of business entities, which are sole proprietorship, partnership, and corporation.

Management is responsible for financial statements. These statements are examined by auditors who express an opinion regarding the statements' conformity to GAAP in the auditor's report. The auditor's report often points out key factors that can affect financial statement analysis. The SEC has begun a program to integrate the Form 10-K requirements with those of the annual report.

A reporting option available to public companies, a summary annual report (a condensed annual report), omits much of the financial information included in a typical annual report.

The EMH relates to the ability of capital markets to generate prices for securities that reflect worth. The market will not be efficient if the market does not have access to relevant information or if fraudulent information is provided.

Individuals in financial positions must be able to recognize ethical issues and resolve them appropriately.

Financial statements of legally separate entities may be issued to show financial position, income, and cash flow as they would appear if the companies were a single entity (consolidated).

The combination of business entities by merger or acquisition is very frequent. An understanding of how a business combination can impact the basic statements is important to the analyst.

Questions

Q 2-1 Name the type of opinion indicated by each of the following situations:

a. There is a material uncertainty.
b. There was a change in accounting principle.
c. There is no material scope limitation or material departure from GAAP.
d. The financial statements do not present fairly the financial position, results of operations, or cash flows of the entity in conformity with GAAP.
e. Except for the effects of the matter(s) to which the qualification relates, the financial statements present fairly, in all material respects, the financial position, results of operations, and cash flows of the entity, in conformity with GAAP.

Q 2-2 What are the roles of management and the auditor in the preparation and integrity of the financial statements?

Q 2-3 What is the purpose of the SEC's integrated disclosure system for financial reporting?

Q 2-4 Why do some unqualified opinions have explanatory paragraphs?

Q 2-5 Describe an auditor's review of financial statements.

Q 2-6 Will the accountant express an opinion on reviewed financial statements? Describe the accountant's report for reviewed financial statements.

Q 2-7 What type of opinion is expressed on a compilation?

Q 2-8 Are all financial statements presented with some kind of an accountant's report? Explain.

Q 2-9 What are the three principal financial statements of a corporation? Briefly describe the purpose of each statement.

Q 2-10 Why are notes to statements necessary?

Q 2-11 What are contingent liabilities? Are lawsuits against the firm contingent liabilities?

Q 2-12 Which of the following events, occurring subsequent to the balance sheet date, would require a note?

a. Major fire in one of the firm's plants
b. Increase in competitor's advertising
c. Purchase of another company
d. Introduction of new management techniques
e. Death of the corporate treasurer

Q 2-13 Describe a proxy statement.

Q 2-14 Briefly describe a summary annual report.

Q 2-15 If a company issues a summary annual report, where can the more extensive financial information be found?

Q 2-16 Comment on the typical number of financial pages in a summary annual report as compared to a full annual report.

Q 2-17 What are the major sections of a statement of cash flows?

Q 2-18 Which two principal financial statements explain the difference between two balance sheet dates? Describe how these financial statements explain the difference between two balance sheet dates.

Q 2-19 What are the three major categories on a balance sheet?

Q 2-20 Can cash dividends be paid from retained earnings? Comment.

Q 2-21 Why should notes to financial statements be reviewed?

Q 2-22 Where do we find a description of a firm's accounting policies?

Q 2-23 Describe the relationship between the terms *ethics* and *morals*.

Q 2-24 What is the relationship between ethics and law?

Q 2-25 Identify the basic accounting equation.

Q 2-26 What is the relationship between the accounting equation and the double-entry system of recording transactions?

Q 2-27 Define the following:

a. Permanent accounts

b. Temporary accounts

Q 2-28 A typical accrual recognition for salaries is as follows:

Salaries Expense	$1,000 (increase)
Salaries Payable	1,000 (increase)

Explain how the matching concept applies in this situation.

Q 2-29 Why are adjusting entries necessary?

Q 2-30 Why aren't all transactions recorded in the general journal?

Q 2-31 Describe the filing deadline for Form 10-K.

Q 2-32 Identify the usual forms of a business entity and describe the ownership characteristic of each.

Q 2-33 Why would the use of insider information be of concern if the market is efficient?

Q 2-34 Considering the EMH, it is best if financial disclosure is made in the body of the financial statements. Comment.

Q 2-35 Considering the EMH, how could abnormal returns be achieved?

Q 2-36 Describe the purchase method of accounting for a business combination.

Q 2-37 Consolidated statements may be issued to show financial position as it would appear if two or more companies were one entity. What is the objective of these statements?

Q 2-38 What is the basic guideline for consolidation?

Q 2-39 Where must a company's code of ethics be made available?

Q 2-40 Describe the Treadway Commission.

Q 2-41 Why is the COSO report on internal control systems important under requirements of the Sarbanes-Oxley Act?

Q 2-42 Under Sarbanes-Oxley, the auditing firm will include which two reports with the audited statements? (*Note:* These two reports can be combined into one report.)

Q 2-43 Under Sarbanes-Oxley, management must include what report with the audited statements?

Q 2-44 Private companies are not under Sarbanes-Oxley. Why do some private companies follow the law?

Q 2-45 Indicate the two approaches to presenting consolidated statements.

Q 2-46 Describe how a company could be required to consolidate another company in which it has no or minor voting stock.

Q 2-47 Consolidation rules are similar between countries. Comment.

Problems

P 2-1 Mike Szabo Company engaged in the following transactions during the month of December:

December 2	Made credit sales of $4,000 (accepted accounts receivable).
6	Made cash sales of $2,500.
10	Paid office salaries of $500.
14	Sold land that originally cost $2,200 for $3,000 cash.
17	Paid $6,000 for equipment.
21	Billed clients $900 for services (accepted accounts receivable).
24	Collected $1,200 on an account receivable.
28	Paid an account payable of $700.

Required Record the transactions, using T-accounts.

P 2-2 Darlene Cook Company engaged in the following transactions during the month of July:

July 1	Acquired land for $10,000. The company paid cash.
8	Billed customers for $3,000. This represents an increase in revenue. The customer has been billed and will pay at a later date. An asset, accounts receivable, has been created.

(*continued*)

(**P 2-2** CONTINUED)

12 Incurred a repair expense for repairs of $600. Darlene Cook Company agreed to pay in 60 days. This transaction involves an increase in accounts payable and repair expense.

15 Received a check for $500 from a customer who was previously billed. This is a reduction in accounts receivable.

20 Paid $300 for supplies. This was previously established as a liability, account payable.

24 Paid wages in the amount of $400. This was for work performed during July.

Required Record the transactions, using T-accounts.

P 2-3 Gaffney Company had these adjusting entry situations at the end of December.

1. On July 1, Gaffney Company paid $1,200 for a one-year insurance policy. The policy was for the period July 1 through June 30. The transaction was recorded as prepaid insurance and a reduction in cash.
2. On September 10, Gaffney Company purchased $500 of supplies for cash. The purchase was recorded as supplies. On December 31, it was determined that various supplies had been consumed in operations and that supplies costing $200 remained on hand.
3. Gaffney Company received $1,000 on December 1 for services to be performed in the following year. This was recorded on December 1 as an increase in cash and as revenue. As of December 31, this needs to be recognized as Unearned Revenue, a liability account.
4. As of December 31, interest charges of $200 have been incurred because of borrowed funds. Payment will not be made until February. A liability for the interest needs to be recognized, as does the interest expense.
5. As of December 31, a $500 liability for salaries needs to be recognized.
6. As of December 31, Gaffney Company had provided services in the amount of $400 for Jones Company. An asset, Accounts Receivable, needs to be recognized along with the revenue.

Required Record the adjusting entries at December 31, using T-accounts.

P 2-4 DeCort Company had these adjusting entry situations at the end of December:

1. On May 1, DeCort Company paid $960 for a two-year insurance policy. The policy was for the period May 1 through April 30 (2 years). This is the first year of the policy. The transaction was recorded as insurance expense.
2. On December 1, DeCort Company purchased $400 of supplies for cash. The purchase was recorded as an asset, supplies. On December 31, it was determined that various supplies had been consumed in operations and that supplies costing $300 remained on hand.
3. DeCort Company holds a note receivable for $4,000. This note is interest-bearing. The interest will be received when the note matures. The note is a one-year note receivable made on June 30, bearing 5% simple interest.
4. DeCort Company owes salaries in the amount of $800 at the end of December.
5. As of December 31, DeCort Company had received $600 for services to be performed. These services had not been performed as of December 31. A liability, Unearned Revenue, needs to be recognized, and revenue needs to be reduced.
6. On December 20, DeCort Company received a $400 bill for advertising in December. The liability account, Accounts Payable, needs to be recognized along with the related expense.

Required Record the adjusting entries at December 31, using T-accounts.

P 2-5
Required Answer the following multiple-choice questions:

a. The balance sheet equation can be defined as which of the following?

1. Assets + Stockholders' Equity = Liabilities
2. Assets + Liabilities = Stockholders' Equity

    3. Assets = Liabilities − Stockholders' Equity
    4. Assets − Liabilities = Stockholders' Equity
    5. None of the above

b. If assets are $40,000 and stockholders' equity is $10,000, how much are liabilities?

    1. $30,000
    2. $50,000
    3. $20,000
    4. $60,000
    5. $10,000

c. If assets are $100,000 and liabilities are $40,000, how much is stockholders' equity?

    1. $40,000
    2. $50,000
    3. $60,000
    4. $30,000
    5. $140,000

d. Which is a permanent account?

    1. Revenue
    2. Advertising Expense
    3. Accounts Receivable
    4. Dividends
    5. Insurance Expense

e. Which is a temporary account?

    1. Cash
    2. Accounts Receivable
    3. Insurance Expense
    4. Accounts Payable
    5. Notes Payable

f. In terms of debits and credits, which accounts have the same normal balances?

    1. Dividends, retained earnings, liabilities
    2. Capital stock, liabilities, expenses
    3. Revenues, capital stock, expenses
    4. Expenses, assets, dividends
    5. Dividends, assets, liabilities

P 2-6
Required Answer the following multiple-choice questions:

a. Audit opinions cannot be classified as which of the following?

    1. All-purpose
    2. Disclaimer of opinion
    3. Adverse opinion
    4. Qualified opinion
    5. Unqualified opinion

b. From the point of view of analysis, which classification of an audit opinion indicates that the financial statements carry the highest degree of reliability?

    1. Unqualified opinion
    2. All-purpose
    3. Disclaimer of opinion
    4. Qualified opinion
    5. Adverse opinion

(*continued*)

(P 2-6 CONTINUED)

c. Which one of the following statements is false?

1. The reliance that can be placed on financial statements that have been reviewed is substantially less than for those that have been audited.
2. An accountant's report described as a compilation presents only financial information as provided by management.
3. A disclaimer of opinion indicates that you should not look to the auditor's report as an indication of the reliability of the statements.
4. A review has substantially less scope than an examination in accordance with generally accepted auditing standards.
5. The typical unqualified opinion has one paragraph.

d. If an accountant performs a compilation and becomes aware of deficiencies in the statements, the accountant's report characterizes the deficiencies by all but one of the following:

1. Omission of substantially all disclosures
2. Omission of statement of cash flows
3. Accounting principles not generally accepted
4. All of the above.
5. None of the above.

e. In addition to the company's principal financial statements, the Form 10-K and shareholder annual reports must include all but one of the following:

1. Information on the market for holders of common stock and related securities, including high and low sales price, frequency and amount of dividends, and number of shares.
2. Five-year summary of selected financial data.
3. Management's discussion and analysis of financial condition and results of operations.
4. Two years of audited balance sheets, three years of audited statements of income, and two years of statements of cash flows.
5. Disclosure of the domestic and foreign components of pretax income.

f. The Form 10-K is submitted to the:

1. American Institute of Certified Public Accountants
2. Securities and Exchange Commission
3. Internal Revenue Service
4. American Accounting Association
5. Emerging Issues Task Force

P 2-7
Required Answer the following multiple-choice questions:

a. Which party has the primary responsibility for the financial statements?

1. Bookkeeper
2. Auditor
3. Management
4. Cost accountant
5. None of the above.

b. Which of the following is a type of audit opinion that a firm would usually prefer?

1. Unqualified opinion
2. Qualified opinion
3. Adverse opinion
4. Clear opinion
5. None of the above.

c. Which of the following statements is true?

1. You are likely to regard an adverse opinion as an immaterial issue as to the reliability of the financial statements.
2. A disclaimer of opinion indicates that you should look to the auditor's report as an indication of the reliability of the statements.⊤
3. A review consists principally of inquiries made to company personal and analytical procedures applied to financial data.
4. When the outside accountant presents only financial information as provided by management, he or she is said to have reviewed the financial statements.
5. None of the above.

d. This item need *not* be provided with a complete set of financial statements:

1. A 20-year summary of operations
2. Note disclosure of such items as accounting policies
3. Balance sheet
4. Income statement
5. Statement of cash flows

e. Which of the following statements is true?

1. Financial statements of legally separate entities may be issued to show financial position, income, and cash flow as they would appear if the companies were a single entity (consolidated).
2. Consolidated statements reflect a legal, rather than an economic, concept of the entity.
3. The financial statements of the parent and the subsidiary are consolidated for all majority-owned subsidiaries.
4. Consolidated statements are rare in the United States.
5. The acceptance of consolidation has been decreasing.

P 2-8 The following are selected accounts of Laura Gibson Company on December 31:

	Permanent (P) or Temporary (T)	Normal Balance (Dr.) or (Cr.)
Cash	_____	_____
Accounts Receivable	_____	_____
Equipment	_____	_____
Accounts Payable	_____	_____
Common Stock	_____	_____
Sales	_____	_____
Purchases	_____	_____
Rent Expense	_____	_____
Utility Expense	_____	_____
Selling Expense	_____	_____

Required In the space provided:

1. Indicate if the account is a permanent (P) or temporary (T) account.
2. Indicate the normal balance in terms of debit (Dr.) or credit (Cr.).

P 2-9 An auditor's report is the formal presentation of all the effort that goes into an audit. Below is a list of the classifications of audit opinions that can be found in an auditor's report as well as a list of phrases describing the opinions.

Classifications of Audit Opinions

a. Unqualified opinion
b. Qualified opinion
c. Adverse opinion
d. Disclaimer of opinion

(*continued*)

(**P 2-9** CONTINUED)

Phrases

_____ 1. This opinion states that the financial statements do not present fairly the financial position, results of operations, or cash flows of the entity, in conformity with generally accepted accounting principles.

_____ 2. This type of report is rendered when the auditor has not performed an audit sufficient in scope to form an opinion.

_____ 3. This opinion states that, except for the effects of the matters to which the qualification relates, the financial statements present fairly, in all material respects, the financial position, results of operations, and cash flows of the entity, in conformity with generally accepted accounting principles.

_____ 4. This opinion states that the financial statements present fairly, in all material respects, the financial position, results of operations, and cash flows of the entity, in conformity with generally accepted accounting principles.

Required Place the appropriate letter identifying each type of opinion on the line in front of the statement or phrase describing the type of opinion.

P 2-10 A company prepares financial statements in order to summarize financial information. Below are a list of financial statements and a list of descriptions.

Financial Statements

a. Balance sheet
b. Income statement
c. Statement of cash flows
d. Statement of stockholders' equity

Descriptions

1. Details the sources and uses of cash during a specified period of time.
2. Summary of revenues and expenses and gains and losses for a specific period of time.
3. Shows the financial condition of an accounting entity as of a specific date.
4. Presents reconciliation of the beginning and ending balances of the stockholders' equity accounts.

Required Match each financial statement with its description.

P 2-11 The Jones Company debits prepaid insurance for insurance premiums paid. During the year insurance expense is computed for interim periods and insurance expense is debited and prepaid insurance is credited. Information for the year ended December 31, 2012 follows:

Prepaid Insurance December 31, 2011	$180,000
Insurance Expense	$320,000
Prepaid Insurance December 31, 2012	$170,000

Required Determine the insurance premiums paid during 2012.

Cases

CASE 2-1 THE CEO RETIRES*

Dan Murphy awoke at 5:45 A.M., just like he did every workday morning. No matter that he went to sleep only four hours ago. The Orange Bowl game had gone late into the evening, and the New Year's Day party was so good, no one wanted to leave. At least Dan could awake easily this morning. Some of his guests had lost a little control celebrating the first day of the new year, and Dan was not a person who ever lost control.

Prepared by Professor William H. Coyle, Babson College.
*Source: "Ethics in the Accounting Curriculum: Cases & Readings," American Accounting Association.

The drive to the office was easier than most days. Perhaps there were a great many parties last night. All the better as it gave Dan time to think. The dawn of a new year, his last year. Dan would turn 65 next December, and the company had a mandatory retirement policy. A good idea he thought, to get new blood in the organization. At least that's what he thought on the climb up. From just another college graduate within the corporate staff, all the way to the chief executive officer's suite. It certainly is a magnificent view from the top.

To be CEO of his own company. Well, not really, as it was the stockholders' company, but he had been CEO for the past eight years. Now he, too, must turn the reins over. "Must," now that's the operative word. He knew it was the best thing for the company. Turnover kept middle management aggressive, but he also knew that he wouldn't leave if he had a choice. So Dan resolved to make his last year the company's best year ever.

It was that thought that kept his attention, yet the focus of consideration and related motivations supporting such a strategy changed as he continued to strategize. At first, Dan thought that it would be a fine way to give something back to a company that had given him so much. His 43 years with the company had given him challenges that filled his life with meaning and satisfaction, provided him with a good living, and made him a man respected and listened to in the business community. But the thought that the company was also forcing him to give all that up made his thoughts turn more inward.

Of course, the company had done many things for him, but what of all the sacrifices he had made? His whole heart and soul were tied to the company. In fact, one could hardly think of Dan Murphy without thinking of the company, in much the same way as prominent corporate leaders and their firms are intrinsically linked. But the company would still be here this time next year, and what of him? Yes, he would leave the company strong, because by leaving it strong, it would strengthen his reputation as a great leader. His legacy would carry and sustain him over the years. But would it? One must also live in a manner consistent with such esteem.

Being the CEO of a major company also has its creature comforts. Dan was accustomed to a certain style of living. How much will that suffer after the salary, bonuses, and stock options are no more?

Arriving at the office by 7:30 A.M., he left a note for his secretary that he was not to be disturbed until 9 A.M. He pulled out the compensation file and examined the incentive clauses in his own contract. The contract was created by the compensation committee of the Board of Directors. All of the committee members were outsiders, that is, not a part of the company's management. This lends the appearance of independence, but most were CEOs of their own companies, and Dan knew that, by and large, CEOs take care of their own. His suspicions were confirmed. If the company's financial results were the best ever this year, then so, too, would be his own personal compensation.

Yet what if there were uncontrollable problems? The general economy appeared fairly stable. However, another oil shock, some more bank failures, or a list of other disasters could turn things into a downward spiral quickly. Economies are easily influenced and consumer and corporate psychology can play a large part in determining outcomes. But even in apparently uncontrollable circumstances, Dan knew he could protect himself and the financial fortunes of his company during the short term, which after all, was the only thing that mattered.

Upon further review of his compensation contract, Dan saw that a large portion of his bonus and stock options was a function of operating income levels, earnings per share, and return on assets. So the trick was to maximize those items. If he did, the company would appear vibrant and poised for future growth at the time of his forced retirement, he reminded himself. Furthermore, his total compensation in the last year of his employment would reach record proportions. Additionally, since his pension is based on the average of his last three years' compensation, Dan will continue to reap the benefits of this year's results for hopefully a long time to come. And who says CEOs don't think long term?

Two remaining issues needed to be addressed. Those were (1) how to ensure a record-breaking year and (2) how to overcome any objections raised in attaining those results. Actually, the former was a relatively simple goal to achieve. Since accounting allows so many alternatives in the way financial events are measured, Dan could just select a package of alternatives, which would maximize the company's earnings and return on assets. Some

(continued)

(**CASE 2-1** CONTINUED)

alternatives may result in changing an accounting method, but since the new auditing standards were issued, his company could still receive an unqualified opinion from his auditors, with only a passing reference to any accounting changes in the auditor's opinion and its effects disclosed in the footnotes. As long as the alternative was allowed by generally accepted accounting principles, and the justification for the change was reasonable, the auditors should not object. If there were objections, Dan could always threaten to change auditors. But still the best avenue to pursue would be a change in accounting estimates, since those changes did not even need to be explicitly disclosed.

So Dan began to mull over what changes in estimates or methods he could employ in order to maximize his firm's financial appearance. In the area of accounting estimates, Dan could lower the rate of estimated default on his accounts receivable, thus lowering bad debt expense. The estimated useful lives of his plant and equipment could be extended, thus lowering depreciation expense. In arguing that quality improvements have been implemented in the manufacturing process, the warranty expense on the products sold could also be lowered. In examining pension expense, he noted that the assumed rate of return on pension assets was at a modest 6.5%, so if that rate could be increased, the corresponding pension expense could be reduced.

Other possibilities occurred to Dan. Perhaps items normally expensed, such as repairs, could be capitalized. Those repairs that could not be capitalized could simply be deferred. The company could also defer short-term expenses for the training of staff. Since research and development costs must now be fully expensed as incurred; a reduction in those expenditures would increase net income. Return on assets would be increased by not acquiring any new fixed assets. Production levels for inventory could be increased, thus spreading fixed costs over a greater number of units and reducing the total average cost per unit. Therefore, gross profit per unit will increase. Inventory levels would be a little bloated, but that should be easily handled by Dan's successor.

The prior examples are subtle changes that could be made. As a last resort, a change in accounting methods could be employed. This would require explicit footnote disclosure and a comment in the auditor's report, but if it came to that, it would still be tolerable. Examples of such changes would be to switch from accelerated to straight-line depreciation or to change from LIFO to FIFO.

How to make changes to the financial results of the company appeared easier than he first thought. Now back to the other potential problem of "getting away with it." At first thought, Dan considered the degree of resistance by the other members of top management. Mike Harrington, Dan's chief financial officer, would have to review any accounting changes that he suggested. Since Dan had brought Mike up the organization with him, Dan didn't foresee any strong resistance from Mike. As for the others, Dan believed he had two things going for him. One was their ambition. Dan knew that they all coveted his job, and a clear successor to Dan had yet to be chosen. Dan would only make a recommendation to the promotion committee of the Board of Directors, but everyone knew his recommendation carried a great deal of weight. Therefore, resistance to any accounting changes by any individual would surely end his or her hope to succeed him as CEO. Secondly, although not as lucrative as Dan's, their bonus package is tied to the exact same accounting numbers. So any actions taken by Dan to increase his compensation will also increase theirs.

Dan was actually beginning to enjoy this situation, even considering it one of his final challenges. Dan realized that any changes he implemented would have the tendency to reverse themselves over time. That would undoubtedly hurt the company's performance down the road, but all of his potential successors were in their mid-to-late 50s, so there would be plenty of time for them to turn things around in the years ahead. Besides, any near-term reversals would merely enhance his reputation as an excellent corporate leader, as problems would arise after his departure.

At that moment, his secretary called to inform him that Mike Harrington wanted to see him. Mike was just the man Dan wanted to see.

What are the ethical issues?

What should Mike do?

Required

    a. Determine the facts—what, who, where, when, and how.

    b. Define the ethical issues.

    c. Identify major principles, rules, and values.

    d. Specify the alternatives.

    e. Compare norms, principles, and values with alternatives to see if a clear decision can be reached.

    f. Assess the consequences.

    g. Make your decision.

CASE 2-2 THE DANGEROUS MORALITY OF MANAGING EARNINGS*

The Majority of Managers Surveyed Say It's Not Wrong to Manage Earnings

Occasionally, the morals and ethics executives use to manage their businesses are examined and discussed. Unfortunately, the morals that guide the timing of nonoperating events and choices of accounting policies have largely been ignored.

The ethical framework used by managers in reporting short-term earnings probably has received less attention than its operating counterpart because accountants prepare financial disclosures consistent with laws and generally accepted accounting principles (GAAP). Those disclosures are reviewed by objective auditors.

Managers determine the short-term reported earnings of their companies by:

- Managing, providing leadership, and directing the use of resources in operations.
- Selecting the timing of some nonoperating events, such as the sale of excess assets or the placement of gains or losses into a particular reporting period.
- Choosing the accounting methods that are used to measure short-term earnings.

Casual observers of the financial reporting process may assume that time, laws, regulation, and professional standards have restricted accounting practices to those that are moral, ethical, fair, and precise. But most managers and their accountants know otherwise—that managing short-term earnings can be part of a manager's job.

To understand the morals of short-term earnings management, we surveyed general managers and finance, control, and audit managers. The results are frightening.

We found striking disagreements among managers in all groups. Furthermore, the liberal definitions revealed in many responses of what is moral or ethical should raise profound questions about the quality of financial information that is used for decision-making purposes by parties both inside and outside a company. It seems many managers are convinced that if a practice is not explicitly prohibited or is only a slight deviation from rules, it is an ethical practice regardless of who might be affected either by the practice or the information that flows from it. This means that anyone who uses information on short-term earnings is vulnerable to misinterpretation, manipulation, or deliberate deception.

The Morals of Managing Earnings

To find a "revealed" consensus concerning the morality of engaging in earnings-management activities, we prepared a questionnaire describing 13 earnings-management situations we had observed either directly or indirectly. The actions described in the incidents were all legal (although some were in violation of GAAP), but each could be construed as involving short-term earnings management.

A total of 649 managers completed our questionnaire. Table 2-1 classifies respondents by job function, and Table 2-2 summarizes the views on the acceptability of various earnings-management practices.

A major finding of the survey was a striking lack of agreement. None of the respondent groups viewed any of the 13 practices unanimously as an ethical or unethical practice. The

(*continued*)

---

*Source: Reprinted from *Management Accounting*, August 1990. Copyright by National Association of Accountants, Montvale, NJ.

(**CASE 2-2** CONTINUED)

dispersion of judgments about many of the incidents was great. For example, here is one hypothetical earnings-management practice described in the questionnaire:

> In September, a general manager realized that his division would need a strong performance in the last quarter of the year in order to reach its budget targets. He decided to implement a sales program offering liberal payment terms to pull some sales that would normally occur next year into the current year. Customers accepting delivery in the fourth quarter would not have to pay the invoice for 120 days.

The survey respondents' judgments of the acceptability of this practice were distributed as follows:

Ethical	279
Questionable	288
Unethical	82
Total	649

TABLE **2-1**	Survey Respondents

Total Sample	
General Managers	119
Finance, Control, & Audit Managers	262
Others or Position Not Known	268
	649

Perhaps you are not surprised by these data. The ethical basis of an early shipment/ liberal payment program may not be something you have considered, but, with the prevalence of such diverse views, how can any user of a short-term earnings report know the quality of the information?

Although the judgments about all earnings-management practices varied considerably, there are some other generalizations that can be made from the findings summarized in Table 2-2.

- On average, the respondents viewed management of short-term earnings by *accounting* methods as significantly less acceptable than accomplishing the same ends by changing or manipulating *operating decisions or procedures.*
- The direction of the effect on earnings matters. *Increasing* earnings is judged less acceptable than *reducing* earnings.
- Materiality matters. Short-term earnings management is judged less acceptable if the earnings effect is *large* rather than *small.*
- The time period of the effect may affect ethical judgments. Managing short-term earnings at the end of an interim *quarterly* reporting period is viewed as somewhat more acceptable than engaging in the same activity at the end of an *annual* reporting period.
- The method of managing earnings has an effect. Increasing profits by offering *extended credit terms* is seen as less acceptable than accomplishing the same end by *selling excess assets or using overtime* to increase shipments.

Managers Interviewed

Were the survey results simply hypothetical, or did managers recognize they can manage earnings and choose to do so? To find the answers, we talked to a large number of the respondents. What they told us was rarely reassuring.

On accounting manipulations, a profit center controller reported:

> Accounting is grey. Very little is absolute.... You can save your company by doing things with sales and expenses, and, if it's legal, then you are justified in doing it.

| TABLE **2-2** | Managing Short-Term Earnings | | | |

Proportion of Managers Who Judge the Practice*

	Ethical	Questionable, or a Minor Infraction	Unethical, a Serious Infraction
1. Managing short-term earnings by changing or manipulating operating decisions or procedures:			
When the result is to reduce earnings	79%	19%	2%
When the result is to increase earnings	57%	31%	12%
2. Managing short-term earnings by changing or manipulating accounting methods:			
When the change to earnings is small	5%	45%	50%
When the change to earnings is large	3%	21%	76%
3. Managing short-term earnings by deferring discretionary expenditures into the next accounting period:			
To meet an interim quarterly budget target	47%	41%	12%
To meet an annual budget target	41%	35%	24%
4. Increasing short-term earnings to meet a budget target:			
By selling excess assets and realizing a profit	80%	16%	4%
By ordering overtime work at year-end to ship as much as possible	74%	21%	5%
By offering customers special credit terms to accept delivery without obligation to pay until the following year	43%	44%	15%

*Percentages are calculated from *Harvard Business Review* readers' sample.

A divisional general manager spoke to us about squeezing reserves to generate additional reported profit:

> If we get a call asking for additional profit, and that's not inconceivable, I would look at our reserves. Our reserves tend to be realistic, but we may have a product claim that could range from $50,000 to $500,000. Who knows what the right amount for something like that is? We would review our reserves, and if we felt some were on the high side, we would not be uncomfortable reducing them.

We also heard about operating manipulations. One corporate group controller noted:

> [To boost sales] we have paid overtime and shipped on Saturday, the last day of the fiscal quarter. If we totally left responsibility for the shipping function to the divisions, it could even slip over to 12:30 A.M. Sunday. There are people who would do that and not know it's wrong.

Managers often recognize that such actions "move" earnings from one period to another. For example, a division controller told us:

> Last year we called our customers and asked if they would take early delivery. We generated an extra $300,000 in sales at the last minute. We were scratching for everything. We made our plans, but we cleaned out our backlog and started in the hole this year. We missed our first quarter sales plan. We will catch up by the end of the second quarter.

And a group vice president said:

> I recently was involved in a situation where the manager wanted to delay the production costs for the advertising that would appear in the fall [so that he could meet his quarterly budget].

Thus, in practice, it appears that a large majority of managers use at least some methods to manage short-term earnings. Though legal, these methods do not seem to be consistent with a strict ethical framework. While the managers' actions have the desired effect on reported earnings, the managers know there are no real positive economic benefits, and the

(continued)

(**CASE 2-2** CONTINUED)

actions might actually be quite costly in the long run. These actions are at best questionable because they involve deceptions that are not disclosed. Most managers who manage earnings, however, do not believe they are doing anything wrong.

We see two major problems. The most important is the generally high tolerance for operating manipulations. The other is the dispersion in managers' views about which practices are moral and ethical.

The Dangerous Allure

The essence of a moral or an ethical approach to management is achieving a balance between individual interests and obligations to those who have a stake in what happens in the corporation (or what happens to a division or group within the corporation). These stakeholders include not only people who work in the firm, but customers, suppliers, creditors, shareholders, and investors as well.

Managers who take unproductive actions to boost short-term earnings may be acting totally within the laws and rules. Also, they may be acting in the best interest of the corporation. But if they fail to consider the adverse effects of their actions on other stakeholders, we may conclude that they are acting unethically.

The managers we interviewed explained that they rated accounting manipulations harshly because in such cases the "truth" has somehow been denied or misstated. The recipients of the earnings reports do not know what earnings would have been if no manipulation had taken place. Even if the accounting methods used are consistent with GAAP, they reason, the actions are not ethical because the interests of major stakeholder groups—including the recipients of the earnings reports—have been ignored.

The managers judge the operating manipulations more favorably because the earnings numbers are indicative of what actually took place. The operating manipulations have changed reality, and "truth" is fairly reported.

We see flaws in that reasoning. One is that the truth has not necessarily been disclosed completely. When sales and profits are borrowed from the future, for example, it is a rare company that discloses the borrowed nature of some of the profits reported.

A second flaw in the reasoning about the acceptability of operating manipulations is that it ignores a few or all of the effects of some types of operating manipulations on the full range of stakeholders. Many managers consider operating manipulations as a kind of "victimless crime."

But victims do exist. Consider, for example, the relatively common operating manipulation of early shipments. As one manager told us:

> Would I ship extra product if I was faced with a sales shortfall? You have to be careful there; you're playing with fire. I would let whatever happened fall to the bottom line. I've been in companies that did whatever they could to make the sales number, such as shipping lower quality product. That's way too short term. You have to draw the line there. You must maintain the level of quality and customer service. You'll end up paying for bad shipments eventually. You'll have returns, repairs, adjustments, ill will that will cause you to lose the account.... [In addition] it's tough to go to your employees one day and say ship everything you can and then turn around the next day and say that the quality standards must be maintained.

Another reported:

> We've had to go to [one of our biggest customers] and say we need an order. That kills us in the negotiations. Our last sale was at a price just over our cost of materials.

These comments point out that customers—and sometimes even the corporation—may be victims.

Without a full analysis of the costs of operating manipulations, the dangers of such manipulations to the corporation are easily underestimated. Mistakes will be made because the quality of information is misjudged. The short term will be emphasized at the expense of the long term. If managers consistently manage short-term earnings, the messages sent to other employees create a corporate culture that lacks mutual trust, integrity, and loyalty.

A Lack of Moral Agreement

We also are troubled by the managers' inability to agree on the types of earnings-management activities that are acceptable. This lack of agreement exists even within corporations.

What this suggests is that many managers are doing their analyses in different ways. The danger is obfuscation of the reality behind the financial reports. Because managers are using different standards, individuals who try to use the information reported may be unable to assess accurately the quality of that information.

If differences in opinions exist, it is likely that financial reporting practices will sink to their lowest and most manipulative level. As a result, managers with strict definitions of what is moral and ethical will find it difficult to compete with managers who are not playing by the same rules. Ethical managers either will loosen their moral standards or fail to be promoted into positions of greater power.

Actions for Concerned Managers

We believe most corporations would benefit if they established clearer accounting and operating standards for all employees to follow. The standard-setting process should involve managers in discussions of the practices related to short-term earnings measurements.

Until these standards are in place, different managers will use widely varying criteria in assessing the acceptability of various earnings-management practices. These variations will have an adverse effect on the quality of the firm's financial information. Companies can use a questionnaire similar to the one in our study to encourage discussion and to communicate corporate standards and the reason for them.

Standards also enable internal and external auditors and management to judge whether the desired quality of earnings is being maintained. In most companies, auditors can depend on good standards to identify and judge the acceptability of the operating manipulations.

Ultimately, the line management chain-of-command, not auditors or financial staff, bears the primary responsibility for controlling operating manipulations. Often managers must rely on their prior experience and good judgment to distinguish between a decision that will have positive long-term benefits and one that has a positive short-term effect but a deleterious long-term effect.

Finally, it is important to manage the corporate culture. A culture that promotes openness and cooperative problem solving among managers is likely to result in less short-term earnings management than one that is more competitive and where annual, and even quarterly, performance shortfalls are punished. A corporate culture that is more concerned with managing for excellence rather than for reporting short-term profits will be less likely to support the widespread use of immoral earnings-management practices.

Required

a. Time, laws, regulation, and professional standards have restricted accounting practices to those that are moral, ethical, fair, and precise. Comment.

b. Most managers surveyed had a conservative, strict interpretation of what is moral or ethical in financial reporting. Comment.

c. The managers surveyed exhibited a surprising agreement as to what constitutes an ethical or unethical practice. Comment.

d. List the five generalizations from the findings in this study relating to managing earnings.

e. Comment on management's ability to manage earnings in the long run by influencing financial accounting.

CASE 2-3 FIRM COMMITMENT?

In the early 1980s, airlines introduced frequent-flier awards to develop passenger loyalty to a single airline. Free tickets and possibly other awards were made available to passengers when they accumulated a certain number of miles or flights on a particular air carrier. These programs were potentially good for the passenger and the airline as long as the awards were

(continued)

(**CASE 2-3** CONTINUED)

not too generous and the airlines could minimize revenue displacement from a paying passenger.

Originally, there were no restrictions. Anyone with the necessary miles could take any flight that had an available seat. In the late 1980s, most airlines changed their no-restriction programs to programs with restrictions and blackout days. The airlines also added partners in frequent-flier programs, such as car rental companies and hotels. These partners handed out frequent-flier miles compensating the airlines in some manner for the miles distributed. Airlines also added triple-mileage deals.

A consequence of these expanding frequent-flier programs was a surge in the number of passengers flying free and a surge in unused miles. To get a handle on the cost and the unused miles, airlines increased the frequent-flier miles needed for a flight and placed time limits on the award miles.

The increased frequent-flier miles needed for a flight and the time limits prompted lawsuits. Many of these lawsuits were filed in state courts. One of the suits filed in the District Court in Chicago in 1989 made its way to the U.S. Supreme Court. In 1995, the Supreme Court ruled that federal airline deregulation law would not bar the breach-of-contract claim in the state court. In June of 1995, a District Court in Dallas ruled in favor of the airline in a case involving an increase in miles needed to earn a trip. Airlines interpret this decision as upholding their right to make changes to their frequent-flier programs.

Required

a. In your opinion, are the outstanding (unused) miles a liability to the airline? (Substantiate your answer.)

b. Comment on the potential problems involved in estimating the dollar amount of any potential liability.

c. 1. What is a contingent liability?

   2. In your opinion, are unused miles a contingent liability to the air carrier?

   3. Recommend the recognition (if any) for unused miles.

CASE 2-4 MULTIPLE COUNTRY ENFORCEMENT*

SEC Charges Royal Ahold and Three Former Top Executives with Fraud; Former Audit Committee Member Charged with Causing Violations of the Securities Laws for Immediate Release
2004-144

Washington, D.C., Oct. 13, 2004—The Securities and Exchange Commission today announced the filing of enforcement actions alleging fraud and other violations against Royal Ahold (Koninklijke Ahold N.V.) (Ahold) and three former top executives: Cees van der Hoeven, former CEO and chairman of executive board; A. Michiel Meurs, former CFO and executive board member; and Jan Andreae, former executive vice president and executive board member. The Commission also charged Roland Fahlin, former member of Ahold's supervisory board and audit committee, with causing violations of the reporting, books and records, and internal controls provisions of the securities laws.

The SEC's complaints, filed in the United States District Court for the District of Columbia, allege that, as a result of the fraudulent inflation of promotional allowances at U.S. Foodservice, Ahold's wholly-owned subsidiary, the improper consolidation of joint ventures through fraudulent side letters, and other accounting errors and irregularities, Ahold's original SEC filings for at least fiscal years 2000 through 2002 were materially false and misleading. For fiscal years 2000 through 2002, Ahold overstated net sales by approximately EUR 33 billion ($30 billion). For fiscal years 2000 and 2001 and the first three quarters of 2002, Ahold overstated operating income by approximately EUR 3.6 billion ($3.3 billion) and net income by approximately EUR 900 million ($829 million).

The Commission has not sought penalties in the enforcement actions against the individuals because the Dutch Public Prosecutor's Office, which is conducting a parallel criminal

*Dr. Thomas Klein, Emeritus, the University of Toledo, assisted with this case.
Source: U.S. Securities and Exchange

investigation in The Netherlands, has requested that the Commission not seek penalties against the individuals because of potential double jeopardy issues under Dutch law. Because of the importance of this case in The Netherlands and the need for continued cooperation between the SEC and regulatory authorities in other countries, the Commission has agreed to the Dutch prosecutor's request.

Required

a. Why can the SEC charge a company in The Netherlands with U.S. security violations?

b. Why is The Netherlands conducting a parallel criminal investigation?

c. Speculate on how many countries may be running a parallel criminal investigation relating to securities sold.

CASE 2-5 MATERIALITY: IN PRACTICE

Professional standards require auditors to make a preliminary judgment about materiality levels during the planning of an audit. Statement of Auditing Standards (SAS) No. 47 states that "the auditor plans the audit to obtain reasonable assurance of detecting misstatements that he/she believes could be large enough, individually or in the aggregate, to be quantitatively material to the financial statements."*

SAS No. 47 indicates that materiality judgments involve both quantitative and qualitative considerations. This statement recognizes that it ordinarily is not practical to design procedures to detect misstatements that could be qualitatively material.

A number of rule-of-thumb materiality calculations have emerged, such as percentages of income, total assets, revenues, and equity. These rule-of-thumb calculations result in differing amounts for audit planning purposes. In fact, sizeable differences can result, depending on the rule of thumb and the industry.

Required

a. It would seem prudent for auditors to give careful consideration to planning materiality decisions. Comment.

b. It is difficult to design procedures to detect misstatements that could be qualitatively material. Comment.

c. It is difficult to design procedures to detect misstatements that could be quantitatively material. Comment.

d. In your opinion, would the application of materiality be a frequent issue in court cases involving financial statements? Comment.

e. Comment on materiality implications of the Sarbanes-Oxley Act as it relates to control weaknesses.

*This case is based on SAS No. 47 as updated and presented in AV312 of the *Codification of Statements on Auditing Standards* (American Institute of Certified Public Accountants, January 1989).
Source: American Institute of Certified Public Accountants, Jan. 1989

CASE 2-6 MANAGEMENT'S RESPONSIBILITY

3M* included these reports with its 2010 annual report:

Management's Responsibility for Financial Reporting

Management is responsible for the integrity and objectivity of the financial information included in this report. The financial statements have been prepared in accordance with accounting principles generally accepted in the United States of America. Where necessary, the financial statements reflect estimates based on management's judgment.

(continued)

*"3M is a diversified technology company with a global presence in the following businesses: Industrial and Transportation; Health Care; Display and Graphics; Consumer and Office; Safety, Security and Protection Services; and Electro and Communications. 3M is among the leading manufacturers of products for many of the markets it serves." 10-K
Source: U.S. Securities and Exchange

(**CASE 2-6** CONTINUED)

Management has established and maintains a system of internal accounting and other controls for the Company and its subsidiaries. This system and its established accounting procedures and related controls are designed to provide reasonable assurance that assets are safeguarded, that the books and records properly reflect all transactions, that policies and procedures are implemented by qualified personnel, and that published financial statements are properly prepared and fairly presented. The Company's system of internal control is supported by widely communicated written policies, including business conduct policies, which are designed to require all employees to maintain high ethical standards in the conduct of Company affairs. Internal auditors continually review the accounting and control system.

3M Company

Management's Report on Internal Control Over Financial Reporting

Management is responsible for establishing and maintaining an adequate system of internal control over financial reporting. Management conducted an assessment of the Company's internal control over financial reporting based on the framework established by the Committee of Sponsoring Organizations of the Treadway Commission in *Internal Control—Integrated Framework*. Based on the assessment, management concluded that, as of December 31, 2010, the Company's internal control over financial reporting is effective.

Management's assessment of the effectiveness of the Company's internal control over financial reporting as of December 31, 2010 excluded Cogent Inc., Arizant Inc. and Attenti Holdings S.A., which were all acquired by the Company in the fourth quarter of 2010 in purchase business combinations. Total assets and total net sales recorded by the Company related to these acquisitions, in the aggregate, represented less than 10 percent of consolidated total assets and less than 1 percent of consolidated net sales of the Company, respectively, as of and for the year ended December 31, 2010. Companies are allowed to exclude acquisitions from their assessment of internal control over financial reporting during the first year of an acquisition while integrating the acquired company under guidelines established by the Securities and Exchange Commission.

The Company's internal control over financial reporting as of December 31, 2010 has been audited by PricewaterhouseCoopers LLP, an independent registered public accounting firm, as stated in their report which is included herein, which expresses an unqualified opinion on the effectiveness of the Company's internal control over financial reporting as of December 31, 2010.

3M Company

Required

  a. Who has the responsibility for the financial statements?

  b. What is the role of the accountant (auditor) as to the financial statements?

  c. Accountants (auditors) are often included as defendants in lawsuits that relate to the financial statements. Speculate as to why this is the case.

  d. Why did 3M include the report "Management's Report on Internal Control Over Financial Reporting"?

CASE 2-7 SAFE HARBOR

In 1995, Congress passed the Private Securities Litigation Reform Act (the "Act"). The principal provisions of the Act are intended to curb abusive litigation and improve the quality of information available to investors through the creation of a safe harbor for forward-looking statements.

Forward-looking statements were defined to include statements relating to projections of revenues and other financial items, plans and objectives, future economic performance, assumptions, reports issued by outside reviewers, or other projections or estimates specified by rule of the SEC. The safe harbor applies to both oral and written statements.

Management frequently uses signals such as "we estimate," "we project," and the like, where forward-looking statements are not otherwise identified as such. The forward-looking

Source: Safe Harbor 2010 10-K

statements must be accompanied by meaningful cautionary statements. The cautionary statement may be contained in a separate risk section elsewhere in the disclosure document.

Southwest Airlines Co.* included this statement with its 2010 form 10-K:

Disclosure Regarding Forward-Looking Information

Some statements in this Form 10-K (or otherwise made by the Company or on the Company's behalf from time to time in other reports, filings with the SEC, news releases, conferences, Internet postings, or otherwise) that are not historical facts may be "forward-looking statements" within the meaning of Section 27A of the Securities Act of 1933, as amended, Section 21E of the Securities Exchange Act of 1934, as amended, and the Private Securities Litigation Reform Act of 1995. Forward-looking statements are based on, and include statements about, the Company's estimates, expectations, beliefs, intentions, or strategies for the future, and the assumptions underlying these forward-looking statements. Specific forward-looking statements can be identified by the fact that they do not relate strictly to historical or current facts and include, without limitation, words such as "anticipates," "believes," "estimates," "expects," "intends," "may," "will," "should," and similar expressions. While management believes these forward-looking statements are reasonable as and when made, forward-looking statements are not guarantees of future performance and involve risks and uncertainties that are difficult to predict. Therefore, actual results may differ materially from what is expressed in or indicated by the Company's forward-looking statements or from historical experience or the Company's present expectations. Factors that could cause these differences include, but are not limited to, those set forth below under "Risk Factors."

Caution should be taken not to place undue reliance on the Company's forward-looking statements, which represent the Company's views only as of the date this report is filed. The Company undertakes no obligation to update publicly or revise any forward-looking statement, whether as a result of new information, future events, or otherwise.

Required

a. Demand for financial reports exists because users believe that the reports help them in decision making. In your opinion, will forward-looking statements as provided by the Private Securities Litigation Reform Act aid users of financial reports in decision making?

b. To some extent, investors' rights are limited by the curb of abusive litigation. In your opinion, is there a net benefit to investors from a safe harbor for forward-looking statements?

*"Southwest Airlines Co. (the "Company" or "Southwest") is a major passenger airline that provides scheduled air transportation in the United States." 10-K

CASE 2-8 ENFORCEMENT

This case includes a news release issued by the Public Company Accounting Oversight Board. This news release comments on the first disciplines of an accounting firm and auditors under the Sarbanes-Oxley Act of 2002.

Board Revokes Firm's Registration, Disciplines Three Accountants for Failure to Cooperate

Washington, DC, May 24, 2005—The Public Company Accounting Oversight Board today revoked the registration of a public accounting firm and barred the firm's managing partner from association with a registered accounting firm after finding that they concealed information from the Board and submitted false information in connection with a PCAOB inspection.

The Board also censured two former partners in the firm, finding that they participated in the misconduct but noting that they promptly alerted the PCAOB and cooperated in the Board's investigation.

"Registered accounting firms and their associated persons have a duty to cooperate in PCAOB inspections," said Claudius Modesti, director of the PCAOB's Division of

Source: U.S. Securities and Exchange

(*continued*)

(**CASE 2-8** CONTINUED)

Enforcement and Investigations. "The findings in this case demonstrate that the Board will not tolerate conduct aimed at thwarting the Board's inspections."

The accounting firm, Goldstein and Morris CPAs, P.C., based in New York City, was notified in September 2004 that the firm would be inspected by the PCAOB in November 2004.

The PCAOB's Division of Registration and Inspections directed a request for information and documents to the firm's managing partner, Edward B. Morris. The Board found that, in responding to the request, Mr. Morris and two partners, Alan J. Goldberger and William A. Postelnik, were aware that the firm had prepared the financial statements of two of its public company audit clients, contrary to auditor independence requirements of federal law. The Board found that Messrs. Morris, Goldberger, and Postelnik took steps to conceal that fact from the Board by omitting certain requested information from the firm's written response to the inspection request.

The Board also found that the partners, after learning of the imminent inspection, formulated and carried out a plan to create and back-date certain documents and place them in the firm's audit files. The Board found that Messrs. Morris, Goldberger, and Postelnik took these steps to conceal from the Board the firm's failure to comply with certain auditing standards.

Messrs. Goldberger and Postelnik notified the PCAOB of the omitted and falsified information. Both resigned from the firm.

The accounting firm and Mr. Morris consented to a Board order making the findings and imposing sanctions, without admitting or denying the findings. The order bars Mr. Morris from association with a registered accounting firm and revokes the firm's registration. Firms that are not registered with the PCAOB are prohibited from auditing the financial statements of public companies.

Messrs. Goldberger and Postelnik each consented to a Board order making the findings and imposing the censures without admitting or denying the findings. The Board limited the sanctions of the two men to censures because they "promptly and voluntarily brought the matter to the Board's attention, disclosed their own misconduct and the misconduct of others, and made affirmative efforts to provide the Board with relevant information."

The Board's orders are available under Enforcement at www.pcaobus.org.

Suspected misconduct by auditors can be reported to the PCAOB Center for Enforcement Tips, Complaints and Other Information by e-mail or by phone to 800-741-3158. Media Inquiries: Public Affairs, 202-207-9227

Required

a. Does it appear that Mr. Morris and the accounting firm can continue to function in public accounting? Comment.

b. It appears that Mr. Morris, Goldberger, and Postelnik can continue to function as certified public accountants. Speculate on what may happen to their ability to function as certified public accountants. (*Hint:* Certification is granted by individual states.)

CASE 2-9 NOTIFY THE SEC

Summary

"This matter involves Hewlett-Packard's failure to disclose the circumstances surrounding a board member's resignation amidst the company's controversial investigation into boardroom leaks. On May 18, 2006, HP's Board of Directors learned the findings of the company's leak investigation and voted to request the resignation of a director believed to have violated HP's policies by providing confidential information to the press. Silicon Valley venture capitalist and fellow director Thomas Perkins (not the source of the leak) voiced his strong objections to the handling of the matter, announced his resignation, and walked out of the Board meeting. Contrary to the reporting requirements of the federal securities laws, HP failed to disclose to investors the circumstances of Mr. Perkins' disagreement with the company."*

*SEC Administrative Proceeding, File No. 3-12643, May 23, 2007.
Source: U.S. Securities and Exchange

Required

a. What form reviewed in this chapter would be used to disclose the resignation of a board member?

b. Comment on why it would be in the public interest to know the circumstances surrounding the resignation of this board member.

Web Case   THOMSON ONE   *Business School Edition*

Please complete the Web case that covers material discussed in this chapter at www.cengagebrain .com. You'll be using Thomson ONE Business School Edition, a powerful tool, that combines a full range of fundamental financial information, earnings estimates, market data, and source documents for 500 publicly traded companies.

To the Net Case

1. Go to the COSO Web site: www.coso.org. What is COSO? List the five major professional associations that sponsored COSO.

2. Consolidated Statement Presentation
   Go to the SEC Web site: www.sec.gov. Under "Filings & Forms (EDGAR)," click on "Search for Company Filings." Click on "Company or fund name."
   a. Under Company Name, enter "Ford Motor Co" (or under Ticker Symbol, enter "F"). Select the 2010 10-K. Review the Sector Statement of Income found a little over half-way through the document. Describe in some detail the consolidation presentation. (Refer to comments in this chapter.)
   b. Type in "Dow Chemical Co" (or under Ticker Symbol, enter "DOW"). Select the 2010 10-K. Review the consolidated statements of income. Describe in some detail the consolidated presentation. (Refer to comments in this chapter.)

3. Proxy
   Go to the SEC Web site: www.sec.gov. Under "Filings & Forms (EDGAR)," click on "Search for Company Filings." Click on "Company or Fund Name Etc." Under Company Name, enter "Gorman-Rupp Company" (or under Ticker Symbol, enter "GRC"). Select the 2010 proxy. Go to Executive Compensation within the proxy. Describe the executive compensation.

4. Audit Report and Auditor's Report on the Firm's Internal Controls
   Go to the SEC Web site: www.sec.gov. Under "Filings & Forms (EDGAR)," click on "Search for Company Filings." Click on "Company or Fund Name Etc." Under Company Name, enter "Bemis Company" (or under Ticker Symbol, enter "BMS"). Select the 2010 10-K.
   Go to Report of Independent Registered Public Accounting Firm. Compare this report with Exhibit 2-5 (Audit Opinion) and Exhibit 2-6 (Auditor's Report on the Firm's Internal Controls). What is the basic difference in presentation?

5. Go to the SEC site (www.sec.gov). Under "Filings & Forms (Edgar)," click on "Search for Company Filings." Click on "Company or fund, etc." Under Company Name, enter "Honeywell International Inc." (or under Ticker Symbol, enter "HON"). Select the 10-K filed February 11, 2011.
   a. "Item 8 Financial Statements and Supplementary Data",
      1. What is the cash and cash equivalents balance at December 31, 2009?
   b. Go to "Consolidated Statement of Cash Flows"
      1. What is the cash and cash equivalents at the beginning of the year ended December 31, 2010?
      2. What is the cash and cash equivalents at the end of the year ended December 31, 2010?
   c. Go to "Consolidated Balance Sheet" December 31, 2010
      1. What is the cash and cash equivalents at December 31, 2010?
   d. From the "Consolidated Balance Sheet":
      1. What is the retained earnings at December 31, 2009?

(continued)

(TO THE NET CONTINUED)

    e. Go to "Consolidated Statement of Operations"

       1. What is the net income attributable to Honeywell for year ended December 31, 2009?

    f. Go to "Consolidated Statement of Shareowners Equity"

       1. What is the beginning balance of retained earnings for year ended December 31, 2010?

       2. What was the net income attributable to Honeywell for the year ended December 31, 2010?

       3. What was the dividends paid on common stock for the year ended December 31, 2010?

       4. What is the ending balance of retained earnings for December 31, 2010?

    g. Go to "Consolidated Balance Sheet" for December 31, 2010

       1. What is the balance for retained earnings at December 31, 2010?

    h. Go to the "Consolidated Statement of Cash Flows"

       1. What was the cash dividend paid for 2010?

    i. What was the dividends paid on common stock for the year ended December 31, 2010 (Consolidated Statement of Shareowners Equity)?

    j. What was the cash dividend paid for 2010 (Consolidated Statement of Cash Flows)? Try to explain the difference between these numbers.

6. Go to www.businessethics.ca. Click on "Business Ethics Articles." Click on "Short Articles on Workplace Ethics" by Cornelius von Baeyer. Select an article and write a summary.

Endnotes

1. www.coso.org.

2. Jaclyne Badal and Phred Dvorak, "Sarbanes-Oxley Gains Adherents," *The Wall Street Journal* (August 14, 2006), p. B3.

3. Charles H. Gibson and Nicholas Schroeder, "How 21 Companies Handled Their Summary Annual Reports," *Financial Executive* (November/December 1989), pp. 45–46.

4. Mary E. Guy, *Ethical Decision Making in Everyday Work Situations* (New York: Quorum Books, 1990), p. 5.

5. Ibid., p. 14.

6. William W. May, ed., *Ethics in the Accounting Curriculum: Cases & Readings* (Sarasota, FL: American Accounting Association, 1990), pp. 1–2.

7. "Regulators Investigate Peat on Its Auditing of S&L," *The New York Times* (May 23, 1991), p. D-1.

8. "S.E.C. Inquiry Is Reported on Loans to Accountants," *The New York Times* (February 7, 1991), p. D-1.

9. "Ernst & Young Settles Negligence Charge," *Business Insurance* (May 6, 1991), p. 2.

10. Ronald Grover, "Curtains for Tinseltown Accounting?" *Business Week* (January 14, 1991), p. 35.

11. Shahram Victory, "Pierce O'Donnell Pans 'Fatal Subtraction,'" *American Lawyer* (March 1991), p. 43.

12. "Buchwald Wins Just $150,000 in Film Lawsuit," *The Wall Street Journal* (March 17, 1992), p. B1.

13. SEC Adopts Rules on Provisions of Sarbanes-Oxley Act, SEC Web site, www.sec.gov/. The SEC News Digest Archive, January 16, 2003.

Chapter

3

Balance Sheet

The principal financial statements are the balance sheet, income statement, and statement of cash flows. This chapter will review the balance sheet in detail. Other titles used for the balance sheet are statement of financial position and statement of financial condition. The title *balance sheet* is the predominant title used.[1]

Another statement, called the statement of stockholders' equity, reconciles the changes in stockholders' equity, a section of the balance sheet. This statement will also be reviewed in this chapter. Many alternative titles are used for the statement of stockholders' equity. The title most frequently used is the *statement of stockholders' equity*. Another frequently used title is the statement of shareholders' equity.[2]

Basic Elements of the Balance Sheet

A balance sheet shows the financial condition of an accounting entity as of a particular date. The balance sheet consists of assets, the resources of the firm; liabilities, the debts of the firm; and stockholders' equity, the owners' interest in the firm.

The assets are derived from two sources, creditors and owners. At any point in time, the assets must equal the contribution of the creditors and owners. The accounting equation expresses this relationship:

$$\text{Assets} = \text{Liabilities} + \text{Stockholders' Equity}$$

On the balance sheet, the assets equal the liabilities plus the stockholders' equity. This may be presented side by side (account form) or with the assets at the top and the liabilities and stockholders' equity at the bottom (report form). Exhibit 3-1 presents a typical report form format, and Exhibit 3-2 presents a typical account form format. The report form is dominant in the United States.[3]

Balance sheet formats differ across nations. For example, nations influenced by British financial reporting report the least liquid assets first and cash last. Nations influenced by the United States report a balance sheet emphasizing liquidity, as illustrated in this chapter.

| EXHIBIT **3-1** | Quaker Chemical Corporation* |

QUAKER CHEMICAL CORPORATION
CONSOLIDATED BALANCE SHEET
Report Form

	December 31,	
	2010	**2009**
	(In thousands, except par value and share amounts)	
ASSETS		
Current Assets		
Cash and cash equivalents	$ 25,766	$ 25,051
Construction fund (restricted cash)	—	2,358
Accounts receivable, net	116,266	108,793
Inventories	60,841	50,040
Current deferred tax assets	4,624	5,523
Prepaid expenses and other current assets	7,985	7,409
Total current assets	215,482	199,174
Property, plant and equipment, net	76,535	67,426
Goodwill	52,758	46,515
Other intangible assets, net	24,030	5,579
Investments in associated companies	9,218	8,824
Non-current deferred tax assets	28,846	28,237
Other assets	42,561	39,537
Total assets	$449,430	$395,292
LIABILITIES AND EQUITY		
Current liabilities		
Short-term borrowings and current portion of long-term debt	$ 890	$ 2,431
Accounts payable	61,192	58,389
Dividends payable	2,701	2,550
Accrued compensation	17,140	16,656
Accrued pension and postretirement benefits	1,672	4,717
Current deferred tax liabilities	181	213
Other current liabilities	17,415	15,224
Total current liabilities	101,191	100,180
Long-term debt	73,855	63,685
Non-current deferred tax liabilities	6,108	5,213
Accrued pension and postretirement benefits	30,016	27,602
Other non-current liabilities	51,161	42,317
Total liabilities	262,331	238,997
Commitments and contingencies	—	—
Equity		
Common stock, $1 par value; authorized 30,000,000 shares; Issued:		
2010-11,492,142 shares, 2009-11,085,549 shares	11,492	11,086
Capital in excess of par value	38,275	27,527
Retained earnings	144,347	123,140
Accumulated other comprehensive loss	(13,736)	(10,439)
Total Quaker shareholders' equity	180,378	151,314
Noncontrolling interest	6,721	4,981
Total equity	187,099	156,295
Total liabilities and shareholders' equity	$449,430	$395,292

*"Quaker develops, produces, and markets a broad range of formulated chemical specialty products for various heavy industrial and manufacturing applications and, in addition, offers and markets chemical management services ("CMS")." 10-K

Source: Quaker Chemical Corporation 2010 10-K

EXHIBIT 3-2 Zebra Technologies Corporation*

Account Form

Zebra Technologies Corporation
Consolidated Balance Sheets
(Amounts in thousands)

ASSETS	December 31, 2010	December 31, 2009
Current Assets:		
Cash and equivalents	$ 47,476	$ 38,943
Restricted cash	1,378	1,725
Investments and marketable securities	125,567	114,064
Accounts receivable, net of allowance of $2,161 in 2010 and $2,186 in 2009	154,146	150,992
Inventories, net	113,742	79,926
Deferred income taxes	19,162	10,792
Income taxes payable	—	4,724
Prepaid expenses and other current assets	14,833	9,771
Total Current Assets	476,304	410,937
Property and equipment at cost, net of accumulated depreciation and amortization:	88,983	77,589
Long term deferred income taxes	21,254	35,842
Goodwill	151,933	153,225
Other intangibles, net	49,706	55,982
Long term investments and marketable securities	85,478	91,989
Other assets	5,206	4,915
Total assets	$878,864	$830,479

LIABILITIES AND STOCKHOLDERS' EQUITY	December 31, 2010	December 31, 2009
Current liabilities:		
Accounts payable	$ 35,304	$ 28,137
Accrued liabilities	68,090	52,591
Deferred revenue	26,757	24,082
Income taxes payable	5,900	—
Total current liabilities	136,051	104,810
Deferred rent	2,406	4,108
Other long-term liabilities	10,375	9,432
Total liabilities	148,832	118,350
Commitments and contingencies (Note 11)		
Stockholders' equity:		
Preferred stock		
Class A Common Stock	722	722
Additional paid capital	129,715	136,104
Treasury stock	(462,029)	(385,831)
Retained earnings	1,070,973	969,195
Accumulated other comprehensive income (loss)	(9,349)	(8,061)
Total stockholders' equity	730,032	712,129
Total liabilities and stockholders' equity	$ 878,864	$ 830,479

*"Zebra delivers products and solutions that improve our customers' ability to put their critical assets to work smarter by identifying, tracking and managing assets, transactions and people." 10-K
Source: Zebra Technologies Corporation 2010 10-K

Assets

Assets are probable future economic benefits obtained or controlled by an entity as a result of past transactions or events.[4] Assets may be *physical*, such as land, buildings, inventory of supplies, material, or finished products. Assets may also be *intangible*, such as patents and trademarks.

Assets are normally divided into two major categories: current and noncurrent (long-term). **Current assets** are assets (1) in the form of cash (2) that will normally be realized in cash or (3) that conserve the use of cash during the operating cycle of a firm or for one year, whichever is longer. The *operating cycle* covers the time between the acquisition of inventory and the realization of cash from selling the inventory. **Noncurrent or long-term assets** take longer than a year or an operating cycle to be converted to cash or to conserve cash. Some industries, such as banking (financial institutions), insurance, and real estate, do not divide assets (or liabilities) into current and noncurrent. Chapter 12 reviews specialized industries.

When a significant subsidiary is consolidated from an industry that does not use the concept of current and noncurrent, then the consolidated statements will not use the concept of current and noncurrent. These companies often present supplementary statements, handling the subsidiary as an investment (nonconsolidated).

For example, General Electric does not use the concept of current and noncurrent. General Electric Company's consolidated financial statements represent the combination of manufacturing and nonfinancial services businesses of General Electric Company (GE) and the accounts of General Electric Capital Services, Inc. (GECS).

Current Assets

Current assets are listed on the balance sheet in order of **liquidity** (the ability to be converted to cash). Current assets typically include cash, marketable securities, short-term receivables, inventories, and prepaids. In some cases, assets other than these may be classified as current. If so, management is indicating that it expects the asset to be converted into cash during the operating cycle or within a year, whichever is longer. An example is land held for immediate disposal. Exhibit 3-3 includes the items that the 2006 edition of *Accounting Trends & Techniques* reported as being disclosed as other current assets. The definition of current assets excludes restricted cash, investments for purposes of control, long-term receivables, the cash surrender value of life insurance, land and other natural resources, depreciable assets, and long-term prepayments.

EXHIBIT **3-3**	Other Current Asset Captions*			
	Number of Entities			
Nature of Asset	**2009**	**2008**	**2007**	**2006**
Deferred and prepaid income taxes	381	371	450	434
Derivatives	232	55	50	56
Property held for sale	79	80	120	120
Unbilled costs	15	13	24	21
Advances or deposits	8	22	23	18
Other – identified	33	48	41	37

*Appearing in either the balance sheet or the notes to financial statements 2008 – 2009 based on 500 entities surveyed; 2006 – 2007 based on 600 entities surveyed.
Source: Accounting Trends & Techniques, copyright © 2010 by American Institute of Certified Public Accountants, Inc., p. 175. Reprinted with permission.

Cash

Cash, the most liquid asset, includes negotiable checks and unrestricted balances in checking accounts, as well as cash on hand. Savings accounts are classified as cash even though the bank may not release the money for a specific period of time. Exhibit 3-4 illustrates the presentation of cash.

| EXHIBIT 3-4 | SeaChange International, Inc.* |

SEACHANGE INTERNATIONAL, INC.
CONSOLIDATED BALANCE SHEET (In Part)
(In thousands, except share data)

	January 31, 2011	January 31, 2010
ASSETS		
Current Assets:		
Cash and cash equivalents	$ 73,145	$ 37,647
Restricted cash	1,332	73
Marketable securities	7,340	2,114
Accounts receivable, net of allowance for doubtful accounts of $995 in 2011 and $852 in 2010, respectively	48,843	50,337
Unbilled receivables	5,644	3,941
Inventories, net	14,393	17,830
Prepaid expenses and other current assets	7,148	7,253
Deferred tax assets	3,775	2,474
Total current assets	161,620	121,669

*"SeaChange International, Inc. ("SeaChange", "we" or "us"), a Delaware corporation founded on July 9, 1993, is a global leader in the delivery of multi-screen video." 10-K
Source: Seachange International, Inc. 2010 10-K

Marketable Securities

Marketable securities (also labeled short-term investments) are characterized by their marketability at a readily determinable market price. A firm holds marketable securities to earn a return on near-cash resources. Management must intend to convert these assets to cash during the current period for them to be classified as marketable securities.

The carrying basis of debt and equity marketable securities is fair value. Refer to Exhibit 3-4 for a presentation of marketable securities.

Accounts Receivable

Accounts receivable are monies due on accounts that arise from sales or services rendered to customers. Accounts receivable are shown net of allowances to reflect their realizable value. This amount is expected to be collected. The most typical allowances are for bad debts (uncollectible accounts). Other allowances may account for expected sales discounts, which are given for prompt payment or for sales returns. These types of allowances recognize expenses in the period of sale, at which time the allowance is established. In future periods, when the losses occur, they are charged to the allowance. All of the allowances are presented in one allowance account. Exhibit 3-4 presents the accounts receivable of SeaChange International, Inc. (less allowances). At January 31, 2011, the firm expects to realize $48,843,000. The gross receivables can be reconciled as follows:

Receivables, net	$48,843,000
Plus: Allowances	995,000
Receivables, gross	$49,838,000

Other receivables may also be included in current assets. These receivables may result from tax refund claims, investees/affiliates, contracts, finance, retained interest in sold receivables, insurance claims, vendors/suppliers, asset disposals, and employees.

Receivables other than trade receivables include tax refund claims, affiliates, contracts, finance, and insurance claims.[5]

Inventories

Inventories are the balance of goods on hand. In a manufacturing firm, they include raw materials, work in process, and finished goods. In a retail firm the inventory is merchandise inventory. Inventories will be carried at cost, expressed in terms of lower-of-cost-or-market.

(Cost methods and lower-of-cost-or-market are covered in Chapter 7.) Refer to Exhibit 3-5 for a presentation of inventory.

Raw Materials These are goods purchased for direct use in manufacturing a product, and they become part of the product. For example, in the manufacture of shirts, the fabric and buttons would be raw materials.

EXHIBIT **3-5**	Simpson Manufacturing Co., Inc.*

Illustration of Inventory

Simpson Manufacturing Co., Inc. and Subsidiaries
Consolidated Balance Sheets (In Part)
(In thousands, except per share data)

	December 31,	
	2010	2009
ASSETS		
Current assets		
Cash and equivalents	$335,049	$250,381
Trade accounts receivable, net	68,256	77,317
Inventories	152,297	163,754
Deferred income taxes	10,189	13,970
Assets held for sale	10,787	7,887
Other current assets	14,678	16,766
Total current assets	591,256	530,075

Notes to Consolidated Financial Statements (In Part)

1. Operations and Summary of Significant Accounting Policies (In Part)

Inventory Valuation
Inventories are stated at lower of cost or net realizable value (market). Cost includes all costs incurred in bringing each product to its present location and condition, as follows:

- Raw materials and purchased finished goods for resale – principally valued at cost determined on a weighted average basis.
- In-process products and finished goods – cost of direct materials and labor plus attributable overhead based on a normal level of activity.

The Company applies net realizable value and obsolescence to the gross value of the inventory. The Company estimates net realizable value based on estimated selling price less further costs to completion and disposal. The Company provides for slow-moving products by comparing inventories on hand to future projected demand. Obsolete inventory is on-hand supply of a product in excess of two years' sales of that product or a supply of that product that the Company believes is no longer marketable. The Company revalues obsolete inventory as having no net realizable value and writes off its full carrying value. The Company has consistently applied this methodology. The Company believes that this approach is prudent and makes suitable provisions for slow-moving and obsolete inventory. When provisions are established, a new cost basis of the inventory is created.

4. Inventories

The components of inventories consisted of the following:

(In thousands)	December 31,	
	2010	2009
Raw materials	$ 61,996	$ 61,408
In-process products	18,364	21,113
Finished products	71,937	81,233
	$152,297	$163,754

*"Simpson Manufacturing Co., Inc., a Delaware Corporation, (the "Company"), through its subsidiary, Simpson Strong-Tie Company Inc. ("Simpson Strong-Tie" or "SST"), designs, engineers and is a leading manufacturer of wood-to-wood, wood-to-concrete and wood-to-masonry connectors, fasteners and fastening systems, and pre-fabricated shearwalls." 10-K
Source: Simpson Manufacturing Co., Inc, 10-K

Work in Process Work in process represents goods started but not ready for sale. Work in process includes the cost of materials, labor costs for workers directly involved in the manufacture, and factory overhead. Factory overhead includes such cost items as rent, indirect wages, and maintenance.

Finished Goods Finished goods are inventory ready for sale. These inventory costs also include the cost of materials, labor costs for workers directly involved in the manufacture, and a portion of factory overhead.

Since retailing and wholesaling firms do not engage in the manufacture of a product but only in the sale, their only inventory item is merchandise. These firms do not have raw materials, work in process, inventory, or finished goods.

Supplies In addition to goods on hand, the firm may have supplies. Supplies could include register tapes, pencils, or sewing machine needles for the shirt factory. Details relating to inventory are usually disclosed in a note.

Prepaids

A **prepaid** is an expenditure made in advance of the use of the service or goods. It represents future benefits that have resulted from past transactions. For example, if insurance is paid in advance for three years, at the end of the first year, two years' worth of the outlay will be prepaid. The entity retains the right to be covered by insurance for two more years.

Typical prepaids include advertising, taxes, insurance, promotion costs, and early payments on long-term contracts. Prepaids are often not disclosed separately. In both Exhibit 3-1 and Exhibit 3-2, the prepaid account is not disclosed separately.

Long-Term Assets

Long-term assets are usually divided into four categories: tangible assets, investments, intangible assets, and other.

Tangible Assets

These are the physical facilities used in the operations of the business. The tangible assets of land, buildings, machinery, and construction in progress will now be reviewed. Accumulated depreciation related to buildings and machinery will also be reviewed.

Land Land is shown at acquisition cost and is not depreciated because land does not get used up. Land containing resources that will be used up, however, such as mineral deposits and timberlands, is subject to depletion. Depletion expense attempts to measure the wearing away of these resources. It is similar to depreciation except that depreciation deals with a tangible fixed asset and depletion deals with a natural resource.

Buildings Structures are presented at cost plus the cost of permanent improvements. Buildings are depreciated (expensed) over their estimated useful life.

Machinery Machinery is listed at historical cost, including delivery and installation, plus any material improvements that extend its life or increase the quantity or quality of service. Machinery is depreciated over its estimated useful life.

Construction in Progress Construction in progress represents cost incurred for projects under construction. These costs will be transferred to the proper tangible asset account upon completion of construction. The firm cannot use these assets while they are under construction. Some analysis is directed at how efficiently the company is using operating assets. This analysis can be distorted by construction in progress, since construction in progress is classified as part of tangible assets. To avoid this distortion, construction in progress should be classified under long-term assets, other.

Accumulated Depreciation Depreciation is the process of allocating the cost of buildings and machinery over the periods benefited. The depreciation expense taken each period is accumulated in a separate account (Accumulated Depreciation). Accumulated depreciation is subtracted from the cost of plant and equipment. The net amount is the **book value** of the asset. It does not represent the current market value of the asset.

There are a number of depreciation methods that a firm can use. Often, a firm depreciates an asset under one method for financial statements and another for income tax returns. A firm often wants to depreciate slowly for the financial statements because this results in the highest immediate income and highest asset balance. The same firm would want to depreciate faster for income tax returns because this results in the lowest immediate income and thus lower income taxes. Over the life of an asset, the total depreciation will be the same regardless of the depreciation method selected.

Three factors are usually considered when computing depreciation: (1) the asset cost, (2) length of the life of the asset, and (3) its salvage value when retired from service. The length of the asset's life and the salvage value must be estimated at the time that the asset is placed in service. These estimates may be later changed if warranted.

Exhibit 3-6 indicates the depreciation methods used for financial reporting purposes by the firms surveyed for the 2010 edition of *Accounting Trends & Techniques*. The most popular method was straight-line. Many firms use more than one depreciation method.

The following assumptions will be made to illustrate some depreciation methods:

1. Cost of asset—$10,000
2. Estimated life of asset—5 years
3. Estimated salvage (or residual) value—$2,000
4. Estimated total hours of use—16,000

EXHIBIT **3-6**	Depreciation Methods			
	Number of Companies			
	2009	**2008**	**2007**	**2006**
Straight-line	488	494	594	592
Declining-balance	10	10	13	16
Sum-of-the-years' digits	3	3	4	5
Accelerated method—not specified	17	21	24	27
Units-of-production	16	14	20	23
Group/Composite	10	7	11	9

2008 – 2009 based on 500 entities surveyed;
2006 – 2007 based on 600 entities surveyed

Source: Accounting Trends & Techniques, Copyright © 2010 by American Institute of Certified Public Accountants, Inc., p. 389. Reprinted with permission.

Straight-Line Method The straight-line method recognizes depreciation in equal amounts over the estimated life of the asset. Compute depreciation using the straight-line method as follows:

$$\frac{\text{Cost} - \text{Salvage Value}}{\text{Estimated Life}} = \text{Annual Depreciation}$$

For the asset used for illustration, the annual depreciation would be computed as follows:

$$\frac{\$10,000 - \$2,000}{5 \text{ years}} = \$1,600$$

The $1,600 depreciation amount would be recognized each year of the five-year life of the asset. Do not depreciate the salvage value.

Declining-Balance Method The declining-balance method, an accelerated method, applies a multiple times the straight-line rate to the declining book value (cost minus accumulated depreciation) to achieve a declining depreciation charge over the estimated life of the asset. This book will use double the straight-line rate, which is the maximum rate that can be used. Compute depreciation using the declining-balance method as follows:

$$\frac{1}{\text{Estimated Life of Asset}} \times 2 \times \text{Book Amount at Beginning of the Year} = \text{Annual Depreciation}$$

For the asset used for illustration, the first year's depreciation would be computed as follows:

$$\frac{1}{5} \times 2 \times (\$10,000 - 0) = \$4,000$$

The declining-balance method results in the following depreciation amounts for each of the five years of the asset's life:

Year	Cost	Accumulated Depreciation at Beginning of Year	Book Amount at Beginning of Year	Depreciation for Year	Book Amount at End of Year
1	$10,000	—	$10,000	$4,000	$6,000
2	10,000	$4,000	6,000	2,400	3,600
3	10,000	6,400	3,600	1,440	2,160
4	10,000	7,840	2,160	160	2,000
5	10,000	8,000	2,000	—	2,000

Estimated salvage value is not considered in the formula, but the asset should not be depreciated below the estimated salvage value. For the sample asset, the formula produced a depreciation amount of $864 in the fourth year. Only $160 depreciation can be used in the fourth year because the $160 amount brings the book amount of the asset down to the salvage value. Once the book amount is equal to the salvage value, no additional depreciation may be taken.

Sum-of-the-Years'-Digits Method The sum-of-the-years'-digits method is an accelerated depreciation method. Thus, the depreciation expense declines steadily over the estimated life of the asset. This method takes a fraction each year times the cost less salvage value. The numerator of the fraction changes each year. It is the remaining number of years of the asset's life. The denominator of the fraction remains constant; it is the sum of the digits representing the years of the asset's life. Compute depreciation using the sum-of-the-years'-digits method as follows:

$$\frac{\text{Remaining Number of Years of Life}}{\text{Sum of the Digits Representing the Years of Life}} \times (\text{Cost} - \text{Salvage}) = \text{Annual Depreciation}$$

For the asset used for illustration, the first year's depreciation would be computed as follows:

$$\frac{5}{(5 + 4 + 3 + 2 + 1) \text{ or } 15} \times (\$10,000 - \$2,000) = \$2,666.67$$

The sum-of-the-years'-digits method results in the following depreciation amounts for each year of the five years of the asset's life:

Year	Cost Less Salvage Value	Fraction	Depreciation for Year	Accumulated Depreciation at End of Year	Book Amount at End of Year
1	$8,000	5/15	$2,666.67	$2,666.67	$7,333.33
2	8,000	4/15	2,133.33	4,800.00	5,200.00
3	8,000	3/15	1,600.00	6,400.00	3,600.00
4	8,000	2/15	1,066.67	7,466.67	2,533.33
5	8,000	1/15	533.33	8,000.00	2,000.00

Unit-of-Production Method The unit-of-production method relates depreciation to the output capacity of the asset, estimated for the life of the asset. The capacity is stated in terms most appropriate for the asset, such as units of production, hours of use, or miles. Hours of use will be used for the asset in our example. For the life of the asset, it is estimated that there will be 16,000 hours of use. The estimated output capacity is divided into the cost of the asset less the salvage value to determine the depreciation per unit of output. For the example asset, the depreciation per hour of use would be $0.50 [(cost of asset, $10,000 − salvage, $2,000) divided by 16,000 hours].

The depreciation for each year is then determined by multiplying the depreciation per unit of output by the output for that year. Assuming that the output was 2,000 hours during the first year, the depreciation for that year would be $1,000 ($0.50 × 2,000). Further depreciation cannot be taken when the accumulated depreciation equals the cost of the asset less the salvage value. For the example asset, this will be when accumulated depreciation equals $8,000.

In Exhibit 3-7, Kelly Services, Inc., presents these assets as property, plant, and equipment at cost. Added detailed information is disclosed in the notes.

Leases

Leases are classified as *operating* leases or *capital* leases. If the lease is in substance an ownership arrangement, it is a capital lease; otherwise, the lease is an operating lease. Assets leased under a capital lease are classified as long-term assets. They are shown net of amortization (depreciation) and listed with plant, property, and equipment. (The discounted value of the obligation, a liability, will be part current and part long term.) Chapter 7 covers the topic of leases in more length.

Investments

Long-term investments, usually stocks and bonds of other companies, are often held to maintain a business relationship or to exercise control. Long-term investments are different from marketable securities, where the intent is to hold for short-term profits and to achieve liquidity. (Financial reports often refer to marketable securities as investments.)

Debt securities under investments are to be classified as held-to-maturity securities or available-for-sale securities. *Held-to-maturity securities* are securities that the firm has the intent and ability to hold to maturity. Debt securities classified as held-to-maturity securities are carried at amortized cost. Debt securities classified as available-for-sale securities are carried at fair value.

Equity securities under investments are to be carried at fair value. An exception for fair value is used for common stock where there is significant influence. For these common stock investments, the investment is carried under the equity method. Under the equity method, the cost is adjusted for the proportionate share of the rise (fall) in retained profits of the subsidiary (investee). For example, a parent company owns 40% of a subsidiary company, purchased at a cost of $400,000. When the subsidiary company earns $100,000, the parent company increases the investment account by 40% of $100,000, or $40,000. When the subsidiary company declares dividends of $20,000, the parent company decreases the investment account by 40% of $20,000, or $8,000. This decrease occurs because the investment account changes in direct proportion to the retained earnings of the subsidiary.

The FASB has given guidance on the use of fair value. Fair value is the price that a company would receive to sell an asset (or transfer a liability) in an orderly transaction between market participants on the date of measurement. With fair value, the firm selects the highest appropriate level for valuation. The levels of input for valuation are as follows:

1. Level 1: Quoted price for identical asset (or liability) in active market.
2. Level 2: Adjusted quoted price for similar asset (or liability). Level 2 inputs are to be used when level 1 inputs are not readily available.
3. Level 3: Unobservable inputs (e.g., present value of expected cash flows). The present value of an asset is the net amount of discounted future cash inflows less the discounted future cash outflows relating to the asset.

EXHIBIT **3-7**	Kelly Services, Inc.*

Properties and Depreciation

CONSOLIDATED BALANCE SHEETS (In Part)
Kelly Services, Inc. and Subsidiaries

	2010	2009
	(In millions of dollars)	
ASSETS		
Current Assets		
Cash and equivalents	$ 80.5	$ 88.9
Trade accounts receivable, less allowances of		
$12.3 million and 15.0 million, respectively	810.9	717.9
Prepaid expenses and other current assets	44.8	70.6
Deferred taxes	22.4	21.0
Total current assets	958.6	898.4
Property and Equipment		
Land and buildings	59.0	58.8
Computer hardware, software and other	260.3	264.0
Accumulated depreciation	(215.3)	(195.7)
Net property and equipment	104.0	127.1
Noncurrent Deferred Taxes	84.0	77.5
Goodwill, net	67.3	67.3
Other Assets	154.5	142.2
Total Assets	$1,368.4	$1,312.5

NOTES TO CONSOLIDATED FINANCIAL STATEMENTS (In Part)
Kelly Services, Inc. and Subsidiaries

1. Summary of Significant Accounting Policies (In Part)

Property and Equipment Property and equipment are stated at cost and are depreciated over their estimated useful lives, principally by the straight-line method. Cost and estimated useful lives of property and equipment by function are as follows:

Category	2010	2009	Life
	(In millions of dollars)		
Land	$ 3.8	$ 3.8	—
Work in progress	7.0	8.2	—
Buildings and improvements	55.2	55.0	15 to 45 years
Computer hardware and software	183.4	181.0	3 to 12 years
Equipment, furniture and fixtures	33.9	36.9	5 years
Leasehold improvements	36.0	37.9	The lesser of the life of the lease or 5 years.
Total property and equipment	$319.3	$322.8	

The Company capitalizes external costs and internal payroll costs incurred in the development of software for internal use as required by the Internal-Use Software Subtopic of the Financial Accounting and Standards Board ("FASB") Accounting Standards Codification ("ASC"). Work in process represents capitalized costs for internal use software not yet in service and is included with computer hardware, software and other on the consolidated balance sheet. Depreciation expense from continuing operations was $31.3 million for 2010, $36.0 million for 2009 and $41.4 million for 2008.

* "We have evolved from a United States-based company concentrating primarily on traditional office staffing into a global workforce solutions leader with a breath of specialty businesses." 10-K

Source: Kelly Services, Inc. 2010 10-K

A company must segregate its fair value measurements into those based on level 1, 2, and 3 inputs. For level 3, the company must include the valuation technique used to measure the fair value, a reconciliation of the changes in fair value during the period, and a related discussion. The investments of Gentex Corporation are illustrated in Exhibit 3-8.

Intangibles

Intangibles are nonphysical assets, such as patents and copyrights. Intangibles are recorded at historical cost. An intangible asset that has a finite life is amortized over its useful life. An intangible asset with an indefinite life are reviewed for impairment. Research and

---

EXHIBIT **3-8**	Gentex Corporation*

Investments

GENTEX CORPORATION AND SUBSIDIARIES
CONSOLIDATED BALANCE SHEETS (In Part)
AS OF DECEMBER 31, 2010 AND 2009

	2010	2009
ASSETS		
CURRENT ASSETS:		
Cash and cash equivalents	$ 348,349,773	$ 336,108,446
Short-term investments	86,447,596	17,123,647
Accounts receivable	95,647,612	71,159,512
Inventories	100,728,730	53,608,996
Prepaid expenses and other	24,095,563	27,412,894
Total current assets	655,269,274	505,413,495
PLANT AND EQUIPMENT:		
Land, buildings and improvements	120,578,714	112,276,501
Machinery and equipment	352,618,391	327,554,073
Construction-in-process	13,351,954	6,973,175
	486,549,059	446,803,749
Less-Accumulated depreciation and amortization	(281,441,303)	(249,273,500)
	205,107,756	197,530,249
OTHER ASSETS:		
Long-term investments	129,091,167	109,155,248
Patents and other assets, net	13,222,442	10,504,497
	142,313,609	119,659,745
	$1,002,690,639	$ 822,603,489

Gentex Corporation and Subsidiaries
Notes to Consolidated Financial Statements (In Part)

(1) Summary of Significant Accounting and Reporting Policies (In Part)

Investments

The Financial Accounting Standards Board (FASB) has issued authoritative guidance at ASC 820 "Fair Value Measurements." This statement establishes a framework for measuring the fair value of assets and liabilities. This framework is intended to provide increased consistency in how fair value determinations are made under various existing accounting standards that permit, or in come cases, require estimates of fair-market value. This standard also expands financial statement disclosure requirements about a company's use of fair value measurements, including the effect of such measure on earnings.

The Company adopted the provisions of ASC 820 related to its financial assets and liabilities in 2008, and to its non-financial assets and liabilities in 2009, neither of which had a material impact on the Company's consolidated financial position, results of operations or cash flows. The Company's investment securities are classified as available for sale and are stated at fair value based on quoted market prices. Adjustments to the fair value of investments are recorded as increases or decreases, net of income taxes, within accumulated other comprehensive income (loss) in shareholders' investment (excluding other-than-temporary impairments). Assets or liabilities that have recurring measurements are shown below as of December 31, 2010.

---

*"Gentex Corporation (the Company) designs, develops, manufactures and markets proprietary products employing electro-optic technology: automatic-dimming rearview automotive mirrors with electronic features and fire protection products. The Company also developed and manufactures variable dimmable windows for the aircraft industry and non-automatic-dimming rearview automotive mirrors with electronic features." 10-K

Source: Gentex Corporation: Investments 2010 10-K

EXHIBIT **3-8**	Gentex Corporation (*continued*)

		Fair Value Measurements at Reporting Date Using		
Description	Total as of December 31, 2010	Quoted Prices in Active Markets for Identical Assets (Level 1)	Significant Other Observable Inputs (Level 2)	Significant Unobservable Inputs (Level 3)
Cash & Cash Equivalents	$348,349,773	$348,349,773	$ —	$ —
Short-Term Investments:				
Government Securities	36,136,760	36,136,760	—	—
U.S. Treasury Notes	50,156,250	—	50,156,250	—
Other	154,586	154,586	—	—
Long-Term Investments:				
Common stocks	63,637,711	63,637,711	—	—
Mutual Funds – Equity	55,234,901	55,234,901	—	—
Limited Partnership – Equity	9,363,555	—	9,363,555	—
Certificate of Deposit	500,000	—	500,000	—
Other – Equity	355,000	355,000	—	—
Total	$563,888,536	$503,868,731	$ 60,019,805	$ —

The Company determines the fair value of its U.S. Treasury Notes by utilizing monthly valuation statements that are provided by its broker. The broker bases the investment valuation by using the bid price in the market. The Company also refers to third party sources to validate valuations. In addition, the Company determines the fair value of its limited partnership equity investments by utilizing monthly valuation statements that are provided by the limited partnership. The limited partnership bases its equity investment valuations on unadjusted quoted prices in active markets. Since valuations are based on quoted prices that are readily and regularly available in an active market, valuation of these securities does not entail a significant degree of judgment.

The amortized cost, unrealized gains and losses, and market value of investment securities are shown as of December 31, 2010 and 2009:

		Unrealized		
2010	Cost	Gains	Losses	Market Value
Short-Term Investments:				
Government Securities	$ 36,137,467	$ 9,254	$ (9,961)	$ 36,136,760
U.S. Treasury Notes	50,095,921	60,329	—	50,156,250
Other	154,586	—	—	154,586
Long-Term Investments:				
Common Stocks	44,899,944	18,819,518	(81,751)	63,637,711
Mutual Funds-Equity	42,106,776	13,128,125	—	55,234,901
Limited Partnership-Equity	7,844,022	1,519,533	—	9,363,555
Certificate of Deposit	500,000	—	—	500,000
Other-Equity	338,506	16,494	—	355,000
Total	$182,077,222	$33,553,253	$(91,712)	$215,538,763

		Unrealized		
2009	Cost	Gains	Losses	Market Value
Short-Term Investments:				
Government Securities	$ 17,058,641	$ 4,924	$ (16,045)	$ 17,047,520
U.S. Treasury Notes	—	—	—	—
Other	76,127	—	—	76,127
Long-Term Investments:				
Common Stocks	42,674,630	15,834,086	(157,625)	58,351,091
Mutual Funds-Equity	34,174,483	7,410,833	(23,738)	41,561,578
Limited Partnership-Equity	7,963,296	937,483	—	8,900,779
Certificate of Deposit	—	—	—	—
Other-Equity	338,506	3,294	—	341,800
Total	$102,285,683	$24,190,620	$(197,408)	$126,278,895

(*continued*)

EXHIBIT **3-8**	Gentex Corporation (*continued*)

Unrealized losses on investments as of December 31, 2010 (excluding other-than-temporary impairments), are as follows:

	Aggregate Unrealized Losses	Aggregate Fair Value
Less than one year	$91,712	$17,007,886
Greater than one year	—	—

ASC 320, "Accounting for Certain Investments in Debt and Equity Securities," as amended and interpreted, provides guidance on determining when an investment is other-than-temporarily impaired. The Company reviews its fixed income and equity investment portfolio for any unrealized losses that would be deemed other-than-temporary and require the recognition of an impairment loss in income. If the cost of an investment exceeds its fair value, the Company evaluates, among other factors, general market conditions, the duration and extent to which the fair value less than cost, and our intent and ability to hold the investments. Management also considers the type of security, related-industry and sector performance, as well as published investments ratings and analyst reports, to evaluate its portfolio. Once a decline in fair value is determined to be other-than-temporary, an impairment charge is recorded and new cost basis in the investment is established. If market, industry, and/or investee conditions deteriorate, the Company may incur future impairments. Management considered equity investment losses of $17,909,901 to be other-than-temporary at December 31, 2008. The Company considered additional equity investment losses of $1,290,590 to be other-than-temporary at March 31, 2009. Accordingly, the losses were recognized in the consolidated statement of income in their respective reporting periods. No investments were considered to be other-than-temporary impaired in 2010.

Fixed income securities as of December 31, 2010, have contractual maturities as follows:

Due within one year	$86,447,596
Due between one and five years	500,000
Due over five years	—
	$86,947,596

Fair Value of Financial Instruments

The Company's financial instruments consist of cash and cash equivalents, investments, accounts receivable and accounts payable. The Company's estimate of the fair values of these financial instruments approximates their carrying amounts at December 31, 2010 and 2009.

---

development costs must be expensed as incurred. Thus, research and development costs in the United States represent an immediate expense, not an intangible. This requirement is not common in many other countries. The following are examples of intangibles that are recorded in the United States.

Goodwill Goodwill arises from the acquisition of a business for a sum greater than the physical asset value, usually because the business has unusual earning power. It may result from good customer relations, a well-respected owner, and so on. Purchased goodwill is not amortized but is subject to annual impairment reviews.[6]

The global treatment of goodwill varies significantly. In some countries, goodwill is not recorded because it is charged to shareholders' equity. In this case, there is no influence to reported income. In other countries, goodwill is expensed in the year acquired. In many countries, goodwill is recorded and amortized.

Patents Patents, exclusive legal rights granted to an inventor for a period of 20 years, are valued at their acquisition cost. The cost of a patent should be amortized over its legal life or its useful life, whichever is shorter.

Trademarks Trademarks are distinctive names or symbols. Rights are granted indefinitely as long as the owner uses it in connection with the product or service and files the paperwork. Since a trademark has an indefinite life, it should not be amortized. Trademarks should be tested for impairment at least annually.

Franchises Franchises are the legal right to operate under a particular corporate name, providing trade-name products or services. The cost of a franchise with a limited life should be amortized over the life of the franchise.

Copyrights Copyrights are rights that authors, painters, musicians, sculptors, and other artists have in their creations and expressions. A copyright is granted for the life of the creator, plus 70 years. The costs of the copyright should be amortized over the period of expected benefit.

Exhibit 3-9 displays the Briggs & Stratton Corporation presentation of intangibles. It consists of goodwill and other intangibles.

EXHIBIT **3-9**	Briggs & Stratton Corporation*

Intangibles

Consolidated Balance Sheet (In Part)
As of June 27, 2010 and June 28, 2009
(in thousands)

ASSETS	2010	2009
CURRENT ASSETS:		
Cash and Cash Equivalents	$ 116,554	$ 15,992
Receivables, Less Reserves of $11,317 and $7,360, Respectively	286,426	262,934
Inventories:		
Finished Products and Parts	278,922	359,429
Work in Process	114,483	109,774
Raw Materials	6,941	8,136
Total Inventories	400,346	477,339
Deferred Income Tax Asset	41,138	51,658
Assets Held for Sale	4,000	4,000
Prepaid Expenses and Other Current Assets	57,179	48,597
Total Current Assets	905,643	860,520
GOODWILL	252,975	253,854
INVESTMENTS	19,706	18,667
DEFERRED LOAN COSTS, Net	525	1,776
OTHER INTANGIBLE ASSETS, Net	90,345	92,190
LONG-TERM DEFERRED INCOME TAX ASSET	72,492	23,165
OTHER LONG-TERM ASSETS, Net	10,608	8,676
PLANT AND EQUIPMENT:		
Land and Land Improvements	17,303	17,559
Buildings	136,725	133,749
Machinery and Equipment	804,362	827,259
Construction in Progress	21,508	13,115
	979,898	991,682
Less – Accumulated Depreciation	642,135	631,507
Total Plant and Equipment, Net	337,763	360,175
	$1,690,057	$1,619,023

Notes to Consolidated Financial Statements (In Part)

For the Fiscal Years Ended June 27, 2010, June 28, 2009 and June 29, 2008

(2) Summary of Significant Accounting Policies (In Part)

Goodwill and Other Intangible Assets: Goodwill reflects the cost of acquisitions in excess of the fair values assigned to identifiable net assets acquired. Goodwill is assigned to reporting units based upon the expected benefit of the synergies of the acquisition. The reporting units are Engine, Home Power Products and Yard Power Products and have goodwill at June 27, 2010 of $136.9 million, $83.3 million, and $32.8 million, respectively. Other Intangible Assets reflect identifiable intangible assets that arose from purchase acquisitions. Other Intangible Assets are comprised of trademarks, patents and customer relationships.

*"Briggs & Stratton (the "Company") is the world's largest producer of air cooled gasoline engines for outdoor power equipment. Briggs & Stratton designs, manufactures, markets and services these products for original equipment manufacturers (OEMs) worldwide." 10-K

Source: Briggs & Stratton Corporation 2010 10-K

(*continued*)

EXHIBIT **3-9** Briggs & Stratton Corporation (*continued*)

Goodwill and trademarks, which are considered to have indefinite lives are not amortized; however, both must be tested for impairment annually. Amortization is recorded on a straight-line basis for other intangible assets with finite lives. Patents have been assigned an estimated weighted average useful life of thirteen years. The customer relationships have been assigned an estimated useful life of twenty-five years. The Company is subject to financial statement risk in the event that goodwill and intangible assets become impaired. The Company performed the required impairment tests in fiscal 2010, 2009 and 2008, and found no impairment of the assets.

(5) Goodwill and Other Intangible Assets:

Goodwill reflects the cost of acquisitions in excess of the fair values assigned to identifiable net assets acquired. Goodwill is assigned to reporting units based upon the expected benefit of the synergies of the acquisition. The reporting units are Engine, Home Power Products and Yard Power Products and have goodwill at June 27, 2010 of $136.9 million, $83.3 million, and $32.8 million, respectively.

The changes in the carrying amount of goodwill for the fiscal years ended June 27, 2010 and June 28, 2009 are as follows (in thousands):

	2010	2009
Beginning Goodwill Balance	$253,854	$248,328
Victa Acquisition	—	8,063
Tax Benefit on Amortization	(1,779)	(1,779)
Reclassification	263	—
Effect of Translation	637	(758)
Ending Goodwill Balance	$252,975	$253,854

The Company's other intangible assets for the years ended June 27, 2010 and June 28, 2009 are as follows (in thousands):

	2010			2009		
	Gross Carrying Amount	Accumulated Amortization	Net	Gross Carrying Amount	Accumulated Amortization	Net
Amortized Intangible Assets:						
Patents	$ 13,601	$ (7,049)	$ 6,552	$ 13,601	$(5,843)	$ 7,758
Customer Relationships	17,910	(4,298)	13,612	17,910	(3,582)	14,328
Miscellaneous	279	(279)	—	279	(277)	—
Effect of Translation	22	—	22	—	—	—
Total Amortized Intangible Assets	31,812	(11,626)	20,186	31,790	(9,704)	22,086
Unamortized Intangible Assets:						
Trademarks/Brand Names	69,841	—	69,841	70,104	—	70,104
Total Unamortized Intangible Assets	69,841	—	69,841	70,104	—	70,104
Effect of Translation	318	—	318	—	—	—
Total Intangible Assets	$101,971	$(11,626)	$90,345	$101,894	$(9,704)	$92,190

Amortization expense of other intangible assets amounts to approximately $1.9 million in each of 2010, 2009, and 2008. The estimated amortization expense of other intangible assets for the next five years is (in thousands):

2011	$1,911
2012	1,911
2013	1,911
2014	1,911
2015	1,860
	$9,504

Other Noncurrent Assets

Firms will occasionally have assets that do not fit into one of the previously discussed classifications. These assets, termed "other," might include noncurrent receivables and noncurrent prepaids. Exhibit 3-10 summarizes types of other assets from a financial statement compilation in *Accounting Trends & Techniques*.

EXHIBIT **3-10**	Other Noncurrent Assets*			
	Number of Entities			
	2009	2008	2007	2006
Deferred income taxes	277	261	287	261
Pension asset	160	169	235	200
Derivatives	150	47	50	46
Segregated cash or securities	103	100	105	82
Software	87	98	116	117
Debt issue costs	68	79	110	104
Property held for sale	43	45	57	68
Cash surrender value of life insurance	42	32	39	43
Assets of nonhomogeneous operations	9	10	10	8
Contracts	8	10	21	16
Estimated insurance recoveries	5	6	9	12
Assets leased to others	5	4	11	13
Other identified noncurrent assets	58	62	68	60

*Appearing either in the balance sheet and/or the notes to financial statements

2008 – 2009 based on 500 entities surveyed;
2006 – 2007 based on 600 entities surveyed

Source: Accounting Trends & Techniques, Copyright © 2010 by American Institute of Certified Public Accountants, Inc., p. 214. Reprinted with permission.

Liabilities

Liabilities are probable future sacrifices of economic benefits arising from present obligations of a particular entity to transfer assets or provide services to other entities in the future as a result of past transactions or events.[7] Liabilities are usually classified as either current or long-term liabilities.

Current Liabilities

Current liabilities are obligations whose liquidation is reasonably expected to require the use of existing current assets or the creation of other current liabilities within a year or an operating cycle, whichever is longer. They include the following items.

Payables

These include short-term obligations created by the acquisition of goods and services, such as accounts payable (for materials or goods bought for use or resale), wages payable, and taxes payable. Payables may also be in the form of a written promissory note, notes payable.

Unearned Income

Payments collected in advance of the performance of service are termed unearned. They include rent income and subscription income. Rather than cash, a future service or good is due the customer.

Other Current Liabilities

Many other current obligations require payment during the year. Exhibit 3-11 displays other current liabilities reported by *Accounting Trends & Techniques* in 2010. Exhibit 3-12 shows the current liabilities of Google, Inc.

Long-Term Liabilities

Long-term liabilities are those due in a period exceeding one year or one operating cycle, whichever is longer. Long-term liabilities are generally of two types: financing arrangements of assets and operational obligations.

Liabilities Relating to Financing Agreements

The long-term liabilities that are financing arrangements of assets usually require systematic payment of principal and interest. They include notes payable, bonds payable, and credit agreements.

EXHIBIT 3-11	Other Current Liabilities*			
	Number of Entities			
	2009	**2008**	**2007**	**2006**
Derivatives	253	88	76	70
Costs related to discontinued operations/restructuring	158	148	172	162
Deferred revenue	140	150	175	161
Interest	123	128	146	143
Deferred taxes	118	122	104	97
Taxes other than federal income taxes	116	122	135	139
Warranties	99	101	126	120
Insurance	86	83	97	101
Advertising	64	63	70	73
Dividends	59	62	75	68
Environmental costs	59	58	68	67
Rebates	55	54	54	59
Customer advances, deposits	54	57	65	68
Litigation	43	39	56	50
Tax uncertainties	33	29	N/C**	N/C**
Billings on uncompleted contracts	26	26	38	29
Due to afflicted companies	23	25	22	22
Royalties	19	20	23	21
Asset retirement obligations	15	18	24	20
Other – described	135	127	146	156

*Appearing in either the balance sheet and/or the notes to financial statements.
**N/C = Not Compiled. Line item was not included in the table for the year shown.

2008 – 2009 based on 500 entities surveyed;
2006 – 2007 based on 600 entities surveyed

Source: *Accounting Trends & Techniques*, Copyright © 2010 by American Institute of Certified Public Accountants, Inc., p. 245. Reprinted with permission.

EXHIBIT 3-12	Google, Inc.*

Current Liabilities – Google, Inc.

Google, Inc.
Consolidated Balance Sheets (In Part)
(In millions)

	As of December 31,	
	2009	**2010**
Current liabilities:		
Accounts payable	$ 216	$ 483
Short-term debt	0	3,465
Accrued compensation and benefits	982	1,410
Accrued expenses and other current liabilities	570	961
Accrued revenue share	694	885
Securities lending payable	0	2,361
Deferred revenue	285	394
Income taxes payable, net	0	37
Total current liabilities	$2,747	$9,996

*"Google is a global technology leader focused on improving the ways people connect with information." 10-K
Source: Google, Inc., 2010 10-K

Notes Payable Promissory notes due in periods greater than one year or one operating cycle, whichever is longer, are classified as long term. If secured by a claim against real property, they are called mortgage notes.

Bonds Payable A bond is a debt security normally issued with $1,000 par per bond and normally requiring semiannual interest payments based on the coupon rate. Bonds payable is similar to notes payable. Bonds payable are usually for a longer duration than notes payable.

Bonds are not necessarily sold at par. They are sold at a premium if the stated rate of interest exceeds the market rate, and they are sold at a discount if the stated rate of interest is less than the market rate. If sold for more than par, a premium on bonds payable arises and increases bonds payable to obtain the current carrying value. Similarly, if sold at less than par, a discount on bonds payable arises and decreases bonds payable on the balance sheet. Each of these accounts, discount or premium, will be gradually written off (amortized) to interest expense over the life of the bond. At the maturity date, the carrying value of bonds payable will be equal to the par value. Amortization of bond discount increases interest expense; amortization of bond premium reduces it. Exhibit 3-13 illustrates bonds sold at par, premium, or discount.

Bonds that are convertible into common stock at the option of the bondholder (creditor) are exchanged for a specified number of common shares, and the bondholder becomes a common stockholder. Often, convertible bonds are issued when the common stock price is low, in management's opinion, and the firm eventually wants to increase its common equity. By issuing a convertible bond, the firm may get more for the specified number of common shares than could be obtained by issuing the common shares. The conversion feature allows the firm to issue the bond at a more favorable interest rate than would be the case with a bond lacking the conversion feature. Also, the tax deductible interest paid on the convertible bond reduces the firm's cost for these funds. If common stock had been issued, the dividend on the common stock would not be tax deductible. Thus, a firm may find that issuing a convertible bond can be an attractive means of raising common equity funds in the long run. However, if the firm's stock price stays depressed after issuing a convertible bond, then the firm will have the convertible bond liability until the bond comes due. Convertible bonds of VeriSign, Inc., and subsidiaries are displayed in Exhibit 3-14.

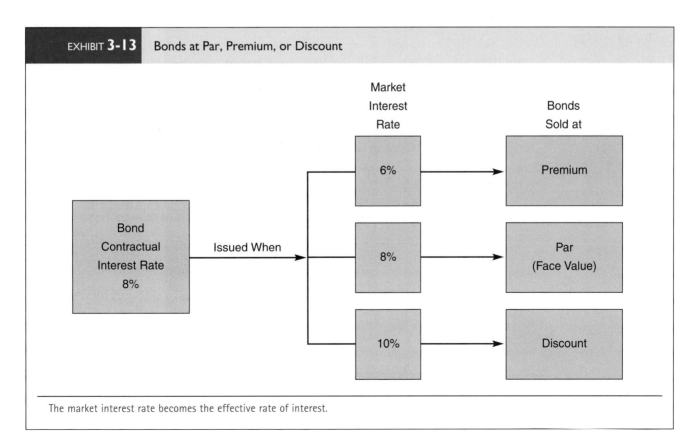

| EXHIBIT **3-13** | Bonds at Par, Premium, or Discount |

The market interest rate becomes the effective rate of interest.

EXHIBIT **3-14**	VeriSign, Inc. and Subsidiaries*

Liabilities (Convertible Bonds)

VeriSign, Inc.
Consolidated Balance Sheets (In Part)
In thousands

	December 31,	
	2010	2009
Liabilities		
Current liabilities:		
Accounts payable and accrued liabilities	$ 195,235	$ 243,967
Deferred revenues	457, 478	642,507
Total current liabilities	652,713	886,474
Long-term deferred revenues	205,560	245,734
Convertible debentures, including contingent interest derivative	581,626	574,378
Long-term deferred tax liabilities	309,696	144,777
Other long-term liabilities	17,981	20,117
Total long-term liabilities	1,114,863	985,006
Total liabilities	$1,767,576	$1,871,480

Notes to Consolidated Financial Statements (In part)

Note 7: Debt and Interest Expense (In part)

Note: There was an extensive description of the terms of the Junior Subordinated Convertible Debentures.
* "We are a provider of Internet infrastructure services." 10-K
Source: Verisign, Inc. and Subsidiaries

Credit Agreements Many firms arrange loan commitments from banks or insurance companies for future loans. Often, the firm does not intend to obtain these loans but has arranged the credit agreement just in case a need exists for additional funds. Such credit agreements do not represent a liability unless the firm actually requests the funds. From the point of view of analysis, the existence of a substantial credit agreement is a positive condition in that it could relieve pressure on the firm if there is a problem in meeting existing liabilities.

In return for giving a credit agreement, the bank or insurance company obtains a fee. This commitment fee is usually a percentage of the unused portion of the commitment. Also, banks often require the firm to keep a specified sum in its bank account, referred to as a compensating balance. Exhibit 3-15 shows credit agreements for Carlisle Companies Incorporated.

Liabilities Relating to Operational Obligations

Long-term liabilities relating to operational obligations include obligations arising from the operation of a business, mostly of a service nature, such as pension obligations, postretirement benefit obligations other than pension plans, deferred taxes, and service warranties. Chapter 7 covers at length pensions and postretirement benefit obligations other than pension plans.

Deferred Taxes Deferred taxes are caused by using different accounting methods for tax and reporting purposes. For example, a firm may use accelerated depreciation for tax purposes and straight-line depreciation for reporting purposes. This causes tax expense for reporting purposes to be higher than taxes payable according to the tax return. The difference is deferred tax. Any situation where revenue or expense is recognized in the financial statements in a different time period than for the tax return will create a deferred tax situation (asset or liability). For example, in the later years of the life of a fixed asset, straight-line depreciation will give higher depreciation and, therefore, lower net income than an accelerated method. Then tax expense for reporting purposes will be lower than taxes payable, and the deferred tax will be reduced (paid). Since firms often buy more and higher-priced assets, however, the increase in deferred taxes may exceed the decrease. In this case, a partial or a total reversal will not occur. The taxes may be deferred for a very long time, perhaps permanently. Chapter 7 covers deferred taxes in more detail.

Warranty Obligations Warranty obligations are estimated obligations arising out of product warranties. Product warranties require the seller to correct any deficiencies in quantity,

EXHIBIT **3-15**	Carlisle Companies Incorporated*

Credit Agreements

Carlisle Companies Incorporated
Consolidated Balance Sheets (In Part)
Dollars in Millions

Liabilities	At December 31,	
Current liabilities:	**2010**	**2009**
Short-term debt, including current maturities	$ 69.0	$ —
Accounts payable	195.4	132.7
Accrued expenses	174.9	143.5
Deferred revenue	17.1	17.3
Current liabilities associated with assets held for sale	—	7.6
Total current liabilities	456.4	301.1
Long-term liabilities:		
Long-term debt	405.1	156.1
Deferred revenue	122.6	113.2
Other long-term liabilities	204.7	125.1
Total long-term liabilities	732.4	394.4

Notes to Consolidated Financial Statements (In Part)

Note 7 Borrowings (In Part)

As of December 31, 2010 and 2009, the Company's borrowings are as follows:

In millions	**2010**	**2009**
5.125% notes due 2020, net of unamortized discount of ($1.1)	$248.9	$ —
6.125% notes due 2016, net of unamortized discount of ($0.6) and ($0.7) respectively	149.4	149.3
8.75% Hawk senior notes due 2014	59.0	
Revolving credit facility	10.0	—
Industrial development and revenue bonds through 2018	6.7	6.7
Other, including capital lease obligations	0.1	0.1
	474.1	156.1
Less revolving credit facility and the Hawk senior notes classified as current	(69.0)	—
Long-term debt	$405.1	$156.1

Revolving Credit Facilities

At December 31, 2010 the Company had $458.5 million available under its $500.0 million revolving credit facility (the "Facility"). Of the amount unavailable for borrowings at December 31, 2010, $10.0 million was borrowed and outstanding in connection with the financing of the Hawk acquisition. Under the terms of the Facility, and at the Company's election, the $10.0 million is payable on January 31, 2011 (30 days from the date of funding) and accordingly has been presented in Short-term debt, including current maturities in the consolidated balance sheet. The Company has the option to roll over amounts payable, at differing tenors and interest rates, until the facility expires in July of 2012. The remainder of the amount unavailable for borrowings relates to issued letters of credit amounting to $31.5 million. At December 31, 2009, the Company had $466.0 million available under the Facility, with the reduction in availability attributable to letters of credit of $34.0 million. Letters of credit are issued primarily to provide security under insurance arrangements and certain borrowings. The revolving credit facility provides for grid-based interest pricing based on the credit rating of the Company's senior unsecured bank debt or other unsecured senior debt and the Company's utilization of the facility. The average interest rate of the revolving credit facility for 2010 and 2009 was 0.65% and 0.85%, respectively.

The Company also maintains a $55.0 million uncommitted line of credit all of which was available for borrowing as of December 31, 2010 and 2009. The average interest rate on the uncommitted line was 1.87% for 2010 and 2.88% for 2009.

*"Carlisle is a diversified manufacturing company consisting of five segments which manufacture and distribute a broad range of products." 10-K
Source: Carlisle Companies Incorporated 2010 10-K

quality, or performance of the product or service for a specific period of time after the sale. Warranty obligations are estimated in order to recognize the obligation at the balance sheet date and to charge the expense to the period of the sale.

Exhibit 3-16 shows the warranty obligations of Ford Motor Company.

EXHIBIT **3-16**	Ford Motor Company and Subsidiaries*

Warranty Obligations

For the Fiscal Year Ended December 31, 2010

NOTE 31. COMMITMENTS AND CONTINGENCIES (In Part)

Guarantees are recorded at fair value at the inception of the guarantee. Litigation and claims are accrued when losses are deemed probable and reasonably estimable.

Estimated warranty costs and additional service actions are accrued for at the time the vehicle is sold to a dealer, including costs for basic warranty coverage on vehicles sold, product recalls, and other customer service actions. Fees or premiums for the issuance of extended service plans are recognized in income over the contract period in proportion to the costs expected to be incurred in performing services under the contract.

Warranty

Included in warranty cost accruals are the costs for basic warranty coverages on products sold. These costs are estimates based primarily on historical warranty claim experience. Warranty accruals accounted for in Accrued liabilities and deferred revenue at December 31 were as follows (in millions):

	2010	2009
Beginning balance	$ 3,147	$ 3,239
Payments made during the period	(2,176)	(2,484)
Changes in accrual related to warranties issued during the period	1,522	1,652
Changes in accrual related to pre-existing warranties	203	584
Foreign currency translation and other	(50)	156
Ending Balance	$ 2,646	$ 3,147

Excluded from the table above are costs accrued for product recalls and customer satisfaction actions.

---

*"We are one of the world's largest producers of cars and trucks." 10-K
Source: Ford Motor Company and Subsidiaries 2010 10-K

Noncontrolling Interest (previously called "Minority Interest")

Noncontrolling interest reflects the ownership of noncontrolling shareholders in the equity of consolidated subsidiaries less than wholly owned. Consider the following simple example. Parent P owns 90% of the common stock of Subsidiary S.

	Parent P Balance Sheet December 31, 2010	Subsidiary S Balance Sheet December 31, 2010
Current assets	$100	$10
Investment in Subsidiary S	18	—
Other long-term assets	382	40
	$500	$50
Current liabilities	100	10
Long-term liabilities	200	20
Total liabilities	$300	$30
Stockholders' equity		
Common stock	50	5
Additional paid in capital	40	5
Retained earnings	110	10
Total stockholders' equity	200	20
Total liabilities and stockholders' equity	$500	$50

This will be shown on the consolidated balance sheet as follows:

Parent P and Subsidiary S
Consolidated Balance Sheet
December 31, 2010

	(In millions)
Current assets	$110
Long-term assets	422
	$532
Current liabilities	$110
Long-term liabilities	220
Total liabilities	330
Stockholders equity	
Common stock	50
Additional paid in capital	40
Retained earnings	110
Noncontrolling interest	2
Total stockholders' equity	202
Total liabilities and stockholders' equity	$532

Prior to the new standard that took effect for fiscal years beginning after December 15, 2008, noncontrolling interest was called minority interest and was usually presented after liabilities and before shareholders' equity. With the new standard, noncontrolling interest is presented with shareholders' equity.

Noncontrolling interest is seldom material. In a firm where noncontrolling interest is material, the analysis can be performed twice, one with noncontrolling interest as a liability to be conservative, and then as a shareholders' equity item. The analysis in this book will leave the noncontrolling interest as a shareholders' equity item. Refer to Exhibit 3-17 for an illustration of noncontrolling interest (minority interest).

Under the new standard, a reconciliation of the beginning and ending balances of both the parent and the noncontrolling interest equity amounts must be presented. This includes net income and owner contributions attributable to each of them. This presentation can be in a note or in a statement of stockholders' equity. The statement of stockholders' equity is illustrated in Chapter 4.

Other Noncurrent Liabilities

Many other noncurrent liabilities may be disclosed. It would not be practical to discuss all of the possibilities. An example would be deferred profit on sales.

Redeemable Preferred Stock

Redeemable preferred stock is subject to mandatory redemption requirements or has a redemption feature outside the control of the issuer. If this feature is coupled with such characteristics as no vote or fixed return, often preferred stock and bond characteristics, then this type of preferred stock is more like debt than equity. For this reason, the SEC directs that the three categories of stock—redeemable preferred stock, nonredeemable preferred stock, and common stock—not be totaled in the balance sheet. Further, the stockholders' equity section should not include redeemable preferred stock. Redeemable preferred stock is illustrated in Exhibit 3-18. Because redeemable preferred stock is more like debt than equity, consider it as part of total liabilities for purposes of financial statement analysis.

Shareholders' or Stockholder's Equity

Shareholders' (Stockholder's) equity is the residual ownership interest in the assets of an entity that remains after deducting its liabilities.[8] Usually divided into two basic categories, paid-in capital and retained earnings, other accounts may appear in shareholders' equity that are usually presented separately from paid-in capital and retained earnings. Other accounts include accumulated other comprehensive income, equity-oriented deferred compensation, and employee stock ownership plans (ESOPs).

EXHIBIT **3-17**	Cummins, Inc. and Subsidiaries*

Noncontrolling Interest

Cummins Inc. and Subsidiaries
Consolidated Balance Sheets (In part)
In millions, except par value

	December 31,	
	2010	2009
LIABILITIES		
Current liabilities		
Loans payable (Note 9)	$ 82	$ 37
Accounts payable (principally trade)	1,362	957
Current portion of accrued product warranty (Note 10)	421	426
Accrued compensation, benefits and retirement costs	468	366
Deferred revenue	182	128
Taxes payable (including taxes on income)	202	94
Other accrued expenses	543	424
Total current liabilities	3,260	2,432
Long-term liabilities		
Long-term debt (Note 9)	709	637
Pensions (Note 11)	195	514
Postretirement benefits other than pensions (Note 11)	439	453
Other liabilities and deferred revenue (Note 12)	803	760
Total liabilities	5,406	4,796
Commitments and contingencies (Note 13)	—	—
EQUITY		
Cummins Inc. shareholders' equity (Note 14)		
Common stock, $2.50 par value, 500 shares authorized, 221.8 and 222.0 shares issued	1,934	1,860
Retained earnings	4,445	3,575
Treasury stock, at cost, 24.0 and 20.7 shares	(964)	(731)
Common stock held by employee benefits trust, at cost, 2.1 and 3.0 shares	(25)	(36)
Accumulated other comprehensive loss		
Defined benefit postretirement plans	(646)	(788)
Other	(74)	(107)
Total accumulated other comprehensive loss	(720)	(895)
Total Cummins Inc. shareholders' equity	4,670	3,773
Noncontrolling interests (Note 17)	326	247
Total equity	4,996	4,020
Total liabilities and equity	$10,402	$8,816

Notes to Consolidated Financial Statements (In Part)

Note 17. NONCONTROLLING INTEREST
Noncontrolling interests in the equity of consolidated subsidiaries are as follows:

	December 31,	
In millions	2010	2009
Cummins India Ltd.	$247	$185
Wuxi Cummins Turbo Technologies Co. Ltd.	60	36
Other	19	26
Total	$326	$247

*"Cummins Inc. was founded in 1919 as a corporation in Columbus, Indiana, as one of the first diesel engine manufacturers. We are a global power leader that designs, manufacturers, distributes and services diesel and natural gas engines, electric power generation systems and engine-related component products, including filtration, exhaust aftertreatment, fuel systems, controls and air handling systems." 10-K
Source: Cummins, Inc. and Subsidiaries 2010 10-K

EXHIBIT **3-18** Nike, Inc.*

Redeemable Preferred Stock

NIKE, INC.
Consolidated Balance Sheet (In Part)

	May 31, 2010	May 31, 2009
	(In millions)	
Total current liabilities	3,364.2	3,277.0
Long-term debt (Note 8)	445.8	437.2
Deferred income taxes and other liabilities (Notes 9 and 18)	855.3	842.0
Commitments and contingencies (Note 15)	—	—
Redeemable Preferred Stock (Note 10)	0.3	0.3
Shareholders' equity:		
Common stock at stated value (Note 11):		
Class A convertible – 90.0 and 95.3 shares outstanding	0.1	0.1
Class B – 394.0 and 390.2 shares outstanding	2.7	2.7
Capital in excess of stated value	3,440.6	2,871.4
Accumulated other comprehensive income (Note 14)	214.8	367.5
Retained earnings	6,095.5	5,451.4
Total shareholders' equity	9,753.7	8,693.1
Total liabilities and shareholders' equity	$14,419.3	$13,249.6

Notes to Consolidated Financial Statements (In Part)

Note 10 – Redeemable Preferred Stock

Sojitz America is the sole owner of the Company's authorized Redeemable Preferred Stock, $1 par value, which is redeemable at the option of Sojitz America or the Company at par value aggregating $0.3 million. A cumulative dividend of $0.10 per share is payable annually on May 31 and no dividends may be declared or paid on the common stock of the Company unless dividends on the Redeemable Preferred Stock have been declared and paid in full. There have been no changes in the Redeemable Preferred Stock in the three years ended May 31, 2010, 2009, and 2008. As the holder of the Redeemable Preferred Stock, Sojitz America does not have general voting rights but does have the right to vote as a separate class on the sale of all or substantially all of the assets of the Company and its subsidiaries, on merger, consolidation, liquidation or dissolution of the Company or on the sale or assignment of the NIKE trademark for athletic footwear sold in the United States.

*"Our principal business activity is the design, development and worldwide marketing of high quality footwear apparel, equipment, and accessory products." 10-K
Source: Nike, Inc. 2010 10-K

Paid-In Capital

The first type of paid-in capital account is capital stock. Two basic types of capital stock are preferred and common.

Both preferred stock and common stock may be issued as par-value stock. (Some states call this *stated value stock*.) The articles of incorporation establish the par value, a designated dollar amount per share. Many states stipulate that the par value of issued stock times the number of shares outstanding constitutes the legal capital. Many states also designate that, if original-issue stock is sold below par value, the buyer is contingently liable for the difference between the par value and the lower amount paid. This does not usually pose a problem because the par value has no direct relationship to market value, the selling price of the stock. To avoid selling a stock below par, the par value is usually set very low in relation to the intended selling price. For example, the intended selling price may be $25.00, and the par value may be $1.00.

Some states allow the issuance of no-par stock (either common or preferred). Some of these states require that the entire proceeds received from the sale of the no-par stock be designated as legal capital.

Additional paid-in capital arises from the excess of amounts paid for stock over the par or stated value of the common and preferred stock. Also included here are amounts over cost from the sale of treasury stock (discussed later in this chapter), capital arising from the donation of assets to the firm, and transfer from retained earnings through stock dividends when the market price of the stock exceeds par.

Common Stock

Common stock shares in all the stockholders' rights and represents ownership that has voting and liquidation rights. Common stockholders elect the board of directors and vote on major corporate decisions. In the event of liquidation, the liquidation rights of common stockholders give them claims to company assets <u>after</u> all creditors' and preferred stockholders' rights have been fulfilled.

Preferred Stock

Preferred stock seldom has voting rights. When preferred stock does have voting rights, it is usually because of missed dividends. For example, the preferred stockholders may possibly receive voting rights if their dividends have been missed two consecutive times. Some other preferred stock characteristics include the following:

- Preference as to dividends
- Accumulation of dividends
- Participation in excess of stated dividend rate
- Convertibility into common stock
- Callability by the corporation
- Redemption at future maturity date (see the previous discussion of redeemable preferred stock)
- Preference in liquidation

Preference as to Dividends

When preferred stock has a preference as to dividends, the current year's preferred dividend must be paid before a dividend can be paid to common stockholders. For par-value (or stated value) stock, the dividend rate is usually stated as a percentage of par. For example, if the dividend rate were 6% and the par were $100 per share, then the dividend per share would be $6. For no-par stock, if the dividend rate is stated as $5, then each share should receive $5 if a dividend is paid. A preference as to dividends does not guarantee that a preferred dividend will be paid in a given year. <u>The board of directors must declare a dividend before a dividend is paid.</u> The lack of a fixed commitment to pay dividends and the lack of a due date on the principal are the primary reasons that many firms elect to issue preferred stock instead of bonds. Preferred stock usually represents an expensive source of funds, compared to bonds. The preferred stock dividends are not tax deductible, whereas interest on bonds is deductible.

Accumulation of Dividends

If the board of directors does not declare dividends in a particular year, a holder of noncumulative preferred stock will never be paid that dividend. To make the preferred stock more attractive to investors, a corporation typically issues cumulative preferred stock. If a corporation fails to declare the usual dividend on the cumulative preferred stock, the amount of passed dividends becomes **dividends in arrears**. Common stockholders cannot be paid any dividends until the preferred dividends in arrears and the current preferred dividends are paid.

To illustrate dividends in arrears, assume a corporation has outstanding 10,000 shares of 8%, $100 par cumulative preferred stock. If dividends are not declared in 2010 and 2011, but are declared in 2012, the preferred stockholders would be entitled to dividends in arrears of $160,000 and current dividends in 2012 of $80,000 before any dividends could be paid to common stockholders.

Participation in Excess of Stated Dividend Rate

When preferred stock is participating, preferred stockholders may receive an extra dividend beyond the stated dividend rate. The terms of the participation depend on the terms included with the stock certificate. For example, the terms may state that any dividend to common stockholders over $10 per share will also be given to preferred stockholders.

To illustrate participating preferred stock, assume that a corporation has 8%, $100 par preferred stock. The terms of the participation are that any dividend paid on common shares over $10 per share will also be paid to preferred stockholders. For the current year, a dividend of $12 per share is declared on the common stock. Therefore, a dividend of $10 must be paid per share of preferred stock for the current year: (8% × $100) + $2.00 = $10.00.

Convertibility into Common Stock

Convertible preferred stock contains a provision that allows the preferred stockholders, at their option, to convert the share of preferred stock at a specific exchange ratio into another security of the corporation. The other security is almost always common stock. The conversion feature is very attractive to investors. For example, the terms may be that each share of preferred stock can be converted to four shares of common stock.

Convertible preferred stock is similar to a convertible bond, except that there are no fixed payout commitments with the convertible preferred stock. The preferred dividend need not be declared, and the preferred stock does not have a due date. The major reason for issuing convertible preferred stock is similar to that for issuing convertible bonds: If the current common stock price is low, in the opinion of management, and the firm eventually wants to increase its common equity, then the firm can raise more money for a given number of common shares by first issuing convertible preferred stock.

A firm usually prefers to issue convertible bonds rather than convertible preferred stock if its capital structure can carry more debt without taking on too much risk. The interest on the convertible bond is tax deductible, while the dividend on the preferred stock is not.

Callability by the Corporation

Callable preferred stock may be retired (recalled) by the corporation at its option. The call price is part of the original stock contract. When the preferred stock is also cumulative, the call terms normally require payment of dividends in arrears before the call is executed.

The call provision favors the company because the company decides when to call. Investors do not like call provisions. Therefore, to make a security that has a call provision marketable, the call provision can normally not be exercised for a given number of years. For example, callable preferred stock issued in 2011 may have a provision that the call option cannot be exercised prior to 2021.

Preference in Liquidation

Should the corporation liquidate, the preferred stockholders normally have priority over common stockholders for settlement of claims. However, the claims of preferred stockholders are secondary to the claims of creditors, including bondholders.

Preference in liquidation for preferred stock over common stock is not usually considered to be an important provision. This is because often, in liquidation, funds are not sufficient to pay claims of preferred stock. Even creditors may receive only a few cents on the dollar in satisfaction of their claims.

Disclosures

Preferred stock may carry various combinations of provisions. The provisions of each preferred stock issue should be disclosed either parenthetically in the stockholders' equity section of the balance sheet or in a note. A company may have various preferred stock issues, each with different provisions. Preferred stock is illustrated in Exhibit 3-19.

Donated Capital

Donated capital may be included in the paid-in capital. Capital is donated to the company by stockholders, creditors, or other parties (such as a city). For example, a city may offer

EXHIBIT 3-19	The Procter & Gamble Company*

Preferred Stock

The Procter & Gamble Company
Consolidated Balance Sheet (In Part)
Amounts in millions

	June 30, 2010	June 30, 2009
SHAREHOLDERS' EQUITY		
Convertible Class A preferred stock, stated value $1 per share (600 shares authorized)	1,277	1,324
Non-voting Class B preferred stock, stated value $1 per share (200 shares authorized)	—	—
Common stock, stated value $1 per share (10,000 shares authorized; shares issued: 2010 – 4,007.6, 2009 – 4,007.3)	4,008	4,007
Additional paid-in capital	61,697	61,118
Reserve for ESOP debt retirement	(1,350)	(1,340)
Accumulated other comprehensive income (loss)	(7,822)	(3,358)
Treasury stock, at cost (shares held: 2010 – 1,164, 2009 – 1,090.3)	(61,309)	(55,961)
Retained earnings	64,614	57,309
Noncontrolling interest	324	283
TOTAL SHAREHOLDERS' EQUITY	$ 61,439	$ 63,382

*"The Procter & Gamble Company is focused on providing branded consumer packaged goods of superior quality and value to improve the lives of the world's consumers." 10-K
Source: The Procter & Gamble Company 2010 10-K

land to a company as an inducement to locate a factory there to increase the level of employment. The firm records the donated land at the appraised amount and records an equal amount as donated capital in stockholders' equity.

Another example would be a company that needs to increase its available cash. A plan is devised, calling for existing common stockholders to donate a percentage of their stock to the company. When the stock is sold, the proceeds are added to the cash account, and the donated capital in stockholders' equity is increased.

Retained Earnings

Retained earnings are the undistributed earnings of the corporation—that is, the net income for all past periods minus the dividends (both cash and stock) that have been declared. Retained earnings, cash dividends, and stock dividends are reviewed in more detail in Chapter 4. Exhibit 3-19 illustrates the presentation of retained earnings.

Quasi-Reorganization

A **quasi-reorganization** is an accounting procedure equivalent to an accounting fresh start. A company with a deficit balance in retained earnings "starts over" with a zero balance rather than a deficit. A quasi-reorganization involves the reclassification of a deficit in retained earnings. It removes the deficit and an equal amount from paid-in capital. A quasi-reorganization may also include a restatement of the carrying values of assets and liabilities to reflect current values.

When a quasi-reorganization is performed, the retained earnings should be dated as of the readjustment date and disclosed in the financial statements for a period of five to ten years. Exhibit 3-20 illustrates a quasi-reorganization of Owens Corning.

Accumulated Other Comprehensive Income

Conceptually, **accumulated other comprehensive income** represents retained earnings from other comprehensive income. In addition to the aggregate amount, companies are required to disclose the separate categories that make up accumulated other comprehensive income.

EXHIBIT **3-20**	Owens Corning*

Quasi-Reorganization
For the Fiscal Year Ended December 31, 2006

Owens Corning and Subsidiaries
Notes to Consolidated Financial Statements (in Part)

3. Fresh-Start Accounting ** **(in Part)**
On the Effective Date, the Company adopted fresh-start accounting in accordance with SoP 90-7. This resulted in a new reporting entity on November 1, 2006, which has a new basis of accounting, a new capital structure and no retained earnings or accumulated losses. The Company was required to implement fresh-start accounting as the holders of existing voting shares immediately before confirmation received less than 50% of the voting shares of the Successor Company. The fresh-start accounting principles pursuant to SoP 90-7 provide, among other things, for the Company to determine the value to be assigned to the equity of the reorganized Company as of a date selected for financial reporting purposes.

The reorganization value represents the amount of resources available for the satisfaction of post-petition liabilities and allowed claims, as negotiated between the Company and its creditors. The Company's total enterprise value at the time of emergence was $5.8 billion, with a total value for common equity of $3.7 billion, including the estimated fair value of the Series A Warrants and Service B Warrants issued on the Effective Date.

In accordance with fresh-start accounting, the reorganization value of the Company was allocated based on the fair market values of the assets and liabilities in accordance with SFAS 141. The fair values represented the Company's best estimates at the Effective Date based on internal and external appraisals and valuations. Liabilities existing at the Effective Date, other than deferred taxes, were stated at present values of amounts to be paid determined at appropriate current interest rates. Any portion not attributed to specific tangible or identified intangible assets was recorded as goodwill. While the Company believes that the enterprise value approximates fair value, differences between the methodology used in testing for goodwill impairment, as discussed in Note 10, and the negotiated value could adversely impact the Company's results of operations.

Pursuant to SoP 90-7, the results of operations of the ten months ended October 31, 2006 include a pre-emergence gain on the cancellation of debt of $5.9 billion resulting from the discharge of liabilities subject to compromise and other liabilities under the Plan; and a pre-emergence gain of $2.2 billion, net of tax, resulting from the aggregate remaining changes to the net carrying value of the Company's pre-emergence assets and liabilities to reflect the fair values under fresh-start accounting.

---

*"Owens Corning, a global company incorporated in Delaware, is headquartered in Toledo, Ohio, and is a leading producer of residential and commercial building materials and glass fiber reinforcements and other similar materials for composite systems." 10-K
**Application of fresh-start accounting at October 31, 2006.
Source: Owens Corning 2010 10-K

The disclosure of the separate components can be made on the face of the balance sheet, in the statement of stockholders' equity, or in the notes. Chapter 4 covers comprehensive income. Exhibit 3-19 illustrates the presentation of accumulated other comprehensive income (loss).

Employee Stock Ownership Plans (ESOPs)

An **employee stock ownership plan (ESOP)** is a qualified stock-bonus, or combination stock-bonus and money-purchase pension plan, designed to invest primarily in the employer's securities. A qualified plan must satisfy certain requirements of the Internal Revenue Code. An ESOP must be a permanent trusteed plan for the exclusive benefit of the employees.

The trust that is part of the plan is exempt from tax on its income, and the employer/sponsor gets a current deduction for contributions to the plan. The plan participants become eligible for favorable taxation of distributions from the plan.

An ESOP may borrow the funds necessary to purchase the employer stock. These funds may be borrowed from the company, its stockholders, or a third party such as a bank. The company can guarantee the loan to the ESOP. Financial leverage—the ability of the ESOP to borrow in order to buy employer securities—is an important aspect.

The Internal Revenue Code favors borrowing for an ESOP. Commercial lending institutions, insurance companies, and mutual funds are permitted an exclusion from income for 50% of the interest received on loans used to finance an ESOP's acquisition of company stock. Thus, these institutions are willing to charge a reduced rate of interest for the loan.

From a company's perspective, an ESOP has both advantages and disadvantages. One advantage is that an ESOP serves as a source of funds for expansion at a reasonable rate. Other possible advantages are as follows:

1. A means to buy the stock from a major shareholder or possibly an unwanted shareholder.
2. Help in financing a leveraged buyout.
3. Reduction of potential of an unfriendly takeover.
4. Help in creating a market for the company's stock.

Some firms do not find an ESOP attractive because it can result in a significant amount of voting stock in the hands of their employees. Existing stockholders may not find an ESOP desirable because it will probably dilute their proportional ownership.

The employer contribution to an ESOP reduces cash, and an unearned compensation item decreases stockholders' equity. The unearned compensation is amortized on the income statement in subsequent periods. When an ESOP borrows funds and the firm (in either an informal or a formal guarantee) commits to future contributions to the ESOP to meet the debt-service requirements, then the firm records this commitment as a liability and as a deferred compensation deduction within stockholders' equity. As the debt is liquidated, the liability and deferred compensation are reduced.

Exhibit 3-21 shows Sara Lee Corporation reporting of the ESOP.

Treasury Stock

A firm creates **treasury stock** when it repurchases its own stock and does not retire it. Since treasury stock lowers the stock outstanding, it is subtracted from stockholders' equity. Treasury stock is, in essence, a reduction in paid-in capital.

A firm may record treasury stock in two ways. One method records the treasury stock at par or stated value, referred to as the *par-value method* of recording treasury stock. This method removes the paid-in capital in excess of par (or stated value) from the original issue. The treasury stock appears as a reduction of paid-in capital.

The other method, referred to as the *cost method*, records treasury stock at the cost of the stock (presented as a reduction of stockholders' equity). Most firms record treasury stock at cost.

Exhibit 3-22 illustrates the presentation of treasury stock for Johnson & Johnson and Subsidiaries. Note that a firm cannot record gains or losses from dealing in its own stock. Any apparent gains or losses related to treasury stock must impact stockholders' equity, such as a reduction in retained earnings.

Stockholders' Equity in Unincorporated Firms

These firms do not have stockholders. Stockholders' equity in an unincorporated firm is termed capital. The amount invested by the owner plus the retained earnings may be shown as one sum. A sole proprietorship form of business has only one owner (one capital account). A partnership form of business has more than one owner (capital account for each owner). Chapter 2 reviewed these forms of business.

Statement of Stockholders' Equity

Firms are required to present reconciliations of the beginning and ending balances of their stockholder accounts. This is accomplished by presenting a "statement of stockholders' equity."

This statement will include all of the stockholders' equity accounts. It is important when performing analysis to be aware of changes in these accounts. For example, common stock will indicate changes in common stock, retained earnings will indicate changes in retained

EXHIBIT **3-21**	The Sara Lee Corporation*

Employee Stock Ownership Program (ESOP)

	July 3, 2010	June 27, 2009
	Dollars in Millions	
Equity		
Sara Lee common stockholders' equity:		
Common stock: (authorized 1,200,000,000 shares; $0.01 par value) Issued and outstanding – 662,118,377 shares in 2010 and 695,658,110 shares in 2009	7	7
Capital surplus	17	17
Retained earnings	2,472	2,721
Unearned stock of ESOP	(97)	(104)
Accumulated other comprehensive income (loss)	(912)	(605)
Total Sara Lee common stockholders' equity	1,487	2,036
Noncontrolling interest	28	34
Total equity	1,515	2,070

Notes to Consolidated Financial Statements (In Part)

Note 10 – Employee Stock Ownership Trust

The corporation maintains an ESOP that holds common stock of the corporation that is used to fund a portion of the corporation's matching program for its 401(k) savings plan for domestic non-union employees. The purchase of the original stock by the Sara Lee ESOP was funded both with debt guaranteed by the corporation and loans from the corporation. The debt guaranteed by the corporation was fully paid in 2004, and only loans from the corporation to the ESOP remain. Each year, the corporation makes contributions that, with the dividends on the common stock held by the Sara Lee ESOP, are used to pay loan interest and principal. Shares are allocated to participants based upon the ratio of the current year's debt service to the sum of the total principal and interest payments over the remaining life of the loan. The number of unallocated shares in the ESOP was 7 million at July 3, 2010 and 8 million at June 27, 2009. Expense recognition for the ESOP is accounted for under the grandfathered provisions contained within US GAAP.

 The expense for the 401(k) recognized by the ESOP amounted to $7 million in 2010, $5 million in 2009 and $7 million in 2008. Payments to the Sara Lee ESOP were $11 million in 2010 and 2009, and $16 million in 2008.

*"Sara Lee Corporation… is a global manufacturer and marketer of high-quality, brand-name products for consumers throughout the world focused primarily on meats, bakery and beverage categories." 10-K
Source: The Sara Lee Corporation, 2010 10-K

earnings, and treasury stock will indicate changes in treasury stock. This statement is illustrated in Chapter 4.

 For many firms, it is important to observe changes to the account Accumulated Other Comprehensive Income (loss). This account is related to comprehensive income, which is covered in Chapter 4.

Problems in Balance Sheet Presentation

Numerous problems inherent in balance sheet presentation may cause difficulty in analysis. First, many assets are valued at cost, so one cannot determine the market value or replacement cost of many assets and should not assume that their balance sheet amount approximates current valuation.

 Second, varying methods are used for asset valuation. For example, inventories may be valued differently from firm to firm and, within a firm, from product to product. Similar problems exist with long-term asset valuation and the related depreciation alternatives.

 A different type of problem exists in that not all items of value to the firm are included as assets. For example, such characteristics as good employees, outstanding management, and a well-chosen location do not appear on the balance sheet. In the same vein, liabilities

EXHIBIT **3-22**	Johnson & Johnson and Subsidiaries*

Treasury Stock

Johnson & Johnson and Subsidiaries
Consolidated Balance Sheets (In Part)
At January 3, 2011 and January 3, 2010
Dollars in Millions Except Share and Per Share Data

Shareholders' equity		
Preferred stock – without par value (authorized and unissued 2,000,000 shares)	—	—
Common stock – par value $1.00 per share (Note 12) (authorized 4,320,000,000 shares; issued 3,119,843,000 shares)	3,120	3,120
Accumulated other comprehensive income (Note 13)	(3,531)	(3,058)
Retained earnings	77,773	70,306
	77,362	70,368
Less: common stock held in treasury, at cost (Note 12) (381,746,000 shares and 365,522,000 shares)	20,783	19,780
Total shareholders' equity	56,579	50,588

*"Johnson & Johnson and its subsidiaries (the "Company") have approximately 114,000 employees worldwide engaged in the research and development, manufacture and sale of a broad range of products in the health care field." 10-K
Source: Johnson & Johnson and Subsidiaries, 2010 10-K

related to contingencies also may not appear on the balance sheet. Chapters 6 and 7 present many of the problems of the balance sheet.

These problems do not make statement analysis impossible. They merely require that qualitative judgment be applied to quantitative data in order to assess the impact of these problem areas.

International Consolidated Balance Sheet (IFRS)

IFRS do not require a standard format for the balance sheet. Usually noncurrent assets are presented first, followed by current assets. For liabilities and owners' equity, "capital and reserves" are usually listed first, then noncurrent liabilities, and last, current liabilities.

The reserves sections of "capital and reserves" would not be part of U.S. GAAP. Reserves may result from upward revaluations of properties and investments. Reserves may also result from currency translation differences, similar to the U.S. GAAP classification of other comprehensive income.

Deloitte Touche Tohmatsu Limited, one of the big four public accounting firms, presents model financial statements under IFRS available on www.deloitte.com. These model financial statements will be used to illustrate statements under IFRS:

International GAAP Holdings Limited
Financial statements for the year ended 31 December 2011

The model financial statements of International GAAP Holdings Limited for the year ended 31 December 2011 are intended to illustrate the presentation and disclosure requirements of International Financial Reporting Standards (IFRSs). They also contain additional disclosures that are considered to be best practice, particularly where such disclosures are included in illustrative examples provided with a specific Standard.

International GAAP Holdings Limited is assumed to have presented financial statements in accordance with IFRSs for a number of years. Therefore, it is not a first-time adopter of IFRSs. Readers should refer to IFRS 1 *First-time Adoption of International Financial Reporting Standards* for specific requirements regarding an entity's first IFRS financial statements, and to the IFRS 1 section of Deloitte's Compliance, Presentation and Disclosure Checklist for details of the particular disclosure requirements applicable for first-time adopters. Deloitte's Compliance, Presentation and Disclosure Checklist can be downloaded from Deloitte's web site www.iasplus.com.

The model financial statements have illustrated the impact of a number of new and revised Standards and Interpretations that are mandatorily effective on 1 January 2011 (see note 2 to the model financial statements for details). The model financial statements have not illustrated the impact of new and revised Standards and Interpretations that are not yet mandatorily effective on 1 January 2011 (e.g. IFRS 9 *Financial Instruments*).

In addition, the model financial statements have been presented without regard to local laws or regulations. Preparers of financial statements will need to ensure that the options selected under IFRSs do not conflict with such sources of regulation (e.g. the revaluation of assets is not permitted in certain regimes – but these financial statements illustrate the presentation and disclosures required when an entity adopts the revaluation model under IAS 16 *Property, Plant and Equipment*). In addition, local laws or securities regulations may specify disclosures in addition to those required by IFRSs (e.g. in relation to directors' remuneration). Preparers of financial statements will consequently need to adapt the model financial statements to comply with such additional local requirements.

The model financial statements do not include separate financial statements for the parent, which may be required by local laws or regulations, or may be prepared voluntarily. Where an entity presents separate financial statements that comply with IFRSs, the requirements of IAS 27 *Consolidated and Separate Financial Statements* will apply. Separate statements of comprehensive income, financial position, changes in equity and cash flows for the parent will generally be required, together with supporting notes.

Suggested disclosures are cross-referenced to the underlying requirements in the texts of the relevant Standards and Interpretations.

For the purposes of presenting the statements of comprehensive income and cash flows, the alternatives allowed under IFRSs for those statements have been illustrated. Preparers should select the alternatives most appropriate to their circumstances and apply the chosen presentation method consistently.

Note that in these model financial statements, we have frequently included line items for which a nil amount is shown, so as to illustrate items that, although not applicable to International GAAP Holdings Limited, are commonly encountered in practice. This does not mean that we have illustrated all possible disclosures. Nor should it be taken to mean that, in practice, entities are required to display line items for such 'nil' amounts."

Disclaimer

Deloitte refers to one or more of Deloitte Touche Tohmatsu Limited, a UK private company limited by guarantee, and its network of member firms, each of which is a legally separate and independent entity. Please see www.deloitte.com/about for a detailed description of the legal structure of Deloitte Touche Tohmatsu Limited and its member firms. "Deloitte" is the band [brand] under which tens of thousands of dedicated professionals in independent firms throughout the world collaborate to provide audit, consulting, financial advisory, risk management, and tax services to selected clients. These firms are member[s] of Deloitte Touche Tohmatsu Limited (DTTL), a UK private company limited by guarantee. Each member firm provides services in a particular geographic area and is subject to the laws and professional regulations of the particular country or countries in which it operates. DTTL does not itself provide services to clients. DTTL and each DTTL member firm are separate and distinct legal entities, which cannot obligate each other. DTTL and each DTTL member firm are liable for only their own acts or omissions and not those of each other. Each DTTL member firm is structured differently in accordance with national laws, regulations, customary practice, and other factors, and may secure the provision of professional services in its territory through subsidiaries, affiliates and/or other entities. This publication contains general information only, and none of Deloitte Touche Tohmatsu Limited, its member firms, or its and their affiliates are, by means of this publication, rendering accounting, business, financial, investment, legal, tax, or other professional advice or services. This publication is not a substitute for such professional advice or services, nor should it be used as a basis for any decision or action that may affect your finances or your business. Before making any decision or taking any action that may affect your finances or your business, you should consult a qualified professional advisor. None of Deloitte Touche Tohmatsu Limited, its member firms, or its and their respective affiliates shall be responsible for any loss whatsoever sustained by any person who relies on this publication.

The model consolidated balance sheet (consolidated statement of financial position) is presented in Exhibit 3-23.

EXHIBIT **3-23**	IFRS Model Consolidated Balance Sheet				

Source	International GAAP Holdings Limited				
IAS 1.10(a),(f),51(b),(c)	Consolidated statement of financial position at 31 December 2011				
IAS 1.113		Notes	31/12/11	31/12/10	01/01/10
IAS 1.51(d), (e)			CU'000	CU'000	CU'000
	Assets				
IAS 1.60	*Non-current assets*				
IAS 1.54(a)	Property, plant and equipment	15	109,783	135,721	161,058
IAS 1.54(b)	Investment property	16	1,968	1,941	170
IAS 1.55	Goodwill	17	20,285	24,060	23,920
IAS 1.54(c)	Other intangible assets	18	9,739	11,325	12,523
IAS 1.54(e)	Investments in associates	20	7,402	7,270	5,706
IAS 1.54(o)	Deferred tax assets	10	2,083	1,964	1,843
IAS 1.55	Finance lease receivables	26	830	717	739
IAS 1.54(d)	Other financial assets	22	10,771	9,655	7,850
IAS 1.55	Other assets	23	—	—	—
	Total non-current assets		162,861	192,653	213,809
IAS 1.60	*Current assets*				
IAS 1.54(g)	Inventories	24	31,213	28,982	29,688
IAS 1.54(h)	Trade and other receivables	25	19,249	14,658	13,550
IAS 1.55	Finance lease receivables	26	198	188	182
IAS 1.55	Amounts due from customers under construction contracts	27	240	230	697
IAS 1.54(d)	Other financial assets	22	8,757	6,949	5,528
IAS 1.54(n)	Current tax assets	10	125	60	81
IAS 1.55	Other assets	23	—	—	—
IAS 1.54(i)	Cash and bank balances	46	23,446	19,778	9,082
			83,228	70,845	58,808
IAS 1.54(j)	Assets classified as held for sale	12	22,336	—	—
	Total current assets		105,564	70,845	58,808
	Total assets		268,425	263,498	272,617

Note: IAS 1.10(f) requires that an entity should present a statement of financial position as at the beginning of the earliest comparative period when it applies an accounting policy retrospectively or makes a retrospective restatement of items in its financial statements, or when it reclassifies items in its financial statements. However, IAS 1 does not provide further clarification as to when an entity is required to present an additional statement of financial position.

IAS 1.31 states that an entity need not provide a specific disclosure required by an IFRS if the information is not material. In determining whether it is necessary to present an additional statement of financial position, entities should consider the materiality of the information that would be contained in the additional statement of financial position and whether this would affect economic decisions made by a user of the financial statements. Specifically, it would be useful to consider factors such as the nature of the change, the alternative disclosures provided and whether the change in accounting policy actually affected the financial position at the beginning of the comparative period. Specific views from regulators should be considered in the assessment.

In this model, the application of new and revised standards does not result in any retrospective restatement of items in the financial statements (see note 2). However, this model does include the additional statement of financial position and the related notes for illustrative purposes only in order to show the level of detail to be disclosed when entities, after considering the specific facts and circumstances and exercising judgement, conclude that the additional statement of financial position and the related notes should be presented.

EXHIBIT **3-23**	IFRS Model Consolidated Balance Sheet *(continued)*

Source	International GAAP Holdings Limited

Consolidated statement of financial position
at 31 December 2011 (Continued)

		Notes	31/12/11	31/12/10	01/01/10
			CU'000	CU'000	CU'000
	Equity and liabilities				
	Capital and reserves				
IAS 1.55	Issued capital	28	32,439	48,672	48,672
IAS 1.55	Reserves	29	4,237	3,376	1,726
IAS 1.55	Retained earnings	30	110,805	94,909	73,824
			147,481	146,957	124,222
IAS 1.55	Amounts recognised directly in equity relating to assets classified as held for sale	12	—	—	—
IAS 1.54(r)	Equity attributable to owners of the Company		147,481	146,957	124,222
IAS 1.54(q)	Non-controlling interests	31	24,316	20,005	17,242
	Total equity		171,797	166,962	141,464
IAS 1.60	*Non-current liabilities*				
IAS 1.55	Borrowings	32	17,868	29,807	25,785
IAS 1.54(m)	Other financial liabilities	34	15,001	—	—
IAS 1.55	Retirement benefit obligation	39	2,861	2,023	2,968
IAS 1.54(o)	Deferred tax liabilities	10	6,729	5,657	4,436
IAS 1.54(l)	Provisions	35	2,294	2,231	4,102
IAS 1.55	Deferred revenue	41	59	165	41
IAS 1.55	Other liabilities	36	180	270	—
	Total non-current liabilities		44,992	40,153	37,332
IAS 1.60	*Current liabilities*				
IAS 1.54(k)	Trade and other payables	37	16,373	21,220	52,750
IAS 1.55	Amounts due to customers under construction contracts	27	36	15	245
IAS 1.55	Borrowings	32	22,446	25,600	33,618
IAS 1.54(m)	Other financial liabilities	34	116	18	—
IAS 1.54(n)	Current tax liabilities	10	5,270	5,868	4,910
IAS 1.54(l)	Provisions	35	3,356	3,195	2,235
IAS 1.55	Deferred revenue	41	265	372	63
IAS 1.55	Other liabilities	36	90	95	—
			47,952	56,383	93,821
IAS 1.54(p)	Liabilities directly associated with assets classified as held for sale	12	3,684	—	—
	Total current liabilities		51,636	56,383	93,821
	Total liabilities		96,628	96,536	131,153
	Total equity and liabilities		268,425	263,498	272,617

Subsequent Events

Subsequent events occur during the time period between the balance sheet data and the date statements are issued. There are two types of subsequent events under GAAP; those that require retroactive recognition (these require balance sheet and income statement recognition), and those that do not require retroactive recognition but require disclosure in the notes to the financial statements. Both types of subsequent events should be material.

Subsequent events that require retroactive recognition usually relate to estimates that were made and the subsequent event indicates that the estimates were substantially incorrect. Possibly a major customer has gone bankrupt and a reasonable amount was not provided for in allowance for doubtful accounts.

The second type of subsequent event does not affect the balance sheet date but does appear to be significant to the users of the financial statements. Possibly the CEO has died and the company is searching for a new CEO. Another example would be the issuance of a significant amount of common stock. This type of subsequent event is illustrated in Exhibit 3-24.

EXHIBIT **3-24**	Best Buy Co., Inc.

Subsequent Event

16. Subsequent Event (Dollars in millions)
In March 2011, we sold $350 principal amount of notes due March 15, 2016 (the "2016 Notes") and $650 principal amount of notes due March 15, 2021 (the "2021 Notes", and together with the 2016 Notes, the "Notes"). The 2016 Notes bear interest at a fixed rate of 3.75% per year, while the 2021 Notes bear interest at a fixed rate of 5.50% per year. Interest on the Notes is payable semi-annually on March 15 and September 15 of each year, beginning September 15, 2011. The Notes were issued at a slight discount to par, which when coupled with underwriting discounts of $6, resulted in net proceeds from the sale of the Notes of $990.

We may redeem some or all of the Notes at any time at a redemption price equal to the greater of (i) 100% of the principal amount of the Notes redeemed and (ii) the sum of the present values of each remaining scheduled payment of principal and interest on the Notes redeemed discounted to the redemption date on a semiannual basis, plus accrued and unpaid interest on the principal amount of the Notes to the redemption date as described in the indenture (including the supplemental indenture) relating to the Notes. Furthermore, if a change of control triggering event occurs, unless we have previously exercised our option to redeem the Notes, we will be required to offer to purchase the Notes at a price equal to 101% of the principal amount of the Notes, plus accrued and unpaid interest to the purchase date.

The Notes are unsecured and unsubordinated obligations and rank equally with all of our other unsecured and unsubordinated debt. The Notes contain covenants that, among other things, limit our ability and the ability of our North American subsidiaries to incur debt secured by liens or to enter into sale and lease-back transactions.

Source: Best Buy, Inc. 2010 10-K

Summary

The balance sheet shows the financial condition of an accounting entity as of a particular date. It is the most basic financial statement, and it is read by various users as part of their decision-making process. This chapter also covered the international consolidating balance sheet (IFRS).

Questions

Q 3-1 Name and describe the three major categories of balance sheet accounts.

Q 3-2 Are the following balance sheet items (A) assets, (L) liabilities, or (E) stockholders' equity?

a. Cash dividends payable

b. Mortgage notes payable

c. Investments in stock

d. Cash

e. Land

f. Inventory

g. Unearned rent

h. Marketable securities

i. Patents

j. Capital stock

k. Retained earnings

l. Accounts receivable

m. Taxes payable

n. Accounts payable

o. Organizational costs

p. Prepaid expenses

q. Goodwill

r. Tools

s. Buildings

Q 3-3 Classify the following as (CA) current asset, (IV) investments, (IA) intangible asset, or (TA) tangible asset:

a. Land

b. Cash

c. Copyrights

d. Marketable securities

e. Goodwill

f. Inventories

g. Tools

h. Prepaids

i. Buildings

j. Accounts receivable

k. Long-term investment in stock

l. Machinery

Q 3-4 Usually, current assets are listed in a specific order, starting with cash. What is the objective of this order of listing?

Q 3-5 Differentiate between marketable securities and long-term investments. What is the purpose of owning each?

Q 3-6 Differentiate between accounts receivable and accounts payable.

Q 3-7 What types of inventory will a retailing firm have? A manufacturing firm?

Q 3-8 What is depreciation? Which tangible assets are depreciated, and which are not? Why?

Q 3-9 For reporting purposes, management prefers higher profits; for tax purposes, lower taxable income is desired. To meet these goals, firms often use different methods of depreciation for tax and reporting purposes. Which depreciation method is best for reporting and which for tax purposes in the short run? Why?

Q 3-10 A rental agency collects rent in advance. Why is the rent collected treated as a liability?

Q 3-11 A bond carries a stated rate of interest of 6% and par of $1,000. It matures in 20 years. It is sold at 83 (83% of $1,000, or $830).

a. Under normal conditions, why would the bond sell at less than par?

b. How would the discount be disclosed on the statements?

Q 3-12 To be conservative, how should noncontrolling interest on the balance sheet be handled for primary analysis?

Q 3-13 Many assets are presented at historical cost. Why does this accounting principle cause difficulties in financial statement analysis?

Q 3-14 Explain how the issuance of a convertible bond can be a very attractive means of raising common equity funds.

Q 3-15 Classify each of the following as a (CA) current asset, (NA) noncurrent asset, (CL) current liability, (NL) noncurrent liability, or (E) equity account. Choose the best or most frequently used classification.

a. Supplies

b. Notes receivable

c. Unearned subscription revenue

d. Accounts payable

e. Retained earnings

f. Accounts receivable

g. Preferred stock

h. Plant

i. Prepaid rent

j. Capital

k. Wages payable

l. Mortgage bonds payable

m. Unearned interest

n. Marketable securities

o. Paid-in capital from sale of treasury stock

p. Land

q. Inventories

r. Taxes accrued

s. Cash

Q 3-16 Explain these preferred stock characteristics:

a. Accumulation of dividends

b. Participation in excess of stated dividend rate

c. Convertibility into common stock

d. Callability by the corporation

e. Preference in liquidation

Q 3-17 Describe the account Unrealized Exchange Gains or Losses.

Q 3-18 What is treasury stock? Why is it deducted from stockholders' equity?

Q 3-19 A firm, with no opening inventory, buys 10 units at $6 each during the period. In which accounts might the $60 appear on the financial statements?

Q 3-20 How is an unconsolidated subsidiary presented on a balance sheet?

Q 3-21 When would noncontrolling interest be presented on a balance sheet?

Q 3-22 DeLand Company owns 100% of Little Florida, Inc. Will DeLand Company show a noncontrolling interest on its balance sheet? Would the answer change if it owned only 60%? Will there ever be a case in which the subsidiary, Little Florida, is not consolidated?

Q 3-23 Describe the item Unrealized Decline in Market Value of Noncurrent Equity Investments.

Q 3-24 What is redeemable preferred stock? Why should it be included with debt for purposes of financial statement analysis?

Q 3-25 Describe fair value as it relates to assets and liabilities.

Q 3-26 With fair value the firm selects the highest appropriate level for valuation. Why the direction to select the highest appropriate level of valuation?

Q 3-27 For level 3 valuation (fair value), the company must include the valuation technique used to measure fair value, a reconciliation of the changes in fair value during the period, and a related discussion. Why the related discussion?

Q 3-28 Describe quasi-reorganization.

Q 3-29 Describe employee stock ownership plans (ESOPs).

Q 3-30 Why are commercial lending institutions, insurance companies, and mutual funds willing to grant loans to an employee stock ownership plan at favorable rates?

Q 3-31 What are some possible disadvantages of an employee stock ownership plan?

Q 3-32 How does a company recognize, in an informal or a formal way, that it has guaranteed commitments to future contributions to an ESOP to meet debt-service requirements?

Q 3-33 Describe depreciation, amortization, and depletion. How do they differ?

Q 3-34 What are the three factors usually considered when computing depreciation?

Q 3-35 An accelerated system of depreciation is often used for income tax purposes but not for financial reporting. Why?

Q 3-36 Which depreciation method will result in the most depreciation over the life of an asset?

Q 3-37 Should depreciation be recognized on a building in a year in which the cost of replacing the building rises? Explain.

Q 3-38 Describe the account Accumulated Other Comprehensive Income.

Q 3-39 Describe donated capital.

Q 3-40 Assume that a city donated land to a company. What accounts would be affected by this donation, and what would be the value?

Q 3-41 Describe the two types of subsequent events under GAAP.

Problems

P 3-1 The following information was obtained from the accounts of Airlines International dated December 31, 2012. It is presented in alphabetical order.

Accounts payable	$ 77,916
Accounts receivable	67,551
Accrued expenses	23,952
Accumulated depreciation	220,541
Allowance for doubtful accounts	248
Capital in excess of par	72,913
Cash	28,837
Common stock (par $0.50, authorized 20,000 shares, issued 14,304 shares)	7,152
Current installments of long-term debt	36,875
Deferred income tax liability (long term)	42,070
Inventory	16,643
Investments and special funds	11,901
Long-term debt, less current portion	393,808
Marketable securities	10,042
Other assets	727
Prepaid expenses	3,963
Property, plant, and equipment at cost	809,980
Retained earnings	67,361
Unearned transportation revenue (airline tickets expiring within one year)	6,808

Required Prepare a classified balance sheet in report form.

P 3-2 The following information was obtained from the accounts of Lukes, Inc., as of December 31, 2012. It is presented in scrambled order.

Common stock, no par value, 10,000 shares authorized, 5,724 shares issued	$ 3,180
Retained earnings	129,950
Deferred income tax liability (long term)	24,000
Long-term debt	99,870
Accounts payable	35,000
Buildings	75,000
Machinery and equipment	300,000
Land	11,000
Accumulated depreciation	200,000
Cash	3,000
Receivables, less allowance of $3,000	58,000
Accrued income taxes	3,000
Inventory	54,000
Other accrued expenses	8,000
Current portion of long-term debt	7,000
Prepaid expenses	2,000
Other assets (long term)	7,000

Required Prepare a classified balance sheet in report form. For assets, use the classifications of current assets, plant and equipment, and other assets. For liabilities, use the classifications of current liabilities and long-term liabilities.

P 3-3 The following information was obtained from the accounts of Alleg, Inc., as of December 31, 2012. It is presented in scrambled order.

Common stock, authorized 21,000 shares at $1 par value, issued 10,000 shares	$ 10,000
Additional paid-in capital	38,000
Cash	13,000
Marketable securities	17,000
Accounts receivable	26,000
Accounts payable	15,000
Current maturities of long-term debt	11,000
Mortgages payable	80,000
Bonds payable	70,000
Inventory	30,000
Land and buildings	57,000
Machinery and equipment	125,000
Goodwill	8,000
Patents	10,000
Other assets	50,000
Deferred income taxes (long-term liability)	18,000
Retained earnings	33,000
Accumulated depreciation	61,000

Required Prepare a classified balance sheet in report form. For assets, use the classifications of current assets, plant and equipment, intangibles, and other assets. For liabilities, use the classifications of current liabilities and long-term liabilities.

P 3-4 The following is the balance sheet of Ingram Industries:

INGRAM INDUSTRIES
Balance Sheet
June 30, 2012

Assets

Current assets:

Cash (including $13,000 in sinking fund for bonds payable)	$ 70,000	
Marketable securities	23,400	
Investment in subsidiary company	23,000	
Accounts receivable	21,000	
Inventories (lower-of-cost-or-market)	117,000	$254,400

(continued)

(**P 3-4** CONTINUED)

Assets

Plant assets:

Land and buildings	$160,000	
Less: Accumulated depreciation	100,000	$ 60,000

Investments:

Treasury stock		4,000

Deferred charges:

Discount on bonds payable	$ 6,000	
Prepaid expenses	2,000	8,000
		$326,400

Liabilities and Stockholders' Equity

Liabilities:

Notes payable to bank	$ 60,000	
Accounts payable	18,000	
Bonds payable	61,000	
Total liabilities		$139,000

Stockholders' equity:

Preferred and common (each $10 par, 5,000 shares preferred and 6,000 shares common)	$110,000	
Capital in excess of par	61,000	
Retained earnings	16,400	
		187,400
Total liabilities and stockholders' equity		$326,400

Required Indicate your criticisms of the balance sheet and briefly explain the proper treatment of any item criticized.

P 3-5 The following is the balance sheet of Rubber Industries:

RUBBER INDUSTRIES
Balance Sheet
For the Year Ended December 31, 2012

Assets

Current assets:

Cash	$ 50,000
Marketable equity securities	19,000
Accounts receivable, net	60,000
Inventory	30,000
Treasury stock	20,000
Total current assets	$179,000

Plant assets:

Land and buildings, net	160,000

Investments:

Short-term U.S. notes	20,000

Other assets:

Supplies	4,000
Total assets	$363,000

Liabilities and Stockholders' Equity

Liabilities:

Bonds payable	$123,000
Accounts payable	40,000
Wages payable	10,000
Total liabilities	$173,000

Stockholders' equity:

Common stock ($20 par, 20,000 shares authorized, 6,000 shares outstanding)	120,000
Retained earnings	50,000
Redeemable preferred stock	20,000
Total liabilities and stockholders' equity	$363,000

Required Indicate your criticisms of the balance sheet and briefly explain the proper treatment of any item criticized.

P 3-6 The following is the balance sheet of McDonald Company:

McDONALD COMPANY
December 31, 2012

Assets

Current assets:

Cash (including $10,000 restricted for payment of note)	$ 40,000	
Marketable equity securities	20,000	
Accounts receivable, less allowance for doubtful accounts of $12,000	70,000	
Inventory	60,000	
Total current assets		$190,000

Plant assets:

Land		$ 40,000	
Buildings, net		100,000	
Equipment	$80,000		
Less: Accumulated depreciation	20,000	60,000	
Patent		20,000	
Organizational costs		15,000	
			235,000

Other assets:

Prepaid insurance	5,000
Total assets	$430,000

Liabilities and Stockholders' Equity

Current liabilities:

Accounts payable	$ 60,000	
Wages payable	10,000	
Notes payable, due July 1, 2014	20,000	
Bonds payable, due December 2018	100,000	
Total current liabilities		$190,000
Dividends payable		4,000
Deferred tax liability, long term		30,000

Stockholders' equity:

Common stock ($10 par, 10,000 shares authorized, 5,000 shares outstanding)	$ 50,000	
Retained earnings	156,000	
Total stockholders' equity		206,000
Total liabilities and stockholders' equity		$430,000

Required Indicate your criticisms of the balance sheet and briefly explain the proper treatment of any item criticized.

P 3-7 You have just started as a staff auditor for a small CPA firm. During the course of the audit, you discover the following items related to a single client firm:

a. During the year, the firm declared and paid $10,000 in dividends.

b. Your client has been named defendant in a legal suit involving a material amount. You have received from the client's counsel a statement indicating little likelihood of loss.

c. Because of cost control actions and general employee dissatisfaction, it is likely that the client will suffer a costly strike in the near future.

d. Twenty days after closing, the client suffered a major fire in one of its plants.

e. The cash account includes a substantial amount set aside for payment of pension obligations.

f. Marketable securities include a large quantity of shares of stock purchased for control purposes.

g. Land is listed on the balance sheet at its market value of $1,000,000. It cost $670,000 to purchase 12 years ago.

h. During the year, the government of Uganda expropriated a plant located in that country. There was substantial loss.

Required How would each of these items be reflected in the year-end balance sheet, including notes?

P 3-8 Corvallis Corporation owns 80% of the stock of Little Harrisburg, Inc. At December 31, 2012, Little Harrisburg had the following summarized balance sheet:

LITTLE HARRISBURG, INC.
Balance Sheet
December 31, 2012

Current assets	$100,000	Current liabilities	$ 50,000
		Long-term debt	150,000
Property, plant, and equipment (net)	400,000	Capital stock	50,000
	$500,000	Retained earnings	250,000
			$500,000

The earnings of Little Harrisburg, Inc., for 2012 were $50,000 after tax.

Required

a. What would be the amount of noncontrolling interest on the balance sheet of Corvallis Corporation?
b. What would be the noncontrolling interest in share of earnings on the income statement of Corvallis Corporation?

P 3-9 Aggarwal Company has had 10,000 shares of 10%, $100 par-value preferred stock and 80,000 shares of $5 stated-value common stock outstanding for the last three years. During that period, dividends paid totaled $0, $200,000, and $220,000 for each year, respectively.

Required Compute the amount of dividends that must have been paid to preferred stockholders and common stockholders in each of the three years, given the following four independent assumptions:

a. Preferred stock is nonparticipating and cumulative.
b. Preferred stock participates up to 12% of its par value and is cumulative.
c. Preferred stock is fully participating and cumulative.
d. Preferred stock is nonparticipating and noncumulative.

P 3-10 Rosewell Company has had 5,000 shares of 9%, $100 par-value preferred stock and 10,000 shares of $10 par-value common stock outstanding for the last two years. During the most recent year, dividends paid totaled $65,000; in the prior year, dividends paid totaled $40,000.

Required Compute the amount of dividends that must have been paid to preferred stockholders and common stockholders in each year, given the following independent assumptions:

a. Preferred stock is fully participating and cumulative.
b. Preferred stock is nonparticipating and noncumulative.
c. Preferred stock participates up to 10% of its par value and is cumulative.
d. Preferred stock is nonparticipating and cumulative.

P 3-11 An item of equipment acquired on January 1 at a cost of $100,000 has an estimated life of 10 years.

Required Assuming that the equipment will have a salvage value of $10,000, determine the depreciation for each of the first three years by the:

a. Straight-line method
b. Declining-balance method
c. Sum-of-the-years'-digits method

P 3-12 An item of equipment acquired on January 1 at a cost of $60,000 has an estimated use of 25,000 hours. During the first three years, the equipment was used 5,000 hours, 6,000 hours, and 4,000 hours, respectively. The estimated salvage value of the equipment is $10,000.

Required Determine the depreciation for each of the three years, using the unit-of-production method.

P 3-13 An item of equipment acquired on January 1 at a cost of $50,000 has an estimated life of five years and an estimated salvage of $10,000.

Required

a. From a management perspective, from among the straight-line method, declining-balance method, and sum-of-the-years'-digits method of depreciation, which method should be chosen for the financial statements if income is to be at a maximum the first year? Which method should be chosen for the income tax returns, assuming that the tax rate stays the same each year? Explain and show computations.

b. Is it permissible to use different depreciation methods in financial statements than those used in tax returns?

P 3-14

Required Answer the following multiple-choice questions:

a. Which of the following accounts would *not appear on a conventional balance sheet?*

   1. Accounts receivable
   2. Accounts payable
   3. Patents
   4. Gain from sale of land
   5. Common stock

b. Current assets typically include all but which of the following assets?

   1. Cash restricted for the retirement of bonds
   2. Unrestricted cash
   3. Marketable securities
   4. Receivables
   5. Inventories

c. The Current Liabilities section of the balance sheet should include

   1. Land.
   2. Cash surrender value of life insurance.
   3. Accounts payable.
   4. Bonds payable.
   5. Preferred stock.

d. Inventories are the balance of goods on hand. In a manufacturing firm, they include all but which of the following?

   1. Raw materials
   2. Work in process
   3. Finished goods
   4. Supplies
   5. Construction in process

e. Which of the following accounts would *not* usually be classified as a current liability?

   1. Accounts payable
   2. Wages payable
   3. Unearned rent income
   4. Bonds payable
   5. Taxes payable

f. For the issuing firm, redeemable preferred stock should be classified where for analysis purposes?

   1. Marketable security
   2. Long-term investment
   3. Intangible
   4. Liabilities
   5. Shareholders' equity

(*continued*)

(P 3-14 CONTINUED)

g. Which of the following accounts would *not* be classified as an intangible?

1. Goodwill
2. Patent
3. Accounts receivable
4. Trademarks
5. Franchises

h. Which of the following is *not* true relating to intangibles?

1. Research and development usually represents a significant intangible on the financial statements.
2. Goodwill arises from the acquisition of a business for a sum greater than the physical asset value.
3. Purchased goodwill is not amortized but is subject to annual impairment reviews.
4. The global treatment of goodwill varies significantly.
5. Intangibles are usually amortized over their useful lives or legal lives, whichever is shorter.

i. Growth Company had total assets of $100,000 and total liabilities of $60,000. What is the balance of the stockholders' equity?

1. $0
2. $40,000
3. $60,000
4. $100,000
5. None of the above.

j. The Current Assets section of the balance sheet should include

1. Inventory.
2. Taxes payable.
3. Land.
4. Patents.
5. Bonds payable.

k. Which of the following is *not* a typical current liability?

1. Accounts payable
2. Wages payable
3. Interest payable
4. Pension liabilities
5. Taxes payable

l. Which of the following is a current liability?

1. Unearned rent income
2. Prepaid interest
3. Land
4. Common stock
5. None of the above.

m. Treasury stock is best classified as a

1. Current liability.
2. Current asset.
3. Reduction of stockholders' equity.
4. Contra asset.
5. Contra liability.

n. Considering IFRSs, which of the following statements would be considered false?

1. IFRSs do not require a standard format for the balance sheet.
2. With IFRSs, usually nonconcurrent assets are presented first, followed by current assets.
3. Under IFRS for liabilities and owners' equity, capital and listed reserves are usually listed first, then noncurrent liabilities, and then current liabilities last.

4. The reserves section of capital and reserves would not be part of U.S. GAAP.
5. All of these items would be considered to be true.

o. Considering IFRSs, which of the following statements would be considered false?

1. When using IFRSs, local laws or securities regulations may specify disclosures in addition to those required by IFRSs.
2. IAS introduced a number of terminology changes. The new titles for the financial statements are not mandatory.
3. The IFRS model consolidated balance sheet, as presented by Deloitte Touche, puts an emphasis on liquidity.
4. Under IFRS, noncontrolling interests are usually presented as the last item in total equity.
5. None of these statements would be considered false.

Cases

CASE 3-1 CONVENIENCE FOODS

Kellogg Company and Subsidiaries*
Consolidated Balance Sheet

(millions, except share data)	2010	2009
Current assets		
Cash and cash equivalents	$ 444	$ 334
Accounts receivable, net	1,190	1,093
Inventories	1,056	910
Other current assets	225	221
Total current assets	$ 2,915	$ 2,558
Property, net	3,128	3,010
Goodwill	3,628	3,643
Other intangibles, net	1,456	1,458
Other assets	720	531
Total assets	$11,847	$11,200
Current liabilities		
Current maturities of long-term debt	$ 952	$ 1
Notes payable	44	44
Accounts payable	1,149	1,077
Other current liabilities	1,039	1,166
Total current liabilities	$ 3,184	$ 2,288
Long-term debt	4,908	4,835
Deferred income taxes	697	425
Pension liability	265	430
Other liabilities	639	947
Commitments and contingencies		
Equity		
Common stock, $.25 par value, 1,000,000,000 shares authorized. Issued: 419,272,027 shares in 2010 and 419,058,168 shares in 2009	105	105
Capital in excess of par value	495	472
Retained earnings	6,122	5,481
Treasury stock at cost: 53,667,635 shares in 2010 and 37,678,215 shares in 2009	(2,650)	(1,820)
Accumulated other comprehensive income (loss)	(1,914)	(1,966)
Total Kellogg Company equity	$ 2,158	$ 2,272
Noncontrolling interests	(4)	3
Total equity	2,154	2,275
Total liabilities and equity	$11,847	$11,200

*"Kellogg Company, founded in 1906 and incorporated in Delaware in 1922, and its subsidiaries are engaged in the manufacture and marketing of ready-to-eat cereal and convenience foods." 10-K

Source: Kellogg Company and Subsidiaries 2010 10-K

(continued)

(**Case 3-1** continued)

Kellogg Company and Subsidiaries
Notes to Consolidated Financial Statements (In Part)

NOTE 1 ACCOUNTING POLICIES (In Part)

Basis of presentation

The consolidated financial statements include the accounts of Kellogg Company and its majority-owned subsidiaries (Kellogg or the Company). Intercompany balances and transactions are eliminated.

The Company's fiscal year normally ends on the Saturday closest to December 31 and as a result, a 53rd week is added approximately every sixth year. The Company's 2010 and 2009 fiscal years each contained 52 weeks and ended on January 1, 2011 and January 2, 2010, respectively. The Company's 2008 fiscal year ended on January 3, 2009, and included a 53rd week. While quarters normally consist of 13-week periods, the fourth quarter of fiscal 2008 included a 14th week.

Use of estimates

The preparation of financial statements in conformity with accounting principles generally accepted in the United States of America requires management to make estimates and assumptions that affect the reported amounts of assets and liabilities, the disclosure of contingent liabilities at the date of the financial statements and the reported amounts of revenues and expenses during the periods reported. Actual results could differ from those estimates.

Cash and cash equivalents

Highly liquid investments with remaining stated maturities of three months or less when purchased are considered cash equivalents and recorded at cost.

Accounts receivable

Accounts receivable consists principally of trade receivables, which are recorded at the invoiced amount, net of allowances for doubtful accounts and prompt payment discounts. Trade receivables do not bear interest. The allowance for doubtful accounts represents management's estimate of the amount of probable credit losses in existing accounts receivable, as determined from a review of past due balances and other specific account data. Account balances are written off against the allowance when management determines the receivable is uncollectible. The Company does not have off-balance sheet credit exposure related to its customers.

Inventories

Inventories are valued at the lower of cost or market. Cost is determined on an average cost basis.

Property

The Company's property consists mainly of plants and equipment used for manufacturing activities. These assets are recorded at cost and depreciated over estimated useful lives using straight-line methods for financial reporting and accelerated methods, where permitted, for tax reporting. Major property categories are depreciated over various periods as follows (in years): manufacturing machinery and equipment 5–20; office equipment 4–5; computer equipment and capitalized software 3–5; building components 15–30; building structures 50. Cost includes interest associated with significant capital projects.

Plant and equipment are reviewed for impairment when conditions indicate that the carrying value may not be recoverable. Such conditions include an extended period of idleness or a plan of disposal. Assets to be disposed of at a future date are depreciated over the remaining period of use. Assets to be sold are written down to realizable value at the time the assets are being actively marketed for sale and a sale is expected to occur within one year. As of year-end 2010 and 2009, the carrying value of assets held for sale was insignificant.

Goodwill and other intangible assets

Goodwill and indefinite-lived intangibles are not amortized, but are tested at least annually for impairment. An intangible asset with a finite life is amortized on a straight-line basis over the estimated useful life.

For the goodwill impairment test, the fair value of the reporting units are estimated based on market multiples. This approach employs market multiples based on earnings before interest, taxes, depreciation and amortization, earnings for companies that are comparable to the Company's reporting units and discounted cash flow. The assumptions used for the impairment test are consistent with those utilized by a market participant performing similar valuations for the Company's reporting units.

Similarly, impairment testing of other intangible assets requires a comparison of carrying value to fair value of that particular asset. Fair values of non-goodwill intangible assets are based primarily on projections of future cash flows to be generated from that asset. For instance, cash flows related to a particular trademark would be based on a projected royalty stream attributable to branded product sales, discounted at rates consistent with rates used by market participants.

These estimates are made using various inputs including historical data, current and anticipated market conditions, management plans, and market comparables.

. . . . .

Research and development

The costs of research and development (R&D) are expensed as incurred and are classified in SGA expense. R&D includes expenditures for new product and process innovation, as well as significant technological improvements to existing products and processes. The Company's R&D expenditures primarily consist of internal salaries, wages, consulting, and supplies attributable to time spent on R&D activities. Other costs include depreciation and maintenance of research facilities and equipment, including assets at manufacturing locations that are temporarily engaged in pilot plant activities.

Income taxes

The Company recognizes uncertain tax positions based on a benefit recognition model. Provided that the tax position is deemed more likely than not of being sustained, the Company recognizes the largest amount of tax benefit that is greater than 50 percent likely of being ultimately realized upon settlement. The tax position is derecognized when it is no longer more likely than not of being sustained. The Company classifies income tax–related interest and penalties as interest expense and SGA expense, respectively, on the Consolidated Statement of Income. The current portion of the Company's unrecognized tax benefits is presented in the Consolidated Balance Sheet in other current assets and other current liabilities, and the amounts expected to be settled after one year are recorded in other assets and other liabilities.

Required
a. 1. The statement is entitled "Consolidated Balance Sheets." What does it mean to have a consolidated balance sheet?
   2. For subsidiaries where control is present, does Kellogg have 100% ownership? Explain.
b. 1. With this information, can the gross receivables be determined? Explain.
   2. What is the estimated amount that will be collected on receivables outstanding at the end of 2010?
c. 1. What is the total amount of inventory at the end of 2010?
   2. What indicates that the inventory is stated on a conservative basis?
   3. What is the trend in inventory balance? Comment.
d. 1. What is the net property and equipment at the end of 2010?
   2. What depreciation method is used for financial reporting purposes? Where permitted, what depreciation methods are used for tax reporting? Comment on why the difference in depreciation methods for financial reporting versus tax reporting.
   3. What is the accumulated depreciation on land at the end of 2010?
e. 1. Describe the treasury stock account.
   2. What method is used to record treasury stock?
   3. Why is treasury stock presented as a reduction in stockholders' equity?

(*continued*)

(**CASE 3-1** CONTINUED)

f. 1. What is the fiscal year?

    2. Comment on the difference in length of fiscal year.

g. Comment on the use of estimates.

h. Does it appear that cash and cash equivalents are presented conservatively?

i. 1. Comment on the source of goodwill.

    2. How are goodwill and indefinite-lived intangibles handled for write-offs?

j. When is research and development expensed?

k. Why is a benefit recognition model used for computing income taxes?

CASE 3-2 WORLD WIDE ENTERTAINMENT

The Walt Disney Company – 2010 Annual Report*

CONSOLIDATED BALANCE SHEETS
(In millions, except per share data)

	October 2, 2010	October 3, 2009
ASSETS		
Current assets		
Cash and cash equivalents	$ 2,722	$ 3,417
Receivables	5,784	4,854
Inventories	1,442	1,271
Television costs	678	631
Deferred income taxes	1,018	1,140
Other current assets	581	576
Total Current Assets	12,225	11,889
Film and television costs	4,773	5,125
Investments	2,513	2,554
Parks, resorts and other property, at cost Attractions,		
buildings and equipment	32,875	32,475
Accumulated depreciation	(18,373)	(17,395)
	14,502	15,080
Projects in progress	2,180	1,350
Land	1,124	1,167
	17,806	17,597
Intangible assets, net	5,081	2,247
Goodwill	24,100	21,683
Other assets	2,708	2,022
	$ 69,206	$ 63,117
LIABILITIES AND EQUITY		
Current Liabilities		
Accounts payable and other accrued liabilities	$ 6,109	$ 5,616
Current portion of borrowings	2,350	1,206
Unearned royalties and other advances	2,541	2,112
Total current liabilities	11,000	8,934
Borrowings	10,130	11,495
Deferred income taxes	2,630	1,819
Other long-term liabilities	6,104	5,444
Commitments and contingencies (note 15)		
Equity		
Preferred stock, $.01 par value		
Authorized – 100 million shares, Issued – none	—	—

*"The Walt Disney Company, together with its subsidiaries, is a diversified worldwide entertaining company with operations in five business segments: Media Networks, Parks and Resorts, Studio Entertainment, and Consumer Products and Interactive Media." 10-K

Source: The Walt Disney Company 2010 10-K

	October 2, 2010	October 3, 2009
Common stock, $.01 par value		
Authorized – 4.6 billion shares at October 2, 2010 and 3.6 billion shares at October 3, 2009		
Issued – 2.7 billion shares at October 2, 2010 and 2.6 billion shares at October 3, 2009	28,736	27,038
Retained earnings	34,327	31,033
Accumulated other comprehensive loss	(1,881)	(1,644)
	61,182	56,427
Treasury stock, at cost, 803.1 million shares at October 2, 2010 and 781.7 million shares at October 3, 2009	(23,663)	(22,693)
Total Disney Shareholder's equity	37,519	33,734
Noncontrolling interests	1,823	1,691
Total Equity	39,342	35,425
Total liabilities and equity	$ 69,206	$ 63,117

NOTES TO CONSOLIDATED FINANCIAL STATEMENTS (In Part)
(Tabular dollars in millions, except per share amounts)

1. Description of the Business and Segment Information (In Part)

The Walt Disney Company, together with the subsidiaries through which businesses are conducted (the Company), is a diversified worldwide entertainment company with operations in the following business segments: Media Networks, Parks and Resorts, Studio Entertainment, Consumer Products and Interactive Media.

2. Summary of Significant Accounting Policies (In Part)

Principles of Consolidation

The consolidated financial statements of the Company include the accounts of The Walt Disney Company and its majority-owned and controlled subsidiaries. Intercompany accounts and transactions have been eliminated in consolidation. In December 1999, DVD Financing, Inc. (DFI), a subsidiary of Disney Vacation Development, Inc. and an indirect subsidiary of the Company, completed a receivable sale transaction that established a facility that permitted DFI to sell receivables arising from the sale of vacation club memberships on a periodic basis. In connection with this facility, DFI prepares separate financial statements, although its separate assets and liabilities are also consolidated in these financial statements. DFI's ability to sell new receivables under this facility ended on December 4, 2008. (See Note 16 for further discussion of this facility)

Reporting Period

The Company's fiscal year ends on the Saturday closest to September 30 and consists of fifty-two weeks with the exception that approximately every six years, we have a fifty-three week year. When a fifty-three week year occurs, the Company reports the additional week in the fourth quarter. Fiscal 2009 was a fifty-three week year beginning on September 28, 2008 and ending on October 3, 2009.

Use of Estimates

The preparation of financial statements in conformity with generally accepted accounting principles requires management to make estimates and assumptions that affect the amounts reported in the financial statements and footnotes thereto. Actual results may differ from those estimates.

Revenue Recognition

Broadcast advertising revenues are recognized when commercials are aired. Revenues from television subscription services related to the Company's primary cable programming services are recognized as services are provided. Certain of the Company's contracts with cable and

(continued)

(**CASE 3-2** CONTINUED)

satellite operators include annual live programming commitments. In these cases, recognition of revenues subject to the commitments is deferred until the annual commitments are satisfied, which generally results in higher revenue recognition in the second half of the year.

Revenues from advance theme park ticket sales are recognized when the tickets are used. For non-expiring, multi-day tickets, revenues are recognized over a three-year time period based on estimated usage, which is derived from historical usage patterns.

Revenues from the theatrical distribution of motion pictures are recognized when motion pictures are exhibited. Revenues from DVD and video game sales, net of anticipated returns and customer incentives, are recognized on the date that video units are made available for sale by retailers. Revenues from the licensing of feature films and television programming are recorded when the content is available for telecast by the licensee and when certain other conditions are met.

Merchandise licensing advances and guarantee royalty payments are recognized based on the contractual royalty rate when the licensed product is sold by the licensee. Non-refundable advances and minimum guarantee royalty payments in excess of royalties earned are generally recognized as revenue at the end of the contract term.

Revenues from our internet and mobile operations are recognized as services are rendered. Advertising revenues at our internet operations are recognized when advertisements are viewed online.

Taxes collected from customers and remitted to governmental authorities are presented in the Consolidated Statements of Income on a net basis.

Allowance for doubtful accounts

The Company maintains an allowance for doubtful accounts to reserve for potentially uncollectible receivables. The allowance for doubtful accounts is estimated based on our analysis of trends in overall receivables aging, specific identification of certain receivables that are at risk of not being paid, past collection experience and current economic trends. In times of domestic or global economic turmoil, the Company's estimates and judgments with respect to the collectability of its receivables are subject to greater uncertainty than in more stable periods.

Advertising Expense

Advertising costs are expensed as incurred. Advertising expense for fiscal 2010, 2009 and 2008 was $2.6 billion, $2.7 billion and $2.9 billion, respectively.

Cash and Cash Equivalents

Cash and cash equivalents consist of cash on hand and marketable securities with original maturities of three months or less.

Inventories

Inventory primarily includes vacation timeshare units, merchandise, materials, and supplies. Carrying amounts of vacation ownership units are recorded at the lower of cost or net realizable value. Carrying amounts of merchandise, materials, and supplies inventories are generally determined on a moving average cost basis and are recorded at the lower of cost or market.

14. Detail of Certain Balance Sheet Accounts (In Part)

	October 2, 2010	October 3, 2009
Current receivables		
Accounts receivable	$5,454	$4,794
Other	656	396
Allowance for doubtful accounts	(326)	(336)
	$5,784	$4,854

Required

a. The statement is entitled "Consolidated Balance Sheets." What does it mean to have a consolidated balance sheet?

b. 1. What is the gross amount of current receivables at October 2, 2010?

2. What is the trend in receivables?

c. 1. Does there appear to be a significant increase in projects in progress?

    2. Are projects in progress and land depreciated?

d. 1. What is the amount of total assets at October 2, 2010?

    2. What is the total current assets at October 2, 2010?

    3. What is the total inventory at October 2, 2010? Does the inventory method appear to be conservative? Comment.

e. Comment on the use of estimates.

f. Why are advertising expenses expensed as incurred?

g. Are cash and cash equivalents presented conservatively? Comment.

h. Revenue recognition; comment on the following:

    1. Broadcast advertising revenues

    2. Revenues from advance theme park ticket sales

    3. Revenues from the theatrical distribution of motion pictures

    4. Merchandise licensing advances and guarantee royalty payments

    5. Revenues from internet and mobile operations

    6. Why the use of several revenue recognition methods?

    7. Are the revenue recognition methods industry-specific?

i. Describe treasury stock and how it is reported.

j. Describe noncontrolling interests.

k. 1. Describe the reporting period.

    2. Does the reporting period create an inconsistency?

CASE 3-3 HEALTH CARE PRODUCTS

Abbott Laboratories and Subsidiaries*

Consolidated Balance Sheet
(dollars in thousands)

	December 31		
	2010	2009	2008
Liabilities and Shareholders' Investment			
Current Liabilities:			
Short-term borrowings	$ 4,349,796	$ 4,978,438	$ 1,691,069
Trade accounts payable	1,535,759	1,280,542	1,351,436
Salaries, wages and commissions	1,328,665	1,117,410	1,011,312
Other accrued liabilities	6,014,772	4,363,032	4,216,742
Dividends payable	680,749	620,640	559,064
Income taxes payable	1,307,723	442,140	805,397
Obligation in connection with conclusion of the TAP Pharmaceutical Products Inc. joint venture	—	36,105	915,982
Current portion of long-term debt	2,044,970	211,182	1,040,906
Total Current Liabilities	17,262,434	13,049,489	11,591,908
Long-term Debt	12,523,517	11,266,294	8,713,327
Post-employment Obligations and Other Long-term Liabilities	7,199,851	5,202,111	4,595,278
Commitments and Contingencies			
Shareholders' Investment:			
Preferred shares, one dollar par value Authorized – 1,000,000 shares, none issued	—	—	—

(continued)

*"Abbott Laboratories is an Illinois corporation, incorporated in 1900. Abbott's principal business is the discovery, development, manufacture, and sale of a broad and diversified line of health care products." 10-K
Source: Abbott Laboratories and Subsidiaries 2010 10-K

(**CASE 3-3** CONTINUED)

| | December 31 | | |
	2010	2009	2008
Common shares, without par value			
Authorized – 2,400,000,000 shares			
Issued at stated capital amount –			
Shares: 2010: 1,619,689,876; 2009:			
1,612,683,987; 2008: 1,601,580,899	8,744,703	8,257,873	7,444,411
Common shares held in treasury, at cost –			
Shares: 2010: 72,705,928; 2009:			
61,516,398; 2008: 49,147,968	(3,916,823)	(3,310,347)	(2,626,404)
Earnings employed in the business	18,927,101	17,054,027	13,825,383
Accumulated other comprehensive income			
(loss)	(1,366,846)	854,074	(1,163,839)
Total Abbott Shareholders' Investment	22,388,135	22,855,627	17,479,551
Noncontrolling Interests in Subsidiaries	88,329	43,102	39,140
Total Shareholders' Investment	22,476,464	22,898,729	17,518,691
	$59,462,266	$52,416,623	$42,419,204

Required

a. The statement is entitled "Consolidated Balance Sheet." What does it mean to have a consolidated balance sheet?

b. 1. What current liability decreased the most?

   2. What current liability increased the most?

c. 1. How many common shares had been issued as of December 31, 2010?

   2. How many shares were held in the treasury at December 31, 2010?

   3. How many shares were outstanding at December 31, 2010?

   4. What is the treasury stock method?

d. Abbott Laboratories discloses the account "Earnings employed in the business." What is this account usually called?

CASE 3-4 BEST

Best Buy Co., Inc.*

Consolidated Balance Sheets (In Part)
$ in millions, except per share and share amounts

	February 26, 2011	February 27, 2010
Assets		
Current Assets		
Cash and cash equivalents	$ 1,103	$ 1,826
Short-term investments	22	90
Receivables	2,348	2,020
Merchandise inventories	5,897	5,486
Other current assets	1,103	1,144
Total current assets	10,473	10,566
Property and Equipment		
Land and buildings	766	757
Leasehold improvements	2,318	2,154
Fixtures and equipment	4,701	4,447
Property under capital lease	120	95
	7,905	7,453
Less accumulated depreciation	4,082	3,383
Net property and equipment	3,823	4,070

*"We are a multinational retailer of consumer electronics, home-office products, entertainment products, appliance and related services." 10-K

Source: Best Buy Co., Inc. 2010 10-K

	February 26, 2011	February 27, 2010
Goodwill	2,454	2,452
Tradenames, Net	133	159
Customer Relationships, Net	203	279
Equity and Other Investments	328	324
Other Assets	435	452
Total Assets	$17,849	$18,302

Notes to Consolidated Financial Statements (In Part)
$ in millions except per share amounts or as otherwise noted

1. Summary of Significant Accounting Policies (In Part)

Basis of Presentation

The consolidated financial statements include the accounts of Best Buy Co., Inc. and its consolidated subsidiaries. Investments in unconsolidated entities over which we exercise significant influence but do not have control are accounted for using the equity method. We have eliminated all intercompany accounts and transactions.

In order to align our fiscal reporting periods and comply with statutory filing requirements in certain foreign jurisdictions, we consolidate the financial results of our Europe, China, Mexico and Turkey operations on a two-month lag. Our policy is to accelerate recording the effect of events occurring in the lag period that significantly affect our consolidated financial statements. Except for our fiscal 2011 restructuring, for which we recorded the effects of certain restructuring charges, no significant intervening event occurred in these operations that would have materially affected our financial condition, results of operations, liquidity or other factors had it been recorded during fiscal 2011. Accordingly, the $171 of restructuring charges related to our International segment were included in our fiscal 2011 results. For further information about our fiscal 2011 restructuring and the nature of the charges we recorded, refer to Note 5, *Restructuring Charges*.

Use of Estimates in the Preparation of Financial Statements

The preparation of financial statements in conformity with accounting principles generally accepted in the U.S. ("GAAP") requires us to make estimates and assumptions. These estimates and assumptions affect the reported amounts in the consolidated balance sheets and statements of earnings, as well as the disclosure of contingent liabilities. Future results could be materially affected if actual results were to differ from these estimates and assumptions.

Fiscal Year

Our fiscal year ends on the Saturday nearest the end of February. Fiscal 2011, 2010 and 2009 each included 52 weeks.

Cash and Cash Equivalents

Cash primarily consists of cash on hand and bank deposits. Cash equivalents consist of money market funds, U.S. Treasury bills, commercial paper and time deposits such as certificates of deposit with an original maturity of three months or less when purchased. The amounts of cash equivalents at February 26, 2011, and February 27, 2010, were $120 and $1,108, respectively, and the weighted-average interest rates were 0.3% and 0.1%, respectively.

Outstanding checks in excess of funds on deposit (book overdrafts) totaled $57 and $108 at February 26, 2011, and February 27, 2010, respectively, and are reflected as accounts payable in our consolidated balance sheets.

Receivables

Receivables consist principally of amounts due from mobile phone network operators for commissions earned; banks for customer credit card, certain debit card and electronic benefits transfer (EBT) transactions; and vendors for various vendor funding programs.

(continued)

(**CASE 3-4** CONTINUED)

We establish allowances for uncollectible receivables based on historical collection trends and write-off history. Our allowances for uncollectible receivables were $107 and $101 at February 26, 2011, and February 27, 2010, respectively.

Merchandise Inventories

Merchandise inventories are recorded at the lower of cost using either the average cost or first-in first-out method, or market. In-bound freight-related costs from our vendors are included as part of the net cost of merchandise inventories. Also included in the cost of inventory are certain vendor allowances that are not a reimbursement of specific, incremental and identifiable costs to promote a vendor's products. Other costs associated with acquiring, storing and transporting merchandise inventories to our retail stores are expensed as incurred and included in cost of goods sold.

Our inventory valuation reflects adjustments for anticipated physical inventory losses (e.g., theft) that have occurred since the last physical inventory. Physical inventory counts are taken on a regular basis to ensure that the inventory reported in our consolidated financial statements is properly stated.

Our inventory valuation also reflects markdowns for the excess of the cost over the amount we expect to realize from the ultimate sale or other disposal of the inventory. Markdowns establish a new cost basis for our inventory. Subsequent changes in facts or circumstances do not result in the reversal of previously recorded markdowns or an increase in that newly established cost basis.

Restricted Assets

Restricted cash and investments in debt securities totaled $490 and $496, at February 26, 2011, and February 27, 2010, respectively, and are included in other current assets or equity and other investments in our consolidated balance sheets. Such balances are pledged as collateral or restricted to use for vendor payables, general liability insurance, workers' compensation insurance and warranty programs.

Property and Equipment

Property and equipment are recorded at cost. We compute depreciation using the straight-line method over the estimated useful lives of the assets. Leasehold improvements are depreciated over the shorter of their estimated useful lives or the period from the date the assets are placed in service to the end of the initial lease term. Leasehold improvements made significantly after the initial lease term are depreciated over the shorter of their estimated useful lives or the remaining lease term, including renewal periods, if reasonably assured. Accelerated depreciation methods are generally used for income tax purposes.

When property is retired or otherwise disposed of, the cost and accumulated depreciation are removed from our consolidated balance sheets and any resulting gain or loss is reflected in our consolidated statements of earnings.

Repairs and maintenance costs are charged directly to expense as incurred. Major renewals or replacements that substantially extend the useful life of an asset are capitalized and depreciated.

Costs associated with the acquisition or development of software for internal use are capitalized and amortized over the expected useful life of the software, from three to seven years. A subsequent addition, modification or upgrade to internal-use software is capitalized to the extent that it enhances the software's functionality or extends its useful life. Capitalized software is included in fixtures and equipment. Software maintenance and training costs are expensed in the period incurred.

Property under capital lease is comprised of buildings and equipment used in our retail operations and corporate support functions. The related depreciation for capital lease assets is included in depreciation expense. The carrying value of property under capital lease was $74 and $54 at February 26, 2011, and February 27, 2010, respectively, net of accumulated depreciation of $45 and $41, respectively.

Estimated useful lives by major asset category are as follows:

Asset	Life (in years)
Buildings	25–50
Leasehold improvements	3–25
Fixtures and equipment	3–20
Property under capital lease	2–20

Required

a. 1. What is the balance in receivables at February 26, 2011 and February 27, 2010?

   2. What is the gross receivables at February 26, 2011 and February 27, 2010?

b. Merchandise Inventories

"Our inventory valuation reflects adjustments for anticipated physical inventory losses (e.g., theft) that have occurred since the last physical inventory."
Why make this adjustment?

c. 1. What does it mean to have a consolidated balance sheet?

   2. Comment on the consolidation policy with regard to Europe, China, Mexico and Turkey.

d. Comment on the use of estimates.

e. Comment on the fiscal year.

f. Cash and cash equivalents – are they presented conservatively?

g. 1. What depreciation methods are generally used for income tax purposes?

   2. What depreciation method is used for financial reporting?

   3. Why the difference in depreciation between financial reporting and tax purposes?

CASE 3-5 OUR PRINCIPAL ASSET IS OUR PEOPLE

Dana Corporation included the following in its 2001 financial report:

Foundation Business: Focused Excellence
Dana's foundation businesses are: axles, drive shafts, structures, brake and chassis products, fluid systems, filtration products, and bearing and sealing products.

These products hold strong market positions—number one or two in the markets they serve. They provide value-added manufacturing, are technically advanced, and each has features that are unique and patented.

Management Statement (in Part)
We believe people are Dana's most important asset. The proper selection, training, and development of our people as a means of ensuring that effective internal controls are fair, uniform reporting are maintained as standard practice throughout the Company.

Required

a. Dana states that "We believe people are Dana's most important asset." Currently, generally accepted accounting principles do not recognize people as an asset. Speculate on why people are not considered to be an asset.

b. Speculate on what concept of an asset Dana is considering when it states "We believe people are Dana's most important asset."

CASE 3-6 BRAND VALUE*

Brand values are expressed in terms of words such as "quality" and "integrity." The Marketing Society rated the brand value of McDonald's in 2008 at $10,417,000,000.*

Required

a. Define an asset.

b. In your opinion, do brands represent a valuable asset? Comment.

c. Under generally accepted accounting principles, should an internally generated brand value be recognized as an asset? Comment.

d. If the brand was purchased, should it be recognized as an asset? Comment.

*Adopted from www.brandfinance.com/docs/50_golden_brands.asp

CASE 3-7 ADVERTISING—ASSET?

Big Car Company did substantial advertising in late December. The company's year-end date was December 31. The president of the firm was concerned that this advertising campaign would reduce profits.

Required
a. Define an asset.
b. Would the advertising represent an asset? Comment.

CASE 3-8 TELECOMMUNICATIONS – PART I

China Unicom (Hong Kong) Limited provides a full range of telecommunications services, including mobile and fixed online services, in China.

They are listed on the New York Stock Exchange and filed a Form 20-F with the SEC for the period ended December 31, 2010.

The following are presented from the Form 20-F filing:

1. Special Note on Our Financial Information and Certain Statistical Information Presented in This Annual Report
2. Audit Report
3. Consolidated Balance Sheets

Special Note on Our Financial Information and Certain Statistical Information Presented in This Annual Report

Our consolidated financial statements as of and for the years ended December 31, 2007, 2008, 2009 and 2010 included in this annual report on Form 20-F have been prepared in accordance with International Financial Reporting Standards, or IFRS, as issued by the International Accounting Standards Board, or the IASB. These financial statements also comply with Hong Kong Financial Reporting Standards, or HKFRS, which collective term includes all applicable individual Hong Kong Financial Reporting Standards, Hong Kong Accounting Standards and Interpretations issued by the Hong Kong Institute of Certified Public Accountants, or HKICPA. As applied to our company, HKFRS is consistent with IFRS in all material respects.

The statistical information set forth in this annual report on Form 20-F relating to the PRC is taken or derived from various publicly available government publications that have not been prepared or independently verified by us. This statistical information may not be consistent with other statistical information from other sources within or outside the PRC.

Report of Independent Registered Public Accounting Firm

TO THE BOARD OF DIRECTORS AND SHAREHOLDERS OF CHINA UNICOM (HONG KONG) LIMITED
In our opinion, the accompanying consolidated balance sheets and the related consolidated statements of income, comprehensive income, changes in equity and cash flows present fairly, in all material respects, the financial position of China Unicom (Hong Kong) Limited and its subsidiaries (together, the "Group") at December 31, 2010 and 2009, and the results of their operations and their cash flows for each of the three years in the period ended December 31, 2010 in conformity with International Financial Reporting Standards as issued by the International Accounting Standards Board and in conformity with Hong Kong Financial Reporting Standards issued by the Hong Kong Institute of Certified Public Accountants. Also in our opinion, the Group maintained, in all material respects, effective internal control over financial reporting as of December 31, 2010, based on criteria established in Internal Control — Integrated Framework issued by the Committee of Sponsoring Organizations of the Treadway

Source: China Unicom 2010 10-K

Commission ("COSO"). The Group's management is responsible for these financial statements, for maintaining effective internal control over financial reporting and for its assessment of the effectiveness of internal control over financial reporting, included in the Management's Annual Report on Internal Control Over Financial Reporting included in Item 15 of this Annual Report on Form 20-F. Our responsibility is to express opinions on these financial statements and on the Group's internal control over financial reporting based on our integrated audits. We conducted our audits in accordance with the standards of the Public Company Accounting Oversight Board (United States). Those standards require that we plan and perform the audits to obtain reasonable assurance about whether the financial statements are free of material misstatement and whether effective internal control over financial reporting was maintained in all material respects. Our audits of the financial statements included examining, on a test basis, evidence supporting the amounts and disclosures in the financial statements, assessing the accounting principles used and significant estimates made by management, and evaluating the overall financial statement presentation. Our audit of internal control over financial reporting included obtaining an understanding of internal control over financial reporting, assessing the risk that a material weakness exists, and testing and evaluating the design and operating effectiveness of internal control based on the assessed risk. Our audits also included performing such other procedures as we considered necessary in the circumstances. We believe that our audits provide a reasonable basis for our opinions.

As discussed in Note 2.25 (a) to the consolidated financial statements, the Group adopted the accounting policy of relative fair value method when accounting for its preferential promotional service packages retrospectively on January 1, 2010.

A company's internal control over financial reporting is a process designed to provide reasonable assurance regarding the reliability of financial reporting and the preparation of financial statements for external purposes in accordance with generally accepted accounting principles. A company's internal control over financial reporting includes those policies and procedures that (i) pertain to the maintenance of records that, in reasonable detail, accurately and fairly reflect the transactions and dispositions of the assets of the company; (ii) provide reasonable assurance that transactions are recorded as necessary to permit preparation of financial statements in accordance with generally accepted accounting principles, and that receipts and expenditures of the company are being made only in accordance with authorizations of management and directors of the company; and (iii) provide reasonable assurance regarding prevention or timely detection of unauthorized acquisition, use, or disposition of the company's assets that could have a material effect on the financial statements.

Because of its inherent limitations, internal control over financial reporting may not prevent or detect misstatements. Also, projections of any evaluation of effectiveness to future periods are subject to the risk that controls may become inadequate because of changes in conditions, or that the degree of compliance with the policies or procedures may deteriorate.

/s/ PricewaterhouseCoopers
Hong Kong
May 24, 2011

CHINA UNICOM (HONG KONG) LIMITED
CONSOLIDATED BALANCE SHEETS
AS OF DECEMBER 31, 2009 AND 2010
(All amounts in Renminbi ("RMB" millions))

		As of December 31		
	Note	2009	2010	2010
		RMB	RMB	US$
ASSETS				
Non-current assets				
Property, plant and equipment	6	351,157	366,060	55,464
Lease prepayments	7	7,729	7,607	1,153
Goodwill	8	2,771	2,771	420

(*continued*)

(**Case 3-8** CONTINUED)

	Note	2009	2010	2010
		RMB	RMB	US$
ASSETS				
Deferred income tax assets	9	5,202	4,840	733
Available-for-sale financial assets	10	7,977	6,214	942
Other assets	12	11,596	11,753	1,780
		386,432	399,245	60,492
Current assets				
Inventories and consumables	13	2,412	3,728	565
Accounts receivable, net	14	8,825	9,286	1,407
Prepayments and other current assets	15	4,252	5,115	775
Amounts due from related parties	40.1	53	50	8
Amounts due from domestic carriers	40.2	1,134	1,261	191
Proceeds receivable for the disposal of the CDMA Business	36, 40.2	5,121	—	—
Short-term bank deposits	16	996	273	41
Cash and cash equivalents	17	7,820	22,495	3,408
		30,613	42,208	6,395
Total assets		417,045	441,453	66,887
EQUITY				
Equity attributable to owners of the parent				
Share capital	18	2,310	2,310	350
Share premium	18	173,435	173,436	26,278
Reserves	19	(18,088)	(18,273)	(2,769)
Retained profits				
- Proposed final dividend	37	3,770	1,885	286
- Others		45,038	46,483	7,043
		206,465	205,841	31,188
Non-controlling interests		2	—	—
Total equity		206,467	205,841	31,188
LIABILITIES				
Non-current liabilities				
Long-term bank loans	20	759	1,462	222
Promissory notes	21	—	15,000	2,273
Convertible bonds	22	—	11,558	1,751
Corporate bonds	23	7,000	7,000	1,061
Deferred income tax liabilities	9	245	22	3
Deferred revenue		2,562	2,171	328
Other obligations	24	187	162	25
		10,753	37,375	5,663
Current liabilities				
Accounts payable and accrued liabilities	25	104,072	97,659	14,795
Taxes payable		912	1,484	225
Amounts due to ultimate holding company	40.1	308	229	35
Amounts due to related parties	40.1	5,438	5,191	787
Amounts due to domestic carriers	40.2	1,136	873	132
Payables in relation to disposal of the CDMA business	40.2	7	—	—
Commercial papers	26	—	23,000	3,485
Short-term bank loans	27	63,909	36,727	5,565
Current portion of long-term bank loans	20	62	58	9
Dividends payable	37	331	431	65
Current portion of deferred revenue		1,397	1,042	158
Current portion of other obligations	24	2,534	2,637	400

As of December 31

	Note	As of December 31		
		2009	2010	2010
		RMB	RMB	US$
Advances from customers		19,719	28,906	4,380
		199,825	198,237	30,036
Total liabilities		210,578	235,612	35,699
Total equity and liabilities		417,045	441,453	66,887
Net current liabilities		(169,212)	(156,029)	(23,641)
Total assets less current liabilities		217,220	243,216	36,851

Required

a. Special Note, etc.

   1. Financial statements were prepared under what reporting standards?

   2. Did they reconcile to GAAP?

   3. The financial statements also comply with Hong Kong Financial Reporting Standards or HKFRS. Does this mean that the standards are identical.

b. Audit Report

   1. How many years are included?

   2. What financial reporting standards were used?

   3. Internal control was guided by what?

   4. Comment on management's responsibility for the statements.

   5. Comment on the auditing standards used.

   6. Proper internal controls will prevent or detect misstatements. Comment.

c. Consolidated Balance Sheet

   1. Why presented in RMB and U.S. $?

   2. Comment on the assets presentation.

   3. Comment on the equity presentation.

   4. Comment on the liabilities presentation.

CASE 3-9 GLOBAL HEALTH CARE

NOTES TO CONSOLIDATED FINANCIAL STATEMENTS (In Part)
Merck & Co., Inc. and Subsidiaries*

($ in millions except per share amounts)
Years Ended December 31
2010 Annual Report

Fair Value Measurements (In Part)

Fair value is defined as the exchange price that would be received for an asset or paid to transfer a liability (an exit price) in the principal or most advantageous market for the asset or liability in an orderly transaction between market participants on the measurement date. Entities are required to use a fair value hierarchy which maximizes the use of observable inputs and minimizes the use of unobservable inputs when measuring fair value. There are three levels of inputs that may be used to measure fair value:

(continued)

---

*"The Company is a global health care company that delivers innovative health solutions through its prescription medicines, vaccines, biologic therapies, animal health, and consumer care products, which it markets directly and through its joint ventures." 10-K
Source: Merck & Co., Inc. and Subsidiaries 2010 10-K

(**CASE 3-9** CONTINUED)

Level 1 — Quoted prices in active markets for identical assets or liabilities. The Company's Level 1 assets include equity securities that are traded in an active exchange market.

Level 2 — Observable inputs other than Level 1 prices, such as quoted prices for similar assets or liabilities, or other inputs that are observable or can be corroborated by observable market data for substantially the full term of the assets or liabilities. The Company's Level 2 assets and liabilities primarily include debt securities with quoted prices that are traded less frequently than exchange-traded instruments, corporate notes and bonds, U.S. and foreign government and agency securities, certain mortgage-backed and asset-backed securities, municipal securities, commercial paper and derivative contracts whose values are determined using pricing models with inputs that are observable in the market or can be derived principally from or corroborated by observable market data.

Level 3 — Unobservable inputs that are supported by little or no market activity and that are financial instruments whose values are determined using pricing models, discounted cash flow methodologies, or similar techniques, as well as instruments for which the determination of fair value requires significant judgment or estimation. The Company's Level 3 assets include certain mortgage-backed securities with limited market activity. At December 31, 2010, $13 million, or approximately 0.4%, of the Company's investment securities were categorized as Level 3 assets.

If the inputs used to measure the financial assets and liabilities fall within more than one level described above, the categorization is based on the lowest level input that is significant to the fair value measurement of the instrument.

Financial Assets and Liabilities Measured at Fair Value on a Recurring Basis**

Financial assets and liabilities measured at fair value on a recurring basis at December 31 are summarized below:

	Fair Value Measurements Using				Fair Value Measurements Using			
	Quoted Prices In Active Markets for Identical Assets (Level 1)	Significant Other Observable Inputs (Level 2)	Significant Unobservable Inputs (Level 3)	Total	Quoted Prices In Active Markets for Identical Assets (Level 1)	Significant Other Observable Inputs (Level 2)	Significant Unobservable Inputs (Level 3)	Total
	2010				2009			
Assets								
Investments								
Corporate notes and bonds	$ —	$1,133	$—	$1,133	$—	$ 205	$—	$ 205
Commercial paper	—	1,046	—	1,046	—	—	—	—
U.S. government and agency securities	—	500	—	500	—	216	—	216
Municipal securities	—	361	—	361	—	187	—	187
Asset-backed securities[1]	—	171	—	171	—	36	—	36
Mortgage-backed securities[1]	—	99	13	112	—	—	—	—
Foreign government bonds	—	10	—	10	—	—	—	—
Equity securities	117	23	—	140	39	39	—	78
Other debt securities	—	3	—	3	—	3	—	3
	117	3,346	13	3,476	39	686	—	725
Other assets								
Securities held for employee compensation	181	—	—	181	108	14	—	122
Other assets	—	—	—	—	—	55	72	127
	181	—	—	181	108	69	72	249
Derivative assets[2]								
Purchased currency options	—	477	—	477	—	292	—	292

**In millions

	Fair Value Measurements Using				Fair Value Measurements Using			
	Quoted Prices In Active Markets for Identical Assets (Level 1)	Significant Other Observable Inputs (Level 2)	Significant Unobservable Inputs (Level 3)	Total	Quoted Prices In Active Markets for Identical Assets (Level 1)	Significant Other Observable Inputs (Level 2)	Significant Unobservable Inputs (Level 3)	Total
	2010				2009			
Forward exchange contracts	—	95	—	95	—	60	—	60
Interest rate swaps	—	56	—	56	—	27	—	27
	—	628	—	628	—	379	—	379
Total assets	$298	$3,974	$13	$4,285	$147	$1,134	$72	$1,353
Liabilities								
Derivative liabilities[2]								
Forward exchange contracts	$ —	$ 54	$—	$ 54	$ —	$ 73	$—	$ 73
Interest rate swaps	—	7	—	7	—	—	—	—
Total liabilities	$ —	$ 61	$—	$ 61	$ —	$ 73	$—	$ 73

[1]*Substantially all of the asset-backed securities are highly-rated (Standard & Poor's rating of AAA and Moody's Investors Service rating of Aaa), secured primarily by credit card, auto loan, and home equity receivables, with weighted-average lives of primarily 5 years or less. Mortgage-backed securities represent AAA-rated securities issued or unconditionally guaranteed as to payment of principal and interest by U.S. government agencies.*

[2]*The fair value determination of derivatives includes an assessment of the credit risk of counterparties to the derivatives and the Company's own credit risk, the effects of which were not significant.*

Required

a. Entities are required to use a fair value hierarchy. Why?

b. There are three levels of inputs that may be used to measure fair value. What are the three levels and describe each.

c. For Merck & Co., Inc. describe the assets and liabilities for each level of inputs.

Web Case THOMSON ONE *Business School Edition*

Please complete the Web case that covers material discussed in this chapter at www.cengagebrain.com. You'll be using Thomson ONE Business School Edition, a powerful tool that combines a full range of fundamental financial information, earnings estimates, market data, and source documents for 500 publicly traded companies.

To the Net Case

1. Go to the SEC Web site (www.sec.gov). Under "Filings & Forms (EDGAR)," click on "Search for Company Filings." Click on "Company or Fund, etc." Under Company Name, enter "Cooper Tire" (or under Ticker Symbol, enter "CTB"). Select the 10-K filed February 25, 2011.

   a. What is the total stockholders' equity at December 31, 2010?

   b. What is the cost of treasury shares at December 31, 2010?

   c. Why is treasury stock subtracted from stockholders' equity?

2. Go to the SEC Web site (www.sec.gov). Under "Filings & Forms (EDGAR)," click on "Search for Company Filings." Click on "Company or Fund, etc." Under Company Name, enter "Yahoo" (or under Ticker Symbol, enter "YHOO"). Select the 10-K filed February 28, 2011.

   a. What is the total current assets at December 31, 2010?

   b. What is the net intangibles at December 31, 2010?

   c. Why are intangibles amortized?

3. Go to the SEC Web site (www.sec.gov). Under "Filings & Forms (EDGAR)," click on "Search for Company Filings." Click on "Company or Fund, etc." Under Company Name, enter "Boeing Co" (or under Ticker Symbol, enter "BA"). Select the 10-K filed February 9, 2011.

(continued)

(**To The Net** CONTINUED)

    a. What is the total for inventories at December 31, 2010?

    b. Go to Note 1, Summary of Significant Accounting Policies. Go to Inventories. Describe the inventory policy, consistent with industry practice, that is unique for this industry. How does this practice impact liquidity appearance?

4. Go to the SEC Web site (www.sec.gov). Under "Filings & Forms (EDGAR)," click on "Search for Company Filings." Click on "Company or Fund, etc." Under Company Name, enter "Dell Inc." (or under ticker symbol, enter "Dell"). Select the 10-K filed March 15, 2011.

    a. What is the balance in accrued warranty at January 28, 2011?

    b. Comment on the subjectivity in determining this balance.

5. Go to the SEC Web site (www.sec.gov). Under "Filings & Forms (EDGAR)," click on "Search for Company Filings." Click on "Company or Fund, etc." Under Company Name, enter "McDonalds" (or under Ticker Symbol, enter "MCD"). Select the 10-K filed February 25, 2011.

    a. What is the total assets at December 31, 2010?

    b. What is the total for investments in and advances to affiliates at December 31, 2010?

    c. In your opinion, are the companies receiving the "investments in and advances to affiliates" consolidated with McDonald's Corporation? Comment.

    d. Considering the balance in "investments in and advances to affiliates" in relation to "total assets," does this relationship of dollars likely represent the importance of affiliates to McDonald's Corporation? Comment.

6. Go to the SEC site (www.sec.gov). Under "Filings & Forms" click on "Search for Company Filings." Click on "Company or fund, etc." Under Company Name, enter "Hershey Food" (or under Ticker Symbol, enter "HSY"). Select the 10-K filed February, 2011.

    a. Note 16 – Capital Stock and Net Income Per Share

        1. Comment on the voting control of Milton Hershey School Trust.

    b. Note 1 – Summary of Significant Accounting Policies

        1. Describe their accounting for investments under the equity method.

        2. Why do they review equity investments for impairment?

7. Go to the SEC site (www.sec.gov). Under "Filings & Forms," click on "Search for Company Filings." Click on "Company or fund, etc." Under Company Name, enter "Terra Industries Inc." (or under Ticker Symbol, enter "TRA"). Select the 10-K filed February 25, 2010.

    a. Go to Note 27 – Subsequent Events

        1. Describe the type of subsequent event and the disclosure requirement.

        2. Describe the particular subsequent event.

Endnotes

1. *Accounting Trends & Techniques* (American Institute of Certified Public Accountants, New York: 2010), p. 147.

2. Ibid., p. 300.

3. Ibid., p. 147.

4. *Statement of Financial Accounting Concepts No. 6*, "Elements of Financial Statements" (Financial Accounting Standards Board, Stamford, CT: 1985), par. 25.

5. *Accounting Trends & Techniques* (American Institute of Certified Public Accountants, New York: 2010), p. 138.

6. SFAS No. 141 (R), "Business Combinations," issued in December 2007, represents the current standard for computing goodwill. SFAS No. 142, "Goodwill and Other Intangible Assets," issued in June 2001, represents the standard relating to when to write down or off goodwill. Prior to SFAS No. 142, goodwill was amortized over a period of 40 years or less.

7. *Statement of Financial Accounting Concepts No. 6*, par. 35.

8. *Statement of Financial Accounting Concepts No. 6*, par. 212.

Chapter 4

Income Statement

The income statement is often considered to be the most important financial statement. Frequently used titles for this statement include statement of operations, statement of income, and statement of earnings. Both the statement of operations and statement of income are very popular titles.[1]

Basic Elements of the Income Statement

An income statement summarizes revenues and expenses and gains and losses, and ends with the net income for a specific period. A multiple-step income statement usually presents separately the gross profit, operating income, income before income taxes, and net income.

A simplified multiple-step income statement might look as follows:

	Net Sales (Revenues)	$XXX
−	*Cost of Goods Sold (cost of sales)*	XXX
	Gross Profit	XXX
−	*Operating Expenses (selling and administrative)*	XXX
	Operating Income	XXX
+(−)	*Other Income or Expense*	XXX
	Income before Income Taxes	XXX
−	*Income Taxes*	XXX
	Net Income	$XXX
	Earnings per Share	$XXX

Some firms use a single-step income statement, which totals revenues and gains (sales, other income, etc.) and then deducts total expenses and losses (cost of goods sold, operating expenses, other expenses, etc.). A simplified single-step income statement might look as follows:

Revenue:	
Net Sales	$XXX
Other Income	XXX
Total Revenue	XXX
Expenses:	
Cost of Goods Sold (cost of sales)	XXX
Operating Expenses (selling and administrative)	XXX
Other Expense	XXX
Income Tax Expense	XXX
Total Expenses	XXX
Net Income	$XXX
Earnings per Share	$XXX

A single-step income statement lists all revenues and gains (usually in order of amount) and then lists all expenses and losses (usually in order of amount). Total expense and loss items deducted from total revenue and gain items determine the net income. Most firms that present a single-step income statement modify it in some way, such as presenting federal income tax expense as a separate item.

Exhibits 4-1 and 4-2 illustrate the different types of income statements. In Exhibit 4-1, Ryder System, Inc., uses a single-step income statement, while in Exhibit 4-2, Intel Corporation uses a multiple-step format.

EXHIBIT 4-1 Ryder System, Inc.*

Single-Step Income Statement

RYDER SYSTEM, INC. AND SUBSIDIARIES
CONSOLIDATED STATEMENTS OF EARNINGS

	Years ended December 31		
	2010	2009	2008
	(In thousands, except per share amounts)		
Revenue	$5,136,435	4,887,254	5,999,041
Operating expense (exclusive of items shown separately)	2,441,924	2,229,539	2,959,518
Salaries and employee-related costs	1,255,659	1,233,243	1,345,216
Subcontracted transportation	261,325	198,860	233,106
Depreciation expense	833,841	881,216	836,149
Gains on vehicle sales, net	(28,727)	(12,292)	(39,020)
Equipment rental	63,228	65,828	78,292
Interest expense	129,994	144,342	152,448
Miscellaneous (income) expense, net	(7,114)	(3,657)	2,564
Restructuring and other charges, net	—	6,406	21,480
	4,950,130	4,743,485	5,589,753
Earnings from continuing operations before income taxes	186,305	143,769	409,288
Provision for income taxes	61,697	53,652	151,709
Earnings from continuing operations	$ 124,608	90,117	257,579
Loss from discontinued operations, net of tax	(6,438)	(28,172)	(57,698)
Net earnings	$ 118,170	61,945	199,881
Earnings (loss) per common share – Basic			
Continuing operations	$ 2.38	1.62	4.54
Discontinued operations	(0.13)	(0.51)	(1.02)
Net earnings	$ 2.25	1.11	3.52
Earnings (loss) per common share – Diluted			
Continuing operations	$ 2.37	1.62	4.51
Discontinued operations	(0.12)	(0.51)	(1.01)
Net earnings	$ 2.25	1.11	3.50

*"Ryder System, Inc. (Ryder), a Florida corporation founded in 1993, is a global leader in transportation and supply chain management solutions." 10-K
Source: Ryder System, Inc. 2010 10-K

| EXHIBIT **4-2** | Intel Corporation |

Multiple-Step Income Statement

INTEL CORPORATION*
CONSOLIDATED STATEMENTS OF INCOME

Three Years Ended December 25, 2010 (In Millions, Except Per Share Amounts)	2010	2009	2008
Net revenue	$43,623	$35,127	$37,586
Cost of sales	15,132	15,566	16,742
Gross margin	28,491	19,561	20,844
Research and development	6,576	5,653	5,722
Marketing, general and administrative	6,309	7,931	5,452
Restructuring and asset impairment charges	—	231	710
Amortization of acquisition-related intangibles	18	35	6
Operating expenses	12,903	13,850	11,890
Operating income	15,588	5,711	8,954
Gains (losses) on equity method investments, net	117	(147)	(1,380)
Gains (losses) on other equity investments, net	231	(23)	(376)
Interest and other, net	109	163	488
Income before taxes	16,045	5,704	7,686
Provision for taxes	4,581	1,335	2,394
Net income	$11,464	$ 4,369	$ 5,292
Basic earnings per common share	$ 2.06	$ 0.79	$ 0.93
Diluted earnings per common share	$ 2.01	$ 0.77	$ 0.92
Weighted average shares outstanding:			
Basic	5,555	5,557	5,663
Diluted	5,696	5,645	5,748

*"We are the world's largest semiconductor chip maker, based on revenue." 10-K
Source: Intel Corporation, 2010 10-K

For firms that have cost of goods sold, cost of goods manufactured, or cost of services, a multiple-step income statement should be used for analysis. The multiple-step format provides intermediate profit figures useful in analysis. You may need to construct the multiple-step format from the single-step. Exhibit 4-3 contains a comprehensive multiple-step income statement illustration. This illustration resembles the vast majority of income statements as presented in the United States. Be familiar with this illustration. It serves as a guide to much of our analysis.

Net Sales (Revenues)

Sales (revenues) represent revenue from goods or services sold to customers. The firm earns revenue from the sale of its principal products. Sales are usually shown net of any discounts, returns, and allowances.

Cost of Goods Sold (Cost of Sales)

This category shows the cost of goods sold to produce revenue. For a retailing firm, the cost of goods sold equals beginning inventory plus purchases minus ending inventory. In a manufacturing firm, the cost of goods manufactured replaces purchases since the goods are produced rather than purchased. A service firm will not have cost of goods sold or cost of sales, but it will often have cost of services.

Other Operating Revenue

Depending on the operations of the business, there may be other operating revenue, such as lease revenue and royalties.

Operating Expenses

Operating expenses consist of two types: selling and administrative. **Selling expenses**, resulting from the company's effort to create sales, include advertising, sales commissions, sales supplies used, and so on. **Administrative expenses** relate to the general administration of the company's operation. They include office salaries, insurance, telephone, bad debt expense, and other costs difficult to allocate.

Other Income or Expense

In this category are secondary activities of the firm that are not directly related to the operations. For example, if a manufacturing firm has a warehouse rented, this lease income would be other income. Dividend and interest income and gains and losses from the sale of assets are also included here. Interest expense is categorized as other expense.

Special Income Statement Items

To comprehend and analyze profits, you need to understand income statement items that require special disclosure. Exhibit 4-3 contains items that require special disclosure. These items are lettered to identify them for discussion. Note that some of these items are presented before tax and some are presented net of tax.

(A) Unusual or Infrequent Item Disclosed Separately

Certain income statement items are either unusual or occur infrequently. They might include such items as a gain on sale of securities, write-downs of receivables, or write-downs of

| EXHIBIT **4-3** | Illustration of Special Items |

G AND F COMPANY
Income Statement (Multiple-Step Format)
For the Year Ended December 31, 2007

	Net sales		$ XXX
	Cost of products sold (cost of sales)		(XXX)
	Gross profit		XXX
	Other operating revenue		XXX
	Operating expenses:		
	Selling expenses	$ XXX	
	General expenses	XXX	(XXX)
	Operating income		XXX
	Other income (includes interest income)		XXX
	Other expenses (includes interest expense)		(XXX)
[A]	Unusual or infrequent item disclosed separately [loss]		(XXX)
[B]	Equity in earnings of nonconsolidated subsidiaries [loss]		XXX
	Income before taxes		XXX
	Income taxes related to operations		(XXX)
	Net income from operations		XXX
[C]	Discontinued operations:		
	Income [loss] from operations of discontinued segment (less applicable income taxes of $XXX)	$(XXX)	
	Income [loss] on disposal of division X (less applicable income taxes of $XXX)	(XXX)	(XXX)
[D]	Extraordinary gain [loss] (less applicable income taxes of $XXX)		(XXX)
[E]	Cumulative effect of change in accounting principle [loss]		XXX
	(less applicable income taxes of $XXX)		
	Net income before noncontrolling interest		$ XXX
[F]	Net income—noncontrolling interest		(XXX)
	Net income		$ XXX
	Earnings per share		$ XXX

Source: U.S. Securities and Exchange

inventory. These items are shown with normal, recurring revenues and expenses, and gains and losses. If material, they will be disclosed separately, before tax. Unusual or infrequent items are typically left in primary analysis because they relate to operations.

In supplementary analysis, unusual or infrequent items should be removed net after tax. Usually, an estimate of the tax effect will be necessary. A reasonable estimate of the tax effect can be made by using the effective income tax rate, usually disclosed in a note, or by dividing income taxes by income before taxes.

Refer to Exhibit 4-4, which illustrates an unusual or infrequent item disclosed separately for Advanced Micro Devices, Inc. The unusual or infrequent item is gain in legal settlement in 2010 and 2009.

EXHIBIT **4-4**	Advanced Micro Devices, Inc.*

Unusual or Infrequent Item

ADVANCED MICRO DEVICES, INC.
CONSOLIDATED STATEMENTS OF OPERATIONS

	Year Ended		
	December 25, 2010	December 26, 2009	December 27, 2008
	(In millions, except per share amounts)		
Net revenue	$6,494	$ 5,403	$ 5,808
Cost of sales	3,533	3,131	3,488
Gross margin	2,961	2,272	2,320
Research and development	1,405	1,721	1,848
Marketing, general and administrative	934	994	1,304
Legal settlement	(283)	(1,242)	—
Amortization of acquired intangible assets	61	70	137
Impairment of goodwill and acquired intangible assets	—	—	1,089
Restructuring charges (reversals)	(4)	65	90
Gain on sale of 200 millimeter equipment	—	—	(193)
Operating income (loss)	848	664	(1,955)
Interest income	11	16	39
Interest expense	(199)	(438)	(391)
Other income (expense), net	311	166	(37)
Income (loss) before equity in net loss of investees and income taxes	971	408	(2,344)
Provision for income taxes	38	112	68
Equity in net loss of investee	(462)	—	—
Income (loss) from continuing operations	471	296	(2,412)
Loss from discontinued operations, net of tax	—	(3)	(684)
Net income (loss)	471	293	(3,096)
Net income (loss) attributable to noncontrolling interest	—	83	(33)
Class B preferred accretion	—	(72)	—
Net income (loss) attributable to AMD common stockholders	$ 471	$ 304	$(3,129)
Net income (loss) attributable to AMD common stockholders per common share			
Basic			
Continuing operations	$ 0.66	$ 0.46	$ (4.03)
Discontinued operations	—	—	(1.12)
Basic net income (loss) attributable to AMD common stockholders per common share	$ 0.66	$ 0.46	$ (5.15)
Diluted			
Continuing operations	$ 0.64	$ 0.45	$ (4.03)

*"We are a global semiconductor company with facilities around the world." 10-K
Source: Advanced Micro Devices, Inc. 2010 10-K

(*continued*)

EXHIBIT **4-4**	Advanced Micro Devices, Inc. (*continued*)

	Year Ended		
	December 25, 2010	December 26, 2009	December 27, 2008
	(In millions, except per share amounts)		
Discontinued operations	—	—	(1.12)
Diluted net income (loss) attributable to AMD common stockholders per common share	$ 0.64	$ 0.45	$ (5.15)
Shares used in per share calculation			
Basic	711	673	607
Diluted	733	678	607

(B) Equity in Earnings of Nonconsolidated Subsidiaries

When a firm accounts for its investments in stocks using the equity method (the investment is not consolidated), the investor reports equity earnings (losses). **Equity earnings** (losses) are the investor's proportionate share of the investee's earnings (losses). If the investor owns 20% of the stock of the investee, for example, and the investee reports income of $100,000, then the investor reports $20,000 on its income statement. In this book, the term *equity earnings* will be used unless equity losses are specifically intended.

To the extent that equity earnings are not accompanied by cash dividends, the investor reports earnings greater than the cash flow from the investment. If an investor company reports material equity earnings, its net income could be much greater than its ability to pay dividends or cover maturing liabilities.

For purposes of analysis, the equity in the net income of nonconsolidated subsidiaries raises practical problems. For example, the equity earnings represent earnings of other companies, not earnings from the operations of the business. Thus, equity earnings can distort the reported results of a business's operations. For each ratio influenced by equity earnings, this book suggests a recommended approach described when the ratio is introduced.

Refer to Exhibit 4-5, which illustrates equity in earnings of nonconsolidated subsidiaries for KB Home. Leaving these accounts in the statements presents a problem for profitability analysis because most of the profitability measures relate income figures to other figures

EXHIBIT **4-5**	KB Home*

Equity Income

KB HOME
CONSOLIDATED STATEMENTS OF OPERATIONS
(In Thousands, Except Per Share Amounts)

	Year Ended November 30,		
	2010	2009	2008
Total revenues	$ 1,589,996	$ 1,824,850	$ 3,033,936
Homebuilding:			
Revenues	$ 1,581,763	$ 1,816,415	$ 3,023,169
Construction and land costs	(1,308,288)	(1,749,911)	(3,314,815)
Selling, general and administrative expenses	(289,520)	(303,024)	(501,027)
Goodwill impairment	—	—	(67,970)
Operating loss	(16,045)	(236,520)	(860,643)

*"KB Home is one of the nation's largest homebuilders and has been building homes for more than 50 years." 10-K
Source: KB Home Equity Income 2010 10-K

EXHIBIT **4-5**	KB Home (*continued*)		
		Year Ended November 30,	
	2010	2009	2008
Interest income	2,098	7,515	34,610
Interest expense, net of amounts capitalized/loss on early redemption of debt	(68,307)	(51,763)	(12,966)
Equity in loss of unconsolidated joint ventures	(6,257)	(49,615)	(152,750)
Homebuilding pretax loss	(88,511)	(330,383)	(991,749)
Financial services:			
Revenues	8,233	8,435	10,767
Expenses	(3,119)	(3,251)	(4,489)
Equity in income of unconsolidated joint venture	7,029	14,015	17,540
Financial services pretax income	12,143	19,199	23,818
Total pretax loss	(76,368)	(311,184)	(967,931)
Income tax benefit (expense)	7,000	209,400	(8,200)
Net loss	$ (69,368)	$ (101,784)	$ (976,131)
Basic and diluted loss per share	$ (.90)	$ (1.33)	$ (12.59)
Basic and diluted average shares outstanding	76,889	76,660	77,509

(usually balance sheet figures). Because these earnings are from nonconsolidated subsidiaries, an inconsistency can result between the numerator and the denominator when computing a ratio. (Chapter 5 presents a detailed discussion of ratios.)

Some ratios are distorted more than others by equity earnings. For example, the ratio that relates income to sales can be distorted because of equity earnings. The numerator of the ratio includes the earnings of the operating company and the equity earnings of nonconsolidated subsidiaries. The denominator (sales) includes only the sales of the operating company. The sales of the unconsolidated subsidiaries will not appear on the investor's income statement because the subsidiary was not consolidated. This causes the ratio to be distorted.

Equity in earnings of nonconsolidated subsidiaries (equity earnings) will be presented before tax. Any tax will be related to the dividend received, and it will typically be immaterial. When removing equity earnings for analysis, do not attempt a tax computation.

Income Taxes Related to Operations

Federal, state, and local income taxes, based on reported accounting profit, are shown here. Income tax expense includes taxes paid and taxes deferred. Income taxes reported here will not include taxes on items presented net of tax.

(C) Discontinued Operations

A common type of unusual item is the disposal of a business or product line. If the disposal meets the criteria of a discontinued operation, then a separate income statement category for the gain or loss from disposal of a segment of the business must be provided. In addition, the results of operations of the segment that has been or will be disposed of are reported in conjunction with the gain or loss on disposal. These effects appear as a separate category after continuing operations.

Discontinued operations pose a problem for profitability analysis. Ideally, income from continuing operations would be the better figure to use to project future income. Several practical problems associated with the removal of a gain or a loss from the discontinued operations occur in the primary profitability analysis. These problems revolve around two points: (1) an inadequate disclosure of data related to the discontinued operations, in order to remove the balance sheet amounts associated with the discontinued operations; and (2) the lack of past profit and loss data associated with the discontinued operations.

Exhibit 4-6 illustrates the presentation of discontinued operations in net income. The best analysis would remove the income statement items that relate to the discontinued operations.

The income statement items that relate to a discontinued operation are always presented net of applicable income taxes. Therefore, the items as presented on the income statement can be removed for primary analysis without further adjustment for income taxes. Supplementary analysis considers discontinued operations in order to avoid disregarding these items.

EXHIBIT **4-6**	Bristol-Myers Squibb Company

Discontinued Operations

BRISTOL-MYERS SQUIBB COMPANY*
CONSOLIDATED STATEMENTS OF EARNINGS
Dollars and Shares in Millions, Except Per Share Data

Item 8. FINANCIAL STATEMENTS AND SUPPLEMENTARY DATA.

	Years Ended December 31,		
	2010	2009	2008
EARNINGS			
Net Sales	$19,484	$18,808	$17,715
Cost of products sold	5,277	5,140	5,316
Marketing, selling and administrative	3,686	3,946	4,140
Advertising and product promotion	977	1,136	1,181
Research and development	3,566	3,647	3,512
Acquired in-process research and development	—	—	32
Provision for restructuring	113	136	215
Litigation expense, net	(19)	132	33
Equity in net income of affiliates	(313)	(550)	(617)
Gain on sale of ImClone shares	—	—	(895)
Other (income)/expense	126	(381)	22
Total Expenses	13,413	13,206	12,939
Earnings from Continuing Operations Before Income Taxes	6,071	5,602	4,776
Provision for income taxes	1,558	1,182	1,090
Net earnings from Continuing Operations	4,513	4,420	3,686
Discontinued Operations:			
Earnings, net of taxes	—	285	578
Gain on disposal, net of taxes	—	7,157	1,979
Net Earnings from Discontinued Operations	—	7,442	2,557
Net Earnings	4,513	11,862	6,243
Net Earnings Attributable to Noncontrolling Interest	1,411	1,250	996
Net Earnings Attributable to Bristol-Myers Squibb Company	$ 3,102	$10,612	$ 5,247
Amounts Attributable to Bristol-Myers Squibb Company:			
Net Earnings from Continuing Operations	$ 3,102	$ 3,239	$ 2,697
Net Earnings from Discontinued Operations	—	7,373	2,550
Net Earnings Attributable to Bristol-Myers Squibb Company	$ 3,102	$10,612	$ 5,247
Earnings per Common Share from Continuing Operations Attributable to Bristol-Myers Squibb Company:			
Basic	$ 1.80	$ 1.63	$ 1.36
Diluted	$ 1.79	$ 1.63	$ 1.35
Earnings per Common Share Attributable to Bristol-Myers Squibb Company:			
Basic	$ 1.80	$ 5.35	$ 2.64
Diluted	$ 1.79	$ 5.34	$ 2.62
Dividends declared per common share	$ 1.29	$ 1.25	$ 1.24

*"We are engaged in the discovery, development, licensing, manufacturing, marketing, distribution and sale of biopharmaceutical products on a global basis." 10-K

Source: Bristol-Myers Squibb Company 2010 10-K

Ideally, the balance sheet accounts that relate to the discontinued operations should be removed for primary analysis. Consider these items on a supplemental basis because they will not contribute to future operating revenue. However, inadequate disclosure often makes it impossible to remove these items from your analysis.

The balance sheet items related to discontinued operations are frequently disposed of when the business or product line has been disposed of prior to the year-end balance sheet date. In this case, the balance sheet accounts related to discontinued operations do not present a problem for the current year.

(D) Extraordinary Items

Extraordinary items are material events and transactions distinguished by their unusual nature and by the infrequency of their occurrence. Examples include a major casualty (such as a fire), prohibition under a newly enacted law, or an expropriation. These items, net of their tax effects, must be shown separately. Some pronouncements have specified items that must be considered extraordinary; an example is a material tax loss carryover. The effect of an extraordinary item on earnings per share must also be shown separately. Exhibit 4-7 presents an extraordinary gain.

In analysis of income for purposes of determining a trend, extraordinary items should be eliminated since the extraordinary item is not expected to recur. In supplementary analysis, these extraordinary items should be considered, as this approach avoids disregarding these items.

Extraordinary items are always presented net of applicable income taxes. Therefore, the items as presented on the income statement are removed without further adjustment for income taxes.

EXHIBIT **4-7**	CenturyLink, Inc.*

Extraordinary Item

CenturyLink, Inc.
Consolidated Statements of Income (In Part)

	Year Ended December 31,		
	2010	2009	2008
INCOME BEFORE INCOME TAX EXPENSE	$1,532,085	814,512	561,387
Income tax expense	582,951	301,881	194,357
INCOME BEFORE NONCONTROLLING INTERESTS AND EXTRAORDINARY ITEM	949,134	512,631	367,030
Noncontrolling interests	(1,429)	(1,377)	(1,298)
NET INCOME BEFORE EXTRAORDINARY ITEM	947,705	511,254	365,732
Extraordinary item, net of income tax expense and noncontrolling interests (see Note 16)	—	135,957	—
NET INCOME ATTRIBUTABLE TO CENTURYLINK, INC.	$ 947,705	647,211	365,732
BASIC EARNINGS PER SHARE			
Before extraordinary item	$ 3.13	2.55	3.53
Extraordinary item	$ —	.68	—
Basic earnings per share	$ 3.13	3.23	3.53
DILUTED EARNINGS PER SHARE			
Before extraordinary item	$ 3.13	2.55	3.52
Extraordinary item	$ —	.68	—
Diluted earnings per share	$ 3.13	3.23	3.52
DIVIDENDS PER COMMON SHARE	$ 2.90	2.80	2.1675
AVERAGE BASIC SHARES OUTSTANDING	300,619	198,813	102,268
AVERAGE DILUTED SHARES OUTSTANDING	301,297	199,057	102,560

*"CenturyLink, together with its subsidiaries, is an integrated communications company engaged primarily in providing a broad array of communications services, including voice, Internet, data and video services." 10-K
Source: Centurylink 2010 10-K

(E) Change in Accounting Principle

At times the company will change from one generally accepted accounting principle to another generally accepted accounting principle or an account principle is made obsolete by a new standard from the FASB.

Current GAAP requires a retrospective approach to changes in accounting principles unless it is impracticable to do so. This means that prior years' financial statements that are presented are revised in the year of change. (The balance sheet is presented for two years, income statement for three years, and statement of cash flows for three years).

The cumulative effect on prior years reported (prior to the change year) is reflected in the company's beginning retained earnings in the change year.

With this standard there is comparability of accounting principles for the statements presented. When using prior annual reports, there will not be comparability. This does present a challenge when doing analysis. It will not be possible to do a consistent analysis if more than one annual report is used.

When it is impracticable to determine the retrospective approach on prior years, then it may be possible to determine the difference to the opening balances in the accounts. Then the opening retained earnings in the year of change will reflect the cumulative effect on prior years.

In this case, prior years' financial statements that are presented are not revised in the year of change.

Prior to the current GAAP, voluntary changes in accounting principle were presented using the prospective method in the United States. With the prospective method, the accounts of each year prior period are not adjusted to reflect the effects of applying the new principle. The new accounting principle is used in the current financial statements, and the effect of using the new principle in prior financial statements is disclosed on the current income statement as a cumulative effect of change in accounting principle, net of tax.

The United States reporting prior to the new standard was inconsistent with the reporting under the International Financial Reporting Standards (IFRS).

The current standard does not rule out the possibility that a new standard could include specific directions on how to report a change in principle. Thus it is possible that the cumulative effect could be directed to be reported in the income statement in the year of change. A standard making the LIFO inventory method obsolete could possibly be handled that way. If such a standard is issued then remove the cumulative effect of accounting change in the primary analysis.

See Exhibit 4-8 for the cumulative effect of accounting change on the income statement.

EXHIBIT **4-8**	Zebra Technologies Corporation*

Cumulative Effect of Change in Accounting Principle

Zebra Technologies Corporation
Consolidated Statements of Earnings (Loss) (In Part)
Amounts in thousands, except per share data

	Year Ended December 31,		
	2008	**2007**	**2006**
Operating income (loss)	(15,346)	$143,185	$ 80,429
Other income (expense):			
Investment income	1,281	23,966	23,182
Foreign exchange gain (loss)	3,518	523	(635)
Other, net	(1,366)	(299)	(1,334)
Total other income	3,433	24,190	21,213
Income (loss) before income taxes and cumulative effect of accounting change	(11,913)	167,375	101,642
Income taxes	26,508	57,262	32,015
Income (loss) before cumulative effect of accounting change	(38,421)	110,113	69,627

*"Zebra delivers products and solutions that improve our customers' ability to help our customers put their critical assets to work smarter by identifying, tracking and managing assets, transactions and people." 10-K
Source: Zebra Technologies Corporations 2010 10-K

EXHIBIT **4-8**	Zebra Technologies Corporation (*continued*)

	Year Ended December 31,		
	2008	2007	2006
Cumulative effect of accounting change, net of income taxes of $694 (see Note 2)	—	—	1,319
Net income (loss)	$(38,421)	$110,113	$ 70,946
Basic earnings (loss) per share before cumulative effect of accounting change	$ (0.60)	$ 1.61	$ 0.99
Diluted earnings (loss) per share before cumulative effect of accounting change	$ (0.60)	$ 1.60	$ 0.98
Basic earnings (loss) per share	$ (0.60)	$ 1.61	$ 1.01
Diluted earnings (loss) per share	$ (0.60)	$ 1.60	$ 1.00
Basic weighted average shares outstanding	64,524	68,463	70,516
Diluted weighted average and equivalent shares outstanding	64,524	68,908	70,956

(F) Net Income—Noncontrolling Interest (previously minority share of earnings)

If a firm consolidates subsidiaries not wholly owned, the total revenues and expenses of the subsidiaries are included with those of the parent. However, to determine the income that would accrue to the parent, it is necessary to deduct the portion of income that would belong to the net income—noncontrolling interest. Prior to December 31, 2009, this was called "minority share of earnings." This item should be presented net of tax.

Noncontrolling interest reflects income from ownership of noncontrolling shareholders in the equity of consolidated subsidiaries less than wholly owned. Exhibit 4-9 illustrates net income attributable to the noncontrolling interest.

Some ratios can be materially distorted because of a net income—noncontrolling interest. For each ratio influenced by a net income—noncontrolling interest, this book suggests a recommended approach.

EXHIBIT **4-9**	Honeywell International, Inc.*

Net Income – Noncontrolling Interest (Minority Interest)

Honeywell International Inc.
Consolidated Statement of Operations

	Year Ended December 31,		
	2010	2009	2008
	(Dollars in millions, except per share amounts)		
Product sales	$26,262	$23,914	$29,212
Service sales	7,108	6,994	7,344
Net sales	33,370	30,908	36,556
Costs, expenses and other			
Cost of products sold	20,701	19,317	25,610
Cost of services sold	4,818	4,695	5,508
	25,519	24,012	31,118
Selling, general and administrative expenses	4,717	4,443	5,130
Other (income) expense	(95)	(55)	(748)
Interest and other financial charges	386	459	456
	30,527	28,859	35,956

*"Honeywell International, Inc. (Honeywell) is a diversified technology and manufacturing company, serving customers worldwide with aerospace products and services, control, sensing and security technologies for buildings, homes and industry, turbochargers, automotive products, specialty chemicals, electronic and advanced materials, process technology for refining and petrochemicals, and energy efficient products and solutions for homes, business and transportation." 10-K
Source: Honeywell International Inc. 2010 10-K

(continued)

EXHIBIT **4-9**	Honeywell International, Inc. (*continued*)		

	Year Ended December 31,		
	2010	2009	2008
	(Dollars in millions, except per share amounts)		
Income before taxes	2,843	2,049	600
Tax expense (benefit)	808	465	(226)
Net income	2,035	1,584	826
Less: Net income attributable to the noncontrolling interest	13	36	20
Net income attributable to Honeywell	$ 2,022	$ 1,548	$ 806
Earnings per share of common stock – basic	$ 2.61	$ 2.06	$ 1.09
Earnings per share of common stock – assuming dilution	$ 2.59	$ 2.05	$ 1.08
Cash dividends per share of common stock	$ 1.21	$ 1.21	$ 1.10

Earnings per Share

In general, **earnings per share** is earnings divided by the number of shares of outstanding common stock. Chapter 9 presents earnings per share in detail and explains its computation. Meanwhile, use the formula of net income divided by outstanding shares of common stock.

Retained Earnings

Retained earnings, an account on the balance sheet, represents the undistributed earnings of the corporation. A reconciliation of retained earnings summarizes the changes in retained earnings. It shows the retained earnings at the beginning of the year, the net income for the year as an addition, the dividends as a subtraction, and concludes with end-of-year retained earnings. It also includes, if appropriate, prior period adjustments (net of tax) and some adjustments for changes in accounting principles (net of tax). These restate beginning retained earnings. Other possible changes to retained earnings are beyond the scope of this book.

Sometimes a portion of retained earnings may be unavailable for dividends because it has been appropriated (restricted). Appropriated retained earnings remain part of retained earnings. The appropriation of retained earnings may or may not have significance.

Appropriations that result from legal requirements (usually state law) and appropriations that result from contractual agreements are potentially significant. The appropriations may leave unappropriated retained earnings inadequate to pay dividends. (*Note:* A corporation will not be able to pay a cash dividend even with an adequate unrestricted balance in retained earnings unless it has adequate cash or ability to raise cash and has complied with the state law where it is incorporated.)

Most appropriations result from management decisions. These are usually not significant because management can choose to remove the appropriation.

Caution should be exercised not to confuse retained earnings or appropriated retained earnings with cash or any other asset. There is no cash or any other asset in retained earnings. The reason for an appropriation will be disclosed either in the reconciliation of retained earnings or in a note. From this disclosure, try to arrive at an opinion as to the significance, if any.

The reconciliation of retained earnings usually appears as part of a statement of stockholders' equity. Sometimes it is combined with the income statement. Exhibit 4-10 gives an example of a reconciliation of retained earnings being presented with a stockholders' equity statement.

Dividends and Stock Splits

Dividends return profits to the owners of a corporation. A cash dividend declared by the board of directors reduces retained earnings by the amount of the dividends declared and creates the current liability, dividends payable. The date of payment occurs after the date of declaration. The dividend payment eliminates the liability, dividends payable, and reduces cash. Note that the date of the declaration of dividends, not the date of the dividend payment, affects retained earnings and creates the liability.

| EXHIBIT **4-10** | Reliance Steel & Aluminum Co.* |

Consolidated Statements of Equity

RELIANCE STEEL & ALUMINUM CO.
CONSOLIDATED STATEMENTS OF EQUITY
(In thousands, except share and per share amounts)

| | Reliance Shareholders | | | | | |
| | Common Stock | | Retained Earnings | Accumulated Other Comprehensive Income (loss) | Non-Controlling Interests | Total |
	Shares	Amount				
Balance at January 1, 2008	74,906,824	$ 646,406	$1,439,598	$ 20,245	$ 1,699	$2,107,948
Net income	—	—	482,777	—	858	483,635
Other comprehensive loss:						
Foreign currency translation loss	—	—	—	(42,624)	—	(42,624)
Unrealized loss on investments, net of tax	—	—	—	(1,163)	—	(1,163)
Minimum pension liability, net of tax	—	—	—	(8,474)	—	(8,474)
Comprehensive income						431,374
Noncontrolling interests acquired	—	—	—	—	2,300	2,300
Payment to noncontrolling interest holder	—	—	—	—	(1,225)	(1,225)
Share based compensation	—	13,189	—	—	—	13,189
Stock options exercised	844,338	17,987	—	—	—	17,987
Share based compensation tax benefits	—	—	9,693	—	—	9,693
Stock repurchased	(2,443,500)	(114,774)	—	—	—	(114,774)
Adjustment to initially apply EITF 06-10	—	—	(2,479)	—	—	(2,479)
Stock issued under incentive bonus plan	5,052	284	—	—	—	284
Cash dividends – $0.40 per share	—	—	(29,229)	—	—	(29,229)
Balance at December 31, 2008	73,312,714	563,092	1,900,360	(32,016)	3,632	2,435,068
Net income	—	—	148,158	—	1,018	149,176
Other comprehensive income:						
Foreign currency translation gain	—	—	—	25,870	—	25,870
Unrealized gain on investments, net of tax	—	—	—	524	—	524
Minimum pension liability, net of tax	—	—	—	4,099	—	4,099
Comprehensive income						179,669
Noncontrolling interests purchased	—	(1,758)	—	—	(903)	(2,661)
Payments to noncontrolling interest holder	—	—	—	—	(2,057)	(2,057)
Share based compensation	—	15,530	—	—	—	15,530
Stock options exercised	427,697	10,490	—	—	—	10,490
Share based compensation tax benefits	—	—	1,208	—	—	1,208
Stock issued under incentive bonus plan	10,360	258	—	—	—	258
Cash dividends – $0.40 per share	—	—	(29,383)	—	—	(29,383)
Balance at December 31, 2009	73,750,771	587,612	2,020,343	(1,523)	1,690	2,608,122
Net income	—	—	194,353	—	3,496	197,849
Other comprehensive income:						
Foreign currency translation gain	—	—	—	9,657	—	9,657
Unrealized gain on investments, net of tax	—	—	—	220	—	220
Minimum pension liability, net of tax	—	—	—	1,921	—	1,921
Comprehensive income						209,647
Issuance of equity interest in subsidiary to noncontrolling interest	—	(1,462)	—	—	1,604	142
Consolidation of a joint venture entity	—	—	—	—	1,370	1,370
Payments to noncontrolling interest holders	—	—	—	—	(1,778)	(1,778)
Share based compensation	61,000	17,334	—	—	—	17,334
Stock options exercised	827,452	21,248	—	—	—	21,248
Share based compensation tax benefits	—	—	3,721	—	—	3,721
Cash dividends – $0.40 per share	—	—	(29,692)	—	—	(29,692)
Balance at December 31, 2010	74,639,223	$ 624,732	$2,188,725	$ 10,275	$ 6,382	$2,830,114

*"We are the largest metals service center company in North America (U.S. and Canada)." 10-K
Source: Reliance Steel & Aluminum Co. 2010 10-K

The board of directors may elect to declare and issue another type of dividend, termed a *stock dividend*. The firm issues a percentage of outstanding stock as new shares to existing shareholders. If the board declares a 10% stock dividend, for example, an owner holding 1,000 shares would receive an additional 100 shares of new stock. The accounting for a stock dividend, assuming a relatively small distribution (less than 25% of the existing stock), requires removing the fair market value of the stock at the date of declaration from retained earnings and transferring it to paid-in capital. With a material stock dividend, the amount removed from retained earnings and transferred to paid-in capital is determined by multiplying the par value of the stock by the number of additional shares. Note that the overall effect of a stock dividend leaves total stockholders' equity and each owner's share of stockholders' equity unchanged. However, the total number of outstanding shares increases.

A stock dividend should reduce the market value of individual shares by the percentage of the stock dividend. Total market value considering all outstanding shares should not change in theory. In practice, the market value change may not be the same percentage as the stock dividend.

A more drastic device to change the market value of individual shares is by declaring a stock split. A 2-for-1 split should reduce the market value per share to one-half the amount prior to the split. The market value per share in practice may not change exactly in proportion to the split. The market value will result from the supply and demand for the stock.

Lowering the market value is sometimes desirable for stocks selling at high prices (as perceived by management). Stocks with high prices are less readily traded. A stock dividend or stock split can influence the demand for the stock.

A stock split merely increases the number of shares of stock. It does not usually change retained earnings or paid-in capital. For example, if a firm had 1,000 shares of common stock, a 2-for-1 stock split would result in 2,000 shares.

For a stock split, the par or stated value of the stock is changed in proportion to the stock split, and no change is made to retained earnings, additional paid-in capital, or capital stock. For example, a firm with $10 par common stock that declares a 2-for-1 stock split would reduce the par value to $5.

Sometimes the company wants to increase the market value of individual shares by declaring a reverse stock split. In this case, the company recalls its present stock and issues a lesser number of shares. This could be one-for-two, one-for-three, one-for-four, one-for-five, one-for-six, etc.

The Sanmina-Sci Corporation did a reverse stock split. They included the following in their 2009 annual report:

"*Reverse Stock Split.* On July 20, 2009, the Board of Directors of the Company authorized a reverse stock split of its common stock at a ratio of one-for-six, effective August 14, 2009. The Company's stockholders previously approved the reverse split in September 2008. As a result of the reverse split, every six shares of common stock outstanding were combined into one share of common stock. The reverse split did not affect the amount of equity the Company has nor did it affect the Company's market capitalization."

Since the number of shares changes under both a stock dividend and stock split, any ratio based on the number of shares must be restated for a meaningful comparison. For example, if a firm had earnings per share of $4 in 2010, a 2-for-1 stock split in 2011 would require restatement of the earnings per share to $2 in 2010 because of the increase in the shares. Restatement will be made for all prior financial statements presented with the current financial statements, including a 5- or 10-year summary.

Source: Sanmina-Sci Corporation 2010 10-K

Legality of Distributions to Stockholders

The legality of distributions to stockholders is governed by applicable state law. Currently, the 50 states may be classified into one of three groups for purposes of distributions to stockholders. These groups are the following:[2]

1. Distributions to stockholders are acceptable as long as the firm has the ability to pay debts as they come due in the normal course of business.

2. Distributions to stockholders are acceptable as long as the firm is solvent and the distributions do not exceed the fair value of net assets.

3. Distributions consist of solvency and balance sheet tests of liquidity and risk.

Thus, the appropriateness of a distribution to stockholders is a legal interpretation. Accountants have not accepted the role of disclosing the firm's capacity to make distributions to stockholders. Accountants have accepted the role of disclosing appropriations (restrictions) of retained earnings. Appropriations can temporarily limit the firm's ability to make distributions. These appropriations are typically directed toward limiting or prohibiting the payment of cash dividends.

During the 1980s and 1990s, many distributions to stockholders exceeded the net book value of the firm's assets. These were often accompanied by debt-financed restructurings. Often, the result was a deficit balance in retained earnings and sometimes a deficit balance in total stockholders' equity.

During 1988, Holiday Corporation (owner of Holiday Inns of America) distributed a $65 per share dividend to prevent a hostile takeover. The result was a substantial deficit to retained earnings and approximately a $770 million deficit to total stockholders' equity.[3]

A similar situation took place at Owens Corning during the 1980s as it made a substantial distribution to stockholders by way of a debt-financed restructuring. Owens Corning also had substantial expenses related to asbestos-related illnesses. At the end of 1995, Owens Corning had a deficit in retained earnings of $781 million and a deficit in total stockholders' equity of $212 million.

An Owens Corning news release of June 20, 1996, stated (in part):

> The Board of Directors has approved an annual dividend policy of 25 cents per share and declared a quarterly dividend of 6-1/4 cents per share payable on October 15, 1996 to shareholders of record as of September 30, 1996.
>
> In reference to the dividend, we were able to initiate this action because debt has been reduced to target levels and cash flow from operations will be in excess of internal funding requirements.
>
> We are delighted to be able to reward our shareholders with a dividend. Reinstating the dividend has been a priority of mine since joining the company and I am pleased that we now are in a position to set the date.

Comprehensive Income

Chapter 1 described the Concept Statements that serve as the basis for evaluating existing standards of financial accounting and reports. Concept Statement Nos. 5 and 6 included the concept of comprehensive income. Comprehensive income was described in SFAC No. 6 as the change in equity of a business enterprise during a period from transactions and other events and circumstances from nonowner sources.

Subsequently, SFAS No. 130 was issued, requiring the reporting of comprehensive income, but using a narrower definition than in SFAC No. 6. Under SFAS No. 130, comprehensive income is net income plus the period's change in accumulated other comprehensive income. Accumulated other comprehensive income is a category within stockholders' equity, described in Chapter 3.

Categories within accumulated other comprehensive income are:

1. *Foreign currency translation adjustments.* The expansion of international business and extensive currency realignment have created special accounting problems. The biggest difficulty has been related to translating foreign financial statements into the financial statements of a U.S. enterprise.

   U.S. financial reporting calls for postponing the recognition of unrealized exchange gains and losses until the foreign operation is substantially liquidated. This postponement is accomplished by creating a separate category within stockholders' equity to carry unrealized exchange gains and losses. This method eliminates the wide fluctuations in earnings from translation adjustments for most firms. For subsidiaries operating in highly inflationary economies, translation adjustments are charged to net earnings. Also, actual foreign currency exchange gains (losses) are included in net earnings.

2. *Unrealized holding gains and losses on available-for-sale marketable securities.* Debt and equity securities classified as available-for-sale securities are carried at fair value.

Unrealized holding gains and losses are included in a separate category within stockholders' equity until realized. Thus, the unrealized holding gains and losses are not included in net earnings. Note that this accounting only applies to securities available for sale. Trading securities are reported at their fair values on the balance sheet date, and unrealized holding gains and losses are included in income of the current period. Debt securities held to maturity are reported at their amortized cost on the balance sheet date.

3. *Changes to stockholders' equity resulting from additional minimum pension liability adjustments.* Accounting standards require a reduction in stockholders' equity for a minimum pension liability under a defined benefit plan. Accounting for a defined benefit plan is reviewed in Chapter 7.

4. *Unrealized gains and losses from derivative instruments.* Derivative instruments are financial instruments or other contracts where rights or obligations meet the definitions of assets or liabilities. The gain or loss for some derivative instruments is reported in current earnings. For other derivative instruments, the gain or loss is reported as a component of other comprehensive income. The gain or loss for these instruments is recognized in subsequent periods in income as the hedged forecasted transactions affect earnings.

Required disclosures are the following:

- Comprehensive income
- Each category of other comprehensive income
- Reclassification adjustments for categories of other comprehensive income
- Tax effects for each category of other comprehensive income
- Balances for each category of accumulated other comprehensive income

The accounting standard provided considerable flexibility in reporting comprehensive income. One format uses a single income statement to report net income and comprehensive income. The second format reports comprehensive income in a separate statement of financial activity. The third format reports comprehensive income within the statement of changes in stockholders' equity. Exhibit 4-10 presents the accumulated other comprehensive income (loss) of Reliance Steel & Aluminum Co. Reliance presents this within its consolidated statements of shareholders' equity.

The first two options were not popular because they require that comprehensive income be closely tied to the income statement. Comprehensive income will typically be more volatile than net income. This is because the items within accumulated other comprehensive income have the potential to be volatile. A good case could be made that comprehensive income is a better indication of long-run profitability than is net income. Some firms elected to disclose comprehensive income as a note to the financial statements.

The FASB and IASB entered into a joint project to improve the presentation of comprehensive income in a manner that is as convergent as possible. At that time the IFRS only provided for comprehensive income to be presented either in a single statement or in two consecutive statements.

The result of this joint project was that the FASB in 2011 issued an amendment of the FASB Accounting Standards Codification which ruled out the option of reporting comprehensive income within the statement of changes in shareholders' equity.

Thus with the effective fiscal year after December 15, 2011, only the following options are available:

1. A single income statement reporting net income and comprehensive income, or
2. Report comprehensive income in a separate statement immediately following the statement of income.

Exhibit 4-11 has illustrations—reporting comprehensive income. Illustration (A)—single income statement to report net income and comprehensive income and illustration (B)—comprehensive income in a separate statement.

This new standard is effective for interim periods. The coverage of comprehensive income in analysis is in Chapter 12.

International Consolidated Income Statement (IFRS)

IFRS and U.S. GAAP for the income statement are similar, with some presentation differences. U.S. GAAP requires either a single-step or multiple-step format. There is no required format under IFRS. Under IFRS, expenses are classified by their nature or function.

Under IFRS, equipment may be revalued. This would result in the adjustment of depreciation expenses. IFRS allows for alternative performance measures to be presented in the income statement that are not allowed by U.S. GAAP.

EXHIBIT **4-11**	Illustrations – Reporting Comprehensive Income

Illustration (A) – Single income statement to report net income and comprehensive income

Convergys Corporation*
Consolidated Statements of Operations and Comprehensive Income (Loss)

	Year Ended December 31,		
(Amounts in millions, except per share amounts)	2010	2009	2008
Revenues	$2,203.4	$2,421.0	$2,526.3
Operating Costs and Expenses:			
Cost of providing services and products sold[1]	1,340.9	1,461.6	1,623.8
Selling, general and administrative expenses	575.7	616.4	561.7
Research and development costs	56.2	74.2	54.9
Depreciation	97.3	110.3	109.7
Amortization	10.1	10.9	11.3
Restructuring charges	38.7	43.3	23.9
Asset impairment	181.1	3.1	—
Total costs and expenses	2,298.0	2,319.8	2,385.3
Operating (Loss) Income	(94.6)	101.2	141.0
Equity in earnings of Cellular Partnerships	47.2	41.0	35.7
Other income (expense), net	8.9	(17.2)	16.2
Interest expense	(19.5)	(28.9)	(22.5)
(Loss) income before income taxes	(58.0)	96.1	170.4
Income tax expense	16.7	11.6	23.9
(Loss) income from continuing operations	(74.7)	84.5	146.5
Income (loss) from discontinued operations, net of tax	21.5	(161.8)	(239.4)
Net (Loss) Income	$ (53.2)	$ (77.3)	$ (92.9)
Other Comprehensive Income (Loss), net of tax:			
Foreign currency translation adjustments	$ 11.7	$ 25.4	$ (59.4)
Change related to pension liability (net of tax benefit (expense) of $2.9, ($2.4), and $12.2)	(3.5)	2.2	(20.3)
Unrealized gain (loss) on hedging activities (net of tax benefit (expense) of $20.0, ($27.9), and $57.5)	33.5	51.8	(107.0)
Total Comprehensive (Loss) Income	$ (11.5)	$ 2.1	$ (279.6)
Basic Earnings (Loss) per share:			
Continuing Operations	$ (0.61)	$ 0.69	$ 1.19
Discontinued operations	0.18	(1.32)	(1.94)
Net basic (loss) earnings per share	$ (0.43)	$ (0.63)	$ (0.75)
Diluted Earnings (Loss) per share:			
Continuing Operations	$ (0.61)	$ 0.68	$ 1.16
Discontinued Operations	0.18	(1.30)	(1.90)
Net diluted (loss) earnings per share	$ (0.43)	$ (0.62)	$ (0.74)
Weighted average common shares outstanding:			
Basic	123.1	122.8	123.5
Diluted	123.1	124.9	125.8

*"Convergys Corporation (the Company or Convergys) is a global leader in relationship management." 10-K
[1]Exclusive of depreciation and amortization, with the exception of amortization of deferred charges.
Source: Convergys Corporation 2010 10-K

(continued)

EXHIBIT **4-11**	Illustrations – Reporting Comprehensive Income (*continued*)

Illustration (B) – Comprehensive income in a separate statement

Zebra Technologies Corporation*
Consolidated Statements of Comprehensive Income (Loss)
(Amounts in thousands)

	Year Ended December 31,		
	2010	2009	2008
Net income (loss)	$101,778	$47,104	$(38,421)
Other comprehensive income (loss):			
Unrealized gain/(loss) on hedging transactions, net of income taxes	(949)	19	5,750
Unrealized holding gains/(losses) on investments, net of income taxes	(406)	737	(543)
Foreign currency translation adjustment	67	3,972	(22,991)
Comprehensive income (loss)	$100,490	$51,832	$(56,205)

*"Zebra delivers products and solutions that improve our customers' ability to put their critical assets to work smarter by identifying, tracking and managing assets, transactions and people." 10-K

Deloitte Touche Tohmatsu Limited, one of the big four public accounting firms, presents model financial statements under IFRS available on www.deloitte.com. These following model financial statements will be used to illustrate statements under IFRS:

International GAAP Holdings Limited

Financial statements for the year ended 31 December 2011

The model financial statements of International GAAP Holdings Limited for the year ended 31 December 2011 are intended to illustrate the presentation and disclosure requirements of International Financial Reporting Standards (IFRSs). They also contain additional disclosures that are considered to be best practice, particularly where such disclosures are included in illustrative examples provided with a specific Standard.

International GAAP Holdings Limited is assumed to have presented financial statements in accordance with IFRSs for a number of years. Therefore, it is not a first-time adopter of IFRSs. Readers should refer to IFRS 1 *First-time Adoption of International Financial Reporting Standards* for specific requirements regarding an entity's first IFRS financial statements, and to the IFRS 1 section of Deloitte's Compliance, Presentation and Disclosure Checklist for details of the particular disclosure requirements applicable for first-time adopters. Deloitte's Compliance, Presentation and Disclosure Checklist can be downloaded from Deloitte's web site www.iasplus.com.

The model financial statements have illustrated the impact of a number of new and revised Standards and Interpretations that are mandatorily effective on 1 January 2011 (see note 2 to the model financial statements for details). The model financial statements have not illustrated the impact of new and revised Standards and Interpretations that are not yet mandatorily effective on 1 January 2011 (e.g. IFRS 9 *Financial Instruments*).

In addition, the model financial statements have been presented without regard to local laws or regulations. Preparers of financial statements will need to ensure that the options selected under IFRSs do not conflict with such sources of regulation (e.g. the revaluation of assets is not permitted in certain regimes – but these financial statements illustrate the presentation and disclosures required when an entity adopts the revaluation model under IAS 16 *Property, Plant and Equipment*). In addition, local laws or securities regulations may specify disclosures in addition to those required by IFRSs (e.g. in relation to directors' remuneration). Preparers of financial statements will consequently need to adapt the model financial statements to comply with such additional local requirements.

The model financial statements do not include separate financial statements for the parent, which may be required by local laws or regulations, or may be prepared voluntarily. Where an entity presents separate financial statements that comply with IFRSs, the requirements of IAS 27 *Consolidated and Separate Financial Statements* will apply. Separate statements of comprehensive income, financial position, changes in equity and cash flows for the parent will generally be required, together with supporting notes.

Suggested disclosures are cross-referenced to the underlying requirements in the texts of the relevant Standards and Interpretations.

For the purposes of presenting the statements of comprehensive income and cash flows, the alternatives allowed under IFRSs for those statements have been illustrated. Preparers should select the alternatives most appropriate to their circumstances and apply the chosen presentation method consistently.

Note that in these model financial statements, we have frequently included line items for which a nil amount is shown, so as to illustrate items that, although not applicable to International GAAP Holdings Limited, are commonly encountered in practice. This does not mean that we have illustrated all possible disclosures. Nor should it be taken to mean that, in practice, entities are required to display line items for such 'nil' amounts.

Disclaimer

Deloitte refers to one or more of Deloitte Touche Tohmatsu Limited, a UK private company limited by guarantee, and its network of member firms, each of which is a legally separate and independent entity. Please see www.deloitte.com/about for a detailed description of the legal structure of Deloitte Touche Tohmatsu Limited and its member firms. "Deloitte" is the band under which tens of thousands of dedicated professionals in independent firms throughout the world collaborate to provide audit, consulting, financial advisory, risk management, and tax services to selected clients. These firms are member of Deloitte Touche Tohmatsu Limited (DTTL), a UK private company limited by guarantee. Each member firm provides services in a particular geographic area and is subject to the laws and professional regulations of the particular country or countries in which it operates. DTTL does not itself provide services to clients. DTTL and each DTTL member firm are separate and distinct legal entities, which cannot obligate each other. DTTL and each DTTL member firm are liable for only their own acts or omissions and not those of each other. Each DTTL member firm is structured differently in accordance with national laws, regulations, customary practice, and other factors, and may secure the provision of professional services in its territory through subsidiaries, affiliates and/or other entities. This publication contains general information only, and none of Deloitte Touche Tohmatsu Limited, its member firms, or its and their affiliates are, by means of this publication, rendering accounting, business, financial, investment, legal, tax, or other professional advice or services. This publication is not a substitute for such professional advice or services, nor should it be used as a basis for any decision or action that may affect your finances or your business. Before making any decision or taking any action that may affect your finances or your business, you should consult a qualified professional advisor. None of Deloitte Touche Tohmatsu Limited, its member firms, or its and their respective affiliates shall be responsible for any loss whatsoever sustained by any person who relies on this publication.

The model income statement in Exhibit 4-12 aggregates expense to their function. The model income statement in Exhibit 4-13 aggregates expenses according to their nature.

Exhibit 4-12 combines the income statement and comprehensive income. This results in an exhibit title of IFRS Model Consolidated Statement of Comprehensive Income.

Exhibit 4-13 presents the Consolidated Income Statement separate from the Consolidated Statement of Comprehensive Income. This results in an exhibit title of IFRS Model Consolidated Income Statement – followed by – Consolidated Statement of Comprehensive Income.

EXHIBIT **4-12**	IFRS Model Consolidated Statement of Comprehensive Income

Source	International GAAP Holdings Limited			
IAS 1.10(b), 51(b),(c)	Consolidated statement of comprehensive income for the year ended 31 December 2011		Year ended 31/12/11	[Alt 1] Year ended 31/12/10
IAS 1.113 IAS 1.51(d),(e)		Notes	CU'000	CU'000
	Continuing operations			
IAS 1.82(a)	Revenue	5	140,918	151,840
IAS 1.99	Cost of sales		(87,897)	(91,840)
IAS 1.85	Gross profit		53,021	60,000
IAS 1.85	Investment income	7	3,608	2,351
IAS 1.85	Other gains and losses	8	647	1,005
IAS 1.99	Distribution expenses		(5,087)	(4,600)
IAS 1.99	Marketing expenses		(3,305)	(2,254)
IAS 1.99	Administration expenses		(13,129)	(17,325)
	Other expenses		(2,801)	(2,612)
IAS 1.82(b)	Finance costs	9	(4,418)	(6,023)
IAS 1.82(c)	Share of profits of associates	20	1,186	1,589
IAS 1.85	Gain recognised on disposal of interest in former associate	20	581	—
IAS 1.85	Other [describe]		—	—
IAS 1.85	Profit before tax		30,303	32,131
IAS 1.82(d)	Income tax expense	10	(11,564)	(11,799)
IAS 1.85	Profit for the year from continuing operations	13	18,739	20,332
	Discontinued operations			
IAS 1.82(e)	Profit for the year from discontinued operations	11	8,310	9,995
IAS 1.82(f)	**Profit for the year**		27,049	30,327
	Other comprehensive income, net of income tax			
IAS 1.82(g)	Exchange differences on translating foreign operations		(39)	85
IAS 1.82(g)	Net gain on available-for-sale financial assets		66	57
IAS 1.82(g)	Net gain on hedging instruments entered into for cash flow hedges		39	20
IAS 1.82(g)	Gain on revaluation of properties		—	1,150
IAS 1.82(h)	Share of other comprehensive income of associates		—	—
IAS 1.85	Other comprehensive income for the year, net of tax		66	1,312
IAS 1.82(i)	**Total comprehensive income for the year**		27,115	31,639
	Profit attributable to:			
IAS 1.83(a)	Owners of the Company		23,049	27,564
IAS 1.83(a)	Non-controlling interests		4,000	2,763
			27,049	30,327
	Total comprehensive income attributable to:			
IAS 1.83(b)	Owners of the Company		23,115	28,876
IAS 1.83(b)	Non-controlling interests		4,000	2,763
			27,115	31,639
	Earnings per share	14		
	From continuing and discontinued operations			
IAS 33.66	Basic (cents per share)		132.2	137.0
IAS 33.66	Diluted (cents per share)		115.5	130.5
	From continuing operations			
IAS 33.66	Basic (cents per share)		84.5	87.3
IAS 33.66	Diluted (cents per share)		74.0	83.2

EXHIBIT **4-12**	IFRS Model Consolidated Statement of Comprehensive Income (*continued*)	

Source	International GAAP Holdings Limited

Note: Alt 1 above illustrates the presentation of comprehensive income in one statement. Alt 2 (see next pages) illustrates the presentation of comprehensive income in two statements.

Whichever presentation is selected, the distinction is retained between items recognised in profit or loss and items recognised in other comprehensive income. The only difference between the one-statement and the two-statement approaches is that, for the latter, a total is struck in the separate income statement at 'profit for the year' (this is the same amount as is presented as a sub-total under the one-statement approach). This 'profit for the year' is then the starting point for the statement of comprehensive income, which is required to be presented immediately following the income statement. Under the two-statement approach, the analysis of 'profit for the year' between the amount attributable to the owners of the parent and the amount attributable to non-controlling interests is presented at the end of the separate income statement.

Irrespective of whether the one-statement or the two-statement approach is followed, for the components of other comprehensive income, additional presentation options are available, as follows.

IAS 1.90
- The individual components may be presented net of tax in the statement of comprehensive income (as illustrated on the previous page), or they may be presented gross with a single line deduction for tax (see Alt 2). Whichever option is selected, the income tax relating to each component of comprehensive income must be disclosed, either in the statement of comprehensive income or in the notes (see note 29).

IAS 1.93
- For reclassification adjustments, an aggregated presentation may be adopted, with separate disclosure of the current year gain or loss and reclassification adjustments in the notes (see previous page and note 29). Alternatively, using a disaggregated presentation, the current year gain or loss and reclassification adjustments are shown separately in the statement of comprehensive income (see Alt 2).

Alt 1 aggregates expenses according to their function.

EXHIBIT **4-13**	IFRS Model Consolidated Income Statement – followed by – Consolidated Statement of Comprehensive Income	

Source	International GAAP Holdings Limited

Consolidated income statement
for the year ended 31 December 2011

		Notes	Year ended 31/12/11 CU'000	[Alt 2] Year ended 31/12/10 CU'000
	Continuing operations			
IAS 1.82(a)	Revenue	5	140,918	151,840
IAS 1.85	Investment income	7	3,608	2,351
IAS 1.85	Other gains and losses	8	647	1,005
IAS 1.99	Changes in inventories of finished goods and work in progress		7,134	2,118
IAS 1.99	Raw materials and consumables used		(84,659)	(85,413)
IAS 1.99	Depreciation and amortisation expenses	13	(11,193)	(13,878)
IAS 1.99	Employee benefits expense	13	(10,113)	(11,527)
IAS 1.82(b)	Finance costs	9	(4,418)	(6,023)
IAS 1.99	Consulting expense		(3,120)	(1,926)
	Other expenses		(10,268)	(8,005)
IAS 1.82(c)	Share of profits of associates	20	1,186	1,589
IAS 1.85	Gain recognised on disposal of interest in former associate	20	581	—
IAS 1.85	Other [describe]		—	—
IAS 1.85	Profit before tax		30,303	32,131
IAS 1.82(d)	Income tax expense	10	(11,564)	(11,799)
IAS 1.85	Profit for the year from continuing operations	13	18,739	20,332

IAS 1.10(b) 81(b),51(b),(c) / IAS 1.113 / IAS 1.51(d),(e)

Source: © 2011 Deloitte Touch Tohmatsu. Deloitte, Deloitte & Touch, Deloitte Touche Tohmatsu, the Deloitte logo, the Deloitte Touch Tohmatsu logo, and certain product names mentioned in this material are trademarks or registered trademarks of Deloitte Touche Tohmatsu, which has no connection to the author or publisher of this book and has no responsibility for its contents.

(*continued*)

EXHIBIT **4-13**	IFRS Model Consolidated Income Statement – followed by – Consolidated Statement of Comprehensive Income (*continued*)

		Notes	Year ended 31/12/11	[Alt 2] Year ended 31/12/10
	Discontinued operations			
IAS 1.82(e)	Profit for the year from discontinued operations	11	8,310	9,995
IAS 1.82(f)	**Profit for the year**		27,049	30,327
	Attributable to:			
IAS 1.83(a)	Owners of the Company		23,049	27,564
IAS 1.83(a)	Non-controlling interests		4,000	2,763
			27,049	30,327
	Earnings per share	14		
	From continuing and discontinued operations			
IAS 33.66, 67A	Basic (cents per share)		132.2	137.0
IAS 33.66, 67A	Diluted (cents per share)		115.5	130.5
	From continuing operations:			
IAS 33.66, 67A	Basic (cents per share)		84.5	87.3
IAS 33.66, 67A	Diluted (cents per share)		74.0	83.2

Note: The format outlined above aggregates expenses according to their nature.
See the previous page for a discussion of the format of the statement of comprehensive income. Note that where the two-statement approach is adopted (above and on the next page), as required by IAS 1.12, the income statement must be displayed immediately before the statement of comprehensive income.

IAS 1.10(b)
81(b), 51(b),(c)

Consolidated statement of comprehensive income
for the year ended 31 December 2011

		Year ended 31/12/11	[Alt 2] Year ended 31/12/10
IAS 1.113			
IAS 1.51(d),(e)		CU'000	CU'000
IAS 182(f)	**Profit for the year**	27,049	30,327
	Other comprehensive income		
IAS 1.82(g)	Exchange differences on translating foreign operations		
	Exchange differences arising during the year	75	121
	Loss on hedging instruments designated in hedges of the net assets of foreign operations	(12)	—
	Reclassification adjustments relating to foreign operations disposed of in the year	(166)	—
	Reclassification adjustments relating to hedges of the net assets of foreign operations disposed of in the year	46	—
		(57)	121
IAS 1.82(g)	Available-for-sale financial assets		
	Net gain on available-for-sale financial assets during the year	94	81
	Reclassification adjustments relating to available-for-sale financial assets disposed of in the year	—	—
		94	81
IAS 1.82(g)	Cash flow hedges		
	Gains arising during the year	436	316
	Reclassification adjustments for amounts recognised in profit or loss	(123)	(86)
	Adjustments for amounts transferred to the initial carrying amounts of hedged items	(257)	(201)
		56	29
IAS 1.82(g)	Gain on revaluation of properties	—	1,643
IAS 1.82(h)	Share of other comprehensive income of associates	—	—
	Income tax relating to components of other comprehensive income	(27)	(562)
IAS 1.82(i)	**Total comprehensive income for the year**	27,115	31,639
	Total comprehensive income attributable to:		
IAS 1.83(b)	Owners of the Company	23,115	28,876
IAS 1.83(b)	Non-controlling interests	4,000	2,763
		27,115	31,639

Summary

The income statement summarizes the profit for a specific period of time. To understand and analyze profitability, the reader must be familiar with the components of income, as well as income statement items that require special disclosure. This chapter presented special income statement items, such as unusual or infrequent items disclosed separately, equity in earnings of nonconsolidated subsidiaries, discontinued operations, extraordinary items, and net income—noncontrolling interest. This chapter also covered the reconciliation of retained earnings, dividends and stock splits, and comprehensive income, and international consolidated income statements (IFRS).

Questions

Q 4-1 What are extraordinary items? How are they shown on the income statement? Why are they shown in that manner?

Q 4-2 Which of the following would be classified as extraordinary?

a. Selling expense
b. Interest expense
c. Gain on the sale of marketable securities
d. Loss from flood
e. Income tax expense
f. Loss from prohibition of red dye
g. Loss from the write-down of inventory

Q 4-3 Give three examples of unusual or infrequent items that are disclosed separately. Why are they shown separately? Are they presented before or after tax? Why or why not?

Q 4-4 Why is the equity in earnings of nonconsolidated subsidiaries sometimes a problem in profitability analysis? Discuss with respect to income versus cash flow.

Q 4-5 A health food distributor selling wholesale dairy products and vitamins decides to discontinue the division that sells vitamins. How should this discontinuance be classified on the income statement?

Q 4-6 Why are unusual or infrequent items disclosed before tax?

Q 4-7 In the future, we should expect few presentations of a "cumulative effect of change in accounting principle." Comment.

Q 4-8 How does the declaration of a cash dividend affect the financial statements? How does the payment of a cash dividend affect the financial statements?

Q 4-9 What is the difference in the impact on financial statements of a stock dividend versus a stock split?

Q 4-10 Why is net income—noncontrolling interest deducted before arriving at net income?

Q 4-11 Explain the relationship between the income statement and the reconciliation of retained earnings.

Q 4-12 List the three types of appropriated retained earnings accounts. Which of these types is most likely not a detriment to the payment of a dividend? Explain.

Q 4-13 A balance sheet represents a specific date, such as "December 31," while an income statement covers a period of time, such as "For the Year Ended December 31, 2011." Why does this difference exist?

Q 4-14 Describe the following items:

a. Net income–noncontrolling interest
b. Equity in earnings of nonconsolidated subsidiaries

Q 4-15 An income statement is a summary of revenues and expenses and gains and losses, ending with net income for a specific period of time. Indicate the two traditional formats for presenting the income statement. Which of these formats is preferable for analysis? Why?

Q 4-16 Melcher Company reported earnings per share in 2011 and 2010 of $2.00 and $1.60, respectively. In 2012, there was a 2-for-1 stock split, and the earnings per share for 2012 were reported to be $1.40. Give a three-year presentation of earnings per share (2010–2012).

Q 4-17 Comment on your ability to determine a firm's capacity to make distributions to stockholders, using published financial statements.

Q 4-18 Management does not usually like to tie comprehensive income closely with the income statement. Comment.

Q 4-19 Review the consolidated income statement, expenses analyzed by function (Exhibit 4-12). Comment on similarities and differences to the U.S. GAAP income statement.

Q 4-20 Review the consolidated income statement, expenses analyzed by nature (Exhibit 4-13). Comment on similarities and differences to the U.S. GAAP income statement.

Problems

P 4-1 The following information for Decher Automotives covers the year ended 2012:

Administrative expense	$ 62,000
Dividend income	10,000 *(continued)*

(**P 4-1** CONTINUED)

Income taxes	$ 100,000
Interest expense	20,000
Merchandise inventory, 1/1	650,000
Merchandise inventory, 12/31	440,000
Flood loss (net of tax)	30,000
Purchases	460,000
Sales	1,000,000
Selling expenses	43,000

Required

a. Prepare a multiple-step income statement.

b. Assuming that 100,000 shares of common stock are outstanding, calculate the earnings per share before extraordinary items and the net earnings per share.

c. Prepare a single-step income statement.

P 4-2 The following information for Lesky Corporation covers the year ended December 31, 2012:

LESKY CORPORATION
Income Statement
For the Year Ended December 31, 2012

Revenue:		
Revenues from sales		$362,000
Rental income		1,000
Interest		2,400
Total revenue		365,400
Expenses:		
Cost of products sold	$242,000	
Selling expenses	47,000	
Administrative and general expenses	11,400	
Interest expense	2,200	
Federal and state income taxes	20,300	
Total expenses		322,900
Net income		$ 42,500

Required Change this statement to a multiple-step format, as illustrated in this chapter.

P 4-3 The accounts of Consolidated Can contain the following amounts at December 31, 2012:

Cost of products sold	$410,000
Dividends	3,000
Extraordinary gain (net of tax)	1,000
Income taxes	9,300
Interest expense	8,700
Other income	1,600
Retained earnings, 1/1	270,000
Sales	480,000
Selling and administrative expense	42,000

Required Prepare a multiple-step income statement combined with a reconciliation of retained earnings for the year ended December 31, 2012.

P 4-4 The following items are from Taperline Corporation on December 31, 2012. Assume a flat 40% corporate tax rate on all items, including the casualty loss.

Sales	$670,000
Rental income	3,600

Gain on the sale of fixed assets	$ 3,000
General and administrative expenses	110,000
Selling expenses	97,000
Interest expense	1,900
Depreciation for the period	10,000
Extraordinary item (casualty loss—pretax)	30,000
Cost of sales	300,000
Common stock (30,000 shares outstanding)	150,000

Required

a. Prepare a single-step income statement for the year ended December 31, 2012. Include earnings per share for earnings before extraordinary items and net income.
b. Prepare a multiple-step income statement. Include earnings per share for earnings before extraordinary items and net income.

P 4-5 The income statement of Rawl Company for the year ended December 31, 2012, shows the following:

Net sales	$360,000
Cost of sales	190,000
Gross profit	170,000
Selling, general, and administrative expense	80,000
Income before unusual write-offs	90,000
Provision for unusual write-offs	50,000
Earnings from operations before income taxes	40,000
Income taxes	20,000
Net earnings from operations before extraordinary charge	20,000
Extraordinary charge, net of tax of $10,000	(50,000)
Net earnings (loss)	$ (30,000)

Required Compute the net earnings remaining after removing unusual write-offs and the extraordinary charge. Remove these items net of tax. Estimate the tax rate for unusual write-offs based on the taxes on operating income.

P 4-6 At the end of 2012, vandals destroyed your financial records. Fortunately, the controller had kept certain statistical data related to the income statement, as follows:

a. Cost of goods sold was $2 million.
b. Administrative expenses were 20% of the cost of sales but only 10% of sales.
c. Selling expenses were 150% of administrative expenses.
d. Bonds payable were $1 million, with an average interest rate of 11%.
e. The tax rate was 48%.
f. 50,000 shares of common stock were outstanding for the entire year.

Required From the information given, reconstruct a multiple-step income statement for the year. Include earnings per share.

P 4-7 The following information applies to Bowling Green Metals Corporation for the year ended December 31, 2012:

Total revenues from regular operations	$832,000
Total expenses from regular operations	776,000
Extraordinary gain, net of applicable income taxes	30,000
Dividends paid	20,000
Number of shares of common stock outstanding during the year	10,000

Required Compute earnings per share before extraordinary items and net earnings. Show how this might be presented in the financial statements.

P 4-8 You were recently hired as the assistant treasurer for Victor, Inc. Yesterday, the treasurer was injured in a bicycle accident and is now hospitalized, unconscious. Your boss, Mr. Fernandes, just informed you that the financial statements are due today. Searching through the treasurer's desk, you find the following notes:

a. Income from continuing operations, based on computations done so far, is $400,000. No taxes are accounted for yet. The tax rate is 30%.
b. Dividends declared and paid were $20,000. During the year, 100,000 shares of stock were outstanding.
c. The corporation experienced an uninsured $20,000 pretax loss from a freak hailstorm. Such a storm is considered to be unusual and infrequent.
d. The company decided to change its inventory pricing method from average cost to the FIFO method. The effect of this change is to increase prior years' income by $30,000 pretax. The FIFO method has been used for 2012. (*Hint:* This adjustment should be placed just prior to net income.)
e. In 2012, the company settled a lawsuit against it for $10,000 pretax. The settlement was not previously accrued and is due for payment in February 2013.
f. In 2012, the firm sold a portion of its long-term securities at a gain of $30,000 pretax.
g. The corporation disposed of its consumer products division in August 2012, at a loss of $90,000 pretax. The loss from operations through August was $60,000 pretax.

Required Prepare an income statement for 2012, in good form, starting with income from continuing operations. Compute earnings per share for income from continuing operations, discontinued operations, extraordinary loss, cumulative effect of a change in accounting principle, and net income.

P 4-9 List the statement on which each of the following items may appear. Choose from (A) income statement, (B) balance sheet, or (C) neither.

a. Net income
b. Cost of goods sold
c. Gross profit
d. Retained earnings
e. Paid-in capital in excess of par
f. Sales
g. Supplies expense
h. Investment in G. Company
i. Dividends
j. Inventory
k. Common stock
l. Interest payable
m. Loss from flood
n. Land
o. Taxes payable
p. Interest income
q. Gain on sale of property
r. Dividend income
s. Depreciation expense
t. Accounts receivable
u. Accumulated depreciation
v. Sales commissions

P 4-10 List where each of the following items may appear. Choose from (A) income statement, (B) balance sheet, or (C) reconciliation of retained earnings.

a. Dividends paid
b. Notes payable
c. Income from noncontrolling interest
d. Accrued payrolls
e. Loss on disposal of equipment
f. Land
g. Adjustments of prior periods
h. Redeemable preferred stock
i. Treasury stock
j. Extraordinary loss
k. Unrealized exchange gains and losses
l. Equity in net income of affiliates
m. Goodwill
n. Unrealized decline in market value of equity investment
o. Cumulative effect of change in accounting principle
p. Common stock
q. Cost of goods sold
r. Supplies

P 4-11 The income statement of Tawls Company for the year ended December 31, 2012, shows the following:

Revenue from sales		$ 980,000
Cost of products sold		510,000
Gross profit		470,000
Operating expenses:		
Selling expenses	$110,000	
General expenses	140,000	250,000
Operating income		220,000
Equity on earnings of nonconsolidated		
subsidiary		60,000
Operating income before income taxes		280,000
Taxes related to operations		100,000
Net income from operations		180,000
Extraordinary loss from flood (less		
applicable taxes of $50,000)		(120,000)
Net income—noncontrolling interest		(40,000)
Net income		$ 20,000

Required
a. Compute the net earnings remaining after removing nonrecurring items.
b. Determine the earnings from the nonconsolidated subsidiary.
c. For the subsidiary that was not consolidated, what amount of income would have been included if this subsidiary had been consolidated?
d. What earnings relate to minority shareholders of a subsidiary that was consolidated?
e. Determine the total tax amount.

P 4-12 The income statement of Jones Company for the year ended December 31, 2012, follows.

Revenue from sales		$ 790,000
Cost of products sold		410,000
Gross profit		380,000
Operating expenses:		
Selling expenses	$ 40,000	
General expenses	80,000	120,000
Operating income		260,000
Equity in earnings of nonconsolidated subsidiaries (loss)		(20,000)
Operating income before income taxes		240,000
Taxes related to operations		(94,000)
Net income from operations		146,000
Discontinued operations:		
Loss from operations of discontinued segment (less applicable		
income tax credit of $30,000)	$(70,000)	
Loss on disposal of segment (less applicable income tax credit		
of $50,000)	(100,000)	(170,000)
Income before cumulative effect of change in accounting		
principle		(24,000)
Cumulative effect of change in accounting principle		
(less applicable income taxes of $25,000)		50,000
Net income		$ 26,000

Required
a. Compute the net earnings remaining after removing nonrecurring items.
b. Determine the earnings (loss) from the nonconsolidated subsidiary.
c. Determine the total tax amount.

P 4-13 Uranium Mining Company, founded in 1982 to mine and market uranium, purchased a mine in 1983 for $900 million. It estimated that the uranium had a market value of $150 per ounce. By 2012, the market value had increased to $300 per ounce. Records for 2012 indicate the following:

Production	200,000 ounces
Sales	230,000 ounces
Deliveries	190,000 ounces
Cash collection	210,000 ounces
Costs of production including depletion*	$50,000,000
Selling expense	$ 2,000,000
Administrative expenses	$ 1,250,000
Tax rate	50%

*Production cost per ounce has remained constant over the last few years, and the company has maintained the same production level.

Required

a. Compute the income for 2012, using each of the following bases:

    1. Receipt of cash
    2. Point of sale
    3. End of production
    4. Based on delivery

b. Comment on when each of the methods should be used. Which method should Uranium Mining Company use?

P 4-14 Each of the following statements represents a decision made by the accountant of Growth Industries:

a. A tornado destroyed $200,000 in uninsured inventory. This loss is included in the cost of goods sold.
b. Land was purchased 10 years ago for $50,000. The accountant adjusts the land account to $100,000, which is the estimated current value.
c. The cost of machinery and equipment is charged to a fixed asset account. The machinery and equipment will be expensed over the period of use.
d. The value of equipment increased this year, so no depreciation of equipment was recorded this year.
e. During the year, inventory that cost $5,000 was stolen by employees. This loss has been included in the cost of goods sold for the financial statements. The total amount of the cost of goods sold was $1 million.
f. The president of the company, who owns the business, used company funds to buy a car for personal use. The car was recorded on the company's books.

Required State whether you agree or disagree with each decision.

P 4-15 The following information for Gaffney Corporation covers the year ended December 31, 2012:

GAFFNEY CORPORATION
Income Statement
For the Year Ended December 31, 2012

Revenue:		
Revenues from sales		$450,000
Other		5,000
Total revenue		455,000
Expenses:		
Cost of products sold	$280,000	
Selling expenses	50,000	
Administrative and general expenses	20,000	
Federal and state income taxes	30,000	
Total expenses		380,000
Net income		75,000

Other comprehensive income

Available-for-sale securities adjustment, net of $5,000 income tax	$ 7,000	
Foreign currency translation adjustment, net of $3,000 income tax	8,000	
Other comprehensive income		15,000
Comprehensive income		$ 90,000

Required

a. Will net income or comprehensive income tend to be more volatile? Comment.
b. Which income figure will be used to compute earnings per share?
c. What is the total tax expense reported?
d. Will the items within other comprehensive income always net out as an addition to net income? Comment.

P 4-16

Required Answer the following multiple-choice questions:

a. Which of the following items would be classified as operating revenue or expense on an income statement of a manufacturing firm?

1. Interest expense
2. Advertising expense
3. Equity income
4. Dividend income
5. Cumulative effect of change in accounting principle

b. Which of the following is a recurring item?

1. Error of a prior period
2. Equity in earnings of nonconsolidated subsidiaries
3. Extraordinary loss
4. Cumulative effect of change in accounting principle
5. Discontinued operations

c. The following relate to the income statement of Growth Company for the year ended 2012. What is the beginning inventory?

Purchases	$180,000
Purchase returns	5,000
Sales	240,000
Cost of goods sold	210,000
Ending inventory	30,000

1. $6,000
2. $65,000
3. $50,000
4. $55,000
5. $70,000

d. Which of the following items are considered to be nonrecurring items?

1. Equity earnings
2. Unusual or infrequent item disclosed separately
3. Discontinued operations
4. Extraordinary item
5. Cumulative effect of change in accounting principle

e. If the investor company owns 30% of the stock of the investee company and the investee company reports profits of $150,000, then the investor company reports equity income of

1. $25,000.
2. $35,000.
3. $45,000.
4. $50,000.
5. $55,000.

(*continued*)

(P 4-16 CONTINUED)

f. Which of the following would be classified as an extraordinary item on the income statement?

1. Loss from tornado
2. Loss on disposal of a segment of business
3. Write-down of inventory
4. Correction of an error of the current period
5. Loss from strike

g. Which of the following is true when a cash dividend is declared and paid?

1. The firm is left with a liability to pay the dividend.
2. Retained earnings is reduced by the amount of the dividend.
3. Retained earnings is increased by the amount of the dividend.
4. Retained earnings is not influenced by the dividend.
5. Stockholders' equity is increased.

h. Which of the following is true when a 10% stock dividend is declared and distributed?

1. Retained earnings is increased.
2. Stockholders' equity is increased.
3. Stockholders' equity is decreased.
4. Authorized shares are increased.
5. The overall effect is to leave stockholders' equity in total and each owner's share of stockholders' equity unchanged; however, the total number of shares increases.

P 4-17

Required Answer the following multiple-choice questions:

a. The following relate to Owens data in 2012. What is the ending inventory?

Purchases	$580,000
Beginning inventory	80,000
Purchase returns	8,000
Sales	900,000
Cost of goods sold	520,000

1. $150,000
2. $132,000
3. $152,000
4. $170,000
5. $142,000

b. Changes in account balances of Gross Flowers during 2012 were as follows:

	Increase
Assets	$400,000
Liabilities	150,000
Capital stock	120,000
Additional paid-in capital	110,000

Assuming there were no charges to retained earnings other than dividends of $20,000, the net income (loss) for 2012 was

1. $(20,000).
2. $(40,000).
3. $20,000.
4. $40,000.
5. $60,000.

c. Which of the following would be classified as an extraordinary item on the income statement?

1. Loss on disposal of a segment of business.
2. Cumulative effect of a change in accounting principle.
3. A sale of fixed assets.
4. An error correction that relates to a prior year.
5. A loss from a flood in a location that would not be expected to flood.

d. Net income–noncontrolling interest comes from which of the following situations?

1. A company has been consolidated with our income statement, and our company owns less than 100% of the other company.
2. A company has been consolidated with our income statement, and our company owns 100% of the other company.
3. Our company owns less than 100% of another company, and the statements are not consolidated.
4. Our company owns 100% of another company, and the statements are not consolidated.
5. None of the above.

e. Which of the following will *not* be disclosed in retained earnings?

1. Declaration of a stock dividend
2. Adjustment for an error of the current period
3. Adjustment for an error of a prior period
4. Net income
5. Net loss

f. Bell Company has 2 million shares of common stock with par of $10. Additional paid-in capital totals $15 million, and retained earnings is $15 million. The directors declare a 5% stock dividend when the market value is $10. The reduction of retained earnings as a result of the declaration will be

2mil × .05 = 100,000 × $10 = 1 mil

1. $0.
2. $1 million.
3. $800,000.
4. $600,000.
5. None of the above.

g. The stockholders' equity of Gaffney Company at November 30, 2012, is presented below.

Common stock, par value $5, authorized 200,000 shares, 100,000 shares issued and outstanding	$500,000
Paid-in capital in excess of par	100,000
Retained earnings	300,000
	$900,000

On December 1, 2012, the board of directors of Gaffney Company declared a 5% stock dividend, to be distributed on December 20. The market price of the common stock was $10 on December 1 and $12 on December 20. What is the amount of the change to retained earnings as a result of the declaration and distribution of this stock dividend?

5% × 100,000 = 5000 × $10 = 50,000

1. $0
2. $40,000
3. $50,000
4. $60,000
5. None of the above.

(*continued*)

(**P 4-17** CONTINUED)

h. Schroeder Company had 200,000 shares of common stock outstanding with a $2 par value and retained earnings of $90,000. In 2010, earnings per share were $0.50. In 2011, the company split the stock 2 for 1. Which of the following would result from the stock split?

1. Retained earnings will decrease as a result of the stock split.
2. A total of 400,000 shares of common stock will be outstanding.
3. The par value would become $4 par.
4. Retained earnings will increase as a result of the stock split.
5. None of the above.

i. Which of the following is *not* a category within accumulated other comprehensive income?

1. Foreign currency translation adjustments.
2. Unrealized holding gains and losses on available-for-sale marketable securities.
3. Changes to stockholders' equity resulting from additional minimum pension liability.
4. Unrealized gains and losses from derivative instruments.
5. Extraordinary item.

Cases

CASE 4-1 HOMEBUILDERS

LENNAR CORPORATION AND SUBSIDIARIES*
CONSOLIDATED STATEMENTS OF OPERATIONS
Years Ended November 30, 2010, 2009 and 2008

	2010	2009	2008
	(Dollars in thousands, except per share amounts)		
Revenues:			
Lennar Homebuilding	$2,705,639	2,834,285	4,263,038
Lennar Financial services	275,786	285,102	312,379
Rialto Investments	92,597	—	—
Total revenues	3,074,022	3,119,387	4,575,417
Costs and expenses:			
Lennar Homebuilding (1)	2,543,323	3,210,386	4,541,881
Lennar Financial services (2)	244,502	249,120	343,369
Rialto Investments	67,904	2,528	—
Corporate general and administrative	93,926	117,565	129,752
Total costs and expenses	2,949,655	3,579,599	5,015,002
Lennar Homebuilding equity in loss from unconsolidated entities (3)	(10,966)	(130,917)	(59,156)
Lennar Homebuilding other income (expense), net (4)	19,135	(98,425)	(172,387)
Other interest expense	(70,245)	(70,850)	(27,594)
Gain on recapitalization of Lennar Homebuilding unconsolidated entity	—	—	133,097
Rialto Investments equity in earnings from unconsolidated entities	15,363	—	—
Rialto Investments other income, net	17,251	—	—
Earnings (loss) before income taxes	94,725	(760,404)	(565,625)
Benefit (provision) for income taxes (5)	25,734	314,345	(547,557)
Net earnings (loss) (including net earnings (loss) attributable to noncontrolling interests)	120,459	(446,059)	(1,113,182)

*"We are one of the nation's largest homebuilders, a provider of financial services and through our Rialto Investments ("Rialto") segment, an investor in distressed real estate assets." 10-K

Source: Lennar Corporation and Subsidiaries Consolidated 2010 10-K

	2010	2009	2008
	(Dollars in thousands, except per share amounts)		
Less: Net earnings (loss) attributable to noncontrolling interests (6)	25,198	(28,912)	(4,097)
Net earnings (loss) attributable to Lennar	$ 95,261	(417,147)	(1,109,085)
Basic earnings (loss) per share	$ 0.51	(2.45)	(7.01)
Diluted earnings (loss) per share	$ 0.51	(2.45)	(7.01)

(1) Lennar Homebuilding costs and expenses include $51.3 million, $373.5 million and $340.5 million, respectively, of valuation adjustments and write-offs of option deposits and pre-acquisition costs for the years ended November 30, 2010, 2009 and 2008.

(2) Lennar Financial Services costs and expenses for the year ended November 30, 2008 include a $27.2 million impairment of goodwill.

(3) Lennar Homebuilding equity in loss from unconsolidated entities includes the Company's share of valuation adjustments related to assets of unconsolidated entities in which the Company has investments of $10.5 million, $101.9 million and $32.2 million, respectively, for the years ended November 30, 2010, 2009 and 2008.

(4) Lennar Homebuilding other income (expense), net includes valuation adjustments to investments in Lennar Homebuilding unconsolidated entities of $1.7 million, $89.0 million and $172.8 million, respectively, for the years ended November 30, 2010, 2009 and 2008.

(5) Benefit (provision) for income taxes for the year ended November 30, 2010 primarily related to settlements with various taxing authorities. For the year ended November 30, 2009, benefit (provision) for income taxes includes a reversal of the Company's deferred tax asset valuation allowance of $351.8 million. For the year ended November 30, 2008, benefit (provision) for income taxes includes a $730.8 million valuation allowance recorded against the Company's deferred tax assets.

(6) Net earnings (loss) attributable to noncontrolling interests for the year ended November 30, 2010 includes $33.2 million related to the FDIC's interest in the portfolio of real estate loans that the Company acquired in partnership with the FDIC. Net earnings (loss) attributable to noncontrolling interests for the year ended November 30, 2009 includes ($13.6) million recorded as a result of $27.2 million of valuation adjustments to inventories of 50%-owned consolidated joint ventures.

Required

a. Would you consider the presentation to be a multiple-step income statement or a single-step income statement? Comment.

b. Does it appear that there is a 100% ownership in all consolidated subsidiaries?

c. If a subsidiary were not consolidated but rather accounted for using the equity method, would this change net earnings (loss)? Explain.

d. Describe equity in loss from unconsolidated entities.

e. Comment on Note 1. Does this note project favorably on the future of Lennar Corporation? Explain.

f. Comment on Note 2. Why take an impairment for goodwill under financial services?

CASE 4-2 COMMUNICATION PRODUCTS

Motorola Solutions, Inc. and Subsidiaries*
Consolidated Statements of Operations

	Years Ended December 31		
(In millions, except per share amounts)	2010	2009	2008
Net sales	$19,282	$18,147	$25,109
Cost of sales	12,384	12,406	18,171
Gross margin	6,898	5,741	6,938
Selling, general and administrative expenses	3,367	3,058	3,912
Research and development expenditures	2,530	2,598	3,399
Other charges	212	577	2,169
Operating earnings (loss)	789	(492)	(2,542)
Other income (expense):			
Interest income (expense), net	(131)	(132)	38
Gains on sales of investments and businesses, net	48	74	76
Other	(29)	47	(425)
Total other income (expense)	(112)	(11)	(311)
Earnings (loss) from continuing operations before income taxes	677	(503)	(2,853)
Income tax expense (benefit)	406	(159)	1,584
Earnings (loss) from continuing operations	271	(344)	(4,437)
Earnings from discontinued operations, net of tax	379	316	197
Net earnings (loss)	650	(28)	(4,240)
Less: Earnings attributable to noncontrolling interests	17	23	4
Net earnings (loss) attributable to Motorola Solutions, Inc.	$ 633	$ (51)	$ (4,244)
Amounts attributable to Motorola Solutions, Inc. common shareholders:			
Earnings (loss) from continuing operations, net of tax	$ 254	$ (367)	$ (4,441)
Earnings from discontinued operations, net of tax	379	316	197
Net earnings (loss)	$ 633	$ (51)	$ (4,244)
Earnings (loss) per common share:			
Basic:			
Continuing operations	$ 0.76	$ (1.12)	$ (13.72)
Discontinued operations	1.14	0.96	0.61
	$ 1.90	$ (0.16)	$ (13.11)
Diluted:			
Continuing operations	$ 0.75	$ (1.12)	$ (13.72)
Discontinued operations	1.12	0.96	0.61
	$ 1.87	$ (0.16)	$ (13.11)
Weighted average common shares outstanding:			
Basic	333.3	327.9	323.6
Diluted	338.1	327.9	323.6
Dividends paid per share	$ —	$ 0.35	$ 1.40

Presentation gives effect to the Reverse Stock Split, which occurred on January 4, 2011.

*"We provide technologies, products, systems and services that make a broad range of mobile experiences possible." 10-K

1. Summary of Significant Accounting Policies (In Part)

Motorola Mobility Separation

On July 1, 2010, an initial registration statement on Form 10 was filed with the U.S. Securities and Exchange Commission ("SEC") in connection with the Company's separation into two independent, publicly traded companies. Amendments to the initial registration

Source: Motorola Solution, Inc. and Subsidiaries Consolidated 2010 10-K

statement were filed on August 31, 2010, October 8, 2010, November 12, 2010 and November 30, 2010. On December 1, 2010, the SEC granted effectiveness to the Form 10.

On January 4, 2011 (the "Distribution Date"), the separation of Motorola Mobility Holdings, Inc. ("Motorola Mobility") from Motorola Solutions (the "Separation") was completed. Motorola Mobility is now an independent public company trading under the symbol "MMI" on the New York Stock Exchange. On January 4, 2011, the stockholders of record as of the close of business on December 21, 2010 (the "Record Date") received one (1) share of Motorola Mobility common stock for each eight (8) shares of Motorola, Inc. common stock held as of the Record Date (the "Distribution"). The Separation was completed pursuant to an Amended and Restated Master Separation and Distribution Agreement, effective as of July 31, 2010, among Motorola, Inc., Motorola Mobility and Motorola Mobility, Inc. All consolidated per share information presented does not give effect to the Distribution.

After the Distribution Date, the Company does not beneficially own any shares of Motorola Mobility common stock and will not consolidate Motorola Mobility financial results for the purpose of its own financial reporting. The financial information presented in this Form 10-K contains the consolidated position of the Company as of December 31, 2010, which includes the results of Motorola Mobility. Beginning in the first quarter of 2011, the historical financial results of Motorola Mobility will be reflected in the Company's consolidated financial statements as discontinued operations.

Changes in Presentation

Reverse Stock Split and Name Change

On November 30, 2010, Motorola Solutions announced the timing and details regarding the Separation and the approval of a reverse stock split at a ratio of 1-for-7. Immediately following the Distribution of Motorola Mobility common stock, the Company completed a 1-for-7 reverse stock split ("the Reverse Stock Split") and changed its name to Motorola Solutions, Inc. All consolidated per share information presented gives effect to the Reverse Stock Split.

Required

a. On January 4, 2011, the stockholders of record as of the close of business on December 21, 2010 (the "Record Date") received one (1) share of Motorola Mobility common stock for each eight (8) shares of Motorola Inc. Describe this distribution.

b. Does the name change?

c. Describe the reverse stock split.

d. Why would they do a reverse split?

CASE 4-3 APPAREL COMPANIES

PERRY ELLIS INTERNATIONAL, INC. AND SUBSIDIARIES*
CONSOLIDATED STATEMENTS OF OPERATIONS
FOR THE YEARS ENDED
(amounts in thousands, except per share data)

	January 29, 2011	January 30, 2010	January 31, 2009
Revenues:			
Net sales	$763,884	$729,217	$825,868
Royalty income	26,404	24,985	25,429
Total revenues	790,288	754,202	851,297
Cost of sales	507,829	505,104	573,046
Gross profit	282,459	249,008	278,251

(continued)

* "We are one of the leading apparel companies in the United States." 10-K
Source: Perry Ellis International, Inc. and Subsidiaries Consolidated 2010 10-K

(**CASE 4-3** CONTINUED)

	January 29, 2011	January 30, 2010	January 31, 2009
Operating expenses			
Selling, general and administrative expenses	220,018	200,356	236,840
Depreciation and amortization	12,211	13,625	14,784
Impairment on long-lived assets	392	254	22,299
Total operating expenses	232,621	214,235	273,923
Operating income	49,838	34,863	4,328
Costs on early extinguishment of debt	730	357	—
Impairment on marketable securities	—	—	2,797
Interest expense	13,203	17,371	17,491
Net income (loss) before income taxes	35,905	17,135	(15,960)
Income tax provision (benefit)	11,393	3,615	(3,682)
Net income (loss)	$ 24,512	$ 13,520	$ (12,278)
Less: Net income attributed to noncontrolling interest	400	353	612
Net income (loss) attributed to Perry Ellis International, Inc.	$ 24,112	$ 13,167	$ (12,890)
Net income (loss) attributed to Perry Ellis International, Inc. per share:			
Basic	$ 1.84	$ 1.04	$ (0.89)
Diluted	$ 1.70	$ 1.01	$ (0.89)
Weighted average number of shares outstanding			
Basic	13,110	12,699	14,416
Diluted	14,149	13,005	14.416

PERRY ELLIS INTERNATIONAL, INC. AND SUBSIDIARIES
FOOTNOTES TO CONSOLIDATED FINANCIAL STATEMENTS (In Part)
FOR THE YEARS ENDED JANUARY 29, 2011, JANUARY 30, 2010 AND
JANUARY 31, 2009

2. Summary of Significant Accounting Policies (In Part)

The following is a summary of the Company's significant accounting policies:

PRINCIPLES OF CONSOLIDATION – The consolidated financial statements include the accounts of Perry Ellis International, Inc. and its wholly-owned and controlled subsidiaries. All intercompany transactions and balances have been eliminated in consolidation. The ownership interest in consolidated subsidiaries of non-controlling shareholders is reflected as noncontrolling interest. The Company's consolidation principles would also consolidate any entity in which the Company would be deemed a primary beneficiary.

USE OF ESTIMATES — The preparation of financial statements in conformity with accounting principles generally accepted in the United States of America requires management to make estimates and assumptions that affect the amounts in the consolidated financial statements and the accompanying footnotes. Actual results could differ from those estimates.

Required

a. 1. Comment on the principles of consolidation.

   2. Does it appear that there is a 100% ownership in all consolidated subsidiaries?

b. Comment on the use of estimates.

c. Would you expect an impairment in marketable securities?

d. What type of "special item" would be "costs on early extinguishment debt"?

CASE 4-4 THE BIG ORDER

On October 15, 1990, United Airlines (UAL Corporation) placed the largest wide-body air-craft order in commercial aviation history—60 Boeing 747-400s and 68 Boeing 777s—with an estimated value of $22 billion. With this order, United became the launch customer for the B777. This order was equally split between firm orders and options.

Required

a. Comment on when United Airlines should record the purchase of these planes.

b. Comment on when Boeing should record the revenue from selling these planes.

c. Speculate on how firm the commitment was on the part of United Airlines to accept delivery of these planes.

d. 1. Speculate on the disclosure for this order in the 1990 financial statements and notes of United Airlines.

   2. Speculate on the disclosure for this order in the 1990 annual report of United Airlines. (Exclude the financial statements and notes.)

e. 1. Speculate on the disclosure for this order in the 1990 financial statements and notes of Boeing.

   2. Speculate on the disclosure for this order in the 1990 annual report of Boeing. (Exclude the financial statements and notes.)

CASE 4-5 CELTICS

Boston Celtics Limited Partnership II and Subsidiaries presented the following consolidated statements of income for 1998, 1997, and 1996.

BOSTON CELTICS LIMITED PARTNERSHIP II AND SUBSIDIARIES
CONSOLIDATED STATEMENTS OF INCOME

	For the Year Ended		
	June 30, 1998	June 30, 1997	June 30, 1996
Revenues:			
Basketball regular season	$39,107,960	$31,813,019	$35,249,625
Ticket sales	28,002,469	23,269,159	22,071,992
Television and radio broadcast rights fees	8,569,485	7,915,626	7,458,651
Other, principally promotional advertising	75,679,914	62,997,804	64,780,268
Costs and expenses:			
Basketball regular season			
Team	40,401,643	40,941,156	27,891,264
Game	2,820,107	2,386,042	2,606,218
General and administrative	13,464,566	13,913,893	15,053,333
Selling and promotional	4,819,478	4,680,168	2,973,488
Depreciation	208,162	189,324	140,894
Amortization of NBA franchise and other intangible assets	165,035	164,702	164,703
	61,878,991	62,275,285	48,829,900
	13,800,923	722,519	15,950,368
Interest expense	(6,017,737)	(5,872,805)	(6,387,598)
Interest income	6,402,366	6,609,541	8,175,184
Net realized gains (losses) on disposition of marketable securities and other short-term investments	(18,235)	361,051	(101,138)
Income from continuing operations before income taxes	14,167,317	1,820,306	17,636,816
Provision for income taxes	1,900,000	1,400,000	1,850,000
Income from continuing operations	12,267,317	420,306	15,786,816

(*continued*)

Source: Boston Celtics Limited Partnership II and Subsidiaries 2010 10-K

(**CASE 4-5** CONTINUED)

	For the Year Ended		
	June 30, 1998	June 30, 1997	June 30, 1996
Discontinued operations:			
Income from discontinued operations (less applicable income taxes of $30,000)			82,806
Gain from disposal of discontinued operations (less applicable income taxes of $17,770,000)			38,330,907
NET INCOME	12,267,317	420,306	54,200,529
Net income applicable to interests of General Partners	306,216	62,246	1,291,014
Net income applicable to interests of Limited Partners	$11,961,101	$ 358,060	$52,909,515
Per unit:			
Income from continuing operations—basic	$ 2.45	$ 0.07	$ 2.68
Income from continuing operations—diluted	$ 2.17	$ 0.06	$ 2.59
Net income—basic	$ 2.45	$ 0.07	$ 9.18
Net income—diluted	$ 2.17	$ 0.06	$ 8.89
Distributions declared	$ 2.00	$ 1.00	$ 1.50

Required

a. Comment on Amortization of NBA Franchise and Other Intangible Assets.

b. Would the discontinued operations be included in projecting the future? Comment.

c. The costs and expenses include team costs and expenses. Speculate on the major reason for the increase in this expense between 1996 and 1997.

d. What were the major reasons for the increase in income from continuing operations between 1997 and 1998?

e. Speculate on why distributions declared were higher in 1998 than 1996. (Notice that net income was substantially higher in 1996.)

CASE 4-6 HOMEBUILDING

D.R. HORTON, INC. AND SUBSIDIARIES*
CONSOLIDATED STATEMENTS OF OPERATIONS

	Year Ended September 30,		
	2010	2009	2008
	(In millions, except per share data)		
Homebuilding:			
Revenues:			
Home sales	$4,302.3	$3,563.6	$ 6,164.3
Land/lot sales	7.4	40.3	354.3
	4,309.7	3,603.9	6,518.6
Cost of sales:			
Home sales	3,558.3	3,096.1	5,473.1
Land/lot sales	4.6	34.9	324.2
Inventory impairments and land option cost write-offs	64.7	407.7	2,484.5
	3,627.6	3,538.7	8,281.8
Gross profit (loss):			
Home sales	744.0	467.5	691.2
Land/lot sales	2.8	5.4	30.1
Inventory impairments and land option cost write-offs	(64.7)	(407.7)	(2,484.5)
	682.1	65.2	(1,763.2)
Selling, general and administrative expense	522.0	523.0	791.8
Goodwill impairment	—	—	79.4

*"D.R. Horton, Inc. is one of the largest homebuilding companies in the United States." 10-K
Note: Net cash provided by operating activities, 2010 $709,400,000; 2009 $1,141,200,000; 2008 $1,876,500,000

	Year Ended September 30,		
	2010	2009	2008
	(In millions, except per share data)		
Interest expense	86.3	100.2	39.0
Loss (gain) on early retirement of debt, net	4.9	(3.9)	2.6
Other (income)	(9.2)	(12.8)	(9.1)
	78.1	(541.3)	(2,666.9)
Financial Services:			
Revenues, net of recourse and reinsurance expense	90.5	53.7	127.5
General and administrative expense	77.2	78.1	100.1
Interest expense	1.9	1.5	3.7
Interest and other (income)	(10.0)	(10.4)	(11.4)
	21.4	(15.5)	35.1
Income (loss) before income taxes	99.5	(556.8)	(2,631.8)
(Benefit from) provision for income taxes	(145.6)	(7.0)	1.8
Net income (loss)	$ 245.1	$ (549.8)	$(2,633.6)
Basic net income (loss) per common share	$ 0.77	$ (1.73)	$ (8.34)
Net income (loss) per common share assuming dilution	$ 0.77	$ (1.73)	$ (8.34)
Cash dividends declared per common share	$ 0.15	$ 0.15	$ 0.45

D.R. HORTON, INC. AND SUBSIDIARIES
Notes to Consolidated Financial Statements (In Part)

Note A – Summary of Significant Accounting Policies (In Part)

Inventories and Cost of Sales (In part)

For those assets deemed to be impaired, the impairment to be recognized is measured as the amount by which the carrying amount of the assets exceeds the fair value of the assets. The Company's determination of fair value is primarily based on discounting the estimated cash flows at a rate commensurate with the inherent risks associated with the assets and related estimated cash flow streams. When an impairment charge for a community is determined, the charge is then allocated to each lot in the community in the same manner land and development costs are allocated to each lot. The inventory within each community is categorized as construction in progress and finished homes, residential land and lots developed and under development, and land held for development, based on the stage of production or plans for future development.

The Company typically does not purchase land for resale. However, when the Company owns land or communities under development that no longer fit into its development and construction plans and it is determined that the best use of the asset is the sale of the asset, the project is accounted for as land held for sale, assuming the land held for sale criteria are met. The Company records land held for sale at the lesser of its carrying value or fair value less estimated costs to sell. In performing impairment evaluation for land held for sale, several factors are considered including, but not limited to, prices for land in recent comparable sales transactions, market analysis studies, which include the estimated price a willing buyer would pay for the land and recent legitimate offers received. If the estimated fair value less costs to sell an asset is less than the current carrying value, the asset is written down to its estimated fair value less costs to sell.

Impairment charges are also recorded on finished homes in substantially completed communities when events or circumstances indicate that the carrying values are greater than the fair values less estimated costs to sell these homes. The key assumptions relating to the valuations are impacted by local market economic conditions and the actions of competitors, and are inherently uncertain. Due to uncertainties in the estimation process, actual results could differ from such estimates. The Company's quarterly assessments reflect management's

(continued)

(**CASE 4-6** CONTINUED)

estimates and it continues to monitor the fair value of held-for-sale assets through the disposition date. See Note D.

Goodwill

Goodwill represents the excess of purchase price over net assets acquired. The Company tests goodwill for potential impairment annually as of September 30, or more frequently if an event occurs or circumstances change that indicate the remaining balance of goodwill may not be recoverable. In analyzing the potential impairment of goodwill, a two-step process is utilized that begins with the estimation of the fair value of the operating segments. If the results of the first step indicate that impairment potentially exists, the second step is performed to measure the amount of the impairment, if any. Impairment is determined to exist when the estimated fair value of goodwill is less than its carrying value.

In performing its goodwill impairment analysis, the Company estimates the fair value of its operating segments utilizing the present values of expected future cash flows. As a result of the analyses performed as of September 30, 2010 and 2009, it was determined that the fair value of the operating segments was greater than their carrying value and therefore, no impairment of goodwill existed. As a result of the analysis performed as of September 30, 2008, the Company recorded a goodwill impairment charge of $79.4 million, all of which related to its Southwest reporting segment. Combined with previous impairments, accumulated goodwill impairment losses at September 30, 2010 and 2009 totaled $553.5 million. As of September 30, 2010 and 2009, the Company's remaining goodwill balance was $15.9 million, all of which related to its South Central reporting segment. The goodwill assessment procedures require management to make comprehensive estimates of future revenues and costs.

Required

a. Does it appear that inventories are a highly liquid asset?

b. Goodwill impairment – what does this imply?

c. Why have early retirement of debt?

CASE 4-7 TELECOMMUNICATIONS – PART 2

China Unicom (Hong Kong) Limited provides a full range of telecommunications services, including mobile and fixed line service, in China.

They are listed on the New York Stock Exchange and filed a Form 20-F with the SEC for the period ended December 31, 2010. The consolidated income statement is presented with this case.

CHINA UNICOM (HONG KONG) LIMITED
CONSOLIDATED STATEMENTS OF INCOME
FOR THE YEARS ENDED DECEMBER 31, 2008, 2009 AND 2010
(All amounts in RMB millions, except per share data)

		Year ended December 31			
	Note	2008	2009	2010	2010
		RMB	RMB	RMB	US$
Continuing operations					
Revenue	5, 28, 40	159,792	153,945	171,298	25,954
Interconnection charges		(13,038)	(12,955)	(13,727)	(2,082)
Depreciation and amortization		(51,847)	(47,587)	(54,433)	(8,247)
Networks, operations and support expenses	29, 43	(18,736)	(23,728)	(26,383)	(3,997)
Employee benefit expenses	30	(20,758)	(21,931)	(23,327)	(3,534)
Other operating expenses	31	(37,997)	(36,723)	(48,269)	(7,313)
Finance costs	32	(3,269)	(1,036)	(1,749)	(265)
Interest income		265	91	142	22
Impairment loss on property, plant and equipment	6	(12,494)	—	—	—

Source: China Unicom Limited 2010 10-K

	Note	Year ended December 31			
		2008	2009	2010	2010
		RMB	RMB	RMB	US$
Realized loss on changes in fair value of derivative component of the convertible bonds	33	—	1,239	—	—
Other income – net	34	2,141	962	1,221	185
Income from continuing operations before income tax		4,059	12,277	4,773	723
Income tax expenses	9	(1,828)	(2,721)	(922)	(140)
Income from continuing operations		2,231	9,556	3,851	583
Discontinued operations					
Income from discontinued operations	36	1,438	—	—	—
Gain on the disposal of discontinued operations	36	26,135	—	—	—
Net income		29,804	9,556	3,851	583
Attributable to:					
Owners of the parent		29,804	9,556	3,851	583
Non-controlling interests		—	—	—	—
		29,804	9,556	3,851	583

Required

a. Consolidated income statement
   1. Why presented in RMB and U.S. $?
   2. Contrast note reference with U.S. GAAP.
   3. Comment on the presentation relating net income to "attributable to."

WEB CASE THOMSON ONE *Business School Edition*

Please complete the Web case that covers material discussed in this chapter at www.cengagebrain.com. You'll be using Thomson ONE Business School Edition, a powerful tool that combines a full range of fundamental financial information, earnings estimates, market data, and source documents for 500 publicly traded companies.

 TO THE NET CASE

1. Go to the SEC site (www.sec.gov). Under "Filings & Forms" click on "Search for Company Filings." Click on "Company or fund, etc." Under Company Name, enter "Freeport-McMoran Copper & Gold Inc." (or under Ticker Symbol, enter "FCX"). Select the 10-K filed February 25, 2011.
   a. What is the amount of net income attributable to noncontrolling interests for 2010?
   b. What is the equity in affiliated companies net earnings for 2010?
   c. Describe equity earnings.
2. Go to the SEC site (www.sec.gov). Under "Filings & Forms," click on "Search for Company Filings." Click on "Company or fund, etc." Under Company Name, enter "Amazon.com Inc." (or under Ticker Symbol, enter "AMZN"). Select the 10-K filed January 28, 2011.
   a. What were the net sales for 2010, 2009 and 2008?
   b. What were the income from operations for 2010, 2009 and 2008?
   c. What were the interest expenses for 2010, 2009 and 2008?
   d. What were the diluted earnings per share for 2010, 2009 and 2008?
   e. Comment considering the data in (a), (b), (c) and (d).

(continued)

(**To the Net** CONTINUED)

3. Go to the SEC site (www.sec.gov). Under "Filings & Forms," click on "Search for Company Filings." Click on "Company or fund, etc." Under Company Name, enter "Alexander & Baldwin, Inc." (or under Ticker Symbol, enter "ALEX"). Select the 10-K filed February 25, 2011.

   a. Determine the business industries of Alexander Baldwin.

   b. Determine the total operating revenue for 2010, 2009 and 2008.

   c. Determine the operating income for 2010, 2009 and 2008.

   d. Comment on the trends in (b) and (c) considering the description of the company in (a).

   e. Determine income from discontinued operations, net of income taxes for 2010, 2009 and 2008.

   f. Comment on how material is income from discontinued operations in relation to net income.

4. Go to the SEC site (www.sec.gov). Under "Filings & Forms," click on "Search for Company Filings." Click of "Company or fund, etc." Under Company Name, enter "Kroger Co." (or under Ticker Symbol, enter "KR"). Select the 10-K filed March 29, 2011.

   a. What is the goodwill account on the balance sheet?

   b. What is the balance on goodwill at January 29, 2011 and January 30, 2010?

   c. Determine the goodwill impairment charge for 2010, 2009 and 2008?

   d. Determine the details for the impairment charge in 2009. Why the change?

   e. Why is the goodwill impairment charge an adjustment to reconcile net earnings to net cash provided by operating activities?

5. Go to the SEC site (www.sec.gov). Under "Filings & Forms," click on "Search for Company Filings." Click on "Company or fund, etc."

   This exercise will review the presentation format for two companies and how they present comprehensive income.

   Firm #1 "Occidental Petroleum Corporation" (or under Ticker Symbol, enter "OXY"). Select the 10-K filed February 24, 2011

   a. Indicate the format presentation selected by Occidental Petroleum Corporation.
      Firm #2 "Arden Group, Inc." (or under Ticker Symbol, enter "ARDNA"). Select the 10-K filed March 10, 2011

   b. Indicate the format presentation selected by Arden Group, Inc.

   c. Which of these two formats presentations is the best for the user of the statement?

Endnotes

1. *Accounting Trends & Techniques* (New York: American Institute of Certified Public Accountants, 2008), p. 311.

2. Michael L. Roberts, William D. Samson, and Michael T. Dugan, "The Stockholders' Equity Section: Form without Substance," *Accounting Horizon* (December 1990), pp. 35–46.

3. Ibid., p. 36.

Basics of Analysis

The analysis of financial data employs various techniques to emphasize the comparative and relative importance of the data presented and to evaluate the position of the firm. These techniques include ratio analysis, common-size analysis, study of differences in components of financial statements among industries, review of descriptive material, and comparisons of results with other types of data. The information derived from these types of analysis should be blended to determine the overall financial position. No one type of analysis supports overall findings or serves all types of users. This chapter provides an introduction to different analyses and uses of financial information.

Financial statement analysis is a judgmental process. One of the primary objectives is identification of major changes (turning points) in trends, amounts, and relationships and investigation of the reasons underlying those changes. Often, a turning point may signal an early warning of a significant shift in the future success or failure of the business. The judgment process can be improved by experience and by use of analytical tools.

Ratio Analysis

Financial ratios are usually expressed as a percent or as times per period. The following ratios will be discussed fully in future chapters.

1. Liquidity ratios measure a firm's ability to meet its current obligations. They may include ratios that measure the efficiency of the use of current assets and current liabilities (Chapter 6).
2. Borrowing capacity (leverage) ratios measure the degree of protection of suppliers of long-term funds (Chapter 7).
3. Profitability ratios measure the earning ability of a firm. Discussion will include measures of the use of assets in general (Chapter 8).
4. Investors are interested in a special group of ratios, in addition to liquidity, debt, and profitability ratios (Chapter 9).
5. Cash flow ratios can indicate liquidity, borrowing capacity, or profitability (Chapter 10).

A ratio can be computed from any pair of numbers. Given the large quantity of variables included in financial statements, a very long list of meaningful ratios can be derived. A standard list of ratios or standard computation of them does not exist. Each author and source on financial analysis uses a different list and often a different computation of the same ratio. This book presents frequently utilized and discussed ratios.

Ratios are interpretable in comparison with (1) prior ratios, (2) ratios of competitors, (3) industry ratios, and (4) predetermined standards. The trend of a ratio and the variability of a ratio are important considerations.

Comparison of income statement and balance sheet numbers, in the form of ratios, can create difficulties due to the timing of the financial statements. Specifically, the income statement covers the entire fiscal period; whereas the balance sheet applies to a single point in time, the end of the period. Ideally, then, to compare an income statement figure such as sales to a balance sheet figure such as receivables, we need to know the average receivables for the year that the sales figure covers. However, these data are not available to the external analyst. In some cases, the analyst uses an average of the beginning and ending balance sheet figures. This approach smooths out changes from beginning to end, but it does not eliminate problems due to seasonal and cyclical changes. It also does not reflect changes that occur unevenly throughout the year.

Be aware that computing averages from two similar balance sheet dates can be misleading. It is possible that a representative average cannot be computed from externally published statements.

A ratio will usually represent a fairly accurate trend, even when the ratio is distorted. If the ratio is distorted, then it does not represent a good absolute number.

Applying the U.S. techniques of ratio analysis to statements prepared in other countries can be misleading. The ratio analysis must be understood in terms of the accounting principles used and the business practices and culture of the country.

Common-Size Analysis (Vertical and Horizontal)

Common-size analysis expresses comparisons in percentages. For example, if cash is $40,000 and total assets is $1 million, then cash represents 4% of total assets. The use of percentages is usually preferable to the use of absolute amounts. An illustration will make this clear. If Firm A earns $10,000 and Firm B earns $1,000, which is more profitable? Firm A is probably your response. However, the total owners' equity of A is $1 million, and B's is $10,000. The return on owners' equity is as follows:

	Firm A	Firm B
$\dfrac{\text{Earnings}}{\text{Owners' Equity}}$	$\dfrac{\$10,000}{\$1,000,000} = 1\%$	$\dfrac{\$1,000}{\$10,000} = 10\%$

The use of common-size analysis makes comparisons of firms of different sizes much more meaningful. Care must be exercised in the use of common-size analysis with small absolute amounts because a small change in amount can result in a very substantial percentage change. For example, if profits last year amounted to $100 and increased this year to $500, this would be an increase of only $400 in profits, but it would represent a substantial percentage increase.

Vertical analysis compares each amount with a base amount selected from the same year. For example, if advertising expenses were $1,000 in 2011 and sales were $100,000, the advertising would have been 1% of sales.

Horizontal analysis compares each amount with a base amount for a selected base year. For example, if sales were $400,000 in 2010 and $600,000 in 2011, then sales increased to 150% of the 2010 level in 2011, an increase of 50%.

Exhibit 5-1 illustrates common-size analysis (vertical and horizontal).

| EXHIBIT **5-1** | Melcher Company |

Income Statement

Illustration of Common-Size Analysis (Vertical and Horizontal)

	For the Years Ended December 31,		
(Absolute dollars)	2011	2010	2009
Revenue from sales	$100,000	$95,000	$91,000
Cost of products sold	65,000	60,800	56,420
Gross profit	35,000	34,200	34,580
Operating expenses			
Selling expenses	14,000	11,400	10,000
General expenses	16,000	15,200	13,650
Total operating expenses	30,000	26,600	23,650
Operating income before income taxes	5,000	7,600	10,930
Taxes related to operations	1,500	2,280	3,279
Net income	$ 3,500	$ 5,320	$ 7,651
Vertical Common Size			
Revenue from sales	100.0%	100.0%	100.0%
Cost of goods sold	65.0	64.0	62.0
Gross profit	35.0	36.0	38.0
Operating expenses			
Selling expenses	14.0	12.0	11.0
General expenses	16.0	16.0	15.0
Total operating expenses	30.0	28.0	26.0
Operating income before income taxes	5.0	8.0	12.0
Taxes related to operations	1.5	2.4	3.6
Net income	3.5%	5.6%	8.4%
Horizontal Common Size			
Revenue from sales	109.9%	104.4%	100.0%
Cost of goods sold	115.2	107.8	100.0
Gross profit	101.2	98.9	100.0
Operating expenses			
Selling expenses	140.0	114.0	100.0
General expenses	117.2	111.4	100.0
Total operating expenses	126.8	112.5	100.0
Operating income before income taxes	45.7	69.5	100.0
Taxes related to operations	45.7	69.5	100.0
Net income	45.7	69.5	100.0

Year-to-Year Change Analysis

Comparing financial statements over two time periods using absolute amounts and percentages can be meaningful. This approach aids in keeping absolute and percentage changes in perspective. For example, a substantial percentage change may not be relevant because of an immaterial absolute change. When performing year-to-year change analysis, follow these rules:

1. When an item has value in the base year and none in the next period, the decrease is 100%.
2. A meaningful percent change cannot be computed when one number is positive and the other number is negative.
3. No percent change is computable when there is no figure for the base year.

These rules are illustrated in Exhibit 5-2.

EXHIBIT **5-2**	Year-To-Year Change Analysis			

Illustrating Rules

Item	Year 1	Year 2	Change Analysis Amount	Percent
Advertising expense	$20,000	$ —	$(20,000)	(100%)
Operating income	6,000	(3,000)	(9,000)	—
Net income	(7,000)	8,000	15,000	—
Other	—	4,000	4,000	—

Financial Statement Variation by Type of Industry

The components of financial statements, especially the balance sheet and the income statement, will vary by type of industry. Exhibits 5-3, 5-4, and 5-5 illustrate, respectively, a merchandising firm (Best Buy Co., Inc.), a service firm (Kelly Services, Inc., and Subsidiaries), and a manufacturing firm (Cooper Tire & Rubber Company).

EXHIBIT **5-3**	Best Buy Co., Inc.*

Merchandising Firm

Consolidated Balance Sheets
$ in millions, except per share and share amounts

	February 26, 2011	February 27, 2010
ASSETS		
Current Assets		
Cash and cash equivalents	$ 1,103	$ 1,826
Short-term investments	22	90
Receivables	2,348	2,020
Merchandise inventories	5,897	5,486
Other current assets	1,103	1,144
Total current assets	10,473	10,566
Property and Equipment		
Land and buildings	766	757
Leasehold improvements	2,318	2,154
Fixtures and equipment	4,701	4,447
Property under capital lease	120	95
	7,905	7,453
Less accumulated depreciation	4,082	3,383
Net property and equipment	3,823	4,070
Goodwill	2,454	2,452
Tradenames, Net	133	159
Customer Relationships, Net	203	279
Equity and Other Investments	328	324
Other Assets	435	452
Total Assets	$17,849	$18,302
LIABILITIES AND EQUITY		
Current Liabilities		
Accounts payable	$ 4,894	$ 5,276

*"We are a multinational retailer of consumer electronics, home office products, entertainment products, appliances and related services." 10-K
Source: Best Buy Co., Inc. 2010 10-K

EXHIBIT **5-3**	Best Buy Co., Inc. (*continued*)

	February 26, 2011	February 27, 2010
Unredeemed gift card liabilities	474	463
Accrued compensation and related expenses	570	544
Accrued liabilities	1,471	1,681
Accrued income taxes	256	316
Short-term debt	557	663
Current portion of long-term debt	441	35
Total current liabilities	8,663	8,978
Long-Term Liabilities	1,183	1,256
Long-Term Debt	711	1,104
Equity		
Best Buy Co., Inc. Shareholders' Equity		
Preferred stock, $1.00 par value: Authorized— 400,000 shares; Issued and outstanding—none	—	—
Common stock, $0.10 par value: Authorized— 1.0 billion shares; Issued and outstanding— 392,590,000 and 418,815,000 shares, respectively	39	42
Additional paid-in capital	18	441
Retained earnings	6,372	5,797
Accumulated other comprehensive income	173	40
Total Best Buy Co., Inc. shareholders' equity	6,602	6,320
Noncontrolling interests	690	644
Total equity	7,292	6,964
Total Liabilities and Equity	$17,849	$18,302

Consolidated Statements of Earnings
$ in millions, except per share amounts

Fiscal Years Ended	February 26, 2011	February 27, 2010	February 28, 2009
Revenue	$50,272	$49,694	$45,015
Cost of goods sold	37,611	37,534	34,017
Restructuring charges – cost of goods sold	24	—	—
Gross profit	12,637	12,160	10,998
Selling, general and administrative expenses	10,325	9,873	8,984
Restructuring charges	198	52	78
Goodwill and tradename impairment	—	—	66
Operating income	2,114	2,235	1,870
Other income (expense)			
Investment income and other	51	54	35
Investment impairment	—	—	(111)
Interest expense	(87)	(94)	(94)
Earnings before income tax expense and equity in income of affiliates	2,078	2,195	1,700
Income tax expense	714	802	674
Equity in income of affiliates	2	1	7
Net earnings including noncontrolling interests	1,366	$ 1,394	$ 1,033
Net earnings attributable to noncontrolling interests	(89)	(77)	(30)
Net earnings attributable to Best Buy Co., Inc.	$ 1,277	$ 1,317	$ 1,003
Earnings per share attributable to Best Buy Co., Inc.			
Basic	$ 3.14	$ 3.16	$ 2.43
Diluted	$ 3.08	$ 3.10	$ 2.39
Weighted-average common shares outstanding (in millions)			
Basic	406.1	416.8	412.5
Diluted	416.5	427.5	422.9

EXHIBIT **5-4**	Kelly Services, Inc. and Subsidiaries*

Service Firm

CONSOLIDATED BALANCE SHEETS
Kelly Services, Inc. and Subsidiaries

	2010	2009
	(In millions of dollars)	
ASSETS		
Current Assets		
Cash and equivalents	$ 80.5	$ 88.9
Trade accounts receivable, less allowances of $12.3 million and $15.0 million, respectively	810.9	717.9
Prepaid expenses and other current assets	44.8	70.6
Deferred taxes	22.4	21.0
Total current assets	958.6	898.4
Property and Equipment		
Land and buildings	59.0	58.8
Computer hardware, software and other	260.3	264.0
Accumulated depreciation	(215.3)	(195.7)
Net property and equipment	104.0	127.1
Noncurrent Deferred Taxes	84.0	77.5
Goodwill, net	67.3	67.3
Other Assets	154.5	142.2
Total Assets	$1,368.4	$1,312.5
LIABILITIES AND STOCKHOLDERS' EQUITY		
Current Liabilities		
Short-term borrowings and current portion of long-term debt	$78.8	$79.6
Accounts payable and accrued liabilities	181.6	182.6
Accrued payroll and related taxes	243.3	208.3
Accrued insurance	31.3	22.9
Income and other taxes	56.0	47.4
Total current liabilities	591.0	540.8
Noncurrent Liabilities		
Long-term debt	—	57.5
Accrued insurance	53.6	54.9
Accrued retirement benefits	85.4	76.9
Other long-term liabilities	14.6	16.0
Total noncurrent liabilities	153.6	205.3
Stockholders' Equity		
Capital stock, $1.00 par value		
Class A common stock, shares issued 36.6 million at 2010 and 2009	36.6	36.6
Class B common stock, shares issued 3.5 million at 2010 and 2009	3.5	3.5
Treasury stock, at cost		
Class A common stock, 3.4 million shares at 2010 and 5.1 million at 2009	(70.3)	(106.6)
Class B common stock	(0.6)	(0.6)
Paid-in capital	28.0	36.9
Earnings invested in the business	597.6	571.5
Accumulated other comprehensive income	29.0	25.1
Total stockholders' equity	623.8	566.4
Total Liabilities and Stockholders' Equity	$1,368.4	$1,312.5

*"We have evolved from a United States-based company concentrating primarily on traditional office staffing into a global workforce solutions leader with a breadth of specialty businesses." 10-K

Source: Kelly Services, Inc. and Subsidiaries 2010 10-K

| EXHIBIT **5-4** | Kelly Services, Inc. and Subsidiaries (*continued*) |

CONSOLIDATED STATEMENTS OF EARNINGS
Kelly Services, Inc. and Subsidiaries

	2010	2009[1]	2008
	(In millions of dollars except per share items)		
Revenue from services	$4,950.3	$4,314.8	$5,517.3
Cost of services	4,155.8	3,613.1	4,539.7
Gross profit	794.5	701.7	977.6
Selling, general and administrative expenses	754.4	794.7	967.4
Asset impairments	2.0	53.1	80.5
Earnings (loss) from operations	38.1	(146.1)	(70.3)
Other expense, net	(5.4)	(2.2)	(3.4)
Earnings (loss) from continuing operations			
before taxes	32.7	(148.3)	(73.7)
Income taxes	6.6	(43.2)	8.0
Earnings (loss) from continuing operations	26.1	(105.1)	(81.7)
Earnings (loss) from discontinued operations,			
net of tax	—	0.6	(0.5)
Net earnings (loss)	$ 26.1	$ (104.5)	$ (82.2)
Basic earnings (loss) per share			
Earnings (loss) from continuing operations	$ 0.71	$ (3.01)	$ (2.35)
Earnings (loss) from discontinued operations	—	0.02	(0.02)
Net earnings (loss)	$ 0.71	$ (3.00)	$ (2.37)
Diluted (loss) earnings per share			
Earnings (loss) from continuing operations	$ 0.71	$ (3.01)	$ (2.35)
Earnings (loss) from discontinued operations	—	0.02	(0.02)
Net (loss) earnings	$ 0.71	$ (3.00)	$ (2.37)
Dividends per share	$ —	$ —	$ 0.54
Average shares outstanding (millions):			
Basic	36.1	34.9	34.8
Diluted	36.1	34.9	34.8

[1]Fiscal year includes 53 weeks.

Merchandising (retail-wholesale) firms sell products purchased from other firms. A principal asset is inventory, which consists of merchandise inventories. For some merchandising firms, a large amount of sales may be for cash. In such cases, the receivables balance will be relatively low. Other merchandising firms have a large amount of sales charged but also accept credit cards such as VISA, so they also have a relatively low balance in receivables. Other firms extend credit and carry the accounts receivable and thus have a relatively large receivables balance. Because of the competitive nature of the industry, profit ratios on the income statement are often quite low, with the cost of sales and operating expenses constituting a large portion of expenses. Refer to Exhibit 5-3, Best Buy Co., Inc.

A service firm generates its revenue from the service provided. Because service cannot typically be stored, inventory is low or nonexistent. In people-intensive services, such as advertising, investment in property and equipment is also low compared with that of manufacturing firms. Refer to Exhibit 5-4, Kelly Services, Inc., and Subsidiaries.

A manufacturing firm will usually have large inventories composed of raw materials, work in process, and finished goods, as well as a material investment in property, plant, and equipment. Notes and accounts receivable may also be material, depending on the terms of sale. The cost of sales often represents the major expense. Refer to Exhibit 5-5, Cooper Tire & Rubber Company.

EXHIBIT **5-5**	Cooper Tire & Rubber Company*

Manufacturing Firm

CONSOLIDATED BALANCE SHEETS
December 31
(Dollar amounts in thousands)

	2009	2010
ASSETS		
Current Assets:		
Cash and cash equivalents	$ 426,981	$ 413,359
Notes receivable	42,599	69,547
Accounts receivable, less allowances of $10,928 in 2009		
and $10,811 in 2010	324,424	414,149
Inventories at lower of cost or market:		
Finished goods	188,323	240,107
Work in progress	22,090	26,735
Raw materials and supplies	88,022	119,985
	298,435	386,827
Other current assets	39,392	56,357
Total current assets	1,131,831	1,340,239
Property, plant and equipment:		
Land and land improvements	33,321	34,355
Buildings	320,021	320,997
Machinery and equipment	1,587,306	1,636,700
Molds, cores and rings	246,395	232,153
	2,187,043	2,224,205
Less accumulated depreciation and amortization	1,336,073	1,371,763
Net property, plant and equipment	850,971	852,442
Intangibles, net of accumulated amortization of $23,165 in 2009		
and $24,455 in 2010	18,546	17,256
Restricted cash	2,219	2,274
Other assets	96,773	93,326
Total assets[1]	$2,100,340	$2,305,537

[1]Assets of consolidated variable interest entities (VIEs) were $204,995 and $204,535 at December 31, 2009 and December 31, 2010, respectively. The assets (principally Property, plant and equipment) of the VIEs can only be used to settle obligations of those VIEs.

	2009	2010
LIABILITIES AND EQUITY		
Current Liabilities:		
Notes payable	$ 156,719	$ 146,947
Accounts payable	300,448	384,464
Accrued liabilities	158,643	152,364
Income taxes	3,955	4,601
Liabilities related to the sale of automotive operations	1,061	——
Current portion of long-term debt	15,515	5,885
Total current liabilities	636,341	694,261
Long-term debt	330,971	320,724
Postretirement benefits other than pensions	244,905	257,657
Pension benefits	272,050	258,321
Other long-term liabilities	145,978	180,082
Long-term liabilities related to the sale of automotive operations	6,043	——
Redeemable noncontrolling shareholders' interests	83,528	71,442
Equity:		
Preferred stock, $1 par value; 5,000,000 shares authorized;		
none issued	——	——

*"Cooper Tire & Rubber Company with its affiliates and subsidiaries ("Cooper" or the "Company") is a leading manufacturer and marketer of replacement tires." 10-K

Source: Cooper Tire & Rubber Company 2010 10-K

EXHIBIT **5-5**	Cooper Tire & Rubber Company (*continued*)		

		2009	2010
Common stock, $1 par value; 300,000,000 shares authorized; 87,850,292 shares issued in 2009 and 2010		87,850	87,850
Capital in excess of par value		70,645	61,444
Retained earnings		1,133,133	1,247,265
Cumulative other comprehensive loss		(470,272)	(468,063)
		821,356	928,496
Less: common shares in treasury at cost (27,327,646 in 2009 and 26,205,336 in 2010)		(490,548)	(467,707)
Total parent stockholders' equity		330,808	460,789
Noncontrolling shareholders' interests in consolidated subsidiaries		49,716	62,261
Total equity		380,524	523,050
Total liabilities and equity[1]		$2,100,340	2,305,537

[1]Liabilities (principally notes payable) of consolidated VIEs were $105,806 and $80,414 at December 31, 2009 and December 31, 2010, respectively, and represent claims against the specific assets of the VIEs.

CONSOLIDATED STATEMENTS OF OPERATIONS
Years ended December 31
(Dollar amounts in thousands except per share amounts)

	2008	2009	2010
Net sales	$2,881,811	$2,778,990	$3,360,984
Cost of products sold	2,805,638	2,359,963	2,940,283
Gross profit	76,173	419,027	420,701
Selling, general and administrative	185,064	206,990	211,678
Impairment of goodwill and indefinite-lived intangible asset	31,340	—	—
Restructuring	76,402	48,718	20,649
Settlement of retiree medical case	—	7,050	—
Operating profit (loss)	(216,633)	156,269	188,374
Interest expense	50,525	47,211	36,647
Interest income	(12,887)	(5,193)	(5,265)
Other – net	3,504	(1,272)	(2,834)
Income (loss) from continuing operations before income taxes	(257,775)	115,523	159,826
Provision (benefit) for income taxes	(30,274)	231	20,057
Income (loss) from continuing operations	(227,501)	115,292	139,769
Income (loss) from discontinued operations, net of income taxes	64	(31,653)	24,118
Net income (loss)	(227,437)	83,639	(163,887)
Net income (loss) attributable to noncontrolling shareholders' interests	(8,057)	31,872	23,438
Net income (loss) attributable to Cooper Tire & Rubber Company	$ (219,380)	$ 51,767	$ 140,449
Basic earnings (loss) per share:			
Income (loss) from continuing operations available to Cooper Tire & Rubber Company common stockholders	$ (3.88)	$ 1.57	$ (1.90)
Income (loss) from discontinued operations	—	(0.53)	0.39

(*continued*)

EXHIBIT **5-5**	Cooper Tire & Rubber Company (*continued*)		
	2008	**2009**	**2010**
Net income (loss) available to Cooper Tire & Rubber Company common stockholders	$ (3.88)	$ 1.04	$ 2.29
Diluted earnings (loss) per share:			
Income (loss) from continuing operations available to Cooper Tire & Rubber Company common stockholders	$ (3.88)	$ 1.54	$ 1.86
Income (loss) from discontinued operations	—	(0.52)	0.38
Net income (loss) available to Cooper Tire & Rubber Company common stockholders	$ (3.88)	$ 1.02	$ 2.24

Review of Descriptive Information

The descriptive information found in an annual report, in trade periodicals, and in industry reviews helps us understand the financial position of a firm. Descriptive material might discuss the role of research and development in producing future sales, present data on capital expansion and the goals related thereto, discuss aspects of employee relations such as minority hiring or union negotiations, or help explain the dividend policy of the firm. In its annual report, a company must present a section called Management Discussion and Analysis (MD&A). This section provides an overview of the previous year and of future goals and new projects. Although the MD&A is unaudited, the information it contains can be very useful.

Comparisons

Absolute figures or ratios appear meaningless unless compared to other figures or ratios. If a person were asked if $10 is a lot of money, the frame of reference would determine the answer. To a small child, still in awe of a quarter, $10 is a lot. To a millionaire, a $10 bill is nothing. Similarly, having 60% of total assets composed of buildings and equipment would be normal for some firms but disastrous for others. One must have a guide to determine the meaning of the ratios and other measures. Several types of comparisons offer insight.

Trend Analysis

Trend analysis studies the financial history of a firm for comparison. By looking at the trend of a particular ratio, one sees whether that ratio is falling, rising, or remaining relatively constant. This helps detect problems or observe good management.

Standard Industrial Classification (SIC) Manual

The Standard Industrial Classification is a statistical classification of business by industry. The National Technical Information Service publishes the classification manual. The manual is the responsibility of the Office of Management and Budget, which is under the executive office of the president.

Use of the SIC promotes comparability of various facets of the U.S. economy and defines industries in accordance with the composition and structure of the economy. An organization's SIC consists of a two-digit major group number, a three-digit industry group number, and a four-digit industry number. These numbers describe the business's identifiable level of industrial detail.

Determining a company's SIC is a good starting point in researching a company, an industry, or a product. Many library sources use the SIC number as a method of classification.

The U.S. Department of Labor provides a Web site that details the SIC manual and provides for searching via key words. The Web site is http://www.osha.gov/oshstats/sicser.html. If you Google "Standard Industrial Classification" (SIC), this Web site will likely be the first one up.

North American Industry Classification System (NAICS)

The North American Industry Classification System (NAICS) was created jointly by the United States, Canada, and Mexico. It is to replace the existing classification of each country: the Standard Industrial Classification of Canada (1980), the Mexican Classification of Activities and Products (1994), and the Standard Industrial Classification (SIC) of the United States (1987).

For the NAICS, economic units with similar production processes are classified in the same industry, and the lines drawn between industries demarcate differences in production processes. This supply-based economic concept was adopted because an industry classification system is a framework for collecting information on both inputs and outputs. This will aid in the collection of statistics on such things as productivity, unit labor costs, and capital intensity.

NAICS provides enhanced industry comparability among the three NAFTA trading partners. It also increases compatibility with the two-digit level of the International Standard Industrial Classification (ISIC Rev. 3) of the United Nations.

NAICS divides the economy into 20 sectors. Industries within these sectors are grouped according to the production criterion. Four sectors are largely goods-producing, and 16 are entirely services-producing industries.

In most sectors, NAICS provides for compatibility at the industry (five-digit) level. For some sectors, the compatibility level is less at four-digit, three-digit, or two-digit levels. Each country can add additional detailed industries, provided the additional detail aggregates to the NAICS level.

The United States adopted the NAICS in 1997 for statistical agencies. Most of the U.S. government agencies now use the NAICS in place of the Standard Industrial Classification. A major exception is the Securities and Exchange Commission (SEC). Companies reporting to the SEC include their SIC. For private companies that publish industry data, some now only use the NAICS, others use the SIC, and still others include both the NAICS and the SIC.

The U.S. Census Bureau provides a Web site that details the NAICS manual and provides for searching via key words. To get to this site, open www.census.gov and under "business and industry" click on NAICS. If you Google "North American Industry Classification System" (NAICS), this Web site will likely be the first one up.

Industry Averages and Comparison with Competitors

The analysis of an entity's financial statements is more meaningful if the results are compared with industry averages and with results of competitors. Several financial services provide composite data on various industries.

The analyst faces a problem when the industries reported do not clearly include the company being examined because the company is diversified into many industrial areas. Since many companies do not clearly fit into any one industry, it is often necessary to use an industry that best fits the firm. The financial services have a similar problem in selecting an industry in which to place a company. Thus, a financial service uses its best judgment as to which industry the firm best fits.

This section briefly describes some financial services. For a more extensive explanation, consult the service's literature. Each service explains how it computes its ratios and the data it provides.

The Department of Commerce Financial Report is a publication of the federal government for manufacturing, mining, and trade corporations. Published by the Economic Surveys Division of the Bureau of the Census, it includes income statement data and balance sheet data in total industry dollars. It also includes an industry-wide common-size vertical income statement (Income Statement in Ratio Format) and an industry-wide common-size vertical balance sheet (Selected Balance Sheet Ratios). This source also includes selected operating and balance sheet ratios. This government publication uses NAICS for classification.

This report, updated quarterly, probably offers the most current source. It typically becomes available within three to four months after the end of the quarter. It is a unique source of industry data in total dollars and would enable a company to compare its dollars (such as sales) with the industry dollars (sales). This service is free and is now on the Internet at www.census.gov/econ/qfr.

Annual Statement Studies is published by the Risk Management Association, the association of lending and credit risk professionals. Submitted by institutional members of the Risk Management Association, the data cover several hundred different industries in manufacturing, wholesaling, retailing, service, agriculture, and construction.

Annual Statement Studies groups the data by industry, using the SIC number, and the NAICS number. It provides common-size balance sheets, income statements, and 16 selected ratios.

The data are sorted by assets and sales and are particularly useful because the financial position and operations of small firms are often quite different from those of larger firms. The presentation also includes a five-year comparison of historical data that presents all firms under a particular NAICS or SIC code.

In each category, the ratios are computed for the median and the upper and lower quartiles. For example:

Number of firms (9)

Ratio—Return on total assets

Results for the nine firms (in order, from highest to lowest):

12%, 11%, 10.5%, 10%, 9.8%, 9.7%, 9.6%, 7.0%, 6.5%

The middle result is the median: 9.8%.

The result halfway between the top result and the median is the upper quartile: 10.5%.

The result halfway between the bottom result and the median is the lower quartile: 9.6%.

For ratios in which a low value is desirable, the results are presented from low values to high—for example, 2% (upper quartile), 5% (median), and 8% (lower quartile). For ratios in which a high value is desirable, the results are presented from high values to low—for example, 10.5% (upper quartile), 9.8% (median), and 9.6% (lower quartile).

Because of the combination of common-size statements, selected ratios, and comparative historical data, *Annual Statement Studies* is one of the most extensively used sources of industry data. Commercial loan officers in banks frequently use this source.

Annual Statement Studies® now contains an industry Z score which indicates the potential for a company to fail compared with the industry. A review of the Z score concept is in Chapter 11 of this text.

Annual Statement Studies® is available in two books; 1) RMA Annual Statement Studies®, and 2) Valu Source's RMA Annual Statement Studies® Valuation Edition.

Valu Source's RMA Annual Statement Studies® Valuation Edition has the same data contained in RMA Annual Statement Studies® plus additional data such as enhanced financial ratios.

Standard & Poor's Industry Surveys contains information of particular interest to investors. This includes a write-up by industry, statistics for companies in an industry, and specific company by industry. Each industry report includes the current environments, industry trends, key industry ratios, and additional industry information.

Almanac of Business and Industrial Financial Ratios, published by CCH Incorporated, is a compilation of corporate tax return data. It includes nearly 200 industries and presents 50 statistics for 13 size categories of firms. Some of the industries include manufacturing, construction, transportation, retail trade, banking, and wholesale trade.

Beginning with the 2002 edition, each *Almanac* industry is cross-referenced to a NAICS number. The IRS's condensed NAICS represents the classification system used in the *Almanac.*

Industry Norms and Key Business Ratios, desktop edition published by Dun & Bradstreet, includes over 800 different lines of business as defined by the SIC code numbers. It includes one-year data consisting of a condensed balance sheet and an income statement in dollars and common size. It also includes working capital and ratios.

There are 14 ratios presented for the upper quartile, median, and lower quartile. The 14 ratios are as follows:

Solvency

    Quick Ratio (Times)

    Current Ratio (Times)

    Current Liabilities to Net Worth (%)

    Current Liabilities to Inventory (%)

    Total Liabilities to Net Worth (%)

    Fixed Assets to Net Worth (%)

Efficiency

    Collection Period (days)

    Sales to Inventory (times)

    Assets to Sales (%)

    Sales to Net Working Capital (times)

    Accounts Payable to Sales (%)

Profitability

    Return on Sales (%)

    Return on Assets (%)

    Return on Equity (%)

Dun & Bradstreet advises that the industry norms and key business ratios are to be used as yardsticks and not as absolutes.

Value Line Investment Survey is in two editions; the Standard Edition and the Small & Mid-Cap Edition. The Standard Edition places companies in 1 of 97 industries. The Small & Mid-Cap Edition places companies in 1 of 84 industries. There are approximately 1,700 stocks in the Standard Edition and approximately 1,800 stocks in the Small & Mid-Cap Edition. The *Value Line Investment Survey* is very popular with investors.

The full-page Ratings & Reports are similar for the Standard Edition and the Small & Mid-Cap Edition. Each stock is rated for timeliness, safety, and technical. The Standard Edition includes an analyst's comments, while the Small & Mid-Cap Edition does not include an analyst's comments.

The data included in *Value Line* for a company are largely for a relatively long period of time (11 to 17 years). The data provided vary somewhat by industry. Some of the data provided for many companies are as follows:

1. Revenues per share
2. Cash flow per share
3. Earnings per share
4. Dividends declared per share
5. Capital spending per share
6. Book value per share
7. Common shares outstanding
8. Average annual P/E ratio
9. Relative P/E ratio
10. Average annual dividend yield
11. Revenues
12. Operating margin
13. Depreciation
14. Net profit

15. Income tax rate
16. Net profit margin
17. Working capital
18. Long-term debt
19. Shareholders' equity
20. Return on total capitalization
21. Return on shareholders' equity
22. Retained to common equity
23. All dividends to net profit

As indicated previously, comparison has become more difficult in recent years as more firms become conglomerates and diversify into many product lines. To counteract this problem, the SEC has implemented line-of-business reporting requirements for companies that must submit their reports to the SEC. These reports are made available to the public. SFAS No. 14 also addresses line-of-business reporting requirements. Such reporting requirements ease the analysis problem created by conglomerates but cannot eliminate it because the entity must decide how to allocate administrative and joint costs.

If industry figures are unavailable or if comparison with a competitor is desired, another firm's statements may be analyzed. Remember, however, that the other firm is not necessarily good or bad, nor does it represent a norm or standard for its industry. It also can be said that industry figures do not necessarily represent good or bad, nor do they represent a standard for its industry.

Alternative accounting methods are acceptable in many situations. Since identical companies may use different valuation or expense methods, it is important to read statements and notes carefully to determine whether the statements are reasonably comparable.

Ideally, the use of all types of comparison would be best. Using trend analysis, industry averages, and comparisons with a major competitor will give support to findings and will provide a concrete basis for analysis.

In analyzing ratios, the analyst will sometimes encounter negative profit figures. **Analysis of ratios that have negative numerators or denominators is meaningless, and the negative sign of the ratio should simply be noted.**

Caution in Using Industry Averages

Financial analysis requires judgment decisions on the part of the analyst. Users of financial statements must be careful not to place undue confidence in ratios or comparisons.

Remember that ratios are simply fractions with a numerator (top) and a denominator (bottom). There are as many ratios for financial analysis as there are pairs of figures. There is no set group, nor is a particular ratio always computed using the same figures. Even the industry ratio formulas vary from source to source. Adequate detailed disclosure of how the industry ratios are computed is often lacking. Major problems can result from analyzing a firm according to the recommendations of a book and then making comparisons to industry ratios that may have been computed differently.

The use of different accounting methods causes a problem. For example, identical firms may use different valuation or revenue recognition methods. Read statements and notes carefully to determine the degree of comparability between statements. Trend analysis for each firm, however, will usually be meaningful. Industry averages group firms together that use different accounting principles.

Different year-ends can also produce different results. Consider the difference in the inventory of two toy stores if one ends November 30 and the other ends December 31. The ratios of firms with differing year-ends are all grouped together in industry averages.

Firms with differing financial policies might be included in the same industry average. Possibly capital-intensive firms are grouped with labor-intensive companies. Firms with large amounts of debt may be included in the same average as firms that prefer to avoid the risk of debt.

Some industry averages come from small samples that may not be representative of the industry. An extreme statement, such as one containing a large loss, can also distort industry data.

Ratios may have alternative forms of computation. In comparing one year to the next, one firm to another, or a company to its industry, meaningful analysis requires that the ratios be computed using the same formula. For example, *Annual Statement Studies* computes income ratios before tax; Dun & Bradstreet profit figures are after tax. The analyst should compute the enterprise ratios on the same basis as is used for industry comparisons, but this is often not possible.

Finally, ratios are not absolute norms. They are general guidelines to be combined with other methods in formulating an evaluation of the financial condition of a firm. Despite the problems with using ratios, they can be very informative if reasonably used.

Relative Size of Firm

Comparisons of firms of different sizes may be more difficult than comparisons of firms of equal size. For example, larger firms often have access to wider and more sophisticated capital markets, can buy in large quantities, and service wider markets. Ratios and common-size analysis help to eliminate some of the problems related to the use of absolute numbers.

Be aware of the different sizes of firms under comparison. These differences can be seen by looking at relative sales, assets, or profit sizes. Investment services such as *Value Line* often make available another meaningful figure—percent of market.

Other Library Sources

The typical business library has many sources of information relating to a particular company, industry, and product. Some of these sources are described here to aid you in your search for information about a company, its industry, and its products.

Ward's Business Directory

Ward's Business Directory covers domestic private and public companies. Up to 20 items of information are provided for each company listed. The data may include names, addresses, telephone numbers, e-mails and URLs, sales, employee figures, and up to five names and titles of executive officers. The directory is a very good service for information on private companies. *Ward's Business Directory* went digital in 2007 under Gale Directory Library.

Standard & Poor's Stock Reports

Standard & Poor's Reports covers companies on the New York Stock Exchange, American Stock Exchange, NASDAQ stock market, and regional exchanges. Arranged alphabetically by stock exchange, it contains a brief narrative analysis of companies regularly traded. It provides key financial data relating to the income statement, balance sheet, and per share data. Other comments cover management, company's business, product lines, and other important factors.

Standard & Poor's Register of Corporations, Directors, and Executives

This annual source is arranged in two volumes. Volume 1 contains an alphabetical list of approximately 75,000 corporations, including such data as ZIP Codes, telephone numbers, and functions of officers, directors, and other principals. The NAICS code is included at the end of each listing.

Volume 2, Section 1 contains an alphabetical list of over 70,000 individuals serving as officers, directors, trustees, partners, and so on. It provides such data as principal business affiliations, business address, and residence address.

Volume 2, Section 2—Indices: Divided into seven subsections:

- *Section 1*—Explains the construction and use of the NAICS code numbers and lists these numbers by major groups and by alphabetical and numerical division of major groups.
- *Section 2*—Lists corporations under the six-digit NAICS codes, which are arranged in numerical order.
- *Section 3*—Lists companies geographically by states and by major cities.

- *Section 4*—Lists and cross-references subsidiaries, divisions, and affiliates in alphabetical sequence and links them to their ultimate parent company listed in Volume 1.
- *Section 5*—Lists the deaths of which publishers have been notified in the past year.
- *Section 6*—Lists individuals whose names appear in the Register for the first time.
- *Section 7*—Lists the companies appearing in the Register for the first time.

This source is published in hard copy and online.

Standard & Poor's Analyst's Handbook

This source contains selected income account and balance sheet items and related ratios as applied to the Standard & Poor's industry group stock price indexes. The progress of a given company may possibly be compared with a composite of its industry groups. Brief monthly updates for selected industries supplement the annual editions of the handbook.

Standard & Poor's Standard Corporation Descriptions, Plus News (Corporation Records)

This source provides background information and detailed financial statistics on U.S. corporations, with extensive coverage for some corporations. The contents and the index are updated throughout the year.

Standard & Poor's Security Owner's Stock Guide

This monthly guide, published by Standard & Poor's, covers over 5,300 common and preferred stocks. It contains trading activity, price range, dividends, and so on, for companies traded on the New York Stock Exchange, American Stock Exchange, over the counter, and regional exchanges. The information is displayed with numerous abbreviations and notes, in order to fit concisely into one single line, for each publicly traded security.

Standard & Poor's Statistical Service

Standard & Poor's Statistical Service includes comprehensive statistics on many industries such as agriculture, metals, building, and transportation. Many additional statistics are included such as price indexes and daily highs, lows, and closes for stock.

Standard & Poor's Net Advantage

Standard & Poor's Net Advantage is available at many academic libraries, public libraries, corporate libraries, and information centers. This source is online only. For Standard & Poor's publications listed in this book under "other library sources," they are all available in print copy. The following publications are also available with Net Advantage:

1. Standard & Poor's Stock Reports
2. Standard & Poor's Register of Corporations, Directors, and Executives
3. Standard & Poor's Standard Corporation Descriptions (Corporation Records)

Mergent Dividend Record and Standard & Poor's Annual Dividend Record

These dividend publications provide a dividend record of payments on virtually all publicly owned American and some foreign companies.

D&B® Million Dollar Directory®

This publication includes many items, including company name, address, telephone number, year founded, annual sales, stock exchange, ticker symbol, and company officers.

The Million Dollar Directory is published in five volumes. The first three contain alphabetical listings, while the fourth and fifth are cross-reference volumes grouped geographically by state and by Standard Industrial Classification (SIC).

The companies must meet at least one of two inclusion requirements:

1. $9 million or more in sales volume
2. 180 or more employees total if the company is a headquarters or single location, 900 or more employees at the location if the company is a branch

Directory of Corporate Affiliations™

This directory gives an in-depth view of companies and their divisions, subsidiaries, and affiliates. It contains an alphabetical index, geographical index, and SIC classifications. The parent company listing consists of address, telephone number, stock ticker symbol, stock exchange(s), approximate sales, number of employees, type of business, and top corporate officers. The database covers more than 180,000 parent companies, affiliates, subsidiaries, and divisions worldwide.

Thomas Register of American Manufacturers

This is a comprehensive reference for products and services (Volumes 1–14), company profiles (Volumes 15 & 16), and a catalog file.

Mergent Industrial Manual and News Reports

Published in two volumes, these manuals cover 2,000 industrial corporations listed on the New York and American stock exchanges and other selected exchanges. Extensive information is provided such as history, business, properties, subsidiaries, financial statements, and SIC codes.

D&B Reference Book of Corporate Managements

Contains profile information on over 200,000 principal corporate officers in over 12,000 companies. The information includes the year of birth, education, military service, present business position, and previous positions. Names and titles of other officers, as well as names of directors who are not officers, are also provided.

Compact Disclosure

This database of textual and financial information on approximately 12,000 public companies can be accessed by a menu-driven screen. The information is taken from annual and periodic reports filed by each company with the Securities and Exchange Commission. A full printout for a company is approximately 14 pages. It includes the major financial statements (annual and quarterly), many financial ratios for the prior three years, institutional holdings, ownership by insiders, president's letter, and financial notes.

A company can be accessed by keying its name or ticker symbol. In addition, the system can be searched by type of business (SIC), geographic area (state, city, ZIP Code, or telephone area code), stock price financial ratios, and much more. Available on CD-ROM database only.

Lexis-Nexis

This service provides accounting, legal, newspaper, and periodical information. Lexis-Nexis includes complete statement portions of annual reports for thousands of publicly traded companies. Many colleges of business, law schools, accounting firms, and law firms subscribe to this service.

The Users of Financial Statements

The financial statements are prepared for a group of diversified users. Users of financial data have their own objectives in analysis.

Management, an obvious user of financial data, must analyze the data from the viewpoints of both investors and creditors. Management must be concerned about the current position of the entity to meet its obligations, as well as the future earning prospects of the firm.

Management is interested in the financial structure of the entity in order to determine a proper mix of short-term debt, long-term debt, and equity from owners. Also of interest is the asset structure of the entity: the combination of cash, inventory, receivables, investments, and fixed assets.

Management must guide the entity toward sound short- and long-term financial policies and also earn a profit. For example, liquidity and profitability are competitive since the most highly liquid assets (cash and marketable securities) are usually the least profitable. It does the entity little good to be guided toward a maximum profitability goal if resources are not available to meet current obligations. The entity would soon find itself in bankruptcy as creditors cut off lines of credit and demand payment. Similarly, management must utilize resources properly to obtain a reasonable return.

The investing public, another category of users, is interested in specific types of analysis. Investors are concerned with the financial position of the entity and its ability to earn future profits. The investor uses an analysis of past trends and the current position of the entity to project the future prospects of the entity.

Credit grantors are interested in the financial statements of the entity. Pure credit grantors obtain a limited return from extending credit: a fixed rate of interest (as in the case of banks) or the profit on the merchandise or services provided (as in the case of suppliers). Since these rewards are limited and the possibility exists that the principal will not be repaid, credit grantors tend to be conservative in extending credit.

The same principle applies to suppliers that extend credit. If merchandise with a 20% markup is sold on credit, it takes five successful sales of the same amount to make up for one sale not collected. In addition, the creditor considers the cost of the funds when extending credit. Extending credit really amounts to financing the entity.

A difference exists between the objectives of short-term grantors of credit and those of long-term grantors. The short-term creditor can look primarily to current resources that appear on the financial statements in order to determine if credit should be extended. Long-term creditors must usually look to the future prospects of earnings in order to be repaid. For example, if bonds are issued that are to be repaid in 30 years, the current resources of the entity will not be an indication of its ability to meet this obligation. The repayment for this obligation will come from future earnings. Thus, the objectives of financial analysis by credit grantors will vary, based on such factors as the term of the credit and the purpose. Profitability of the entity may not be a major consideration, as long as the resources for repayment can be projected.

The financial structure of the entity is of interest to creditors because the amount of equity capital in relation to debt indicates the risk that the owners bear in relation to the creditors. The equity capital provides creditors with a cushion against loss. When this equity cushion is small, creditors are bearing the risk of the entity.

Many other parties are interested in analyzing financial statements. Unions that represent employees are interested in the ability of the entity to grant wage increases and fringe benefits, such as pension plans. The government also has an interest in analyzing financial statements for tax purposes and for ensuring compliance with antitrust laws.

Summary

Financial analysis consists of the quantitative and qualitative aspects of measuring the relative financial position among firms and industries. Analysis can be done in different ways, depending on the type of firm or industry and the specific needs of the user. Financial statements will vary by size of firm and among industries.

The SIC and NAICS classification systems have been developed to promote comparability of firms. Determining a company's SIC and/or NAICS is a good starting point in researching a company, an industry, or a product.

The analysis of an entity's financial statements is more meaningful if the results are compared with industry averages and with results of competitors. At the same time, caution must be exercised in using industry averages and results of competitors.

Many library services are available that relate to individual companies, industries, and products. These sources can be a valuable aid in researching a firm.

Financial statements are prepared for a group of diversified users. These users have various needs and uses for the financial statements.

Questions

Q 5-1 What is a ratio? How do ratios help to alleviate the problem of size differences among firms?

Q 5-2 What does each of the following categories of ratios attempt to measure? (a) liquidity; (b) long-term

borrowing capacity; (c) profitability. Name a group of users who might be interested in each category.

Q 5-3 Brown Company earned 5.5% on sales in 2011. What further information would be needed to evaluate this result?

Q 5-4 Differentiate between absolute and percentage changes. Which is generally a better measure of change? Why?

Q 5-5 Differentiate between horizontal and vertical analysis. Using sales as a component for each type, give an example that explains the difference.

Q 5-6 What is trend analysis? Can it be used for ratios? For absolute figures?

Q 5-7 Suppose you are comparing two firms within an industry. One is large and the other is small. Will relative or absolute numbers be of more value in each case? What kinds of statistics can help evaluate relative size?

Q 5-8 Are managers the only users of financial reports? Discuss.

Q 5-9 Briefly describe how each of these groups might use financial reports: managers, investors, and creditors.

Q 5-10 Refer to Exhibits 5-3, 5-4, and 5-5 to answer the following questions:

a. For each of the firms illustrated, what is the single largest asset category? Does this seem typical of this type of firm?

b. Which of the three firms has the largest amount in current assets in relation to the amount in current liabilities? Does this seem logical? Explain.

Q 5-11 Differentiate between the types of inventory typically held by a retailing firm and a manufacturing firm.

Q 5-12 Sometimes manufacturing firms have only raw materials and finished goods listed on their balance sheets. This is true of Avon Products, a manufacturer of cosmetics, and it might be true of food canners also. Explain the absence of work in process.

Q 5-13 Using these results for a given ratio, compute the median, upper quartile, and lower quartile. 14%, 13.5%, 13%, 11.8%, 10.5%, 9.5%, 9.3%, 9%, 7%

Q 5-14 You want profile information on the president of a company. Which reference book should be consulted?

Q 5-15 Answer the following concerning the *Almanac of Business and Industrial Financial Ratios*:

a. This service presents statistics for how many size categories of firms?

b. Indicate some of the industries covered by this service.

Q 5-16 Using *The Department of Commerce Financial Report* discussion in the text, answer the following:

a. Could we determine the percentage of total sales income after income taxes that a particular firm had in relation to the total industry sales? Explain.

b. Could we determine the percentage of total assets that a particular firm had in relation to the total industry? Explain.

Q 5-17

a. What is the SIC number? How can it aid in the search of a company, industry, or product?

b. What is the NAICS number? How can it aid in the search of a company, industry, or product?

Q 5-18 You want to know if there have been any reported deaths of officers of a company you are researching. What library source will aid you in your search?

Q 5-19 You want to compare the progress of a given company with a composite of that company's industry group for selected income statement and balance sheet items. Which library source will aid you?

Q 5-20 You are considering buying the stock of a large publicly traded company. You need an opinion of timeliness of the industry and the company. Which publication could you use?

Q 5-21 You want to know the trading activity (volume of its stock sold) for a company. Which service provides this information?

Q 5-22 Indicate some sources that contain a dividend record of payments.

Q 5-23 What source includes comprehensive statistics on many industries?

Q 5-24 You would like to determine the principal business affiliations of the president of a company you are analyzing. Which reference service may have this information?

Q 5-25 Indicate some sources that contain an appraisal of the outlook for particular industries.

Q 5-26 What source contains a comprehensive reference for products and services, company profiles, and a catalog file?

Problems

P 5-1 Best Buy Co., Inc.'s consolidated balance sheets from its 2011 annual report are presented in Exhibit 5-3.

Required

a. Using the balance sheets, prepare a vertical common-size analysis for 2011 and 2010. Use total assets as a base.

(continued)

(**P 5-1** CONTINUED)

   b. Using the balance sheets, prepare a horizontal common-size analysis for 2011 and 2010. Use 2010 as the base.

   c. Comment on significant trends that appear in (a) and (b).

P 5-2 Best Buy Co., Inc.'s consolidated statements of earnings from its 2011 annual report are presented in Exhibit 5-3.

Required

   a. Using the statement of earnings, prepare a vertical common-size analysis for 2011, 2010, and 2009. Use revenue as a base.

   b. Using the statement of earnings, prepare a horizontal common-size analysis for 2011, 2010, and 2009. Use 2009 as the base.

   c. Comment on significant trends that appear in (a) and (b).

P 5-3 The Kelly Services, Inc., and Subsidiaries balance sheets from its 2010 annual report are presented in Exhibit 5-4.

Required

   a. Using the balance sheets, prepare a vertical common-size analysis for 2010 and 2009. Use total assets as a base.

   b. Using the balance sheets, prepare a horizontal common-size analysis for 2010 and 2009. Use 2009 as the base.

   c. Comment on significant trends that appear in (a) and (b).

P 5-4 The Kelly Services, Inc., and Subsidiaries statements of earnings from its 2010 annual report are presented in Exhibit 5-4.

Required

   a. Using the statements of earnings, prepare a vertical common-size analysis for 2010, 2009, and 2008. Use revenues as the base.

   b. Using the statements of earnings, prepare a horizontal common-size analysis for 2010, 2009, and 2008. Use 2008 as the base.

   c. Comment on significant trends that appear in (a) and (b).

P 5-5

			Change Analysis	
Item	Year 1	Year 2	Amount	Percent
1	—	3,000		
2	6,000	(4,000)		
3	(7,000)	4,000		
4	4,000	—		
5	8,000	10,000		

Required Determine the absolute change and the percentage for these items.

P 5-6

			Change Analysis	
Item	Year 1	Year 2	Amount	Percent
1	4,000	—		
2	5,000	(3,000)		
3	(9,000)	2,000		
4	7,000	—		
5	—	15,000		

Required Determine the absolute change and the percentage for these items.

P 5-7

| | Rapid Retail Comparative Statements of Income | | | |
| | December 31 | | Increase (Decrease) | |
(In thousands of dollars)	2011	2010	Dollars	Percent
Net sales	$30,000	$28,000		
Cost of goods sold	20,000	19,500		
Gross profit	10,000	8,500		
Selling, general and				
administrative expense	3,000	2,900		
Operating income	7,000	5,600		
Interest expense	100	80		
Income before taxes	6,900	5,520		
Income tax expense	2,000	1,600		
Net income	$ 4,900	$ 3,920		

Required

a. Complete the increase (decrease) in dollars and percent.
b. Comment on trends.

P 5-8

Required Answer the following multiple-choice questions:

a. Which of the following statements is incorrect?

1. Ratios are fractions expressed in percent or times per year.
2. A ratio can be computed from any pair of numbers.
3. A very long list of meaningful ratios can be derived.
4. There is one standard list of ratios.
5. Comparison of income statement and balance sheet numbers, in the form of ratios, should not be done.

b. A figure from this year's statement is compared with a base selected from the current year.

1. Vertical common-size statement
2. Horizontal common-size statement
3. Funds statement
4. Absolute figures
5. Balance sheet

c. Fremont Electronics has income of $1 million. Columbus Electronics has income of $2 million. Which of the following statements is a correct statement?

1. Columbus Electronics is getting a higher return on assets employed.
2. Columbus Electronics has higher profit margins than does Fremont Electronics.
3. Fremont Electronics could be more profitable than Columbus Electronics in relation to resources employed.
4. No comparison can be made between Fremont Electronics and Columbus Electronics.
5. Fremont Electronics is not making good use of its resources.

d. Industry ratios should *not* be considered as absolute norms for a given industry because of all but which of the following?

1. The firms have different accounting methods.
2. Many companies have varied product lines.

(*continued*)

(**P 5-8** CONTINUED)

  3. Companies within the same industry may differ in their method of operations.
  4. The fiscal year-ends of the companies may differ.
  5. The financial services may be private independent firms.

 e. Which of the following is a publication of the federal government for manufacturing, mining, and trade corporations?

  1. *Annual Statement Studies*
  2. *Standard & Poor's Industry Surveys*
  3. *Almanac of Business and Industrial Financial Ratios*
  4. *Industry Norms and Key Business Ratios*
  5. *The Department of Commerce Financial Report*

 f. Which service represents a compilation of corporate tax return data?

  1. *Annual Statement Studies*
  2. *Standard & Poor's Industry Surveys*
  3. *Almanac of Business and Industrial Financial Ratios*
  4. *Industry Norms and Key Business Ratios*
  5. *The Department of Commerce Financial Report*

 g. Which service includes over 800 different lines of business?

  1. *Annual Statement Studies*
  2. *Standard & Poor's Industry Surveys*
  3. *Almanac of Business and Industrial Financial Ratios*
  4. *Industry Norms and Key Business Ratios*
  5. *The Department of Commerce Financial Report*

 h. Which analysis compares each amount with a base amount for a selected base year?

  1. Vertical common-size
  2. Horizontal common-size
  3. Funds statement
  4. Common-size statement
  5. None of these

 i. Suppose you are comparing two firms in the coal industry. Which type of numbers would be most meaningful for statement analysis?

  1. Relative numbers would be most meaningful for both firms, especially for interfirm comparisons.
  2. Relative numbers are not meaningful.
  3. Absolute numbers would be most meaningful.
  4. Absolute numbers are not relevant.
  5. It is not meaningful to compare two firms.

 j. Management is a user of financial analysis. Which of the following comments does *not* represent a fair statement as to the management perspective?

  1. Management is not interested in the view of investors.
  2. Management is interested in liquidity.
  3. Management is interested in profitability.
  4. Management is interested in the debt position.
  5. Management is interested in the financial structure of the entity.

WEB CASE THOMSON ONE   *Business School Edition*

Please complete the Web case that covers material discussed in this chapter at www.cengagebrain.com. You'll be using Thomson ONE Business School Edition, a powerful tool that combines a full range of fundamental financial information, earnings estimates, market data, and source documents for 500 publicly traded companies.

TO THE NET CASE

1. Go to the SEC Web site (www.sec.gov). Under "Filings & Forms (EDGAR)," click on "Search for Company Filings." Click on "Company or Fund, etc." Under Company Name, enter "Alexander & Baldwin" (or under Ticker Symbol, enter "ALEX"). Select the 10-K filed February 25, 2011. For the following partial consolidated statements of income, compute horizontal and vertical common-size analysis. Use December 31, 2008, for the base on the horizontal common-size analysis. Use total revenue for the vertical common-size analysis. Comment on the results.

	Years Ended December 31,		
	2010	2009	2008
Operating revenue:			
Ocean transportation			
Logistics services			
Real estate leasing			
Real estate sales			
Agribusiness			
Total operating revenue			

2. Go to the SEC site (www.sec.gov). Under "Filings & Forms" click on "Search for Company Filings." Click on "Company or fund, etc." Under Company Name, enter "Best Buy Co" (or under Ticker Symbol, enter "BBT"). Select the 10-K filed April 25, 2011. For the following partial consolidated statements of earnings, compute horizontal and vertical common-size analysis. Use February 28, 2009 as the base in the horizontal common-size analysis. Use revenue for the vertical common-size analysis. Comment on the results.

	Consolidated Statements of Earnings		
	February 26, 2011	February 27, 2010	February 28, 2009
Revenue			
Cost of goods sold			
Restructuring charges – cost of goods sold			
Gross profit			
Selling, general and administrative expenses			
Restructuring charges			
Goodwill and tradename impairment			
Operating income			

3. Go to the SEC Web site (www.sec.gov). Under "Filings & Forms (EDGAR)," click on "Search for Company Filings." Click on "Company or Fund, etc." Under Company Name, enter "Amazoncom Inc" (or under Ticker Symbol, enter "AMZN"). Select the 10-K filed January 28, 2011. For the following partial consolidated balance sheets, compute horizontal and vertical common-size analyses. Use December 31, 2009, for the base in the horizontal common-size analysis. Use total liabilities and stockholders' equity for the vertical common-size analysis. Comment on the results.

	December 31,	
	2010	2009
Liabilities and stockholders' equity		
Total current liabilities		
Long-term liabilities		
Commitments and contingencies		
Stockholders' equity		
Preferred stock		
Common stock		
Treasury stock, at cost		
Additional paid-in capital		
Accumulated other comprehensive income (loss)		
Retained earning		
Total stockholders' equity		
Total liabilities and stockholders' equity		

(continued)

(**To The Net** CONTINUED)

4. Go to the SEC Web site (www.sec.gov). Under "Filings & Forms (EDGAR)," click on "Search for Company Filings." Click on "Company or fund, etc." Under Company Name, enter "Kroger Co" (or under Ticker Symbol, enter "KR"). Select the 10-K filed March 29, 2011. For the following partial consolidated statement of income, prepare a horizontal common-size analysis with change in dollars. Use the year ended January 30, 2010, as the base. Comment on the results.

Consolidated Statement of Income (In Part)
Years Ended January 29, 2011, and January 30, 2010
(In millions)

	Jan. 29, 2011 52 Weeks	Jan. 30, 2010 52 Weeks	Increase (Decrease) Dollars	Percent
Sales				
Merchandise costs, including advertising, warehousing, and transportation, excluding items shown separately below				
Operating, general and administrative				
Rent				
Depreciation and amortization				
Goodwill impairment charge				
Operating profit				

5. Go to the SEC Web site (www.sec.gov). Under "Filings & Forms (EDGAR)," click on "Search for Company Filings." Click on "Company or Fund, etc." Under Company Name, enter "Yahoo Inc." (or under Ticker Symbol, enter "YHOO"). Select the 10-K filed February 28, 2011. For the following partial consolidated statements of operations, prepare a horizontal common-size analysis with change in dollars. Use the year ended December 31, 2009, as the base. Comment on the results.

Yahoo! Inc.
Consolidated Statements of Income
Years Ended December 31, 2009, and December 31, 2010 (In thousands)

	Dec. 31, 2009	Dec. 31, 2010	Increase (Decrease) Dollars	Percent
Revenues				
Cost of revenues				
Gross profit				
Operating expenses:				
Sales and Marketing				
Product development				
General and administrative				
Amortization of intangibles				
Restructuring changes, net				
Goodwill impairment change				
Total operating expense				
Income from operations				

Chapter

6

Liquidity of Short-Term Assets; Related Debt-Paying Ability

An entity's ability to maintain its short-term debt-paying ability is important to all users of financial statements. If the entity cannot maintain a short-term debt-paying ability, it will not be able to maintain a long-term debt-paying ability, nor will it be able to satisfy its stockholders. Even a very profitable entity will find itself bankrupt if it fails to meet its obligations to short-term creditors. The ability to pay current obligations when due is also related to the cash-generating ability of the firm. This topic will be discussed in Chapter 10.

When analyzing the short-term debt-paying ability of the firm, we find a close relationship between the current assets and the current liabilities. Generally, the current liabilities will be paid with cash generated from the current assets. As previously indicated, the profitability of the firm does not determine the short-term debt-paying ability. In other words, using accrual accounting, the entity may report very high profits but may not have the ability to pay its current bills because it lacks available funds. If the entity reports a loss, it may still be able to pay short-term obligations.

This chapter suggests procedures for analyzing short-term assets and the short-term debt-paying ability of an entity. The procedures require an understanding of current assets, current liabilities, and the notes to financial statements.

This chapter also includes a detailed discussion of four very important assets—cash, marketable securities, accounts receivable, and inventory. Accounts receivable and inventory, two critical assets, often substantially influence the liquidity and profitability of a firm.

Chapters 6 through 10 will extensively use the 2011 financial statements of Nike, Inc. (Nike) to illustrate the technique of financial analysis. This will aid readers in viewing financial analysis as a whole. Nike, Inc.'s 2011 financial statements are presented following Chapter 10. With the Nike statements is an analysis that summarizes and expands on the Nike analysis in Chapters 6 through 10.

Current Assets, Current Liabilities, and the Operating Cycle

Current assets (1) are in the form of cash, (2) will be realized in cash, or (3) conserve the use of cash *within the operating cycle of a business or one year, whichever is longer.*[1]

The five categories of assets usually found in current assets, listed in their order of liquidity, include cash, marketable securities, receivables, inventories, and prepayments. Other assets may also be classified in current assets, such as assets held for sale. This chapter will examine in detail each type of current asset.

The operating cycle for a company is the time period between the acquisition of goods and the final cash realization resulting from sales and subsequent collections. For example, a food store purchases inventory and then sells the inventory for cash. The relatively short time that the inventory remains an asset of the food store represents a very short operating cycle. In another example, a car manufacturer purchases materials and then uses labor and overhead to convert these materials into a finished car. A dealer buys the car on credit and then pays the manufacturer. Compared to the food store, the car manufacturer has a much longer operating cycle, but it is still less than a year. Only a few businesses have an operating cycle longer than a year. For example, if a business is involved in selling resort property, the average time period that the property is held before sale, plus the average collection period, is typically longer than a year.

Cash

Cash is a medium of exchange that a bank will accept for deposit and a creditor will accept for payment. To be classified as a current asset, cash must be free from any restrictions that would prevent its deposit or use it to pay creditors classified as current. If restricted for specific short-term creditors, many firms still classify this cash under current assets, but they disclose the restrictions. Cash restricted for short-term creditors should be eliminated along with the related amount of short-term debt when determining the short-term debt-paying ability. Cash should be available to pay general short-term creditors to be considered as part of the firm's short-term debt-paying ability.

It has become common for banks to require a portion of any loan to remain on deposit in the bank for the duration of the loan period. These deposits, termed compensating balances, reduce the amount of cash available to the borrower to meet obligations, and they increase the borrower's effective interest rate.

Compensating balances against short-term borrowings are separately stated in the current asset section or notes. Compensating balances for long-term borrowings are separately stated as noncurrent assets under either investments or other assets.

The cash account on the balance sheet is usually entitled *cash, cash and equivalents*, or *cash and certificates of deposit*. The cash classification typically includes currency and unrestricted funds on deposit with a bank.

Two major problems are encountered when analyzing a current asset: determining a fair valuation for the asset and determining the liquidity of the asset. These problems apply to the cash asset only when it has been restricted. Thus, it is usually a simple matter to decide on the amount of cash to use when determining the short-term debt-paying ability of an entity.

Marketable Securities

The business entity has varying cash needs throughout the year. Because an inferred cost arises from keeping money available, management does not want to keep all of the entity's cash needs in the form of cash throughout the year. The available alternative turns some of the cash into productive use through short-term investments (marketable securities), which can be converted into cash as the need arises.

To qualify as a marketable security, the investment must be readily marketable, and it must be the intent of management to convert the investment to cash within the current operating cycle or one year, whichever is longer. The key element of this test is managerial intent.

It is to management's advantage to show investments under marketable securities, instead of long-term investments, because this classification improves the liquidity appearance of the firm. When the same securities are carried as marketable securities year after year, they are likely held for a business purpose. For example, the other company may be a major supplier or customer of the firm being analyzed. The firm would not want to sell these securities to pay short-term creditors. Therefore, to be conservative, it is better to reclassify them as investments for analysis purposes.

Investments classified as marketable securities should be temporary. Examples of marketable securities include treasury bills, short-term notes of corporations, government bonds, corporate bonds, preferred stock, and common stock. Investments in preferred stock and common stock are referred to as *marketable equity securities.*

Debt and equity securities are to be carried at fair value. An exception is that debt securities can be carried at amortized cost if classified as held-to-maturity securities, but these debt securities would be classified under investments (not classified under current assets).[2]

A security's liquidity must be determined in order for it to be classified as a marketable security. The analyst must assume that securities classified as marketable securities are readily marketable.

Exhibit 6-1 presents the marketable securities on the 2011 annual report of Nike, Inc. It discloses the detail of the marketable securities account. Many companies do not disclose this detail.

EXHIBIT 6-1   Nike, Inc.*

Marketable Securities (Short-Term Investments)

NIKE, INC.
CONSOLIDATED BALANCE SHEETS (In Part)

	May 31,	
	2011	**2010**
	(In millions)	
ASSETS		
Current Assets:		
Cash and cash equivalents	$ 1,955	$ 3,079
Short-term investments (Note 6)	2,583	2,067
Accounts receivable, net (Note 1)	3,138	2,650
Inventories (Notes 1 and 2)	2,715	2,041
Deferred income taxes (Note 9)	312	249
Prepaid expenses and other current assets	594	873
Total current assets	11,297	10,959
Property, plant and equipment, net (Note 3)	2,115	1,932
Identifiable intangible assets, net (Note 4)	487	467
Goodwill (Note 4)	205	188
Deferred income taxes and other assets (Notes 9 and 17)	894	873
Total assets	$14,998	$14,419

Nike, Inc.

Notes to Consolidated Financial Statements (In Part)

Note 1 – Summary of Significant Accounting Policies (In Part)

Short-term Investments
Short-term investments consist of highly liquid investments, including commercial paper, U.S. Treasury, U.S. agency, and corporate debt securities, with maturities over three months from the date of purchase. Debt securities that the Company has the ability and positive intent to hold to maturity are carried at amortized cost. At May 31, 2011 and 2010, the Company did not hold any short-term investments that were classified as held-to-maturity.

At May 31, 2011 and 2010, short-term investments consisted of available-for-sale securities. Available-for-sale securities are recorded at fair value with unrealized gains and losses reported, net of tax, in other comprehensive income, unless unrealized losses are determined to be other than temporary. The Company considers all available-for-sale securities, including those with maturity dates beyond 12 months, as available to support current operational liquidity needs and therefore classifies all securities with maturity dates beyond three months at the date of purchase as current assets within short-term investments on the consolidated balance sheet.

Note 6 This note includes more information on the Company's short-term investments.

*"Our principal business activity is the design, development and worldwide marketing and selling of high quality footwear, apparel, equipment, and accessory products." 10-K
Source: Nike, Inc. 2010 10-K

Receivables

An entity usually has a number of claims to future inflows of cash. These claims are usually classified as **accounts receivable** and **notes receivable** on the financial statements. The primary claim that most entities have comes from the selling of merchandise or services on account to customers, referred to as *trade receivables*, with the customer promising to pay within a limited period of time, such as 30 days. Other claims may be from sources such as loans to employees or a federal tax refund.

Claims from customers, usually in the form of accounts receivable, neither bear interest nor involve claims against specific resources of the customer. In some cases, however, the customer signs a note instead of being granted the privilege of having an open account. Usually, the interest-bearing note will be for a longer period of time than an account receivable. In some cases, a customer who does not pay an account receivable when due signs a *note receivable* in place of the account receivable.

The common characteristic of receivables is that the company expects to receive cash some time in the future. This causes two valuation problems. First, a period of time must pass before the receivable can be collected, so the entity incurs costs for the use of these funds. Second, collection might not be made.

The valuation problem from waiting to collect is *ignored in the valuation of receivables and of notes classified as current assets* because of the short waiting period and the immaterial difference in value. The waiting period problem is not ignored if the receivable or note is long term and classified as an investment. The stipulated rate of interest is presumed to be fair, except when:

1. No interest is stated.
2. The stated rate of interest is clearly unreasonable.
3. The face value of the note is materially different from the cash sales price of the property, goods, or services, or the market value of the note at the date of the transaction.[3]

Under the condition that the face amount of the note does not represent the fair value of the consideration exchanged, *the note is recorded as a present value amount on the date of the original transaction*. The note is recorded at less than (or more than) the face amount, taking into consideration the time value of money. The difference between the recorded amount and the face amount is subsequently amortized as interest income (note receivable) or as interest expense (note payable).

The second problem in valuing receivables or notes is that collection may not be made. Usually, an allowance provides for estimated uncollectible accounts. Estimated losses must be accrued against income, and the impairment of the asset must be recognized (or liability recorded) under the following conditions:

1. Information available prior to the issuance of the financial statements indicates that it is probable that an asset has been impaired, or a liability has been incurred at the date of the financial statements.
2. The amount of the loss can be reasonably estimated.[4]

Both of these conditions are normally met with respect to the uncollectibility of receivables, and the amount subject to being uncollectible is usually material. Thus, in most cases, the company must estimate bad debt expense and indicate the impairment of the receivable. The expense is placed on the income statement, and the impairment of the receivable is disclosed by the use of an account, **allowance for doubtful accounts**, which is subtracted from the gross receivable account. Later, a specific customer's account, identified as being uncollectible, is charged against allowance for doubtful accounts and the gross receivable account on the balance sheet. (This does not mean that the firm will stop efforts to collect.)

It is difficult for the firm to estimate the collectibility of any individual receivable, but when it considers all of the receivables in setting up the allowance, the total estimate should be reasonably accurate. The problem of collection applies to each type of receivable, including notes. The company normally provides for only one allowance account as a matter of convenience, but it considers possible collection problems with all types of receivables and notes when determining the allowance account.

The impairment of receivables may come from causes other than uncollectibility, such as cash discounts allowed, sales returns, and allowances given. Usually, the company considers all of the causes that impair receivables in allowance for doubtful accounts, rather than setting up a separate allowance account for each cause.

Nike presented its receivable account for May 31, 2011 and 2010, as follows:

	2011	2010
Accounts receivable, net	$3,138,000,000	$2,650,000,000

This indicates that net receivables were $3,138,000,000 at May 31, 2011 and $2,650,000,000 at May 31, 2010, after subtracting allowances for doubtful accounts.

NIKE, INC.
Notes to Consolidated Balance Statements (In Part)
Note 1 – Summary of Significant Accounting Policies (In Part)

Allowance for Uncollectible Accounts Receivable

Accounts receivable consists primarily of amounts receivable from customers. We make ongoing estimates relating to the collectability of our accounts receivable and maintain an allowance for estimated losses resulting from the inability of our customers to make required payments. In determining the amount of the allowance, we consider our historical level of credit losses and make judgments about the creditworthiness of significant customers based on ongoing credit evaluations. Accounts receivable with anticipated collection dates greater than 12 months from the balance sheet date and related allowances are considered non-current and recorded in other assets. The allowance for uncollectible accounts receivable was $124 million and $117 million at May 31, 2011 and 2010, respectively, of which $50 million and $43 million was classified as long-term and recorded in other assets.

Using this note, the allowance for uncollectible accounts receivable presented with accounts receivable, net can be computed as follows:

	2011	2010
Total allowance for uncollectible accounts	$124,000,000	$117,000,000
Less: Recorded in other assets	50,000,000	43,000,000
Presented with accounts receivable	$ 74,000,000	$ 74,000,000

The use of the allowance for doubtful accounts approach results in the bad debt expense being charged to the period of sale, thus matching this expense with its related revenue. It also results in recognition of the impairment of the asset. The later charge-off of a specified account receivable does not influence the income statement or net receivables on the balance sheet. The charge-off reduces accounts receivable and allowance for doubtful accounts.

When both conditions specified are not met, or the receivables are immaterial, the entity recognizes bad debt expense using the direct write-off method. With this method, bad debt expense is recognized when a specific customer's account is identified as being uncollectible. At this time, the bad debt expense is recognized on the income statement, and gross accounts receivable is decreased on the balance sheet. This method recognizes the bad debt expense in the same period for both the income statement and the tax return.

The direct write-off method frequently results in the bad debt expense being recognized in the year subsequent to the sale, and thus does not result in a proper matching of expense with revenue. This method reports gross receivables, which does not recognize the impairment of the asset from uncollectibility.

Some companies have trade receivables and installment receivables. Installment receivables will usually be for a relatively long period of time. Installment receivables due within a year are classified under current assets. Installment receivables due after a year are classified below current assets.

Installment receivables classified under current assets are normally much longer than the typical trade receivables. The analyst should make special note of this when making comparisons with competitors. For example, a retail company that has substantial installment receivables is not comparable to a retail company that does not have installment receivables.

Installment receivables are usually considered to be of lower quality than other receivables because of the length of time needed to collect the installment receivables. More importantly, the company with installment receivables should have high standards when granting credit and should closely monitor its receivables.

Exhibit 6-2 indicates the disclosure by CA, Inc., and Subsidiaries.

Customer concentration can be an important consideration in the quality of receivables. When a large portion of receivables is from a few customers, the firm can be highly dependent on those customers. Nike's Form 10-K disclosed that "no customer accounted for 10% or more of our net sales during fiscal 2011."

The liquidity of the trade receivables for a company can be examined by making *two computations*. *The first computation* determines the number of days' sales in receivables at the end of the accounting period, and *the second computation* determines the accounts receivable turnover. The turnover figure can be computed to show the number of times per year receivables turn over or to show how many days on the average it takes to collect the receivables.

Days' Sales in Receivables

The number of days' sales in receivables relates the amount of the accounts receivable to the average daily sales on account. For this computation, the accounts receivable amount should include trade notes receivable. Other receivables not related to sales on account should not be included in this computation. Compute the days' sales in receivables as follows:

$$\text{Days' Sales in Receivables} = \frac{\text{Gross Receivables}}{\text{Net Sales}/365}$$

EXHIBIT **6-2**	CA, Inc. and Subsidiaries*

CA, Inc. and Subsidiaries
Consolidated Balance Sheets (In Part)

	March 31,	
(IN MILLIONS, EXCEPT SHARE AMOUNTS)	2011	2010
Assets		
Current Assets		
Cash and cash equivalents	$ 3,049	$ 2,583
Marketable securities – current	75	—
Trade and installment accounts receivable, net	849	931
Deferred income taxes – current	246	360
Other current assets	152	116
Total Current Assets	4,371	3,990
Marketable securities – noncurrent	104	—
Installment accounts receivable, due after one year, net	—	46
Property and equipment, net of accumulated depreciation of $632 and $538, respectively	437	452
Goodwill	5,688	5,605
Capitalized software and other intangible assets, net	1,284	1,215
Deferred income taxes – noncurrent	284	348
Other noncurrent assets, net	246	232
Total assets	$12,414	$11,888

Note 6. Trade and Installment Accounts Receivable.
Note: A detailed description was included with the statements.

*"CA Technologies is the leading independent enterprise information technology (IT) management software and solutions company with expertise across IT environments – from mainframe and physical to virtual and cloud." 10-K
Source: CA, Inc. and Subsidiaries 2010 10-K

EXHIBIT **6-3**	Nike, Inc.		

Days' Sales in Receivables

Years Ended May 31, 2011 and 2010

(In millions)	2011	2010
Accounts receivable, net	$3,138	$2,650
Allowance for uncollectible accounts	74	74
Gross receivables (net plus allowance) (A)	3,212	2,724
Net sales	20,862	19,014
Average daily sales on account (net sales on account divided by 365) (B)	57.16	52.09
Days' sales in receivables (A ÷ B)	56.19 days	52.29 days

Source: Nike, Inc. 2010 10-K

This formula divides the number of days in a year into net sales on account and then divides the resulting figure into gross receivables. Exhibit 6-3 presents this computation for Nike at the end of 2011 and 2010. The increase in days' sales in receivables from 52.29 days at the end of 2010 to 56.19 days at the end of 2011 indicates a negative trend in the control of receivables.

An internal analyst compares days' sales in receivables with the company's credit terms as an indication of how efficiently the company manages its receivables. For example, if the credit term is 30 days, days' sales in receivables should not be materially over 30 days. If days' sales in receivables are materially more than the credit terms, the company has a collection problem. An effort should be made to keep the days' sales in receivables close to the credit terms.

Consider the effect on the quality of receivables from a change in the *credit terms*. Shortening the credit terms indicates that there will be less risk in the collection of future receivables, and lengthening the credit terms indicates a greater risk. Credit term information is readily available for internal analysis and may be available in notes.

Right of return privileges can also be important to the quality of receivables. Liberal right of return privileges can be a negative factor in the quality of receivables and on sales that have already been recorded. Particular attention should be paid to any change in the right of return privileges. Right of return privileges can readily be determined for internal analysis, and this information should be available in a note if considered to be material.

The net sales figure includes collectible and uncollectible accounts. The uncollectible accounts *would not exist* if there were an accurate way, prior to sale, of determining which credit customers would not pay. Firms make an effort to determine credit standing when they approve a customer for credit, but this process does not eliminate uncollectible accounts. Since the net sales figure includes both collectible and uncollectible accounts (gross sales), the comparable receivables figure should include gross receivables, rather than the net receivables figure that remains after the allowance for doubtful accounts is deducted.

The days' sales in receivables indicates the length of time that the receivables have been outstanding at the end of the year. *The indication can be misleading if sales are seasonal and/ or the company uses a natural business year.* If the company uses a natural business year for its accounting period, the days' sales in receivables will tend to be understated because the actual sales per day at the end of the year will be low when compared to the average sales per day for the year. The understatement of days' sales in receivables can also be explained by the fact that gross receivables will tend to be below average at that time of year.

The following is an example of how days' sales in receivables will tend to be understated when a company uses a natural business year:

Average sales per day for the entire year	$ 2,000
Sales per day at the end of the natural business year	1,000
Gross receivables at the end of the year	100,000

Days' sales in receivables based on the formula:

$$\frac{\$100,000}{\$2,000} = 50 \text{ days}$$

Days' sales in receivables based on sales per day at the end of the natural business year:

$$\frac{\$100,000}{\$1,000} = 100 \text{ days}$$

The liquidity of a company that uses a natural business year tends to be overstated. However, the only positive way to know if a company uses a natural business year is through research. The information may not be readily available.

It is unlikely that a company that has a seasonal business will close the accounting year during peak activity. At the peak of the business cycle, company personnel are busy and receivables are likely to be at their highest levels. If a company closed during peak activity, the days' sales in receivables would tend to be overstated and the liquidity understated.

The length of time that the receivables have been outstanding indicates their collectibility. The days' sales in receivables should be compared for several years. A comparison should also be made between the days' sales in receivables for a particular company and comparable figures for other firms in the industry and industry averages. This type of comparison can be made when doing either internal or external analysis.

Assuming that the days' sales in receivables computation is *not* distorted because of a seasonal business and/or the company's use of a natural business year, consider the following reasons to explain why the days' sales in receivables appears to be abnormally high:

1. Sales volume expands materially late in the year.
2. Receivables are uncollectible and should have been written off.
3. The company seasonally dates invoices. (An example would be a toy manufacturer that ships in August with the receivable due at the end of December.)
4. A large portion of receivables are on the installment basis.

Assuming that the distortion is *not* from a seasonal situation or the company's use of a natural business year, the following should be considered as possible reasons why the days' sales in receivables appears to be abnormally low:

1. Sales volume decreases materially late in the year.
2. A material amount of sales are on a cash basis.
3. The company has a factoring arrangement in which a material amount of the receivables is sold. (With a factoring arrangement, the receivables are sold to an outside party.)

When doing external analysis, many of the reasons why the days' sales in receivables is abnormally high or low cannot be determined without access to internal information.

Accounts Receivable Turnover

Another computation, accounts receivable turnover, indicates the liquidity of the receivables. Compute the accounts receivable turnover measured in times per year as follows:

$$\text{Accounts Receivable Turnover} = \frac{\text{Net Sales}}{\text{Average Gross Receivables}}$$

Exhibit 6-4 presents this computation for Nike at the end of 2011 and 2010. The turnover of receivables increased between 2010 and 2011 from 6.69 times per year to 7.03 times per year. For Nike, this would be a positive trend.

Computing the average gross receivables based on beginning-of-year and end-of-year receivables can be misleading if the business has seasonal fluctuations or if the company uses a natural business year. To avoid problems of seasonal fluctuations or of comparing a company that uses a natural business year with one that uses a calendar year, the monthly balances (or even weekly balances) of accounts receivable should be used in the computation. This is feasible when performing internal analysis, but not when performing external analysis. In

EXHIBIT **6-4** Nike, Inc.		
Accounts Receivable Turnover		

Years Ended May 31, 2011 and 2010

(In millions)	2011	2010
Net sales (A)	$20,862	$19,014
End-of-year receivables, net	3,138	2,650
Beginning-of-year receivables, net	2,650	2,884
Allowance for doubtful accounts:		
End of 2011 $74.0		
End of 2010 $74.0		
End of 2009 $73.9		
Ending gross receivables (net plus allowance)	3,212	2,724
Beginning gross receivables (net plus allowance)	2,724	2,958
Average gross receivables (B)	2,968	2,841
Accounts receivables turnover (A ÷ B)	7.03 times	6.69 times

Source: Nike, Inc. 2010 10-K

the case of external analysis, quarterly figures can be used to help eliminate these problems. If these problems cannot be eliminated, companies not on the same basis should not be compared. The company with the natural business year tends to overstate its accounts receivable turnover, thus overstating its liquidity.

Accounts Receivable Turnover in Days

The accounts receivable turnover can be expressed in terms of days instead of times per year. Turnover in number of days also gives a comparison with the number of days' sales in the ending receivables. The accounts receivable turnover in days also results in an answer directly related to the firm's credit terms. Compute the accounts receivable turnover in days as follows:

$$\text{Accounts Receivable Turnover in Days} = \frac{\text{Average Gross Receivables}}{\text{Net Sales}/365}$$

This formula is the same as that for determining number of days' sales in receivables, except that the accounts receivable turnover in days is computed using the average gross receivables. Exhibit 6-5 presents the computation for Nike at the end of 2011 and 2010. Accounts receivable turnover in days decreased from 54.54 days in 2010 to 51.92 days in 2011. This would represent a positive trend.

The accounts receivable turnover in times per year and days can both be computed by alternative formulas, using Nike's 2011 figures, as follows:

1. Accounts Receivable Turnover in Times per Year

$$\frac{365}{\begin{array}{c}\text{Accounts Receivable}\\\text{Turnover in Days}\end{array}} = \frac{365}{51.92} = 7.03 \text{ Times per Year}$$

2. Accounts Receivable Turnover in Days

$$\frac{365}{\begin{array}{c}\text{Accounts Receivable}\\\text{Times per Year}\end{array}} = \frac{365}{7.03} = 51.92 \text{ Days per Year}$$

The answers obtained for both accounts receivable turnover in number of times per year and accounts receivable turnover in days, using the alternative formulas, may differ slightly from the answers obtained with the previous formulas. The difference is due to rounding.

EXHIBIT **6-5**	Nike, Inc.	

Accounts Receivable Turnover in Days

Years Ended May 31, 2011 and 2010

(In millions)	2011	2010
Net sales	$20,862	$19,014
Average gross receivables [A]	2,968	2,841
Sales per day (net sales divided by 365) [B]	57.16	52.09
Accounts receivable turnover in days [A ÷ B]	51.92 days	54.54 days

Source: Nike, Inc. 2010 10-K

Credit Sales versus Cash Sales

A difficulty in computing receivables' liquidity is the problem of credit sales versus cash sales. Net sales includes both credit sales and cash sales. To have a realistic indication of the liquidity of receivables, only the credit sales should be included in the computations. If cash sales are included, the liquidity will be overstated.

The internal analyst determines the credit sales figure and eliminates the problem of credit sales versus cash sales. The external analyst should be aware of this problem and should not be misled by the liquidity figures. The distinction between cash sales and credit sales is not usually a major problem for the external analyst because certain types of businesses tend to sell only on cash terms, and others sell only on credit terms. For example, a manufacturer usually sells only on credit terms. Some businesses, such as a retail department store, have a mixture of credit sales and cash sales.

In cases of mixed sales, the proportion of credit and cash sales tends to stay rather constant. Therefore, the liquidity figures are comparable (but overstated), enabling the reader to compare figures from period to period as well as figures of similar companies.

Inventories

Inventory is often the most significant asset in determining the short-term debt-paying ability of an entity. Often, the inventory account is more than half of the total current assets. Because of the significance of inventories, a special effort should be made to analyze properly this important area.

To be classified as **inventory**, the asset should be for sale in the ordinary course of business, or used or consumed in the production of goods. A trading concern purchases merchandise in a form to sell to customers. Inventories of a trading concern, whether wholesale or retail, usually appear in one inventory account (Merchandise Inventory). A manufacturing concern produces goods to be sold. Inventories of a manufacturing concern are normally classified in three distinct inventory accounts: inventory available to use in production (raw materials inventory), inventory in production (work-in-process inventory), and inventory completed (finished goods inventory).

Usually, it is much more difficult to determine the inventory figures in a manufacturing concern than in a trading concern. The manufacturing concern deals with materials, labor, and overhead when determining the inventory figures, while the trading concern only deals with purchased merchandise. The overhead portion of the work-in-process inventory and the finished goods inventory is often a problem when determining a manufacturer's inventory. The overhead consists of all the costs of the factory other than direct materials and direct labor. From an analysis viewpoint, however, many of the problems of determining the proper inventory value are solved before the entity publishes financial statements.

Inventory is particularly sensitive to changes in business activity, so management must keep inventory in balance with business activity. Failure to do so leads to excessive costs (such as storage cost), production disruptions, and employee layoffs. For example, it is difficult for automobile manufacturers to balance inventories with business activities. When sales decline rapidly, the industry has difficulty adjusting production and the resulting inventory to match the decline. Manufacturers have to use customer incentives, such as price rebates, to get the large inventory buildup back to a manageable level. When business activity increases, inventory shortages can lead to overtime costs. The increase in activity can also lead to cash shortages because of the length of time necessary to acquire inventory, sell the merchandise, and collect receivables.

Inventory quantities and costs may be accounted for using either the **perpetual** or **periodic** system. Using the perpetual system, the company maintains a continuous record of physical quantities in its inventory. When the perpetual system includes costs (versus quantities only), then the company updates its inventory and cost of goods sold continually as purchases and sales take place. (The inventory needs to be verified by a physical count at least once a year.)

Using the periodic system, physical counts are taken periodically, which should be at least once a year. The cost of the ending inventory is determined by attaching costs to the physical quantities on hand based on the cost flow assumption used. The cost of goods sold is calculated by subtracting the ending inventory from the cost of goods available for sale.

Inventory Cost

The most critical problem that many entities face is determining which cost to use, since the cost prices have usually varied over time. If it were practical to determine the specific cost of an item, this would be a good cost figure to use. It would also substantially reduce inventory valuation problems. In practice, because of the different types of inventory items and the constant flow of these items, it is not practical to determine the specific costs. Exceptions to this are large items and/or expensive items. For example, it would be practical to determine the specific cost of a new car in the dealer's showroom or the specific cost of an expensive diamond in a jewelry store. When specific costs are used, this is referred to as the **specific identification** method.

Because the cost of specific items is not usually practical to determine and because other things are considered (such as the income result), companies typically use a cost flow assumption. The most common cost flow assumptions are first-in, first-out (FIFO), last-in, first-out (LIFO), or some average computation. These assumptions can produce substantially different results because of changing prices.

The **FIFO method** assumes that the first inventory acquired is the first sold. This means that the cost of goods sold account consists of beginning inventory and the earliest items purchased. The latest items purchased remain in inventory. These latest costs are fairly representative of the current costs to replace the inventory. If the inventory flows slowly (low turnover), or if there has been substantial inflation, even FIFO may not produce an inventory figure for the balance sheet representative of the replacement cost. Part of the inventory cost of a manufacturing concern consists of overhead, some of which may represent costs from several years prior, such as depreciation on the plant and equipment. Often, the costs transferred to cost of goods sold under FIFO are low in relation to current costs, so current costs are not matched against current revenue. During a time of inflation, the resulting profit is overstated. To the extent that inventory does not represent replacement cost, an understatement of the inventory cost occurs.

The **LIFO method** assumes that the costs of the latest items bought or produced are matched against current sales. Usually, this assumption materially improves the matching of current costs against current revenue, so the resulting profit figure is fairly realistic. The first items (and oldest costs) in inventory can materially distort the reported inventory figure in comparison with its replacement cost. A firm that has been on LIFO for many years may have some inventory costs that go back 20 years or more. Because of inflation, the resulting inventory figure will not reflect current replacement costs. LIFO accounting was started in the United States. It is now accepted in a few other countries.

Averaging methods lump the costs to determine a midpoint. An average cost computation for inventories results in an inventory amount and a cost of goods sold amount somewhere between FIFO and LIFO. During times of inflation, the resulting inventory is more than LIFO and less than FIFO. The resulting cost of goods sold is less than LIFO and more than FIFO.

Exhibit 6-6 summarizes the inventory methods used by the companies surveyed for *Accounting Trends & Techniques*. The table covers the years 2009, 2008, 2007, and 2006.

EXHIBIT **6-6**	Inventory Cost Determination			

| | Number of Companies | | | |
	2009	2008	2007	2006
Methods				
First-in first-out (FIFO)	325	323	391	385
Last-in first-out (LIFO)	176	179	213	228
Average cost	147	146	155	159
Other	18	17	24	30
Use of LIFO				
All inventories	4	7	14	11
50% or more of inventories	82	86	91	109
Less than 50% of inventories	78	72	88	88
Not determinable	12	14	20	20
Entities using LIFO	176	179	213	228

Note: 2008 – 2009 based on 500 entities surveyed; 2006 – 2007 based on 600 entities surveyed.
Source: Accounting Trends & Techniques, copyright © 2010 by American Institute of Certified Public Accountants, Inc. p. 169.
Reprinted with permission.

Exhibit 6-6 indicates that the most popular inventory methods are FIFO and LIFO. It is perceived that LIFO requires more cost to administer than FIFO. LIFO is not as popular during times of relatively low inflation. During times of relatively high inflation, LIFO becomes more popular because LIFO matches the latest costs against revenue. LIFO results in tax benefits because of the matching of recent higher costs against revenue.

Exhibit 6-6 includes a summary of companies that use LIFO for all inventories, 50% or more of inventories, less than 50% of inventories, and not determinable. This summary indicates that only a small percentage of companies that use LIFO use it for all of their inventories.

For the following illustration, the periodic system is used with the inventory count at the end of the year. The same answer would result for FIFO and specific identification under either the perpetual or periodic system. A different answer would result for LIFO or average cost, depending on whether a perpetual or periodic system is used.

To illustrate the major costing methods for determining which costs apply to the units remaining in inventory at the end of the year and which costs are allocated to cost of goods sold, consider the following:

Date	Description	Number of Units	Cost per Unit	Total Cost
January 1	Beginning inventory	200	$ 6	$ 1,200
March 1	Purchase	1,200	7	8,400
July 1	Purchase	300	9	2,700
October 1	Purchase	400	11	4,400
		2,100		$16,700

A physical inventory count on December 31 indicates 800 units on hand. There were 2,100 units available during the year, and 800 remained at the end of the year; therefore, 1,300 units were sold.

Four cost assumptions will be used to illustrate the determination of the ending inventory costs and the related cost of goods sold: *first-in, first-out (FIFO); last-in, first-out (LIFO); average cost;* and *specific identification.*

First-In, First-Out Method (FIFO) The cost of ending inventory is found by attaching cost to the physical quantities on hand, based on the FIFO cost flow assumption. The cost of goods sold is calculated by subtracting the ending inventory cost from the cost of goods available for sale.

		Number of Units		Cost per Unit	Inventory Cost	Cost of Goods Sold
October 1	Purchase	400	@	$11	$4,400	
July 1	Purchase	300	@	9	2,700	
March 1	Purchase	100	@	7	700	
Ending inventory		800			$7,800	
Cost of goods sold ($16,700 − $7,800)						$8,900

Last-In, First-Out Method (LIFO) The cost of the ending inventory is found by attaching costs to the physical quantities on hand, based on the LIFO cost flow assumption. The cost of goods sold is calculated by subtracting the ending inventory cost from the cost of goods available for sale.

		Number of Units		Cost per Unit	Inventory Cost	Cost of Goods Sold
January 1	Beginning inventory	200	@	$6	$1,200	
March 1	Purchase	600	@	7	4,200	
Ending inventory		800			$5,400	
Cost of goods sold ($16,700 − $5,400)						$11,300

Average Cost There are several ways to compute the average cost. The weighted average divides the total cost by the total units to determine the average cost per unit. The average cost per unit is multiplied by the inventory quantity to determine inventory cost. The cost of goods sold is calculated by subtracting the ending inventory cost from the cost of goods available for sale.

	Inventory Cost	Cost of Goods Sold
Total cost $\frac{\$16,700}{2,100} = \$7.95$ Total units		
Ending inventory (800 × $7.95)	$6,360	
Cost of goods sold ($16,700 − $6,360)		$10,340

Specific Identification With the specific identification method, the items in inventory are identified as coming from specific purchases. For this example, assume that the 800 items in inventory can be identified with the March 1 purchase. The cost of goods sold is calculated by subtracting the ending inventory cost from the cost of goods available for sale.

	Inventory Cost	Cost of Goods Sold
Ending inventory (800 × $7.00)	$5,600	
Cost of goods sold ($16,700 − $5,600)		$11,100

The difference in results for inventory cost and cost of goods sold from using different inventory methods may be material or immaterial. The major impact on the results usually comes from the rate of inflation. In general, the higher the inflation rate, the greater the differences between the inventory methods.

Because the inventory amounts can be substantially different under the various cost flow assumptions, the analyst should be cautious when comparing the liquidity of firms that have different inventory cost flow assumptions. Caution is particularly necessary when one of the firms is using the LIFO method because LIFO may prove meaningless with regard to the firm's short-term debt-paying ability. If two firms that have different cost flow assumptions need to be compared, this problem should be kept in mind to avoid being misled by the indicated short-term debt-paying ability.

Since the resulting inventory amount will not be equal to the cost of replacing the inventory, regardless of the cost method, another problem needs to be considered when determining the short-term debt-paying ability of the firm: the inventory must be sold for more than cost in order to realize a profit. To the extent that the inventory is sold for more than cost, the short-term debt-paying ability has been understated. However, the extent of the understatement is materially reduced by several factors. One, the firm will incur substantial selling and administrative costs in addition to the inventory cost, thereby reducing the understatement of liquidity to the resulting net profit. Two, the replacement cost of the inventory usually exceeds the reported inventory cost, even if FIFO is used. Therefore, more funds will be required to replace the inventory sold. This will reduce the future short-term debt-paying ability of the firm. Also, since accountants support the conservatism concept, they would rather have a slight understatement of the short-term debt-paying ability of the firm than an overstatement.

The impact on the entity of the different inventory methods must be understood. Since the extremes in inventory costing are LIFO and FIFO, the following summarizes these methods. This summary assumes that the entity faces a period of inflation. The conclusions arrived at in this summary would be reversed if the entity faces a deflationary period.

1. LIFO generally results in a lower profit than does FIFO, as a result of a higher cost of goods sold. This difference can be substantial.

2. Generally, reported profit under LIFO is closer to reality than profit reported under FIFO because the cost of goods sold is closer to replacement cost under LIFO. This is the case under both inflationary and deflationary conditions.

3. FIFO reports a higher inventory ending balance (closer to replacement cost). However, this figure falls short of true replacement cost.

4. The cash flow under LIFO is greater than the cash flow under FIFO because of the difference in tax liability between the two methods; this is an important reason why a company selects LIFO.

5. Some companies use a periodic inventory system, which updates the inventory in the general ledger once a year. Purchases made late in the year become part of the cost of goods sold under LIFO. If prices have increased during the period, the cost of goods sold will increase and profits will decrease. It is important that accountants inform management that profits will be lower if substantial purchases of inventory are made near the end of the year, and a periodic inventory system is used.

6. A company using LIFO could face a severe tax problem and a severe cash problem if sales reduce or eliminate the amount of inventory normally carried. The reduction in inventory would result in older costs being matched against current sales. This distorts profits on the high side. Because of the high reported profit, income taxes would increase. When the firm needs to replenish the inventory, it has to use additional cash. These problems can be reduced by planning and close supervision of production and purchases. A method called dollar-value LIFO is now frequently used by companies that use LIFO. The dollar-value LIFO method uses price indexes related to the inventory instead of units and unit costs. With dollar-value LIFO, inventory each period is determined for pools of inventory dollars. (See an intermediate accounting book for a detailed explanation of dollar-value LIFO.)

7. LIFO would probably not be used for inventory that has a high turnover rate because there would be an immaterial difference in the results between LIFO and FIFO.

8. LIFO results in a lower profit figure than does FIFO, the result of a higher cost of goods sold.

A firm using LIFO must disclose a LIFO reserve account, most often in a note to the financial statement. Usually, the amount disclosed must be added to inventory to approximate the inventory at FIFO. An inventory at FIFO is usually a reasonable approximation of the current replacement cost of the inventory.

Lower-of-Cost-or-Market Rule We have reviewed the inventory cost-based measurements of FIFO, LIFO, average, and specific identification. These cost-based measurements are all considered to be historical cost approaches. The accounting profession decided that a "departure from the cost basis of inventory pricing is required when the utility of the goods is no longer as great as its cost." Utility of the goods has been measured through market values. When the market value of inventory falls below cost, it is necessary to write the inventory down to the lower market value. This is known as the **lower-of-cost-or-market (LCM) rule**. Market is defined in terms of current replacement cost, either by purchase or manufacture.

Following the LCM rule, inventories can be written down below cost but never up above cost. The LCM rule provides for the recognition of the loss in utility during the period in which the loss occurs. The LCM rule is consistent with both the matching and the conservatism assumptions.

The LCM rule is used by many countries other than the United States. As indicated, market is defined in the United States in terms of current replacement cost. Market in other countries may be defined differently, such as "net realizable value."

Nike uses the FIFO inventory method. The Gorman-Rupp Company will be used to illustrate LIFO. Selected balance sheet and notes from the 2008 annual report of the Gorman-Rupp Company are in Exhibit 6-7.

The approximate current costs of the Gorman-Rupp inventory at December 31, 2010 and 2009 follow.

	2010	2009
Balance per balance sheet	$51,449,000	$40,506,000
Additional amount in note	47,100,000	47,600,000
Approximate current costs	$98,549,000	$88,106,000

Liquidity of Inventory Analysis of the liquidity of the inventories can be approached in a manner similar to that taken to analyze the liquidity of accounts receivable. One computation determines the *number of days' sales in inventory* at the end of the accounting period,

---

EXHIBIT **6-7**	The Gorman-Rupp Company*

Illustration of LIFO

Consolidated Balance Sheets (In Part)

(Thousands of dollars)	December 31,	
	2010	2009
Inventories:		
Raw materials and in-process	20,128	22,087
Finished parts	27,005	16,026
Finished products	4,316	2,393
	$51,449	$40,506

Notes to Consolidated Financial Statements (In Part)

Note A – Summary of Major Accounting Policies (In Part)

Inventories

Inventories are stated at the lower of cost or market. The costs for approximately 82% of inventories at December 31, 2010 and 90% at December 31, 2009 are determined using the last-in, first-out (LIFO) method, with the remainder determined using the first-in, first-out (FIFO) method. Cost components include materials inbound freight costs, labor and allocations of fixed cost, and variable overhauls costs are absorption costing basis.

Note C – Inventories

The excess of replacement costs over LIFO cost is approximately $47.1 million and $47.6 million at December 31, 2010 and 2009, respectively. Replacement cost approximates current cost. Some inventory quantities were reduced during 2010 and 2009, resulting in liquidation of some LIFO quantities carried at lower costs from earlier years versus current year costs. The related effect increased net income by $829,000 in 2010 ($0.05 per share) and $1.9 million ($0.12 per share) in 2009. Allowances for excess and obsolete inventory totaled $2.7 million and $2.2 million at December 31, 2010 and 2009, respectively.

---

*"The Gorman-Rupp company... designs, manufactures and globally sell pumps and related equipment (pump and motor controls) for use in water, wastewater, construction, industrial, petroleum, original equipment, agriculture, fire protection, heating, ventilating and air conditioning ("HVAC"), military and other liquid-handling applications." 10-K
Source: The Gorman-Rupp Company 2010 10-K

another computation determines the *inventory turnover in times per year*, and a third determines the *inventory turnover in days*.

Days' Sales in Inventory The number of days' sales in inventory ratio relates the amount of the ending inventory to the average daily cost of goods sold. All of the inventory accounts should be included in the computation. The computation gives an indication of the length of time that it will take to use up the inventory through sales. This can be misleading if sales are seasonal or if the company uses a natural business year.

If the company uses a natural business year for its accounting period, the number of days' sales in inventory will tend to be understated because the average daily cost of goods sold will be at a low point at this time of year. If the days' sales in inventory is understated, the liquidity of the inventory is overstated. The same caution should be observed here as was suggested for determining the liquidity of receivables, when one company uses a natural business year and the other uses a calendar year.

If the company closes its year during peak activity, the number of days' sales in inventory would tend to be overstated and the liquidity would be understated. As indicated with receivables, no good business reason exists for closing the year when activities are at a peak, so this situation should rarely occur.

Compute the number of days' sales in inventory as follows:

$$\text{Days' Sales in Inventory} = \frac{\text{Ending Inventory}}{\text{Cost of Goods Sold}/365}$$

The formula divides the number of days in a year into the cost of goods sold and then divides the resulting figure into the ending inventory. Exhibit 6-8 presents the number of days' sales in inventory for Nike for May 31, 2011, and May 31, 2010. The number of days' sales in inventory has increased from 72.94 days at the end of 2010 to 87.27 days at the end of 2011. This represents a negative trend.

If sales are approximately constant, then the lower the number of days' sales in inventory, the better the inventory control. An inventory buildup can be burdensome if business volume decreases. However, it can be good if business volume expands, since the increased inventory would be available for customers. The days' sales in inventory estimates the number of days that it will take to sell the current inventory. For several reasons, this estimate may not be very accurate. The cost of goods sold figure is based on last year's sales, divided by the number of days in a year. Sales next year may not be at the same pace as last year. Also, the ending inventory figure may not be representative of the quantity of inventory actually on hand, especially if using LIFO.

A seasonal situation, with inventory unusually low or high at the end of the year, would also result in an unrealistic days' sales in inventory computation. Also, a natural business year with low inventory at the end of the year would result in an unrealistic days' sales in inventory. Therefore, the resulting answer should be taken as a rough estimate, but it helps when comparing periods or similar companies. The number of days' sales in inventory could become too low, resulting in lost sales. Good knowledge of the industry and the company is required to determine if the number of days' sales in inventory is too low.

EXHIBIT **6-8** Nike, Inc.		
Days' Sales in Inventory		
Years Ended May 31, 2011 and 2010		
(In millions)	2011	2010
Inventories, end of year [A]	$ 2,715	$ 2,041
Cost of goods sold	11,354	10,214
Average daily cost of goods sold (cost of goods sold divided by 365) [B]	31.11	27.98
Number of days' sales in inventory [A ÷ B]	87.27 days	72.94 days

Source: Nike, Inc. 2010 10-K

In some cases, not only will the cost of goods sold not be reported separately, but the figure reported will not be a close approximation of the cost of goods sold. This, of course, presents a problem for the external analyst. In such cases, net sales should be used in place of the cost of goods sold. The result will not be a realistic number of days' sales in inventory, but it can be useful in comparing periods within one firm and in comparing one firm with another. Using net sales produces a much lower number of days' sales in inventory, which materially over-states the liquidity of the ending inventory. Therefore, only the trend determined from compar-ing one period with another and one firm with other firms should be taken seriously (not actual absolute figures). When you suspect that the days' sales in inventory computation does not result in a reasonable answer, consider using this ratio only to indicate a trend.

If the dollar figures for inventory and/or the cost of goods sold are not reasonable, the ratios calculated with these figures may be distorted. These distortions can be eliminated to some extent by using quantities rather than dollars in the computation. The use of quantities in the computation may work very well for single products or groups of similar products. It does not work very well for a large diversified inventory because of possible changes in the mix of the inventory. Also, using quantities rather than dollars will not be feasible when using externally published statements.

An example of the use of quantities, instead of dollars, follows:

Ending inventory	50 units
Cost of goods sold	500 units

$$\text{Days' sales in inventory} = \frac{50}{500/365} = 36.50 \text{ days}$$

Inventory Turnover Inventory turnover indicates the liquidity of the inventory. This com-putation is similar to the accounts receivable turnover computation.

The inventory turnover formula follows:

$$\text{Inventory Turnover} = \frac{\text{Cost of Goods Sold}}{\text{Average Inventory}}$$

Exhibit 6-9 presents the inventory turnover using the 2011 and 2010 figures for Nike. For Nike, the inventory turnover increased from 4.64 to 4.77.

Computing the average inventory based on the beginning-of-year and end-of-year inven-tories can be misleading if the company has seasonal fluctuations or if the company uses a natural business year. The solution to the problem is similar to that used when computing the receivables turnover—that is, use the monthly (or even weekly) balances of inventory. Monthly estimates of inventory are available for internal analysis, but not for external analy-sis. Quarterly figures may be available for external analysis. If adequate information is not available, it is important to avoid comparing a company on a natural business year with a company on a calendar year. The company with the natural business year tends to overstate inventory turnover and therefore the liquidity of its inventory.

EXHIBIT **6-9**	Nike, Inc.

Merchandise Inventory Turnover

Years Ended May 31, 2011 and 2010		
(In millions)	2011	2010
Cost of goods sold [A]	$11,354	$10,214
Inventories:		
Beginning of year	2,041	2,357
End of year	2,715	2,041
Total	4,756	4,398
Average inventory [B]	2,378	2,199
Merchandise inventory turnover [A ÷ B]	4.77 times per year	4.64 times per year

Source: Nike, Inc. 2010 10-K

Over time, the difference between the inventory turnover for a firm that uses LIFO and one that uses a method that results in a higher inventory figure can become very material. The LIFO firm will have a much lower inventory and therefore a much higher turnover. Also, it may not be reasonable to compare firms in different industries.

When you suspect that the inventory turnover computation does not result in a reasonable answer because of unrealistic inventory and/or cost of goods sold dollar figures, the computation should be performed using quantities rather than dollars. As with the days' sales in inventory, this alternative is feasible only when performing internal analysis. (It may not be feasible even for internal analysis because of product line changes.)

Inventory Turnover in Days The inventory turnover figure can be expressed in number of days instead of times per year. This is comparable to the computation that expressed accounts receivable turnover in days. Compute the inventory turnover in days as follows:

$$\text{Inventory Turnover in Days} = \frac{\text{Average Inventory}}{\text{Cost of Goods Sold}/365}$$

This is the same formula for determining the days' sales in inventory, except that it uses the average inventory. Exhibit 6-10 uses the 2011 and 2010 Nike data to compute the inventory turnover in days. There was a decrease in inventory turnover in days for Nike in 2011. This represents a favorable trend.

The inventory turnover in days can be used to compute the inventory turnover per year, as follows:

$$\frac{365}{\text{Inventory Turnover in Days}} = \text{Inventory Turnover per Year}$$

Using the 2011 Nike data, the inventory turnover is as follows:

$$\frac{365}{\text{Inventory Turnover in Days}} = \frac{365}{76.44} = 4.77 \text{ times per year}$$

Operating Cycle The operating cycle represents the period of time that elapses between the acquisition of goods and the final cash realization resulting from sales and subsequent collections. An approximation of the operating cycle can be determined from the receivables liquidity figures and the inventory liquidity figures. Compute the operating cycle as follows:

Operating Cycle = Accounts Receivable Turnover in Days + Inventory Turnover in Days

Exhibit 6-11 uses the 2011 and 2010 Nike data to compute the operating cycle. For Nike, the operating cycle decreased, which is a positive trend.

The estimate of the operating cycle is not realistic if the accounts receivable turnover in days and the inventory turnover in days are not realistic. Remember that the accounts receivable turnover in days and the inventory turnover in days are understated, and thus the liquidity is overstated, if the company uses a natural business year and computed the averages based on beginning-of-year and end-of-year data. It should also be remembered that the

EXHIBIT **6-10**	Nike, Inc.		
Inventory Turnover in Days			
Years Ended May 31, 2011 and 2010			
(In millions)		**2011**	**2010**
Cost of goods sold		$11,354	$10,210
Average inventory [A]		2,378	2,199
Sales of inventory per day (cost of goods sold divided by 365) [B]		31.11	27.97
Inventory turnover in days [A ÷ B]		76.44 days	78.62 days

Source: Nike, Inc. 2010 10-K

EXHIBIT **6-11**	Nike, Inc.

Operating Cycle

Years Ended May 31, 2011 and 2010

	2011	2010
Accounts receivable turnover in days [A]	51.92	54.54
Inventory turnover in days [B]	76.44	78.62
Operating cycle [A + B]	128.36	133.16

Source: Nike, Inc. 2010 10-K

inventory turnover in days is understated, and the liquidity of the inventory overstated, if the company uses LIFO inventory. In addition, it should be noted that accounts receivable turnover in days is understated, and liquidity of receivables overstated, if the sales figures used included cash and credit sales.

The operating cycle should be helpful when comparing a firm from period to period and when comparing a firm with similar companies. This would be the case, even if understated or overstated, as long as the figures in the computation are comparable.

Related to the operating cycle figure is a computation that indicates how long it will take to realize cash from the ending inventory. This computation consists of combining the number of days' sales in ending receivables and the number of days' sales in ending inventory. The 2011 Nike data produced a days' sales in ending receivables of 56.19 days and a days' sales in ending inventory of 87.27 days, for a total of 143.46 days. In this case, there is an increase, considering the year-end numbers. This indicates less liquidity at the end of the year than during the year.

Prepayments

Prepayments consist of unexpired costs for which payment has been made. These current assets are expected to be consumed within the operating cycle or one year, whichever is longer. Prepayments normally represent an immaterial portion of the current assets. Therefore, they have little influence on the short-term debt-paying ability of the firm.

Since prepayments have been paid for and will not generate cash in the future, they differ from other current assets. Prepayments relate to the short-term debt-paying ability of the entity because they conserve the use of cash.

Because of the nature of prepayments, the problems of valuation and liquidity are handled in a simple manner. Valuation is taken as the cost that has been paid. Since a prepayment is a current asset that has been paid for in a relatively short period before the balance sheet date, the cost paid fairly represents the cash used for the prepayment. Except in rare circumstances, a prepayment will not result in a receipt of cash; therefore, no liquidity computation is needed. An example of a circumstance where cash is received would be an insurance policy canceled early. No liquidity computation is possible, even in this case.

Other Current Assets

Current assets other than cash, marketable securities, receivables, inventories, and prepayments may be listed under current assets. These other current assets may be very material in any one year and, unless they are recurring, may distort the firm's liquidity.

These assets will, in management's opinion, be realized in cash or conserve the use of cash within the operating cycle of the business or one year, whichever is longer. Examples of other current assets include property held for sale and advances or deposits, often explained in a note.

Current Liabilities

Current liabilities are "obligations whose liquidation is reasonably expected to require the use of existing resources properly classifiable as current assets or the creation of other current liabilities."[5] Thus, the definition of current liabilities correlates with the definition of current assets.

Typical items found in current liabilities include accounts payable, notes payable, accrued wages, accrued taxes, collections received in advance, and current portions of long-term liabilities. The 2011 Nike annual report listed current liabilities as follows:

	(In millions)
Current liabilities:	
Current portion of long-term debt	$ 200
Notes payable	187
Accounts payable	1,469
Accrued liabilities	1,985
Income taxes payable	117
Total current liabilities	$3,958

For a current liability, liquidity is not a problem, and the valuation problem is immaterial and is disregarded. Theoretically, the valuation of a current liability should be the present value of the required future outlay of money. Since the difference between the present value and the amount that will be paid in the future is immaterial, the current liability is carried at its face value.

Current Assets Compared with Current Liabilities

A comparison of current assets with current liabilities indicates the short-term debt-paying ability of the entity. Several comparisons can be made to determine this ability:

1. Working capital
2. Current ratio
3. Acid-test ratio
4. Cash ratio

Working Capital

The working capital of a business is an indication of the short-run solvency of the business. Compute working capital as follows:

$$\text{Working Capital} = \text{Current Assets} - \text{Current Liabilities}$$

Exhibit 6-12 presents the working capital for Nike at the end of 2011 and 2010. Nike had $7,339,000,000 in working capital in 2011 and $7,595,000,000 in working capital in 2010. These figures tend to be understated because some of the current assets, such as inventory, may be understated, based on the book figures.

The inventory as reported may be much less than its replacement cost. The difference between the reported inventory amount and the replacement amount is normally material when the firm is using LIFO inventory. The difference may also be material when using one of the other cost methods.

The current working capital amount should be compared with past amounts to determine if working capital is reasonable. Because the relative size of a firm may be expanding

EXHIBIT **6-12**	Nike, Inc.

Working Capital

Years Ended May 31, 2011 and 2010

(In millions)	2011	2010
Current assets [A]	$11,297	$10,959
Current liabilities [B]	3,958	3,364
Working capital [A − B]	$ 7,339	$ 7,595

Source: Nike, Inc. 2010 10-K

or contracting, comparing the working capital of one firm with that of another firm is usually meaningless because of their size differences. If the working capital appears to be out of line, the reasons should be found by analyzing the individual current asset and current liability accounts.

Current Ratio

Another indicator, the current ratio, determines short-term debt-paying ability and is computed as follows:

$$\text{Current Ratio} = \frac{\text{Current Assets}}{\text{Current Liabilities}}$$

Exhibit 6-13 presents the current ratio for Nike at the end of 2011 and 2010. For Nike, the current ratio was 2.85 at the end of 2011 and 3.26 at the end of 2010. This indicates a negative trend considering liquidity.

For many years, the guideline for the minimum current ratio has been 2.00. Until the mid-1960s, the typical firm successfully maintained a current ratio of 2.00 or better. Since that time, the current ratio of many firms has declined to a point below the 2.00 guideline. Currently, many firms are not successful in staying above a current ratio of 2.00. This indicates a decline in the liquidity of many firms. It also could indicate better control of receivables and/or inventory.

A comparison with industry averages should be made to determine the typical current ratio for similar firms. In some industries, a current ratio substantially below 2.00 is adequate, while other industries require a much larger ratio. In general, the shorter the operating cycle, the lower the current ratio. The longer the operating cycle, the higher the current ratio.

A comparison of the firm's current ratio with prior periods, and a comparison with industry averages, will help to determine if the ratio is high or low. These comparisons do not indicate why it is high or low. Possible reasons can be found from an analysis of the individual current asset and current liability accounts. Often, the major reasons for the current ratio being out of line will be found in a detailed analysis of accounts receivable and inventory.

The current ratio is considered to be more indicative of the short-term debt-paying ability than the working capital. Working capital only determines the absolute difference between the current assets and current liabilities. The current ratio shows the relationship between the size of the current assets and the size of the current liabilities, making it feasible to compare the current ratio, for example, between IBM and Intel. A comparison of the working capital of these two firms would be meaningless because IBM is a larger firm than Intel.

LIFO inventory can cause major problems with the current ratio because of the understatement of inventory. The result is an understated current ratio. Extreme caution should be exercised when comparing a firm that uses LIFO and a firm that uses some other costing method.

Before computing the current ratio, the analyst should compute the accounts receivable turnover and the merchandise inventory turnover. These computations enable the analyst to

EXHIBIT **6-13**	Nike, Inc.

Current Ratio

Years Ended May 31, 2011 and 2010

(In millions)	2011	2010
Current assets [A]	$11,297	$10,959
Current liabilities [B]	3,958	3,364
Current ratio [A ÷ B]	2.85	3.26

Source: Nike, Inc. 2010 10-K

formulate an opinion as to whether liquidity problems exist with receivables and/or inventory. An opinion as to the quality of receivables and inventory should influence the analyst's opinion of the current ratio. If liquidity problems exist with receivables and/or inventory, the current ratio needs to be much higher.

Acid-Test Ratio (Quick Ratio)

The current ratio evaluates an enterprise's overall liquidity position, considering current assets and current liabilities. At times, it is desirable to access a more immediate position than that indicated by the current ratio. The acid-test (or quick) ratio relates the most liquid assets to current liabilities.

Inventory is removed from current assets when computing the acid-test ratio. Some of the reasons for removing inventory are that inventory may be slow-moving or possibly obsolete, and parts of the inventory may have been pledged to specific creditors. For example, a winery's inventory requires considerable time for aging and, therefore, a considerable time before sale. To include the wine inventory in the acid-test computation would overstate the liquidity. A valuation problem with inventory also exists because it is stated at a cost figure that may be materially different from a fair current valuation.

Compute the acid-test ratio as follows:

$$\text{Acid-Test Ratio} = \frac{\text{Current Assets} - \text{Inventory}}{\text{Current Liabilities}}$$

Exhibit 6-14 presents the acid-test ratio for Nike at the end of 2011 and 2010. For Nike, the acid-test ratio was 2.17 at the end of 2011 and 2.65 at the end of 2010. This represents a negative trend.

It may also be desirable to exclude some other items from current assets that may not represent current cash flow, such as prepaid and miscellaneous items. Compute the more conservative acid-test ratio as follows:

$$\text{Acid-Test Ratio} = \frac{\text{Cash Equivalents} + \text{Marketable Securities} + \text{Net Receivables}}{\text{Current Liabilities}}$$

Usually, a very immaterial difference occurs between the acid-test ratios computed under the first method and this second method. Frequently, the only difference is the inclusion of prepayments in the first computation.

Exhibit 6-15 presents the conservative acid-test ratio for Nike at the end of 2011 and 2010. This approach resulted in an acid-test ratio of 1.94 at the end of 2011 and 2.32 at the end of 2010.

From this point on in this book, the more conservative computations will be used for the acid-test ratio. When a company needs to view liquidity with only inventory removed, the alternative computation should be used.

For many years, the guideline for the minimum acid-test ratio was 1.00. A comparison should be made with the firm's past acid-test ratios and with major competitors and the

EXHIBIT **6-14**	Nike, Inc.	
Acid-Test Ratio		
Years Ended May 31, 2011 and 2010		
(In millions)	2011	2010
Current assets	$11,297	$10,959
Less: Ending inventory	2,715	2,041
Remaining current assets [A]	$ 8,582	$ 8,918
Current liabilities [B]	$ 3,958	$ 3,369
Acid-test ratio [A ÷ B]	2.17	2.65

Source: Nike, Inc. 2010 10-K

EXHIBIT **6-15**	Nike, Inc.	

Acid-Test Ratio (Conservative Approach)

Years Ended May 31, 2011 and 2010

(In millions)	2011	2010
Cash, including short-term investments	$4,538	$5,146
Net receivables	3,138	2,650
Total quick assets [A]	$7,676	$7,796
Current liabilities [B]	$3,958	$3,364
Acid-test ratio [A ÷ B]	1.94 times	2.32 times

Source: Nike, Inc. 2010 10-K

industry averages. Some industries find that a ratio less than 1.00 is adequate, while others need a ratio greater than 1.00. For example, a grocery store may sell only for cash and not have receivables. This type of business can have an acid-test ratio substantially below the 1.00 guideline and still have adequate liquidity.

Before computing the acid-test ratio, the accounts receivable turnover should be calculated. An opinion as to the quality of receivables should help the analyst form an opinion of the acid-test ratio.

There has been a major decline in the liquidity of companies in the United States, as measured by the current ratio and the acid-test ratio. Exhibit 6-16 shows the dramatically

EXHIBIT **6-16**	Trends in Current Ratio and Acid-Test Ratio

All U.S. Manufacturing Companies, 1964–2010

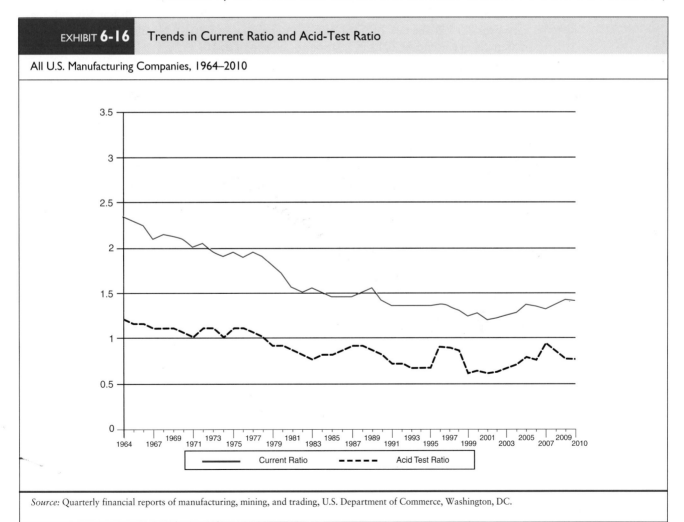

Source: Quarterly financial reports of manufacturing, mining, and trading, U.S. Department of Commerce, Washington, DC.

reduced liquidity of U.S. companies. Reduced liquidity leads to more bankruptcies and greater risk for creditors and investors.

Cash Ratio

Sometimes an analyst needs to view the liquidity of a firm from an extremely conservative point of view. For example, the company may have pledged its receivables and its inventory, or the analyst suspects severe liquidity problems with inventory and receivables. The best indicator of the company's short-run liquidity may be the cash ratio. Compute the cash ratio as follows:

$$\text{Cash Ratio} = \frac{\text{Cash Equivalents} + \text{Marketable Securities}}{\text{Current Liabilities}}$$

The analyst seldom gives the cash ratio much weight when evaluating the liquidity of a firm because it is not realistic to expect a firm to have enough cash equivalents and marketable securities to cover current liabilities. If the firm must depend on cash equivalents and marketable securities for its liquidity, its solvency may be impaired.

Analysts should consider the cash ratio of companies that have naturally slow-moving inventories and receivables and companies that are highly speculative. For example, a land development company in Florida may sell lots paid for over a number of years on the installment basis, or the success of a new company may be in doubt.

The cash ratio indicates the immediate liquidity of the firm. A high cash ratio indicates that the firm is not using its cash to its best advantage; cash should be put to work in the operations of the company. Detailed knowledge of the firm is required, however, before drawing a definite conclusion. Management may have plans for the cash, such as a building expansion program. A cash ratio that is too low could indicate an immediate problem with paying bills.

Exhibit 6-17 presents this ratio for Nike at the end of 2011 and 2010. For Nike, the cash ratio was 1.15 at the end of 2011 and 1.53 at the end of 2010. Nike's cash ratio decreased materially at the end of 2011 in relation to the end of 2010.

Other Liquidity Considerations

Another ratio that may be useful to the analyst is the sales to working capital ratio. In addition, there may be liquidity considerations that are not on the face of the statements. This ratio and other liquidity considerations are discussed in this section.

Sales to Working Capital (Working Capital Turnover)

Relating sales to working capital gives an indication of the turnover in working capital per year. The analyst needs to compare this ratio with the past, with competitors, and with industry averages in order to form an opinion as to the adequacy of the working capital turnover. Like many ratios, no rules of thumb exist as to what it should be. Since this ratio relates a balance sheet number (working capital) to an income statement number (sales), a problem exists if the balance sheet number is not representative of the year. To avoid this

EXHIBIT **6-17** Nike, Inc.		
Cash Ratio		
Years Ended May 31, 2011 and 2010		
(In millions)	**2011**	**2010**
Cash, including short-term investments [A]	$4,538	$5,146
Current liabilities [B]	$3,958	$3,364
Cash ratio [A ÷ B]	1.15	1.53
Source: Nike, Inc. 2010 10-K		

problem, use the average monthly working capital figure when available. Compute the working capital turnover as follows:

$$\text{Sales to Working Capital} = \frac{\text{Sales}}{\text{Average Working Capital}}$$

A low working capital turnover ratio tentatively indicates an unprofitable use of working capital. In other words, sales are not adequate in relation to the available working capital. A high ratio tentatively indicates that the firm is undercapitalized (overtrading). An undercapitalized firm is particularly susceptible to liquidity problems when a major adverse change in business conditions occurs.

Exhibit 6-18 presents this ratio for Nike at the end of 2011 and 2010. The sales to working capital ratio increased from 2010 to 2011. (Working capital in 2011 was lower in relation to sales than it was in 2010.) This tentatively indicates a slightly more profitable use of working capital in 2011 in relation to 2010.

Liquidity Considerations Not on the Face of the Statements

A firm may have a better liquidity position than indicated by the face of the financial statements. The following list presents several examples:

1. Unused bank credit lines would be a positive addition to liquidity. They are frequently disclosed in notes.
2. A firm may have some long-term assets that could be converted to cash quickly. This would add to the firm's liquidity. Extreme caution is advised if there is any reliance on long-term assets for liquidity. For one thing, the long-term assets are usually needed in operations. Second, even excess long-term assets may not be easily converted into cash in a short period of time. An exception might be investments, depending on the nature of the investments.
3. A firm may be in a very good long-term debt position and therefore have the capability to issue debt or stock. Thus, the firm could relieve a severe liquidity problem in a reasonable amount of time.

A firm may not be in as good a position of liquidity as indicated by the ratios, as the following examples show:

1. A firm may have notes discounted on which the other party has full recourse against the firm. Discounted notes should be disclosed in a note. (A company that discounts a customer note receivable is in essence selling the note to the bank with recourse.)
2. A firm may have major contingent liabilities that have not been recorded, such as a disputed tax claim. Unrecorded contingencies that are material are disclosed in a note.
3. A firm may have guaranteed a bank note for another company. This would be disclosed in a note.

EXHIBIT **6-18**	Nike, Inc.

Sales to Working Capital

Years Ended May 31, 2011 and 2010

(In millions)	2011	2010
Net sales [A]	$20,862	$19,014
Working capital at beginning of year	7,595	6,457
Working capital at end of year	7,339	7,595
Average working capital [B]	7,467	7,026
Sales to working capital [A ÷ B]	2.79 times per year	2.71 times per year

Source: Nike, Inc. 2010 10-K

Summary

The ratios related to the liquidity of short-term assets and the short-term debt-paying ability follow:

$$\text{Days' Sales in Receivables} = \frac{\text{Gross Receivables}}{\text{Net Sales}/365}$$

$$\text{Accounts Receivable Turnover} = \frac{\text{Net Sales}}{\text{Average Gross Receivables}}$$

$$\text{Accounts Receivable Turnover in Days} = \frac{\text{Average Gross Receivables}}{\text{Net Sales}/365}$$

$$\text{Days' Sales in Inventory} = \frac{\text{Ending Inventory}}{\text{Cost of Goods Sold}/365}$$

$$\text{Inventory Turnover} = \frac{\text{Cost of Goods Sold}}{\text{Average Inventory}}$$

$$\text{Inventory Turnover in Days} = \frac{\text{Average Inventory}}{\text{Cost of Goods Sold}/365}$$

$$\text{Operating Cycle} = \text{Accounts Receivable Turnover in Days} + \text{Inventory Turnover in Days}$$

$$\text{Working Capital} = \text{Current Assets} - \text{Current Liabilities}$$

$$\text{Current Ratio} = \frac{\text{Current Assets}}{\text{Current Liabilities}}$$

$$\text{Acid-Test Ratio} = \frac{\text{Cash Equivalents} + \text{Marketable Securities} + \text{Net Receivables}}{\text{Current Liabilities}}$$

$$\text{Cash Ratio} = \frac{\text{Cash Equivalents} + \text{Marketable Securities}}{\text{Current Liabilities}}$$

$$\text{Sales to Working Capital} = \frac{\text{Sales}}{\text{Average Working Capital}}$$

Questions

Q 6-1 It is proposed at a stockholders' meeting that the firm slow its rate of payments on accounts payable in order to make more funds available for operations. It is contended that this procedure will enable the firm to expand inventory, which will in turn enable the firm to generate more sales. Comment on this proposal.

Q 6-2 Jones Wholesale Company has been one of the fastest growing wholesale firms in the United States for the last five years in terms of sales and profits. The firm has maintained a current ratio above the average for the wholesale industry. Mr. Jones has asked you to explain possible reasons why the firm is having difficulty meeting its payroll and its accounts payable. What would you tell Mr. Jones?

Q 6-3 What is the reason for separating current assets from the rest of the assets found on the balance sheet?

Q 6-4 Define the operating cycle.

Q 6-5 Define current assets.

Q 6-6 List the major categories of items usually found in current assets.

Q 6-7 Rachit Company has cash that has been frozen in a bank in Cuba. Should this cash be classified as a current asset? Discuss.

Q 6-8 A. B. Smith Company has guaranteed a $1 million bank note for Alender Company. How would this influence the liquidity ratios of A. B. Smith Company? How should this situation be considered?

Q 6-9 Arrow Company has invested funds in a supplier to help ensure a steady supply of needed materials. Would this investment be classified as a marketable security (current asset)?

Q 6-10 List the two computations that are used to determine the liquidity of receivables.

Q 6-11 List the two computations that are used to determine the liquidity of inventory.

Q 6-12 Would a company that uses a natural business year tend to overstate or understate the liquidity of its receivables? Explain.

Q 6-13 T. Melcher Company uses the calendar year. Sales are at a peak during the holiday season, and T. Melcher Company extends 30-day credit terms to customers. Comment on the expected liquidity of its receivables, based on the days' sales in receivables and the accounts receivable turnover.

Q 6-14 A company that uses a natural business year, or ends its year when business is at a peak, will tend to distort the liquidity of its receivables when end-of-year and beginning-of-year receivables are used in the computation. Explain how a company that uses a natural business year or ends its year when business is at a peak can eliminate the distortion in its liquidity computations.

Q 6-15 If a company has substantial cash sales and credit sales, is there any meaning to the receivable liquidity computations that are based on gross sales?

Q 6-16 Describe the difference in inventories between a firm that is a retail company and a firm that is a manufacturing concern.

Q 6-17 During times of inflation, which of the inventory costing methods listed below would give the most realistic valuation of inventory? Which method would give the least realistic valuation of inventory? Explain.

a. LIFO
b. Average
c. FIFO

Q 6-18 The number of days' sales in inventory relates the amount of the ending inventory to the average daily cost of goods sold. Explain why this computation may be misleading under the following conditions:

a. The company uses a natural business year for its accounting period.
b. The company closes the year when activities are at a peak.
c. The company uses LIFO inventory, and inflation has been a problem for a number of years.

Q 6-19 The days' sales in inventory is an estimate of the number of days that it will take to sell the current inventory.

a. What is the ideal number of days' sales in inventory?
b. In general, does a company want many days' sales in inventory?
c. Can days' sales in inventory be too low?

Q 6-20 Some firms do not report the cost of goods sold separately on their income statements. In such a case, how should you proceed to compute days' sales in inventory? Will this procedure produce a realistic days' sales in inventory?

Q 6-21 One of the computations used to determine the liquidity of inventory determines the inventory turnover. In this computation, usually the average inventory is determined by using the beginning-of-the-year and the end-of-the-year inventory figures, but this computation can be misleading if the company has seasonal fluctuations or uses a natural business year. Suggest how to eliminate these distortions.

Q 6-22 Explain the influence of the use of LIFO inventory on the inventory turnover.

Q 6-23 Define working capital.

Q 6-24 Define current liabilities.

Q 6-25 Several comparisons can be made to determine the short-term debt-paying ability of an entity. Some of these are:

a. Working capital

b. Current ratio

c. Acid-test ratio

d. Cash ratio

   1. Define each of these terms.

   2. If the book figures are based on cost, will the results of the preceding computations tend to be understated or overstated? Explain.

   3. What figures should be used in order to avoid the problem referred to in (2)?

Q 6-26 Discuss how to use working capital in analysis.

Q 6-27 Both current assets and current liabilities are used in the computation of working capital and the current ratio, yet the current ratio is considered to be more indicative of the short-term debt-paying ability. Explain.

Q 6-28 In determining the short-term liquidity of a firm, the current ratio is usually considered to be a better guide than the acid-test ratio, and the acid-test ratio is considered to be a better guide than the cash ratio. Discuss when the acid-test ratio would be preferred over the current ratio and when the cash ratio would be preferred over the acid-test ratio.

Q 6-29 Discuss some benefits that may accrue to a firm from reducing its operating cycle. Suggest some ways that may be used to reduce a company's operating cycle.

Q 6-30 Discuss why some firms have longer natural operating cycles than other firms.

Q 6-31 Would a firm with a relatively long operating cycle tend to charge a higher markup on its inventory cost than a firm with a short operating cycle? Discuss.

Q 6-32 Is the profitability of the entity considered to be of major importance in determining the short-term debt-paying ability? Discuss.

Q 6-33 Does the allowance method for bad debts or the direct write-off method result in the fairest presentation of receivables on the balance sheet and the fairest matching of expenses against revenue?

Q 6-34 When a firm faces an inflationary condition and the LIFO inventory method is based on a periodic basis, purchases late in the year can have a substantial influence on profits. Comment.

Q 6-35 Why could a current asset such as Net Assets of Business Held for Sale distort a firm's liquidity, in terms of working capital or the current ratio?

Q 6-36 Before computing the current ratio, the accounts receivable turnover and the inventory turnover should be computed. Why?

Q 6-37 Before computing the acid-test ratio, compute the accounts receivable turnover. Comment.

Q 6-38 Which inventory costing method results in the highest balance sheet amount for inventory? (Assume inflationary conditions.)

Q 6-39 Indicate the single most important factor that motivates a company to select LIFO.

Q 6-40 A relatively low sales to working capital ratio is a tentative indication of an efficient use of working capital. Comment. A relatively high sales to working capital ratio is a tentative indication that the firm is undercapitalized. Comment.

Q 6-41 List three situations in which the liquidity position of the firm may be better than that indicated by the liquidity ratios.

Q 6-42 List three situations in which the liquidity position of the firm may not be as good as that indicated by the liquidity ratios.

Q 6-43 Indicate the objective of the sales to working capital ratio.

Q 6-44 Why does LIFO result in a very unrealistic ending inventory figure in a period of rising prices?

Q 6-45 The cost of inventory at the close of the calendar year of the first year of operation is $40,000, using LIFO inventory, resulting in a profit before tax of $100,000. If the FIFO inventory would have been $50,000, what would the reported profit before tax have been? If the average cost method would have resulted in an inventory of $45,000, what would the reported profit before tax have been? Should the inventory costing method be disclosed? Why?

Problems

P 6-1 In this problem, compute the acid-test ratio as follows:

$$\frac{\text{Current Assets} - \text{Inventory}}{\text{Current Liabilities}}$$

Required Determine the cost of sales of a firm with the following financial data.

Current ratio	2.5
Quick ratio or acid-test	2.0
Current liabilities	$400,000
Inventory turnover	3 times

P 6-2 Hawk Company wants to determine the liquidity of its receivables. It has supplied you with the following data regarding selected accounts for December 31, 2011, and 2010:

	2011	2010
Net sales	$1,180,178	$2,200,000
Receivables, less allowance for losses and discounts		
Beginning of year (allowance for losses and discounts, 2011—$12,300; 2010—$7,180)	240,360	230,180
End of year (allowance for losses and discounts, 2011—$11,180; 2010—$12,300)	220,385	240,360

Required

a. Compute the number of days' sales in receivables at December 31, 2011, and 2010.
b. Compute the accounts receivable turnover for 2011 and 2010. (Use year-end gross receivables.)
c. Comment on the liquidity of Hawk Company receivables.

P 6-3 Mr. Williams, the owner of Williams Produce, wants to maintain control over accounts receivable. He understands that days' sales in receivables and accounts receivable turnover will give a good indication of how well receivables are being managed. Williams Produce does 60% of its business during June, July, and August. Mr. Williams provided the following pertinent data:

	For Year Ended December 31, 2011	For Year Ended July 31, 2011
Net sales	$800,000	$790,000
Receivables, less allowance for doubtful accounts		
Beginning of period (allowance January 1, $3,000; August 1, $4,000)	50,000	89,000
End of period (allowance December 31, $3,500; July 31, $4,100)	55,400	90,150

Required

a. Compute the days' sales in receivables for July 31, 2011, and December 31, 2011, based on the accompanying data.
b. Compute the accounts receivable turnover for the period ended July 31, 2011, and December 31, 2011. (Use year-end gross receivables.)
c. Comment on the results from (a) and (b).

P 6-4 L. Solomon Company would like to compare its days' sales in receivables with that of a competitor, L. Konrath Company. Both companies have had similar sales results in the past, but L. Konrath Company has had better profit results. L. Solomon Company suspects that one reason for the better profit results is that L. Konrath Company did a better job of managing receivables. L. Solomon Company uses a calendar year that ends on December 31, while L. Konrath Company uses a fiscal year that ends on July 31. Information related to sales and receivables of the two companies follows:

	For Year Ended December 31, 20XX
L. Solomon Company	
Net sales	$1,800,000
Receivables, less allowance for doubtful accounts of $8,000	110,000

(continued)

(**P 6-4** CONTINUED)

	For Year Ended July 31, 20XX
L. Konrath Company	
Net sales	$1,850,000
Receivables, less allowance for doubtful accounts of $4,000	60,000

Required
a. Compute the days' sales in receivables for both companies. (Use year-end gross receivables.)
b. Comment on the results.

P 6-5a P. Gibson Company has computed its accounts receivable turnover in days to be 36.
Required Compute the accounts receivable turnover per year.

P 6-5b P. Gibson Company has computed its accounts receivable turnover per year to be 12.
Required Compute the accounts receivable turnover in days.

P 6-5c P. Gibson Company has gross receivables at the end of the year of $280,000 and net sales for the year of $2,158,000.
Required Compute the days' sales in receivables at the end of the year.

P 6-5d P. Gibson Company has net sales of $3,500,000 and average gross receivables of $324,000.
Required Compute the accounts receivable turnover.

P 6-6 J. Shaffer Company has an ending inventory of $360,500 and a cost of goods sold for the year of $2,100,000. It has used LIFO inventory for a number of years because of persistent inflation.
Required
a. Compute the days' sales in inventory.
b. Is J. Shaffer Company's days' sales in inventory as computed realistic in comparison with the actual days' sales in inventory?
c. Would the days' sales in inventory computed for J. Shaffer Company be a helpful guide?

P 6-7 D. Szabo Company had an average inventory of $280,000 and a cost of goods sold of $1,250,000.
Required Compute the following:
a. The inventory turnover in days
b. The inventory turnover

P 6-8 The inventory and sales data for this year for G. Rabbit Company are as follows:

	End of Year	Beginning of Year
Net sales	$3,150,000	
Gross receivables	180,000	$160,000
Inventory	480,000	390,000
Cost of goods sold	2,250,000	

Required Using the above data from G. Rabbit Company, compute the following:
a. The accounts receivable turnover in days
b. The inventory turnover in days
c. The operating cycle

P 6-9 Anna Banana Company would like to estimate how long it will take to realize cash from its ending inventory. For this purpose, the following data are submitted:

Accounts receivable, less allowance for doubtful accounts of $30,000	$ 560,000
Ending inventory	680,000
Net sales	4,350,000
Cost of goods sold	3,600,000

Required Estimate how long it will take to realize cash from the ending inventory.

P 6-10 Laura Badora Company has been using LIFO inventory. The company is required to disclose the replacement cost of its inventory and the replacement cost of its cost of goods sold on its annual statements. Selected data for the year ended 2011 are as follows:

Ending accounts receivable, less allowance for doubtful accounts of $25,000	$ 480,000
Ending inventory, LIFO (estimated replacement $900,000)	570,000
Net sales	3,650,000
Cost of goods sold (estimated replacement cost $3,150,000)	2,850,000

Required
a. Compute the days' sales in receivables.
b. Compute the days' sales in inventory, using the cost figure.
c. Compute the days' sales in inventory, using the replacement cost for the inventory and the cost of goods sold.
d. Should replacement cost of inventory and cost of goods sold be used, when possible, when computing days' sales in inventory? Discuss.

P 6-11 A partial balance sheet and income statement for King Corporation follow:

KING CORPORATION
Partial Balance Sheet
December 31, 2011

Assets	
Current assets:	
Cash	$ 33,493
Marketable securities	215,147
Trade receivables, less allowance of $6,000	255,000
Inventories, LIFO	523,000
Prepaid expenses	26,180
Total current assets	$1,052,820
Liabilities	
Current liabilities:	
Trade accounts payable	$ 103,689
Notes payable (primarily to banks) and commercial paper	210,381
Accrued expenses and other liabilities	120,602
Income taxes payable	3,120
Current maturities of long-term debt	22,050
Total current liabilities	$ 459,842

KING CORPORATION
Partial Income Statement
For Year Ended December 31, 2011

Net sales	$3,050,600
Miscellaneous income	45,060
	$3,095,660
Costs and expenses:	
Cost of sales	$2,185,100
Selling, general, and administrative expenses	350,265
Interest expense	45,600
Income taxes	300,000
	2,880,965
Net income	$ 214,695

Note: The trade receivables at December 31, 2010, were $280,000, net of an allowance of $8,000, for a gross receivables figure of $288,000. The inventory at December 31, 2010, was $565,000.

(continued)

(**P 6-11** CONTINUED)

Required Compute the following:

a. Working capital
b. Current ratio
c. Acid-test ratio
d. Cash ratio
e. Days' sales in receivables

f. Accounts receivable turnover in days
g. Days' sales in inventory
h. Inventory turnover in days
i. Operating cycle

P 6-12 Individual transactions often have a significant impact on ratios. This problem will consider the direction of such an impact.

	Total Current Assets	Total Current Liabilities	Net Working Capital	Current Ratio
a. Cash is acquired through issuance of additional common stock.	___	___	___	___
b. Merchandise is sold for cash. (Assume a profit.)	___	___	___	___
c. A fixed asset is sold for more than book value.	___	___	___	___
d. Payment is made to trade creditors for previous purchases.	___	___	___	___
e. A cash dividend is declared and paid.	___	___	___	___
f. A stock dividend is declared and paid.	___	___	___	___
g. Cash is obtained through long-term bank loans.	___	___	___	___
h. A profitable firm increases its fixed assets depreciation allowance account.	___	___	___	___
i. Current operating expenses are paid.	___	___	___	___
j. Ten-year notes are issued to pay off accounts payable.	___	___	___	___
k. Accounts receivable are collected.	___	___	___	___
l. Equipment is purchased with short-term notes.	___	___	___	___
m. Merchandise is purchased on credit.	___	___	___	___
n. The estimated taxes payable are increased.	___	___	___	___
o. Marketable securities are sold below cost.	___	___	___	___

Required Indicate the effects of the previous transactions on each of the following: total current assets, total current liabilities, net working capital, and current ratio. Use + to indicate an increase, − to indicate a decrease, and 0 to indicate no effect. Assume an initial current ratio of more than 1 to 1.

P 6-13 Current assets and current liabilities for companies D and E are summarized as follows:

	Company D	Company E
Current assets	$400,000	$900,000
Current liabilities	200,000	700,000
Working capital	$200,000	$200,000

Required Evaluate the relative solvency of companies D and E.

P 6-14 Current assets and current liabilities for companies R and T are summarized as follows.

	Company R	Company T
Current assets	$400,000	$800,000
Current liabilities	200,000	400,000
Working capital	$200,000	$400,000

Required Evaluate the relative solvency of companies R and T.

P 6-15 The following financial data were taken from the annual financial statements of Smith Corporation:

	2009	2010	2011
Current assets	$ 450,000	$ 400,000	$ 500,000
Current liabilities	390,000	300,000	340,000
Sales	1,450,000	1,500,000	1,400,000
Cost of goods sold	1,180,000	1,020,000	1,120,000
Inventory	280,000	200,000	250,000
Accounts receivable	120,000	110,000	105,000

Required

a. Based on these data, calculate the following for 2010 and 2011:

1. Working capital
2. Current ratio
3. Acid-test ratio
4. Accounts receivable turnover
5. Merchandise inventory turnover
6. Inventory turnover in days

b. Evaluate the results of your computations in regard to the short-term liquidity of the firm.

P 6-16 Anne Elizabeth Corporation is engaged in the business of making toys. A high percentage of its products are sold to consumers during November and December. Therefore, retailers need to have the toys in stock prior to November. The corporation produces on a relatively stable basis during the year in order to retain its skilled employees and to minimize its investment in plant and equipment. The seasonal nature of its business requires a substantial capacity to store inventory.

The gross receivables balance at April 30, 2010, was $75,000, and the inventory balance was $350,000 on this date. Sales for the year ended April 30, 2011, totaled $4,000,000, and the cost of goods sold totaled $1,800,000.

Anne Elizabeth Corporation uses a natural business year that ends on April 30. Inventory and accounts receivable data are given in the following table for the year ended April 30, 2011:

Month	Month-End Balance	
	Gross Receivables	Inventory
May 2010	$ 60,000	$525,000
June 2010	40,000	650,000
July 2010	50,000	775,000
August 2010	60,000	900,000
September 2010	200,000	975,000
October 2010	800,000	700,000
November 2010	1,500,000	400,000
December 2010	1,800,000	25,000
January 2011	1,000,000	100,000
February 2011	600,000	150,000
March 2011	200,000	275,000
April 2011	50,000	400,000

Required

a. Using averages based on the year-end figures, compute the following:

1. Accounts receivable turnover in days
2. Accounts receivable turnover per year
3. Inventory turnover in days
4. Inventory turnover per year

(*continued*)

(**P 6-16** CONTINUED)

b. Using averages based on monthly figures, compute the following:

1. Accounts receivable turnover in days
2. Accounts receivable turnover per year
3. Inventory turnover in days
4. Inventory turnover per year

c. Comment on the difference between the ratios computed in (a) and (b).
d. Compute the days' sales in receivables.
e. Compute the days' sales in inventory.
f. How realistic are the days' sales in receivables and the days' sales in inventory that were computed in (d) and (e)?

P 6-17 The following data relate to inventory for the year ended December 31, 2011:

Date	Description	Number of Units	Cost per Unit	Total Cost
January 1	Beginning inventory	400	$5.00	$ 2,000
March 1	Purchase	1,000	6.00	6,000
August 1	Purchase	200	7.00	1,400 .
November 1	Purchase	200	7.50	1,500
		1,800		$10,900

A physical inventory on December 31, 2011, indicates that 400 units are on hand and that they came from the March 1 purchase.
Required Compute the cost of goods sold for the year ended December 31, 2011, and the ending inventory under the following cost assumptions:

a. First-in, first-out (FIFO)
b. Last-in, first-out (LIFO)
c. Average cost (weighted average)
d. Specific identification

P 6-18 The following data relate to inventory for the year ended December 31, 2011. A physical inventory on December 31, 2011, indicates that 600 units are on hand and that they came from the July 1 purchase.

Date	Description	Number of Units	Cost per Unit	Total Cost
January 1	Beginning inventory	1,000	$4.00	$ 4,000
February 20	Purchase	800	4.50	3,600
April 1	Purchase	900	4.75	4,275
July 1	Purchase	700	5.00	3,500
October 22	Purchase	500	4.90	2,450
December 10	Purchase	500	5.00	2,500
		4,400		$20,325

Required Compute the cost of goods sold for the year ended December 31, 2011, and the ending inventory under the following cost assumptions:

a. First-in, first-out (FIFO)
b. Last-in, first-out (LIFO)
c. Average cost (weighted average)
d. Specific identification

P 6-19 J.A. Appliance Company has supplied you with the following data regarding working capital and sales for the years 2011, 2010, and 2009.

	2011	2010	2009
Working capital	$270,000	$260,000	$240,000
Sales	$650,000	$600,000	$500,000
Industry average for the ratio sales to working capital	4.10 times	4.05 times	4.00 times

Required

a. Compute the sales to working capital ratio for each year.
b. Comment on the sales to working capital ratio for J.A. Appliance in relation to the industry average and what this may indicate.

P 6-20 Depoole Company manufactures industrial products and employs a calendar year for financial reporting purposes. Items (a) through (e) present several of Depoole's transactions during 2011. The total of cash equivalents, marketable securities, and net receivables exceeded total current liabilities both before and after each transaction described. Depoole had positive profits in 2011 and a credit balance throughout 2011 in its retained earnings account.

Required Answer the following multiple-choice questions:

a. Payment of a trade account payable of $64,500 would

1. Increase the current ratio, but the acid-test ratio would not be affected.
2. Increase the acid-test ratio, but the current ratio would not be affected.
3. Increase both the current and acid-test ratios.
4. Decrease both the current and acid-test ratios.
5. Have no effect on the current and acid-test ratios.

b. The purchase of raw materials for $85,000 on open account would

1. Increase the current ratio.
2. Decrease the current ratio.
3. Increase net working capital.
4. Decrease net working capital.
5. Increase both the current ratio and net working capital.

c. The collection of a current accounts receivable of $29,000 would

1. Increase the current ratio.
2. Decrease the current ratio.
3. Increase the acid-test ratio.
4. Decrease the acid-test ratio.
5. Not affect the current or acid-test ratios.

d. Obsolete inventory of $125,000 was written off during 2009. This would

1. Decrease the acid-test ratio.
2. Increase the acid-test ratio.
3. Increase net working capital.
4. Decrease the current ratio.
5. Decrease both the current and acid-test ratios.

e. The early liquidation of a long-term note with cash would

1. Affect the current ratio to a greater degree than the acid-test ratio.
2. Affect the acid-test ratio to a greater degree than the current ratio.
3. Affect the current and acid-test ratios to the same degree.
4. Affect the current ratio, but not the acid-test ratio.
5. Affect the acid-test ratio, but not the current ratio.

Source: Adapted from past CMA Examinations. Used by Permission of The Institute of Certified Management Accountants.

(CMA Adapted)

P 6-21 Information from Greg Company's balance sheet follows:

Current assets:	
Cash	$ 2,100,000
Marketable securities	7,200,000
Accounts receivable	50,500,000
Inventories	65,000,000
Prepaid expenses	1,000,000
Total current assets	$125,800,000
Current liabilities:	
Notes payable	$ 1,400,000
Accounts payable	18,000,000
Accrued expenses	11,000,000
Income taxes payable	600,000
Payments due within one year on long-term debt	3,000,000
Total current liabilities	$ 34,000,000

Required Answer the following multiple-choice questions:

a. What is the acid-test ratio for Greg Company?

    1. 1.60
    2. 1.76
    3. 1.90
    4. 2.20

b. What is the effect of the collection of accounts receivable on the current ratio and net working capital, respectively?

	Current Ratio	Net Working Capital
1.	No effect	No effect
2.	Increase	Increase
3.	Increase	No effect
4.	No effect	Increase

P 6-22 The following data apply to items (a) and (b). Mr. Sparks, the owner of School Supplies, Inc., wants to maintain control over accounts receivable. He understands that accounts receivable turnover will give a good indication of how well receivables are being managed. School Supplies, Inc., does 70% of its business during June, July, and August. The terms of sale are 2/10, net/60.
    Net sales for the year ended December 31, 2011, and receivables balances follow:

Net sales	$1,500,000
Receivables, less allowance for doubtful accounts of $8,000 at January 1, 2011	72,000
Receivables, less allowance for doubtful accounts of $10,000 at December 31, 2011	60,000

Required Answer the following multiple-choice questions:

a. The average accounts receivable turnover calculated from the previous data is

    1. 20.0 times.
    2. 25.0 times.
    3. 22.7 times.
    4. 18.75 times.
    5. 20.8 times.

b. The average accounts receivable turnover computed for School Supplies, Inc., in item (a) is

    1. Representative for the entire year.
    2. Overstated.
    3. Understated.

Source: Adapted from past CMA Examinations. Used by Permission of The Institute of Certified Management Accountants.

(CMA Adapted)

P 6-23 Items (a) through (d) are based on the following information:

SHARKEY CORPORATION
Selected Financial Data

	As of December 31,	
	2011	2010
Cash	$ 8,000	$ 60,000
Marketable securities	32,000	8,000
Accounts receivable	40,000	110,000
Inventory	80,000	140,000
Net property, plant, and equipment	240,000	280,000
Accounts payable	60,000	100,000
Short-term notes payable	30,000	50,000
Cash sales	1,500,000	1,400,000
Credit sales	600,000	900,000
Cost of goods sold	1,260,000	1,403,000

Required Answer the following multiple-choice questions:

a. Sharkey's acid-test ratio as of December 31, 2011, is

1. 0.63.
2. 0.70.
3. 0.89.
4. 0.99.

b. Sharkey's receivables turnover for 2011 is

1. 8 times.
2. 6 times.
3. 12 times.
4. 14 times.

c. Sharkey's inventory turnover for 2011 is

1. 11.45 times.
2. 10.50 times.
3. 9.85 times.
4. 8.45 times.

d. Sharkey's current ratio at December 31, 2011, is

1. 1.40.
2. 2.60.
3. 1.90.
4. 1.78.

e. If current assets exceed current liabilities, payments to creditors made on the last day of the year will

1. Decrease current ratio.
2. Increase current ratio.
3. Decrease working capital.
4. Increase working capital.

P 6-24
Required Answer the following multiple-choice questions:

a. A company's current ratio is 2.2 to 1 and quick (acid-test) ratio is 1.0 to 1 at the beginning of the year. At the end of the year, the company has a current ratio of 2.5 to 1 and a quick ratio of 0.8 to 1. Which of the following could help explain the divergence in the ratios from the beginning to the end of the year?

(*continued*)

(**P 6-24** CONTINUED)

      1. An increase in inventory levels during the current year.
      2. An increase in credit sales in relationship to cash sales.
      3. An increase in the use of trade payables during the current year.
      4. An increase in the collection rate of accounts receivable.
      5. The sale of marketable securities at a price below cost.

b. If, just prior to a period of rising prices, a company changed its inventory measurement method from FIFO to LIFO, the effect in the next period would be to

      1. Increase both the current ratio and inventory turnover.
      2. Decrease both the current ratio and inventory turnover.
      3. Increase the current ratio and decrease inventory turnover.
      4. Decrease the current ratio and increase inventory turnover.
      5. Leave the current ratio and inventory turnover unchanged.

c. Selected year-end data for Bayer Company are as follows:

Current liabilities	$600,000
Acid-test ratio	2.5
Current ratio	3.0
Cost of sales	$500,000

Bayer Company's inventory turnover based on these year-end data is

      1. 1.20.
      2. 2.40.
      3. 1.67.
      4. Some amount other than those given.
      5. Not determinable from the data given.

d. If a firm has a high current ratio but a low acid-test ratio, one can conclude that

      1. The firm has a large outstanding accounts receivable balance.
      2. The firm has a large investment in inventory.
      3. The firm has a large amount of current liabilities.
      4. The cash ratio is extremely high.
      5. The two ratios must be recalculated because both conditions cannot occur simultaneously.

e. Investment instruments used to invest temporarily idle cash balances should have which of the following characteristics?

      1. High expected return, low marketability, and a short term to maturity.
      2. High expected return, readily marketable, and no maturity date.
      3. Low default risk, low marketability, and a short term to maturity.
      4. Low default risk, readily marketable, and a long term to maturity.
      5. Low default risk, readily marketable, and a short term to maturity.

f. The primary objective in the management of accounts receivable is

      1. To achieve a combination of sales volume, bad-debt experience, and receivables turnover that maximizes the profits of the corporation.
      2. To realize no bad debts because of the opportunity cost involved.
      3. To provide the treasurer of the corporation with sufficient cash to pay the company's bills on time.
      4. To coordinate the activities of manufacturing, marketing, and financing so that the corporation can maximize its profits.
      5. To allow the most liberal credit acceptance policy because increased sales mean increased profits.

g. A firm requires short-term funds to cover payroll expenses. These funds can come from

      1. Trade credit.
      2. Collections of receivables.
      3. Bank loans.

4. Delayed payments of accounts payable.
5. All of the above.

Source: Adapted from past CMA Examinations. Used by Permission of The Institute of Certified Management Accountants.

(CMA Adapted)

P 6-25 Consecutive five-year balance sheets and income statements of Anne Gibson Corporation follow:

ANNE GIBSON CORPORATION
Balance Sheet
December 31, 2007 through December 31, 2011

(Dollars in thousands)	2011	2010	2009	2008	2007
Assets:					
Current assets					
Cash	$ 47,200	$ 46,000	$ 45,000	$ 44,000	$ 43,000
Marketable securities	2,000	2,500	3,000	3,000	3,000
Accounts receivable, less allowance of $1,000, December 31, 2011; $900, December 31, 2010; $900, December 31, 2009; $800, December 31, 2008; $1,200, December 31, 2007	131,000	128,000	127,000	126,000	125,000
Inventories	122,000	124,000	126,000	127,000	125,000
Prepaid expenses	3,000	2,500	2,000	1,000	1,000
Total current assets	305,200	303,000	303,000	301,000	297,000
Property, plant and equipment, net	240,000	239,000	238,000	237,500	234,000
Other assets	10,000	8,000	7,000	6,500	7,000
Total assets	$555,200	$550,000	$548,000	$545,000	$538,000
Liabilities and stockholders' equity:					
Current liabilities					
Accounts payable	$ 72,000	$ 73,000	$ 75,000	$ 76,000	$ 78,500
Accrued compensation	26,000	25,000	25,500	26,000	26,000
Income taxes	11,500	12,000	13,000	12,500	11,000
Total current liabilities	109,500	110,000	113,500	114,500	115,500
Long-term debt	68,000	60,000	58,000	60,000	62,000
Deferred income taxes	25,000	24,000	23,000	22,000	21,000
Stockholders' equity	352,700	356,000	353,500	348,500	339,500
Total liabilities and stockholders' equity	$555,200	$550,000	$548,000	$545,000	$538,000

ANNE GIBSON CORPORATION
Statement of Earnings
For Years Ended December 31, 2007–2011

(In thousands, except per share)	2011	2010	2009	2008	2007
Net sales	$880,000	$910,000	$840,000	$825,000	$820,000
Cost of goods sold	740,000	760,000	704,000	695,000	692,000
Gross profit	140,000	150,000	136,000	130,000	128,000
Selling and administrative expense	53,000	52,000	50,000	49,800	49,000
Interest expense	6,700	5,900	5,800	5,900	6,000
Earnings from continuing operations before income taxes	80,300	92,100	80,200	74,300	73,000
Income taxes	26,000	27,500	28,000	23,000	22,500
Net earnings	$ 54,300	$ 64,600	$ 52,200	$ 51,300	$ 50,500
Earnings per share	$ 1.40	$ 1.65	$ 1.38	$ 1.36	$ 1.33

(continued)

(**P 6-25** CONTINUED)

Required

a. Using year-end balance sheet figures, compute the following for the maximum number of years, based on the available data:

    1. Days' sales in receivables
    2. Accounts receivable turnover
    3. Accounts receivable turnover in days
    4. Days' sales in inventory
    5. Inventory turnover
    6. Inventory turnover in days
    7. Operating cycle
    8. Working capital
    9. Current ratio
    10. Acid-test ratio
    11. Cash ratio
    12. Sales to working capital

b. Using average balance sheet figures, as suggested in the chapter, compute the following for the maximum number of years, based on the available data:

    1. Days' sales in receivables
    2. Accounts receivable turnover
    3. Accounts receivable turnover in days
    4. Days' sales in inventory
    5. Inventory turnover
    6. Inventory turnover in days
    7. Operating cycle
    8. Working capital
    9. Current ratio
    10. Acid-test ratio
    11. Cash ratio
    12. Sales to working capital

c. Comment on trends indicated in short-term liquidity.

P 6-26 Allowance for Uncollectible Accounts—Ethics vs. Conservatism
To aid in determining the balance for the allowance for uncollectible accounts, an aging schedule is often prepared. The Arrow Company prepared the following aging schedule for December 31, 2011:

ARROW COMPANY
Aging Schedule of Accounts Receivable

Age of Accounts	Receivable Balance	Estimate Percent Uncollectible	Estimated Uncollectible Accounts
Current	$120,000	1.5%	$1,800
1–30 days past due	40,000	2.0	800
31–60 days past due	30,000	3.0	900
61–90 days past due	20,000	4.0	800
Over 90 days past due	25,000	7.0	1,750
Total	$235,000		$6,050

The current balance in allowance for uncollectible accounts is $2,000. The president of Arrow Company directs that the allowance be adjusted to $12,000. His reasoning is that 2011 has been a bad year for profits. Additional expenses this year will hardly be noticed, and this will help profits in future years.

Required
a. 1. If the allowance for uncollectible accounts is adjusted to $6,050, how much will this add to expense for 2011?
   2. If the allowance for uncollectible accounts is adjusted to $12,000, how much will this add to expense for 2011?

b. Is the president's direction an example of conservatism or unethical? Comment.

P 6-27 Accounts Receivable—Note Receivable—Ethics

Eric Page, the CEO of Marvick Enterprises, has been concerned with the firm's days' sales in receivables, which are running substantially higher than the past. He directs the CFO to get on top of the situation and reduce days' sales in receivables.

The CFO reviews the receivables and finds that the problem is substantially with one customer that owes $10 million to Marvick Enterprises that was 120 days old. The CFO contacts the customer who informs him that they had a temporary liquidity problem relating to a storm that disrupted the business of several of their customers.

The CFO agrees to help out by converting the receivable to a one-year note, paying 6%. This should give the customer adequate time and result in additional revenue for Marvick Enterprises. The customer agrees to those terms and signs the note.

Required
a. Will the substitution of the note receivable for the account receivable reduce days' sales in receivable?
b. Will the substitution of the note receivable for the account receivable improve the liquidity of Marvick Enterprises?
c. Do you consider this situation to be ethical? Comment.

Cases

CASE 6-1 STRENGTH OF STEEL

AK STEEL HOLDING CORPORATION*
CONSOLIDATED BALANCE SHEETS
December 31, 2010 and 2009
(dollars in millions, except per share amounts)

	2010	2009
ASSETS		
Current Assets:		
Cash and cash equivalents	$ 216.8	$ 461.7
Accounts receivable, net	482.8	463.1
Inventories, net	448.7	416.7
Deferred tax asset, current	225.7	223.9
Other current assets	30.1	64.7
Total Current Assets	1,404.1	1,630.1
Property, Plant and Equipment	5,668.2	5,385.1
Accumulated depreciation	(3,635.0)	(3,409.1)
Property, Plant and Equipment, net	2,033.2	1,976.0
Other Non-current Assets:		
Investment in AFSG Holdings, Inc.	55.6	55.6
Other investments	57.0	52.1
Goodwill	37.1	37.1
Other intangible assets	0.2	0.2

(*continued*)

*"AK Steel Corporation ("AK Holding") is a corporation formed under the laws of Delaware in 1993 and is a fully-integrated producer of flat-rolled carbon, stainless and electrical steels and tubular products through its wholly-owned subsidiary." 10-K

Source: AK Steel Holding Corporation Consolidated Balance Sheets 2010 10-K

(**CASE 6-1** CONTINUED)	2010	2009
Other Non-current Assets: *(continued)*		
Deferred tax asset, non-current	581.5	514.7
Other non-current assets	19.9	8.9
Total Other Non-current Assets	751.3	668.6
TOTAL ASSETS	$ 4,188.6	$ 4,274.7
LIABILITIES AND STOCKHOLDERS' EQUITY		
Current Liabilities:		
Accounts payable	$ 553.1	$ 438.9
Accrued liabilities	145.0	157.0
Current portion of long-term debt	0.7	0.7
Current portion of pension and other postretirement		
benefit obligations	145.7	144.1
Total Current Liabilities	844.5	740.7
Non-current Liabilities:		
Long-term debt	650.6	605.8
Pension and other postretirement benefit obligations	1,706.0	1,856.2
Other non-current liabilities	346.4	191.9
Total Non-current Liabilities	2,703	2,653.9
TOTAL LIABILITIES	3,547.5	3,394.6
Commitments and Contingencies (see Note 8)		
Stockholders' Equity:		
Preferred stock, authorized 25,000,000 shares	—	—
Common stock, authorized 200,000,000 shares of $.01		
par value each; issued 2010, 122,829,975 shares;		
2009, 121,881,816 shares; outstanding 2010,		
109,986,790 shares; 2009, 109,394,455 shares	1.2	1.2
Additional paid-in capital	1,909.4	1,911.4
Treasury stock, common shares at cost, 2010,		
12,843,185; 2009, 12,487,361 shares	(170.1)	(162.2)
Accumulated deficit	(1,188.4)	(1,037.5)
Accumulated other comprehensive income	92.6	167.9
Total AK Steel Holding Corporations Stockholders'		
Equity	644.7	880.8
Noncontrolling interest	(3.6)	(0.7)
TOTAL STOCKHOLDERS' EQUITY	641.1	880.1
TOTAL LIABILITIES AND STOCKHOLDERS' EQUITY	$ 4,188.6	$ 4,274.7

AK STEEL HOLDING CORPORATION

NOTES TO CONSOLIDATED FINANCIAL STATEMENTS (In Part)

(dollars in millions, except per share amounts)

1. Summary of Significant Accounting Policies (In Part)

Inventories: Inventories are valued at the lower of cost or market. The cost of the majority of inventories is measured on the last in, first out ("LIFO") method. Other inventories are measured principally at average cost and consist mostly of foreign inventories and certain raw materials.

	2010	2009
Inventories on LIFO:		
Finished and semi-finished	$ 679.8	$ 597.4
Raw materials and supplies	265.0	205.5
Adjustment to state inventories at LIFO value	(514.2)	(405.2)
Total	430.6	397.7
Other inventories	18.1	19.0
Total inventories	$ 448.7	$ 416.7

During 2010, 2009 and 2008, liquidation of LIFO layers generated income of $13.0, $96.8 and $181.9, respectively.

Required

a. What is the working capital at the end of 2010?

b. What is the balance in the LIFO reserve account at the end of 2010? Describe this account.

c. If the LIFO reserve account was added to the inventory at LIFO, what would be the resulting inventory number at the end of 2010? Which inventory amount do you consider to be more realistic?

d. Does the use of LIFO or FIFO produce higher, lower, or the same income during (1) price increases; (2) price decreases; and (3) constant prices? (Assume no decrease or increase in inventory quantity).

e. Does the use of LIFO or FIFO produce higher, lower, or the same amount of cash flow during (1) price increases; (2) price decreases; and (3) constant costs? Answer the question for both pretax cash flows and after-tax cash flows. (Assume no decrease or increase in inventory quantity).

f. Assume that the company purchased inventory on the last day of the year, beginning inventory equaled ending inventory, and inventory records for the item purchases were maintained periodically on the LIFO basis. Would that purchase be included on the income statement or the balance sheet at year-end?

g. Explain how liquidation of LIFO layers generates income.

CASE 6-2 RISING PRICES, A TIME TO SWITCH OFF LIFO?

The following information was taken directly from the annual report of a firm that wishes to remain anonymous. (The dates have been changed.)

FINANCIAL SUMMARY

Effects of LIFO Accounting

For a number of years, the corporation has used the last-in, first-out (LIFO) method of accounting for its steel inventories. In periods of extended inflation, coupled with uncertain supplies of raw materials from foreign sources, and rapid increases and fluctuations in prices of raw materials such as nickel and chrome nickel scrap, earnings can be affected unrealistically for any given year.

Because of these factors, the corporation will apply to the Internal Revenue Service for permission to discontinue using the LIFO method of accounting for valuing those inventories for which this method has been used. If such application is granted, the LIFO reserve at December 31, 2011, of $12,300,000 would be eliminated, which would require a provision for income taxes of approximately $6,150,000. The corporation will also seek permission to pay the increased taxes over a 10-year period. If the corporation had not used the LIFO method of accounting during 2010, net earnings for the year would have been increased by approximately $1,500,000.

The 2011 annual report also disclosed the following:

		2011	2010
1.	Sales and revenues	$536,467,782	$487,886,449
2.	Earnings per common share	$3.44	$3.58

Required

a. The corporation indicates that earnings can be affected unrealistically by rapid increases and fluctuations in prices when using LIFO. Comment.

b. How much taxes will need to be paid on past earnings from the switch from LIFO? How will the switch from LIFO influence taxes in the future?

c. How will a switch from LIFO affect 2011 profits?

d. How will a switch from LIFO affect future profits?

e. How will a switch from LIFO affect 2011 cash flow?

f. How will a switch from LIFO affect future cash flow?

g. Speculate on the real reason that the corporation wishes to switch from LIFO.

CASE 6-3 IMAGING

Eastman Kodak Company*
CONSOLIDATED STATEMENT OF OPERATIONS

(in millions, except per share data)	For the Year Ended December 31,		
	2010	2009	2008
Net sales			
Products	$ 5,507	$ 6,323	$ 8,130
Services	776	788	793
Licensing & royalties	904	495	493
Total net sales	$ 7,187	$ 7,606	$ 9,416
Cost of sales			
Products	$ 4,638	$ 5,243	$ 6,647
Services	598	595	600
Total cost of sales	$ 5,236	$ 5,838	$ 7,247
Gross profit	$ 1,951	$ 1,768	$ 2,169
Selling, general and administrative expenses	1,277	1,302	1,606
Research and development costs	321	356	478
Restructuring costs, rationalization and other	70	226	140
Other operating expenses (income), net	619	(88)	766
Loss from continuing operations before interest expense, other income (charges), net and income taxes	(336)	(28)	(821)
Interest expense	149	119	108
Loss on early extinguishment of debt, net	102	—	—
Other income (charges), net	26	30	55
Loss from continuing operations before income taxes	(561)	(117)	(874)
Provision (benefit) for income taxes	114	115	(147)
Loss from continuing operations	(675)	(232)	(727)
(Loss) earnings from discontinued operations, net of income taxes	(12)	17	285
Extraordinary item, net of tax	—	6	—
NET LOSS	(687)	(209)	(442)
Less: Net earnings attributable to noncontrolling interests	—	(1)	—
NET LOSS ATTRIBUTABLE TO EASTMAN KODAK COMPANY	$ (687)	$ (210)	$ (442)
Basic and diluted net (loss) earnings per share attributable to Eastman Kodak Company common shareholders:			
Continuing operations	$ (2.51)	$ (0.87)	$ (2.58)
Discontinued operations	(0.05)	0.07	1.01
Extraordinary item	—	0.02	—
Total	$ (2.56)	$ (0.78)	$ (1.57)

*"Eastman Kodak Company… helps consumers, businesses, and creative professionals unleash the power of pictures and printing to enrich their lives." 10-K

Eastman Kodak Company
CONSOLIDATED STATEMENT OF FINANCIAL POSITION

(In millions, except share and per share data)	As of December 31,	
	2010	2009
ASSETS		
CURRENT ASSETS		
Cash and cash equivalents	$ 1,624	$ 2,024
Receivables, net	1,259	1,395
Inventories, net	696	679
Deferred income taxes	120	121
Other current assets	100	84
Total current assets	3,799	4,303

(continued)

Source: Eastman Kodak Company 2010 10-K

(In millions, except share and per share data)	As of December 31, 2010	2009
Property, plant and equipment, net	1,037	1,254
Goodwill	294	907
Other long-term assets	1,109	1,227
TOTAL ASSETS	$ 6,239	$ 7,691
LIABILITIES AND EQUITY		
CURRENT LIABILITIES		
Accounts payable, trade	$ 959	$ 919
Short-term borrowings and current portion of long-term debt	50	62
Accrued income taxes	343	23
Other current liabilities	1,481	1,892
Total current liabilities	2,833	2,896
Long-term debt, net of current portion	1,195	1,129
Pension and other postretirement liabilities	2,661	2,694
Other long-term liabilities	625	1,005
Total liabilities	7,314	7,724
Commitments and Contingencies (Note 10)		
EQUITY (DEFICIT)		
Common stock, $2.50 par value, 950,000,000 shares authorized; 391,292,760 shares issued as of December 31, 2010 and 2009; 268,898,978 and 268,630,514 shares outstanding as of December 31, 2010 and 2009	978	978
Additional paid in capital	1,105	1,093
Retained earnings	4,969	5,676
Accumulated other comprehensive (loss)	(2,135)	(1,760)
	4,917	5,987
Treasury stock, at cost; 122,393,782 shares as of December 31, 2010 and 122,662,246 shares as of December 31, 2009	(5,994)	(6,022)
Total Eastman Kodak Company shareholders' (deficit) equity	(1,077)	(35)
Noncontrolling interests	2	2
Total (deficit) equity	(1,075)	(33)
TOTAL LIABILITIES AND EQUITY (DEFICIT)	$ 6,239	$ 7,691

Eastman Kodak Company

Notes to Financial Statements (In Part)

NOTE 2: RECEIVABLES, NET

(In millions)	As of December 31, 2010	2009
Trade receivables	$1,137	$1,238
Miscellaneous receivables	122	157
Total (net of allowances of $77 and $98 as of December 31, 2010 and 2009, respectively)	$1,259	$1,395

Approximately $224 million and $218 million of the total trade receivable amounts as of December 31, 2010 and 2009, respectively, are expected to be settled through customer deductions in lieu of cash payments. Such deductions represent rebates owed to the customer and are included in other current liabilities in the accompanying Consolidated Statement of Financial Position at each respective balance sheet date.

(*continued*)

(**CASE 6-3** CONTINUED)

NOTE 7: OTHER CURRENT LIABILITIES

	As of December 31,	
(In millions)	2010	2009
Accrued employment-related liabilities	$ 420	$ 501
Accrued customer rebates, advertising and promotional expenses	322	369
Deferred revenue	178	275
Accrued restructuring liabilities	42	95
Other	519	652
Total	$1,481	$1,892

The other component above consists of other miscellaneous current liabilities that, individually, are less than 5% of the total current liabilities component within the Consolidated Statement of Financial Position, and therefore, have been aggregated in accordance with Regulation S-X.

NOTE 8: SHORT-TERM BORROWINGS AND LONG-TERM DEBT (In Part)

SHORT-TERM BORROWINGS AND CURRENT PORTION OF LONG-TERM DEBT

The Company's current portion of long-term debt was $50 million and $62 million as of December 31, 2010 and 2009, respectively. There were no amounts outstanding under short-term bank borrowings as of December 31, 2010 and 2009.

Required
a. Based on these data, calculate the following for 2010 and 2009:
   1. Days' sales in receivables (use trade receivables)
   2. Accounts receivable turnover (use gross trade receivables at year-end)
   3. Days' sales in inventory
   4. Inventory turnover (use year-end inventory)
   5. Working capital
   6. Current ratio
   7. Acid-test ratio
b. Comment on each ratio individually
c. Why are portions of long-term debt included in short-term borrowings?
d. Prepare a vertical common-size analysis for the balance sheets using 2010 and 2009. (Use total assets as the base.)
e. Comment on the vertical common-size analysis

CASE 6-4 TECHNOLOGY

Consolidated Statement of Income
3M Company and Subsidiaries*
Years ended December 31

(Millions, except per share amounts)	2010	2009	2008
Net sales	$26,662	$23,123	$25,269
Operating expenses			
Cost of sales	13,831	12,109	13,379
Selling, general and administrative expenses	5,479	4,907	5,245

(*continued*)

*"3M is a diversified technology company with a global presence in the following businesses: Industrial and Transportation; Health Care; Display and Graphics; Consumer and Office; Safety, Security and Protection Services; and Electro and Communications. 3M is among the leading manufacturers of products for many of the markets it serves. Most 3M products involve expertise in product development, manufacturing and marketing, and are subject to competition from products manufactured and sold by other technologically oriented companies." 10-K
Source: 3M Company and Subsidiaries 2010 10-K

(Millions, except per share amounts)	2010	2009	2008
Research, development and related expenses	1,434	1,293	1,404
Loss from sale of business	—	—	23
Total operating expenses	20,744	18,309	20,051
Operating income	5,918	4,814	5,218
Interest expense and income			
Interest expense	201	219	215
Interest income	(38)	(37)	(105)
Total interest expense (income)	163	182	110
Income before income taxes	5,755	4,632	5,108
Provision for income taxes	1,592	1,388	1,588
Net income including noncontrolling	$ 4,163	$ 3,244	$ 3,520
Less: Net income attributable to noncontrolling assets	78	51	60
Net income attributable to 3M	$ 4,085	3,193	3,460
Weighted average 3M common shares outstanding – basic	713.7	700.5	699.2
Earnings per share attributable to 3M common			
shareholders – basic	5.72	4.56	4.95
Weighted average 3M common shares outstanding –			
diluted	$ 725.5	$ 706.7	$ 707.2
Earnings per share attributable to 3M common			
shareholders – basic	5.63	4.52	4.89
Cash dividends paid per 3M common share	$ 2.10	$ 2.04	$ 2.00

Consolidated Balance sheet
3M Company and Subsidiaries
At December 31

(Dollars in millions, except per share amount)	2010	2009
Assets		
Current Assets:		
Cash and cash equivalents	$ 3,377	$ 3,040
Marketable securities – current	1,101	744
Accounts receivable – net of allowances of $98 and $109	3,615	3,250
Inventories		
Finished goods	1,476	1,255
Work in progress	950	815
Raw materials and supplies	729	569
Total inventories	3,155	2,639
Other current assets	967	1,122
Total current assets	12,215	10,795
Marketable securities – non current	540	825
Investments	146	103
Property, plant and equipment	20,253	19,440
Less: Accumulated Depreciation	(12,974)	(12,440)
Property, plant and equipment – net	7,279	7,000
Goodwill	6,820	5,832
Intangible assets – net	1,820	1,342
Prepaid pension benefits	74	78
Other assets	1,262	1,275
Total assets	$ 30,156	$ 27,250
Liabilities		
Current liabilities		
Short-term borrowings and current portion of long-term debt	$ 1,269	$ 613
Accounts payable	1,662	1,453
Accrued payroll	778	680
Accrued income taxes	358	252

(*continued*)

(**CASE 6-4** CONTINUED)

(Dollars in millions, except per share amount)	2010	2009
Other current liabilities	2,022	1,899
Total current liabilities	6,089	4,897
Long-term debt	4,183	5,097
Pension and postretirement benefits	2,013	2,227
Other liabilities	1,854	1,727
Total liabilities	$ 14,139	$ 13,948
Commitments and contingencies (Note 14)		
Equity		
3M Company shareholders' equity:		
Common stock, par value $.01 per share	$ 9	$ 9
Shares outstanding – 2010: 711,977,608		
Shares outstanding – 2009: 710,599,119		
Additional paid-in capital	3,468	3,153
Retained earnings	25,995	23,753
Treasury stock	(10,266)	(10,397)
Accumulated other comprehensive income (loss)	(3,543)	(3,754)
Total 3M Company shareholders' equity	15,663	12,764
Noncontrolling interest	354	538
Total equity	$ 16,017	$ 13,302
Total liabilities and equity	$ 30,156	$ 27,250

NOTES TO CONSOLIDATED FINANCIAL STATEMENTS (IN PART)

Note I Significant Accounting Policies (In Part)

Cash and Cash Equivalents: Cash and cash equivalents consist of cash and temporary investments with maturities of three months or less when acquired.

Inventories: Inventories are stated at the lower of cost or market, with cost generally determined on a first-in, first-out basis.

Accounts Receivable and Allowances: Trade accounts receivable are recorded at the invoiced amount and do not bear interest. The Company maintains allowances for bad debts, cash discounts, product returns and various other items. The allowance for doubtful accounts and product returns is based on the best estimate of the amount of probable credit losses in existing accounts receivable and anticipated sales returns. The Company determines the allowances based on historical write-off experience by industry and regional economic data and historical sales returns. The Company reviews the allowance for doubtful accounts monthly. The Company does not have any significant off-balance-sheet credit exposure related to its customers.

Required

a. Based on these data, calculate the following for 2010 and 2009:
   1. Days' sales in receivables
   2. Accounts receivable turnover (gross receivables at year-end)
   3. Days' sales in inventory
   4. Inventory turnover (use inventory at year-end)
   5. Working capital
   6. Current ratio
   7. Acid-test ratio
b. Comment on each ratio individually
c. Comment on the apparent total liquidity

Case 6-5 BOOMING RETAIL

The Grand retail firm reported the following financial data for the past several years:

(Amounts in thousands)	Year				
	5	4	3	2	1
Sales	$1,254,131	$1,210,918	$1,096,152	$979,458	$920,797
Net accounts receivable	419,731	368,267	312,776	272,450	230,427

The Grand retail firm had a decentralized credit operation allowing each store to administer its credit operation. Many stores provided installment plans allowing the customer up to 36 months to pay. Gross profits on installment sales were reflected in the financial statements in the period when the sales were made.

Required

a. Using Year 1 as the base, prepare horizontal common-size analysis for sales and net accounts receivable.

b. Compute the accounts receivable turnover for Years 2–5. (Use net accounts receivable.)

c. Would financial control of accounts receivable be more important with installment sales than with sales on 30-day credit? Comment.

d. Comment on what is apparently happening at The Grand retail firm.

Note: Data from an actual retail company.

Case 6-6 GREETINGS

American Greetings*
CONSOLIDATED STATEMENTS OF OPERATIONS
Years ended February 28, 2011, 2010 and 2009
Thousands of dollars except share and per share amounts

	2011	2010	2009
Net sales	$ 1,560,213	$ 1,598,292	$ 1,646,399
Other revenue	32,355	37,566	44,339
Total revenue	1,592,568	1,635,858	1,690,738
Material, labor and other production costs	682,368	713,075	809,956
Selling, distribution and marketing expenses	478,227	507,960	618,899
Administrative and general expenses	260,476	276,031	226,317
Goodwill and other intangible assets impairment	—	—	290,166
Other operating income – net	(3,205)	(310)	(1,396)
Operating income (loss)	174,702	139,102	(253,204)
Interest expense	25,389	26,311	22,854
Interest income	(853)	(1,676)	(3,282)
Other non-operating (income) expense – net	(5,841)	(6,487)	2,157
Income (loss) before income tax expense (benefit)	156,007	120,954	(274,933)
Income tax expense (benefit)	68,989	39,380	(47,174)
(Loss) income from continuing operations			(227,759)
Net income (loss)	$ 87,018	$ 81,574	$ (227,759)
Earnings (loss) per share – basic	$ 2.18	$ 2.07	$ (4.89)
Earnings (loss) per share – assuming dilution	$ 2.11	$ 2.03	$ (4.89)
Average number of shares outstanding	39,982,784	39,467,811	46,543,780
Average number of shares outstanding – assuming dilution	41,244,903	40,159,651	46,543,780
Dividends declared per share	$ 0.56	$ 0.36	$ 0.60

*"Founded in 1906, American Greetings operates predominantly in a single industry: the design, manufacture and sale of everyday and seasonal greeting cards and other social expression products." 10-K

(*continued*)

Source: American Greetings 2010 10-K

(**CASE 6-6** CONTINUED)

CONSOLIDATED STATEMENT OF FINANCIAL POSITION
February 28, 2011 and 2010
Thousands of dollars except share and per share amounts

	2011	2010
ASSETS		
CURRENT ASSETS		
Cash and cash equivalents	$ 215,838	$ 137,949
Trade accounts receivable, net	119,779	135,758
Inventories	179,730	163,956
Deferred and refundable income taxes	50,051	78,433
Assets held for sale	7,154	15,147
Prepaid expenses and other	128,372	148,048
Total current assets	700,924	679,291
GOODWILL	28,903	31,106
OTHER ASSETS	436,137	428,161
DEFERRED AND REFUNDABLE INCOME TAXES	124,789	148,210
PROPERTY, PLANT AND EQUIPMENT – NET	241,649	242,883
	$1,532,402	$1,529,651
LIABILITIES AND SHAREHOLDERS' EQUITY		
CURRENT LIABILITIES		
Debt due within one year	$ —	$ 1,000
Accounts payable	87,105	95,434
Accrued liabilities	69,824	78,245
Accrued compensation and benefits	72,379	85,092
Income taxes payable	10,951	13,901
Other current liabilities	102,286	94,915
Total current liabilities	342,545	368,587
LONG-TERM DEBT	232,545	328,723
OTHER LIABILITIES	176,522	168,098
DEFERRED INCOME TAXES AND NONCURRENT INCOME TAXES PAYABLE	31,736	28,179
SHAREHOLDERS' EQUITY		
Common shares – par value $1 per share:		
Class A – 82,181,659 shares issued less 44,711,736 treasury shares in 2011 and 80,884,505 shares issued less 44,627,298 treasury shares in 2010	37,470	36,257
Class B – 6,066,092 shares issued less 3,128,841 treasure shares in 2011 and 6,066,092 shares issued less 2,843,190 treasury shares in 2010	2,937	3,223
Capital in excess of par value	492,048	461,076
Treasury stock	(952,206)	(946,724)
Accumulated other comprehensive loss	(2,346)	(29,815)
Retained earnings	1,171,008	1,112,047
Total shareholders' equity	748,911	636,064
	$1,532,402	$1,529,651

NOTES TO CONSOLIDATED FINANCIAL STATEMENTS (In Part)
Years ended February 28, 2011, 2010 and 2009
Thousands of dollars except per share amounts

NOTE I – SIGNIFICANT ACCOUNTING POLICIES (In Part)

Cash Equivalents: The Corporation considers all highly liquid instruments purchased with an original maturity of less than three months to be cash equivalents.

Allowance for Doubtful Accounts: The Corporation evaluates the collectibility of its accounts receivable based on a combination of factors. In circumstances where the Corporation is aware of a customer's inability to meet its financial obligations, a specific allowance for bad debts against amounts due is recorded to reduce the receivable to the amount the Corporation reasonably expects will be collected. In addition, the Corporation recognizes allowances for bad debts based on estimates developed by using standard quantitative measures incorporating historical write-offs. See Note 6 for further information.

Customer Allowances and Discounts: The Corporation offers certain of its customers allowances and discounts including cooperative advertising, rebates, marketing allowances and various other allowances and discounts. These amounts are recorded as reductions of gross accounts receivable or included in accrued liabilities and are recognized as reductions of net sales when earned. These amounts are earned by the customer as product is purchased from the Corporation and are recorded based on the terms of individual customer contracts. See Note 6 for further information.

Concentration of Credit Risks: The Corporation sells primarily to customers in the retail trade, including those in the mass merchandise, drug store, discount retailer, supermarket and other channels of distribution. These customers are located throughout the United States, Canada, the United Kingdom, Australia, New Zealand and Mexico. Net sales from continuing operations to the Corporation's five largest customers accounted for approximately 42%, 39% and 36% of total revenue in 2011, 2010 and 2009, respectively. Net sales to Wal-Mart Stores, Inc. and its subsidiaries accounted for approximately 15%, 14% and 15% of total revenue in 2011, 2010 and 2009, respectively. Net sales to Target Corporation accounted for approximately 14% and 13% of total revenue in 2011 and 2010, respectively, and less than 10% in 2009.

The Corporation conducts business based on periodic evaluations of its customers' financial condition and generally does not require collateral to secure their obligation to the Corporation. While the competitiveness of the retail industry presents an inherent uncertainty, the Corporation does not believe a significant risk of loss exists from a concentration of credit.

Inventories: Finished products, work in process and raw materials inventories are carried at the lower of cost or market. The last-in, first-out (LIFO) cost method is used for certain domestic inventories, which approximate 80% of the total pre-LIFO consolidated inventories at February 28, 2011 and 2010, respectively. International inventories and the remaining domestic inventories principally use the first-in, first-out (FIFO) method except for display material and factory supplies which are carried at average cost. The Corporation allocates fixed production overhead to inventory based on the normal capacity of the production facilities. Abnormal amounts of idle facility expense, freight, handling costs and wasted material are treated as a current period expense. See Note 7 for further information.

NOTE 6 – CUSTOMER ALLOWANCES AND DISCOUNTS

Trade accounts receivable are reported net of certain allowances and discounts. The most significant of these are as follows:

	February 28, 2011	February 28, 2010
Allowance for seasonal sales returns	$34,058	$ 36,443
Allowance for outdated products	8,264	10,438
Allowance for doubtful accounts	5,374	2,963
Allowance for cooperative advertising and marketing funds	25,631	24,061
Allowance for rebates	24,920	29,338
	$98,247	$103,243

(*continued*)

(**CASE 6-6** CONTINUED)

Certain customer allowances and discounts are settled in cash. These accounts, primarily rebates, which are classified as "Accrued liabilities" on the Consolidated Statement of Financial Position, totaled $11,913 and $15,326 as of February 28, 2011 and 2010, respectively.

NOTE 7 – INVENTORIES

	February 28, 2011	February 28, 2010
Raw materials	$ 21,248	$ 18,609
Work in process	6,476	6,622
Finished products	212,056	194,283
	239,780	219,514
Less LIFO reserve	78,358	75,491
	161,422	144,023
Display material and factory supplies	18,308	19,933
	$179,730	$163,956

There were no material LIFO liquidations in 2011 and 2009. During 2010, inventory quantities declined resulting in the liquidation of LIFO inventory layers carried at lower costs compared with current year purchases. The income statement effect of such liquidation on material, labor and other production costs was approximately $13,000. Inventory held on location for retailers with SBT arrangements, which is included in finished products, totaled approximately $42,000 and $38,000 as of February 28, 2011 and 2010, respectively.

Required

a. Based on these data, calculate the following for 2011 and 2010:
   1. Days' sales in receivables
   2. Accounts receivable turnover (gross receivables at year-end)
   3. Days' sales in inventory
   4. Inventory turnover (use inventory at year-end)
   5. Working capital
   6. Current ratio
   7. Acid-test ratio
b. Comment on each ratio individually.
c. 1. Describe the individual allowance consideration.
   2. Are some of these allowance considerations normal for most companies?
d. What would be the inventory balance at February 28, 2011 if the LIFO reserve were removed?
e. Were there material LIFO liquidations in 2011, 2010 or 2009?
f. Comment on the apparent total liquidity.

CASE 6-7 LIFO – TAX, U.S. GAAP AND IFRS IMPLICATIONS

The LIFO method assumes that the costs of the latest items bought or produced are matched against current sales. Usually, this assumption materially improves the matching of current costs against current revenue.

In the United States, LIFO is accepted GAAP as it is in some other countries. IFRS does not allow LIFO.

LIFO is used in many industries in the United States. In some industries, 50% or more of the firms use LIFO.

Source: U.S. Securities and Exchange

For some United States companies, their LIFO reserve account is very material. Some companies with substantial LIFO reserves are as follows:

Company	LIFO Reserve	Financial Statement Date
Exxon Mobil Corp.	$21,300,000,000	12-31-2010
Caterpillar	2,575,000,000	12-31-2010
Deere & Co.	1,398,000,000	10-31-2010
Ford Motor Co.	865,000,000	12-31-2010
Kroger	827,000,000	1-29-2011
	$26,965,000,000	

In the United States, if LIFO is used for federal taxes, then it must be used for financial reporting. Many firms that use LIFO would likely not use LIFO except for this conformity requirement.

During periods of rising prices, the firm should benefit on taxes as long as the inventory does not decline. The tax benefit may be reduced or eliminated if inventory quantities decline and old lower costs are matched against current sales.

Required

a. If the United States firms adopt IFRS, what implications will this have for United States firms that use LIFO?

b. Assume that the United States tax rate is 40% including federal, state and local income taxes. What is the potential tax liability (in total) for the firms listed in this case?

CASE 6-8 SPECIALTY RETAILER – LIQUIDITY REVIEW

1. **Abercrombie & Fitch Co.**
   (January 29, 2011 – 52-week; January 30, 2010 – 52-week; January 31, 2009 – 52-week)
   "Abercrombie & Fitch Co. ("A&F"), a company incorporated in Delaware in 1996, through its subsidiaries (collectively, A&F and its subsidiaries are referred to as "Abercrombie & Fitch" or the "Company"), is a specialty retailer that operates stores and direct-to-consumer operations." 10-K

   Source: Abercrombie & Fitch 2010 10-K

2. **Limited Brands, Inc.**
   (January 29, 2011 – 52-week; January 30, 2010 – 52-week; January 31, 2009 – 52-week)
   "We operate in the highly competitive specialty retail business. Founded in 1963 in Columbus, Ohio, we have evolved from an apparel-based specialty retailer to an approximately $10 billion segment leader focused on women's intimate and other apparel, beauty and personal care product categories that make customers feel sexy, sophisticated and forever young." 10-K

   Source: Limited Brands 2010 10-K

3. **Gap, Inc.**
   (January 29, 2011 – 52-week; January 30, 2010 – 52-week; January 31, 2009 – 52-week)
   "The Gap, Inc. (the "Company," "we," and "our") was incorporated in the State of California in July 1969 and was reincorporated under the laws of the State of Delaware in May 1988. We are a global specialty retailer offering apparel, accessories, and personal care products for men, women, children, and babies under the Gap, Old Navy, Banana Republic, Piperlime, and Athleta brands." 10-K

   Source: Gap Inc 2010 10-K

	Abercrombie & Fitch		Limited Brands, Inc.		GAP, Inc.	
Data Reviewed	2011	2010	2011	2010	2011	2010
Current ratio	2.56	2.73	1.72	2.46	1.87	2.19
Acid test	1.62	1.77	.91	1.53	.79	1.21

Required

a. For each company, indicate the trend in liquidity.

b. How would you rank these companies, considering liquidity?

CASE 6-9 EAT AT MY RESTAURANT – LIQUIDITY REVIEW

With this case, we review the liquidity of several restaurant companies. The restaurant companies reviewed and the year-end dates are as follows:

1. **Yum Brands, Inc.**
   (December 25, 2010; December 26, 2009)
   "YUM consist of six operating segments: KFC – U.S., Pizza Hut – U.S., Taco Bell – U.S. Long John Silver's ("LJS") – U.S. and A&W All American Food Restaurants ("A&W") – U.S., YUM Restaurants International ("YRI" or "International Division") and YUM Restaurants China ("China Division")." 10-K

   Source: Yum! Brands, Inc. and Subsidiaries 2010 10-K

2. **Panera Bread**
   (December 28, 2010; December 29, 2009)
   "Panera Bread Company and its subsidiaries, referred to as "Panera Bread," "Panera," the "Company," "we," "us," and "our," is a national bakery-café concept with 1,453 Company-owned and franchise-operated bakery-café locations in 40 states, the District of Columbia, and Ontario, Canada." 10-K

   Source: Panera Bread 2010 10-K

3. **Starbucks**
   (October 3, 2010; September 27, 2009)
   "Starbucks is the premier roaster and retailer of specialty coffee in the world, operating in more than 50 countries." 10-K

   Source: Starbucks 2010 10-K

Data Reviewed	Yum Brands, Inc.		Panera Bread		Starbucks	
	2010	2009	2010	2009	2010	2009
Current ratio	.94	.73	1.56	2.26	1.55	1.29
Acid test	.69	.36	1.27	1.93	.98	.59

Required

a. For each company, indicate the trend in liquidity

b. Give your opinion as to the relative liquidity of each of these companies. How would you rank these companies, considering liquidity?

WEB CASE THOMSON ONE *Business School Edition*

Please complete the Web case that covers material discussed in this chapter at www.cengagebrain .com. You'll be using Thomson ONE Business School Edition, a powerful tool that combines a full range of fundamental financial information, earnings estimates, market data, and source documents for 500 publicly traded companies.

 TO THE NET CASE

---

1. Go to the SEC Web site (www.sec.gov). Under "Filings & Forms (EDGAR)," click on "Search for Company Filings." Click on "Company or Fund, etc."

   a. Under Company Name, enter "Quaker" (or under Ticker Symbol, enter "KWR"). Select the 10-K filed March 2, 2011.

      1. Copy the first sentence in the "Item 1. Business" section.

      2. Compute the current ratio for December 31, 2010 and 2009.

   b. Under Company Name, enter "Kroger Co" (or under Ticker Symbol, enter "KR"). In the Form Type box, enter "10–K." Select the 10-K filed March 29, 2011.

      1. Copy the first sentence in the "Item 1. Business" section.

      2. Compute the current ratio for January 29, 2011, and January 30, 2010.

   c. Consider the nature of the business of these companies. Comment on why Quaker has a higher current ratio than Kroger Co.

2. Go to the SEC Web site (www.sec.gov). Under "Filings & Forms (EDGAR)," click on "Search for Company Filings." Click on "Company or Fund, etc." Under Company Name, enter "Kroger Co" (or under Ticker Symbol, enter "KR"). Select the 10-K filed March 29, 2011.

   a. Copy the first sentence in the "Item 1. Business" section.

   b. Determine the net inventory balances at January 29, 2011.

   c. Determine the replacement cost of inventory at January 29, 2011.

   d. Comment on why the inventory balance is lower than replacement cost.

3. Go to the SEC Web site (www.sec.gov). Under "Filings & Forms (EDGAR)," click on "Search for Company Filings." Click on "Company or Fund, etc." Under Company Name, enter "Dynatronics Corp" (or under Ticker Symbol, enter "DYNT"). Select the 10-K SB filed September 22, 2010.

   a. Copy the third paragraph in the "Item 1. Business" section.

   b. What is the net trade receivable at June 30, 2010?

   c. What is the gross receivable at June 30, 2010?

   d. Describe the inventory method.

4. Go to the SEC site (www.sec.gov). Under "Filings & Forms (EDGAR)," click on "Search for Company Filings." Click on "Company or Fund, etc." Under Company Name, enter "TASER International" (or under Ticker Symbol, enter "TASR"). Select the 10-K filed March 14, 2011.

   a. Copy the first two sentences in the "Item 1 Business" section.

   b. What is the net receivables at December 31, 2010?

   c. What is the gross receivables at December 31, 2010?

   d. Notes to Financial Statements (in Part)

      1. Organization and Summary of Significant Accounting Policies (in Part) Inventory (in Part): "Provisions are made to reduce potentially excess, obsolete, or slow-moving inventories to their net realizable value." What does management consider to arrive at the net realizable value?

   e. For December 31, 2010 and December 31, 2009, what percentage is "Cash and cash equivalents" in relation to total current assets and total assets. Why do they have this balance in "Cash and cash equivalents"?

5. Go to the SEC Web site (www.sec.gov). Under "Filings & Forms (EDGAR)," click on "Search for Company Filings." Click on "Company or Fund, etc." Under Company Name, enter "Dell Inc" (or under Ticker Symbol, enter "DELL"). Select the 10-K filed March 15, 2011.

   a. Copy the first two sentences in the "Item 1. Business" section.

   b. Speculate why inventories are relatively low in relation to accounts receivable, net.

   c. Speculate why accounts receivable, net is relatively low in relation to accounts payable.

   d. Speculate why the amounts in cash and cash equivalents and short-term investments are large in relation to total current assets.

Endnotes

1. *Accounting Research Bulletin No. 43,* "Restatement and Revision of Accounting Research Bulletins," 1953, Chapter 3, Section A, par. 4.

2. *Statement of Financial Accounting Standards No. 115,* "Accounting for Certain Investments in Debt and Equity Securities" (Financial Accounting Standards Board, Norwalk, CT: 1993).

3. *Opinions of the Accounting Principles Board No. 21,* "Interest on Receivables and Payables" (American Institute of Certified Public Accountants, New York: 1971), par. 11.

4. *Statement of Financial Accounting Standards No. 5,* "Accounting for Contingencies" (Financial Accounting Standards Board, Stamford, CT: 1975), par. 8.

5. Committee on Accounting Procedure, American Institute of Certified Public Accountants, "Accounting Research and Terminology Bulletins" (American Institute of Certified Public Accountants, New York: 1961), p. 21.

Long-Term Debt-Paying Ability

R. Sherwood Veith/iStockphoto.com

This chapter covers two approaches to viewing a firm's long-term debt-paying ability. One approach views the firm's ability to carry the debt as indicated by the income statement, and the other considers the firm's ability to carry debt as indicated by the balance sheet.

In the long run, a relationship exists between the reported income resulting from the use of accrual accounting and the ability of the firm to meet its long-term obligations. Although the reported income does not agree with the cash available in the short run, the revenue and expense items eventually do result in cash movements. Because of the close relationship between the reported income and the ability of the firm to meet its long-run obligations, the entity's profitability is an important factor when determining long-term debt-paying ability.

In addition to the profitability of the firm, the amount of debt in relation to the size of the firm should be analyzed. This analysis indicates the amount of funds provided by outsiders in relation to those provided by owners of the firm. If outsiders have provided a high proportion of the resources, the risks of the business have been substantially shifted to the outsiders. A large proportion of debt in the capital structure increases the risk of not meeting the principal or interest obligation because the company may not generate adequate funds to meet these obligations.

Income Statement Consideration When Determining Long-Term Debt-Paying Ability

The firm's ability to carry debt, as indicated by the income statement, can be viewed by considering the times interest earned and the fixed charge coverage.

Times Interest Earned

The times interest earned ratio indicates a firm's long-term debt-paying ability from the income statement view. If the times interest earned is adequate, little danger exists that the firm will not be able to meet its interest obligation. If the firm has good coverage of the interest obligation, it should also be able to refinance the principal when it comes due. In effect, the funds will probably never be required to pay off the principal if the company has a good record of covering the interest expense. A relatively high, stable coverage of interest over the years indicates a good record; a low, fluctuating coverage from year to year indicates a poor record.

Companies that maintain a good record can finance a relatively high proportion of debt in relation to shareholders' equity and, at the same time, obtain funds at favorable rates. Utility companies have traditionally been examples of companies that have a high debt structure in relation to shareholders' equity. They accomplished this because of their relatively high, stable coverage of interest over the years. This stability evolved in an industry with a regulated profit and a relatively stable demand. During the 1970s, 1980s, and 1990s, utilities experienced a severe strain on their profits, as rate increases did not keep pace with inflation. In addition, the demand was not as predictable as in prior years. The strain on profits and the uncertainty of demand influenced investors to demand higher interest rates from utilities than had been previously required in relation to other companies.

A company issues debt obligations to obtain funds at an interest rate less than the earnings from these funds. This is called **trading on the equity or leverage.** With a high interest rate, the added risk exists that the company will not be able to earn more on the funds than the interest cost on them.

Compute times interest earned as follows:

$$\text{Times Interest Earned} = \frac{\begin{array}{c}\text{Recurring Earnings, Excluding Interest}\\ \text{Expense, Tax Expense, Equity Earnings,}\\ \text{and Noncontrolling Interest}\end{array}}{\text{Interest Expense, Including Capitalized Interest}}$$

The income statement contains several figures that might be used in this analysis. In general, the primary analysis of the firm's ability to carry the debt as indicated by the income statement should include only income expected to occur in subsequent periods. Thus, the following nonrecurring items should be excluded:

1. Discontinued operations
2. Extraordinary items

In addition to these nonrecurring items, other items that should be excluded for the times interest earned computation include:

1. INTEREST EXPENSE. This is added back to net income because the interest coverage would be understated by one if interest expense were deducted before computing times interest earned.
2. INCOME TAX EXPENSE. Income taxes are computed after deducting interest expense, so they do not affect the safety of the interest payments.
3. EQUITY EARNINGS (LOSSES) OF NONCONSOLIDATED SUBSIDIARIES. These are excluded because they are not available to cover interest payments, except to the extent that they are accompanied by cash dividends.
4. NET INCOME—NONCONTROLLING INTEREST. This adjustment at the bottom of the income statement should be excluded; use income before Net income–Noncontrolling interest. Net income–Noncontrolling interest results from consolidating a firm in which a company has control but less than 100% ownership. All of the interest expense of the firm consolidated is included in the consolidated income statement. Therefore, all of the income of the firm consolidated should be considered in the coverage.

Capitalization of interest results in interest being added to a fixed asset instead of expensed. The interest capitalized should be included with the total interest expense in the denominator of the times interest earned ratio because it is part of the interest payment. The capitalized interest must be added to the interest expense disclosed on the income statement or in notes.

An example of capitalized interest would be interest during the current year on a bond issued to build a factory. As long as the factory is under construction, this interest would be added to the asset account, Construction in Process, on the balance sheet. This interest does not appear on the income statement, but it is as much of a commitment as the interest expense deducted on the income statement.

When the factory is completed, the annual interest on the bond issued to build the factory will be expensed. When expensed, interest appears on the income statement.

Capitalized interest is usually disclosed in a note. Some firms describe the capitalized interest on the face of the income statement.

Exhibit 7-1 shows the computation for times interest earned for the years 2011 and 2010. These are very high numbers, and the coverage decreased in 2011.

To evaluate the adequacy of coverage, the times interest earned ratio should be computed for a period of three to five years and compared to competitors and the industry average. Computing interest earned for three to five years provides insight on the stability of the interest coverage. Because the firm needs to cover interest in the bad years as well as the good years, the lowest times interest earned in the period is used as the primary indication of the interest coverage. A cyclical firm may have a very high times interest earned ratio in highly profitable years, but interest may not be covered in low profit years.

Interest coverage on long-term debt is sometimes computed separately from the normal times interest earned. For this purpose only, use the interest on long-term debt, thus focusing on the long-term interest coverage. Since times interest earned indicates long-term debt-paying ability, this revised computation helps focus on the long-term position. For external analysis, it is usually not practical to compute times interest coverage on long-term debt because of the lack of data. However, this computation can be made for internal analysis.

In the long run, a firm must have the funds to meet all of its expenses. In the short run, a firm can often meet its interest obligations even when the times interest earned is less than 1.00. Some of the expenses, such as depreciation expense, amortization expense, and depletion expense, do not require funds in the short run. The airline industry has had several bad periods when the times interest earned was less than 1.00, but it was able to maintain the interest payments.

To get a better indication of a firm's ability to cover interest payments in the short run, the noncash expenses such as depreciation, depletion, and amortization can be added back to the numerator of the times interest earned ratio. The resulting ratio, which is less conservative, gives a type of cash basis times interest earned useful for evaluating the firm in the short run.

EXHIBIT **7-1**	Nike, Inc.		
Times Interest Earned			
Years Ended May 31, 2011 and 2010			
(In millions)		**2011**	**2010**
Income before income taxes		$2,844	$2,517
Plus: Interest expense		34*	36*
Adjusted income (A)		$2,878	$2,553
Interest expense		$ 34*	$ 36*
Capitalized interest		**	**
Total interest expense (B)		$ 34	$ 36
Times interest earned (A ÷ B)		84.65	70.92

*Interest expense includes both expensed and capitalized.
**Per Note 3—Property, plant and equipment.
"Capitalized interest was not material for the years ended May 31, 2011, 2010 and 2009." 10-K
Source: Nike, Inc. 2010 10-K

Fixed Charge Coverage

The fixed charge coverage ratio, an extension of the times interest earned ratio, also indicates a firm's long-term debt-paying ability from the income statement view. The fixed charge coverage ratio indicates a firm's ability to cover fixed charges. It is computed as follows:

$$\text{Fixed Charge Coverage} = \frac{\begin{array}{c}\text{Recurring Earnings, Excluding Interest Expense,}\\\text{Tax Expense, Equity Earnings, and}\\\text{Noncontrolling Interest} + \text{Interest Portion of Rentals}\end{array}}{\begin{array}{c}\text{Interest Expense, Including Capitalized Interest}\\+ \text{Interest Portion of Rentals}\end{array}}$$

A difference of opinion occurs in practice as to what should be included in the fixed charges. When assets are leased, the lessee classifies leases as either capital leases or operating leases. The lessee treats a capital lease as an acquisition and includes the leased asset in fixed assets and the related obligation in liabilities. Part of the lease payment is considered to be interest expense. Therefore, the interest expense on the income statement includes interest related to capital leases.

A portion of operating lease payments is an item frequently included in addition to interest expense. Operating leases are not on the balance sheet, but they are reflected on the income statement in the rent expense. An operating lease for a relatively long term is a type of long-term financing, so part of the lease payment is really interest. When a portion of operating lease payments is included in fixed charges, it is an effort to recognize the true total interest that the firm pays.

SEC reporting may require a more conservative computation than the times interest earned ratio in order to determine the firm's long-term debt-paying ability. The SEC refers to its ratio as the **ratio of earnings to fixed charges**. The major difference between the times interest earned computation and the ratio of earnings to fixed charges is that the latter computation includes a portion of the operating leases.

Usually, one-third of the operating leases' rental charges is included in the fixed charges because this is an approximation of the proportion of lease payment that is interest. The SEC does not accept the one-third approximation automatically, but requires a more specific estimate of the interest portion based on the terms of the lease. Individuals interested in a company's ratio of earnings to fixed charges can find this ratio on the face of the income statement included with the SEC registration statement (Form S-7) when debt securities are registered.

Nike discloses that the interest component of leases includes one-tenth of rental expense, which approximates the interest component of operating leases. When working problems and the like in this book, use the one-third of operating leases' rental charges as an approximation of the proportion of lease payment that is interest when the interest component of leases is not disclosed.

The same adjusted earnings figure is used in the fixed charge coverage ratio as is used for the times interest earned ratio, except that the interest portion of operating leases (rentals) is added to the adjusted earnings for the fixed charge coverage ratio. The interest portion of operating leases is added to the adjusted earnings because it was previously deducted on the income statement as rental charges.

Exhibit 7-2 shows the fixed charge coverage for Nike for 2011 and 2010, with the interest portion of rentals considered. This figure, though more conservative than the times interest earned, is still very good for Nike.

Among the other items sometimes considered as fixed charges are depreciation, depletion and amortization, debt principal payments, and pension payments. Substantial preferred dividends may also be included, or a separate ratio may be computed to consider preferred dividends. The more items considered as fixed charges, the more conservative the ratio. The trend is usually similar to that found for the times interest earned ratio.

EXHIBIT **7-2**	Nike, Inc.	

Fixed Charge Coverage

	Years Ended May 31, 2011 and 2010	
(In millions)	**2011**	**2010**
Income before income taxes	$2,844	$2,517
Plus: Interest expense	34*	36*
Interest portion of leases	45	42
Earnings adjusted (A)	$2,923	$2,595
Interest expense	34*	36*
Capitalized interest	**	**
Interest portion of leases	45***	42
Adjusted interest (B)	$ 79.0	$ 78.0
Fixed charge coverage (A ÷ B)	37.00 Times per year	33.27 Times per year

*Interest expense includes both expensed and capitalized.
**Per Note 3—Property, plant and equipment.
***See Exhibit 12-1 in the Summary material following chapter 10.
"Capitalized interest was not material for the years ended May 31, 2011, 2010 and 2009" 10-K
Source: Nike, Inc. 2010 10-K

Balance Sheet Consideration When Determining Long-Term Debt-Paying Ability

The firm's ability to carry debt, as indicated by the balance sheet, can be viewed by considering the debt ratio and the debt/equity ratio.

Debt Ratio

The debt ratio indicates the firm's long-term debt-paying ability. It is computed as follows:

$$\text{Debt Ratio} = \frac{\text{Total Liabilities}}{\text{Total Assets}}$$

Total liabilities includes short-term liabilities, reserves, deferred tax liabilities, noncontrolling interests, redeemable preferred stock, and any other noncurrent liability. It does not include shareholders' equity.

The debt ratio indicates the percentage of assets financed by creditors, and it helps to determine how well creditors are protected in case of insolvency. If creditors are not well protected, the company is not in a position to issue additional long-term debt. From the perspective of long-term debt-paying ability, the lower this ratio, the better the company's position.

Exhibit 7-3 shows the debt ratio for Nike for May 31, 2011, and May 31, 2010. The exhibit indicates that substantially less than one-half of the Nike assets were financed by outsiders in both 2011 and 2010. This debt ratio is a conservative computation because all of the liabilities and near liabilities have been included. At the same time, the assets are understated because no adjustments have been made for assets that have a fair market value greater than book value.

The debt ratio should be compared with competitors and industry averages. Industries that have stable earnings can handle more debt than industries that have cyclical earnings. This comparison can be misleading if one firm has substantial hidden assets, or liabilities that other firms do not (such as substantial land carried at historical cost).

In practice, substantial disagreement occurs on the details of the formula to compute the debt ratio. Some of the disagreement revolves around whether short-term liabilities should be included. Some firms exclude short-term liabilities because they are not long-term sources of funds and are, therefore, not a valid indication of the firm's long-term debt position. Other firms include short-term liabilities because these liabilities become part of the total

EXHIBIT **7-3**	Nike, Inc.

Debt Ratio

Years Ended May 31, 2011 and 2010

(In millions)	2011	2010
Total liabilities compiled:		
Current liabilities	$ 3,958	$ 3,364
Long-term debt	276	446
Deferred income taxes and other liabilities	921	855
Redeemable preferred stock	0	0
Total liabilities [A]	$ 5,155	$ 4,665
Total assets [B]	$14,998	$14,419
Debt ratio [A ÷ B]	34.37%	32.35%

Source: Nike, Inc. 2010 10-K

source of outside funds in the long run. For example, individual accounts payable are relatively short term, but accounts payable in total becomes a rather permanent part of the entire sources of funds. This book takes a conservative position that includes the short-term liabilities in the debt ratio.

Another issue involves whether certain other items should be included in liabilities. Under current GAAP, some liabilities clearly represent a commitment to pay out funds in the future, whereas other items may never result in a future payment. Items that present particular problems as to a future payment of funds include reserves, deferred taxes, noncontrolling interests, and redeemable preferred stock. Each of these items will be reviewed in the sections that follow.

Reserves

The reserve accounts classified under liabilities (some short-term and some long-term) result from an expense charge to the income statement and an equal increase in the reserve account on the balance sheet. These reserve accounts do not represent definite commitments to pay out funds in the future, but they are estimates of funds that will be paid out.

Reserve accounts are used infrequently in U.S. financial reporting. It is thought that they provide too much discretion in determining the amount of the reserve and the related impact on reported income. When the reserve account is increased, income is reduced. A reduction in a reserve account represents a balance sheet entry. Reserve accounts are popular in some other countries like Germany. This book takes a conservative position that includes the reserves in liabilities in the debt ratio.

Deferred Taxes (Interperiod Tax Allocation)

In the United States, a firm may recognize certain income and expense items in one period for the financial statements and in another period for the federal tax return. This can result in financial statement income in any one period that is substantially different from tax return income. For many other countries, this is not the case. For example, there are few timing differences in Germany, and there are no timing differences in Japan. For these countries, deferred taxes are not a substantial issue or are not an issue at all. In the United States, taxes payable based on the tax return can be substantially different from income tax expense based on financial statement income. Current GAAP directs that the tax expense for the financial statements be based on the tax-related items on the financial statements. Taxes payable are based on the actual current taxes payable, determined by the tax return. (The Internal Revenue Code specifies the procedures for determining taxable income.) The tax expense for the financial statements often does not agree with the taxes payable. The difference between tax expense and taxes payable is recorded as deferred income taxes. The concept that results in deferred income taxes is called **interperiod tax allocation**.

As an illustration of deferred taxes, consider the following facts related to a machinery purchase for $100,000:

Three-year write-off for tax purposes:

1st year	$ 25,000
2nd year	38,000
3rd year	37,000
	$100,000

Five-year write-off for financial statements:

1st year	$ 20,000
2nd year	20,000
3rd year	20,000
4th year	20,000
5th year	20,000
	$100,000

For both tax and financial statement purposes, $100,000 was written off for the equipment. The write-off on the tax return was three years, while the write-off on the financial statements was five years. The faster write-off on the tax return resulted in lower taxable income than the income reported on the income statement during the first three years. During the last two years, the income statement income was lower than the tax return income.

In addition to temporary differences, the tax liability can be influenced by an **operating loss carryback** and/or **operating loss carryforward**. The tax code allows a corporation reporting an operating loss for income tax purposes in the current year to carry this loss back and forward to offset reported taxable income. The company may first carry an operating loss back two years in sequential order, starting with the earliest of the two years. If the taxable income for the past two years is not enough to offset the operating loss, then the remaining loss is sequentially carried forward 20 years and offset against future taxable income.

A company can elect to forgo a carryback and, instead, only carry forward an operating loss. A company would not normally forgo a carryback because an operating loss carryback results in a definite and immediate income tax refund. A carryforward will reduce income taxes payable in future years to the extent of earned taxable income. A company could possibly benefit from forgoing a carryback if prospects in future years are good and an increase in the tax rate is anticipated.

Interperiod tax allocation should be used for all temporary differences. A temporary difference between the tax basis of an asset or a liability and its reported amount in the financial statements will result in taxable or deductible amounts in future years when the reported amount of the asset or liability is recovered or settled, respectively.

A corporation usually reports deferred taxes in two classifications: a net current amount and a net noncurrent amount. The net current amount could result in a current asset or a current liability being reported. The net noncurrent amount could result in a noncurrent asset or a noncurrent liability being reported.

Classification as current or noncurrent is usually based on the classification of the asset or liability responsible for the temporary difference. For example, a deferred tax liability resulting from the excess of tax depreciation over financial reporting depreciation would be reported as a noncurrent liability. This is because the temporary difference is related to non-current assets (fixed assets).

When a deferred tax asset or liability is not related to an asset or a liability, the deferred tax asset or liability is classified according to the expected reversal date of the temporary difference. For example, a deferred tax amount resulting from an operating loss carryforward would be classified based on the expected reversal date of the temporary difference.

There should be a valuation allowance against a deferred tax asset if sufficient uncertainty exists about a corporation's future taxable income. A valuation allowance reduces the deferred tax asset to its expected realizable amount. At the time that the valuation allowance is recognized, tax expense is increased.

A more likely than not criterion is used to measure uncertainty. If more likely than not a deferred asset will not be realized, a valuation allowance would be required.

Nike discloses deferred taxes in current assets, long-term assets, and long-term liabilities. For many firms, the long-term liability, deferred taxes, has grown to a substantial amount, which often increases each year. This occurs because of the growth in the temporary differences that cause the timing difference.

Deferred taxes must be accounted for, using the liability method, which focuses on the balance sheet. Deferred taxes are recorded at amounts at which they will be settled when underlying temporary differences reverse. Deferred taxes are adjusted for tax rate changes. A change in tax rates can result in a material adjustment to the deferred account and can substantially influence income in the year of the tax rate change.

Some individuals disagree with the concept of deferred taxes (interperiod tax allocation). It is uncertain that the deferred tax will be paid. If it will be paid (received), it is uncertain when it will be paid (or received). The deferred tax accounts are, therefore, often referred to as **soft accounts**.

Because of the uncertainty over whether (and when) a deferred tax liability (asset) will be paid (received), some individuals elect to exclude deferred tax liabilities and assets when performing analysis. This is inconsistent with GAAP, which recognize deferred taxes.

Some revenue and expense items, referred to as **permanent differences**, never go on the tax return, but do go on the income statement. Examples would be premiums on life insurance and life insurance proceeds. Federal tax law does not allow these items to be included in expense and revenue, respectively. These items never influence either the tax expense or the tax liability, so they never influence the deferred tax accounts.

Noncontrolling Interest

The account, noncontrolling interest, results when the firm has consolidated another company of which it owns less than 100%. The proportion of the consolidated company that is not owned appears on the balance sheet as part of shareholders' equity.

Some firms exclude the noncontrolling interest when computing debt ratios because this amount does not represent a commitment to pay funds to outsiders. Other firms include the noncontrolling interest when computing debt ratios because these funds came from outsiders and are part of the total funds that the firm uses. This book takes the conservative position of including noncontrolling interest in the primary computation of debt ratios. To review noncontrolling interest, refer to the section of Chapter 3 on noncontrolling interest.

Redeemable Preferred Stock

Redeemable preferred stock is subject to mandatory redemption requirements or has a redemption feature outside the issuer's control. Some redeemable preferred stock agreements require the firm to purchase certain amounts of the preferred stock on the open market. The Securities and Exchange Commission dictates that redeemable preferred stock not be disclosed under shareholders' equity.

The nature of redeemable preferred stock leaves open to judgment how it should be handled when computing debt ratios. One view excludes it from debt and includes it in shareholders' equity, on the grounds that it does not represent a normal debt relationship. A conservative position includes it as debt when computing the debt ratios. This book uses the conservative approach and includes redeemable preferred stock in debt for the primary computation of debt ratios. For a more detailed review, refer to the section of Chapter 3 that describes redeemable preferred stock.

Debt/Equity Ratio

The **debt/equity ratio** is another computation that determines the entity's long-term debt-paying ability. This computation compares the total debt with the total shareholders' equity. The debt/equity ratio also helps determine how well creditors are protected in case of insolvency. From the perspective of long-term debt-paying ability, the lower this ratio is, the better the company's debt position.

In this book, the computation of the debt/equity ratio is conservative because all of the liabilities and near liabilities are included, and the shareholders' equity is understated to the

EXHIBIT **7-4**	Nike, Inc.	

Debt/Equity Ratio

Years Ended May 31, 2011 and 2010		
(In millions)	**2011**	**2010**
Total liabilities [Exhibit 7-3] [A]	$5,155	$4,665
Shareholders' equity [B]	$9,843	$9,754
Debt/equity ratio [A ÷ B]	52.37%	47.83%

Source: Nike, Inc. 2010 10-K

extent that assets have a value greater than book value. This ratio should also be compared with industry averages and competitors. Compute the debt/equity ratio as follows:

$$\text{Debt/Equity Ratio} = \frac{\text{Total Liabilities}}{\text{Shareholders' Equity}}$$

Exhibit 7-4 shows the debt/equity ratio for Nike for May 31, 2011, and May 31, 2010. Using a conservative approach to computing debt/equity, Exhibit 7-4 indicates the debt/equity ratio was 52.37% at the end of 2011, down from 47.83% at the end of 2010.

The debt ratio and the debt/equity ratio have the same objectives. Therefore, these ratios are alternatives to each other if they are computed in the manner recommended here. Because some financial services may be reporting the debt ratio and others may be reporting the debt/equity ratio, the reader should be familiar with both.

As indicated previously, a problem exists with the lack of uniformity in the way some ratios are computed. This especially occurs with the debt ratio and the debt/equity ratio. When comparing the debt ratio and the debt/equity ratio with industry ratios, try to determine how the industry ratios were computed. A reasonable comparison may not be possible because the financial sources sometimes do not indicate what elements of debt the computations include.

Debt to Tangible Net Worth Ratio

The debt to tangible net worth ratio also determines the entity's long-term debt-paying ability. This ratio also indicates how well creditors are protected in case of the firm's insolvency. As with the debt ratio and the debt/equity ratio, from the perspective of long-term debt-paying ability, it is better to have a lower ratio.

The debt to tangible net worth ratio is a more conservative ratio than either the debt ratio or the debt/equity ratio. It eliminates intangible assets, such as goodwill, trademarks, patents, and copyrights, because they do not provide resources to pay creditors—a very conservative position. Compute the debt to tangible net worth ratio as follows:

$$\text{Debt to Tangible Net Worth Ratio} = \frac{\text{Total Liabilities}}{\text{Shareholders' Equity} - \text{Intangible Assets}}$$

In this book, the computation of the debt to tangible net worth ratio is conservative. All of the liabilities and near liabilities are included, and the shareholders' equity is understated to the extent that assets have a value greater than book value.

Exhibit 7-5 shows the debt to tangible net worth ratios for Nike for May 31, 2011, and May 31, 2010. This is a conservative view of the debt-paying ability. There was a substantial increase in debt to tangible net work in 2011.

Other Long-Term Debt-Paying Ability Ratios

A number of additional ratios indicate perspective on the long-term debt-paying ability of a firm.

The current debt/net worth ratio indicates a relationship between current liabilities and funds contributed by shareholders. The higher the proportion of funds provided by current liabilities, the greater the risk.

EXHIBIT **7-5**	Nike, Inc.	

Debt to Tangible Net Worth Ratio

	Years Ended May 31, 2011 and 2010	
(In millions)	2011	2010
Total liabilities [Exhibit 7-3] [A]	$5,155	$4,665
Shareholders' equity	$9,843	$9,754
Less: Intangible assets	(692)	(655)
Adjusted shareholders' equity [B]	$9,151	$9,099
Debt to tangible net worth ratio [A ÷ B]	56.33%	51.27%

Source: Nike, Inc. 2010 10-K

Another ratio, the **total capitalization ratio**, compares long-term debt to total capitalization. Total capitalization consists of long-term debt, preferred stock, and common shareholders' equity. The lower the ratio, the lower the risk.

Another ratio, the **fixed asset/equity ratio**, indicates the extent to which shareholders have provided funds in relation to fixed assets. Some firms subtract intangibles from shareholders' equity to obtain tangible net worth. This results in a more conservative ratio. The higher the fixed assets in relation to equity, the greater the risk.

Exhibit 7-6 indicates the trend in current liabilities, total liabilities, and owners' equity of firms in the United States between 1964 and 2010. It shows that a major shift has taken place in the capital structure of firms, toward a higher proportion of debt in relation to total assets. This indicates a substantial increase in risk as management more frequently faces debt coming due. It also indicates that short-term debt is a permanent part of the financial structure of firms. This supports the decision to include short-term liabilities in the ratios determining long-term debt-paying ability (debt ratio, debt/equity ratio, and debt to tangible net worth ratio).

EXHIBIT **7-6**	Trends in Current Liabilities, Long-Term Liabilities, and Owners' Equity, 1964–2010

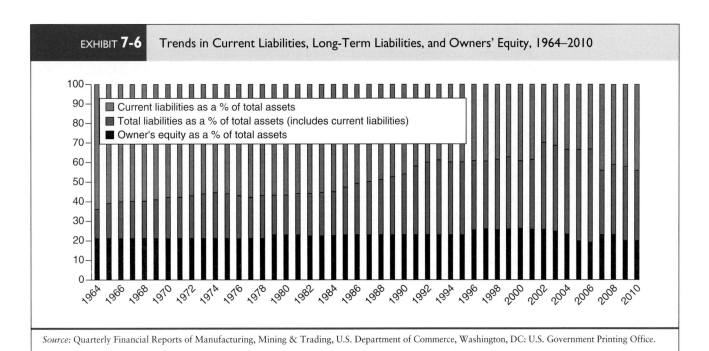

Source: Quarterly Financial Reports of Manufacturing, Mining & Trading, U.S. Department of Commerce, Washington, DC: U.S. Government Printing Office.

Special Items That Influence a Firm's Long-Term Debt-Paying Ability

A number of special items influence a firm's long-term debt-paying ability. These items are now reviewed.

Long-Term Assets versus Long-Term Debt

The specific assets of the firm are important if the firm becomes unprofitable and the assets are sold. Therefore, consider the assets of the firm when determining the long-term debt-paying ability. The assets are insurance should the firm become unprofitable. The ability to analyze the assets, in relation to the long-term debt-paying ability, is limited, based on the information reported in the published financial statements. The statements do not extensively disclose market or liquidation values; they disclose only unrecovered cost for many items. The market value figure reported for some investments has been an exception.

A review of the financial statements is often of value if the firm liquidates or decides to reduce the scope of its operations. Examples of assets that may have substantial value would be land, timberlands, and investments.

When Penn Central Company went bankrupt, it had substantial debt and operating losses. Yet because of assets that had substantial market values, creditors were repaid. In other cases, creditors receive nothing or only nominal amounts when a firm goes bankrupt.

Substantial assets that have a potential value higher than the book figures may also indicate an earnings potential that will be realized later. For example, knowing that a railroad owns land that contains millions or billions of tons of coal could indicate substantial profit potential, even if the coal is not economical to mine at the present time. In future years, as the price of competitive products such as oil and gas increases, the coal may become economical to mine. This happened in the United States in the late 1970s. Several railroads that owned millions or billions of tons of unmined coal found that the coal became very valuable as the price of oil and gas increased.

Long-Term Leasing

Earlier, this chapter explained the influence of long-term leasing in relation to the income statement. Now we will consider the influence of long-term leasing from the balance sheet perspective.

First, we will review some points made previously. The lessee classifies leases as either capital leases or operating leases. A capital lease is handled as if the lessee acquired the asset. The leased asset is classified as a fixed asset, and the related obligation is included in liabilities. Operating leases are not reflected on the balance sheet but in a note and on the income statement as rent expense.

Operating leases for a relatively long term (a type of long-term financing) should be considered in a supplemental manner as to their influence on the debt structure of the firms. Capital leases have already been considered in the debt ratios computed because the capital leases were part of the total assets and also part of the total liabilities on the balance sheet.

The capitalized asset amount will not agree with the capitalized liability amount because the liability is reduced by payments and the asset is reduced by depreciation taken. Usually, a company depreciates capital leases faster than payments are made. This would result in the capitalized asset amount being lower than the related capitalized liability amount. On the original date of the capital lease, the capitalized asset amount and the capitalized liability amount are the same.

The Nike note relating to long-term leases indicates the minimum future rentals under operating leases for years subsequent to May 31, 2011. These figures do not include an amount for any possible contingent rentals because they are not practicable to estimate.

Note 15—Commitments and Contingencies (In Part)

The Company leases space for certain of its offices, warehouses and retail stores under leases expiring from 1 to 24 years after May 31, 2011. Rent expense was $446 million,

EXHIBIT 7-7	Nike, Inc.

Adjusted Debt Ratio and Debt/Equity Considering Operating Leases

(In millions)	May 31, 2011
Adjusted debt ratio:	
Unadjusted total liabilities (Exhibit 7-3)	$ 5,155
Plus: Estimated for operating leases ($1,844 × 90%)	1,660
Adjusted liabilities [A]	$ 6,815
Unadjusted total assets	$14,998
Plus: Estimated for operating leases	1,660
Adjusted assets [B]	$16,658
Adjusted debt ratio [A ÷ B]	40.91%
Unadjusted debt ratio (Exhibit 7-3)	34.37%
Adjusted debt/equity:	
Adjusted liabilities [A]	$ 6,815
Shareholders' equity [B]	9,843
Adjusted debt/equity [A ÷ B]	69.24%
Unadjusted debt/equity (Exhibit 7-4)	52.37%

Source: Nike, Inc. 2010 10-K

$416 million, and $397 million for the years ended May 31, 2011, 2010 and 2009, respectively. Amounts of minimum future annual rental commitments under non-cancelable operating leases in each of the five years ending May 31, 2012 through 2016 are $374 million, $310 million, $253 million, $198 million, $174 million, respectively, and $535 million in later years.

If these leases had been capitalized, the amount added to fixed assets and the amount added to liabilities would be the same at the time of the initial entry. As indicated previously, the amounts would not be the same, subsequently, because the asset is depreciated at some selected rate, while the liability is reduced as payments are made. When incorporating the operating leases into the debt ratios, use the liability amount and assume that the asset and the liability amount would be the same since no realistic way exists to compute the difference.

It would not be realistic to include the total future rentals that relate to operating leases in the lease commitments note ($1,844) because part of the commitment would be an interest consideration. Earlier, this chapter indicated that some firms estimate that one-third of the operating lease commitment is for interest. With a one-third estimate for interest, two-thirds is estimated for principal. Nike estimated the interest component of leases includes one-tenth of rental expense and approximates the interest component of operating leases. This would mean the estimate for principal would be 90%. This amount can be added to fixed assets and long-term liabilities in order to obtain a supplemental view of the debt ratios that relate to the balance sheet. Exhibit 7-7 shows the adjusted debt ratio and debt/equity ratio for Nike at May 31, 2011; this increases the debt position by a material amount.

In Chapter 1 it was indicated that the FASB and the IASB were working on the convergence of U.S. GAAP and International Financial Reporting Standards. A major convergence project involves leases. This project is fairly broad and will likely eliminate operating leases. Many of these leases will be recorded as an asset and liability. Also, contingent rents will be reviewed for capitalization on a basis of most likely estimated future payments.

When this standard is issued and effective, it will result in increased assets and liabilities. The new standard will reduce rent and increase interest expense. It will also increase depreciation expense.

The note on operating leases will be eliminated. Thus the adjustment of the debt ratio and debt/equity will be eliminated.

Pension Plans

The Employee Retirement Income Security Act (ERISA) became law in 1974 and substantially influenced the administration of pension plans, while elevating their liability status for the firm. This act includes provisions requiring minimum funding of plans, minimum rights to employees upon termination of their employment, and the creation of a special federal agency, the Pension Benefit Guaranty Corporation (PBGC), to help fund employee benefits when pension plans are terminated. The PBGC receives a fee for every employee covered by a pension plan subject to PBGC. The PBGC has the right to impose a lien against a covered firm of 30% of the firm's net worth. This lien has the status of a tax lien and, therefore, ranks high among creditor claims. In practice, the PBGC has been reluctant to impose this lien except when a firm is in bankruptcy proceedings. As a result, the PBGC has received a relatively small amount of assets when it has imposed the lien.

An important provision in a pension plan is the vesting provision. An employee vested in the pension plan is eligible to receive some pension benefits at retirement, regardless of whether the employee continues working for the employer. ERISA has had a major impact on reducing the vesting time. The original ERISA has been amended several times to increase the responsibility of firms regarding their pension plans.

In 1980, Congress passed the Multiemployer Pension Plan Amendment Act. Multiemployer pension plans are plans maintained jointly by two or more unrelated employers. This act provides for significant increased employer obligations for multiemployer pension plans and makes the PBGC coverage mandatory for multiemployer plans.

When a firm has a multiemployer pension plan, it normally covers union employees. Such a firm usually has other pension plans that cover nonunion employees. When disclosing a multiemployer pension plan, the firm normally includes the cost of the plan with the cost of the other pension plans. It is usually not practical to isolate the cost of these plans because of commingling. These plans usually operate on a pay-as-you-go basis, so no liability arises unless a payment has not been made. A potential significant liability arises if the company withdraws from the multiemployer plan. Unfortunately, the amount of this liability often cannot be ascertained from the pension note.

The Kroger Company included the following comment in its January 29, 2011, annual report (in millions):

Multi-Employer Plans

The Company also contributes to various multi-employer pension plans based on obligations arising from most of its collective bargaining agreements. These plans provide retirement benefits to participants based on their service to contributing employers. The benefits are paid from assets held in trust for that purpose. Trustees are appointed in equal number by employers and unions. The trustees typically are responsible for determining the level of benefits to be provided to participants as well as for such matters as the investment of the assets and the administration of the plans.

The Company recognizes expense in connection with these plans as contributions are funded. The Company made contributions to these funds, and recognized expense, of $262 million in 2010, $233 million in 2009, and $219 million in 2008.

Based on the most recent information available to it, the Company believes that the present value of actuarial accrued liabilities in most or all of these multi-employer plans substantially exceeds the value of the assets held in trust to pay benefits. Moreover, if the Company were to exit certain markets or otherwise cease making contributions to these funds, the Company could trigger a substantial withdrawal liability. Any adjustment for withdrawal liability will be recorded when it is probable that a liability exists and can be reasonably estimated.

Source: Kroger Company 2010 10-K

Defined Contribution Plan

A company-sponsored pension plan is either a defined contribution plan or a defined benefit plan. A **defined contribution plan** defines the contributions of the company to the pension plan. Once this defined contribution is paid, the company has no further obligation to the pension plan. This type of plan shifts the risk to the employee as to whether the pension funds will grow to provide for a reasonable pension payment upon retirement. With this type of plan, which gained popularity during the 1980s, there is no problem estimating the company's pension liability or pension expense. Thus, defined contribution plans do not present major financial reporting problems.

A **401(k)** is a type of defined contribution plan. Such a plan may or may not require a company's contribution. It may provide for an employee's contribution. When a company makes a required contribution, this ends any pension liability.

For firms with defined contribution plans, try to grasp the significance of these plans by doing the following:

1. For a three-year period, compare pension expense with operating revenue. This will indicate the materiality of pension expense in relation to operating revenue and the trend.
2. For a three-year period, compare pension expense with income before income taxes. This will indicate the materiality of pension expense in relation to income and the trend.
3. Note any balance sheet items. (There will usually not be a balance sheet item because the firm is paying on a pay-as-you-go basis.)

Nike – Note 13 – Benefit Plans (In Part)

The Company recognized $31 million, $24 million, and $18 million of selling and administrative expense related to cash awards under" a Long-Term Incentive Plan (LTIP) during the years ended May 31, 2011, 2010, and 2009, respectively.

. . . . .

The Company has pension plans in various countries worldwide. The pension plans are only available to local employees and are generally government mandated. The liability related to the unfunded pension liabilities of the plans was $93 million and $113 million at May 31, 2011 and 2010, respectively, which was primarily classified as long-term in other liabilities.

. . . . .

The Company has various 401(k) employee savings plans available to U.S.-based employees. The Company matches a portion of employee contributions. Company contributions to the savings plans were $39 million, $34 million, and $38 million for the years ended May 31, 2011, 2010, and 2009, respectively, and are included in selling and administrative expense.

The 401(k) employee savings plans expenses as a percentage of revenues were 0.19%, 0.18%, and 0.20% in 2011, 2010 and 2009, respectively.

Defined Benefit Plan

A defined benefit plan defines the benefits to be received by the participants in the plan. For example, the plan may call for the participant to receive 40% of his or her average pay for the three years before retirement. This type of plan leaves the company with the risk of having insufficient funds in the pension fund to meet the defined benefit. This type of plan was the predominant type of plan prior to the 1980s. Most companies still have a defined benefit plan, partly because of the difficulties involved in switching to a defined contribution plan. Some companies have terminated their defined benefit plan by funding the obligations of the plan and starting a defined contribution plan. In some cases, this has resulted in millions of dollars being transferred to the company from the pension plan after the defined benefit plan obligations have been met. The U.S. Congress added an excise tax on "reversions" in 1990. This excise tax can be as high as 50%, thereby substantially slowing down the "reversions."

A number of assumptions about future events must be made regarding a defined benefit plan. Some of these assumptions that relate to the future are interest rates, employee turnover, mortality rates, compensation, and pension benefits set by law. Assumptions about future events contribute materially to the financial reporting problems in the pension area. Two firms with the same plan may make significantly different assumptions, resulting in major differences in pension expense and liability.

There are many technical terms associated with defined benefit plans. A description of all of these terms is beyond the scope of this book.

For firms with defined benefit plans, try to grasp the significance of these plans by doing the following:

1. For a three-year period, compare pension expense with operating revenue. This will indicate the materiality of pension expense in relation to operating revenue and the trend.

2. For a three-year period, compare pension expense with income before income taxes. This will indicate the materiality of pension expense in relation to income and the trend.

3. Compare the benefit obligations with the value of plan assets. This can indicate significant underfunding or overfunding. Underfunding represents a potential liability. Overfunding represents an opportunity to reduce future pension expense. Overfunding can also be used to reduce related costs, such as disability benefits, retiree health costs, and staff downsizings. Overfunding can also be used to take credits to the income statement.

4. Note the net balance sheet liability (asset) recognized.

Exhibit 7-8 shows selected items from the Vulcan Materials Company pension note. It also includes selected items from the statement of earnings and the balance sheet.

We note that the Vulcan Materials Company pension plans in Exhibit 7-8 are defined benefit plans. Observe the following relating to the Vulcan Materials Company plans:

1. Pension expense (cost) in relation to operating revenue: (defined benefit)

(Amounts in thousands)	2010	2009	2008
Pension cost [A]	$ 16,928	$ 16,185	$ 8,173
Operating revenue [B]	2,558,862	2,690,490	3,651,438
Pension expense/operating revenue [A] ÷ [B]	0.66%	0.60%	0.22%

Note: Pension cost increased materially in 2009 and then increased moderately in 2010.

2. Pension expense (cost) in relation to earnings from continuing operations before income taxes: (defined benefit)

(Amounts in thousands)	2010	2009	2008
Pension cost [A]	$ 16,928	$ 16,185	$ 8,173
Earnings (loss) from continuing operations before income taxes [B]	(192,206)	(19,221)	75,058
Pension expense (cost)/earnings (loss) from continuing operations before income taxes [A] ÷ [B]	**	**	10.89%

Note: **Earnings from continuing operations before income taxes were negative in 2010 and 2009. Pension expense was material in 2008 in relation to earnings from continuing operations before income taxes. Pension cost increased materially in 2009 in absolute terms and increased moderately in 2010 in absolute terms.

3. Comparison of benefit obligation with fair value of assets at end of year: (defined benefit)

(Amounts in thousands)	2010	2009	2008
Benefit obligation	$ 761,384	$ 709,783	$ 620,845
Fair value of assets	630,303	493,646	418,977
Fair value of assets (under) over benefit obligation	$(131,081)	$(216,137)	$(201,868)

Note: Fair value of assets (under) over benefit obligation increased materially in 2009 and decreased materially in 2010.

4. Amounts recognized in the consolidated balance sheets: (defined benefit)

(Amounts in thousands)	2010	2009	2008
Noncurrent assets	$ 1,083	$ 0	$ 0
Current liabilities	(5,028)	(4,104)	(3,453)
Noncurrent liabilities	(127,136)	(212,033)	(198,415)
Net amount recognized	$(131,081)	$(216,137)	$(201,868)

Note: Net amount recognized increased substantially in 2009 and decreased materially in 2010.

Postretirement Benefits Other Than Pensions

Some benefits other than pensions, such as medical insurance and life insurance contracts, accrue to employees upon retirement. These benefits can be substantial. Many firms have obligations in the millions of dollars. Prior to 1993, most firms did not have these obligations funded; therefore, for these firms, a potential for a significant liability existed.

Source: Nike, Inc. 2010 10-K

EXHIBIT **7-8**	Vulcan Materials Company*

Pension Benefits—Defined Benefit Pension Plans

Consolidated Statements of Earnings (In Part)
Vulcan Materials Company and Subsidiary Companies
For the Years Ended December 31
Amounts in thousands

	2010	2009	2008
Net sales	$2,405,916	$2,543,707	$3,453,081
Delivery revenues	152,946	146,783	198,357
Total revenues	$2,558,862	$2,690,490	$3,651,438
Earnings (loss) from continuing operations before income taxes	$(192,206)	$(19,221)	$75,058

Consolidated Balance Sheets (In Part)
Amounts in Thousands

	2010	2009
Total current assets	$ 772,106	$ 732,889
Total assets	8,337,891	8,524,871
Total current liabilities	565,672	856,695
Total liabilities	4,372,911	4,487,634
Total shareholders' equity	3,964,980	4,037,237
Total liabilities and shareholders' equity	$8,337,891	$8,524,871

Note 10 Benefit Plans (defined benefit) (In Part)
Amounts in Thousands

	2010	2009	2008
Benefit obligation at end of year	$ 761,384	$ 709,783	$ 620,845
Fair value of assets at end of year	630,303	493,646	418,977
Funded status	$(131,081)	$(216,137)	$(201,868)

Note 10 Benefit Plans (defined benefit) (In Part)
Amounts Recognized in the Consolidated Balance Sheets
Amounts in Thousands

	2010	2009	2008
Noncurrent assets	$ 1,083	$ 0	$ 0
Current liabilities	(5,028)	(4,104)	(3,453)
Noncurrent liabilities	(127,136)	(212,033)	(198,415)
Net amount recognized	$(131,081)	$(216,137)	$(201,868)

Note 10 Benefit Plans (defined benefit) (In Part)
Amounts in Thousands

	2010	2009	2008
Net periodic pension benefit cost	$16,928	$16,185	$8,173

*"Vulcan Materials Company is a New Jersey corporation and the nation's largest producer of construction aggregates: primarily crushed stone, sand, and gravel." 10-K
Source: Vulcan Materials Company 2010 10-K

Beginning in 1993, firms were required to accrue, or set up a reserve for, future postretirement benefits other than pensions (rather than deduct these costs when paid). Firms can usually spread the catch-up accrual costs over 20 years or take the charge in one lump sum. The amount involved is frequently material, so this choice can represent a major problem when comparing the financial results of two or more firms. For some firms, the catch-up charge for medical insurance was so material that it resulted in a deficit in retained earnings or even a deficit to the entire shareholders' equity section.

Many firms reduce costs by changing their plans to limit health care benefits to retirees to a maximum fixed amount. This type of plan, in contrast to open-ended medical benefits, could materially reduce the firm's health care costs for retirees. Review the notes closely to determine how the firm records health care costs for retirees.

For firms with postretirement benefits other than pensions, you should try to grasp the significance using the same basic approach as was used for defined benefit plans for pensions.

Exhibit 7-9 shows selected items from the Vulcan Materials Company postretirement benefits other than pensions. It also includes selected items from the statement of earnings and the balance sheet.

Observe the following relating to the Vulcan Materials Company postretirement benefits other than pensions.

1. Expense (cost) in relation to operating revenue:

(Amounts in thousands)	2010	2009	2008
Net periodic postretirement benefit cost [A]	$ 11,075	$ 10,732	$ 12,315
Total revenues [B]	2,558,862	2,690,490	3,651,438
Net periodic postretirement benefit cost/total revenues [A] ÷ [B]	0.43%	0.40%	0.34%

2. Expense (cost) in relation to income before taxes:

(Amounts in thousands)	2010	2009	2008
Net periodic postretirement benefit cost [A]	$ 11,075	$ 10,732	$ 12,315
Earnings (loss) from continuing operations before income taxes [B]	(192,206)	(19,221)	75,058
Net periodic postretirement benefit cost/earnings from continuing operations before income taxes [A] ÷ [B]	**	**	16.41%

Note: ** Earnings from continuing operations before income taxes were negative in 2010 and 2009.
Net periodic postretirement benefit cost was material in 2008 in relation to earnings from continuing operations before income taxes.
Net periodic postretirement benefit cost decreased materially in 2009 and then increased moderately in 2010. Comparison of net periodic postretirement benefit cost in relation to earnings from continuing operations before income taxes was not made in 2009 and 2010 because of the negative earnings.

3. Comparison of benefit obligations with the fair value of the plan assets:

(Amounts in thousands)	2010	2009
Benefit obligation	$ 133,717	$118, 313
Fair value of assets	0	0
Excess of obligations over plan assets	$(133,717)	$(118,313)

Note: Benefit obligation is not funded. Dividing the 2010 benefit obligation by total liabilities of $4.4 billion results in a rate of not funded benefit obligation to total liabilities of 3.1%, which is substantial.

4. Amounts recognized in the consolidated balance sheet:

(Amounts in thousands)	2010	2009
Current liabilities	$ (9,100)	$ (8,323)
Noncurrent liabilities	(124,617)	(109,990)
Net amount recognized	$(133,717)	$(118,313)

Note: Net liabilities increased materially.

EXHIBIT **7-9**	Vulcan Materials Company*

Postretirement Plans—Other Than Pensions

Consolidated Statements of Earnings (In Part)
(Amounts in thousands)

For the years ended December 31,	2010	2009	2008
Net sales	$2,405,916	$2,543,707	$3,453,081
Delivery revenues	152,946	146,783	198,357
Total revenues	$2,558,862	$2,690,490	$3,651,438
Earnings (loss) from continuing operations before income taxes	$ (192,206)	$ (19,221)	$ 75,058

Consolidated Balance Sheets (In Part)
Amounts in Thousands

	2010	2009
Total current assets	$ 772,106	$ 732,889
Total assets	8,337,891	8,524,871
Total current liabilities	565,672	856,695
Total liabilities	4,372,911	4,487,634
Total shareholders' equity	3,964,980	4,037,237
Total liabilities and shareholders' equity	$8,337,891	$8,524,871

Note 10: Benefit Plans (In Part)
Postretirement Plans—Other than Pensions (In Part)
Amounts in Thousands

	2010	2009
Benefit obligation at end of year	$ 133,717	$ 118,313
Fair value of assets at end of year	0	0
Funded status (under funded)	$(133,717)	$(118,313)

Amounts Recognized in the Consolidated Balance Sheets and
Net Periodic Postretirement Benefit Cost
Postretirement Plans—Other than Pensions
Amounts in Thousands

	2010	2009
Current liabilities	$ (9,100)	$ (8,322)
Noncurrent liabilities	(124,617)	(109,990)
Net amount recognized	$(133,717)	$(118,313)

	2010	2009	2008
Net periodic postretirement benefit cost	$11,075	$10,732	$12,315

*"Vulcan Materials Company is a New Jersey corporation and the nation's largest producer of construction aggregates: primarily crushed stone, sand, and gravel." 10-K
Source: Vulcan Materials Company 2010 10-K

Joint Ventures

A **joint venture** is an association of two or more businesses established for a special purpose. Some joint ventures are in the form of partnerships or other unincorporated forms of business. Others are in the form of corporations jointly owned by two or more other firms.

The accounting principles for joint ventures are flexible because of their many forms. The typical problem concerns whether a joint venture should be carried as an investment or consolidated. Some joint ventures are very significant in relation to the parent firm. There is typically a question as to whether the parent firm has control or only significant influence. When the parent firm has control, it usually consolidates joint ventures by using a pro-rata share. Other joint ventures are usually carried in an investment account by using the equity method. In either case, disclosure of significant information often appears in a note.

When a firm enters into a joint venture, it frequently makes commitments such as guaranteeing a bank loan for the joint venture or a long-term contract to purchase materials with the joint venture. This type of action can give the company significant potential liabilities or commitments that do not appear on the face of the balance sheet. This potential problem exists with all joint ventures, including those that have been consolidated. To be aware of these significant potential liabilities or commitments, read the note that relates to the joint venture. Then consider this information in relation to the additional liabilities or commitments to which the joint venture may commit the firm.

Exhibit 7-10 details a joint venture of Hasbro, Inc.

EXHIBIT **7-10**	Hasbro, Inc. and Subsidiaries*

Joint Ventures (2010 Annual Report)

HASBRO, INC. AND SUBSIDIARIES
Notes to Consolidated Financial Statements (In Part)
(Thousands of Dollars and Shares Except Per Share Data)

(5) Equity Method Investment

In the second quarter of 2009, the Company acquired a 50% interest in a joint venture, Hub Television Networks, LLC ("THE HUB", formerly known as DHJV company LLC), with Discovery Communications, Inc. ("Discovery"). THE HUB, formerly known as the Discovery Kids Network, was established to create a television network in the United States dedicated to high-quality children's and family entertainment and educational programming. The Company purchased its 50% share in THE HUB for a payment of $300,000 and certain future payments based on the value of certain tax benefits expected to be received by the Company. The present value of the expected future payments at the acquisition date totaled approximately $67,900 and was recorded as a component of the Company's investment in the joint venture. The balance of the associated liability, including imputed interest, was $72,665 and $71,234 at December 26, 2010 and December 27, 2009, respectively, and is included as a component of other liabilities in the accompanying balance sheet.

Voting control of the joint venture is shared 50/50 between the Company and Discovery. The Company has determined that it does not meet the control requirements to consolidate the joint venture, and accounts for the investment using the equity method of accounting. The Company's share in the earnings (loss) of the joint venture for the years ended December 26, 2010 and December 27, 2009 totaled $(9,323) of loss and $3,856 of earnings, respectively, and is included as a component of other (income) expense in the accompanying consolidated statements of operations.

The Company has entered into a license agreement with the joint venture that will require the payment of royalties by the Company to the joint venture based on a percentage of revenue derived from products related to television shows broadcast by the joint venture. The license agreement includes a minimum royalty guarantee of $125,000, payable in 5 annual installments of $25,000 per year, commencing in 2009, which can be earned out over approximately a 10 year period. During 2010 and 2009, the Company paid the first two annual installments of $25,000 each. The Company and the joint venture are also parties to an agreement under which the Company will provide the joint venture with an exclusive first look in the U.S. to license certain types of programming developed by the Company based on its intellectual property. In the event the joint venture licenses the programming from the Company to air on the network, the joint venture is required to pay the Company a license fee.

As of December 26, 2010, the Company's interest in the joint venture totaled $354,612 and is a component of other assets. The Company enters into certain transactions with the joint venture including the licensing of television programming and the purchase of advertising. During 2010 and 2009, these transactions were not material.

*"We are a worldwide leader in children's and family leisure time products and services with a broad portfolio of brands and entertainment properties." 10-K
Source: Hasbro, Inc. And Subsidiaries 2010 10-K

Contingencies

A **contingency** is an existing condition, situation, or set of circumstances involving uncertainty as to possible gain or loss to an enterprise that will ultimately be resolved when one or more future events occur or fail to occur.[1]

A contingency is characterized by an existing condition, uncertainty as to the ultimate effect, and its resolution depending on one or more future events. A loss contingency should be accrued if two conditions are met:[2]

1. Information prior to issuance of the financial statements indicates that it is *probable* that an asset has been impaired or a liability has been incurred at the date of the financial statements.
2. The amount of the loss can be *reasonably estimated*.

If a contingency loss meets one, but not both, of the criteria for recording and is, therefore, not accrued, disclosure by note is made when it is at *least reasonably possible* that there has been an impairment of assets or that a liability has been incurred. Examples of contingencies include warranty obligations and collectibility of receivables. If the firm guarantees the indebtedness of others, the contingency is usually disclosed in a note.

When examining financial statements, a note that describes contingencies should be closely reviewed for possible significant liabilities not disclosed on the face of the balance sheet.

The following covers gain contingencies:

1. Contingencies that might result in gains usually are not reflected in the accounts because to do so might be to recognize revenue prior to its realization.
2. Adequate disclosure shall be made of contingencies that might result in gains, but care shall be exercised to avoid misleading implications as to the likelihood of realization.[3]

The notes of the firm should be reviewed for gain contingencies. Exhibit 7-11 discusses an income tax gain contingency for Air Products and Chemicals, Inc.

EXHIBIT **7-11**	Air Products and Chemicals, Inc.*

Gain Contingencies (2010 Annual Report)

Notes to Consolidated Financial Statements (In Part)
22 Income taxes (In Part) Millions of dollars

A reconciliation of the beginning and ending amount of the unrecognized tax benefits is as follows:

Unrecognized Tax Benefits	2010	2009	2008
Balance at beginning of year	$194.9	$184.1	$116.5
Additions for tax positions of the current year	37.3	25.6	58.3
Additions for tax positions of prior years	13.1	39.0	20.1
Reductions for tax positions of prior years	(1.1)	(45.2)	(5.2)
Settlements	—	(5.4)	(4.6)
Statute of limitations expiration	(6.3)	(5.4)	(3.4)
Foreign currency translation	(4.2)	2.2	2.4
Balance at End of Year	$233.7	$194.9	$184.1

*"Air Products and Chemicals, Inc. (the Company or Air Products), a Delaware corporation originally founded in 1940, serves technology, energy, industrial, and healthcare customers globally with a unique portfolio of products, services, and solutions that include atmospheric gases, process and specialty gases, performance materials, equipment, and services." 10-K
Source: Air Products and Chemicals, Inc. 2010 10-K

Financial Instruments with Off-Balance-Sheet Risk and Financial Instruments with Concentrations of Credit Risk

Credit and market risk for all financial instruments with off-balance-sheet risk require the following disclosure:

1. The face or contract amount.

2. The nature and terms, including, at a minimum, a discussion of credit and market risk, cash requirements, and accounting policies.[4]

Disclosure is also required of the following regarding financial instruments with off-balance-sheet credit risk:

1. The amount of accounting loss the entity would incur if any party failed completely to perform according to the terms of the contract and the collateral or other security, if any, proved worthless.
2. The entity's policy of requiring collateral and a brief description of the collateral it currently holds.[5]

Accounting loss represents the worst-case loss if everything related to a contract went wrong. This includes the possibility that a loss may occur from the failure of another party to perform according to the terms of a contract, as well as the possibility that changes in market prices may make a financial instrument less valuable or more troublesome.

In addition to requiring disclosure of matters relating to off-balance-sheet financial instruments, disclosure is required of credit risk concentration. This disclosure includes information on the extent of risk from exposures to individuals or groups of counterparties in the same industry or region. The activity, region, or economic characteristic that identifies a concentration requires a narrative description. The provision of requiring disclosure of credit risk concentration can be particularly significant to small companies. Examples are a retail store whose receivables are substantially with local residents and a local bank with a loan portfolio concentrated with debtors dependent on the local tourist business.

Exhibit 7-12 presents financial instruments with off-balance-sheet risk and financial instruments with concentrations of credit risk for Nordson Corporation as disclosed in its 2010 annual report.

Disclosures about Fair Value of Financial Instruments

Disclosure is required about the fair value of financial instruments. This includes financial instruments recognized and not recognized in the balance sheet (both assets and liabilities). When estimating fair value is not practicable, then descriptive information pertinent to estimating fair value should be disclosed.

The disclosure about fair value of financial instruments can be either in the body of the financial statements or in the notes.[6] This disclosure could possibly indicate significant opportunity or additional risk to the company. For example, long-term debt disclosed at a fair value above the carrying amount increases the potential for a loss.

EXHIBIT **7-12**	Nordson Corporation*

Off-Balance-Sheet Risk and Concentrations of Credit Risk (2010 Annual Report)

NOTES TO CONSOLIDATED FINANCIAL STATEMENTS (In Part) (In thousands)

Note 9 – Financial instruments (In Part)

We operate internationally and enter into intercompany transactions denominated in foreign currencies. Consequently, we are subject to market risk arising from exchange rate movements between the dates foreign currency transactions occur and the dates they are settled. We regularly use foreign currency forward contracts to reduce our risks related to most of these transactions. These contracts usually have maturities of 90 days or less and generally require us to exchange foreign currencies for U.S. dollars at maturity, at rates stated in the contracts. These contracts are not designated as hedging instruments under U.S. GAAP. Accordingly, the changes in the fair value of the hedges of balance sheet positions are recognized in each accounting period in "Other—net" on the Consolidated Statement of Income together with the transaction gain or loss from the hedged balance sheet position. Gains of $7,970 and $3,817 were recognized from changes in fair value of these contracts in 2010 and 2009, respectively. A loss of $2,033 was recognized from changes in fair value of these contracts in 2008. We do not use financial instruments for trading or speculative purposes.

---

* "We are one of the world's leading manufacturers of equipment used for precision material dispensing, testing and inspection, surface preparation and curing." 10-K
Source: Nordson Corporation 2010 10-K

| EXHIBIT **7-12** | Nordson Corporation (*continued*) |

At October 31, 2010, we had outstanding forward exchange contracts that mature at various dates through January 2011. The following table summarizes, by currency, forward exchange contracts outstanding at October 31, 2010 and 2009:

	Sell		Buy	
	National Amounts	Fair Market Value	National Amounts	Fair Market Value
October 31, 2010 contract amounts:				
Euro	$17,145	$17,601	$171,870	$181,430
British pound	—	—	25,832	26,576
Japanese yen	12,947	13,260	18,678	19,490
Others	6,357	6,545	28,361	29,854
Total	$36,449	$37,406	$244,741	$257,350
October 31, 2009 contract amounts:				
Euro	$ 7,663	$ 7,698	$178,983	$181,831
British pound	491	493	12,015	11,997
Japanese yen	2,876	2,911	20,862	21,342
Others	8,678	8,580	26,143	26,489
Total	$19,708	$19,682	$238,003	$241,659

Exhibit 7-13 presents the fair value of financial instruments for Nordson Corporation, as disclosed in its 2010 annual report.

| EXHIBIT **7-13** | Nordson Corporation* |

Fair Value of Financial Instruments (2010 Annual Report)

NOTES TO CONSOLIDATED FINANCIAL STATEMENTS (In Part)
(In thousands)

Note 9 – Financial instruments (In Part)

The carrying amounts and fair values of financial instruments, other than receivables and accounts payable, are shown in the table below. The carrying values of receivables and accounts payable approximate fair value due to the short-term nature of these instruments:

	2010		2009	
	Carrying Amount	Fair Value	Carrying Amount	Fair Value
Cash and cash equivalents	$ 42,329	$ 42,329	$ 18,781	$ 18,781
Marketable securities	7,840	7,840	43	43
Notes payable	(2,160)	(2,160)	(1,287)	(1,287)
Long-term debt	(110,260)	(112,495)	(156,550)	(159,706)
Forward exchange contracts (net)	11,653	11,653	3,683	3,683

We used the following methods and assumptions in estimating the fair value of financial instruments:

- Cash, cash equivalents and notes payable are valued at their carrying amounts due to the relatively short period to maturity of the instruments.
- Marketable securities are valued at quoted market prices, which are considered to be Level 1 inputs under the fair value hierarchy.
- Long-term debt is valued by discounting future cash flows at currently available rates for borrowing arrangements with similar terms and conditions, which are considered to be Level 2 inputs under the fair value hierarchy.
- Forward exchange contracts are estimated using quoted exchange rates, which are considered to be Level 2 inputs under the fair value hierarchy.

*"We are one of the world's leading manufacturers of equipment used for precision material dispensing, testing and inspection, surface preparation and curing." 10-K
Source: Nordson Corporation 2010 10-K

Summary

This chapter covered two approaches to a firm's long-term debt-paying ability. One approach considers the firm's ability to carry debt as indicated by the income statement, and the other approach views it as indicated by the balance sheet. The ratios related to debt include the following:

$$\text{Times Interest Earned} = \frac{\text{Recurring Earnings, Excluding Interest Expense, Tax Expense, Equity Earnings, and Noncontrolling Interest}}{\text{Interest Expense, Including Capitalized Interest}}$$

$$\text{Fixed Charge Coverage} = \frac{\text{Recurring Earnings, Excluding Interest Expense, Tax Expense, Equity Earnings, and Noncontrolling Interest} + \text{Interest Portion of Rentals}}{\text{Interest Expense, Including Capitalized Interest} + \text{Interest Portion of Rentals}}$$

$$\text{Debt Ratio} = \frac{\text{Total Liabilities}}{\text{Total Assets}}$$

↓ smaller better

$$\text{Debt/Equity Ratio} = \frac{\text{Total Liabilities}}{\text{Shareholders' Equity}}$$ ↓

$$\text{Debt to Tangible Net Worth Ratio} = \frac{\text{Total Liabilities}}{\text{Shareholders' Equity} - \text{Intangible Assets.}}$$ ↓

Questions

Q 7-1 Is profitability important to a firm's long-term debt-paying ability? Discuss.

Q 7-2 List the two approaches to examining a firm's long-term debt-paying ability. Discuss why each of these approaches gives an important view of a firm's ability to carry debt.

Q 7-3 What type of times interest earned ratio would be desirable? What type would not be desirable?

Q 7-4 Would you expect an auto manufacturer to finance a relatively high proportion of its long-term funds from debt? Discuss.

Q 7-5 Would you expect a telephone company to have a high debt ratio? Discuss.

Q 7-6 Why should capitalized interest be added to interest expense when computing times interest earned?

Q 7-7 Discuss how noncash charges for depreciation, depletion, and amortization can be used to obtain a short-run view of times interest earned.

Q 7-8 Why is it difficult to determine the value of assets?

Q 7-9 Is it feasible to get a precise measurement of the funds that could be available from long-term assets to pay long-term debts? Discuss.

Q 7-10 One of the ratios used to indicate long-term debt-paying ability compares total liabilities to total assets.

What is the intent of this ratio? How precise is this ratio in achieving its intent?

Q 7-11 For a given firm, would you expect the debt ratio to be as high as the debt/equity ratio? Explain.

Q 7-12 Explain how the debt/equity ratio indicates the same relative long-term debt-paying ability as does the debt ratio, only in a different form.

Q 7-13 Why is it important to compare long-term debt ratios of a given firm with industry averages?

Q 7-14 How should lessees account for operating leases? Capital leases? Include both income statement and balance sheet accounts.

Q 7-15 A firm with substantial leased assets that have not been capitalized may be overstating its long-term debt-paying ability. Explain.

Q 7-16 Capital leases that have not been capitalized will decrease the times interest earned ratio. Comment.

Q 7-17 Indicate the status of pension liabilities under the Employee Retirement Income Security Act.

Q 7-18 Why is the vesting provision an important provision of a pension plan? How has the Employee Retirement Income Security Act influenced vesting periods?

Q 7-19 Indicate the risk to a company if it withdraws from a multiemployer pension plan or if the multiemployer pension plan is terminated.

Q 7-20 Operating leases are not reflected on the balance sheet, but they are reflected on the income statement in the rent expense. Comment on why an interest expense figure that relates to long-term operating leases should be considered when determining a fixed charge coverage.

Q 7-21 What portion of net worth can the federal government require a company to use to pay for pension obligations?

Q 7-22 Consider the debt ratio. Explain a position for including short-term liabilities in the debt ratio. Explain a position for excluding short-term liabilities from the debt ratio. Which of these approaches would be more conservative?

Q 7-23 Consider the accounts of bonds payable and reserve for rebuilding furnaces. Explain how one of these accounts could be considered a firm liability and the other could be considered a soft liability.

Q 7-24 Explain why deferred taxes that are disclosed as long-term liabilities may not result in actual cash outlays in the future.

Q 7-25 A firm has a high current debt/net worth ratio in relation to prior years, competitors, and the industry. Comment on what this tentatively indicates.

Q 7-26 Comment on the implications of relying on a greater proportion of short-term debt in relation to long-term debt.

Q 7-27 When a firm guarantees a bank loan for a joint venture in which it participates and the joint venture is handled as an investment, then the overall potential debt position will not be obvious from the face of the balance sheet. Comment.

Q 7-28 When examining financial statements, a note that describes contingencies should be reviewed closely for possible significant liabilities that are not disclosed on the face of the balance sheet. Comment.

Q 7-29 There is a chance that a company may be in a position to have large sums transferred from the pension fund to the company. Comment.

Q 7-30 Indicate why comparing firms for postretirement benefits other than pensions can be difficult.

Q 7-31 Speculate on why the disclosure of the concentrations of credit risk is potentially important to the users of financial reports.

Q 7-32 Comment on the significance of disclosing the off-balance-sheet risk of accounting loss.

Q 7-33 Comment on the significance of disclosing the fair value of financial instruments.

Problems

P 7-1 Consider the following operating figures:

Net sales	$1,079,143
Cost and deductions:	
Cost of sales	792,755
Selling and administration	264,566
Interest expense, net	4,311
Income taxes	5,059
	1,066,691
	$ 12,452

Note: Depreciation expense totals $40,000.

Required
  a. Compute the times interest earned.
  b. Compute the cash basis times interest earned.

P 7-2 Jones Petro Company reports the following consolidated statement of income:

Operating revenues	$2,989
Costs and expenses:	
Cost of rentals and royalties	543
Cost of sales	314
Selling, service, administrative, and general expense	1,424
Total costs and expenses	2,281

(*continued*)

(**P 7-2** CONTINUED)

Operating income	708
Other income	27
Other deductions (interest)	60
Income before income taxes	675
Income taxes	309
Income before outside shareholders' interests	366
Outside shareholders' interests	66
Net income	$ 300

Note: Depreciation expense totals $200; operating lease payments total $150; and preferred dividends total $50. Assume that one-third of operating lease payments is for interest.

Required

a. Compute the times interest earned.
b. Compute the fixed charge coverage.

P 7-3 Sherwill's statement of consolidated income is as follows:

Net sales	$658
Other income	8
	666
Costs and expenses:	
Cost of products sold	418
Selling, general, and administrative expenses	196
Interest	16
	630
Income before income taxes and extraordinary charges	36
Income taxes	18
Income before extraordinary charge	18
Extraordinary charge—losses on tornado damage (net)	4
Net income	$ 14

Note: Depreciation expense totals $200; operating lease payments total $150; and preferred dividends total $50. Assume that one-third of operating lease payments is for interest.

Required

a. Compute the times interest earned.
b. Compute the fixed charge coverage.

P 7-4 Kaufman Company's balance sheet follows.

Assets	
Current assets	
Cash	$ 13,445
Short-term investments—at cost (approximate market)	5,239
Trade accounts receivable, less allowance of $1,590	88,337
Inventories—at lower of cost (average method) or market:	
Finished merchandise	113,879
Work in process, raw materials, and supplies	47,036
	160,915
Prepaid expenses	8,221
Total current assets	276,157
Other assets:	
Receivables, advances, and other assets	4,473
Intangibles	2,324
Total other assets	6,797
Property, plant, and equipment:	
Land	5,981
Buildings	78,908
Machinery and equipment	162,425
	247,314
Less allowances for depreciation	106,067
Net property, plant, and equipment	141,247
Total assets	$424,201

Liabilities and Shareholders' Equity

Current liabilities:

Notes payable	$ 2,817
Trade accounts payable	23,720
Pension, interest, and other accruals	33,219
Taxes, other than income taxes	4,736
Income taxes	3,409
Total current liabilities	67,901
Long-term debt, 12% debentures	86,235
Deferred income taxes	8,768
Minority interest in subsidiaries	12,075
Total liabilities	174,979

Stockholders' equity:

Serial preferred	9,154
Common $5.25 par value	33,540
Additional paid-in capital	3,506
Retained earnings	203,712
	249,912
Less cost of common shares in treasury	690
Total shareholders' equity	249,222
Total liabilities and shareholders' equity	$424,201

Required

a. Compute the debt ratio.
b. Compute the debt/equity ratio.
c. Compute the ratio of total debt to tangible net worth.
d. Comment on the amount of debt that Kaufman Company has.

P 7-5 Individual transactions often have a significant impact on ratios. This problem will consider the direction of such an impact.

Ratio Transaction	Times Interest Earned	Debt Ratio	Debt/Equity Ratio	Debt to Tangible Net Worth
a. Purchase of buildings financed by mortgage.				
b. Purchase of inventory on short-term loan at 1% over prime rate.				
c. Declaration and payment of cash dividend.				
d. Declaration and payment of stock dividend.				
e. Firm increases profits by cutting cost of sales.				
f. Appropriation of retained earnings.				
g. Sale of common stock.				
h. Repayment of long-term bank loan.				
i. Conversion of bonds to common stock outstanding.				
j. Sale of inventory at greater than cost.				

Required Indicate the effect of each of the transactions on the ratios listed. Use + to indicate an increase, − to indicate a decrease, and 0 to indicate no effect. Assume an initial times interest earned of more than 1, and a debt ratio, debt/equity ratio, and a total debt to tangible net worth of less than 1.

P 7-6 Mr. Parks has asked you to advise him on the long-term debt-paying ability of Arodex Company. He provides you with the following ratios:

	2011	2010	2009
Times interest earned	8.2	6.0	5.5
Debt ratio	40%	39%	40%
Debt to tangible net worth	80%	81%	81%

(*continued*)

(**P 7-6** CONTINUED)

Required

a. Give the implications and the limitations of each item separately and then the collective influence that could be drawn from them about Arodex Company's long-term debt position.

b. What warnings should you offer Mr. Parks about the limitations of ratio analysis for the purpose stated here?

P 7-7 For the year ended June 30, 2011, A.E.G. Enterprises presented the financial statements below.

Early in the new fiscal year, the officers of the firm formalized a substantial expansion plan. The plan will increase fixed assets by $190 million. In addition, extra inventory will be needed to support expanded production. The increase in inventory is purported to be $10 million.

The firm's investment bankers have suggested the following three alternative financing plans:

Plan A: Sell preferred stock at par, 5%.

Plan B: Sell common stock at $10 per share.

Plan C: Sell long-term bonds, due in 20 years, at par ($1,000), with a stated interest rate of 8%.

A.E.G. ENTERPRISES
Balance Sheet for June 30, 2011 (in thousands)

Assets		
Current assets:		
Cash	$ 50,000	
Accounts receivable	60,000	
Inventory	106,000	
Total current assets		$216,000
Property, plant, and equipment	$504,000	
Less: Accumulated depreciation	140,000	364,000
Patents and other intangible assets		20,000
Total assets		$600,000
Liabilities and Stockholders' Equity		
Current liabilities:		
Accounts payable	$ 46,000	
Taxes payable	15,000	
Other current liabilities	32,000	
Total current liabilities		$ 93,000
Long-term debt		100,000
Stockholders' equity:		
Preferred stock ($100 par, 5% cumulative, 500,000 shares authorized and issued)		50,000
Common stock ($1 par, 200,000,000 shares authorized, 100,000,000 issued)		100,000
Premium on common stock		120,000
Retained earnings		137,000
Total liabilities and stockholders' equity		$600,000

A.E.G. ENTERPRISES
Income Statement
For the Year Ended June 30, 2011
(in thousands except earnings per share)

Sales		$936,000
Cost of sales		671,000
Gross profit		$265,000
Operating expenses:		
Selling	$62,000	
General	41,000	103,000
Operating income		$162,000

Other items:	
Interest expense	20,000
Earnings before provision for income tax	$142,000
Provision for income tax	56,800
Net income	$ 85,200
Earnings per share	$ 0.83

Required

a. For the year ended June 30, 2011, compute:

1. Times interest earned
2. Debt ratio
3. Debt/equity ratio
4. Debt to tangible net worth ratio

b. Assuming the same financial results and statement balances, except for the increased assets and financing, compute the same ratios as in (a) under each financing alternative. Do not attempt to adjust retained earnings for the next year's profits.

c. Changes in earnings and number of shares will give the following earnings per share: Plan A—0.73, Plan B—0.69, and Plan C—0.73. Based on the information given, discuss the advantages and disadvantages of each alternative.

d. Why does the 5% preferred stock cost the company more than the 8% bonds?

P 7-8 The consolidated statement of earnings of Anonymous Corporation for the year ended December 31, 2011, is as follows:

Net sales	$1,550,010,000
Other income, net	10,898,000
	1,560,908,000
Costs and expenses:	
Cost of goods sold	1,237,403,000
Depreciation and amortization	32,229,000
Selling, general, and administrative	178,850,000
Interest	37,646,000
	1,486,128,000
Earnings from continuing operations before income taxes and equity earnings	74,780,000
Income taxes	37,394,000
Earnings from continuing operations before equity earnings	37,386,000
Equity in net earnings of unconsolidated subsidiaries and affiliated companies	27,749,000
Earnings from continuing operations	65,135,000
Earnings (losses) from discontinued operations, net of applicable income taxes	6,392,000
Net earnings	$ 71,527,000

Required

a. Compute the times interest earned for 2011.
b. Compute the times interest earned for 2011, including the equity income in the coverage.
c. What is the impact of including equity earnings from the coverage? Why should equity income be excluded from the times interest earned coverage?

P 7-9 Allen Company and Barker Company are competitors in the same industry. Selected financial data from their 2011 statements follow.

Balance Sheet
December 31, 2011

	Allen Company	Barker Company
Cash	$ 10,000	$ 35,000
Accounts receivable	45,000	120,000
Inventory	70,000	190,000
Investments	40,000	100,000
Intangibles	11,000	20,000
Property, plant, and equipment	180,000	520,000
Total assets	$356,000	$985,000

(*continued*)

(**P 7-9** CONTINUED)

	Allen Company	Barker Company
Accounts payable	$ 60,000	$165,000
Bonds payable	100,000	410,000
Preferred stock, $1 par	50,000	30,000
Common stock, $10 par	100,000	280,000
Retained earnings	46,000	100,000
Total liabilities and capital	$356,000	$985,000

Income Statement
For the Year Ended December 31, 2011

	Allen Company	Barker Company
Sales	$1,050,000	$2,800,000
Cost of goods sold	725,000	2,050,000
Selling and administrative expenses	230,000	580,000
Interest expense	10,000	32,000
Income taxes	42,000	65,000
Net income	$ 43,000	$ 73,000
Industry Averages:		
Times interest earned		7.2 times
Debt ratio		40.3%
Debt/equity		66.6%
Debt to tangible net worth		72.7%

Required

a. Compute the following ratios for each company:

1. Times interest earned
2. Debt ratio
3. Debt/equity ratio
4. Debt to tangible net worth

b. Is Barker Company in a position to take on additional long-term debt? Explain.
c. Which company has the better long-term debt position? Explain.

P 7-10 Consecutive five-year balance sheets and income statements of Laura Gibson Corporation are shown below and on the following page.
Required

a. Compute the following for the years ended December 31, 2007–2011:

1. Times interest earned
2. Fixed charge coverage
3. Debt ratio
4. Debt/equity ratio
5. Debt to tangible net worth

b. Comment on the debt position and the trends indicated in the long-term debt-paying ability.

LAURA GIBSON CORPORATION
Balance Sheets
December 31, 2007 through December 31, 2011

(Dollars in thousands)	2011	2010	2009	2008	2007
Assets					
Current assets:					
Cash	$ 27,000	$ 26,000	$ 25,800	$ 25,500	$ 25,000
Accounts receivable, net	135,000	132,000	130,000	129,000	128,000
Inventories	128,000	130,000	134,000	132,000	126,000
Total current assets	290,000	288,000	289,800	286,500	279,000
Property, plant, and equipment, net	250,000	248,000	247,000	246,000	243,000
Intangibles	20,000	18,000	17,000	16,000	15,000
Total assets	$560,000	$554,000	$553,800	$548,500	$537,000

(Dollars in thousands)	2011	2010	2009	2008	2007
Liabilities and shareholders' equity					
Current liabilities:					
Accounts payable	$ 75,000	$ 76,000	$ 76,500	$ 77,000	$ 78,000
Income taxes	13,000	13,500	14,000	13,000	13,500
Total current liabilities	88,000	89,500	90,500	90,000	91,500
Long-term debt	170,000	168,000	165,000	164,000	262,000
Shareholders' equity	302,000	296,500	298,300	294,500	183,500
Total liabilities and shareholders' equity	$560,000	$554,000	$553,800	$548,500	$537,000

LAURA GIBSON CORPORATION
Statement of Earnings
For the Years Ended December 31, 2007–2011

(In thousands, except per share)	2011	2010	2009	2008	2007
Net sales	$920,000	$950,000	$910,000	$850,000	$800,000
Cost of goods sold	640,000	648,000	624,000	580,000	552,000
Gross margin	280,000	302,000	286,000	270,000	248,000
Selling and administrative expense	156,000	157,000	154,000	150,000	147,000
Interest expense	17,000	16,000	15,000	14,500	23,000
Earnings from continuing operations before income taxes	$107,000	$129,000	$117,000	$105,500	$ 78,000
Income taxes	36,300	43,200	39,800	35,800	26,500
Earnings from continuing operations	70,700	85,800	77,200	69,700	51,500
Discontinued operating earnings (loss), net of taxes:					
From operations	(1,400)	1,300	1,400	1,450	1,600
On disposal	(900)	—	—	—	—
Earnings (loss) from discontinued operation	(2,300)	1,300	1,400	1,450	1,600
Net earnings	$ 68,400	$ 87,100	$ 78,600	$ 71,150	$ 53,100
Earnings (loss) per share:					
Continuing operations	$ 1.53	$ 1.69	$ 1.46	$ 1.37	$ 1.25
Discontinued operations	(0.03)	0.01	0.01	0.01	0.01
Net earnings per share	$ 1.50	$ 1.70	$ 1.47	$ 1.38	$ 1.26

Note: Operating lease payments were as follows: 2011, $30,000; 2010, $27,000; 2009, $28,500; 2008, $30,000; 2007, $27,000 (dollars in thousands).

P 7-11

Required Answer the following multiple-choice questions:

a. Which of the following ratios can be used as a guide to a firm's ability to carry debt from an income perspective?

1. Debt ratio
2. Debt to tangible net worth
3. Debt/equity
4. Times interest earned
5. Current ratio

b. There is disagreement on all but which of the following items as to whether it should be considered a liability in the debt ratio?

1. Short-term liabilities
2. Reserve accounts
3. Deferred taxes
4. Noncontrolling income (loss)
5. Preferred stock

(*continued*)

(**P 7-11** CONTINUED)

c. A firm may have substantial liabilities that are not disclosed on the face of the balance sheet from all but which of the following?

1. Leases
2. Pension plans
3. Joint ventures
4. Contingencies
5. Bonds payable

d. In computing the debt ratio, which of the following is subtracted in the denominator?

1. Copyrights
2. Trademarks
3. Patents
4. Marketable securities
5. None of the above.

e. All but which of these ratios are considered to be debt ratios?

1. Times interest earned
2. Debt ratio
3. Debt/equity
4. Fixed charge ratio
5. Current ratio

f. Which of the following statements is false?

1. The debt to tangible net worth ratio is more conservative than the debt ratio.
2. The debt to tangible net worth ratio is more conservative than the debt/equity ratio.
3. Times interest earned indicates an income statement view of debt.
4. The debt/equity ratio indicates an income statement view of debt.
5. The debt ratio indicates a balance sheet view of debt.

g. Sneider Company has long-term debt of $500,000, while Abbott Company has long-term debt of $50,000. Which of the following statements best represents an analysis of the long-term debt position of these two firms?

1. Sneider Company's times interest earned should be lower than Abbott Company's.
2. Abbott Company's times interest earned should be lower than Sneider Company's.
3. Abbott Company has a better long-term borrowing ability than does Sneider Company.
4. Sneider Company has a better long-term borrowing ability than does Abbott Company.
5. None of the above.

h. A times interest earned ratio of 0.20 to 1 means

1. That the firm will default on its interest payment.
2. That net income is less than the interest expense (including capitalized interest).
3. That cash flow exceeds the net income.
4. That the firm should reduce its debt.
5. None of the above.

i. In computing debt to tangible net worth, which of the following is *not* subtracted in the denominator?

1. Patents
2. Goodwill
3. Land
4. Bonds payable
5. Both 3 and 4

j. The ratio fixed charge coverage

   1. Is a cash flow indication of debt-paying ability.
   2. Is an income statement indication of debt-paying ability.
   3. Is a balance sheet indication of debt-paying ability.
   4. Will usually be higher than the times interest earned ratio.
   5. None of the above.

k. Under the Employee Retirement Income Security Act, a company can be liable for its pension plan up to

   1. 30% of its net worth.
   2. 30% of pension liabilities.
   3. 30% of liabilities.
   4. 40% of its net worth.
   5. None of the above.

l. Which of the following statements is correct?

   1. Capitalized interest should be included with interest expense when computing times interest earned.
   2. A ratio that indicates a firm's long-term debt-paying ability from the balance sheet view is the times interest earned.
   3. Some of the items on the income statement that are excluded in order to compute times interest earned are interest expense, income taxes, and interest income.
   4. Usually, the highest times interest coverage in the most recent five-year period is used as the primary indication of the interest coverage.
   5. None of the above.

m. Which of these items does *not* represent a definite commitment to pay out funds in the future?

   1. Notes payable
   2. Bonds payable
   3. Noncontrolling interests
   4. Wages payable
   5. None of the above.

Cases

CASE 7-1 OUTSOURCED SERVICES

THE GEO GROUP, INC.*
CONSOLIDATED STATEMENTS OF INCOME
Fiscal Years Ended January 2, 2011, January 3, 2010, and December 28, 2008

	2010	2009	2008
	(In thousands, except per share data)		
Revenues	$1,269,968	$1,141,090	$1,043,006
Operating Expenses	975,020	897,099	822,053
Depreciation and Amortization	48,111	39,306	37,406
General and Administrative Expenses	106,364	69,240	69,151
Operating Income	140,473	135,445	114,396
Interest Income	6,271	4,943	7,045

(*continued*)

*"We are a leading provider of government-outsourced services specializing in the management of correctional, detention, mental health residential treatment and re-entry facilities, and the provision of community based services and youth services in the United States, Australia, South Africa, the United Kingdom and Canada." 10-K
Source: The Geo Group, Inc. 2010 10-K

(**CASE 7-1** CONTINUED)

	2010	2009	2008
	\(In thousands, except per share data)		
Interest Expense	(40,707)	(28,518)	(30,202)
Loss on Extinguishment of Debt	(7,933)	(6,839)	—
Income Before Income Taxes, Equity in Earnings of Affiliates, and Discontinued Operations	98,104	105,031	91,239
Provision for Income Taxes	39,532	42,079	34,033
Equity in Earnings of Affiliates, net of income tax provision (benefit) of $2,212, $1,368, and ($805)	4,218	3,517	4,623
Income from Continuing Operations	62,790	66,469	61,829
Loss from Discontinued Operations, net of income tax provision (benefit) of $0, ($216), and $236	—	(346)	(2,551)
Net Income	$ 62,790	$ 66,123	$ 59,278
Loss (Earnings) Attributable to Noncontrolling Interests	678	(169)	(376)
Net Income Attributable to The GEO Group, Inc.	$ 63,468	$ 65,954	$ 58,902
Weighted Average Common Shares Outstanding:			
Basic	55,379	50,879	50,539
Diluted	55,989	51,922	51,830
Income per Common Share Attributable to the GEO Group, Inc.:			
Basic:			
Income from continuing operations	$ 1.15	$ 1.30	$ 1.22
Loss from discontinued operations	—	—	(0.05)
Net income per share – basic	$ 1.15	$ 1.30	$ 1.17
Diluted:			
Income from continuing operations	$ 1.13	$ 1.28	$ 1.19
Loss from discontinued operations	—	(0.01)	(0.05)
Net income per share - diluted	$ 1.13	$ 1.27	$ 1.14
Comprehensive Income (Loss):			
Net income	$ 62,790	$ 66,123	$ 59,278
Total other comprehensive income (loss), net of tax	4,645	12,174	(14,361)
Total comprehensive income	67,435	78,297	44,917
Comprehensive (income) loss attributable to noncontrolling interests	608	428	(210)
Comprehensive income attributable to the GEO Group, Inc.	$ 68,043	$ 78,725	$ 44,707

6. Property and Equipment (In Part)

Property and equipment consist of the following at fiscal year end:

	Useful Life	2010	2009
	(Years)	(In thousands)	
Land	—	$ 97,393	$ 60,331
Buildings and improvements	2 to 50	1,131,895	797,185
Leasehold improvements	1 to 29	260,167	95,696
Equipment	3 to 10	77,906	63,382
Furniture and fixtures	3 to 7	18,453	11,731
Facility construction in progress		120,584	129,956
		$1,706,398	$1,158,281
Less accumulated depreciation and amortization		(195,106)	(159,721)
Property and equipment, net		$1,511,292	$ 998,560

The Company depreciates its leasehold improvements over the shorter of their estimated useful lives or the terms of the leases including renewal periods that are reasonably assured. The Company's construction in progress primarily consists of development costs associated with the Facility Construction & Design segment for contracts with various federal, state and local agencies for which we have management contracts. Interest capitalized in property and equipment was $4.1 million and $4.9 million for the fiscal years ended January 2, 2011 and January 3, 2010, respectively.

Required

a. What is the gross interest expense for 2010 and 2009?

b. What is the interest reported on the income statement for 2010, 2009 and 2008?

c. What was the interest added to property and equipment during 2010 and 2009?

d. When is capitalized interest recognized as an expense? Describe.

e. What was the effect on income from capitalizing interest? Describe.

f. Compute times interest earned for 2010 and 2009. Comment on the absolute amounts and the trend.

CASE 7-2 GLOBAL PROVIDER

THE SHAW GROUP, INC.*

This case includes data from The Shaw Group, Inc. annual report for the year ended August 31, 2010.

Note 6 – Property and Equipment:

Property and equipment consisted of the following (in thousands):

	August 31,	
	2010	2009
Transportation equipment	$ 10,899	$ 20,977
Furniture, fixtures, and software	162,446	146,905
Machinery and equipment	263,759	219,753
Buildings and improvements	233,353	151,708
Assets acquired under capital leases	3,612	5,561
Land	14,269	12,404
Construction in progress	89,401	79,004
	777,739	636,402
Less: accumulated depreciation	(293,098)	(250,796)
Property and equipment, net	$ 484,641	$ 385,606

Assets acquired under capital leases, net of accumulated depreciation, were $1.6 million and $2.0 million at August 31, 2010, and 2009, respectively. If the assets acquired under capital leases transfer title at the end of the lease term or contain a bargain purchase option, the assts are amortized over their estimated useful lives; otherwise, the assets are amortized over the respective lease term. Depreciation expense of $59.8 million, $52.3 million, and $43.7 million for the fiscal years ended August 31, 2010, 2009, and 2008, respectively, is included in cost of revenues and general and administrative expenses in the accompanying consolidated statements of operations.

At August 31, 2010, construction in progress consisted primarily of deposits on heavy equipment to be used on some of our power projects. At August 31, 2009, construction in progress consisted primarily of cost related to the construction of our module fabrication and assembly facility in Lake Charles, Louisiana.

In fiscal year 2009, we recorded an asset impairment charge of $5.5 million for a consolidated joint venture. The impairment charge reduced the property, plant, and equipment to its salvage value.

(continued)

---

*The Shaw Group Inc. (Shaw, we, us, and our) is a leading global provider of technology, engineering, procurement, construction, maintenance, fabrication, manufacturing, consulting, remediation and facilities management services to a diverse client base that includes multinational and national oil companies and industrial corporations, regulated utilities, independent and merchant power producers, and government agencies.
Source: The Shaw Group, Inc. 2010 10-K

(**Case 7-2** continued)

Note 9 – Debt and Revolving Lines of Credit (in part):

Our debt (including capital lease obligations) consisted of the following (in thousands):

	August 31, 2010		August 31, 2009	
	Short-term	Long-term	Short-term	Long-term
Notes payable on purchases of equipment; 0% to 1.3% interest; payments discounted at imputed rate of 5.9% interest; due September 2010 through April 2011	$ 4,079	$ —	$ 10,610	$2,146
Notes payable on purchases of equipment; 5.2% to 6.0% interest; due June 2011 through July 2012, and paid in full October 2009	—	—	1,188	1,824
Other notes payable	—	—	2,805	2,277
Capital lease obligations	400	979	796	1,380
Subtotal	4,479	979	15,399	7,627
Westinghouse Bonds (see description below)	1,520,674	—	1,387,954	—
Total	$1,525,153	$979	$1,403,353	$7,627

The notes payable on purchases of equipment are collateralized by the purchased equipment. The carrying amount of the equipment pledged as collateral was approximately $18.8 million at August 31, 2010.

Annual scheduled maturities of debt and minimum lease payments under capital lease obligations during each year ending August 31 are as follows (in thousands):

	Capital Lease Obligations	Debt
2011	$ 475	$ 4,079
2012	399	—
2013	399	1,520,674
2014	266	—
2015	—	—
Thereafter	—	—
Subtotal	1,539	1,524,753
Less: amount representing interest	(160)	—
Total	$1,379	$1,524,753

Note 13 – Operating Leases

We lease certain office buildings, fabrication and warehouse facilities, machinery, and equipment under various lease arrangements. Leases that do not qualify as capital leases are classified as operating leases and the related lease payments are expensed on a straight-line basis over the lease term, including, as applicable, any free-rent period during which we have the right to use the asset. For leases with renewal options where the renewal is reasonably assured, the lease term, including the renewal period, is used to determine the appropriate lease classification and to compute periodic rental expense.

Certain of our operating lease agreements are non-cancelable and expire at various times and require various minimum rentals. The non-cancelable operating leases with initial non-cancelable periods in excess of twelve months that were in effect as of August 31, 2010, require us to make the following estimated future payments:

For the year ending August 31 (in thousands)	
2011	$ 72,805
2012	61,677
2013	51,381
2014	45,791
2015	35,883
Thereafter	91,845
Total future minimum lease payments	$359,382

Future minimum lease payments as of August 31, 2010 have not been reduced by minimum non-cancelable sublease rentals aggregating approximately $0.8 million.

In 2002, we entered into a 10-year non-cancelable operating lease for our Corporate Headquarters building in Baton Rouge, Louisiana. In connection with this lease, we purchased an option for $12.2 million for the right to acquire additional office space and undeveloped land for approximately $150 million. The option expires the earlier of January 2012, or upon renewal of the existing Corporate Headquarters lease. The cost of the option is included in other assets. The book value of the option is assessed for impairment annually based on appraisals of the additional office space and undeveloped land subject to the option. If we renew the lease rather than exercise the option, the option value will be expensed over the term of the new Corporate Headquarters building lease.

We also enter into lease agreements for equipment needed to fulfill the requirements of specific jobs. Any payments owed or committed under these lease arrangements as of August 31, 2010, are not included as part of total minimum lease payments shown above.

The total rental expense for the fiscal years ended August 31, 2010, 2009, and 2008 was approximately $178.8 million, $178.1 million, and $170.6 million, respectively. Deferred rent payable (current and long-term) aggregated $32.0 million and $30.3 million at August 31, 2010 and 2009, respectively.

Required

a. For August 31, 2010:
   1. What was the gross amount for property and equipment?
   2. What was the net amount for property and equipment?
   3. What was the gross amount for assets acquired under capital leases?
   4. What was the net amount for assets acquired under capital leases?
   5. How material are assets acquired under capital leases in relation to total property and equipment?

b. How material are capital lease obligations in relation to total debt and revolving lines of credit at August 31, 2010?

c. Operating leases:
   1. What was the total future minimum lease payments as of August 31, 2010?
   2. Using two-thirds of future minimum lease payments representing principal, what would be the estimate for principal at August 31, 2010?
   3. How material are operating leases in relation to capital leases?

CASE 7-3 COMMITTED TO SAVING PEOPLE MONEY

WAL-MART STORES, INC.*
Consolidated Balance Sheets

(Amounts in millions except per share data)	As of January 31, 2011	As of January 31, 2010 As adjusted
ASSETS		
Current assets:		
Cash and cash equivalents	$ 7,395	$ 7,907
Receivables, net	5,089	4,144
Inventories	36,318	32,713
Prepaid expenses and other	2,960	3,128
Current assets of discontinued operations	131	140
Total current assets	51,893	48,032
Property and equipment:		
Land	24,386	22,591
Buildings and improvements	79,051	73,657
Fixtures and equipment	38,290	34,035
Transportation and equipment	2,595	2,355

(continued)

*Wal-Mart Stores, Inc. ("Walmart," the "Company" or "we") operates retail stores in various formats around the world and is committed to saving people money so they can live better.
Source: Wal-Mart Stores, Inc 2010 10-K

(**Case 7-3** CONTINUED)

(Amounts in millions except per share data)	As of January 31,	
	2011	**2010 As adjusted**
Property and equipment: (continued)		
Construction in process	4,262	5,210
Property and equipment	148,584	137,848
Less accumulated depreciation	(43,486)	(38,304)
Property and equipment, net	105,098	99,544
Property under capital leases:		
Property under capital leases	5,905	5,669
Less accumulated amortization	(3,125)	(2,906)
Property under capital leases, net	2,780	2,763
Goodwill	16,763	16,126
Other assets and deferred charges	4,129	3,942
Total assets	$180,663	$170,407
LIABILITIES AND EQUITY		
Current liabilities:		
Short-term borrowings	$ 1,031	$ 523
Accounts payable	33,557	30,451
Accrued liabilities	18,701	18,734
Accrued income taxes	157	1,347
Long-term debt due within one year	4,655	4,050
Obligations under capital leases due within one year	336	346
Current liabilities of discontinued operations	47	92
Total current liabilities	58,484	55,543
Long-term debt	40,692	33,231
Long-term obligations under capital leases	3,150	3,170
Deferred income taxes and other	6,682	5,508
Redeemable noncontrolling interest	408	307
Commitments and contingencies		
Equity:		
Preferred stock ($0.10 par value; 100 shares authorized, none issued)	—	—
Common stock ($0.10 par value; 11,000 shares authorized, 3,516 and 3,786 issued and outstanding at January 31, 2011 and 2010, respectively)	352	378
Capital in excess of par value	3,577	3,803
Retained earnings	63,967	66,357
Accumulated other comprehensive income (loss)	646	(70)
Total Walmart shareholder's equity	68,452	70,468
Noncontrolling interest	2,705	2,180
Total equity	71,247	72,648
Total liabilities and equity	$180,663	$170,407

Required

a. Observe that the accumulated amortization is deducted from property under capital lease. Why is this described as amortization instead of depreciation?

b. Why do the assets under capital leases not equal the liabilities under capital leases?

CASE 7-4 LOCKOUT

The Celtics Basketball Holdings, L.P. and Subsidiary included the following note in its 1998 annual report:

Note G—Commitments and Contingencies (in Part)

National Basketball Association ("NBA") players, including those that play for the Boston Celtics, are covered by a collective bargaining agreement between the NBA and the NBA Players Association (the "NBPA") that was to be in effect through June 30, 2001 (the "Collective Bargaining Agreement"). Under the terms of the Collective Bargaining Agreement, the NBA had the right to terminate the Collective Bargaining Agreement after the 1997–1998 season if it

Source: The Celtics Basketball Holdings, L.P and Subsidiary 2010 10-K

was determined that the aggregate salaries and benefits paid by all NBA teams for the 1997–1998 season exceeded 51.8% of projected Basketball Related Income, as defined in the Collective Bargaining Agreement ("BRI"). Effective June 30, 1998, the Board of Governors of the NBA voted to exercise that right and reopen the Collective Bargaining Agreement, as it had been determined that the aggregate salaries and benefits paid by the NBA teams for the 1997–1998 season would exceed 51.8% of projected BRI. Effective July 1, 1998, the NBA commenced a lockout of NBA players in support of its attempt to reach a new collective bargaining agreement. The NBA and the NBPA have been engaged in negotiations regarding a new collective bargaining agreement, but as of September 18, 1998, no agreement has been reached. In the event that the lockout extends into the 1998–1999 season, NBA teams, including the Boston Celtics, will refund amounts paid by season ticket holders (plus interest) for any games that are canceled as a result of the lockout. In addition, as a result of the lockout, NBA teams have not made any payments due to players with respect to the 1998–1999 season. The NBPA has disputed the NBA's position on this matter, and both the NBA and the NBPA have presented their cases to an independent arbitrator, who will make his ruling no later than the middle of October 1998. As of September 18, 1998, the arbitrator has not ruled on this matter.

Although the ultimate outcome of this matter cannot be determined at this time, any loss of games as a result of the absence of a collective bargaining agreement or the continuation of the lockout will have a material adverse effect on the Partnership's financial condition and its results of operations. Further, if NBA teams, including the Boston Celtics, are required to honor the player contracts for the 1998–99 season and beyond without agreeing to a new collective bargaining agreement or without ending the lockout, which would result in the loss of games, the Partnership's financial condition and results of operations will be materially and adversely affected.

The Partnership has employment agreements with officers, coaches and players of the basketball team (Celtics Basketball). Certain of the contracts provide for guaranteed payments which must be paid even if the employee is injured or terminated. Amounts required to be paid under such contracts in effect as of September 18, 1998, including option years and $8,100,000 included in accrued expenses at June 30, 1998, but excluding deferred compensation commitments disclosed in Note E—Deferred Compensation, are as follows:

Years ending June 30, 1999	$32,715,000
2000	33,828,000
2001	27,284,000
2002	20,860,000
2003	19,585,000
2004 and thereafter	10,800,000

Commitments for the year ended June 30, 1999, include payments due to players under contracts for the 1998–1999 season in the amount of $18,801,000, which are currently not being paid as a result of the lockout described above.

Celtics Basketball maintains disability and life insurance policies on most of its key players. The level of insurance coverage maintained is based on management's determination of the insurance proceeds which would be required to meet its guaranteed obligations in the event of permanent or total disability of its key players.

Required Discuss how to incorporate the contingency note into an analysis of Celtics Basketball Holdings, L.P. and Subsidiary.

Case 7-5 SAFE – MANY EMPLOYERS

SAFEWAY INC. AND SUBSIDIARIES*
Note K: Employee Benefit Plans and Collective Bargaining Agreements (in part)
Multi-Employer Pension Plans

Safeway participates in various multi-employer retirement plans, covering substantially all Company employees not covered under the Company's non-contributory retirement plans.

(continued)

---

*"Safeway Inc. is one of the largest food and drug retailers in North America, with 1,694 stores at year-end 2010." 10-K
Source: Safeway Inc. and Subsidiaries 2010 10-K

(**CASE 7-5** CONTINUED)

These multi-employer retirement plans are generally defined benefit plans and are pursuant to agreements between the Company and various unions. In many cases, specific benefit levels are not negotiated with contributing employers or in some cases even known by contributing employers. Contributions of $292.3 million in 2010, $278.1 million in 2009 and $286.9 million in 2008 were made and charged to expense.

Required

a. What were the contributions to multi-employer plans for 2010, 2009 and 2008? Comment on the trend.

b. Determine the total liability for multi-employer pension plans at the end of 2010.

c. What control does Safeway Inc. have over multi-employer pension plans?

CASE 7-6 SAFE – RETIREMENT BENEFITS

SAFEWAY INC. AND SUBSIDIARIES*

Notes to Consolidated Financial Statements (In Part)
Note K: Employee Benefit Plans and Collective Bargaining Agreements (In part)

Pension Plans

The Company maintains defined benefit, non-contributory retirement plans for substantially all of its employees not participating in multi-employer pension plans. Safeway recognizes the funded status of its retirement plans on its consolidated balance sheet.

Other Post-Retirement Benefits

In addition to the Company's pension plans, the Company sponsors plans that provide post-retirement medical and life insurance benefits to certain employees. Retirees share a portion of the cost of the postretirement medical plans. Safeway pays all the costs of the life insurance plans. The Company also sponsors a Retirement Restoration Plan that provides death benefits and supplemental income payments for senior executives after retirement. All of these Other Post-Retirement Benefit Plans are unfunded.

The following table provides a reconciliation of the changes in the retirement plans' benefit obligation and fair value of assets over the two-year period ended January 1, 2011 and a statement of the funded status as of year-end 2010 and year-end 2009. Activity for 2009 includes the removal of the Canadian money purchase plan which had been previously presented within the table but has since been determined to be a defined contribution plan (in millions):

	Pension		Other Post-Retirement Benefits	
	2010	2009	2010	2009
Change in projected benefit obligation:				
Beginning balance	$2,095.5	$2,009.0	$ 121.7	$ 111.0
Service cost	36.1	39.4	2.3	1.5
Interest cost	125.8	116.0	7.2	6.6
Plan amendments	—	(15.1)	—	—
Actuarial loss	108.6	157.1	6.8	4.7
Plan participant contributions	—	—	1.8	2.3
Benefit payments	(129.5)	(121.4)	(9.3)	(10.0)
Reclassification of money purchase plan component	—	(138.1)	—	—
Currency translation adjustment	20.7	48.6	2.3	5.6
Ending balance	$2,257.2	$2,095.5	$ 132.8	$ 121.7

* "Safeway Inc. is one of the largest food and drug retailers in North America, with 1,694 stores at year-end 2010."
10-K
Source: Safeway Inc. and Subsidiaries 2010 10-K

	Pension		Other Post-Retirement Benefits	
	2010	2009	2010	2009
Change in fair value of plan assets:				
Beginning balance	$1,572.1	$1,512.7	$ —	$ —
Actual return on plan assets	183.6	252.8	—	—
Employer contributions	10.2	16.7	7.5	7.7
Plan participant contributions	—	—	1.8	2.3
Benefit payments	(129.5)	(121.4)	(9.3)	(10.0)
Reclassification of money purchase plan component	—	(129.6)	—	—
Currency translation adjustment	15.8	40.9	—	—
Ending balance	$1,652.2	$1,572.1	$ —	$ —
Components of net amount recognized in financial position:				
Other accrued liabilities (current liability)	$ (1.5)	$ (1.4)	$ (8.4)	$ (8.3)
Pension and postretirement benefit obligations (non-current liability)	(603.5)	(522.0)	(124.4)	(113.4)
Funded status	$ (605.0)	$ (523.4)	$(132.8)	$(121.7)

Amounts recognized in accumulated other comprehensive income consist of the following (in millions):

	Pension		Other Post-Retirement Benefits	
	2010	2009	2010	2009
Net actuarial loss	$583.5	$592.4	$26.1	$21.9
Prior service cost (credit)	47.1	64.4	(1.5)	(1.6)
	$630.6	$656.8	$ 24.6	$20.3

Safeway expects approximately $62.2 million of the net actuarial pension loss and $15.9 million of the prior service cost to be recognized as a component of net periodic benefit cost in 2011.

Information for Safeway's pension plans, all of which have an accumulated benefit obligation in excess of plan assets as of year-end 2010 and 2009, is shown below (in millions):

	2010	2009
Projected benefit obligation	$2,257.2	$2,095.5
Accumulated benefit obligation	2,171.9	2,028.4
Fair value of plan assets	$1,652.2	$1,572.1

Required

a. 1. Determine the projected benefit obligation at the end of 2010 and 2009 (pension and other post-retirement benefits).
   2. Determine the fair value of plan assets at the end of 2010 and 2009 (pension and other post-retirement benefits).
   3. Determine the funded status at the end of 2010 and 2009 (pension and other post-retirement benefits).
   4. Why is the funded status of the other post-retirement benefits equal to the projected benefit obligation?
   5. Do all of the pension plans have an accumulated benefit obligation in excess of plan assets?

b. Comment on the trend in projected benefit obligation and the funded status (pension and other post-retirement benefits).

CASE 7-7 SPECIALTY COFFEE

STARBUCKS CORPORATION*
NOTES TO CONSOLIDATED FINANCIAL STATEMENTS (In Part)
Fiscal Years ended October 3, 2010, September 27, 2009
and September 28, 2008
Note 14 Employee Stock and Benefit Plans (In Part)

Defined Contribution Plans

We maintain voluntary defined contribution plans, both qualified and non-qualified, covering eligible employees as defined in the plan documents. Participating employees may elect to defer and contribute a portion of their eligible compensation to the plans up to limits stated in the plan documents, not to exceed the dollar amounts set by applicable laws.

Our matching contributions to all US and non-US plans were $23.5 million, $19.7 million and $25.3 million in fiscal years 2010, 2009 and 2008, respectively.

Required

a. "Participating employees may elect to defer and contribute a portion of their eligible compensation to the plans up to limits in the plan documents." Comment.

b. Comment on the company liability for this type of plan.

c. Company contributions to all U.S. and non-U.S. plans were "$23.5 million, $19.7 million and $25.3 million in fiscal years 2010, 2009 and 2008, respectively." Why the fluctuations in company contributions?

d. Total net revenues for the Starbucks Corporation were $10,707,400,000, $9,774,000,000 and $10,383,000,000 in fiscal years 2010, 2009 and 2008, respectively. Comment on the materiality of company contributions in relation to net revenues.

*"Starbucks is the premier roaster and retailer of specialty coffee in the world, operating in more than 50 countries." 10-K
Source: Starbucks Corporation 2010 10-K

CASE 7-8 TRANSACTION PRINTERS

TRANSACT TECHNOLOGIES INCORPORATED*
NOTES TO CONSOLIDATED FINANCIAL STATEMENTS (In Part)

9. Retirement savings plan

We maintain a 401(k) plan under which all full-time employees are eligible to participate at the beginning of each month immediately following their date of hire. We match employees' contributions at a rate of 50% of employees' contributions up to the first 6% of the employees' compensation contributed to the 401(k) plan. Our matching contributions were $223,000, $237,000 and $244,000 in 2010, 2009 and 2008, respectively.

TRANSACT TECHNOLOGIES INCORPORATED
CONSOLIDATED STATEMENTS OF INCOME
(In thousands, except per share data)

	Year Ended December 31,		
	2010	2009	2008
Net sales	$63,194	$58,346	$62,207
Net income	$ 3,904	$ 2,140	$ 1,444

Required

a. In general, what type of retirement savings plan does TransAct Technologies have?

b. Give your opinion as to the materiality of the pension plan.

c. Give your opinion as to the control of pension expense.

*"TransAct designs, develops, assembles, markets and services world-class transaction-based printers under the Epic and Ithaca® brand names." 10-K
Source: Transact Technologies Incorporated 2010 10-K

Case 7-9 READY-TO-EAT

KELLOGG COMPANY AND SUBSIDIARIES*

NOTES TO CONSOLIDATED FINANCIAL STATEMENTS (In Part)
Note 11 Derivative Instruments and Fair Value Measurements (In Part)

Credit risk concentration

The Company is exposed to credit loss in the event of nonperformance by counterparties on derivative financial and commodity contracts. Management believes a concentration of credit risk with respect to derivative counterparties is limited due to the credit ratings of the counterparties and the use of master netting and reciprocal collateralization agreements.

Master netting agreements apply in situations where the Company executes multiple contracts with the same counterparty. Certain counterparties represent a concentration of credit risk to the Company. If those counterparties fail to perform according to the terms of derivative contracts, this would result in a loss to the Company of $50 million as of January 1, 2011.

For certain derivative contracts, reciprocal collateralization agreements with counterparties call for the posting of collateral in the form of cash, treasury securities or letters of credit if a fair value loss position to the Company or our counterparties exceeds a certain amount. There were no collateral balance requirements at January 1, 2011.

Management believes concentrations of credit risk with respect to accounts receivable is limited due to the generally high credit quality of the Company's major customers, as well as the large number and geographic dispersion of smaller customers. However, the Company conducts a disproportionate amount of business with a small number of large multinational grocery retailers, with the five largest accounts encompassing approximately 30% of consolidated trade receivables at January 1, 2011.

Required

a. In some situations, the company executes multiple contracts with the same counterparty. Indicate the loss as of January 1, 2011 if those counterparties fail to perform according to the terms of derivative contracts.

b. What were the collateral balance requirements at January 1, 2011?

c. The company is exposed to credit loss in the event of nonperformance by counterparties on derivative financial and commodity contracts. Why does management believe the risk is limited?

d. Why does management believe that concentrations of credit risk with respect to accounts receivable is limited?

*"Kellogg Company, founded in 1906 and incorporated in Delaware in 1922 and its subsidiaries are engaged in the manufacture and marketing of ready-to-eat cereal and convenience foods." 10-K
Source: Kellogg Company and Subsidiaries 2010 10-K

Case 7-10 SPECIALTY RETAILER – DEBT VIEW

In this case, we review the debt of several specialty retail stores. The companies reviewed and the year-end dates are as follows:

1. **Abercrombie & Fitch Co.**
   (52-week fiscal year ended January 29, 2011; 52-week fiscal year ended January 30, 2010; 52-week fiscal year ended January 31, 2009)
   "Abercrombie & Fitch Co … is a specialty retailer that operates stores and direct-to-consumer operations." 10-K
   Source: Abercrombie & Fitch 2010 10-K

2. **Limited Brands, Inc.**
   (52-week fiscal year ended January 29, 2011; 52-week fiscal year ended January 30, 2010; 52-week fiscal year ended January 31, 2009)
   "We operate in the highly competitive specialty retail business." 10-K
   Source: Limited Brands 2010 10-K

3. **Gap Inc.**
   (52-week fiscal year ended January 29, 2011; 52-week fiscal year ended January 30, 2010; 52-week fiscal year ended January 31, 2009)
   Source: Gap Inc 2010 10-K

(*continued*)

(**CASE 7-10** CONTINUED)

"We are a global specialty retailer offering apparel, accessories, and personal care products..." 10-K

	Abercrombie & Fitch		Limited Brands		GAP	
	2011	**2010**	**2011**	**2010**	**2011**	**2010**
Times interest earned (times per year)	××	××	7.01	3.74	××	××
Fixed charge coverage (times per year)	××	××	4.29	2.60	××	××
Debt ratio (%)	35.86	35.22	77.10	69.55	42.25	38.75
Debt/equity ratio (%)	55.91	54.38	336.76	228.43	73.16	63.26
Debt to tangible net worth ratio (%)	55.91*	54.38*	✓✓✓	3,370.95	76.07	65.40

Note: *Apparently no intangible assets

××Disclosure not adequate to compute

✓✓✓Negative stockholders' equity after subtracting intangible assets

Required

a. Comment on the relative times interest earned results.

b. Comment on the relative fixed charge coverage results.

c. Comment on the relative times interest earned vs. the fixed charge coverage. Why is the times interest earned materially higher than the fixed charge coverage?

d. Why is the debt/equity materially more than the debt ratio?

e. Considering the debt ratio, comment on the relative debt position of these companies.

f. Why is the debt to tangible net worth usually higher than the debt/equity ratio?

CASE 7-11 EAT AT MY RESTAURANT – DEBT VIEW

In this case, we review the debt of several restaurant companies. The restaurant companies reviewed and the year-end dates are as follows:

1. **Yum Brands, Inc.**

 (December 25, 2010; December 26, 2009) (52 weeks)

 "YUM consists of six operating segments: KFC-U.S., Pizza Hut-US, Taco Bell-U.S., Long John Silver's ("LJS")-U.S. and A & W All American Food Restaurants ("A&W")-U.S., YUM Restaurants International ("YRI" or "International Division") and YUM Restaurants China ("China Division")." 10-K

 Source: Yum! Brands, Inc. and Subsidiaries 2010 10-K

2. **Panera Bread**

 (December 28, 2010; December 29, 2009) (52 weeks)

 "Panera Bread Company and its subsidiaries, referred to as "Panera Bread," "Panera," the "Company," "we," "us," and "our," is a national bakery-café concept with 1,453 Company-owned and franchise-operated bakery-café locations in 40 states, the District of Columbia, and Ontario, Canada." 10-K

 Source: Panera Bread 2010 10-K

3. **Starbucks**

 (October 3, 2010; September 27, 2009) (Fiscal year 2010 included 53 weeks, while fiscal year 2009 included 52 weeks).

 "Starbucks is the premier roaster and retailer of specialty coffee in the world, operating in more than 50 countries." 10-K

 Source: Starbucks Corporation 2010 10-K

	Yum Brands, Inc.		Panera Bread		Starbucks	
	2010	**2009**	**2010**	**2009**	**2010**	**2009**
Times interest earned (times per year)	7.52	6.10	267.91	200.89	35.08	11.35
Fixed charge coverage (times per year)	4.10	3.75	256.86	193.56	5.75	2.58
Debt ratio (%)	79.93	84.42	35.58	28.68	42.34	45.19
Debt/equity ratio (%)	398.26	541.65	55.23	40.22	73.57	82.74
Debt to tangible net worth ratio (%)	1,242.43	5,028.33	72.66	48.97	80.91	92.70

Required

   a. Comment on the relative times interest earned between the companies.

   b. Comment on the relative fixed charge coverage for each company.

   c. Comment on the relative times interest earned vs. the fixed charge coverage. Why is the times interest earned materially higher than the fixed charge coverage?

   d. Why is the debt/equity materially more than the debt ratio?

   e. Considering the debt ratio, comment on the relative debt position of these companies.

   f. Why is the debt to tangible net worth usually higher than the debt/equity ratio?

WEB CASE THOMSON ONE *Business School Edition*

Please complete the Web case that covers material discussed in this chapter at www.cengagebrain.com. You'll be using Thomson ONE Business School Edition, a powerful tool that combines a full range of fundamental financial information, earnings estimates, market data, and source documents for 500 publicly traded companies.

TO THE NET CASE

1. Go to the SEC site (www.sec.gov). Under "Filings & Forms (Edgar)," click on "Search for Company Filings." Click on "Company or fund, etc." Under Company Name, enter "Walt Disney" (or under Ticker Symbol, enter "DIS"). Select the 10-K filed November 24, 2010.

   a. Copy the first sentence in the "Item 1. Business" section.

   b. "Note 2 – Summary of Significant Accounting Policies – reporting period." Comment on the reporting period. Will the reporting period cause a comparability issue?

   c. "Note 15 – Commitments and Contingencies" (see notes to financial statements). Legal matters. Comment on Celador International Ltd. v. The Walt Disney.

   d. "Item 9 – Changes and Disagreements with Accountants on Accounting and Financial Disclosure." Comment on these disclosures or lack of disclosures.

   e. "Item 11 – Executive Compensation." Where is the "Board Compensation" and "Executive Compensation" disclosed?

2. Go to the SEC site (www.sec.gov). Under "Filings & Forms (Edgar)," click on "Search for Company Filings." Click on "Company or fund, etc." Under Company Name, enter "The Dow Chemical Company and Subsidiaries" (or under Ticker Symbol, enter "DOW"). Select the 10-K filed February 18, 2011.

   a. Note Q – Determine the net periodic cost of defined benefit pension plans and other postretirement benefits for the year ended December 31, 2010. How material is the cost in relation to net sales? How material are these costs in relation to income from continuing operations before income taxes?

   b. Determine the projected benefit obligation for defined benefit pension plans and other postretirement benefits at December 31, 2010. Determine the funded status at end of year for these plans. Comment.

   c. Determine the amounts recognized in the Consolidated Balance Sheets at December 31, 2010 for defined benefit pensions plans and other postretirement benefits.

3. Go to the SEC site (www.sec.gov). Under "Filings & Forms (Edgar)," click on "Search for Company Filings." Click on "Company or fund, etc." Under Company Name, enter "Flowers Food Inc." (or under Ticker Symbol, enter "FLO"). Select the 10-K filed February 23, 2011.

   a. Compute the times interest earned ratio for the fiscal year ended January 1, 2011.

   b. Compute the debt ratio for the year ended January 1, 2011.

   c. Compute the operating cash flow/total debt for the year ended January 1, 2011.

   d. Comment on the above ratios.

(continued)

(To The Net CONTINUED)

4. Go to the SEC site (www.sec.gov). Under "Filings & Forms (Edgar)," click on "Search for Company Filings." Click on "Company or fund, etc." Under Company Name, enter "Amgen Inc." (or under Ticker Symbol, enter "AMGN"). Select the 10-K filed February 25, 2011.

   a. Compute the times interest earned ratio for the years ended December 31, 2010, 2009, and 2008.

   b. Compute the debt ratio for the years ended December 31, 2010, 2009, and 2008.

   c. Compute the operating cash flow for the years ended December 31, 2010, 2009, and 2008.

   d. Comment on the above ratios.

Endnotes

1. *Statement of Financial Accounting Standards No. 5*, "Accounting for Contingencies" (Stamford, CT: Financial Accounting Standards Board, 1975), par. 1.

2. *Statement of Financial Accounting Standards No. 5*, par. 8.

3. *Statement of Financial Accounting Standards No. 5*, par. 17.

4. *Statement of Financial Accounting Standards No. 105*, "Disclosure of Information about Financial Instruments with Off-Balance-Sheet Risk and Financial Instruments with Concentrations of Credit Risk" (Stamford, CT: Financial Accounting Standards Board, 1990), par. 17.

5. *Statement of Financial Accounting Standards No. 105*, par. 18.

6. *Statement of Financial Accounting Standards No. 107*, "Disclosure about Fair Value of Financial Instruments" (Stamford, CT: Financial Accounting Standards Board, 1991), par. 10.

Chapter 8

Profitability

Profitability is the ability of a firm to generate earnings. Analysis of profit is of vital concern to stockholders because they derive revenue in the form of dividends. Further, increased profits can cause a rise in market price, leading to capital gains. Profits are also important to creditors because profits are one source of funds for debt coverage. Management uses profit as a performance measure.

In profitability analysis, absolute figures are less meaningful than earnings measured as a percentage of a number of bases: the productive assets, the owners' and creditors' capital employed, and sales.

Profitability Measures

The income statement contains several figures that might be used in profitability analysis. In general, the primary financial analysis of profit ratios should include only the types of income arising from the normal operations of the business. This excludes the following:

1. Discontinued operations
2. Extraordinary items

Exhibit 4-3 in Chapter 4 illustrates an income statement with these items. Review this section on special income statement items in Chapter 4 before continuing with the discussion of profitability. Equity in earnings of nonconsolidated subsidiaries and the noncontrolling interest share of earnings are also important to the analysis of profitability. Chapter 4 covers these items, and Exhibits 4-5 and 4-9 illustrate the concepts.

Trend analysis should also consider only income arising from the normal operations of the business. An illustration will help justify this reasoning. XYZ Corporation had net income of $100,000 in Year 1 and $150,000 in Year 2. Year 2, however, included an extraordinary gain of $60,000. In reality, XYZ suffered a drop in profit from operating income.

Net Profit Margin

A commonly used profit measure is return on sales, often termed net profit margin. If a company reports that it earned 6% last year, this statistic usually means that its profit was 6% of sales. Calculate **net profit margin** as follows:

$$\text{Net Profit Margin} = \frac{\text{Net Income Before Noncontrolling Interest,}}{\text{Net Sales}}$$

This ratio gives a measure of net income dollars generated by each dollar of sales. Although it is desirable for this ratio to be high, competitive forces within an industry, economic conditions, use of debt financing, and operating characteristics such as high fixed costs will cause the net profit margin to vary between and within industries.

Exhibit 8-1 shows the net profit margin using the 2011 and 2010 figures for Nike. This analysis shows that Nike's net profit margin increased slightly in 2011, but would still be considered high.

EXHIBIT **8-1**	Nike, Inc.	
Net Profit Margin		
Years Ended May 31, 2011 and 2010		
(In millions)	**2011**	**2010**
Net income [A]	$ 2,133.0	$ 1,907.0
Net sales [B]	$20,862.0	$19,014.0
Net profit margin [A ÷ B]	10.22%	10.03%

Source: Nike, Inc. 2010 10-K

Several refinements to the net profit margin ratio can make it more accurate than the ratio computation in this book. Numerator refinements include removing "other income" and "other expense" items from net income. These items do not relate to net sales (denominator). Therefore, they can cause a distortion in the net profit margin.

This book does not adjust the net profit margin ratio for these items because this often requires an advanced understanding of financial statements beyond the level intended. Also, this chapter covers operating income margin, operating asset turnover, and return on operating assets. These ratios provide a look at the firm's operations.

When working the problems in this book, do not remove "other income" or "other expense" when computing the net profit margin unless otherwise instructed by the problem. In other analyses, if you elect to refine a net profit margin computation by removing "other income" or "other expense" items from net income, remove them net of the firm's tax rate. This is a reasonable approximation of the tax effect.

If you do not refine a net profit margin computation for "other income" and "other expense" items, at least observe whether the company has a net "other income" or a net "other expense." A net "other income" distorts the net profit margin on the high side, while a net "other expense" distorts the profit margin on the low side.

The Nike statement can be used to illustrate the removal of items that do not relate to net sales. Exhibit 8-2 shows the net profit margin computed with these items removed for 2011 and 2010. The adjusted computation results in the 2011 net profit margin being decreased by 0.10% and the 2010 net profit margin decrease by 0.17%. Both of these decreases are likely to be considered immaterial.

Total Asset Turnover

Total asset turnover measures the activity of the assets and the ability of the firm to generate sales through use of the assets. Compute **total asset turnover** as follows:

$$\text{Total Asset Turnover} = \frac{\text{Net Sales}}{\text{Average Total Assets}}$$

EXHIBIT **8-2**	Nike, Inc.

Net Profit Margin (Revised Computation)

Years Ended May 31, 2011 and 2010

(In millions)	2011	2010
Net income	$ 2,133.0	$ 1,907.0
Tax rate: Effective Tax rate (Note 9)	25.0%	24.2%
Items not related to net sales:		
Interest expense (income), net	4.0	6.0
Other (income) expense, net	(33.0)	(49.0)
Net (income) expense not related to net sales	29.0	(43.0)
Net (income) expense not related to net sales × (1 − Tax rate)	(21.8)	(32.6)
Net income minus net of tax items not related to net sales [C]	2,111.2	1,874.4
Net sales [D]	20,862.0	19,014.0
Adjusted net profit margin [C ÷ D]	10.12%	9.86%

Source: Nike, Inc. 2010 10-K

EXHIBIT **8-3**	Nike, Inc.

Total Asset Turnover

Years Ended May 31, 2011 and 2010

(In millions)	2011	2010
Net sales [A]	$20,862.0	$19,014.0
Average total assets:		
Beginning of year	$14,419.0	$13,249.6
End of year	14,998.0	14,419.0
Total	$29,417.0	$27,668.6
Average [B]	$14,708.5	$13,834.3
Total asset turnover [A ÷ B]	1.42 times	1.37 times

Source: Nike, Inc. 2010 10-K

Exhibit 8-3 shows total asset turnover for Nike for 2011 and 2010. The total asset turnover increased from 1.37 to 1.42. This increase would be considered to be moderate.

The total asset turnover computation has refinements that relate to assets (denominator) but do not relate to net sales (numerator). Examples would be the exclusion of investments and construction in progress. This book does not make these refinements. This chapter covers operating income margin, operating asset turnover, and return on operating assets.

If the refinements are not made, observe the investment account, Construction in Progress, and other assets that do not relate to net sales. The presence of these accounts distorts the total asset turnover on the low side. (Actual turnover is better than the computation indicates.)

Return on Assets

Return on assets measures the firm's ability to utilize its assets to create profits by comparing profits with the assets that generate the profits. Compute the **return on assets** as follows:

$$\text{Return on Assets} = \frac{\text{Net Income Before Noncontrolling Interest and Nonrecurring Items}}{\text{Average Total Assets}}$$

Exhibit 8-4 shows the 2011 and 2010 return on assets for Nike. The return on total assets for Nike increased moderately in 2011.

EXHIBIT **8-4**	Nike, Inc.	

Return on Assets

Years Ended May 31, 2011 and 2010		
(In millions)	**2011**	**2010**
Net income [A]	$ 2,133.0	$ 1,907.0
Average total assets [B]	$14,708.5	$13,834.3
Return on assets [A ÷ B]	14.50%	13.78%

Source: Nike, Inc. 2010 10-K

Theoretically, the best average would be based on month-end figures, which are not available to the outside user. Computing an average based on beginning and ending figures provides a rough approximation that does not consider the timing of interim changes in assets. Such changes might be related to seasonal factors.

However, even a simple average based on beginning and ending amounts requires two figures. Ratios for two years require three years of balance sheet data. Since an annual report only contains two balance sheets, obtaining the data for averages may be a problem. If so, ending balance sheet figures may be used consistently instead of averages for ratio analysis. Similar comments could be made about other ratios that utilize balance sheet figures.

DuPont Return on Assets

Net profit margin, total asset turnover, and return on assets are usually reviewed together because of the direct influence that the net profit margin and the total asset turnover have on return on assets. This book reviews these ratios together; when reviewed together, they are collectively termed the **DuPont return on assets**.

The rate of return on assets can be broken down into two component ratios: the net profit margin and the total asset turnover. These ratios allow for improved analysis of changes in the return on assets percentage. E. I. DuPont de Nemours and Company developed this method of separating the rate of return ratio into its component parts. Compute the DuPont return on assets as follows:

$$\frac{\text{Net Income Before Noncontrolling Interest and Nonrecurring Items}}{\text{Average Total Assets}} = \frac{\text{Net Income Before Noncontrolling Interest and Nonrecurring Items}}{\text{Net Sales}} \times \frac{\text{Net Sales}}{\text{Average Total Assets}}$$

Exhibit 8-5 shows the DuPont return on assets for Nike for 2011 and 2010. Separating the ratio into the two elements allows for discussion of the causes for the increase in the percentage of return on assets. This exhibit indicates that Nike's return on assets increased both because of an increase in net profit margin and an increase in total asset turnover.

EXHIBIT **8-5**	Nike, Inc.	

DuPont Return on Assets

Years Ended May 31, 2011 and 2010					
	Return on Assets*	=	**Net Profit Margin**	×	**Total Asset Turnover**
2011	14.50%	=	10.22%	×	1.42 times
2010	13.78%	=	10.03%	×	1.37 times

*There are some minor differences due to rounding.
Source: Nike, Inc. 2010 10-K

Interpretation Through DuPont Analysis

The following examples help to illustrate the use of this analysis:

Example 1

	Return on Assets	=	Net Profit Margin	×	Total Asset Turnover
Year 1	10%	=	5%	×	2.0
Year 2	10%	=	4%	×	2.5

Example 1 shows how a more efficient use of assets can offset rising costs such as labor or materials.

Example 2

	Return on Assets	=	Net Profit Margin	×	Total Asset Turnover
Firm A					
Year 1	10%	=	4.0%	×	2.5
Year 2	8%	=	4.0%	×	2.0
Firm B					
Year 1	10%	=	4.0%	×	2.5
Year 2	8%	=	3.2%	×	2.5

Example 2 shows how a trend in return on assets can be better explained through the breakdown into two ratios. The two firms have identical returns on assets. Further analysis shows that Firm A suffers from a slowdown in asset turnover. It is generating fewer sales for the assets invested. Firm B suffers from a reduction in the net profit margin. It is generating less profit per dollar of sales.

Variation in Computation of DuPont Ratios Considering Only Operating Accounts

It is often argued that only operating assets should be considered in the return on asset calculation. Operating assets exclude construction in progress, long-term investments, intangibles, and the other assets category from total assets. Similarly, operating income—the profit generated by manufacturing, merchandising, or service functions—that equals net sales less the cost of sales and operating expenses should also be used instead of net income.

The DuPont analysis, considering only operating accounts, requires a computation of operating income and operating assets. Exhibit 8-6 shows the computations of operating income and operating assets for Nike. This includes operating income for 2011 and 2010 and operating assets for 2011, 2010, and 2009.

The operating ratios may give significantly different results from net earnings ratios if a firm has large amounts of nonoperating assets. For example, if a firm has heavy investments in unconsolidated subsidiaries, and if these subsidiaries pay large dividends, then other income may be a large portion of net earnings. The profit picture may not be as good if these earnings from other sources are eliminated by analyzing operating ratios. Since earnings from investments are not derived from the primary business, the lower profit figures that represent normal earnings will typically be more meaningful.

Operating Income Margin

The operating income margin includes only operating income in the numerator. Compute the operating income margin as follows:

$$\text{Operating Income Margin} = \frac{\text{Operating Income}}{\text{Net Sales}}$$

Exhibit 8-7 indicates the operating income margin for Nike in 2011 and 2010. It shows a moderate increase in 2011 in the operating income margin percentage.

EXHIBIT **8-6**	Nike, Inc.

Operating Income and Operating Assets

Years Ended May 31, 2011 and 2010

(In millions)	2011	2010
Operating income:		
Net sales [A]	$20,862.0	$19,014.0
Operating expenses:		
Cost of products sold	$11,354.0	$10,214.0
Selling, general, and administrative	6,693.0	6,326.0
Total operating expenses [B]	$18,047.0	$16,540.0
Operating income [A − B]	$ 2,815.0	$ 2,474.0

	2011	2010	2009
Operating assets:			
Total assets [A]	$14,998.0	$14,419.0	$13,249.6
Less: Construction in progress, identifiable intangible assets, net, goodwill, deferred income taxes and other assets [B]	1,713.0	1,705.0	1,721.7
Operating assets [A − B]	$13,285.0	$12,714.0	$11,527.9

Source: Nike, Inc. 2010 10-K

EXHIBIT **8-7**	Nike, Inc.

Operating Income Margin

Years Ended May 31, 2011 and 2010

(In millions)	2011	2010
Operating income [A]	$ 2,815.0	$ 2,474.0
Net sales [B]	$20,862.0	$19,014.0
Operating income margin [A ÷ B]	13.49%	13.01%

Source: Nike, Inc. 2010 10-K

Operating Asset Turnover

This ratio measures the ability of operating assets to generate sales dollars. Compute operating asset turnover as follows:

$$\text{Operating Asset Turnover} = \frac{\text{Net Sales}}{\text{Average Operating Assets}}$$

Exhibit 8-8 shows the operating asset turnover for Nike in 2011 and 2010. It indicates a moderate increase from 2010 to 2011. This moderate increase is similar to the moderate increase in total asset turnover.

Return on Operating Assets

Adjusting for nonoperating items results in the following formula for **return on operating assets**:

$$\text{Return on Operating Assets} = \frac{\text{Operating Income}}{\text{Average Operating Assets}}$$

EXHIBIT **8-8**	Nike, Inc.	

Operating Asset Turnover

Years Ended May 31, 2011 and 2010

(In millions)	2011	2010
Net sales [A]	$20,862.0	$19,014.0
Average operating assets:		
Beginning of year	$12,714.0	$11,527.9
End of year	13,285.0	12,714.0
Total [B]	$25,999.0	$24,241.9
Average [B ÷ 2] = [C]	$12,999.5	$12,121.0
Operating asset turnover [A ÷ C]	1.60 times per year	1.57 times per year

Source: Nike, Inc. 2010 10-K

Exhibit 8-9 shows the return on operating assets for Nike for 2011 and 2010. It indicates a moderate increase in the return on operating assets from 2010 to 2011.

The return on operating assets can be viewed in terms of the DuPont analysis that follows:

DuPont Return on Operating Assets = Operating Income Margin × Operating Asset Turnover

EXHIBIT **8-9**	Nike, Inc.	

Return on Operating Assets

Years Ended May 31, 2011 and 2010

(In millions)	2011	2010
Operating income [A]	$ 2,815.0	$ 2,474.0
Average operating assets [B]	$12,999.5	$12,121.0
Return on operating assets [A ÷ B]	21.65%	20.41%

Source: Nike, Inc. 2010 10-K

Exhibit 8-10 indicates the DuPont return on operating assets for Nike for 2011 and 2010. This figure supports the conclusion that a minor increase in operating income margin and a moderate increase in operating asset turnover resulted in a moderate increase in return on operating assets.

EXHIBIT **8-10**	Nike, Inc.	

DuPont Analysis with Operating Accounts

Years Ended May 31, 2011 and 2010

	Return on Operating Assets*	=	Operating Income Margin	×	Operating Asset Turnover
2011	21.65%	=	13.49%	×	1.60
2010	20.41%	=	13.01%	×	1.57

*There are some differences due to rounding.
Source: Nike, Inc. 2010 10-K

Sales to Fixed Assets

This ratio measures the firm's ability to make productive use of its property, plant, and equipment by generating sales dollars. Since construction in progress does not contribute to current sales, it should be excluded from net fixed assets. This ratio may not be meaningful because of old fixed assets or a labor-intensive industry. In these cases, the ratio is substantially higher because of the low fixed asset base. Compute the sales to fixed assets as follows:

$$\text{Sales to Fixed Assets} = \frac{\text{Net Sales}}{\text{Average Net Fixed Assets (Exclude Construction in Progress)}}$$

Exhibit 8-11 shows the sales to fixed assets for Nike for 2011 and 2010. It increased moderately between 2010 and 2011. Sales increases more than kept up with net fixed assets increases.

EXHIBIT **8-11**	Nike, Inc.	
Sales to Fixed Assets (Exclude Construction in Progress)		
Years Ended May 31, 2011 and 2010		
(In millions)	**2011**	**2010**
Net sales [A]	$20,862.0	$19,014.0
Net fixed assets: (exclude Construction in Progress)		
Beginning of year	$ 1,755.0	$ 1,793.9
End of year	1,988.0	1,755.0
Total [B]	$ 3,743.0	$ 3,548.9
Average [B ÷ 2] = [C]	$ 1,871.5	$ 1,774.5
Sales to fixed assets [A ÷ C]	11.15 times per year	10.72 times per year
Source: Nike, Inc. 2010 10-K		

Return on Investment (ROI)

The **return on investment (ROI)** applies to ratios measuring the income earned on the invested capital. These types of measures are widely used to evaluate enterprise performance. Since return on investment is a type of return on capital, this ratio measures the ability of the firm to reward those who provide long-term funds and to attract providers of future funds. Compute the return on investment as follows:

$$\text{Return on Investment} = \frac{\begin{array}{c}\text{Net Income Before Noncontrolling Interest and Nonrecurring Items} \\ + \ [(\text{Interest Expense}) \times (1 - \text{Tax Rate})]\end{array}}{\text{Average (Long-Term Liabilities} + \text{Equity)}}$$

This ratio evaluates the earnings performance of the firm without regard to the way the investment is financed. It measures the earnings on investment and indicates how well the firm utilizes its asset base. Exhibit 8-12 shows the return on investment for Nike for 2011 and 2010. This ratio increased moderately between 2010 and 2011.

Return on Total Equity

The **return on total equity** measures the return to both common and preferred stockholders. Compute the return on total equity as follows:

$$\text{Return on Total Equity} = \frac{\begin{array}{c}\text{Net Income Before Nonrecurring Items} - \\ \text{Dividends on Redeemable Preferred Stock}\end{array}}{\text{Average Total Equity}}$$

Preferred stock subject to mandatory redemption is termed redeemable preferred stock. The SEC requires that redeemable preferred stock be categorized separately from other equity securities because the shares must be redeemed in a manner similar to the repayment of debt. Most companies do not have redeemable preferred stock. For those firms that do, the redeemable preferred stock is excluded from total equity and considered part of debt.

EXHIBIT **8-12**	Nike, Inc.

Return on Investment

Years Ended May 31, 2011 and 2010

(In millions)	2011	2010
Interest expense [A]*	$ 34.0	$ 36.0
Net income	$ 2,133.0	$ 1,907.0
Tax rate (see note 9 in 10-K)	25.0%	24.2%
1 − Tax rate [B]	75.0%	75.8%
(Interest expense*) × (1 − Tax rate) [A × B]	$ 25.5	$ 27.3
Net income + [(Interest expense*) × (1 − Tax rate)] [C]	$ 2,158.5	$ 1,934.3
Long-term liabilities and shareholders' equity		
Beginning of year:		
Long-term liabilities	$ 1,301.0	$ 1,279.2
Total shareholders' equity	9,754.0	8,693.1
End of year:		
Long-term liabilities	1,197.0	1,301.0
Total shareholders' equity	9,843.0	9,754.0
Total [D]	$22,095.0	$21,027.3
Average [D ÷ 2] = [E]	$11,047.5	$10,513.7
Return on investment [C ÷ E]	19.54%	18.40%

*Interest expense includes both expensed and capitalized.
"Per note 3 property, plant, and equipment "capitalized interest" was not material for the years ended May 31, 2011, 2010, and 2009." (10-K)
Source: Nike, Inc. 2010 10-K

Similarly, the dividends must be deducted from income. They have not been deducted on the income statement, despite the similarity to debt and interest, because they are still dividends and payable only if declared.

Exhibit 8-13 shows the return on total equity for Nike for 2011 and 2010. It increased moderately from 20.68% in 2010 to 21.77% in 2011.

EXHIBIT **8-13**	Nike, Inc.

Return on Total Equity

Years Ended May 31, 2011 and 2010

(In millions)	2011	2010
Net income	$ 2,133.0	$ 1,907.0
Less: Redeemable preferred dividends	0.0	0.0
Adjusted income [A]	$ 2,133.0	$ 1,907.0
Total equity:		
Beginning of year	$ 9,754.0	$ 8,693.1
End of year	9,843.0	9,754.0
Total equity [B]	$19,597.0	$18,447.1
Average [B ÷ 2] = [C]	$ 9,798.5	$ 9,223.6
Return on total equity [A ÷ C]	21.77%	20.68%

Source: Nike, Inc. 2010 10-K

Return on Common Equity

This ratio measures the return to the common stockholder, the residual owner. Compute the return on common equity as follows:

$$\text{Return on Common Equity} = \frac{\text{Net Income Before Nonrecurring Items} - \text{Preferred Dividends}}{\text{Average Common Equity}}$$

The net income appears on the income statement. The preferred dividends appear most commonly on the statement of stockholders' equity. Common equity includes common capital stock and retained earnings less common treasury stock. This amount equals total equity minus the preferred capital and any noncontrolling interest included in the equity section.

Exhibit 8-14 shows the return on common equity for Nike for 2011 and 2010. Nike's return on common equity is the same as its return on total equity.

EXHIBIT **8-14**	Nike, Inc.	

Return on Common Equity

Years Ended May 31, 2011 and 2010

(In millions)	2011	2010
Net income	$ 2,133.0	$ 1,907.0
Less: Redeemable preferred dividends	0.0	0.0
Adjusted income [A]	$ 2,133.0	$ 1,907.0
Total common equity:		
Beginning of year	$ 9,754.0	$ 8,693.1
End of year	9,843.0	9,754.0
Total [B]	$19,597.0	$18,447.1
Average common equity [B ÷ 2] = [C]	$ 9,798.5	$ 9,223.6
Return on common equity [A ÷ C]	21.77%	20.68%

Source: Nike, Inc. 2010 10-K

The Relationship Between Profitability Ratios

Technically, a ratio with a profit figure in the numerator and some type of "supplier of funds" figure in the denominator is a type of return on investment. Another frequently used measure is a variation of the return on total assets. Compute this return on total assets variation as follows:

$$\text{Return on Total Assets Variation} = \frac{\text{Net Income} + \text{Interest Expense}}{\text{Average Total Assets}}$$

This ratio includes the return to all suppliers of funds, both long- and short-term, by both creditors and investors. It differs from the return on assets ratio previously discussed because it adds back the interest. It differs from the return on investment in that it does not adjust interest for the income tax effect, it includes short-term funds, and it uses the average investment. It will not be discussed or utilized further here because it does not lend itself to DuPont analysis.

Rates of return have been calculated on a variety of bases. The interrelationship between these ratios is of importance in understanding the return to the suppliers of funds. Exhibit 8-15 displays a comparison of profitability measures for Nike.

The return on assets measures the return to all providers of funds since total assets equal total liabilities and equity. This ratio will usually be the lowest since it includes all of the assets. The return on investment measures the return to long-term suppliers of funds, and it is usually higher than the return on assets because of the relatively low amount paid for short-term funds. This is especially true of accounts payable.

The rate of return on total equity will usually be higher than the return on investment because the rate of return on equity measures return only to the shareholders. A profitable use of long-term sources of funds from creditors provides a higher return to shareholders than the return on investment. In other words, the profits made on long-term funds from creditors were greater than the interest paid for use of the funds.

EXHIBIT **8-15**	Nike, Inc.

Comparison of Profitability Measures

Years Ended May 31, 2011 and 2010

	2011	2010
Return on assets	14.50%	13.78%
Return on investment	19.54%	18.40%
Return on total equity	21.77%	20.68%
Return on common equity	21.77%	20.68%

Source: Nike, Inc. 2010 10-K

Common stockholders absorb the greatest degree of risk and, therefore, usually earn the highest return. For the return on common equity to be the highest, the return on funds obtained from preferred stockholders must be more than the funds paid to the preferred stockholders. For Nike the return on total equity and the return on common equity are the same because they do not have preferred equity.

Gross Profit Margin

Gross profit equals the difference between net sales revenue and the cost of goods sold. The cost of goods sold is the beginning inventory plus purchases minus the ending inventory. It is the cost of the product sold during the period. Changes in the cost of goods sold, which represents such a large expense for merchandising and manufacturing firms, can have a substantial impact on the profit for the period. Comparing gross profit with net sales is termed the **gross profit margin**. Compute the gross profit margin as follows:

$$\text{Gross Profit Margin} = \frac{\text{Gross Profit}}{\text{Net Sales}}$$

This ratio should then be compared with industry data or analyzed by trend analysis. Exhibit 8-16 illustrates trend analysis. In this illustration, the gross profit margin has declined substantially over the three-year period. This could be attributable to a number of factors:

1. The cost of buying inventory has increased more rapidly than have selling prices.
2. Selling prices have declined due to competition.
3. The mix of goods has changed to include more products with lower margins.
4. Theft is occurring. If sales are not recorded, the cost of goods sold figure in relation to the sales figure is very high. If inventory is being stolen, the ending inventory will be low and the cost of goods sold will be high.

Gross profit margin analysis helps a number of users. Managers budget gross profit levels into their predictions of profitability. Gross profit margins are also used in cost control. Estimations utilizing gross profit margins can determine inventory levels for interim

EXHIBIT **8-16**	Example Gross Profit Margin

Years Ended May 31, 2011, 2010, and 2009

	2011	2010	2009
Net sales [B]	$5,000,000	$4,500,000	$4,000,000
Less: Cost of goods sold	3,500,000	2,925,000	2,200,000
Gross profit [A]	$1,500,000	$1,575,000	$1,800,000
Gross profit margin [A ÷ B]	30.00%	35.00%	45.00%

statements in the merchandising industries. Gross profit margins can also be used to estimate inventory involved in insured losses. In addition, gross profit measures are used by auditors and the Internal Revenue Service to judge the accuracy of accounting systems.

Gross profit margin analysis requires an income statement in multiple-step format. Otherwise, the gross profit must be computed, which is the case with Nike. Exhibit 8-17 presents Nike's gross profit margin, which decreased slightly in 2011 after increasing moderately in 2010.

EXHIBIT **8-17** Nike, Inc.			
Gross Profit Margin			
Years Ended May 31, 2011, 2010, and 2009			
(In millions)	**2011**	**2010**	**2009**
Net sales [B]	$20,862.0	$19,014.0	$19,176.0
Less: Cost of products sold	11,354.0	10,214.0	10,572.0
Gross profit [A]	$ 9,508.0	$ 8,800.0	$ 8,604.0
Gross profit margin [A ÷ B]	45.58%	46.25%	44.87%

Source: Nike, Inc. 2010 10-K

Trends in Profitability

Exhibit 8-18 shows profitability trends for manufacturing for the period 1975–2010. Operating profit compared with net sales and net income compared with net sales both fluctuated substantially over this period. Net income compared with net sales fluctuated substantially. Notice the material decline in this ratio in 1992 and 2001 and the substantial increase in this ratio for 2002, 2003, 2004, and 2006, followed by a substantial decrease in 2007, and then a material decrease in 2008.

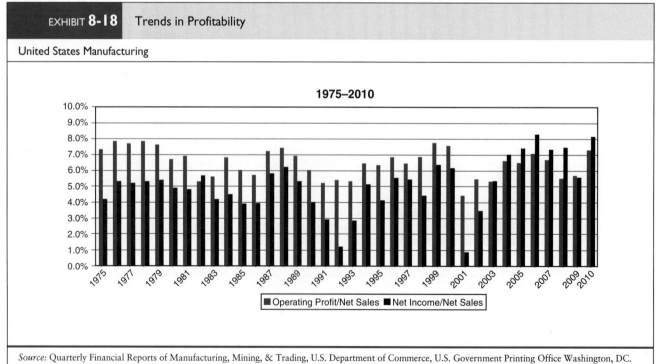

EXHIBIT **8-18** Trends in Profitability

United States Manufacturing

Source: Quarterly Financial Reports of Manufacturing, Mining, & Trading, U.S. Department of Commerce, U.S. Government Printing Office Washington, DC.

Segment Reporting

A public business enterprise reports financial and descriptive information about reportable operating segments. Operating segments are segments about which separate financial information is available that is evaluated by the chief operating decision maker in deciding how to allocate resources and in assessing performance. It requires information about the countries in which the firm earns revenues and holds assets, as well as about major customers.

Descriptive information must be disclosed about the way the operating segments were determined. Disclosure is required for products and services by the operating segments. Disclosure is also required about the differences between the measurements used in reporting segment information and those used in the firm's general-purpose financial information.

Segment data can be analyzed in terms of both trends and ratios. Vertical and horizontal common-size analyses can be used for trends. Examples of ratios would be relating profits to sales or identifiable assets.

Segment trends would be of interest to management and investors. The maximum benefits from this type of analysis come when analyzing a nonintegrated company in terms of product lines, especially with segments of relatively similar size.

Nike reported operating segments and related information in Note 18, which is partially included in Exhibit 8-19. These data should be reviewed, and consideration should be given to using vertical and horizontal analyses and to computing ratios that appear meaningful. This type of review is illustrated in Exhibits 8-20 and 8-21.

Exhibit 8-20 presents some Nike information in vertical common-size analysis. Revenue, earnings before interest and taxes, additions to long-lived assets and property, plant and equipment, net are included.

Based on revenue, the North America segment is the dominant segment, followed by Western Europe, and then emerging markets. There was a material increase in emerging markets. Western Europe, Central & Eastern Europe and Japan all had material decreases.

Earnings before interest and taxes changed materially by segment. Material increases were in North America, greater China, and emerging markets. Material decreases were in Western Europe, Central & Eastern Europe, and Japan.

Additions to long-lived assets were dominant in North America, Western Europe, and greater China. Nominal additions were in Central & Eastern Europe and Japan.

Material property, plant and equipment, net were in North America, Western Europe, and Japan. Immaterial property, plant and equipment, net were in Central & Eastern Europe, and emerging markets.

A review of Exhibit 8-21 (segment information – ratio analysis) indicates that the most profitable segment (based on earnings before interest and taxes/revenue) was greater in China and that profits had increased in this segment.

Revenues by Major Product Lines

Exhibit 8-22 shows revenues by major product lines presented by Nike. Revenues by Major Product Lines—Horizontal Common-Size Analysis is presented in Exhibit 8-23. Footwear is the dominate segment representing over half the revenues. The fastest growth was experienced in the other segment.

Gains and Losses from Prior Period Adjustments

Prior period adjustments result from certain changes in accounting principles, the realization of income tax benefits of preacquisition operating loss carryforwards of purchased subsidiaries, a change in accounting entity, and corrections of errors in prior periods. Prior period adjustments are charged to retained earnings.

EXHIBIT **8-19**	NIKE, INC.

Segment Information

Note 18 Operating Segments and Related Information (In part)

	Year Ended May 31,		
	2011	2010	2009
	(In millions)		
Revenue			
North America	$ 7,578	$ 6,696	$ 6,778
Western Europe	3,810	3,892	4,139
Central & Eastern Europe	1,031	993	1,247
Greater China	2,060	1,742	1,743
Japan	766	882	926
Emerging Markets	2,736	2,199	1,828
Global Brand Divisions	123	105	96
Total NIKE Brand	18,104	16,509	16,757
Other Businesses	2,747	2,530	2,419
Corporate	11	(25)	—
Total NIKE Consolidated Revenues	$20,862	$19,014	$19,176
Earnings Before Interest and Taxes			
North America	$ 1,750	$ 1,538	$ 1,429
Western Europe	721	856	939
Central & Eastern Europe	233	253	394
Greater China	777	637	575
Japan	114	180	205
Emerging Markets	688	521	364
Global Brand Divisions	(998)	(867)	(811)
Total NIKE Brand	$ 3,285	$ 3,118	$ 3,095
Additions to Long-lived Assets			
North America	$ 79	$ 45	$ 99
Western Europe	75	59	70
Central & Eastern Europe	5	4	7
Greater China	43	80	59
Japan	9	12	10
Emerging Markets	21	11	12
Global Brand Divisions	44	30	37
Total NIKE Brand	276	241	294
Other Businesses	38	52	90
Corporate	118	42	72
Total Additions to Long-lived Assets	$ 432	$ 335	$ 456
Property, Plant and Equipment, net			
North America	$ 330	$ 325	
Western Europe	338	282	
Central & Eastern Europe	13	11	
Greater China	179	146	
Japan	360	333	
Emerging Markets	58	48	
Global Brand Divisions	116	99	
Total NIKE Brand	1,394	1,244	
Other Businesses	164	167	
Corporate	557	521	
Total Property, Plant and Equipment, net	$ 2,115	$ 1,932	

Source: Nike, Inc. 2010 10-K

EXHIBIT **8-20**	NIKE, INC.

Segment Information (in part)

Vertical Common-Size Analysis*

	Year Ended May 31,		
	2011	**2010**	**2009**
Revenue			
North America	36.3	35.2%	35.3%
Western Europe	18.3	20.5	21.6
Central & Eastern Europe	4.9	5.2	6.5
Greater China	9.9	9.2	9.1
Japan	3.7	4.6	4.8
Emerging Markets	13.1	11.6	9.5
Global Brand Divisions	.6	.6	.5
Total NIKE Brand	86.8	86.8	87.4
Other Businesses	13.2	13.3	12.6
Corporate	.0	.1	.0
Total NIKE Consolidated Revenues	100.0%	100.0%	100.0%
Earnings Before Interest and Taxes			
North America	53.3	49.3	46.2
Western Europe	21.9	27.5	30.3
Central & Eastern Europe	7.1	8.1	12.7
Greater China	23.7	20.4	18.6
Japan	3.5	5.8	6.6
Emerging Markets	20.9	16.7	11.8
Global Brand Divisions	(30.4)	(27.8)	(26.2)
Total NIKE Brand	100.0%	100.0%	100.0%
Additions to Long-lived Assets			
North America	18.3	13.4	21.7
Western Europe	17.4	17.6	15.4
Central & Eastern Europe	1.2	1.2	1.5
Greater China	10.0	23.9	12.9
Japan	2.1	3.6	2.2
Emerging Markets	4.9	3.3	2.6
Global Brand Divisions	10.2	10.0	8.1
Total NIKE Brand	63.9	71.9	64.5
Other Businesses	8.8	15.5	19.7
Corporate	27.3	12.5	15.8
Total Additions to Long-lived Assets	100.0%	100.0%	100.0%
Property, Plant and Equipment, net			
North America	15.6	16.8	
Western Europe	16.0	14.6	
Central & Eastern Europe	.6	.6	
Greater China	8.5	7.6	
Japan	17.0	17.2	
Emerging Markets	2.7	2.5	
Global Brand Divisions	5.5	5.1	
Total NIKE Brand	65.9	64.4	
Other Businesses	7.8	8.6	
Corporate	26.3	27.0	
Total Property, Plant and Equipment, net	100.0%	100.0%	

*There are some rounding differences.
Source: Nike, Inc. 2010 10-K

EXHIBIT **8-21**	NIKE, INC.

Segment Information – Ratio Analysis

	Year Ended May 31,		
	2011	2010	2009
Earnings Before Interest and Taxes/Revenue			
North America	23.1	23.0	21.1
Western Europe	18.9	22.0	22.7
Central & Eastern Europe	22.6	25.5	31.6
Greater China	37.7	36.6	33.0
Japan	14.9	20.4	22.1
Emerging Markets	25.1	23.7	19.9

Note: Did not compute Global Brand Divisions or Total NIKE Brand.
Source: Nike, Inc. 2010 10-K

EXHIBIT **8-22**	Nike, Inc.

Segment Information
Revenues by Major Product Lines (10-K)

	Year Ended May 31,		
(In millions)	2011	2010	2009
Footwear	$11,493	$10,332	$10,307
Apparel	5,475	5,037	5,245
Equipment	1,013	1,035	1,110
Other[1]	2,881	2,610	2,514
Total revenues	$20,862	$19,014	$19,176

[1]Other revenues to external customers primarily include external sales by Cole Haan, Converse, Hurley, Nike Golf, and
  Umbro.
Source: Nike, Inc. 2010 10-K

EXHIBIT **8-23**	Nike, Inc.

Segment Information
Revenues by Major Product Lines (10-K)
Horizontal Common-Size Analysis

	Year Ended May 31,		
	2011	2010	2009
Footwear	111.5%	100.2%	100.0%
Apparel	104.4	96.0	100.0
Equipment	91.3	93.2	100.0
Other	114.6	103.8	100.0
Total revenues	108.8	99.2	100.0

Source: Nike, Inc. 2010 10-K

These items are a type of gain or loss, but they never go through the income statement. They are not recognized on the income statement. If material, they should be considered in analysis. Current period ratios would not be revised because these items relate to prior periods.

A review of the retained earnings account presented in the statement of stockholders' equity will reveal prior period adjustments.

Exhibit 8-24 presents a prior period adjustment of the Standard Register Company.

| EXHIBIT **8-24** | The Standard Register Company* |

Prior Period Adjustment

The Standard Register Company included this information in its financial statements for the year ended December 28, 2008.

Note: In addition to the note, the Consolidated Statements of Shareholders' Equity disclosed the cumulative effect of restatement in prior years.

THE STANDARD REGISTER COMPANY
NOTES TO CONSOLIDATED FINANCIAL STATEMENTS (In Part)
(Dollars in thousands, except per share amounts)

NOTE 1—Summary of Significant Accounting Policies (In Part)

Prior Period Adjustment

During 2008, we discovered an error on our 2004 income tax return related to the classification of gains reported on the sale of a business unit. The error in classification caused us not to utilize capital loss carryforwards available on our 2004 tax return. The capital loss carryforward available to the Company was included in our deferred tax assets with a full valuation allowance in 2004. As a result of this error, we understated our deferred tax assets and income tax benefit by $1,420 in 2004. An amended return was filed in 2008.

For financial reporting purposes, this error has been accounted for as a prior period adjustment in accordance with Statement of Financial Accounting Standard (SFAS) No. 154, "Accounting Changes and Error Corrections." We do not believe that any of our prior period financial statements were materially misstated as a result of not adjusting our deferred tax assets as described above. We have restated the December 30, 2007, balance sheet and the Statement of Shareholders' Equity for 2006 and 2007 to appropriately reflect the deferred tax asset. The effect of the restatement on periods prior to 2006 has been recorded as an adjustment of $1,420 to beginning retained earnings.

*"Standard Register is a leading provider of custom-printed documents and related services in the United States." 10-K
Source: The Standard Register Company 2010 10-K

Comprehensive Income

Chapter 4 explained that the categories within accumulated other income are: (1) foreign currency translation adjustments, (2) unrealized holding gains and losses on available-for-sale marketable securities, (3) changes to stockholders' equity resulting from additional minimum pension liability adjustments, and (4) unrealized gains and losses from derivative instruments.

There has been considerable flexibility in reporting comprehensive income. One format used a single income statement to report net income and comprehensive income. A second format reported comprehensive income in a separate statement of financial activity. A third format reported comprehensive income within the statement of changes in shareholders' equity.

Most companies selected the third format reporting comprehensive income within the statement of changes in shareholders' equity. Nike selected this third format for its May 31, 2011 financial statements.

Nike reported four items in comprehensive income in its 2011 financial report. These items were as follows:

	(in millions)
Other comprehensive income (Notes 14 and 17):	
Foreign currency translation and other (net of tax expense of $121)	263
Net loss on cash flow hedges (net of tax benefit of $66)	(242)
Net loss on net investment hedges (net of tax benefit of $28)	(57)
Reclassification to net income of previously deferred net gains related to hedge derivatives (net of tax expense of $24)	(84)
Total comprehensive income	(120)

Note that comprehensive income includes items not in net income. Our traditional profitability analysis includes items that related to net income. This excludes other comprehensive income items. Ratios in which you may want to consider including comprehensive income are: (1) return on assets, (2) return on investment, (3) return on total equity, and (4) return on common equity. For some firms, these ratios will change materially.

For Nike, the change to these ratios for 2011 would not be material as net income was $2,133,000,000 and net comprehensive loss was $120,000,000.

In Chapter 4, it was indicated that the FASB and IASB entered into a joint project to improve the presentation of comprehensive income in a manner that is as convergent as possible. At that time, the IFRS only provided for comprehensive income to be presented either in a single statement or in two consecutive statements.

The result of this joint project was that the FASB in 2011 issued an amendment of the FASB Accounting Standards Codification which ruled out the option of reporting comprehensive income within the statement of changes in shareholders' equity.

Thus with the effective fiscal year after December 15, 2011, only the following options are available:

1. A single income statement reporting net income and comprehensive income, or
2. Report comprehensive income in a separate statement immediately following the statement of income

This new standard is effective for interim periods. The coverage of comprehensive income in analysis is in Chapter 12.

Pro-Forma Financial Information

Pro-forma financial information is a hypothetical or projected amount. Synonymous with "what if" analysis, pro-forma data indicate what would have happened under specified circumstances.

Used properly, pro-forma financial information makes a positive contribution to financial reporting—for example, what would be the net income if additional shares were issued?

Used improperly, pro-forma financial information can be a negative contribution to financial reporting. For example, releasing pro-forma earnings can be misleading if not explained.

It became popular in the United States for companies to release pro-forma earnings at approximately the time that financial results were released that used GAAP. Typically, how the company arrived at the pro-forma earnings was not adequately disclosed. It was inferred that this was the better number for investors to follow. Many investors did make decisions based on the pro-forma earnings as opposed to the GAAP earnings.

The Sarbanes-Oxley Act required the Commission (SEC) to adopt rules requiring that if a company publicly discloses non-GAAP financial measures or includes them in a Commission filing:

1. The company must reconcile those non-GAAP financial measures to a company's financial condition and results of operations under GAAP.
2. Any public disclosure of a non-GAAP financial measure may not contain an untrue statement of a material fact or omit to state a material fact necessary in order to make the non-GAAP financial measure, in light of circumstances under which it is presented, not misleading.[1]

A June 2004 article in *Accounting Horizons* compared S&P Companies' own reported earnings data (pro forma) with U.S. GAAP net income, 1990–2003. In each year, the pro-forma earnings were higher. In some years, the pro-forma earnings were materially more than the U.S. GAAP net income.[2]

The Wall Street Journal made the following comment in a September 2003 article:

> If you thought the Sarbanes-Oxley Act, that sweeping package of overhauls adopted in response to U.S. corporate scandals, got rid of the "pro forma"-like tactics by which companies were able to make their earnings look better, you thought wrong.[3]

One example in the article was "Sanmina-SCI Corp., which strips restructuring costs out of its GAAP earnings to help reach its pro-forma earnings—and has done so every quarter for the past 2 1/2 years. 'Restructuring' costs might seem to imply a one-time event, but Sanmina has stripped out restructuring costs in each of its last 10 quarters, back to 2001."[4]

Source: The Wall Street Journal

Interim Reports

Interim reports are an additional source of information on profitability. These are reports that cover fiscal periods of less than one year. The SEC requires that limited financial data be provided on Form 10-Q. The SEC also requires that these companies disclose certain quarterly information in notes to the annual report.

The same reporting principles used for annual reports should be employed for interim reports, with the intent that the interim reporting be an integral part of the annual report. For interim financial reports, timeliness of data offsets lack of detail. Some data included are:

1. Income statement amounts:
   a. Sales or gross revenues
   b. Provision for income taxes
   c. Extraordinary items and tax effect
   d. Cumulative effect of an accounting change
   e. Net income
2. Earnings per share
3. Seasonal information
4. Significant changes in income tax provision or estimate
5. Disposal of segments of business and unusual items material to the period
6. Contingent items
7. Changes in accounting principles or estimates
8. Significant changes in financial position

Interim reports contain more estimates in the financial data than in the annual reports. Interim reports are also unaudited. For these reasons, they are less reliable than annual reports.

Income tax expense is an example of a figure that can require considerable judgment and estimation for the interim period. The objective with the interim income tax expense is to use an annual effective tax rate, which may require considerable estimation. Some reasons for this are foreign tax credits and the tax effect of losses in an interim period.

Interim statements must disclose the seasonal nature of the firm's activities. It is also recommended that firms that are seasonal in nature supplement their interim report by including information for 12-month periods ended at the interim date for the current and preceding years.

Interim statements can help the analyst determine trends and identify trouble areas before the year-end report is available. The information obtained (such as a lower profit margin) may indicate that trouble is brewing.

Nike included a section called "Selected Quarterly Financial Data" in its annual reports. It indicates that it's fourth fiscal quarter had the highest volume and was most profitable. This would be the months of March, April, and May. Revenue was up in each quarter compared to the prior year, especially in the 4th quarter. Profits were up also in each quarter compared to the prior year, especially in the 2nd quarter.

Summary

Profitability is the ability of a firm to generate earnings. It is measured relative to a number of bases, such as assets, sales, and investment.

The ratios related to profitability covered in this chapter follow:

$$\text{Net Profit Margin} = \frac{\text{Net Income Before Noncontrolling Interest, Equity Income and Nonrecurring Items}}{\text{Net Sales}} \quad \uparrow \quad \%$$

efficiency

$$\text{Total Asset Turnover} = \frac{\text{Net Sales}}{\text{Average Total Assets}} \quad \uparrow \quad \text{times}$$

$$\text{Return on Assets} = \frac{\text{Net Income Before Noncontrolling Interest of Earnings and Nonrecurring Items}}{\text{Average Total Assets}} \quad \uparrow \quad \%$$

$$\frac{\text{Net Income Before Noncontrolling Interest and Nonrecurring Items}}{\text{Average Total Assets}} = \frac{\text{Net Income Before Noncontrolling Interest and Nonrecurring Items}}{\text{Net Sales}} \times \frac{\text{Net Sales}}{\text{Average Total Assets}}$$

$$\text{Operating Income Margin} = \frac{\text{Operating Income}}{\text{Net Sales}}$$

$$\text{Operating Asset Turnover} = \frac{\text{Net Sales}}{\text{Average Operating Assets}}$$

$$\text{Return on Operating Assets} = \frac{\text{Operating Income}}{\text{Average Operating Assets}}$$

$$\text{DuPont Return on Operating Assets} = \text{Operating Income Margin} \times \text{Operating Asset Turnover}$$

$$\text{Sales to Fixed Assets} = \frac{\text{Net Sales}}{\text{Average Net Fixed Assets (Exclude Construction in Progress)}} \quad \uparrow \quad \text{times}$$

$$\text{Return on Investment} = \frac{\text{Net Income Before Noncontrolling Interest and Nonrecurring Items} + [(\text{Interest Expense}) \times (1 - \text{Tax Rate})]}{\text{Average (Long-Term Liabilities} + \text{Equity})}$$

$$\text{Return on Total Equity} = \frac{\text{Net Income Before Nonrecurring Items} - \text{Dividends on Redeemable Preferred Stock}}{\text{Average Total Equity}} \quad \uparrow \quad \%$$

$$\text{Return on Common Equity} = \frac{\text{Net Income Before Nonrecurring Items} - \text{Preferred Dividends}}{\text{Average Common Equity}} \quad \uparrow \quad \%$$

$$\text{Gross Profit Margin} = \frac{\text{Gross Profit}}{\text{Net Sales}}$$

Questions

Q 8-1 Profits might be compared with sales, assets, or stockholders' equity. Why might all three bases be used? Will trends in these ratios always move in the same direction?

Q 8-2 What is the advantage of segregating extraordinary items in the income statement?

Q 8-3 If profits as a percent of sales decline, what can be said about expenses?

Q 8-4 Would you expect the profit margin in a quality jewelry store to differ from that of a grocery store? Comment.

Q 8-5 The ratio return on assets has net income in the numerator and total assets in the denominator. Explain how each part of the ratio could cause return on assets to fall.

Q 8-6 What is the DuPont analysis, and how does it aid in financial analysis?

Q 8-7 How does operating income differ from net income? How do operating assets differ from total assets? What is the advantage in removing nonoperating items from the DuPont analysis?

Q 8-8 Why are equity earnings usually greater than cash flow generated from the investment? How can these equity earnings distort profitability analysis?

Q 8-9 Explain how return on assets could decline, given an increase in net profit margin.

Q 8-10 How is return on investment different from return on total equity? How does return on total equity differ from return on common equity?

Q 8-11 What is return on investment? What are some of the types of measures for return on investment? Why is the following ratio preferred?

$$\frac{\text{Net Income Before Noncontrolling Interest and Nonrecurring Items} + [(\text{Interest Expense}) \times (1 - \text{Tax Rate})]}{\text{Average (Long-Term Debt} + \text{Equity})}$$

Why is the interest multiplied by $(1 - \text{Tax Rate})$?

Q 8-12 G. Herrich Company and Thomas, Inc., are department stores. For the current year, they reported a net income after tax of $400,000 and $600,000, respectively. Is Thomas, Inc., a more profitable company than G. Herrich Company? Discuss.

Q 8-13 Since interim reports are not audited, they are not meaningful. Comment.

Q 8-14 Speculate on why accounting standards do not mandate full financial statements in interim reports.

Q 8-15 Why may comprehensive income fluctuate substantially more than net income?

Q 8-16 Why can pro-forma financial information be misleading?

Problems

P 8-1 Ahl Enterprise lists the following data for 2011 and 2010:

	2011	2010
Net income	$ 52,500	$ 40,000
Net sales	1,050,000	1,000,000
Average total assets	230,000	200,000
Average common equity	170,000	160,000

Required Calculate the net profit margin, return on assets, total asset turnover, and return on common equity for both years. Comment on the results. (For return on assets and total asset turnover, use end-of-year total assets; for return on common equity, use end-of-year common equity.)

P 8-2 Income statement data for Starr Canning Corporation are as follows:

	2011	2010
Sales	$1,400,000	$1,200,000
Cost of goods sold	850,000	730,000
Selling expenses	205,000	240,000
General expenses	140,000	100,000
Income tax expense	82,000	50,000

Required
a. Prepare an income statement in comparative form, stating each item for both years as a percent of sales (vertical common-size analysis).
b. Comment on the findings in (a).

P 8-3 The balance sheet for Schultz Bone Company at December 31, 2011 had the following account balances:

Total current liabilities (non-interest-bearing)	$450,000
Bonds payable, 6% (issued in 1982; due in 2018)	750,000
Preferred stock, 5%, $100 par	300,000
Common stock, $10 par	750,000
Premium on common stock	150,000
Retained earnings	600,000

Income before income tax was $200,000, and income taxes were $80,000 for the current year.

Required Calculate each of the following:

a. Return on assets (using ending assets)
b. Return on total equity (using ending total equity)
c. Return on common equity (using ending common equity)
d. Times interest earned

P 8-4 Revenue and expense data for Vent Molded Plastics and for the plastics industry as a whole follow:

	Vent Molded Plastics	Plastics Industry
Sales	$462,000	100.3%
Sales returns	4,500	0.3
Cost of goods sold	330,000	67.1
Selling expenses	43,000	10.1
General expenses	32,000	7.9
Other income	1,800	0.4
Other expense	7,000	1.3
Income tax	22,000	5.5

Required Convert the dollar figures for Vent Molded Plastics into percentages based on net sales. Compare these with the industry average, and comment on your findings.

P 8-5 Day Ko Incorporated presented the following comparative income statements for 2011 and 2010:

	For the Years Ended	
	2011	2010
Net sales	$1,589,150	$1,294,966
Other income	22,334	20,822
	1,611,484	1,315,788
Costs and expenses:		
Material and manufacturing costs of products sold	651,390	466,250
Research and development	135,314	113,100
General and selling	526,680	446,110
Interest	18,768	11,522
Other	15,570	7,306
	1,347,722	1,044,288
Earnings before income taxes and noncontrolling interest	263,762	271,500
Provision for income taxes	114,502	121,740
Earnings before noncontrolling interest	149,260	149,760
Noncontrolling interest	11,056	12,650
Net earnings	$ 138,204	$ 137,110

Other relevant financial information follows:

	For the Years Ended	
	2011	**2010**
Average common shares issued	29,580	29,480
Total long-term debt	$ 209,128	$ 212,702
Total stockholders' equity (all common)	810,292	720,530
Total assets	1,437,636	1,182,110
Operating assets	1,411,686	1,159,666
Dividends per share	1.96	1.86
Stock price (December 31)	533/4	761/8

Required

a. How did 2011 net sales compare with 2010?
b. How did 2011 net earnings compare with 2010?
c. Calculate the following for 2011 and 2010:

    1. Net profit margin
    2. Return on assets (using ending assets)
    3. Total asset turnover (using ending assets)
    4. DuPont analysis
    5. Operating income margin
    6. Return on operating assets (using ending assets)
    7. Operating asset turnover (using ending assets)
    8. DuPont analysis with operating ratios
    9. Return on investment (using ending liabilities and equity)
    10. Return on equity (using ending common equity)

d. Based on the previous computations, summarize the trend in profitability for this firm.

P 8-6 Dorex, Inc., presented the following comparative income statements for 2011, 2010, and 2009:

	For the Years Ended		
	2011	**2010**	**2009**
Net sales	$1,600,000	$1,300,000	$1,200,000
Other income	22,100	21,500	21,000
	1,622,100	1,321,500	1,221,000
Costs and expenses:			
Material and manufacturing costs of products sold	740,000	624,000	576,000
Research and development	90,000	78,000	71,400
General and selling	600,000	500,500	465,000
Interest	19,000	18,200	17,040
Other	14,000	13,650	13,800
	$1,463,000	$1,234,350	$1,143,240

	For the Years Ended		
	2011	**2010**	**2009**
Earnings before income taxes and noncontrolling interest	$159,100	$87,150	$77,760
Provision for income taxes	62,049	35,731	32,659
Earnings before noncontrolling interest	97,051	51,419	45,101
Noncontrolling interest	10,200	8,500	8,100
Net earnings	86,851	42,919	37,001

(*continued*)

(**P 8-6** CONTINUED)

	For the Years Ended		
	2011	2010	2009
Other relevant financial information:			
Average common shares issued	29,610	29,100	28,800
Average long-term debt	$ 211,100	$ 121,800	$ 214,000
Average stockholders' equity (all common)	811,200	790,100	770,000
Average total assets	1,440,600	1,220,000	1,180,000
Average operating assets	1,390,200	1,160,000	1,090,000

Required

a. Calculate the following for 2011, 2010, and 2009:

 1. Net profit margin
 2. Return on assets
 3. Total asset turnover
 4. DuPont analysis
 5. Operating income margin
 6. Return on operating assets
 7. Operating asset turnover
 8. DuPont analysis with operating ratios
 9. Return on investment
 10. Return on total equity

b. Based on the previous computations, summarize the trend in profitability for this firm.

P 8-7 Selected financial data for Squid Company are as follows:

	2011	2010	2009
Summary of operations:			
Net sales	$1,002,100	$980,500	$900,000
Cost of products sold	520,500	514,762	477,000
Selling, administrative, and general expenses	170,200	167,665	155,700
Nonoperating income	9,192	8,860	6,500
Interest expense	14,620	12,100	11,250
Earnings before income taxes	287,588	277,113	249,550
Provision for income taxes	116,473	113,616	105,560
Net earnings	171,115	163,497	143,990
Financial information:			
Working capital	$ 190,400	$189,000	$180,000
Average property, plant, and equipment	302,500	281,000	173,000
Average total assets	839,000	770,000	765,000
Average long-term debt	120,000	112,000	101,000
Average stockholders' equity	406,000	369,500	342,000

Required

a. Compute the following for 2011, 2010, and 2009:

 1. Net profit margin
 2. Return on assets
 3. Total asset turnover
 4. DuPont analysis
 5. Return on investment
 6. Return on total equity
 7. Sales to fixed assets

b. Discuss your findings in (a).

P 8-8 D. H. Muller Company presented the following income statement in its 2011 annual report:

	For the Years Ended		
(Dollars in thousands except per-share amounts)	2011	2010	2009
Net sales	$297,580	$256,360	$242,150
Cost of sales	206,000	176,300	165,970
Gross profit	91,580	80,060	76,180
Selling, administrative, and other expenses	65,200	57,200	56,000
Operating earnings	26,380	22,860	20,180
Interest expense	(5,990)	(5,100)	(4,000)
Other deductions, net	(320)	(1,100)	(800)
Earnings before income taxes, noncontrolling interests, and extraordinary items	20,070	16,660	15,380
Income taxes	(8,028)	(6,830)	(6,229)
Net earnings of subsidiaries applicable to noncontrolling interests	(700)	(670)	(668)
Earnings before extraordinary items	11,342	9,160	8,483
Extraordinary items:			
Gain on sale of investment, net of federal and state income taxes of $520	—	1,050	—
Loss due to damages to South American facilities, net of noncontrolling interest of $430	—	(1,600)	—
Net earnings	$ 11,342	$ 8,610	$ 8,483
Earnings per common share:			
Earnings before extraordinary items	$ 2.20	$ 1.82	$ 1.65
Extraordinary items	—	(0.06)	—
Net earnings	$ 2.20	$ 1.76	$ 1.65

The asset side of the balance sheet is summarized as follows:

(Dollars in thousands)	2011	2010	2009
Current assets	$ 89,800	$ 84,500	$ 83,100
Property, plant, and equipment	45,850	40,300	39,800
Other assets (including investments, deposits, deferred charges, and intangibles)	10,110	12,200	13,100
Total assets	$145,760	$137,000	$136,000

Required
a. Based on these data, compute the following for 2011, 2010, and 2009:

1. Net profit margin
2. Return on assets (using total assets)
3. Total asset turnover (using total assets)
4. DuPont analysis
5. Operating income margin
6. Return on operating assets (using end-of-year operating assets)
7. Operating asset turnover (using end-of-year operating assets)
8. DuPont analysis with operating ratios
9. Gross profit margin

b. Discuss your findings.

P 8-9 The following financial information is for A. Galler Company for 2011, 2010, and 2009:

	2011	2010	2009
Income before interest	$4,400,000	$4,000,000	$3,300,000
Interest expense	800,000	600,000	550,000
Income before tax	3,600,000	3,400,000	2,750,000
Tax	1,500,000	1,450,000	1,050,000
Net income	$2,100,000	$1,950,000	$1,700,000

	2011	2010	2009
Current liabilities	$ 2,600,000	$2,300,000	$2,200,000
Long-term debt	7,000,000	6,200,000	5,800,000
Preferred stock (14%)	100,000	100,000	100,000
Common equity	$10,000,000	9,000,000	8,300,000

Required

a. For 2011, 2010, and 2009, determine the following:

1. Return on assets (using end-of-year total assets)
2. Return on investment (using end-of-year long-term liabilities and equity)
3. Return on total equity (using ending total equity)
4. Return on common equity (using ending common equity)

b. Discuss the trend in these profit figures.
c. Discuss the benefit from the use of long-term debt and preferred stock.

P 8-10 Dexall Company recently had a fire in its store. Management must determine the inventory loss for the insurance company. Since the firm did not have perpetual inventory records, the insurance company has suggested that it might accept an estimate using the gross profit test. The beginning inventory, as determined from the last financial statements, was $10,000. Purchase invoices indicate purchases of $100,000. Credit and cash sales during the period were $120,000. Last year, the gross profit for the firm was 40%, which was also the industry average.

Required

a. Based on these data, estimate the inventory loss.
b. If the industry average gross profit was 50%, why might the insurance company be leery of the estimated loss?

P 8-11 Transactions affect various financial statement amounts.

	Net Profit	Retained Earnings	Total Stockholders' Equity
a. A stock dividend is declared and paid.	_____	_____	_____
b. Merchandise is purchased on credit.	_____	_____	_____
c. Marketable securities are sold above cost.	_____	_____	_____
d. Accounts receivable are collected.	_____	_____	_____
e. A cash dividend is declared and paid.	_____	_____	_____
f. Treasury stock is purchased and recorded at cost.	_____	_____	_____
g. Treasury stock is sold above cost.	_____	_____	_____
h. Common stock is sold.	_____	_____	_____
i. A fixed asset is sold for less than book value.	_____	_____	_____
j. Bonds are converted into common stock.	_____	_____	_____

Required Indicate the effects of the previous transactions on each of the following: net profit, retained earnings, total stockholders' equity. Use + to indicate an increase, − to indicate a decrease, and 0 to indicate no effect.

P 8-12 Consecutive five-year balance sheets and income statements of Mary Lou Szabo Corporation are as follows:

MARY LOU SZABO CORPORATION
Balance Sheets
December 31, 2007, through December 31, 2011

(Dollars in thousands)	2011	2010	2009	2008	2007
Assets					
Current assets:					
Cash	$ 24,000	$ 25,000	$ 26,000	$ 24,000	$ 26,000
Accounts receivable, net	120,000	122,000	128,000	129,000	130,000
Inventories	135,000	138,000	141,000	140,000	137,000
Total current assets	279,000	285,000	295,000	293,000	293,000
Property, plant, and equipment, net	500,000	491,000	485,000	479,000	470,000
Goodwill	80,000	85,000	90,000	95,000	100,000
Total assets	$859,000	$861,000	$870,000	$867,000	$863,000
Liabilities and Stockholders' Equity					
Current liabilities:					
Accounts payable	$180,000	$181,000	$181,500	$183,000	$184,000
Income taxes	14,000	14,500	14,000	12,000	12,500
Total current liabilities	194,000	195,500	195,500	195,000	196,500
Long-term debt	65,000	67,500	79,500	82,000	107,500
Redeemable preferred stock	80,000	80,000	80,000	80,000	—
Total liabilities	339,000	343,000	355,000	357,000	304,000
Stockholders' equity:					
Preferred stock	70,000	70,000	70,000	70,000	120,000
Common stock	350,000	350,000	350,000	350,000	350,000
Paid-in capital in excess of par, common stock	15,000	15,000	15,000	15,000	15,000
Retained earnings	85,000	83,000	80,000	75,000	74,000
Total stockholders' equity	520,000	518,000	515,000	510,000	559,000
Total liabilities and stockholders' equity	$859,000	$861,000	$870,000	$867,000	$863,000

MARY LOU SZABO CORPORATION
Statement of Earnings
Years Ended December 31, 2007–2011

(Dollars in thousands)	2011	2010	2009	2008	2007
Net sales	$ 980,000	$ 960,000	$ 940,000	$ 900,000	$ 880,000
Cost of goods sold	625,000	616,000	607,000	580,000	566,000
Gross profit	355,000	344,000	333,000	320,000	314,000
Selling and administrative expense	(240,000)	(239,000)	(238,000)	(239,000)	(235,000)
Interest expense	(6,500)	(6,700)	(8,000)	(8,100)	(11,000)
Earnings from continuing operations before income taxes	108,500	98,300	87,000	72,900	68,000
Income taxes	35,800	33,400	29,200	21,700	23,100
Earnings from continuing operations	72,700	64,900	57,800	51,200	44,900
Extraordinary loss, net of taxes	—	—	—	—	(30,000)
Net earnings	$ 72,700	$ 64,900	$ 57,800	$ 51,200	$ 14,900
Earnings (loss) per share:					
Continuing operations	$ 2.00	$ 1.80	$ 1.62	$ 1.46	$ 1.28
Extraordinary loss	—	—	—	—	(0.85)
Net earnings per share	$ 2.00	$ 1.80	$ 1.62	$ 1.46	$ 0.43

Note: Dividends on preferred stock were as follows:

Redeemable preferred stock		Preferred stock	
2008–2011	$6,400	2008–2011	$ 6,300
		2007	10,800

(*continued*)

(**P 8-12** CONTINUED)

Required
a. Compute the following for the years ended December 31, 2009–2011:

1. Net profit margin
2. Total asset turnover
3. Return on assets
4. DuPont return on assets
5. Operating income margin
6. Operating asset turnover
7. Return on operating assets
8. DuPont return on operating assets
9. Sales to fixed assets
10. Return on investment
11. Return on total equity
12. Return on common equity
13. Gross profit margin

Note: For ratios that call for using average balance sheet figures, compute the rate using average balance sheet figures and year-end balance sheet figures.

b. Briefly comment on profitability and trends indicated in profitability. Also comment on the difference in results between using the average balance sheet figures and year-end figures.

P 8-13
Required Answer the following multiple-choice questions:

a. Which of the following is *not* considered to be a nonrecurring item?

1. Discontinued operations
2. Extraordinary items
3. Cumulative effect of change in accounting principle
4. Interest expense
5. None of the above.

b. Ideally, which of these ratios will indicate the highest return for an individual firm?

1. Return on assets
2. Return on assets variation
3. Return on investments
4. Return on total equity
5. Return on common equity

c. If a firm's gross profit has declined substantially, this could be attributed to all but which of the following reasons?

1. The cost of buying inventory has increased more rapidly than selling prices.
2. Selling prices have declined due to competition.
3. Selling prices have increased due to competition.
4. The mix of goods has changed to include more products with lower margins.
5. Theft is occurring.

d. Gross profit analysis could be of value for all but which of the following?

1. Projections of profitability
2. Estimating administrative expenses
3. Inventory for interim statements
4. Estimating inventory for insurance claims
5. Replacing the physical taking of inventory on an annual basis

e. Total asset turnover measures

1. Net income dollars generated by each dollar of sales.
2. The ability of the firm to generate sales through the use of the assets.

   3. The firm's ability to make productive use of its property, plant, and equipment through generation of profits.
   4. The relationship between the income earned on the capital invested.
   5. Return to the common shareholders.

f. Equity earnings can represent a problem in analyzing profitability because

   1. Equity earnings may not be related to cash flow.
   2. Equity earnings are extraordinary.
   3. Equity earnings are unusual.
   4. Equity earnings are not from operations.
   5. Equity earnings are equal to dividends received.

g. Which of the following is *not* a type of operating asset?

   1. Intangibles
   2. Receivables
   3. Land
   4. Inventory
   5. Building

h. Earnings based on percent of holdings by outside owners of consolidated subsidiaries are termed

   1. Equity earnings.
   2. Earnings of subsidiaries.
   3. Investment income.
   4. Noncontrolling interest.
   5. None of the above.

i. Net profit margin × total asset turnover measures

   1. DuPont return on assets.
   2. Return on investment.
   3. Return on stockholders' equity.
   4. Return on common equity.
   5. None of the above.

j. Return on assets cannot rise under which of the following circumstances?

	Net profit margin	Total asset turnover
1.	Decline	Rise
2.	Rise	Decline
3.	Rise	Rise
4.	Decline	Decline
5.	The ratio could rise under all of the above.	

k. A reason that equity earnings create a problem in analyzing profitability is because

   1. Equity earnings are nonrecurring.
   2. Equity earnings are extraordinary.
   3. Equity earnings are usually less than the related cash flow.
   4. Equity earnings relate to operations.
   5. None of the above.

l. Which of the following ratios will usually have the highest percent?

   1. Return on investment
   2. Return on total equity
   3. Return on common equity
   4. Return on total assets
   5. There is not enough information to tell.

(*continued*)

(**P 8-13** CONTINUED)

m. Which of the following ratios will usually have the lowest percent?

1. Return on investment
2. Return on total equity
3. Return on common equity
4. Return on total assets
5. There is not enough information to tell.

n. Which of the following items will be reported on the income statement as part of net income?

1. Prior period adjustment
2. Unrealized decline in market value of investments
3. Foreign currency translation
4. Gain from selling land
5. None of the above.

o. Noncontrolling interest in earnings is

1. The total earnings of unconsolidated subsidiaries.
2. Earnings based on the percent of holdings by the parent of unconsolidated subsidiaries.
3. Total earnings of unconsolidated subsidiaries.
4. Earnings based on the percent of holdings by outside owners of unconsolidated subsidiaries.
5. None of the above.

p. Which of the following could cause return on assets to decline when net profit margin is increasing?

1. Purchase of land at year-end
2. Increase in book value
3. A stock dividend
4. Increased turnover of operating assets
5. None of the above.

P 8-14 Warranty Obligations—Ethics Consideration

The Bishop Company has a balance in the warranty obligation account of $400,000. An analysis of the products sold under warranty indicates that a balance of $900,000 should be adequate for this year-end.

The president of Bishop Company directs that the balance be adjusted to $600,000. If more is needed, it will be adjusted next quarter. The president indicates that there is not adequate liquidity currently to pay more than $600,000.

Required

a. 1. Adjusting to $600,000 will add how much to expense for the current year?
   2. Adjusting to $900,000 will add how much to expense for the current year?

b. If the balance in the warranty obligation account is not adequate, will this prevent subsequent payments? Comment.

c. Comment on the ethics of not providing a balance that is reasonably close to what the analysis indicates.

Cases

CASE 8-1 JEFF'S SELF-SERVICE STATION

John Dearden and his wife, Patricia, have been taking a vacation to Stowe, Vermont, each summer. They like the area very much and would like to retire someday in this vicinity. While in Stowe during the summer, they notice a "for sale" sign in front of a self-service station. John is 55 and is no longer satisfied with commuting to work in New York City. He decides to inquire about the asking price of the station. He is aware that Stowe is considered a good vacation area during the entire year, especially when the ski season is in progress.

On inquiry, John determines that the asking price of the station is $70,000, which includes two pumps, a small building, and 1/8 acre of land.

John asks to see some financial statements and is shown profit and loss statements for 2011 and 2010 that have been prepared for tax purposes by a local accountant.

JEFF'S SELF-SERVICE STATION
STATEMENT OF EARNINGS
For the Years Ended December 31, 2011 and 2010

	2011	2010
Revenue	$185,060	$175,180
Expenses:		
Cost of goods sold	160,180	153,280
Depreciation (a)	1,000	1,000
Real estate and property taxes	1,100	1,050
Repairs and maintenance	1,470	1,200
Other expenses	680	725
Total expenses	164,430	157,255
Profit	$ 20,630	$ 17,925
(a) Building and equipment cost	$ 30,000	
Original estimated life	30 years	
Depreciation per year	$ 1,000	

John is also given an appraiser's report on the property. The land is appraised at $50,000, and the equipment and building are valued at $20,000. The equipment and building are estimated to have a useful life of 10 years.

The station has been operated by Jeff Anderson without additional help. He estimates that if help were hired to operate the station, it would cost $10,000 per year. John anticipates that he will be able to operate the station without additional help. John intends to incorporate. The anticipated tax rate is 50%.

Required

a. Determine the indicated return on investment if John Dearden purchases the station. Include only financial data that will be recorded on the books. Consider 2011 and 2010 to be representative years for revenue and expenses.

b. Determine the indicated return on investment if help were hired to operate the station.

c. Why is there a difference between the rates of return in (a) and (b)? Discuss.

d. Determine the cash flow for 2012 if John serves as the manager and 2012 turns out to be the same as 2011. Do not include the cost of the hired help. No inventory is on hand at the date of purchase, but an inventory of $10,000 is on hand at the end of the year. There are no receivables or liabilities.

e. Indicate some other considerations that should be analyzed.

f. Should John purchase the station?

CASE 8-2 DIVERSIFIED MANUFACTURER

Crane Co.**

Notes to Consolidated Financial Statements (In Part)
Note 13 – Segment Information (In Part)

Information by geographic segments follows:

(in thousands)	2010	2009	2008
Net sales*			
United States	$1,319,793	$1,322,433	$1,567,002
Canada	248,380	227,091	306,886
Europe	531,037	544,561	596,785
Other international	118,615	102,258	133,634
TOTAL NET SALES	$2,217,825	$2,196,343	$2,604,307
Assets*			
United States	$1,110,668	$ 998,827	$1,122,561
Canada	259,957	288,793	189,229
Europe	435,406	422,844	626,297
Other international	264,055	186,244	79,310
Corporate	636,611	816,190	757,091
TOTAL ASSETS	$2,706,697	$2,712,898	$2,774,488

*Net sales and assets by geographic region are based on the location of the business unit.

Required

a. Using 2008 as the base, prepare a horizontal common-size analysis for the following:
   1. Net sales
   2. Assets
b. Comment on each of the horizontal common-size in (a).

**"We are a diversified manufacturer of highly engineered industrial products." 10-K
Source: Diversified Manufacturer, Crane Co. 2010 10-K

CASE 8-3 LEADING ROASTER

Starbucks presented the following in its 2010 annual report:

Starbucks Corporation*

Notes to Consolidated Financial Statements (In Part)
Note 19 Segment Reporting (In Part)

Revenue mix by product type (*in millions*):

Fiscal Year Ended	Oct 3, 2010		Sep 27, 2009		Sep 28, 2008	
Beverage	$ 6,750.3	63%	$6,238.4	64%	$ 6,663.3	64%
Food	1,878.7	18%	1,680.2	17%	1,511.7	15%
Whole bean and soluble coffees	1,131.3	10%	965.2	10%	987.8	9%
Other[1]	947.1	9%	890.8	9%	1,220.2	12%
Total	$10,707.4	100%	$9,774.6	100%	$10,383.0	100%

[1]Other includes royalty and licensing revenues, beverage-related accessories and equipment

Information by geographic area (*in millions*):

Fiscal Year Ended	Oct 3, 2010	Sep 27, 2009	Sep 28, 2008
Net revenues from external customers:			
United States	$ 8,335.4	$7,787.7	$ 8,227.0
Other countries	2,372.0	1,986.9	2,156.0
Total	$10,707.4	$9,774.6	$10,383.0

*"Starbucks is the premier roaster and retailer of specialty coffee in the world." 10-K
Source: Starbucks Corporation 2010 10-K

No customer accounts for 10% or more of revenues. Revenues are shown based on the geographic location of our customers. Revenues from countries other than the US consist primarily of revenues from Canada and the UK, which together account for approximately 64% of net revenues from other countries for fiscal 2010.

Fiscal Year Ended	Oct 3, 2010	Sep 27, 2009	Sep 28, 2008
Long-lived assets:			
United States	$2,807.9	$2,776.7	$3,099.9
Other countries	821.6	764.3	824.8
Total	$3,629.5	$3,541.0	$3,924.7

Management evaluates the performance of its operating segments based on net revenues and operating income. The accounting policies of the operating segments are the same as those described in the summary of significant accounting policies in Note 1. Operating income represents earnings before net interest income and other, interest expense and income taxes. Management does not evaluate the performance of its operating segments using asset measures. The identifiable assets by segment disclosed in this note are those assets specifically identifiable within each segment and include net property, plant and equipment, equity and cost investments, goodwill, and other intangible assets. Corporate assets are primarily comprised of cash and investments, assets of the corporate headquarters and roasting facilities, and inventory.

Required

a. Comment on the vertical common-size presentation for "Beverage, Food, Whole bean and soluble coffees and Other."

b. 1. Prepare a horizontal common-size analysis of revenue with September 28, 2008 as the base for "Beverage, Food, Whole Bean and Soluble Coffees, and Other"

   2. Comment on b(1).

c. For net revenues from external customers:

   1. Prepare a vertical common-size analysis for United States and other countries. Use total as the base.

   2. Comment on c(1).

   3. Prepare a horizontal common-size analysis, with September 28, 2008 as the base, for United States and other countries.

   4. Comment on c(3).

d. 1. Prepare a vertical common-size analysis for long-lived assets. Use total as the base.

   2. Comment on d(1).

   3. Prepare a horizontal common-size analysis, with September 28, 2008 as the base, for long-lived assets.

   4. Comment on d(3).

CASE 8-4 CERTIFIED ORGANIC

Whole Foods Market, Inc. included these statements in its 2010 annual report.*

WHOLE FOODS MARKET, INC.
Consolidated Balance Sheets
(in thousands)
September 26, 2010 and September 27, 2009

Assets	2010	2009
Current Assets:		
Cash and cash equivalents	$ 131,996	$ 430,130
Short-term investments – available-for-sale securities	329,738	—
Restricted cash	86,802	71,023
Accounts receivable	133,346	104,731

(continued)

*"Whole Foods Market is the world's leading natural and organic foods supermarket and America's first national "Certified Organic" grocer." 10-K
Source: Whole Foods Market, Inc. 2010 10-K

(**CASE 8-4** CONTINUED)

Assets	2010	2009
Merchandise inventories	$ 323,487	$ 310,602
Prepaid expenses and other current assets	54,686	51,137
Deferred income taxes	101,464	87,757
Total current assets	1,161,519	1,055,380
**Property and equipment, net of accumulated depreciation and amortization	1,886,130	1,897,853
Long-term investments – available-for-sale securities	96,146	—
Goodwill	665,224	658,254
Intangible assets, net of accumulated amortization	69,064	73,035
Deferred income taxes	99,156	91,000
Other assets	9,301	7,866
Total assets	$3,986,540	$3,783,388

Liabilities and Shareholders Equity	2010	2009
Current Liabilities:		
Current installments of long-term debt and capital lease obligations	$ 410	$ 389
Accounts payable	213,212	189,597
Accrued payroll, bonus and other benefits due team members	244,427	207,983
Dividends payable	—	8,217
Other current liabilities	289,823	277,838
Total current liabilities	747,872	684,024
Long-term debt and capital lease obligations, less current installments	508,288	738,848
Deferred lease liabilities	294,291	250,326
Other long-term liabilities	62,831	69,262
Total liabilities	1,613,282	1,742,460
Series A redeemable preferred stock, $0.10 par value, 425 shares authorized; zero and 425 shares issued and outstanding at 2010 and 2009, respectively	—	413,052
Shareholders' equity:		
Common stock, no par value, 300,000 shares authorized; 172,033 and 140,542 shares issued and outstanding at 2010 and 2009, respectively	1,773,897	1,283,028
Accumulated other comprehensive income (loss)	791	(13,367)
Retained earnings	598,570	358,215
Total shareholders' equity	2,373,258	1,627,876
Commitments and contingencies		
Total liabilities and shareholders' equity	$3,986,540	$3,783,388

**Property and equipment include construction in progress and equipment not yet in service (2010 – $120,845; 2009 – $130,068)

WHOLE FOODS MARKET, INC.
CONSOLIDATED STATEMENTS OF OPERATIONS
(in thousands, except per share amounts)
Fiscal years ended September 26, 2010, September 27, 2009 and September 28, 2008

	2010	2009	2008
Sales	$9,005,794	$8,031,620	$7,953,912
Cost of goods sold and occupancy costs	5,870,393	5,277,310	5,247,207
Gross profit	3,135,401	2,754,310	2,706,705
Direct store expenses	2,375,716	2,145,809	2,107,940
General and administrative expenses	272,449	243,749	270,428
Pre-opening expenses	38,044	49,218	55,554
Relocation, store closure and lease termination costs	11,217	31,185	36,545
Operating income	437,975	284,349	236,238
Interest expense	(33,048)	(36,856)	(36,416)

	2010	2009	2008
Investment and other income	$ 6,854	$ 3,449	$ 6,697
Income before income taxes	411,781	250,942	206,519
Provision for income taxes	165,948	104,138	91,995
Net income	245,833	146,804	114,524
Preferred stock dividends	5,478	28,050	—
Income available to common shareholders	$ 240,355	$ 118,754	$ 114,524
Basic earnings per share	$ 1.45	$ 0.85	$ 0.82
Weighted average shares outstanding	166,244	140,414	139,886
Diluted earnings per share	$ 1.43	$ 0.85	$ 0.82
Weighted average shares outstanding, diluted basis	171,710	140,414	140,011
Dividends declared per common share	$ —	$ —	$ 0.60

Required

a. Compute the following for 2010 and 2009:
   1. Net profit margin
   2. Total asset turnover (use year-end assets)
   3. Return on assets (use year-end assets)
   4. Operating income margin
   5. Return on operating assets (use year-end assets)
   6. Sales to fixed assets (use year-end fixed assets)
   7. Return on investment (use year-end balance sheet accounts)
   8. Return on total equity (use year-end equity)
   9. Gross profit margin
b. Comment on the trends in (a).

CASE 8-5 DIGITAL MEDIA

Yahoo! Inc.* included these statements in its 2010 annual report:

YAHOO! INC.
CONSOLIDATED STATEMENTS OF INCOME

	Years Ended December 31,		
	2008	2009	2010
	(In thousands, except per share amounts)		
Revenues			
Cost of revenues	$7,208,502	$6,460,315	$6,324,651
Gross profit	3,023,362	2,871,746	2,627,545
	4,185,140	3,588,746	3,697,106
Operating expenses:			
Sales and marketing	1,563,313	1,245,350	1,264,491
Product development	1,221,787	1,210,168	1,082,176
General and administrative	705,136	580,352	488,332
Amortization of intangibles	87,550	39,106	31,626
Restructuring charges, net	106,854	126,901	57,957
Goodwill impairment charge	487,537	—	—
Total operating expenses	4,172,177	3,201,877	2,924,582
Income from operations	12,963	386,692	772,524
Other income, net	73,750	187,528	297,869
Income before income taxes and earnings in equity interests	86,713	574,220	1,070,393
Provision for income taxes	(259,006)	(219,321)	(221,523)
Earnings in equity interests	596,979	250,390	395,758
Net income	424,686	605,289	1,244,628
			(continued)

*"Yahoo! Inc., together with its consolidated subsidiaries . . . is a premier digital media company that delivers personalized digital content and experiences, across devices and around the globe, to vast audiences." 10-K
Source: Yahoo! Inc. 2010 10-K

(**CASE 8-5** CONTINUED)

	Years Ended December 31,		
	2008	2009	2010
Less: Net income attributable to noncontrolling interests	(5,765)	(7,297)	(12,965)
Net income attributable to Yahoo! Inc.	$ 418,921	$ 597,992	$1,231,663
Net income attributable to Yahoo! Inc. common stockholders per share – basic	$ 0.31	$ 0.43	$ 0.91
Net income attributable to Yahoo! Inc. common stockholders per share – diluted	$ 0.29	$ 0.42	$ 0.90
Shares used in per share calculation – basic	1,369,476	1,397,652	1,354,118
Shares used in per share calculation – diluted	1,391,230	1,415,658	1,364,612
Stock-based compensation expense by function:			
Cost of revenues	$ 13,813	$ 10,759	$ 3,275
Sales and marketing	182,826	141,537	71,154
Product development	178,091	205,971	106,665
General and administrative	63,113	79,820	42,384
Restructuring expense reversals	(30,236)	11,062	(4,211)

YAHOO! INC.
CONSOLIDATED BALANCE SHEETS

	December 31,	
	2009	2010
	(In thousands, except par values)	
ASSETS		
Current assets:		
Cash and cash equivalents	$ 1,275,430	$ 1,526,427
Short-term marketable debt securities	2,015,655	1,357,661
Accounts receivable, net of allowance of $41,003 and $22,975 as of December 31, 2009 and 2010, respectively	1,003,362	1,028,090
Prepaid expenses and other current assets	300,325	432,560
Total current assets	4,594,772	4,345,548
Long-term marketable debt securities	1,226,919	744,594
Property and equipment, net **	1,426,862	1,653,422
Goodwill	3,640,373	3,681,645
Intangible assets, net	355,883	255,870
Other long-term assets	194,933	235,136
Investments in equity interests	3,496,288	4,011,889
Total assets	$14,936,030	$14,928,104
LIABILITIES AND EQUITY		
Current liabilities:		
Accounts payable	$ 136,769	$ 162,424
Accrued expenses and other current liabilities	1,169,815	1,208,792
Deferred revenue	411,144	254,656
Total current liabilities	1,717,728	1,625,872
Long-term deferred revenue	122,550	56,365
Capital lease and other long-term liabilities	83,021	142,799
Deferred and other long-term tax liabilities, net	494,095	506,658
Total liabilities	2,417,394	2,331,694
Commitments and contingencies (Note 12)	—	—
Yahoo! Inc. stockholders' equity:		
Preferred stock, $0.001 par value, 10,000 shares authorized; none issued or outstanding	—	—
Common stock, $0.001 par value; 5,000,000 shares authorized; 1,413,718 shares issued and 1,406,075 shares outstanding as of December 31, 2009 and 1,308,836 shares issued and 1,308,836 shares outstanding as of December 31, 2010	1,410	1,306

** *"Assets not yet in use $142,899 (2009); $175,830 (2010)." 10-K

	December 31,	
	2009	2010
Additional paid-in capital	10,640,367	10,109,913
Treasury stock at cost, 7,643 shares as of December 31, 2009 and zero shares as of December 31, 2010	(117,331)	—
Retained earnings	1,599,638	1,942,656
Accumulated other comprehensive income	369,236	504,254
Total Yahoo! Inc. stockholders' equity	12,493,320	12,558,129
Noncontrolling interests	25,316	38,281
Total equity	12,518,636	12,596,410
Total liabilities and equity	$14,936,030	$14,928,104

Required

a. Compute the following for 2009 and 2010:
   1. Net profit margin
   2. Total asset turnover (use year-end total assets)
   3. Return on assets (use year-end total assets)
   4. Operating income margin
   5. Return on operating assets (use year-end operating assets)
   6. Sales to fixed assets (use year-end operating assets)
   7. Return on total equity (use year-end total equity)
   8. Gross profit margin

b. Comment on the trends in (a).

c. 1. Prepare a horizontal common-size consolidated statement of operations for 2008–2010. Use 2008 as the base.
   2. Comment on the results in (1).

CASE 8-6 RETURN ON ASSETS – INDUSTRY COMPARISON

With this case, a comparison is made between two firms in different industries using net profit margin, total asset turnover, and return on assets.

JOHNSON & JOHNSON AND SUBSIDIARIES*
CONSOLIDATED STATEMENT OF EARNINGS

(Dollars in Millions, Except Per Share Figures) (Note 1)

	2010
Sales to customers	$ 61,587
Cost of products sold	18,792
Gross profit	42,795
Selling, marketing and administrative expenses	19,424
Research and development expense	6,844
Interest income	(107)
Interest expense, net of portion capitalized (Note 4)	455
Other (income) expense, net	(768)
Earnings before provision for taxes on income	16,947
Provision for taxes on income (Note 8)	3,613
Net earnings	**$ 13,334**
Basic net earnings per share (Notes 1 and 15)	**$ 4.85**
Diluted net earnings per share (Notes 1 and 15)	**$ 4.78**
Cash dividends per share	**$ 2.110**
Basic average shares outstanding (Notes 1 and 15)	**2,751.4**
Diluted average shares outstanding (Notes 1 and 15)	**2,788.8**

(continued)

---

* "Johnson & Johnson and its subsidiaries have approximately 114,000 employees worldwide engaged in the research and development, manufacture and sale of a broad range of products in the health care field." 10-K
  Source: Johnson & Johnson and Subsidiaries 2010 10-K

(**Case 8-6** continued)

Johnson & Johnson and Subsidiaries
From Consolidated Balance Sheets
Total Assets
Dollars in millions

January 2, 2011	$102,908
January 3, 2010	$ 94,682

BEST BUY CO. INC.**
CONSOLIDATED STATEMENTS OF EARNINGS (IN PART)
Dollars in millions, except per share amounts

Fiscal Year Ended	February 26, 2011
Revenue	$50,272
Cost of goods sold	36,611
Restructuring charges – cost of goods sold	24
Gross profit	12,637
Selling, general and administrative expenses	10,325
Restructuring charges	198
Goodwill and tradename impairment	—
Operating income	2,114
Other income (expense)	
Investment income and other	51
Interest expense	(87)
Earnings before income tax expense and equity in income of affiliates	2,078
Income tax expense	714
Equity in income of affiliates	2
Net earnings including noncontrolling interests	$ 1,366
Net earnings attributable to noncontrolling interests	(89)
Net earnings attributable to Best Buy Co., Inc.	$ 1,277

**"We are a multinational retailer of consumer electronics, home office products, entertainment products, appliances and related services." 10-K

Best Buy Co. Inc.
From Consolidated Balance Sheets
Total Assets
Dollars in Millions

February 26, 2011	$17,849
February 27, 2010	$18,302

Required

a. Compute the following ratios for Johnson & Johnson:

1. Net profit margin

2. Total asset turnover

3. Return on assets

b. Compute the following ratios for Best Buy Co.:

1. Net profit margin

2. Total asset turnover

3. Return on assets

c. Comment on the effect of the industry on these ratios.

Source: Best Buy Co., Inc. 2010 10-K

Case 8-7 NAME THE INDUSTRY

With this case, a comparison is made between three firms in different industries using net profit margin, total asset turnover and current ratio.

	Net Profit Margin	Total Asset Turnover	Current Ratio
Firm A	1.67%	3.40 times	1.16
Firm B	21.48%	1.06 times	2.01
Firm C	4.44%	1.49 times	1.71

1. **Apple**
   Fiscal year 2010 ended September 25, 2010, and consisted of 52 weeks
   "Apple, Inc. and its wholly-owned subsidiaries (collectively "Apple" or the "Company")
   designs, manufactures and markets a range of personal computers, mobile
   communication and media devices, and portable digital music players, and sells a variety
   of related software, services, peripherals, networking solutions, and third-party digital
   content and applications." 10-K
   Source: Apple, 2010 10-K

2. **Costco Wholesale Corporation**
   Fiscal year ended August 29, 2010, and consisted of 52 weeks
   "We operate membership warehouses based on the concept that offering our members
   low prices on a limited selection of nationally branded and selected private-label
   products in a wide range of merchandise categories will produce high sales volumes and
   rapid inventory turnover." 10-K
   Source: Costco Wholesale Corporation 2010 10-K

3. **Target Corporation**
   Fiscal year 2010 ended January 29, 2011, and consisted of 52 weeks
   "Our Retail Segment includes all of our merchandising operations, including our fully
   integrated online business. We offer everyday essentials and fashionable, differentiated
   merchandise at discounted prices." 10-K
   Source: Target Corporation 2010 10-K

Required

a. Which firm is Firm A? Comment on your reasons.

b. Which firm is Firm B? Comment on your reasons.

c. Which firm is Firm C? Comment on your reasons.

CASE 8-8 SPECIALTY RETAILER – PROFITABILITY VIEW

1. **Abercrombie & Fitch Co.**
   (52 week fiscal year ended January 29, 2011; 52 week fiscal year ended January 30, 2010)
   "Abercrombie & Fitch Co . . . is a specialty retailer that operates stores and direct-to-
   consumer operations." 10-K
   Source: Abercrombie & Fitch 2010 10-K

2. **Limited Brands, Inc.**
   (52 week fiscal year ended January 29, 2011; 52 week fiscal year ended January 30, 2010)
   "We operate in the highly competitive specialty retail business." 10-K
   Source: Limited Brands 2010 10-K

3. **GAP, Inc.**
   (52 week fiscal year ended January 29, 2011; 52 week fiscal year ended January 30,
   2010)
   "We are a global specialty retailer offering apparel, accessories, and personal care
   products." 10-K
   Source: Gap Inc 2010 10-K

Data reviewed	Abercrombie & Fitch		Limited Brands		GAP	
	2010	2009	2010	2009	2010	2009
Net profit margin	4.33	2.70	8.37	5.19	8.21	7.76
Return on assets	5.21	2.78	11.82	7.07	16.00	14.17
Return on total equity	8.08	4.30	43.98	21.63	26.84	23.76

Required

a. Comment on the net profit margin for these companies. Consider absolute amounts and
   trend.

b. Comment on the return on assets for these companies. Consider absolute amounts and trend.

c. Comment on the return on total equity for these companies. Consider absolute amounts
   and trend.

d. Comment on the relative profitability of these companies.

CASE 8-9 EAT AT MY RESTAURANT – PROFITABILITY VIEW

With this case, we review the profitability of several restaurant companies. The restaurant companies reviewed and the year-end dates are as follows:

1. **Yum Brands, Inc.**
   December 25, 2010; December 26, 2009 (52 weeks)
   "YUM consists of six operating segments: KFC – U.S., Pizza Hut – U.S., Taco Bell – U.S., Long John Silver's ("LJS") – U.S., and A&W All American Food Restaurants ("A&W") – U.S., YUM Restaurants International ("YRI" or "International Division") and YUM Restaurants China ("China Division")." 10-K
   Source: Yum! Brands, Inc. and Subsidiaries 2010 10-K

2. **Panera Bread Company**
   December 28, 2010; December 29, 2009 (52 weeks)
   "Panera Bread Company and it subsidiaries, referred to as "Panera Bread," "Panera," the "Company," "we," "us," and "our," is a national bakery-café concept with 1,453 company-owned and franchise-operated bakery-café locations in 40 states, the District of Columbia, and Ontario, Canada." 10-K
   Source: Panera Bread 2010 10-K

3. **Starbucks Corporation**
   October 3, 2010; September 27, 2009 (Fiscal year 2010 included 53 weeks, while fiscal year ended 2009 included 52 weeks)
   "Starbucks is the premier roaster and retailer of specialty coffee in the world, operating in more than 50 countries." 10-K
   Source: Starbucks Corporation 2010 10-K

Ratio	Yum Brands, Inc.		Panera Bread		Starbucks	
	2010	2009	2010	2009	2010	2009
Net profit margin %	10.21	9.88	7.25	6.36	8.83	4.00
Return on assets %	14.98	15.66	12.70	11.39	15.81	6.95
Return on total equity %	83.22	210.00	18.71	15.85	28.14	14.11

Required

a. Comment on the *net profit margin* for these companies.
b. Comment on the *return on assets* for these companies.
c. Comment on the *return on total equity* for these companies.
d. Comment on the *relative profitability* of these companies.

CASE 8-10 EAT AT MY RESTAURANT – PROFITABILITY VIEW – COMPREHENSIVE INCOME INCLUDED

With this case, we review the profitability of Yum Brands, Panera Bread and Starbucks, including comprehensive income for 2010 and 2009.

Ratio	Yum Brands, Inc.		Panera Bread		Starbucks	
	2010	2009	2010	2009	2010	2009
Net profit margin %	10.18	11.67	7.26	6.40	8.75	4.17
Return on assets %	14.94	18.50	12.71	11.47	15.67	7.25
Return on total equity %	83.00	248.04	18.72	16.98	27.90	14.73

Required

a. Which company appears to have the better net profit margin?
b. Which company appears to have the best return on assets?

Source: Yum! Brands, Inc. and Subsidiaries 2010 10-K
Source: Panera Bread 2010 10-K
Source: Starbucks Corporation 2010 10-K

c. Which company appears to have the better return on total equity?

d. 1. Considering the data in Case 8-9 and Case 8-10, comment on the impact of considering comprehensive income for each company for the years 2010 and 2009:
   Yum Brands
   Panera Bread
   Starbucks

   2. Would the impact be the same in future years?

WEB CASE THOMSON ONE *Business School Edition*

Please complete the Web case that covers material discussed in this chapter at www.cengagebrain.com. You'll be using Thomson ONE Business School Edition, a powerful tool that combines a full range of fundamental financial information, earnings estimates, market data, and source documents for 500 publicly traded companies.

TO THE NET CASE

1. Go to the SEC site (www.sec.gov). Under "Filings & Forms," click on "Search for Company Filings." Click on "Company or fund, etc." Under Company Name, enter "Google Inc." (or under Ticker Symbol, enter "GOOG"). Select the 10-K filed February 11, 2011.

   a. Copy the first sentence in the "Item 1. Business Overview" section.

   b. Prepare a horizontal common-size analysis for the following (use 2008 as the base):

	2008	2009	2010
Revenue			
Income from operations			
Net income			

   c. Comment on the trends in (b).

2. Go to the SEC site (www.sec.gov). Under "Filings & Forms," click on "Search for Company Filings." Click on "Company or fund, etc." Under Company Name, enter "Flowers Foods Inc." (or under Ticker Symbol, enter "FLO"). Select the 10-K filed February 23, 2011.

   a. Copy the first sentence in the "Item 1. Business"

   b. Complete this schedule:

   FLOWERS FOODS, INC. AND SUBSIDIARIES
   Consolidated Statements of Income (In Part)

	For the 52 weeks ended		For the 53 weeks ended
(Amounts in thousands)	January 1, 2011	January 2, 2010	January 3, 2009
Sales			
Materials, supplies, labor and other production costs (exclusive of depreciation and amortization shown separately below)			
Selling, distribution and administrative expenses			
Depreciation and amortization			
Income from operations			

   c. Complete the schedule in (b) using horizontal common-size analysis. Use January 3, 2009 as the base.

   d. Comment on the comparability of these years.

   e. Comment on the trends observed in (b) and (c).

3. Go to the SEC site (www.sec.gov). Under "Filings & Forms," click on "Search for Company Filings." Click on "Company or fund, etc." Under Company Name, enter "Intel Corp" (or under Ticker Symbol, enter "INTC"). Select the 10-K filed February 18, 2011.

   a. Copy the first sentence in the "Industry" subsection from the "Item 1 Business" section.

   b. Complete the following schedule:

(continued)

(**To the Net** CONTINUED)

INTEL CORPORATION
Consolidated Statements of Income (In Part)
Three Years Ended December 25, 2010

(In millions)	2010	2009	2008
Net revenue			
Cost of sales			
Gross margin			
Operating income			

c. Complete the schedule in (b) using horizontal common-size analysis. Use 2008 as the base.

d. Comment on the comparability of these years.

e. Comment on the trends observed in (b) and (c).

4. Go to the SEC site (www.sec.gov). Under "Filings & Forms," click on "Search for Company Filings." Click on "Company or fund, etc." Under Company Name, enter "Advanced Micro Devices Inc" (or under Ticker Symbol, enter "AMD"). Select the 10-K filed February 18, 2011.

a. Copy the first sentence in the "General" subsection from the "Item Business" section.

b. Complete the following schedule:

ADVANCED MICRO DEVICES, INC.
Consolidated Statements of Operations (In Part)
Three Years Ended December 25, 2010

(In millions)	2010	2009	2008
Net revenue			
Cost of sales			
Gross margin			
Operating income (loss)			

c. Complete the schedule in (b) using horizontal common-size analysis. Use 2008 as the base.

d. Comment on the trends observed in (b) and (c).

5. Which firm, Intel Corp. or Advanced Micro Devices, Inc. appears to have performed better? Comment.

Endnotes

1. Release No. 33-8176, January 22, 2003, Conditions for Use of Non-GAAP Financial Measures Release Nos.: 34-47226; FR-65. www.sec.gov, "Regulatory Actions, Final Rule Releases."

2. Richard Barker, "Reporting Financial Performance," *Accounting Horizons* (June 2004), p. 159.

3. Michael Rapoport, "Pro Forma Proves a Hard Habit to Break on Earning Reports," *The Wall Street Journal* (September 18, 2003), p. B38.

4. Ibid., p. B38.

Chapter

9

For the Investor

Certain types of analysis particularly concern investors. While this chapter is not intended as a comprehensive guide to investment analysis, it will introduce certain types of analysis useful to the investor. In addition to the analysis covered in this chapter, an investor would also be interested in the liquidity, debt, and profitability ratios covered in prior chapters.

Leverage and Its Effects on Earnings

The use of debt, called *financial leverage*, has a significant impact on earnings. The existence of fixed operating costs, called *operating leverage*, also affects earnings. The higher the percentage of fixed operating costs, the greater the variation in income as a result of a variation in sales (revenue).

This book does not compute a ratio for operating leverage because it cannot be readily computed from published financial statements. This book does compute financial leverage because it is readily computed from published financial statements.

The expense of debt financing is interest, a fixed charge dependent on the amount of financial principal and the rate of interest. Interest is a contractual obligation created by the borrowing agreement. In contrast to dividends, interest must be paid regardless of whether the firm is in a highly profitable period. An advantage of interest over dividends is its tax deductibility. Because the interest is subtracted to calculate taxable income, income tax expense is reduced.

Definition of Financial Leverage and Magnification Effects

The use of financing with a fixed charge (such as interest) is termed financial leverage. Financial leverage is successful if the firm earns more on the borrowed funds than it pays to use them. It is not successful if the firm earns less on the borrowed funds than it pays to use them. Using financial leverage results in a fixed financing charge that can materially affect the earnings available to the common shareholders.

Exhibit 9-1 illustrates financial leverage and its magnification effects. In this illustration, earnings before interest and tax for Dowell Company are $1,000,000. Further, the firm has an interest expense of $200,000 and a tax rate of 40%. The statement illustrates the effect of leverage on the return to the common stockholder. At earnings before interest and tax (EBIT) of $1,000,000, the net income is $480,000. If EBIT increases by 10% to $1,100,000, as in the exhibit, the net income rises by 12.5%. This magnification is caused by the fixed nature of interest expense. While earnings available to pay interest rise, interest remains the same, thus leaving more for the residual owners. Note that since the tax rate remains the same, earnings before tax change at the same rate as earnings after tax. Hence, this analysis could be made with either profit figure.

If financial leverage is used, a rise in EBIT will cause an even greater rise in net income, and a decrease in EBIT will cause an even greater decrease in net income. Looking again at the statement for Dowell Company in Exhibit 9-1, when EBIT declined 20%, net income dropped from $480,000 to $360,000—a decline of $120,000, or 25%, based on the original $480,000. The use of financial leverage, termed **trading on the equity**, is only successful if the rate of earnings on borrowed funds exceeds the fixed charges.

EXHIBIT **9-1**	Dowell Company		
Financial Leverage—Partial Income Statement to Illustrate Magnification Effects			
	Base Year Figures	20% Decrease in Earnings Before Interest and Tax	10% Increase in Earnings Before Interest and Tax
Earnings before interest and tax	$1,000,000	$ 800,000	$1,100,000
Interest	(200,000)	(200,000)	(200,000)
Earnings before tax	800,000	600,000	900,000
Income tax (40%)	(320,000)	(240,000)	(360,000)
Net income	$ 480,000	$ 360,000	$ 540,000
Percentage change in net income [A]		25.0%	12.5%
Percentage change in earnings before interest and tax [B]		20.0%	10.0%
Degree of financial leverage [A ÷ B]		1.25	1.25

Source: Dowell Company 2010 10-K

Computing the Degree of Financial Leverage

The degree of financial leverage is the multiplication factor by which the net income changes as compared with the change in EBIT. One way of computing it follows:

$$\frac{\%\ \text{Change Net Income}}{\%\ \text{Change EBIT}}$$

For Dowell Company:

$$\frac{12.5\%}{10.0\%} = 1.25, = \frac{25.0\%}{20.0\%} = 1.25$$

The degree of financial leverage is 1.25. From a base EBIT of $1,000,000, any change in EBIT will be accompanied by 1.25 times that change in net income. If net income before interest and tax rises 4%, earnings to the stockholder will rise 5%. If net income before interest and tax falls 8%, earnings to the stockholder will decline 10%. The degree of financial leverage (DFL) can be computed more easily as follows:

$$\text{Degree of Financial Leverage} = \frac{\text{Earnings Before Interest and Tax}}{\text{Earnings Before Tax}}$$

Again referring to Dowell Company:

$$\text{Degree of Financial Leverage at Earnings Before Interest and Tax on \$1,000,000} = \frac{\$1,000,000}{\$800,000} = 1.25$$

Note that the degree of financial leverage represents a particular base level of income. The degree of financial leverage may differ for other levels of income or fixed charges.

The degree of financial leverage formula will not work precisely when the income statement includes any of the following items:

1. Noncontrolling interest
2. Equity income
3. Nonrecurring items
   a. Discontinued operations
   b. Extraordinary items

When any of these items are included, they should be eliminated from the numerator and denominator. The all-inclusive formula follows:

$$\text{All-Inclusive Degree of Financial Leverage} = \frac{\text{Earnings Before Interest, Tax, Noncontrolling Interest, Equity Income, and Nonrecurring Items}}{\text{Earnings Before Tax, Noncontrolling Interest, Equity Income, and Nonrecurring Items}}$$

This formula results in the ratio by which earnings before interest, tax, noncontrolling interest, equity income, and nonrecurring items will change in relation to a change in earnings before tax, noncontrolling interest, equity income, and nonrecurring items. In other words, it eliminates the noncontrolling interest, equity income, and nonrecurring items from the degree of financial leverage.

Exhibit 9-2 shows the degree of financial leverage for Nike for 2011 and 2010. The degree of financial leverage is 1.01 for 2011 and 1.01 for 2010. This is a very low degree of financial leverage. Therefore, the financial leverage at the end of 2011 indicates that as earnings before interest changes, net income will change by 1.01 times that amount. If earnings before interest increases, the financial leverage will be favorable. If earnings before interest decreases, the financial leverage will be unfavorable. In periods of relatively low or declining interest rates, financial leverage looks more favorable than in periods of high or increasing interest rates. (*Note:* Essentially, Nike has minor financial leverage in 2011 and 2010.)

EXHIBIT **9-2**	Nike, Inc.	

Degree of Financial Leverage

Base Years 2011 and 2010		
(In millions)	2011	2010
Income before income taxes [B]	$2,844.0	$2,517.0
Interest	34.0*	36.0*
Earnings before interest and tax [A]	$2,878.0	$2,553.0
Degree of financial leverage [A ÷ B]	1.01	1.01

*Interest expense includes both expensed and capitalized.
Per notes—property, plant, and equipment, capitalized interest was not material for the years ended May 31, 2011, 2010 and 2009 (10-K).
Source: Nike, Inc. 2010 10-K

Summary of Financial Leverage

Two things are important in looking at financial leverage as part of financial analysis. First, how high is the degree of financial leverage? This is a type of risk (or opportunity) measurement from the viewpoint of the stockholder. The higher the degree of financial leverage, the greater the multiplication factor. Second, does the financial leverage work for or against the owners?

Earnings per Common Share

Earnings per share—the amount of income earned on a share of common stock during an accounting period—applies only to common stock and to corporate income statements. Nonpublic companies, because of cost-benefit considerations, do not have to report earnings per share. Because earnings per share receives much attention from the financial community, investors, and potential investors, it will be described in some detail.

Fortunately, we do not need to compute earnings per share. A company is required to present it at the bottom of the income statement. Per share amounts for discontinued operations and extraordinary items must be presented on the face of the income statement or in the notes to the financial statements. Earnings per share for recurring items is the most significant for primary analysis.

Computing earnings per share initially involves net income, preferred stock dividends declared and accumulated, and the weighted average number of shares outstanding, as follows:

$$\text{Earnings per Share} = \frac{\text{Net Income} - \text{Preferred Dividends}}{\text{Weighted Average Number of Common Shares Outstanding}}$$

Since earnings pertain to an entire period, they should be related to the common shares outstanding during the period. Thus, the denominator of the equation is the weighted average number of common shares outstanding.

To illustrate, assume that a corporation had 10,000 shares of common stock outstanding at the beginning of the year. On July 1, it issued 2,000 shares, and on October 1, it issued another 3,000 shares. The weighted average number of shares outstanding would be computed as follows:

Months Shares Are Outstanding	Shares Outstanding	×	Fraction of Year Outstanding	=	Weighted Average
January–June	10,000		6/12		5,000
July–September	12,000		3/12		3,000
October–December	15,000		3/12		3,750
					11,750

When the common shares outstanding increase as a result of a stock dividend or stock split, retroactive recognition must be given to these events for all comparative earnings per share presentations. Stock dividends and stock splits do not provide the firm with more funds; they only change the number of outstanding shares. Earnings per share should be related to the outstanding common stock after the stock dividend or stock split. In the weighted average common shares illustration, if we assume that a 2-for-1 stock split took place on December 31, the denominator of the earnings per share computation becomes 23,500 (11,750 × 2). The denominator of prior years' earnings per share computations would also be doubled. If we assume that net income is $100,000 and preferred dividends total $10,000 in this illustration, then the earnings per common share would be $3.83 [($100,000 − $10,000)/23,500].

The current earnings per share guidelines call for the presentation of basic earnings per share and diluted earnings per share. Basic earnings per share is computed by dividing net income less preferred dividends by the weighted average number of shares of common stock outstanding during the period. Diluted earnings per share is computed by dividing net income less preferred dividends by the weighted average number of shares of common stock outstanding plus the dilutive effect of potentially dilutive securities. Potentially dilutive securities are convertible securities, warrants, options, or other rights that upon conversion or exercise could in the aggregate dilute earnings per common share.

Exhibit 9-3 presents the earnings per share of Nike for the years 2009, 2010, and 2011. There was a material increase in earnings per share for 2010 and 2011. This was especially true of 2010.

EXHIBIT **9-3**	Nike, Inc.		
Earnings per Share			
Years Ended May 31, 2011, 2010, and 2009			
	2011	2010	2009
Basic earnings per common share	$4.48	$3.93	$3.07
Diluted earnings per common share	$4.39	$3.86	$3.03
Source: Nike, Inc. 2010 10-K			

Price/Earnings Ratio

The **price/earnings (P/E) ratio** expresses the relationship between the market price of a share of common stock and that stock's current earnings per share. Compute the P/E ratio as follows:

$$\text{Price/Earnings Ratio} = \frac{\text{Market Price per Share}}{\text{Diluted Earnings per Share, Before Nonrecurring Items}}$$

Using diluted earnings per share results in a higher price/earnings ratio, a conservative computation of the ratio. Ideally, the P/E ratio should be computed using diluted earnings per share for continuing earnings per share. This gives an indication of what is being paid for a dollar of recurring earnings.

P/E ratios are available from many sources, such as *The Wall Street Journal* and *Standard & Poor's Industry Surveys*. Exhibit 9-4 shows the P/E ratio for Nike for 2011 and 2010. The P/E ratio was 19.24 at the end of 2011 and 18.75 at the end of 2010. This indicates that the stock has been selling for about 19 times earnings. You can get a perspective on this ratio by comparing it with competitors ratio, average P/E ratio for the industry, and an average

EXHIBIT **9-4**	Nike, Inc.		
Price/Earnings Ratio			
May 31, 2011 and 2010			
		2011	2010
Market price per common share (May 31, close) [A]		$84.45	$72.38
Diluted earnings per share before nonrecurring items [B]		$ 4.39	$ 3.86
Price/earnings ratio [A ÷ B]		19.24	18.75
Source: Nike, Inc. 2010 10-K			

for all of the stocks on an exchange, such as the New York Stock Exchange. These averages will vary greatly over several years.

Investors view the P/E ratio as a gauge of future earning power of the firm. Companies with high-growth opportunities generally have high P/E ratios; firms with low-growth tend to have lower P/E ratios. However, investors may be wrong in their estimates of growth potential. One fundamental of investing is to be wiser than the market. An example would be buying a stock that has a relatively low P/E ratio when the prospects for the company are much better than reflected in the P/E ratio.

P/E ratios do not have any meaning when a firm has abnormally low profits in relation to the asset base or when a firm has losses. The P/E ratio in these cases would be abnormally high or negative.

Percentage of Earnings Retained

The proportion of current earnings retained for internal growth is computed as follows:

$$\text{Percentage of Earnings Retained} = \frac{\text{Net Income Before Nonrecurring Items} - \text{All Dividends}}{\text{Net Income Before Nonrecurring Items}}$$

The percentage of earnings retained is better for trend analysis if nonrecurring items are removed. This indicates what is being retained of recurring earnings. Determine dividends from the statement of cash flows.

A problem occurs because the percentage of earnings retained implies that earnings represent a cash pool for paying dividends. Under accrual accounting, earnings do not represent a cash pool. Operating cash flow compared with cash dividends gives a better indication of the cash from operations and the dividends paid. Chapter 10 introduces this ratio.

Many firms have a policy on the percentage of earnings that they want retained—for example, between 60% and 75%. In general, new firms, growing firms, and firms perceived as growth firms will have a relatively high percentage of earnings retained. Many new firms, growing firms, and firms perceived as growing firms do not pay dividends.

In the *Almanac of Business and Industrial Financial Ratios*, the percentage of earnings retained is called the *ratio of retained earnings to net income*. The phrase *retained earnings* as used in the ratio in the *Almanac* is a misnomer. Retained earnings in this ratio does not mean accumulated profits but rather that portion of income retained in a single year. Hence, this ratio has two different names.

Exhibit 9-5 shows the percentage of earnings retained by Nike using 2011 and 2010 figures. Nike retains a substantial proportion of its profits for internal use. The percentage of earnings retained has been consistent [2001 (78.01%); 2002 (80.71%); 2003 (81.38%); 2004 (81.05%); 2005 (80.46%); 2006 (79.10%); 2007 (76.96%); 2008 (78.08%); 2009 (68.61%); 2010 (73.52%); 2011 (73.98%)]. The year 2009 was the low year in those years because of some significant charges to operations.

EXHIBIT **9-5** Nike, Inc.		
Percentage of Earnings Retained		
Years Ended May 31, 2011 and 2010		
(In millions)	**2011**	**2010**
Net income before nonrecurring items [B]	$ 2,133.0	$ 1,907.0
Less: Dividends	(555.0)	(505.0)
Earnings retained [A]	$ 1,378.0	$ 1,402.0
Percentage of earnings retained [A ÷ B]	73.98%	73.52%
Source: Nike, Inc. 2010 10-K		

Dividend Payout

The dividend payout measures the portion of current earnings per common share being paid out in dividends. Compute the dividend payout ratio as follows:

$$\text{Dividend Payout} = \frac{\text{Dividends per Common Share}}{\text{Diluted Earnings per Share Before Nonrecurring Items}}$$

Earnings per share are diluted in the formula because this is the most conservative viewpoint. Ideally, diluted earnings per share should not include nonrecurring items since directors normally look at recurring earnings to develop a stable dividend policy.

The dividend payout ratio has a similar problem as the percentage of earnings retained. Investors may assume that dividend payout implies that earnings per share represent cash. Under accrual accounting, earnings per share do not represent a cash pool.

Most firms hesitate to decrease dividends since this tends to have adverse effects on the market price of the company's stock. No rule of thumb exists for a correct payout ratio. Some stockholders prefer high dividends; others prefer to have the firm reinvest the earnings in hopes of higher capital gains. In the latter case, the payout ratio would be a relatively smaller percentage.

Exhibit 9-6 presents Nike's 2011 and 2010 dividend payout ratios, which increased from 27.46% in 2010 to 27.33% in 2011. These are conservative payout ratios. Often, to

EXHIBIT **9-6**	Nike, Inc.		
Dividend Payout			
Years Ended May 31, 2011 and 2010			
		2011	2010
Dividends per share [A]		$ 1.20	$ 1.06
Diluted earnings per share before nonrecurring items [B]		$ 4.39	$ 3.86
Dividend payout ratio [A ÷ B]		27.33%	27.46%
Source: Nike, Inc. 2010 10-K			

attract the type of stockholder who looks favorably on a low dividend payout ratio, a company must have a good return on common equity. The dividend payout has been fairly consistent but did turn up in 2009 [2001 (22.22%); 2002 (19.51%); 2003 (19.49%); 2004 (21.08%); 2005 (21.21%); 2006 (22.35%); 2007 (24.23%)]; 2008 (23.40%); 2009 (32.34%); 2010 (27.46%); 2011 (27.33%)].

Industry averages of dividend payout ratios are available in *Standard & Poor's Industry Surveys.* Although no correct payout exists, even within an industry, the outlook for the industry often makes the bulk of the ratios in a particular industry similar.

In general, new firms, growing firms, and firms perceived as growth firms have a relatively low dividend payout. Nike would be considered a growing firm.

Dividend Yield

The dividend yield indicates the relationship between the dividends per common share and the market price per common share. Compute the dividend yield as follows:

$$\text{Dividend Yield} = \frac{\text{Dividends per Common Share}}{\text{Market Price per Common Share}}$$

For this ratio, multiply the fourth quarter dividend declared by 4. This indicates the current dividend rate. Exhibit 9-7 shows the dividend yield for Nike for 2011 and 2010. The dividend yield has been relatively low. Investors were likely satisfied with the dividend yield for Nike.

Since total earnings from securities include both dividends and price appreciation, no rule of thumb exists for dividend yield. The yield depends on the firm's dividend policy and the market price. If the firm successfully invests the money not distributed as dividends, the price should rise. If the firm holds the dividends at low amounts to allow for reinvestment of profits, the dividend yield is likely to be low. A low dividend yield satisfies many investors if the company has a record of above-average return on common equity. Investors that want current income prefer a high dividend yield.

EXHIBIT **9-7**	Nike, Inc.		
Dividend Yield			
May 31, 2011 and 2010			
		2011	2010
Dividends per share [A]		$ 1.20	$ 1.06
Market price per share [B]		$ 84.45	$ 72.38
Dividend yield [A ÷ B]		1.42%	1.46%
Source: Nike, Inc. 2010 10-K			

Book Value per Share

A figure frequently published in annual reports is book value per share, which indicates the amount of stockholders' equity that relates to each share of outstanding common stock. The formula for book value per share follows:

$$\text{Book Value per Share} = \frac{\text{Total Shareholders' Equity} - \text{Preferred Stock Equity}}{\text{Number of Common Shares Outstanding}}$$

Preferred stock equity should be stated at liquidation price, if other than book, because the preferred stockholders would be paid this value in the event of liquidation. Liquidation value is sometimes difficult to locate in an annual report. If this value cannot be found, the book figure that relates to preferred stock may be used in place of liquidation value. Exhibit 9-8 shows the book value per share for Nike for 2011 and 2010. The book value increased from $20.15 in 2010 to $21.03 in 2011.

EXHIBIT **9-8**	Nike, Inc.	

Book Value per Share

May 31, 2011 and 2010

(In millions)	2011	2010
Shareholders' equity	$9,843.0	$9,754.0
Less: Preferred stock*	—	—
Adjusted shareholders' equity [A]	$9,843.0	$9,754.0
Shares outstanding [B]	468	484
Book value per share [A ÷ B]	$ 21.03	$ 20.15

*Redeemable preferred stock classified above shareholders' equity.
Source: Nike, Inc. 2010 10-K

The market price of the securities usually does not approximate the book value. These historical dollars reflect past unrecovered cost of the assets. The market value of the stock, however, reflects the potential of the firm as seen by the investor. For example, land will be valued at cost, and this asset value will be reflected in the book value. If the asset were purchased several years ago and is now worth substantially more, however, the market value of the stock may recognize this potential.

Book value is of limited use to the investment analyst since it is based on the book numbers. When market value is below book value, investors view the company as lacking potential. A market value above book value indicates that investors view the company as having enough potential to be worth more than the book numbers. Note that Nike was selling materially above book value (Market 2011, $84.45).

When investors are pessimistic about the prospects for stocks, the stocks sell below book value. On the other hand, when investors are optimistic about stock prospects, the stocks sell above book value. There have been times when the majority of stocks sold below book value. There have also been times when the majority of stocks sold at a multiple of five or six times book value.

Stock Options (Stock-Based Compensation)

Corporations frequently provide stock options (or other stock-based compensation) for employees and officers of the company. Setting aside shares for options (or other stock-based compensation) is very popular in the United States.

A basic understanding of stock option accounting (or other stock-based compensation) is needed in order to assess the disclosure of a company.

In December 2004, the FASB issued SFAS No. 123, revised (R), which is a revision of SFAS No. 123, "Accounting for Stock-Based Compensation." Prior to SFAS No. 123 (R), a company could elect to present the effect of stock-based compensation expense in the body of the income statement or in the notes. Under SFAS No. 123 (R), the effect of stock-based compensation must be presented in the income statement (disclosure detail can be in the notes).

The Securities and Exchange Commission accepted SFAS No. 123 (R), except for the compliance dates. In April 2005, the Commission issued revised compliance dates. The Commission rule allows companies to implement SFAS No. 123 (R) at the beginning of their fiscal year, instead of the next reporting period, which begins after June 15, 2005 (or December 15, 2005 for small-business issuers).

SFAS No. 123 (R) resulted in greater international comparability in the accounting for share-based transactions. In February 2004, the IASB issued a reporting standard that requires all entities to recognize an expense for all employee services received in share-based payment transactions, using a fair-value-based method that is similar in most respects to the fair-value–based method established in SFAS No. 123 (R).

SFAS No. 123 (R) essentially carried forward the reporting of noncompensatory plans. A noncompensatory plan attempts to raise capital or encourage widespread ownership of the corporation's stock among officers and employees. Because the officers and employees purchase the stock at only a slight discount (usually 5% or less) from the market price, there is not a substantial dilution of the position of existing stockholders or a substantial compensation issue. For those plans, no compensation expense is recognized when these options are exercised, and the shares are issued slightly below the market price.

Two terms that are particularly important to understanding SFAS No. 123 (R) are *grant date* and *vested*. The **grant date** is the date at which an employer and an employee reach a mutual understanding of the key terms and conditions of a share-based payment award. The employer becomes contingently obligated on the grant date to issue equity instruments or transfer assets to an employee who renders the requisite service.[1] A share-based payment award becomes vested at the date that the employee's right to receive or retain shares, other instruments, or cash under the award is no longer contingent on satisfaction of either a service condition or a performance condition.[2]

Key provisions of SFAS No. 123 (R) are as follows:

1. It requires a public entity to measure the cost of employee services received in exchange for an award of equity instruments based on the grant-date fair value of the award.
2. The option expense will be recognized over the period during which an employee is required to provide service in exchange for the award (usually the vesting period).
3. A public entity will initially measure the cost of employee services received in exchange for an award of liability instruments based on its current fair value.
4. The notes to financial statements of both public and nonpublic entities will disclose information to assist users of financial information to understand the nature of share-based payment transactions and the effects of these transactions on the financial statements.

Warren E. Buffett, one of the world's richest persons and likely the world's most famous investor, had been critical of firms that do not recognize option expense in the body of the income statement. His view was that option expense needed to be considered when evaluating the performance of a company.

When stock prices decline, is there a value to holding stock options? A decline in stock prices could make the existing stock options worthless. But many companies rewrite the options with a lower price when the stock declines. Thus, for the holders of the options, it becomes a situation of "tails I win, heads I win." Buffett tells the following story relating to stock options:

> A gorgeous woman slinks up to a CEO at a party and through moist lips purrs, "I'll do anything—anything—you want. Just tell me what you would like." With no hesitation, he replies, "Reprice my options."[3]

> Warren Buffett

Nike disclosed $105, $159, and $171 (in millions) in total stock-based compensation for the years ended May 31, 2011, 2010, and 2009, respectively (Exhibit 9-9).

The impact of option expense can be substantial, resulting in lower net income and earnings per share. It can have a particularly material impact on high-tech companies that are rewarding employees with substantial stock-based compensation.

To assist in determining the materiality of options, use the following ratio:

$$\text{Materiality of Options} = \frac{\substack{\text{Net Income Before Nonrecurring Items Not Including} \\ \text{Option Expense} - \text{Net Income Before Nonrecurring Items} \\ \text{Including Option Expense}}}{\substack{\text{Net Income Before Nonrecurring Items Not} \\ \text{Including Option Expense}}}$$

Using data from Exhibits 9-5 and 9-9 for Nike, the materiality of options is computed for 2011. The total stock-based compensation expense was adjusted for estimated taxes.

$$\text{Materiality of Options} = \frac{(\$2{,}133 + \$77) - \$2{,}133}{\$2{,}133 + \$77}$$

$$= 3.48\%$$

For Nike, the impact of option expense appears to be moderate.

EXHIBIT **9-9** Nike, Inc.

Stock-Based Compensation Expense

Note 11—Common Stock and Stock-Based Compensation (In Part)

The authorized number of shares of Class A Common Stock, no par value, and Class B Common Stock, no par value, are 175 million and 750 million, respectively. Each share of Class A Common Stock is convertible into one share of Class B Common Stock. Voting rights of Class B Common Stock are limited in certain circumstances with respect to the election of directors.

In 1990, the Board of Directors adopted, and the shareholders approved, the NIKE, Inc. 1990 Stock Incentive Plan (the "1990 Plan"). The 1990 Plan provides for the issuance of up to 163 million previously unissued shares of Class B Common Stock in connection with stock options and other awards granted under the plan. The 1990 Plan authorizes the grant of non-statutory stock options, incentive stock options, stock appreciation rights, restricted stock, restricted stock units, and performance-based awards. The exercise price for stock options and stock appreciation rights may not be less than the fair market value of the underlying shares on the date of grant. A committee of the Board of Directors administers the 1990 Plan. The committee has the authority to determine the employees to whom awards will be made, the amount of the awards, and the other terms and conditions of the awards. Substantially all stock option grants outstanding under the 1990 plan were granted in the first quarter of each fiscal year, vest ratably over four years, and expire 10 years from the date of grant.

The following table summarizes the Company's total stock-based compensation expense recognized in selling and administrative expense:

	Year Ended May 31,		
	2011	2010	2009
	(In millions)		
Stock options[1]	$ 77	$135	$129
ESPPs	14	14	14
Restricted stock	14	10	8
Subtotal	$105	$159	$151
Stock options and restricted stock expense—restructuring[2]	—	—	20
Total stock-based compensation expense	$105	$159	$171

[1]Expense for stock options includes the expense associated with stock appreciation rights. Accelerated stock option expense is recorded for employees eligible for accelerated stock option vesting upon retirement. In the first quarter of fiscal 2011, the Company changed the accelerated vesting provisions of its stock option plan. Under the new provisions, accelerated stock option expense for year ended May 31, 2011 was $12 million. The accelerated stock option expense for the years ended May 31, 2010 and 2009 was $74 million and $59 million, respectively.

[2]In connection with the restructuring activities that took place during fiscal 2009, the Company recognized stock-based compensation expense relating to the modification of stock option agreements, allowing for an extended post-termination exercise period, and accelerated vesting of restricted stock as part of severance packages. See Note 16—Restructuring Charges for further details.

As of May 31, 2011, the Company had $111 million of unrecognized compensation costs from stock options, net of estimated forfeitures, to be recognized as selling and administrative expense over a weighted average period of 2.2 years.

Source: Nike, Inc. 2010 10-K

Restricted Stock

In July 2003, Microsoft Corporation announced that it would stop issuing stock options to employees and instead give them restricted stock. This was a defining event in the popularity of restricted stock and the reduction in stock option plans.

With restricted stock, employees cannot sell their shares until a certain amount of time passes, and employees may have to forfeit their shares if they leave before vesting. Often, a portion of the shares vest each year for three, four, or five years. For some restricted stock, an employee forfeits the shares if certain financial targets are not met. With restricted stock, the expense is booked by companies in a manner similar to the new requirement for expensing options.

Some employees prefer restricted stock over options because they receive actual shares of stock. Usually, the employee receives dividends. This may occur before the stock has vested.

Traditionally, restricted stock was only awarded to top executives, possibly along with options. In anticipation of a standard requiring expensing of options, firms started to issue restricted stock to a broad group of employees instead of options, sometimes in conjunction with options.

For Nike, as shown in Exhibit 9-9, restricted stock was included in the total stock-based compensation expense.

Stock Appreciation Rights

Some firms grant key employees **stock appreciation rights** instead of stock options or in addition to stock options. Stock appreciation rights give the employee the right to receive compensation in cash or stock (or a combination of these) at some future date, based on the difference between the market price of the stock at the date of exercise over a preestablished price.

The accounting for stock appreciation rights directs that the compensation expense recognized each period be based on the difference between the quoted market value at the end of each period and the option price. This compensation expense is then reduced by previously recognized compensation expense on the stock appreciation right. For example, assume that the option price is $10.00 and the market value is $15.00 at the end of the first period of the stock appreciation right. Compensation expense would be recognized at $5.00 ($15.00 − $10.00) per share included in the plan. If 100,000 shares are in the plan, then the expense to be charged to the income statement would be $500,000 ($5.00 × 100,000 shares). If the market value is $12.00 at the end of the second period of the stock appreciation right, expenses are reduced by $3.00 per share. This is because the total compensation expense for the two years is $2.00 ($12.00 − $10.00). Since $5.00 of expense was recognized in the first year, $3.00 of negative compensation is considered in the second year in order to total $2.00 of expense. With 100,000 shares, the reduction to expenses in the second year would be $300,000 ($3.00 × 100,000 shares). Thus, stock appreciation rights can have a material influence on income, dictated by changing stock prices.

A company with outstanding stock appreciation rights describes them in a note to the financial statements. If the number of shares is known, a possible future influence on income can be computed, based on assumptions made regarding future market prices. For example, if the note discloses that the firm has 50,000 shares of stock appreciation rights outstanding, and the stock market price was $10.00 at the end of the year, the analyst can assume a market price at the end of next year and compute the compensation expense for next year. With these facts and an assumed market price of $15.00 at the end of next year, the compensation expense for next year can be computed to be $250,000 [($15.00 − $10.00) × 50,000 shares]. This potential charge to earnings should be considered as the stock is evaluated as a potential investment.

Stock appreciation rights tied to the future market price of the stock can represent a material potential drain on the company. Even a relatively small number of stock appreciation rights outstanding could be material. This should be considered by existing and potential stockholders. Some firms have placed limits on the potential appreciation in order to control the cost of appreciation rights.

The General Electric Company 2001 annual report indicated that "at year-end 2001, there were 131 thousand stock appreciation rights outstanding at an average exercise price of $7.68." The General Electric Company stock price during 2001 ranged from a low of $28.25 to a high of $52.90.

Apparently, stock appreciation rights were not outstanding as of May 31, 2011 for Nike.

Summary

This chapter has reviewed certain types of analysis that particularly concern investors. Ratios relevant to this analysis include the following:

$$\text{Degree of Financial Leverage} = \frac{\text{Earnings Before Interest and Tax}}{\text{Earnings Before Tax}}$$

$$\text{All-Inclusive Degree of Financial Leverage} = \frac{\text{Earnings Before Interest, Tax, Noncontrolling Interest, Equity Income, and Nonrecurring Items}}{\text{Earnings Before Tax, Noncontrolling Interest, Equity Income, and Nonrecurring Items}}$$

$$\text{Earnings per Share} = \frac{\text{Net Income} - \text{Preferred Dividends}}{\text{Weighted Average Number of Common Shares Outstanding}}$$

$$\text{Price/Earnings Ratio} = \frac{\text{Market Price per Share}}{\text{Diluted Earnings per Share, Before Nonrecurring Items}}$$

$$\text{Percentage of Earnings Retained} = \frac{\text{Net Income Before Nonrecurring Items} - \text{All Dividends}}{\text{Net Income Before Nonrecurring Items}}$$

$$\text{Dividend Payout} = \frac{\text{Dividends per Common Share}}{\text{Diluted Earnings per Share Before Nonrecurring Items}}$$

$$\text{Dividend Yield} = \frac{\text{Dividends per Common Share}}{\text{Market Price per Common Share}}$$

$$\text{Book Value per Share} = \frac{\text{Total Shareholders' Equity} - \text{Preferred Stock Equity}}{\text{Number of Common Shares Outstanding}}$$

$$\text{Materiality of Options} = \frac{\text{Net Income Before Nonrecurring Items Not Including Option Expense} - \text{Net Income Before Nonrecurring Items Including Option Expense}}{\text{Net Income Before Nonrecurring Items Not Including Option Expense}}$$

Questions

Q 9-1 Give a simple definition of *earnings per share.*

Q 9-2 Assume that a corporation is a nonpublic company. Comment on the requirement for this firm to disclose earnings per share.

Q 9-3 Keller & Fink, a partnership, engages in the wholesale fish market. How would this company disclose earnings per share?

Q 9-4 Dividends on preferred stock total $5,000 for the current year. How would these dividends influence earnings per share?

Q 9-5 The denominator of the earnings per share computation includes the weighted average number of common shares outstanding. Why use the weighted average instead of the year-end common shares outstanding?

Q 9-6 Preferred dividends decreased this year because some preferred stock was retired. How would this influence the earnings per share computation this year?

Q 9-7 Retroactive recognition is given to stock dividends and stock splits on common stock when computing earnings per share. Why?

Q 9-8 Why do many firms try to maintain a stable percentage of earnings retained?

Q 9-9 Define *financial leverage.* What is its effect on earnings? When is the use of financial leverage advantageous and disadvantageous?

Q 9-10 Given a set level of earnings before interest and tax, how will a rise in interest rates affect the degree of financial leverage?

Q 9-11 Why is the price/earnings ratio considered a gauge of future earning power?

Q 9-12 Why does a relatively new firm often have a low dividend payout ratio? Why does a firm with a substantial growth record and/or substantial growth prospects often have a low dividend payout ratio?

Q 9-13 Why would an investor ever buy stock in a firm with a low dividend yield?

Q 9-14 Why is book value often meaningless? What improvements to financial statements would make it more meaningful?

Q 9-15 Why should an investor read the note concerning stock options? How might stock options affect profitability?

Q 9-16 Why can a relatively small number of stock appreciation rights prove to be a material drain on future earnings and cash of a company?

Q 9-17 Explain how outstanding stock appreciation rights could increase reported income in a particular year.

Problems

P 9-1 McDonald Company shows the following condensed income statement information for the current year:

Revenue from sales		$ 3,500,000
Cost of products sold		(1,700,000)
Gross profit	1,800,000	
Operating expenses:		
Selling expenses	$ 425,000	
General expenses	350,000	(775,000)
Operating income		1,025,000
Other income		20,000
Interest		(70,000)
Operating income before income taxes		975,000
Taxes related to operations		(335,000)
Income from operations		640,000
Extraordinary loss (less applicable income taxes of $40,000)		(80,000)
Income before noncontrolling interest		560,000
Noncontrolling interest (loss)		(50,000)
Net income		$ 510,000

Required Calculate the degree of financial leverage.

P 9-2 A firm has earnings before interest and tax of $1,000,000, interest of $200,000, and net income of $400,000 in Year 1.

Required
a. Calculate the degree of financial leverage in base Year 1.
b. If earnings before interest and tax increase by 10% in Year 2, what will be the new level of earnings, assuming the same tax rate as in Year 1?
c. If earnings before interest and tax decrease to $800,000 in Year 2, what will be the new level of earnings, assuming the same tax rate as in Year 1?

P 9-3 The following information was in the annual report of Rover Company:

	2011	2010	2009
Earnings per share	$ 1.12	$ 1.20	$ 1.27
Cash dividends per share (common)	$ 0.90	$ 0.85	$ 0.82
Market price per share	$ 12.80	$ 14.00	$ 16.30
Total common dividends	$ 21,700,000	$ 19,500,000	$ 18,360,000
Shares outstanding, end of year	24,280,000	23,100,000	22,500,000
Total assets	$1,280,100,000	$1,267,200,000	$1,260,400,000
Total liabilities	$ 800,400,000	$ 808,500,000	$ 799,200,000
Nonredeemable preferred stock	$ 15,300,000	$ 15,300,000	$ 15,300,000
Preferred dividends	$ 910,000	$ 910,000	$ 910,000
Net income	$ 31,200,000	$ 30,600,000	$ 29,800,000

(*continued*)

(P 9-3 CONTINUED)

Required

a. Based on these data, compute the following for 2011, 2010, and 2009:

 1. Percentage of earnings retained
 2. Price/earnings ratio
 3. Dividend payout
 4. Dividend yield
 5. Book value per share

b. Discuss your findings from the viewpoint of a potential investor.

P 9-4 The following data relate to Edger Company:

	2011	2010	2009
Earnings per share	$ 2.30	$ 3.40	$ 4.54
Dividends per share	$ 1.90	$ 1.90	$ 1.90
Market price, end of year	$ 41.25	$ 35.00	$ 29.00
Net income	$ 9,100,000	$ 13,300,000	$ 16,500,000
Total cash dividends	$ 6,080,000	$ 5,900,000	$ 6,050,000
Order backlog at year-end	$5,490,800,000	$4,150,200,000	$3,700,100,000
Net contracts awarded	$2,650,700,000	$1,800,450,000	$3,700,100,000

Note: The stock was selling at 120.5%, 108.0%, and 105.0% of book value in 2011, 2010, and 2009, respectively.

Required

a. Compute the following for 2011, 2010, and 2009:

 1. Percentage of earnings retained
 2. Price/earnings ratio
 3. Dividend payout
 4. Dividend yield
 5. Book value per share

b. Comment on your results from (a). Include in your discussion the data on backlog and new contracts awarded.

P 9-5 Dicker Company has the following pattern of financial data for Years 1 and 2:

	Year 1	Year 2
Net income	$ 40,000	$ 42,000
Preferred stock (5%)	$450,000	$550,000
Weighted average number of common shares outstanding	38,000	38,000

Required Calculate earnings per share and comment on the trend.

P 9-6 Assume the following facts for the current year:

 Common shares outstanding on January 1: 50,000 shares
 July 1: 2-for-1 stock split
 October 1: a stock issue of 10,000 shares

Required Compute the denominator of the earnings per share computation for the current year.

P 9-7 XYZ Corporation reported earnings per share of $2.00 in 2010. In 2011, XYZ Corporation reported earnings per share of $1.50. On July 1, 2011, and December 31, 2011, 2-for-1 stock splits were declared.

Required Present the earnings per share for a two-year comparative income statement that includes 2011 and 2010.

P 9-8 Cook Company shows the following condensed income statement information for the year ended December 31, 2011:

Income before extraordinary gain	$30,000
Plus: Extraordinary gain, net of tax expense of $2,000	5,000
Net income	$35,000

The company declared dividends of $3,000 on preferred stock and $5,000 on common stock. At the beginning of 2011, 20,000 shares of common stock were outstanding. On July 1, 2011, the company issued 1,000 additional common shares. The preferred stock is not convertible.

Required
a. Compute the earnings per share.
b. How much of the earnings per share appears to be recurring?

P 9-9 Assume the following facts for the current year:

Net income	$200,000
Common dividends	$ 20,000
Preferred dividends (The preferred stock is not convertible.)	$ 10,000
Common shares outstanding on January 1	20,000 shares
Common stock issued on July 1	5,000 shares
2-for-1 stock split on December 31	

Required
a. Compute the earnings per share for the current year.
b. Earnings per share in the prior year was $8.00. Use the earnings per share computed in (a) and present a two-year earnings per share comparison for the current year and the prior year.

P 9-10 Smith and Jones, Inc. is primarily engaged in the worldwide production, processing, distribution, and marketing of food products. The following information is from its 2011 annual report:

	2011	2010
Earnings per share	$ 1.08	$ 1.14
Cash dividends per common share	$ 0.80	$ 0.76
Market price per common share	$ 12.94	$ 15.19
Common shares outstanding	25,380,000	25,316,000
Total assets	$1,264,086,000	$1,173,924,000
Total liabilities	$ 823,758,000	$ 742,499,000
Nonredeemable preferred stock	$ 16,600,000	$ 16,600,000
Preferred dividends	$ 4,567,000	$ 930,000
Net income	$ 32,094,000	$ 31,049,000

Required
a. Based on these data, compute the following for 2011 and 2010:

1. Percentage of earnings retained
2. Price/earnings ratio
3. Dividend payout
4. Dividend yield
5. Book value per share

b. Discuss your findings from the viewpoint of a potential investor.

P 9-11 On December 31, 2011, Farley Camera, Inc., issues 5,000 stock appreciation rights to its president to entitle her to receive cash for the difference between the market price of its stock and a preestablished price of $20. The date of exercise is December 31, 2012, and the required service period is the entire three years. The market price fluctuates as follows: 12/31/12—$23.00; 12/31/13—$21.00; 12/31/14—$26.00. Farley Camera accrued the following compensation expense:

2012	$15,000	2013	$(10,000)	2014	$25,000

Required
a. What is the executive's main advantage of receiving stock appreciation rights over stock options?
b. In 2012, a $15,000 expense is recorded. What is the offsetting account?
c. What is the financial impact on the company of the exercise of the stock appreciation rights in 2014? How does this impact affect financial statement analysis?

P 9-12a A company has only common stock outstanding.

Required Answer the following multiple-choice question. Total stockholders' equity minus preferred stock equity divided by the number of shares outstanding represents the

1. Return on equity.
2. Stated value per share.
3. Book value per share.
4. Price/earnings ratio.

P 9-12b Maple Corporation's stockholders' equity at June 30, 2011 consisted of the following:

Preferred stock, 10%, $50 par value; liquidating value, $55 per share; 20,000 shares issued and outstanding	$1,000,000
Common stock, $10 par value; 500,000 shares authorized; 150,000 shares issued and outstanding	1,500,000
Retained earnings	500,000

Required Answer the following multiple-choice question. The book value per share of common stock is

1. $10.00.
2. $12.67.
3. $13.33.
4. $17.65.

P 9-13 Consecutive five-year balance sheets and income statements of Donna Szabo Corporation are shown below and on the following page.

Required

a. Compute or determine the following for the years 2007–2011:

1. Degree of financial leverage
2. Earnings per common share
3. Price/earnings ratio
4. Percentage of earnings retained
5. Dividend payout
6. Dividend yield
7. Book value per share
8. Materiality of options (use stock options outstanding)

b. Comment from the perspective of an investor.

DONNA SZABO CORPORATION
BALANCE SHEETS
December 31, 2007 through December 31, 2011

(Dollars in thousands)	2011	2010	2009	2008	2007
Assets					
Current assets:					
Cash	$ 26,000	$ 27,000	$ 29,000	$ 28,000	$ 27,000
Accounts receivable, net	125,000	126,000	128,000	130,000	128,000
Inventories	140,000	143,000	145,000	146,000	144,000
Total current assets	291,000	296,000	302,000	304,000	299,000
Property, plant, and equipment, net	420,000	418,000	417,000	418,000	415,000
Total assets	$ 711,000	$ 714,000	$ 719,000	$ 722,000	$ 714,000
Liabilities and Stockholders' Equity					
Current liabilities:					
Accounts payable	$ 120,000	$ 122,000	$ 122,500	$ 124,000	$ 125,000
Income taxes	12,000	13,000	13,500	13,000	12,000
Total current liabilities	132,000	135,000	136,000	137,000	137,000
Long-term debt	90,000	65,000	67,000	68,000	69,000

(Dollars in thousands)	2011	2010	2009	2008	2007
Stockholders' equity:					
Preferred stock	49,000	76,000	80,000	82,000	75,000
Common stock	290,000	290,000	290,000	290,000	290,000
Paid-in capital in excess of par, common stock	70,000	70,000	70,000	70,000	70,000
Retained earnings	80,000	78,000	76,000	75,000	73,000
Total stockholders' equity	489,000	514,000	516,000	517,000	508,000
Total liabilities and stockholders' equity	$711,000	$714,000	$719,000	$722,000	$714,000

DONNA SZABO CORPORATION
STATEMENT OF EARNINGS
Years Ended December 31, 2007–2011

(In thousands, except per share)	2011	2010	2009	2008	2007
Net sales	$ 890,000	$ 870,000	$ 850,000	$ 935,000	$ 920,000
Cost of goods sold	(540,000)	(530,700)	(522,750)	(579,000)	(570,000)
Gross profit	350,000	339,300	327,250	356,000	350,000
Selling and administrative expense	(230,000)	(225,000)	(220,000)	(225,000)	(224,000)
Interest expense	(9,500)	(6,600)	(6,800)	(6,900)	(7,000)
Earnings from continuing operations before income taxes	110,500	107,700	100,450	124,100	119,000
Income taxes	(33,000)	(33,300)	(32,100)	(30,400)	(37,400)
Earnings from continuing operations	77,500	74,400	68,350	93,700	81,600
Extraordinary gains, net of taxes	20,000	—	—	—	—
Net earnings	$ 97,500	$ 74,400	$ 68,350	$ 93,700	$ 81,600
Earnings per share:					
Continuing operations	$ 2.67	$ 2.57	$ 2.36	$ 3.23	$ 2.81
Extraordinary gain	0.69	—	—	—	—
Net earnings per share	$ 3.36	$ 2.57	$ 2.36	$ 3.23	$ 2.81

Note: Additional data:

1. Preferred stock dividends (in thousands):

2011	$3,920
2010	$6,100
2009	$6,400
2008	$6,600
2007	$6,000

2. Common shares outstanding, 29,000,000 (actual) (2007–2011)
3. Stock options outstanding, 1,000,000 (actual) (2007–2011)
4. Dividends per common share (actual):

2011	$3.16
2010	$2.29
2009	$2.10
2008	$2.93
2007	$2.80

5. Market price per common share (actual):

2011	$24.00
2010	$22.00
2009	$21.00
2008	$37.00
2007	$29.00

P 9-14 Answer the following multiple-choice questions:

a. In 2009 and 2010, Zoret Company reported earnings per share of $0.80 and $1.00, respectively. In 2011, Zoret Company declared a 4-for-1 stock split. For the year 2011, Zoret Company reported earnings of $0.30 per share. The appropriate earnings per share presentation for a three-year comparative analysis that includes 2009, 2010, and 2011 would be

	2011	2010	2009
1.	$0.30	$0.25	$0.80
2.	$0.30	$4.00	$3.20
3.	$0.30	$0.25	$0.20
4.	$1.20	$0.25	$0.20
5.	$1.20	$4.00	$3.20

b. The degree of financial leverage for Zorro Company was 1.50 when EBIT was reported at $1,000,000. If EBIT goes to $2,000,000, the accompanying change in net income will be

1. $2,500,000.
2. $3,000,000.
3. $2,000,000.
4. $1,500,000.
5. $1,000,000.

c. In 2012, Zello Company declared a 10% stock dividend. In 2011, earnings per share was $1.00. When the 2011 earnings per share is disclosed in the 2012 annual report, it will be disclosed at

1. $1.00.
2. $1.10.
3. $1.20.
4. $0.91.
5. $0.81.

d. Which of the following ratios usually reflects investors' opinions of the future prospects for the firm?

1. Dividend yield
2. Book value per share
3. Price/earnings ratio
4. Earnings per share
5. Dividend payout

e. Which of the following ratios gives a perspective on risk in the capital structure?

1. Book value per share
2. Dividend yield
3. Dividend payout
4. Degree of financial leverage
5. Price/earnings ratio

f. The earnings per share ratio is computed for

1. Convertible bonds.
2. Redeemable preferred stock.
3. Common stock.
4. Nonredeemable preferred stock.
5. None of the above.

g. Increasing financial leverage can be a risky strategy from the viewpoint of stockholders of companies having

1. Steady and high profits.
2. Low and falling profits.
3. Relatively high and increasing profits.
4. A low debt/equity ratio and relatively high profits.
5. None of the above.

h. A firm has a degree of financial leverage of 1.3. If earnings before interest and tax increase by 10%, then net income

1. Will increase by 13.0%.
2. Will increase by 13.
3. Will decrease by 13.0%.
4. Will decrease by 13.
5. None of the above.

i. The ratio that represents dividends per common share in relation to market price per common share is

1. Dividend payout.
2. Dividend yield.
3. Price/earnings.
4. Book value per share.
5. Percentage of earnings retained.

j. Book value per share may not approximate market value per share because

1. Investments may have a market value substantially above the original cost.
2. Land may have substantially increased in value.
3. Market value reflects future potential earning power.
4. The firm owns patents that have substantial value.
5. All of the above.

Cases

CASE 9-1 FOREST PRODUCTS

WEYERHAEUSER COMPANY*
CONSOLIDATED STATEMENT OF OPERATIONS
for the three-year period ended December 31, 2010

DOLLAR AMOUNTS IN MILLIONS, EXCEPT PER SHARE FIGURES

	2010	2009	2008
Net sales and revenues	$ 6,552	$ 5,528	$ 8,100
Cost of products sold	5,392	5,127	7,508
Gross margin	1,160	401	592
Selling, general and administrative expenses	677	709	996
Research and development expenses	34	51	66
Alternative fuel mixture credits (Note 21)	—	(344)	—
Charges for restructuring, closures and impairments (Note 19)	149	698	2,118
Other operating costs (income), net (Note 20)	(168)	(266)	13
Operating income (loss)	468	(447)	(2,601)
Interest income and other	83	74	366
Impairment of investments and other related charges (Note 19)	(3)	(7)	(160)
Interest expense, net of capitalized interest	(452)	(462)	(414)
Earnings (loss) from continuing operations before income taxes	96	(842)	(2,809)
Income tax benefit (Note 21)	1,187	274	900
Earnings (loss) from continuing operations	1,283	(568)	(1,909)
Earnings from discontinued operations, net of income taxes (Note 4)	—	—	667
Net earnings (loss)	1,283	(568)	(1,242)
Less: net (earnings) loss attributable to noncontrolling interests	(2)	23	66

(continued)

*We are a forest products company that grows and harvests trees, builds homes and makes a range of forest products essential to everyday lives.
Source: Forest Products, Weyerhaeuser Company 2010 10-K

(**CASE 9-1** CONTINUED)

DOLLAR AMOUNTS IN MILLIONS, EXCEPT PER SHARE FIGURES

	2010	2009	2008
Net earnings (loss) attributable to Weyerhaeuser common shareholders	$ 1,281	$ (545)	$ (1,176)
Basic earnings (loss) per share attributable to Weyerhaeuser common shareholders (Note 5):			
Continuing operations	$ 4.00	$ (2.58)	$ (8.72)
Discontinued operations	—	—	3.15
Net earnings (loss) per share	$ 4.00	$ (2.58)	$ (5.57)
Diluted earnings (loss) per share attributable to Weyerhaeuser common shareholders (Note 5):			
Continuing operations	$ 3.99	$ (2.58)	$ (8.72)
Discontinued operations	—	—	3.15
Net earnings (loss) per share	$ 3.99	$ (2.58)	$ (5.57)
Dividends paid per share (Note 2)	$ 26.61	$ 0.60	$ 2.40
Weighted average shares outstanding (in thousands) (Note 5)			
Basic	319,976	211,342	211,258
Diluted	321,096	211,342	211,258

CONSOLIDATED BALANCE SHEET (In Part)
LIABILITIES AND EQUITY

Dollar amounts in millions, except per-share figures	December 31, 2010	December 31, 2009
Total liabilities	$ 8,815	$11,196
Equity:		
Weyerhaeuser shareholders' interest (Notes 2, 17 and 18):		
Common shares: $1.25 par value, authorized 1,360,000,000 and 400,000,000 shares; issued and outstanding: 535,975,518 and 211,358,955 shares	670	264
Other capital	4,552	1,786
Retained earnings	181	2,658
Cumulative other comprehensive loss	(791)	(664)
Total Weyerhaeuser shareholders' interest	4,612	4,044
Noncontrolling interests	2	10
Total equity	4,614	4,054
Total liabilities and equity	$13,429	$15,250

CONSOLIDATED STATEMENT OF CHANGES IN EQUITY AND
COMPREHENSIVE INCOME (In Part)
FOR THE THREE-YEAR PERIOD ENDED DECEMBER 31, 2010

DOLLAR AMOUNTS IN MILLIONS

	2010	2009	2008
Common Shares:			
Balance at beginning of year	$264	$264	$262
Issued for exercise of stock options	1	—	—
Retraction or redemption of exchangeable shares	—	—	2
Special Dividend (Note 17)	405	—	—
Balance at end of year	$670	$264	$264

Required

a. 1. How many shares of common stock had been issued as of December 31, 2010?

   2. How many shares of common stock were outstanding as of December 31, 2010?

3. What share number is used to compute basic earnings per share for 2010? Describe the computation of this number.

4. What share number was used to compute diluted earnings per share for 2010? Describe the computation of this number.

5. Why the substantial difference in shares outstanding at December 31, 2010 and the weighted average shares outstanding at December 31, 2010?

b. What earnings per share number would analysts likely put more emphasis on for the year-end period ended December 31, 2010?

c. Compute the book value for December 31, 2010.

CASE 9-2 INTEGRATED ELECTRONICS

Fiscal year ended October 2, 2010

SANMINA-SCI CORPORATION*
CONSOLIDATED STATEMENTS OF OPERATIONS (In Part)

	Year Ended		
	October 2, 2010	October 3, 2009	September 27, 2008
	(In thousands, except per share amounts)		
Income (loss) from continuing operations	122,435	(137,822)	(512,936)
Income from discontinued operations, net of tax	—	—	24,987
Net income (loss)	$122,435	$(137,822)	$(487,949)
Basic earnings (loss) per share:			
Continuing operations	$ 1.55	$ (1.67)	$ (5.80)
Discontinued operations	$ —	$ —	$ 0.28
Net income (loss)	$ 1.55	$ (1.67)	$ (5.52)
Diluted earnings (loss) per share:			
Continuing operations	$ 1.48	$ (1.67)	$ (5.80)
Discontinued operations	$ —	$ —	$ 0.28
Net income (loss)	$ 1.48	$ (1.67)	$ (5.52)
Weighted-average shares used in computing per share amounts:			
Basic	79,195	82,528	88,454
Diluted	82,477	82,528	88,454

Fiscal year ended October 3, 2009

SANMINA-SCI CORPORATION*
CONSOLIDATED STATEMENTS OF OPERATIONS (In Part)

	Year Ended		
	October 3, 2009	September 27, 2008	September 29, 2007
	(In thousands, except per share amounts)		
Loss from continuing operations	(136,222)	(511,336)	(1,141,493)
Income from discontinued operations, net of tax	—	24,987	6,836
Net loss	$(136,222)	$(486,349)	$(1,134,657)
Basic and diluted earnings (loss) per share:			
Continuing operations	$ (1.65)	$ (5.78)	$ (12.99)
Discontinuing operations	$ —	$ 0.28	$ 0.08
Net loss	$ (1.65)	$ (5.50)	$ (12.91)
Weighted-average shares used in computing basic and diluted share amounts:	82,528	88,454	87,853

(*continued*)

Source: Sanmina-Sci Corporation Consolidated 2010 10-K

(**CASE 9-2** CONTINUED)

Fiscal year ended October 3, 2009
Notes to Consolidated Financial Statements (In Part)

Note 11. Stockholders Equity (In Part)

Reverse Stock Split. On July 20, 2009, the Board of Directors of the Company authorized a reverse split of its common stock at a ratio of one for six, effective August 14, 2009. The Company's stockholders previously approved the reverse split in September 2008. As a result of the reverse split, every six shares of common stock outstanding were combined into one share of common stock. The reverse split did not affect the amount of equity the Company has nor did it affect the Company's market capitalization.

Fiscal year ended September 27, 2008

SANMINA-SCI CORPORATION*
CONSOLIDATED STATEMENTS OF OPERATIONS (In Part)

	Year Ended		
	September 27, 2008	September 29, 2007	September 30, 2006
	(In thousands, except per share amounts)		
Loss from continuing operations	(511,336)	(1,141,493)	(161,465)
Income from discontinued operations, net of tax	24,987	6,836	19,908
Net loss	$(486,349)	$(1,134,657)	$(141,557)
Basic and diluted earnings (loss) per share:			
Continuing operations			
Loss before cumulative effect of accounting changes	$ (0.96)	$ (2.17)	$ (0.31)
Cumulative effect of accounting changes	—	—	—
Loss from continuing operations	$ (0.96)	(2.17)	(0.31)
Discontinued operations	$ 0.05	$ 0.01	$ 0.04
Net loss	$ (0.92)	$ (2.15)	$ (0.27)
Weighted-average shares used in computing basic and diluted per share amounts:	530,721	527,117	525,967

*"We are an independent global provider of customized, integrated electronics manufacture services, or EMS." 10-K

Required

a. For the year ended September 27, 2008, determine the loss from continuing operations from the following consolidated statements of operations (use the amounts reported):
   1. October 2, 2010
   2. October 3, 2009
   3. September 27, 2008
   4. Describe the difference in the number presented.
b. For the year ended September 27, 2008, determine the diluted earnings (loss) per share for continuing operations from the following consolidated statements of operations:
   1. October 2, 2010
   2. October 3, 2009
   3. September 27, 2008
   4. Describe the difference in the number presented.
c. For the year ended September 27, 2008, determine the weighted-average shares used in computing diluted per share from the following consolidated statements of operations:
   1. October 2, 2010
   2. October 3, 2009
   3. September 27, 2008
   4. Describe the difference in the number presented.

CASE 9-3 GLOBAL DIVERSIFIED FINANCIAL SERVICES

The Wall Street Journal—Digital Network
Tuesday, May 10, 2011
by Matt Phillips and Randall Smith

"Citigroup Inc. became a $40 stock for the first time since late 2007, as its share price appeared to rise more than 830% from Friday's close....

    Through a reverse split, Citigroup was able to ax a huge number of shares outstanding by turning every 10 shares into a single share."

    Wall Street Journal, Digital Network, Tuesday, May 10, 2011 by Matt Phillips and Randall Smith

CITIGROUP INC. AND SUBSIDIARIES*
CONSOLIDATED FINANCIAL STATEMENT OF INCOME (IN PART)
For the fiscal year ended December 21, 2010

In millions of dollars, except per-share amounts	2010	2009	2008
Citigroup's Net Income (loss)	$ 10,602	$ (1,606)	$(27,684)
Basic earnings per share[2]			
Income (loss) from continuing operations	$ 0.37	$ (0.76)	$ (6.39)
Income (loss) from discontinued operations, net of taxes	(0.01)	(0.04)	0.76
Net income (loss)	$ 0.36	$ (0.80)	$ (5.63)
Weighted average common shares outstanding	28,776.0	11,568.3	5,265.4
Diluted earnings per share[2]			
Income (loss) from continuing operations	$ 0.35	$ (0.76)	$ (6.39)
Income (loss) from discontinued operations, net of taxes	—	(0.04)	0.76
Net income (loss)	$ 0.35	$ (0.80)	$ (5.63)
Adjusted weighted average common shares outstanding	$29,678.1	$12,099.3	$5,768.9

(1) As of January 1, 2009, the Company adopted ASC 320-10-65, Investments—Debt and Equity Securities. The Company disclosed comparable information with the prior year in its 2009 periodic reports.

(2) The Diluted EPS calculation for 2009 and 2008 utilizes Basic shares and Income available to common shareholders (Basic) due to the negative Income available to common shareholders. Using actual Diluted shares and Income available to common shareholders (Diluted) would result in anti-dilution.

*"Citigroup is a global diversified financial services holding company whose businesses provide consumers, corporations, governments and institutions with a broad range of financial products and services." 10-K
Source: CitiGroup Inc. and Subsidiaries 2010 10-K

Required

  a. What would happen to the stock price on the date that the reverse split was effective?

  b. Citigroup's net income (loss) for 2010, 2009 and 2008 would be reported at what amount after the reverse split?

  c. Restate the earnings per share for 2010, 2009 and 2008 after the reverse split.

CASE 9-4 FAMILY STYLE

Selected data from the 2010 annual report of Frisch's Restaurants, Inc. follow:

FRISCH'S RESTAURANTS, INC. AND SUBSIDIARIES*
CONSOLIDATED BALANCE SHEET (In Part)

	June 1, 2010	June 2, 2009
Shareholders' Equity		
Capital stock		
Preferred stock—authorized, 3,000,000 shares without par value; none issued	—	—
Common stock—authorized, 12,000,000 shares without par value; issued 7,585,764 and 7,582,347 shares—stated value—$1	7,585,764	7,582,347
		(continued)

*"The registrant, Frisch's Restaurants, Inc. (together with its wholly owned subsidiaries, referred to as the "Company" or the "Registrant"), is a regional company that operates full service family-style restaurants under the name Frisch's Big Boy." 10-K
Source: Frisch's Restaurants, Inc. 2010 10-K

(**CASE 9-4** CONTINUED)

	June 1, 2010	June 2, 2009
Additional contributed capital	65,222,878	64,721,328
	72,808,642	72,303,675
Accumulated other comprehensive loss	(7,856,427)	(6,634,422)
Retained earnings	89,701,652	82,306,488
	81,845,225	75,672,066
Less cost of treasury stock (2,525,174 and 2,482,233 shares)	(34,559,851)	(33,598,597)
Total shareholders' equity	120,094,016	114,377,144
Total liabilities and shareholders' equity	$189,252,646	$176,975,948

FRISCH'S RESTAURANTS, INC. AND SUBSIDIARIES
CONSOLIDATED STATEMENT OF EARNINGS
Three years ended June 1, 2010

	2010	2009	2008
Sales	$292,872,174	$297,860,951	$299,562,346
Cost of sales			
Food and paper	99,651,072	105,859,982	106,895,380
Payroll and related	97,918,797	97,678,114	98,347,394
Other operating costs	64,987,881	66,082,244	66,382,911
	262,557,750	269,620,340	271,625,685
Gross profit	30,314,424	28,240,611	27,936,661
Administrative and advertising	15,127,522	14,637,943	14,130,762
Franchise fees and other revenue	(1,266,368)	(1,281,940)	(1,277,707)
Gains on sale of assets	—	(1,163,173)	(524,354)
Litigation settlement	—	(889,579)	—
Impairment of long-lived assets	—	—	4,660,093
Operating profit	16,453,270	16,937,360	10,947,867
Interest expense	1,748,542	2,000,442	2,359,369
Earnings before income taxes	14,704,728	14,936,918	8,588,498
Income taxes			
Current			
Federal	6,035,179	4,626,721	5,469,816
Less tax credits	(951,592)	(1,010,762)	(904,475)
State and municipal	579,963	406,403	582,012
Deferred	(957,753)	193,701	(2,505,066)
Total income taxes	4,705,797	4,216,063	2,642,287
NET EARNINGS	$ 9,998,931	$ 10,720,855	$ 5,946,211
Earnings per share (EPS) of common stock:			
Basic net earnings per share	$ 1.96	$ 2.10	$ 1.16
Diluted net earnings per share	$ 1.93	$ 2.08	$ 1.14

Fiscal years 2010 and 2009 each contained 52 weeks consisting of 364 days. Fiscal year 2008 contained 53 weeks consisting of 371 days.

Other selected data:

	Year Ended	
	June 1, 2010	June 2, 2009
1. Market price per common share	$ 20.87	$ 28.00
2. Dividends paid in total	$2,603,767	$2,449,347
3. Dividends paid per share	$ 0.51	$ 0.48

Required

a. Compute the following for 2010 and 2009:

1. Degree of financial leverage

2. Price/earnings ratio

3. Percentage of earnings retained

4. Dividend yield

5. Common stock—authorized
6. Common stock—issued
7. Treasury stock
8. Common stock outstanding
9. Book value per share
   b. Comment on the ratios computed under (a).
   c. 1. Identify special items on the income statement for the years 2010 and 2009.
      2. How would these special items be removed from net earnings?

CASE 9-5 DELICIOUS APPLE

Apple, Inc.* presented this selected financial data with its 2010 annual report:

CONSOLIDATED STATEMENTS OF OPERATIONS
(In millions, except share amounts which are reflected in thousands and per share amounts)

Three years ended September 25, 2010	2010	2009	2008
Net sales	$ 65,225	$ 42,905	$ 37,491
Cost of sales	39,541	25,683	24,294
Gross margin	25,684	17,222	13,197
Operating expenses:			
Research and development	1,782	1,333	1,109
Selling, general and administrative	5,517	4,149	3,761
Total operating expenses	7,299	5,482	4,870
Operating income	18,385	11,740	8,327
Other income and expense	155	326	620
Income before provision for income taxes	18,540	12,066	8,947
Provision for income taxes	4,527	3,831	2,828
Net income	$ 14,013	$ 8,345	$ 6,119
Earnings per common share:			
Basic	$ 15.41	$ 9.22	$ 6.94
Diluted	$ 15.15	$ 9.08	$ 6.78
Shares used in computing earnings per share:			
Basic	909,461	893,016	881,592
Diluted	924,712	907,005	902,139

Fiscal Years

"The Company's fiscal year is the 52 or 53-week period that ends on the last Saturday of September. The Company's fiscal years 2010, 2009 and 2008 ended on September 25, 2010, September 26, 2009 and September 27, 2008, respectively, and included 52 weeks each. An additional week is included in the first fiscal quarter approximately every six years to realign fiscal quarters with calendar quarters." 10-K

Other:
Market price per share:

September 25, 2010	$292.32
September 26, 2009	$182.37
September 27, 2008	$128.24

Total dividends paid:

2010	0
2009	0
2008	0

(continued)

*"Apple, Inc. and its wholly-owned subsidiaries (collectively "Apple" or the "Company") designs, manufactures and markets a range of personal computers, mobile communication and media devices, and portable digital music players, and sells a variety of related software, services, peripherals, networking solutions, and third-party digital content and applications." 10-K
Source: Apple, Inc 2010 10-K

(**CASE 9-5** CONTINUED)

Dividends declared per share:

2010	0
2009	0
2008	0

Required

a. 1. For consolidated statements of operations, prepare a horizontal common-size analysis for 2008–2010. Use 2008 as the base.

 2. Comment on the results in (1).

b. 1. For consolidated statements of operations, prepare a vertical common-size analysis for 2008–2010. Use net sales as the base.

 2. Comment on the results in (1).

c. Based on these data, compute the following for 2008–2010.

 1. Price/earnings ratio

 2. Dividend yield

 3. Comment on the results in (1) and (2)

CASE 9-6 SPECIALTY RETAILER—INVESTOR VIEW

1. **Abercrombie & Fitch Co.**
(52-week fiscal year ended January 29, 2011; 52-week fiscal year ended January 30, 2010; 52-week fiscal year ended January 31, 2009)
"Abercrombie & Fitch Co ... is a specialty retailer that operates stores and direct-to-consumer operations." 10-K
Source: Abercrombie & Fitch 2010 10-K

2. **Limited Brands, Inc.**
(52-week fiscal year ended January 29, 2011; 52-week fiscal year ended January 30, 2010; 52-week fiscal year ended January 31, 2009)
"We operate in the highly competitive specialty retail business" 10-K
Source: Limited Brands 2010 10-K

3. **Gap, Inc.**
(52-week fiscal year ended January 29, 2011; 52-week fiscal year ended January 30, 2010; 52-week fiscal year ended January 31, 2009)
"We are a global specialty retailer offering apparel, accessories, and personal care products" 10-K
Source: Gap Inc 2010 10-K

Data reviewed	Abercrombie & Fitch		Limited Brands		GAP	
	2010	2009	2010	2009	2010	2009
All-inclusive degree of financial coverage	*	*	1.17	1.36	*	*
Diluted earnings per share before nonrecurring items	$ 1.67	$ .89	$ 2.42	$ 1.37	$ 1.88	$ 1.58
Percentage of earnings retained	58.97%	22.11%	**	56.92%	79.07%	78.77%
Dividend yield	1.45%	2.22%	15.91%***	3.15%	2.08%	1.78%
Price/earnings ratio	28.96	35.44	11.95	13.88	10.21	12.08
Market price per share	$ 48.36	$ 31.54	$ 28.92	$ 19.02	$ 19.20	$ 19.08

*Disclosure not adequate to compute
**Dividends more than earnings
***Special dividends of $4.00 per share are included

Required

a. Comment on all data reviewed for each individual company.

b. Based on the above, which firm would you select?

CASE 9-7 EAT AT MY RESTAURANT—INVESTOR VIEW

With this case, we review the profitability of several restaurant companies. The restaurant companies reviewed and the year-end dates are as follows:

1. **Yum Brands, Inc.**
   December 25, 2010; December 26, 2009 (52 weeks each year)
   "YUM consists of six operating segments: KFC—U.S., Pizza Hut—U.S., Taco Bell–U.S., Long John Silver's ("LJS")—U.S., and A&W All American Food Restaurants ("A&W")—U.S., YUM Restaurants International ("YRI" or "International Division") and YUM Restaurants China ("China Division")." 10-K
   Source: Yum! Brands, Inc. and Subsidiaries 2010 10-K

2. **Panera Bread**
   December 28, 2010; December 29, 2009 (52 weeks each year)
   "Panera Bread Company and it subsidiaries, referred to as "Panera Bread," "Panera," the "Company," "we," "us," and "our," is a national bakery-café concept with 1,453 company-owned and franchise-operated bakery-café locations in 40 states, the District of Columbia, and Ontario, Canada." 10-K
   Source: Panera Bread 2010 10-K

3. **Starbucks**
   October 3, 2010; September 27, 2009 (Fiscal year 2010 included 53 weeks, while fiscal year ended 2009 included 52 weeks)
   "Starbucks is the premier roaster and retailer of specialty coffee in the world, operating in more than 50 countries." 10-K
   Source: Starbucks Corporation 2010 10-K

Data reviewed	Yum Brands, Inc.		Panera Bread		Starbucks	
	2010	2009	2010	2009	2010	2009
All-inclusive degree of financial leverage	*	*	100.37	100.50	102.28	107.00
Diluted earnings per share before nonrecurring items	$ 2.38	$ 2.22	$ 3.62	$ 2.78	$ 1.24	$ 0.52
Percentage of earnings retained	64.42%	66.20%	100.00%	100.00%	81.97%	100.00%
Dividend yield	1.85%	2.26%	0	0	1.39%	0
Price/earnings ratio	20.87	15.94	28.21	24.69	20.92	38.13
Market price per share	$ 49.66	$ 35.38	$ 102.11	$ 68.63	$ 25.94	$ 19.83

*Disclosure not adequate to compute

Required

a. Comment on the data reviewed for each individual company for 2010 and 2009.

b. Based on the above, which firm would you select?

WEB CASE THOMSON ONE *Business School Edition*

Please complete the Web case that covers material covered in this chapter at www.cengagebrain.com. You'll be using Thomson ONE Business School Edition, a powerful tool that combines a full range of fundamental financial information, earnings estimates, market data, and source documents for 500 publicly traded companies.

TO THE NET CASE

1. Go to the SEC site (www.sec.gov). Under "Filings and Forms" click on "Search for Company Filings." Click on "Company or Fund, etc." Under Company Name, enter "Belden" (or enter stock symbol "BDC"). Select the 10-K submitted February 25, 2011. For the years ended 2010, 2009 and 2008, compute or find the following:

   a. Earnings per common share (basic and diluted)

   b. Price/earnings ratio

(*continued*)

(**To the Net** CONTINUED)

 c. Percentage of earnings retained

 d. Dividend payout

 e. Dividend yield
  Note:
  Market Price—December 31

2010	$36.82
2009	$21.92
2008	$20.88

  Dividends per share 2010, 2009 and 2008. ($.20 per share each year)

2. Go to the SEC site (www.sec.gov). Under "Filings and Forms" click on "Search for Company Filings." Click on "Company or Fund, etc." Under Company Name, enter "Motorola Solutions, Inc." (or enter stock symbol "MSI"). Select the 10-K submitted February 18, 2011. Review the consolidated statements of operations for the years ended December 31, 2010, 2009, and 2008. In your opinion, what items make it difficult to form an opinion on the results of Motorola Solutions?

3. Go to the SEC site (www.sec.gov). Under "Filings and Forms" click on "Search for Company Filings." Click on "Company or Fund, etc." Under Company Name, enter "Boeing Co." (or enter stock symbol, enter "BA"). Select the 10-K submitted February 9, 2011. For the years ended December 31, 2010, 2009, and 2008, find the following:

 a. Earnings per common share (basic and diluted)

 b. Price/earnings ratio

 c. Percentage of earnings retained

 d. Dividend payout

 e. Dividend yield
  Note:
  Market Price—December 31

2010	$65.26
2009	$54.13
2008	$42.67

4. Go to the SEC site (www.sec.gov). Under "Filings and Forms" click on "Search for Company Filings." Click on "Company or Fund, etc." Under Company Name, enter "Whole Foods Market" (or enter stock symbol, enter "WFMI"). Select the 10-K submitted November 24, 2010. For September 26, 2010 and September 27, 2009, find the following:

 a. Total assets

 b. Shareholders' equity

 c. Common stock shares issued and outstanding

 d. Compute the total capitalization at September 26, 2010 and September 27, 2009

 e. Why is the total capitalization different from the total shareholders' equity?
  Note:
  Market Price—December 31

September 26, 2010	$37.07
September 27, 2009	$28.77

Endnotes

1. FASB No. 123 (revised 2004), Glossary, Grant date.

2. Ibid., Glossary, Vest, Vesting, or Vested.

3. Copyrighted material—reproduced with permission of the author.

Chapter

10

Statement of Cash Flows

Considering the importance of cash, it is not surprising that the statement of cash flows has become one of the primary financial statements. The statement of cash flows gives managers, equity analysts, commercial lenders, and investment bankers a thorough explanation of the changes that occurred in the firm's cash balances.

The statement of cash flows provides an explanation of the changes that occurred in the firm's cash balances for a specific period. Cash is considered to be the lifeblood of the firm. Understanding the flow of cash is critical to having a handle on the pulse of the firm.

Quote the Banker, "Watch Cash Flow"

Once upon a midnight dreary as I pondered weak and weary
Over many a quaint and curious volume of accounting lore,
Seeking gimmicks (without scruple) to squeeze through some new tax loophole,
Suddenly I heard a knock upon my door,
   Only this, and nothing more.

Then I felt a queasy tingling and I heard the cash a-jingling
As a fearsome banker entered whom I'd often seen before.
His face was money-green and in his eyes there could be seen
Dollar-signs that seemed to glitter as he reckoned up the score.
   "Cash flow," the banker said, and nothing more.

I had always thought it fine to show a jet black bottom line,
But the banker sounded a resounding, "No,
Your receivables are high, mounting upward toward the sky;
Write-offs loom. What matters is cash flow."
   He repeated, "Watch cash flow."

Then I tried to tell the story of our lovely inventory
Which, though large, is full of most delightful stuff.
But the banker saw its growth, and with a mighty oath

He waved his arms and shouted, "Stop! Enough!
    Pay the interest, and don't give me any guff!"

Next I looked for non-cash items which could add ad infinitum
To replace the ever-outward flow of cash,
But to keep my statement black I'd held depreciation back,
And my banker said that I'd done something rash.
    He quivered, and his teeth began to gnash.

When I asked him for a loan, he responded, with a groan,
That the interest rate would be just prime plus eight,
And to guarantee my purity he'd insist on some security—
All my assets plus the scalp upon my pate.
    Only this, a standard rate.

Though my bottom line is black, I am flat upon my back.
My cash flows out and customers pay slow.
The growth of my receivables is almost unbelievable;
The result is certain—unremitting woe!
And I hear the banker utter an ominous low mutter,
    "Watch cash flow."

—HERBERT S. BAILEY
Reprinted with permission.

Basic Elements of the Statement of Cash Flows

The statement of cash flows is prepared using a concept of cash that includes not only cash itself but also short-term, highly liquid investments. This is referred to as the "cash and cash equivalent" focus. The category cash and cash equivalents includes cash on hand, cash on deposit, and investments in short-term, highly liquid investments. The cash flow statement analysis explains the change in these focus accounts by examining all the accounts on the balance sheet other than the focus accounts.

Management may use the statement of cash flows to determine dividend policy, cash generated by operations, and investing and financing policy. Outsiders, such as creditors or investors, may use it to determine such things as the firm's ability to increase dividends, its ability to pay debt with cash from operations, and the percentage of cash from operations in relation to the cash from financing.

The statement of cash flows must report all transactions affecting cash flow. A company will occasionally have investing and/or financing activities that have no direct effect on cash flow. For example, a company may acquire land in exchange for common stock. This is an investing transaction (acquiring the land) and a financing transaction (issuing the common stock). The conversion of long-term bonds into common stock involves two financing activities with no effect on cash flow. Since transactions such as these will have future effects on cash flows, these transactions are to be disclosed in a separate schedule presented with the statement of cash flows.

The statement of cash flows classifies cash receipts and cash payments into operating, investing, and financing activities.[1] In brief, operating activities involve income statement items. Investing activities generally result from changes in long-term asset items. Financing activities generally relate to long-term liability and stockholders' equity items. A description of these activities and typical cash flows are as follows:

1. OPERATING ACTIVITIES. Operating activities include all transactions and other events that are not investing or financing activities. Cash flows from operating activities are generally the cash effects of transactions and other events that enter into the determination of net income.
   Typical cash inflows:
     From sale of goods or services
     From return on loans (interest)
     From return on equity securities (dividends)

Typical cash outflows:
   Payments for acquisitions of inventory
   Payments to employees
   Payments to governments (taxes)
   Payments of interest expense
   Payments to suppliers for other expenses

2. INVESTING ACTIVITIES. Investing activities include lending money and collecting on those loans and acquiring and selling investments and productive long-term assets.
   Typical cash inflows:
      From receipts from loans collected
      From sales of debt or equity securities of other corporations
      From sale of property, plant, and equipment
   Typical cash outflows:
      Loans to other entities
      Purchase of debt or equity securities of other entities
      Purchase of property, plant, and equipment

3. FINANCING ACTIVITIES. Financing activities include cash flows relating to liability and owners' equity.
   Typical cash inflows:
      From sale of equity securities
      From sale of bonds, mortgages, notes, and other short- or long-term borrowings
   Typical cash outflows:
      Payment of dividends
      Reacquisition of the firm's capital stock
      Payment of amounts borrowed

The statement of cash flows presents cash flows from operating activities first, followed by investing activities and then financing activities. The individual inflows and outflows from investing and financing activities are presented separately. The operating activities section can be presented using the *direct method* or the *indirect method*. (The indirect method is sometimes referred to as the *reconciliation method*.) The direct method essentially presents the income statement on a cash basis, instead of an accrual basis. The indirect method adjusts net income for items that affected net income but did not affect cash.

SFAS No. 95 encourages enterprises to use the direct method to present cash flows from operating activities. However, if a company uses the direct method, the standard requires a reconciliation of net income to net cash provided by operating activities in a separate schedule. If a firm uses the indirect method, it must make a separate disclosure of interest paid and income taxes paid during the period. Exhibit 10-1 presents skeleton formats of a statement of cash flows using the direct method and the indirect method.

EXHIBIT 10-1 | Jones Company Example

Statement of Cash Flows—Comparison of Presentation of Direct Method and Indirect Method (Operating Activities) For Year Ended December 31, 20XX

Direct Method

Cash flows from operating activities:	
Cash received from customers	$ 370,000
Cash paid to suppliers and employees	(310,000)
Interest received	10,000
Interest paid (net of amount capitalized)	(4,000)
Income taxes paid	(15,000)
Net cash provided by operations	51,000

(*continued*)

| EXHIBIT 10-1 | Jones Company Example (*continued*) |

Direct Method

Cash flows from investing activities:	
Capital expenditures	$ (30,000)
Proceeds from property, plant, and equipment disposals	6,000
Net cash used in investing activities	(24,000)
Cash flows from financing activities:	
Net proceeds from repayment of commercial paper	(4,000)
Proceeds from issuance of long-term debt	6,000
Dividends paid	(5,000)
Net cash used in financing activities	(3,000)
Net increase in cash and cash equivalents	24,000
Cash and cash equivalents at beginning of period	8,000
Cash and cash equivalents at end of period	$ 32,000
Reconciliation of net earnings to cash provided by operating activities:	
Net earnings	$ 40,000
Provision for depreciation	6,000
Provision for allowance for doubtful accounts	1,000
Deferred income taxes	1,000
Loss on property, plant, and equipment disposals	2,000
Changes in operating assets and liabilities:	
Receivables increase	(2,000)
Inventories increase	(4,000)
Accounts payable increase	5,000
Accrued income taxes increase	2,000
Net cash provided by operating activities	$ 51,000
Supplemental schedule of noncash investing and financing activities:	
Land acquired (investing) by issuing bonds (financing)	$ 10,000

Indirect Method

Operating activities:	
Net earnings	$ 40,000
Provision for depreciation	6,000
Provision for allowance for doubtful accounts	1,000
Deferred income taxes	1,000
Loss on property, plant, and equipment disposals	2,000
Changes in operating assets and liabilities:	
Receivables increase	(2,000)
Inventories increase	(4,000)
Accounts payable increase	5,000
Accrued income taxes increase	2,000
Net cash provided by operating activities	$ 51,000
Cash flows from investing activities:	
Capital expenditures	(30,000)
Proceeds from property, plant, and equipment disposals	6,000
Net cash used in investing activities	(24,000)
Cash flows from financing activities:	
Net proceeds from repayment of commercial paper	(4,000)
Proceeds from issuance of long-term debt	6,000
Dividends paid	(5,000)
Net cash used in financing activities	(3,000)
Net increase in cash and cash equivalents	24,000
Cash and cash equivalents at beginning of period	8,000
Cash and cash equivalents at end of period	$ 32,000
Supplemental disclosure of cash flow information:	
Interest paid	$ 500
Income taxes paid	10,000
Supplemental schedule of noncash investing and financing activities:	
Land acquired (investing) and issuing bonds (financing)	$ 10,000

The 1986 SFAS Exposure Draft, "Statement of Cash Flows," indicates that:

The principal advantage of the direct method is that it shows the operating cash receipts and payments. Knowledge of where operating cash flows came from and how cash was used in past periods may be useful in estimating future cash flows. The indirect method of reporting has the advantage of focusing on the differences between income and cash flow from operating activities.[2]

Source: U.S. Securities and Exchange

The statement of cash flows has now been a required financial statement for over 20 years. The financial community is in agreement as to the importance of this statement. Unfortunately, the statement of cash flows has not proven as useful as many expected. A major reason for this is the failure to require the direct method of presenting operating activities. Many ratios relating to the cash flow have been developed by companies, financial services, articles, and books. There is little agreement on what ratios to compute and how to compute these ratios. Also, the direct method allows for analysis that cannot be done with the indirect method.

Exhibit 10-2 presents the 2011 Nike consolidated statement of cash flows. This statement presents cash from operations using the indirect method. The statement closely follows the standard format.

In addition to reviewing the flow of funds on a yearly basis, reviewing the flow of funds for a three-year period may be helpful. This can be accomplished by adding a total column to the statement that represents the total of each item for the three-year period. This has been done for Nike in Exhibit 10-2.

EXHIBIT 10-2 Nike, Inc.

Consolidated Statements of Cash Flows, with Three-Year Total (Total Column Added)

NIKE, INC.
CONSOLIDATED STATEMENT OF CASH FLOWS

	Total	2011	2010	2009
Cash provided by operations:		(In millions)		
Net income	$ 5,527	$ 2,133	$ 1,907	$ 1,487
Income charges (credits) not affecting cash:				
Depreciation	994	335	324	335
Deferred income taxes	(362)	(76)	8	(294)
Stock-based compensation (Note 11)	435	105	159	171
Impairment of goodwill, intangibles and other assets (Note 4)	401	—	—	401
Amortization and other	143	23	72	48
Changes in certain working capital components and other assets and liabilities excluding the impact of acquisition and divestitures:				
(Increase) decrease in accounts receivable	(329)	(273)	182	(238)
(Increase) decrease in inventories	(234)	(551)	285	32
(Increase) decrease in prepaid expenses and other current assets	(91)	(35)	(70)	14
(Increase) decrease in accounts payable, accrued liabilities and income taxes payable	228	151	297	(220)
Cash provided by operations	6,712	1,812	3,164	1,736
Cash used by investing activities:				
Purchase of short-term investments	(14,249)	(7,616)	(3,724)	(2,909)
Maturities of short-term investments	7,927	4,313	2,334	1,280
Sales of short-term investments	4,329	2,766	453	1,110
Additions to property, plant and equipment	(1,223)	(432)	(335)	(456)
Disposals of property, plant and equipment	94	1	10	33
Increase in other assets, net of other liabilities	(88)	(30)	(11)	(47)
Settlement of net investment hedges	173	(23)	5	191
Cash used by investing activities	(3,087)	(1,021)	(1,268)	(798)

Source: Nike, Inc. 2010 10-K *(continued)*

EXHIBIT 10-2	Nike, Inc. *(continued)*				

			Year Ended May 31,		
		Total	2011	2010	2009
			(In millions)		
Cash used by financing activities:					
Reductions in long-term debt, including current portion		$ (47)	$ (8)	$ (32)	$ (7)
Increase (decrease) in notes payable		13	41	(205)	177
Proceeds from exercise of stock options and other stock					
issuances		896	345	364	187
Excess tax benefits from share-based payment arrangements		147	64	58	25
Repurchase of common stock		(3,249)	(1,859)	(741)	(649)
Dividends – common and preferred		(1,327)	(555)	(505)	(467)
Cash used by financing activities		(3,767)	(1,972)	(1,061)	(734)
Effect of exchange rate changes		(37)	57	(47)	(47)
Net (decrease) increase in cash and equivalents		(179)	(1,124)	788	157
Cash and equivalents, beginning of year		2,134	3,079	2,291	2,134
Cash and equivalents, end of year		$ 1,955	$ 1,955	$ 3,079	$ 2,291
Supplemental disclosure of cash flow information:					
Cash paid during the year for:					
Interest, net of capitalized interest		$ 127	$ 32	$ 48	$ 47
Income taxes		2,038	736	537	765
Dividends declared and not paid		397	145	131	121

Some observations on the 2011 Nike statement of cash flows, considering the three-year period ended May 31, 2011, follow:

1. Cash provided by operations was the major source of cash. This operating cash flow approximately offsets the cash outflow for investing activities and the outflow for financing activities.
2. Cash flow from operations related to net income and depreciation represented substantially all of the cash flow from operations.
3. Cash used for additions to property, plant, and equipment represented the major use of cash used by investing activities (except for purchases, maturities and sales of short-term investment).
4. Cash used for repurchase of common stock represented the major use of cash for financing activities. Possibly some of the repurchase of stock was related to the proceeds from exercise of stock options and other stock issuances. One of the reasons for expensing stock options is that typically a company will repurchase stock and then issue stock with the exercise of options.

Exhibit 10-3 presents the 2011 cash flow statement of Tech Data Corporation, with a total column for the three-year period. This firm presented the cash flows from operating activities using the direct method. Note the following with regard to the direct method in Exhibit 10-3.

1. Net cash provided by operations represented the major source of cash.
2. Acquisition of business, net of cash acquired represented the major outflow of funds under investing activities.
3. Cash paid for purchase of treasury stock represented the major outflow of funds under financing activities.
4. Capital contributions and net borrowings from joint venture parties represented the major inflow of funds under financing activities.

EXHIBIT 10-3 Tech Data Corporation*

TECH DATA CORPORATION AND SUBSIDIARIES
CONSOLIDATED STATEMENT OF CASH FLOWS
(In thousands)
(Total column added)

	Year ended January 31,			
	Three-Year Total	2011	2010	2009
Cash flows from operating activities:				
Cash received from customers	$ 70,175,744	$ 24,258,805	$ 21,927,372	$ 23,989,567
Cash paid to vendors and employees	(69,022,849)	(24,065,824)	(21,320,637)	(23,636,388)
Interest paid, net	(50,324)	(15,927)	(14,015)	(20,382)
Income taxes paid	(124,988)	(73,211)	(48,790)	(52,987)
Net cash provided by operating activities	927,583	103,843	543,930	279,810
Cash flows from investing activities:				
Acquisition of business, net of cash acquired	(227,557)	(141,138)	(8,153)	(78,266)
Proceeds from sale of property and equipment	5,491	0	5,491	0
Expenditures for property and equipment	(50,372)	(18,614)	(14,486)	(17,272)
Software and software development costs	(42,942)	(13,288)	(14,379)	(15,275)
Net cash used in investing activities	(315,380)	(173,040)	(31,527)	(110,813)
Cash flows from financing activities:				
Proceeds from the issuance of treasury stock	44,494	5,005	37,959	1,530
Cash paid for purchase of treasury stock	(300,000)	(200,000)	0	(100,000)
Capital contributions and net borrowings from joint venture partner	68,574	34,556	23,208	10,810
Net (repayments) borrowings on revolving credit loans	(22,927)	(46,645)	(19,116)	42,834
Principal payments on long-term debt	(7,894)	(454)	(5,654)	(1,786)
Excess tax benefit from stock-based compensation	(2,143)	1,180	963	0
Net cash (used in) provided by financing activities	(215,610)	(206,358)	37,360	(46,612)
Effect of exchange rate changes on cash and cash equivalents	(3,999)	(1,090)	38,793	(41,702)
Net (decrease) increase in cash and cash equivalents	392,594	(276,645)	588,556	80,683
Cash and cash equivalents at beginning of year	447,340	1,116,579	528,023	447,340
Cash and cash equivalents at end of year	$ 839,934	$ 839,934	$ 1,116,579	$ 528,023
Reconciliation of net income to net cash provided by operating activities:				
Net income attributable to shareholders of Tech Data Corporation	$ 511,676	$ 214,243	$ 180,155	$ 117,278
Net income (loss) attributable to noncontrolling interest:	3,843	4,620	1,045	(1,822)
Consolidated net income	515,519	218,863	181,200	115,456
Adjustments to reconcile net income to net cash provided by (used in) operating activities:				
Depreciation and amortization	144,473	47,285	45,594	51,234
Provision for losses on accounts receivable	37,470	11,517	10,953	15,000
Stock-based compensation expense	33,102	9,887	11,225	11,990
Accretion of debt discount on convertible senior debentures	30,834	10,278	10,278	10,278
Deferred income taxes	22,652	6,972	(2,541)	18,221
Excess tax benefit from stock-based compensation	(2,143)	(1,180)	(963)	—
Changes in operating assets and liabilities, net of acquisitions:				
Accounts receivable	(367,878)	(113,303)	(168,152)	(86,423)
Inventories	(494,860)	(349,429)	116,543	(261,974)
Prepaid expenses and other assets	(32,072)	(34,601)	21,290	(18,761)
Accounts payable	989,639	278,356	336,587	374,696
Accrued expenses and other liabilities	50,847	19,198	(18,444)	50,093
Total adjustments	412,064	(115,020)	362,730	164,354
Net cash provided by operating activities	$ 927,583	$ 103,843	$ 543,930	$ 279,810

*"Tech Data Corporation … is the world's second largest wholesale distributor of technology products." 10-K
Source: Tech Data Corporation and Subsidiaries 2010 10-K

Note the following with regard to the indirect method in Exhibit 10-3. (The indirect method represents "Reconciliation of net income to net cash provided by operating activities.")

1. Net income plus depreciation and amortization make up most of the cash flow (remember that net income does not represent cash flow and that depreciation and amortization are not cash flow items).
2. Notice how changes in operating assets and liabilities make up approximately 44% of net cash provided by operating activities.
3. Acquisition of business, net of cash acquired represented the major outflow of funds in investing activities.

Exhibit 10-4 restates the 2011 cash flows for Tech Data Corporation, viewing inflows and outflows separately. Some observations regarding Exhibit 10-4 follow:

1. Approximately 100% of the total inflows came from operations.
2. Approximately 98% of total cash outflows related to operations.
3. The only significant inflow or outflow for investing activities was an outflow for acquisition of business, net of cash acquired.
4. The only significant inflow or outflow for financing activities was an outflow for purchase of treasury stock.

EXHIBIT **10-4**   Tech Data Corporation*

Viewing Inflows and Outflows Separately
Year Ended January 31, 2011

(In thousands)	Inflows	Outflows	Percent Inflow	Percent Outflow
Cash flows from operating activities:				
Cash received from customers	$24,258,805		99.83	
Cash paid to vendors and employees		$24,065,824		97.92
Interest paid, net		15,927		.06
Income taxes paid		73,211		.30
Net cash provided by operating activities	24,258,805	24,154,962	99.83	98.29
Cash flows from investing activities:				
Acquisition of businesses, net of cash acquired		141,138		.57
Proceeds from sale of property and equipment	0			
Expenditures for property and equipment		18,614		.08
Software and software development costs		13,288		.05
Net cash used in investing activities	0	173,040	0	.70
Cash flows from financing activities:				
Proceeds from the reissuance of treasury stock	5,005		.02	
Cash paid for purchase of treasury stock		200,000		.81
Capital contributions and net borrowings from joint venture partner	34,556		0.14	
Net (repayments) borrowings on revaluing credit loans		46,645		.19
Principal payments on long-term debt		454		.00
Excess tax benefit from stock-based compensation	1,180		.00	
Net cash (used in) provided by financing activities	40,741	247,099	.17	1.01
Effect of exchange rate changes on cash and cash equivalents		1,090		.00
Changes in cash (inflows and outflows):	24,299,546	24,576,191	100.00	100.00
Total cash inflows		24,299,546		
Net decrease in cash		$ 276,645		

*"Tech Data Corporation ("Tech Data," "we," "our," "us," or the "Company"), is the world's second largest wholesale distributor of technology products." 10-K
Source: Tech Data Corporation and Subsidiaries 2010 10-K

Financial Ratios and the Statement of Cash Flows

Financial ratios that relate to the statement of cash flows were slow in being developed. This was related to several factors. For one thing, most financial ratios traditionally related an income statement item(s) to a balance sheet item(s). This became the normal way of approaching financial analysis, and the statement of cash flows did not become a required statement until 1987. Thus, it took a while for analysts to become familiar with the statement.

Ratios have now been developed that relate to the cash flow statement. Some of these ratios are as follows:

1. Operating cash flow/current maturities of long-term debt and current notes payable
2. Operating cash flow/total debt
3. Operating cash flow per share
4. Operating cash flow/cash dividends

Operating Cash Flow/Current Maturities of Long-Term Debt and Current Notes Payable

The **operating cash flow/current maturities of long-term debt and current notes payable** is a ratio that indicates a firm's ability to meet its current maturities of debt. The higher this ratio, the better the firm's ability to meet its current maturities of debt. The higher this ratio, the better the firm's liquidity. This ratio relates to the liquidity ratios discussed in Chapter 6.

The formula for operating cash flow/current maturities of long-term debt and current notes payable follows:

$$\frac{\text{Operating Cash Flow}}{\text{Current Maturities of Long-Term Debt and Current Notes Payable}}$$

It is computed for Nike for 2011 and 2010 in Exhibit 10-5. For Nike, this ratio substantially declined in 2011. Both years represent material coverage.

EXHIBIT **10-5**	Nike, Inc.	
Operating Cash Flow/Current Maturities of Long-Term Debt and Current Notes Payable		
Years Ended May 31, 2011 and 2010		
(In millions)	2011	2010
Operating cash flow [A]	$1,812.0	$3,164.0
Current maturities of long-term debt and current notes payable [B]	$ 387.0	$ 146.0
Operating cash flow/current maturities of long-term debt and current notes payable [A ÷ B]	4.68 times	21.67 times

Source: Nike, Inc. 2010 10-K

Operating Cash Flow/Total Debt

The **operating cash flow/total debt** indicates a firm's ability to cover total debt with the yearly operating cash flow. The higher the ratio, the better the firm's ability to carry its total debt. From a debt standpoint, this is considered to be important. It relates to the debt ratios presented in Chapter 7. It is a type of income view of debt, except that operating cash flow is the perspective instead of an income figure.

The operating cash flow is the same cash flow amount that is used for the operating cash flow/current maturities of long-term debt and current notes payable. The total debt figure is the same total debt amount that was computed in Chapter 7 for the debt ratio and the debt/equity ratio. For the primary computation of the operating cash flow/total debt ratio, all possible balance sheet debt items are included, as was done for the debt ratio and the debt/equity ratio. This is the more conservative approach to computing the ratio. In practice, many firms are more selective about what is included in debt. Some include only short-term liabilities and long-term items, such as bonds payable. The formula for operating cash flow/total debt is as follows:

$$\frac{\text{Operating Cash Flow}}{\text{Total Debt}}$$

The operating cash flow/total debt ratio is computed in Exhibit 10-6 for Nike for the years ended May 31, 2011 and 2010. It indicates that cash flow is significant in relation to total debt in both years, but the coverage materially declined in 2011.

EXHIBIT **10-6**	Nike, Inc.		
Operating Cash Flow/Total Debt			
Years Ended May 31, 2011 and 2010			
(In millions)		**2011**	**2010**
Operating cash flow [A]		$1,812.0	$3,164.0
Total debt [B]		$5,155.0	$4,665.0
Operating cash flow/total debt [A ÷ B]		35.15%	67.82%

Source: Nike, Inc. 2010 10-K

Operating Cash Flow per Share

Operating cash flow per share indicates the funds flow per common share outstanding. It is usually substantially higher than earnings per share because depreciation has not been deducted.

In the short run, operating cash flow per share is a better indication of a firm's ability to make capital expenditure decisions and pay dividends than is earnings per share. This ratio should not be viewed as a substitute for earnings per share in terms of a firm's profitability. For this reason, firms are prohibited from reporting cash flow per share on the face of the statement of cash flows or elsewhere in their financials. However, it is a complementary ratio that relates to the ratios of relevance to investors (discussed in Chapter 9).

The operating cash flow per share formula is as follows:

$$\frac{\text{Operating Cash Flow} - \text{Preferred Dividends}}{\text{Diluted Weighted Average Common Shares Outstanding}}$$

The operating cash flow amount is the same figure that was used in the two previous cash flow formulas in this chapter. For common shares outstanding, use the shares that were used for the purpose of computing earnings per share on the most diluted basis. This figure is available when doing internal analysis. It is also in a firm's 10-K annual report. Some companies disclose these shares in the annual report. This share number cannot be computed from information in the annual report, except for very simple situations.

EXHIBIT **10-7**	Nike, Inc.		
Operating Cash Flow per Share			
Years Ended May 31, 2011 and 2010			
(In millions)		**2011**	**2010**
Operating cash flow		$1,812.00	$3,164.00
Less: Redeemable preferred dividends		0.03	0.03
Operating cash flow after preferred dividends [A]		$1,811.97	$3,163.97
Diluted weighted average common shares outstanding [B]		485.70	493.90
Operating cash flow per share [A ÷ B]		$ 3.73	$ 6.41

Source: Nike, Inc. 2010 10-K

When these share amounts are not available, use the outstanding shares of common stock. This will result in an approximation of the operating cash flow per share. The advantage of using the number of shares used for earnings per share is that this results in an amount that can be compared with earnings per share, and it avoids distortions.

Operating cash flow per share is computed for Nike for 2011 and 2010 in Exhibit 10-7. Operating cash flow per share was materially more than earnings per share in 2010 and materially less than earnings per share in 2011.

Operating Cash Flow/Cash Dividends

The **operating cash flow/cash dividends** indicates a firm's ability to cover cash dividends with the yearly operating cash flow. The higher the ratio, the better the firm's ability to cover cash dividends. This ratio relates to the investor ratios discussed in Chapter 9.

The operating cash flow/cash dividends formula is as follows:

$$\frac{\text{Operating Cash Flow}}{\text{Cash Dividends}}$$

The operating cash flow amount is the same figure that was used in the three previous formulas in this chapter. Operating cash flow/cash dividends is computed for Nike for 2011 and 2010 in Exhibit 10-8. It indicates material coverage of cash dividends in both 2011 and 2010, although there was a material decline in 2011.

EXHIBIT **10-8**	Nike, Inc.	
Operating Cash Flow/Cash Dividends		
Years Ended May 31, 2011 and 2010		
(In millions)	**2011**	**2010**
Operating cash flow [A]	$1,812.0	$3,164.0
Cash dividends [B]	$ 555.0	$ 505.0
Operating cash flow/cash dividends [A ÷ B]	3.26 times per year	6.27 times per year

Source: Nike, Inc. 2010 10-K

Alternative Cash Flow

There is no standard definition of cash flow in the financial literature. Often, cash flow is used to mean net income plus depreciation expense. This definition of cash flow could be used to compute the cash flow amount for the formulas introduced in this chapter. However, this is a narrow definition of cash flow, and it is considered less useful than the net cash flow from operating activities.

Procedures for Development of the Statement of Cash Flows

Cash inflows and outflows are determined by analyzing all balance sheet accounts other than the cash and cash equivalent accounts. The following account balance changes indicate cash inflows:

1. Decreases in assets (e.g., the sale of land for cash)
2. Increases in liabilities (e.g., the issuance of long-term bonds)
3. Increases in stockholders' equity (e.g., the sale of common stock)

Cash outflows are indicated by the following account balance changes:

1. Increases in assets (e.g., the purchase of a building for cash)

2. Decreases in liabilities (e.g., retirement of long-term debt)

3. Decreases in stockholders' equity (e.g., the payment of a cash dividend)

Transactions within any individual account may result in both a source and a use of cash. For example, the land account may have increased, but analysis may indicate that there was both an acquisition and a disposal of land.

Exhibit 10-9 contains the data needed for preparing a statement of cash flows for ABC Company for the year ended December 31, 2011. These data will be used to illustrate the preparation of the statement of cash flows.

Three techniques may be used to prepare the statement of cash flows: (1) the visual method, (2) the T-account method, and (3) the worksheet method. The visual method can be used only when the financial information is not complicated. When the financial information is complicated, either the T-account method or the worksheet method must be used. This book illustrates only the visual method because of the emphasis on using financial accounting information, not on preparing financial statements. For an explanation of the T-account method and the worksheet method, consult an intermediate accounting textbook.

EXHIBIT 10-9	ABC Company

Financial Information for Statement of Cash Flows

Balance Sheet Information

	Balances		
Accounts	December 31, 2010	December 31, 2011	Category
Assets:			
Cash	$ 2,400	$ 3,000	Cash
Accounts receivable, net	4,000	3,900	Operating
Inventories	5,000	6,000	Operating
Total current assets	11,400	12,900	
Land	10,000	19,500	Investing
Equipment	72,000	73,000	Investing
Accumulated depreciation	(9,500)	(14,000)	Operating
Total assets	$83,900	91,400	
Liabilities:			
Accounts payable	$ 4,000	$ 2,900	Operating
Taxes payable	1,600	2,000	Operating
Total current liabilities	5,600	4,900	
Bonds payable	35,000	40,000	Financing
Stockholders' Equity:			
Common stock, $10 par	36,000	39,000	Financing
Retained earnings	7,300	7,500	*
Total liabilities and stockholders' equity	$83,900	$ 91,400	

**Income Statement Information
For the Year Ended December 31, 2011**

		Category
Sales	$22,000	Operating
Operating expenses	17,500	Operating
Operating income	4,500	
Gain on sale of land	1,000	Investing
Income before tax expense	5,500	
Tax expense	2,000	Operating
Net income	$ 3,500	*

*Retained earnings is decreased by cash dividends, $3,300 (financing), and increased by net income, $3,500. Net income can be a combination of operating, investing, and financing activities. In this exhibit, all of the net income relates to operating activities, except for the gain on sale of land (investing).

Source: ABC Company 2010 10-K

EXHIBIT 10-9	ABC Company *(continued)*

Supplemental Information	Category
(a) Dividends declared and paid are $3,300.	Financing
(b) Land was sold for $1,500.	Investing
(c) Equipment was purchased for $1,000.	Investing
(d) Bonds payable were retired for $5,000.	Financing
(e) Common stock was sold for $3,000.	Financing
(f) Operating expenses include depreciation expense of $4,500.	Operating
(g) The land account and the bonds payable account increased by $10,000 because of a noncash exchange.	Investing and Financing

Following the steps in developing the statement of cash flows, first compute the change in cash and cash equivalents. For ABC Company, this is the increase of $600 in the cash account—the net increase in cash.

For the second step, compute the net change in each balance sheet account other than the cash account. The changes in the balance sheet accounts for ABC Company follow:

Assets:

Accounts receivable decrease	$ 100	Operating
Inventories increase	1,000	Operating
Land increase	9,500	Investing
Equipment increase	1,000	Investing
Accumulated depreciation increase	4,500	Operating
(contra-asset—a change would be similar to a change in liabilities)		

Liabilities:

Accounts payable decrease	1,100	Operating
Taxes payable increase	400	Operating
Bonds payable increase	5,000	Financing

Stockholders' equity:

Common stock increase	3,000	Financing
Retained earnings increase	200	*

*This is a combination of operating, financing, and investing activities.

For the third step, consider the changes in the balance sheet accounts along with the income statement for the current period and the supplementary information. The cash flows are segregated into cash flows from operating activities, cash flows from investing activities, and cash flows from financing activities. Noncash investing and/or financing activities should be shown in a separate schedule with the statement of cash flows.

To illustrate the direct and indirect methods of presenting operating activities, the ABC Company income statement is used, along with the relevant supplemental information and balance sheet accounts. For the direct approach, the income statement is adjusted to present the revenue and expense accounts on a cash basis. Exhibit 10-10 illustrates the accrual basis income statement adjusted to a cash basis. Exhibit 10-11 shows the statement of cash flows for ABC Company, using the direct approach for presenting cash flows from operations.

When the cash provided by operations is presented using the direct approach, the income statement accounts are usually described in terms of receipts or payments. For example, "sales" on the accrual basis income statement is usually described as "receipts from customers" when presented on a cash basis.

EXHIBIT 10-10	ABC Company

Schedule of Change from Accrual Basis to Cash Basis Income Statement

	Accrual Basis	Adjustments*	Add (Subtract)	Cash Basis
Sales	$22,000	Decrease in receivables	100	$22,100
Operating expenses	17,500	Depreciation expense	(4,500)	
		Increase in inventories	1,000	
		Decrease in accounts payable	1,100	15,100
Operating income	4,500			7,000
Gain on sale of land	1,000	This gain is related to investing activities.	(1,000)	—
Income before tax expense	5,500			7,000
Tax expense	2,000	Increase in taxes payable	(400)	1,600
Net income	$ 3,500			$ 5,400

*Adjustments are for noncash flow items in the income statement, changes in balance sheet accounts related to cash flow from operations, and the removal of gains and losses on the income statement that are related to investing or financing activities.

The noncash flow items in the income statement are removed from the account. For example, depreciation expense may be in the cost of goods sold, and this expense would be removed from the cost of goods sold.

Changes in balance sheet accounts related to cash flow from operations are adjusted to the related income statement account as follows:

Revenue accounts	$ XXX
Add decreases in asset accounts and increases in liability accounts	+XXX
Deduct increases in asset accounts and decreases in liability accounts	−XXX
Cash inflow	$ XXX
Expense accounts	
Add increases in asset accounts and decreases in liability accounts	+XXX
Deduct decreases in asset accounts and increases in liability accounts	−XXX
Cash outflow	$ XXX

Source: ABC Company 2010 10-K

EXHIBIT 10-11	ABC Company*

Direct Approach for Presenting Cash Flows from Operations

Statement of Cash Flows
For the Year Ended December 31, 2011

Cash flows from operating activities:		
Receipts from customers	$ 22,100	
Payments to suppliers	(15,100)	
Income taxes paid	(1,600)	
Net cash provided by operating activities		$ 5,400
Cash flows from investing activities:		
Proceeds from sale of land	1,500	
Purchase of equipment	(1,000)	
Net cash provided by investing activities		500
Cash flows from financing activities:		
Dividends declared and paid	(3,300)	
Retirement of bonds payable	(5,000)	
Proceeds from common stock	3,000	
Net cash used for financing activities		(5,300)
Net increase in cash		$ 600

Source: ABC Company 2010 10-K

EXHIBIT **10-11**	ABC Company (*continued*)	

Reconciliation of net income to net cash provided by operating activities:	
Net income	$ 3,500
Adjustments to reconcile net income to net cash provided by operating activities:	
Decrease in accounts receivable	100
Depreciation expense	4,500
Increase in inventories	(1,000)
Decrease in accounts payable	(1,100)
Gain on sale of land	(1,000)
Increase in taxes payable	400
Net cash provided by operating activities	$ 5,400
Supplemental schedule of noncash investing and financing activities:	
Land acquired by issuing bonds	$10,000

Exhibit 10-12 shows the statement of cash flows for ABC Company using the indirect approach. To compute cash flows from operations, we start with net income and add back or deduct adjustments necessary to change the income on an accrual basis to income on a cash basis, after eliminating gains or losses that relate to investing or financing activities. Notice on the ABC Company schedule of change from accrual basis to cash basis income statement (Exhibit 10-10) that the adjustments include noncash flow items on the income statement, changes in balance sheet accounts related to operations, and gains and losses on the income statement related to investing or financing activities.

EXHIBIT **10-12**	ABC Company		

Indirect Approach for Presenting Cash Flows from Operations

Statement of Cash Flows
For the Year Ended December 31, 2011

Cash flows from operating activities:		
Net income	$ 3,500	
Add (deduct) items not affecting operating activities:		
Depreciation expense	4,500	
Decrease in accounts receivable	100	
Increase in inventories	(1,000)	
Decrease in accounts payable	(1,100)	
Increase in taxes payable	400	
Gain on sale of land	(1,000)	
Net cash provided by operating activities		$ 5,400
Cash flows from investing activities:		
Proceeds from sale of land	1,500	
Purchase of equipment	(1,000)	
Net cash provided by investing activities		500
Cash flows from financing activities:		
Dividends declared and paid	(3,300)	
Retirement of bonds payable	(5,000)	
Proceeds from common stock	3,000	
Net cash used for financing activities		(5,300)
Net increase in cash		$ 600
Supplemental disclosure of cash flow information:		
Cash paid during the year for:		
Interest net of amount capitalized		$ 0
Income taxes		1,600
Supplemental schedule of noncash investing and financing activities:		
Land acquired by issuing bonds		$10,000

Source: ABC Company 2010 10-K

For the indirect approach, follow these directions when adjusting the net income (or loss) to net cash flows from operating activities:

Net income (loss)	$XXX
Noncash flow items:	
Add expense	+XXX
Deduct revenues	−XXX
Changes in balance sheet accounts related to operations:*	
Add decreases in assets and increases in liabilities	+XXX
Deduct increases in assets and decreases in liabilities	−XXX
Gains and losses on the income statement that are related to investing or financing activities:	
Add losses	+XXX
Deduct gains	−XXX
Net cash provided by operating activities	$XXX

*These are usually the current asset and current liability accounts.

The remaining changes in balance sheet accounts (other than those used to compute cash provided by operating activities) and the remaining supplemental information are used to determine the cash flows from investing activities and cash flows from financing activities. These accounts are also used to determine noncash investing and/or financing.

Some observations on the ABC Company statement of cash flows follow:

1.	Net cash provided by operating activities	$5,400
2.	Net cash provided by investing activities	$ 500
3.	Net cash used for financing activities	$5,300
4.	Net increase in cash	$ 600

As previously indicated, when the operations section has been presented using the direct method, additional observations can be determined by preparing the statement of cash flows to present inflows and outflows separately. This has been done in Exhibit 10-13. Some observations from the summary of cash flows in Exhibit 10-13 follow:

EXHIBIT 10-13 ABC Company

Statement of Cash Flows
For the Year Ended December 31, 2011
(Inflows and Outflows, by Activity—Inflows Presented on Direct Basis)

	Inflows	Outflows	Inflow Percent	Outflow Percent
Operating activities:				
Receipts from customers	$22,100		83.1%	
Payments to suppliers		$15,100		58.1%
Income taxes paid	—	1,600	—	6.2
Cash flow from operating activities	22,100	16,700	83.1	64.3
Investing activities:				
Proceeds from sale of land	1,500		5.6	
Purchase of equipment	—	1,000	—	3.8
Cash flow from investing activities	1,500	1,000	5.6	3.8
Financing activities:				
Dividends declared and paid		3,300		12.7
Retirement of bonds payable		5,000		19.2
Proceeds from common stock	3,000	—	11.3	—
Cash flow from financing activities	3,000	8,300	11.3	31.9
Total cash inflows/outflows	26,600	$26,000	100.0%	100.0%
Total cash outflows	26,000			
Net increase in cash	$ 600			

Source: ABC Company 2010 10-K

Inflows:

    1. Receipts from customers represent approximately 83% of total cash inflow.

    2. Proceeds from common stock sales approximate 11% of total cash inflow.

    3. Proceeds from sales of land approximate 6% of total cash inflow.

Outflows:

    1. Payments to suppliers represent approximately 58% of total cash outflow.

    2. Retirement of bonds payable approximates 19% of total cash outflow.

    3. Dividends paid approximate 13% of total cash outflow.

Summary

The statement of cash flows provides cash flow information that is critical for users to make informed decisions. The statement of cash flows should be reviewed for several time periods in order to determine the major sources of cash and the major uses of cash.

The ratios related to the statement of cash flows are the following:

The formula for **operating cash flow/current maturities of long-term debt and current notes payable** is:

$$\frac{\text{Operating Cash Flow}}{\text{Current Maturities of Long-Term Debt and Current Notes Payable}}$$

The formula for **operating cash flow/total debt** is:

$$\frac{\text{Operating Cash Flow}}{\text{Total Debt}}$$

The formula for **operating cash flow per share** is:

$$\frac{\text{Operating Cash Flow} - \text{Preferred Dividends}}{\text{Diluted Weighted Average Common Shares Outstanding}}$$

The formula for **operating cash flow/cash dividends** is:

$$\frac{\text{Operating Cash Flow}}{\text{Cash Dividends}}$$

Questions

Q 10-1 If a firm presents an income statement and a balance sheet, why is it necessary that a statement of cash flows also be presented?

Q 10-2 Into what three categories are cash flows segregated on the statement of cash flows?

Q 10-3 Using the descriptions of assets, liabilities, and stockholders' equity, summarize the changes to these accounts for cash inflows and changes for cash outflows.

Q 10-4 The land account may be used only to explain a use of cash, but not a source of cash. Comment.

Q 10-5 Indicate the three techniques that may be used to complete the steps in developing the statement of cash flows.

Q 10-6 There are two principal methods of presenting cash flow from operating activities—the direct method and the indirect method. Describe these two methods.

Q 10-7 Depreciation expense, amortization of patents, and amortization of bond discount are examples of items that are added to net income when using the indirect method of presenting cash flows from operating activities. Amortization of premium on bonds and a reduction in deferred taxes are examples of items that are deducted from net income when using the indirect method of presenting cash flows from operating activities. Explain why these adjustments to net income are made to compute cash flows from operating activities.

Q 10-8 What is the meaning of the term *cash* in the statement of cash flows?

Q 10-9 What is the purpose of the statement of cash flows?

Q 10-10 Why is it important to disclose certain noncash investing and financing transactions, such as exchanging common stock for land?

Q 10-11 Would a write-off of uncollectible accounts against allowance for doubtful accounts be disclosed on a cash flow statement? Explain.

Q 10-12 Fully depreciated equipment costing $60,000 was discarded, with no salvage value. What effect would this have on the statement of cash flows?

Q 10-13 For the current year, a firm reported net income from operations of $20,000 on its income statement and an increase of $30,000 in cash from operations on the statement of cash flows. Explain some likely reasons for the greater increase in cash from operations than net income from operations.

Q 10-14 A firm owed accounts payable of $150,000 at the beginning of the year and $250,000 at the end of the year. What influence will the $100,000 increase have on cash from operations?

Q 10-15 A member of the board of directors is puzzled by the fact that the firm has had a very profitable year but does not have enough cash to pay its bills on time. Explain to the director how a firm can be profitable, yet not have enough cash to pay its bills and dividends.

Q 10-16 Depreciation is often considered a major source of funds. Do you agree? Explain.

Q 10-17 Pickerton started the year with $50,000 in accounts receivable. The firm ended the year with $20,000 in accounts receivable. How did this decrease influence cash from operations?

Q 10-18 Aerco Company acquired equipment in exchange for $50,000 in common stock. Should this transaction be on the statement of cash flows?

Q 10-19 Operating cash flow per share is a better indicator of profitability than is earnings per share. Do you agree? Explain.

Q 10-20 Hornet Company had operating cash flow of $60,000 during a year in which it paid dividends of $11,000. What does this indicate about Hornet's dividend-paying ability?

Q 10-21 The Mason Company, a retail business had $100,000 in cash sales and $450,000 in credit sales for 2012. The accounts receivable balances were $50,000 and $60,000 on December 31, 2011 and 2012, respectively. What was the cash receipts from sales in 2012?

Problems

P 10-1 The following material relates to Darrow Company:

Data	Operating Activity	Investing Activity	Financing Activity	Increase	Decrease	Noncash Trans- actions
	Cash Flows Classification			**Effect on Cash**		
a. Net loss						
b. Increase in inventory						
c. Decrease in receivables						
d. Increase in prepaid insurance						
e. Issuance of common stock						
f. Acquisition of land, using notes payable						
g. Purchase of land, using cash						
h. Paid cash dividend						
i. Payment of income taxes						
j. Retirement of bonds, using cash						
k. Sale of equipment for cash						

Required Place an X in the appropriate columns for each of the situations.

P 10-2

Data	Operating Activity	Investing Activity	Financing Activity	Increase	Decrease	Noncash Trans- actions
	Cash Flows Classification			**Effect on Cash**		
a. Net income						
b. Paid cash dividend						
c. Increase in receivables						
d. Retirement of debt—paying cash						
e. Purchase of treasury stock						
f. Purchase of equipment						

	Cash Flows Classification			Effect on Cash		Noncash Trans-actions
Data	Operating Activity	Investing Activity	Financing Activity	Increase	Decrease	
g. Sale of equipment	_____	_____	_____	_____	_____	_____
h. Decrease in inventory	_____	_____	_____	_____	_____	_____
i. Acquisition of land, using common stock	_____	_____	_____	_____	_____	_____
j. Retired bonds, using common stock	_____	_____	_____	_____	_____	_____
k. Decrease in accounts payable	_____	_____	_____	_____	_____	_____

Required Place an X in the appropriate columns for each of the situations.

P 10-3 BBB Company's balance sheet and income statement follow:

BBB COMPANY
Balance Sheet
December 31, 2011 and 2010

	December 31,	
	2011	2010
Assets		
Cash	$ 4,500	$ 4,000
Marketable securities	2,500	2,000
Accounts receivable	6,800	7,200
Inventories	7,500	8,000
Total current assets	21,300	21,200
Land	11,000	12,000
Equipment	24,000	20,500
Accumulated depreciation—equipment	(3,800)	(3,000)
Building	70,000	70,000
Accumulated depreciation—building	(14,000)	(12,000)
Total assets	$108,500	$108,700
Liabilities and Stockholders' Equity		
Accounts payable	$ 7,800	$ 7,000
Wages payable	1,050	1,000
Taxes payable	500	1,500
Total current liabilities	9,350	9,500
Bonds payable	30,000	30,000
Common stock, $10 par	32,000	30,000
Additional paid-in capital	21,000	19,200
Retained earnings	16,150	20,000
Total liabilities and stockholders' equity	$108,500	$108,700

BBB COMPANY
Income Statement
For Year Ended December 31, 2011

Sales		$38,000
Operating expenses:		
Depreciation expense	$ 2,800	
Other operating expenses	35,000	37,800
Operating income		200
Gain on sale of land		800
Income before tax expense		1,000
Tax expense		500
Net income		$ 500

(*continued*)

(P 10-3 CONTINUED)

Supplemental information:

Dividends declared and paid	$ 4,350
Land sold for cash	1,800
Equipment purchased for cash	3,500
Common stock sold for cash	3,800

Required

a. Prepare a statement of cash flows for the year ended December 31, 2011. (Present the cash flows from operations using the indirect method.)

b. Comment on the statement of cash flows.

P 10-4 The income statement and other selected data for Frish Company follow:

FRISH COMPANY
Income Statement
For Year Ended December 31, 2011

Net sales	$640,000
Expenses:	
Cost of goods sold	360,000
Selling and administrative expense	43,000
Other expense	2,000
Total expenses	405,000
Income before income tax	235,000
Income tax	92,000
Net income	$143,000

Other data:

a. Cost of goods sold, including depreciation expense of $15,000

b. Selling and administrative expense, including depreciation expense of $5,000

c. Other expense, representing amortization of patent, $3,000, and amortization of bond premium, $1,000

d. Increase in accounts receivable	$ 27,000
e. Increase in accounts payable	15,000
f. Increase in inventories	35,000
g. Decrease in prepaid expenses	1,000
h. Increase in accrued liabilities	3,000
i. Decrease in income taxes payable	10,000

Required

a. Prepare a schedule of change from accrual basis to cash basis income statement.

b. Using the schedule of change from accrual basis to cash basis income statement computed in (a), present the cash provided by operations, using (1) the direct approach and (2) the indirect approach.

P 10-5 The income statement and other selected data for Boyer Company follow:

BOYER COMPANY
Income Statement
For Year Ended December 31, 2011

Sales		$19,000
Operating expenses:		
Depreciation expense	$ 2,300	
Other operating expenses	12,000	14,300
Operating income		4,700
Loss on sale of land		1,500
Income before tax expense		3,200
Tax expense		1,000
Net income		$ 2,200

Supplemental information:

a. Dividends declared and paid	$ 800
b. Land purchased	3,000
c. Land sold	500
d. Equipment purchased	2,000
e. Bonds payable retired	2,000
f. Common stock sold	1,400
g. Land acquired in exchange for common stock	3,000
h. Increase in accounts receivable	400
i. Increase in inventories	800
j. Increase in accounts payable	500
k. Decrease in income taxes payable	400

Required

a. Prepare a schedule of change from an accrual basis to a cash basis income statement.

b. Using the schedule of change from accrual basis to cash basis income statement computed in (a), present the cash provided by operations, using (1) the direct approach and (2) the indirect approach.

P 10-6 Sampson Company's balance sheets for December 31, 2011 and 2010, as well as the income statement for the year ended December 31, 2011, are shown next.

SAMPSON COMPANY
Balance Sheet
December 31, 2011 and 2010

	2011	2010
Assets		
Cash	$ 38,000	$ 60,000
Net receivables	72,000	65,000
Inventory	98,000	85,000
Plant assets	195,000	180,000
Accumulated depreciation	(45,000)	(35,000)
Total assets	$358,000	$355,000
Liabilities and Stockholders' Equity		
Accounts payable	$ 85,000	$ 80,000
Accrued liabilities (related to cost of sales)	44,000	61,000
Mortgage payable	11,000	—
Common stock	180,000	174,000
Retained earnings	38,000	40,000
Total liabilities and stockholders' equity	$358,000	$355,000

SAMPSON COMPANY
Income Statement
For Year Ended December 31, 2011

Net sales	$145,000
Cost of sales	108,000
Gross profit	37,000
Other expenses	6,000
Profit before taxes	31,000
Tax expense	12,000
Net income	$ 19,000

Other data:

1. Dividends paid in cash during 2011 were $21,000.
2. Depreciation is included in the cost of sales.
3. The change in the accumulated depreciation account is the depreciation expense for the year.

(*continued*)

(**P 10-6** CONTINUED)

Required

a. Prepare the statement of cash flows for the year ended December 31, 2011, using the indirect method for net cash flow from operating activities.

b. Prepare the statement of cash flows for the year ended December 31, 2011, using the direct method for net cash flow from operating activities.

c. Comment on significant items disclosed in the statement of cash flows.

P 10-7 Arrowbell Company is a growing company. Two years ago, it decided to expand in order to increase its production capacity. The company anticipates that the expansion program can be completed in another two years. Financial information for Arrowbell is as follows.

ARROWBELL COMPANY
Sales and Net Income

Year	Sales	Net Income
2007	$2,568,660	$145,800
2008	2,660,455	101,600
2009	2,550,180	52,650
2010	2,625,280	86,800
2011	3,680,650	151,490

ARROWBELL COMPANY
Balance Sheet
December 31, 2011 and 2010

	2011	2010
Assets		
Current assets:		
Cash	$ 250,480	$ 260,155
Accounts receivable (net)	760,950	690,550
Inventories at lower-of-cost-or-market	725,318	628,238
Prepaid expenses	18,555	20,250
Total current assets	1,755,303	1,599,193
Plant and equipment:		
Land, buildings, machinery, and equipment	3,150,165	2,646,070
Less: Accumulated depreciation	650,180	525,650
Net plant and equipment	2,499,985	2,120,420
Other assets:		
Cash surrender value of life insurance	20,650	18,180
Other	40,660	38,918
Total other assets	61,310	57,098
Total assets	$4,316,598	$3,776,711
Liabilities and Stockholders' Equity		
Current liabilities:		
Notes and mortgages payable, current portion	$ 915,180	$ 550,155
Accounts payable and accrued liabilities	1,160,111	851,080
Total current liabilities	2,075,291	1,401,235
Long-term notes and mortgages payable, less current portion above	550,000	775,659
Total liabilities	2,625,291	2,176,894
Stockholders' equity:		
Capital stock, par value $1.00; authorized, 800,000; issued and outstanding, 600,000 (2011 and 2010)	600,000	600,000
Paid in excess of par	890,000	890,000
Retained earnings	201,307	109,817
Total stockholders' equity	1,691,307	1,599,817
Total liabilities and stockholders' equity	$4,316,598	$3,776,711

ARROWBELL COMPANY
Statement of Cash Flows
For Years Ended December 31, 2011 and 2010

	2011	2010
Cash flows from operating activities:		
Net income	$ 151,490	$ 86,800
Noncash expenses, revenues, losses, and gains included in income:		
Depreciation	134,755	102,180
Increase in accounts receivable	(70,400)	(10,180)
Increase in inventories	(97,080)	(15,349)
Decrease in prepaid expenses in 2011, increase in 2010	1,695	(1,058)
Increase in accounts payable and accrued liabilities	309,031	15,265
Net cash provided by operating activities	429,491	177,658
Cash flows from investing activities:		
Proceeds from retirement of property, plant, and equipment	10,115	3,865
Purchases of property, plant, and equipment	(524,435)	(218,650)
Increase in cash surrender value of life insurance	(2,470)	(1,848)
Other	(1,742)	(1,630)
Net cash used for investing activities	(518,532)	(218,263)
Cash flows from financing activities:		
Retirement of long-term debt	(225,659)	(50,000)
Increase in notes and mortgages payable	365,025	159,155
Cash dividends	(60,000)	(60,000)
Net cash provided by financing activities	79,366	49,155
Net increase (decrease) in cash	$ (9,675)	$ 8,550

Required

a. Comment on the short-term debt position, including computations of current ratio, acid-test ratio, cash ratio, and operating cash flow/current maturities of long-term debt and current notes payable.

b. If you were a supplier to this company, what would you be concerned about?

c. Comment on the long-term debt position, including computations of the debt ratio, debt/equity, debt to tangible net worth, and operating cash flow/total debt. Review the statement of operating cash flows.

d. If you were a banker, what would you be concerned about if this company approached you for a long-term loan to continue its expansion program?

e. What should management consider doing at this point with regard to the company's expansion program?

P 10-8 The balance sheet for December 31, 2011, income statement for the year ended December 31, 2011, and the statement of cash flows for the year ended December 31, 2011, of Bernett Company are shown in the following balance sheet.

The president of Bernett Company cannot understand why Bernett is having trouble paying current obligations. He notes that business has been very good, as sales have more than doubled, and the company achieved a profit of $69,000 in 2011.

BERNETT COMPANY
Balance Sheet
December 31, 2011 and 2010

	2011	2010
Assets		
Cash	$ 5,000	$ 28,000
Accounts receivable, net	92,000	70,000
Inventory	130,000	85,000
Prepaid expenses	4,000	6,000
Land	30,000	10,000

(continued)

(**P 10-8** CONTINUED)

	2011	2010
Assets		
Building	$170,000	$ 30,000
Accumulated depreciation	(20,000)	(10,000)
Total assets	$411,000	$219,000
Liabilities and Stockholders' Equity		
Accounts payable	$ 49,000	$ 44,000
Income taxes payable	5,000	4,000
Accrued liabilities	6,000	5,000
Bonds payable (current $10,000 at 12/31/11)	175,000	20,000
Common stock	106,000	96,000
Retained earnings	70,000	50,000
Total liabilities and stockholders' equity	$411,000	$219,000

BERNETT COMPANY
Income Statement
For Year Ended December 31, 2011

Sales	$500,000
Less expenses:	
Cost of goods sold (includes depreciation of $4,000)	310,000
Selling and administrative expenses (includes depreciation of $6,000)	80,000
Interest expense	11,000
Total expenses	401,000
Income before taxes	99,000
Income tax expense	30,000
Net income	$ 69,000

BERNETT COMPANY
Statement of Cash Flows
For Year Ended December 31, 2011

Net cash flow from operating activities:		
Net income	$ 69,000	
Noncash expenses, revenues, losses, and gains included in income:		
Depreciation	10,000	
Increase in receivables	(22,000)	
Increase in inventory	(45,000)	
Decrease in prepaid expenses	2,000	
Increase in accounts payable	5,000	
Increase in income taxes payable	1,000	
Increase in accrued liabilities	1,000	
Net cash flow from operating activities		$ 21,000
Cash flows from investing activities:		
Increase in land	$ (20,000)	
Increase in buildings	(140,000)	
Net cash used by investing activities		(160,000)
Cash flows from financing activities:		
Bond payable increase	$ 155,000	
Common stock increase	10,000	
Cash dividends paid	(49,000)	
Net cash provided by financing activities		116,000
Net decrease in cash		$ (23,000)

Required

a. Comment on the statement of cash flows.
b. Compute the following liquidity ratios for 2011:

  1. Current ratio
  2. Acid-test ratio
  3. Operating cash flow/current maturities of long-term debt and current notes payable
  4. Cash ratio

c. Compute the following debt ratios for 2011:

    1. Times interest earned
    2. Debt ratio
    3. Operating cash flow/total debt

d. Compute the following profitability ratios for 2011:

    1. Return on assets (using average assets)
    2. Return on common equity (using average common equity)

e. Compute the following investor ratio for 2011: Operating cash flow/cash dividends.
f. Give your opinion as to the liquidity of Bernett.
g. Give your opinion as to the debt position of Bernett.
h. Give your opinion as to the profitability of Bernett.
i. Give your opinion as to the investor ratio.
j. Give your opinion of the alternatives Bernett has in order to ensure that it can pay bills as they come due.

P 10-9 Zaro Company's balance sheets for December 31, 2011 and 2010, income statement for the year ended December 31, 2011, and the statement of cash flows for the year ended December 31, 2011, follow:

ZARO COMPANY
Balance Sheet
December 31, 2011 and 2010

	2011	2010
Assets		
Cash	$ 30,000	$ 15,000
Accounts receivable, net	75,000	87,000
Inventory	90,000	105,000
Prepaid expenses	3,000	2,000
Land	25,000	25,000
Building and equipment	122,000	120,000
Accumulated depreciation	(92,000)	(80,000)
Total assets	$253,000	$274,000
Liabilities and Stockholders' Equity		
Accounts payable	$ 25,500	$ 32,000
Income taxes payable	2,500	3,000
Accrued liabilities	5,000	5,000
Bonds payable (current $20,000 at 12/31/11)	90,000	95,000
Common stock	85,000	85,000
Retained earnings	45,000	54,000
Total liabilities and stockholders' equity	$253,000	$274,000

ZARO COMPANY
Income Statement
For Year Ended December 31, 2011

Sales	$400,000
Less expense:	
Cost of goods sold (includes depreciation of $5,000)	$280,000
Selling and administrative expenses (includes depreciation expenses of $7,000)	78,000
Interest expense	8,000
Total expenses	$366,000
Income before taxes	34,000
Income tax expense	14,000
Net income	$ 20,000

(*continued*)

(**P 10-9** CONTINUED)

ZARO COMPANY
Statement of Cash Flows
For Year Ended December 31, 2011

Net cash flow from operating activities:		
Net income	$ 20,000	
Noncash expenses, revenues, losses, and gains included in income:		
Depreciation	12,000	
Decrease in accounts receivable	12,000	
Decrease in inventory	15,000	
Increase in prepaid expenses	(1,000)	
Decrease in accounts payable	(6,500)	
Decrease in income taxes payable	(500)	
Net cash flow from operating activities		$ 51,000
Cash flows from investing activities:		
Increase in buildings and equipment	$ (2,000)	
Net cash used by investing activities		(2,000)
Cash flows from financing activities:		
Decrease in bonds payable	$ (5,000)	
Cash dividends paid	(29,000)	
Net cash used for financing activities		(34,000)
Net increase in cash		$ 15,000

The president of Zaro Company cannot understand how the company was able to pay cash dividends that were greater than net income and at the same time increase the cash balance. He notes that business was down slightly in 2011.

Required

a. Comment on the statement of cash flows.
b. Compute the following liquidity ratios for 2011:

1. Current ratio
2. Acid-test ratio
3. Operating cash flow/current maturities of long-term debt and current notes payable
4. Cash ratio

c. Compute the following debt ratios for 2011:

1. Times interest earned
2. Debt ratio

d. Compute the following profitability ratios for 2011:

1. Return on assets (using average assets)
2. Return on common equity (using average common equity)

e. Give your opinion as to the liquidity of Zaro.
f. Give your opinion as to the debt position of Zaro.
g. Give your opinion as to the profitability of Zaro.
h. Explain to the president how Zaro was able to pay cash dividends that were greater than net income and at the same time increase the cash balance.

P 10-10 The Ladies Store presented the following statement of cash flows for the year ended December 31, 2011:

THE LADIES STORE
Statement of Cash Flows
For Year Ended December 31, 2011

Cash received:	
From sales to customers	$150,000
From sales of bonds	100,000
From issuance of notes payable	40,000
From interest on bonds	5,000
Total cash received	295,000

Cash payments:

For merchandise purchases	$110,000
For purchase of truck	20,000
For purchase of investment	80,000
For purchase of equipment	45,000
For interest	2,000
For income taxes	15,000
Total cash payments	272,000
Net increase in cash	$ 23,000

Note: Depreciation expense was $15,000.

Required

a. Prepare a statement of cash flows in proper form.
b. Comment on the major flows of cash.

P 10-11 Answer the following multiple-choice questions:

a. Which of the following could lead to cash flow problems?

1. Tightening of credit by suppliers.
2. Easing of credit by suppliers.
3. Reduction of inventory.
4. Improved quality of accounts receivable.
5. Selling of bonds.

b. Which of the following would not contribute to bankruptcy of a profitable firm?

1. Substantial increase in inventory.
2. Substantial increase in receivables.
3. Substantial decrease in accounts payable.
4. Substantial decrease in notes payable.
5. Substantial decrease in receivables.

c. Which of the following current asset or current liability accounts is not included in the computation of cash flows from operating activities?

1. Change in accounts receivable.
2. Change in inventory.
3. Change in accounts payable.
4. Change in accrued wages.
5. Change in notes payable to banks.

d. Which of the following items is not included in the adjustment of net income to cash flows from operating activities?

1. Increase in deferred taxes.
2. Amortization of goodwill.
3. Depreciation expense for the period.
4. Amortization of premium on bonds payable.
5. Proceeds from selling land.

e. Which of the following represents an internal source of cash?

1. Cash inflows from financing activities.
2. Cash inflows from investing activities.
3. Cash inflows from selling land.
4. Cash inflows from operating activities.
5. Cash inflows from issuing stock.

f. How would revenue from services be classified?

1. Investing inflow
2. Investing outflow

(*continued*)

(**P 10-11** CONTINUED)

    3. Operating inflow
    4. Operating outflow
    5. Financing outflow

g. What type of account is inventory?

    1. Investing
    2. Financing
    3. Operating
    4. Noncash
    5. Sometimes operating and sometimes investing.

h. How would short-term investments in marketable securities be classified?

    1. Operating activities
    2. Financing activities
    3. Investing activities
    4. Noncash activities
    5. Cash and cash equivalents

i. Which of the following is *not* a typical cash flow under operating activities?

    1. Cash inflows from sale of goods or services.
    2. Cash inflows from interest.
    3. Cash outflows to employees.
    4. Cash outflows to suppliers.
    5. Cash inflows from sale of property, plant, and equipment.

j. A transaction that will increase working capital is

    1. Purchase of marketable securities.
    2. Payment of accounts payable.
    3. Collection of accounts receivable.
    4. Sale of common stock.
    5. None of the above.

k. Working capital is defined as

    1. Current assets less current liabilities.
    2. Cash equivalent accounts less current liabilities.
    3. Current assets less notes payable.
    4. Total assets less current liabilities.
    5. Current assets less cash equivalent accounts.

l. Management should use the statement of cash flows for which of the following purposes?

    1. Determine the financial position.
    2. Determine cash flow from investing activities.
    3. Determine the balance in accounts payable.
    4. Determine the balance in accounts receivable.
    5. None of the above.

m. The purchase of land by the issuance of bonds payable should be presented in a statement of cash flows in which of the following sections?

    1. Cash flows from operating activities.
    2. Supplemental schedule of noncash investing and financing activities.
    3. Cash flows from investing activities.

4. Cash flows from financing activities.
5. None of the above.

P 10-12 Szabo Company presented the following data with its 2011 financial statements:

DONNA SZABO COMPANY
Statements of Cash Flows
For Years Ended December 31, 2011, 2010, and 2009

	2011	2010	2009
Increase (decrease) in cash:			
Cash flows from operating activities:			
Cash received from customers	$ 173,233	$ 176,446	$ 158,702
Cash paid to suppliers and employees	(150,668)	(157,073)	(144,060)
Interest received	132	105	89
Interest paid	(191)	(389)	(777)
Income taxes paid	(6,626)	(4,754)	(845)
Net cash provided by operations	15,880	14,335	13,109
Cash flows from investing activities:			
Capital expenditures	(8,988)	(5,387)	(6,781)
Proceeds from property, plant, and equipment disposals	1,215	114	123
Net cash used in investing activities	(7,773)	(5,273)	(6,658)
Cash flows from financing activities:			
Net increase (decrease) in short-term debt	—	5,100	7,200
Increase in long-term debt	4,100	3,700	5,200
Dividends paid	(6,050)	(8,200)	(8,000)
Purchase of common stock	(8,233)	(3,109)	(70)
Net cash used in financing activities	(10,183)	(2,509)	4,330
Net increase (decrease) in cash and cash equivalents	(2,076)	6,553	10,781
Cash and cash equivalents at beginning of year	24,885	18,332	7,551
Cash and cash equivalents at end of year	$ 22,809	$ 24,885	$ 18,332

Reconciliation of Net Income to Net Cash Provided by Operating Activities

	2011	2010	2009
Net income	$ 7,610	$ 3,242	$ 506
Provision for depreciation and amortization	12,000	9,700	9,000
Provision for losses on accounts receivable	170	163	140
Gain on property, plant, and equipment disposals	(2,000)	(1,120)	(1,500)
Changes in operating assets and liabilities:			
Accounts receivable	(2,000)	(1,750)	(1,600)
Inventories	(3,100)	(2,700)	(2,300)
Other assets	—	—	(57)
Accounts payable	—	5,100	7,200
Accrued income taxes	1,200	—	—
Deferred income taxes	2,000	1,700	1,720
Net cash provided by operating activities	$15,880	$14,335	$13,109

Required

a. Prepare a statement of cash flows with a three-year total column for 2009–2011.
b. Comment on significant trends you detect in the statement prepared in (a).
c. Prepare a statement of cash flows, with inflow/outflow for the year ended December 31, 2011.
d. Comment on significant trends you detect in the statement prepared in (c).

P 10-13 Consider the following data for three different companies:

	($000 Omitted)		
	Owens	Arrow	Alpha
Net cash provided (used) by:			
Operating activities	$(2,000)	$2,700	$(3,000)
Investing activities	(6,000)	(600)	(400)
Financing activities	9,000	(400)	(2,600)
Net increase (decrease) in cash	$ 1,000	$1,700	$(6,000)

The patterns of cash flows for these firms differ. One firm is a growth firm that is expanding rapidly, another firm is in danger of bankruptcy, while another firm is an older firm that is expanding slowly.

Required Select the growth firm, the firm in danger of bankruptcy, and the firm that is the older firm expanding slowly. Explain your selection.

P 10-14 The following information was taken from the 2011 financial statements of Jones Corporation:

Accounts receivable, January 1, 2011	$ 30,000
Accounts receivable, December 31, 2011	40,000
Sales (all credit sales)	480,000

Note: No accounts receivable were written off or recovered during the year.

Required
   a. Determine the cash collected from customers by Jones Corporation in 2011.
   b. Comment on why cash collected from customers differed from sales.

P 10-15 Webster Corporation's statement of cash flows for the year ended December 31, 2011, was prepared using the indirect method, and it included the following items:

Net income	$100,000
Noncash adjustments:	
Depreciation expense	20,000
Decrease in accounts receivable	8,000
Decrease in inventory	25,000
Increase in accounts payable	10,000
Net cash flows from operating activities	$163,000

Note: Webster Corporation reported revenues from customers of $150,000 in its 2011 income statement.

Required
   a. What amount of cash did Webster receive from customers during the year ended December 31, 2011?
   b. Did depreciation expense provide cash inflow? Comment.

Cases

CASE 10-1 TRAVEL COMPANY

The data in this case come from the financial reports of Priceline.com.*

Priceline.com Incorporated
Selected Consolidated Balance Sheet Items
(In thousands, except per share data)

	December 31,	
	2010	2009
Total current assets	$1,957,464	$1,022,941
Total assets	2,905,953	1,834,224
Total current liabilities	471,168	408,765
Total liabilities	1,046,828	476,610
Accumulated earnings (deficit)	69,110	(454,673)
Stockholders' Equity	1,813,336	1,321,629

Priceline.com Incorporated
Selected Consolidated Statements of Operations
(In thousands, except per share data)

	December 31,		
	2010	2009	2008
Total revenues	$3,084,905	$2,338,212	$1,884,806
Gross profit	1,908,991	1,260,763	955,971
Operating income	786,797	470,835	289,474
Net income	528,142	489,472	185,624
Per diluted common share	$ 10.35	$ 9.88	$ 3.74

Priceline.com Incorporated
Selected Consolidated Statements of Cash Flows
(In thousands)

	2010	2009	2008
Net cash provided by operating activities	$ 777,297	$ 509,665	$ 315,553
Net cash (used in) provided by investing activities	(841,098)	(501,460)	(151,905)
Net cash (used in) provided by financing activities	212,957	(168,960)	(168,848)
Cash and cash equivalents, end of period	358,967	202,141	364,550

Required

a. 1. Compute the current ratio for 2010 and 2009. Comment.

   2. Compute the debt ratio for 2010 and 2009. Comment.

   3. Total revenues – Prepare a horizontal common-size – use 2008 as the base. Comment.

   4. Gross profit – Prepare a horizontal common-size – use 2008 as the base. Comment.

   5. Net income – Prepare a horizontal common-size – use 2008 as the base. Comment.

   6. Per diluted common share – Prepare a horizontal common-size – use 2008 as the base. Comment.

   7. Net cash provided by operating activities – Prepare a horizontal common-size – use 2008 as the base. Comment.

b. Give an overall comment.

*"Priceline.com Incorporated is a leading online travel company that offers our customers hotel room reservations at over 150,000 hotels worldwide through the Booking.com, priceline.com and Agoda brands." 10-K
Source: Priceline.com 2010 10-K

Case 10-2 CASH FLOW – THE DIRECT METHOD

ARDEN GROUP, INC. AND CONSOLIDATED SUBSIDIARIES*
CONSOLIDATED STATEMENTS OF CASH FLOWS

(In thousands)	Fifty-Two Weeks Ended January 1, 2011	Fifty-Two Weeks Ended January 2, 2010	Fifty-Three Weeks Ended January 3, 2009
Cash flows from operating activities:			
Cash received from customers	$ 417,580	$ 431,108	$ 479,578
Cash paid to suppliers and employees	(384,624)	(391,957)	(437,970)
Interest and dividends received	1,580	565	2,513
Interest paid	(94)	(87)	(109)
Income taxes paid	(11,354)	(13,895)	(15,545)
Net cash provided by operating activities	23,088	25,734	28,467
Cash flows from investing activities:			
Capital expenditures	(2,597)	(2,890)	(5,159)
Purchases of investments	(29,861)	(30,164)	(25,130)
Sales of investments	51,926	13,127	35,556
Proceeds from the sale of property, plant and equipment	16	48	21
Net cash provided by (used) in investing activities	19,484	(19,879)	5,288
Cash flows from financing activities:			
Cash dividends paid	(3,161)	(3,161)	(82,188)
Net cash used in financing activities	(3,161)	(3,161)	(82,188)
Net increase (decrease) in cash and cash equivalents	39,411	2,694	(48,433)
Cash and cash equivalents at beginning of year	13,180	10,486	58,919
Cash and cash equivalents at end of year	$ 52,591	$ 13,180	$ 10,486
Reconciliation of Net Income to Net Cash Provided by Operating Activities:			
Net income	$ 18,085	$ 21,624	$ 24,667
Adjustments to reconcile net income to net cash provided by operating activities:			
Depreciation and amortization	5,307	5,599	6,110
Provision for losses on accounts receivable	44	94	169
Deferred income taxes	1,129	108	1,923
Net loss from the disposal of property, plant and equipment	8	54	89
Realized loss on investments, net	66	0	907
Amortization of premium on investments	960	472	259
Stock appreciation rights compensation expense (income)	(394)	(273)	1,823
Changes in assets and liabilities net of effects from noncash investing and financing activities:			
(Increase) decrease in assets:			
Accounts and notes receivable	799	(246)	527
Inventories	(1,302)	972	3,712
Other current assets	95	204	(281)
Other assets	27	16	(69)
Increase (decrease) in liabilities:			
Accounts payable, trade and other current liabilities:	(1,090)	(2,402)	(9,148)
Federal and state income taxes payable	(237)	668	(608)
Deferred rent	(61)	99	154
Other liabilities	(348)	(1,255)	(1,767)
Net cash provided by operating activities	$ 23,088	$ 25,734	$ 28,467

*"The Registrant, Arden Group, Inc. (Company or Arden), is a holding company which conducts operations through its wholly-owned subsidiary, Arden-Mayfair, Inc. (Arden-Mayfair) and Arden-Mayfair's wholly-owned subsidiary, Gelson's Markets (Gelson's), which operates supermarkets in Southern California. The Company also owns certain real estate properties through a subsidiary, Mayfair Realty, Inc. (Mayfair Realty) which is wholly-owned by the Company and Arden-Mayfair. The Company is a Delaware Corporation organized in 1988." 10-K

Source: ARDEN GROUP, INC. AND CONSOLIDATED SUBSIDIARIES, 2010 10-K

Required

a. Prepare the statement of cash flows with a total column for the three-year period. (Do not include reconciliation of net income to net cash provided by operating activities).

b. Comment on significant cash flow items in the statement prepared in (a).

c. Prepare the statement of cash flows for the 52 weeks ended January 1, 2011, with inflows separated from outflows. Present the data in dollars and percentages. Do not include reconciliation of net income to net cash provided by operating activities.

d. Comment on significant cash flow items on the statement prepared in (c).

CASE 10-3 WEB SITE

Google, Inc.*
CONSOLIDATED STATEMENTS OF CASH FLOWS
(In millions)

	Year Ended December 31,		
	2008	2009	2010
Operating activities			
Net income	$ 4,227	$ 6,520	$ 8,505
Adjustments:			
Depreciation and amortization of property and equipment	1,212	1,240	1,067
Amortization of intangibles and other assets	288	284	329
Stock-based compensation	1,120	1,164	1,376
Excess tax benefits from stock-based award activity	(159)	(90)	(94)
Deferred income taxes	(225)	(268)	9
Impairment of equity investments	1,095	0	0
Other	(32)	(20)	(12)
Changes in assets and liabilities, net of effects of acquisitions and divestiture:			
Accounts receivable	(334)	(504)	(1,129)
Income taxes, net	626	217	102
Prepaid revenue share, expenses and other assets	(147)	262	(414)
Accounts payable	(212)	34	272
Accrued expenses and other liabilities	339	243	745
Accrued revenue share	14	158	214
Deferred revenue	41	76	111
Net cash provided by operating activities	7,853	9,316	11,081
Investing activities			
Purchases of property and equipment	(2,359)	(810)	(4,018)
Purchases of marketable securities	(15,356)	(29,139)	(43,985)
Maturities and sales of marketable securities	15,763	22,103	37,099
Investments in non-marketable equity securities	(47)	(65)	(320)
Cash collateral received from securities lending	0	0	2,361
Investments in reverse repurchase agreements	0	0	(750)
Acquisitions, net of cash acquired and proceeds received from divestiture, and purchases of intangible and other assets	(3,320)	(108)	(1,067)
Net cash used in investing activities	(5,319)	(8,019)	(10,680)
Financing activities			
Net proceeds (payments) from stock-based award activities	(72)	143	294
Excess tax benefits from stock-based award activities	159	90	94
Repurchase of common stock in connection with acquisitions	0	0	(801)
Proceeds from issuance of short-term debt	0	0	5,246
Repayment of short-term debt	0	0	(1,783)
Net cash provided by financing activities	87	233	3,050

(continued)

*"Google is a global technology leader focused on improving the ways people connect with information. We aspire to build products that improve the lives of billions of people globally." 10-K
Source: Google, Inc., 2010 10-K

(**CASE 10-3** CONTINUED)

	Year Ended December 31,		
	2008	2009	2010
Effect of exchange rate changes on cash and cash equivalents	(46)	11	(19)
Net increase in cash and cash equivalents	2,575	1,541	3,432
Cash and cash equivalents at beginning of year	6,082	8,657	10,198
Cash and cash equivalents at end of year	8,657	10,198	13,630
Supplemental disclosures of cash flow information			
Cash paid for taxes	$ 1,224	$ 1,896	$ 2,175
Non-cash financing activity:			
Fair value of common stock issued and vested options			
assumed in connection with acquisitions	0	0	750

Required

a. 1. For net income and net cash provided by operating activities, perform a horizontal common-size analysis. Use 2008 as the base.

2. Comment.

b. Why is depreciation and amortization of property and equipment added back to net income?

c. Investing activities – is there an indication of external growth?

d. Why is the non-cash activity listed at the bottom of the statement?

CASE 10-4 THE RETAIL MOVER

This case represents an actual retail company. The dates and format have been changed.

Required

a. Compute and comment on the following for 2007, 2008, and 2011:

1. Working capital

2. Current ratio

b. Comment on the difference between net income and net cash outflow from operating activities for the years ended December 31, 2008, and December 31, 2011.

c. This company reported a loss of $177,340,000 for 2012. Reviewing the balance sheet data, speculate on major reasons for this loss.

d. Considering (a), (b), and (c), comment on the wisdom of the short-term bank loan in 2012. (Consider the company's perspective and the bank's perspective.)

I. Selected Balance Sheet Data	December 31, 2008	December 31, 2007
Total current assets	$719,478,441	$628,408,895
Total current liabilities	458,999,682	366,718,656

THE RETAIL MOVER
STATEMENT OF CASH FLOWS
Year Ended December 31, 2008

Net cash flow from operating activities:	
Net income	$ 39,577,000
Noncash expenses, revenues, losses, and gains included in income:	
Increase in equity in Zeller's Limited	(2,777,000)
Depreciation and amortization	9,619,000
Net increase in reserves	74,000
Increase in deferred federal income taxes	232,000
Net increase in receivables	(51,463,995)

Net increase in inventories	$(38,364,709)
Net increase in prepaid taxes, rents, etc.	(209,043)
Increase in accounts payable	9,828,348
Increase in salaries, wages, and bonuses	470,054
Increase in taxes withheld from employees' compensation	301,035
Decrease in taxes other than federal income taxes	(659,021)
Increase in federal income taxes payable	4,007,022
Increases in deferred credits, principally income taxes related to installment sales (short-term)	14,045,572
Rounding difference in working capital	520
Net cash outflow from operating activities	(15,319,217)
Cash flows from investing activities:	
Investment in properties, fixtures, and improvements	(16,141,000)
Investment in Zeller's Limited	(436,000)
Increase in sundry accounts (net)	(48,000)
Net cash outflow from investing activities	(16,625,000)
Cash flows from financing activities:	
Sales of common stock to employees	5,219,000
Dividends to stockholders	(20,821,000)
Purchase of treasury stock	(13,224,000)
Purchase of preferred stock for cancellation	(948,000)
Retirement of 4 3/4% sinking fund debentures	(1,538,000)
Increase in short-term notes payable	56,323,016
Increase in bank loans	7,965,000
Net cash inflow from financing activities	32,976,016
Net increase in cash and short-term securities	$ 1,031,799

II. Selected Balance Sheet Data	December 31, 2011
Total current assets	$1,044,689,000
Total current liabilities	661,058,000

THE RETAIL MOVER
STATEMENT OF CASH FLOWS
Year Ended December 31, 2011

Net cash flow from operating activities:	
Net income	$ 10,902,000
Noncash expenses, revenues, losses, and gains included in income:	
Undistributed equity in net earnings of unconsolidated subsidiaries	(3,570,000)
Depreciation and amortization of properties	13,579,000
Increase in deferred federal income taxes—noncurrent	2,723,000
Decrease in deferred contingent compensation and other liabilities	(498,000)
Net receivables increase	(52,737,000)
Merchandise inventories increase	(51,104,000)
Other current assets increase	(8,935,000)
Accounts payable for merchandise decrease	(2,781,000)
Salaries, wages, and bonuses decrease	(3,349,000)
Other accrued expenses increase	3,932,000
Taxes withheld from employees increase	2,217,000
Sales and other taxes increase	448,000
Federal income taxes payable decrease	(8,480,000)
Increase in deferred income taxes related to installment sales	4,449,000
Net cash flow from operating activities	(93,204,000)
Cash flows from investing activities:	
Investments on properties, fixtures, and improvements	(23,143,000)
Increase in other assets—net	(642,000)
Investment in Granjewel Jewelers & Distributors, Inc.	(5,700,000)
Net cash outflow from investing activities	(29,485,000)

(*continued*)

(**Case 10-4** CONTINUED)

Cash flows from financing activities:

Increase in short-term notes payable to banks	$100,000,000
Receipts from employees under stock purchase contracts	2,584,000
Short-term commercial notes	73,063,000
Cash dividends to stockholders	(21,122,000)
Decrease in long-term debt	(6,074,000)
Purchase of cumulative preferred stock, for cancellation	(618,000)
Purchase of treasury common stock	(136,000)
Bank loans decreased	(10,000,000)
Net cash inflow from financing activities	137,697,000
Net increase in cash	$ 15,008,000

III.

Income Statement Data related to 2011 and 2012 (in Part)

	2012	2011
Net earnings (loss)	$(177,340,000)	$10,902,000

Balance Sheet Data related to 2011 and 2012 (in Part)

	December 31, 2012	December 31, 2011
Assets		
Current assets:		
Cash notes	$ 79,642,000	$ 45,951,000
Customers' installment accounts receivable	518,387,000	602,305,000
Less:		
Allowance for doubtful accounts	(79,510,000)	(16,315,000)
Unearned credit insurance premiums	(1,386,000)	(4,923,000)
Deferred finance income	(37,523,000)	(59,748,000)
	399,968,000	521,319,000
Merchandise inventories	407,357,000	450,637,000
Other accounts receivable, refundable taxes, and claims	31,223,000	19,483,000
Prepaid expenses	6,591,000	7,299,000
Total current assets	$924,781,000	$1,044,689,000
Liabilities		
Current liabilities:		
Bank loans	$600,000,000	$ —
Short-term commercial notes	—	453,097,000
Current portion of long-term debt	995,000	—
Accounts payable for merchandise	50,067,000	58,192,000
Salaries, wages, and bonuses	10,808,000	14,678,000
Other accrued expenses	49,095,000	14,172,000
Taxes withheld from employees	1,919,000	4,412,000
Sales and other taxes	17,322,000	13,429,000
Federal income taxes payable	17,700,000	—
Deferred income taxes related to installment sales	2,000,000	103,078,000
Total current liabilities	749,906,000	661,058,000
Other liabilities		
Long-term debt	216,341,000	220,336,000
Deferred federal income taxes	—	14,649,000
Deferred contingent compensation and other liabilities	2,183,000	4,196,000
Total other liabilities	218,524,000	239,181,000
Total liabilities	$968,430,000	$ 900,239,000

CASE 10-5 NONCASH CHARGES

Owens Corning Fiberglass Corporation

For Immediate Release (February 6, 1992)

Owens Corning Takes $800 Million Non-Cash Charge to Accrue for Future Asbestos Claims

"This action demonstrates our desire to put the asbestos situation behind us," new chairman and CEO Glen H. Hiner says.

Toledo, Ohio, February 6, 1992—Owens Corning Fiberglass Corp. (NYSE:OCF) today announced that its results for the fourth quarter and year ended December 31, 1991, include a special non-cash charge of $800 million to accrue for the estimated uninsured cost of future asbestos claims the Company may receive through the balance of the decade. "This action demonstrates our desire to put the asbestos situation behind us," said Glen Hiner, Owens Corning's new chairman and chief executive officer. "After a thorough review of the situation with outside consultants, we believe this accrual will be sufficient to cover the company's uninsured costs for cases received until the year 2000. We will, of course, make adjustments to our reserves if that becomes appropriate, but this is our best estimate of these uninsured costs. With this action," Mr. Hiner continued, "everyone can now focus once again on the fundamental strengths of the Company. We generate considerable amounts of cash, our operating divisions are leaders in every market they serve throughout the world, and we have taken a number of steps in the last few years to strengthen our competitive position even further."

Owens Corning Fiberglass Corporation

For Immediate Release (June 20, 1996)

Owens Corning Initiates Federal Lawsuit, Records Post-1999 Asbestos Provisions and Announces Dividend

NEW YORK, New York, June 20, 1996—A federal lawsuit aimed at fraudulent testing procedures for asbestos-related illnesses, involving tens of thousands of pending cases, was filed yesterday by Owens Corning. The Company also announced the quantification of liabilities related to post-1999 asbestos claims, the reinstatement of an annual dividend and a sales goal of $5 billion by 1999.

The specific announcements are as follows:

- A lawsuit, alleging falsified medical test results in tens of thousands of asbestos claims, was filed on June 19, 1996, in the U.S. District Court for the Eastern District of Louisiana against the owners and operators of three pulmonary function testing laboratories. Overall, a total of 40,000 cases may be impacted by the investigation for fraudulent testing procedures. The lawsuit is the subject of a separate press release also disseminated this morning.

- A net, after-tax charge of $545 million, or $9.56 per fully diluted share for asbestos claims—received after 1999—will be recorded in the second quarter of 1996, as detailed in a Form 8-K filed this morning with the SEC. Cash payments associated with this charge will begin after the year 2000 and will be spread over 15 years or more.

- The Board of Directors has approved an annual dividend policy of 25 cents per share and declared a quarterly dividend of 6-1/4 cents per share payable on October 15, 1996, to shareholders of record as of September 30, 1996.

- The company expects to reach its sales goal of $5 billion in 1999—a full year ahead of the original goal.

"The asbestos charge quantifies what we expect to be the cost to Owens Corning of post-1999 claims," stated Glen H. Hiner, chairman and chief executive officer. "We further believe that the present value of the Owens Corning asbestos liability, including the current charge, is less than the current discount in our stock price."

In addition to these developments, Owens Corning announced it is engaged in substantive discussions with 30 of the principal plaintiff law firms in an effort to obtain further resolution of its asbestos liability. These discussions have encompassed the possibility of global as well as individual law firm settlements.

Source: Owens Corning Fiberglass Corporation, 2010 10-K

(continued)

(**CASE 10-5** CONTINUED)

"These meetings are by mutual consent," stated Hiner. "The discussions will continue and we expect to know by year end whether we can achieve further agreement. Plaintiff attorneys involved in the talks stated they will not serve any more non-malignancy claims on Owens Corning while negotiations continue."

In reference to the dividend, Hiner stated, "we were able to initiate this action because debt has been reduced to target levels and cash flow from operations will be in excess of internal funding requirements."

"We are delighted to be able to reward our shareholders with a dividend," said Hiner. "Reinstating the dividend has been a priority of mine since joining the company and I am pleased that we now are in a position to set the date."

The Toledo-based company had 1995 sales of $3.6 billion and employs 18,000 people in more than 30 countries.

OWENS CORNING
CONSOLIDATED STATEMENT OF CASH FLOWS (IN PART)
For the years ended December 31, 1997, 1996 and 1995

(In millions of dollars)	1997	1996	1995
Net Cash Flow from Operations			
Net income (loss)	$ 47	$(284)	$ 231
Reconciliation of net cash provided by operating activities:			
Noncash items:			
Provision for asbestos litigation claims (Note 22)	—	875	—
Cumulative effect of accounting change (Note 6)	15		—
Provision for depreciation and amortization	173	141	132
Provision (credit) for deferred income taxes (Note 11)	110	(258)	142
Other (Note 4)	49	(2)	(2)
(Increase) decrease in receivables (Note 13)	57	20	36
(Increase) decrease in inventories	60	(71)	(15)
Increase (decrease) in accounts payable and accrued Liabilities	(60)	103	(50)
Disbursements (funding) of VEBA trust	19	45	(64)
Proceeds from insurance for asbestos litigation claims, excluding Fibreboard (Note 22)	97	101	251
Payments for asbestos litigation claims, excluding Fibreboard (Note 22)	(300)	(267)	(308)
Other	(136)	(68)	(68)
Net cash flow from operations	131	335	285

April 29, 1998

Owens Corning opened a new front in its battle to avoid being swamped by tens of thousands of damage claims filed by people who say they got sick from exposure to asbestos-containing insulation produced by the company. Owens Corning charged in U.S. District Court in Toledo, Ohio, that Allstate Insurance Co. is guilty of breach of contract by failing to provide coverage.

Owens Corning announced in March 1998 that it might have to spend more than expected to resolve asbestos claims because of growing damage awards to people with a severe form of asbestos-linked cancer called mesothelioma.

Required

a. In the long run, cash receipts from operations is equal to revenue from operations. Comment.

b. February 6, 1992—Owens Corning announced a special noncash charge of $800 million to accrue for the estimated uninsured cost of future asbestos claims the company may receive through the balance of the decade. How much will the noncash charge reduce gross earnings in 1992? Over what period of time is the expected outflow?

   c. June 20, 1996—Owens Corning announced a net, after-tax charge of $545 million for asbestos claims received after 1999. How much will this charge reduce net income in 1996? Over what period of time is the cash outflow expected?

   d. Assume Owens Corning receives money related to the federal lawsuit alleging falsified medical tests. In what period will the cash inflow be recorded? When will the related revenue be recorded?

   e. April 29, 1998—Owens Corning filed suit against Allstate Insurance Co. related to asbestos exposure coverage. What are the apparent implications if Owens Corning does not win the suit?

   f. Owens Corning announced in March 1998 that it might have to spend more than expected to resolve asbestos claims. What does this imply as to future expenses and cash outflow related to asbestos claims?

   g. Owens Corning, consolidated statement of cash flows, for the years ended December 31, 1997, 1996, and 1995.

     1. What year has a charge for asbestos litigation claims?

     2. What years have cash inflow from proceeds from insurance for asbestos litigation claims?

     3. What years have payments for asbestos litigation claims?

CASE 10-6 CASH MOVEMENTS AND PERIODIC INCOME DETERMINATION

"The estimating of income, under conditions of uncertainty as well as of certainty, requires that the accountant trace carefully the relation between income flows and cash movements."

"While it is true that there may not be an equality between the amount of revenue and the amount of cash receipts for any period less than the duration of enterprise existence, receipts are the elements with which we construct all measures of revenue. A dollar is received at some time during the life of the enterprise for each dollar of revenue exhibited during the fiscal period. The sum of the annual revenues for all fiscal periods is equal to the amount of ultimate total revenue. There may be no equality between the amount of expense and the amount of cash disbursements for the fiscal period and yet the two sums are equal for the life of the enterprise. A dollar is disbursed at some time during the enterprise existence for each dollar exhibited as expense of the fiscal period."*

"The accountant's problem is essentially one of reconciling cash receipts with revenues and cash disbursements with expenses. That is, for every revenue recognized but not received in cash during the current period, an asset of equal value must be recorded (or a liability must be amortized); for every expense recognized but not paid in cash in the current period, a liability of equal value must be recognized but not paid in cash in the current period, a liability of equal value must be recognized (or an asset must be amortized)."

Required

   a. Income determination is an exact science. Comment.

   b. Cash flow must be estimated. Comment.

   c. In the long run, cash receipts from operations is equal to revenue from operations. Comment.

   d. Assume that a firm has a negative cash flow from operations in the short run. How could this negative cash flow from operations be compensated for in the short run? Discuss.

   e. Assume that the reported operating income has been substantially more than the cash flow from operations for the past two years. Comment on what will need to happen to future cash flow from operations in order for the past reported income to hold up.

*Source: Excerpts from "Cash Movements and Periodic Income Determination," Reed K. Story, *The Accounting Review*, Vol. XXXV, No. 3 (July, 1960), pp. 449–454.

CASE 10-7 THE BIG.COM

The data in this case come from the financial reports of Amazon.com, Inc.*

SELECTED CONSOLIDATED BALANCE SHEET ITEMS
(In millions, except market price)

December 31,

	2010	2009	2008	2007	2006	2005	2004	2003	2002	2001	2000	1999
Total current assets	$13,947	$ 9,797	$6,157	$5,164	$3,373	$2,929	$2,539	$ 1,821	$ 1,616	$ 1,208	$1,361	$1,012
Total assets	18,797	13,813	8,314	6,485	4,363	3,696	3,249	2,162	1,990	1,637	2,135	2,471
Total current liabilities	10,372	7,364	4,746	3,714	2,532	1,899	1,620	1,253	1,066	921	975	739
Long-term debt and other	1,561	1,192	896	1,574	1,400	1,551	1,855	1,945	2,277	2,156	2,127	1,466
Total liabilities	11,933	8,556	5,642	5,288	3,932	3,450	3,475	3,198	3,343	3,077	3,102	2,205
Stockholders' (deficit) equity	6,864	5,257	2,672	1,197	431	246	(227)	(1,036)	(1,353)	(1,440)	(967)	266
Total liabilities and stockholders' equity	18,797	13,813	8,314	6,485	4,363	3,696	3,249	2,162	1,990	1,637	2,135	2,471
Outstanding shares of common stock	451	444	428	416	414	416	410	403	388	373	357	345
Market price-common stock	180.00	134.52	51.28	92.64	39.46	47.15	44.29	52.62	18.89	10.82	15.56	76.12

SELECTED CONSOLIDATED STATEMENT OF OPERATIONS ITEMS
(In millions, except fully diluted earnings per share)

Year Ended December 31,

	2010	2009	2008	2007	2006	2005	2004	2003	2002	2001	2000	1999	1998
Net sales	$34,204	$24,509	$19,166	$14,835	$10,711	$8,490	$6,921	$5,264	$3,933	$3,122	$ 2,762	$1,640	$ 610
Gross profit	7,643	5,531	4,270	3,353	2,456	2,039	1,602	1,257	993	799	656	291	114
Net income (loss)	1,152	902	645	476	190	359	588	35	(149)	(567)	(1,411)	(720)	(125)
Fully diluted earnings per share	2.53	2.04	1.49	1.12	.45	.78	1.39	.08	(.40)	(1.53)	(4.02)	(2.20)	(.42)

SELECTED CONSOLIDATED STATEMENT OF CASH FLOW ITEMS
(In millions)

Year Ended December 31,

	2010	2009	2008	2007	2006	2005	2004	2003	2002	2001	2000	1999	1998
Net cash provided (used) in operating activities	$3,495	$ 3,293	$ 1,697	$1,405	$ 702	$ 703	$ 566	$ 393	$ 174	$ 120	$(130)	$ (91)	$ 31
Net cash provided (used) in investing activities	3,360	(2,337)	(1,199)	42	(333)	(778)	(317)	236	(122)	(253)	164	(932)	(324)
Net cash provided (used) in financing activities	181	(280)	(198)	50	(400)	(193)	(97)	(332)	107	107	693	1,140	254
Cash and cash equivalents, end of period	3,777	3,444	2,769	2,539	1,022	1,013	1,303	1,102	738	540	822	133	72

*"Amazon.com opened its virtual doors on the World Wide Web in July 1995 and offers Earth's Biggest Selection. We seek to be Earth's most customer-centric company for three primary customer sets: consumers, sellers and enterprises. In addition, we generate revenue through other marketing and promotional services, such as online advertising, and co-branded credit card agreements." 10-K
Source: Amazon.com Inc., 2010 10-K

Required

a. Amazon had a deficit in stockholders' equity from 2000–2004. During this time period, Amazon increased cash and cash equivalents, end of period. Comment on how this was accomplished.

b. Compute the debt ratio for the period 1999–2010. Comment on the results.

c. Comment on the importance of net cash provided by financing activities 1998–2002.

d. Comment on the trend in net cash provided by operating activities 2000–2010.

e. Comment on the trend in net sales vs. the trend in net income (loss).

f. Comment on the market decline between 1999 and 2001.

   1. Compute the total stock market price (outstanding shares of common X market price per share) for the period 1999–2010.

   2. Compare the total stock market price on f(1) with the stockholders' equity. Comment.

g. Compute the price/earnings ratio for the period 1999–2010.

h. Does the future look good for Amazon.com? Comment.

Case 10-8 GLASS CONTAINERS

The data in this case come from the 2010 and 2009 annual report of Owens-Illinois.*

Selected Consolidated Balance Sheet Items – December 31
(In millions, except outstanding shares of common stock)

	2010	2009	2008
Total current assets	$2,738	$2,797	$2,444.7
Total assets	9,754	8,727	7,876.5
Total current liabilities	2,079	2,034	2,003.3
Long-term debt	3,924	3,258	2,940.3
Deferred taxes	203	186	77.6
Pension benefits	576	578	741.8
Nonpension postretirement benefits	259	267	239.7
Other liabilities	381	343	360.1
Asbestos-related liabilities	306	310	320.3
Liabilities of discontinued operations	—	15	—
Total liabilities	7,728	6,991	6,683.1

Note (from 2010 statement 10-K):

Common stock, par value $0.01 per share, 250,000,000 shares authorized, 180,808,992 and 179,923,309 shares issued (included treasury shares), respectively. Treasury stock, at cost, 17,093,509 and 11,322,544 shares, respectively.

(This is from the consolidated balance sheet December 31, 2010 and 2009.)

Note: Common stock market price:

December 31, 2010	$30.70
December 31, 2009	$32.87
December 31, 2008	$27.33

Selected Consolidated Results of Operations
(Dollars in millions, except outstanding shares of common stock)

	Years Ended December 31,		
	2010	2009	2008
Net sales	$6,633	$6,652	$7,540
Gross profit	1,350	1,335	1,546
Net earnings (loss) attribute to the Company	(47)	162	258
Diluted earnings per share of common stock from continuing operations	1.55	0.65	1.03

(continued)

*"The Company is the largest manufacturer of glass containers in the world, based on revenues, with leading positions in Europe, North America, South America and Asia Pacific." 10-K
Source: Owens-Illinois 2010 10-K

(**CASE 10-8** CONTINUED)

Owens-Illinois, Inc.
Consolidated Cash Flows (In Part)
(Dollars in millions)

	Years Ended December 31,		
	2010	2009	2008
Operating activities:			
Net earnings	$ (5)	$ 198	$ 328
Earnings from discontinued operations	(31)	(66)	(96)
(Gain) loss on disposal of discontinued operations	331	—	(7)
Non-cash charges (credits):			
Depreciation	369	364	420
Amortization of intangibles and other deferred items	22	21	29
Amortization of finance fees and debt discount	19	10	8
Deferred tax benefit	(56)	52	21
Non-cash tax benefit	(8)	(48)	—
Restructuring and asset impairment	13	207	133
Charges for acquisition-related costs	26	—	—
Future asbestos-related costs	170	180	250
Other	142	61	63
Asbestos-related payments	(179)	(190)	(210)
Cash paid for restructuring activities	(61)	(65)	(49)
Change in non-current operating assets	(19)	28	8
Reduction of non-current liabilities	(62)	(179)	(90)
Change in components of working capital	(71)	156	(148)
Cash provided by continuing operating activities	600	729	660
Cash provided by (utilized in) discontinued operating activities	(8)	71	97
Total cash provided by operating activities	592	800	757
Investing activities:			
Cash utilized in investing activities	(1,314)	(418)	(377)
Financing activities:			
Cash provided by (utilized in) financing activities	547	114	(365)
Cash at end of year	640	812	380

Required

a. Compute the following ratios for 2008–2010:
   1. Current ratio
   2. Debt ratio
   3. Gross profit margin
   4. Operating cash flow/total debt

b. Comment on the ratios in (a)

c. Asbestos-related
   1. For the three-year period 2008–2010, how much was recognized in expense for asbestos-related costs?
   2. For the three-year period 2008–2010, how much was paid for asbestos-related payments?
   3. Why is there a difference between the expense and the cash payments for asbestos-related payments for the period 2008–2010?
   4. Compute by year (2008–2010) the impact that asbestos charges (expense and payments) had on net cash provides (used) in operating activities.

d. 1. Compute the total capitalization for 2010 and 2009 (outstanding shares of common stock X market price).
   2. Compare the total shareowners' equity related to common stock, with the capitalization. Comment on the difference.

CASE 10-9 SPECIALTY RETAILER

With this case, we review the cash flow of several specialty retail stores. The companies reviewed and the year-end dates are as follows:

1. **Abercrombie & Fitch Co.**
   (52-week fiscal year ended January 29, 2011; 52-week fiscal year ended January 30, 2010; 52-week fiscal year ended January 31, 2009)
   "Abercrombie & Fitch Co ... is a specialty retailer that operates stores and direct-to-consumer operations." 10-K

   Source: Abercrombie & Fitch 2010 10-K

2. **Limited Brands, Inc.**
   (52-week fiscal year ended January 29, 2011; 52-week fiscal year ended January 30, 2010; 52-week fiscal year ended January 31, 2009)
   "We operate in the highly competitive specialty retail business." 10-K

   Source: Limited Brands 2010 10-K

3. **Gap, Inc.**
   (52-week fiscal year ended January 29, 2011; 52-week fiscal year ended January 30, 2010; 52-week fiscal year ended January 31, 2009)
   "We are a global specialty retailer offering apparel, accessories, and personal care products." 10-K

   Source: Gap Inc 2010 10-K

	Abercrombie & Fitch		Limited Brands		GAP	
Data reviewed	2010	2009	2010	2009	2010	2009
Net cash provided by operating activities	$391,789,000	$395,487,000	$1,284,000,000	$1,174,000,000	$1,744,000,000	$1,928,000,000
Net income	$150,283,000	$254,000	$805,000,000	$448,000,000	$1,204,000,000	$1,102,000,000
Operating cash flow/current maturities of long-term debt and current notes payable	*	*	*	*	*	*
Operating cash flow/total debt	37.06%	39.79%	25.81%	23.53%	58.43%	62.31%
Operating cash flow per share	$4.36	$4.46	$3.86	$3.59	$2.72	$2.76
Operating cash flow/cash dividends	6.35 times	6.43 times	.86 times	6.08 times	6.92 times	8.24 times

*No current maturities of long-term debt and current notes payable.

Required

a. Comment on the difference between net cash provided by operating activities and net income. Speculate on which number is likely to be the better indicator of long-term profitability.

b. Comment on the data reviewed for each item

c. Do any of these firms appear to have a cash flow problem? Comment.

CASE 10-10 EAT AT MY RESTAURANT – CASH FLOW

With this case, we review the cash flow of several restaurant companies. The restaurant companies reviewed and the year-end dates are as follows:

1. **Yum Brands, Inc.**
   December 25, 2010; December 26, 2009 (52 weeks each year)
   "YUM consists of six operating segments: KFC – U.S., Pizza Hut – U.S., Taco Bell – U.S., Long John Silver's ("LJS") – U.S., and A&W All American Food Restaurants ("A&W") – U.S., YUM Restaurants International ("YRI" or "International Division") and YUM Restaurants China ("China Division")." 10-K

   Source: Yum! Brands, Inc. and Subsidiaries 2010 10-K

2. **Panera Bread**
   December 28, 2010; December 29, 2009 (52 weeks each year)
   "Panera Bread Company and it subsidiaries, referred to as "Panera Bread," "Panera," the "Company," "we," "us," and "our," is a national bakery-café concept with 1,453

(*continued*)

(**CASE 10-10** CONTINUED)

company-owned and franchise-operated bakery-café locations in 40 states, the District of Columbia, and Ontario, Canada." 10-K

Source: Panera Bread 2010 10-K

3. **Starbucks**

October 3, 2010; September 27, 2009 (Fiscal year 2010 included 53 weeks, while fiscal year ended 2009 included 52 weeks)

"Starbucks is the premier roaster and retailer of specialty coffee in the world, operating in more than 50 countries." 10-K

Source: Starbucks Corporation 2010 10-K

Note: All three of these companies had net income – including noncontrolling interest. The net income – noncontrolling interest was considered to be immaterial.

Data reviewed	Yum Brands, Inc.		Panera Bread		Starbucks	
	2010	2009	2010	2009	2010	2009
Net cash provided by operating activities	$1,968,000,000	$1,404,000,000	$237,634,000	$214,904,000	$1,704,900,000	$1,389,000,000
Net income – including noncontrolling interest	$1,178,000,000	$1,083,000,000	$111,599,000	$86,851,000	$948,300,000	$391,500,000
Operating cash flow/current maturities of long-term debt and current notes payable	2.92	23.80	No current long-term debt and current notes payable		No current long-term debt and current notes payable	
Operating cash flow/total debt	30.57%	23.27%	72.23%	89.50%	63.06%	55.12%
Operating cash flow per share	$4.05	$2.91	$7.68	$6.94	$2.23	$1.86
Operating cash flow/cash dividends	4.78	3.88	No dividends		9.97	No dividends

Required

a. Comment on the difference between net cash provided by operating activities and net income including noncontrolling interest. Speculate on which number is likely to be the better indicator of long-term profitability.

b. Comment on the data reviewed for each firm.

c. Do any of these firms appear to have a cash flow problem? Comment.

WEB CASE THOMSON ONE *Business School Edition*

Please complete the Web case that covers material discussed in this chapter at www.cengagebrain.com. You'll be using Thomson ONE Business School Edition, a powerful tool that combines a full range of fundamental financial information, earnings estimates, market data, and source documents for 500 publicly traded companies.

 TO THE NET CASE

1. Go to the SEC site (www.sec.gov). Under "Filings & Forms," click on "Search for Company Filings." Click on "Company or fund, etc." Under Company Name, enter "Northrop Grumman Corp" (or under Ticker Symbol, enter "NOC"). Select the 10-K filed February 9, 2011.

   a. Copy the first sentence in the "Item 1. Business" section (History).

   b. Review the consolidated statements of cash flows. Under what method are the operating activities presented? What advantage does this presentation have over the alternative presentation?

   c. Why are the noncash investing and financing activities presented at the bottom of the statement? Why would liabilities assumed by the company be presented under noncash investing and financing activities?

2. Go to the SEC site (www.sec.gov). Under "Filings & Forms," click on "Search for Company Filings." Click on "Company or fund, etc." Under Company Name, enter "Intel Corporation" (or under Ticker Symbol, enter "INTC"). Select the 10-K filed February 18, 2011.

   a. Describe this type of form for cash flows.

   b. Determine the following for 2010:

    1. Net income

    2. Depreciation

    3. Share-based compensation

    4. Net cash provided by operating activities

    5. Comment on why the depreciation and share-based compensation are added to net income

  c. Describe this type of form for cash flows.

  d. Determine the following for 2009:

    1. Net income

    2. Depreciation

    3. Share-based compensation

    4. Net cash provided by operating activities

    5. Comment on why the depreciation, share-based compensation are added to net income

3. Go to the SEC site (www.sec.gov). Under "Filings & Forms," click on "Search for Company Filings." Click on "Company or fund, etc." Under Company Name, enter "Molson Coors Brewing Company" (or under Ticker Symbol, enter "TAP"). Select the 10-K filed February 22, 2011.

  a. "Item 1. Business" – copy the "history"

  b. Prepare the following ratios for the years ended December 25, 2010 and December 26, 2009:

    1. Operating cash flow/current maturities of long-term debt and current notes payable

    2. Operating cash flow/total debt

    3. Operating cash flow per share

    4. Operating cash flow/cash dividend

  c. Comment on the results in (b)

4. Go to the SEC site (www.sec.gov). Under "Filings & Forms," click on "Search for Company Filings." Click on "Company or fund, etc." Under Company Name, enter "Ann Taylor Stores Corp" (or under Ticker Symbol, enter "ANN"). Select the 10-K filed March 11, 2011.

  a. Copy the first sentence in the "General" subsection from the "Item 1 Business."

  b. Determine the numbers for the following:

	Fiscal Year Ended		
	January 29, 2011	January 30, 2010	January 31, 2009
Net sales			
Gross Margin			
Operating Income (less)			
Net cash provided by operating activities			

  c. Comment on the trends in (b)

  d. Review the consolidated statements of cash flows

    1. Why is the depreciation and amortization added back into net income?

    2. Why is the change in inventories added to net income (loss) for the year ended January 30, 2010?

    3. Why is the change in inventories subtracted from net income for the year ended January 29, 2011?

Endnotes

1. The effect of exchange rate changes on cash is presented separately at the bottom of the statement.

2. *Exposure Draft*, "Statement of Cash Flows" (Stamford, CT: Financial Accounting Standards Board, 1986), p. 21.

Summary Analysis Nike, Inc. (Includes 2011 Financial Statements of Form 10-K)

U sers must be able to apply and understand financial statement analysis. They must study ratio and trend analysis for meaning. This analysis is the difficult aspect of interpreting financial statements. Chapters 6 through 10 have illustrated the technique of calculating ratios for the analysis of Nike, Inc.

This summary analysis brings together the analysis in Chapters 6 through 10 relating to Nike. It adds information on a selected competitor and the industry. It also adds some common-size analysis.

Nike–Background Information

Bill Bowerman, head track coach at the University of Oregon, teamed up with Philip Knight, a former student, to form Blue Ribbon Sports in 1964. Blue Ribbon Sports became Nike in 1972. The name "Nike" was chosen because Nike was the Greek goddess of victory.

Nike specialized in athletic footwear until 1979. In 1979, the Nike apparel line was launched, and in 1996, the Nike equipment division formed.

By 1999, Nike was the world's largest supplier of athletic footwear and one of the world's largest suppliers of athletic apparel. Nike products are sold in many countries. Nike and Adidas are possibly the only equipment, sports footwear, and apparel companies with the infrastructure to sell extensively worldwide.

Bill Bowerman retired from the board in June 1999 and passed away in December 1999. Philip Knight is the chairman of the board. He stepped down as chief executive officer at the end of 2004. Mark G. Parker is the chief executive officer and president of Nike. He has been president, chief executive officer, and a director since January 2006. He has been employed by Nike since 1979 with primary responsibilities in product research, design and development, marketing, and brand management. (Proxy filed July 26, 2011.)

Management's Discussion and Analysis of Financial Condition and Results of Operations (See 10-K, Item 7, In Part)

Selected Highlights

NIKE designs, develops, markets and sells high quality footwear, apparel, equipment and accessory products worldwide. We are the largest seller of athletic footwear and apparel in the world. We sell our products to retail accounts, through NIKE-owned retail stores and internet sales, which we refer to as our "Direct to Consumer" operations, and through a mix of independent distributors and licensees, worldwide. Our goal is to deliver value to our shareholders by building a profitable global portfolio of branded footwear, apparel, equipment and accessories businesses. Our strategy is to achieve long-term revenue growth by creating innovative, "must have" products, building deep personal consumer connections with our brands, and delivering compelling retail presentation and experiences.

. . . . .

Our fiscal 2011 results demonstrated our continued focus toward meeting our financial goals, while positioning ourselves for sustainable, profitable long-term growth. Despite the uncertain macroeconomic environment in fiscal 2011, we delivered record high revenues and diluted earnings per share. Our revenues grew 10% to $20.9 billion, net income increased 12% to $2.1 billion, and we delivered diluted earnings per share of $4.39, a 14% increase from fiscal 2010.

. . . . .

Futures Orders

Futures and advance orders for NIKE Brand footwear and apparel scheduled for delivery from June through November 2011 were 15% higher than the orders reported for the comparable prior year period. This futures and advance order amount is calculated based upon our forecast of the actual exchange rates under which our revenues will be translated during this period, which approximate current spot rates. Excluding the impact of currency changes, futures orders increased 12%, primarily driven by a high single-digit percentage increase in unit sales volume and a low single-digit percentage increase in average price per unit for both footwear and apparel products.

Note: Item 7 of the Nike 10-K is approximately 30 pages. It is suggested that you read the 10-K, Item 7 before proceeding with this summary. After reviewing the summary, read Item 7 of the 10-K again. This will give you a very good understanding of Nike's financial statements.

Vertical Common-Size Statement of Income (Exhibit 1)

Highlights
- Income before income taxes increased materially in 2010 and slightly in 2011.
- Income taxes increased materially in 2010 and moderately in 2011.
- Net income increased materially in 2010 and slightly in 2011.
- The material increase in income before income taxes, incomes taxes, and net income in 2010 were related to the following charges in 2009:
    Restructuring charges
    Goodwill impairment
    Intangible and other asset impairment

Horizontal Common-Size Statement of Income (Exhibit 2)

Highlights
- Material increases in 2011 in revenues, cost of sales, gross margins, income before income taxes, income taxes, and net income.
- There was also material increases in 2010 in income before income taxes, income taxes, and net income. These increases were related to the charges in 2009 that were not present in 2010.

EXHIBIT 1	Nike, Inc.

Vertical Common-Size Statement of Income

	Year Ended May 31,		
	2011	2010	2009
Revenues	100.0%	100.0%	100.0%
Cost of sales	54.4	53.7	55.1
Gross margin	45.6	46.3	44.9
Demand creation expense	11.7	12.4	12.3
Operating overhead expense	20.3	20.9	19.8
Total selling and administrative expense	32.1	33.3	32.1
Restructuring charges (Note 16)	.0	.0	1.0
Goodwill impairment (Note 4)	.0	.0	1.0
Intangible and other asset impairment (Note 4)	.0	.0	1.0
Interest expense (income), net (Notes 6, 7 and 8)	.0	.0	(.1)
Other (income), net (Note 17)	(.2)	(.3)	(.5)
Income before income taxes	13.6	13.2	10.2
Income taxes (Note 9)	3.4	3.2	2.5
Net income	10.2	10.0	7.8

Note: There are some rounding differences.

EXHIBIT 2	Nike, Inc.

Horizontal Common-Size Statement of Income Along with Actual Statement of Income

	Year Ended May 31,			Year Ended May 31,		
	2011	2010	2009	2011	2010	2009
				(In millions, except per share data)		
Revenues	108.8	99.2	100.0	$20,862	$19,014	$19,176
Cost of sales	107.4	96.6	100.0	11,354	10,214	10,572
Gross margin	110.5	102.3	100.0	9,508	8,800	8,604
Demand creation expense	104.1	100.2	100.0	2,448	2,356	2,352
Operating overhead expense	111.8	104.5	100.0	4,245	3,970	3,798
Total selling and administrative expense	108.8	102.9	100.0	6,693	6,326	6,150
Restructuring charges*	—	—	100.0	—	—	195
Goodwill impairment*	—	—	100.0	—	—	199
Intangible and other asset impairment*	—	—	100.0	—	—	202
Interest expense (income), net**	—	—	100.0	4	6	(10)
Other (income), net***	37.1	55.1	100.0	(33)	(49)	(89)
Income before income taxes	145.3	128.6	100.0	2,844	2,517	1,957
Income taxes	151.3	129.8	100.0	711	610	470
Net income	143.4	128.2	100.0	2,133	1,907	1,487

*These items were only present in 2009.

**Interest expense (income), net

2009	(Income)	$10,000,000
2010	Expense	$ 6,000,000
2011	Expense	$ 4,000,000

***Other (income), net

2009	$89,000,000
2010	$49,000,000
2011	$33,000,000

Liquidity

- Days' sales in receivables declined materially in 2010 and then in 2011 came back to approximately the same days' sales in receivables as for 2009.
- Accounts receivable turnover times per year improved slightly in 2010 and moderately in 2011.
- Accounts receivable turnover in days declined slightly in 2010 and moderately in 2011.
- Days' sales in inventory declined materially in 2010 and then increased materially in 2011. The 2011 days' sales in inventory was substantially higher than the 2009 level.
- Inventory turnover times per year increased moderately in both 2010 and 2011.
- Inventory turnover days decreased slightly in 2010 and substantially in 2011.
- Operating cycle decreased slightly in 2010 and moderately in 2011. There was a substantial improvement between 2009 and 2011.
- Working capital increased materially in 2010 and declined slightly in 2011.
- Current ratio increased materially in 2010 and then decreased materially in 2011.
- Acid-test ratio increased materially in 2010 and then decreased materially in 2011.
- The cash ratio increased materially in 2010 and then decreased materially in 2011.
- Sales to working capital decreased materially in 2010 and then increased slightly in 2011.
- The ratio of operating cash flow/current maturities of long-term debt and current notes payable increased very materially in 2010 and then decreased very materially in 2011.

Summary—Liquidity

Liquidity indicators fluctuated between 2009 and 2011 for receivables and inventory, ending with reasonable indicators. There was a substantial improvement in the operating cycle between 2009 and 2011.

The current ratio, acid-test ratio, and cash ratio appear to be very good at the end of 2011. They did decline materially in 2011.

Sales to working capital declined materially.

The ratio of operating cash flow/current maturities of long-term debt and current notes payable increased very materially in 2010 and then decreased very materially in 2011, ending with a reasonable coverage. Liquidity appears to be good to very good.

Long-Term Debt-Paying Ability

- Times interest earned was very good in all three years. It increased materially each year.
- Fixed charge coverage was very good in all three years. It increased moderately each year.
- Debt ratio was very good in all three years. It decreased moderately in 2010 and increased moderately in 2011.
- Debt/equity was very good in all three years. It decreased substantially in 2010 and increased substantially in 2011.
- Debt to tangible net worth was very good in all three years. Intangibles had a substantial influence on the long-term debt position.
- Operating cash flow/total debt was very good in all three years. It had a very material increase in 2010 and then settled back to approximately the same level as 2009.

Summary—Long-Term Debt-Paying Ability

The long-term debt-paying ability was very good.

Profitability

- Net profit margin increased materially in 2010 and slightly in 2011.
- Total asset turnover decreased substantially in 2010 and increased slightly in 2011.
- Return on assets increased materially in 2010 and moderately in 2011.
- Operating income margin increased slightly in 2010 and increased slightly again in 2011.
- Return on operating assets decreased substantially in 2010 and increased moderately in 2011.
- Sales to fixed assets decreased slightly in 2010 and increased moderately in 2011.
- Return on investment increased materially in 2010 and moderately in 2011.
- Return on total equity increased materially in 2010 and moderately in 2011.
- Return on common equity increased at the same rates as return on total equity.
- Gross profit margin increased slightly in 2010 and decreased slightly in 2011.

Summary—Profitability

A number of ratios increased materially in 2010 and then increased slightly or moderately in 2011 (net profit margin, return on assets, return on investment, return on total equity, and return on common equity).

Two asset turnover ratios decreased materially in 2010 and then increased slightly in 2011 (total asset turnover and operating asset turnover).

Operating ratios were not as impressive as many of the other ratios (operating income margin, operating asset turnover and return on operating assets).

Two ratios did not change significantly (sales to fixed assets and gross profit margin). Profitability overall was very good.

Investor Analysis

- Degree of financial leverage was very low.
- Diluted earnings per share increased materially in 2010 and 2011.
- Price/earnings ratio decreased slightly in 2010 and increased slightly in 2011.
- Percentage of earnings retained increased moderately in 2010 and slightly in 2011.
- Dividend payout decreased materially in 2010 and decreased slightly in 2011.
- Dividend yield decreased materially in 2010 and slightly in 2011.
- Book value per share increased materially in 2010 and moderately in 2011.
- Materiality of option compensation expense decreased materially in both 2010 and 2011.
- Operating cash flow per share increased very materially in 2010 and decreased very materially in 2011.
- Operating cash flow/cash dividends increased very materially in 2010 and decreased very materially in 2011.
- Year-end market price increased very materially in 2010 and 2011.

Summary—Investor Analysis

In general, investor analysis is good, although there was a mixture of results.

The impressive year-end market price increase appears to be responding to the significant diluted earnings per share increase and a favorable profitability perspective, as well as improved overall stock market conditions.

Three-Year Ratio Comparison (Exhibit 3)

The use of ratios can be very helpful in analysis, but caution must be exercised in drawing conclusions. Many potential problems were discussed in previous chapters. Keep these potential problems in mind when using ratios. Nike uses a year ended May 31 and has somewhat of a seasonal business. This could influence some of the ratios, particularly liquidity ratios.

EXHIBIT **3**	Nike, Inc.				
Three-year Ratio Comparison					
	Unit	2011	2010	2009
Liquidity:				
Days' sales in receivables	Days	56.19	52.29	56.30
Accounts receivable turnover	Times per year	7.03	6.69	6.62
Accounts receivable turnover	Days	51.92	54.54	55.15
Days' sales in inventory	Days	87.27	72.94	81.39
Inventory turnover	Times per year	4.77	4.64	4.41
Inventory turnover	Days	76.44	78.62	82.79

EXHIBIT **3**	Nike, Inc. *(continued)*

	Unit	2011	2010	2009
Operating cycle	Days	128.36	133.16	137.94
Working capital (in millions)	$	7,339	7,595	6,457
Current ratio	N/A	2.85	3.26	2.97
Acid-test ratio	N/A	1.94	2.32	1.93
Cash ratio	N/A	1.15	1.53	1.05
Sales to working capital	Times per year	2.79	2.71	3.20
Operating cash flow/current maturities of long-term debt and current notes payable	Times per year	4.68	21.67	4.63
Long-term debt-paying ability:				
Times interest earned	Times per year	84.65	70.92	49.55
Fixed charge coverage	Times per year	37.00	33.27	25.46
Debt ratio	%	34.37	32.35	34.39
Debt/equity	%	52.37	47.83	52.42
Debt to tangible net worth	%	56.33	51.27	56.73
Operating cash flow/total debt	%	35.15	67.82	38.10
Profitability:				
Net profit margin	%	10.22	10.03	7.75
Total asset turnover	Times per year	1.42	1.37	1.49
Return on assets	%	14.50	13.78	11.57
Operating income margin	%	13.49	13.01	12.80
Operating asset turnover	Times per year	1.60	1.57	1.74
Return on operating assets	%	21.65	20.41	22.25
Sales to fixed assets	Times per year	11.15	10.72	10.99
Return on investment	%	19.54	18.40	15.89
Return on total equity	%	21.77	20.68	18.00
Return on common equity	%	21.77	20.68	18.00
Gross profit margin	%	45.58	46.28	44.87
Investor analysis:				
Degree of financial leverage	N/A	1.01	1.01	1.02
Diluted earnings per share	$	4.39	3.86	3.03
Price/earnings ratio	N/A	19.24	18.75	18.83
Percentage of earnings retained	%	73.98	73.52	68.61
Dividend payout	%	27.33	27.46	32.34
Dividend yield	%	1.42	1.46	1.72
Book value per share	$	21.03	20.15	17.91
Materiality of option compensation expense	%	3.48	6.61	7.97
Operating cash flow per share	$	3.73	6.41	3.54
Operating cash flow/cash dividends	Times per year	3.26	6.27	3.72
Year-end market price	$	84.45	72.38	57.05

For 2009, the restructuring charges, goodwill impairment, and intangible and other asset impairment negatively impact the profitability ratios for 2009. 2009 is part of our three-year ratio comparison.

Ratio Comparison with Selected Competitor (Exhibit 4)

Nike has substantial competition which is illustrated by the following comments (in part) in its 2011 10-K:

Competition

The athletic footwear, apparel, and equipment industry is keenly competitive in the United States and on a worldwide basis. We compete internationally with a significant number of athletic and leisure shoe companies, athletic and leisure apparel companies, sports equipment companies, and large companies having diversified lines of athletic and leisure shoes, apparel, and equipment, including Adidas, Puma, and others. The intense competition and the rapid changes in technology and consumer preferences in the markets for athletic and leisure footwear and apparel, and athletic equipment, constitute significant risk factors in our operations.

EXHIBIT 4	Nike Inc.

Ratio Comparison with Selected Competitor

Year Ended May 31, 2011 (Nike), Year Ended December 31, 2010 (Skechers U.S.A.)

	Unit	Nike 2011	Skechers 2010
Liquidity:			
Days' sales in receivables	Days	56.19	51.97
Accounts receivable turnover	Times per year	7.03	7.72
Accounts receivable turnover	Days	51.92	47.29
Days' sales in inventory	Days	87.27	132.87
Inventory turnover	Times per year	4.77	3.52
Inventory turnover in days	Days	76.44	103.78
Operating cycle	Days	128.36	151.07
Working capital (in millions)	$	7,339	666.1
Current ratio	N/A	2.85	3.17
Acid-test ratio	N/A	1.94	1.63
Cash ratio	N/A	1.15	.76
Sales to working capital	Times per year	2.79	3.28
Operating cash flow/current maturities of long-term debt and current notes payable	Times per year	4.68	*
Long-term debt-paying ability:			
Times interest earned	Times per year	84.60	14.24
Fixed charge coverage	Times per year	37.00	3.26
Debt ratio	%	34.37	27.51
Debt/equity	%	52.37	37.95
Debt to tangible net worth	%	56.33	38.25
Operating cash flow/total debt	%	35.15	*
Profitability:			
Net profit margin	%	10.22	6.78
Total asset turnover	Times per year	1.42	1.74
Return on assets	%	14.50	11.84
Operating income margin	%	13.49	9.80
Operating asset turnover	Times per year	1.60	1.78
Return on operating assets	%	21.65	17.66
Sales to fixed assets	Times per year	11.15	8.62
Return on investment	%	19.54	15.69
Return on total equity	%	21.77	16.06
Return on common equity	%	21.77	16.06
Gross profit margin	%	45.58	45.44
Investor analysis:			
Degree of financial leverage	N/A	1.01	1.02
Diluted earnings per share	$	4.39	2.78
Price/earnings ratio	N/A	19.24	7.19
Percentage of earnings retained	%	73.98	No dividends
Dividend payout	%	27.33	No dividends
Dividend yield	%	1.42	No dividends
Book value per share	$	21.03	19.62
Materiality of option compensation expense	%	3.57	.01
Operating cash flow per share	$	3.73	*
Operating cash flow/cash dividends	Times per year	3.26	No dividends
Year-end market price	$	84.45	20.00

*Negative operating cash flow.

Selected Competitor

Adidas has the closest resemblance to Nike. Adidas is a German company, and financial statements using U.S. GAAP are not available for Adidas.

Skechers U.S.A., Inc., was selected as the closest competitor filing a 10-K.

Nike has a SIC 3021 – Rubber & Plastics Footwear, while Skechers U.S.A. has a SIC 3140 – Footwear (no rubber). Skechers U.S.A. describes its business in its December 31, 2010 10-K (in part) as follows:

General

We design and market Skechers-branded lifestyle and athletic footwear for men, women and children under several unique lines. Our footwear reflects a combination of style, quality and value that appeals to a broad range of consumers. In addition to Skechers-branded lines, we also offer several uniquely branded fashion and street-focused footwear lines for men, women and children. These lines are branded and marketed separately from Skechers and appeal to specific audiences. Our brands are sold through department and specialty stores, athletic and independent retailers, and boutiques as well as catalog and Internet retailers. Along with wholesale distribution, our footwear is available at our e-commerce websites and our own retail stores. As of February 15th, 2011 we operated 105 concept stores, 99 factory outlet stores and 40 warehouse outlet stores in the United States, and 28 concept stores and 16 factory outlets internationally. Our objective is to profitably grow our operations worldwide while leveraging our recognizable Skechers brand through our strong product lines, innovative advertising and diversified distribution channels.

Skechers U.S.A. is much smaller than Nike as indicated by the following revenue and assets:

Revenue:
Nike $20,862,000,000   (Year ended May 31, 2011)
Skechers U.S.A. $ 2,006,868,000   (Year ended December 31, 2010)
Total Assets:
Nike $14,998,000,000   (At May 31, 2011)
Skechers U.S.A. $ 1,304,794,000   (At December 31, 2010)

Again, caution must be exercised in drawing conclusions from the absolute numbers and ratios as well as the analysis in general. Keep potential problems in mind when drawing conclusions. Some of the potential problems on this comparison are the different year-ends, somewhat seasonal nature of the business, and different size of firms. In this case, we would likely be particularly concerned about the different year-ends and different size of firms.

Liquidity

- In the receivable area, Skechers is materially ahead of Nike, with days' sales in receivables (days), accounts receivables turnover (times per year), and accounts receivable turnover (days), all being better.
- In the inventory area, Nike is materially ahead of Skechers, with days' sales in inventory (days), inventory turnover (times per year), and inventory turnover in days (days), all being materially better.

They do have somewhat different inventory methods, which could account for some of the difference. The following information is derived from the Skechers 10-K:

Inventories

Inventories, principally finished goods, are stated at the lower of cost (based on the first-in, first-out method) or market. The Company provides for estimated losses from obsolete or slow-moving inventories and writes down the cost of inventory at the time such determinations are made. Reserves are estimated based upon inventory on hand, historical sales activity, and the expected net realizable value. The net realizable value is determined based upon estimated sales prices of such inventory through off-price or discount store channels.

The following indicates the inventory methods derived from the Nike 10-K:

Inventory Valuation

Inventories are stated at lower of cost or market and valued on a first-in, first-out ("FIFO") or moving average cost basis.

- Skechers has a moderately higher operating cycle, which favors Nike.
- Working capital cannot be compared. Nike is materially bigger than Skechers.
- Skechers' current ratio is moderately higher than Nike's. This is not necessarily good because the Nike current ratio is very good, and Skechers possibly has too much inventory.
- Nike's acid-test ratio is materially better than Skechers'.
- Nike's cash ratio is materially better than Skechers'.
- Skechers' sales to working capital is materially better than Nike's, even with the apparent high inventory.
- Nike's operating cash flow/current maturities of long-term debt and current notes payable is materially better than Skechers'.

Summary–Liquidity

In general, both firms appear to be in a good liquidity position, with the exception that Nike should review its receivables closely while Skechers should review its inventory closely. Also, Nike has a materially better operating cash flow/current maturities of long-term debt and current notes payable.

Long-Term Debt-Paying Ability

- Nike has a materially better times interest earned and fixed charge coverage than Skechers, but the Skechers coverage is good.
- Skechers has a materially better debt ratio, debt/equity, and debt to tangible net worth, but the Nike ratios are good. Nike has a materially better operating cash flow/total debt.

Summary–Long-Term Debt-Paying Ability

Both firms appear to be in a good or very good debt position. The exception to this is the low fixed charge coverage for Skechers.

Profitability

- Nike has a number of profitability indicators that are materially better than Skechers. Included here are net profit margin, return on assets, operating income margin, return on operating assets, sales to fixed assets, return on investment, return on total equity, and return on common equity.
- Skechers has a number of profitability indicators that are materially better than Nike. Included here are total asset turnover and operating asset turnover.
- Gross profit margin was approximately the same.

Summary—Profitability

Many of Nike's profitability indicators were materially better than Skechers'. Skechers did have a materially better total asset turnover and operating asset turnover.

Investor Analysis

- Neither company has a high degree of financial leverage.
- Price/earnings ratio was materially better for Nike.
- Skechers did not pay a dividend as indicated by percentage of earnings retained, dividend payout, dividend yield, and operating cash flow/cash dividends.
- Book value per share was moderately higher for Nike.
- Materiality of option compensation expense was materially higher for Nike.
- Diluted earnings per share was materially higher for Nike as was operating cash flow per share.
- Year-end market price was materially higher for Nike.
- Skechers had negative cash flow from operations.

Summary—Investor Analysis

The investor analysis favors Nike. This is likely related to the profitability comparison and somewhat related to the dividends paid by Nike.

Ratio Comparison with Industry (Exhibit 5)

Comparison with the industry is frequently a problem as to the quality of the comparison. The companies in the industry will typically be using different accounting methods. An example would be costing of inventory, with some companies using LIFO, some using FIFO, and some using an average. Industry ratios frequently do not address issues such as income statement unusual or infrequent items, equity earnings, discontinued operations, extraordinary items, or noncontrolling interest.

A problem with using industry data at a library is that commercial publications sometimes send the material to a library several months after general distribution. This brings a time issue to be considered. The U.S. Department of Commerce Quarterly Financial Report is online and represents relatively recent data. These data may be of limited or no use, depending on the company that is being analyzed.

The industry ratios available are frequently of a broader industry coverage than the ideal. Nike is under SIC Rubber and Plastics Footwear (3021). Robert Morris Associates Annual Statement Studies publishes some industry material using SIC 3052 Manufacturing Rubber and Plastics, Hose and Belting. Dun & Bradstreet Industry Norms and Key Business Ratios publishes SIC 30 Rubber and Plastics. The U.S. Department of Commerce publishes Quarterly Financial Report for manufacturing, mining, and the trade corporations. They have dropped SIC in favor of NAICS. They combine subsectors 315 and 316, apparel and leather products. For Nike, the NAICS is 316211, Rubber and Plastics Footwear Manufacturing.

In Nike's performance graph presented in the 2009 10-K, Nike compared its stock performance for the period May 2006 – May 2011 with the S&P 500 Index, Total Returns, Dow Jones U.S. Footwear Index, S&P 500 Apparel, Accessories and Luxury Goods. For stock performance, Nike closely resembled Dow Jones U.S. Footwear Index. Nike was up approximately 222%, while Dow Jones U.S. Footwear Index was up 170%.

Although there are problems with using industry comparison, the effort is usually beneficial. It is necessary to be cautious when drawing conclusions. You may want to review "Caution in Using Industry Averages" in Chapter 5.

Consider picking out four or five close competitors of the firm that you are analyzing and compute the industry average. This will likely result in a more meaningful comparison than using published industry data.

Liquidity

- Nike's receivables appear to be materially less liquid than the industry. Part of this can likely be explained by the May 31 year-end for Nike. The difference between the Nike ratios and the industry is so material that it is likely that most firms in the industry are using shorter credit terms.
- Nike's inventory appears to be materially more liquid than the industry. Part of this can likely be explained by the May 31 year-end for Nike. Possibly, many firms in the industry are using a different inventory costing method than Nike uses.
- The current ratio, acid-test, and cash ratio are materially better for Nike than the industry. These were influenced by less liquid receivables but more liquid inventory. They are also influenced by the materially better cash ratio of Nike.
- Sales to working capital is materially less for Nike than the industry.

Summary—Liquidity

We do not have a good industry comparison with Nike in the liquidity area. It is possible that Nike has substantially different policies in the receivables and inventory areas than the industry.

Long-Term Debt-Paying Ability

- Nike's time interest earned, debt ratio, and debt/equity are materially better than the industry.

Summary—Long-Term Debt-Paying Ability

Nike's long-term debt-paying ability appears to be materially better than the industry.

EXHIBIT **5**	Nike, Inc.

Ratio Comparison with Industry

Ratio	Unit	2011 Nike	Industry Ratio	Source
Liquidity:				
Days' sales in receivables	Days	56.19	38.72	DC
Accounts receivable turnover	Times per year	7.03	9.48	DC
Accounts receivable turnover	Days	51.92	38.50	DC
Days' sales in inventory	Days	87.27	Not available	—
Merchandise inventory turnover	Times per year	4.77	3.8	ABI
Inventory turnover	Days	76.44	96.05	ABI
Operating cycle	Days	128.36	Not available	—
Working capital (in millions)	$	7,339	N/A	—
Current ratio	N/A	2.85	2.47	DC
Acid-test ratio	N/A	1.94	1.21	DC
Cash ratio	N/A	1.15	.50	DC
Sales to working capital	Times per year	2.79	4.57	DC
Operating cash flow/current maturities of long-term debt and notes payable	Times per year	4.68	Not available	—
Long-term debt-paying ability:				
Times interest earned	Times per year	84.60	8.42	DC
Fixed charge coverage	Times per year	37.00	Not available	—
Debt ratio	%	34.37	48.71	DC
Debt/equity	%	52.37	94.96	DC
Debt to tangible net worth	%	56.33	Not available	—
Operating cash flow/total debt	%	35.15	Not available	—
Profitability:				
Net profit margin	%	10.22	7.91	DC
Total asset turnover	Times per year	1.42	1.29	DC
Return on assets	%	14.50	10.18	DC
Operating income margin	%	13.49	8.41	DC
Operating asset turnover	Times per year	1.60	2.18	DC
Return on operating assets	%	21.65	18.33	DC
Sales to fixed assets	Times per year	11.15	4.24	DC
Return on investment	%	19.54	16.19	DC
Return on total equity	%	21.77	19.97	DC
Return on common equity	%	21.77	Not available	—
Gross profit margin	%	45.58	Not available	—
Investor analysis:				
Degree of financial leverage	N/A	1.01	1.13	DC
Diluted earning per share	$	4.39	N/A	—
Price/earnings ratio	N/A	19.24	13.43	S&P
Percentage of earnings retained	%	73.98	66.04	DC
Dividend payout ratio	%	27.33	Not available	—
Dividend yield	%	1.42	1.86	S&P
Book value per share	$	21.03	N/A	—
Materiality of option compensation expense	%	3.57	Not available	—
Operating cash flow per share	$	3.73	N/A	—
Operating cash flow/cash dividends	Times per year	3.26	Not available	—
Year-end market price	$	84.45	N/A	—

Index: Industry statistics are directly from or computed from the following sources:
DC = *U.S. Department of Commerce – Quarterly Financial Report for Manufacturing, Mining, and Trade Corporations*
S&P = *Standard and Poor's 500, the Outlook, 500 Composite*
ABI = *The Almanac of Business and Industrial Financial Ratios, NAICS 316115*
Note: *Industry ratios in general were not available that compute the ratios consistent with this book. Also, industry data is subject to revision and the SIC is somewhat different.*

Profitability

All of the profitability ratios were materially better for Nike than the industry, except for operating asset turnover. Operating asset turnover was materially better for the industry.

Summary—Profitability

Nike had an outstanding profit year in relation to the industry.

Investor Analysis

- The degree of financial leverage is materially lower for Nike than for the industry.
- The price/earnings ratio is materially higher for Nike than the 500 composite. Considering the profitability ratios for Nike, a higher price/earnings ratio is justified.
- Nike retained a materially higher percentage of earnings than did the industry.
- The dividend yield was materially lower for Nike than for the industry.

Summary—Investor Analysis

Only a few comparisons are possible in the investor area. The comparisons are favorable toward Nike, except for dividend yield.

Orders

Worldwide futures and advance orders for NIKE Brand athletic footwear and apparel, scheduled for delivery from June through November 2011, were $10.3 billion compared to $8.8 billion for the same period last year. 10-K

Summary

In general, the years 2009–2011 appear to be very good for Nike in terms of liquidity. The long-term debt-paying ability was very good. This appears to be the case from both an income statement and a balance sheet viewpoint. Profitability appears to be very good. Impressive year-end market price increase appears to be responding to an impressive diluted earnings per share increase and a favorable profitability perspective.

Nike 2011 (Exhibit 12-1)

The Nike 2011 financial statements and notes are presented along with Nike Exhibit 12-1, which shows the computation of the ratio earnings to total fixed charges. Exhibit 12-1 found in the Nike documents, discloses the interest expense:

| EXHIBIT 12-1 | Nike, Inc. computation of ratio of earnings to fixed charges |

	Year Ended May 31,				
	2011	**2010**	**2009**	**2008**	**2007**
			(In millions)		
Net income	$2,133	$1,907	$1,487	$1,883	$1,492
Income taxes	711	610	470	620	708
Income before income taxes	2,844	2,517	1,957	2,503	2,200
Add fixed charges					
Interest expense[1]	34	36	40	41	50
Interest component of leases[2]	45	42	40	34	28
Total fixed charges	79	78	80	75	78
Earnings before income taxes and fixed charges[3]	$2,923	$2,595	$2,037	$2,578	$2,278
Ratio of earnings to total fixed charges	37.0	33.3	25.5	34.4	29.2

[1]Interest expense includes interest both expensed and capitalized.

[2]Interest component of leases includes one-tenth of rental expense which approximates the interest component of operating leases.

[3]Earnings before income taxes and fixed charges is exclusive of capitalized interest.

The following pages (labeled 56–87) is derived from the Nike 10-k:

NIKE, INC.
CONSOLIDATED STATEMENTS OF INCOME

	Year Ended May 31,		
	2011	2010	2009
	(In millions, except per share data)		
Revenues	$20,862	$19,014	$19,176
Cost of sales	11,354	10,214	10,572
Gross margin	9,508	8,800	8,604
Demand creation expense	2,448	2,356	2,352
Operating overhead expense	4,245	3,970	3,798
Total selling and administrative expense	6,693	6,326	6,150
Restructuring charges (Note 16)	—	—	195
Goodwill impairment (Note 4)	—	—	199
Intangible and other asset impairment (Note 4)	—	—	202
Interest expense (income), net (Notes 6, 7 and 8)	4	6	(10)
Other (income), net (Note 17)	(33)	(49)	(89)
Income before income taxes	2,844	2,517	1,957
Income taxes (Note 9)	711	610	470
Net income	$ 2,133	$ 1,907	$ 1,487
Basic earnings per common share (Notes 1 and 12)	$ 4.48	$ 3.93	$ 3.07
Diluted earnings per common share (Notes 1 and 12)	$ 4.39	$ 3.86	$ 3.03
Dividends declared per common share	$ 1.20	$ 1.06	$ 0.98

The accompanying notes to consolidated financial statements are an integral part of this statement.

56

Source: Nike, Inc. 2011 10-K

NIKE, INC.
CONSOLIDATED BALANCE SHEETS

	May 31,	
	2011	**2010**
	(In millions)	
ASSETS		
Current assets:		
Cash and equivalents	$ 1,955	$ 3,079
Short-term investments (Note 6)	2,583	2,067
Accounts receivable, net (Note 1)	3,138	2,650
Inventories (Notes 1 and 2)	2,715	2,041
Deferred income taxes (Note 9)	312	249
Prepaid expenses and other current assets	594	873
Total current assets	11,297	10,959
Property, plant and equipment, net (Note 3)	2,115	1,932
Identifiable intangible assets, net (Note 4)	487	467
Goodwill (Note 4)	205	188
Deferred income taxes and other assets (Notes 9 and 17)	894	873
Total assets	$14,998	$14,419
LIABILITIES AND SHAREHOLDERS' EQUITY		
Current liabilities:		
Current portion of long-term debt (Note 8)	$ 200	$ 7
Notes payable (Note 7)	187	139
Accounts payable (Note 7)	1,469	1,255
Accrued liabilities (Notes 5 and 17)	1,985	1,904
Income taxes payable (Note 9)	117	59
Total current liabilities	3,958	3,364
Long-term debt (Note 8)	276	446
Deferred income taxes and other liabilities (Notes 9 and 17)	921	855
Commitments and contingencies (Note 15)	—	—
Redeemable Preferred Stock (Note 10)	—	—
Shareholders' equity:		
Common stock at stated value (Note 11):		
Class A convertible — 90 and 90 shares outstanding	—	—
Class B — 378 and 394 shares outstanding	3	3
Capital in excess of stated value	3,944	3,441
Accumulated other comprehensive income (Note 14)	95	215
Retained earnings	5,801	6,095
Total shareholders' equity	9,843	9,754
Total liabilities and shareholders' equity	$14,998	$14,419

The accompanying notes to consolidated financial statements are an integral part of this statement.

57

NIKE, INC.
CONSOLIDATED STATEMENTS OF CASH FLOWS

	Year Ended May 31,		
	2011	**2010**	**2009**
		(In millions)	
Cash provided by operations:			
Net income	$ 2,133	$ 1,907	$ 1,487
Income charges (credits) not affecting cash:			
Depreciation	335	324	335
Deferred income taxes	(76)	8	(294)
Stock-based compensation (Note 11)	105	159	171
Impairment of goodwill, intangibles and other assets (Note 4)	—	—	401
Amortization and other	23	72	48
Changes in certain working capital components and other assets and liabilities excluding the impact of acquisition and divestitures:			
(Increase) decrease in accounts receivable	(273)	182	(238)
(Increase) decrease in inventories	(551)	285	32
(Increase) decrease in prepaid expenses and other current assets	(35)	(70)	14
Increase (decrease) in accounts payable, accrued liabilities and income taxes payable	151	297	(220)
Cash provided by operations	1,812	3,164	1,736
Cash used by investing activities:			
Purchases of short-term investments	(7,616)	(3,724)	(2,909)
Maturities of short-term investments	4,313	2,334	1,280
Sales of short-term investments	2,766	453	1,110
Additions to property, plant and equipment	(432)	(335)	(456)
Disposals of property, plant and equipment	1	10	33
Increase in other assets, net of other liabilities	(30)	(11)	(47)
Settlement of net investment hedges	(23)	5	191
Cash used by investing activities	(1,021)	(1,268)	(798)
Cash used by financing activities:			
Reductions in long-term debt, including current portion	(8)	(32)	(7)
Increase (decrease) in notes payable	41	(205)	177
Proceeds from exercise of stock options and other stock issuances	345	364	187
Excess tax benefits from share-based payment arrangements	64	58	25
Repurchase of common stock	(1,859)	(741)	(649)
Dividends — common and preferred	(555)	(505)	(467)
Cash used by financing activities	(1,972)	(1,061)	(734)
Effect of exchange rate changes	57	(47)	(47)
Net (decrease) increase in cash and equivalents	(1,124)	788	157
Cash and equivalents, beginning of year	3,079	2,291	2,134
Cash and equivalents, end of year	$ 1,955	$ 3,079	$ 2,291
Supplemental disclosure of cash flow information:			
Cash paid during the year for:			
Interest, net of capitalized interest	$ 32	$ 48	$ 47
Income taxes	736	537	765
Dividends declared and not paid	145	131	121

The accompanying notes to consolidated financial statements are an integral part of this statement.

58

NIKE, INC.
CONSOLIDATED STATEMENTS OF SHAREHOLDERS' EQUITY

	Common Stock				Capital in Excess of Stated Value	Accumulated Other Comprehensive Income	Retained Earnings	Total
	Class A		Class B					
	Shares	Amount	Shares	Amount				
					(In millions, except per share data)			
Balance at May 31, 2008	97	$ —	394	$ 3	$ 2,498	$ 251	$ 5,073	$ 7,825
Stock options exercised			4		167			167
Conversion to Class B Common Stock	(2)		2					—
Repurchase of Class B Common Stock			(11)		(6)		(633)	(639)
Dividends on Common stock ($0.98 per share)							(475)	(475)
Issuance of shares to employees			1		45			45
Stock-based compensation (Note 11):					171			171
Forfeiture of shares from employees			—		(4)		(1)	(5)
Comprehensive income:								
Net income							1,487	1,487
Other comprehensive income:								
Foreign currency translation and other (net of tax benefit of $178)						(335)		(335)
Net gain on cash flow hedges (net of tax expense of $168)						454		454
Net gain on net investment hedges (net of tax expense of $55)						106		106
Reclassification to net income of previously deferred net gains related to hedge derivatives (net of tax expense of $40)						(108)		(108)
Total comprehensive income						117	1,487	1,604
Balance at May 31, 2009	95	$ —	390	$ 3	$ 2,871	$ 368	$ 5,451	$ 8,693
Stock options exercised			9		380			380
Conversion to Class B Common Stock	(5)		5					—
Repurchase of Class B Common Stock			(11)		(7)		(747)	(754)
Dividends on Common stock ($1.06 per share)							(515)	(515)
Issuance of shares to employees			1		40			40
Stock-based compensation (Note 11):					159			159
Forfeiture of shares from employees			—		(2)		(1)	(3)
Comprehensive income:								
Net income							1,907	1,907
Other comprehensive income (Notes 14 and 17):								
Foreign currency translation and other (net of tax benefit of $72)						(159)		(159)
Net gain on cash flow hedges (net of tax expense of $28)						87		87
Net gain on net investment hedges (net of tax expense of $21)						45		45
Reclassification to net income of previously deferred net gains related to hedge derivatives (net of tax expense of $42)						(122)		(122)
Reclassification of ineffective hedge gains to net income (net of tax expense of $1)						(4)		(4)
Total comprehensive income						(153)	1,907	1,754
Balance at May 31, 2010	90	$ —	394	$ 3	$ 3,441	$ 215	$ 6,095	$ 9,754
Stock options exercised			7		368			368
Repurchase of Class B Common Stock			(24)		(14)		(1,857)	(1,871)
Dividends on Common stock ($1.20 per share)							(569)	(569)
Issuance of shares to employees			1		49			49
Stock-based compensation (Note 11):					105			105
Forfeiture of shares from employees			—		(5)		(1)	(6)
Comprehensive income:								
Net income							2,133	2,133
Other comprehensive income (Notes 14 and 17):								
Foreign currency translation and other (net of tax expense of $121)						263		263
Net loss on cash flow hedges (net of tax benefit of $66)						(242)		(242)
Net loss on net investment hedges (net of tax benefit of $28)						(57)		(57)
Reclassification to net income of previously deferred net gains related to hedge derivatives (net of tax expense of $24)						(84)		(84)
Total comprehensive income						(120)	2,133	2,013
Balance at May 31, 2011	90	$ —	378	$ 3	$ 3,944	$ 95	$ 5,801	$ 9,843

The accompanying notes to consolidated financial statements are an integral part of this statement.

59

NIKE, INC.
NOTES TO CONSOLIDATED FINANCIAL STATEMENTS

Note 1 — Summary of Significant Accounting Policies

Description of Business

NIKE, Inc. is a worldwide leader in the design, marketing and distribution of athletic and sports-inspired footwear, apparel, equipment and accessories. Wholly-owned NIKE subsidiaries include Cole Haan, which designs, markets and distributes dress and casual shoes, handbags, accessories and coats; Converse Inc., which designs, markets and distributes athletic and casual footwear, apparel and accessories; Hurley International LLC, which designs, markets and distributes action sports and youth lifestyle footwear, apparel and accessories; and Umbro International Limited, which designs, distributes and licenses athletic and casual footwear, apparel and equipment, primarily for the sport of soccer.

Basis of Consolidation

The consolidated financial statements include the accounts of NIKE, Inc. and its subsidiaries (the "Company"). All significant intercompany transactions and balances have been eliminated.

Recognition of Revenues

Wholesale revenues are recognized when title passes and the risks and rewards of ownership have passed to the customer, based on the terms of sale. This occurs upon shipment or upon receipt by the customer depending on the country of the sale and the agreement with the customer. Retail store revenues are recorded at the time of sale. Provisions for sales discounts, returns and miscellaneous claims from customers are made at the time of sale. As of May 31, 2011 and 2010, the Company's reserve balances for sales discounts, returns and miscellaneous claims were $423 million and $371 million, respectively.

Shipping and Handling Costs

Shipping and handling costs are expensed as incurred and included in cost of sales.

Demand Creation Expense

Demand creation expense consists of advertising and promotion costs, including costs of endorsement contracts, television, digital and print advertising, brand events, and retail brand presentation. Advertising production costs are expensed the first time an advertisement is run. Advertising placement costs are expensed in the month the advertising appears, while costs related to brand events are expensed when the event occurs. Costs related to retail brand presentation are expensed when the presentation is completed and delivered. A significant amount of the Company's promotional expenses result from payments under endorsement contracts. Accounting for endorsement payments is based upon specific contract provisions. Generally, endorsement payments are expensed on a straight-line basis over the term of the contract after giving recognition to periodic performance compliance provisions of the contracts. Prepayments made under contracts are included in prepaid expenses or other assets depending on the period to which the prepayment applies.

Through cooperative advertising programs, the Company reimburses retail customers for certain costs of advertising the Company's products. The Company records these costs in selling and administrative expense at the point in time when it is obligated to its customers for the costs, which is when the related revenues are recognized. This obligation may arise prior to the related advertisement being run.

Total advertising and promotion expenses were $2,448 million, $2,356 million, and $2,352 million for the years ended May 31, 2011, 2010 and 2009, respectively. Prepaid advertising and promotion expenses recorded in prepaid expenses and other assets totaled $291 million and $261 million at May 31, 2011 and 2010, respectively.

60

NIKE, INC.
NOTES TO CONSOLIDATED FINANCIAL STATEMENTS — (Continued)

Cash and Equivalents

Cash and equivalents represent cash and short-term, highly liquid investments with maturities of three months or less at date of purchase. The carrying amounts reflected in the consolidated balance sheet for cash and equivalents approximate fair value.

Short-Term Investments

Short-term investments consist of highly liquid investments, including commercial paper, U.S. treasury, U.S. agency, and corporate debt securities, with maturities over three months from the date of purchase. Debt securities that the Company has the ability and positive intent to hold to maturity are carried at amortized cost. At May 31, 2011 and 2010, the Company did not hold any short-term investments that were classified as trading or held-to-maturity.

At May 31, 2011 and 2010, short-term investments consisted of available-for-sale securities. Available-for-sale securities are recorded at fair value with unrealized gains and losses reported, net of tax, in other comprehensive income, unless unrealized losses are determined to be other than temporary. The Company considers all available-for-sale securities, including those with maturity dates beyond 12 months, as available to support current operational liquidity needs and therefore classifies all securities with maturity dates beyond three months at the date of purchase as current assets within short-term investments on the consolidated balance sheet.

See Note 6 — Fair Value Measurements for more information on the Company's short term investments.

Allowance for Uncollectible Accounts Receivable

Accounts receivable consists primarily of amounts receivable from customers. We make ongoing estimates relating to the collectability of our accounts receivable and maintain an allowance for estimated losses resulting from the inability of our customers to make required payments. In determining the amount of the allowance, we consider our historical level of credit losses and make judgments about the creditworthiness of significant customers based on ongoing credit evaluations. Accounts receivable with anticipated collection dates greater than 12 months from the balance sheet date and related allowances are considered non-current and recorded in other assets. The allowance for uncollectible accounts receivable was $124 million and $117 million at May 31, 2011 and 2010, respectively, of which $50 million and $43 million was classified as long-term and recorded in other assets.

Inventory Valuation

Inventories are stated at lower of cost or market and valued on a first-in, first-out ("FIFO") or moving average cost basis.

Property, Plant and Equipment and Depreciation

Property, plant and equipment are recorded at cost. Depreciation for financial reporting purposes is determined on a straight-line basis for buildings and leasehold improvements over 2 to 40 years and for machinery and equipment over 2 to 15 years. Computer software (including, in some cases, the cost of internal labor) is depreciated on a straight-line basis over 3 to 10 years.

Impairment of Long-Lived Assets

The Company reviews the carrying value of long-lived assets or asset groups to be used in operations whenever events or changes in circumstances indicate that the carrying amount of the assets might not be recoverable. Factors that would necessitate an impairment assessment include a significant adverse change in the

61

Source: Nike, Inc. 2011 10-K

NIKE, INC.
NOTES TO CONSOLIDATED FINANCIAL STATEMENTS — (Continued)

extent or manner in which an asset is used, a significant adverse change in legal factors or the business climate that could affect the value of the asset, or a significant decline in the observable market value of an asset, among others. If such facts indicate a potential impairment, the Company would assess the recoverability of an asset group by determining if the carrying value of the asset group exceeds the sum of the projected undiscounted cash flows expected to result from the use and eventual disposition of the assets over the remaining economic life of the primary asset in the asset group. If the recoverability test indicates that the carrying value of the asset group is not recoverable, the Company will estimate the fair value of the asset group using appropriate valuation methodologies which would typically include an estimate of discounted cash flows. Any impairment would be measured as the difference between the asset groups carrying amount and its estimated fair value.

Identifiable Intangible Assets and Goodwill

The Company performs annual impairment tests on goodwill and intangible assets with indefinite lives in the fourth quarter of each fiscal year, or when events occur or circumstances change that would, more likely than not, reduce the fair value of a reporting unit or an intangible asset with an indefinite life below its carrying value. Events or changes in circumstances that may trigger interim impairment reviews include significant changes in business climate, operating results, planned investments in the reporting unit, or an expectation that the carrying amount may not be recoverable, among other factors. The impairment test requires the Company to estimate the fair value of its reporting units. If the carrying value of a reporting unit exceeds its fair value, the goodwill of that reporting unit is potentially impaired and the Company proceeds to step two of the impairment analysis. In step two of the analysis, the Company measures and records an impairment loss equal to the excess of the carrying value of the reporting unit's goodwill over its implied fair value should such a circumstance arise.

The Company generally bases its measurement of fair value of a reporting unit on a blended analysis of the present value of future discounted cash flows and the market valuation approach. The discounted cash flows model indicates the fair value of the reporting unit based on the present value of the cash flows that the Company expects the reporting unit to generate in the future. The Company's significant estimates in the discounted cash flows model include: its weighted average cost of capital; long-term rate of growth and profitability of the reporting unit's business; and working capital effects. The market valuation approach indicates the fair value of the business based on a comparison of the reporting unit to comparable publicly traded companies in similar lines of business. Significant estimates in the market valuation approach model include identifying similar companies with comparable business factors such as size, growth, profitability, risk and return on investment, and assessing comparable revenue and operating income multiples in estimating the fair value of the reporting unit.

The Company believes the weighted use of discounted cash flows and the market valuation approach is the best method for determining the fair value of its reporting units because these are the most common valuation methodologies used within its industry; and the blended use of both models compensates for the inherent risks associated with either model if used on a stand-alone basis.

Indefinite-lived intangible assets primarily consist of acquired trade names and trademarks. In measuring the fair value for these intangible assets, the Company utilizes the relief-from-royalty method. This method assumes that trade names and trademarks have value to the extent that their owner is relieved of the obligation to pay royalties for the benefits received from them. This method requires the Company to estimate the future revenue for the related brands, the appropriate royalty rate and the weighted average cost of capital.

Foreign Currency Translation and Foreign Currency Transactions

Adjustments resulting from translating foreign functional currency financial statements into U.S. dollars are included in the foreign currency translation adjustment, a component of accumulated other comprehensive income in shareholders' equity.

62

Source: Nike, Inc. 2011 10-K

NIKE, INC.

NOTES TO CONSOLIDATED FINANCIAL STATEMENTS — (Continued)

The Company's global subsidiaries have various assets and liabilities, primarily receivables and payables, that are denominated in currencies other than their functional currency. These balance sheet items are subject to remeasurement, the impact of which is recorded in other (income), net, within our consolidated statement of income.

Accounting for Derivatives and Hedging Activities

The Company uses derivative financial instruments to limit exposure to changes in foreign currency exchange rates and interest rates. All derivatives are recorded at fair value on the balance sheet and changes in the fair value of derivative financial instruments are either recognized in other comprehensive income (a component of shareholders' equity), debt or net income depending on the nature of the underlying exposure, whether the derivative is formally designated as a hedge, and, if designated, the extent to which the hedge is effective. The Company classifies the cash flows at settlement from derivatives in the same category as the cash flows from the related hedged items. For undesignated hedges and designated cash flow hedges, this is within the cash provided by operations component of the consolidated statements of cash flows. For designated net investment hedges, this is generally within the cash used by investing activities component of the cash flow statement. As our fair value hedges are receive-fixed, pay-variable interest rate swaps, the cash flows associated with these derivative instruments are periodic interest payments while the swaps are outstanding, which are reflected in net income within the cash provided by operations component of the cash flow statement.

See Note 17 — Risk Management and Derivatives for more information on the Company's risk management program and derivatives.

Stock-Based Compensation

The Company estimates the fair value of options and stock appreciation rights granted under the NIKE, Inc. 1990 Stock Incentive Plan (the "1990 Plan") and employees' purchase rights under the Employee Stock Purchase Plans ("ESPPs") using the Black-Scholes option pricing model. The Company recognizes this fair value, net of estimated forfeitures, as selling and administrative expense in the consolidated statements of income over the vesting period using the straight-line method.

See Note 11 — Common Stock and Stock-Based Compensation for more information on the Company's stock programs.

Income Taxes

The Company accounts for income taxes using the asset and liability method. This approach requires the recognition of deferred tax assets and liabilities for the expected future tax consequences of temporary differences between the carrying amounts and the tax basis of assets and liabilities. United States income taxes are provided currently on financial statement earnings of non-U.S. subsidiaries that are expected to be repatriated. The Company determines annually the amount of undistributed non-U.S. earnings to invest indefinitely in its non-U.S. operations. The Company recognizes interest and penalties related to income tax matters in income tax expense.

See Note 9 — Income Taxes for further discussion.

Earnings Per Share

Basic earnings per common share is calculated by dividing net income by the weighted average number of common shares outstanding during the year. Diluted earnings per common share is calculated by adjusting weighted average outstanding shares, assuming conversion of all potentially dilutive stock options and awards.

63

Source: Nike, Inc. 2011 10-K

NIKE, INC.

NOTES TO CONSOLIDATED FINANCIAL STATEMENTS — (Continued)

See Note 12 — Earnings Per Share for further discussion.

Management Estimates

The preparation of financial statements in conformity with generally accepted accounting principles requires management to make estimates, including estimates relating to assumptions that affect the reported amounts of assets and liabilities and disclosure of contingent assets and liabilities at the date of financial statements and the reported amounts of revenues and expenses during the reporting period. Actual results could differ from these estimates.

Recently Adopted Accounting Standards

In January 2010, the Financial Accounting Standards Board ("FASB") issued guidance to amend the disclosure requirements related to recurring and nonrecurring fair value measurements. The guidance requires additional disclosures about the different classes of assets and liabilities measured at fair value, the valuation techniques and inputs used, the activity in Level 3 fair value measurements, and the transfers between Levels 1, 2, and 3 of the fair value measurement hierarchy. This guidance became effective for the Company beginning March 1, 2010, except for disclosures relating to purchases, sales, issuances and settlements of Level 3 assets and liabilities, which will be effective for the Company beginning June 1, 2011. As this guidance only requires expanded disclosures, the adoption did not and will not impact the Company's consolidated financial position or results of operations.

In June 2009, the FASB issued a new accounting standard that revised the guidance for the consolidation of variable interest entities ("VIE"). This new guidance requires a qualitative approach to identifying a controlling financial interest in a VIE, and requires an ongoing assessment of whether an entity is a VIE and whether an interest in a VIE makes the holder the primary beneficiary of the VIE. This guidance became effective for the Company beginning June 1, 2010. The adoption of this guidance did not have an impact on the Company's consolidated financial position or results of operations.

Recently Issued Accounting Standards

In June 2011, the FASB issued new guidance on the presentation of comprehensive income. This new guidance requires the components of net income and other comprehensive income to be either presented in one continuous statement, referred to as the statement of comprehensive income, or in two separate, but consecutive statements. This new guidance eliminates the current option to report other comprehensive income and its components in the statement of shareholders' equity. While the new guidance changes the presentation of comprehensive income, there are no changes to the components that are recognized in net income or other comprehensive income under current accounting guidance. This new guidance is effective for the Company beginning June 1, 2012. As this guidance only amends the presentation of the components of comprehensive income, the adoption will not have an impact on the Company's consolidated financial position or results of operations.

In April 2011, the FASB issued new guidance to achieve common fair value measurement and disclosure requirements between U.S. GAAP and International Financial Reporting Standards. This new guidance, which is effective for the Company beginning June 1, 2012, amends current U.S. GAAP fair value measurement and disclosure guidance to include increased transparency around valuation inputs and investment categorization. The Company does not expect the adoption will have a material impact on its consolidated financial position or results of operations.

64

NIKE, INC.

NOTES TO CONSOLIDATED FINANCIAL STATEMENTS — (Continued)

In October 2009, the FASB issued new standards that revised the guidance for revenue recognition with multiple deliverables. These new standards impact the determination of when the individual deliverables included in a multiple-element arrangement may be treated as separate units of accounting. Additionally, these new standards modify the manner in which the transaction consideration is allocated across the separately identified deliverables by no longer permitting the residual method of allocating arrangement consideration. These new standards are effective for the Company beginning June 1, 2011. The Company does not expect the adoption will have a material impact on its consolidated financial position or results of operations.

Note 2 — Inventories

Inventory balances of $2,715 million and $2,041 million at May 31, 2011 and 2010, respectively, were substantially all finished goods.

Note 3 — Property, Plant and Equipment

Property, plant and equipment included the following:

	As of May 31,	
	2011	2010
	(In millions)	
Land	$ 237	$ 223
Buildings	1,124	952
Machinery and equipment	2,487	2,217
Leasehold improvements	931	821
Construction in process	127	177
	4,906	4,390
Less accumulated depreciation	2,791	2,458
	$2,115	$1,932

Capitalized interest was not material for the years ended May 31, 2011, 2010, and 2009.

Note 4 — Identifiable Intangible Assets, Goodwill and Umbro Impairment

Identified Intangible Assets and Goodwill

The following table summarizes the Company's identifiable intangible asset balances as of May 31, 2011 and 2010:

	May 31, 2011			May 31, 2010		
	Gross Carrying Amount	Accumulated Amortization	Net Carrying Amount	Gross Carrying Amount	Accumulated Amortization	Net Carrying Amount
			(In millions)			
Amortized intangible assets:						
Patents	$ 80	$ (24)	$ 56	$ 69	$ (21)	$ 48
Trademarks	44	(25)	19	40	(18)	22
Other	47	(22)	25	32	(18)	14
Total	$ 171	$ (71)	$ 100	$ 141	$ (57)	$ 84
Unamortized intangible assets — Trademarks			387			383
Identifiable intangible assets, net			$ 487			$ 467

65

NIKE, INC.

NOTES TO CONSOLIDATED FINANCIAL STATEMENTS — (Continued)

The effect of foreign exchange fluctuations for the year ended May 31, 2011 increased unamortized intangible assets by approximately $4 million.

Amortization expense, which is included in selling and administrative expense, was $16 million, $14 million, and $12 million for the years ended May 31, 2011, 2010, and 2009, respectively. The estimated amortization expense for intangible assets subject to amortization for each of the years ending May 31, 2012 through May 31, 2016 are as follows: 2012: $16 million; 2013: $14 million; 2014: $12 million; 2015: $8 million; 2016: $7 million.

All goodwill balances are included in the Company's "Other" category for segment reporting purposes. The following table summarizes the Company's goodwill balance as of May 31, 2011 and 2010:

	Goodwill	Accumulated Impairment (In millions)	Goodwill, net
May 31, 2009	$ 393	$ (199)	$ 194
Other[1]	(6)	—	(6)
May 31, 2010	387	(199)	188
Umbro France[2]	10	—	10
Other[1]	7	—	7
May 31, 2011	$ 404	$ (199)	$ 205

[1] Other consists of foreign currency translation adjustments on Umbro goodwill.

[2] In March 2011, Umbro acquired the remaining 51% of the exclusive licensee and distributor of the Umbro brand in France for approximately $15 million.

Umbro Impairment in Fiscal 2009

The Company performs annual impairment tests on goodwill and intangible assets with indefinite lives in the fourth quarter of each fiscal year, or when events occur or circumstances change that would, more likely than not, reduce the fair value of a reporting unit or intangible assets with an indefinite life below its carrying value. As a result of a significant decline in global consumer demand and continued weakness in the macroeconomic environment, as well as decisions by Company management to adjust planned investment in the Umbro brand, the Company concluded sufficient indicators of impairment existed to require the performance of an interim assessment of Umbro's goodwill and indefinite lived intangible assets as of February 1, 2009. Accordingly, the Company performed the first step of the goodwill impairment assessment for Umbro by comparing the estimated fair value of Umbro to its carrying amount, and determined there was a potential impairment of goodwill as the carrying amount exceeded the estimated fair value. Therefore, the Company performed the second step of the assessment which compared the implied fair value of Umbro's goodwill to the book value of goodwill. The implied fair value of goodwill is determined by allocating the estimated fair value of Umbro to all of its assets and liabilities, including both recognized and unrecognized intangibles, in the same manner as goodwill was determined in the original business combination.

The Company measured the fair value of Umbro by using an equal weighting of the fair value implied by a discounted cash flow analysis and by comparisons with the market values of similar publicly traded companies. The Company believes the blended use of both models compensates for the inherent risk associated with either model if used on a stand-alone basis, and this combination is indicative of the factors a market participant would consider when performing a similar valuation. The fair value of Umbro's indefinite-lived trademark was

66

NIKE, INC.

NOTES TO CONSOLIDATED FINANCIAL STATEMENTS — (Continued)

estimated using the relief from royalty method, which assumes that the trademark has value to the extent that Umbro is relieved of the obligation to pay royalties for the benefits received from the trademark. The assessments of the Company resulted in the recognition of impairment charges of $199 million and $181 million related to Umbro's goodwill and trademark, respectively, for the year ended May 31, 2009. A tax benefit of $55 million was recognized as a result of the trademark impairment charge. In addition to the above impairment analysis, the Company determined an equity investment held by Umbro was impaired, and recognized a charge of $21 million related to the impairment of this investment. These charges are included in the Company's "Other" category for segment reporting purposes.

The discounted cash flow analysis calculated the fair value of Umbro using management's business plans and projections as the basis for expected cash flows for the next 12 years and a 3% residual growth rate thereafter. The Company used a weighted average discount rate of 14% in its analysis, which was derived primarily from published sources as well as our adjustment for increased market risk given current market conditions. Other significant estimates used in the discounted cash flow analysis include the rates of projected growth and profitability of Umbro's business and working capital effects. The market valuation approach indicates the fair value of Umbro based on a comparison of Umbro to publicly traded companies in similar lines of business. Significant estimates in the market valuation approach include identifying similar companies with comparable business factors such as size, growth, profitability, mix of revenue generated from licensed and direct distribution, and risk of return on investment.

Holding all other assumptions constant at the test date, a 100 basis point increase in the discount rate would reduce the adjusted carrying value of Umbro's net assets by an additional 12%.

Note 5 — Accrued Liabilities

Accrued liabilities included the following:

	May 31,	
	2011	2010
	(In millions)	
Compensation and benefits, excluding taxes	$ 628	$ 599
Endorser compensation	284	267
Taxes other than income taxes	214	158
Fair value of derivatives	186	164
Dividends payable	145	131
Advertising and marketing	139	125
Import and logistics costs	98	80
Other[1]	291	380
	$1,985	$1,904

---

[1] Other consists of various accrued expenses and no individual item accounted for more than 5% of the balance at May 31, 2011 and 2010.

Note 6 — Fair Value Measurements

The Company measures certain financial assets and liabilities at fair value on a recurring basis, including derivatives and available-for-sale securities. Fair value is a market-based measurement that should be determined based on the assumptions that market participants would use in pricing an asset or liability. As a basis for

67

NIKE, INC.

NOTES TO CONSOLIDATED FINANCIAL STATEMENTS — (Continued)

considering such assumptions, the Company uses a three-level hierarchy established by the FASB that prioritizes fair value measurements based on the types of inputs used for the various valuation techniques (market approach, income approach, and cost approach).

The levels of hierarchy are described below:

- Level 1: Observable inputs such as quoted prices in active markets for identical assets or liabilities.

- Level 2: Inputs other than quoted prices that are observable for the asset or liability, either directly or indirectly; these include quoted prices for similar assets or liabilities in active markets and quoted prices for identical or similar assets or liabilities in markets that are not active.

- Level 3: Unobservable inputs in which there is little or no market data available, which require the reporting entity to develop its own assumptions.

The Company's assessment of the significance of a particular input to the fair value measurement in its entirety requires judgment and considers factors specific to the asset or liability. Financial assets and liabilities are classified in their entirety based on the most stringent level of input that is significant to the fair value measurement.

The following table presents information about the Company's financial assets and liabilities measured at fair value on a recurring basis as of May 31, 2011 and 2010 and indicates the fair value hierarchy of the valuation techniques utilized by the Company to determine such fair value.

	May 31, 2011				
	Fair Value Measurements Using			Assets /Liabilities at Fair Value	Balance Sheet Classification
	Level 1	Level 2	Level 3		
	(In millions)				
Assets					
Derivatives:					
Foreign exchange forwards and options	$ —	$ 38	$ —	$ 38	Other current assets and other long-term assets
Interest rate swap contracts	—	15	—	15	Other current assets and other long-term assets
Total derivatives	—	53	—	53	
Available-for-sale securities:					
U.S. Treasury securities	125	—	—	125	Cash equivalents
Commercial paper and bonds	—	157	—	157	Cash equivalents
Money market funds	—	780	—	780	Cash equivalents
U.S. Treasury securities	1,473	—	—	1,473	Short-term investments
U.S. Agency securities	—	308	—	308	Short-term investments
Commercial paper and bonds	—	802	—	802	Short-term investments
Total available-for-sale securities	1,598	2,047	—	3,645	
Total Assets	$ 1,598	$ 2,100	$ —	$ 3,698	
Liabilities					
Derivatives:					
Foreign exchange forwards and options	$ —	$ 197	$ —	$ 197	Accrued liabilities and other long-term liabilities
Total Liabilities	$ —	$ 197	$ —	$ 197	

68

NIKE, INC.
NOTES TO CONSOLIDATED FINANCIAL STATEMENTS — (Continued)

	May 31, 2010				
	Fair Value Measurements Using			Assets /Liabilities at Fair Value	Balance Sheet Classification
	Level 1	Level 2	Level 3		
	(In millions)				
Assets					
Derivatives:					
Foreign exchange forwards and options	$ —	$ 420	$ —	$ 420	Other current assets and other long-term assets
Interest rate swap contracts	—	15	—	15	Other current assets and other long-term assets
Total derivatives	—	435	—	435	
Available-for-sale securities:					
U.S. Treasury securities	1,232	—	—	1,232	Cash equivalents
Commercial paper and bonds	—	462	—	462	Cash equivalents
Money market funds	—	685	—	685	Cash equivalents
U.S. Treasury securities	1,085	—	—	1,085	Short-term investments
U.S. Agency securities	—	298	—	298	Short-term investments
Commercial paper and bonds	—	684	—	684	Short-term investments
Total available-for-sale securities	2,317	2,129	—	4,446	
Total Assets	$ 2,317	$ 2,564	$ —	$ 4,881	
Liabilities					
Derivatives:					
Foreign exchange forwards and options	$ —	$ 165	$ —	$ 165	Accrued liabilities and other long-term liabilities
Total Liabilities	$ —	$ 165	$ —	$ 165	

Derivative financial instruments include foreign currency forwards, option contracts and interest rate swaps. The fair value of these derivatives contracts is determined using observable market inputs such as the forward pricing curve, currency volatilities, currency correlations and interest rates, and considers nonperformance risk of the Company and that of its counterparties. Adjustments relating to these risks were not material for the years ended May 31, 2011 and 2010.

Available-for-sale securities are primarily comprised of investments in U.S. Treasury and agency securities, commercial paper, bonds and money market funds. These securities are valued using market prices on both active markets (level 1) and less active markets (level 2). Level 1 instrument valuations are obtained from real-time quotes for transactions in active exchange markets involving identical assets. Level 2 instrument valuations are obtained from readily-available pricing sources for comparable instruments.

As of May 31, 2011 and 2010, the Company had no material Level 3 measurements and no assets or liabilities measured at fair value on a non-recurring basis.

Short-Term Investments

As of May 31, 2011 and 2010, short-term investments consisted of available-for-sale securities. As of May 31, 2011, the Company held $2,253 million of available-for-sale securities with maturity dates within one year and $330 million with maturity dates over one year and less than five years within short-term investments. As of May 31, 2010, the Company held $1,900 million of available-for-sale securities with maturity dates within one year and $167 million with maturity dates over one year and less than five years within short-term investments.

NIKE, INC.

NOTES TO CONSOLIDATED FINANCIAL STATEMENTS — (Continued)

Short-term investments classified as available-for-sale consist of the following at fair value:

	As of May 31,	
	2011	2010
	(In millions)	
Available-for-sale investments:		
U.S. treasury and agencies	$1,781	$1,383
Commercial paper and bonds	802	684
Total available-for-sale investments	$2,583	$2,067

Included in interest expense (income), net for the years ended May 31, 2011, 2010, and 2009 was interest income of $30 million, $30 million, and $50 million, respectively, related to cash and equivalents and short-term investments.

For fair value information regarding notes payable and long-term debt, refer to Note 7 — Short-Term Borrowings and Credit Lines and Note 8 — Long-Term Debt.

Note 7 — Short-Term Borrowings and Credit Lines

Notes payable to banks and interest-bearing accounts payable to Sojitz Corporation of America ("Sojitz America") as of May 31, 2011 and 2010, are summarized below:

	May 31,			
	2011		2010	
	Borrowings	Interest Rate	Borrowings	Interest Rate
	(In millions)			
Notes payable:				
U.S. operations	35	—[1]	18	—[1]
Non-U.S. operations	152	7.05%[1]	121	6.35%[1]
	$ 187		$ 139	
Sojitz America	$ 111	0.99%	$ 88	1.07%

[1] Weighted average interest rate includes non-interest bearing overdrafts.

The carrying amounts reflected in the consolidated balance sheet for notes payable approximate fair value.

The Company purchases through Sojitz America certain athletic footwear, apparel and equipment it acquires from non-U.S. suppliers. These purchases are for the Company's operations outside of the United States, Europe and Japan. Accounts payable to Sojitz America are generally due up to 60 days after shipment of goods from the foreign port. The interest rate on such accounts payable is the 60-day London Interbank Offered Rate ("LIBOR") as of the beginning of the month of the invoice date, plus 0.75%.

As of May 31, 2011 and 2010, the Company had no amounts outstanding under its commercial paper program.

In December 2006, the Company entered into a $1 billion revolving credit facility with a group of banks. The facility matures in December 2012. Based on the Company's current long-term senior unsecured debt ratings of A+ and A1 from Standard and Poor's Corporation and Moody's Investor Services, respectively, the interest

70

NIKE, INC.

NOTES TO CONSOLIDATED FINANCIAL STATEMENTS — (Continued)

rate charged on any outstanding borrowings would be the prevailing LIBOR plus 0.15%. The facility fee is 0.05% of the total commitment. Under this agreement, the Company must maintain, among other things, certain minimum specified financial ratios with which the Company was in compliance at May 31, 2011. No amounts were outstanding under this facility as of May 31, 2011 and 2010.

Note 8 — Long-Term Debt

Long-term debt, net of unamortized premiums and discounts and swap fair value adjustments, is comprised of the following:

	May 31,	
	2011	2010
	(In millions)	
5.66% Corporate bond, payable July 23, 2012	$ 26	$ 27
5.40% Corporate bond, payable August 7, 2012	16	16
4.70% Corporate bond, payable October 1, 2013	50	50
5.15% Corporate bond, payable October 15, 2015	114	112
4.30% Japanese Yen note, payable June 26, 2011	130	116
1.52% Japanese Yen note, payable February 14, 2012	62	55
2.60% Japanese Yen note, maturing August 20, 2001 through November 20, 2020	54	53
2.00% Japanese Yen note, maturing August 20, 2001 through November 20, 2020	24	24
Total	476	453
Less current maturities	200	7
	$276	$446

The scheduled maturity of long-term debt in each of the years ending May 31, 2012 through 2016 are $200 million, $48 million, $58 million, $8 million and $109 million, at face value, respectively.

The Company's long-term debt is recorded at adjusted cost, net of amortized premiums and discounts and interest rate swap fair value adjustments. The fair value of long-term debt is estimated based upon quoted prices for similar instruments. The fair value of the Company's long-term debt, including the current portion, was approximately $482 million at May 31, 2011 and $453 million at May 31, 2010.

In fiscal years 2003 and 2004, the Company issued a total of $240 million in medium-term notes of which $190 million, at face value, were outstanding at May 31, 2011. The outstanding notes have coupon rates that range from 4.70% to 5.66% and maturity dates ranging from July 2012 to October 2015. For each of these notes, except the $50 million note maturing in October 2013, the Company has entered into interest rate swap agreements whereby the Company receives fixed interest payments at the same rate as the notes and pays variable interest payments based on the six-month LIBOR plus a spread. Each swap has the same notional amount and maturity date as the corresponding note. At May 31, 2011, the interest rates payable on these swap agreements ranged from approximately 0.3% to 1.0%.

In June 1996, one of the Company's wholly owned Japanese subsidiaries, NIKE Logistics YK, borrowed ¥10.5 billion (approximately $130 million as of May 31, 2011) in a private placement with a maturity of June 26, 2011. Interest is paid semi-annually. The agreement provides for early retirement of the borrowing.

In July 1999, NIKE Logistics YK assumed a total of ¥13.0 billion in loans as part of its agreement to purchase a distribution center in Japan, which serves as collateral for the loans. These loans mature in equal quarterly installments during the period August 20, 2001 through November 20, 2020. Interest is also paid quarterly. As of May 31, 2011, ¥6.3 billion (approximately $78 million) in loans remain outstanding.

71

NIKE, INC.

NOTES TO CONSOLIDATED FINANCIAL STATEMENTS — (Continued)

In February 2007, NIKE Logistics YK entered into a ¥5.0 billion (approximately $62 million as of May 31, 2011) term loan that replaced certain intercompany borrowings and matures on February 14, 2012. The interest rate on the loan is approximately 1.5% and interest is paid semi-annually.

Note 9 — Income Taxes

Income before income taxes is as follows:

	Year Ended May 31,		
	2011	2010	2009
	(In millions)		
Income before income taxes:			
United States	$1,084	$ 699	$ 846
Foreign	1,760	1,818	1,111
	$2,844	$2,517	$1,957

The provision for income taxes is as follows:

	Year Ended May 31,		
	2011	2010	2009
	(In millions)		
Current:			
United States			
Federal	$289	$200	$ 410
State	57	50	46
Foreign	441	349	308
	787	599	764
Deferred:			
United States			
Federal	(61)	18	(251)
State	—	(1)	(8)
Foreign	(15)	(6)	(35)
	(76)	11	(294)
	$711	$610	$ 470

A reconciliation from the U.S. statutory federal income tax rate to the effective income tax rate follows:

	Year Ended May 31,		
	2011	2010	2009
Federal income tax rate	35.0%	35.0%	35.0%
State taxes, net of federal benefit	1.3%	1.3%	1.2%
Foreign earnings	-10.2%	-13.6%	-14.9%
Other, net	-1.1%	1.5%	2.7%
Effective income tax rate	25.0%	24.2%	24.0%

The effective tax rate for the year ended May 31, 2011 of 25.0% increased from the fiscal 2010 effective tax rate of 24.2% due primarily to the change in geographic mix of earnings. A larger percentage of our earnings before income taxes in the current year are attributable to operations in the United States where the statutory tax rate is generally higher than the tax rate on operations outside of the U.S. This impact was partially offset by

72

NIKE, INC.

NOTES TO CONSOLIDATED FINANCIAL STATEMENTS — (Continued)

changes to uncertain tax positions. Our effective tax rate for the year ended May 31, 2010 of 24.2% increased from the fiscal 2009 effective rate of 24.0%. The effective tax rate for fiscal 2009 includes a tax benefit related to charges recorded for the impairment of Umbro's goodwill, intangible and other assets.

Deferred tax assets and (liabilities) are comprised of the following:

	May 31,	
	2011	2010
	(In millions)	
Deferred tax assets:		
Allowance for doubtful accounts	$ 19	$ 17
Inventories	63	47
Sales return reserves	72	52
Deferred compensation	152	144
Stock-based compensation	148	145
Reserves and accrued liabilities	66	86
Foreign loss carry-forwards	60	26
Foreign tax credit carry-forwards	236	148
Hedges	21	1
Undistributed earnings of foreign subsidiaries	—	128
Other	86	37
Total deferred tax assets	923	831
Valuation allowance	(51)	(36)
Total deferred tax assets after valuation allowance	872	795
Deferred tax liabilities:		
Undistributed earnings of foreign subsidiaries	(40)	—
Property, plant and equipment	(151)	(99)
Intangibles	(97)	(99)
Hedges	(1)	(72)
Other	(20)	(8)
Total deferred tax liability	(309)	(278)
Net deferred tax asset	$ 563	$ 517

The following is a reconciliation of the changes in the gross balance of unrecognized tax benefits:

	May 31,		
	2011	2010	2009
		(In millions)	
Unrecognized tax benefits, as of the beginning of the period	$282	$ 274	$251
Gross increases related to prior period tax positions	13	87	53
Gross decreases related to prior period tax positions	(98)	(122)	(62)
Gross increases related to current period tax positions	59	52	72
Gross decreases related to current period tax positions	(6)	—	—
Settlements	(43)	(3)	(29)
Lapse of statute of limitations	(8)	(9)	(4)
Changes due to currency translation	13	3	(7)
Unrecognized tax benefits, as of the end of the period	$212	$ 282	$274

73

NIKE, INC.

NOTES TO CONSOLIDATED FINANCIAL STATEMENTS — (Continued)

As of May 31, 2011, the total gross unrecognized tax benefits, excluding related interest and penalties, were $212 million, $93 million of which would affect the Company's effective tax rate if recognized in future periods. Total gross unrecognized tax benefits, excluding interest and penalties, as of May 31, 2010 and 2009 was $282 million and $274 million, respectively.

The Company recognizes interest and penalties related to income tax matters in income tax expense. The liability for payment of interest and penalties increased $10 million, $6 million, and $2 million during the years ended May 31, 2011, 2010, and 2009, respectively. As of May 31, 2011 and 2010, accrued interest and penalties related to uncertain tax positions was $91 million and $81 million, respectively (excluding federal benefit).

The Company is subject to taxation primarily in the U.S., China and the Netherlands as well as various state and other foreign jurisdictions. The Company has concluded substantially all U.S. federal income tax matters through fiscal year 2009. The Company is currently under audit by the Internal Revenue Service for the 2010 tax year. The Company's major foreign jurisdictions, China and the Netherlands, have concluded substantially all income tax matters through calendar 2000 and fiscal 2005, respectively. The Company estimates that it is reasonably possible that the total gross unrecognized tax benefits could decrease by up to $69 million within the next 12 months as a result of resolutions of global tax examinations and the expiration of applicable statutes of limitations.

The Company has indefinitely reinvested approximately $4.4 billion of the cumulative undistributed earnings of certain foreign subsidiaries. Such earnings would be subject to U.S. taxation if repatriated to the U.S. Determination of the amount of unrecognized deferred tax liability associated with the indefinitely reinvested cumulative undistributed earnings is not practicable.

A portion of the Company's foreign operations are benefitting from a tax holiday that will phase out in 2019. The decrease in income tax expense for the year ended May 31, 2011 as a result of this arrangement was approximately $36 million ($0.07 per diluted share) and $30 million ($0.06 per diluted share) for the year ended May 31, 2010.

Deferred tax assets at May 31, 2011 and 2010 were reduced by a valuation allowance relating to tax benefits of certain subsidiaries with operating losses where it is more likely than not that the deferred tax assets will not be realized. The net change in the valuation allowance was an increase of $15 million and $10 million for the years ended May 31, 2011 and 2010, respectively and a decrease of $15 million for the year ended May 31, 2009.

The Company does not anticipate that any foreign tax credit carry-forwards will expire. The Company has available domestic and foreign loss carry-forwards of $183 million at May 31, 2011. Such losses will expire as follows:

	Year Ending May 31,						
	2013	2014	2015	2016	2017-2028	Indefinite	Total
				(In millions)			
Net Operating Losses	$ 7	$10	$ 4	$10	$ 91	$ 61	$183

During the years ended May 31, 2011, 2010, and 2009, income tax benefits attributable to employee stock-based compensation transactions of $68 million, $57 million, and $25 million, respectively, were allocated to shareholders' equity.

74

NIKE, INC.
NOTES TO CONSOLIDATED FINANCIAL STATEMENTS — (Continued)

Note 10 — Redeemable Preferred Stock

Sojitz America is the sole owner of the Company's authorized Redeemable Preferred Stock, $1 par value, which is redeemable at the option of Sojitz America or the Company at par value aggregating $0.3 million. A cumulative dividend of $0.10 per share is payable annually on May 31 and no dividends may be declared or paid on the common stock of the Company unless dividends on the Redeemable Preferred Stock have been declared and paid in full. There have been no changes in the Redeemable Preferred Stock in the three years ended May 31, 2011, 2010, and 2009. As the holder of the Redeemable Preferred Stock, Sojitz America does not have general voting rights but does have the right to vote as a separate class on the sale of all or substantially all of the assets of the Company and its subsidiaries, on merger, consolidation, liquidation or dissolution of the Company or on the sale or assignment of the NIKE trademark for athletic footwear sold in the United States.

Note 11 — Common Stock and Stock-Based Compensation

The authorized number of shares of Class A Common Stock, no par value, and Class B Common Stock, no par value, are 175 million and 750 million, respectively. Each share of Class A Common Stock is convertible into one share of Class B Common Stock. Voting rights of Class B Common Stock are limited in certain circumstances with respect to the election of directors.

In 1990, the Board of Directors adopted, and the shareholders approved, the NIKE, Inc. 1990 Stock Incentive Plan (the "1990 Plan"). The 1990 Plan provides for the issuance of up to 163 million previously unissued shares of Class B Common Stock in connection with stock options and other awards granted under the plan. The 1990 Plan authorizes the grant of non-statutory stock options, incentive stock options, stock appreciation rights, restricted stock, restricted stock units, and performance-based awards. The exercise price for stock options and stock appreciation rights may not be less than the fair market value of the underlying shares on the date of grant. A committee of the Board of Directors administers the 1990 Plan. The committee has the authority to determine the employees to whom awards will be made, the amount of the awards, and the other terms and conditions of the awards. Substantially all stock option grants outstanding under the 1990 Plan were granted in the first quarter of each fiscal year, vest ratably over four years, and expire 10 years from the date of grant.

The following table summarizes the Company's total stock-based compensation expense recognized in selling and administrative expense:

	Year Ended May 31,		
	2011	**2010**	**2009**
		(in millions)	
Stock options[1]	$ 77	$135	$129
ESPPs	14	14	14
Restricted stock	14	10	8
Subtotal	105	159	151
Stock options and restricted stock expense — restructuring [2]	—	—	20
Total stock-based compensation expense	$105	$159	$171

---

[1] Expense for stock options includes the expense associated with stock appreciation rights. Accelerated stock option expense is recorded for employees eligible for accelerated stock option vesting upon retirement. In the first quarter of fiscal 2011, the Company changed the accelerated vesting provisions of its stock option plan. Under the new provisions, accelerated stock option expense for year ended May 31, 2011 was $12 million. The accelerated stock option expense for the years ended May 31, 2010 and 2009 was $74 million and $59 million, respectively.

75

Source: Nike, Inc. 2011 10-K

NIKE, INC.

NOTES TO CONSOLIDATED FINANCIAL STATEMENTS — (Continued)

(2) In connection with the restructuring activities that took place during fiscal 2009, the Company recognized stock-based compensation expense relating to the modification of stock option agreements, allowing for an extended post-termination exercise period, and accelerated vesting of restricted stock as part of severance packages. See Note 16 — Restructuring Charges for further details.

As of May 31, 2011, the Company had $111 million of unrecognized compensation costs from stock options, net of estimated forfeitures, to be recognized as selling and administrative expense over a weighted average period of 2.2 years.

The weighted average fair value per share of the options granted during the years ended May 31, 2011, 2010, and 2009, as computed using the Black-Scholes pricing model, was $17.68, $23.43, and $17.13, respectively. The weighted average assumptions used to estimate these fair values are as follows:

	Year Ended May 31,		
	2011	**2010**	**2009**
Dividend yield	1.6%	1.9%	1.5%
Expected volatility	31.5%	57.6%	32.5%
Weighted average expected life (in years)	5.0	5.0	5.0
Risk-free interest rate	1.7%	2.5%	3.4%

The Company estimates the expected volatility based on the implied volatility in market traded options on the Company's common stock with a term greater than one year, along with other factors. The weighted average expected life of options is based on an analysis of historical and expected future exercise patterns. The interest rate is based on the U.S. Treasury (constant maturity) risk-free rate in effect at the date of grant for periods corresponding with the expected term of the options.

The following summarizes the stock option transactions under the plan discussed above:

	Shares[1] (In millions)	Weighted Average Option Price
Options outstanding May 31, 2008	36.6	$ 40.14
Exercised	(4.0)	35.70
Forfeited	(1.3)	51.19
Granted	7.5	58.17
Options outstanding May 31, 2009	38.8	$ 43.69
Exercised	(8.6)	37.64
Forfeited	(0.6)	51.92
Granted	6.4	52.79
Options outstanding May 31, 2010	36.0	$ 46.60
Exercised	(7.0)	42.70
Forfeited	(0.5)	58.08
Granted	6.3	69.20
Options outstanding May 31, 2011	34.8	$ 51.29
Options exercisable at May 31,		
2009	21.4	$ 36.91
2010	20.4	41.16
2011	20.1	$ 44.05

[1] Includes stock appreciation rights transactions.

76

NIKE, INC.
NOTES TO CONSOLIDATED FINANCIAL STATEMENTS — (Continued)

The weighted average contractual life remaining for options outstanding and options exercisable at May 31, 2011 was 6.0 years and 4.5 years, respectively. The aggregate intrinsic value for options outstanding and exercisable at May 31, 2011 was $1,154 million and $811 million, respectively. The aggregate intrinsic value was the amount by which the market value of the underlying stock exceeded the exercise price of the options. The total intrinsic value of the options exercised during the years ended May 31, 2011, 2010, and 2009 was $267 million, $239 million, and $108 million, respectively.

In addition to the 1990 Plan, the Company gives employees the right to purchase shares at a discount to the market price under employee stock purchase plans ("ESPPs"). Employees are eligible to participate through payroll deductions up to 10% of their compensation. At the end of each six-month offering period, shares are purchased by the participants at 85% of the lower of the fair market value at the beginning or the end of the offering period. Employees purchased 0.8 million shares during the years ended May 31, 2011 and 2010, and 1.0 million shares during the year ended May 31, 2009.

From time to time, the Company grants restricted stock and unrestricted stock to key employees under the 1990 Plan. The number of shares granted to employees during the years ended May 31, 2011, 2010, and 2009 were 0.2 million, 0.5 million, and 0.1 million with weighted average values per share of $70.23, $53.16, and $56.97, respectively. Recipients of restricted shares are entitled to cash dividends and to vote their respective shares throughout the period of restriction. The value of all of the granted shares was established by the market price on the date of grant. During the years ended May 31, 2011, 2010, and 2009, the fair value of restricted shares vested was $15 million, $8 million, and $10 million, respectively, determined as of the date of vesting.

Note 12 — Earnings Per Share

The following is a reconciliation from basic earnings per share to diluted earnings per share. Options to purchase an additional 0.2 million, 0.2 million, and 13.2 million shares of common stock were outstanding at May 31, 2011, 2010, and 2009, respectively, but were not included in the computation of diluted earnings per share because the options were anti-dilutive.

	Year Ended May 31,		
	2011	2010	2009
	(In millions, except per share data)		
Determination of shares:			
Weighted average common shares outstanding	475.5	485.5	484.9
Assumed conversion of dilutive stock options and awards	10.2	8.4	5.8
Diluted weighted average common shares outstanding	485.7	493.9	490.7
Basic earnings per common share	$ 4.48	$ 3.93	$ 3.07
Diluted earnings per common share	$ 4.39	$ 3.86	$ 3.03

Note 13 — Benefit Plans

The Company has a profit sharing plan available to most U.S.-based employees. The terms of the plan call for annual contributions by the Company as determined by the Board of Directors. A subsidiary of the Company also has a profit sharing plan available to its U.S.-based employees. The terms of the plan call for annual contributions as determined by the subsidiary's executive management. Contributions of $39 million, $35 million, and $28 million were made to the plans and are included in selling and administrative expense for the years ended May 31, 2011, 2010, and 2009, respectively. The Company has various 401(k) employee savings

77

NIKE, INC.

NOTES TO CONSOLIDATED FINANCIAL STATEMENTS — (Continued)

plans available to U.S.-based employees. The Company matches a portion of employee contributions. Company contributions to the savings plans were $39 million, $34 million, and $38 million for the years ended May 31, 2011, 2010, and 2009, respectively, and are included in selling and administrative expense.

The Company also has a Long-Term Incentive Plan ("LTIP") that was adopted by the Board of Directors and approved by shareholders in September 1997 and later amended in fiscal 2007. The Company recognized $31 million, $24 million, and $18 million of selling and administrative expense related to cash awards under the LTIP during the years ended May 31, 2011, 2010, and 2009, respectively.

The Company has pension plans in various countries worldwide. The pension plans are only available to local employees and are generally government mandated. The liability related to the unfunded pension liabilities of the plans was $93 million and $113 million at May 31, 2011 and 2010, respectively, which was primarily classified as long-term in other liabilities.

Note 14 — Accumulated Other Comprehensive Income

The components of accumulated other comprehensive income, net of tax, are as follows:

	May 31,	
	2011	2010
	(In millions)	
Cumulative translation adjustment and other	$ 168	$ (95)
Net deferred gain on net investment hedge derivatives	50	107
Net deferred (loss) gain on cash flow hedge derivatives	(123)	203
	$ 95	$215

Note 15 — Commitments and Contingencies

The Company leases space for certain of its offices, warehouses and retail stores under leases expiring from 1 to 24 years after May 31, 2011. Rent expense was $446 million, $416 million, and $397 million for the years ended May 31, 2011, 2010 and 2009, respectively. Amounts of minimum future annual rental commitments under non-cancelable operating leases in each of the five years ending May 31, 2012 through 2016 are $374 million, $310 million, $253 million, $198 million, $174 million, respectively, and $535 million in later years.

As of May 31, 2011 and 2010, the Company had letters of credit outstanding totaling $99 million and $101 million, respectively. These letters of credit were generally issued for the purchase of inventory.

In connection with various contracts and agreements, the Company provides routine indemnifications relating to the enforceability of intellectual property rights, coverage for legal issues that arise and other items where the Company is acting as the guarantor. Currently, the Company has several such agreements in place. However, based on the Company's historical experience and the estimated probability of future loss, the Company has determined that the fair value of such indemnifications is not material to the Company's financial position or results of operations.

In the ordinary course of its business, the Company is involved in various legal proceedings involving contractual and employment relationships, product liability claims, trademark rights, and a variety of other matters. The Company does not believe there are any pending legal proceedings that will have a material impact on the Company's financial position or results of operations.

78

NIKE, INC.
NOTES TO CONSOLIDATED FINANCIAL STATEMENTS — (Continued)

Note 16 — Restructuring Charges

During fiscal 2009, the Company took necessary steps to streamline its management structure, enhance consumer focus, drive innovation more quickly to market and establish a more scalable, long-term cost structure. As a result, the Company reduced its global workforce by approximately 5% and incurred pre-tax restructuring charges of $195 million, primarily consisting of severance costs related to the workforce reduction. As nearly all of the restructuring activities were completed in fiscal 2009, the Company did not recognize additional costs relating to these actions. The restructuring charge is reflected in the corporate expense line in the segment presentation of earnings before interest and taxes in Note 18 — Operating Segments and Related Information. The restructuring accrual included in accrued liabilities in the consolidated balance sheet was $3 million and $8 million as of May 31, 2011 and 2010, respectively.

Note 17 — Risk Management and Derivatives

The Company is exposed to global market risks, including the effect of changes in foreign currency exchange rates and interest rates, and uses derivatives to manage financial exposures that occur in the normal course of business. The Company does not hold or issue derivatives for trading purposes.

The Company formally documents all relationships between formally designated hedging instruments and hedged items, as well as its risk management objective and strategy for undertaking hedge transactions. This process includes linking all derivatives to either specific firm commitments or forecasted transactions. The Company also enters into foreign exchange forwards to mitigate the change in fair value of specific assets and liabilities on the balance sheet, which are not designated as hedging instruments under the accounting standards for derivatives and hedging. Accordingly, changes in the fair value of these non-designated instruments of recorded balance sheet positions are recognized immediately in other (income), net, on the income statement together with the transaction gain or loss from the hedged balance sheet position. The Company classifies the cash flows at settlement from these undesignated instruments in the same category as the cash flows from the related hedged items, generally within the cash provided by operations component of the cash flow statement.

The majority of derivatives outstanding as of May 31, 2011 are designated as cash flow, fair value or net investment hedges. All derivatives are recognized on the balance sheet at their fair value and classified based on the instrument's maturity date. The total notional amount of outstanding derivatives as of May 31, 2011 was $7 billion, which is primarily comprised of cash flow hedges for Euro/U.S. Dollar, British Pound/Euro, and Japanese Yen/U.S. Dollar currency pairs.

79

NIKE, INC.

NOTES TO CONSOLIDATED FINANCIAL STATEMENTS — (Continued)

The following table presents the fair values of derivative instruments included within the consolidated balance sheet as of May 31, 2011 and 2010:

| | Asset Derivatives | | | Liability Derivatives | | |
	Balance Sheet Location	May 31, 2011	May 31, 2010	Balance Sheet Location	May 31, 2011	May 31, 2010
			(in millions)			
Derivatives formally designated as hedging instruments:						
Foreign exchange forwards and options	Prepaid expenses and other current assets	$ 22	$ 316	Accrued liabilities	$ 170	$ 25
Foreign exchange forwards and options	Deferred income taxes and other long-term assets	7	—	Deferred income taxes and other long-term liabilities	10	—
Interest rate swap contracts	Deferred income taxes and other long-term assets	15	15	Deferred income taxes and other long-term liabilities	—	—
Total derivatives formally designated as hedging instruments		44	331		180	25
Derivatives not designated as hedging instruments:						
Foreign exchange forwards and options	Prepaid expenses and other current assets	$ 9	$ 104	Accrued liabilities	$ 16	$ 139
Foreign exchange forwards and options	Deferred income taxes and other long-term assets	—	—	Deferred income taxes and other long-term liabilities	1	1
Total derivatives not designated as hedging instruments		9	104		17	140
Total derivatives		$ 53	$ 435		$ 197	$ 165

The following tables present the amounts affecting the consolidated statements of income for years ended May 31, 2011, 2010 and 2009:

| | Amount of Gain (Loss) Recognized in Other Comprehensive Income on Derivatives[1] | | | Amount of Gain (Loss) Reclassified From Accumulated Other Comprehensive Income into Income[1] | | | |
| | Year Ended May 31, | | | Location of Gain (Loss) Reclassified From Accumulated Other Comprehensive Income Into Income[1] | Year Ended May 31, | | |
Derivatives formally designated	2011	2010	2009		2011	2010	2009
				(in millions)			
Derivatives designated as cash flow hedges:							
Foreign exchange forwards and options	$ (87)	$ (30)	$ 106	Revenue	$ (30)	$ 51	$ 93
Foreign exchange forwards and options	(152)	89	350	Cost of sales	103	60	(14)
Foreign exchange forwards and options	(4)	5	—	Selling and administrative expense	1	1	1
Foreign exchange forwards and options	(65)	51	165	Other (income), net	34	56	68
Total designated cash flow hedges	$ (308)	$ 115	$ 621		$ 108	$ 168	$ 148
Derivatives designated as net investment hedges:							
Foreign exchange forwards and options	$ (85)	$ 66	$ 161	Other (income), net	$ —	$ —	$ —

[1] For the year ended May 31, 2011 and 2009, the Company recorded an immaterial amount of ineffectiveness from cash flow hedges in other (income), net. For the year ended May 31, 2010, $5 million of ineffectiveness from cash flow hedges was recorded in other (income), net.

80

NIKE, INC.

NOTES TO CONSOLIDATED FINANCIAL STATEMENTS — (Continued)

	Amount of Gain (Loss) recognized in Income on Derivatives Year Ended May 31, (in millions)			Location of Gain (Loss) Recognized in Income on Derivatives
	2011	2010	2009	
Derivatives designated as fair value hedges:				
Interest rate swaps[1]	$ 6	$ 7	$ 2	Interest expense (income), net
Derivatives not designated as hedging instruments:				
Foreign exchange forwards and options	$(30)	$(91)	$(83)	Other (income), net

[1] All interest rate swap agreements meet the shortcut method requirements under the accounting standards for derivatives and hedging. Accordingly, changes in the fair values of the interest rate swap agreements are exactly offset by changes in the fair value of the underlying long-term debt. Refer to section "Fair Value Hedges" for additional detail.

Refer to Note 5 — Accrued Liabilities for derivative instruments recorded in accrued liabilities, Note 6 —Fair Value Measurements for a description of how the above financial instruments are valued, Note 14 — Accumulated Other Comprehensive Income and the consolidated statements of shareholders' equity for additional information on changes in other comprehensive income for the years ended May 31, 2011, 2010 and 2009.

Cash Flow Hedges

The purpose of the Company's foreign currency hedging activities is to protect the Company from the risk that the eventual cash flows resulting from transactions in foreign currencies, including revenues, product costs, selling and administrative expense, investments in U.S. dollar-denominated available-for-sale debt securities and intercompany transactions, including intercompany borrowings, will be adversely affected by changes in exchange rates. It is the Company's policy to utilize derivatives to reduce foreign exchange risks where internal netting strategies cannot be effectively employed. Hedged transactions are denominated primarily in Euros, British Pounds and Japanese Yen. The Company hedges up to 100% of anticipated exposures typically 12 months in advance, but has hedged as much as 34 months in advance.

All changes in fair values of outstanding cash flow hedge derivatives, except the ineffective portion, are recorded in other comprehensive income until net income is affected by the variability of cash flows of the hedged transaction. In most cases, amounts recorded in other comprehensive income will be released to net income some time after the maturity of the related derivative. The consolidated statement of income classification of effective hedge results is the same as that of the underlying exposure. Results of hedges of revenue and product costs are recorded in revenue and cost of sales, respectively, when the underlying hedged transaction affects net income. Results of hedges of selling and administrative expense are recorded together with those costs when the related expense is recorded. Results of hedges of forecasted purchases of U.S. dollar-denominated available-for-sale securities are recorded in other (income), net when the securities are sold. Results of hedges of forecasted intercompany transactions are recorded in other (income), net when the transaction occurs. The Company classifies the cash flows at settlement from these designated cash flow hedge derivatives in the same category as the cash flows from the related hedged items, generally within the cash provided by operations component of the cash flow statement.

Premiums paid on options are initially recorded as deferred charges. The Company assesses the effectiveness of options based on the total cash flows method and records total changes in the options' fair value to other comprehensive income to the degree they are effective.

81

NIKE, INC.
NOTES TO CONSOLIDATED FINANCIAL STATEMENTS — (Continued)

As of May 31, 2011, $120 million of deferred net losses (net of tax) on both outstanding and matured derivatives accumulated in other comprehensive income are expected to be reclassified to net income during the next 12 months as a result of underlying hedged transactions also being recorded in net income. Actual amounts ultimately reclassified to net income are dependent on the exchange rates in effect when derivative contracts that are currently outstanding mature. As of May 31, 2011, the maximum term over which the Company is hedging exposures to the variability of cash flows for its forecasted and recorded transactions is 15 months.

The Company formally assesses both at a hedge's inception and on an ongoing basis, whether the derivatives that are used in the hedging transaction have been highly effective in offsetting changes in the cash flows of hedged items and whether those derivatives may be expected to remain highly effective in future periods. Effectiveness for cash flow hedges is assessed based on forward rates. When it is determined that a derivative is not, or has ceased to be, highly effective as a hedge, the Company discontinues hedge accounting.

The Company discontinues hedge accounting prospectively when (1) it determines that the derivative is no longer highly effective in offsetting changes in the cash flows of a hedged item (including hedged items such as firm commitments or forecasted transactions); (2) the derivative expires or is sold, terminated, or exercised; (3) it is no longer probable that the forecasted transaction will occur; or (4) management determines that designating the derivative as a hedging instrument is no longer appropriate.

When the Company discontinues hedge accounting because it is no longer probable that the forecasted transaction will occur in the originally expected period, but is expected to occur within an additional two-month period of time thereafter, the gain or loss on the derivative remains in accumulated other comprehensive income and is reclassified to net income when the forecasted transaction affects net income. However, if it is probable that a forecasted transaction will not occur by the end of the originally specified time period or within an additional two-month period of time thereafter, the gains and losses that were accumulated in other comprehensive income will be recognized immediately in net income. In all situations in which hedge accounting is discontinued and the derivative remains outstanding, the Company will carry the derivative at its fair value on the balance sheet, recognizing future changes in the fair value in other (income), net. For the year ended May 31, 2011 an immaterial amount of ineffectiveness was recorded to other (income), net. For the years ended May 31, 2010 and 2009, the Company recorded in other (income), net $5 million gain and an immaterial amount of ineffectiveness from cash flow hedges, respectively.

Fair Value Hedges

The Company is also exposed to the risk of changes in the fair value of certain fixed-rate debt attributable to changes in interest rates. Derivatives currently used by the Company to hedge this risk are receive-fixed, pay-variable interest rate swaps. As of May 31, 2011, all interest rate swap agreements are designated as fair value hedges of the related long-term debt and meet the shortcut method requirements under the accounting standards for derivatives and hedging. Accordingly, changes in the fair values of the interest rate swap agreements are exactly offset by changes in the fair value of the underlying long-term debt. The cash flows associated with the Company's fair value hedges are periodic interest payments while the swaps are outstanding, which are reflected in net income within the cash provided by operations component of the cash flow statement. No ineffectiveness has been recorded to net income related to interest rate swaps designated as fair value hedges for the years ended May 31, 2011, 2010, and 2009.

In fiscal 2003, the Company entered into a receive-floating, pay-fixed interest rate swap agreement related to a Japanese Yen denominated intercompany loan with one of the Company's Japanese subsidiaries. This interest rate swap was not designated as a hedge under the accounting standards for derivatives and hedging.

82

NIKE, INC.
NOTES TO CONSOLIDATED FINANCIAL STATEMENTS — (Continued)

Accordingly, changes in the fair value of the swap were recorded to net income each period through maturity as a component of interest expense (income), net. Both the intercompany loan and the related interest rate swap matured during the year ended May 31, 2009.

Net Investment Hedges

The Company also hedges the risk of variability in foreign-currency-denominated net investments in wholly-owned international operations. All changes in fair value of the derivatives designated as net investment hedges, except ineffective portions, are reported in the cumulative translation adjustment component of other comprehensive income along with the foreign currency translation adjustments on those investments. The Company classifies the cash flows at settlement of its net investment hedges within the cash used by investing component of the cash flow statement. The Company assesses hedge effectiveness based on changes in forward rates. The Company recorded no ineffectiveness from its net investment hedges for the years ended May 31, 2011, 2010, and 2009.

Credit Risk

The Company is exposed to credit-related losses in the event of non-performance by counterparties to hedging instruments. The counterparties to all derivative transactions are major financial institutions with investment grade credit ratings. However, this does not eliminate the Company's exposure to credit risk with these institutions. This credit risk is limited to the unrealized gains in such contracts should any of these counterparties fail to perform as contracted. To manage this risk, the Company has established strict counterparty credit guidelines that are continually monitored and reported to senior management according to prescribed guidelines. The Company also utilizes a portfolio of financial institutions either headquartered or operating in the same countries the Company conducts its business.

The Company's derivative contracts contain credit risk related contingent features aiming to protect against significant deterioration in counterparties' creditworthiness and their ultimate ability to settle outstanding derivative contracts in the normal course of business. The Company's bilateral credit related contingent features require the owing entity, either the Company or the derivative counterparty, to post collateral should the fair value of outstanding derivatives per counterparty be greater than $50 million. Additionally, a certain level of decline in credit rating of either the Company or the counterparty could trigger collateral requirements. As of May 31, 2011, the Company was in compliance with all such credit risk related contingent features. The aggregate fair value of derivative instruments with credit risk related contingent features that are in a net liability position at May 31, 2011 was $160 million. The Company, or any counterparty, were not required to post any collateral as a result of these contingent features. As a result of the above considerations, the Company considers the impact of the risk of counterparty default to be immaterial.

Note 18 — Operating Segments and Related Information

Operating Segments. The Company's operating segments are evidence of the structure of the Company's internal organization. The major segments are defined by geographic regions for operations participating in NIKE Brand sales activity excluding NIKE Golf. Each NIKE Brand geographic segment operates predominantly in one industry: the design, development, marketing and selling of athletic footwear, apparel, and equipment. In fiscal 2009, the Company initiated a reorganization of the NIKE Brand into a new model consisting of six geographies. Effective June 1, 2009, the Company's new reportable operating segments for the NIKE Brand are: North America, Western Europe, Central and Eastern Europe, Greater China, Japan, and Emerging Markets. Previously, NIKE Brand operations were organized into the following four geographic regions: U.S., Europe, Middle East and Africa (collectively, "EMEA"), Asia Pacific, and Americas. The Company's NIKE Brand Direct to Consumer operations are managed within each geographic segment.

83

NIKE, INC.
NOTES TO CONSOLIDATED FINANCIAL STATEMENTS — (Continued)

The Company's "Other" category is broken into two components for presentation purposes to align with the way management views the Company. The "Global Brand Divisions" category primarily represents NIKE Brand licensing businesses that are not part of a geographic operating segment, selling, general and administrative expenses that are centrally managed for the NIKE Brand and costs associated with product development and supply chain operations. The "Other Businesses" category primarily consists of the activities of our affiliate brands; Cole Haan, Converse Inc., Hurley International LLC and Umbro International Limited; and NIKE Golf. Activities represented in the "Other" category are immaterial for individual disclosure.

Revenues as shown below represent sales to external customers for each segment. Intercompany revenues have been eliminated and are immaterial for separate disclosure.

Corporate consists of unallocated general and administrative expenses, which includes expenses associated with centrally managed departments, depreciation and amortization related to the Company's headquarters, unallocated insurance and benefit programs, including stock-based compensation, certain foreign currency gains and losses, including hedge gains and losses, certain corporate eliminations and other items.

Effective June 1, 2009, the primary financial measure used by the Company to evaluate performance of individual operating segments is Earnings Before Interest and Taxes (commonly referred to as "EBIT") which represents net income before interest expense (income), net and income taxes in the consolidated statements of income. Reconciling items for EBIT represent corporate expense items that are not allocated to the operating segments for management reporting. Previously, the Company evaluated performance of individual operating segments based on pre-tax income or income before income taxes.

As part of the Company's centrally managed foreign exchange risk management program, standard foreign currency rates are assigned to each NIKE Brand entity in our geographic operating segments and are used to record any non-functional currency revenues or product purchases into the entity's functional currency. Geographic operating segment revenues and cost of sales reflect use of these standard rates. For all NIKE Brand operating segments, differences between assigned standard foreign currency rates and actual market rates are included in Corporate together with foreign currency hedge gains and losses generated from the centrally managed foreign exchange risk management program and other conversion gains and losses. Prior to June 1, 2010, foreign currency results, including hedge results and other conversion gains and losses generated by the Western Europe and Central & Eastern Europe geographies were recorded in their respective geographic results.

Additions to long-lived assets as presented in the following table represent capital expenditures.

Accounts receivable, inventories and property, plant and equipment for operating segments are regularly reviewed by management and are therefore provided below.

Certain prior year amounts have been reclassified to conform to fiscal 2011 presentation, as South Africa became part of the Emerging Markets operating segment beginning June 1, 2010. Previously, South Africa was part of the Central & Eastern Europe operating segment.

NIKE, INC.

NOTES TO CONSOLIDATED FINANCIAL STATEMENTS — (Continued)

	Year Ended May 31,		
	2011	**2010**	**2009**
		(In millions)	
Revenue			
North America	$ 7,578	$ 6,696	$ 6,778
Western Europe	3,810	3,892	4,139
Central & Eastern Europe	1,031	993	1,247
Greater China	2,060	1,742	1,743
Japan	766	882	926
Emerging Markets	2,736	2,199	1,828
Global Brand Divisions	123	105	96
Total NIKE Brand	18,104	16,509	16,757
Other Businesses	2,747	2,530	2,419
Corporate	11	(25)	—
Total NIKE Consolidated Revenues	$20,862	$19,014	$19,176
Earnings Before Interest and Taxes			
North America	$ 1,750	$ 1,538	$ 1,429
Western Europe	721	856	939
Central & Eastern Europe	233	253	394
Greater China	777	637	575
Japan	114	180	205
Emerging Markets	688	521	364
Global Brand Divisions	(998)	(867)	(811)
Total NIKE Brand	3,285	3,118	3,095
Other Businesses[1]	334	299	(193)
Corporate[2]	(771)	(894)	(955)
Total NIKE Consolidated Earnings Before Interest and Taxes	2,848	2,523	1,947
Interest expense (income), net	4	6	(10)
Total NIKE Consolidated Earnings Before Taxes	$ 2,844	$ 2,517	$ 1,957
Additions to Long-lived Assets			
North America	$ 79	$ 45	$ 99
Western Europe	75	59	70
Central & Eastern Europe	5	4	7
Greater China	43	80	59
Japan	9	12	10
Emerging Markets	21	11	12
Global Brand Divisions	44	30	37
Total NIKE Brand	276	241	294
Other Businesses	38	52	90
Corporate	118	42	72
Total Additions to Long-lived Assets	$ 432	$ 335	$ 456
Depreciation			
North America	$ 70	$ 65	$ 64
Western Europe	52	57	51
Central & Eastern Europe	4	4	4
Greater China	19	11	7
Japan	22	26	30
Emerging Markets	14	12	10
Global Brand Divisions	39	33	43
Total NIKE Brand	220	208	209
Other Businesses	44	46	38
Corporate	71	70	88
Total Depreciation	$ 335	$ 324	$ 335

85

NIKE, INC.

NOTES TO CONSOLIDATED FINANCIAL STATEMENTS — (Continued)

---

(1) During the year ended May 31, 2009, the Other category included a pre-tax charge of $401 million for the impairment of goodwill, intangible and other assets of Umbro, which was recorded in the third quarter of fiscal 2009. See Note 4 — Identifiable Intangible Assets, Goodwill and Umbro Impairment for more information.

(2) During the year ended May 31, 2009, Corporate expense included pre-tax charges of $195 million for the Company's restructuring activities, which were completed in the fourth quarter of fiscal 2009. See Note 16 — Restructuring Charges for more information.

	Year Ended May 31,	
	2011	2010
	(In millions)	
Accounts Receivable, net		
North America	$ 1,069	$ 848
Western Europe	500	402
Central & Eastern Europe	290	271
Greater China	140	129
Japan	153	167
Emerging Markets	466	350
Global Brand Divisions	23	22
Total NIKE Brand	2,641	2,189
Other Businesses	471	442
Corporate	26	19
Total Accounts Receivable, net	$ 3,138	$ 2,650
Inventories		
North America	$ 1,034	$ 768
Western Europe	434	347
Central & Eastern Europe	145	102
Greater China	152	104
Japan	82	68
Emerging Markets	429	285
Global Brand Divisions	25	20
Total NIKE Brand	2,301	1,694
Other Businesses	414	347
Corporate	—	—
Total Inventories	$ 2,715	$ 2,041
Property, Plant and Equipment, net		
North America	$ 330	$ 325
Western Europe	338	282
Central & Eastern Europe	13	11
Greater China	179	146
Japan	360	333
Emerging Markets	58	48
Global Brand Divisions	116	99
Total NIKE Brand	1,394	1,244
Other Businesses	164	167
Corporate	557	521
Total Property, Plant and Equipment, net	$ 2,115	$ 1,932

86

NIKE, INC.
NOTES TO CONSOLIDATED FINANCIAL STATEMENTS — (Continued)

Revenues by Major Product Lines.   Revenues to external customers for NIKE Brand products are attributable to sales of footwear, apparel and equipment. Other revenues to external customers primarily include external sales by Cole Haan, Converse, Hurley, NIKE Golf, and Umbro.

	Year Ended May 31,		
	2011	2010	2009
		(In millions)	
Footwear	$11,493	$10,332	$10,307
Apparel	5,475	5,037	5,245
Equipment	1,013	1,035	1,110
Other	2,881	2,610	2,514
	$20,862	$19,014	$19,176

Revenues and Long-Lived Assets by Geographic Area.   Geographical area information is similar to what was shown previously under operating segments with the exception of the Other activity, which has been allocated to the geographical areas based on the location where the sales originated. Revenues derived in the United States were $8,956 million, $7,914 million, and $8,020 million for the years ended May 31, 2011, 2010, and 2009, respectively. The Company's largest concentrations of long-lived assets primarily consist of the Company's world headquarters and distribution facilities in the United States and distribution facilities in Japan, Belgium and China. Long-lived assets attributable to operations in the United States, which are comprised of net property, plant & equipment, were $1,115 million, $1,070 million, and $1,143 million at May 31, 2011, 2010, and 2009, respectively. Long-lived assets attributable to operations in Japan were $363 million, $336 million, and $322 million at May 31, 2011, 2010 and 2009, respectively. Long-lived assets attributable to operations in Belgium were $182 million, $164 million, and $191 million at May 31, 2011, 2010, and 2009, respectively. Long-lived assets attributable to operations in China were $175 million, $144 million, and $76 million at May 31, 2011, 2010, and 2009, respectively.

Major Customers.   No customer accounted for 10% or more of the Company's net sales during the years ended May 31, 2011, 2010, and 2009.

87

Chapter

11

Expanded Analysis

This chapter reviews special areas related to the usefulness of ratios and financial analyses. These special areas are as follows: (1) financial ratios as perceived by commercial loan departments, (2) financial ratios as perceived by corporate controllers, (3) financial ratios as perceived by certified public accountants, (4) financial ratios as perceived by chartered financial analysts, (5) financial ratios used in annual reports, (6) degree of conservatism and quality of earnings, (7) forecasting financial failure, (8) analytical review procedures, (9) management's use of analysis, (10) use of LIFO reserves, (11) graphing financial information, (12) management of earnings, (13) the housing bust, and (14) valuation.

Financial Ratios as Perceived by Commercial Loan Departments

Financial ratios can be used by a commercial loan department to aid the loan officers in deciding whether to grant a commercial loan and in maintaining control of a loan once it is granted.[1] In order to gain insights into how commercial loan departments view financial ratios, a questionnaire was sent to the commercial loan departments of the 100 largest banks in the United States. Usable responses were received from 44% of them.

A list of 59 financial ratios was drawn from the financial literature, textbooks, and published industry data for this study. The study set three objectives: (1) the significance of each ratio, in the opinion of commercial loan officers, (2) how frequently each ratio is included in loan agreements, and (3) what a specific financial ratio primarily measures, in the opinion of commercial loan officers. For the primary measure, the choices were liquidity, long-term debt-paying ability, profitability, or other. Exhibit 11-1 lists the ratios included in this study.

Most Significant Ratios and Their Primary Measure

Exhibit 11-2 displays the 10 financial ratios given the highest significance rating by the commercial loan officers, as well as the primary measure of these ratios. The highest rating is a 9, and the lowest rating is a 0.

Most of the ratios given a high significance rating were regarded primarily as measures of liquidity or debt. Only 2 of the top 10 ratios measure profitability, 5 measure debt, and

| EXHIBIT 11-1 | Ratios Rated by Commercial Loan Officers |

Ratio	Ratio
Cash ratio	Sales/fixed assets
Accounts receivable turnover in days	Sales/working capital
Accounts receivable turnover—times per year	Sales/net worth
Days' sales in receivables	Cash/sales
Quick ratio (acid-test)	Quick assets/sales
Inventory turnover in days	Current assets/sales
Inventory turnover—times per year	Return on assets:
Days' sales in inventory	before interest and tax
Current debt/inventory	before tax
Inventory/current assets	after tax
Inventory/working capital	Return on operating assets
Current ratio	Return on total invested:
Inventory/current assets	before tax
Inventory/working capital	after tax
Current ratio	Return on equity:
Net fixed assets/tangible net worth	before tax
Cash/total assets	after tax
Quick assets/total assets	Net profit margin:
Current assets/total assets	before tax
Retained earnings/total assets	after tax
Debt/equity ratio	Retained earnings/net income
Total debt as a % of net working capital	Cash flow/current maturities of
Total debt/total assets	long-term debt
Short-term debt as a % of total invested capital	Cash flow/total debt
Long-term debt as a % of total invested capital	Times interest earned
Funded debt/working capital	Fixed charge coverage
Total equity/total assets	Degree of operating leverage
Fixed assets/equity	Degree of financial leverage
Common equity as a % of total invested capital	Earnings per share
Current debt/net worth	Book value per share
Net worth at market value/total liabilities	Dividend payout ratio
Total asset turnover	Dividend yield
Sales/operating assets	Price/earnings ratio
	Stock price as a % of book value

| EXHIBIT 11-2 | Commercial Loan Departments |

Most Significant Ratios and Their Primary Measures

Ratio	Significance Rating	Primary Measure
Debt/equity	8.71	Debt
Current ratio	8.25	Liquidity
Cash flow/current maturities of long-term debt	8.08	Debt
Fixed charge coverage	7.58	Debt
Net profit margin after tax	7.56	Profitability
Times interest earned	7.50	Debt
Net profit margin before tax	7.43	Profitability
Degree of financial leverage	7.33	Debt
Inventory turnover in days	7.25	Liquidity
Accounts receivable turnover in days	7.08	Liquidity

3 measure liquidity. The two profitability ratios were two different computations of the net profit margin: (1) net profit margin after tax and (2) net profit margin before tax. Two of the top three ratios were measures of debt, and the other ratio was a measure of liquidity. The debt/equity ratio was given the highest significance rating, with the current ratio the second highest. We can assume that the financial ratios rated most significant by commercial loan officers would have the greatest influence on a loan decision.

Ratios Appearing Most Frequently in Loan Agreements

A commercial bank may elect to include a ratio as part of a loan agreement. This would be a way of using ratios to control an outstanding loan. Exhibit 11-3 contains a list of the 10 financial ratios that appear most frequently in loan agreements, along with an indication of what each ratio primarily measures. For the two ratios that do not have a primary measure indicated, there was no majority opinion as to what the ratio primarily measured. Six of the ratios that appear most frequently in loan agreements primarily measure debt, two primarily measure liquidity, and none primarily measure profitability.

The two top ratios, debt/equity and current ratio, were given the highest significance rating. The dividend payout ratio was the third most likely ratio to appear in loan agreements, but it was not rated as a highly significant ratio. Logically, this ratio appears in loan agreements as a means of controlling the outflow of cash for dividends.

EXHIBIT 11-3	Commercial Loan Departments	
Ratios Appearing Most Frequently in Loan Agreements		
Ratio	Percentage of Banks Including Ratio in 26% or More of Their Loan Agreements	Primary Measure
Debt/equity	92.5	Debt
Current ratio	90.0	Liquidity
Dividend payout ratio	70.0	*
Cash flow/current maturities of long-term debt	60.3	Debt
Fixed charge coverage	55.2	Debt
Times interest earned	52.6	Debt
Degree of financial leverage	44.7	Debt
Equity/assets	41.0	*
Cash flow/total debt	36.1	Debt
Quick ratio (acid-test)	33.3	Liquidity

*No majority primary measure indicated in this survey.

Financial Ratios as Perceived by Corporate Controllers

To get the views of corporate controllers on important issues relating to financial ratios, a questionnaire was sent to the controllers of the companies included in the *Fortune 500* list of the largest industrials.[2] The study excluded companies 100% owned or controlled by another firm. The survey received a usable response rate of 19.42%. The questionnaire used the same ratios used for the commercial loan department survey. The three objectives of this study were the determination of: (1) the significance of a specific ratio as perceived by controllers, (2) which financial ratios are included as corporate objectives, and (3) the primary measure of each ratio.

Most Significant Ratios and Their Primary Measure

Exhibit 11-4 displays the 10 financial ratios given the highest significance rating by the corporate controllers, along with the primary measure of these ratios. The highest rating is a 9 and the lowest is a 0.

The financial executives gave the profitability ratios the highest significance ratings. The highest rated debt ratio was debt/equity, while the highest rated liquidity ratio was the

EXHIBIT 11-4	Corporate Controllers

Most Significant Ratios and Their Primary Measures

Ratio	Significance Rating	Primary Measure
Earnings per share	8.19	Profitability
Return on equity after tax	7.83	Profitability
Net profit margin after tax	7.47	Profitability
Debt/equity ratio	7.46	Debt
Net profit margin before tax	7.41	Profitability
Return on total invested capital after tax	7.20	Profitability
Return on assets after tax	6.97	Profitability
Dividend payout ratio	6.83	Other*
Price/earnings ratio	6.81	Other*
Current ratio	6.71	Liquidity

*Primary measure indicated to be other than liquidity, debt, or profitability. The ratios rated this way tend to be related to stock analysis.

current ratio. In comparing the responses of the commercial loan officers and the controllers, the controllers rate the profitability ratios as having the highest significance, while the commercial loan officers rate the debt and liquidity ratios the highest.

Key Financial Ratios Included as Corporate Objectives

Many firms have selected key financial ratios to be included as part of their corporate objectives. The next section of the survey was designed to determine what ratios the firms used in their corporate objectives. Exhibit 11-5 lists the 10 ratios most likely to be included in corporate objectives according to the controllers. Nine of the ratios included in Exhibit 11-5 were also included in Exhibit 11-4. One ratio, accounts receivable turnover in days, appears in the top 10 ratios in relation to corporate objectives but not in the top 10 significant ratios. One ratio, the price/earnings ratio, appears in the top 10 ratios in relation to significance but not in the top 10 ratios used for corporate objectives.

Logically, there would be a high correlation between the ratios rated as highly significant and those included in corporate objectives. The debt/equity ratio and the current ratio are rated higher on the objectives list than on the significance list. This makes sense since a firm has to have some balance in its objectives between liquidity, debt, and profitability.

EXHIBIT 11-5	Ratios Appearing in Corporate Objectives and Their Primary Measures

Ratio	Percentage of Firms Indicating That the Ratio Was Included in Corporate Objectives	Primary Measure
Earnings per share	80.6	Profitability
Debt/equity ratio	68.8	Debt
Return on equity after tax	68.5	Profitability
Current ratio	62.0	Liquidity
Net profit margin after tax	60.9	Profitability
Dividend payout ratio	54.3	Other
Return on total invested capital after tax	53.3	Profitability
Net profit margin before tax	52.2	Profitability
Accounts receivable turnover in days	47.3	Liquidity
Return on assets after tax	47.3	Profitability

Financial Ratios as Perceived by Certified Public Accountants

A questionnaire was sent to one-third of the members of the Ohio Society of Certified Public Accountants who were registered as a partner in a CPA firm.[3] A total of 495 questionnaires were sent, and the usable response rate was 18.8%.

This questionnaire used the same ratios as were used for the commercial loan department and corporate controllers. The specific objectives of this study were to determine the following from the viewpoint of the CPA:

1. The specific financial ratios that CPAs view primarily as a measure of liquidity, debt, and profitability.
2. The relative importance of the financial ratios viewed as a measure of liquidity, debt, or profitability.

Exhibit 11-6 displays the 10 financial ratios given the highest significance rating by the CPAs and the primary measure of these ratios. The highest rating is a 9 and the lowest is a 0.

The CPAs gave the highest significance rating to two liquidity ratios—the current ratio and the accounts receivable turnover in days. The highest rated profitability ratio was after-tax return on equity, and the highest rated debt ratio was debt/equity.

EXHIBIT 11-6	CPAs	
Most Significant Ratios and Their Primary Measures		
Ratio	Significance Rating	Primary Measure
Current ratio	7.10	Liquidity
Accounts receivable turnover in days	6.94	Liquidity
After-tax return on equity	6.79	Profitability
Debt/equity ratio	6.78	Debt
Quick ratio (acid-test)	6.77	Liquidity
Net profit margin after tax	6.67	Profitability
Net profit margin before tax	6.63	Profitability
Return on assets after tax	6.39	Profitability
Return on total invested capital after tax	6.30	Profitability
Inventory turnover in days	6.09	Liquidity

Financial Ratios as Perceived by Chartered Financial Analysts[4]

Exhibit 11-7 displays the 10 financial ratios given the highest significance rating by chartered financial analysts (CFAs) and the primary measure of these ratios. Again, the highest rating is a 9 and the lowest rating is a 0.

The surveyed CFAs gave the highest significance ratings to profitability ratios, with the exception of the price/earnings ratio. Return on equity after tax received the highest significance by a wide margin. Four of the next five most significant ratios were also profitability ratios—earnings per share, net profit margin after tax, return on equity before tax, and net profit margin before tax.

The price/earnings ratio—categorized by the analysts as an "other" measure—received the second highest significance rating. CFAs apparently view profitability and what is being paid for those profits before turning to liquidity and debt.

The two highest rated debt ratios were fixed charge coverage and times interest earned, rated seventh and tenth, respectively. Both of these ratios indicate a firm's ability to carry debt. The highest rated debt ratio relating to the balance sheet was the debt/equity ratio, rated as the eleventh most significant. Surprisingly, more significance was placed on debt ratios relating to the ability to carry debt than on those relating to the ability to meet debt obligations.

EXHIBIT 11-7	**Chartered Financial Analysts**	

Most Significant Ratios and Their Primary Measures

Ratio	Significance Rating	Primary Measure
Return on equity after tax	8.21	Profitability
Price/earnings ratio	7.65	*
Earnings per share	7.58	Profitability
Net profit margin after tax	7.52	Profitability
Return on equity before tax	7.41	Profitability
Net profit margin before tax	7.32	Profitability
Fixed charge coverage	7.22	Debt
Quick ratio (acid-test)	7.10	Liquidity
Return on assets after tax	7.06	Profitability
Times interest earned	7.06	Debt

*Primary measure indicated to be other than liquidity, debt, or profitability. The ratios rated this way tend to be related to stock analysis.

The highest rated liquidity ratio was the acid-test ratio, rated eighth. The second highest liquidity ratio was the current ratio, rated twentieth.[5]

Financial Ratios Used in Annual Reports

Financial ratios are used to interpret and explain financial statements.[6] Used properly, they can be effective tools in evaluating a company's liquidity, debt position, and profitability. Probably no tool is as effective in evaluating where a company has been financially and projecting its financial future as the proper use of financial ratios.

A firm can use its annual report effectively to relate financial data by the use of financial ratios. To determine how effectively firms use ratios to communicate financial data, the annual reports of 100 firms identified in the *Fortune 500* industrial companies were reviewed. The 100 firms represented the first 20 of each 100 in the *Fortune 500* list. The objective of this research project was to determine (1) which financial ratios were frequently reported in annual reports, (2) where the ratios were disclosed in the annual reports, and (3) what computational methodology was used to compute these ratios.

Exhibit 11-8 indicates the ratios disclosed most frequently in the annual reports reviewed and the section of the annual report where the ratios were located. The locations were the president's letter, management discussion, management highlights, financial review, and financial summary. In many cases, the same ratio was located in several sections, so the numbers under the sections in Exhibit 11-8 do not add up to the total number of annual reports where the ratio was included.

Seven ratios appeared more than 50% of the time in one section or another. These ratios and the number of times found were earnings per share (100), dividends per share (98), book value per share (84), working capital (81), return on equity (62), profit margin (58), and effective tax rate (50). The current ratio was found 47 times, and the next ratio in order of disclosure, the debt/capital ratio, appeared 23 times. From this listing, we can conclude that profitability ratios and ratios related to investing were the most popular. Exhibit 11-8 excludes ratios not disclosed at least five times.

Logically, profitability ratios and ratios related to investing were the most popular for inclusion in the annual report. Including ratios related to investing in the annual report makes sense because one of the annual report's major objectives is to inform stockholders.

A review of the methodology used indicated that wide differences of opinion exist on how some of the ratios should be computed. This is especially true of the debt ratios. The two debt ratios most frequently disclosed were the debt/capital ratio and the debt/equity

EXHIBIT 11-8	Ratios Disclosed Most Frequently in Annual Reports*					
	Number Included	President's Letter	Management Discussion	Management Highlights	Financial Review	Financial Summary
Earnings per share	100	66	5	98	45	93
Dividends per share	98	53	10	85	49	88
Book value per share	84	10	3	53	18	63
Working capital	81	1	1	50	23	67
Return on equity	62	28	3	21	23	37
Profit margin	58	10	3	21	23	35
Effective tax rate	50	2	1	2	46	6
Current ratio	47	3	1	16	12	34
Debt/capital	23	9	0	4	14	23
Return on capital	21	6	2	8	8	5
Debt/equity	19	5	0	3	8	8
Return on assets	13	4	1	2	5	10
Dividend payout	13	3	0	0	6	6
Gross profit	12	0	1	0	11	3
Pretax margin	10	2	0	3	6	6
Total asset turnover	7	1	0	0	4	4
Price/earnings ratio	7	0	0	0	1	6
Operating margin	7	1	0	2	6	1
Labor per hour	5	0	2	2	2	2

*Numbers represent both absolute numbers and percentages, since a review was made of the financial statements of 100 firms.

ratio. This book does not cover the debt/capital ratio. It is similar to the debt/equity ratio, except that the denominator includes sources of capital, in addition to stockholders' equity.

The annual reports disclosed the debt/capital ratio 23 times and used 11 different formulas. One firm used average balance sheet amounts between the beginning and the end of the year, while 22 firms used ending balance sheet figures. The debt/equity ratio was disclosed 19 times, and 6 different formulas were used. All firms used the ending balance sheet accounts to compute the debt/equity ratio.

In general, no major effort is being made to explain financial results by the disclosure of financial ratios in annual reports. Several financial ratios that could be interpreted as important were not disclosed or were disclosed very infrequently. This is particularly important for ratios that cannot be reasonably computed by outsiders because of a lack of data such as accounts receivable turnover.

At present, no regulatory agency such as the SEC or the FASB accepts responsibility for determining either the content of financial ratios or the format of presentation for annual reports, except for the ratio earnings per share. Many practical and theoretical issues relate to the computation of financial ratios. As long as each firm can exercise its opinion as to the practical and theoretical issues, there will be a great divergence of opinion on how a particular ratio should be computed.

Degree of Conservatism and Quality of Earnings

A review of financial statements, including the notes, indicates their conservatism with regard to accounting policies. Accounting policies that result in the slowest reporting of income are the most conservative. When a firm has conservative accounting policies, it is said that its earnings are of high quality. This section reviews a number of areas that often indicate a firm's degree of conservatism in reporting income.

Inventory

Under inflationary conditions, the matching of current cost against the current revenue results in the lowest income for a period of time. The LIFO inventory method follows this procedure.

FIFO, the least conservative method, uses the oldest costs and matches them against revenue. Other inventory methods fall somewhere between the results of LIFO and FIFO.

For a construction firm that has long-term contracts, the two principal accounting methods that relate to inventory are the completed-contract method and the percentage-of-completion method. The conservative completed-contract method recognizes all of the income when the contract is completed; the percentage-of-completion method recognizes income as work progresses on the contract.

Fixed Assets

Two accounting decisions related to fixed assets can have a significant influence on income: the method of depreciation and the period of time selected to depreciate an asset.

The conservative methods, sum-of-the-years'-digits and declining-balance, recognize a large amount of depreciation in the early years of the asset's life. The straight-line method, the least conservative method, recognizes depreciation in equal amounts over each year of the asset's life.

Sometimes a material difference in the asset's life used for depreciation occurs between firms. Comparing the lives used for depreciation for similar firms can be a clue as to how conservative the firms are in computing depreciation. The shorter the period of time used, the lower the income.

Intangible Assets

Intangible assets include goodwill, patents, and copyrights. Research and development (R&D) costs are a type of intangible asset, but they are expensed as incurred. The shorter the period of time used to recognize the cost of the intangible asset, the more conservative the accounting. (Goodwill is not amortized, but it is tested for impairment.)

Some firms spend very large sums on R&D, and others spend little or nothing. Because of the requirement that R&D costs be expensed in the period incurred, the income of a firm that does considerable research is reduced substantially in the period that the cost is incurred. This results in more conservative earnings.

Pensions

Two points relating to pensions should be examined when the firm has a defined benefit plan. One is the assumed discount rate used to compute the actuarial present value of the accumulated benefit obligation and the projected benefit obligation. The higher the interest rate used, the lower the present value of the liability and the lower the immediate pension cost. The other item is the rate of compensation increase used in computing the projected benefit obligations. If the rate is too low, the projected benefit obligation is too low. If the rate is too high, the projected benefit obligation is too high.

Forecasting Financial Failure

There have been many academic studies on the use of financial ratios to forecast financial failure. Basically, these studies try to isolate individual ratios or combinations of ratios that can be observed as trends that may forecast failure.

A reliable model that can be used to forecast financial failure can also be used by management to take preventive measures. Such a model can aid investors in selecting and disposing of stocks. Banks can use it to aid in lending decisions and in monitoring loans. Firms can use it in making credit decisions and in monitoring accounts receivable. In general, many sources can use such a model to improve the allocation and control of resources. A model that forecasts financial failure can also be valuable to an auditor. It can aid in the determination of audit procedures and in making a decision as to whether the firm will remain as a going concern.

Financial failure can be described in many ways. It can mean liquidation, deferment of payments to short-term creditors, deferment of payments of interest on bonds, deferment of payments of principal on bonds, or the omission of a preferred dividend. One of the problems in examining the literature on forecasting financial failure is that different authors use different criteria to indicate failure. When reviewing the literature, always determine the criteria used to define financial failure.

This book reviews two of the studies that deal with predicting financial failure. Based on the number of references to these two studies in the literature, they appear to be particularly significant on the subject of forecasting financial failure.

Univariate Model

William Beaver reported his univariate model in a study published in *The Accounting Review* in January 1968.[7] A univariate model uses a single variable. Such a model would use individual financial ratios to forecast financial failure. The Beaver study classified a firm as failed when any one of the following events occurred in the 1954–1964 period: bankruptcy, bond default, an overdrawn bank account, or nonpayment of a preferred stock dividend.

Beaver paired 79 failed firms with a similar number of successful firms drawn from *Moody's Industrial Manuals.* For each failed firm in the sample, a successful one was selected from the same industry. The Beaver study indicated that the following ratios were the best for forecasting financial failure (in the order of their predictive power):

1. Cash flow/total debt
2. Net income/total assets (return on assets)
3. Total debt/total assets (debt ratio)

Beaver speculated as to the reason for these results:

My interpretation of the finding is that the cash flow, net income, and debt positions cannot be altered and represent permanent aspects of the firm. Because failure is too costly to all involved, the permanent, rather than the short-term, factors largely determine whether or not a firm will declare bankruptcy or default on a bond payment.[8]

Source: William Beaver, The Accounting Review

Assuming that the ratios identified by Beaver are valid in forecasting financial failure, it would be wise to pay particular attention to trends in these ratios when following a firm. Beaver's reasoning for seeing these ratios as valid in forecasting financial failure appears to be very sound.

These three ratios for Nike for 2011 have been computed earlier. Cash flow/total debt was 35.15%, which appears to be very good. Net income/total assets (return on assets) was 14.50%, which appears to be very good. The debt ratio was 34.37%, which again is very good. Thus, Nike appears to have minimal risk of financial failure.

The Beaver study also computed the mean values of 13 financial statement items for each year before failure. Several important relationships were indicated among the liquid asset items.[9]

1. Failed firms have less cash but more accounts receivable.
2. When cash and receivables are added together, as they are in quick assets and current assets, the difference between failed and successful firms is obscured because the cash and receivables differences are working in opposite directions.
3. Failed firms tend to have less inventory.

These results indicate that particular attention should be paid to three current assets when forecasting financial failure: cash, accounts receivable, and inventory. The analyst should be alert for low cash and inventory and high accounts receivable.

Multivariate Model

Edward I. Altman and Thomas P. McGough developed a multivariate model to predict bankruptcy.[10] His model uses five financial ratios weighted in order to maximize the predictive power of the model. The model produces an overall discriminant score, called a Z score. The Altman model is as follows:

$$Z = .012 X_1 + .014 X_2 + .033 X_3 + .006 X_4 + .010 X_5$$

$$X_1 = \text{Working Capital/Total Assets}$$

This computation is a measure of the net liquid assets of the firm relative to the total capitalization.

$$X_2 = \text{Retained Earnings (balance sheet)/Total Assets}$$

This variable measures cumulative profitability over time.

$$X_3 = \text{Earnings Before Interest and Taxes/Total Assets}$$

This variable measures the productivity of the firm's assets, extracting any tax or leverage factors.

$$X_4 = \text{Market Value of Equity/Book Value of Total Debt}$$

This variable measures how much the firm's assets can decline in value before the liabilities exceed the assets and the firm becomes insolvent. Equity is measured by the combined market value of all shares of stock, preferred and common, while debt includes both current and long-term debts.

$$X_5 = \text{Sales/Total Assets}$$

This variable measures the sales-generating ability of the firm's assets.

When computing the Z score, the ratios are expressed in absolute percentage terms. Thus, X_1 (working capital/total assets) of 25% is noted as 25.

The Altman model was developed using manufacturing companies whose asset size was between \$1 million and \$25 million. The original sample by Altman and the test samples used the period 1946–1965. The model's accuracy in predicting bankruptcies in more recent years (1970–1973) was reported in a 1974 article.[11] Not all of the companies included in the test were manufacturing companies, although the model was initially developed by using only manufacturing companies.

With the Altman model, the lower the Z score, the more likely that the firm will go bankrupt. By computing the Z score for a firm over several years, it can be determined whether the firm is moving toward a more likely or less likely position with regard to bankruptcy. In a later study that covered the period 1970–1973, a Z score of 2.675 was established as a practical cutoff point. Firms that scored below 2.675 are assumed to have characteristics similar to those of past failures.[12] Current GAAP recognize more liabilities than the GAAP used at the time of this study. Thus, we would expect firms to score somewhat less than in the time period 1970–1973. The Altman model is substantially less significant if there is no firm market value for the stock (preferred and common), because variable X_4 in the model requires that the market value of the stock be determined.

Nike Z Score

The Z Score for Nike for 2011 follows:

$$\begin{aligned}
Z = \ &.012 \,(\text{working capital} / \text{total assets}) \\
&+ .014 \,(\text{retained earnings [balance sheet]} / \text{total assets}) \\
&+ .033 \,(\text{earnings before interest and taxes} / \text{total assets}) \\
&+ .006 \,(\text{market value of equity} / \text{book value of total debt}) \\
&+ .010 \,(\text{sales} / \text{total assets}) \\
Z = \ &.012 \,(\$7,339,000,000 / \$14,998,000,000) \\
&+ .014 \,(\$5,801,000,000 / \$14,998,000,000) \\
&+ .033 \,(\$2,878,000,000 / \$14,998,000,000) \\
&+ .006 \,((\$468,000,000 \times \$84.45) / \$5,155,000,000) \\
&+ .010 \,(\$20,862,000,000 / \$14,998,000,000) \\
Z = \ &.012 \,(48.93) \\
&+ .014 \,(38.68) \\
&+ .033 \,(19.19) \\
&+ .006 \,(766.68) \\
&+ .010 \,(139.10) \\
Z = \ &7.75
\end{aligned}$$

The Z Score for Nike for 2011 was 7.75. Considering that higher scores are better and that companies with scores below 2.675 are assumed to have characteristics similar to those of past failures, Nike is a very healthy company.

There are many academic studies on the use of ratios to forecast financial failure. These studies help substantiate that firms with weak ratios are more likely to go bankrupt than firms with strong ratios. Since no conclusive model has yet been developed, the best approach is probably an integrated one. As a supplemental measure, it may also be helpful to compute some of the ratios that appear useful in forecasting financial failure.

Analytical Review Procedures

Statement of Auditing Standards No. 23, "Analytical Review Procedures," provides guidance for the use of such procedures in audits. The objective of analytical review procedures is to isolate significant fluctuations and unusual items in operating statistics.

Analytical review procedures may be performed at various times, including the planning stage, during the audit itself, and near the completion of the audit. Some examples of analytical review procedures that may lead to special audit procedures follow:

1. Horizontal common-size analysis of the income statement may indicate that an item, such as selling expenses, is abnormally high for the period. This could lead to a close examination of the selling expenses.
2. Vertical common-size analysis of the income statement may indicate that the cost of goods sold is out of line in relation to sales, in comparison with prior periods.
3. A comparison of accounts receivable turnover with the industry data may indicate that receivables are turning over much slower than is typical for the industry. This may indicate that receivables should be analyzed closely.
4. Cash flow in relation to debt may have declined significantly, indicating a materially reduced ability to cover debt from internal cash flow.
5. The acid-test ratio may have declined significantly, indicating a materially reduced ability to pay current liabilities with current assets less inventories.

When the auditor spots a significant trend in a statement or ratio, follow-up procedures should be performed to determine the reason. Such an investigation can lead to significant findings.

Management's Use of Analysis

Management can use financial ratios and common-size analysis as aids in many ways. Analysis can indicate the relative liquidity, debt, and profitability of a firm. Analysis can also indicate how investors perceive the firm and can help detect emerging problems and strengths in a firm. As indicated previously, financial ratios can also be used as part of the firm's corporate objectives. Using financial ratios in conjunction with the budgeting process can be particularly helpful. An objective of the budgeting process is to determine the firm's game plan. The budget can consist of an overall comprehensive budget and many separate budgets, such as a production budget.

The comprehensive budget relating to financial statements indicates how a firm plans to get from one financial position (balance sheet) to another. The income statement details how the firm changed internally from one balance sheet position to another in terms of revenue and expenses. The statement of cash flows indicates how the firm's cash changed from one balance sheet to another.

A proposed comprehensive budget should be compared with financial ratios that have been agreed upon as part of the firm's corporate objectives. For example, if corporate objectives include a current ratio of 2:1, a debt equity of 40%, and a return on equity of 15%, then the proposed comprehensive budget should be compared with these corporate objectives before the budget is accepted as the firm's overall game plan. If the proposed comprehensive budget will not result in the firm achieving its objectives, management should attempt to change the game plan in order to achieve its objectives. If management cannot change the proposed comprehensive budget satisfactorily to achieve the corporate objectives, they should know this when the comprehensive budget is accepted.

Use of LIFO Reserves

A firm that uses LIFO usually discloses a LIFO reserve account in a note on the face of the balance sheet. If a LIFO reserve account is not disclosed, there is usually some indication of an amount that approximates current cost. Nike uses first-in, first-out or moving average; therefore, it does not have a LIFO reserve. Thus, Sherwin-Williams Company was selected to illustrate LIFO reserve analysis.

In its 2010 annual report, Sherwin-Williams Company disclosed that the excess of FIFO over LIFO was $277,164,00 and $250,454,000 for 2010 and 2009, respectively. This information can be used for supplemental analysis of inventory and (in general) the analysis of liquidity, debt, and profitability. Supplemental analysis using this additional inventory information can be particularly significant when there is a substantial LIFO reserve and/or a substantial change in the reserve.

For Sherwin-Williams Company, an approximation of the increase or decrease in income if inventory is at approximate current acquisition costs could be computed by comparing the change in inventory, net of any tax effect. For 2010, compute the approximation of the income if the inventory were at approximate current acquisition costs as follows:

		In thousands
2010 Net Income		$462,485
Inventory reserve:		
2010	$277,164	
2009	250,454	
(a) Net increase	26,710	
(b) Effective tax rate	× 31.8%	
(c) Change in taxes [a × b]	$ 8,494	
(d) Net increase in income [a−c]		18,216
Estimated income if the inventory were presented at approximate current acquisitions cost		$480,701

Specific liquidity and debt ratios can be recomputed, taking into consideration the adjusted inventory figure. To make these computations, add the gross inventory reserve to the inventory disclosed in current assets. Add the approximate additional taxes to the current liabilities.

Estimate the additional tax figure by multiplying the gross LIFO reserve by the effective tax rate. This tax figure relates to the additional income that would have been reported in the current year and all prior years if the higher inventory amounts had been reported. The additional tax amount is a deferred tax amount that is added to current liabilities, to be conservative. The difference between the additional inventory amount and the additional tax amount is added to retained earnings because it represents the total prior influence on net income. The adjusted figures for Sherwin-Williams Company at the end of 2010 follow:

Inventory:	Thousands
As disclosed on the balance sheet	$ 917,701
Increase in inventory	277,164
	$1,194,865
Deferred current tax liability:	
Effective tax rate (31.8%) × increase in inventory ($277,164)	$ 88,138
Retained earnings:	
As disclosed on the balance sheet	$4,824,489
Increase in retained earnings ($277,164 − $88,138)	189,026
	$5,013,515

An adjusted cost of goods sold can also be estimated using the change in the inventory reserve. A net increase in the inventory reserve would reduce the cost of goods sold. A net decrease in inventory reserve would increase the cost of goods sold.

The adjusted liquidity, debt, and profitability ratios could possibly be considered to be more realistic than the unadjusted price computations because of the use of current acquisition costs for inventory.

For many of the ratios, we cannot generalize about whether the ratio will improve or decline when the LIFO reserve is used. For example, if the current ratio is above 2.00, then it may not improve when the firm has a high tax rate. When the current ratio and/or tax rate is low, the current ratio will likely improve.

The Sherwin-Williams Company inventory disclosure on its December 21, 2010 annual report follows:

Consolidated Balance Sheets (In Part)
(thousands of dollars)

Inventories:	
Finished goods	$743,953
Work in process and raw materials	173,748
	$917,701

Note: Note 4 below is in thousands of dollars, except per share amounts.

Note 4—Inventories

Inventories were stated at the lower of cost or market with cost determined principally on the last-in, first-out (LIFO) method. The following presents the effect on inventories, net income and net income per share had the company used the first-in, first-out (FIFO) inventory valuation method adjusted for income taxes at the statutory rate and assuming no other adjustments. Management believes that the use of LIFO results in a better matching of costs and revenues. This information is presented to enable the reader to make comparisons with companies using the FIFO method of inventory valuation. During 2009, certain inventories accounted for on the LIFO method were reduced, resulting in the liquidation of certain quantities carried at costs prevailing in prior years. The impact on net income of such liquidation was $8,634.

	2010	2009	2008
Percentage of total inventories on LIFO	76%	83%	86%
Excess of FIFO over LIFO	$277,164	$250,454	$321,280
(Decrease) increase in net income due to LIFO	(16,394)	43,650	(49,184)
(Decrease) increase in net income per common share due to LIFO	(.15)	.38	(.41)

Note: Notice that Note 4 discloses a decrease in net income due to LIFO of $16,394 (in thousands), while our prior estimate was $18,216 (in thousands).

Note: When LIFO inventories are reduced, this brings out lower cost inventory to cost of goods sold. This increases profits for the year when the LIFO inventory was reduced. This is referred to as the LIFO layers effect.

"During 2009 certain inventories accounted for on the LIFO method were reduced, resulting in the liquidation of certain quantities carried at costs prevailing in prior years. The impact on net income of such liquidation was $8,634,000."

Graphing Financial Information

It has become popular to use graphs in annual reports to present financial information. Graphs make it easier to grasp key financial information. They can be a better communication device than a written report or a tabular presentation because they communicate by means of pictures and, thus, create more immediate mental images.

There are many forms of graphs. Some popular forms used by accountants are line, column, bar, and pie graphs. These forms will be briefly described here, but a detailed description of those and other forms can be found in reference books and articles.[13]

The line graph uses a set of points connected by a line to show change over time. It is important for the vertical axis to start at zero and that it not be broken. Not starting the vertical axis at zero and/or breaking the vertical axis can result in a very misleading presentation. Exhibit 11-9 illustrates a line graph.

A column graph has vertical columns. As for a line graph, it is important that the vertical axis start at zero and that it not be broken. A column graph is often the best form of graph for presenting accounting data. Exhibit 11-10 presents a column graph.

A bar graph is similar to a column graph, except that the bars are horizontal. Exhibit 11-11 illustrates a bar graph.

A pie graph is divided into segments. This type of graph makes a comparison of the segments, which must add up to 100%. A pie graph can mislead if it creates an optical illusion. Also, some accounting data do not fit on a pie graph. Exhibit 11-12 illustrates a pie graph.

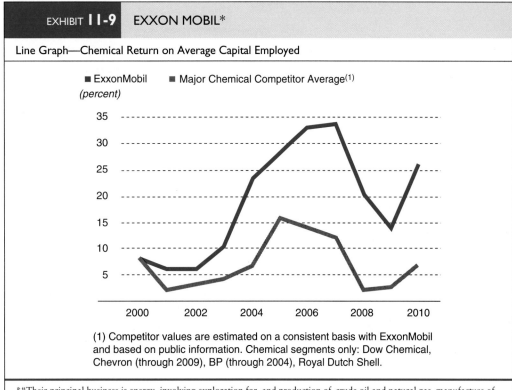

EXHIBIT **11-9**   EXXON MOBIL*

Line Graph—Chemical Return on Average Capital Employed

■ ExxonMobil   ■ Major Chemical Competitor Average(1)
(percent)

(1) Competitor values are estimated on a consistent basis with ExxonMobil and based on public information. Chemical segments only: Dow Chemical, Chevron (through 2009), BP (through 2004), Royal Dutch Shell.

*"Their principal business is energy, involving exploration for, and production of, crude oil and natural gas, manufacture of petroleum products and transportation and sale of crude oil, natural gas and petroleum products." 10-K
Source: Courtesy of ExxonMobil

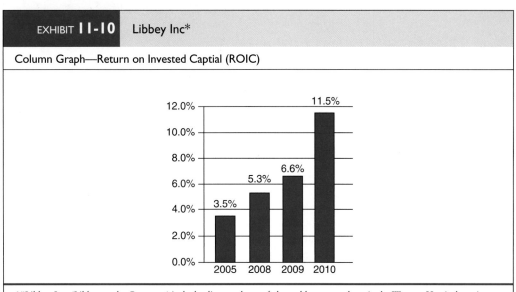

EXHIBIT **11-10**   Libbey Inc*

Column Graph—Return on Invested Captial (ROIC)

*"Libbey Inc. (Libbey or the Company) is the leading producer of glass tableware products in the Western Hemisphere, in addition to supplying to key markets throughout the world. 10-K.
Source: Libbey Inc, 2010 10-K

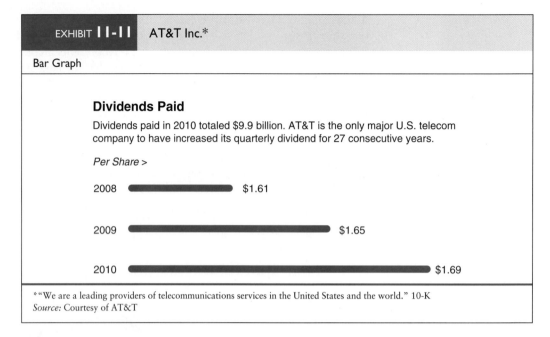

EXHIBIT 11-11 AT&T Inc.*

Bar Graph

Dividends Paid

Dividends paid in 2010 totaled $9.9 billion. AT&T is the only major U.S. telecom company to have increased its quarterly dividend for 27 consecutive years.

Per Share >

2008 $1.61

2009 $1.65

2010 $1.69

*"We are a leading providers of telecommunications services in the United States and the world." 10-K
Source: Courtesy of AT&T

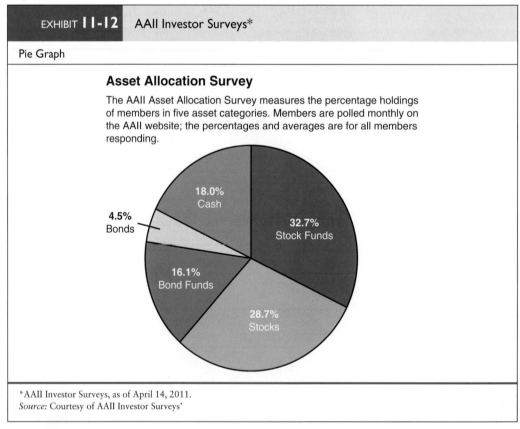

EXHIBIT 11-12 AAII Investor Surveys*

Pie Graph

Asset Allocation Survey

The AAII Asset Allocation Survey measures the percentage holdings of members in five asset categories. Members are polled monthly on the AAII website; the percentages and averages are for all members responding.

18.0% Cash
4.5% Bonds
32.7% Stock Funds
16.1% Bond Funds
28.7% Stocks

*AAII Investor Surveys, as of April 14, 2011.
Source: Courtesy of AAII Investor Surveys'

Management of Earnings

Chapter 1 describes cash basis as recognizing revenue when cash is received and recognizing expenses when cash is paid. It was indicated that the cash basis usually does not provide reasonable information about the entity's earnings capability in the short run. Because of the shortcomings of the cash basis, the accrual basis has been adopted for income reporting for most firms.

With the accrual basis, revenue is recognized when realized (realization concept) and expenses are recognized when incurred (matching concept). As indicated in Chapter 1, use of the accrual basis complicates the accounting process, but the end result is more representative than the cash basis of an entity's financial condition. Without the accrual basis, accountants would not usually be able to make the time period assumption—that the entity can be accounted for with reasonable accuracy for a particular period of time.

Nike includes the following comment in its Management Discussion and Analysis of Financial Condition and Results of Operation in its 2011 annual report:

Critical Accounting Policies

Our previous discussion and analysis of our financial condition and results of operations are based upon our consolidated financial statements, which have been prepared in accordance with accounting principles generally accepted in the United States of America. The preparation of these financial statements requires us to make estimates and judgments that affect the reported amounts of assets, liabilities, revenues and expenses, and related disclosure of contingent assets and liabilities.

We believe that the estimates, assumptions and judgments involved in the accounting policies described below have the greatest potential impact on our financial statements, so we consider these to be our critical accounting policies. Because of the uncertainty inherent in these matters, actual results could differ from the estimates we use in applying the critical accounting policies. Certain of these critical accounting policies affect working capital account balances, including the policies for endorsement contracts. These policies require that we make estimates in the preparation of our financial statements as of a given date. However, since our business cycle is relatively short, actual results related to these estimates are generally known within the six-month period following the financial statement date. Thus, these policies generally affect only the timing of reported amounts across two to three fiscal quarters.

Within the context of these critical accounting policies, we are not currently aware of any reasonably likely events or circumstances that would result in materially different amounts being reported.

The accounting policies described in detail were the following:

- *Revenue recognition*
- *Allowance for uncollectible accounts receivable*
- *Inventory reserves*
- *Contingent payments under endorsement contracts*
- *Property, plant and equipment and definite-lived assets*
- *Goodwill and indefinite-lived intangible assets*
- *Hedge accounting for derivatives*
- *Stock-based compensation*
- *Taxes*
- *Other contingencies*

Thus, Nike describes the proper use of estimates and judgments to prepare its financial statements under generally accepted accounting principles.

Some firms have used estimates and judgments to improperly manipulate their financial statements. Other firms have deliberately made errors to manipulate their financial statements. This results in financial statements that are not a proper representation of financial condition and results of operations, this created a substantial problem during the 1990s. The former chairman of the Securities and Exchange Commission, Arthur Levitt, had this to say as part of his address entitled the "Numbers Game," at the New York University Center for Law and Business on September 28, 1998:

Increasingly, I have become concerned that the motivation to meet Wall Street earnings expectations may be overriding common sense business practices. Too many corporate managers, auditors, and analysts are participants in a game of nods and winks. In the zeal to satisfy consensus earnings estimates and project a smooth earnings path, wishful thinking may be winning the day over faithful representation.

Source: Arthur Levitt at the New York University Center for Law and Business, Sept. 28, 1998

As a result, I fear that we are witnessing an erosion in the quality of earnings, and therefore, the quality of financial reporting. Managing may be giving way to manipulations; integrity may be losing out to illusion.

Many in corporate America are just as frustrated and concerned about this trend as we, at the SEC, are. They know how difficult it is to hold the line on good practices when their competitors operate in the gray area between legitimacy and outright fraud.

A gray area where the Accounting is being perverted; where managers are cutting corners; and, where earnings reports reflect the desires of management rather than the underlying financial performance of the company.[14]

Thus, both the former chairman of the Securities and Exchange Commission and the financial community were concerned about the apparent increase in the inappropriate management of earnings during the 1990s. We can speculate on why there was an increase in the improper management of earnings during the 1990s. Some of the likely reasons are as follows: (1) conviction that the capital markets would pay more for a stock that represented smooth earnings rather than peaks and valleys of earnings, (2) increase in the awarding of stock options as a means of compensation as opposed to cash, (3) substantial negative market reaction when a company would not meet its numbers, and (4) possibly an all-time high in greed.

The general public did not appear to be overly concerned about the increase in the improper management of earnings until the Enron situation developed in 2001. A possible reason for this lack of concern was the substantial increase in stock prices during the 1990s. Starting in 2000, stock prices experienced substantial declines. These declines in stock prices likely influenced the general public to be concerned about the improper management of earnings.

There are many ways to manage earnings improperly. We don't know of all the possibilities, but the ways that we do know would require us to write a separate book. We do know that revenue recognition is often involved in the manipulation of financial reports. The General Accounting Office, Congress's investigative arm, reported in an October 2002 report to the Senate Banking Committee that earnings restatements cost investors $100 billion in the prior five years. Earnings restatements rose by about 145% from 1997 through June 2002. Revenue-recognition issues arose in 38% of the cases studied.[15]

Revenue recognition often also involves inventory, accounts receivable, and cash flow. For example, early recognition of revenue could involve moving inventory from the balance sheet to cost of goods sold on the income statement, the booking of accounts receivable, and lack of cash flow. An understanding of financial reporting and analysis would help in detecting the problem.

Enron and WorldCom substantially influenced financial reporting in the United States. These cases crystallized views of the U.S. House and Senate that resulted in the Sarbanes-Oxley Act of 2002. Hopefully, the Sarbanes-Oxley Act will lead to constructive improvement in financial reporting.

Enron was one of the largest corporations in the world. In October 2001 it announced that it was reducing after-tax net income by approximately $500 million and shareholders' equity by $1.2 billion. In November, it announced that it was restating reported net income for the years 1997–2000. In December 2001, Enron filed for bankruptcy.

The Enron situation involved many financial reporting issues that were poorly disclosed or not disclosed at all. Some of the issues were accounting for investments in subsidiaries and special-purpose entities, sales of investments to special-purpose entities, revenue for fees, and fair value of investments.[16] The Enron financial statements, including the notes, were complicated and difficult to comprehend. The lesson here is that if a reasonable understanding of financial reporting and analysis is not adequate to understand the financial report, then consider this when investing.

In June 2002 WorldCom announced that it had inflated profits by $3.8 billion over the previous five quarters. WorldCom was the largest corporate accounting fraud in history. Soon after this announcement, WorldCom declared bankruptcy.[17] In November 2002, a special bankruptcy court examiner reported that the improper accounting would exceed $7.2 billion.[18]

The WorldCom fraud was uncovered by three accountants working in the internal auditing department. Their findings were communicated to the audit committee of the board, and later the entire board was informed. The internal discovery and reporting of the fraud represents a positive aspect of the WorldCom fraud.[19]

The WorldCom problem apparently started in 2000 when business declined. Initially, WorldCom moved dollars from reserve accounts to hold up profits. When this was no longer sufficient, it then turned to shifting operating costs to capital accounts. Shifting operating costs (expenses on the income statement) to capital accounts (assets on the balance sheet) would make the company look more profitable in the short run. As capital expenditures, these costs would be depreciated in subsequent years. Apparently, WorldCom had planned a write-down. This would remove these accounts from the balance sheet. Hopefully, Wall Street would overlook the write-down when looking to the future.[20]

Although the WorldCom fraud was discovered by internal auditors, the Securities and Exchange Commission sent a "Request for Information" to WorldCom on March 7, 2002. The SEC apparently thought that the WorldCom profit figures were suspicious, considering that WorldCom's closest competitors, including AT&T Corp., were losing money throughout 2001. A lesson from WorldCom is that if the numbers look too good, that may be because they *are* too good.[21]

Following Enron and WorldCom, many cases have been brought against companies and individuals for improper management of earnings. As of 2005, the largest company subsequent to Enron and WorldCom charged with improper management of earnings has been American International Group, Inc. (AIG). AIG is the world's biggest publicly traded seller of property-casualty insurance to businesses and the largest life insurer in the United States in terms of premiums.[22]

The SEC, the Justice Department, and the U.S. Attorney's Office in New York City were all investigating AIG's accounting issues. New York's attorney general and insurance commissioner sued AIG and two former top executives, accusing them of manipulating AIG's financial results.[23] The New York prosecutor's office presented evidence to a grand jury weighing criminal charges against individuals during the summer of 2005.[24]

On May 31, 2005, AIG restated its financial results for a five-year period. "The accounting adjustments tallied in the document slashed AIG's previously reported net income for 2004 by 12%, or $1.32 billion, to $9.73 billion, and reduced AIG's book value by $2.26 billion to $80.61 billion. Overall, the restatement reduced AIG's net income from 2000 through 2004 by $3.9 billion, or 10%."[25]

A U.S. Government Accountability Office (GAO) study dated July 2006 disclosed that "over the period of January 1, 2002 through September 30, 2005, the total number of restating companies (1,084) represents 16% of the average number of listed companies from 2002 to 2005, as compared to almost 8% during the 1997–2001 period."[26]

This study concluded that "a variety of factors appear to have contributed to the increased trend in restatements, including increased accountability requirements on the part of company executives; increased auditor and regulatory scrutiny … and a general unwillingness on the part of public companies to risk failing to restate regardless of the significance of the event."[27]

In an August 2006 correspondence, the GAO made this comment related to its July 2006 study: "Although there are many reasons for restatements, most restatements involve more routine reporting issues … and are not symptomatic of financial reporting fraud and/or accounting errors."[28]

It was noted in Chapter 4 that a FASB standard issued in May 2005 requires retrospective application to prior periods' financial statements of a voluntary change in accounting principle unless it is impracticable. This standard will contribute to additional retrospective application to prior periods.

The SEC issued Staff Bulletin No. 108 in September 2006 that requires retroactive revision of prior-period numbers presented in financial reporting. This relates to accounting for immaterial adjustments waived over time that become cumulatively material at a point in time. This bulletin will also contribute to additional retrospective application to prior periods.

Restatements have become a substantial problem in analysis of financial statements. It is important to review companies that are being analyzed for restatements during the period of time that is being analyzed. A similar review should be made for companies with which the company is being compared. It is impossible to guard against some unreliable industry data.

The Housing Bust

The housing bust led to a worldwide recession or possibly depression, depending on how it finally plays out. A few comments are in order to explain its origins and implications.

The Federal National Mortgage Association (Fannie Mae) and Federal Home Mortgage Corporation (Freddie Mac) control a substantial portion of the mortgage market in the United States. Fannie Mae was created in 1938 to raise levels of home ownership. It was in effect a U.S. government organization.

In 1968, Fannie Mae was privatized, removing it from the national budget. It began operating as a government-sponsored enterprise with the implied protection of the federal government. As a government-sponsored enterprise, it does not pay taxes or report to the SEC. It is subject to congressional oversight, which has proven to be ineffective. The federal government created a second government-sponsored enterprise in 1970, the Freddie Mac.

Because of the implied protection of the federal government, the rating agencies (Standard & Poor's, Moody's, Fitch) gave their mortgage securities a AAA rating. With this rating, the securities were sold to banks, mutual funds, governments, and individuals throughout the world.

In 1977, Congress passed the Community Reinvestment Act, which required banks to meet the credit needs of the local communities. The objective of this Act was to reduce discriminatory credit practices against low-income neighborhoods. Banks sold many of their mortgages to either Fannie Mae or Freddie Mac.

Fannie Mae and Freddie Mac controlled trillions of dollars of mortgages either by holding the mortgages or selling the mortgages. Many individuals warned of the dangers of Fannie Mae and Freddie Mac to the world economy because of their size, their securities given a AAA rating, and the way they operated with loose government oversight that was often political.

Both Fannie Mae and Freddie Mac contributed substantial sums to politicians that took many forms, including sponsored travel for congressional staff. They have paid millions in fines for violating federal election laws. Individual executives at both Fannie Mae and Freddie Mac were paid millions annually.

Government auditors in 2003 and 2004 found that both Fannie Mae and Freddie Mac manipulated accounting rules to look more profitable and help ensure that executives would receive substantial bonuses.

By the time that the mortgage market blew up in 2007 and 2008, Fannie Mae and Freddie Mac had polluted the world with high-risk mortgages. As housing prices declined in the United States, in some cities by over 50%, mortgages that were high quality became troubled mortgages because the outstanding mortgage on many homes became substantially more than the value of the home.

Financial institutions such as Lehman Brothers, Merrill Lynch, American International Group, Goldman Sachs, J. P. Morgan Chase, and Bear Stearns had taken substantial financial risk (these are only example firms as the list would be very long). In some cases, financial institutions had taken on obligations that were 30 or 40 times their equity. Hundreds of banks failed.

The collapse of the housing market and of many financial institutions led to a worldwide stock market collapse. An analysis of a company that was done only a few weeks earlier was of little use.

This points out the importance of keeping track of investments and being ready to revise the analysis. Companies such as Nike, which had a very good analysis, did experience declines in market value, but they did survive. Material problems on the mortgage market were still present in 2012. Mortgage market problems will likely continue for many more years.

Valuation

Valuation is a process of estimating the value of a firm or some component of a firm. There are many approaches to valuation. Those approaches can be summarized as fundamental analysis and multiperiod discounted valuation approaches. In practice, a wide variety of valuation approaches are employed.

With fundamental analysis, the basic accounting measures are used to assess the firm's future operating cash flows or earnings. Fundamental analysis makes use of the financial statements. This approach considers items such as reported earnings, cash flow, and book value.

The multiperiod discounted valuation approach projects either earnings or cash flow and discounts these numbers to the present value (intrinsic value).

Multiples

Fundamental valuation typically uses one or more multiples. Multiples frequently used are price-to-earnings (PE), price-to-book, price-to-operating cash flow, and price-to-sales. Perceived risk will reduce a multiple, while perceived growth will increase a multiple. When using a multiple approach, it is important to compare results with similar firms.

Multiples use conventional financial statements. For example, PE uses earnings, price-to-book uses the book value, and price-to-operating cash flow uses operating cash flow, while price-to-sales uses sales. Often, the analysis will use several multiples.

The use of multiples and conventional financial reports is not well accepted by the traditional financial literature or many valuation books. However, there is ample evidence proving that security analysts and fund managers prefer the use of multiples.

Multiperiod Discounted Valuation Models

The financial literature and valuation books strongly support use of the multiperiod discounted valuation model in terms of either earnings or cash flow. Discounted cash flow is preferred.

Multiperiod Discounted Earnings Models

There are many multiperiod discounted earnings models. These models rely on accrual accounting to produce results that are closer to the firm's underlying economic performance in the short run than are cash flows.

The two most popular discounted earnings models appear to be discounted abnormal earnings (DAE) and residual income (RI).

Discounted Abnormal Earnings

With this approach, the value of the firm's equity is the sum of its book value and discounted forecasts of abnormal earnings.

Residual Income

This approach discounts future expected earnings. The focus is on earnings as a periodic measure of shareholder wealth creation.

Multiperiod Discounted Cash Flow Models

There are many multiperiod discounted cash flow models. The three most popular seem to be free cash flow (FCF), dividend discount model (DDM), and discounted cash flow (DCF).

Free Cash Flow

The free cash flow model states that the intrinsic value (discounted free cash flow) equals the sum of the stream of expected free cash flows discounted to the present.

There are different definitions of free cash flow, but they are along these lines for common stock: operating cash flows minus interest, minus cash outlays for operating capacity (buildings, equipment, etc.), minus repayments, minus preferred dividends.

Dividend Discount Model (DDM)

The dividend discount model discounts the projected dividend stream to present value. It considers only the dividend stream to common shareholders.

Discounted Cash Flow (DCF)

The discounted cash flow model involves a multiple-year forecast of cash flows. The forecasts are discounted at the firm's estimated cost of capital to arrive at an estimated present value.

What They Use

"Three recent studies have dealt with the issue of what models are actually used by analysts: Barker (1999), Demirakos et al. (2004), and Asquith et al. (2005). All these studies agree that multiperiod discounted valuation models do not seem to play a significant role in analysts' normal valuation activity. Simple price-earnings multiples seem to be the predominant technique. Hence, any cost of equity capital discounted valuation model may not be an adequate representation of the reality of valuation."[29]

Let's review the three studies sited: Barker, Demirakos et al., and Asquith et al.

Barker

The Barker study states that the value of a share is given by the dividend discount model, but the actual determination of the share value is rarely based on the direct estimation of the future dividends.[30]

Barker references prior studies of valuation models used by market participants, which indicated that the strongest and most consistent finding in the behavioral literature is that the price-to-earnings is of primary importance.[31] A further finding was that discounted cash flow models are of little practical importance to investment decisions.[32]

The Barker study itself dealt with analysts and fund managers in the United Kingdom. The valuation models selected for study were price-earnings, dividend yield, price-cash flow (PCF), net asset value (NAV), sales/market capitalization, discounted cash flow, and dividend discount.[33] Analysts and fund managers were asked to rate the importance of these valuation models. Both groups picked the PE method as the preferred method of valuation. The PE, dividend yield, and price-cash flow were significantly more important than all other valuation models. (The discounted cash flow model and the dividend discount model were both of little practical importance.)[34]

The analysts were asked to rank the importance of selected financial ratios: the profit and loss account (ratios) were perceived to be of greater relevance than the balance sheet (ratios).[35]

For both the analysts and fund managers, "a consistent finding from these interviews was that valuation models are perceived to be important in the context of one another, and not just in isolation."[36] This also applied to financial ratios.

Source: Financial Restatements, July 2006, GAO-06-678, P4.

It was found that analysts anchor their process in accounting information combined with other sources that are considered relevant to the reliably foreseeable future.[37] This indicates the importance of financial reports.

Analysts and fund managers consider almost all information received directly from companies to be very important.[38] They both "perceive their own assessment of company management to be at the heart of investment decision-making."[39] If management makes the correct decisions, the firm will generate future cash flow streams.

Source: Financial Restatements, July 2006, GAO-06-678, P4.

Demirakos et al.

The Demirakos et al. study examined the valuation practices of financial analysts at international investment banks. The firms consisted of 26 large U.K.-listed companies drawn from the beverages, electronics, and pharmaceuticals sectors.

Descriptive analysis "shows that almost all the sampled reports contain some form of valuation by reference to a multiple of earnings.[40] The attention given to PE models varies systematically across sectors in understandable ways."[41]

> *Source:* Demirakos et al. study
>
> The main message to emerge from this content analysis of financial analysts' reports is that analysts appear to tailor their valuation methodologies to the circumstances of the industry. PE models remain the mainstay of valuation practice, but other forms of analysis complement those as circumstances demand. In some cases, discounted cash flow (DCF) models are used and in others, more detailed analysis of price-to-sales multiples, growth options, or profitability analysis are used. Another finding is that use of the residual income valuation (RIV) model is extremely limited, but analysts frequently use accounting data in single-period comparative and hybrid models.[42]
>
> *Source:* Demirakos et al. study

Asquith et al.

The Asquith et al. study catalogued the complete contents of *Institutional Investor* All-American analyst reports and examined the market reactions to their release. This study found that analysts use market-to-book value as their asset multiple.[43] No information reported in this study indicated that discounted cash flow was used.

International Aspects

The Barker study dealt with analysts and fund managers in the United Kingdom. The Demirakos study examined the valuation practices of financial analysts at international investment banks. Twenty-six large U.K. firms were examined. The Asquith study examined the contents of *Institutional Investor* All-American analyst reports. Did the varied international aspects of these studies influence the results?

Marco Trombetta in his paper "Discussion of Implied Cost of Equity Capital in Earnings-Based Valuation: International Evidence" commented as follows:

> The kind of training that financial analysts are likely to receive around the world is probably fairly similar, especially if we focus on those countries with a significant

important stock market. Moreover the globalization of capital markets and investment strategies calls into question the assumption that financial analysis is a national activity.[44]

Source: Marco Trombetta, "Discussion of Implied Cost of Equity Capital in Earnings-Based Valuation: International Evidence"

Valuation as Seen by Management Consultants

This section comments on a book, *Valuation, Measuring, and Managing the Value of Companies,* that now is in its fifth edition. Because the three authors (Tom Copeland, Tim Koller, and Jack Murrin) are all current or former partners of McKinsey & Company, Inc., and co-leaders of its corporate finance practice, it reflects practice as viewed by consultants. Individuals interested in valuation from a firm's perspective would benefit from a review of this book.

From Page V

McKinsey & Company, Inc., is an international top management consulting firm. Founded in 1926, McKinsey advises leading companies around the world.

This book is written from the perspective of creating value for the firm. The firm should be managed to increase its value. Its "premise is that the value of a company derives from its ability to generate cash flows and cash-flow-based returns on investment."[45]

The authors' position follows closely the theory of valuation. Discounted cash flows provide a more reliable picture of a company's value than an earnings-multiple approach.[46] Discounted cash flows drive the value of a company.

The firm should focus on long-term rather than short-term cash flows. Short-term cash flows are easy to manipulate, such as delaying research.[47]

Copeland et al. examine mergers and acquisitions (M&A) and observe that the market is often unimpressed with the acquirers' deals. Reviewing the results of academic studies of transactions involving public companies in mergers and acquisitions showed that "shareholders of acquiring companies, on average, earned small returns that are not even statistically different from zero."[48] On the other hand, shareholders of acquired companies are often big winners "receiving on average a 20% premium in a friendly merger and a 35% premium in a hostile takeover."[49] Many acquisitions turn out badly because the purchaser paid too much.[50]

The authors observed that the acquirers overpaid for the following reasons:[51]

1. Overoptimistic appraisal of market potential
2. Overestimation of synergies
3. Poor due diligence
4. Overbidding

Dot.coms

The authors maintain that the correct way to value dot.coms is to use the classic discounted cash flow approach to valuating, reinforcing the continued importance of basic economics and finance.[52]

E-commerce firms have investments in customer acquisition, which is expensed in the income statement. Thus, as more customers are acquired, the values balloon as the losses balloon.[53]

Amazon.com built a customer base and expanded its offerings. Amazon.com started with private equity financing and sold convertible preferred in 1996, which was converted to common in 1997.

Some data from the Amazon.com financial statements are given in Exhibit 11-13. Amazon.com had a market capitalization in the billions by the end of 2000, yet it had never made a profit.

According to the Copeland et al. approach to discounted cash flow for "high-growth companies like Amazon.com, don't be constrained by current performance. Instead of starting from the present—the usual practice in DCF valuations—start by thinking about what the industry and the company could look like when they evolve from today's very high-growth, unstable condition to a substantial, moderate growth rate in the future, and then extrapolate back to current performance."[54]

Copeland et al. also recommend a customer value analysis when valuing very high-growth companies. Five factors that drive the customer-value analysis of a retailer like Amazon.com are as follows:[55]

EXHIBIT **11-13**	Selected Data from the Amazon.com Financial Statements, 1997–2000			
$millions	**1997**	**1998**	**1999**	**2000**
Income statements:				
Sales	148	610	1,640	2,762
Operating loss	(33)	(109)	(606)	(864)
Net loss	(31)	(125)	(720)	(1,411)
Balance sheets:				
Current liabilities	44	162	739	975
Long-term debt	77	348	1,466	2,127
Stockholders' equity:				
Common stock	66	300	1,148	1,326
Accumulated deficit	(38)	(162)	(882)	(2,293)
Total	28	138	266	(967)
Total liabilities & stockholders' equity	149	648	2,471	2,135
Cash flow statements:				
Net cash provided (used) in operating activities	1	31	(91)	(130)
Proceeds from long-term debt	75	326	1,264	681
Proceeds of capital stock and exercise of stock options	53	14	64	45

Selected Data from the Amazon.com financial statements 1997–2000
Source: Amazon.com 2010 10-K

1. The average revenue per customer per year from purchases by its customers as well as revenues from advertisements on its site and from retailers that rent space on it to sell their own products

2. The total number of customers

3. The contribution margin per customer (before the cost of acquiring customers)

4. The average cost of acquiring a customer

5. The customer churn rate (that is, the proportion of customers lost each year)

Any analysis should consider a company's ability to survive long enough for the projections to take place. Amazon.com was able to raise substantial capital prior to the dot.com crash in 2000. Apparently, Amazon.com raised more capital than needed in 1999 and 2000, which allowed it to operate on plan without making major adjustments because of inadequate capital. Note the proceeds from long-term debt: 1997 ($75,000,000), 1998 ($326,000,000), 1999 ($1,264,000,000), and 2000 ($681,000,000).

Summary

This chapter reviewed special areas related to financial statements. It was noted that commercial loan departments give a high significance rating to selected ratios that primarily measure liquidity or debt. The debt/equity ratio received the highest significance rating, and the current ratio was the second highest rated by the commercial loan officers. A commercial bank may elect to include a ratio as part of a loan agreement. The two ratios most likely to be included in a loan agreement are the debt/equity and the current ratio.

Financial executives give the profitability ratios the highest significance ratings. They rate earnings per share and return on investment the highest. Many firms have selected key financial ratios, such as profitability ratios, to be included as part of their corporate objectives.

Certified public accountants give the highest significance rating to two liquidity ratios: the current ratio and the accounts receivable turnover in days. The highest rated profitability ratio was the after-tax net profit margin, while the highest rated debt ratio was debt/equity.

A firm could use its annual report to relate financial data effectively by the use of financial ratios. In general, no major effort is being made to explain financial results by the disclosure of financial ratios in annual reports. A review of the methodology used to compute the ratios disclosed in annual reports indicated that wide differences of opinion exist on how many of the ratios should be computed.

A review of the financial statements, including the notes, indicates the conservatism of the statements in terms of accounting policies. When a firm has conservative accounting policies, it is said that its earnings are of high quality.

There have been many academic studies on the use of financial ratios to forecast financial failure. No conclusive model has yet been developed to forecast financial failure.

Auditors use financial analysis as part of their analytical review procedures. By using financial analysis, they can detect significant fluctuations and unusual items in operating statistics. This can result in a more efficient and effective audit.

Management can use financial analysis in many ways to manage a firm more effectively. A particularly effective use of financial analysis is to integrate ratios that have been accepted as corporate objectives into comprehensive budgeting.

It has become popular to use graphs in annual reports to present financial information. Graphs make it easier to grasp key financial information. Graphs can communicate better than a written report or a tabular presentation.

Many companies are restating their financial statements. This represents a substantial problem when analyzing financial statements.

The improper management of earnings has become a very hot topic. Hopefully, this improper manipulation of earnings is under control.

The collapse of the housing market and of many financial institutions led to a worldwide stock market collapse. Analysis of a company that was done only a few years earlier was of little use.

The objective with valuation is to determine a value for the firm's equity. In theory, the value of a company derives from its ability to generate cash flows and cash-flow-based returns on investment. Research indicates that multiperiod discounted valuation models do not seem to play a significant role in analysts' or fund managers' normal valuation activity. A simple price-earnings multiple seems to be predominant. The multiperiod discounted valuation models appear to play a significant role for a management consulting firm reviewed.

Questions

Q 11-1 Commercial loan officers regard profitability financial ratios as very significant. Comment.

Q 11-2 Which two financial ratios do commercial loan officers regard as the most significant? Which two financial ratios appear most frequently in loan agreements?

Q 11-3 The commercial loan officers did not list the dividend payout ratio as a highly significant ratio, but they did indicate that the dividend payout ratio appeared frequently in loan agreements. Speculate on the reason for this apparent inconsistency.

Q 11-4 Corporate controllers regard profitability financial ratios as very significant. Comment.

Q 11-5 List the top five financial ratios included in corporate objectives according to the study reviewed in this book. Indicate what each of these ratios primarily measures.

Q 11-6 CPAs regard which two financial ratios as the most significant? The highest rated profitability ratio? The highest debt ratio?

Q 11-7 Financial ratios are used extensively in annual reports to interpret and explain financial statements. Comment.

Q 11-8 List the sections of annual reports where ratios are most frequently located, in order of use.

Q 11-9 According to a study of annual reports reviewed in this chapter, what type or types of financial ratios are most likely to be included in annual reports? Speculate on the probable reason for these ratios appearing in annual reports.

Q 11-10 The study of annual reports reviewed in this chapter showed that earnings per share was disclosed in every annual report. Why?

Q 11-11 The study of annual reports reviewed in this chapter indicated that wide differences of opinion exist on how many ratios should be computed. Comment.

Q 11-12 What types of accounting policies are described as conservative?

Q 11-13 Indicate which of the following accounting policies are conservative by placing an X under Yes or No. Assume inflationary conditions exist.

	Conservative	
	Yes	No
a. LIFO inventory		
b. FIFO inventory		
c. Completed-contract method		
d. Percentage-of-completion method		
e. Accelerated depreciation method		
f. Straight-line depreciation method		
g. A relatively short estimated life for a fixed asset		
h. Short period for expensing intangibles		
i. Amortization of patent over five years		
j. High interest rate used to compute the present value of accumulated benefit obligation		
k. High rate of compensation increase used in computing the projected benefit obligation		

Q 11-14 All firms are required to expense R&D costs incurred each period. Some firms spend very large sums on R&D, while others spend little or nothing on this area. Why is it important to observe whether a firm has substantial or immaterial R&D expenses?

Q 11-15 Indicate some possible uses of a reliable model that can be used to forecast financial failure.

Q 11-16 Describe what is meant by a firm's *financial failure*.

Q 11-17 According to the Beaver study, which ratios should be watched most closely, in order of their predictive power?

Q 11-18 According to the Beaver study, three current asset accounts should be given particular attention in order to forecast financial failure. List each of these accounts and indicate whether they should be abnormally high or low.

Q 11-19 What does a Z score below 2.675 indicate, according to the Altman model?

Q 11-20 Indicate a practical problem with computing a Z score for a closely held firm.

Q 11-21 No conclusive model has been developed to forecast financial failure. This indicates that financial ratios are not helpful in forecasting financial failure. Comment.

Q 11-22 You are the auditor of Piedmore Corporation. You determine that the accounts receivable turnover has been much slower this period than in prior periods and that it is also materially lower than the industry average. How might this situation affect your audit plan?

Q 11-23 You are in charge of preparing a comprehensive budget for your firm. Indicate how financial ratios can help determine an acceptable comprehensive budget.

Q 11-24 List four popular forms of graphs used by accountants.

Q 11-25 List two things that can make a line graph misleading.

Q 11-26 Indicate two possible problems with a pie graph for accounting data.

Q 11-27 The surveyed CFAs gave the highest significance rating to which type of financial ratio?

Q 11-28 CFAs gave liquidity ratios a high significance rating. Comment.

Q 11-29 Describe a proper management of earnings. Describe an improper management of earnings.

Q 11-30 In valuation of stock equity, fundamental analysis makes extensive use of multiperiod discounted cash flow. Comment.

Q 11-31 The use of multiples and conventional financial reports is not well accepted by the traditional financial literature or many valuation books. Comment.

Q 11-32 Multiperiod discounted valuation models do not seem to play a significant role in analysts' normal valuation activity. Comment.

Q 11-33 Comment on the importance of an assessment of company management when valuing a company from the perspective of analysts and fund managers.

Q 11-34 We are interested in the future when valuing the stock equity of a company. Therefore, traditional financial statements are of little use in this endeavor. Comment.

Q 11-35 It appears that most restatements are symptomatic of financial reporting fraud. Comment.

Problems

P 11-1

Required Answer the following multiple-choice questions:

a. Notes to financial statements are beneficial in meeting the disclosure requirements of financial reporting. The notes should not be used to

   1. Describe significant accounting policies.
   2. Describe depreciation methods employed by the company.
   3. Describe principles and methods peculiar to the industry in which the company operates when these principles and methods are predominately followed in that industry.
   4. Disclose the basis of consolidation for consolidated statements.
   5. Correct an improper presentation in the financial statements.

b. Which one of the following would be a source of funds under a cash concept of funds but would not be listed as a source under the working capital concept?

   1. Sale of stock
   2. Sale of machinery
   3. Sale of treasury stock
   4. Collection of accounts receivable
   5. Proceeds from long-term bank borrowing

c. The concept of conservatism is often considered important in accounting. The application of this concept means that in the event some doubt occurs as to how a transaction should be recorded, it should be recorded so as to

1. Understate income and overstate assets.
2. Overstate income and overstate assets.
3. Understate income and understate assets.
4. Overstate income and understate assets.
5. Overstate cash and overstate assets.

d. Early in a period in which sales were increasing at a modest rate and plant expansion and start-up costs were occurring at a rapid rate, a successful business would likely experience

1. Increased profits and increased financing requirements because of an increasing cash shortage.
2. Increased profits and decreased financing requirements because of an increasing cash surplus.
3. Increased profits and no change in financing requirements.
4. Decreased profits and increased financing requirements because of an increasing cash shortage.
5. Decreased profits and decreased financing requirements because of an increasing cash surplus.

e. Which of the following ratios would best disclose effective management of working capital by a given firm relative to other firms in the same industry?

1. A high rate of financial leverage relative to the industry average.
2. A high number of days' sales uncollected relative to the industry average.
3. A high turnover of net working capital relative to the industry average.
4. A high number of days' sales in inventory relative to the industry average.
5. A high proportion of fixed assets relative to the industry average.

P 11-2

Required Answer the following multiple-choice questions:

a. If business conditions are stable, a decline in the number of days' sales outstanding from one year to the next (based on a company's accounts receivable at year-end) might indicate

1. A stiffening of the company's credit policies.
2. That the second year's sales were made at lower prices than the first year's sales.
3. That a longer discount period and a more distant due date were extended to customers in the second year.
4. A significant decrease in the volume of sales of the second year.

b. Trading on equity (financial leverage) is likely to be a good financial strategy for stockholders of companies having

1. Cyclical high and low amounts of reported earnings.
2. Steady amounts of reported earnings.
3. Volatile fluctuation in reported earnings over short periods of time.
4. Steadily declining amounts of reported earnings.

c. The ratio of total cash, trade receivables, and marketable securities to current liabilities is

1. The acid-test ratio.
2. The current ratio.
3. Significant if the result is 2-to-1 or below.
4. Meaningless.

(*continued*)

(**P 11-2** CONTINUED)

d. The times interest earned ratio is a primary measure of

1. Liquidity.
2. Long-term debt-paying ability.
3. Activity.
4. Profitability.

e. The calculation of the number of times bond interest is earned involves dividing

1. Net income by annual bond interest expense.
2. Net income plus income taxes by annual bond interest expense.
3. Net income plus income taxes and bond interest expense by annual bond interest expense.
4. Sinking fund earnings by annual bond interest expense.

P 11-3

Required Answer the following multiple-choice questions:

a. Which of the following would not be an example of the use of a multiple when valuing common equity?

1. Multiperiod discounted earnings models
2. Price-to-earnings (PE)
3. Price-to-book
4. Price-to-operating cash flow

b. The two most popular discounted earnings models appear to be

1. Discounted abnormal earnings and residual income.
2. Free cash flow and dividend discount model.
3. Sales/market capitalization and price-earnings.
4. Price-cash flow and dividend discount.

c. Shareholders of acquired companies are often big winners, receiving on average a premium of what in a friendly merger?

1. 10%
2. 20%
3. 30%
4. 35%

d. Which of the following was not given as a reason for acquirers paying too much in an acquisition?

1. Overuse of conventional financial statements
2. Overbidding
3. Overoptimistic appraisal of market potential
4. Overestimation of synergies

e. Which of the following would likely be very useful when valuing a dot.com?

1. Discounted cash flow
2. Price-earnings
3. Net asset value
4. Dividend yield

P 11-4 Thorpe Company is a wholesale distributor of professional equipment and supplies. The company's sales have averaged about $900,000 annually for the three-year period 2009–2011. The firm's total assets at the end of 2011 amounted to $850,000.

The president of Thorpe Company has asked the controller to prepare a report that summarizes the financial aspects of the company's operations for the past three years. This report will be presented to the board of directors at its next meeting.

In addition to comparative financial statements, the controller has decided to present a number of relevant financial ratios that can assist in the identification and interpretation of trends. At the request of the controller, the accounting staff has calculated the following ratios for the three-year period 2009–2011:

Ratio	2009	2010	2011
Current ratio	2.00	2.13	2.18
Acid-test (quick) ratio	1.20	1.10	0.97
Accounts receivable turnover	9.72	8.57	7.13
Inventory turnover	5.25	4.80	3.80
Percent of total debt to total assets	44.00%	41.00%	38.00%
Percent of long-term debt to total assets	25.00%	22.00%	19.00%
Sales to fixed assets (fixed asset turnover)	1.75	1.88	1.99
Sales as a percent of 2009 sales	100.00%	103.00%	106.00%
Gross profit percentage	40.0%	33.6%	38.5%
Net income to sales	7.8%	7.8%	8.0%
Return on total assets	8.5%	8.6%	8.7%
Return on stockholders' equity	15.1%	14.6%	14.1%

In preparing his report, the controller has decided first to examine the financial ratios independently of any other data to determine whether the ratios themselves reveal any significant trends over the first three-year period.

Required

a. The current ratio is increasing, while the acid-test (quick) ratio is decreasing. Using the ratios provided, identify and explain the contributing factor(s) for this apparently divergent trend.

b. In terms of the ratios provided, what conclusion(s) can be drawn regarding the company's use of financial leverage during the 2009–2011 period?

c. Using the ratios provided, what conclusion(s) can be drawn regarding the company's net investment in plant and equipment?

(CMA Adapted)

P 11-5 L. Konrath Company is considering extending credit to D. Hawk Company. L. Konrath Company estimated that sales to D. Hawk Company would amount to $2 million each year. L. Konrath Company, a wholesaler, sells throughout the Midwest. D. Hawk Company, a retail chain operation, has a number of stores in the Midwest. L. Konrath Company has had a gross profit of approximately 60% in recent years and expects to have a similar gross profit on the D. Hawk Company order. The D. Hawk Company order is approximately 15% of L. Konrath Company's present sales. Data from recent statements of D. Hawk Company follow:

(In millions)	2009	2010	2011
Assets			
Current assets:			
Cash	$ 2.6	$ 1.8	$ 1.6
Government securities (cost)	0.4	0.2	—
Accounts and notes receivable (net)	8.0	8.5	8.5
Inventories	2.8	3.2	2.8
Prepaid assets	0.7	0.6	0.6
Total current assets	14.5	14.3	13.5
Property, plant, and equipment (net)	4.3	5.4	5.9
Total assets	$18.8	$19.7	$19.4
Liabilities and Equities			
Current liabilities	$ 6.9	$ 8.5	$ 9.3
Long-term debt, 6%	3.0	2.0	1.0
Total liabilities	9.9	10.5	10.3
Shareholders' equity	8.9	9.2	9.1
Total liabilities and equities	$18.8	$19.7	$19.4

(continued)

(P 11-5 CONTINUED**)**

(In millions)	2009	2010	2011
Income			
Net sales	$24.2	$24.5	$24.9
Cost of goods sold	16.9	17.2	18.0
Gross margin	7.3	7.3	6.9
Selling and administrative expenses	6.6	6.8	7.3
Earnings (loss) before taxes	0.7	0.5	(0.4)
Income taxes	0.3	0.2	(0.2)
Net income	$ 0.4	$ 0.3	$ (0.2)

Required

a. Calculate the following for D. Hawk Company for 2011:

   1. Rate of return on total assets
   2. Acid-test ratio
   3. Return on sales
   4. Current ratio
   5. Inventory turnover

b. As part of the analysis to determine whether L. Konrath Company should extend credit to D. Hawk Company, assume the ratios were calculated from D. Hawk Company statements. For each ratio, indicate whether it is a favorable, an unfavorable, or a neutral statistic in the decision to grant D. Hawk Company credit. Briefly explain your choice in each case.

Ratio	2009	2010	2011
Rate of return on total assets	1.96%	1.12%	(.87)%
Return on sales	1.69%	.99%	(.69)%
Acid-test ratio	1.73	1.36	1.19
Current ratio	2.39	1.92	1.67
Inventory turnover (times per year)	4.41	4.32	4.52
Equity relationships:			
Current liabilities	36.0%	43.0%	48.0%
Long-term liabilities	16.0	10.5	5.0
Shareholders' equity	48.0	46.5	47.0
	100.0%	100.0%	100.0%
Asset relationships:			
Current assets	77.0%	72.5%	69.5%
Property, plant, and equipment	23.0	27.5	30.5
	100.0%	100.0%	100.0%

c. Would you grant credit to D. Hawk Company? Support your answer with facts given in the problem.
d. What additional information, if any, would you want before making a final decision?

(CMA Adapted)

P 11-6 Your company is considering the possible acquisition of Growth, Inc. The financial statements of Growth, Inc., follow:

GROWTH, INC.
Balance Sheet
December 31, 2011 and 2010

	2011	2010
Assets		
Current assets:		
Cash	$ 64,346	$ 11,964
Accounts receivable, less allowance of $750 for doubtful accounts	99,021	83,575
Inventories, FIFO	63,414	74,890
Prepaid expenses	834	1,170
Total current assets	227,615	171,599

	2011	2010
Assets		
Investments and other assets	$ 379	$ 175
Property, plant, and equipment:		
Land and land improvements	6,990	6,400
Buildings	63,280	59,259
Machinery and equipment	182,000	156,000
	252,270	221,659
Less: Accumulated depreciation	110,000	98,000
Net property, plant, and equipment	142,270	123,659
Total assets	$370,264	$295,433
Liabilities and Stockholders' Equity		
Current liabilities:		
Accounts payable	$ 32,730	$ 26,850
Federal income taxes	5,300	4,800
Accrued liabilities	30,200	24,500
Current portion of long-term debt	5,500	5,500
Total current liabilities	73,730	61,650
Long-term debt	76,750	41,900
Other long-term liabilities	5,700	4,300
Deferred federal income taxes	16,000	12,000
Total liabilities	172,180	119,850
Stockholders' equity:		
Capital stock	44,000	43,500
Retained earnings	154,084	132,083
Total stockholders' equity	198,084	175,583
Total liabilities and stockholders' equity	$370,264	$295,433

GROWTH, INC.
Statement of Income
Years Ended December 31, 2011, 2010, and 2009

	2011	2010	2009
Revenues	$578,530	$523,249	$556,549
Costs and expenses:			
Cost of products sold	495,651	457,527	482,358
Selling, general, and administrative	35,433	30,619	29,582
Interest and debt expense	4,308	3,951	2,630
	535,392	492,097	514,570
Income before income taxes	43,138	31,152	41,979
Provision for income taxes	20,120	12,680	17,400
Net income	$ 23,018	$ 18,472	$ 24,579
Net income per share	$ 2.27	$ 1.85	$ 2.43

Partial notes: Under the LIFO method, inventories have been reduced by approximately $35,300 and $41,100 at December 31, 2011 and 2010, respectively, from current cost, which would be reported under the first-in, first-out method.

The effective tax rates were 36.6%, 30.7%, and 31.4%, respectively, for the years ended December 31, 2011, 2010, and 2009.

Required

a. Compute the following for 2011, without considering the LIFO reserve:

Liquidity

1. Days' sales in inventory
2. Merchandise inventory turnover
3. Inventory turnover in days
4. Operating cycle
5. Working capital

(*continued*)

(**P 11-6** CONTINUED)

    6. Current ratio
    7. Acid-test ratio
    8. Cash ratio

Debt

    1. Debt ratio
    2. Debt/equity ratio
    3. Times interest earned

Profitability

    1. Net profit margin
    2. Total asset turnover
    3. Return on assets
    4. Return on total equity

  b. Compute the ratios in part (a), considering the LIFO reserve.
  c. Comment on the apparent liquidity, debt, and profitability, considering both sets of ratios.

P 11-7

Required For each of the following numbered items, you are to select the lettered item(s) that indicate(s) its effect(s) on the corporation's statements. If more than one effect is applicable to a particular item, be sure to indicate *all* applicable letters. (Assume that the state statutes do not permit declaration of nonliquidating dividends except from earnings.)

Item	Effect
1. Declaration of a cash dividend due in one month on noncumulative preferred stock	a. Reduces working capital
	b. Increases working capital
2. Declaration and payment of an ordinary stock dividend	c. Reduces current ratio
	d. Increases current ratio
3. Receipt of a cash dividend, not previously recorded, on stock of another corporation	e. Reduces the dollar amount of total capital stock
4. Passing of a dividend on cumulative preferred stocks	f. Increases the dollar amount of total capital stock
5. Receipt of preferred shares as a dividend on stock held as a temporary investment. This was not a regularly recurring dividend.	g. Reduces total retained earnings
	h. Increases total retained earnings
	i. Reduces equity per share of common stock
6. Payment of dividend mentioned in (1)	
7. Issue of new common shares in a 5-for-1 stock split	j. Reduces equity of each common stockholder

P 11-8 Argo Sales Corporation has in recent years maintained the following relationships among the data on its financial statements:

Gross profit rate on net sales	40%
Net profit rate on net sales	10%
Rate of selling expenses to net sales	20%
Accounts receivable turnover	8 per year
Inventory turnover	6 per year
Acid-test ratio	2-to-1
Current ratio	3-to-1
Quick-asset composition: 8% cash, 32% marketable securities, 60% accounts receivable	
Asset turnover	2 per year
Ratio of total assets to intangible assets	20-to-1
Ratio of accumulated depreciation to cost of fixed assets	1-to-3
Ratio of accounts receivable to accounts payable	1.5-to-1
Ratio of working capital to stockholders' equity	1-to-1.6
Ratio of total debt to stockholders' equity	1-to-2

The corporation had a net income of $120,000 for 2011, which resulted in earnings of $5.20 per share of common stock. Additional information includes the following:

> Capital stock authorized, issued (all in 2000), and outstanding:
>   Common, $10 per share par value, issued at 10% premium
>   Preferred, 6% nonparticipating, $100 per share par value, issued at a 10% premium
> Market value per share of common at December 31, 2011: $78
> Preferred dividends paid in 2011: $3,000
> Times interest earned in 2011: 33
> The amounts of the following were the same at December 31, 2011 as at January 1, 2011: inventory, accounts receivable, 5% bonds payable—due 2020, and total stockholders' equity.
> All purchases and sales were on account.

Required

a. Prepare in good form the condensed balance sheet and income statement for the year ending December 31, 2011, presenting the amounts you would expect to appear on Argo's financial statements (ignoring income taxes). Major captions appearing on Argo's balance sheet are current assets, fixed assets, intangible assets, current liabilities, long-term liabilities, and stockholders' equity. In addition to the accounts divulged in the problem, you should include accounts for prepaid expenses, accrued expenses, and administrative expenses. Supporting computations should be in good form.

b. Compute the following for 2011. (Show your computations.)

1. Rate of return on stockholders' equity
2. Price/earnings ratio for common stock
3. Dividends paid per share of common stock
4. Dividends paid per share of preferred stock
5. Yield on common stock

(CMA Adapted)

P 11-9 Warford Corporation was formed five years ago through a public subscription of common stock. Lucinda Street, who owns 15% of the common stock, was one of the organizers of Warford and is its current president. The company has been successful but currently is experiencing a shortage of funds. On June 10, Street approached Bell National Bank, asking for a 24-month extension on two $30,000 notes, which are due on June 30, 2011 and September 30, 2011. Another note of $7,000 is due on December 31, 2011, but Street expects no difficulty in paying this note on its due date. Street explained that Warford's cash flow problems are due primarily to the company's desire to finance a $300,000 plant expansion over the next two fiscal years through internally generated funds.

The commercial loan officer of Bell National Bank requested financial reports for the last two fiscal years. These reports follow:

WARFORD CORPORATION
Statement of Financial Position
March 31, 2010 and 2011

	2010	2011
Assets:		
Cash	$ 12,500	$ 16,400
Notes receivable	104,000	112,000
Accounts receivable (net)	68,500	81,600
Inventories (at cost)	50,000	80,000
Plant and equipment (net of depreciation)	646,000	680,000
Total assets	$881,000	$970,000
Liabilities and Owners' Equity:		
Accounts payable	$ 72,000	$ 69,000
Notes payable	54,500	67,000
Accrued liabilities	6,000	9,000

(continued)

(**P 11-9** CONTINUED)

	2010	2011
Common stock (60,000 shares, $10 par)	600,000	600,000
Retained earnings*	148,500	225,000
Total liabilities and owners' equity	$881,000	$970,000

*Cash dividends were paid at the rate of $1.00 per share in fiscal year 2010 and $1.25 per share in fiscal year 2011.

WARFORD CORPORATION
Income Statement
For the Fiscal Years Ended March 31, 2010 and 2011

	2010	2011
Sales	$2,700,000	$3,000,000
Cost of goods sold*	1,720,000	1,902,500
Gross profit	980,000	1,097,500
Operating expenses	780,000	845,000
Net income before taxes	200,000	252,500
Income taxes (40%)	80,000	101,000
Income after taxes	$ 120,000	$ 151,500

*Depreciation charges on the plant and equipment of $100,000 and $102,500 for fiscal years ended March 31, 2010 and 2011, respectively, are included in cost of goods sold.

Required

a. Calculate the following items for Warford Corporation:

1. Current ratio for fiscal years 2010 and 2011
2. Acid-test (quick) ratio for fiscal years 2010 and 2011
3. Inventory turnover for fiscal year 2011
4. Return on assets for fiscal years 2010 and 2011
5. Percentage change in sales, cost of goods sold, gross profit, and net income after taxes from fiscal year 2010 to 2011

b. Identify and explain what other financial reports and/or financial analyses might be helpful to the commercial loan officer of Bell National Bank in evaluating Street's request for a time extension on Warford's notes.

c. Assume that the percentage changes experienced in fiscal year 2011, as compared with fiscal year 2010, for sales, cost of goods sold, gross profit, and net income after taxes, will be repeated in each of the next two years. Is Warford's desire to finance the plant expansion from internally generated funds realistic? Explain.

d. Should Bell National Bank grant the extension on Warford's notes, considering Street's statement about financing the plant expansion through internally generated funds? Explain.

(CMA Adapted)

P 11-10 The following data apply to items (a) through (g):

JOHANSON COMPANY
Statement of Financial Position
December 31, 2010 and 2011

(In thousands)	2010	2011
Assets		
Current assets:		
Cash and temporary investments	$ 380	$ 400
Accounts receivable (net)	1,500	1,700
Inventories	2,120	2,200
Total current assets	4,000	4,300
Long-term assets:		
Land	500	500
Building and equipment (net)	4,000	4,700
Total long-term assets	4,500	5,200
Total assets	$8,500	$9,500

(In thousands)	2010	2011
Liabilities and Equities		
Current liabilities:		
Accounts payable	$ 700	$1,400
Current portion of long-term debt	500	1,000
Total current liabilities	1,200	2,400
Long-term debt	4,000	3,000
Total liabilities	5,200	5,400
Stockholders' equity:		
Common stock	3,000	3,000
Retained earnings	300	1,100
Total stockholders' equity	3,300	4,100
Total liabilities and equities	$8,500	$9,500

JOHANSON COMPANY
Statement of Income and Retained Earnings
For the Year Ended December 31, 2011

(In thousands)		
Net sales		$28,800
Less: Cost of goods sold	$15,120	
Selling expenses	7,180	
Administrative expenses	4,100	
Interest	400	
Income taxes	800	27,600
Net income		1,200
Retained earnings, January 1		300
Subtotal		1,500
Cash dividends declared and paid		400
Retained earnings, December 31		$ 1,100

Required Answer the following multiple-choice questions:

a. The acid-test ratio for 2011 is

    1. 1.1-to-1.
    2. 0.9-to-1.
    3. 1.8-to-1.
    4. 0.2-to-1.
    5. 0.17-to-1.

b. The average number of days' sales outstanding in 2011 is

    1. 18 days.
    2. 360 days.
    3. 20 days.
    4. 4.4 days.
    5. 80 days.

c. The times interest earned ratio for 2011 is

    1. 3.0 times.
    2. 1.0 time.
    3. 72.0 times.
    4. 2.0 times.
    5. 6.0 times.

d. The asset turnover in 2011 is

    1. 3.2 times.
    2. 1.7 times.
    3. 0.4 time.

(*continued*)

(**P 11-10** CONTINUED)

    4. 1.1 times.
    5. 0.13 time.

e. The inventory turnover in 2011 is

    1. 13.6 times.
    2. 12.5 times.
    3. 0.9 time.
    4. 7.0 times.
    5. 51.4 times.

f. The operating income margin in 2011 is

    1. 2.7%.
    2. 91.7%.
    3. 52.5%.
    4. 95.8%.
    5. 8.3%.

g. The dividend payout ratio in 2011 is

    1. 100%.
    2. 36%.
    3. 20%.
    4. 8.8%.
    5. 33.3%.

(CMA Adapted)

P 11-11 The statement of financial position for Paragon Corporation at November 30, 2011, the end of its current fiscal year, follows. The market price of the company's common stock was $4 per share on November 30, 2011.

(In thousands)
Assets
Current assets:

Cash		$ 6,000	
Accounts receivable	$ 7,000		
Less: Allowance for doubtful accounts	400	6,600	
Merchandise inventory		16,000	
Supplies on hand		400	
Prepaid expenses		1,000	
Total current assets			$30,000
Property, plant, and equipment:			
Land		27,500	
Building	$36,000		
Less: Accumulated depreciation	13,500	22,500	
Total property, plant, and equipment			50,000
Total assets			$80,000

Liabilities and Stockholders' Equity
Current liabilities:

Accounts payable		$ 6,400	
Accrued interest payable		800	
Accrued income taxes payable		2,200	
Accrued wages payable		600	
Deposits received from customers		2,000	
Total current liabilities			$12,000
Long-term debt:			
Bonds payable—20-year, 8% convertible debentures			
due December 1, 2016 (Note 7)		20,000	
Less: Unamortized discount		200	19,800
Total liabilities			31,800

(In thousands)
Stockholders' equity:

Common stock—authorized 40,000,000 shares of $1 par value; 20,000,000 shares issued and outstanding	20,000	
Paid-in capital in excess of par value	12,200	
Total paid-in capital	32,200	
Retained earnings	16,000	
Total stockholders' equity		48,200
Total liabilities and stockholders' equity		$80,000

All items are to be considered independent of one another, and any transactions given in the items are to be considered the only transactions to affect Paragon Corporation during the just-completed current or coming fiscal year. Average balance sheet account balances are used in computing ratios involving income statement accounts. Ending balance sheet account balances are used in computing ratios involving only balance sheet items.

Required Answer the following multiple-choice questions:

a. If Paragon paid back all of the deposits received from customers, its current ratio would be

   1. 2.50-to-1.00.
   2. 2.80-to-1.00.
   3. 2.33-to-1.00.
   4. 3.00-to-1.00.
   5. 2.29-to-1.00.

b. If Paragon paid back all of the deposits received from customers, its quick (acid-test) ratio would be

   1. 1.06-to-1.00.
   2. 1.00-to-1.00.
   3. 0.88-to-1.00.
   4. 1.26-to-1.00.
   5. 1.20-to-1.00.

c. A 2-for-1 common stock split by Paragon would

   1. Result in each $1,000 bond being convertible into 600 new shares of Paragon common stock.
   2. Decrease the retained earnings due to the capitalization of retained earnings.
   3. Not affect the number of common shares outstanding.
   4. Increase the total paid-in capital.
   5. Increase the total stockholders' equity.

d. Paragon Corporation's building is being depreciated using the straight-line method, salvage value of $6,000,000, and life of 20 years. The number of years the building has been depreciated by Paragon as of November 30, 2011 is

   1. 7.5 years.
   2. 12.5 years.
   3. 9.0 years.
   4. 15.0 years.
   5. None of these.

e. Paragon's book value per share of common stock as of November 30, 2011 is

   1. $4.00.
   2. $1.61.
   3. $1.00.
   4. $2.41.
   5. None of these.

(*continued*)

(P 11-11 CONTINUED)

f. If, during the current fiscal year ending November 30, 2011, Paragon had sales of $90,000,000 with a gross profit of 20% and an inventory turnover of five times per year, the merchandise inventory balance on December 1, 2010 was

1. $14,400,000.
2. $12,800,000.
3. $18,000,000.
4. $20,000,000.
5. $16,000,000.

g. If Paragon has a payout ratio of 80% and declared and paid $4,000,000 of cash dividends during the current fiscal year ended November 30, 2011, the retained earnings balance on December 1, 2010 was

1. $20,000,000.
2. $17,000,000.
3. $15,000,000.
4. $11,000,000.
5. None of these.

(CMA Adapted)

P 11-12 Calcor Company has been a wholesale distributor of automobile parts for domestic automakers for 20 years. Calcor has suffered through the recent slump in the domestic auto industry, and its performance has not rebounded to the levels of the industry as a whole.

Calcor's single-step income statement for the year ended November 30, 2011, follows:

CALCOR COMPANY
Income Statement
For the Year Ended November 30, 2011 (thousands omitted)

Net sales	$8,400
Expenses:	
Cost of goods sold	6,300
Selling expense	780
Administrative expense	900
Interest expense	140
Total	8,120
Income before income taxes	280
Income taxes	112
Net income	$ 168

Calcor's return on sales before interest and taxes was 5% in fiscal 2011 compared with the industry average of 9%. Calcor's turnover of average assets of four times per year and return on average assets before interest and taxes of 20% are both well below the industry average.

Joe Kuhn, president of Calcor, wishes to improve these ratios and raise them nearer to the industry averages. He established the following goals for Calcor Company for fiscal 2012:

Return on sales before interest and taxes	8%
Turnover of average assets	5 times per year
Return on average assets before interest and taxes	30%

For fiscal 2012, Kuhn and the rest of Calcor's management team are considering the following actions, which they expect will improve profitability and result in a 5% increase in unit sales:

1. Increase selling prices 10%.
2. Increase advertising by $420,000 and hold all other selling and administrative expenses at fiscal 2011 levels.
3. Improve customer service by increasing average current assets (inventory and accounts receivable) by a total of $300,000, and hold all other assets at fiscal 2011 levels.
4. Finance the additional assets at an annual interest rate of 10% and hold all other interest expense at fiscal 2011 levels.

5. Improve the quality of products carried; this will increase the units of goods sold by 4%.
6. Calcor's 2012 effective income tax rate is expected to be 40%—the same as in fiscal 2011.

Required
a. Prepare a single-step pro forma income statement for Calcor Company for the year ended November 30, 2012, assuming that Calcor's planned actions would be carried out and that the 5% increase in unit sales would be realized.
b. Calculate the following ratios for Calcor Company for the 2011–2012 fiscal year and state whether Kuhn's goal would be achieved:

1. Return on sales before interest and taxes.
2. Turnover of average assets.
3. Return on average assets before interest and taxes.

c. Would it be possible for Calcor Company to achieve the first two of Kuhn's goals without achieving his third goal of a 30% return on average assets before interest and taxes? Explain your answer.

(CMA Adapted)

P 11-13 The following data are for the A, B, and C Companies:

	Company		
Variables	A	B	C
Current assets	$150,000	$170,000	$180,000
Current liabilities	$ 60,000	$ 50,000	$ 30,000
Total assets	$300,000	$280,000	$250,000
Retained earnings	$ 80,000	$ 90,000	$ 60,000
Earnings before interest and taxes	$ 70,000	$ 60,000	$ 50,000
Market price per share	$ 20.00	$ 18.75	$ 16.50
Number of shares outstanding	9,000	9,000	9,000
Book value of total debt	$ 30,000	$ 50,000	$ 80,000
Sales	$430,000	$400,000	$200,000

Required
a. Compute the Z score for each company.
b. According to the Altman model, which of these firms is most likely to experience financial failure?

P 11-14 General Company's financial statements for 2011 follow here and on the following pages:

GENERAL COMPANY
Statement of Income
Years Ended December 31, 2011, 2010, and 2009

	2011	2010	2009
Net sales	$860,000	$770,000	$690,000
Cost and expenses:			
Cost of products sold	730,000	630,000	580,000
Selling, general, and administrative	46,000	40,000	38,000
Interest and debt expense	4,000	3,900	6,500
	780,000	673,900	624,500
Income before income taxes	80,000	96,100	65,500
Provision for income taxes	33,000	24,000	21,000
Net income	$ 47,000	$ 72,100	$ 44,500
Net income per share	$ 2.67	$ 4.10	$ 2.54

(continued)

(**P 11-14** CONTINUED)

GENERAL COMPANY
Statement of Cash Flows
Years Ended December 31, 2011, 2010, and 2009

	2011	2010	2009
Operating activities:			
Net income	$ 47,000	$ 72,100	$ 44,500
Adjustments to reconcile net income to net cash provided by operating activities:			
Depreciation and amortization	21,000	20,000	19,000
Deferred taxes	3,800	2,500	2,000
Increase in accounts receivable	(4,000)	(3,000)	(3,000)
Decrease (increase) in inventories	(3,000)	(2,500)	1,000
Decrease (increase) in prepaid expenses	(300)	(200)	100
Increase (decrease) in accounts payable	6,000	5,000	(1,000)
Increase (decrease) in income taxes	100	300	(100)
Increase (decrease) in accrued liabilities	6,000	3,000	(1,000)
Net cash provided by operating activities	76,600	97,200	61,500
Investing activities:			
Additions to property, plant, and equipment	(66,500)	$(84,400)	(52,500)
Financing activities:			
Payment on long-term debt	(1,000)	(2,000)	(1,500)
Issuance of other long-term liabilities	9,200	1,000	(1,000)
Issuance of capital stock	1,000	—	—
Dividend paid	(10,300)	(9,800)	(9,500)
Net cash used in financing activities	(1,100)	(10,800)	(12,000)
Increase (decrease) in cash	9,000	2,000	(3,000)
Cash at beginning of year	39,000	37,000	40,000
Cash at end of year	$ 48,000	$ 39,000	$ 37,000

GENERAL COMPANY
Balance Sheet December 31, 2011

	2011	2010
Assets		
Current assets:		
Cash	$ 48,000	$ 39,000
Accounts receivable, less allowance for doubtful accounts of $2,000 in 2011 and $1,400 in 2010	125,000	121,000
Inventories	71,000	68,000
Prepaid expenses	2,500	2,200
Total current assets	246,500	230,200
Property, plant, and equipment:		
Land and land improvements	12,000	10,500
Buildings	98,000	89,000
Machinery and equipment	303,000	247,000
	413,000	346,500
Less: Accumulated depreciation	165,000	144,000
Net property, plant, and equipment	248,000	202,500
Total assets	$494,500	$432,700
Liabilities and Stockholders' Equity		
Current liabilities:		
Accounts payable	$ 56,000	$ 50,000
Income taxes	3,700	3,600
Accrued liabilities	34,000	28,000
Total current liabilities	93,700	81,600
Long-term debt	63,000	64,000
Other long-term liabilities	16,000	6,800
Deferred federal income taxes	27,800	24,000
Total liabilities	200,500	176,400

	2011	2010
Stockholders' equity:		
Capital stock	46,000	45,000
Retained earnings	248,000	211,300
Total stockholders' equity	294,000	256,300
Total liabilities and stockholders' equity	$494,500	$432,700

Note: The market price of the stock at the end of 2011 was $30.00 per share. There were 23,000 common shares outstanding at December 31, 2011.

Required
  a. Compute the Z score of General Company at the end of 2011.
  b. According to the Altman model, does the Z score of General Company indicate a high probability of financial failure?

P 11-15

LIFO reserves: Rhodes Company
Reported year for analysis, 2011

2011 Net income as reported	$ 90,200,000
2011 Inventory reserve	50,000,000
2010 Inventory reserve	46,000,000
2011 Income taxes	55,000,000
2011 Income before income taxes	145,200,000

Required Compute the approximate income if inventory had been valued at approximate current cost.

P 11-16

LIFO reserves: Lion Company
Reported year for analysis, 2011

2011 Net income as reported	$45,000,000
2011 Inventory reserve	20,000,000
2010 Inventory reserve	28,000,000
2011 Income taxes	14,000,000
2011 Income before income taxes	59,000,000

Required Compute the approximate income if inventory had been valued at approximate current cost.

P 11-17 An airline presented this graph with its annual report.

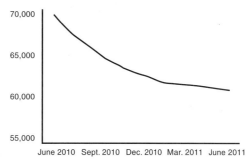

Staffing Levels
Full-Time Equivalent Employees

At Quarter-End

Required Indicate the misleading feature in this graph.

P 11-18 Provision for Obsolete Inventory—Ethical?
The Jones Company is having a very good year with sales running 50% above projections. At the end of the year the CFO decides that this is a good time to provide for possible obsolete

(*continued*)

(**P 11-18** CONTINUED)

inventory and sets up a $15 million reserve account for obsolete inventory. As time permits, next year there will be close examination of inventory to determine inventory that is obsolete.

Required
a. How will the reserve impact current earnings?
b. Next year when the obsolete inventory is identified, how will this impact earnings?
c. Was setting up the reserve ethical? Comment.

P 11-19 Push for Year End Sales—Ethical?

The Boyer Company manufactures snow blowers. It has been a warm fall and sales have declined materially. This has resulted in a buildup of inventory.

Required
a. In early December the Boyer Company embarks on a sales promotion giving a special 10% discount for orders received by December 15. Comment on the ethics of this promotion.
b. In early December the Boyer Company embarks on a sales promotion giving a guaranteed return up to March 31. These orders must be received by December 15 and this promotion only applies to the first $2,000,000 in orders received. Comment on the ethics of this promotion.

Cases

CASE 11-1 SMOKE AND SMOKELESS

REYNOLDS AMERICAN INC.*
CONSOLIDATED STATEMENTS OF INCOME
(Dollars in Millions, Except Per Share Amounts)

	For the Years Ended December 31,		
	2010	2009	2008
Net sales[1]	$8,170	$8,015	$8,377
Net sales, related party	381	404	468
Net sales	8,551	8,419	8,845
Costs and expenses:			
Cost of products sold[1][2][3][4]	4,544	4,485	4,863
Selling, general and administrative expenses	1,493	1,508	1,500
Amortization expense	25	28	22
Asset impairment and exit charges	38	—	—
Trademark impairment charge	6	567	318
Goodwill impairment charge	26	—	—
Restructuring charge	—	56	90
Operating income	2,419	1,775	2,052
Interest and debt expense	232	251	275
Interest income	(12)	(19)	(60)
Gain on termination of joint venture	—	—	(328)
Other expense, net	7	9	37
Income from continuing operations before income taxes	2,192	1,534	2,128
Provision for income taxes	863	572	790
Income from continuing operations	1,329	962	1,338
Losses from discontinued operations, net of tax	(216)	—	—
Net income	$1,113	$ 962	$1,338

* "Reynolds American Inc., referred to as RAI, is a holding company whose operating subsidiaries include the second largest cigarette manufacturer in the United States, R. J. Reynolds Tobacco Company, and the second largest smokeless tobacco products manufacturer in the United States, American Snuff Company, LLC (formerly known as Conwood Company, LLC), referred to as American Snuff Co." 10-K

Source: Reynolds American Inc. 2010 10-K

| | For the Years Ended December 31, | | |
	2010	2009	2008
Basic income per share[5]:			
Income from continuing operations	$ 2.28	$ 1.65	$ 2.28
Losses from discontinued operations	(0.37)	—	—
Net income	$ 1.91	$ 1.65	$ 2.28
Diluted income per share:			
Income from continuing operations	$ 2.27	$ 1.65	$ 2.28
Losses from discontinued operations	(0.37)	—	—
Net income	$ 1.90	$ 1.65	$ 2.28
Dividends declared per share	$ 1.84	$ 1.73	$ 1.70

[1]Excludes excise taxes of $4,340 million, $3,927 million and $1,890 million for the years ended December 31, 2010, 2009 and 2008, respectively.

[2]Includes Master Settlement Agreement, referred to as MSA, and other state settlement agreements with the states of Mississippi, Florida, Texas and Minnesota, together with the MSA, collectively referred to as the State Settlement Agreements, expense of $2,496 million, $2,540 million and $2,703 million for the years ended December 31, 2010, 2009 and 2008, respectively.

[3]Includes federal tobacco quote buyout expenses of $243 million, $240 million and $249 million for the years ended December 31, 2010, 2009 and 2008, respectively.

[4]Includes U.S. Food and Drug Administration, referred to FDA, user fees of $75 million and $22 million for the years ended December 31, 2010 and 2009, respectively.

[5]All per share amounts have been retroactively adjusted to reflect the November 15, 2010, two-for-one stock split. See note 1 for additional information.

REYNOLDS AMERICAN INC.
CONSOLIDATED BALANCE SHEETS
(Dollars in Millions)

| | December 31, | |
	2010	2009
Assets		
Current assets:		
Cash and cash equivalents	$ 2,195	$ 2,723
Accounts receivable	118	109
Accounts receivable, related party	48	96
Notes receivable	34	36
Other receivables	10	15
Inventories	1,055	1,219
Deferred income taxes, net	946	956
Prepaid expenses and other	195	341
Assets held for sale	201	—
Total current assets	4,082	5,495
Property, plant and equipment, at cost:		
Land and land improvements	89	88
Buildings and leasehold improvements	656	661
Machinery and equipment	1,700	1,759
Construction-in-process	157	87
Total property, plant and equipment	2,602	2,595
Less accumulated depreciation	1,600	1,570
Property, plant and equipment, net	1,002	1,025
Trademarks and other intangible assets, net of accumulated amortization (2010 − $672; 2009 − $647)	2,675	2,718
Goodwill	8,010	8,185
Other assets and deferred charges	589	586
	$17,078	$18,009
Liabilities and shareholders' equity		
Current liabilities:		
Accounts payable	$ 179	$ 196
Tobacco settlement accruals	2,589	2,611
Due to related party	4	3
Deferred revenue, related party	53	57
Current maturities of long-term debt	400	300

(*continued*)

(**CASE 11-1** CONTINUED)

	December 31,	
	2010	2009
Current liabilities: *(continued)*		
Other current liabilities	1,147	1,173
Total current liabilities	4,372	4,340
Long-term debt (less current maturities)	3,701	4,136
Deferred income taxes, net	518	441
Long-term retirement benefits (less current portion)	1,668	2,218
Other noncurrent liabilities	309	376
Commitments and contingencies:		
Shareholders' equity:		
Common stock (shares issued: 2010 – 583,043,872; 2009 – 582,848,102)	—	—
Paid-in capital	8,535	8,498
Accumulated deficit	(547)	(579)
Accumulated other comprehensive loss – (Defined benefit pension and post-retirement plans: 2010 – $(1,446) and 2009 – $(1,376), net of tax)	(1,478)	(1,421)
Total shareholders' equity	6,510	6,498
	$17,078	$18,009

NOTES TO CONSOLIDATED FINANCIAL STATEMENTS (IN PART)

Note 1 Business and Summary of Significant Accounting Policies (In Part)

Stock Split

On October 12, 2010, RAI's Board of Directors approved a two-for-one stock split of RAI's common stock, which was issued on November 15, 2001, to shareholders of record on November 1, 2010. Shareholders on the record date received one additional share of RAI common stock for each share owned. All current and prior period share and per share amounts have been adjusted to reflect this stock split.

Inventories

Inventories are stated at the lower of cost or market. The cost of tobacco inventories is determined principally under the last-in, first-out, or LIFO, method and is calculated at the end of each year. The cost of work in process and finished goods includes materials, direct labor, variable costs and overhead, and full absorption of fixed manufacturing overhead. Stocks of tobacco, which have an operating cycle that exceeds 12 months due to aging requirements, are classified as current assets, consistent with recognized industry practice.

Note 9—Inventories

The major components of inventories at December 31 were as follows:

	2010	2009
Leaf tobacco	$ 997	$1,052
Other raw materials	44	65
Work in progress	64	80
Finished products	122	180
Other	25	32
Total	1,252	1,409
Less LIFO allowance	197	190
	$1,055	$1,219

Inventories valued under the LIFO method were $600 million and $473 million at December 31, 2010 and 2009, respectively, net of the LIFO allowance. The LIFO allowance reflects the excess of the current cost of LIFO inventories at December 31, 2010 and 2009, over the amount at which these inventories were carried on the consolidated balance sheets. RAI recorded expense of $7 million, $78 million and income of $61 million from LIFO inventory changes during 2010, 2009 and 2008, respectively.

Note 11 Income Taxes (In Part)

The differences between the provision for income taxes from continuing operations and income taxes computed at statutory U.S. federal income tax rates for the years ended December 31 were as follows:

	2010	2009	2008
Income taxes computed at statutory U.S. federal income tax rates	$ 767	$ 537	$ 745
State and local income taxes, net of federal tax benefits	100	81	73
Favorable resolution of federal tax matters	—	—	(2)
Domestic manufacturing deduction	(54)	(41)	(41)
Other items, net	50	(5)	15
Provision for income taxes from continuing operations	$ 863	$ 572	$ 790
Effective tax rate	39.4%	37.3%	37.1%

The effective tax rate for 2010 was unfavorably impacted by a $27 million increase in tax attributable to the Patient Protection and Affordable Care Act of 2010 and the Health Care and Education Reconciliation Act of 2010. The effective tax rates for 2008 and 2009 were unfavorably impacted by increases in unrecognized income tax benefits and increases in tax attributable to accumulated and undistributed foreign earnings.

As of December 31, 2010, there were $438 million of accumulated and undistributed foreign earnings. Of this amount, RAI has invested $77 million and has plans to invest $10 million overseas. RAI has recorded deferred income taxes of $125 million on the $351 million of accumulated earnings in excess of its historical and planned overseas investments.

Note to the case:

The FABER REPORT, May 25, 2011 reported that JP Morgan did an analysis of 519 companies and found a collective $1.375 trillion in undistributed foreign earnings.

United States companies are taxed at a rate of up to 35% when they repatriate off share earnings.

Required

a. Determine the change in net income for 2010 in comparison with the reported net income if FIFO had been used for all inventory.

b. Compute the following for 2010 with no adjustments for LIFO reserve:
   1. Days' sales in inventory
   2. Working capital
   3. Current ratio
   4. Acid-test ratio
   5. Debt ratio

c. Compute the measures in (b) considering the LIFO reserve (eliminate the LIFO reserve):
   1. Days' sales in inventory
   2. Working capital
   3. Current ratio
   4. Acid-test ratio
   5. Debt ratio

d. Comment on the different results of the ratios computed in (b) and (c).

e. For the 2009 financial statements, what was the diluted income per share for 2009 and 2008?

f. How much deferred taxes have been recognized by Reynolds American Inc. for undistributed foreign earnings. Is this conservative?

CASE 11-2 ACCOUNTING HOCUS-POCUS

This case is an excerpt from a presentation given by former Chairman Arthur Levitt, Securities and Exchange Commission, the "Numbers Game," to New York University Center for Law and Business, September 28, 1998.

(continued)

Source: U.S. Securities and Exchange

(**Case 11-2** CONTINUED)

Accounting Hocus-Pocus

Our accounting principles weren't meant to be a straitjacket. Accountants are wise enough to know they cannot anticipate every business structure or every new and innovative transaction, so they develop principles that allow for flexibility to adapt to changing circumstances. That's why the highest standards of objectivity, integrity and judgment can't be the exception. They must be the rule.

Flexibility in accounting allows it to keep pace with business innovations. Abuses such as earnings management occur when people exploit this pliancy. Trickery is employed to obscure actual financial volatility. This, in turn, masks the true consequences of management's decisions. These practices aren't limited to smaller companies struggling to gain investor interest. It's also happening in companies whose products we know and admire.

So what are these illusions? Five of the more popular ones I want to discuss today are "big bath" restructuring charges, creative acquisition accounting, "cookie jar reserves," "immaterial" misapplications of accounting principles and the premature recognition of revenue.

"Big-Bath" Charges

Let me first deal with "Big Bath" restructuring charges.

Companies remain competitive by regularly assessing the efficiency and profitability of their operations. Problems arise, however, when we see large charges associated with companies restructuring. These charges help companies "clean up" their balance sheet—giving them a so-called "big bath."

Why are companies tempted to overstate these charges? When earnings take a major hit, the theory goes Wall Street will look beyond a one-time loss and focus only on future earnings.

And if these charges are conservatively estimated with a little extra cushioning, that so-called conservative estimate is miraculously reborn as income when estimates change or future earnings fall short.

When a company decides to restructure, management and employees, investors and creditors, customers and suppliers all want to understand the expected effects. We need, of course, to ensure that financial reporting provides this information. But this should not lead to flushing all the associated costs—and maybe a little extra—through the financial statements.

Creative Acquisition Accounting

Let me turn now to the second gimmick.

In recent years, whole industries have been remade through consolidations, acquisitions and spin-offs. Some acquirers, particularly those using stock as an acquisition currency, have used this environment as an opportunity to engage in another form of "creative accounting." I call it "merger magic."

I am not talking tonight about the pooling versus purchase problem. Some companies have no choice but to use purchase accounting—which can result in lower future earnings. But that's a result some companies are unwilling to tolerate.

So what do they do? They classify an ever-growing portion of the acquisition price as "in-process" Research and Development, so—you guessed it—the amount can be written off in a "one-time" charge—removing any future earnings drag. Equally troubling is the creation of large liabilities for future operating expenses to protect future earnings—all under the mask of an acquisition.

Miscellaneous "Cookie Jar Reserves"

A third illusion played by some companies is using unrealistic assumptions to estimate liabilities for such items as sales returns, loan losses or warranty costs. In doing so, they stash accruals in cookie jars during the good times and reach into them when needed in the bad times.

I'm reminded of one U.S. company who took a large one-time loss to earnings to reimburse franchisees for equipment. That equipment, however, which included literally the kitchen sink, had yet to be bought. And, at the same time, they announced that future earnings would grow an impressive 15% per year.

"Materiality"

Let me turn now to the fourth gimmick—the abuse of materiality—a word that captures the attention of both attorneys and accountants. Materiality is another way we build flexibility into financial reporting. Using the logic of diminishing returns, some items may be so insignificant that they are not worth measuring and reporting with exact precision.

But some companies misuse the concept of materiality. They intentionally record errors within a defined percentage ceiling. They then try to excuse that fib by arguing that the effect on the bottom line is too small to matter. If that's the case, why do they work so hard to create these errors? Maybe because the effect can matter, especially if it picks up that last penny of the consensus estimate. When either management or the outside auditors are questioned about these clear violations of GAAP, they answer sheepishly...."It doesn't matter. It's immaterial."

In markets where missing an earnings projection by a penny can result in a loss of millions of dollars in market capitalization, I have a hard time accepting that some of these so-called non-events simply don't matter.

Revenue Recognition

Lastly, companies try to boost earnings by manipulating the recognition of revenue. Think about a bottle of fine wine. You wouldn't pop the cork on that bottle before it was ready. But some companies are doing this with their revenue—recognizing it before a sale is complete, before the product is delivered to a customer, or at a time when the customer still has options to terminate, void or delay the sale.

Required

a. "Big Bath"—Comment on how a "Big Bath" would have enabled WorldCom to cover up its fraud.

b. Why would writing off "in-process" Research and Development be similar to a "Big Bath"?

c. How could a company use "allowance for doubtful accounts" as "Cookie Jar Reserves"?

d. Speculate on how a company could use "Materiality" or disregard or partially disregard a specific accounting standard.

CASE 11-3 TURN A CHEEK

June 1996, *The New York Times* columnist Bob Herbert wrote a pair of opinion editorials accusing Nike Corp. of cruelly exploiting cheap Asian labor. Nike CEO Philip Knight replied in a letter to the editor, which the *The New York Times* published. Some of the information in the Knight letter included that Nike has, on average, paid double the minimum wage as defined in countries where its products are produced under contract.[56]

In 1998, Marc Kasky, a resident of California, sued Nike, alleging that the Knight letter violated California's consumer protection laws against deceptive advertising and unfair business practices.[57] In effect, the position was that *The New York Times* editorials were under the First Amendment, but that the Nike reply was under the Fifth Amendment. The First Amendment covers freedom of speech, while the Fifth Amendment covers commercial speech.

The California Supreme Court ruled in May 2002 that the Nike reply had to be viewed under the Fifth Amendment. The Supreme Court stated it was "commercial speech because it is both more readily verifiable by its speaker and more hardy than noncommercial speech, can be effectively regulated to suppress false and actually or inherently misleading messages without undue risk of chilling public debate."[58]

Nike appealed the decision to the U.S. Supreme Court. The Supreme Court agreed to hear the case. In June 2003, the Supreme Court changed its mind and dismissed the matter on procedural grounds.[59] Usually, the justices consider cases only after the state courts render a final decision; here, the state court had only said the speech was a commercial

(*continued*)

(**CASE 11-3** CONTINUED)

speech and sent the case back down for further proceedings—likely including a trial on whether the statements were indeed misleading.[60]

A trial did not take place, as Nike settled on September 2003, agreeing to pay $1.5 million over a three-year period to the Fair Labor Association, a Washington worker-rights group.[61]

Required

a. Write a position paper on why the Nike reply should be viewed under the First Amendment.

b. Write a position paper on why the Nike reply should be viewed under the Fifth Amendment.

Good reference materials for this case are:
Note: Roger Parloff, "Can We Talk," *Fortune* (September 2, 2002), pp. 102–104, 106, 108, 110.
Note: Kasky v. Nike, Inc. Cite as 45 P. 3d 243 (Cal 2002).
Note: Nike Web site www.Nike.com.

CASE 11-4 BOOKS UNLIMITED*—PART 1

Borders Group, Inc., presented this information in its 10-Ks:

CONSOLIDATED STATEMENTS OF OPERATIONS
(Dollars in millions except per share data)

	Jan. 31, 2009	Feb. 2, 2008	Feb. 3, 2007
Sales	$3,242.1	$3,555.1	$3,532.3
Other revenue	33.3	42.3	37.1
Total revenue	$3,275.4	$3,597.4	$3,569.4
Cost of merchandise sold (includes occupancy)	2,484.8	2,668.3	2,615.7
Gross margin	790.6	929.1	953.7
Selling, general, and administrative expenses	839.6	907.0	879.8
Pre-opening expense	2.8	5.0	8.1
Goodwill impairment	40.3	—	—
Asset impairments and other write-downs	57.1	13.0	60.6
Operating income (loss)	(149.2)	4.1	5.2
Interest expense, net	5.3	43.1	29.9
Loss before income tax	(154.5)	(39.0)	(24.7)
Income tax provision (benefit)	30.2	(19.1)	(2.8)
Loss from continuing operations	$ (184.7)	$ (19.9)	$ (21.9)
Loss from operations of discontinued operations (net of income tax benefit of $0.9, $2.9 and $15.2)	(1.7)	(8.7)	(129.4)
Loss from disposal of discontinued operations (net of income tax benefit of $3.1, $7.6 and $0.0)	(0.3)	(128.8)	—
Loss from discontinued operations (net of tax)	(2.0)	(137.5)	(129.4)
Net loss	$ (186.7)	$ (157.4)	$ (151.3)
Loss per common share data (Note 2)			
Basic:			
Loss from continuing operations per common share	$ (3.07)	$ (0.34)	$ (0.35)
Loss from discontinued operations per common share	$ (0.03)	$ (2.34)	$ (2.09)
Net loss per common share	$ (3.10)	$ (2.68)	$ (2.44)
Weighted-average common shares outstanding	60.2	58.7	61.9

*"Borders Group, Inc., through our subsidiaries, Borders, Inc. ("Borders"), Walden Book Company, Inc. ("Walden-books"), and others (individually and collectively, "we," "our" or the "Company"), is an operator of book, music and movie superstores and mall-based bookstores." 10-K
Source: Borders Group, Inc 2010 10-K

CONSOLIDATED BALANCE SHEETS
(Dollars in millions except share amounts)

	Fiscal Year Ended	
	Jan. 31, 2009	**Feb. 2, 2008**
Assets		
Current assets:		
Cash and cash equivalents	$ 53.6	$ 58.5
Merchandise inventories	915.2	1,242.0
Accounts receivable and other current assets	102.4	103.5
Current assets of discontinued operations	—	102.0
Total current assets	1,071.2	1,506.0
Property and equipment, net	494.2	592.8
Other assets	39.4	64.9
Deferred income taxes	4.0	44.9
Goodwill	0.2	40.5
Noncurrent assets of discontinued operations	—	53.6
Total assets	$1,609.0	$2,302.7
Liabilities, Minority Interest and Stockholders' Equity		
Current liabilities:		
Short-term borrowings and current portion of long-term debt	$ 329.8	$ 548.6
Trade accounts payable	350.0	511.9
Accrued payroll and other liabilities	279.8	321.6
Taxes, including income taxes	30.1	18.3
Deferred income taxes	4.0	9.9
Current liabilities of discontinued operations	—	57.5
Total current liabilities	993.7	1,467.8
Long-term debt	6.4	5.4
Other long-term liabilities	345.8	325.0
Noncurrent liabilities of discontinued operations	—	25.4
Contingencies (Note 8)	—	—
Total liabilities	1,345.9	1,823.6
Minority interest	0.5	2.2
Total liabilities and minority interest	1,346.4	1,825.8
Stockholders' equity:		
Common stock, 300,000,000 shares authorized; 59,903,232 and 58,794,224 shares issued and outstanding at January 31, 2009 and February 2, 2008, respectively	186.9	184.0
Accumulated other comprehensive income	11.9	42.4
Retained earnings	63.8	250.5
Total stockholders' equity	262.6	476.9
Total liabilities, minority interest and stockholders' equity	$1,609.0	$2,302.7

CONSOLIDATED STATEMENTS OF CASH FLOWS
(Dollars in millions)

	Fiscal Year Ended,		
	Jan. 31, 2009	**Feb. 2, 2008**	**Feb. 3, 2007**
Cash provided by (used for):			
Net loss	$(186.7)	$(157.4)	$(151.3)
Net loss from discontinued operations	(2.0)	(137.5)	(129.4)
Net loss from continuing operations	(184.7)	(19.9)	(21.9)
Operations			
Adjustments to reconcile net loss from continuing operations to operating cash flows:			
Depreciation	107.1	103.7	111.2
Gain on sale of investments	—	—	(5.0)
Loss on disposal of assets	1.9	0.5	2.0
Stock-based compensation cost	3.0	5.1	4.1

(continued)

(**CASE 11-4** CONTINUED)

	Fiscal Year Ended,		
	Jan. 31, 2009	Feb. 2, 2008	Feb. 3, 2007
Operations *(continued)*			
Decrease in minority interest	—	0.4	0.6
Decrease (increase) in deferred income taxes	34.5	(3.7)	(24.7)
Decrease (increase) in other long-term assets	23.6	0.3	(1.3)
(Decrease) increase in other long-term			
liabilities	(14.9)	4.5	8.8
Goodwill impairment	40.3	—	—
Asset impairments and other write-downs	57.1	13.0	60.6
Cash provided by (used for) current assets and			
current liabilities:			
Decrease (increase) in inventories	321.4	52.2	(23.3)
Decrease (increase) in accounts receivable	10.2	13.3	(7.5)
Decrease (increase) in prepaid expenses	9.8	(1.0)	10.4
Decrease in accounts payable	(160.2)	(59.2)	(55.7)
Increase (decrease) in taxes payable	13.7	(36.4)	(70.0)
(Decrease) increase in accrued payroll and			
other liabilities	(29.2)	32.2	50.8
Net cash provided by operating activities of			
continuing operations	233.6	105.0	39.1
Investing			
Capital expenditures	(79.9)	(131.3)	(165.6)
Investment in Paperchase	(3.6)	(0.8)	—
Proceeds from the sale of discontinued operations	97.3	20.4	—
Proceeds from sale of investments	—	—	21.6
Net cash provided by (used for) investing			
activities of continuing operations	13.8	(111.7)	(144.0)
Financing			
Proceeds from the excess tax benefit of options			
exercised	0.5	0.9	4.3
Net (repayment of) funding from credit facility	(261.7)	43.4	303.4
Funding from short-term note financing	42.5	—	—
Issuance of long-term debt	1.2	0.4	—
Repayment of long-term debt	(1.4)	—	—
Repayment of long-term capital lease obligations	(0.4)	(0.4)	(0.1)
Issuance of common stock	(0.4)	3.1	21.9
Repurchase of common stock	(0.2)	(0.6)	(148.7)
Payment of cash dividends	(6.5)	(19.4)	(25.2)
Net cash (used for) provided by financing			
activities of continuing operations	(226.4)	27.4	155.6
Effect of exchange rates on cash and cash			
equivalents of continuing operations	(0.9)	0.8	(0.6)
Net cash (used for) provided by operating activities			
of discontinued operations	(21.3)	(0.7)	16.2
Net cash used for investing activities of			
discontinued operations	(6.5)	(17.8)	(41.9)
Net cash (used for) provided by financing activities			
of discontinued operations	—	(41.9)	13.9
Effect of exchange rates on cash and cash			
equivalents of discontinued operations	2.8	(0.2)	0.5
Net cash used for discontinued operations	(25.0)	(60.6)	(11.3)
Net increase (decrease) in cash and cash equivalents	(4.9)	(39.1)	38.8
Cash and cash equivalents at beginning of year	58.5	97.6	58.8
Cash and cash equivalents at end of year	$ 53.6	$ 58.5	$ 97.6
Supplemental cash flow disclosures:			
Interest paid	$ 36.3	$ 43.8	$ 32.8
Income taxes (received) paid	$ (34.6)	$ 12.4	$ 63.5

Required

a. Compute the following liquidity ratios for 2009 and 2008:
1. Days' sales in inventory
2. Inventory turnover (use ending inventory)
3. Working capital
4. Current ratio
5. Cash ratio
6. Sales to working capital (use ending working capital)
7. Operating cash flow/current maturities of long-term debt and current notes payable

b. Compute the following long-term debt-paying ability for 2009 and 2008:
1. Debt ratio
2. Operating cash flow/total debt

c. Compute the following profitability ratios for 2009 and 2008:
1. Net profit margin
2. Return on assets (use end of year total assets)
3. Return on total equity (use end of year total equity)
4. Gross profit margin

d. Compute or obtain the following investor analysis:
1. Earnings per common share
2. Operating cash flow/cash dividends

e. Comment on the results in (a), (b), (c) and (d).

f. Comment on the trend in net income (loss).

g. Comment on significant trends (items) in the Consolidated Statement of Cash Flows.

h. Using these ratios for 2009 and 2008, comment using the Beaver Study on possible financial failure:
1. Cash flow/total debt
2. Net income/total assets (return on assets)
3. Total debt/total assets (debt ratio)

Case 11-5 BOOKS UNLIMITED—PART 2

Borders Group, Inc. presented this information in its 10-K:*

CONSOLIDATED STATEMENTS OF OPERATIONS
(Dollars in millions except per share data)

	Jan. 30, 2010	Jan. 31, 2009	Feb. 2, 2008
Sales	$2,791.1	$3,242.1	$3,555.1
Other revenue	32.8	33.3	42.3
Total revenue	$2,823.9	$3,275.4	$3,597.4
Cost of merchandise sold (includes occupancy)	2,191.3	2,484.8	2,668.3
Gross margin	632.6	790.6	929.1
Selling, general and administrative expenses	711.3	842.4	912.0
Goodwill impairment	—	40.3	—
Asset impairments and other writedowns	16.2	57.1	13.0
Operating income (loss)	(94.9)	(149.2)	4.1
Interest expense	24.1	45.4	43.1
Warrant/put expense (income)	20.7	(40.1)	—
Total interest expense	44.8	5.3	43.1

(continued)

*"Borders Group, Inc., through our subsidiaries including Borders, Inc. ("Borders") (individually and collectively, "we," "our" or the "Company"), is an operator of book and movie superstores and mall-based bookstores." 10-K
Source: Borders Group, Inc 2010 10-K

(**CASE 11-5** CONTINUED)

	Jan. 30, 2010	Jan. 31, 2009	Feb. 2, 2008
Loss before income tax	(139.7)	(154.5)	(39.0)
Income tax provision (benefit)	(29.5)	30.2	(19.1)
Loss from continuing operations	$ (110.2)	$ (184.7)	$ (19.9)
Loss from operations of discontinued operations (net of income tax benefit of $—, $0.9 and $2.9)	—	(1.7)	(8.7)
Gain (loss) from disposal of discontinued operations (net of income tax benefit of $—, $3.1 and $7.6)	0.8	(0.3)	(128.8)
Gain (loss) from discontinued operations (net of tax)	0.8	(2.0)	(137.5)
Net loss	$ (109.4)	$ (186.7)	$ (157.4)
Loss per common share data (Note 2)			
Basic:			
Loss from continuing operations per common share	$ (1.83)	$ (3.07)	$ (0.34)
Gain (loss) from discontinued operations per common share	$ 0.01	$ (0.03)	$ (2.34)
Net loss per common share	$ (1.82)	$ (3.10)	$ (2.68)
Weighted-average common shares outstanding (in millions)	60.1	60.2	58.7

CONSOLIDATED BALANCE SHEETS
(Dollars in millions except share amounts)

	Fiscal Year Ended	
	Jan. 30, 2010	Jan. 31, 2009
Assets		
Current assets:		
Cash and cash equivalents	$ 37.0	$ 53.6
Merchandise inventories	873.8	915.2
Accounts receivable and other current assets	76.5	102.4
Deferred income taxes	1.0	—
Total current assets	988.3	1,071.2
Property and equipment, net	392.8	494.2
Other assets	39.9	39.4
Deferred income taxes	3.9	4.0
Goodwill	0.3	0.2
Total assets	$1,425.2	$1,609.0
Liabilities and Stockholders' Equity		
Current liabilities:		
Short-term borrowings and current portion of long-term debt	$ 275.4	$ 329.8
Trade accounts payable	350.8	350.0
Accrued payroll and other liabilities	257.4	279.8
Taxes, including income taxes	44.1	30.1
Deferred income taxes	—	4.0
Total current liabilities	927.7	993.7
Long-term debt	6.6	6.4
Other long-term liabilities	332.6	345.8
Contingencies (Note 8)	—	—
Total liabilities	1,266.9	1,345.9
Stockholders' equity:		
Common stock, 300,000,000 shares authorized; 59,869,384 and 59,903,232 shares issued and outstanding at January 31, 2010 and January 31, 2009, respectively	187.2	187.4
Accumulated other comprehensive income	16.7	11.9
Retained earnings (deficit)	(45.6)	63.8
Total stockholders' equity	158.3	263.1
Total liabilities and stockholders' equity	$1,425.2	$1,609.0

CONSOLIDATED STATEMENTS OF CASH FLOWS
(Dollars in millions)

	Fiscal Year Ended,		
	Jan. 30, 2010	Jan. 31, 2009	Feb. 2, 2008
Cash provided by (used for):			
Net loss	$(109.4)	$(186.7)	$(157.4)
Net income (loss) from discontinued operations	0.8	(2.0)	(137.5)
Loss from continuing operations	(110.2)	(184.7)	(19.9)
Operations			
Adjustments to reconcile net loss from continuing operations to operating cash flows:			
Depreciation	98.8	107.1	103.7
Loss on disposal of assets	3.8	1.9	0.5
Stock-based compensation cost (income)	(0.3)	3.0	5.1
Increase in warranty liability	8.8	0.8	—
Increase (decrease) in deferred income taxes	(4.8)	34.5	(3.7)
Decrease in other long-term assets	0.2	23.6	0.3
(Decrease) increase in other long-term liabilities	(22.5)	(15.7)	4.9
Goodwill impairment	—	40.3	—
Write-off intangible asset	16.2	—	—
Asset impairments and other writedowns	16.2	57.1	13.0
Cash provided by (used for) current assets and current liabilities:			
Decrease in inventories	43.9	321.4	52.2
Decrease in accounts receivable	10.4	10.2	13.3
Decrease (increase) in prepaid expenses	3.9	9.8	(1.0)
Increase (decrease) in accounts payable	0.2	(160.2)	(59.2)
Increase (decrease) in taxes payable	13.4	13.7	(36.4)
Increase (decrease) in accrued payroll and other liabilities	(21.9)	(29.2)	32.2
Net cash provided by operating activities of continuing operations	56.1	233.6	105.0
Investing			
Capital expenditures	(17.9)	(79.9)	(131.3)
Investment in Paperchase	—	(3.6)	(0.8)
Proceeds from the sale of discontinued operations	—	97.3	20.4
Net cash provided by (used for) investing activities of continuing operations	(17.9)	13.8	(111.7)
Financing			
Proceeds from the excess tax benefit of options exercised	—	0.5	0.9
Net funding from (repayment of) credit facility	(54.5)	(261.7)	43.4
Funding from short-term note financing	—	42.5	—
Issuance of long-term debt	—	1.2	0.4
Repayment of long-term debt	(0.3)	(1.4)	—
Repayment of long-term capital lease obligations	(1.2)	(0.4)	(0.4)
Issuance of common stock	0.1	(0.4)	3.1
Repurchase of common stock	—	(0.2)	(0.6)
Payment of cash dividends	—	(6.5)	(19.4)
Net cash provided by (used for) financing activities of continuing operations	(55.9)	(226.4)	27.4
Effect of exchange rates on cash and cash equivalents of continuing operations	0.3	(0.9)	0.8
Net cash provided by (used for) operating activities of discontinued operations	0.8	(21.3)	(0.7)
Net cash used for investing activities of discontinued operations	—	(6.5)	(17.8)
Net cash used for financing activities of discontinued operations	—	—	(41.9)

(continued)

(**CASE 11-5** CONTINUED)

	Fiscal Year Ended,		
	Jan. 30, 2010	Jan. 31, 2009	Feb. 2, 2008
Effect of exchange rates on cash and cash equivalents of discontinued operations	—	2.8	(0.2)
Net cash provided by (used for) discontinued operations	0.8	(25.0)	(60.6)
Net decrease in cash and cash equivalents	(16.6)	(4.9)	(39.1)
Cash and cash equivalents at beginning of year	53.6	58.5	97.6
Cash and cash equivalents at end of year	$ 37.0	$ 53.6	$ 58.5
Supplemental cash flow disclosures:			
Interest paid	$ 16.6	$ 36.3	$ 43.8
Net income taxes (received) paid	$ (42.5)	$ (34.6)	$ 12.4

REPORT OF INDEPENDENT REGISTERED PUBLIC ACCOUNTING FIRM ON CONSOLIDATED FINANCIAL STATEMENTS

The Board of Directors and Stockholders of Borders Group, Inc.

We have audited the accompanying consolidated balance sheets of Borders Group, Inc. and subsidiaries as of January 30, 2010 and January 31, 2009 and the related consolidated statements of operations, stockholders' equity, and cash flows for each of the three years in the period ended January 30, 2010. Our audits also included the financial statement schedule listed in the Index at Item 15(a)(2). These financial statements and schedule are the responsibility of the Company's management. Our responsibility is to express an opinion on these financial statements and schedule based on our audits.

We conducted our audits in accordance with the standards of the Public Company Accounting Oversight Board (United States). Those standards require that we plan and perform the audit to obtain reasonable assurance about whether the financial statements are free of material misstatement. An audit includes examining, on a test basis, evidence supporting the amounts and disclosures in the financial statements. An audit also includes assessing the accounting principles used and significant estimates made by management, as well as evaluating the overall financial statement presentation. We believe that our audits provide a reasonable basis for our opinion.

In our opinion, the financial statements referred to above present fairly, in all material respects, the consolidated financial position of Borders Group, Inc. and subsidiaries at January 30, 2010 and January 31, 2009 and the consolidated results of their operations and their cash flows for each of the three years in the period ended January 30, 2010, in conformity with U.S. generally accepted accounting principles. Also, in our opinion, the related financial statement schedule, when considered in relation to the basic financial statements taken as a whole, presents fairly in all material respects the information set forth therein.

As discussed in Note 7 to the consolidated financial statements, in 2007 the Company adopted the required provisions of the guidance originally issued in Financial Accounting Standards Board Interpretation No. 48, Accounting for Uncertainty in Income Taxes (codified in FASB ASC Topic 740, Income Taxes).

We also have audited, in accordance with the standards of the Public Company Accounting Oversight Board (United States), Borders Group, Inc.'s internal control over financial reporting as of January 30, 2010, based on criteria established in Internal Control-Integrated Framework issued by the Committee of Sponsoring Organizations of the Treadway Commission and our report dated April 1, 2010 expressed an unqualified opinion thereon.

/s/ ERNST & YOUNG LLP

Detroit, Michigan
April 1, 2010

Required

a. Perform a horizontal common-size analysis of the consolidated statements of operations using sales through gross margin for 2008, 2009, and 2010. Use the fiscal year ended February 2, 2008 as the base. Comment.

b. Perform a vertical common-size analysis of the consolidated statements of operations using sales through gross margin for 2008, 2009, and 2010. Use sales as the base. Comment.

c. For the years ended January 31, 2009 and January 30, 2010, compute the following ratios. Comment.

    1. Cash flow/total debt

    2. Net income/total assets (return on assets)

    3. Total debt/total assets (debt ratio)

    Note: These are the ratios that the Beaver study indicated were the best for forecasting failure (in the order of their predictive power).

d. For the consolidated statements of cash flows for the fiscal year ended February 2, 2008, January 31, 2009 and January 30, 2010, comment on the significance of the decrease in inventories on the net cash provided by operating activities of continuing operations.

e. Consolidated Statements of Cash Flows (dollars in millions) (In Part):

| | Fiscal year ended | | |
	January 30, 2010	January 31, 2009	February 2, 2008
Supplemental cash flow disclosures:			
Interest paid	$ 16.6	$ 36.3	$43.8
Net income taxes (received) paid	$(42.5)	$(34.6)	$12.4

f. Comment on the audit report dated April 1, 2010.

CASE 11-6 VALUE—NIKE, INC.

Selected data from Nike's financial statements for the period 2007–2011 follow:

Item 6 Selected Financial Data (In Part)

Financial History

	2011	2010	2009	2008	2007
	(In millions, except per share data and financial ratios)				
Year Ended May 31,					
Revenues	$20,862	$19,014	$19,176	$18,627	$16,326
Gross margin	9,058	8,800	8,604	8,387	7,161
Gross margin %	45.6%	46.3%	44.9%	45.0%	43.9%
Restructuring charges	—	—	195	—	—
Goodwill impairment	—	—	199	—	—
Intangible and other asset impairment	—	—	202	—	—
Net income	2,133	1,907	1,487	1,883	1,492
Basic earnings per common share	4.48	3.93	3.07	3.80	2.96
Diluted earnings per common share	4.39	3.86	3.03	3.74	2.93
Weighted average common shares outstanding	475.5	485.5	484.9	495.6	503.8
Diluted weighted average common shares outstanding	485.7	493.9	490.7	504.1	509.9
Cash dividends declared per common share	1.20	1.06	0.98	0.875	0.71
Cash flow from operations	1,812	3,164	1,736	1,936	1,879
Price range of common stock					
High	92.30	78.55	70.28	70.60	57.12
Low	67.21	50.16	38.24	51.50	37.76

(continued)

Source: Nike, Inc. 2010 10-K

(**Case 11-6** CONTINUED)

	2011	2010	2009	2008	2007
	(In millions, except per share data and financial ratios)				
At May 31,					
Cash and equivalents	$ 1,955	$ 3,079	$ 2,291	$ 2,134	$ 1,857
Short-term investments	2,583	2,067	1,164	642	990
Inventories	2,715	2,041	2,357	2,438	2,122
Working capital	7,339	7,595	6,457	5,518	5,493
Total assets	14,998	14,419	13,250	12,443	10,688
Long-term debt	276	446	437	441	410
Redeemable Preferred Stock	0.3	0.3	0.3	0.3	0.3
Shareholders' equity	9,843	9,754	8,693	7,825	7,025
Year-end stock price	84.45	72.38	57.05	68.37	56.75
Market capitalization	39,523	35,032	27,698	33,577	28,472
Financial Ratios:					
Return on equity	21.8%	20.7%	18.0%	25.4%	22.4%
Return on assets	14.5%	13.8%	11.6%	16.3%	14.5%
Inventory turns	4.8	4.6	4.4	4.5	4.4
Current ratio at May 31	2.9	3.3	3.0	2.7	3.1
Price/Earnings ratio at May 31	19.2	18.8	18.8	18.3	19.4

Note: There are many approaches to valuing a company. The analysts would likely review a company using several approaches.

Required

a. Liquidity
   1. Review the summary analysis for Nike, Inc. from 2009–2011. Give your opinion of the liquidity position (refer back to Exhibit 3, Summary Analysis).
   2. Review the current ratio in this case (2007–2011). Comment.
   3. Review cash provided by operations (2007–2011). Comment.

b. Long-term debt-paying ability
   1. Review the summary analysis for Nike, Inc. from 2009–2011. Give your opinion of the debt position (refer back to Exhibit 3, Summary Analysis).
   2. Review the debt ratio for 2009–2011. Comment.

c. Profitability
   1. Review the summary analysis for Nike, Inc. from 2009–2011. Give your opinion of the profitability (refer back to Exhibit 3, Summary Analysis).
   2. Review the trend in revenues (2007–2011). Comment.
   3. Review the trend in gross profit margin (2007–2011). Comment.

d. Investor Analysis
   1. Review the absolute amount and trend in the price/earnings for 2007–2011. Considering liquidity, debt, and profitability, is there a reasonable probability that the price/earnings may increase?
   2. Comment on the trend in market capitalization (2007–2011) (share price x number of outstanding shares).
   3. Review cash dividends declared per common share (2007–2011). Is there a likely chance that dividends will be increased during the year ending May 31, 2012?
   4. Give your opinion of the stock price of Nike, Inc. on May 31, 2013. In practice, many things would be considered that are not presented in this case. Base your opinion on the summary analysis (2009–2011) and the financial history (2007–2011).

e. Other
   1. This case has used a fundamental financial statement approach to valuing Nike. In your opinion, would an analyst likely use this type of approach for valuing Nike? Comment.

WEB CASE THOMSON ONE *Business School Edition*

Please complete the Web case that covers material discussed in this chapter at www.cengagebrain.com. You'll be using Thomson ONE Business School Edition, a powerful tool that combines a full range of fundamental financial information, earnings estimates, market data, and source documents for 500 publicly traded companies.

 TO THE NET CASE

1. Go to the SEC site (www.sec.gov). Under Filings and Forms (EDGAR), click on "Search for Company Filings." Click on "Companies and Other Filers." Under Company Name, enter "Kimberly-Clark Company" (or enter stock symbol "KMB"). Select the 10-K filed February 23, 2011.

   Determine:

   a. Item 1 Business. Copy the first sentence.

   b.

	December 31,	
	2010	2009
	Millions of Dollars	
Inventory balance		
Inventory valuation adjustment		

   c. 2010 net income.

   d. 2010 effective tax rate.

   e. The approximate income for 2010 if inventory had been valued at approximate current cost.

2. Go to the SEC site (www.sec.gov). Under Filings and Forms (EDGAR), click on "Search for Company Filings." Click on "Companies and Other Filers." Under Company Name, enter "Omnova Solutions" (or enter stock symbol "OMN"). Select the 10-K filed January 25, 2011.

   a. Determine the business description. Copy the second paragraph under introduction.

   b. What were the inventories November 30, 2010 and 2009, respectively, per the consolidated balance sheets?

   c. For November 30, 2010, what was the percentage of inventories valued using the last-in, first-out ("LIFO") method?

   d. 1. For November 30, 2010, what was the acquired cost of inventories?

      2. For November 30, 2010, what was the excess of acquired cost over LIFO cost?

      3. During 2010 there was a partial liquidation of LIFO inventory. How much did this decrease the cost of products sold for 2010?

      4. During 2009 there was a partial liquidation of LIFO inventory. How much did this decrease the cost of products sold for 2009?

Endnotes

1. C. H. Gibson, "Financial Ratios as Perceived by Commercial Loan Officers," *Akron Business and Economic Review* (Summer 1983), pp. 23–27.

2. The basis of the comments in this section is a study by Dr. Charles Gibson in 1981. The research was done under a grant from the Deloitte Haskins & Sells Foundation.

3. C. H. Gibson, "Ohio CPA's Perceptions of Financial Ratios," *The Ohio CPA Journal* (Autumn 1985), pp. 25–30. © 1985. Reprinted with permission of *The Ohio CPA Journal.*

4. C. H. Gibson, "How Chartered Financial Analysts View Financial Ratios," *Financial Analysts Journal* (May–June 1987), pp. 74–76.

5. Ibid.

6. C. H. Gibson, "Financial Ratios in Annual Reports," *The CPA Journal* (September 1982), pp. 18–29.

7. W. H. Beaver, "Alternative Accounting Measures as Predictors of Failure," *The Accounting Review* (January 1968), pp. 113–122.

8. Ibid., p. 117.

9. Ibid., p. 119.

10. E. I. Altman, "Financial Ratios, Discriminant Analysis and the Prediction of Corporate Bankruptcy," *Journal of Finance* (September 1968), pp. 589–609.

11. Edward I. Altman and Thomas P. McGough, "Evaluation of a Company as a Going Concern," *The Journal of Accountancy* (December 1974), pp. 50–57.

12. Ibid., p. 52.

13. Suggested reference sources: Anker V. Andersen, "Graphing Financial Information: How Accountants Can Use Graphs to Communicate," *National Association of Accountants* (1983), p. 50; Edward Bloches, Robert P. Moffie, and Robert W. Smud, "How Best to Communicate Numerical Data," *The Internal Auditor* (February 1985), pp. 38–42; Deanna Qxender Burgess, "Graphical Sleight of Hand: How Can Auditors Spot Altered Exhibits That Appear in Annual Reports?" *Journal of Accountancy* (February 2002), pp. 45–50; Charles H. Gibson and Nicholas Schroeder, "Improving Your Practice—Graphically," *The CPA Journal* (August 1990), pp. 28–37; Johnny R. Johnson, Richard R. Rice, and Roger A. Roemmich, "Pictures That Lie: The Abuse of Graphs in Annual Reports," *Management Accounting* (October 1980), pp. 50–56; Robert Lefferts, *How to Prepare Charts and Graphs for Effective Reports* (New York: Barnes & Noble Books, 1982), p. 166; David Lynch and Steven Galen, "Got the Picture? CPAs Can Use Some Simple Principles to Create Effective Charts and Graphs for Financial Reports and Presentations," *Journal of Accountancy* (May 2002), pp. 183–187; Calvin F. Schmid and Stanton E. Schmid, *Handbook of Graphic Presentation*, 2nd ed. (New York: Ronald Press, 1979), p. 308.

14. www.sec.gov.

15. "Restatements of Profits Prove Costly to Investors," *The Wall Street Journal* (October 24, 2002), p. D2.

16. George J. Benoton and Al L. Hartgraves, "Enron: What Happened and What We Can Learn from It," *Journal of Accounting and Public Policy* (August 2002), pp. 105–127.

17. Susan Pulliam and Deborah Solomon, "How Three Unlikely Sleuths Discovered Fraud at WorldCom," *The Wall Street Journal* (October 30, 2002), p. A6.

18. Jared Sandberg and Susan Pulliam, "Report by WorldCom Examiner Finds New Fraudulent Activities," *The Wall Street Journal* (November 5, 2002), p. 1.

19. Pulliam and Solomon, "How Three Unlikely Sleuths Discovered Fraud at WorldCom."

20. Ibid.

21. Ibid.

22. Theo Francis, "AIG Issues Report, and Caution," *The Wall Street Journal* (June 1, 2005), p. C1.

23. Ibid., p. C3.

24. Ibid.

25. Ibid.

26. Financial Restatements, July 2006, GAO-06-678, P4.

27. Ibid., p. 48.

28. United States Government Accountability Office, Washington, DC, Letter addressed to the Honorable Paul S. Sarbanes, Ranking Minority Member, Committee on Banking, Housing, and Urban Affairs, United States Senate, August 31, 2006. Enclosure I, pg. 5, GAO-06-1053a Financial Restatement Database.

29. Marco Trombetta, "Discussion of Implied Cost of Equity Capital in Earnings-Based Valuation: International Evidence," *Accounting and Business Research* (2004, 34:4), p. 345.

30. Richard G. Barker, "The Role of Dividends in Valuation Models Used by Analysts and Fund Managers," *The European Accounting Review* (1999, 8:2), p. 195.

31. Ibid., p. 197.

32. Ibid.

33. Ibid., pp. 200–201.

34. Ibid., p. 200.

35. Ibid., p. 202.

36. Ibid.

37. Ibid., p. 204.

38. Ibid., p. 205.

39. Ibid., p. 214.

40. Efthimios G. Demirakos, Norman C. Strong, and Martin Walker, "What Valuation Models Do Analysts Use?," *Accounting Horizons* (December 2004, 18:4), p. 229.

41. Ibid.

42. Ibid., p. 237.

43. Paul Asquith, Michael B. Mikhail, and Andrea S. Au, "Information Content of Equity Analyst Reports," *Journal of Financial Economics* (2005, 75), p. 278.

44. Trombetta, "Discussion of Implied Cost of Equity Capital," p. 345.

45. Tom Copeland, Tim Koller, and Jack Murrin, *Valuation, Measuring, and Managing the Value of Companies,* 3rd ed. (New York: John Wiley & Sons, 2000), p. preface 1x.

46. Ibid., p. 62.

47. Ibid., p. 67.

48. Ibid., p. 113.

49. Ibid.

50. Ibid., p. 115.

51. Ibid., p. 116.

52. Ibid., p. 315.

53. Ibid.

54. Ibid., p. 317.

55. Ibid., p. 321.

56. Roger Parloff, "Can We Talk," *Fortune* (September 2, 2002), pp. 102–103.

57. Ibid., p. 103.

58. *Kasky v. Nike, Inc.* Cite as 45 P. 3d 243 (Cal 2002).

59. Eugene Valokh, "Nike and the Free-Speech Knot," *The Wall Street Journal* (June 30, 2003), p. A16.

60. Ibid.

61. Stephanie Kang, "Nike Settles Case with an Activist for $1.5 Million," *The Wall Street Journal* (September 15, 2003), p. 10.

Chapter

12

Special Industries: Banks, Utilities, Oil and Gas, Transportation, Insurance, and Real Estate Companies

The preceding chapters covered material most applicable to manufacturing, retailing, wholesaling, and service industries. This chapter covers six specialized industries: banks, utilities, oil and gas, transportation, insurance, and real estate companies. The chapter notes the differences in statements and suggests changes or additions to analysis.

Banks

Banks operate under either a federal or a state charter. National banks are required to submit uniform accounting statements to the Comptroller of the Currency. State banks are controlled by their state banking departments. In addition, the Federal Deposit Insurance Corporation and the Board of Governors of the Federal Reserve System receive financial and operating statements from all members of the Federal Reserve System. Member banks are required to keep reserves with their district Federal Reserve bank. State banking laws also dictate the geographical area within which a bank may function. The range runs from within one county to interstate.

Banking systems usually involve two types of structures: individual banks and bank holding companies. Bank holding companies consist of a parent that owns one or many banks. In addition, the holding company may own bank-related financial services and non-financial subsidiaries. In financial report analysis, we must determine the extent of the business generated by banking services. In order for the specific industry ratios to be meaningful, a large proportion of the services should be bank related.

Exhibit 12-1 presents part of the 2010 annual report of the BancFirst Corporation.

Balance Sheet

The balance sheet of a commercial bank is sometimes termed the *report of condition*. Two significant differences exist between the traditional balance sheet and that of a bank. First, the accounts of banks may seem the opposite of those of other types of firms. Checking accounts or demand deposits are liabilities to a bank, since it owes the customers money in

| EXHIBIT **12-1** | BancFirst Corporation* |

Selected Data from 2010 Annual Report

BANCFIRST CORPORATION
Consolidated Balance Sheets
(Dollars in thousands, except per share data)

	December 31,	
	2010	2009
ASSETS		
Cash and due from banks	$ 93,059	$ 106,856
Interest-bearing deposits with banks	1,111,020	929,654
Federal funds sold	41,207	5,000
Securities (market value: $746,972 and $418,112, respectively)	746,343	417,172
Loans:		
Total loans (net of unearned interest)	2,811,964	2,738,654
Allowance for loan losses	(35,745)	(36,383)
Loans, net	2,776,219	2,702,271
Premises and equipment, net	97,796	91,794
Other real estate owned, net	22,956	9,505
Intangible assets, net	11,610	7,144
Goodwill	44,548	34,684
Accrued interest receivable	21,914	21,670
Other assets	93,577	90,365
Total assets	$5,060,249	$4,416,115
LIABILITIES AND STOCKHOLDERS' EQUITY		
Deposits:		
Noninterest-bearing	$1,318,431	$1,157,688
Interest-bearing	3,185,323	2,771,328
Total deposits	4,503,754	3,929,016
Short-term borrowings	7,250	100
Accrued interest payable	3,235	3,886
Long-term borrowings	34,265	—
Other liabilities	24,285	25,559
Junior subordinated debentures	28,866	26,804
Total liabilities	4,601,655	3,985,365
Commitments and contingent liabilities (Note (19))		
Stockholders' equity:		
Senior preferred stock, $1.00 par; 10,000,000 shares authorized; none issued	—	—
Cumulative preferred stock, $5.00 par, 900,000 shares authorized; none issued	—	—
Common stock, $1.00 par, 20,000,000 shares authorized; shares issued and outstanding: 15,368,717 and 15,308,741, respectively	15,639	15,309
Capital surplus	73,040	69,725
Retained earnings	361,680	334,693
Accumulated other comprehensive income, net of income tax of $4,551 and $5,915, respectively	8,505	11,023
Total stockholders' equity	458,594	430,750
Total liabilities and stockholders' equity	$5,060,249	$4,416,115

*"BancFirst Corporation (the "Company") is an Oklahoma business corporation and a financial holding company under Federal law." 10-K
Source: Bancfirst Corporation 2010 10-K

(*continued*)

EXHIBIT **12-1**   BancFirst Corporation (*continued*)

BANCFIRST CORPORATION
Consolidated Statements of Income and Comprehensive Income
(Dollars in thousands, except per share data)

	Year Ended December 31,		
	2010	2009	2008
INTEREST INCOME			
Loans, including fees	$154,822	$152,731	$172,234
Securities:			
Taxable	12,378	13,436	16,387
Tax-exempt	1,243	1,398	1,439
Federal funds sold	12	1	7,315
Interest-bearing deposits with banks	2,462	2,240	549
Total interest income	170,917	169,806	197,924
INTEREST EXPENSE			
Deposits	26,081	36,508	56,384
Short-term borrowings	6	11	458
Long-term borrowings	61	—	9
Junior subordinated debentures	1,993	1,966	1,966
Total interest expense	28,141	38,485	58,817
Net interest income	142,776	131,321	139,107
Provision for loan losses	2,954	10,389	10,676
Net interest income after provision for loan losses	139,822	120,932	128,431
NONINTEREST INCOME			
Trust revenue	6,288	5,826	5,972
Service charges on deposits	39,343	37,096	33,060
Securities transactions	324	336	6,938
Income from sales of loans	2,942	2,779	2,127
Insurance commissions	8,543	6,979	6,913
Cash management	6,536	8,476	10,796
Gain on sale of other assets	379	213	2,971
Other	5,564	5,159	5,608
Total noninterest income	69,919	66,864	74,385
NONINTEREST EXPENSE			
Salaries and employee benefits	82,359	79,019	79,886
Occupancy and fixed assets expense, net	9,050	8,346	8,956
Depreciation	7,424	7,520	7,647
Amortization of intangible assets	1,107	920	902
Data processing services	4,352	3,636	3,297
Net expense from other real estate owned	948	366	179
Marketing and business promotion	5,887	5,529	6,271
Deposit insurance	5,722	7,833	489
Other	27,246	25,948	27,379
Total noninterest expense	144,095	139,117	135,006
Income before taxes	65,646	48,679	67,810
Income tax expense	23,337	16,070	23,452
Net income	42,309	32,609	44,358
Other comprehensive (loss) income, net of tax of $(1,417), $(1,988) and $4,161, respectively			
Unrealized (losses) gains on securities	(2,729)	(3,872)	3,218
Reclassification adjustment for gains included in net income	211	218	4,510
Comprehensive income	$ 39,791	$ 28,955	$ 52,086
NET INCOME FOR COMMON SHARE			
Basic	$ 2.76	$ 2.13	$ 2.91
Diluted	$ 2.70	$ 2.09	$ 2.85

| EXHIBIT **12-1** | BancFirst Corporation (*continued*) |

BANCFIRST CORPORATION
Consolidated Statements of Stockholders' Equity
(Dollars in thousands, except share data)

	Year Ended December 31,					
	2010		**2009**		**2008**	
	Shares	**Amount**	**Shares**	**Amount**	**Shares**	**Amount**
COMMON STOCK						
Issued at beginning of period	15,308,741	$ 15,309	15,281,141	$ 15,281	15,217,230	$ 15,217
Shares issued	76,476	76	27,600	28	103,911	104
Shares acquired and canceled	(16,500)	(16)	—	—	(40,000)	(40)
Issued at end of period	15,368,717	$ 15,369	15,308,741	$ 15,309	15,281,141	$ 15,281
CAPITAL SURPLUS						
Balance at beginning of period		$ 69,725		$ 67,975		$ 63,917
Common stock issued		1,581		460		1,763
Tax effect of stock options		516		252		1,103
Stock option expense		1,218		1,038		1,192
Balance at end of period		$ 73,040		$ 69,725		$ 67,975
RETAINED EARNINGS						
Balance at beginning of period		$334,693		$315,858		$285,879
Net income		42,309		32,609		44,358
Dividends on common stock ($0.96, $0.90 and $0.84 per share, respectively)		(14,733)		(13,774)		(12,785)
Common stock acquired and canceled		(589)		—		(1,594)
Balance at end of period		$361,680		$334,693		$315,858
ACCUMULATED OTHER COMPREHENSIVE INCOME/(LOSS)						
Unrealized gains (losses) on securities:						
Balance at beginning of period		$ 11,023		$ 14,677		$ 6,949
Net change		(2,518)		(3,654)		7,728
Balance at end of period		$ 8,505		$ 11,023		$ 14,677
Total stockholders' equity		$458,594		$430,750		$413,791

these cases. Similarly, loans to customers are assets—receivables. Furthermore, the balance sheet accounts are not subdivided into current and noncurrent accounts.

Some banks provide a very detailed disclosure of their assets and liabilities. Other banks provide only general disclosure. The quality of review that can be performed can be no better than the disclosure.

Representative assets of a bank may include cash on hand or due from other banks, investment securities, loans, bank premises, and equipment. Closely review the disclosure of a bank's assets. This review may indicate risk or opportunity. For example, a review of the assets may indicate that the bank has a substantial risk if interest rates increase. The general rule is that for 20-year fixed obligations, a gain or loss of 8% of principal arises when interest rates change by 1%. Thus, an investment of $100 million in 20-year bonds would lose approximately $32 million in principal if interest rates increased by 4%. A similar example would be a bank that holds long-term fixed-rate mortgages. The value of these mortgages could decline substantially if interest rates increased. Many bank annual reports do not disclose the amount of fixed-rate mortgages.

Review the stockholders' equity section of the balance sheet to determine whether significant accumulated other comprehensive income (loss) exists. BancFirst Corporation had accumulated comprehensive income of $8,505,000 at December 31, 2010, and an accumulated comprehensive income of $11,023,000 at December 31, 2009. The decline came from an unrealized loss on securities.

Subprime residential real estate loans became a major issue with financial institutions. There is no standard definition of subprime residential real estate loans. For these loans there is a perceived risk spread to other residential real estate loans.

BancFirst apparently did not specifically comment on residential real estate loans but did make the following comment as to their loans:

Composition

The Company's loan portfolio was diversified among various types of commercial and individual borrowers. Commercial loans were comprised principally of loans to companies in light manufacturing, retail and service industries. Consumer loans were comprised primarily of loans to individuals for automobiles. Student loans have decreased to $56.3 million at December 31, 2010 down from $148.2 million at December 31, 2009 and $131.2 million at December 31, 2008. On March 21, 2010, Congress passed student loan reform legislation centralizing student lending in a governmental agency, which as of June 30, 2010 resulted in an end to the student loan programs provided by the Company. The Company sold all student loans held for sale of $144.5 million in October 2010. The Company did not have any credit card receivables at year end 2010, 2009 or 2008.

Loans secured by real estate including farmland, multifamily, commercial, one to four family housing and construction and development loans, have been a large portion of the Company's loan portfolio. The Company is subject to risk of future market fluctuations in property values relating to these loans. The Company attempts to manage this risk through rigorous loan underwriting standards.

LOANS BY CATEGORY

	2010	
	Amount	% of Total
Commercial, financial and other	$ 777,576	27.65%
Real estate – construction	230,367	8.19
Real estate – one to four family	608,786	21.65
Real estate – farmland, multifamily and commercial	921,958	32.79
Consumer	273,277	9.72
Total	$2,811,964	100.00%

. . . . .

Source: Bancfirst Corporation 2010 10-K

In recent years, less developed country (LDC) loans have become a national issue. In general LDC loans are perceived as being more risky than domestic loans. BancFirst Corporation apparently did not have international loans at the end of either 2010 or 2009.

As part of the review of assets, review the disclosure that describes related-party loans. Observe the maturity and the trend of these loans.

BancFirst included the following as to related-party loans (from Note 5):

Related Party Loans

The Company has made loans in the ordinary course of business to the executive officers and directors of the Company and to certain affiliates of these executive officers and directors. Management believes that all such loans were made on substantially the same terms as those prevailing at the time for comparable transactions with other persons and do not represent more than a normal risk of collectability or present other unfavorable features. A summary of these loans is as follows:

Year Ended December 31,	Balance Beginning of the Period	Additions	Collections/ Terminations	Balance End of the Period
		(dollars in thousands)		
2010	$20,222	$36,968	$(35,903)	$21,287
2009	21,918	35,132	(36,828)	20,222
2008	15,808	50,282	(44,172)	21,918

. . . . .

Source: Bancfirst Corporation 2010 10-K

Review the disclosure of allowance for loan losses. It may indicate a significant change and/or significant losses charged.

BancFirst included the following as to allowance for loan losses (note: this is part of a five year presentation):

ANALYSIS FOR ALLOWANCE FOR LOAN LOSSES (In Part)

	Year Ended December 31,		
	2010	2009	2008
	(Dollars in thousands)		
Balance at beginning of period	$ 36,383	$ 34,290	$ 29,127
Charge-offs:			
Commercial	(584)	(4,940)	(1,901)
Real estate	(2,851)	(2,182)	(3,326)
Consumer	(689)	(1,008)	(897)
Other	(56)	(823)	(151)
Total charge-offs	(4,180)	(8,953)	(6,275)
Recoveries:			
Commercial	151	172	187
Real Estate	141	137	118
Consumer	185	252	221
Other	111	96	236
Total recoveries	588	657	762
Net charge-offs	(3,592)	(8,296)	(5,513)
Provision charged to operations	2,954	10,389	10,676
Additions from acquisitions	—	—	—
Balance at end of period	$ 35,745	$ 36,383	$ 34,290
Average loans	$2,761,986	$2,749,544	$2,612,553
Total loans	$2,811,964	$2,738,654	$2,757,854
Net charge-offs to average loans	0.13%	0.30%	0.21%
Allowance to total loans	1.27%	1.33%	1.24%

Review the disclosure of nonperforming assets and restricted assets. In general, nonperforming assets are those for which the bank is not receiving income or is receiving reduced income.

The following was presented by BancFirst relating to nonperforming and restructured assets (note: this was part of a five year presentation):

Source: Bancfirst Corporation 2010 10-K

NONPERFORMING AND RESTRUCTURED ASSETS (In Part)

	Year Ended December 31,		
	2010	2009	2008
	(Dollars in thousands)		
Past due over 90 days and still accruing	$ 1,096	$ 853	$ 1,346
Nonaccrual	26,701	37,133	21,359
Restructured	294	1,970	1,022
Total nonperforming and restructured loans	28,091	39,956	23,727
Other real estate owned and repossessed assets	23,179	9,881	3,997
Total nonperforming and restructured assets	$51,270	$49,837	$27,724
Nonperforming and restructured loans to total loans	1.00%	1.46%	0.86%
Nonperforming and restructured assets to total assets	1.01%	1.13%	0.72%

Potential problem loans are performing loans to borrowers with a weakened financial condition, or which are experiencing unfavorable trends in their financial condition, which causes management to have concerns as to the ability of such borrowers to comply with the existing repayment terms. BancFirst had approximately $60.3 million, $73.6 million and $66.8 million of these loans at December 31, 2010, 2009 and 2008,

Source: Bancfirst Corporation 2010 10-K

respectively, which were not included in nonperforming and restructured assets. In general, these loans are adequately collateralized and have no specific identifiable probable loss. Loans which are considered to have identifiable probable loss potential are placed on nonaccrual status, are allocated a specific allowance for loss or are directly charged-down, and are reported as nonperforming. The Company's nonaccrual loans are primarily commercial and real estate loans.

. . . . .

Review the disclosure of allowance for loan losses. The following was presented by BancFirst relating to allowance for loan losses (note: this was part of a five year presentation):

ANALYSIS OF ALLOWANCE FOR LOAN LOSSES (In Part)

	Year Ended December 31,		
	2010	2009	2008
	(Dollars in thousands)		
Balance at beginning of period	$ 36,383	$ 34,290	$ 29,127
Charge-offs:			
Commercial	(584)	(4,940)	(1,901)
Real estate	(2,851)	(2,182)	(3,326)
Consumer	(689)	(1,008)	(897)
Other	(56)	(823)	(151)
Total charge-offs	(4,180)	(8,953)	(6,275)
Recoveries:			
Commercial	151	172	187
Real Estate	141	137	118
Consumer	185	252	221
Other	111	96	236
Total recoveries	588	657	762
Net charge-offs	(3,592)	(8,296)	(5,513)
Provision charged to operations	2,954	10,389	10,676
Additions from acquisitions	—	—	—
Balance at end of period	$ 35,745	$ 36,383	$ 34,290
Average loans	$2,761,986	$2,749,544	$2,612,553
Total loans	$2,811,964	$2,738,654	$2,757,854
Net charge-offs to average loans	0.13%	0.30%	0.21%
Allowance to total loans	1.27%	1.33%	1.24%
Allocation of the allowance by category of loans:			
Commercial, financial and other	$ 10,558	$ 9,789	$ 9,520
Real estate – construction	3,884	3,447	3,231
Real estate – mortgage	18,060	18,533	17,421
Consumer	3,243	4,614	4,118
Total	$ 35,745	$ 36,383	$ 34,290
Percentage of loans in each category to total loans:			
Commercial, financial and other	29.54%	26.90%	27.76%
Real estate – construction	10.86	9.47	9.42
Real estate – mortgage	50.52	503.95	50.81
Consumer	9.08	12.68	12.01
Total	100.00%	100.00%	100.00%

Liabilities

Review liabilities for favorable or unfavorable trends. Deposits are typically the dominant liability.

The liability presentation of BancFirst Corporation for December 31, 2010 and December 31, 2009 follows:

Source: Bancfirst Corporation 2010 10-K

| | Dollars in thousands December 31, | |
	2010	2009
Liabilities		
Deposits:		
Noninterest-bearing	$1,318,431	$1,157,688
Interest-bearing	3,185,323	2,771,328
Total deposits	4,503,754	3,929,016
Short-term borrowings	7,250	100
Accrued interest payable	3,235	3,886
Long-term borrowings	34,265	—
Other liabilities	24,285	25,559
Junior subordinated debentures	28,866	26,804
Total liabilities	$4,601,655	$3,985,365

A very favorable trend was the increase in deposits. Noninterest-bearing deposits increased 13.9%, while interest-bearing deposits increased 14.9%.

Borrowings increased materially as short-term borrowings increased from $100,000 to $7,250,000, while long-term borrowings increased from $0 to $34,265,000.

As part of the review of liabilities, look for a note that describes commitments and contingent liabilities. This note may reveal significant commitments and contingent liabilities. BancFirst included the following note:

Source: Bancfirst Corporation 2010 10-K

(19) COMMITMENTS AND CONTINGENT LIABILITIES (In Part)

The Company is a party to financial instruments with off-balance-sheet risk in the normal course of business to meet the financing needs of its customers. These financial instruments include loan commitments and standby letters of credit which involve elements of credit and interest-rate risk to varying degrees. The Company's exposure to credit loss in the event of nonperformance by the other party to the instrument is represented by the instrument's contractual account. To control this credit risk, the Company uses the same underwriting standards as it uses for loans recorded on the balance sheet. The amounts of financial instruments with off-balance-sheet risk are as follows:

| | December 31, | |
	2010	2009
	(dollars in thousands)	
Loan commitments	$625,970	$638,652
Stand-by letters of credit	55,339	61,718

Loan commitments are agreements to lend to a customer, as long as there is no violation of any condition established in the contract. Stand-by letters of credit are conditional commitments issued by the Company to guarantee the performance of a customer to a third party. These instruments generally have fixed expiration dates or other termination clauses and may require payment of a fee. Since many of the instruments are expected to expire without being drawn upon, the total amounts do not necessarily represent commitments that will be funded in the future.

Shareholders' Equity

The shareholders' equity of a bank resembles that of other types of firms, except that the total shareholders' equity is usually very low in relation to total assets. A general guide for many years was that a bank's shareholders' equity should be approximately 10% of total assets, but very few banks in recent years have had that much shareholders' equity. Currently, shareholders' equity of 6% to 7% would probably be considered favorable. Banc-First had approximately 9.1% shareholders' equity at the end of 2010. In general, the lower the proportion of shareholders' equity in relation to total assets, the greater the risk of failure. A higher shareholders' equity in relation to total assets would probably improve safety, but the bank would perhaps be less profitable because of the additional capital requirement.

As part of the analysis of shareholders' equity, review the statement of shareholders' equity and the related notes for any significant changes. BancFirst had a substantial decrease in total shareholders' equity in relation to total assets, but a substantial increase in absolute amount. Retained earnings also had a substantial increase in absolute amount.

The current approach by bank regulators is to view not only the adequacy of shareholders' equity in relation to total assets, but also to view it in relation to risk-adjusted assets. BancFirst disclosed the following as part of Note 15 Shareholders' Equity:

> The Company and BancFirst are subject to risk-based capital guidelines issued by the Board of Governors of the Federal Reserve System and FDIC. These guidelines are used to evaluate capital adequacy and involve both quantitative and qualitative evaluations of the Company's and BancFirst's assets, liabilities, and certain off-balance-sheet items calculated under regulatory practices. Failure to meet the minimum capital requirements can initiate certain mandatory or discretionary actions by the regulatory agencies that could have a direct material effect on the Company's financial statements. Management believes, as of December 31, 2010, that the Company and BancFirst met all capital adequacy requirements to which they are subject. The required capital amounts and the Company's and BancFirst's respective ratios are shown in the following table:" (table not presented)

> "As of December 31, 2010, the most recent notification from the Federal Reserve Bank of Kansas City and the FDIC categorized BancFirst as "well capitalized" under the regulatory framework for prompt corrective action. To be well capitalized under federal bank regulatory agency definitions, a depository institution must have a Tier 1 Ratio of at least 6%, a combined Tier 1 and Tier 2 Ratio of at least 10%, and a Leverage Ratio of at least 5%. There are no conditions or events since the most recent notification of BancFirst's capital category that management believes would change its category.

Income Statement

A bank's principal revenue source is usually interest income from loans and investment securities. The difference between interest income and interest expense is termed *net interest income* or *net interest margin*.

The net interest margin is important to a bank's profitability. Usually, falling interest rates are positive for a bank's interest margin because the bank will be able to reduce the interest rate that it pays for deposits before the average rate of return earned on loans and investments declines. Increasing interest rates are usually negative for a bank's interest margin because the bank will need to increase the interest rate on deposits, which is usually done before rates on loans and investments are adjusted.

Bank income statements include a separate section for other income (noninterest income). Typical other income includes trust department fees, service charges on deposit accounts, trading account profits (losses), and securities transactions.

The importance of other income has substantially increased for banks. For example, service charges have increased in importance in recent years since many banks have set service charges at a level to make the service profitable. This has frequently been the result of improved cost analysis. In addition, banks have been adding nontraditional sources of income, such as mortgage banking, sales of mutual funds, sales of annuities, and computer services for other banks and financial institutions.

BancFirst had net interest income after provision for loan losses of $139,822,000 and $120,932,000, respectively, for 2010 and 2009.

The noninterest income increased from $66,864,000 in 2009 to $69,919,000 in 2010. The noninterest expense increased from $139,117,000 to $144,095,000.

Ratios for Banks

Because of the vastly different accounts and statement formats, few of the traditional ratios are appropriate for banks. Exceptions include return on assets, return on equity, and most of the investment-related ratios. The following sections present meaningful ratios for bank analysis, but this is not a comprehensive treatment. The investment firm of Keefe, Bruyette & Woods, Inc., in its *Bankbook Report on Performance*, lists 21 financial ratios. This is an excellent source of industry averages for banks.

Earning Assets to Total Assets

Earning assets includes loans, leases, investment securities, and money market assets. It excludes cash and nonearning deposits plus fixed assets. This ratio shows how well bank management puts bank assets to work. High-performance banks have a high ratio.

Banks typically present data on an average annual basis. This is used to compute a number of ratios. In this book the year-end amounts are used. Exhibit 12-2 presents BancFirst's earning assets to total assets ratio, which increased between 2009 and 2010.

Interest Margin to Average Earning Assets

This is a key determinant of bank profitability, for it provides an indication of management's ability to control the spread between interest income and interest expense. Exhibit 12-3 presents this ratio for BancFirst.

Loan Loss Coverage Ratio

The loan loss coverage ratio, computed by dividing pretax income plus provision for loan losses by net charge-offs, helps determine the asset quality and the level of protection of loans. Exhibit 12-4 presents this ratio for BancFirst. This ratio increased materially in 2010, which is a positive indicator.

EXHIBIT 12-2	BancFirst		
Earning Assets to Total Assets 2010 and 2009			
(In thousands of dollars)		**2010**	**2009**
Average earning assets [A]		$4,262,056	$3,862,494
Average total assets [B]		4,595,551	4,172,979
Earning assets to total assets [A ÷ B]		92.74%	92.56%
Source: Bancfirst Corporation 2010 10-K			

EXHIBIT 12-3	BancFirst		
Interest Margin to Average Earning Assets **For the Years Ended December 31, 2010 and 2009**			
(In thousands of dollars)		**2010**	**2009**
Interest margin [A]		$ 142,776	$ 131,321
Average earning assets [B]		$4,262,056	$4,172,979
Interest margin to average earning assets [A ÷ B]		3.35%	3.15%
Note: Their consolidated average balance sheets and interest margin analysis reports net margin of 3.37% for 2010 and 3.42% for 2009. *Source:* Bancfirst Corporation 2010 10-K			

EXHIBIT 12-4	BancFirst		
Loan Loss Coverage Ratio **For the Years Ended December 31, 2010 and 2009**			
(In thousands of dollars)		**2010**	**2009**
Pretax income		$65,646	$48,679
Provision for loan losses		2,954	10,389
[A]		$68,600	$59,068
Net charge-offs [B]		$ 2,954	$10,389
Loan loss coverage ratio [A ÷ B]		23.22 times	5.69 times
Source: Bancfirst Corporation 2010 10-K			

Equity Capital to Total Assets

This ratio, also called funds to total assets, measures the extent of equity ownership in the bank. This ownership provides the cushion against the risk of using debt and leverage. Exhibit 12-5 presents this ratio, computed by using year-end figures, for BancFirst. This ratio decreased in 2010 to 9.38% from 10.20% in 2009. Both of these ratios appear to be very good.

Deposits Times Capital

The ratio of deposits times capital concerns both depositors and stockholders. To some extent, it is a type of debt/equity ratio, indicating a bank's debt position. More capital implies a greater margin of safety, while a larger deposit base gives a prospect of higher return to stockholders, since more money is available for investment purposes. Exhibit 12-6 presents this ratio for BancFirst, based on year-end figures. Deposits times capital increased in 2010 to 9.48 from 8.65 in 2009.

Loans to Deposits

Average total loans to average deposits is a type of asset to liability ratio. Loans make up a large portion of the bank's assets, and its principal obligations are the deposits that can be withdrawn on request—within time limitations. This is a type of debt coverage ratio, and it measures the bank's position with regard to taking risks. Exhibit 12-7 shows this ratio for BancFirst. Loans to deposits decreased in 2010, indicating a decrease in risk from a debt standpoint.

EXHIBIT **12-5**	BancFirst	

Equity Capital to Total Assets
For the Years Ended December 31, 2010 and 2009

(In millions of dollars)	2010	2009
Average equity [A]	$ 444,672	$ 422,271
Average total assets [B]	$4,738,182	$4,141,660
Equity capital to total assets [A ÷ B]	9.38%	10.20%

Source: Bancfirst Corporation 2010 10-K

EXHIBIT **12-6**	BancFirst	

Deposits Times Capital
For the Years Ended December 31, 2010 and 2009

(In millions of dollars)	2010	2009
Average deposits [A]	$4,216,385	$3,653,312
Average shareholders' equity [B]	$ 444,672	$ 422,271
Deposits times capital [A ÷ B]	9.48 times	8.65 times

Source: Bancfirst Corporation 2010 10-K

EXHIBIT **12-7**	BancFirst	

Loans to Deposits
For the Years Ended December 31, 2010 and 2009

(In millions of dollars)	2010	2009
Average total loans [A]	$2,775,309	$2,748,259
Average deposits [B]	$4,216,385	$3,653,312
Loans to deposits [A ÷ B]	65.82%	75.23%

Source: Bancfirst Corporation 2010 10-K

Regulated Utilities

Regulated utilities render a unique service on which the public depends. Regulated utilities are basically monopolies subject to government regulation, including rate regulation. In recent years, laws have been enacted that greatly reduce the monopoly aspect.

Uniformity of accounting is prescribed by the Federal Energy Regulatory Commission for interstate electric and gas companies and by the Federal Communications Commission for telephone and telegraph companies, as well as by state regulatory agencies.

This section includes comments on regulated utilities. In recent years, most utilities have added nonregulated businesses. In many cases, the nonregulated businesses have become more than the regulated businesses. These utilities usually do not present financial reports like a regulated utility, especially the form of the balance sheet. These balance sheets may appear like a normal balance sheet. The ratios introduced in this section may not be feasible to be computed for utilities with substantial nonregulated businesses.

Financial Statements

Balance sheets for utilities differ from business balance sheets mainly in the order that accounts for utilities are presented. Plant and equipment are the first assets listed, followed by investments and other assets, current assets, and deferred charges. Note that Wisconsin Energy Corporation combines deferred charges and other assets. Under liabilities and equity, the first section is capitalization. The capitalization section usually includes all sources of long-term capital, such as common stock, preferred stock, and long-term debt. The capitalization section is followed by current liabilities, and then deferred credits and other.

The income statement for utilities is set up by operating revenues, less operating expenses to arrive at net operating income. Net operating income is adjusted by other income (deductions) to arrive at income before interest charges. Interest charges are then deducted to arrive at income before income taxes.

Exhibit 12-8 presents a part of the 2010 annual report of Wisconsin Energy Corporation. Review Exhibit 12-8 to become familiar with the form of utility financial statements.

EXHIBIT 12-8	Wisconsin Energy Corporation*

Selected Financial Data

WISCONSIN ENERGY CORPORATION
Consolidated Income Statements
Year Ended December 31

	2010	2009	2008
	(Millions of Dollars, Except Per Share Amounts)		
Operating Revenues	$4,202.5	$4,100.9	$4,402.4
Operating Expenses			
Fuel and purchases power	1,099.9	1,059.7	1,238.1
Cost of gas sold	751.5	912.0	1,220.9
Other operation and maintenance	1,327.5	1,246.1	1,346.2
Depreciation and amortization	305.6	343.0	323.6
Property and revenue taxes	106.0	110.5	106.5
Total Operating Expenses	3,590.5	3,671.3	4,235.3
Amortization of Gain	198.4	230.7	488.1
Operating income	810.4	660.3	655.2
Equity in Earnings of Transmission Affiliate	60.1	59.1	51.8

* "Wisconsin Energy Corporation was incorporated in the state of Wisconsin in 1981 and became a diversified holding company in 1986. We maintain our principal executive offices in Milwaukee, Wisconsin. Unless qualified by their context when used in this document, the terms Wisconsin Energy, the Company, our, us or we refer to the holding company and all of its subsidiaries.

We conduct our operations primarily in two operating segments: a utility energy segment and a non-utility energy segment. Our primary subsidiaries are Wisconsin Electric, Wisconsin Gas LLC (Wisconsin Gas) and W.E. Power, LLC (We Power)." 10-K

Source: Wisconsin Energy Corporations 2010 10-K

(*continued*)

EXHIBIT **12-8**	Wisconsin Energy Corporation *(continued)*

	2010	2009	2008
	(Millions of Dollars, Except Per Share Amounts)		
Other Income and Deductions, net	40.2	28.5	16.9
Interest Expense, net	206.4	156.7	153.7
Income from Continuing Operations Before Income Taxes	704.3	591.2	570.2
Income Taxes	249.9	215.5	215.1
Income from Continuing Operations	454.4	375.7	355.1
Income from Discontinued Operations, Net of Tax	2.1	6.7	4.0
Net income	$ 456.5	382.4	359.1
Earnings Per Share (Basic)			
Continuing Operations	$ 3.89	3.21	3.04
Discontinued Operations	0.02	0.06	0.03
Total Earnings Per Share (Basic)	$ 3.91	3.27	3.07
Earnings Per Share (Diluted)			
Continuing Operations	$ 3.84	3.19	3.00
Discontinued Operations	0.02	0.05	0.04
Total Earnings Per Share (Diluted)	$ 3.86	3.24	3.04
Weighted Average Common Shares Outstanding (Millions)			
Basic	116.9	116.9	116.9
Diluted	118.4	117.9	118.2

The following pro forma information reflects the impact of the two-for-one stock split, which will be effective March 2011. See Note T – Subsequent Events for further information.

	2010	2009	2008
Pro Forma Earnings Per Share (Diluted)			
Continuing Operations	$ 1.92	$ 1.59	$ 1.50
Discontinued Operations	0.01	0.03	0.02
Total Pro Forma Earnings Per Share (Diluted)	$ 1.93	$ 1.62	$ 1.52

WISCONSIN ENERGY CORPORATION
Consolidated Balance Sheets
December 31

Assets	2010	2009
	(Millions of Dollars)	
Property, Plant and Equipment		
In service	$11,590.8	$10,192.1
Accumulated depreciation	(3,624.0)	(3,431.9)
	7,966.8	6.760.2
Construction work in progress	1,569.9	2,185.1
Leased facilities, net	64.8	70.5
Net Property, Plant and Equipment	9,601.5	9.015.8
Investments		
Equity investment in transmission affiliate	330.5	314.6
Other	45.8	44.1
Total Investments	376.3	358.7
Current Assets		
Cash and cash equivalents	24.5	20.2
Restricted cash	8.3	194.5
Accounts receivable, net of allowance for doubtful accounts of $58.1 and $57.9	344.6	298.7
Accrued revenues	280.3	288.7
Materials, supplies and inventories	379.1	378.1
Regulatory assets	54.4	58.9
Prepayments and other	239.9	290.2
Total Current Assets	1,331.1	1,529.3

EXHIBIT 12-8	Wisconsin Energy Corporation *(continued)*

	2010	2009
Assets	(Millions of Dollars)	
Deferred Charges and Other Assets		
Regulatory assets	1,090.1	1,180.5
Goodwill	441.9	441.9
Other	218.9	171.7
Total Deferred Charges and Other Assets	1,750.9	1,794.1
Total Assets	$13,059.8	$12,697.9

	2010	2009
Capitalization and Liabilities	(Millions of Dollars)	
Capitalization		
Common equity	$ 3,802.1	$ 3,566.9
Preferred stock of subsidiary	30.4	30.4
Long-term debt	3,392.0	3,875.8
Total Capitalization	7,764.5	7,473.1
Current Liabilities		
Long-term debt due currently	473.4	295.7
Short-term debt	657.9	825.1
Accounts payable	315.4	290.6
Regulatory liabilities	15.3	222.8
Other	259.1	259.9
Total Current Liabilities	1,721.1	1,894.1
Deferred Credits and Other Liabilities		
Regulatory liabilities	883.8	876.0
Asset retirement obligations	52.6	57.9
Deferred income taxes – long-term	1,154.8	1,017.9
Accumulated deferred investment tax credits	34.0	37.7
Deferred revenue, net	805.5	739.1
Pension and other benefit obligations	353.2	318.7
Other long-term liabilities	290.3	283.4
Total Deferred Credits and Other Liabilities	3,574.2	3,330.7
Commitments and Contingencies (Note R)	—	—
Total Capitalization and Liabilities	$13,059.8	$12,697.9

A. SUMMARY OF SIGNIFICANT ACCOUNTING POLICIES

Property and Depreciation: We record property, plant and equipment at cost. Cost includes material, labor, overheads and capitalized interest. Utility property also includes AFUDC – Equity, Additions to and significant replacements of property are charged to property, plant and equipment at cost; minor items are charged to maintenance expense. The cost of depreciable utility property less salvage value is charged to accumulated depreciation when property is retired.

We recorded the following property in service by segment as of December 31:

	2010	2009
Property in Service	(Millions of Dollars)	
Utility Energy	$ 9,221.1	$ 8,998.3
Non-Utility Energy	2,283.4	1,111.6
Other	86.3	82.2
Total	$11,590.8	$10,192.1

Our utility depreciation rates are certified by the PSCW and MPSC and include estimates for salvage value and removal costs. Depreciation as a percent of average depreciable utility plant was 2.8% in 2010 and 3.7% in 2009 and 2008.

PWGS 1 and PWGS 2 are being depreciated over an estimated useful life of 37 years. OC 1 is being depreciated over an estimated useful life of 45 years.

For assets other than our regulated assets, we accrue depreciation expense at straight-line rates over the estimated useful lives of the assets. Estimated useful lives for non-regulated assets are 3 to 40 years for furniture and equipment, 2 to 5 years for software and 30 to 40 years for buildings.

(continued)

EXHIBIT 12-8	Wisconsin Energy Corporation (continued)

Our regulated utilities collect in their rates amounts representing future removal costs for many assets that do not have an associated Asset Retirement Obligation (ARO). We record a regulatory liability on our balance sheet for the estimated amounts we have collected in rates for future removal costs less amounts we have spent in removal activities. This regulatory liability was $723.9 million as of December 31, 2010 and $718.7 million as of December 31, 2009.

We recorded the following Construction Work in Progress (CWIP) by segment as of December 31:

CWIP	2010	2009
	(Millions of Dollars)	
Utility Energy	$ 806.9	$ 386.2
Non-Utility Energy	761.3	1,794.8
Other	1.7	4.1
Total	$1,569.9	$2,185.1

Allowance For Funds Used During Construction − Regulated: AFUDC is included in utility plant accounts and represents the cost of borrowed funds (AFUDC − Debt) used during plant construction, and a return on stockholders' capital (AFUDC − Equity) used for construction purposes. AFUDC − Debt is recorded as a reduction of interest expense, and AFUDC − Equity is recorded in Other Income and Deductions, net.

During 2009 and 2008, Wisconsin Electric accrued AFUDC at a rate of 9.09% as authorized by the PSCW. Consistent with the PSCW's 2008 rate order, Wisconsin Electric accrued AFUDC on 50% of all utility CWIP projects except the Oak Creek AQCS project which accrued AFUDC on 100% of CWIP. Wisconsin Electric's rates are set to provide a current return on CWIP that does not accrue AFUDC. Based on the 2010 PSCW rate order, effective January 1, 2010 Wisconsin Electric is recording AFUDC on 100% of CWIP associated with the Oak Creek AQCS project, the Edgewater Unit 5 Selective Catalytic Reduction project, and the Glacier Hills Wind Park. Wisconsin Electric will record AFUDC on 50% of all other electric, gas, and steam utility CWIP. The AFUDC rate starting January 1, 2010 is 8.83%.

During 2009 and 2008, Wisconsin Gas accrued AFUDC at a rate of 10.80% on 50% of its CWIP as authorized by the PSCW in its 2008 rate order. Wisconsin Gas' rates are set to provide a current return on CWIP that does not accrue AFUDC. Based on the 2010 PSCW rate order, effective January 1, 2010 Wisconsin Gas is recording AFUDC on 50% of all CWIP using an AFUDC rate of 9.05%.

Our regulated segment recorded the following AFUDC for the years ended December 31:

	2010	2009	2008
	(Millions of Dollars)		
AFUDC – Debt	$13.5	$ 6.7	$3.3
AFUDC – Equity	$32.5	$16.0	$7.8

Capitalized Interest and Carrying Costs − Non-Regulated Energy: As part of the construction of the electric generating units under our PTF program, we capitalized interest during construction. As allowed under the lease agreements, we were able to collect the carrying costs during the construction of the PTF generating units from our utility customers. We have deferred these carrying costs collected on our balance sheet while the PTF units were under construction and we are amortizing the deferred carrying costs to revenue after the assets were placed in service over the individual lease terms. For further information on the accounting for capitalized interest and deferred carrying costs associated with the construction of our PTF power plants, see Note E.

· · · · ·

E – ACCOUNTING AND REPORTING FOR POWER THE FUTURE GENERATING UNITS

Background: As part of our PTF strategy, our non-utility subsidiary, We Power, has built four new generating units, PWGS 1, PWGS 2, OC 1 and OC 2, which are leased to our utility subsidiary, Wisconsin Electric, under long-term leases that have been approved by the PSCW. The leases are designed to recover the capital costs of the plant, including a return. PWGS 1, PWGS 2, OC 1 and OC 2 were placed in service in July 2005, May 2008, February 2010 and January 2011, respectively. The accompanying consolidated financial statements eliminate all intercompany transactions between We Power and Wisconsin Electric and reflect the cash inflows from Wisconsin Electric customers and the cash outflows to our vendors and suppliers.

The Oak Creek expansion includes common projects that benefit the existing units at this site as well as the new units. These projects include a coal handling facility and a water intake system, which were placed in service in November 2007 and January 2009, respectively.

During Construction: Under the terms of each lease, we collect in current rates amounts representing our pre-tax cost of capital (debt and equity) associated with capital expenditures for our PTF units. Our pre-tax cost of capital is approximately 14%. The carrying costs that we collected in rates were recorded as deferred revenue and started being amortized to revenue

EXHIBIT **12-8**	Wisconsin Energy Corporation (*continued*)

over the term of each lease once the respective unit was placed into service. During the construction of our PTF units, we capitalized interest costs at an overall weighted-average pre-tax cost of interest, which was approximately 5% for the years ended December 31, 2010 and 2009. Capitalized interest is included in the total cost of the PTF units.

Plant in Service: Now that the PTF units are placed in service, we expect to continue to recover in rates the lease costs which reflect the authorized cash construction costs of the units plus a return on the investment. The authorized cash costs are established by the PSCW. The authorized cash costs exclude capitalized interest since carrying costs were recovered during the construction of the units. The lease payments are expected to be levelized, except that OC 1 and OC 2 will be recovered on a levelized basis that has a one time 10.6% escalation after the first five years of the leases. The leases established a set return on equity component of 12.7% after tax. The interest component of the return under each lease has been determined at rates in effect at the time of commercial operation.

We recognize revenues (consisting of the lease payments included in rates and the amortization of the deferred revenue) on a levelized basis over the term of the lease. We depreciate the PTF assets on a straight-line basis over their expected service life.

Inventories are not a problem for electric utilities. Traditionally, receivables have not been a problem because the services are essential and could be cut off for nonpayment and because often a prepayment is required of the customer. In recent years, receivables have been a problem for some utilities because some utility commissions have ruled that services could not be cut off during the winter.

Wisconsin Energy Corporation had $379,100,000 in materials, supplies, and inventories on December 31, 2010. It is partly a regulated and a nonregulated energy company.

A few accounts on the financial statements of a utility are particularly important to the understanding of the statements. On the balance sheet, many utilities have a construction work-in-progress (CWIP) account. Exhibit 12-8 discloses that Wisconsin Energy had construction work in progress of $1,569,900,000 and $2,185,100,000 in 2010 and 2009, respectively.

Utilities that have substantial construction work in progress are usually viewed as being more risky investments than utilities that do not. Most utility commissions allow no construction work in progress or only a small amount in the rate base. Therefore, the utility rates essentially do not reflect the construction work in progress.

The utility intends to have the additional property and plant considered in the rate base when the construction work is completed. However, the utility commission may not allow all of this property and plant in the rate base. If the commission rules that inefficiency caused part of the cost, it may disallow the cost. The commission may also disallow part of the cost on the grounds that the utility used bad judgment and provided for excess capacity. Costs disallowed are in effect charged to the stockholders, as future income will not include a return on disallowed cost. In the long run, everybody pays for inefficiency and excess capacity because disallowed costs are a risk that can drive the stock price down and interest rates up for the utility. This increases the cost of capital for the utility, which in turn may force utility rates up.

For the costs allowed, the risk exists that the utility commission will not allow a reasonable rate of return. It is important to observe what proportion of total property and plant is represented by construction work in progress. Also, be familiar with the political climate of the utility commission that will be ruling on the construction work in progress costs.

The income statement accounts—allowance for equity funds and allowance for borrowed funds used during construction—relate to construction work-in-progress costs on the balance sheet. Both of these accounts, sometimes jointly referred to as the allowance for funds used during construction, have been added to construction work-in-progress costs. Wisconsin Energy Corporation did not disclose these accounts separately on the income statement. It did describe them in a note.

The account allowance for equity funds used during construction represents an assumed rate of return on equity funds used for construction. The account allowance for borrowed funds used during construction represents the cost of borrowed funds that are used for construction.

By increasing the balance sheet account, Construction Work in Progress, for an assumed rate of return on equity funds, the utility builds into the cost base an amount for an assumed rate of return on equity funds. As explained previously, the utility commission may not accept this cost base. The costs that have been added into the cost base have also been added to income, through the allowance for equity funds. Sometimes the account allowance for equity funds used during construction represents a significant portion of the utility's net income.

The income statement account, Allowance for Borrowed Funds Used during Construction, charges to the balance sheet account, Construction in Progress, the interest on borrowed funds used for construction in progress. Thus, this interest is added to the cost base.

Utilities with substantial construction work in progress can have significant cash flow problems. Their reported net income can be substantially higher than the cash flow related to the income statement. Sometimes these utilities issue additional bonds and stocks to obtain funds to pay interest and dividends.

Wisconsin Energy also had capitalized interest related to nonregulated energy. This would be part of its construction work in progress.

Ratios for Regulated Utilities

Because of the vastly different accounts and statement formats, few of the traditional ratios are appropriate for regulated utilities. Exceptions are the return on assets, return on equity, debt/equity, and times interest earned. Investor-related ratios are also of value in analyzing utilities. For example, the cash flow per share ratio can be a particularly important indicator of the utility's ability to maintain and increase dividends. Standard & Poor's *Industry Survey* is a good source for composite industry data on utilities.

The ratios reviewed here would often apply to the regulated and nonregulated as long as the nonregulated is associated with the utility business.

Operating Ratio

The operating ratio measures efficiency by comparing operating expenses to operating revenues. A profitable utility holds this ratio low. A vertical common-size analysis of the income statement will aid in conclusions regarding this ratio. Exhibit 12-9 presents the operating ratio for Wisconsin Energy. This ratio decreased moderately in 2010, thus having a positive influence on profitability.

EXHIBIT 12-9	Wisconsin Energy Corporation

Operating Ratio
For the Years Ended December 31, 2010 and 2009

(In millions of dollars)	2010	2009
Operating expenses [A]	$ 3,590.5	$ 3,671.3
Operating revenues [B]	$ 4,202.5	$ 4,100.9
Operating ratio [A ÷ B]	85.44%	89.52%

Source: Wisconsin Energy Corporations 2010 10-K

Funded Debt to Operating Property

A key ratio, the comparison of funded debt to net fixed operating property, is sometimes termed LTD (long-term debt) to *net property* because funded debt is long-term debt. Operating property consists of property and plant less the allowance for depreciation and any allowance for nuclear fuel amortization. Construction in progress is included since it has probably been substantially funded by debt. This ratio measures debt coverage and indicates how funds are supplied. It resembles debt to total assets, with only specialized debt and the specific assets that generate the profits to cover the debt charges. Exhibit 12-10 presents funded debt to operating property for Wisconsin Energy. This ratio decreased slightly in 2010, indicating a less risky debt position.

EXHIBIT 12-10	Wisconsin Energy Corporation

Funded Debt to Operating Property
For the Years Ended December 31, 2010 and 2009

(In millions of dollars)	2010	2009
Funded debt* [A]	$ 4,406.3	$ 4,171.5
Operating property [B]**	$ 9,536.7	$ 8,945.3
Funded debt to operating property [A ÷ B]	46.20%	46.63%

*Included long-term debt and current maturities of long-term debt.
**Excluded leased facilities, net from net property, plant, and equipment.
Source: Wisconsin Energy Corporations 2010 10-K

Percent Earned on Operating Property

This ratio, sometimes termed *earnings on net property*, relates net earnings to the assets primarily intended to generate earnings—net property and plant. Exhibit 12-11 presents this ratio for Wisconsin Energy. Note that this ratio increased substantially in 2010, which is a favorable trend.

EXHIBIT 12-11	Wisconsin Energy Corporation

Percent Earned on Operating Property
For the Years Ended December 31, 2010 and 2009

(In millions of dollars)	2010	2009
Net income* [A]	$ 394.3	$ 316.6
Operating property** [B]	$8,031.6	$6,830.7
Percent earned on operating property [A ÷ B]	4.91%	4.63%

*Excluded discontinued operations and equity earnings.
**Excluded construction work in progress.
Source: Wisconsin Energy Corporations 2010 10-K

Operating Revenue to Operating Property

This ratio is basically an operating asset turnover ratio. In public utilities, the fixed plant is often much larger than the expected annual revenue, and this ratio will be less than 1. Exhibit 12-12 presents this ratio for Wisconsin Energy, which indicates a material decrease in the operating revenue to operating property and represents an unfavorable trend.

EXHIBIT 12-12	Wisconsin Energy Corporation

Operating Revenue to Operating Property
For the Years Ended December 31, 2010 and 2009

(In millions of dollars)	2010	2009
Operating revenues [A]	$ 4,202.5	$ 4,100.9
Operating property* [B]	$ 8,031.6	$ 6,830.7
Operating revenue to operating property [A ÷ B]	52.32%	60.04%

*Removed construction work in progress.
Source: Wisconsin Energy Corporations 2010 10-K

Oil and Gas

Oil and gas companies' financial statements are affected significantly by the method they choose to account for costs associated with exploration and production. The method chosen is some variation of the successful-efforts or full-costing methods, which will be explained along with their effects on the financial statements. The financial statements of oil and gas companies are also unique because they are required to disclose, in a note, supplementary information on oil and gas exploration, development, and production activities. This requirement will be explained in this section.

Cash flow is important to all companies, but particularly to oil and gas companies. Therefore, cash flow must be part of the analysis of an oil or a gas company. In addition, most of the traditional financial ratios apply to oil and gas companies. This section will not cover special ratios that relate to oil and gas companies.

The 2010 financial statements of ConocoPhillips will be used to illustrate oil and gas financial statements. ConocoPhillips is an integrated international energy company.

Successful-Efforts versus Full-Costing Methods

A gas company uses a variation of two costing methods to account for exploration and production costs: the successful-efforts method and the full-costing method.

The **successful-efforts method** places only exploration and production costs of successful wells on the balance sheet under property, plant, and equipment. Exploration and production costs of unsuccessful (or dry) wells are expensed when it is determined that there is a dry hole. With the **full-costing method**, exploration and production costs of all the wells (successful and unsuccessful) are placed on the balance sheet under property, plant, and equipment.

Under both methods, exploration and production costs placed on the balance sheet are subsequently amortized as expense to the income statement. Amortization costs that relate to natural resources are called *depletion expense*.

The costing method used for exploration and production can have a very significant influence on the balance sheet and the income statement. Under both methods, exploration and production costs are eventually expensed, but a significant difference exists in the timing of the expense.

In theory, the successful-efforts method takes the position that a direct relationship exists between costs incurred and specific reserves discovered. These costs should be placed on the balance sheet. Costs associated with unsuccessful efforts are a period expense and should be charged to expense. In theory, the full-costing method takes the position that the drilling of all wells, successful and unsuccessful, is part of the process of finding successful wells. Therefore, all of the cost should be placed on the balance sheet.

In practice, the decision to use the successful-efforts method or the full-costing method is probably not significantly influenced by theory but by practicalities. Most relatively small oil and gas companies select a variation of the full-costing method. This results in a much larger balance sheet. In the short run, it also usually results in higher reported profits. Small oil companies speculate that the larger balance sheet and the increased reported profits can be used to influence some banks and limited partners, which the small companies tend to use as sources of funds.

Large oil and gas companies tend to select a variation of the successful-efforts method. This results in a lower balance sheet amount and lower reported income in the short run. The large companies usually depend on bonds and stock as their primary sources of outside capital. Investors in bonds and stock are not likely to be influenced by the larger balance sheet and higher income that result from capitalizing dry wells.

The method used can have a significant influence on the balance sheet and the income statement. The successful-efforts method is more conservative. Review Exhibit 12-13 for a description of ConocoPhillips' method of accounting for exploration and production costs.

Supplementary Information on Oil and Gas Exploration, Development, and Production Activities

As part of your review of an oil or a gas company, note the supplemental oil and gas information. Review Exhibit 12-14 for a brief summary of the supplementary information presented by ConocoPhillips.

EXHIBIT **12-13**	ConocoPhillips*

Note 1 to Consolidated Financial Statements (In Part)

Oil and Gas Exploration and Development – Oil and gas exploration and development costs are accounted for using the successful efforts method of accounting.

Property Acquisition Costs – Oil and gas leasehold acquisition costs are capitalized and included in the balance sheet caption properties, plants and equipment. Leasehold impairment is recognized based on exploratory experience and management's judgment. Upon achievement of all conditions necessary for reserves to be classified as proved, the associated leasehold costs are reclassified to proved properties.

Exploratory Costs – Geological and geophysical costs and the costs of carrying and retaining undeveloped properties are expensed as incurred. Exploratory well costs are capitalized, or "suspended," on the balance sheet pending further evaluation of whether economically recoverable reserves have been found. If economically recoverable reserves are not found, exploratory well costs are expensed as dry holes. If exploratory wells encounter potentially economic quantities of oil and gas, the well costs remain capitalized on the balance sheet as long as sufficient progress assessing the reserves and the economic and operating viability of the project is being made. For complex exploratory discoveries, it is not unusual to have exploratory wells remain suspended on the balance sheet for several years while we perform additional appraisal drilling and seismic work on the potential oil and gas field or while we seek government or co-venturer approval of development plans or seek environmental permitting. Once all required approvals and permits have been obtained, the projects are moved into the development phase, and the oil and gas resources are designated as proved reserves.

Management reviews suspended well balances quarterly, continuously monitors the results of the additional appraisal drilling and seismic work, and expenses the suspended well costs as dry holes when it judges the potential field does not warrant further investment in the near term. See Note 8—Suspended Wells, for additional information on suspended wells.

Development Costs – Costs incurred to drill and equip development wells, including unsuccessful development wells, are capitalized.

Depletion and Amortization – Leasehold costs of producing properties are depleted using the unit-of-production method based on estimated proved oil and gas reserves. Amortization of intangible development costs is based on the unit-of-production method using estimated proved developed oil and gas reserves.

*"ConocoPhillips is an international, integrated energy company." 10-K
Source: Conocophillips 2010 10-K

EXHIBIT **12-14**	ConocoPhillips*

Oil and Operations (Unaudited) (In Part)
2010 Annual Report

ConocoPhillips presented supplemental data (unaudited) using 27 pages in 2010 its annual report. Exhibit 12-14 represents only a small part of the disclosure.

Oil and Gas Operations (Unaudited) (In Part)

In accordance with Financial Accounting Standards Board (FASB) Accounting Standards Codification Topic 932, "Extractive Activities—Oil and Gas," and regulations of the U.S. Securities and Exchange Commission (SEC), we are making certain supplemental disclosures about our oil and gas exploration and production operations.

These disclosures include information about our consolidated oil and gas activities and our proportionate share of our equity affiliates' oil and gas activities, covering both those in our Exploration and Production (E'P) segment, as well as in our LUKOIL Investment segment. As a result, amounts reported as Equity Affiliates in Oil and Gas Operations may differ from those shown in the individual segment disclosures reported elsewhere in this report.

Our proved reserves include estimated quantities related to production sharing contracts (PSCs), which are reported under the "economic interest" method and are subject to fluctuations in prices of crude oil, natural gas and natural gas liquids; recoverable operating expenses; and capital costs. If costs remain stable, reserve quantities attributable to recovery of costs will change inversely to changes in commodity prices. For example, if prices increase, then our applicable reserve quantities would decline. At December 31, 2010, approximately 12 percent of our total proved reserves were under PSCs, primarily in our Asia Pacific/Middle East geographic reporting area.

Our disclosures by geographic area include the United States, Canada, Europe (primarily Norway and the United Kingdom), Russia, Asia Pacific/Middle East, Africa, and Other Areas. Other Areas primarily consists of the Caspian Region.

· · · · ·

*"ConocoPhillips is an international, integrated energy company." 10-K
Source: Conocophillips 2010 10-K

(*continued*)

EXHIBIT **12-14**	ConocoPhillips (*continued*)

The major headings in this disclosure follow:

- Reserves Governance
- Proved Reserves
- Proved Undeveloped Reserves
- Results of Operations
- Statistics
- Costs Incurred
- Capitalized Costs
- Standardized Measure of Discounted Future Net Cash Flows Relating to Proved Oil and Gas Reserve Quantities

Cash Flow

Monitoring cash flow can be particularly important when following an oil or a gas company. The potential for a significant difference exists between the reported income and cash flow from operations. One reason is that large sums can be spent for exploration and development, years in advance of revenue from the found reserves. The other reason is that there can be significant differences between when expenses are deducted on the financial statements and when they are deducted on the tax return. Therefore, observe the operating cash flow.

Cash from operating activities for a three-year period will be disclosed on the statement of cash flows. For ConocoPhillips, net cash provided by operating activities was $17,045,000,000, $12,479,000,000, and $22,658,000,000 for 2010, 2009, and 2008, respectively. Net income (loss) attributable to ConocoPhillips was $11,358,000,000, $4,414,000,000, and ($16,349,000,000) for 2010, 2009, and 2008, respectively.

Transportation

Three components of the transportation industry will be discussed: air carriers, railroads, and the motor carrier industry. The Civil Aeronautics Board, which requires the use of a uniform system of accounts and reporting, regulates interstate commercial aviation. The Interstate Commerce Commission, which also has control over a uniform system of accounts and reporting, regulates interstate railroads. The Interstate Commerce Commission also regulates interstate motor carriers whose principal business is transportation services.

Financial Statements

The balance sheet format for air carriers, railroads, and motor carriers resembles that for manufacturing or retailing firms. As in a heavy manufacturing firm, property and equipment make up a large portion of assets. Also, supplies and parts comprise the basic inventory items. The income statement format resembles that of a utility. The system of accounts provides for the grouping of all revenues and expenses in terms of both major natural objectives and functional activities. There is no cost of goods sold calculation; rather, there is operating income: revenue (categorized) minus operating expenses. In essence, the statements are a prescribed, categorized form of single-step income statement. They cannot be converted to multiple-step format.

Ratios

Most of the traditional ratios also apply in the transportation field. Exceptions are inventory turnovers (because there is no cost of goods sold) and gross profit margin. The ratios discussed in the subsections that follow are especially suited to transportation. They are derived from the 2010 statement of income and balance sheet for Southwest Airlines Co., presented in Exhibit 12-15.

EXHIBIT 12-15	Southwest Airlines Co.*

Selected Financial Data

SOUTHWEST AIRLINES CO.
Consolidated Balance Sheet
(In millions, except share data)

	December 31, 2010	December 31, 2009
		(As adjusted-Note 3)
ASSETS		
Current assets:		
Cash and cash equivalents	$ 1,261	$ 1,114
Short-term investments	2,277	1,479
Accounts and other receivables	195	169
Inventories of parts and supplies, at cost	243	221
Deferred income taxes	214	291
Prepaid expenses and other current assets	89	84
Total current assets	4,279	3,358
Property and equipment, at cost:		
Flight equipment	13,991	13,719
Ground property and equipment	2,122	1,922
Deposits on flight equipment purchase contracts	230	247
	16,343	15,888
Less allowance for depreciation and amortization	5,765	5,254
	10,578	10,634
Other assets	606	277
	$15,463	$14,269
LIABILITIES AND STOCKHOLDERS' EQUITY		
Current liabilities:		
Accounts payable	$ 739	$ 732
Accrued liabilities	863	729
Air traffic liability	1,198	1,044
Current maturities of long-term debt	505	190
Total current liabilities	3,305	2,695
Long-term debt less current maturities	2,875	3,325
Deferred income taxes	2,493	2,200
Deferred gains from sale and leaseback of aircraft	88	102
Other noncurrent liabilities	465	493
Commitments and contingencies		
Stockholders' equity:		
Common stock, $1.00 par value: 2,000,000,000 shares authorized; 807,611,634 shares issued in 2010 and 2009	808	808
Capital in excess of par value	1,183	1,216
Retained earnings	5,399	4,971
Accumulated other comprehensive loss	(262)	(578)
Treasury stock, at cost: 60,177,362 and 64,820,703 shares in 2010 and 2009, respectively	(891)	(963)
Total stockholders' equity	6,237	5,454
	$15,463	$14,269

*"Southwest Airlines Co. (the "Company" or "Southwest") is a major passenger airline that provides scheduled air transportation in the United States." 10-K
Source: Southwest airlines Co. 2010 10-K

(*continued*)

| EXHIBIT **12-15** | Southwest Airlines Co. (*continued*) |

Southwest Airlines Co.
Consolidated Statement of Income
(In millions, except per share amounts)

	Years Ended December 31,		
	2010	**2009**	**2008**
OPERATING REVENUES:			
Passenger	$11,489	$ 9,829	$10,549
Freight	125	118	145
Other	490	340	329
Total operating revenues	12,104	10,350	11,023
OPERATING EXPENSES:			
Salaries, wages, and benefits	3,704	3,468	3,340
Fuel and oil	3,620	3,044	3,713
Maintenance materials and repairs	751	719	721
Aircraft rentals	180	186	154
Landing fees and other rentals	807	718	662
Depreciation and amortization	628	616	599
Other operating expenses	1,426	1,337	1,385
Total operating expenses	11,116	10,088	10,574
OPERATING INCOME			
OTHER EXPENSES (INCOME):			
Interest expense	167	186	130
Capitalized interest	(18)	(21)	(25)
Interest income	(12)	(13)	(26)
Other (gains) losses, net	106	(54)	92
Total other expenses (income)	243	98	171
INCOME BEFORE INCOME TAXES	745	164	278
PROVISION FOR INCOME TAXES	286	65	100
NET INCOME	$ 459	$ 99	$ 178
NET INCOME PER SHARE, BASIC	$ .62	$ .13	$ .24
NET INCOME PER SHARE, DILUTED	$ .61	$ .13	$ .24
Cash dividends declared per common share	$ .0180	$ .0180	$ .0180

The traditional sources of industry averages cover transportation. The federal government accumulates numerous statistics for regulated industries, including transportation. An example is the Interstate Commerce Commission's *Annual Report* on transport statistics in the United States.

For the motor carrier industry, a particularly good source of industry data is the annual publication *Financial Analysis of the Motor Carrier Industry*, published by the American Trucking Association, Inc. This publication includes an economic and industry overview, distribution of revenue by carrier type, and industry issues. It also includes definitions of terminology that relate to the motor carrier industry.

There are hundreds of motor carrier firms, most of which are relatively small. The American Trucking Association compiles data by composite carrier groups. For example, Group A includes composite data for several hundred general freight carriers with annual revenues of less than $5 million. One of the groups includes composite data for the publicly held carriers of general freight.

The very extensive composite data in the American Trucking Association publication include industry total dollars for the income statement and balance sheet. It also includes vertical common-size analyses for the income statement and the balance sheet. This publication also includes approximately 36 ratios and other analytical data, such as total tons.

Operating Ratio

The operating ratio is computed by comparing operating expenses with operating revenues. It measures cost and should be kept low, but external conditions, such as the level of business activity, may affect this ratio. Operating revenues vary from year to year because of differences in rates, classification of traffic, volume of traffic carried, and the distance traffic is transported. Operating expenses change because of variations in the price level, traffic carried, type of service performed, and effectiveness of operating and maintaining the properties. Common-size analysis of revenues and expenses is needed to explain changes in the operating ratio.

Exhibit 12-16 presents the operating ratio for Southwest Airlines Co. The operating ratio for Southwest Airlines decreased from 97.47% in 2009 to 91.84 in 2010. The operating ratio can dramatically affect the profitability of a carrier. This trend in the operating ratio is favorable for Southwest Airlines.

EXHIBIT 12-16	Southwest Airlines Co.		
Operating Ratio For the Years Ended December 31, 2010 and 2009			
(In millions)		2010	2009
Operating expenses [A]		$ 11,116	$ 10,088
Operating revenues [B]		$ 12,104	$ 10,350
Operating ratio [A ÷ B]		91.84%	97.47%
Source: Southwest airlines Co. 2010 10-K			

Long-Term Debt to Operating Property

Because of the transportation companies' heavy investment in operating assets, such as equipment, the long-term ratios increase in importance. Long-term borrowing capacity is also a key consideration. The ratio of long-term debt to operating property ratio gives a measure of the sources of funds with which property is obtained. It also measures borrowing capacity. Operating property is defined as long-term property and equipment. Exhibit 12-17 presents this ratio for Southwest Airlines. For Southwest Airlines, the long-term debt to operating property ratio decreased materially in 2010 to 27.18% from 31.27%. This represents a positive trend.

EXHIBIT 12-17	Southwest Airlines Co.		
Long-Term Debt to Operating Property For the Years Ended December 31, 2010 and 2009			
(In millions)		2010	2009
Long-term debt less current maturities [A]		$ 2,875	$ 3,325
Operating property [B]		$ 10,578	$ 10,634
Long-term debt to operating property [A ÷ B]		27.18%	31.27%
Source: Southwest airlines Co. 2010 10-K			

Operating Revenue to Operating Property

This ratio measures turnover of operating assets. The objective is to generate as many dollars in revenue per dollar of property as possible. Exhibit 12-18 presents this ratio for Southwest Airlines. The operating revenue to operating property increased materially between 2009 and 2010.

Per-Mile, Per-Person, and Per-Ton Passenger Load Factors

For transportation companies, additional insight can be gained by looking at revenues and expenses on a per unit of usage basis. Examples would be per mile of line or per 10 miles for

EXHIBIT 12-18	Southwest Airlines Co.

Operating Revenue to Operating Property
For the Years Ended December 31, 2010 and 2009

(In millions)	2010	2009
Operating revenue [A]	$ 12,104	$ 10,350
Operating property [B]	$ 10,578	$ 10,634
Operating revenue to operating property [A ÷ B]	114.43%	97.33%

Source: Southwest airlines Co. 2010 10-K

railroads, or a per passenger mile for air carriers. Although this type of disclosure is not required, it is often presented in highlights.

This type of disclosure is illustrated in Exhibit 12-19, which shows statistics for Southwest Airlines Co.

EXHIBIT 12-19	Southwest Airlines Co.

Selected Financial Data
For the Years Ended December 31, 2006–2010

Item 6. Selected Financial Data (In Part)

	2010	2009	2008	2007	2006
Operating Data:					
Revenue passengers carried	88,191,322	86,310,229	88,529,234	88,713,482	83,814,823
Enplaned passengers	114,213,010	101,338,228	101,920,598	101,910,809	96,276,907
Revenue passenger miles (RPMs) (000s)	78,046,967	74,456,710	73,491,687	72,318,812	67,691,289
Available seat miles (ASMs) (000s)	98,437,092	98,001,550	103,271,343	99,635,967	92,663,023
Load factor[1]	79.3%	76.0%	71.2%	72.6%	73.1%
Average length of passenger haul (miles)	885	863	830	815	808
Average aircraft stage length (miles)	648	639	636	629	622
Trips flown	1,114,451	1,125,111	1,191,151	1,160,699	1,092,331
Average passenger fare	$ 130.27	$ 114.61	$ 119.16	$ 106.60	$ 104.40
Passenger revenue yield per RPM	14.72¢	13.29¢	14.35¢	13.08¢	12.93¢
Operating revenue yield per ASM	12.30¢	10.56¢	10.67¢	9.90¢	9.81¢
Operating expense per ASM	11.29¢	10.29¢	10.24¢	9.10¢	8.80¢
Fuel costs per gallon, including taxes (average)	$ 2.51	$ 2.12	$ 2.44	$ 1.80	$ 1.64
Fuel consumed, in gallons (millions)	1,437	1,428	1,511	1,489	1,389
Fulltime equivalent Employees at period-end	34,901	34,726	35,499	34,378	32,664
Aircraft in service at period-end[2]	548	537	537	520	481

[1]Revenue passenger miles divided by available seat miles.
[2]Includes leased aircraft.
Source: Southwest airlines Co. 2010 10-K

Insurance

Insurance companies provide two types of services. One is an identified contract service—mortality protection or loss protection. The second is investment management service.

There are basically four types of insurance organizations:

1. STOCK COMPANIES. A stock company is a corporation organized to earn profits for its stockholders. The comments in this insurance section relate specifically to stock companies. Many of the comments are also valid for the other types of insurance organizations.

2. MUTUAL COMPANIES. A mutual company is an incorporated entity, without private ownership interest, operating for the benefit of its policyholders and their beneficiaries.

3. FRATERNAL BENEFIT SOCIETIES. A fraternal benefit society resembles a mutual insurance company in that, although incorporated, it does not have capital stock, and it operates for the benefit of its members and beneficiaries. Policyholders participate in the earnings of the society, and the policies stipulate that the society has the power to assess them in case the legal reserves become impaired.

4. ASSESSMENT COMPANIES. An assessment company is an organized group with similar interests, such as a religious denomination.

The regulation of insurance companies started at the state level. Beginning in 1828, the State of New York required that annual reports be filed with the state controller. Subsequently, other states followed this precedent, and all 50 states have insurance departments that require annual statements of insurance companies. The reports are filed with the state insurance departments in accordance with statutory accounting practices (SAP). The National Association of Insurance Commissioners (NAIC), a voluntary association, has succeeded in achieving near uniformity among the states, so there are no significant differences in SAP among the states.[1]

Statutory accounting emphasizes the balance sheet. In its concern for protecting policyholders, statutory accounting focuses on the financial solvency of the insurance corporation. After the annual reports are filed with the individual state insurance departments, a testing process is conducted by the NAIC. This process is based on ratio calculations concerning the financial position of a company. If a company's ratio is outside the prescribed limit, the NAIC brings that to the attention of the state insurance department.

A.M. Best Company publishes *Best's Insurance Reports*, which are issued separately for life-health companies and property-casualty companies. *Best's Insurance Reports* evaluate the financial condition of more than 3,000 insurance companies. The majority of companies are assigned a Best's Rating, ranging from A+ (Superior) to C– (Fair). The other companies are classified as "Not Assigned." The "Not Assigned" category has 10 classifications to identify why a company has not been assigned a Best's Rating.

Some of the items included in Best's data include a balance sheet, summary of operations, operating ratios, profitability ratios, leverage ratios, and liquidity ratios. Most of the ratios are industry-specific. It is not practical to describe and explain them in this book. It should be noted that the financial data, including the ratios, are based on the data submitted to the state insurance departments and are thus based on SAP. GAAP for insurance companies developed much later than SAP. The annual reports of insurance companies are based on GAAP.

The 1934 Securities and Exchange Act established national government regulation, in addition to the state regulation of insurance companies. Stock insurance companies with assets of $1 million and at least 500 stockholders must register with the SEC and file the required forms, such as the annual Form 10-K. Reports filed with the SEC must conform with GAAP.

Exhibit 12-20 contains the income statement and balance sheet from the 2010 annual report of the Chubb Corporation. These statements were prepared using GAAP. Review them to observe the unique nature of insurance company financial statements.

Balance Sheet Under GAAP

The balance sheet for an insurance company is not classified by current assets and current liabilities (nonclassified balance sheet). Instead, its basic sections are assets, liabilities, and shareholders' equity.

Assets

The assets section starts with investments, a classification in which most insurance companies maintain the majority of their assets. Many of the investments have a high degree of liquidity, so that prompt payment can be assured in the event of a catastrophic loss. The majority of the investments are typically in bonds, with stock investments being much lower.

| EXHIBIT **12-20** | The Chubb Corporation* |

2010 Annual Report – Selected Financial Data

THE CHUBB CORPORATION
Consolidated Statements of Income

| | In Millions, Except for Per Share Amounts | | |
| | Years Ended December 31 | | |
	2010	2009	2008
Revenues			
Premiums Earned	$11,215	$11,331	$11,828
Investment income	1,665	1,649	1,732
Other Revenues	13	13	32
Realized Investment Gains (Losses), Net			
Total Other-Than-Temporary Impairment Losses on Investments	(6)	(132)	(446)
Other-Than-Temporary Impairment Losses on Investments			
Recognized in Other Comprehensive Income	(5)	20	—
Other Realized Investment Gains, Net	437	135	75
TOTAL REVENUES	13,319	13,016	13,221
Losses and Expenses			
Losses and Loss Expenses	6,499	6,268	6,898
Amortization of Deferred Policy Acquisition Costs	3,067	3,021	3,123
Other Insurance Operating costs and Expenses	425	416	441
Investment Expenses	35	39	32
Other Expenses	15	16	36
Corporate Expenses	290	294	284
TOTAL LOSSES AND EXPENSES	10,331	10,054	10,814
INCOME BEFORE FEDERAL AND FOREIGN INCOME TAX	2,988	2,962	2,407
Federal and Foreign Income Tax	814	779	603
NET INCOME	$ 2,174	$ 2,183	$ 1,804
Net Income Per Share			
Basic	$ 6.81	$ 6.24	$ 5.00
Diluted	6.76	6.18	4.92

THE CHUBB CORPORATION
Consolidated Balance Sheets

| | In Millions December 31, | |
	2010	2009
Assets		
Invested Assets		
Short Term Investments	$ 1,905	$ 1,918
Fixed Maturities		
Tax Exempt (cost $19,072 and $18,720)	19,774	19,587
Taxable (cost $15,989 and $16,470)	16,745	16,991
Equity Securities (cost $1,285 and $1,215)	1,550	1,433
Other Invested Assets	2,239	2,075
TOTAL INVESTED ASSETS	42,213	42,004
Cash	70	51
Accrued Investment Income	447	460
Premiums Receivable	2,098	2,101
Reinsurance Recoverable on Unpaid Losses and Loss Expenses	1,817	2,053

*"The Chubb Corporation (Chubb) was incorporated as a business corporation under the laws of the State of New Jersey in June 1967. Chubb and its subsidiaries are referred to collectively as the Corporation. Chubb is a holding company for a family of property and casualty insurance companies known informally as the Chubb Group of Insurance Companies (the P&C Group)." 10-K

Note: See accompanying notes.

Source: The Chubb Corporation 2010 10-K

EXHIBIT 12-20   The Chubb Corporation (*continued*)

	In Millions December 31,	
	2010	2009
Prepaid Reinsurance Premiums	325	308
Deferred Policy Acquisition Costs	1,562	1,533
Deferred Income Tax	98	272
Goodwill	467	467
Other Assets	1,152	1,200
TOTAL ASSETS	$50,249	$50,449
Liabilities		
Unpaid Losses and Loss Expense	$22,718	$22,839
Unearned Premiums	6,189	6,153
Long Term Debt	3,975	3,975
Dividend Payable to Shareholders	112	118
Accrued Expenses and Other Liabilities	1,725	1,730
TOTAL LIABILITIES	34,719	34,815
Commitments and Contingent Liabilities (Note 6 and 13)		
Shareholders' Equity		
Preferred Stock – Authorized 8,000,000 Shares; $1 Par Value;		
Issued – None	—	—
Common Stock – Authorized 1,200,000,000 Shares; $1 Par		
Value; Issued 371,980,460	372	372
Paid-In Surplus	208	224
Retained Earnings	17,943	16,235
Accumulated Other Comprehensive Income	790	720
Treasury Stock, at Cost – 74,707,547 and 39,972,796 shares	(3,783)	(1,917)
TOTAL SHAREHOLDERS' EQUITY	15,530	15,634
TOTAL LIABILITIES AND SHAREHOLDERS' EQUITY	$50,249	$50,449

THE CHUBB CORPORATION
Consolidated Statement of Shareholders' Equity (In Part)

	(In Millions) Years Ended December 31,		
	2010	2009	2008
Accumulated Other Comprehensive Income (Loss)			
Unrealized Appreciation (Depreciation) of Investments Including			
Unrealized Other-Than-Temporary Impairment Losses			
Balance, Beginning of Year	$1,044	$ (143)	$ 526
Cumulative Effect, as of April 1, 2009, of Change in Accounting			
Principle, Net of Tax	—	(30)	—
Change During Year, Net of Tax	76	1,217	(669)
Balance, End of Year	1,120	1,044	(143)
Foreign Currency Translations Gains (Losses)			
Balance, Beginning of Year	160	(10)	216
Change During Year, Net of Tax	(18)	170	(226)
Balance, End of Year	142	160	(10)
Postretirement Benefit Costs Not Yet Recognized in Net Income			
Balance, Beginning of Year	(484)	(582)	(298)
Change During Year, Net of Tax	12	98	(284)
Balance, End of Year	(472)	(484)	(582)
Accumulated Other Comprehensive Income (Loss), End of Year	790	720	(735)

Real estate investments are usually present for both property-casualty insurance companies and life insurance companies. Because liabilities are relatively short term for property-casualty companies, the investment in real estate for these companies is usually immaterial. For life insurance companies, the investment in real estate may be much greater than for property-casualty companies because of the generally longer-term nature and predictability of their liabilities.

For debt and equity investments, review the disclosure to determine whether there are significant differences between the fair value and the cost or amortized cost. Also review the stockholders' equity section of the balance sheet to determine whether there is significant unrealized appreciation of investments (gains or losses).

Assets—Other Than Investments

A number of asset accounts other than investments may be on an insurance company's balance sheet. Some of the typical accounts are described in the paragraphs that follow.

Real estate used in operations is reported at cost, less accumulated depreciation. Under SAP, real estate used in operations is expensed.

Deferred policy acquisition costs represent the cost of obtaining policies. Under GAAP, these costs are deferred and charged to expense over the premium-paying period. This is one of the major differences between GAAP reporting and SAP reporting. Under SAP reporting, these costs are charged to expense as they are incurred.

Goodwill is an intangible account resulting from acquiring other companies. The same account can be found on the balance sheet of companies other than insurance companies. Under GAAP, the goodwill account is accounted for as an asset. Under SAP, neither the goodwill account nor other intangibles are recognized.

Liabilities

Generally, the largest liability is for loss reserves. Reserving for losses involves estimating the ultimate value, considering the present value of the commitments. The quantification process is subject to a number of subjective estimates, including inflation, interest rates, and judicial interpretations. Mortality estimates are also important for life insurance companies. These reserve accounts should be adequate to pay policy claims under the terms of the insurance policies.

Another liability account found on an insurance company's balance sheet is policy and contract claims. This account represents claims that have accrued as of the balance sheet date. These claims are reported net of any portion that can be recovered.

Many other liability accounts, such as notes payable and income taxes payable, are found on an insurance company's balance sheet. These are typically reported in the same manner as other industries report them, except there is no current liability classification.

Shareholders' Equity

The shareholders' equity usually resembles the shareholders' equity section for companies in other industries. The account Accumulated Other Comprehensive Income (loss) can be particularly large for insurance companies. For the Chubb Corporation, the details of the account Accumulated Other Comprehensive Income are in the Consolidated Statements of Shareholders' Equity. For the Chubb Corporation, the account Accumulated Other Comprehensive Income (loss) contains unrealized appreciation (depreciation) of investments, foreign currency translations gains (losses), and postretirement benefit costs not yet recognized in net income.

Income Statement Under GAAP

The manner of recognizing revenue on insurance contracts is unique for the insurance industry. In general, the duration of the contract governs the revenue recognition.

For contracts of short duration, revenue is ordinarily recognized over the period of the contract in proportion to the amount of insurance protection provided. When the risk differs significantly from the contract period, revenue is recognized over the period of risk in proportion to the amount of insurance protection.[2]

Policies relating to loss protection typically fall under the short-duration contract. An example would be casualty insurance in which the insurance company retains the right to cancel the contract at the end of the policy term.

For long-duration contracts, revenue is recognized when the premium is due from the policyholder. Examples would be whole-life contracts and single-premium life contracts.[3] Likewise, acquisition costs are capitalized and expensed in proportion to premium revenue.

Long-duration contracts that do not subject the insurance enterprise to significant risks arising from policyholder mortality or morbidity are referred to as *investment contracts*. Amounts received on these contracts are not to be reported as revenues but rather as liabilities and accounted for in the same way as interest-bearing instruments.[4] The contracts are regarded as investment contracts since they do not incorporate significant insurance risk. Interestingly, many of the life insurance policies currently being written are of this type.

With the investment contracts, premium payments are credited to the policyholder balance. The insurance company assesses charges against this balance for contract services and credits the balance for income earned. The insurer can adjust the schedule for contract services and the rate at which income is credited.

Investment contracts generally include an assessment against the policyholder on inception of the contract and an assessment when the contract is terminated. The inception fees are booked as recoveries of capitalized acquisition costs, and the termination fees are booked as revenue at the time of termination.

In addition to their insurance activities, insurance companies are substantially involved with investments. Realized gains and losses from investments are reported in operations in the period incurred.

Ratios

As previously indicated, many of the ratios relating to insurance companies are industry-specific. An explanation of industry-specific ratios is beyond the scope of this book. The industry-specific ratios are frequently based on SAP financial reporting to the states, rather than the GAAP financial reporting that is used for the annual report and SEC requirements.

Ratios computed from the GAAP-based financial statements are often profitability- and investor-related. Examples of such ratios are return on common equity, price/earnings ratio, dividend payout, and dividend yield. These ratios are explained in other sections of this book.

Insurance companies tend to have a stock market price at a discount to the average market price (price/earnings ratio). This discount is typically 10% to 20%, but at times it is much more. There are likely many reasons for this relatively low market value. Insurance is a highly regulated industry that some perceive as having low-growth prospects. It is also an industry with substantial competition. The regulation and the competition put pressure on the premiums that can be charged. The accounting environment likely also contributes to the relatively low market price for insurance company stocks. The existence of two sets of accounting principles, SAP and GAAP, contributes to the lack of understanding of insurance companies' financial statements. Also, many of the accounting standards are complex and industry-specific.

The nature of the insurance industry leads to standards that allow much subjectivity and possible manipulation of reported profit. For example, insurance companies are perceived to underreserve during tough years and overreserve during good years.

Insurance company financial fraud led to the April 2005 announcement from the Securities and Exchange Commission that it was increasing its enforcement of accounting rules. "The Securities and Exchange Commission, using its power as an enforcer of accounting rules, is asserting for the first time in decades a key role for federal officials overseeing the insurance industry."[5]

"The federal government's ability to regulate the insurance industry is still limited by law. The McCarran-Ferguson Act of 1945 gave primacy in regulating and taxing insurers for states.... Because of the law, even the SEC can only go so far with its accounting cudgel. Its mandate extends only to companies with publicly offered securities, while some of the largest U.S. insurers—including the biggest, State Farm—are either owned by policyholders or closely held."[6]

Real Estate Companies

Real estate companies typically construct and operate income-producing real properties. Examples of such properties are shopping centers, hotels, and office buildings. A typical project would involve selecting a site, arranging financing, arranging for long-term leases, construction, and subsequently operating and maintaining the property.

Real estate companies contend that conventional accounting—recognizing depreciation but not the underlying value of the property—misleads investors. In some cases, these companies have taken the drastic step of selling major parts or all of the companies' assets to realize greater benefits for stockholders. Some real estate companies have attempted to reflect value by disclosing current value in addition to the conventional accounting.

Summary

Financial statements vary among industries, and they are especially different for banks, utilities, transportation companies, and insurance companies. In each case, the accounting for these firms is subject to a uniform accounting system. Changes in analysis are necessitated by the differences in accounting presentation.

Oil and gas companies' financial statements are affected significantly by the method that they choose to account for costs associated with exploration and production. Another important aspect of the financial statements of oil and gas companies is the note requirement that relates to supplementary information on oil and gas exploration, development, and production activities. Cash flow is also particularly significant to oil and gas companies.

Real estate companies emphasize the underlying value of the property and earnings before depreciation and deferred taxes from operations.

Special industry ratios were reviewed in this chapter. The following ratios are helpful when analyzing a bank:

$$\text{Earning Assets to Total Assets} = \frac{\text{Average Earning Assets}}{\text{Average Total Assets}}$$

$$\text{Interest Margin to Average Earning Assets} = \frac{\text{Interest Margin}}{\text{Average Earning Assets}}$$

$$\text{Loan Loss Coverage Ratio} = \frac{\text{Pretax Income} + \text{Provision for Loan Losses}}{\text{Net Charge-Offs}}$$

$$\text{Equity Capital to Total Assets} = \frac{\text{Average Equity}}{\text{Average Total Assets}}$$

$$\text{Deposits Times Capital} = \frac{\text{Average Deposits}}{\text{Average Shareholders' Equity}}$$

$$\text{Loans to Deposits} = \frac{\text{Average Total Loans}}{\text{Average Deposits}}$$

The following ratios are helpful in analyzing utility performance:

$$\text{Operating Ratio} = \frac{\text{Operating Expense}}{\text{Operating Revenue}}$$

$$\text{Funded Debt to Operating Property} = \frac{\text{Funded Debt}}{\text{Operating Property}}$$

$$\text{Percent Earned on Operating Property} = \frac{\text{Net Income}}{\text{Operating Property}}$$

$$\text{Operating Revenue to Operating Property} = \frac{\text{Operating Revenue}}{\text{Operating Property}}$$

The ratios that follow are especially suited to transportation. Additional insight can be gained by looking at revenues and expenses on a per unit of usage basis.

$$\text{Operating Ratio} = \frac{\text{Operating Expense}}{\text{Operating Revenue}}$$

$$\text{Long-Term Debt to Operating Property} = \frac{\text{Long-Term Debt}}{\text{Operating Property}}$$

$$\text{Operating Revenue to Operating Property} = \frac{\text{Operating Revenue}}{\text{Operating Property}}$$

Questions

Q 12-1 What are the main sources of revenue for banks?

Q 12-2 Why are loans, which are usually liabilities, treated as assets for banks?

Q 12-3 Why are savings accounts liabilities for banks?

Q 12-4 Why are banks concerned with their loans/deposits ratios?

Q 12-5 To what agencies and other users of financial statements must banks report?

Q 12-6 Why must the user be cautious in analyzing bank holding companies?

Q 12-7 What is usually the biggest expense item for a bank?

Q 12-8 What does the ratio total deposits times capital measure?

Q 12-9 What ratios are used to indicate profitability for banks?

Q 12-10 Why are banks concerned about the percentage of earning assets to total assets?

Q 12-11 What does the loan loss coverage ratio measure?

Q 12-12 What type of ratio is deposits times capital?

Q 12-13 Give an example of why a review of bank assets may indicate risk or opportunity of which you were not aware.

Q 12-14 Why review the disclosure of the market value of investments versus the book amount of investments for banks?

Q 12-15 Why review the disclosure of foreign loans for banks?

Q 12-16 Why review the disclosure of allowance for loan losses for a bank?

Q 12-17 Why review the disclosure of nonperforming assets for banks?

Q 12-18 Why could a review of savings deposit balances be important when reviewing a bank's financial statements?

Q 12-19 Why review the note that describes commitments and contingent liabilities for a bank?

Q 12-20 Utilities are usually very highly leveraged. How is it that they are able to carry such high levels of debt?

Q 12-21 How does demand for utilities differ from demand for other products or services?

Q 12-22 For regulated utilities, why are plant and equipment usually listed first for utilities?

Q 12-23 Are inventory ratios meaningful for utilities? Why?

Q 12-24 What does the funded debt to operating property ratio measure for a utility?

Q 12-25 Is times interest earned meaningful for utilities? Why or why not?

Q 12-26 For regulated utilities, are current liabilities usually presented first in utility reporting? Comment.

Q 12-27 For regulated utilities, why review the account Construction Work in Progress?

Q 12-28 For regulated utilities, describe the income statement accounts, allowance for equity funds used during construction, and allowance for borrowed funds used during construction.

Q 12-29 Differentiate between successful-efforts and full-costing accounting as applied to the oil and gas industry.

Q 12-30 Some industries described in this chapter are controlled by federal regulatory agencies. How does this affect their accounting systems?

Q 12-31 When reviewing the financial statements of oil and gas companies, why is it important to note the method of costing (expensing) exploration and production costs?

Q 12-32 Oil and gas companies must disclose quantity estimates for proved oil and gas reserves and the major factors causing changes in these resource estimates. Briefly indicate why this disclosure can be significant.

Q 12-33 For oil and gas companies, there is the potential for a significant difference between the reported income and cash flows from operations. Comment.

Q 12-34 Is it more desirable to have the operating ratios increasing or decreasing for utilities and transportation companies?

Q 12-35 What type of ratio is operating revenue to operating property? Will it exceed 1:1 for a utility?

Q 12-36 What is the most important category of assets for transportation firms?

Q 12-37 Briefly describe the revenue section of the income statement for a transportation firm.

Q 12-38 In a transportation firm, what types of things will change operating revenues? Operating expenses?

Q 12-39 If a transportation firm shows a rise in revenue per passenger mile, what does this increase imply?

Q 12-40 How is the passenger load factor of a bus company related to profitability?

Q 12-41 Explain how the publication *Financial Analysis of the Motor Carrier Industry* could be used to determine the percentage of total revenue a firm has in relation to similar trucking firms.

Q 12-42 Are annual reports filed with state insurance departments in accordance with U.S. GAAP?

Q 12-43 Annual reports that insurance companies issue to the public are in accordance with what accounting standards?

Q 12-44 Why could an insurance company with substantial investments in real estate represent a risk?

Q 12-45 For an insurance company, describe the difference between GAAP reporting and SAP reporting of deferred policy acquisition costs.

Q 12-46 Briefly describe the difference between accounting for intangibles for an insurance company under GAAP and under SAP.

Q 12-47 Briefly describe the unique aspects of revenue recognition for an insurance company.

Q 12-48 Insurance industry-specific financial ratios are usually prepared from financial statements prepared under what standards?

Q 12-49 Insurance companies tend to have a stock market price at a discount to the average market price (price/earnings ratio). Indicate some perceived reasons for this relatively low price/earnings ratio.

Q 12-50 Real estate companies contend that conventional accounting does not recognize the underlying value of the property and that this misleads investors. Discuss.

Problems

P 12-1 The following are statistics from the annual report of McEttrick National Bank:

	2011	2010
Average loans	$16,000,000	$13,200,000
Average total assets	26,000,000	22,000,000
Average total deposits	24,000,000	20,000,000
Average total capital	1,850,000	1,600,000
Interest expenses	1,615,000	1,512,250
Interest income	1,750,000	1,650,000

Required
   a. Calculate the following for 2010 and 2011:

   1. Total deposits times capital for each year.
   2. Loans to total deposits for each year.
   3. Capital funds to total assets for each year.
   4. Interest margin to average total assets for each year.

   b. Comment on the trends in the ratios computed in (a).

P 12-2 The following are statistics from the annual report of Dover Bank:

	2011	2010	2009
Average earning assets	$50,000,000	$45,000,000	$43,000,000
Average total assets	58,823,529	54,216,867	52,000,000
Income before securities transactions	530,000	453,000	420,000
Interest margin	2,550,000	2,200,000	2,020,000
Pretax income before securities transactions	562,000	480,500	440,000
Provision for loan losses	190,000	160,000	142,000
Net charge-offs	180,000	162,000	160,000
Average equity	4,117,600	3,524,000	3,120,000
Average net loans	32,500,000	26,000,000	22,500,000
Average deposits	52,500,000	42,500,000	37,857,000

Required

a. Calculate the following for 2011, 2010, and 2009:

    1. Earning assets to total assets
    2. Interest margin to average earning assets
    3. Loan loss coverage ratio
    4. Equity to total assets
    5. Deposits times capital
    6. Loans to deposits

b. Comment on trends found in the ratios computed in (a).

P 12-3 Super Power Company reported the following statistics in its statements of income:

	2011	2010
Electric revenues:		
Residential	$11,800,000	$10,000,000
Commercial and industrial	10,430,000	10,000,000
Other	600,000	500,000
	22,830,000	20,500,000
Operating expenses and taxes*	20,340,000	18,125,000
Operating income	2,490,000	2,375,000
Other income	200,000	195,000
Income before interest deductions	2,690,000	2,570,000
Interest deductions	1,200,000	1,000,000
Net income	$ 1,490,000	$ 1,570,000

*Includes taxes of $3,200,000 in 2011 and $3,000,000 in 2010.

Required

a. Calculate the operating ratio and comment on the results.
b. Calculate the times interest earned and comment on the results.
c. Perform a vertical common-size analysis of revenues, using total revenue as the base, and comment on the relative size of the component parts.

P 12-4 The following statistics relate to Michgate, an electric utility:

	2011	2010	2009
(In thousands of dollars, except per share)			
Operating expenses	$ 850,600	$ 820,200	$ 780,000
Operating revenues	1,080,500	1,037,200	974,000
Earnings per share	3.00	2.90	2.60
Cash flow per share	3.40	3.25	2.30
Operating property	3,900,000	3,750,000	3,600,000
Funded debt (long-term)	1,500,000	1,480,000	1,470,000
Net income	280,000	260,000	230,000

Required

a. Calculate the following for 2011, 2010, and 2009:

    1. Operating ratio
    2. Funded debt to operating property
    3. Percent earned on operating property
    4. Operating revenue to operating property

b. Comment on trends found in the ratios computed in (a).
c. Comment on the trend between earnings per share and cash flow per share.

P 12-5 Local Airways had the following results in the past two years:

	2011	2010
Operating revenues	$ 624,000	$ 618,000
Operating expenses	$ 625,000	$ 617,000
Operating property	$ 365,000	$ 360,000
Long-term debt	$ 280,000	$ 270,000
Estimated passenger miles	7,340,000	7,600,000

(continued)

(**P 12-5** CONTINUED)

Required Calculate the following for 2011 and 2010:

a. The operating ratio and comment on the trend.
b. The long-term debt to operating property ratio. What does this tell about debt use?
c. The operating revenue to operating property and comment on the trend.
d. The revenue per passenger mile. What has caused this trend?

P 12-6 Chihi Airways had the following results for the past three years:

	2011	2010	2009
(In thousands of dollars)			
Operating expenses	$1,550,000	$1,520,000	$1,480,000
Operating revenues	1,840,000	1,670,400	1,620,700
Long-term debt	910,000	900,500	895,000
Operating property	995,000	990,000	985,000
Passenger load factor	66.5%	59.0%	57.8%

Required
a. Calculate the following for 2011, 2010, and 2009:

1. Operating ratio
2. Long-term debt to operating property
3. Operating revenue to operating property

b. Comment on trends found in the ratios computed in (a).
c. Comment on the passenger load factor.

P 12-7
Required Answer the following multiple-choice questions related to insurance financial reporting:

a. Which of the following does not represent a basic type of insurance organization?

1. Stock companies
2. Bond companies
3. Mutual companies
4. Fraternal benefit societies
5. Assessment companies

b. Which of these statements is not correct?

1. The balance sheet is a classified balance sheet.
2. The assets section starts with investments.
3. The majority of the investments are typically in bonds.
4. For life insurance companies, the investment in real estate may be much greater than that for property-casualty companies.
5. Real estate investments are reported at cost less accumulated depreciation and an allowance for impairment in value.

c. Generally, the largest liability is for loss reserves. The quantification process is subject to a number of estimates. Which of the following would not be one of the estimates?

1. Investment gains/losses
2. Inflation rate
3. Interest rates
4. Judicial interpretations
5. Mortality estimates

d. The manner of recognizing revenue on insurance contracts is unique for the insurance industry. Which of the following statements is not true?

1. In general, the duration of the contract governs the revenue recognition.
2. When the risk differs significantly from the contract period, revenue is recognized over the period of risk in proportion to the amount of insurance protection.

3. For long-duration contracts, revenue is recognized when the premium is due from policyholders.
4. Realized gains and losses from investments are reported in operations in the period incurred.
5. For investment contracts, termination fees are booked as revenue over the period of the contract.

e. Which of the following statements is not true?

1. Statutory accounting has emphasized the balance sheet in its concern for protecting the policyholders by focusing on the financial solvency of the insurance corporation.
2. All 50 states have insurance departments that require annual statements of insurance companies. These annual reports are filed with the state insurance departments in accordance with SAP.
3. After the annual reports are filed with the individual state insurance departments, a testing process is conducted by the NAIC. If a company's ratio is outside the prescribed limit, the NAIC brings that to the attention of the company.
4. A.M. Best Company publishes *Best's Insurance Reports*, which are published separately for life-health companies and property-casualty companies. The financial data, including the ratios, are based on the data submitted to the state insurance departments and are thus based on SAP.
5. Many stock insurance companies must register with the Securities and Exchange Commission and file the required forms, such as the annual Form 10-K. Reports filed with the SEC must conform with GAAP.

f. Insurance companies tend to have a stock market price at a discount to the average market price (price/earnings ratio). Which of the following is a likely reason for this relatively low market value?

1. Insurance is a highly regulated industry.
2. The insurance industry has substantial competition.
3. The accounting environment likely contributes to the relatively low market price for insurance company stocks.
4. The nature of the industry leads to standards that provide for much judgment and possible manipulation of reported profit.
5. All of the above.

P 12-8

Required Answer the following multiple-choice questions related to bank financial reporting:

a. All but which of the following would be a representative asset of a bank?

1. Investment securities
2. Loans
3. Equipment
4. Cash on hand
5. Savings accounts

b. All but which of the following would be considered an earning asset of a bank for the earning assets to total assets ratio?

1. Loans
2. Leases
3. Cash
4. Investment securities
5. Money market assets

c. The ratio for a bank that provides an indication of management's ability to control the spread between interest income and interest expense is the

1. Loan loss coverage ratio.
2. Earning assets to total assets.

(continued)

(**P 12-8** CONTINUED)

      3. Return on earning assets.
      4. Interest margin to average total assets.
      5. Equity capital to total assets.

  d. All but which of the following would be a representative liability of a bank?

      1. Savings
      2. Demand deposits
      3. Cash on hand
      4. Long-term debt
      5. Time deposits

  e. Typically, the largest expense for a bank will be

      1. Employer benefits.
      2. Occupancy expense.
      3. Salaries.
      4. Provision for loan losses.
      5. Interest expense.

  f. The ratio that indicates the extent of equity ownership in a bank is the

      1. Interest margin to average total assets.
      2. Loss coverage ratio.
      3. Loans to deposits.
      4. Equity capital to total assets.
      5. Deposits times capital.

P 12-9

Required Answer the following multiple-choice questions:

  a. A ratio that indicates how funds are supplied to a utility is

      1. Return on assets.
      2. Percent earned on operating property.
      3. Operating ratio.
      4. Funded debt to operating property.
      5. Operating revenue to operating property.

  b. A ratio that relates net earnings to the assets primarily intended to generate earnings for a utility is

      1. Return on assets.
      2. Percent earned on operating property.
      3. Operating ratio.
      4. Funded debt to operating property.
      5. Operating revenue to operating property.

  c. For a utility, the ratio that is basically an operating asset turnover ratio is

      1. Return on assets.
      2. Percent earned on operating property.
      3. Operating ratio.
      4. Funded debt to operating property.
      5. Operating revenue to operating property.

  d. A ratio that indicates a measure of operating efficiency for a utility is

      1. Operating revenue to operating property.
      2. Funded debt to operating property.
      3. Operating ratio.
      4. Percent earned on operating property.
      5. Long-term debt to operating property.

e. For a transportation firm, which ratio gives a measure of the source of funds with which property is obtained?

1. Operating ratio
2. Operating revenue to operating property
3. Long-term debt to operating property
4. Per mile-per person-per ton
5. Return on equity

f. Which ratio is a measure of turnover of operating assets for a transportation firm?

1. Operating ratio
2. Long-term debt to operating property
3. Per mile-per person-per ton
4. Return on investment
5. Operating revenue to operating property

g. Which of these industries does not have a uniform system of accounts?

1. Banks
2. Utilities
3. Transportation
4. Oil and gas
5. 1, 2, and 3

h. Which of the following has a balance sheet similar in format to a manufacturing firm?

1. Banks
2. Insurance companies
3. Regulated utilities
4. 1 and 2
5. None of the above

Cases

CASE 12-1 AFUDC EQUITY AND DEBT

PG&E Corporation*
CONSOLIDATED STATEMENTS OF INCOME
(in millions, except per share amounts)

	Year Ended December 31,		
	2010	2009	2008
Operating Revenues			
Electric	$10,645	$10,257	$10,738
Natural gas	3,196	3,142	3,890
Total operating revenues	13,841	13,399	14,628
Operating Expenses			
Cost of electricity	3,898	3,711	4,425
Cost of natural gas	1,291	1,291	2,090
Operating and maintenance	4,439	4,346	4,201
Depreciation, amortization, and decommissioning	1,905	1,752	1,651
Total operating expenses	11,533	11,100	12,367

(*continued*)

*"PG&E Corporation, incorporated in California in 1995, is a holding company whose primary purpose is to hold interests in energy-based businesses." 10-K
Source: AFUDC Equity and Debt, PG&E Corporation 2010 10-K

(**Case 12-1** CONTINUED)

	Year Ended December 31,		
	2010	2009	2008
Operating Income	2,308	2,299	2,261
Interest income	9	33	94
Interest expense	(684)	(705)	(728)
Other income (expense), net	27	67	(4)
Income Before Income Taxes	1,660	1,694	1,623
Income tax provision	547	460	425
Income From Continuing Operations	1,113	1,234	1,198
Discontinued Operations			
NEGT income tax benefit	—	—	154
Net Income	1,113	1,234	1,352
Preferred stock dividend requirement of subsidiary	14	14	14
Income Available for Common Shareholders	$ 1,099	$ 1,220	$ 1,338
Weighted Average Common Shares Outstanding, Basic	382	368	357
Weighted Average Common Shares Outstanding, Diluted	392	386	358
Earnings Per Common Share from Continuing Operations, Basic	$ 2.86	$ 3.25	$ 3.23
Net Earnings Per Common Share, Basic	$ 2.86	$ 3.25	$ 3.64
Earnings Per Common Share from Continuing Operations, Diluted	$ 2.82	$ 3.20	$ 3.22
Net Earnings Per Common Share, Diluted	$ 2.82	$ 3.20	$ 3.63
Dividends Declared Per Common Share	$ 1.82	$ 1.68	$ 1.56

PG&E Corporation
CONSOLIDATED BALANCE SHEETS
(in millions, except per share data)

	Balance at December 31,	
	2010	2009
ASSETS		
Current Assets		
Cash and cash equivalents	$ 291	$ 527
Restricted cash ($38 and $39 related to energy recovery bonds at December 31, 2010 and 2009, respectively)	563	633
Accounts receivable:		
Customers (net of allowance for doubtful accounts of $81 and $68 at December 31, 2010 and 2009, respectively)	944	859
Accrued unbilled revenue	649	671
Regulatory balancing accounts	1,105	1,109
Other	794	750
Regulatory assets	599	427
Inventories		
Gas stored underground and fuel oil	152	114
Materials and supplies	205	200
Income taxes receivable	47	127
Other	193	240
Total current assets	5,542	5,657
Property, Plant, and Equipment		
Electric	33,508	30,481
Gas	11,382	10,697
Construction work in progress	1,384	1,888
Other	15	14
Total property, plant, and equipment	46,289	43,080
Accumulated depreciation	(14,840)	(14,188)
Net property, plant, and equipment	31,449	28,892

	Balance at December 31,	
	2010	2009
Other Noncurrent Assets		
Regulatory assets ($735 and $1,124 related to energy recovery bonds at December 31, 2010 and 2009, respectively)	5,846	5,522
Nuclear decommissioning trusts	2,009	1,899
Income taxes receivable	565	596
Other	614	379
Total other noncurrent assets	9,034	8,396
TOTAL ASSETS	$46,025	$42,945

PG&E Corporation
CONSOLIDATED BALANCE SHEETS
(in millions, except share amounts)

	Balance at December 31,	
	2010	2009
LIABILITIES AND EQUITY		
Current Liabilities		
Short-term borrowings	$ 853	$ 833
Long-term debt, classified as current	809	342
Energy recovery bonds, classified as current	404	386
Accounts payable		
Trade creditors	1,129	984
Disputed claims and customer refunds	745	773
Regulatory balancing accounts	256	281
Other	379	349
Interest payable	862	818
Income taxes payable	77	214
Deferred income taxes	113	332
Other	1,558	1,501
Total current liabilities	7,185	6,813
Noncurrent liabilities		
Long-term debt	10,906	10,381
Energy recovery bonds	423	827
Regulatory liabilities	4,525	4,125
Pension and other postretirement benefits	2,234	1,773
Asset retirement obligations	1,586	1,593
Deferred income taxes	5,547	4,732
Other	2,085	2,116
Total noncurrent liabilities	27,306	25,547
Commitments and Contingencies (Note 15)		
Equity		
Shareholders' Equity		
Preferred stock	—	—
Common stock, no par value, authorized 800,000,000 shares, 395,227,205 shares outstanding at December 31, 2010 and 371,272,457 shares outstanding at December 31, 2009	6,878	6,280
Reinvested earnings	4,606	4,213
Accumulated other comprehensive loss	(202)	(160)
Total shareholders' equity	11,282	10,333
Noncontrolling Interest – Preferred Stock of Subsidiary	252	252
Total equity	11,534	10,585
TOTAL LIABILITIES AND EQUITY	$46,025	$42,945

(continued)

(CASE 12-1 CONTINUED)

Note 2 Summary of Significant Accounting Policies (In Part)

Property, Plant, and Equipment

Property, plant, and equipment are reported at their original cost. These original costs include labor and materials, construction overhead, and allowance for funds used during construction ("AFUDC").

The Utility's balances at December 31, 2010 are as follows:

	Gross Plant as of December 31, 2010	Accumulated Depreciation as of December 31, 2010	Net Plant as of December 31, 2010
Electricity generating facilities[1]	$ 6,012	$ (1,404)	$ 4,608
Electricity distribution facilities	20,991	(7,161)	13,830
Electricity transmission	6,505	(1,829)	4,676
Natural gas distribution facilities	7,443	(2,819)	4,624
Natural gas transportation and storage	3,939	(1,613)	2,326
Construction work in progress	1,384	—	1,384
Total	$46,274	$(14,826)	$31,448

[1]Balance includes nuclear fuel inventories. Stored nuclear fuel inventory is stated at weighted average cost. Nuclear fuel in the reactor is expensed as it is used based on the amount of energy output (see Note 15 below.)

The Utility's balances at December 31, 2009 are as follows:

	Gross Plant as of December 31, 2009	Accumulated Depreciation as of December 31, 2009	Net Plant as of December 31, 2009
Electricity generating facilities[1]	$ 4,777	$ (1,279)	$ 3,498
Electricity distribution facilities	19,924	(6,924)	13,000
Electricity transmission	5,780	(1,751)	4,029
Natural gas distribution facilities	7,069	(2,667)	4,402
Natural gas transportation and storage	3,628	(1,554)	2,074
Construction work in progress	1,888	—	1,888
Total	$43,066	$(14,175)	$28,891

[1]Balance includes nuclear fuel inventories. Stored nuclear fuel inventory is stated at weighted average cost. Nuclear fuel in the reactor is expensed as it is used based on the amount of energy output (see Note 15 below.)

AFUDC

AFUDC is a method used to compensate the Utility for the estimated cost of debt (interest) and equity funds used to finance regulated plant additions and is capitalized as part of the cost of construction projects. AFUDC is recoverable from customers through rates over the life of the related property once the property is placed in service. The portion of AFUDC related to the cost of debt is recorded as a reduction to interest expense. AFUDC related to the cost of equity is recorded in other income. The Utility recorded AFUDC of $110 million and $50 million during 2010, $95 million and $44 million during 2009, $70 million and $44 million during 2008, related to equity and debt, respectively.

Required

a. Describe AFUDC as used by PG&E.

b. How does capitalizing interest on borrowed funds affect income in the year of capitalization versus not capitalizing this interest? Explain.

c. Would net income tend to be higher than cash flow if there is substantial capitalization of interest on the borrowed funds during the current period?

    d. How does capitalizing the allowance for equity funds used during construction affect income in the year of capitalization versus not capitalizing these charges?

    e. Would net income tend to be higher than cash flow if there is substantial capitalization of the allowance for equity funds during construction for the current year?

    f. Compute the following for the years 2010 and 2009 and comment on these ratios:

       1. Operating ratio

       2. Funded debt to operating property

       3. Percent earned on operating property

       4. Operating revenue to operating property

CASE 12-2 RESULTS OF OPERATIONS FOR OIL AND GAS PRODUCING ACTIVITIES

Hess Corporation* included information in this case as part of the supplementary oil and gas data. This case only represents a small portion of the supplementary oil and gas data.

Results of Operations for Oil and Gas Producing Activities

The results of operations shown below exclude non-oil and gas producing activities, primarily gains on sales of oil and gas properties, interest expense, gains and losses resulting from foreign exchange transactions and other non-operating income. Therefore, these results are on a different basis than the net income from Exploration and Production operations reported in Management's Discussion and Analysis of Financial Condition and Results of Operations and in Note 18, Segment Information, in the notes to the financial statements.

For the Years Ended December 31	Total	United States	Europe	Africa	Asia and Other
2010		(Millions of Dollars)			
Sales and other operating revenues					
Unaffiliated customers	$8,601	$2,310	$2,251	$2,750	$1,290
Inter-company	143	143	—	—	—
Total revenues	8,744	2,453	2,251	2,750	1,290
Costs and expenses					
Production expenses, including related taxes	1,924	489	727	455	253
Exploration expenses, including dry holes and lease impairment	865	364	49	143	309
General, administrative and other expenses	281	161	48	20	52
Depreciation, depletion, amortization	2,222	649	463	772	338
Asset impairments	532	—	—	532	—
Total costs and expenses	5,824	1,663	1,287	1,922	952
Results of operations before income taxes	2,920	790	964	828	338
Provision for income taxes	1,583	305	477	580	221
Results of operations	$1,337	$ 485	$ 487	$ 248	$ 117

Required

    a. Prepare a vertical common-size analysis for results of operations for oil and gas producing activities for 2010. Use total revenues as the base.

    b. Prepare a horizontal common-size analysis for 2010. Use total as the base.

    c. Comment on the common-size analysis in (a) and (b).

*"Hess Corporation (the Registrant) is a Delaware corporation, incorporated in 1920. The Registrant and its subsidiaries (collectively referred to as the Corporation or Hess) is a global integrated energy company that operates in two segments, Exploration and Production (E&P) and Marketing and Refining (M&R)." 10-K
Source: Hess Corporation, 2010 10-K

CASE 12-3 FINANCIAL SERVICES PROVIDER

Camden National Corporation included the following in its 2010 annual report:

CAMDEN NATIONAL CORPORATION*
NOTES TO CONSOLIDATED FINANCIAL STATEMENTS (In Part)
(Amounts in Tables Expressed in Thousands, Except Number of Shares and per Share Data)

3. Loans and Allowances for Loan Losses (In Part)

The following is a summary of activity in the allowance for loan losses:

	December 31,		
	2010	**2009**	**2008**
Balance at beginning of year	$20,246	$17,691	$13,653
Loans charged off	(5,547)	(6,456)	(5,553)
Recoveries	1,269	849	825
Net charge-offs	(4,278)	(5,607)	(4,728)
Acquired from Union Trust	—	—	4,369
Provision for loan losses	6,325	8,162	4,397
Balance at end of year	$22,293	$20,246	$17,691

Required

a. Give your opinion of trends in the allowance for loan losses.

*"The Company, as a diversified financial services provider, pursues the objective of achieving long-term sustainable growth by balancing growth opportunities against profit, while mitigating risks inherent in the financial services industry." 10-K

Source: Camden National Corporation 2010 10-K

CASE 12-4 ATTRACTING DEPOSITS

Santander Holdings USA, Inc.*
included the following in its 2010 10-K
Consolidated Balance Sheets

	AT DECEMBER 31,	
(IN THOUSANDS)	**2010**	**2009**
Assets		
Cash and amounts due from depository institutions	$ 1,705,895	$ 2,323,290
Investment securities available for sale	13,371,848	13,609,398
Other investments	614,241	692,240
Loans held for investments	65,017,884	57,552,177
Allowance for loan losses	(2,197,450)	(1,818,224)
Net loans held for investment	62,820,434	55,733,953
Loans held for sale	150,063	118,994
Premises and equipment	595,951	477,812
Accrued interest receivable	406,617	345,122
Goodwill	4,124,351	4,135,540
Core deposit and other intangibles, net of accumulated amortization of $997,671 in 2010 and $934,270 in 2009	188,940	245,641
Bank owned life insurance	1,519,462	1,810,511
Other assets	4,154,013	3,460,714
Total Assets	$89,651,815	$82,953,215

(*continued*)

*"SHUSA is the parent company of Sovereign Bank ("Sovereign Bank" or "the Bank"), a federally chartered savings bank. SHUSA had approximately 700 community banking offices, over 2,300 ATMs and 11,714 team members as of December 31, 2010 with principal markets in the Northeastern United States." 10-K

Source: Santander Holdings USA 2010 10-K

(IN THOUSANDS)	AT DECEMBER 31,	
	2010	2009
Liabilities		
Deposits and other customer accounts	$42,673,293	$44,428,065
Borrowings and other debt obligations	33,630,117	27,235,151
Advance payments by borrowers for taxes and insurance	104,125	87,445
Other liabilities	1,983,610	1,815,019
Total Liabilities	78,391,145	73,565,680
Stockholders' Equity		
Preferred stock; no par value; $25,000 liquidation preference; 7,500,000 shares authorized; 8,000 shares outstanding in 2010 and 2009	195,445	195,445
Common stock; no par value; 800,000,000 shares authorized; 517,107,043 issued in 2010 and 511,107,043 issued in 2009	11,117,328	10,381,500
Warrants and employee stock options issued	285,435	285,435
Noncontrolling interest	25,636	22,397
Accumulated other comprehensive loss	(234,190)	(349,869)
Retained (deficit)/earnings	(128,984)	(1,147,373)
Total Stockholders' Equity	11,260,670	9,387,535
Total Liabilities and Stockholders' Equity	$89,651,815	$82,953,215

Consolidated Statements of Operations

(IN THOUSANDS)	FOR THE YEAR ENDED DECEMBER 31,		
	2010	2009	2008
Interest Income:			
Interest-earning deposits	$ 3,320	$ 8,114	$ 5,820
Investment securities:			
Available for sale	466,141	383,926	554,351
Other	1,235	1,761	23,786
Interest on loans	4,313,793	4,029,785	3,339,207
Total interest income	4,784,489	4,423,586	3,923,164
Interest Expense:			
Deposits and other customer accounts	228,633	640,549	951,588
Borrowings and other debt obligations	1,157,217	1,139,533	1,089,134
Total interest expense	1,385,850	1,780,082	2,040,722
Net interest income	3,398,639	2,643,504	1,882,442
Provision for credit losses	1,627,026	1,984,537	911,000
Net interest income after provision for credit losses	1,771,613	658,967	971,442
Non-interest Income:			
Consumer banking fees	531,337	369,845	312,627
Commercial banking fees	180,295	187,276	213,945
Mortgage banking (expense)/revenue	47,955	(129,504)	(13,226)
Capital markets (expense)/revenue	7,972	(1,753)	23,810
Bank-owned life insurance	54,112	58,829	75,990
Miscellaneous income	7,242	15,451	23,292
Total fees and other income	828,913	500,144	636,438
Total other-than-temporary impairment losses	(58,526)	(604,489)	(887,730)
Portion of loss recognized in other comprehensive income (before taxes)	53,763	424,293	—
Gains/(Losses) on the sale of investment securities	205,139	22,349	(567,451)
Net gain/(loss) on investment securities recognized in earnings	200,556	(157,847)	(1,455,181)
Total non-interest income	1,029,469	342,297	(818,743)

(continued)

(CASE 12-4 CONTINUED)

	FOR THE YEAR ENDED DECEMBER 31,		
(IN THOUSANDS)	2010	2009	2008
General and administrative expenses:			
Compensation and benefits	707,593	716,418	755,379
Occupancy and equipment	312,295	318,706	310,535
Technology expense	112,058	107,100	102,591
Outside services	123,958	119,238	64,474
Marketing expense	37,177	36,318	78,995
Other administrative	280,019	222,680	172,332
Total general and administrative expenses	1,573,100	1,520,460	1,484,306
Other Expenses:			
Amortization of intangibles	63,401	75,692	103,643
Deposit insurance premiums and other costs	93,225	138,747	37,506
Equity method investments	26,613	21,412	128,530
Transaction related and integration charges and other restructuring costs	—	299,119	32,348
Loss on debt extinguishment	25,758	68,733	—
Total other expenses	208,997	603,703	302,027
Income/(Loss) before income taxes	1,018,985	(1,122,899)	(1,633,634)
Income tax provision/(benefit)	(40,390)	(1,284,464)	723,576
NET INCOME/(LOSS)	$1,059,375	$ 161,565	$(2,357,210)
Less:			
Net income attributable to noncontrolling interest	$ 37,239	$ 17,809	$ —
Net income/(loss) attributable to SHUSA	$1,022,136	$ 143,756	$(2,357,210)

Notes to Consolidated Financial Statements

Note 7 – Loans (In Part)

The activity in the allowance for credit losses is as follows (in thousands):

	FOR THE YEAR ENDED DECEMBER 31,		
	2010	2009	2008
Allowance for loan losses balance, beginning of period	$1,818,224	$1,102,753	$ 709,444
Allowance established in connection with reconsolidation of previously unconsolidated securitized assets	5,991	—	—
Acquired allowance for loan losses due to SCUSA contribution from Santander	—	347,302	—
Provision for loan losses[1]	1,585,545	1,790,559	874,140
Allowance released in connection with loan sales or securitizations	—	—	(3,745)
Charge-offs:			
Commercial	650,888	518,468	238,470
Consumer	861,269	1,232,070	353,244
Total charge-offs	1,512,157	1,750,538	591,714
Recoveries:			
Commercial	54,768	11,288	13,378
Consumer	245,079	316,860	101,250
Total recoveries	299,847	328,148	114,628
Charge-offs, net of recoveries	1,212,310	1,422,390	477,086
Allowance for loan losses balance, end of period	2,197,450	1,818,224	1,102,753

	FOR THE YEAR ENDED DECEMBER 31,		
	2010	2009	2008
Reserve for unfunded lending commitments, beginning of period	259,140	65,162	28,302
Provision for unfunded lending commitments[1]	41,481	193,978	36,860
Reserve for unfunded lending commitments, end of period	300,621	259,140	65,162
Total allowance for credit losses	$2,498,071	$2,077,364	$1,167,915

[1]SHUSA defines the provision for credit losses on the consolidated statement of operations as the sum of the total provision for loan losses and provision for unfunded lending commitment.

Impaired and past due loans are summarized as follows (in thousands):

	AT DECEMBER 31,	
	2010	2009
Impaired loans with a related allowance	$1,836,993	$1,193,095
Impaired loans without a related allowance	299,501	283,652
Total impaired loans	$2,136,494	$1,476,747
Allowance for impaired loans	$ 417,873	$ 363,059
Total loans past due 90 days as to interest or principal and accruing interest	$ 169	$ 27,321

Notes to Consolidated Financial Statements (In Part)

Note 1 – Summary of Significant Accounting Policies (In Part)

Santander Holdings USA, Inc. ("SHUSA" or "the Company"), formerly Sovereign Bancorp Inc., is a Virginia corporation and is the holding company of Sovereign Bank ("Sovereign Bank" or "the Bank"). SHUSA is headquartered in Boston, Massachusetts and Sovereign Bank is headquartered in Wyomissing, Pennsylvania. On January 30, 2009, SHUSA was acquired by Santander and as such, is a wholly owned subsidiary of Santander.

Required

  a. Prepare a horizontal common-size analysis for 2010, 2009, and 2008 for the following items from the Consolidated Statements of Operations (use 2008 as the base).

    1. Total interest income

    2. Total interest expense

    3. Provision for credit losses

    4. Total fees and other income

    5. Total general and administrative expenses

    6. Total other expenses

    7. Net income/(loss)

  b. Comment on the trends indicated in (a).

  c. Using Note 7 – Loans, comment on the following:

    1. Total charge-offs

    2. Charge-offs, net of recoveries

    3. Allowance for loan losses balance, end of period

    4. Total impaired loans

    5. Allowance for impaired loans

    6. Total loans past due 90 days as to interest or principal and accruing interest

  d. Compute the following for 2010 and 2009 (use ending balance sheet accounts):

    1. Earning assets to total assets

    2. Interest margin to average earning assets (use end of year earning assets)

    3. Loan loss coverage ratio

(*continued*)

(**CASE 12-4** CONTINUED)

   4. Equity to total assets (use year-end numbers)

   5. Deposits times capital (use year-end numbers)

   6. Loans to deposits (use year-end numbers)

e. Comment on the trends indicated by the ratios computed in (d).

CASE 12-5 COVERED

Exhibit 12-20 includes the consolidated statement of income for the Chubb Corporation.

Required

a. Prepare a horizontal common-size analysis of the consolidated statement of income. Use 2008 as the base.

b. Comment on the trends found in (a).

Source: Chubb Corporation 2010 10-K

WEB CASE THOMSON ONE *Business School Edition*

Please complete the Web case that covers material discussed in this chapter at www.cengagebrain.com. You'll be using Thomson ONE Business School Edition, a powerful tool that combines a full range of fundamental financial information, earnings estimates, market data, and source documents for 500 publicly traded companies.

TO THE NET CASE

1. Go to the SEC site (www.sec.gov). Under "Filings & Forms (Edgar)," click on "Search for Company Filings." Click on "Company or fund name, etc." Under Company Name, enter "Independent Bank Corp" (or under Ticker Symbol, enter "INDB"). Select the 10-K filed March 8, 2011.

   a. Copy the first sentence in the "Market Area and Competition" subsection from the "Item 1. Business" section.

   b. Comment on the trend in Table 7 "Nonperforming Assets" and Table 11 "Summary of Allocation of Allowance for Loan Losses" from the "Item 7. Management's Discussion and Analysis of Financial Condition and Results of Operation" section for Table 11. Only comment on 2010.

2. Go to the SEC site (www.sec.gov). Under "Filings & Forms (Edgar)," click on "Search for Company Filings." Click on "Company or fund name, etc." Under Company Name, enter "Columbia Bancorp" (or under Ticker Symbol, enter "CBBC"). Select the 10-K filed March 26, 2009.

   a. Copy the first paragraph under Item 1 Business, General.

   b. Go to "Note 5 Loans and Allowance for Loan Losses" found in the "Item 8 Financial Statements and Supplementary Data" section and answer the following:

      1. Comment on the trend in total loan portfolio.

      2. Comment on the trend in allowance for loan losses.

      3. Comment on the trend in investment in impaired loans.

3. Go to the SEC site (www.sec.gov). Under "Filings & Forms (Edgar)," click on "Search for Company Filings." Click on "Company or fund name, etc." Under Company Name, enter "Alliant Energy Corp" (or under Ticker Symbol, enter "LNT"). Select the 10-K filed February 28, 2011.

   a. Copy the first two sentences under Item 1, Business, A. General.

   b. Determine the construction work in progress for December 31, 2010 and December 31, 2009.

   c. Determine the allowance for funds used during construction for 2010, 2009, and 2008.

   d. Determine the income from continuing operations before income taxes for 2010, 2009, and 2008.

   e. Does the allowance for funds used during construction appear to be material?

4. Go to the SEC site (www.sec.gov). Under "Filings & Forms (Edgar)," click on "Search for Company Filings." Click on "Company or fund name, etc." Under Company Name, enter "Exxon Mobil" (or under Ticker Symbol, enter "XOM"). Select the 10-K filed February 25, 2011.

   a. Copy the first three sentences under 1. Business.

   b. Notes to consolidated financial statements

      1. Summary of accounting policies (In Part) – Comment on revenue recognition.

Endnotes

1. Arthur Andersen & Co., *Insurance* (Essex, England: Saffron Press Ltd., 1983), p. 87.

2. *Statement of Financial Accounting Standards No. 60*, "Accounting and Reporting by Insurance Enterprises" (Stamford, CT: Financial Accounting Standards Board, 1982), par. 13.

3. *Statement of Financial Accounting Standards No. 60*, par. 15.

4. *Statement of Financial Accounting Standards No. 97*, "Accounting and Reporting by Insurance Enterprises for Certain Long-Duration Contracts and for Realized Gains and Losses from the Sale of Investments" (Stamford, CT: Financial Accounting Standards Board, 1987), par. 15.

5. "SEC Broadens Role to Investigate Insurance Industry," *The Blade* (April 8, 2005), Sec. B, p. 14.

6. Ibid.

Chapter

13

Personal Financial Statements and Accounting for Governments and Not-for-Profit Organizations

This chapter briefly covers three types of financial reporting that have not been discussed in previous chapters: (1) personal financial statements, (2) governments, and (3) not-for-profit organizations other than governments.

Personal Financial Statements

Personal financial statements of individuals, husband and wife, or a larger family group are prepared for obtaining credit, income tax planning, retirement planning, and estate planning. *Statement of Position 82-1* (SOP 82-1) covers guidelines for the preparation of personal financial statements.[1] According to SOP 82-1:

> The primary users of personal financial statements normally consider estimated current value information to be more relevant for their decisions than historical cost information. Lenders require estimated current value information to assess collateral, and most personal loan applications require estimated current value information. Estimated current values are required for estate, gift, and income tax planning, and estimated current value information about assets is often required in federal and state filings of candidates for public office.[2]

Source: Financial Accounting Standards Board

SOP 82-1 concludes that personal financial statements should present assets at their estimated current values and liabilities at their estimated current amounts at the date of the financial statements. This contrasts with commercial financial statements, which predominantly use historical cost information. SOP 82-1 provides guidelines for determining the estimated current value of an asset and the estimated current amount of a liability.[3]

Form of the Statements

The basic and most important statement prepared for personal financial statements, a statement of financial condition, resembles a balance sheet. It states assets at estimated current values and liabilities at estimated current amounts. A tax liability is estimated on the difference between the stated amounts of the assets and liabilities and the tax basis of these assets and liabilities. For example, land may cost $10,000, which would be the tax basis, but may have an estimated current value of $25,000. The estimated tax liability on the difference between the $10,000 and the $25,000 would be estimated.

The difference between the total assets and total liabilities, designated net worth, is equivalent to the equity section in a commercial balance sheet. The statement of financial condition is prepared on the accrual basis. Assets and liabilities are presented in order of liquidity and maturity, without classification as current and noncurrent.

The optional statement of changes in net worth presents the major changes (sources of increases and decreases) in net worth. This statement combines income and other changes because of the mix of business and personal items. Examples of changes in net worth would be income, increases in the estimated current value of assets, and decreases in estimated income taxes. The statement of changes in net worth presents changes in terms of realized increases (decreases) and unrealized increases (decreases). Examples of realized increases (decreases) are salary, dividends, income taxes, and personal expenditures. Examples of unrealized increases (decreases) are an increase in the value of securities, an increase in the value of a residence, a decrease in the value of a boat, and estimated income taxes on the differences between the estimated current values of assets and the estimated current amounts of liabilities and their tax bases. Comparative financial statements may be more informative than statements of only one period.

For personal financial statements, the statement of changes in net worth replaces the income statement. SOP 82-1 includes guidelines on disclosure. These guidelines are not all-inclusive. Examples of disclosure include the methods used in determining current values of major assets, descriptions of intangible assets, and assumptions used to compute the estimated income taxes.

Most individuals do not maintain a complete set of records, so the necessary data must be gathered from various sources. These sources include brokers' statements, income tax returns, safe deposit boxes, insurance policies, real estate tax returns, checkbooks, and bank statements.

Suggestions for Reviewing the Statement of Financial Condition

1. Usually the most important figure, the net worth amount indicates the level of wealth.
2. Determine the amount of the assets that you consider to be very liquid (cash, savings accounts, marketable securities, and so on). These assets are readily available.
3. Observe the due date of the liabilities. In general, analysts would prefer the liabilities to be relatively long term. Long-term liabilities do not represent an immediate pressing problem.
4. When possible, compare specific assets with their related liabilities. This will indicate the net investment in the asset. For example, a residence with a current value of $90,000 and a $40,000 mortgage represents a net investment of $50,000.

Suggestions for Reviewing the Statement of Changes in Net Worth

1. Review realized increases in net worth. Determine the principal sources of realized net worth.
2. Review realized decreases in net worth. Determine the principal items in realized decreases in net worth.
3. Observe whether the net realized amount increased or decreased and by how much.
4. Review unrealized increases in net worth. Determine the principal sources of the increases.
5. Review unrealized decreases in net worth. Determine the principal sources of the decreases.
6. Observe whether the net unrealized amount increased or decreased and the amount.
7. Observe whether the net change increased or decreased and the amount.
8. Observe the net worth at the end of the year. (This indicates the level of wealth.)

Illustration of Preparation of the Statement of Financial Condition

For Bill and Mary, assume that assets and liabilities, effective income tax rates, and the amount of estimated income taxes are as follows at December 31, 2012:

Account	Tax Bases	Estimated Current Value	Excess of Estimated Current Values over Tax Bases	Effective Income Tax Rates	Amount of Estimated Income Taxes
Cash	$ 8,000	$ 8,000	—	—	—
Savings accounts	20,000	20,000	—	—	—
Marketable securities	50,000	60,000	$10,000	28%	$ 2,800
Options	0	20,000	20,000	28%	5,600
Royalties	0	10,000	10,000	28%	2,800
Auto	15,000	10,000	(5,000)	—	—
Boat	12,000	8,000	(4,000)	—	—
Residence	110,000	130,000	20,000	28%	5,600*
Furnishings	30,000	25,000	(5,000)	—	—
Mortgage payable	(60,000)	(60,000)	—	—	—
Auto loan	(5,000)	(5,000)	—	—	—
Credit cards	(5,000)	(4,000)	—	—	—
Total estimated income tax					$16,800

*The residence may not be taxed.

Bill and Mary
Statement of Financial Condition
December 31, 2012

Assets:	
Cash	$ 8,000
Savings accounts	20,000
Marketable securities	60,000
Options	20,000
Royalties	10,000
Auto	10,000
Boat	8,000
Residence	130,000
Furnishings	25,000
Total assets	$291,000
Liabilities:	
Credit cards	$ 4,000
Auto loan	5,000
Mortgage payable	60,000
Total liabilities	69,000
Estimated income taxes on the difference between the estimated current values of assets and the estimated current amounts of liabilities and their tax bases	16,800
Net worth	205,200
Total liabilities and net worth	$291,000

Comments

1. Many would consider the net worth, $205,200, a relatively high amount.

2. Liquid assets total $88,000 (cash, $8,000; savings accounts, $20,000; and marketable securities, $60,000).

3. Most of the liabilities appear to be long term (mortgage payable, $60,000).

4. Compare specific assets with related liabilities:

Auto:		Residence:	
Current value	$10,000	Current value	$130,000
Auto loan	5,000	Mortgage payable	60,000
Net investment	$ 5,000	Net investment	$ 70,000

Illustration of Preparation of the Statement of Changes in Net Worth

For Bill and Mary, the data relating to changes in net worth for the year ended December 31, 2012, follow:

Realized increases in net worth:	
Salary	$ 70,000
Dividend income	5,000
Interest income	6,000
Gain on sale of marketable securities	2,000
Realized decreases in net worth:	
Income taxes	20,000
Real estate taxes	2,000
Personal expenditures	28,000
Unrealized increases in net worth:	
Marketable securities	11,000
Residence	3,000
Unrealized decreases in net worth:	
Boat	2,000
Furnishings	4,000
Estimated income taxes on the differences between the estimated current values of assets and current amounts of liabilities and their tax bases	12,000
Net worth at the beginning of year	176,200

Bill and Mary
Statement of Changes in Net Worth
For the Year Ended December 31, 2012

Realized increases in net worth:	
Salary	$ 70,000
Dividend income	5,000
Interest income	6,000
Gain on sale of marketable securities	2,000
	83,000
Realized decreases in net worth:	
Income taxes	20,000
Real estate taxes	2,000
Personal expenditures	28,000
	50,000
Net realized increase in net worth	33,000
Unrealized increases in net worth:	
Marketable securities	11,000
Residence	3,000
	14,000
Unrealized decreases in net worth:	
Boat	2,000
Furnishings	4,000
Estimated income taxes on the differences between the estimated current values of assets and the estimated current amounts of liabilities and their tax base	12,000
	18,000
Net unrealized decreases in net worth	4,000
Net increase in net worth	29,000
Net worth at the beginning of year	176,200
Net worth at the end of the year	$205,200

Comments

1. Most of the realized increase in net worth is salary ($70,000).

2. The major decreases in realized net worth are income taxes ($20,000) and personal expenditures ($28,000).

3. The net realized increase in net worth totaled $33,000.

4. The principal unrealized increase in net worth is marketable securities ($11,000).

5. The principal unrealized decreases in net worth are estimated income taxes on the differences between the estimated current value of assets and the estimated current amounts of liabilities and their tax bases ($12,000).

6. The net unrealized decreases in net worth totaled $4,000.

7. The net increase in net worth totaled $29,000.

8. The net worth at the end of the year totaled $205,200.

Accounting for Governments

The accounting terminology utilized by governments differs greatly from that used by profit-oriented enterprises. Governments use such terms as *appropriations* and *general fund*. Definitions of some of the terms that will be encountered follow:

- Appropriations: Provision for necessary resources and the authority for their disbursement.
- Debt service: Cash receipts and disbursements related to the payment of interest and principal on long-term debt.
- Capital projects: Cash receipts and disbursements related to the acquisition of long-lived assets.
- Special assessments: Cash receipts and disbursements related to improvements or services for which special property assessments have been levied.
- Enterprises: Operations that are similar to private businesses in which service users are charged fees.
- Internal services: Service centers that supply goods or services to other governmental units on a cost reimbursement basis.
- General fund: All cash receipts and disbursements not required to be accounted for in another fund.
- Proprietary funds: Funds whose purpose is to maintain the assets through cost reimbursement by users or partial cost recovery from users and periodic infusion of additional assets.
- Fiduciary funds (nonexpendable funds): Funds whose principal must remain intact (revenues earned may be distributed).
- Encumbrances: Future commitments for expenditures.

Thousands of state and local governments in the United States account for a large segment of the gross national product. State and local governments have a major impact on the citizens. No organization had a clear responsibility for providing accounting principles for state and local governments. The AICPA, the National Council on Governmental Accounting, and the Municipal Finance Officers Association provided significant leadership in establishing accounting principles for state and local governments.

During the early 1980s, many thought that governmental accounting could benefit from the establishment of a board similar to the FASB. A group of government accountants and CPAs organized a committee known as the Governmental Accounting Standards Board Organizing Committee. The Committee recommended the establishment of a separate standard-setting body for governmental accounting.

In April 1984, the Financial Accounting Foundation amended its articles of incorporation to accommodate a Governmental Accounting Standards Board (GASB). Thus, the GASB became a branch of the Financial Accounting Foundation. The GASB has a seven-member board. A simple majority of four votes is needed to issue a pronouncement.

Governmental Accounting Standards Board Statement No. 1, Appendix B, addresses the jurisdictional hierarchy of the GASB and the FASB. It establishes the following priorities for governmental units[4]:

1. Pronouncements of the Governmental Accounting Standards Board.
2. Pronouncements of the Financial Accounting Standards Board.
3. Pronouncements of bodies composed of expert accountants that follow a due process procedure, including broad distribution of proposed accounting principles for public comment, for the intended purpose of establishing accounting principles or describing existing practices that are generally accepted.
4. Practices or pronouncements that are widely recognized as being generally accepted because they represent prevalent practice in a particular industry or the knowledgeable application to specific circumstances of pronouncements that are generally accepted.
5. Other accounting literature.

Governmental Accounting Standards Board Statement No. 1 also adopts the National Council on Governmental Accounting pronouncements and the American Institute of Certified Public Accountants audit guide, entitled *Audits of State and Local Governmental Units*, as the basis for currently existing GAAP for state and local governmental units.

In 1984, the GASB codified all existing governmental accounting and financial reporting standards, interpretations, and technical bulletins in a joint effort with the Government Finance Officers Association (GFOA). This book, *Codification of Governmental Accounting and Financial Reporting Standards*, is periodically updated to accommodate subsequent changes.

State and local governments serve as stewards over public funds. This stewardship responsibility dominates state and local government accounting.

State and local government accounting revolves around fund accounting. A **fund** is defined as an:

Independent fiscal and accounting entity with a self-balancing set of accounts recording cash and/or other resources together with all related liabilities, obligations, reserves, and equities which are segregated for the purpose of carrying on specific activities or attaining certain objectives in accordance with special regulations, restrictions, or limitations.[5]

Source: Government Accounting, Auditing, and Financial Reporting (Chicago: Municipal Finance Officers Association of the United States and Canada, 1968), p. 6

Government transactions are recorded in one or more funds designed to emphasize control and budgetary limitations. Examples of funds, established for a specific purpose, are highway maintenance, parks, debt repayment, endowment, and welfare. The number of funds utilized depends on the responsibilities of the particular state or local government and the grouping of these responsibilities. For example, highway maintenance and bridge maintenance may be grouped together.

Some governments do their accounting using a method that resembles a cash basis, others use a modified accrual basis, and some use an accrual basis. A single government unit may use more than one basis, depending on the fund. The trend is away from the cash basis and toward the modified accrual basis or accrual basis.

Under the GASB, the most substantial pronouncement has been GASB Statement No. 34, which was issued in 1999. GASB Statement No. 34 redefines what constitutes basic financial statements for state and local governments. This includes states, cities, towns, and special-purpose governments such as school districts.

GASB Statement No. 34 provides minimum requirements for general-purpose external financial statements. Exhibit 13-1 shows a diagram illustrating the minimum requirements.

The basic financial statements are to be preceded by the management's discussion and analysis (MD&A). The "MD&A should provide an objective and easily readable analysis of the government's financial activities based on currently known facts, decisions, or conditions."[6] The "MD&A provides financial managers with the opportunity to present both a short-term and a long-term analysis of the government's activities."[7]

Source: Governmental Accounting Standards Board Statement

The MD&A must include[8]:

- An objective discussion of the basic financial statements and condensed financial information comparing current and prior years
- An analysis of the overall financial position and results of operations

Source: Governmental Accounting Standards Board Statement

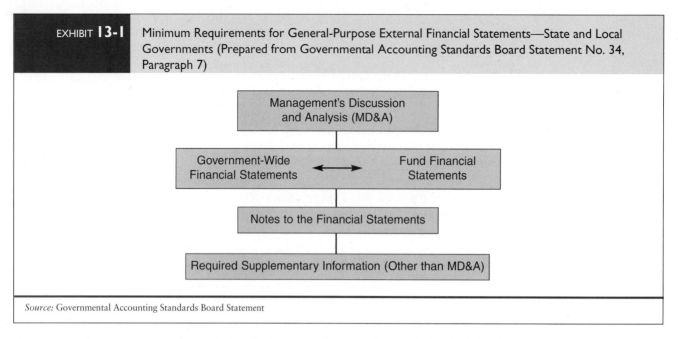

| EXHIBIT **13-1** | Minimum Requirements for General-Purpose External Financial Statements—State and Local Governments (Prepared from Governmental Accounting Standards Board Statement No. 34, Paragraph 7) |

Source: Governmental Accounting Standards Board Statement

- An analysis of balances and transactions of individual funds
- An analysis of significant variations between the original and final budget and the final budget and actual results for the general fund
- A description of significant capital–asset and long-term debt activity during the year
- Known facts, decisions, or conditions expected to have a significant impact on financial position or results of operations

GASB Statement No. 34 makes it clear that neither government-wide statements nor fund statements are considered superior or subordinate to the other. For the government-wide statements, governmental activities are to be presented separately from the financial statements of business-type activities. Examples of governmental activities are police and fire departments; examples of business-type activities are airports and utilities.

The government-wide financial statements are to be prepared on an accrual basis for all of the government's activities. These government-wide financial statements help users:[9]

- Assess the finances of the government in its entirety, including the year's operating results
- Determine whether the government's overall financial position improved or deteriorated
- Evaluate whether the government's current-year revenues were sufficient to pay for current-year services
- See the cost of providing services to its citizenry
- See how the government finances its programs—through user fees and other program revenues versus general tax revenues
- Understand the extent to which the government has invested in capital assets, including roads, bridges, and other infrastructure assets
- Make better comparisons between governments

As indicated previously, the government entity will continue to present fund statements. The government entity uses funds to maintain its financial records during the year. The funds enable the government entity to segregate transactions related to certain functions or activities in separate funds in order to aid financial management and to demonstrate legal compliance.

As indicated earlier, a fund is defined as a fiscal and accounting entity with a self-balancing set of accounts. The three categories of funds are governmental, proprietary, and fiduciary.

Governmental funds are those through which most governmental functions are financed. These funds are used to account for the general operations of government.

Proprietary funds focus on maintaining capital or producing income, or both. Fiduciary funds focus on assets held in a trustee or agency capacity on behalf of others external to the government entity.

Government funds use the modified accrual basis of accounting. Proprietary and fiduciary funds use the accrual basis of accounting. The differences in the accrual and modified accrual bases of accounting come from the recognition of revenue, from the recording of deferred revenue, and from the presentation of expenses versus expenditures.

A required reconciliation is to be presented reconciling the "government-wide financial statements at the bottom of the fund financial statements or in an accompanying schedule."[10]

Source: Journal of Accountancy

Notes to the financial statements are similar to notes of corporate statements in that they provide information to aid the user's understanding of the basic financial statements. In addition, the notes must contain budgetary information that includes the original budget and revised budgets. The budget, being a detailed plan of operations for each period, includes an item-by-item estimate of expenditures when the representatives of the citizens (city council, town meeting, and so on) approve the budget. The individual expenditures then become limits. An increase in an approved expenditure will require approval by the same representatives who set up a legal control over expenditures. This differs from the budget for a commercial business, which is merely a plan of future revenues and expenses.

In addition to the notes to the financial statements, the typical governmental entity provides a statistical section. This statistical section includes important information that aids in the understanding of the governmental entity. It also often presents historical, financial, analytical, economic, and demographic information that may be useful for analysis. Exhibit 13-2 includes parts of Table 2 of the statistical section from the 2010 comprehensive annual financial report of the City of Toledo, Ohio. It includes expenses for business-type activities. A review of this schedule provides insight into revenue for areas such as water, sewer and storm utilities.

Exhibit 13-3 shows Table 12 of the statistical section from the 2010 comprehensive annual financial report of the City of Toledo, Ohio. It includes the ratio of net general bonded debt to assessed value and net bonded debt per capita.

The comprehensive annual financial report will include a "Report of Independent Auditors." Review this report in detail. It could include important information relating to the financial statements and the internal controls of the government entity.

In addition to the primary financial statements, the government entity will report on any "component units," which are legally separate organizations that hold the elected officials of the primary government financially accountable. The financial data of the component units

---

EXHIBIT 13-2	Table 2, City of Toledo, Ohio

Changes in Net Assets by Component (In Part) Last Eight Fiscal Years
(Accrual Basis of Accounting)
(Amounts in Thousands)

	Revenues							
	2003	2004	2005	2006	2007	2008	2009	2010
Business-type activities:								
Charges for services:								
Water	$32,578	$34,258	$ 37,326	$34,790	$ 38,627	$ 38,070	$ 35,913	$ 42,487
Sewer	35,370	39,919	43,551	44,377	48,901	56,064	54,189	57,354
Storm Utility	8,315	7,710	8,637	8,132	8,620	9,034	10,069	9,798
Utilities administration	8,085	7,829	10,288	7,802	9,676	10,564	8,696	10,071
Parking	1,356	1,382	1,435	1,486	1,403	1,509	1,459	1,383
Property management	886	277	264	(688)	266	262	208	470
Small business development	52	77	38	(2)	—	—	—	177
Tow lot	—	—	527	2,225	2,315	2,549	1,418	1,911
Capital grants	1,577	—	—	—	—	—	—	5,423
Total business-type activities revenues	$88,219	$91,452	$102,066	$98,122	$109,808	$118,052	$111,952	$129,074

Source: City of Toledo, Finance Department, Comprehensive Annual Report, for the Year Ended December 31, 2010, p. 174.

EXHIBIT 13-3	Table 12, City of Toledo, Ohio

Ratio of Net General Bonded Debt to Assessed Value and Net Bonded Debt per Capita Last Ten Fiscal Years

Fiscal Year	Population[1]	Assessed Value[2]	Gross General Bonded Debt[2]	Less Balance in Debt Service Fund[2][3]	Net General Bonded Debt[2]	Ratio of Net Bonded Debt to Assessed Value	Net Bonded Debt Per Capita
2010	287,208	3,805,777	143,832	(190)	143,642	3.8%	$500.13
2009	313,619	4,128,523	152,563	(118)	152,445	3.7%	486.08
2008	313,619	4,297,595	136,904	(90)	136,814	3.2%	436.24
2007	313,619	4,592,047	131,821	(58)	131,763	2.9%	420.14
2006	313,619	4,813,232	126,683	(45)	126,638	2.6%	403.80
2005	313,619	4,369,616	128,474	(38)	128,436	2.9%	409.53
2004	313,619	4,423,240	127,241	(38)	127,203	2.9%	405.60
2003	313,619	4,411,593	125,978	(29)	125,949	2.9%	401.60
2002	313,619	4,009,940	127,805	(215)	127,590	3.2%	406.83
2001	313,619	4,025,806	123,810	(579)	123,231	3.1%	392.93

[1]Source: U.S. Bureau of the Census

[2]Amounts shown in thousands of dollars. Personal property starting in 2010 is not part of this calculation. Source: Lucas County Auditor.

[3]The City has paid its general bonded debt service for the tax years shown from current income tax revenues. The amount required is transferred to the debt service funds from the capital improvement fund.

Source: City of Toledo, Financial Department, Comprehensive Annual Report for the Year Ended December 31, 2010, p. 186.

are also included because of the significance of their operational or financial relationships with the government entity.

To determine whether the government entity has one or more component units, review the management's discussion and analysis, government-wide financial statements, fund financial statements, and notes for disclosure of component units. Also, review the Report of Independent Auditors. "Financial statements of component units should be on an accrual basis of accounting."[11] The 2010 comprehensive annual financial report of the City of Toledo, Ohio, did not disclose component units, but the comprehensive annual financial report of Lucas County, Ohio, did reveal component units.

The Lucas County report provides a separate statement combining statements of net assets of discretely presented component units and a separate statement of activities of discretely presented component units. The government-wide financial statements include a separate component unit column to emphasize that they are legally separate from the county. Note 2 describes the component units in detail. One of the component units is the Toledo Mud Hens Baseball Club, Inc. Partial disclosure of the Toledo Mud Hens Baseball Club is as follows:

Note 2 Summary of Significant Accounting Policies (In Part)

Discretely Presented Component Units

Toledo Mud Hens Baseball club, Inc. (the "Mud Hens")

The Mud Hens were organized to own, manage, and operate a professional baseball club. Upon dissolution, any remaining net assets become property of the Board of County Commissioners and new appointments to the board of directors require concurrence of the commissioners. The county receives rent from the Mud Hens to retire non-tax revenue bonds issued to finance the construction of the baseball stadium. The Mud Hens are reported on a fiscal year ending October 31.

The Report of Independent Auditors includes this comment:

"We conducted our audit in accordance with auditing standards generally accepted in the United States of America and the standards applicable to financial audits contained in Government Auditing Standards, issued by the Comptroller General of the United

Source: Report of Independent Auditors

States. Those standards require that we plan and perform the audit to obtain reasonable assurance about whether the financial statements are free of material misstatement. The financial statements of the discretely presented component units audited by other auditors were not audited in accordance with Government Auditing Standards."

Review a governmental accounting book for a detailed discussion of state and local government accounting procedures. A typical governmental comprehensive annual financial report will be 200 pages or longer. A detailed review of the contents of these financial reports is beyond the scope of this book.

A great variance exists in the quality of disclosure in the financial reporting of state and local governments. Some poorly reported items have been pension liabilities, marketable securities, inventories, fixed assets, and lease obligations.

The Government Finance Officers Association of the United States and Canada presents a Certificate of Achievement for Excellence in Financial Reporting to governmental units and public employee retirement systems whose comprehensive annual financial reports are judged to conform substantially to program standards. These standards are considered to be very rigorous.

The municipal bond rating of the governmental unit should also be determined. Standard & Poor's, Fitch, and Moody's evaluate and grade the quality of a bond relative to the probability of default. One rating is assigned to all general obligation bonds (backed by the full faith and credit of the governmental unit). Bonds not backed by the full faith and credit of the governmental unit, such as industrial revenue bonds, are rated individually. These ratings do not represent the probability of default by the governmental unit.

When reviewing a governmental financial statement, the following suggestions are helpful:

1. Determine if a Certificate of Achievement has been received.
2. a. Determine the bond rating of the governmental unit for its general obligation bonds. Since the rating from Standard & Poor's, Fitch, and Moody's may differ, determine the rating from each.
   b. Determine the bond rating of bonds not backed by the full faith and credit of the governmental unit. Again, determine the rating from Standard & Poor's, Fitch, and Moody's.
3. Review the Report of Independent Auditors.
4. Review the management's discussion and analysis.
5. Review the notes to the financial statements.
6. Review the government-wide financial statements.
7. Review the fund financial statements.
8. Review the supplementary information.
9. Look for component units. If component units are present, then determine the obligation of the government unit to the component unit.
10. Review the statistical section.

Accounting for Not-for-Profit Organizations Other Than Governments

Not-for-profit organizations account for a substantial portion of economic activity in the United States. There are over 20,000 not-for-profit organizations in the United States.[12] Examples of not-for-profit organizations include hospitals, religious institutions, professional organizations, universities, and museums.

Not-for-profit accounting principles were derived from numerous not-for-profit industry accounting manuals and audit guides. Examples were AICPA audit guides for Colleges and Universities, Audits of Voluntary Health and Welfare Organizations, and audits of providers of Health Care Services.

The FASB was concerned about the lack of uniformity in the accounting for not-for-profit organizations and the lack of overall quality of not-for-profit organizations' financial reporting. To address this concern, the FASB issued four accounting standards relating to not-for-profits. These standards are: (1) SFAS No. 93, "Recognition of Depreciation by Not-for-Profit Organizations," (2) SFAS No. 116, "Accounting for Contributions Received and Contributions Made," (3) SFAS No. 117, "Financial Statements of Not-for-Profit Organizations," and (4) SFAS No. 124, "Accounting for Certain Investments Held by Not-for-Profit Organizations." A brief description of these accounting standards and how they impact financial reports follows:

1. SFAS No. 93, "Recognition of Depreciation by Not-for-Profit Organizations"[13]

Prior to SFAS No. 93, most not-for-profit organizations did not recognize depreciation. SFAS No. 93 requires not-for-profit organizations to recognize depreciation on long-lived tangible assets. SFAS No. 93 includes these requirements relating to depreciation.

1. Disclose the amount of depreciation expense for each period.
2. Disclose depreciable assets by major classes as of the balance sheet date.
3. Disclose accumulated depreciation for each asset class or in total as of the balance sheet date.
4. Disclose the methods used to calculate depreciation.

SFAS No. 93 exempts individual works of art or historical treasures from the depreciation requirements. For this exemption, two requirements must be met:

1. The asset must have "cultural, aesthetic, or historical value that is worth preserving perpetually."
2. The organization that owns the artwork or historical treasure must be able to preserve the asset so that its potentially unlimited service potential will remain intact.

2. SFAS No. 116, "Accounting for Contributions Received and Contributions Made"[14]

SFAS No. 116 applies to *all not-for-profit organizations as well as to any entity that receives or makes contributions*. Some key aspects of SFAS No. 116 are summarized.

Contributions Received

Contributions received are to be recognized as revenues or gains in the period received. In addition, these contributions are to be recognized as assets, as decreases in liabilities, or as expenses in the same period. Contributions received are to be measured at their fair values and reported as restricted support or unrestricted support.

Contributed services received are to be recognized if one of the following conditions holds:

1. The service creates or enhances nonfinancial assets
2. The services involve specialized skills that would most likely be paid for if they were not donated (i.e., electrical services, plumbing services, accounting services, etc.)

Contributed services recognized should be disclosed by nature and amount for the period. Service contributions are to be valued at the fair value of the services or the resulting increase in assets.

Under SFAS No. 116, donated works of art, historical treasures, or similar assets can be excluded if the following conditions are met:

1. Contributed items are held for public service purposes rather than for financial gain.
2. Contributed items must be protected, kept unencumbered, cared for, and preserved.
3. The organization must have a policy of using funds from the sales of collected items to purchase additional collection pieces.

Contributions received are to be segregated into permanent restrictions, temporary restrictions, and unrestricted support imposed by donors. Restricted contributions shall be reported as an increase in either permanently restricted net assets or temporarily restricted net assets. Unrestricted contributions received are to be reported as unrestricted support and increases in unrestricted net assets. Contributions received are to be measured at fair value.

Conditional promises are to be recognized in the financial statements when the condition(s) has been substantially met. If the nature of the conditional promise is ambiguous, it should be interpreted as conditional.

Contributions Made

Contributions made are to be recognized as expenses in the period in which they are made. These contributions are to be reported as decreases in assets or increases in liabilities. Contributions made are to be measured at the fair value of the asset contributed or the liability discharged. Conditional promises to give are recognized when the conditions are substantially met.

3. SFAS No. 117, "Financial Statements of Not-for-Profit Organizations"[15]

Prior to SFAS No. 117, there were significant differences in the financial reports of not-for-profit organizations. The intent of SFAS No. 117 is to provide consistency in the financial statements of not-for-profit organizations. SFAS No. 117 addresses financial statements, the content of financial statements, and the classification of financial statement information.

Not-for-profit organizations are to present three aggregated financial statements. These include a statement of financial position, a statement of activities, and a statement of cash flows. SFAS No. 117 specifies the content of each of these required financial statements.

Concerning the statement of financial position, SFAS No. 117 directs that it is to include aggregated information about the assets, liabilities, and net assets. SFAS No. 117 requires the statement of activity to provide information concerning the effects of transactions on the amount and nature of net assets, the interrelationships between those transactions and other events, and how the organization uses the resources to provide services. The statement of activity is also to disclose the changes in the amounts of permanently restricted net assets, temporarily restricted net assets, and unrestricted net assets.

With regard to the content of the statement of cash flows, SFAS No. 117 requires that not-for-profit organizations comply with SFAS No. 95, "Statement of Cash Flows." In addition, SFAS No. 117 amends SFAS No. 95 concerning its description of financing activities. Financing activities now include receipts of donations restricted for acquiring, constructing, or improving long-lived assets or establishing or increasing permanent or term endowments.

For the statement of financial position, SFAS No. 117 requires that assets and liabilities should be reported in relatively homogeneous groups. They should also be classified to provide information about their interrelationships, liquidity, and financial flexibility. New assets are to be classified as either permanently restricted, temporarily restricted, or unrestricted. Revenues, expenses, gains, and losses are to be separated into reasonably homogeneous groups for the statement of activities. They also are to be classified as affecting permanently restricted, temporarily restricted, or unrestricted net assets.

4. SFAS No. 124, "Accounting for Certain Investments Held By Not-for-Profit Organizations"[16]

This statement applies to investments in equity securities that have a readily determinable fair value and to all investments in debt securities. These investments are to be shown at their fair values in the statement of financial position. This statement does not apply to investments in equity securities that are accounted for under the equity method or to investments in consolidated subsidiaries. Disclosure requirements in the statement of financial position include the aggregate carrying value of investments by major categories and the basis for determining the carrying values of equity securities without readily determinable fair market values. Any shortfall in the fair value of donor-restricted endowment funds below the amount required by donor stipulations or by law must also be disclosed.

For the statement of activities, any realized or unrealized gains and losses are to be shown. Some of the disclosure requirements for the statement of activities include the composition of the investment return, which consists of investment income, realized gains and losses on investments not reported at fair value, and net gains and losses on investments that are reported at fair value.

Applicability of GAAP to Not-for-Profit Organizations

Some individuals believed that the applicability of GAAP to not-for-profit organizations was unclear. SOP 94-2 was issued to address the applicability of GAAP to not-for-profit organizations.[17]

SOP 94-2 concludes that not-for-profit organizations should follow the guidance in effective provisions of ARBs, APB Opinions, and FASB Statements and Interpretations unless the specific pronouncement explicitly exempts not-for-profit organizations or their subject matter precludes such applicability (SOP 94-2, paragraph .09).

Exhibit 13-4 contains the consolidated statement of financial position and the consolidated statement of activities for the Ohio Society of Certified Public Accountants. These statements are for the year ended April 30, 2011. Not included in Exhibit 13-4 are the independent auditors' report, consolidated statements of cash flows, notes to consolidated financial statements, independent auditors' report on supplementary information, consolidating statement of financial position, and consolidating statement of activities.

Budgeting by Objectives and/or Measures of Productivity

Accounting for not-for-profit institutions differs greatly from accounting for a profit-oriented enterprise. The accounting for a profit-oriented business centers on the entity concept and the efficiency of the entity. The accounting for governments and accounting for not-for-profit organizations do not include an entity concept or efficiency. The accounting for a profit-oriented business has a bottom-line net income. The accounting for governments and accounting for not-for-profit organizations do not have a bottom line.

Some governments and not-for-profit organizations have added budgeting by objectives and/or measures of productivity to their financial reporting to incorporate measures of efficiency. The article, "Budgeting by Objectives: Charlotte's Experience," reported several

---

EXHIBIT 13-4	The Ohio Society of Certified Public Accountants

CONSOLIDATED STATEMENT OF FINANCIAL POSITION
April 30, 2011
(with Comparative Totals at April 30, 2010)

	2011	2010
ASSETS		
Cash and cash equivalents	$ 315,000	$ 51,000
Accounts receivable, net	37,000	40,000
Pledges receivable, net	495,000	715,000
Prepaid expenses and deposits	181,000	158,000
Prepaid pension	269,000	213,000
Investments	5,405,000	4,601,000
Property, net	1,454,000	1,501,000
TOTAL ASSETS	$8,156,000	$7,279,000
LIABILITIES AND NET ASSETS		
LIABILITIES		
Accounts payable and accrued liabilities	$1,060,000	$ 915,000
Deferred revenue	1,018,000	777,000
Short-term borrowings	—	257,000
Mortgage payable	1,052,000	1,090,000
Total liabilities	3,130,000	3,039,000
NET ASSETS		
Unrestricted	2,686,000	2,061,000
Temporarily restricted	276,000	258,000
Permanently restricted	2,064,000	1,921,000
Total net assets	5,026,000	4,240,000
TOTAL LIABILITIES AND NET ASSETS	$8,156,000	$7,279,000

Source: © 2011, the Ohio Society of Certified Public Accountants. All rights reserved.

EXHIBIT 13-4	The Ohio Society of Certified Public Accountants (*continued*)

CONSOLIDATED STATEMENT OF ACTIVITIES
Year Ended April 30, 2011
(with Comparative Totals at April 30, 2010)

	Unrestricted	Temporarily Restricted	Permanently Restricted	2011 Total	2010 Total
REVENUE					
Dues	$ 4,705,000			$ 4,705,000	$ 4,665,000
Education and training course fees	3,495,000			3,495,000	3,431,000
Peer review fees	502,000			502,000	376,000
Public relations and publications	386,000			386,000	418,000
Investment income, net	311,000	$ 5,000	$ 61,000	377,000	622,000
Member Connections and sections	258,000			258,000	274,000
Other	196,000			196,000	193,000
Foundation contributions	53,000	65,000		118,000	93,000
Membership affinity programs	49,000			49,000	70,000
Released from restrictions – scholarships	28,000	7,000	(35,000)		
–net assets	35,000	(35,000)			
Total revenue	10,018,000	42,000	26,000	10,086,000	10,142,000
EXPENSES					
Education and training programs	3,792,000			3,792,000	3,628,000
Public relations and publications	1,713,000			1,713,000	1,709,000
General and administrative	1,254,000			1,254,000	1,190,000
Governmental affairs	769,000			769,000	703,000
Membership	701,000			701,000	773,000
Peer review	553,000			553,000	601,000
Member Connections and sections	550,000			550,000	607,000
Interest	72,000			72,000	72,000
Foundation scholarships	39,000			39,000	47,000
Total expenses	9,443,000			9,443,000	9,330,000
Increase from operating activity before non-operating activity	575,000	42,000	26,000	643,000	812,000
NON-OPERATING ACTIVITY					
Centennial Campaign – contributions			24,000	24,000	136,000
Investment gain, net		26,000	93,000	119,000	153,000
Released from restrictions – Centennial Campaign	50,000	(50,000)			
Increase (decrease) from non-operating activity	50,000	(24,000)	117,000	143,000	289,000
CHANGE IN NET ASSETS	625,000	18,000	143,000	786,000	1,101,000
NET ASSETS – BEGINNING OF YEAR	2,061,000	258,000	1,921,000	4,240,000	3,139,000
NET ASSETS – END OF YEAR	$ 2,686,000	$276,000	$2,064,000	$ 5,026,000	$ 4,240,00

objectives incorporated in the budget of Charlotte, North Carolina. Four primary objectives guided the budget: (1) the property tax rate should not increase, (2) continued emphasis should be placed on making the best use of city employees and the present computer capability, (3) any budget increase should be held to a minimum, and (4) a balanced program of services should be presented.[18]

This article also reports measures of productivity that Charlotte has used. These measures of productivity include (1) customers served per $1,000 of sanitation expense, (2) number of tons of refuse per $1,000 expense, and (3) street miles flushed per $1,000 expense.[19]

Budgeting by objectives and/or measures of productivity could be added to the financial reporting of any not-for-profit institution. The objectives and measures of productivity should be applicable to the particular not-for-profit institution.

Summary

This chapter reviewed financial reporting for personal financial statements and accounting for governments and other not-for-profit organizations. Accounting for these areas differs greatly from accounting for profit-oriented businesses. This difference has been narrowed substantially for not-for-profit organizations other than governments.

Statement of Position 82-1 presents guidelines for the preparation of personal financial statements. SOP 82-1 concludes that personal financial statements should present assets at their estimated current values and liabilities at their estimated current amounts at the date of the financial statements. This differs from commercial financial statements that predominantly use historical information.

GASB Statement No. 34 redefines what constitutes basic financial statements for state and local governments.

Minimum requirements for general-purpose external financial statements—state and local governments include management discussion and analysis (MD&A), government-wide financial statements, fund financial statements, and required supplementary information (other than MD&A).

Not-for-profit accounting for organizations, other than governments, has changed substantially. It now resembles accounting for profit organizations. A major difference is that not-for-profit organizations issue a statement of activities instead of an income statement.

Some not-for-profit institutions have added budgeting by objectives and/or measures of productivity to their financial reporting to incorporate measures of efficiency.

Questions

Q 13-1 May personal financial statements be prepared only for an individual? Comment.

Q 13-2 What is the basic personal financial statement?

Q 13-3 Is a statement of changes in net worth required when presenting personal financial statements?

Q 13-4 Are comparative financial statements required when presenting personal financial statements?

Q 13-5 When preparing a personal statement of financial condition, should assets and liabilities be presented on the basis of historical cost or estimated current value?

Q 13-6 In a personal statement of financial condition, what is the equity section called?

Q 13-7 What personal financial statement should be prepared when an explanation of changes in net worth is desired?

Q 13-8 Is the presentation of a personal income statement appropriate?

Q 13-9 GAAP as they apply to personal financial statements use the cash basis. Comment.

Q 13-10 Is the concept of working capital used with personal financial statements? Comment.

Q 13-11 List some sources of information that may be available when preparing personal financial statements.

Q 13-12 Give examples of disclosure in notes with personal financial statements.

Q 13-13 If quoted market prices are not available, a personal financial statement cannot be prepared. Comment.

Q 13-14 List some objectives that could be incorporated into the financial reporting of a professional accounting organization.

Q 13-15 Do not-for-profit organizations, other than governments, use fund accounting? Comment.

Q 13-16 The accounting for governments is centered on the entity concept and the efficiency of the entity. Comment.

Q 13-17 For governmental accounting, define the following types of funds:

1. General fund
2. Proprietary fund
3. Fiduciary fund

Q 13-18 How many funds will be used by a state or local government?

Q 13-19 The budget for a state or local government is not as binding as a budget for a commercial business. Comment.

Q 13-20 Which organization provides a service whereby it issues a certificate of conformance to governmental units with financial reports that meet its standards?

Q 13-21 The rating on an industrial revenue bond is representative of the probability of default of bonds issued with the full faith and credit of a governmental unit. Comment.

Q 13-22 The accounting for not-for-profit institutions does not typically include the concept of efficiency. Indicate how the concept of efficiency can be incorporated in the financial reporting of a not-for-profit institution.

Q 13-23 Could a profit-oriented enterprise use fund accounting practices? Comment.

Q 13-24 How many members serve on the GASB? How many votes are needed to issue a pronouncement?

Q 13-25 What is the purpose of the book, *Codification of Governmental Accounting and Financial Reporting Standards*?

Q 13-26 Under GASB, which statement has been the most substantial pronouncement?

Q 13-27 For the government-wide statements, governmental activities are to be presented separately from the financial statements of business-type activities. Give one example of a governmental activity and one example of a business-type activity.

Q 13-28 Why are the financial data of a component unit included with the government entities reporting entity?

Problems

P 13-1 For each of these situations, indicate the amount to be placed on a statement of financial condition at December 31, 2012.

a. Bill and Pat Konner purchased their home at 2829 Willow Road in Stow, Ohio, in August 1994 for $80,000. The unpaid mortgage is $20,000. Immediately after purchasing the home, Bill and Pat added several improvements totaling $10,000. Real estate prices in Stow have increased 40% since the time of purchase.

From the facts given, determine the estimated current value of the home.

b. Joe Best drives a Toyota, for which he paid $20,000 when it was new. Joe believes that since he maintains the car in good condition, he could sell it for $12,000. The average selling price for this model of Toyota is $9,000.

From the facts given, determine the estimated current value of Joe's car.

c. Sue Bell is 40 years old and has an IRA with a balance of $20,000. The IRS penalty for early withdrawal is 10%. The marginal tax rate for Sue Bell is 30% (tax on gross amount).

What is the estimated current value of the IRA and the estimated income taxes on the difference between the estimated current values of assets and the estimated current amounts of liabilities and their tax bases?

d. Bill Kell guaranteed a loan of $8,000 for his girlfriend to buy a car. She is behind in payments on the car.

What liability should be shown on Bill Kell's statement of financial condition?

e. Dick Better bought a home in 1996 for $70,000. Currently, the mortgage on the home is $45,000. Because of the current high interest rates, the bank has offered to retire the mortgage for $40,000.

What is the estimated current value of this liability?

P 13-2 For each of these situations, indicate the amount to be placed on a statement of financial condition at December 31, 2012.

a. Raj Reel owns the following securities:
1,000 shares of Ree's
2,000 shares of Bell's
Ree's is traded on the New York Stock Exchange. The prices from the most recent trade day follow:

Open	19
High	20½
Low	19
Close	20

Bell's is a local company whose stock is sold by brokers on a workout basis. (The broker tries to find a buyer.) The most recent selling price was $8.

What is the estimated current value of these securities? (Assume that the commission on Ree's would be $14 and the commission on Bell's would be $17.)

(continued)

(**P 13-2** CONTINUED)

    b. Charlie has a certificate of deposit with a $10,000 balance. Accrued interest is $500. The penalty for early withdrawal would be $300.

    What is the estimated current value of the certificate of deposit?

    c. Jones has an option to buy 500 shares of ABC Construction at a price of $20 per share. The option expires in one year. ABC Construction shares are presently selling for $25.

    What is the estimated current value of these options?

    d. Carl Jones has a whole-life insurance policy with the face amount of $100,000, cash value of $50,000, and a loan outstanding against the policy of $20,000. Susan Jones is the beneficiary.

    What is the estimated current value of the insurance policy?

    e. Larry Solomon paid $60,000 for a home 10 years ago. The unpaid mortgage on the home is $30,000. Larry estimates the current value of the home to be $90,000. This estimate is partially based on the selling price of homes recently sold in the neighborhood. Larry's home is assessed for tax purposes at $50,000. Assessments in the area average one-half of market value. The house has not been inspected for assessment during the past two years. Larry would sell through a broker, who would charge 5% of the selling price.

    What is the estimated current value of the home?

P 13-3 For Barb and Carl, the assets and liabilities and the effective income tax rates at December 31, 2012, follow:

Accounts	Tax Bases	Estimated Current Value	Excess of Estimated Current Values over Tax Bases	Effective Income Tax Rates	Amount of Estimated Income Taxes
Cash	$ 20,000	$ 20,000	$ —	—	_____
Marketable securities	45,000	50,000	5,000	28%	_____
Life insurance	50,000	50,000	—	—	_____
Residence	100,000	125,000	25,000	28%	_____
Furnishings	40,000	25,000	(15,000)	—	_____
Jewelry	20,000	20,000	—	—	_____
Autos	20,000	12,000	(8,000)	—	_____
Mortgage payable	(90,000)	(90,000)	—	—	_____
Note payable	(30,000)	(30,000)	—	—	_____
Credit cards	(10,000)	(10,000)	—	—	_____

Required

    a. Compute the estimated tax liability on the differences between the estimated current value of the assets and liabilities and their tax bases.

    b. Present a statement of financial condition for Barb and Carl at December 31, 2012.

    c. Comment on the statement of financial condition.

P 13-4 For Mary Lou and Ernie, the assets and liabilities and the effective income tax rates at December 31, 2012, follow:

Accounts	Tax Bases	Estimated Current Value	Excess of Estimated Current Values over Tax Bases	Effective Income Tax Rates	Amount of Estimated Income Taxes
Cash	$ 20,000	$ 20,000	$ —	—	_____
Marketable securities	80,000	100,000	20,000	28%	_____
Options	0	30,000	30,000	28%	_____
Residence	100,000	150,000	50,000	28%	_____
Royalties	0	20,000	20,000	28%	_____
Furnishings	40,000	20,000	(20,000)	—	_____
Auto	20,000	15,000	(5,000)	—	_____
Mortgage	(70,000)	(70,000)	—	—	_____
Auto loan	(10,000)	(10,000)	—	—	_____

Required

a. Compute the estimated tax liability on the differences between the estimated current value of the assets and liabilities and their tax bases.

b. Present a statement of financial condition for Mary Lou and Ernie at December 31, 2012.

c. Comment on the statement of financial condition.

P 13-5 For Mike Szabo, the changes in net worth for the year ended December 31, 2012, follow:

Realized increases in net worth:	
Salary	$ 60,000
Dividend income	2,500
Interest income	2,000
Gain on sale of marketable securities	500
Realized decreases in net worth:	
Income taxes	20,000
Interest expense	6,000
Personal expenditures	29,000
Unrealized increases in net worth:	
Stock options	3,000
Land	7,000
Residence	5,000
Unrealized decreases in net worth:	
Boat	3,000
Jewelry	1,000
Furnishings	4,000
Estimated income taxes on the differences between the estimated current values of assets and the estimated current amounts of liabilities and their tax bases	15,000
Net worth at the beginning of year	150,000

Required

a. Prepare a statement of changes in net worth for the year ended December 31, 2012.

b. Comment on the statement of changes in net worth.

P 13-6 For Jim and Carrie, the changes in net worth for the year ended December 31, 2012, are as follows.

Realized increases in net worth:	
Salary	$ 50,000
Interest income	6,000
Realized decreases in net worth:	
Income taxes	15,000
Interest expense	3,000
Personal property taxes	1,000
Real estate taxes	1,500
Personal expenditures	25,000
Unrealized increases in net worth:	
Marketable securities	2,000
Land	5,000
Residence	3,000
Stock options	4,000
Unrealized decreases in net worth:	
Furnishings	3,000
Estimated income taxes on the differences between the estimated current values of assets and the estimated current amounts of liabilities and their tax bases	12,000
Net worth at the beginning of year	130,000

(continued)

(**P 13-6** CONTINUED)

Required

a. Prepare a statement of changes in net worth for the year ended December 31, 2012.

b. Comment on the statement of changes in net worth.

P 13-7 Use Exhibit 13-2, City of Toledo, Ohio, Revenues, Business-type Activities.

Required

a. Prepare a horizontal common-size statement for 2003–2010. Use 2003 as the base.

b. Comment on significant items in the horizontal common-size analysis.

P 13-8 Use Exhibit 13-2, City of Toledo, Ohio, Revenues, Business-type Activities.

Required

a. Prepare a vertical common-size statement. Use total business-type activities as the base.

b. Comment on significant items in the vertical common-size analysis.

P 13-9 Use Exhibit 13-3, City of Toledo, Ohio, Ratio of Net General Bonded Debt to Assessed Value and Net Bonded Debt per Capita, Last 10 Fiscal Years.

Required

a. Prepare a vertical common-size statement. Use 2001 as the base. Include assessed value, net general bonded debt, and net bonded debt per capita.

b. Comment on significant items in the vertical common-size analysis.

P 13-10 Use Exhibit 13-4, the Ohio Society of Certified Public Accountants' financial report.

Required

a. Prepare a vertical common-size analysis for the consolidated statement of financial position. For April 30, 2011, use total assets as the base and stop with total expenses. Comment on significant items in total assets, liabilities, and net assets.

b. Prepare a vertical common-size analysis for the consolidated statement of activities. Work up the vertical common-size analysis for unrestricted and total. Use total expenses as the base. Comment on significant items.

P 13-11 The Ohio Society of Certified Public Accountants' financial report for the year ended April 30, 2011, included this note:

Note 1. Organization (In Part)

The Ohio Society of Certified Public Accountants was organized in 1908 as a not-for-profit corporation. The mission of the society is to act on behalf of its members and provide necessary support to assure that members serve the public by performing quality professional services.

Required Using Exhibit 13-4, the Ohio Society of Certified Public Accountants' Consolidated Statement of Activities, comment on items that indicate that the society is achieving its mission.

P 13-12

Required Answer the following multiple-choice questions related to personal financial statements:

a. For the personal financial statement, statement of changes in net worth, which of the following would be a realized increase in net worth?

1. Dividend income
2. Change in value of land
3. Decrease in value of house
4. Personal expenditures
5. None of the above.

b. For the personal financial statement, statement of changes in net worth, which of the following would be an unrealized increase in net worth?

1. Increase in value of land
2. Decrease in value of furnishings
3. Personal expenditures
4. Salary
5. None of the above.

c. Which of the following is *not* a suggestion for reviewing the statement of financial condition?

1. Review realized decreases in net worth.
2. Review the net worth amount.
3. Determine the amount of the assets that you consider to be very liquid.
4. Observe the due period of the liabilities.
5. Compare specific assets with any related liabilities.

d. Which of the following would be a source of information for personal financial statements?

1. Bank statements
2. Checkbooks
3. Real estate tax returns
4. Insurance policies
5. All of the above.

e. Which of the following would *not* be an acceptable presentation on the statement of financial condition?

1. A car may be presented at cost.
2. Payables and other liabilities are presented at the discounted amounts of cash to be paid.
3. Investments in real estate should be presented at their estimated current values.
4. The liability for income taxes payable should include unpaid income taxes for completed tax years and an estimated amount for income taxes accrued for the elapsed portion of the current tax year to the date of the financial statements.
5. All of the above.

P 13-13

Required Answer the following multiple-choice questions related to state and local governments:

a. Proprietary funds are a type of funds used by governments. A reasonable definition of proprietary funds would be

1. Funds whose purpose is to maintain the assets through cost reimbursement by users or partial cost recovery from users and periodic infusion of additional assets.
2. Funds whose principal must remain intact.
3. Funds that handle all cash receipts and disbursements not required to be accounted for in another fund.
4. Funds that handle cash receipts and disbursements related to the payment of interest and principal on long-term debt.
5. None of the above.

b. Government transactions are recorded in one or more funds designed to emphasize control and budgetary limitations. A fund may be established for which of the following specific purposes?

1. Highway maintenance
2. Parks
3. Debt repayment
4. Endowment fund
5. All of the above.

c. Which of the following is *not* a minimum requirement for general-purpose external financial statements—state and local governments?

1. Statement of cash flow
2. Management discussion and analysis
3. Government-wide financial statements
4. Fund financial statements
5. Notes to the financial statements

(continued)

(P 13-13 CONTINUED)

   d. For state and local governments, the MD&A must include all but which of the following?

      1. An objective discussion of the basic financial statements and condensed financial information comparing current and prior years.
      2. An analysis of the overall financial position and results of operations.
      3. An analysis of balances and transactions of individual funds.
      4. An analysis of significant variations between the original and final budget and the final budget and actual results for the general fund.
      5. Known facts, decisions, or conditions expected to have an impact on financial position or results of operations.

   e. Which of the following statements is *not* true?

      1. The government-wide financial statements are to be prepared on an accrual basis for all of the government's activities.
      2. Under GASB Statement No. 34, the government entity will continue to present fund statements.
      3. Under GASB Statement No. 34, government-wide statements are superior to fund statements.
      4. Government-wide financial statements are prepared on an accrual basis.
      5. Government transactions are recorded in one or more funds designed to emphasize central and budgetary limitations.

P 13-14

Required Answer the following multiple-choice questions:

   a. Which of the following is *not* true?

      1. SFAS No. 93 requires not-for-profit organizations to recognize depreciation on long-lived tangible assets.
      2. Under SFAS No. 116, "Accounting for Contributions Received and Contributions Made," contributions are to be segregated into permanent restrictions, temporary restrictions, and unrestricted support imposed by donors.
      3. Prior to SFAS No. 117, "Financial Statements of Not-for-Profit Organizations," there were significant differences in the financial reports of not-for-profit organizations.
      4. Not-for-profit organizations are to present two aggregated financial statements.
      5. According to SFAS No. 124, "Accounting for Certain Investments Held by Not-for-Profit Organizations," equity securities should be shown at their fair values in the statement of financial position.

   b. Which of the following is an example of a profit institution?

      1. Bank
      2. State government
      3. Church
      4. University
      5. None of the above.

   c. Which of the following is *not* true?

      1. SOP 94-2 concludes that not-for-profit organizations should follow the guidance in effective provisions of GAAP, unless the specific pronouncement explicitly exempts not-for-profit organizations or their subject matter precludes such applicability.
      2. Not-for-profit organizations account for a substantial portion of economic activity in the United States.
      3. Prior to SOP 94-2, not-for-profit accounting principles were derived solely from AICPA audit guides.
      4. Under SFAS No. 116, "Accounting for Contributions Received and Contributions Made," contributions received are to be recognized as revenues or gains in the period received.
      5. For a not-for-profit organization, the statement of activities should show realized or unrealized gains and losses.

    d. Which of the following is *not* true?

       1. The accounting for a not-for-profit institution does not include an entity concept or efficiency.

       2. The accounting for a not-for-profit institution has a bottom-line net income.

       3. Some not-for-profit institutions have added budgeting by objectives and/or productivity to their financial reporting to incorporate measures of efficiency.

       4. Budgeting by objectives and/or measures of productivity could be added to the financial reporting of any not-for-profit institution.

       5. Accounting for not-for-profit institutions differs greatly from accounting for a profit-oriented enterprise.

Cases

CASE 13-1 DEFICIT BUDGET?

In July 2003, the Medical College of Ohio (MCO) (now part of the University of Toledo) approved its first deficit budget of $3.4 million, but no programs or faculty members were cut.

    MCO announced a "mission-based" study of all programs and an examination of how financially viable they are, as well as how essential they are.

    MCO was projected to lose money because of recognizing depreciation expense. Without depreciation expense, MCO would have a $5 million profit for fiscal year 2004.

    In recognizing depreciation expense, MCO was adopting a new accounting standard passed in 2000 that requires colleges (universities) to account for depreciation. Many colleges adopted the new standard by disclosing in a note in their audited financial statements, not their operating budgets.

Required

  a. In your opinion, should colleges and universities recognize depreciation expense? Comment.

  b. Is recognizing depreciation expense in a note equivalent to recognizing depreciation expense in the statements? Comment.

  c. Should the standard be explicit on how a college or university recognizes depreciation expense? Comment.

Note: Information relating to this case comes from "**MCO Board Votes Its 1st Deficit Budget,**" *The Blade,* Toledo, Ohio, July 29, 2003, Section B, pp. 1–2.

Source: "MCO Board Votes Its 1st Deficit Budget," The Blade, Toledo, Ohio, July 29, 2003, Section B, pp. 1–2.

CASE 13-2 MY MUD HENS

Toledo Mud Hens Baseball Club, Inc., is a not-for-profit organization that is a separate legal entity and can be sued in its own right.

    The Toledo Mud Hens are probably the most famous team in all of minor league baseball. They have been named the Toledo Mud Hens since 1896 when the team played at Bay View Park. The surrounding marshland was frequented by these strange birds.

    Famous people such as Casey Stengel, Jamie Farr, and Bob Costas have helped bring the team nationwide fame. Players who have contributed to the team's fame include Moses Fleetwood Walker, Addie Joss, Tony Clark, Kirby Puckett, Travis Fryman, and Kirk Gibson.

    An Ohio Historical Marker in Toledo, Ohio, reads as follows:

Moses Fleetwood Walker Square
In honor of baseball's first
African-American
Major League Player
Toledo Blue Stockings—1889
Ohio Historical Marker
Moses Fleetwood Walker

(continued)

Source: "Square Is Named for Walker," The Blade (October 2, 2002), SEc. B, P1; Lucas County, Ohio, Ohio and "The Toledo Mud Hens – History in the Making,"

(**Case 13-2** CONTINUED)

Moses Fleetwood Walker was born on October 7, 1856, in Ohio to Moses M. Walker, a physician, and Caroline, a midwife. He attended and played baseball at Oberlin College and the University of Michigan. In 1883, Walker joined the newly formed Toledo Blue Stockings and became the first African-American major league baseball player when Toledo joined the major league–sanctioned American Association the following year. As a bare-handed catcher, his biggest assets were his catching ability, powerful throwing arm, and aggressive base running. He endured racial prejudice from teammates, opponents, and baseball fans and eventually left to become a writer, inventor, civil rights advocate, and entrepreneur. Walker was elected to the Ohio Baseball Hall of Fame in 1991. He died in 1924 and is buried in Steubenville, Ohio, in the family plot at Union Cemetery.

There is now a Moses Fleetwood Walker Society in Toledo, Ohio. It has an annual dinner after the World Series. The dinner and dues help raise money to buy baseball items for underprivileged kids. On August 1, 2011, the Toledo Mud Hens honored the first African-American to play Major League Baseball. Moses Fleetwood Walker played for the Toledo Blue Stockings in 1884.

By 1889 blacks were barred from the high minor leagues and the major leagues. It remained that way until 1947 when Jackie Robinson joined the Brooklyn Dodgers.

Casey Stengel skippered six Toledo teams, including the 1927 squad that won the Junior World Series.

In 2002, the team moved into a new facility. The County issued $20 million in economic development revenue bonds and $6 million in economic development revenue anticipation notes in March 2001. The County retired the notes in March 2002 after receiving revenue for the naming rights (Fifth Third Field) and the lease of the luxury suites.

Lucas County receives rent from the Mud Hens that in the County's opinion is substantially below market rate. The board of the Mud Hens is approved by the Board of County Commissioners.

The Mud Hens' ball park was named by *Newsweek Magazine* as the best minor league park. The largest video board in minor league baseball was added to the park in 2005. Another large video board was added in 1909.

The Lucas County, Ohio, comprehensive annual financial report included the Toledo Mud Hens Baseball Club, Inc., financial information for the fiscal year ended December 31, 2010.

LUCAS COUNTY, OHIO
STATEMENTS OF NET ASSETS*
Discretely Presented Component Unit
December 31, 2010

	Toledo Mud Hens Baseball Club, Inc.
Assets	
Equity in pooled cash and investments	$ 9,513,986
Receivables (net of allowances for uncollectibles): Accounts	355,459
Materials and supplies inventory	156,082
Prepayments	83,808
Other assets	20,015
Capital assets:	
Nondepreciable capital assets	118,250
Depreciable capital assets, net	3,334,616
Total capital assets, net	3,452,866
Total assets	$13,582,216
Liabilities	
Accounts payable	$ 121,074
Accrued liabilities	2,699,253
Unearned revenue	613,124

*Adapted from Lucas County, Ohio, combining Statements of Net Assets, Discretely Presented Component Units, December 31, 2010.

	Toledo Mud Hens Baseball Club, Inc.
Long-term liabilities:	
Due in more than one year	145,383
Total liabilities	3,578,834
Net assets	
Invested in capital assets, net of related debt	$ 3,452,866
Unrestricted	6,550,516
Total net assets	$10,003,382

LUCAS COUNTY, OHIO
STATEMENT OF ACTIVITIES*
Discretely Presented Component Units
For the Year Ended December 31, 2010

	Expenses	Program Revenues Charges for Services and Sales	Toledo Mud Hens Baseball Club, Inc.
Component Units:			
Toledo Mud Hens Baseball Club, Inc.	$10,437,265	$11,697,987	$ 1,260,722
Total			1,260,722
General Revenues:			
Investment earnings			15,060
Miscellaneous			24,218
Total General Revenues			39,278
Change in net assets			1,300,000
Net assets at beginning of year			8,703,382
Net assets at end of year			$10,003,382

*Adapted from Lucas County, Ohio, Statement of Activities, Discretely Presented Component Units For the Year Ended December 31, 2010.

Source: "Square Is Named for Walker," The Blade (October 2, 2002), Sec. B, P1; Lucas County, Ohio, and "The Toledo Mud Hens – History in the Making", provided by Toledo Mud Hens Baseball Club, Inc. The source also includes Lucas County, Ohio, comprehensive annual financial report, for fiscal year ended December 31, 2010.

Required

a. What form would the Mud Hens statement take?

b. Why does Lucas County, Ohio include financial and descriptive information relating to the Mud Hens in its financial report?

c. Based on the Statement of Activities, did the Mud Hens have a good year in 2010? Comment.

d. Based on the Statement of Net Assets, does it appear that the Mud Hens were in good financial condition at December 31, 2010? Comment.

CASE 13-3 JEEP

DaimlerChrysler completed its first year of production of the Jeep Liberty in 2001. This production was in a new plant that cost $1.2 billion.

DaimlerChrysler was assisted in financing this new plant by the federal government, state government, the City of Toledo, and Lucas County. The county pledged $2 million by 2002 to help the City of Toledo acquire and improve the site for the new plant.

Required How would the county account for its $2 million expenditure?

Source: Jeep 2010 10-K

CASE 13-4 GOVERNOR LUCAS—THIS IS YOUR COUNTY

Lucas County, Ohio presented the following table in its comprehensive annual financial report for the fiscal year ended December 31, 2010:

Table 5
Lucas County, Ohio
Revenues by Source
Last Ten Fiscal Years
(Amounts in 000's)

Fiscal Year	General & Tangible Personal Property Tax[1]	Sales Tax	Lodging Tax	Investment Income	Charges for Services	Fines & Forfeitures	Licenses & Permits	Special Assessments	Intergovernmental Revenue	Other	Total
2001	$ 90,518	70,480	3,398	13,525	24,608	666	34	2,581	194,753	43,382	443,945
2002	$103,604	68,211	4,040	8,321	24,727	601	37	2,303	178,345	38,431	428,620
2003	$105,815	67,007	3,608	4,016	25,809	677	54	1,763	184,601	47,504	440,854
2004	$107,041	69,958	3,616	3,171	28,383	648	72	2,035	196,518	22,456	433,898
2005	$108,466	70,601	3,759	7,061	28,503	724	33	2,525	201,485	19,837	442,994
2006	$103,745	70,824	3,920	11,576	29,579	807	30	2,370	234,084	19,606	476,541
2007	$ 97,075	71,377	3,689	14,158	34,618	679	30	7,580	229,917	66,563	525,686
2008	$ 88,193	71,333	6,393	15,050	33,722	744	26	3,415	260,776	18,339	497,992
2009	$ 97,555	64,341	4,160	5,057	32,723	973	727	2,137	258,441	36,158	502,272
2010	$ 91,873	68,074	4,487	4,695	35,914	674	810	3,193	246,625	30,893	487,238

[1]General and tangible personal property taxes included rollbacks, homestead, and other revenues from the state of Ohio prior to 2007. These were reclassified as intergovernmental revenues beginning in 2007.

Note: For years 2001 – 2009, lodging tax has been reclassified out of general and tangible personal property tax.

Required

a. Complete a horizontal common-size analysis. Use the total column as the base.

b. Comment on the results of the horizontal common-size analysis.

c. Complete a vertical common-size analysis. Use 2001 as the base.

d. Comment on the results of the vertical common-size analysis.

CASE 13-5 COUNTY-WIDE

Lucas County, Ohio presented the following within its management's discussion and analysis with its comprehensive annual financial report for the fiscal year ended December 31, 2010. It was presented as part of the county-wide financial analysis.

Net Assets

	Governmental Activities 2010	Business-type Activities 2010	Governmental Activities 2009	Business-type Activities 2009	2010 Total	2009 Total
Assets:						
Current and other assets	$391,961,270	$ 18,153,258	$395,033,258	$ 17,278,558	$410,114,528	$412,311,816
Capital assets, net	319,262,002	108,502,158	318,307,304	106,456,627	427,764,160	424,763,931
Total assets	711,223,272	126,655,416	713,340,562	123,735,185	837,878,688	837,075,747
Liabilities:						
Current and other liabilities	162,688,647	3,418,957	252,857,094	1,105,366	166,107,604	253,962,480
Long-term liabilities	153,471,494	27,473,032	100,095,739	27,339,983	180,944,526	127,435.722
Total liabilities	316,160,141	30,891,989	352,952,833	28,445,349	347,052,130	381,398,182
Net Assets:						
Invested in capital assets, net of related debt	175,461,604	80,658,885	156,501,240	79,709,579	256,120,489	236,210,819
Restricted	173,835,725	—	162,435,877	—	173,836,725	162,435,877
Unrestricted	45,765,802	15,104,542	41,450,612	15,580,257	60,870,344	57,030,869
Total net assets	$395,063,131	$ 95,763,427	$360,387,729	$ 95,289,836	$490,826,568	$455,677,565

Source: Lucas County Auditor, comprehensive annual report for the fiscal year ended December 31, 2020, p. 16.

Required Prepare a descriptive county-wide financial analysis.

Source: Governor Lucas

TO THE NET CASE

1. Go to the GASB site (www.gasb.org). Click on "About GASB." Click on "Facts About GASB." Be prepared to discuss the following:
   a. What is the GASB?
   b. Why is the GASB's work important?
   c. How does the GASB set standards?
   d. How can one access GASB information and communications?

2. Go to the GASB site (http://www.gasb.org). Click on "About GASB." Click on "Strategic Plan." Click on "Summary of the Plan." Be prepared to discuss the following:
   a. Vision
   b. Mission
   c. Core values
   d. Goals

3. Go to the GASB site (www.gasb.org). Click on "About GASB." Click on "Rules of Procedure." Under the Mission of the Governmental Accounting Standards Board, be prepared to discuss the following:
   a. Mission statement
   b. Uses and users of governmental accounting and financial reporting
   c. How the mission is accomplished
   d. Guiding principles
   e. Due process

Endnotes

1. *Statement of Position 82-1*, "Accounting and Financial Reporting for Personal Financial Statements" (New York: American Institute of Certified Public Accountants, October 1982).

2. *Statement of Position 82-1*, p. 6.

3. A good article on this subject is Michael D. Kinsman and Bruce Samuelson, "Personal Financial Statements: Valuation Challenges and Solutions," *Journal of Accountancy* (September 1987), p. 138.

4. *Governmental Accounting Standards Board Statement No. 1* (July 1984), Appendix B, par. 4.

5. *Governmental Accounting, Auditing, and Financial Reporting* (Chicago: Municipal Finance Officers Association of the United States and Canada, 1968), p. 6.

6. *Governmental Accounting Standards Board Statement No. 34*, "Basic Financial Statements— Management's Discussion and Analysis—For State and Local Governments" (Governmental Accounting Standards Board, 1999), par. 8.

7. Ibid., par. 8.

8. Edward M. Klasny and James M. Williams, "Government Reporting Faces an Overhaul," *Journal of Accountancy* (January 2000), pp. 49–51.

9. Ibid., preface.

10. Ibid., preface.

11. Ibid., par. 107.

12. Walter Robbins and Paul Polinski, "Financial Reporting by Nonprofits," *National Public Accountant* (October 1995), p. 29.

13. *Statement of Financial Accounting Standards No. 93*, "Recognition of Depreciation by Not-for-Profit Organizations" (Stamford, CT: Financial Accounting Standards Board, 1987).

14. *Statement of Financial Accounting Standards No. 116*, "Accounting for Contributions Received and Contributions Made" (Norwalk, CT: Financial Accounting Standards Board, 1993).

15. *Statement of Financial Accounting Standards No. 117*, "Financial Statements of Not-for-Profit Organizations" (Norwalk, CT: Financial Accounting Standards Board, 1993).

16. *Statement of Financial Accounting Standards No. 124*, "Accounting for Certain Investments Held by Not-for-Profit Organizations" (Norwalk, CT: Financial Accounting Standards Board, 1995).

17. *Statement of Position 94-2*, "The Application of the Requirements of Accounting Research Bulletins, Opinions of the Accounting Principles Board and Statements of Interpretations of the Financial Accounting Standards Board to Not-for-Profit Organizations" (New York: American Institute of Certified Public Accountants, September 1994).

18. Charles H. Gibson, "Budgeting by Objectives: Charlotte's Experience," *Management Accounting* (January 1978), p. 39.

19. Ibid., pp. 39, 48.

Thomson ONE Basics and Tutorial

Thomson ONE is a web-based portal product that provides integrated access to Thomson Financial content for the purpose of financial analysis. As such, it delivers a broad range of financial content. The following Thomson ONE basics and tutorial are designed to help you learn how to use important features of this tool geared toward various types of financial analyses. While the product you are using is the Thomson ONE – Business School Edition, you are likely to use this or a similar program in your professional career.

Logging On to Thomson ONE

In Exhibit A-1, you see the welcome screen for Thomson ONE. You can log on to Thomson ONE at www.cengage.com/thomsonone. To do this for the first time, you will need to click on the "Register" button to register the access code from the access card packaged with your textbook. Once you have registered this code, you can create a username and password so that you will be able to return to the site for subsequent research sessions by hitting the "Enter" button.

EXHIBIT A-1

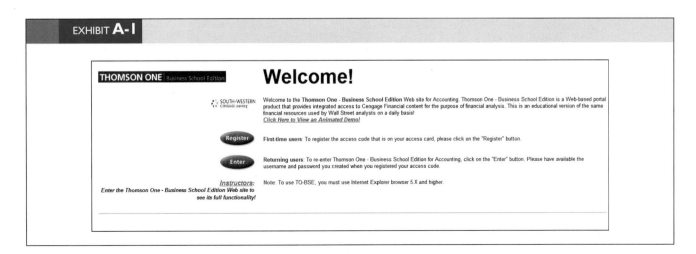

THOMSON ONE | Business School Edition

Welcome!

SOUTH-WESTERN CENGAGE Learning

Welcome to the **Thomson One - Business School Edition** Web site for Accounting. Thomson One - Business School Edition is a Web-based portal product that provides integrated access to Cengage Financial content for the purpose of financial analysis. This is an educational version of the same financial resources used by Wall Street analysts on a daily basis!
Click Here to View an Animated Demo!

Register

First-time users: To register the access code that is on your access card, please click on the "Register" button.

Enter

Returning users: To re-enter Thomson One - Business School Edition for Accounting, click on the "Enter" button. Please have available the username and password you created when you registered your access code.

Instructors:
Enter the Thomson One - Business School Edition Web site to see its full functionality!

Note: To use TO-BSE, you must use Internet Explorer browser 5.X and higher.

After Logging On

After logging on to Thomson ONE, you will see the screen shown in Exhibit A-2. If you click on "What companies can I access…," you will see a list of 500 companies and their ticker symbols available for access under this edition of the database. However, if you already know what company you are looking for and are ready to begin your financial analysis, then you would click the hyperlink that says: "Click Here to Access Thomson ONE – Business School Edition Now!"

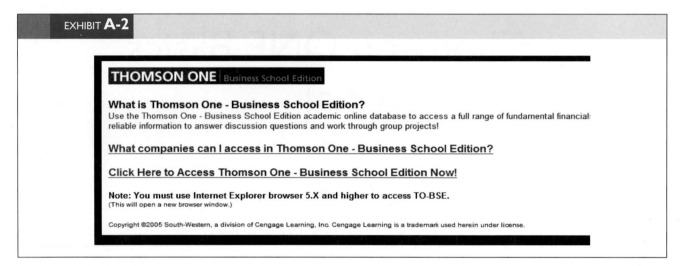
Company Search

Once Thomson ONE is accessed, on the upper left-hand side of your screen, you should see an input field for your company query, followed by a box that says "Portfolios" and a series of folders that will allow you to search for diverse types of financial information (Exhibit A-3). Let's begin our search with an overview about a company (the default mode for this database). To enter your company, you can either enter a ticker symbol (to look up the company) or the name of the company in the top box on the left.

EXHIBIT **A-3**

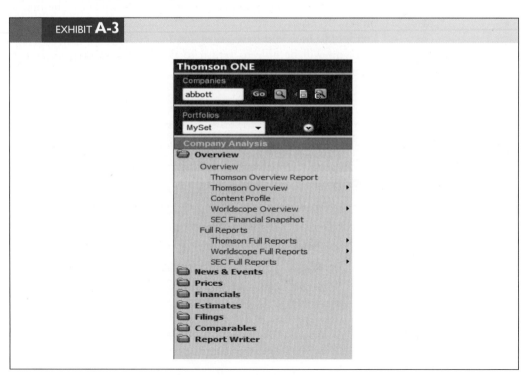

Let's say that you want to access information about Abbott Laboratories, Inc. in the USA. You can access this in a couple different ways:

1. Type "abbott" in the box and hit "Go," or
2. Type "abbott" in the box and do a Ticker Lookup using the magnifying glass icon.

At that point you will see a "Company Screening" page (Exhibit A-4).

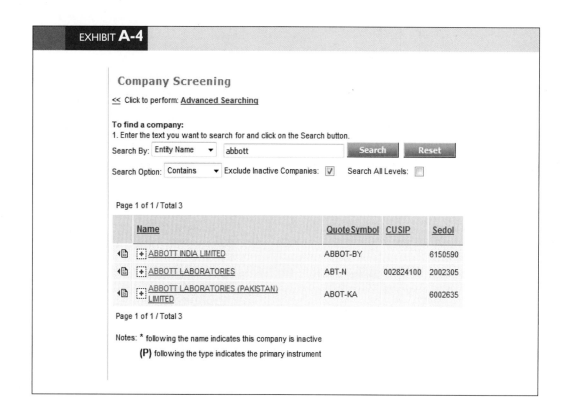

EXHIBIT **A-4**

This page pops up if there is *more than one* company listing that matches your query. In this case, you need to choose between:

- ABBOTT INDIA LIMITED,
- ABBOTT LABORATORIES in the USA, and
- ABBOTT LABORATORIES (PAKISTAN) LIMITED

before Thomson ONE will go to the Overview Report.

If there was only one company matching your query, then the Overview Report would pop up immediately.

Types of Information

When you select the **Company Analysis** mode and have a company identifier in the **Companies** text box, the **Company Overview** information page is displayed by default. In Exhibit A-5, notice that the main modes include: (1) Company Analysis, (2) Indices, (3) Comparables, (4) Screening and Targeting, and (5) Tools.

EXHIBIT **A-5**

Thomson ONE

Companies

ABT-N   Go

Portfolios

MySet

Company Analysis

📁 **Overview**
   Overview
      Thomson Overview Report
      Thomson Overview   ▶
      Content Profile
      Worldscope Overview   ▶
      SEC Financial Snapshot
   Full Reports
      Thomson Full Reports   ▶
      Worldscope Full Reports ▶
      SEC Full Reports   ▶
📁 **News & Events**
📁 **Prices**
📁 **Financials**
📁 **Estimates**
📁 **Filings**
📁 **Comparables**
📁 **Report Writer**

Indices

Comparables

Screening & Targeting

Tools

For most accounting courses, your research will probably come from the Company Analysis mode, which is the focus of this tutorial. Within Company Analysis, there are 8 folders. Many of these folders have sub-menu options and are summarized below.

The first folder, **"Overview,"** includes the following information:

- Address and website of the company,
- A Business Description Summary,
- Industry, Sector, and Stock Exchange,
- The three most recent years of key financials,
- Earnings Per Share (EPS) Forecasts, and
- Key Executives and links to compensation and members of Board Committees and Directors.

The second folder, **"News & Events,"** includes news items that are fed into Thomson ONE every 20 minutes. The split screen view shows relevant news for the company being researched in terms of both the:

- Top market news stories and links (in one frame) and
- Global news coverage (in the other frame).

The third folder, **"Prices,"** focuses on detailed stock quotes, performance overviews, price history reports, & interactive charts.

The fourth folder, "**Financials**," provides a wide variety of financial statements, financial ratios, and comparative financials charts. As you go through the sub-menu options you will notice that financial statements and ratios are drawn from several sources including: Worldscope, Thomson Financials, and the SEC. In addition, this folder has many options that allow users to download PDF and Excel formats of data, as well as printable reports. There are also a variety of options to facilitate comparability. These include the CURRENCY option shown by the $\$$ icon and the SCALE option shown by the ⚖ icon at the top of the open window. The CURRENCY option allows users to recast the financial statements in various currencies, including U.S. dollars, British Pounds, Euros, Japanese yen, and more. The SCALE option allows users to recast financial statement in terms of thousands, millions, and billions.

As you will find in your research, the definition of financial ratios may vary. However, Thomson ONE provides a wealth of information about the definition of financial ratios, defined for the various Thomson ONE sources and for various industries.

As an example, let's look at Abbott Laboratories again. You are interested in the company's return on total assets, so you first open Financials> Financial Ratios> SEC Ratios> Annual Ratios. You find Net Income/Total Assets is equal to 0.12% for 12/31/08. To make sure that it is calculated the way you understand it, you can double-click on the amount and a new window pops up to show the definition. According to this:

> The SEC Item Name: **NET INCOME TO TOTAL ASSETS** is calculated as:
> = Net Income/Total Assets
> This Profitability ratio assesses the profitability of a business in relation to its assets at a given point in time. Generally, the higher the return on assets, the more skillfully management is using its resources.

As you continue your research, you are interested in what the other sources show for this ratio. Are they the same or is there some type of adjustment that might help you in your analysis? If you open Financials> Financial Ratios> Thomson Ratios> Annual Ratios, you see that the first Profitability Ratio is Return on Assets. Is that the same as the SEC ratio? When you look at the amount for 12/31/08, the number is dramatically different. How did they calculate it? Just like before, you would double-click on the amount, which is 13.22, and a new window pops up to show that the definition is much different and varies with industries:

> **Definition:** Worldscope Item Name: **RETURN ON ASSETS**; Profitability Ratio, Annual/Interim Item; Field 08326
>
> For Industrial Companies Annual Time Series, the ratio is computed as:
> (**Net Income before Preferred Dividends** + ((**Interest Expense on Debt-Interest Capitalized**) * (1−**Tax Rate**))) / **Last Year's Total Assets** * 100
>
> For Banks, the ratio is computed as:
> **Net Income before Preferred Dividends** + ((**Interest Expense on Debt-Interest Capitalized**) * (1−**Tax Rate**))) / (**Last Year's Total Assets** − **Last Year's Customer Liabilities on Acceptances**) * 100. (Customer Liabilities on Acceptances only subtracted when included in Total Assets.)
>
> For Insurance Companies, the ratio is computed as:
> (**Net Income before Preferred Dividends** + ((**Interest Expense on Debt-Interest Capitalized**) *(1−**Tax Rate**))) + **Policyholders' Surplus**) / **Last Year's Total Assets** * 100
>
> For Other Financial Companies, the ratio is computed as:
> (**Net Income before Preferred Dividends** + ((**Interest Expense on Debt-Interest Capitalized**) * (1−**Tax Rate**))) / (**Last Year's Total Assets** − **Last Year's Custody Securities**) * 100
>
> There are some *exceptions* noted for U.S. Companies due to the Standard Tax Rate Used in Calculations: In 1986 and prior years: 46% tax rate; In 1987 to 1994: 34% tax rate; In 1995 and subsequent years: 35% tax rate

For All Industries Interim Time Series:
$$((\text{Trailing 12 Months Net Profit} + (\text{Trailing 12 Months Interest Expense On Debt} *$$
$$(1 - \text{Tax Rate}/100)))) / \text{Last Year's Total Assets} * 100$$

The fifth folder under Company Analysis is "**Estimates.**" This folder includes information about:

- Yearly and quarterly Earnings Per Share data,
- Price Earnings ratios, and
- Broker recommendations about the company's stock.

The sixth folder, "**Filings,**" maintains downloadable SEC filings for the company. These include PDF, Microsoft Word, and html formats.

The seventh folder is the "**Comparables**" folder. As you experiment with Thomson ONE, you will find that there are many types of comparative reports that may be of interest to you in your research. In particular, the "Comparables" setting can be activated to allow users to display key financial data for the **peers** or competitors for the company selected. Once your company is opened in Overview, go to Comparables and select peers according to SIC Code, industry, sectors, etc. This peer group listing will appear in a separate window on the left of the screen, as well as be noted as a portfolio option (see Exhibit A-6).

Notice that the Portfolio option provides a way to build a number of sets of companies for comparison purposes and creates reports on items such as: profitability, performance, liquidity analysis, etc. Both default and custom peer sets can be saved to your Portfolio User Folder. For example, if we wanted to create a working portfolio of just Abbott Laboratories, Bayer AG, and ELI Lilly & Company, we would select each company's box on the far left and then click on the "New" button (just above the check boxes). This would create our new working portfolio, which would be listed in the drop-down Portfolios choices.

Finally, the eighth folder under Company Analysis is "**Report Writer.**" This tool allows users to prepare customized reports for a single company or tabular format reports that can include multiple companies.

Conclusion

While this has been a quick look at Thomson ONE, be sure to take advantage of all the hyperlinks and pull-down menus that the database offers but may not have been mentioned. By leveraging the easy-to-use technology and spreadsheet formatting of this one-stop database, you will be able to save time by drilling down and mastering the concepts explained in your text, as well as advancing your understanding of financial accounting, SEC filings, and market research.

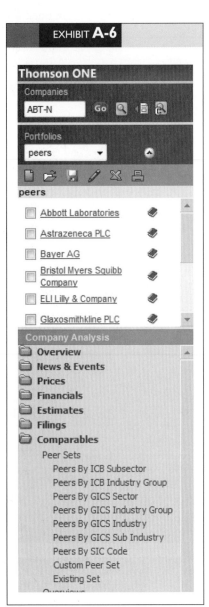

EXHIBIT **A-6**

Glossary

Many of the terms in this glossary are explained in the text. Terms not explained in the text are included because they represent terms frequently found in annual reports and the financial literature.

A

Accelerated Cost Recovery System (ACRS): Depreciation method introduced for tax purposes in 1981 and subsequently modified. *See* Modified Accelerated Cost Recovery System (MACRS).

Accelerated depreciation: Any depreciation method in which the charges in earlier periods exceed those in later periods.

Account: A record used to classify and summarize transactions.

Accountant: One who performs accounting services.

Account form of balance sheet: A balance sheet that presents assets on the left-hand side and liabilities and owners' equity on the right-hand side.

Accounting: The systematic process of measuring the economic activity of an entity to provide useful information to those who make business and economic decisions.

Accounting changes: A term used to describe the use of a different accounting principle, estimate, or reporting entity than used in a prior year.

Accounting controls: Procedures concerned with safeguarding the assets or the reliability of the financial statements.

Accounting cycle: A series of steps used for analyzing, recording, classifying, and summarizing transactions.

Accounting equation: Assets = Liabilities + Owners' Equity.

Accounting errors: Mistakes resulting from mathematical errors, improper application of accounting principles, or omissions of material facts.

Accounting period: The time to which an accounting report is related. The time is usually annual, quarterly, or monthly.

Accounting policies: The accounting principles and practices adopted by a company to report its financial results.

Accounting Principles Board (APB): A board established by the AICPA that issued opinions establishing accounting standards during the period 1959–1973.

Accounting process: The procedures used for analyzing, recording, classifying, and summarizing the information to be presented in accounting reports.

Accounting Research Bulletins (ARBs): Publications of the Committee on Accounting Procedure of the AICPA that established accounting standards during the years 1939–1959.

Accounting system: The procedures and methods used to collect and report accounting data.

Accounts payable: Amounts owed for inventory, goods, or services acquired in the normal course of business.

Accounts receivable (trade receivables): Monies due on accounts from customers arising from sales or services rendered.

Accounts receivable aging: A procedure that uses an aging schedule to determine the year-end balance needed in the allowance for uncollectible accounts.

Accounts receivable factoring: The sale of receivables without recourse for cash to a third party.

Accrual basis: The accrual basis of accounting dictates that revenue is recognized when realized (realization concept) and expenses are recognized when incurred (matching concept).

Accrued expenses: Expenses incurred but not recognized in the accounts.

Accrued liability: A liability resulting from the recognition of an expense before the payment of cash.

Accrued pension cost: The difference between the amount of pension recorded as an expense and the amount of the funding payment.

Accrued revenues: Revenues for services performed or for goods delivered that have not been recorded.

Accumulated benefit obligation (ABO): The present value of pension benefits earned to date based on employee service and compensations to that date.

Accumulated depreciation: Depreciation allocates the cost of buildings and machinery over the periods of benefits. The depreciation expense taken each period accumulates in the Accumulated Depreciation account.

Accumulated other comprehensive income: This is reported in the stockholders' equity. Other comprehensive income (loss) might include four items:
- Unrealized increases (gains) or decreases (losses) in the fair value of investments in available-for-sale securities
- Translation adjustments from converting the financial statements of a company's foreign operations into U.S. dollars
- Certain gains and losses on "derivative" financial instruments
- Certain pension plan gains, losses, and prior service cost adjustments

Accumulated postretirement benefit obligation (APBO): The present value of postretirement benefits earned to date based on employee service to that date.

Acquisition: A business combination in which one corporation acquires control over the operations of another entity.

Acquisition cost: The amount that includes all of the cost normally necessary to acquire an asset and prepare it for its intended use.

Acquisitions: Companies that have been acquired.

Actuarial assumptions: Assumptions about future events based on historic data such as employee turnover, service lives, and longevity that are used to estimate future costs such as pension benefits.

Actuarial present value: The present value of pension obligations determined by using stated actuarial assumptions and estimates.

Additional paid-in capital: The investment by stockholders in excess of the stocks' par or stated value as well as invested capital from other sources, such as donations of property or sale of treasury stock.

Additions: Enlargements and extensions of existing facilities.

Adjusting entries: Entries made at the end of each accounting period to update the accounts.

Administrative controls: Procedures concerned with efficient operation of the business and adherence to managerial policies.

Administrative expense: Expense that results from the general administration of the company's operation.

Adverse opinion: An audit opinion issued whenever financial statements contain departures from GAAP that are too material to warrant only a qualification. This opinion states that the financial statements do not present fairly the financial position, results of operations, or cash flows of the entity in conformity with GAAP.

Aging of accounts receivables: A method of reviewing for uncollectible trade receivables by which an estimate of the bad debts expense is determined. The receivable balances are classified into age categories, and then an estimate of noncollection is applied.

Aging schedule: A form used to categorize the various individual accounts receivable according to the length of time each has been outstanding.

AICPA: *See* American Institute of Certified Public Accountants.

Allowance for funds used during construction (AFUDC): The recording of AFUDC is a utility accounting practice prescribed by the state utility commission. It represents the estimated debt and equity costs of financing construction work in progress. AFUDC does not represent a current source of cash, but under regulatory rate practices, a return on and recovery of AFUDC is permitted in determining rates charged for utility services. Some utilities report the estimated debt and equity costs of financing construction work in progress in separate accounts.

Allowance for uncollectible accounts: A contra accounts receivable account showing an estimate of the accounts receivable that will not be collected.

Allowance method: A method of estimating bad debts on the basis of either the net credit sales of the period or the accounts receivable at the end of the period.

American Accounting Association (AAA): An organization of accounting professors and practicing accountants (http://aaahq.org).

American Institute of Certified Public Accountants (AICPA): The national professional organization for certified public accountants (www.aicpa.org).

Amortization: The periodic allocation of the cost of an intangible asset over its useful life.

Analyze: To evaluate the condition of an accounting-related item and possible reasons for discrepancies.

Annualize: To extend an item to an annual basis.

Annual report: A formal presentation containing financial statements and other important information prepared by the management of a corporation once a year.

Annuity: A series of equal payments (receipts) over a specified number of equal time periods.

Antidilution of earnings: Assumed conversion of convertible securities or exercise of stock options that results in an increase in earnings per share or a decrease in loss per share.

Antidilutive securities: Securities whose assumed conversion or exercise results in an increase in earnings per share or a decrease in loss per share.

Appreciation: An increase in the value of an asset.

Appropriated retained earnings: A restriction of retained earnings that indicates that a portion of a company's assets are to be used for purposes other than paying dividends.

Appropriations (government accounting): Budget authorizations of expenditures.

Arm's-length transaction: Transactions that are conducted by independent parties, each acting in its own self-interest.

Asset impairment: Condition in which a resource's expected future cash flow is less than its reported book value. The income statement reports losses on impaired assets.

Assets: Probable future economic benefits obtained or controlled by a particular entity as a result of past transactions or events.

Assignment of receivables: The borrowing of money with receivables pledged as security.

Attestation: Any service performed by a CPA resulting in a written communication that expresses a conclusion about the reliability of a written assertion.

Audit committee: A committee of the board of directors comprised mainly of outside directors having no management ties to the organization.

Audit report: The mechanism for communicating the results of an audit.

Auditing: A systematic process of objectively obtaining and evaluating evidence regarding assertions and communicating the results to interested users.

Auditor: A person who conducts an audit.

Authorized stock: The maximum number of shares a corporation may issue without changing its charter with the state.

Available-for-sale securities: Stocks and bonds that are not classified as either held-to-maturity or trading securities.

Average cost method (inventory): Averaging methods that lump the costs of inventory to determine an average.

B

Bad debt: An account or note receivable that proves to be entirely or partially uncollectible.

Bad debt expense: An account on the income statement representing estimated uncollectible credit sales for the current accounting period.

Bad debt recovery: Represents an account receivable previously written off as uncollectible and is now collected.

Balance: Sum of debit entries minus the sum of credit entries in an account.

Balance sheet (classified): A form that segregates the assets and liabilities between current and noncurrent.

Balance sheet (financial position form): A form that deducts current liabilities from current assets to show working capital. The form adds remaining assets and deducts the remaining liabilities to derive the residual stockholders' equity.

Balance sheet (statement of financial position): The financial statement that shows the financial position of an accounting entity as of a specific date. The balance sheet lists assets, the resources of the firm; liabilities, the debts of the firm; and stockholders' equity, the owners' interest in the firm.

Balance sheet (unclassified): A form that does not segregate the assets and liabilities between current and noncurrent.

Balancing equation: Assets = Liabilities + Stockholders' Equity.

Bankruptcy protection: Legal arrangement in which creditor claims are suspended while a court-appointed trustee reorganizes the bankrupt firm.

Bargain purchase option: Provision granting the lessee the right, but not the obligation, to purchase leased property at a price that, at the inception date, is sufficiently below the expected fair value of the property at exercise date to provide reasonable assurance of exercise.

Bargain renewal option: Provision granting the lessee the right, but not the obligation, to renew the lease at a rental that, at inception, is sufficiently below the expected fair rental at exercise date to provide reasonable assurance of renewal.

Basic earnings per share: The amount of earnings for the period available to each share of common stock outstanding during the reporting period.

Basis: A figure or value that is the starting point in computing gain or loss.

Bearer (coupon) bonds: Bonds whose ownership is determined by possession and for which interest is paid to the holder (bearer) of an interest coupon.

Benchmark: In the content of outcomes and performance discussion, the term refers to desired program results. It may include a target or standard for the program to achieve. It is also used to denote best practices.

BestCalls.com: This site has live broadcasts and recordings of earnings announcements and management interviews (www .bestcalls.com).

Big bath: The concept that a company expecting to have a series of hits to earnings in future years is better off to try to recognize all of the bad news in one year, leaving future years unencumbered by continuing losses.

Blue sky laws: State laws that regulate the issuance of securities.

Board of directors: A body of individuals who are elected by the stockholders to be their representatives in managing the company.

Bond: A security, usually long-term, representing money borrowed by a corporation. Normally issued with $1,000 face value.

Bond discount: The difference between the face value and the sales price when bonds are sold below their face value.

Bond indenture: The contract between the issuing entity and the bondholders specifying the terms, rights, and obligations of the contracting parties.

Bond issue price: The present value of the annuity interest payments plus the present value of the principal.

Bond premium: The difference between the face value and the sales price when bonds are sold above their face value.

Bond refinancing: Issuing new bonds to replace outstanding bonds either at maturity or prior to maturity.

Bond sinking fund: A fund established by the segregation of assets over the life of the bond issue to pay the bondholders at maturity.

Bonds (serial): A bond issue that matures in installments.

Book value: The original cost of an asset less any accumulated depreciation (depletion or amortization) taken to date.

Book value per share: The dollar amount of the net assets of a company per share of common stock.

Bottom line: The financial vernacular for net income.

Budget: A quantitative plan of activities and programs expressed in terms of assets, liabilities, revenues, and expenses.

Buildings: A structure used in a business operation.

Business combination: One or more businesses that are merged together as one accounting entity.

Business entity: The viewpoint that the business (or entity) for which the financial statements are prepared is separate and distinct from the owners of the entity.

Business (source) document: Business record used as the basis for analyzing and recording transactions; examples include invoices, check stubs, receipts, and similar business papers.

C

Calendar year: The accounting year that ends on December 31.

Call loan (demand loan): Loan repayable on demand.

Callable bonds: Bonds that a corporation has the option of buying back and retiring at a given price before maturity.

Callable obligation: A debt instrument payable on demand of the company that issued the obligation.

Callable preferred stock: Preferred stock that may be redeemed and retired by the corporation at its option.

Capital: Owners' equity in an unincorporated firm.

Capital expenditures: Costs that increase the future economic benefits of an asset above those originally expected.

Capital lease: Long-term lease in which the risk of ownership lies with the lessee and whose terms resemble a purchase or sale; recorded as an asset with a corresponding liability at the present value of the lease payments.

Capital stock: The portion of the contribution by stockholders assignable to the shares of stock as par or stated value.

Capital structure: Amount, types, and proportion of an entity's liabilities and shareholders' equity.

Capitalization: The process of assigning value to a balance sheet account (asset or liability).

Capitalized interest: Interest added to the cost of a fixed asset instead of being expensed.

Carrying value: The face of a bond plus the amount of unamortized premium or minus the amount of unamortized discount.

Cash: The most liquid asset that includes negotiable checks, unrestricted balances in checking accounts, and cash on hand.

Cash basis accounting: A system of accounting that records revenues when received and expenses when paid.

Cash dividend: The payment (receipt) of a dividend in cash.

Cash equivalents: A company's highly liquid short-term investments considered to be cash equivalents and usually classified with cash on the balance sheet.

Cash flows from financing activities: Cash flows relating to liability and owners' equity accounts.

Cash flows from investing activities: Cash flows relating to lending money and to acquiring and selling investments and productive long-term assets.

Cash flows from operating activities: Generally, the cash effects of transactions and other events that determine net income.

Cash (sales) discount: A reduction in sales price allowed if payment is received within a specified period, usually offered to customers to encourage prompt payment.

Cash surrender value: The investment portion of a life insurance policy, payable to the policyholder if the policyholder cancels the policy.

Certified internal auditor (CIA): Internal auditor who has satisfied the examination requirements of the Institute of Internal Auditors.

Certified management accountant (CMA): An accountant who has met the admission criteria and demonstrated the competency of technical knowledge in management accounting required by the Institute of Management Accountants.

Certified public accountant (CPA): An accountant who has received a certificate stating that he or she has met the requirements of state law.

Change in an accounting estimate: A change in the estimation of the effects of future events.

Change in an accounting principle: Adoption of a generally accepted accounting principle different from the one used previously for reporting purposes.

Change in reporting entity: An accounting change that reflects financial statements for a different unit of accountability.

Chart of accounts: A listing of all accounts used by a company.

Chief accountant of the SEC: An appointed official of the Securities and Exchange Commission.

Chief financial officer (CFO): Executive responsible for overseeing the financial operations of an organization.

Classified balance sheet: A balance sheet that segregates the assets and liabilities as current and noncurrent.

Closing entries: Temporary account balances that are transferred to the permanent stockholders' equity account, Retained Earnings.

Collateral: Security for loans or other forms of indebtedness.

Commercial paper: Short-term obligations or promissory notes, unsecured, interest bearing, with flexible maturities.

Commitment fee: A fee for committing to holding a credit facility available over a period of time to a borrower.

Common-size analysis (horizontal): Common-size analysis expresses comparisons in percentages. Horizontal analysis indicates proportionate change over a period of time.

Common-size analysis (vertical): Common-size analysis expresses comparisons in percentages. Vertical analysis indicates the proportionate expression of each item in a given period to a base figure selected from that same period.

Common stock (capital stock): The stock representing the most basic rights to ownership of a corporation.

Common stock equivalent shares: A security that is not in the form of a common stock but that contains provisions that enable its holder to acquire common stock.

Comparability: For accounting information, the quality that allows a user to analyze two or more companies and look for similarities and differences.

Comparative statements: Financial statements for two or more periods.

Compensated absences: Payments to employees for vacation, holiday, illness, or other personal activities.

Compensating balance requirements: Provisions in loan agreements requiring the borrower to maintain minimum cash balances with the lending institution.

Compensatory option plans: Stock option plans offered to a select group of employees.

Compilation: A professional service in which the CPA presents information that is the representation of management without undertaking to express any assurance on the statements.

Completed-contract method: A method that recognizes revenues on long-term construction contracts only when the contract is completed.

Complex capital structure: Capital structure that has potentially dilutive securities such as convertible debt, preferred stock, and options.

Composite depreciation: A depreciation method that aggregates dissimilar assets and computes depreciation for the aggregation based on a weighted average life expectancy.

Compound interest: The process of earning interest on interest from previous periods.

Comprehensive income: Net income plus the period's change in accumulated other comprehensive income (accumulated other comprehensive income is a category within stockholders' equity).

Conglomerates: Complex companies that operate in multiple industries.

Conservatism: The concept that directs that the measurement with the least favorable effect on net income and financial position in the current period be selected.

Conservative analysis: This perspective represents a relatively strict interpretation of the value of assets and what constitutes debt.

Consigned goods: Inventory physically located at a dealer but another company retains title until the consignee sells the inventory.

Consignment: A transfer of property without a transfer of title and risk of ownership. The recipient of the property (consignee) acts as a selling agent on behalf of the owner (consignor).

Consistency: The concept requiring the entity to give the same treatment to comparable transactions from period to period.

Consolidated financial statements: The combined financial statements of a parent company and its subsidiary.

Constant dollar accounting (price-level accounting): The method of reporting financial statement elements in dollars having similar purchasing power. Constant dollar accounting measures general changes in prices of goods and services.

Construction-in-process: Fixed asset account in which construction costs are recorded until construction is completed.

Contingencies: Conditions that may result in gains and losses and that will be resolved by the occurrence of future events.

Contingent asset: An asset that may arise in the future if certain events occur.

Contingent liabilities: Liabilities whose payment is dependent on a particular occurrence such as settlement of litigation or a ruling of a tax court.

Continuing operations: Operations expected to remain active.

Contra account: An account used to offset a primary account in order to show a net valuation, for example, Accounts Receivable (primary account) less Allowance for Doubtful Accounts (contra account).

Contributed capital: The sum of the capital stock accounts and the capital in excess of par (or stated) value accounts.

Contributory pension plan: A pension plan in which employees make contributions to the plan and thus bear part of the cost.

Control account: The general ledger account that is supported by a subsidiary ledger.

Controller: The chief accounting officer for a company. This individual usually reports to the chief financial officer (CFO).

Convertible bonds: Bonds that may be exchanged for other securities of the corporation, usually common stock.

Convertible preferred stock: Preferred stock that can be converted into common stock.

Convertible securities: Securities whose terms permit the holder to convert the investment into common stock of the issuing companies.

Copyright: An exclusive right granted by the federal government to publish and sell literary, musical, and other artistic materials.

Corporate officers: Senior executive managers of the company identified by title and name.

Corporation: A separate legal entity having its own rights, privileges, and liabilities distinct from those of its owners.

COSO: Refers to the Committee of Sponsoring Organizations of the Treadway Commission.

Cost accounting: Determines product costs and other relevant information used.

Cost/benefit: The process of determining that the benefit of an act or series of acts exceeds the cost of performing the act(s).

Cost of goods manufactured: The total cost of goods completed in the manufacturing process during an accounting period.

Cost of goods sold: Cost of goods available for sale minus ending inventory.

Cost of goods sold or cost of sales: The cost of goods sold during an accounting period.

Cost principle: The accounting principle that records historical cost as the appropriate basis of initial accounting recognition of all acquisitions, liabilities, and owners' equity.

Cost recovery: A revenue recognition method that requires recovery of the total cost prior to the recognition of revenue.

Coupon rate: The stated interest rate in a bond contract. Also referred to as the nominal, stated, or face rate.

Covenants: Conditions placed in a loan or credit agreement by the lender to protect its position as a creditor of the borrowing.

Credit: An entry on the right side of an account.

Credit agreement: A contractual arrangement between a lender and a borrower that sets the terms and conditions for borrowing.

Credit ratings: Formal credit risk evaluations by credit rating agencies of a company's ability to repay principal and interest on its debt obligations.

Credit risk: Uncertainty that the party on the other side of an agreement will abide by the terms of the agreement.

Creditor: A party who lends money to a company.

Cumulative effect of change in accounting principle: The effect that a new accounting principle would have had on net income of prior periods if it had been used instead of the old principle.

Cumulative preferred stock: Preferred stock on which unpaid dividends accumulate over time and must be satisfied in any given year before a dividend may be paid to common stockholders.

Currency swap: An exchange of two currencies as part of an agreement to reverse the exchange on a specific future date.

Current assets: Current assets are assets (1) in the form of cash, (2) that will normally be realized in cash, or (3) that conserve the use of cash during the operating cycle of a firm or for one year, whichever is longer.

Current cost: The current replacement cost of the same asset owned, adjusted for the value of any operating advantages or disadvantages.

Current liabilities: Obligations whose liquidation is reasonably expected to require the use of existing resources properly classifiable as current assets or the creation of other current liabilities.

Current market value: The amount of cash, or its equivalent, that could be obtained by selling an asset in an orderly liquidation.

Current maturity of long-term debt: The portion of a long-term debt payable within the next operating cycle or one year, whichever is longer.

Current replacement cost: The estimated cost of acquiring the best asset available to undertake the function of the asset owned.

Current value: The amount of cash, or its equivalent, that could be received by selling an asset currently.

D

Debenture bonds: Bonds issued on the general credit of a company.

Debit: An entry on the left side of an account.

Debt: Considered to be funds a company has borrowed from a creditor.

Debt securities: Investments in debt instruments such as commercial paper or bonds.

Debt service: A term used by bankers, which refers to a borrower's requirement to make payment of the current maturities on outstanding debt.

Decentralization: The freedom for managers at lower levels of an organization to make decisions.

Decision usefulness: The overriding quality or characteristic of accounting information.

Declining-balance method: The declining-balance method applies double the straight-line depreciation rate times the declining book value (cost minus accumulated depreciation) to achieve a declining depreciation charge over the estimated life of the asset.

Default: A failure of a debtor to meet principal or interest payment on a debt at the due date.

Default risk: The probability that a company will be unable to meet its obligations.

Defeasance: A method of early retirement of debt in which risk-free securities are purchased and then placed in a trust account to be used to retire the outstanding debt at its maturity.

Deferral: Postponement of the recognition of an expense already paid or of a revenue already received.

Deferred charge: A long-term expense prepayment amortized to expense.

Deferred expense: An asset resulting from the payment of cash before the incurrence of expense.

Deferred financing costs, net: An asset account usually classified under other assets; costs associated with the issuance of long-term bonds that have not been amortized.

Deferred revenue: A liability resulting from the receipt of cash before the recognition of revenue.

Deferred taxes: A balance sheet account; classified as an asset or a liability depending on the nature of the timing differences. The differences are the result of any situation that recognizes revenue or expense in a different time period for tax purposes than for the financial statements.

Deficiency: An additional tax liability that the IRS deems to be owed by a taxpayer.

Deficit: A negative (debit) balance in retained earnings.

Defined benefit pension plan: A pension plan that defines the benefits that employees will receive at retirement.

Defined contribution pension plan: A pension plan that specifies the employer's contributions and bases benefits solely on the amount contributed.

Deflation: A general decrease in prices.

Demand loan (call loan): Loan repayable on demand.

Depletion: Recognition of the wearing away or using up of a natural resource.

Depreciable cost: The cost of a fixed asset less salvage value.

Depreciation expense: The process of allocating the cost of buildings, machinery, and equipment over the periods benefited.

Derivative: A financial instrument derived from some other asset, event, or value.

Derivative instruments: Financial instruments or other contracts in which rights or obligations meet the definitions of assets or liabilities.

Devaluation: A downward adjustment of the exchange rate between two currencies.

Diluted earnings per share: The amount of earnings for the period available to each share of common stock outstanding during the reporting period and to each share that would have been outstanding assuming the issuance of common shares for all dilutive potential common shares outstanding during the reporting period.

Dilution: Refers to the effect on earnings calculations when the number of shares issued increases disproportionately to the growth in the earnings.

Direct financing type lease: A capital lease in which the lessor receives income only from financing the "purchase" of the leased asset.

Direct method: For preparing the operating activities section of the statement of cash flows, the approach in which cash receipts and cash payments are reported.

Direct write-off method: A method of recognizing specific accounts receivable determined to be uncollectible.

Disbursement: A payment by cash or check.

Disclaimer of opinion: Inability to render an audit opinion because of lack of sufficient evidence or lack of independence.

Discontinued operations: The disposal of a major segment of a business.

Discount on bonds: A bond is issued below its face amount, indicating that the coupon rate is lower than the market rate for similar bonds.

Discount on notes payable: A contra liability that represents interest deducted from a loan in advance.

Discount rate: The interest rate used to compute the present value.

Discounted cash flow (DCF): Measures all expected future cash inflows and outflows as if they occurred at a single point in time.

Discounted note: A non–interest-bearing note for which the interest charge has been deducted from the principal in advance.

Discounting: The process of selling a promissory note.

Discussion memorandum (DM): A document issued by the FASB that identifies the principal issues involved with financial accounting and reporting topics. It includes a discussion of the various points of view as to the resolution of issues but does not reach a specific conclusion.

Dissolution: Termination of a business.

Divestitures: Companies that have been disposed of.

Dividends (cash): Cash payment from current or past income to the owners of a corporation.

Dividends in arrears: The accumulated unpaid dividends from prior years on cumulative preferred stock.

Dividends payable: A current liability on the balance sheet resulting from the declaration of dividends by the board of directors.

Dividends (stock): A percentage of outstanding stock issued as new shares to existing shareholders.

Dollar-value LIFO: An adaptation of LIFO that measures inventory by total dollar amount rather than by individual units. LIFO increment layers are determined based on total dollar changes.

Domestic corporation: A company established under U.S. or state law.

Donated assets: Receipt of assets without being required to give goods or services in return.

Donated capital: Assets donated to the company by stockholders, creditors, or other parties.

Double-declining-balance depreciation: A method of calculating depreciation by which a percentage equal to twice the straight-line percentage is multiplied by the declining book value to determine the depreciation expense for the period (salvage value is ignored when calculating).

Double-entry accounting: A system of recording transactions in a way that maintains the equality of the equation: Assets = Liabilities + Stockholders' Equity.

Dry holes: Wells drilled in which commercial quantities of oil or gas are not found.

E

Early extinguishment of debt: The retirement of debt prior to the maturity date.

Earnings: A term used interchangeably with income and profit.

Earnings management: The ability of a company's management to select, or "manipulate," its profits.

Earnings per share: A company's bottom line stated on a per share basis.

Earnings smoothing: Provides an earnings stream with less variability.

Economic substance: The "real" nature of a transaction, as opposed to its legal form.

EDGAR system: The SEC's electronic data-gathering analysis and retrieval system.

Effective rate of interest: The yield or true rate of interest.

Effective tax rate: Income taxes expressed as a percentage (income taxes vs. net income before taxes).

Efficient market hypothesis: A theory to explain the functioning of capital markets in which share prices reflect all publicly available information.

Emerging Issues Task Force (EITF): A task force of representatives from the accounting profession created by the FASB to deal with emerging issues of financial reporting.

Employee Retirement Income Security Act (ERISA): A legislative act passed by Congress in 1974 that made significant changes in requirements for employer pension plans. This act has been amended several times since 1974.

Employee stock ownership plans (ESOPs): A qualified stock-bonus, or combination stock-bonus and money purchase, pension plan designed to invest primarily in the employer's securities.

Enterprise funds (governmental accounting): Funds used to report any activity for which a fee is charged to external users for goods or services.

Entity assumption: Accounting records are kept for the business entity as distinct from the entity's owners.

Equipment: Assets used in the production of goods or in providing services.

Equity: The residual interest in the assets of an entity that remains after deducting its liabilities. Synonymous with the expression *shareholders' equity*.

Equity in earnings of nonconsolidated subsidiaries: When a firm has investments in stocks, uses the equity method of accounting, and the investment is not consolidated, then the investor firm reports equity earnings (the proportionate share of the earnings of the investee).

Equity method: A method to value intercorporate equity investments by adjusting the investor's cost basis for the percentage ownership in the investee's earnings (or losses) and for any dividends paid by the investee.

Equity-oriented deferred compensation: The amount of compensation cost deferred and amortized to future periods as the services are provided.

Equity securities: Securities issued by corporations as a form of ownership in the business.

ERISA: The acronym for the Employee Retirement Income Security Act of 1974.

Escrow: Money on property put into the custody of a third party for delivery to a grantee after fulfillment of specified conditions.

Estimated economic life of leased property: The useful life of leased property estimated at inception under conditions of normal maintenance and repairs.

Estimated liability: An obligation of the entity whose exact amount cannot be determined until a later date.

Estimated residual value of leased property: The expected fair or market value of leased property at the end of the lease term.

Estimated useful life: The period of time that a company establishes in order to depreciate a fixed asset.

Ethics: A set of principles referring to ideals of character and conduct.

Event: A happening of consequence to an entity.

Exchange rate: The rate at which one unit of currency may be purchased by another unit of currency.

Executory costs: Insurance, maintenance, and local and property taxes on leased property.

Expectations gap: The disparity between users' and CPAs' perceptions of professional services, especially audit services.

Expenses: Outflows or uses of assets or incurrences of liabilities (or a combination of both) during the process of an entity's revenue-generating operations.

Exposure draft (ED): A proposed Statement of Financial Accounting Standards.

External expansion: Occurs as firms take over, or merge with, other existing firms.

Extinguishment of debt: Get rid of a liability.

Extraordinary items: Material events and transactions distinguished by their unusual nature and infrequent occurrence.

F

Face amount, maturity value: The amount that will be paid on a bond (note) at the maturity date.

Face rate of interest: The rate of interest on the bond certificate.

Factor: Selling accounts receivable for cash.

Fair value: The amount at which an asset (liability) could be bought (incurred) or sold (settled) in a current transaction between willing parties.

FASB: *See* Financial Accounting Standards Board.

Feedback value: An ingredient of relevant accounting information.

Fiduciary duty: Management's obligation to protect the interests of equity investors.

Fiduciary funds (governmental accounting): Funds used to report assets held in a trustee or an agency capacity for others.

FIFO method: An inventory costing method that assigns the most recent costs to ending inventory.

Financial accounting: Recording and communication of financial information under GAAP.

Financial Accounting Standards Board (FASB): A body that has responsibility for developing and issuing rules on accounting practice in the United States (www.fasb.org).

Financial analysis: Describes the process of studying a company's financial report.

Financial leverage: The amount of debt financing in relation to equity financing.

Financial news: For a wealth of information about the economy and specific companies and industries (*The Wall Street Journal*, www.wsj.com; *The New York Times*, www .nyt.com; *Financial Times*, www.ft.com; *Investor's Business Daily*, www.investors.com).

Financial portals: These sites have financial news, information about companies, and other financial information. There are many such sites. Some popular sites are Microsoft's Money Central (http://money.msn.com/), Yahoo! Finance (http:// finance.yahoo.com), and The Street.com (www.thestreet.com).

Financial Reporting Release (FRR): SEC statement dealing with reporting and disclosure requirements in documents filed with the SEC.

Financial statement (report) analysis: The process of reviewing, analyzing, and interpreting the basic financial reports.

Financial statements: Generally considered to be the balance sheet, income statement, and statement of cash flows.

Financial summary: A section of the annual report that provides a 5-, 10-, or 11-year summary of selected financial data.

Financing activities: Activities concerned with the raising and repayment of funds in the form of debt and equity.

Finished goods: A manufacturer's inventory that is complete and ready for sale.

First-in, first-out (FIFO) (inventory): The flow pattern that assumes that the first unit purchased is the first sold.

Fiscal year: Any 12-month accounting period used by an economic entity that closes at the end of a month other than December.

Fixed assets: Tangible, long-lived assets, primarily property, plant, and equipment. They are expected to provide service benefit for more than one year.

Fixed cost: Cost that remains unchanged in total for a given time period, despite wide changes in the related level of total activity or volume.

Forecasted transaction: A transaction that is expected to occur for which there is no firm commitment.

Foreclosure: Seizure of collateral by a creditor.

Foreign Corrupt Practices Act: Legislation intended to increase the accountability of management for accurate records and reliable financial statements.

Foreign currency: A currency other than the entity's functional currency.

Foreign currency transactions: Transactions that are settled with a nondomestic currency.

Foreign exchange rate: Specifies the number of U.S. dollars (from a U.S. perspective) that are needed to obtain one unit of a specific foreign currency.

Foreign operations: Operational activities that take place in a foreign country.

Forgery: The act of fabricating or producing something falsely.

Form 8-K: A special SEC filing required when a material event or transaction occurs between Form 10-Q filing dates.

Form 10-K: A form that is like an annual report but with more detail. It is provided to the SEC.

Form 10-Q: An SEC form required to be filed at the end of a company's first, second, and third fiscal year quarters. It contains interim information on a company's operations and financial position.

Form 20-F: The annual financial report filing with the SEC required of all foreign companies whose debt or equity capital is available for purchase/sale on a U.S. exchange.

Form S-1: Form filed with the Securities and Exchange Commission listing securities to be traded on a national stock market.

Form S-4: Form filed with the Securities and Exchange Commission that registers securities used to effect a business combination.

Form versus substance: Form refers to the legal nature of a transaction or event; substance refers to the economic aspects of the transaction or event.

Forward contract: Agreement to purchase or sell commodities, securities, or currencies on a specified future date at a specified price.

Forward exchange rate: A rate quoted currently for the exchange of currency at some future specified date.

Fractional share: A unit of stock that is less than one full share.

Franchise: A contractual privilege granted by one person to another permitting the sale of a product, use of trade name, or provision of a service within a specified territory and/or in a specified manner.

Fraud: Intent to deceive.

Fraudulent transfer: A transfer of an interest or an obligation incurred by the debtor within one year prior to the date of filing a bankruptcy petition with the intent to defraud creditors.

Fringe benefit: The compensation or other benefit provided by the employer to the employee at no charge that is above and beyond salary or wages.

Full-costing method: The method of accounting that capitalizes all costs of exploring for and developing oil and gas reserves within a defined area subject only to the limitation that costs attributable to developed reserves should not exceed their estimated present value.

Full disclosure: Accounting reports must disclose all facts that may influence the judgment of an informed reader.

Functional currency: The currency a company uses to conduct its business.

Fund accounting: Accounting procedures in which a self-balancing group of accounts is provided for each accounting entity established by legal, contractual, or voluntary action.

Funded debt: The long-term debt of a business.

Fund financial statements (governmental accounting): Consist of a series of statements that focus on information about the government's major governmental and enterprise funds, including its blended component units.

Funding payment: A payment made by the employer to the pension fund.

Furniture and fixtures: A noncurrent depreciable asset consisting of office or store equipment.

Future contract: Exchange-traded contract for future acceptance or delivery of a standardized quantity of a commodity or financial instrument on a specified future date at a specified price.

Future value of an annuity: Amount accumulated in the future when a series of payments is invested and accrues interest.

G

Gain or loss on redemption: The difference between the carrying value and the redemption price at the time bonds are redeemed.

Gains: Profits realized from activities that are incidental to a firm's primary operating activities.

General fund (governmental accounting): A fund that is used to account for all financial resources not accounted for in another fund.

General journal: A journal used to record transactions not maintained in special journals.

General ledger: A record of all accounts used by a company.

General partnership: An association in which each partner has unlimited liability.

Generally accepted accounting principles (GAAP): Accounting principles that have substantial authoritative support.

Generally accepted auditing standards (GAAS): Standards governing the conduct of independent audits of nonpublic companies by CPAs.

Going concern or continuity: Assumes that the entity being accounted for will remain in business for an indefinite period of time.

Golden parachute agreement: A highly lucrative contract giving a senior corporate executive monetary or other benefits if his or her job is lost in a merger or an acquisition.

Goodwill: An intangible asset representing the unrecorded assets of a firm. It appears in the accounting records only if the firm is acquired for a price in excess of the fair market value of its net assets.

Government-wide financial statements: These financial statements consist of a statement of net assets and a statement of activities. These statements should report all of the assets, liabilities, revenues, expenses, and gains and losses of the government.

Governmental Accounting Standards Board (GASB): The standards-setting body for governmental accounting and financial reporting.

Governmental funds: General, special revenue, project, debt service, and special assessment funds; each designed for a specific purpose and used by a state or local government to account for its normal operations.

Grant date: The date at which an employer and an employee reach a mutual understanding of the key terms and conditions of a share-based payment award.

Gross profit margin: Gross profit margin equals the difference between net sales revenue and the cost of goods sold.

Group depreciation: A depreciation method that groups like assets together and computes depreciation for the group rather than for individual assets.

Guarantee of employee stock ownership plan (ESOPs): An employee stock bonus plan used as a financing vehicle for an employer that borrows money to purchase its own stock. The stock is security for the loan, and the ESOP repays the loan from employer contributions.

Guaranteed residual value: A guarantee by lessee of a minimum value for the residual value of a leased asset. If the residual value is less than the guarantee, the lessee must pay the difference to the lessor.

H

Harmonization of accounting principles: The attempt by various organizations (e.g., the FASB, IASB) to establish a common set of international accounting and reporting standards.

Hedge: A process of buying or selling commodities, forward contracts, or options for the explicit purpose of reducing or eliminating foreign exchange risk.

Hedging contract: A contract to buy or sell foreign currencies in the forward market to protect against the risks of foreign exchange rate fluctuations.

Held-to-maturity securities: Investments in bonds of other companies in which the investor has the positive intent and the ability to hold the securities to maturity.

Historical cost: The cash equivalent price of goods or services at the date of acquisition.

Horizontal analysis: A comparison of financial statement items over a period of time.

Human resource accounting: Attempts to account for the services of employees.

Hybrid securities: A security that is neither clearly debt nor clearly equity.

I

IAS: *See* International Accounting Standards.

IASB: *See* International Accounting Standards Board.

IFRS: *See* International Financial Reporting Standards.

Impairment: A temporary or permanent reduction in asset value.

Implicit interest rate: The interest rate that would discount the minimum lease payments to the fair market value of the leased asset at the lease signing date.

Imputed interest rate: A rate of interest applied to a note when the effective rate was either not evident or determinable by other factors involved in the exchange.

Income smoothing: An accounting practice that attempts to present a stable measure of income (usually an increasing amount).

Income statement (statement of earnings): A statement that summarizes revenues and expenses.

Income summary: A temporary account in which revenues and expenses are closed at the end of the year.

Income taxes: Taxes levied by federal, state, and local governments on reported accounting profit. Income tax expense includes both tax paid and deferred.

Inconsistency: A change in accounting principle from one period to the next, requiring an explanatory paragraph following the opinion paragraph of the auditor's report.

Incorporated: A legal state of existence signifying that a corporate entity has been recognized.

Incorporation by reference: Direction of the reader's attention to information included in a source other than the Form 10-K, rather than reporting such information in Form 10-K.

Incremental borrowing rate: The interest rate at which the lessee could borrow the amount of money necessary to purchase the leased asset, taking into consideration the lessee's financial situation and the current conditions in the marketplace.

Indentures: Provisions and restrictions attached to a bond that make the bond more attractive for investors.

Indexed bond: An obligation with interest payments tied to an inflation index.

Indirect cost: An expense that is difficult to trace directly to a specific costing object.

Indirect method: For preparing the operating activities section of the statement of cash flows, the approach in which net income is reconciled to net cash flow from operations.

Industry practices: Practices leading to accounting reports that do not conform to the general theory that underlies accounting.

Industry ratios: Financial ratios for a particular industry.

Industry segment: A component of an organization providing a product or related products (or services) to outside parties.

Inflation: An increase in the general price level of goods and services.

Information overload: Amount of data that unnecessarily complicates analysis.

Initial direct costs: Costs such as commissions, legal fees, and preparation of documents that are incurred by the lessor or negotiating and completing a lease transaction.

Initial public offering (IPO): The first or initial sale of voting stock to the general market by a previously privately held concern.

Insolvent: A condition in which a company is unable to pay its debts.

Installment method: The method in which revenue is recognized at the time cash is collected.

Installment sales: A type of sale that requires periodic payments over an extended length of time.

Institute of Management Accountants (IMA): An organization of management accountants concerned with the internal use of accounting data.

In-substance defeasance of debt: The debtor irrevocably places cash or other assets in a trust to be used solely for satisfying the payments of both interest and principal on a specific debt obligation.

Intangibles: Nonphysical assets, such as legal rights, recorded at historical cost, then reduced by systematic amortization.

Intercompany profit: The profit resulting when one related company sells to another related company.

Intercompany receivables and payables: Receivables and payables among a parent company and its subsidiary(ies).

Interest: The cost for the use of money. It is a cost to the borrower and revenue to the lender.

Interest-bearing note: A debt instrument (note) that pays interest at a stated rate for a stated period.

Interest rate: A rate, usually expressed as a percentage per annum, charged on money borrowed or lent.

Interest rate risk: Uncertainty about future interest rates and their impact on future cash flows as well as on the fair value of existing assets and liabilities.

Interest rate swaps: An agreement to exchange variable rate interest payments based on a specific index for a fixed rate or a variable rate stream of payments based on another index.

Interim reports: Financial reports that cover fiscal periods of less than one year.

Internal auditing: The department responsible in a company for the review and appraisal of its accounting and administrative controls.

Internal control: The process effected by an entity to provide reasonable assurance regarding the achievement of objectives. It consists of three parts—operations controls, financial reporting controls, and compliance controls.

Internal event: An event occurring entirely within an entity.

Internal financing: Financing provided from cash generated from business operations.

Internal reporting: Represents financial data or other information accumulated by one individual to be communicated to another within the business entity.

Internal Revenue Service (IRS): U.S. government agency responsible for administering U.S. income tax rules.

International Accounting Standards (IAS): The accounting standards adopted by the IASC and later by the IASB.

International Accounting Standards Board (IASB): Established in January 2001 to replace the IASC. The new structure has characteristics similar to that of the FASB. The IASB sets global financial accounting and reporting standards (www.ifrs.org/Home.htm).

International Accounting Standards Committee (IASC): An organization established in 1973 by the leading professional groups of the major industrial countries.

International Federation of Accountants (IFAC): An association of professional accounting organizations founded in 1977.

International Financial Reporting Standards: Standards issued by the International Accounting Standards Board (IASB).

Interperiod: Of or related to more than one reporting period.

Interperiod tax allocation: The process of allocating the taxes paid by a company over the periods in which the taxes are recognized for accounting purposes.

Intraperiod: Of or related to one reporting period.

Intrinsic value method: Method of accounting for stock-based compensation in which the difference between the exercise price and the market price per share at the grant date is used to measure compensation expense.

Introductory paragraph: The first paragraph of the standard audit report, which identifies the financial statements covered by the audit report and clearly differentiates management's responsibility for preparing the financial statements from the auditor's responsibility for expressing an opinion on them.

Inventories: The balance of goods on hand.

Inventory-lower-of-cost-or-market (LCM) rule: An inventory pricing method that prices the inventory at an amount below cost if the replacement (market) value is less than cost.

Investing activities: Describes a firm's uses of cash to acquire other assets. A category shown on the cash flow statement.

Investments: Usually stocks and bonds of other companies held for the purpose of maintaining a business relationship or exercising control. To be classified as long term, it must be the intent of management to hold these assets as such. Long-term investments are differentiated from marketable securities, where the intent is to hold the assets for short-term profits and to achieve liquidity.

Investors: Owners and potential owners of a company.

Invoice: Form sent by the seller to the buyer as evidence of a sale.

Issued stock: The shares of stock sold or otherwise transferred to stockholders.

J

Joint venture: An association of two or more businesses established for a special purpose; some in the form of partnerships and unincorporated joint ventures; others in the form of corporations jointly owned by two or more other firms.

Journalizing: The act of recording journal entries.

Journals: Initial recordings of a company's transactions.

Junk bonds: High-risk, high-yield bonds issued by companies in a weak financial condition.

K

Kiting: A type of misrepresentation fraud used to conceal bank overdrafts or cash misappropriations.

L

Labor intensive: Activities, companies, and industries that are dominated by human effort.

Land: Realty used for business purposes. It is shown at acquisition cost and not depreciated. Land containing resources that will be used up, however, such as mineral deposits and timberlands, is subject to depletion.

Land improvements: Expenditures incurred in the process of putting land into a usable condition, for example, clearing, grading, paving.

Lapping: A form of concealment that involves crediting current customer remittances to the accounts of customers who have remitted previously.

Last-in, first-out (LIFO) (inventory): The flow pattern that assumes that those units purchased last are sold first.

Lease: An agreement conveying the right to use property, plant, or equipment (land and/or depreciable assets) for a stated period of time.

Lease improvement: An improvement to leased property that becomes the property of the lessor at the end of the lease.

Lease term: The noncancelable period of a lease designated in the lease contract plus the period of any bargain renewal periods over which the lease is likely to be renewed.

Leasehold: A payment made to secure the right to a lease.

Ledger: Summarizes the effects of transactions upon individual accounts.

Lessee: The party to a lease who acquires the right to use the property, plant, and equipment.

Lessor: The party to a lease giving up the right to use the property, plant, and equipment.

Letter to the shareholders: A section of the annual report that presents a message from the company's chairman of the board or president.

Leverage: The use of borrowed funds and amounts contributed by preferred stockholders to earn an overall return higher than the cost of these funds.

Leveraged buyout (LBO): A purchase of a company where a substantial amount of the purchase price is debt financed.

Liabilities: Future sacrifices of economic benefits arising from present obligations to other entities.

License: Rights to engage in a particular activity.

Life cycle: Progression of a product, company, or industry from inception, through growth, to maturity, and into decline.

LIFO conformity rule: A federal tax regulation that requires the use of LIFO for financial reporting purposes if LIFO is used for income tax purposes.

LIFO inventory pool: A group of inventory items having common characteristics and assumed to be the same when applying LIFO.

LIFO layer: An incremental group of LIFO inventory items created in any year in which the number of units purchased or produced exceeds the number sold.

LIFO liquidation: The reduction or elimination of old LIFO layers because total purchases or production in the current period is less than sales.

LIFO method: An inventory method that assigns the most recent costs to the cost of goods sold.

LIFO reserves (LIFO valuation adjustment): The amount that would need to be added back to the LIFO inventory in order for the inventory account to approximate current cost.

Limited liability: The concept that stockholders in a corporation are not held personally liable.

Line of credit: A prearranged loan allowing borrowing up to a certain maximum amount.

Liquid assets: Current assets that either are in cash or can be readily converted to cash.

Liquidating dividend: A dividend that exceeds the balance in retained earnings.

Liquidation: The process of selling off the assets of a business, paying any outstanding debts, and distributing any remaining cash to the owners.

Liquidity: The nearness to cash of the assets and liabilities.

Listed company: A company whose shares or bonds have been accepted for trading on a securities exchange.

Loan covenant: Provision of a loan contract restricting the actions of the borrower or allowing for some monitoring of the borrower's actions.

Loan defaults: Violations of loan agreements that could result in loan principal and interest becoming immediately due.

Loan (mortgage) amortization: The process by which payments on a loan are allocated between principal and interest components.

Loan restructuring: Revision of loan terms in a manner mutually acceptable to the lender and borrower.

Long-term liabilities: Long-term liabilities are those due in a period exceeding one year or one operating cycle, whichever is longer.

Loss on sale of asset: The amount by which selling price is less than book value.

Losses: Losses realized from activities that are incidental to a firm's primary activities.

Lower of cost or market: A method to value inventories and marketable securities.

M

Machinery: An asset listed at historical cost, including delivery and installation, plus any material improvements that extend its life or increase the quantity or quality of service; depreciated over its estimated useful life.

Maintenance: Expenditures made to maintain plant assets in good operating condition.

Management accounting: The branch of accounting concerned with providing management with information to facilitate planning and control.

Management report: Management statements to shareholders that acknowledge management's responsibility for the preparation and integrity of financial statements.

Management's discussion and analysis (MD&A): Part of the annual report package required by the Securities and Exchange Commission. Management comments on the results of operations, liquidity, and capital resources for the years under review in the financial statements.

Market capitalization: Total value of an entity's outstanding shares at a point in time which reflects the value investors place on a company. It is computed by multiplying the number of common shares outstanding by the share price.

Market value (stock): The price investors are willing to pay for a share of stock.

Marketable securities: Ownership and debt instruments of the government and other companies that can be readily converted into cash.

Matching: The concept that determines the revenue and then matches the appropriate cost incurred in generating this revenue.

Materiality: The concept that exempts immaterial items from the concepts and principles that bind the accountant, and allows these items to be handled in the most economical and expedient manner possible.

Maturity date: Date on which the principal of a note becomes due.

Maturity value: The amount of cash the maker is to pay the payee on the maturity of the note.

Merchandise inventory: The account wholesalers and retailers use to report inventory held for sale.

Merger: A combination of one or more companies into a single corporate entity.

Minimum lease payments: The lease payments required over the lease term plus any amount to be paid for the residual value through either a bargain purchase option or a guarantee of residual value.

Minority interest (balance sheet account): The ownership of minority shareholders in the equity of consolidated subsidiaries that are less than wholly owned.

Minority share of earnings: The portion of income that belongs to the minority owners of a firm that has been consolidated.

Misappropriation: The fraudulent transfer of assets from the firm to one or more employees.

Modified Accelerated Cost Recovery System (MACRS): The accelerated cost recovery system as revised by the Tax Reform Act of 1986.

Monetary assets: Cash and other assets that represent the right to receive a specific amount of cash.

Monetary liabilities: Accounts payable and other liabilities that represent the obligation to pay a specific amount of cash.

Monetary unit: The unit used to measure financial transactions.

Mortgage: A loan backed by an asset with the asset title pledged to the lender.

Mortgage payable: A liability secured by real property.

Moving average: The name given to an average cost method when it is used with a perpetual inventory system.

Multinational enterprise: Entity engages in transnational business activities.

Multiple-step income statement: Form of the income statement that arrives at net income in steps.

Municipal debt: Debt securities issued by state, county, and local governments and their agencies.

N

NASDAQ (OTC): The National Association of Securities Dealers Automated Quotations. Represents a computerized communication network that handles the securities transactions of the over-the-counter market (www.nasdaq.com).

Natural business year: A 12-month period ending on a date that coincides with the end of an operating cycle.

Natural resources: Assets produced by nature such as petroleum, minerals, and timber.

Negative goodwill: Term used to describe the amount paid for another company that is less than the fair value of the company's net identifiable assets.

Negligence: An accountant's failure to conduct an audit with "due care."

Negotiable notes: Notes that are legally transferable by endorsement and delivery.

Net assets: Total assets less total liabilities (equivalent to shareowners' equity).

Net income: Amount by which total revenues exceed total expenses. The bottom line on the income statement.

Net of tax: Indicates that expected tax effects have already been considered as part of a particular calculation or figure. Indicates that taxes have been deducted from a particular financial component.

Net operating loss carryback: When tax-deductible expenses exceed taxable revenues, a company may carry the net operating loss back three years and receive refunds for income taxes paid in those years.

Net operating loss carryforward: When tax-deductible expenses exceed taxable revenues, a company may carry an operating loss forward and offset future taxable income.

Net periodic pension expense: The amount recognized in an employer's financial statements as an expense of a pension plan for a period.

Net realizable value: The nondiscounted amount of cash, or its equivalent, into which an asset is expected to be converted less direct costs necessary to make that conversion.

Net sales: Gross sales revenue less any allowances or discounts.

Net worth: Synonymous with shareholders' equity.

Neutrality: A qualitative characteristic of accounting information that involves the faithful reporting of business activity without bias to one or another view.

New York Stock Exchange (NYSE): The world's largest securities exchange (www.nyse.com).

Nominal accounts: The name given to revenue, expense, and dividend accounts because they are temporary and are closed at the end of the period.

Noncancelable: A lease contract that can be canceled only under very unlikely circumstances or with extremely expensive penalties to the lessee.

Noncash investing and financing activities: A category of investing and financing activities that does not involve cash flows.

Noncontributory pension plans: Plans in which the employer bears the total cost of the plan.

Noncontrolling interest (balance sheet account): Noncontrolling interest reflects the ownership of noncontrolling shareholders in the equity of consolidated subsidiaries less than wholly owned.

Noncontrolling interest in earnings: The portion of income that belongs to the minority owners of a firm that has been consolidated.

Noncumulative preferred stock: Preferred stock that has no claim on any prior-year dividends that may have been "passed."

Noncurrent or long-term assets: Assets that do not qualify as current assets. In general, they take longer than a year to be converted to cash or to conserve cash in the long run.

Nondetachable warrants: Stock warrants that cannot be traded separately from the security with which they were originally issued.

Nonprofit accounting: Accounting policies, procedures, and techniques employed by nonprofit organizations.

Nonpublic company: A company whose equity or debt securities are not publicly traded on a stock exchange or in the over-the-counter market.

Nonrecurring: Earnings that do not represent the normal, recurring earnings from operations.

Nontrade notes payable: Notes issued to nontrade creditors for purposes other than to purchase goods or services.

Nontrade receivables: Any receivables arising from transactions that are not directly associated with the normal operating activities of a business.

Not sufficient funds (NSF) check: A check that is not honored by a bank because of insufficient cash in the maker's account.

Note: A written promise to pay signed by the debtor.

Note payable: Payables in the form of a written promissory note.

Note receivable: An asset resulting from the acceptance of a promissory note from another company.

Notes: Present additional information on items included in the financial statements and additional financial information.

Notes to the financial statements: Information that clarifies and extends the material presented in the financial statements with narrative and detail.

O

Objective acceleration clause: A clause in a debt agreement that identifies specific conditions that will cause the debt to be callable immediately.

Objectivity: Represents freedom from subjective valuation and bias in making an accounting decision.

Obsolescence: This represents a major factor in depreciation, resulting from technological or market changes.

Off-balance-sheet financing: Refers to a company taking advantage of debt-like resources without these obligations appearing as debt on the face of the balance sheet.

On account: Purchases or sales on credit.

Operating activities: One of three major categories included in a statement of cash flows; includes transactions and events that normally enter into the determination of net income, including interest and taxes.

Operating cycle: The period of time elapsing between the acquisition of goods and the final cash realization resulting from sales and subsequent collections.

Operating expenses: Consist of two types: selling and administrative. Selling expenses result from the company's effort to create sales. Administrative expenses relate to the general administration of the company's operation.

Operating lease (lessee): Periodic payment for the right to use an asset, recorded in a manner similar to the recording of rent expense payments.

Opportunity cost: This represents revenue forfeited by rejecting an alternative use of time or facilities.

Option: A financial instrument that conveys to its owner the right, but not the obligation, to buy or sell a security, commodity, or currency at a specific price over a specified time period or at a specific date.

Organization costs: The costs of forming a corporation.

Organizational costs: The legal costs incurred when organizing a business; carried as an asset and usually written off over a period of five years or longer.

Original entry: Represents recording a business transaction in a journal.

Other assets: Represents a balance sheet category for minor assets not classified under the typical headings.

Other income and expenses: Income and expenses from secondary activities of the firm not directly related to the operations.

Outstanding shares: The number of authorized shares of capital stock sold to stockholders that are currently in the possession of stockholders (issues shares less treasury shares).

Owners' equity (stockholders' equity, shareholders' equity): The residual ownership interest in the assets of an entity that remains after deducting its liabilities.

P

Paid-in capital in excess of par value (or stated value): The proceeds from the sale of capital stock in excess of the par value (or stated value) of the capital stock.

Par value: An amount set by the firm's board of directors and approved by the state. (The par value does not relate to the market value.)

Parent: Tax term applied to the buyer company in a business combination.

Parent company: A company that owns a controlling interest in another company.

Participating preferred stock: Preferred stock that provides for additional dividends to be paid to preferred stockholders after dividends of a specified amount are paid to common stockholders.

Partnership: An unincorporated business owned by two or more individuals.

Patent: Exclusive legal rights granted to an inventor for a period of 20 years.

Payables (trade): Short-term obligations created by the acquisition of goods and services, such as accounts payable, wages payable, and taxes payable.

Payee: The party that will receive the money from a promissory note at some future date.

Pension Benefit Guaranty Corporation: A U.S. government agency that insures the pension benefits of workers.

Pension fund: A fund established through contributions from an employer and sometimes from employees that pays pension benefits to employees after retirement.

Pension plan: An arrangement whereby an employer provides benefits (payments) to employees after they retire for services they provided while they were working.

Pension plan—contributory: A pension plan in which the employees bear part of the cost of the stated benefits or voluntarily make payments to increase their benefits.

Pension plan—funded: A pension plan in which the employer sets funds aside for future pension benefits by making payments to a funding agency that is responsible for accumulating the assets of the pension fund and for making payments to the recipients as the benefits become due.

Pension plan—noncontributory: A pension plan in which the employer bears the entire cost.

Pension plan—qualified: A pension plan in accord with federal income tax requirements that permits deductibility of the employer's contributions to the pension fund and tax-free status of earnings from pension fund assets.

Percentage-of-completion method: A revenue recognition method that recognizes profit each period during the life of the contract in proportion to the amount of the contract completed during the period.

Period cost: Cost that is recognized as an expense during the period in which it is incurred.

Periodic inventory method: A method of accounting for inventory that determines inventory at the end of the period.

Permanent accounts: All balance sheet accounts.

Permanent differences: Nondeductible expenses or nontaxable revenues that are recognized for financial reporting purposes but that are never part of taxable income.

Perpetual inventory method: A method of accounting for inventory that records continuously the sales and purchases of individual items of inventory.

Personal financial statements: Financial statements of individuals, husband and wife, or a larger family group.

Petty cash (fund): Small quantity of funds kept on hand for incidental expenditures requiring quick cash.

Pledging: Using assets as collateral for a bank loan.

Pooling of interest: A method of accounting for a business combination that combines all asset, liability, and stockholders' equity accounts.

Post-balance sheet event: Event occurring between the balance sheet date and the date financial statements are issued and made available to external users (also called subsequent event).

Posting: Transcribing the amounts from journal entries into the general ledger.

Postretirement benefits other than pensions: Benefits other than pensions that accrue to employees upon retirement, such as medical insurance and life insurance contracts.

Predictive value: Helps a decision maker predict future consequences based on information about past transactions and events.

Preferred stock: Stock that has some preference over common stock.

Premium: An amount paid in excess of the face value of a security (stock or bond).

Prepaid: An expenditure made in advance of the use of the service or goods.

Present value consideration: The characteristic that money to be received or paid out in the future is not worth as much as money available today. Accountants consider the time value of money when preparing the financial statements for such areas as long-term leases, pensions, and other long-term situations in which the future payments or receipts are not indicative of the present value of the asset or the obligation.

Present value factor: Using multiplication, converts a future value to its present value.

Present value of an annuity: The amount at a present time that is equivalent to a series of payments and interest in the future.

Primary earnings per share: Net income applicable to common stock divided by the sum of the weighted-average common stock and common stock equivalents.

Prime loan: A type of loan that is offered at a rate considered to be prime to individuals who qualify for a prime rate loan (considered to be a high-quality loan).

Principal: The original or base amount of a loan or an investment.

Prior-period adjustments: Reported as restatements of retained earnings. They include corrections of errors of prior periods, a change in accounting entity, certain changes in accounting principles, and adjustments that result from the realization of income tax benefits of preacquisition operating loss carryforwards of purchased subsidiaries.

Prior service cost: When a defined pension plan is adopted or amended, credit is often given to employees for years of service provided before the date of adoption or amendment. The cost of taking on this added commitment is called the prior service cost.

Privatization: The sale of all or part of a previously government-controlled entity to the general public.

Pro-forma amount: Hypothetical or projected amount. Synonymous with "what-if" analyses. Pro-forma statements indicate what would have happened under specified circumstances.

Productive-output depreciation: A depreciation method in which the depreciable cost is divided by the total estimated output to determine the depreciation rate per unit of output.

Profitability: The relative success of a company's operations.

Projected benefit obligation (PBO): The present value of pension benefits earned to date based on past service and an estimate of future compensation levels for pay-related plans.

Promissory note: A formal written promise to pay a certain amount of money at a specified future date.

Property dividend: A dividend in a form of an asset other than cash.

Property, plant, and equipment: Tangible assets of a long-term nature used in the continuing operation of the business.

Proportionate consolidation: A method of consolidating the financial results of a parent company and its subsidiary in which only the proportion of net assets owned by the parent are consolidated.

Proprietary funds (governmental accounting): Funds used to report assets held in a trustee or an agency capacity for others.

Proprietorship: A business owned by one person. The owner and business are not separate legal entities but are separate accounting entities.

Prospectus: A document describing the nature of a business and its recent financial history.

Proxy: A legal document granting another party the right to vote for a shareholder on matters involving a shareholder vote.

Proxy statement: Information provided in a formal written form to shareholders prior to a company's regular annual meeting.

Public company: A company whose voting shares are listed for trading on a recognized securities exchange or are otherwise available for purchase by public investors.

Public Company Accounting Oversight Board (PCAOB): The PCAOB is a regulatory body created by the Sarbanes-Oxley Act of 2002. It regulates audits of SEC registrants. The PCAOB operates under the U.S. Securities and Exchange Commission. It has the authority for registration, inspection, and discipline of firms auditing SEC registrants and sets standards for public company audits (www.pcaobus.org).

Purchase accounting: The assets and liabilities of an acquired company accounted for on the books of the acquiring company at their relative fair market values to the acquiring company at the date of acquisition.

Put option: Contract giving the owner the right, but not the obligation, to sell an asset at a specified price.

Q

Qualified opinion: An audit opinion rendered under circumstances of one or more material scope restrictions or departures from GAAP.

Qualitative characteristics: Standards for judging the information accountants provide to decision makers; the primary criteria are relevance and reliability.

Quarterly statements: Interim financial statements on a quarterly basis.

Quasi-reorganization: An accounting procedure equivalent to an accounting fresh start. A company with a deficit balance in retained earnings "starts over" with a zero balance rather than a deficit. A quasi-reorganization may also include a restatement of the carrying values of assets and liabilities to reflect current values.

R

Ratio analysis: A comparison of relationships among account balances.

Raw materials: Goods purchased for direct use in manufacturing that become part of the product.

Real accounts: The name given to balance sheet accounts because they are permanent and are not closed at the end of the period.

Realization (revenue recognition): A concept that generally recognizes revenue when (1) the earning process is virtually complete and (2) the exchange value can be objectively determined.

Receivables: Claims arising from the selling of merchandise or services on account to customers are referred to as trade receivables. Other claims may be from sources such as loans to employees or a federal tax refund.

Recognition: Recording a transaction on the accounting records.

Recourse: The right of one company to collect money from another company in the event that a third party fails to pay its obligation to the first company.

Redeemable preferred stock: Preferred stock subject to mandatory redemption requirements, or with a redemption feature that is outside the control of the issuer.

Registrar: An independent agent that maintains a record of the number of a company's shares of capital stock that have been issued and to whom.

Relevance: Qualitative characteristic requiring that accounting information bear directly on the economic decision for which it is to be used; one of the primary qualitative characteristics of accounting information.

Reliability: Qualitative characteristic requiring that accounting information be faithful to the original data and that it be neutral and verifiable; one of the primary qualitative characteristics of accounting information.

Repairs: Expenditures made to restore assets to good operating condition upon their breakdown or to restore and replace broken parts.

Replacement cost: The cost to reproduce or replace an asset.

Report form of balance sheet: A balance sheet presentation that presents assets, liabilities, and stockholders' equity in a vertical format.

Reporting currency: The currency used to measure and report.

Representational faithfulness: The agreement of information with what it is supposed to represent.

Research and Development (R&D): Funds spent to improve existing products and develop new ones.

Reserves: Accounts classified under liabilities resulting from an expense to the income statement and an equal increase in the reserve account on the balance sheet. These reserve accounts do not represent definite commitments to pay out funds in the future, but they do represent an estimate of funds that will be paid out in the future.

Residual value (salvage value): The estimated net scrap or trade-in value of a tangible asset at the date of disposal.

Restrictive covenants: Limitations imposed by a creditor on a debtor's actions. Covenants are often based on accounting measurements of assets, liabilities, and/or income.

Restructure: The term used to describe corporate downsizing and refocus of operations.

Retail inventory method: An inventory method that converts the retail value of inventory to an estimated cost.

Retained earnings: The undistributed earnings of a corporation consisting of the net income for all past periods minus the dividends that have been declared.

Retained earnings restricted: The amount of retained earnings that has been restricted for specific purposes.

Retroactively: The method of accounting for accounting principle changes whereby past years' financial statements are restated to reflect the use of the new method.

Revenue recognition: A basic accounting concept that is applied to determine when revenue should be recognized (recorded). Generally, under this principle, revenues are recognized when two criteria are met; the earnings process is substantially complete, and the revenues are realized, or realizable.

Revenues: Inflows or other enhancements of assets of an entity or settlements of its liabilities (or a combination of both) from delivering or producing goods, rendering services, or other activities that constitute the entity's ongoing major or central operations.

Risk: The uncertainty surrounding estimates of future cash flows.

Royalties: Payment for a right over some natural resource or payment to an author or composer.

S

S Corporation: A corporation which is not subject to federal income taxes. (Taxable income is passed through to its stockholders.)

Sale and leaseback: Sale of an asset with the purchaser concurrently leasing the asset to the seller.

Sales discounts: Contra-revenue account used to record discounts given to customers for early payment of their accounts.

Sales or revenues: Income from the sale of goods or services and lease or royalty payments.

Sales returns and allowances: Contra-revenue account used to record both refunds to customers and reduction of their accounts.

Sales-type lease: A capital lease that generates two income streams: one from the sale of the asset and a second from the financing of the asset.

Salvage value (residual value): The estimated net scrap or trade-in value of a tangible asset at the date of disposal.

Scope paragraph: That paragraph of the audit report that tells what the auditor did. Specifically, it states whether or not the audit was conducted in accordance with GAAS.

SEC EDGAR database: Contains electronic copies of SEC filings by publicly traded companies (www.edgar-online.com and www.tenkwizard.com).

Secured bonds: Bonds for which assets are pledged to guarantee repayment.

Secured loan: A loan backed by certain assets as collateral.

Securities Act of 1933: A federal statute governing the registration of new securities issues traded in interstate commerce.

Securities Act of 1934: A federal statute establishing recurring reporting requirements for public companies once their securities have been registered with the SEC.

Securities and Exchange Commission (SEC): An agency of the federal government that has the legal power to set and enforce accounting practices (www.sec.gov).

Segment reporting (product segment information): When operations are diversified, the firm may report results on a segmented basis.

Self-insurance: A coverage borne by the person or company itself against the risk of loss that may occur if property is destroyed or damaged from some cause.

Selling expenses: Result from the company's efforts to create sales.

Senior debt: Debt obligations that would have a prior claim over junior debt and equity holders on the assets of a company in liquidation.

Serial bonds: Bonds that do not all have the same due date; a portion of the bonds comes due each time period.

Service cost: A component of net periodic pension expense representing the actuarial present value of benefits accruing to employees for services rendered during that period.

Service lives: Working years of employees prior to retirement, as used in accounting for postretirement benefit obligations.

Short selling: A technique used by investors who try to profit from the falling price of a stock.

Short selling (naked): The short seller sells shares without owning them. Later these shares are purchased and delivered.

Short-term debt: Represents money payable by the debtor to the creditor within one year.

Shrinkage: The amount of inventory that is lost, stolen, or spoiled.

Simple capital structure: A corporate structure that includes only common and nonconvertible preferred stock and has no convertible securities, stock options, warrants, or other rights outstanding.

Simple interest: Interest computed on the principal amount only.

Single-employer pension plans: Pension plans established for a single employer.

Single-step income statement: Form of the income statement that arrives at net income in a single step.

Sinking fund: An accumulation of cash or securities in a special fund dedicated to paying, or redeeming, an issue of bonds or preferred stock.

Social accounting: Attempts to account for the benefits to the social environment within which the firm operates.

Sole proprietorship: A business with a single owner.

Solvency: The ability of a company to remain in business over the long term.

Special journal: An accounting record used to list a particular type of frequently recurring transaction.

Specific identification (inventory): Identifies the items in inventory as coming from specific purchases.

Spinoff: A parent company transfers a portion of a subsidiary's stock as other assets to its stockholders.

Staff accounting bulletin (SAB): Accounting interpretations made by the staff of the SEC. SABs do not necessarily represent official positions of the SEC.

Stakeholders: All parties interested in the performance of a company.

Standard audit report: The form of audit report recommended by the Auditing Standards Board of the AICPA. This report is rendered at the conclusion of an audit in which the auditor encountered no material scope limitations, and the financial statements conform to GAAP in all material respects.

Stated (contract) rate: The rate of interest printed on a bond.

Stated value: A value assigned by a company's board of directors to no-par stock.

Statement of cash flows: A statement that provides detailed information on cash flows resulting from operating, investing, and financing activities.

Statement of owners' equity (statement of shareholders' equity): An accounting statement describing transactions affecting the owners' equity.

Statement of retained earnings: A summary of the changes to retained earnings for an accounting period.

Statements of financial accounting concepts (SFACs): Statements issued by the Financial Accounting Standards Board that provide the Board with a common foundation and basic reasons for considering the merits of various alternative accounting principles.

Statements of financial accounting standards (SFASs): Statements that establish generally accepted accounting principles (GAAP) for specific accounting issues.

Statements of position (SOPs): Statements issued by the Accounting Standards Division of the AICPA to influence the development of accounting standards.

Stock appreciation rights: Give the holder the right to receive compensation at some future date based on the market price of the stock at the date of exercise over a preestablished price.

Stock certificate: A document issued to a stockholder indicating the number of shares of stock owned.

Stock dividend: A dividend in the form of additional shares of a company's stock.

Stock options: Allow the holder to purchase a company's stock at favorable terms.

Stock rights: Rights issued to existing shareholders to buy shares of stock in order to maintain their proportionate ownership interests.

Stock split: Increase in the number of shares of a class of capital stock, with no change in the total dollar amount of the class, but with a converse reduction in the par or stated value of the shares.

Stockholder (shareholder): The owner of one or more shares of stock in an incorporated business.

Stockholders' (shareholders') equity: Total owners' equity of a corporation.

Straight-line amortization of bonds: Writes off an equal amount of bond premium or discount each period.

Straight-line method: A method of depreciation that allocates the cost of a tangible asset in a constant over the life of the asset.

Sub prime loan: A type of loan that is offered at a rate above prime to individuals who do not qualify for prime rate loans (considered to be a high-risk loan).

Subordinated debt: A form of long-term debt that is "junior," or in a secondary position vis-à-vis the claim on a company's assets for the payment of its other debt obligations.

Subscription: A contract between the purchaser of stock and the issuer in which the purchaser promises to buy shares of the issuing company's stock.

Subsequent events: Events that occur after the balance sheet date but before the statements are issued.

Subsidiary: An entity economically controlled by another company, despite its independent legal status.

Subsidiary account: One of the accounts in a particular subsidiary ledger.

Subsidiary ledger: Provides detailed information regarding a particular general ledger account.

Successful-efforts method: The method of accounting which capitalizes only the costs that result in the discovery of oil and gas reserves.

Sum-of-the-years'-digits method: A method of depreciation that takes a fraction each year times the cost less salvage value. The numerator of the fraction is the remaining number of years of life. The denominator remains constant and is the sum of the digits of the years of life.

Summary annual report: A simplified annual report in which data required by the SEC is supplied in the proxy statement and the Form 10-K.

Summary of significant accounting policies: A description of all significant accounting policies of the company. An integral part of the financial statements, this information is typically presented as the first footnote.

Supplies: Items used indirectly in the production of goods or services.

T

T-account: A form of ledger page used to record (or illustrate) the entry of debits and credits into ledger accounts.

Take-or-pay contract: An executory contract by which one party agrees to pay for the product regardless of whether or not the product is physically received.

Tangible assets: The physical facilities used in the operation of a business.

Tax benefit: A reduction in taxes, or a tax credit or refund, due to a particular action or expense incurred by a taxable entity.

Taxable income: Income determined in accordance with income tax regulation.

Taxes payable: Represents unpaid taxes that are owed to a governmental unit.

Technical analysis: A method of predicting stock prices based on historical price and trading patterns.

Temporal method of translation: A method of translating foreign financial statements in which cash, receivables, and payables are translated at the exchange rate in effect at the balance sheet date. Other assets and liabilities are translated at historical rates, while revenues and expenses are translated at the weighted average rate for the period.

Temporary accounts: Accounts closed at the end of an accounting period; includes all income statement accounts and the dividends account.

Temporary differences: Revenue and expense recognized in one period for financial reporting but recognized in an earlier or a later period for income tax purposes.

10-K report: Mandatory report filed by a company on an annual basis with the Securities and Exchange Commission.

10-Q report: Mandatory report filed by a company on a quarterly basis with the Securities and Exchange Commission.

Term bonds: Bonds that mature in one lump sum at a specified future date.

Time period: Assumes that the entity can be accounted for with reasonable accuracy for a particular period of time.

Time value of money: The concept that money earns interest over time. This implies that a dollar to be received a year from now is worth less than a dollar received today.

Timeliness: The qualitative characteristic indicating that accounting information should reach the user in time to help in making a decision.

Trading on equity: Financial leverage, or the use of borrowed funds, particularly long-term debt, in the capital structure of a firm.

Trading securities: Securities held by firms for brief periods of time that are intended to generate profits from short-term differences in price.

Transaction approach: The recording of events that affect the financial position of the entity and that can be reasonably determined in monetary terms.

Translation adjustments (foreign currency translation adjustment): An account classified under stockholders' equity that represents foreign currency translation gains and losses that have not been charged to the income statement.

Translation gains and losses: Gains and losses due to fluctuations in exchange rates.

Treadway Commission: Popular name for the National Commission on Fraudulent Reporting, which has issued a number of recommendations for the prevention of fraud in financial reports, ethics, and effective internal controls.

Treasurer: The officer in a firm who is responsible for the safeguarding and efficient use of a company's liquid assets.

Treasury stock: Capital stock of a company, either common or preferred, that has been issued and reacquired by the issuing company but has not been reissued or retired. It reduces stockholders' equity.

Trend analysis: Analysis over more than one accounting period to identify the trend of a company's results.

Trial balance: A listing of all general ledger accounts and their balances for the purpose of verifying that total debits equal total credits.

Troubled debt restructuring: A concession by creditors to allow debtors to eliminate or modify debt obligations.

U

Unappropriated retained earnings: The unrestricted retained earnings.

Unaudited: A term applied to information in the annual or quarterly reports that is outside the audit conducted by the auditors.

Unconsolidated subsidiaries: Subsidiaries whose financial statements are not combined with those of the parent company.

Understandability: A user-specific quality directing that accounting information be understandable to users who have a reasonable knowledge of business and economic activities and who are willing to study the information with reasonable diligence.

Unearned income: A liability, either current or long-term, for income received prior to the delivery of goods or the rendering of services (also described as deferred income).

Unexpended industrial revenue bond proceeds: An asset account, classified under other assets, representing funds that have not yet been used for the purpose indicated when the bonds were issued.

Unit-of-production method: Relates depreciation to the output capacity of the asset, estimated for the life of the asset.

Unlimited liability: Each partner is liable for all partnership debts. Limited partners in a limited partnership, which is allowed in some states, do not have unlimited liability.

Unlisted securities: Securities that are not listed on an organized stock exchange.

Unqualified opinion: An audit opinion not qualified for any material scope restrictions or departures from GAAP.

Unrealized decline in market value of noncurrent equity investments: A stockholders' equity account that results from adjusting long-term equity securities to the lower of cost or market value.

Unrealized (gain) loss: A (gain) loss recognized in the financial statements but not associated with an asset sale.

Unsecured (debenture) bonds: Bonds for which no specific collateral has been pledged.

Unusual or infrequent item: Certain income statement items that are unusual or occur infrequently, but not both.

Useful life: Length of time over which a long-term asset is forecasted to provide economic benefits.

V

Valuation: A process of estimating the value of a firm or some component of a firm.

Venture capital: Funding by investment firms that specialize in financing unproven but potentially profitable businesses.

Verifiability: The qualitative characteristic indicating that accounting information can be confirmed or duplicated by independent parties using the same measurement technique.

Vertical analysis: A comparison of various financial statement items within a single period with the use of common-size statements.

Vertical integration: The combination of firms with operations in different but successive stages of production and/or distribution.

Vested benefit obligation (VBO): The portion of the pension benefit obligation that does not depend on future employee service.

Vesting: The accrual to an employee of pension rights arising from employer contributions that are not contingent on the employee's continuing service with the employer.

W

Warrant: A security that gives the holder the right to purchase shares of common stock in accordance with the terms of the instrument, usually upon payment of a specified amount.

Warranties: Obligations of a company to provide free service on units failing to perform satisfactorily or to replace defective goods.

Warranty obligations: Estimated obligations arising out of product warranties.

Weighted average cost method: An inventory costing method that assigns the same unit cost to all units available for sale during the period.

Weighted average of outstanding common stock: Gives the proportional shares outstanding in their fraction of the fiscal year.

Work in process: Goods started, but not ready for sale.

Working capital: The excess of current assets over current liabilities.

Write-off: A write-off recognizes that the asset no longer has any value to the firm.

Y

Yield: Dividends or interest expressed as a percentage of the cost of the security.

Z

Zero coupon bond: A bond that does not pay periodic interest but promises to pay a fixed amount at the maturity date.

Z score: Statistically derived combination of weighted ratios to predict the likelihood of bankruptcy.

Bibliography

1. Introduction to Financial Reporting

Aguilar, Luis A. "Reinvigorating the Enforcement Program to Restore Investor Confidence," Introductory Remarks Before the District of Columbia Bar, Washington, D.C. (March 18, 2009), http://www.sec.gov/, Speeches & Public Statements.

Aier, Jagadison K. Joseph Comprix, Matthew T. Gunlock, and Deanna Lee. "The Financial Expertise of CFOs and Accounting Restatements," *Accounting Horizons* (September 2005), 123–135.

American Accounting Association's Financial Accounting Standards Committee. "The FASB's Conceptual Framework for Financial Reporting: A Critical Analysis," *Accounting Horizons* (June 2007), 229–238.

Armstrong, C., M. Barth, A. Jagolinzer, and E. Riedl. "Market Reaction to the Adoption of IFRS in Europe," *The Accounting Review* (January 2010), 31–61.

Ashbaugh, H., R. LaFond, and B. W. Mayhew. "Do Nonaudit Services Compromise Auditor Independence? Further Evidence," *The Accounting Review* (78: 2003), 611–639.

Bae, K. H., H. Tan, and M. Welker. "International GAAP Differences: The Impact on Foreign Analysts," *The Accounting Review* (May 2008), 593–628.

Ball, Ray. "What is the Actual Economic Role of Financial Reporting?" *Accounting Horizons* (December 2008), 427–432.

Bannister, James W., and Harry A. Newman. "Analysis of Corporate Disclosures on Relative Performance Evaluation," *Accounting Horizons* (September 2003), 235–246.

Bartley, Jon. "Are You Prepared for XBLL?," *Financial Executive* (October 2010), 30–33.

Beckwith, George. "Is a Separate FASB for Private Company GAAP Coming?" *Financial Executive* (October 2010), 66–67.

Beneish, M., and T. Yohn. "Information Friction and Investor Home Bias: A Perspective on the Effect of Global IFRS Adoption on the Extent of Equity Home Bias," Journal of Accounting and Public Policy (November 2008), 433–443.

Beresford, Dennis. "How to Succeed as a Standard Setter by Trying Really Hard," *Accounting Horizons* (September 1997), 79–90.

Bloomfield, Robert J. "Accounting as the Language of Business," *Accounting Horizons* (December 2008), 433–436.

Bradshaw, M., and G. Miller. "Will Harmonizing Accounting Standards Really Harmonize Accounting? Evidence from Non-U.S. Firms Adopting US GAAP," *Journal of Accounting, Auditing and Finance* (Spring 2008), 233–263.

Brody, Richard G., D. Jordan Lowe, and Kurt Pany. "Could $51 Million Be Immaterial When Enron Reports Income of $10.5 Million?" *Accounting Horizons* (June 2003), 153–160.

Cain, A. "Simplified Accounting Principles on the Horizon for Small Firms," *Internal Auditor* (April 2007), 20–20.

Carpenter, Tina D., M. G. Fennema, Phillip Z. Fretwell, and William Hillson. "A Changing Corporate Culture," *Journal of Accountancy* (March 2004), 57–61.

Chen, Shimin, Zzheng Sun, and Yuetang Wang. "Evidence from China on Whether Harmonized Accounting Standards Harmonize Accounting Practices," *Accounting Horizons* (September 2002), 183–197.

Cheney, Glen. "Differential Problems & Possibilities," *Financial Executive* (March/April 2004), 20–22.

Cheney, Glen. "If IFRS Offer the Answer, They Sure Raise a Lot of Questions," *Financial Executive* (November 2007), 21–23.

Cotter, J., and I. Zimmer. "Disclosure Versus Recognition: The Case of Asset Revaluations," *Asia Pacific Journal of Accounting and Economics* (June 2003), 81–99.

Cox, Christopher. "Chairman's Address to the SEC Roundtable on International Financial Reporting Standards," (March 6, 2007), http://www.sec.gov/news/speech/2007/spch030607cc.htm.

Cox, Christopher. "Remarks Before the AICPA National Conference on Current SEC and PCAOB Developments," Washington, D.C. (December 8, 2008), http://www.sec.gov/, Speeches & Public Statements.

Cox, Christopher. "Securing America's Competitiveness," Remarks by the SEC Chairman to the U.S. Chamber of Commerce (March 14, 2007), http://www.sec.gov/news/speech/2007/spch031407cc.htm.

Davidson, Ronald A., Alexander M. G. Gelardi, and Fangyue Li. "Analysis of the Conceptual Framework of China's New Accounting System," *Journal of Accounting* (March 1996), 58–74.

DeFelice, Alexandra. "Private Company Financial Reporting," *Journal of Accounting* (February 2011), 34–36.

de Mesa Graziano, Cheryl, and William M. Sinnett. "How Low Can Sarbanes-Oxley Section 404 Costs Go?" *Financial Executive* (July/August 2007), 61–63.

Dye, Ronald A., and Shyam Sunder. "Why Not Allow FASB and IASB Standards to Compete in the U.S." *Accounting Horizons* (September 2001), 257–271.

Farber, David B., Marilyn F. Johnson, and Kathy R. Petroni. "Congressional Intervention in the Standard-Setting Process: An Analysis of the Stock Option Accounting Reform Act of 2004," *Accounting Horizons* (March 2007), 1–2.

Ford, Caroline O., and C. William Thomas. "Test-Driving the Codification," *Journal of Accounting* (December 2008), 62–66.

Fornaro, James M. "SEC Guidance on Disclosure Related to Climate Change," *Journal of Accounting* (January 2011), 42–44.

Gannon, D. J. "Achieving a Single Global Standard," *CPA Journal* (August 2010), (Vol. 80 Issue 8), 11–12.

Gannon, D. J., and Alex Ashwal. "Financial Reporting Goes Global," *Journal of Accounting* (September 2004), 43–47.

Ge, Weili, and Sarah McVay. "The Disclosure of Material Weaknesses in Internal Control After the Sarbanes-Oxley Act," *Accounting Horizons* (September 2005), 137–158.

Geiger, Marshall A., and K. Raghunandan. "Going-Concern Opinions in the New Legal Environment," *Accounting Horizons* (March 2002), 17–26.

Geiger, Marshall A., and Dasaratha V. Rama. "Audit Firm Size and Going-Concern Reporting Accuracy," *Accounting Horizons* (March 2006), 1–17.

Geiger, Marshall A., and Porcher L. Taylor III. "CEO and CFO Certifications of Financial Information," *Accounting Horizons* (December 2003), 357–368.

Gerboth, Dale L. "The Conceptual Framework: Not Definitions, But Professional Values," *Accounting Horizons* (September 1987), 1–8.

Gill, M. Lawrence. "IFRS: Coming to America," *Journal of Accountancy* (June 2007), 70–71.

Goldwasser, D. L. "Independence in a Changing Accounting Profession: Is It Possible to Achieve?," *The CPA Journal* (October 1999), 46–51.

Grady, Robert E. "The Sarbox Monster," *The Wall Street Journal* (April 26, 2007), A29.

Grant, C. Terry, Chauncey M. DePree, and Gerry H. Grant. "Earnings Management and the Abuse of Materiality," *Journal of Accountancy* (September 2000), 41–44.

Gray, Sidney J., Cheryl L. Linthicum, and Donna L. Streat. "Have European and US GAAP Measures of Income and Equity Converged Under IFRS? Evidence from European Companies Listed in the U.S.," *Accounting & Business Research* (Vol. 39, 2009), 431–447.

Hail, Luzi, Christian Leuz, and Peter Wysocki. "Global Accounting Convergence and the Potential Adoption of IFRS by the U.S. (Part II): Political Factors and Future Scenarios for U.S. Accounting Standards," *Accounting Horizons* (December 2010), 567–588.

Heffes, Ellen M., and Cheryl deMesa Graziano. "Accounting Without Borders: Has Its Time Come?," *Financial Executive* (September 2007), 22–26.

Heffes, Ellen M. "IFRS in the U.S. Raises Questions: 'Convergence' or 'Conversion'?" *Financial Executive* (Vol. 25, Issue 5), 111–115.

Henry, Elaine, Stephen Lin, and Ya-Wen Yeng. "The European U.S. GAAP; IFRS to U.S.," *Accounting Horizons* (June 2009), 121–150.

Herrmann, Don, and Ian P. N. Hague. "Convergence in Search of the Best," *Journal of Accounting* (January 2006), 69–73.

Hirshleifer, D., S. Lim, and S. Teoh. "Limited Attention, Information Disclosure, and Financial Reporting," *Journal of Accounting and Economics* (36: 2003), 332–386.

Holder-Webb, Lora M., and Michael S. Wilkins. "The Incremental Information Content of SAS No. 559 Going-Concern Opinions," *Journal of Accounting Research* (Spring 2000), 209–219.

James, Kevin L. "The Effects of Internal Audit Structure on Perceived Financial Statement Fraud Prevention," *Accounting Horizons* (December 2003), 315–327.

Kahn, Jeremy. "Accounting's White Knight," *Fortune* (September 30, 2002), 117, 118, 120, 122.

King, Ronald R. "The PCAOB Meets the Constitution: The Supreme Court to Decide on the PCAOB's Conformity with the Separation of Powers Doctrine and Appointments Clause," *Accounting Horizons* (March 2010), 79–83.

Klein, April. "Likely Effects of Stock Exchange Governance Proposals and Sarbanes-Oxley on Corporate Boards and Financial Reporting," *Accounting Horizons* (December 2003), 343–355.

Kranacher, Mary-Jo. "Bringing the World Together on One Standard," *CPA Journal* (October 2010), 16–23.

Lamoreaux, Mathew G., and Kim Nilsen. "Convergence Milestone," *Journal of Accountancy* (August 2010), 26–31.

Leug, Christian. "Different Approaches to Corporate Reporting Regulation: How Jurisdictions Differ and Why," *Accounting & Business Research* (Special Issue 2010), 229–256.

Levitt, A. "The Importance of High Quality Accounting Standards," *Accounting Horizons* (March 1998), 79–82.

Li, S. "Does Mandatory Adoption of International Financial Reporting Standards in the European Union Reduce the Cost of Equity Capital?" *The Accounting Review* (March 2010), 607–636.

Lobo, Gerald J., and Jian Zhou. "Did Conservatism in Financial Reporting Increase After the Sarbanes-Oxley Act? Initial Evidence," *Accounting Review* (March 2006), 57–73.

Martin, Alyssa. "How Section 404 Can Help Deter Fraud," *Financial Executive* (May 2005), 45–47.

McAnally, Mary Lea, McGuire, Sean T., and Weaver, Connie D. "Assessing the Financial Reporting Consequences of Conversion to IFRS: The Case of Equity-Based Compensation," *Accounting Horizons* (December 2010), 589–621.

McEwen, Ruth Ann, Thomas J. Joey, and John A. Brozousky. "The FASB's Codification Project: A Critical Step Toward Simplification," *Accounting Horizons* (December 2006), 391–398.

McKinnon, John D. "U.S., EU to Streamline Accounting," *The Wall Street Journal* (May 1, 2007), A8.

Meeks, G., and G. Swann. "Accounting Standards and the Economics of Standards," *Accounting and Business Research* (Vol. 39, Issue 3, 2009), 191–210.

Mercer, Molly. "How Do Investors Assess the Credibility of Management Disclosures?," *Accounting Horizons* (September 2004), 185–196.

Mosso, David. "Transparency Unveiled: Financial Crisis Prevention Through Accounting Reform," *Accounting Horizons* (March 2010), 95–107.

Munter, Paul. "Accounting Standard-Setting: Convergence Drives More Change," *Financial Executive* (January – February 2011), 22–25.

Nelson, M. "Behavioral Evidence on the Effects of Principles and Rules Bases Standards," *Accounting Horizons* (March 2003), 91–104.

Nobes, Christopher W. "Rules-Based Standards and the Lack of Principles in Accounting," *Accounting Horizons* (March 2005), 25–34.

Orenstein, Edith. "Ask FERF About... International Standard-Setting Organization," *Financial Executive* (March 2005), 64.

Parfet, W. V. "Accounting Subjectivity and Earnings Management: A Prepared Perspective," *Accounting Horizons* (December 2000), 481–488.

Pickard, Geoffrey. "Simplify Global Accounting," *Journal of Accountancy* (July 2007), 36–38.

Plumlee, M., and D. Plumlee. "Information Lost: A Descriptive Analysis of IFRS Firms' 20-F Reconciliations," *Journal of Applied Research in Accounting and Finance* (January 2008), 15–31.

Practer, Paul. "Should U.S. Private Companies Use IFRS for SMEs?" *Financial Executive* (October 2007), 16–17.

Pratt, Mary K. "Get Ready for Global Accounting," *Computer World* (February 8, 2010), 21–23.

Price, Jennifer Tisone. "A Brave New World: The Future of Audit Standards," *Catalyst* (September/October 2003), 8–10.

Qu, Xiaohu, and Guohua Zhang. Measuring the Convergence of National Accounting Standards with International Financial Reporting Standards: The Application of Fuzzy Clustering Analysis," *International Journal of Accounting* (September 2010), 334–355.

Ramos, Michael. "Section 404 Compliance in the Annual Report," *Journal of Accountancy* (October 2004), 43–48.

Ratnatunga, Janek, Stewart Jones, and Kashi R. Balachandran. "The Valuation and Reporting of Organizational Capability in Carbon Emissions Management," *Accounting Horizons* (March 2011), 127–142.

Reed, Ronald O., William M. Sinnett, Thomas Buchman, and Richard Wobbekind. "Should Private Companies Implement Sarbanes-Oxley?," *Financial Executive* (April 2005), 54–57.

Reilly, David. "What's Better in Accounting, Rules or 'Feel'?" *The Wall Street Journal* (April 30, 2007), C1–2.

Reither, Cheri L. "How the FASB Approaches a Standard-Setting Issue," *Accounting Horizons* (December 1997), 91–104.

Response to the SEC Release, "Acceptance from Foreign Private Issuers of Financial Statements Prepared in Accordance with International Financial Reporting Standards without Reconciliation to US GAAP, File No. 57-13-07."

Rogero, L. H. "Characteristics of High Quality Accounting Standards," *Accounting Horizons* (June 1998), 177–183.

SEC's Congressionally Mandated Study on Mark-to-Market Accounting, (December 30, 2008), http://www.sec.gov, Special Studies.

SEC Special Studies Archive, "Report and Recommendations Pursuant to Section 401(c) of the Sarbanes-Oxley Act of 2002 on Arrangements with Off-Balance Sheet Implications, Special Purpose Entities, and Transparency of Filings by Issuers," (June 15, 2005), http://www.sec.gov/news/studies/soxoffbalancerpt.pdf.

Sinnett, William M., and Ellen M. Heffes. "Section 404 Implementation: Is the Gain Worth the Pain?," *Financial Executive* (May 2005), 30–32.

Stamp, Edward. "Why Can Accounting Not Become a Science Like Physics?" *Abacus* (Spring 1981), 13–27.

Sunder, S. "Adverse Effects of Uniform Written Reporting Standards on Accounting Practice, Education, and Research," *Journal of Accounting and Public Policy* (March 2010), 99–114.

Sutton, Michael H. "Financial Reporting in U.S. Capital Markets: International Dimensions," *Accounting Horizons* (June 1997), 96–102.

Swieringa, Robert J. "Robert T. Sprouse and Fundamental Concepts of Financial Accounting," *Accounting Horizons* (March 2011), 207–220.

Tie, Robert. "The Case for Private Company GAAP," *Journal of Accountancy* (May 2005), 27–29.

Vorhies, James Brady. "The New Importance of Materiality," *Journal of Accountancy* (May 2005), 53–59.

Wallace, Wanda A., and John Walsh. "Apples-to-Apples Profits Abroad," *Financial Executives* (May/June 1995), 28–31.

Watts, Ross L. "Conservatism in Accounting Part I" Explanations and Implications," *Accounting Horizons* (September 2003), 207–221.

Watts, Ross L. "Conservationism in Accounting Part II: Evidence and Research Opportunities," *Accounting Horizons* (December 2003), 287–301.

Wyatt, Arthur R. "Accounting Professionalism – They Just Don't Get It!," *Accounting Horizons* (March 2004), 45–53.

Wyatt, Arthur. "Accounting Standards: Conceptual or Political?," *Accounting Horizons* (September 1990), 83–88.

Zeff, Stephen A. "How the U.S. Accounting Profession Got Where It Is Today: Part I," *Accounting Horizons* (September 2003), 189–205.

Zeff, Stephen A. "Political Lobbying on Proposed Standards: A Challenge to the IASB," *Accounting Horizons* (March 2002), 45–54.

2. Introduction to Financial Statements and Other Financial Reporting Topics

Atkins, Paul S. "Is Excessive Regulation and Litigation Eroding U.S. Financial Competitiveness?," Remarks by SEC Commissioner, Conference Co-Sponsored by the American Enterprise Institute and the Brookings Institution, Washington, D.C. (April 20, 2007), http://www.sec.gov/news/speech/2007/spch042007psa.htm.

Bauer, Christopher. "A Preventative Maintenance Approach to Ethics," *Financial Executive* (May 2005), 18–20.

Benston, Gi, and A. Hartgraves. "Enron: What Happened and What We Can Learn From It," *Journal of Accounting and Public Policy* (August 2002), 105–127.

Bruns, William J., and Kenneth A. Merchant. "The Dangerous Morality of Managing Earnings," *Management Accounting* (August 1990), 22–25.

Campos, Roel C. "SEC Regulation Outside the United States," Remarks by SEC Commissioner Before the Governance for Owners Conference in London, England (March 8, 2007), http://www.sec.gov/news/speech/2007/spch030807rcc.htm.

Cook, J. Michael, and Michael H. Sutton. "Summary Annual Reporting: A Cure for Information Overload," *Financial Executive* (January/February 1995), 12–15.

Copeland, Jr., James E. "Ethics as an Imperative," *Accounting Horizons* (March 2005), 35–43.

DeFond, M., K. Raghunandan, and K. Jubramanyam. "Do Non-Audit Service Fees Impair Auditor Independence? Evidence from Going Concern Audit Opinions," *Journal of Accounting Research* (September 2002), 1247–1274.

Duska, Ronald F., and Brenda Shay Duska. "Accounting Ethics," (Cambridge, MA: Blackwell, 2003).

Epstein, Marc J., and Moses L. Pava. "Profile of an Annual Report," *Financial Executive* (January/February 1994), 41–43.

Erickson, Merle, Brian W. Mayhew, and William L. Felix, Jr. "Why Do Audits Fail? Evidence from Lincoln Savings and Loan," *Journal of Accounting Research* (Spring 2000), 165–194.

Ettredge, Michael, James Heintz, Chan Li, and Susan Scholz. "Auditor Realignments Accompanying Implementation of SOX 404 ICFR Reporting Requirements," *Accounting Horizons* (March 2011), 17–39.

Firth, Michael. "Auditor-Provided Consultancy Services and Their Associations with Audit Fees and Audit Opinions," *Journal of Business Finance & Accounting* (June/July 2002), 661–694.

Frankel, R., M. Johnson, and K. Nelson. "The Relation Between Auditor's Fees for Non-Audit Services and Earnings Quality," *The Accounting Review* (77 Supplement 2002), 71–105.

Gibson, A. M., and A. H. Frakes. "Truth or Consequences: A Study of Critical Issues and Decision Making in Accounting," *Journal of Business Ethics* (16 (2) 1997), 161–171.

Graham, Roger C., Raymond D. King, and Cameron K. J. Merrill. "Decision Usefulness of Alternative Joint Venture Reporting Methods," *Accounting Horizons* (June 2003), 123–137.

Hartgraves, Al L., and George J. Benston. "The Evolving Accounting Standards for Special Purpose Entities and Consolidations," *Accounting Horizons* (September 2002), 245–258.

Heiman, V. "Auditors' Assessments of the Likelihood of Analytical Review Explanations," *The Accounting Review* (65: 1990), 875–890.

Heiman-Hoffman, V. B., K. P. Morgan, and J. M. Patton. "The Warning Signs of Fraudulent Financial Reporting," *Journal of Accountancy* (October 1996), 75–77.

Hermanson, Dana R., Jagan Krishnan, and Zhongxia Ye. "Adverse Section 404 Opinions and Shareholder Dissatisfaction Toward Auditors," *Accounting Horizons* (December 2009), 391–409.

Hitlebeitel, K. M., and S. K. Jones. "Initial Evidence on the Impact of Integrating Ethics into Accounting Education," *Issues in Accounting Education* (6: 1991), 262–275.

Huss, H. Fenwick, and Denise M. Palterson. "Ethics in Accounting: Values Education Without Indoctrination," *Journal of Business Ethics* (March 1993), 235–243.

Ingberman, M., and G. H. Sorter. "The Role of Financial Statements in an Efficient Market," *Journal of Accounting, Auditing and Finance* (Fall 1978), 58–62.

Krall, Karen M. "More Talk, More Action," *Journal of Accountancy* (May 2005), 67–70; 72–74.

Krishnan, Jayanthi, and Joon S. Yang. "Recent Trends in Audit Report and Earnings Announcements Lags," *Accounting Horizons* (December 2009), 265–288.

Lee, Charles, and Dale Morse. "Summary Annual Reports," *Accounting Horizons* (March 1990), 39–50.

Lowe, Herman J. "Ethics in Our 100-Year History," *Journal of Accountancy* (May 1987), 78–87.

McEnroe, John E., and Stanley C. Martens. "Auditors' and Investors' Perceptions of the Expectation Gap," *Accounting Horizons* (December 2001), 345–358.

Meiers, Donald H. "The MD&A Challenge," *Journal of Accountancy* (January 2006), 59–60, 62, 64, 66.

Millman, Gregory J. "New Scandals, Old Lessons: Financial Ethics After Enron," *Financial Executive* (July/August 2002), 16–19.

Nagy, Albert L. "Mandatory Audit Firm Turnover, Financial Reporting Quality, and Client Bargaining Power: The Case of Arthur Anderson," *Accounting Horizons* (June 2005), 51–68.

Nagy, Albert L. "Section 404 Compliance and Financial Reporting Quality," *Accounting Horizons* (September 2010), 441–454.

Nair, R. D., and Larry E. Rittenberg. "Summary Annual Reports: Background and Implications for Financial Reporting and Auditing," *Accounting Horizons* (March 1990), 25–38.

Perera, M. H. "Towards a Framework to Analyzing the Impact of Culture on Accounting," *International Journal of Accounting* (1989), 42–56.

Ponemon, L., and A. Glazer. "Accounting Education and Ethical Development; The Influence of Liberal Learning on Students and Alumni in Accounting Practice," *Issues in Accounting Education* (5: 1990), 195–208.

Price, Jennifer Tisone. "A Brave New World: The Future of Audit Standards," *Catalyst* (September/October 2003), 8–10.

Raghunandan, K., William J. Read, and J. Scott Whisenant. "Initial Evidence on the Association Between Nonaudit Fees and Restated Financial Statements," *Accounting Horizons* (September 2003), 223–224.

Rama, Dasaratha V., and William J. Read. "Resignations by the Big 4 and the Market for Audit Services," *Accounting Horizons* (June 2006), 97–109.

Sainty, Barbara J., Gary K. Taylor, and David D. Williams. "Investor Dissatisfaction Toward Auditors," *Journal of Accounting, Auditing, & Finance* (Spring 2002), 111–136.

Schroeder, Nicholas W., and Charles H. Gibson. "Are Summary Annual Reports Successful?" *Accounting Horizons* (June 1992), 28–37.

Schroeder, Nicholas W., and Charles H. Gibson. "Improving Annual Reports by Improving the Readability of Footnotes," *The Woman CPA* (April 1988), 13–16.

Shafer, William E., D. Jordan Lowe, and Timothy J. Fogarty. "The Effects of Corporate Ownership on Public Accountants' Professionalism and Ethics," *Accounting Horizons* (June 2002), 109–124.

Smith, Dr. L. Murphy. "A Fresh Look at Accounting Ethics (or Dr. Smith Goes to Washington)," *Accounting Horizons* (March 2003), 47–49.

Snyder, Lisa A. "Streamlining Ethics Enforcement," *Journal of Accountancy* (August 2003), 51–56.

Wells, Joseph T. "So That's Why It's Called a Pyramid Scheme," *Journal of Accountancy* (October 2000), 91–95.

Wells, Joseph T. "Timing Is of the Essence," *Journal of Accountancy* (May 2001), 78; 81-82; 85–87.

Wilks, T. Jeffery, and Mark F. Zimbelman. "Using Game Theory and Strategic Reasoning Concepts to Prevent and Detect Fraud," *Accounting Horizons* (September 2004), 173–184.

3. Balance Sheet

Bahnam, Russ. "Valuing IP Post-Sarbanes-Oxley," *Journal of Accounting* (November 2005), 72–78.

Barron, Orie E., Donal Byard, Charles Kite, and Edward J. Riedl. "High-Technology Intangibles and Analysts' Forecasts," *Journal of Accounting Research* (May 2002), 289–320.

Botosan, Christine A., Lisa Koonce, Stephen G. Ryan, Mary S. Stone, and James M. Wahlen. "Accounting for Liabilities: Conceptual Issues, Standard Setting, and Evidence from Academic Research," *Accounting Horizons* (September 2005), 159–186.

Donohue, James, and Cynthia Waller Vallario. "A New Scorecard for Intellectual Property," *Journal of Accountancy* (April 2002), 75–79.

Flamholtz, Eric G., D. Gerald Searfoss, and Russell Coff. "Developing Human Resource Accounting as a Human Resource Decision Support System," *Accounting Horizons* (September 1988), 1–9.

Frischmann, Peter J., Paul D. Kimmel, and Terry D. Warfield. "Innovation in Preferred Stock: Current Developments and Implications for Financial Reporting," *Accounting Horizons* (September 1999), 201–218.

Gibson, Charles H. "Quasi-Reorganizations in Practice," *Accounting Horizons* (September 1988), 83–89.

Healy, Paul M., Stewart C. Myers, and Christopher D. Howe. "The R & D Accounting and the Tradeoff Between Relevance and Objectivity," *Journal of Accounting Research* (June 2002), 677–710.

Kim, M., and G. Moore. "Economics vs. Accounting Depreciation," *Journal of Accounting and Economics* (April 1988), 111–125.

Leu, Baruch. "Intangibles at a Crossroads: What's Next?," *Financial Executive* (March/April 2002), 34–36, 38–39.

Luft, Joan. "Nonfinancial Information and Accounting: A Reconsideration of Benefits," *Accounting Horizons* (December 2009), 307–325.

Moehrle, Stephen R., Jennifer A. Reynolds-Moehrle, and James S. Wallace. "How Informative Are Earnings Numbers That Exclude Goodwill Amortization," *Accounting Horizons* (September 2001), 243–255.

Mueller, Jennifer M. "Amortization of Certain Intangible Assets," *Journal of Accountancy* (December 2004), 74–78.

Murry, Dennis. "What Are the Essential Features of a Liability?," *Accounting Horizons* (December 2010), 623–633.

Sanders, George, Paul Munter, and Tommy Moures. "Software-The Unrecorded Asset," *Management Accounting* (August 1994), 57–61.

Sundar, Shyam. "Econometrics of Fair Values," *Accounting Horizons* (March 2008), 111–125.

Trott, Edward W. "Accounting for Debt Instruments Held as Assets," *Accounting Horizons* (December 2009), 457–469.

4. Income Statement

Asquith, Paul, Paul Healy, and Krishna Palepu. "Earnings and Stock Splits," *The Accounting Review* (July 1989), 387–403.

Bauman, Mark P. "The Impact and Valuation of Off-Balance-Sheet Activities Concealed by Equity Method Accounting," *Accounting Horizons* (December 2003), 303–314.

Burgstahler, David, James Jiambolvo, and Terry Shevlin. "Do Stock Prices Fully Reflect the Implications of Special Items for Future Earnings?," *Journal of Accounting Research* (June 2002), 585–612.

Cheng, Q. "What Determines Residual Income?," *The Accounting Review* (January 2005), 85–112.

Elliott, J. A., and D. R. Philbrick. "Accounting Changes and Earnings Predictability," *The Accounting Review* (January 1990), 157–174.

Hirst, D. Eric, and Lisa Koonce. "Management Earnings Forecasts: A Review and Framework," *Accounting Horizons* (September 2008), 315–338.

Lilien, Steven, Martin Mellman, and Victor Pastena. "Accounting Changes: Successful Versus Unsuccessful Firms," *The Accounting Review* (October 1988), 642–656.

McGough, Eugene. "Anatomy of a Stock Split," *Management Accounting* (September 1993), 58–61.

Moore, Lovella. "Economic 'Reality' and the Myth of the Bottom Line," *Accounting Horizons* (September 2009), 327–340.

Pincus, Morton, and Charles Wasley. "The Incidence of Accounting Changes and Characteristics of Firms Making Accounting Changes," *Journal of Accountancy* (June 1994), 1–24.

5. Basics of Analysis

Chang, L. S., K. S. Most, and C. W. Brain. "The Utility of Annual Reports: An International Study," *Journal of International Business Studies* (Spring/Summer 1983), 63–84.

Gibson, C. H., and P. A. Boyer. "Need for Disclosure of Uniform Financial Ratios," *Journal of Accountancy* (May 1980), 78.

Wells, Joseph T. "Irrational Ratios," *Journal of Accountancy* (August 2001), 80–83.

Wittington, G. "Some Basic Properties of Accounting Ratios," *Journal of Business Finance and Accounting* (Summer 1980), 219–232.

6. Liquidity of Short-Term Assets; Related Debt-Paying Ability

Boer, Germain. "Managing the Cash GAP," *Journal of Accountancy*, (October 1999), 27–32.

Davis, H. Z., N. Kahn, and E. Rosen. "LIFO Inventory Liquidations: An Empirical Study," *Journal of Accounting Research* (Autumn 1984), 480–496.

Dopuch, N., and M. Pincus. "Evidence on the Choice of Inventory Accounting Methods: LIFO Versus FIFO," *Journal of Accounting Research* (Spring 1988), 28–59.

Heath, L. C. "Is Working Capital Really Working?," *Journal of Accountancy* (August 1980), 55–62.

Hunt, H. G. III. "Potential Determinants of Corporate Inventory Accounting Decisions," *Journal of Accounting Research* (Autumn 1985), 448–467.

Payne, Stephen. "Working Capital Optimization Can Yield Real Gains," *Financial Executive* (September 2002), 40–42.

7. Long-Term Debt-Paying Ability

Boatsman, James, and Xiaobo Dong. "Equity Value Implications of Lease Accounting," *Accounting Horizons* (March 2011), 1–16.

Deakin, Edward B. "Accounting for Contingencies: The Pennzoil-Texaco Case," *Accounting Horizons* (March 1989), 21–28.

Desir, Rosemond, Kirsten Fanning, and Ray J. Pfeiffer. "Are Revisions to SFAS No. 5 Needed?," *Accounting Horizons* (December 2010), 525–545.

Dietrich, J., and R. S. Kaplan. "Empirical Analysis of the Commercial Loan Classification Decision," *Accounting Review* (January 1982), 18–38.

Heian, James B., and James B. Thies. "Consolidation of Finance Subsidiaries: $230 Billion in Off-Balance-Sheet Financing Comes Home to Roost," *Accounting Horizons* (March 1989), 1–9.

Hepp, John, and Rahul Gupta. "Preparing for the New Lease Accounting," *Financial Executive* (October 2010), 49–54.

Leib, Barclay. "Questioning the Basic Assumptions," *Financial Executive* (September 2002), 35–38.

Schipper, Katherine, and Teri Lombardi Yohn. "Standard-Setting Issues and Academic Research Related to the Accounting for Financial Asset Transfers," *Accounting Horizons* (March 2007), 59–80.

Thomas, J. K. "Why Do Firms Terminate Their Overfunded Pension Plans?," *Journal of Accounting and Economics* (November 1989), 361–398.

Williams, Georgina, and Thomas J. Phillips. "Cleaning Up Our Act: Accounting for Environmental Liabilities," *Management Accounting* (February 1994), 30–33.

8. Profitability

Albrecht, David W., and Niranjan Chipalkalti. "New Segment Reporting," *The CPA Journal* (May 1998), 46–52.

Bhattacharya, Nilabhra, Ervin L. Black, Theodore E. Christensen, and C. R. Larson. "Assessing the Relative Informativeness and Performance of Pro Forma Earnings and GAAP Operating Earnings," *Journal of Accounting and Economics* (36: 2003), 285–319.

Bhattacharya, Nilabhra, Ervin L. Black, Theodore E. Christensen, and Richard D. Mergenthaler. "Empirical Evidence on Recent Trends in Pro Forma Reporting," *Accounting Horizons* (March 2004), 27–43.

Bradshaw, Mark T., and Richard G. Sloan. "GAAP versus the Street: An Empirical Assessment of Two Alternative Definitions of Earnings," *Journal of Accounting Research* (March 2002), 41–66.

Entwistle, G. M., G. D. Feltham, and C. Mbagwu. "Financial Reporting Regulation and the Reporting of Pro Forma Earnings," *Accounting Horizons* (March 2006), 39–55.

Glover, Jonathan C., Yuja Ijiri, Carolyn B. Levine, and Pierre Jinghong Liang. "Separating Facts from Forecasts in Financial Statements," *Accounting Horizons* (December 2005), 267–282.

Guidry, F., A. J. Leone, and S. Rock. "Earnings-Based Bonus Plans and Earnings Management by Business-Unit Managers," *Journal of Accounting and Economics* (26: 1999), 113–142.

Healy, P. M., and J. M. Wahlen. "A Review of the Earnings Management Literature and Its Implications for Standard Setting," *Accounting Horizons* (October 13, 1999), 365–383.

Hodge, Frank D. "Investors' Perceptions of Earnings Quality, Auditor Independence, and the Usefulness of Audited Financial Information," *Accounting Horizons* (2003 Supplement), 37–48.

Leibowitz, M. "Market-to-Book Ratios and Positive and Negative Returns on Equity," *Journal of Financial Statement Analysis* (Winter 1999), 21–30.

Liv, Jing, and Jacob Thomas. "Stock Returns and Accounting Earnings," *Journal of Accounting Research* (Spring 2000), 71–102.

Lougee, B. A., and C. A. Marquardt. "Earnings Informativeness and Strategic Disclosure: An Empirical Examination of 'Pro Forma' Earnings," *The Accounting Review* (2004), 769–795.

MacDonald, Elizabeth. "Accounting in the Danger Zone," *Forbes* (September 2, 2002), 138.

McNichols, M., and G. P. Wilson. "Evidence of Earnings Management from the Provision for Bad Debts," *Journal of Accounting Research* (Supplement 26, 1988), 1–31.

Moses, D. "Income Smoothing and Incentives: Empirical Tests Using Accounting Changes," *The Accounting Review* (April 1987), 358–377.

Nelson, M. W., J. A. Elliot, and R. L. Tarpley. "Evidence from Auditors About Managers' and Auditors' Earnings Management Decisions," *The Accounting Review* (Supplement 2002), 175–202.

Nelson, Mark W., John A. Elliot, and Robin L. Tarpley. "How Are Earnings Managed? Examples from Auditors," *Accounting Horizons* (2003 Supplement), 17–35.

Phillips, T., M. Luehlfing, and C. Vallario. "Hazy Reporting," *Journal of Accountancy* (August 2002), 47–50.

Worthy, F. S. "Manipulating Profits: How It's Done," *Fortune* (June 15, 1984), 50–54.

9. For the Investor

Aguilar, Luis A. "Empowering the Markets Watchdog to Effect Real Results," North American Securities Administrators Association's Winter Enforcement Conference, San Diego, California (January 10, 2009), http://www.sec.gov, Speeches & Public Statements.

Aguilar, Luis A. "Increasing Accountability and Transparency to Investors," Remarks at "The SEC Speaks in 2009," Washington, D.C. (February 6, 2009), http://www.sec.gov, Speeches & Public Statements.

Aharony, J., and A. Dotan. "A Comparative Analysis of Auditor, Manager, and Financial Analyst Interpretations of SFAS No. 5 Disclosure Guidelines," *Journal of Business Finance & Accounting* (April-May), 475–504.

Arnott, Robert D., and Clifford S. Asness. "Surprise! Higher Dividends = Higher Earnings Growth," *AIMR* (2003), 70–87.

Ball, Ray. "The Earnings-Price Anomaly," *Journal of Accounting and Economics* (June/September 1992), 319–346.

Balsam, Steven, Sebastian O'Keefe, and Mark M. Wiedemer. "Frontline Reaction to FASB 123(R)," *Journal of Accountancy* (April 2007), 55–56.

Beaver, W., and D. Morse. "What Determines Price-Earnings Ratios?," *Financial Analysts Journal* (July-August 1978), 65–76.

Bens, Daniel A., Venky Nagar, and M. H. Franco Wong. "Real Investment Implications of Employee Stock Options Exercises," *Journal of Accounting Research* (May 2002), 359–406.

Block, Frank E. "A Study of the Price to Book Relationship," *Financial Analysts Journal* (January/February 1995), 63–73.

Block, Stanley. "The Dividend Puzzle: The Relationship Between Payout Rates and Growth," *AAII Journal* (May 2009), 5–7.

Botosan, Christine, A., and Marlene A. Plumlee. "Stock Options Expense: The Sword of Damocles Revealed," *Accounting Horizons* (December 2001), 311–327.

Butler, Kirt C., Larry H. P. Lang. "The Forecast Accuracy of Individual Analysts: Evidence of Systematic Optimism and Pessimism," *Journal of Accounting Research* (Spring 1991), 150–156.

CFA, Ping Zhou, and William Ruland. "Dividend Payout and Future Earnings Growth," *CFA Institute* (May/June 2006), 58–69.

Chambers, A. E., and S. H. Penman. "Timeliness of Reporting and the Stock Price Reaction to Earnings Announcements," *Journal of Accounting Research* (Spring 1984), 21–47.

Clarkson, P., Y. La, and G. Richardson. "The Market Valuation of Environmental Capital Expenditures by Pulp and Paper Companies," *The Accounting Review* (April 2004), 329–345.

Clemente, Holly A. "What Wall Street Sees When It Looks at Your P/E Ratio," *Financial Executive* (May/June 1990), 40–44.

Coggin, T. D., and J. E. Hunter. "Analysts EPS Forecasts Nearer Actual Than Statistical Models," *The Journal of Business Forecasting* (Winter 1982–1983), 20–23.

Cole, Kevin, Jean Helwege, and David Laster. "Stock Market Valuation Indicators: Is This Time Different?," *Financial Analysts Journal* (May/June 1996), 56–64.

Comiskey, Eugene E., Jonathan E. Clark, and Charles W. Mulford. "Is Negative Goodwill Valued by Investors," *Accounting Horizons* (September 2010), 333–353.

Core, John, and Wayne Guay. "Estimating the Value of Employee Stock Option Portfolios and Their Sensitivities to Price and Volatility," *Journal of Accounting Research* (June 2002), 613–630.

Duan, Ying, Gang Hu, and R. David McLean. "When Is Stock Picking Likely to Be Successful? Evidence from Mutual Funds," *Financial Analysts Journal* (March/April 2009), 1–12.

Eaton, Tim V., and Brian A. Pruryk. "No Longer an 'Option,'" *Journal of Accountancy* (April 2005), 63–68.

Farber, David B., Marilyn F. Johnson, and Kathy R. Petroni. "Congressional Intervention in the Standard-Setting Process: An Analysis of the Stock Option Accounting Reforms Act of 2004," *Accounting Horizons* (March 2007), 1–22.

Griffin, P. A. "Got Information? Investor Response to Form 10-K and Form 10-Q EDGAR Filing," *Review of Accounting Studies* (8: 2003), 433–460.

Holthausen, Robert W., and D. F. Larcker. "The Prediction of Stock Returns Using Financial Statement Information," *Journal of Accounting and Economics* (June/September 1992), 373–411.

Kaustia, Markku, Heidi Laukkanen, and Vesa Puttonen. "Should Good Stocks Have High Prices or High Returns?," *Financial Analysts Journal* (May/June 2009), 1–8.

Klarman, Seth A., and Jason Zweig. "Opportunities for Patient Investors," *Financial Analysts Journal* (September/October 2010), 18–28.

Levitt, A. "The Numbers Game. Remarks Delivered at the NYU Center for Law and Business," New York, NY (September 28, 1998), http://www.sec.gov (press release, 1998).

Liv, Jing, Doron Nissim, and Jacob Thomas. "Equity Valuation Using Multiples," *Journal of Accounting Research* (March 2002), 135–173.

MacDonald, Elizabeth. "An Expensive Option," *Forbes* (August 16, 2004), 116–117.

Mangano, Janet J. "The Little Book of Big Dividends: A Sage Formula for Guaranteed Returns," *Financial Analysts Journal* (March/April 2011), 76.

Molodovsky, Nicholas. "A Theory of Price-Earnings Ratios," *Financial Analysts Journal* (January/February 1995), 29–43.

Nichols, D. Craig, and James M. Wahlen. "How Do Earnings Numbers Relate to Stock Returns? A Review of Classic Accounting Research with Updated Evidence," *Accounting Horizons* (December 2004), 263–286.

Ou, Jane A., and Stephen H. Penman. "Financial Statement Analysis and the Prediction of Stock Returns," *Journal of Accounting and Economics* (November 1989), 295–329.

Ou, Jane A., and James F. Jepen. "Analysts Earnings Forecasts and the Roles of Earnings and Book Value in Equity Valuation," *Journal of Business Finance & Accounting* (April/May 2002), 287–316.

Roberts, David, and Thomas Roberts. "New Option Expensing Rulings Spawn New Options," *Financial Executive* (May 2005), 26–28.

Schilit, H. *Financial Shenanigans: How to Detect Accounting Gimmicks and Fraud in Financial Reports*, New York: McGraw-Hill, 1993.

Skinner, D., and R. Sloan. "Earning Surprises, Growth Expectations, and Stock Returns or Don't Let an Earnings Torpedo Sink Your Portfolio," *Review of Accounting Studies* (7: 2002), 289–312.

Tong, Yen H, and Bin Miao. "Are Dividends Associated with the Quality of Earnings?," *Accounting Horizons* (March 2011), 183–205.

Wallace, W. "Pro Forma Before and After the SEC's Warning: A Quantification of Reporting Variances from GAAP," 2002. Morristown, NJ: FEI. Research Foundation.

Walter, Elisse B., "Restoring Investor Trust Through Corporate Governance," Remarks Before the Practicing Law Institute, New York, New York (February 18, 2009), http://www.sec.gov/, Speeches & Public Statements.

Weil, J. "Companies Pollute Earnings Reports Leaving P/E Ratios Hard to Calculate" *Wall Street Journal* (August 21, 2001), 1A.

Zarowin, P. "What Determines Earnings-Price Ratios Revisited," *Journal of Accounting Auditing and Finance* (Summer 1990), 439–454.

Zhang, X. "Conservative Accounting and Equity Valuation," *Journal of Accounting & Economics* (29: 2000), 125–149.

Zhou, Ping, and William Ruland. "Dividend Payout and Future Earnings Growth," *Financial Analysts Journal* (May/June 2006), 58–69.

10. Statement of Cash Flows

Adhikari, Ajay, and Augustine Duru. "Voluntary Disclosure of Free Cash Flow Information," *Accounting Horizons* (December 2006), 311–332.

Casey, C. J., and N. J. Bartczak. "Cash Flow—It's Not the Bottom Line," *Harvard Business Review* (July/August 1984), 61–66.

Chludek, Astrid K. "Perceived Versus Actual Cash Flow Implications of Deferred Taxes – An Analysis of Value Relevance and Reversal Under IFRS," *Journal of International Research* (Vol. 10, 2011), 1–25.

Comiskey, Eugene E. "The Classification by Real Estate Investment Trusts of Distributions from Unconsolidated Entities," *Accounting Horizons* (June 2006), 111–132.

DeFond, M., and M. Hung. "An Empirical Analysis of Analysts' Cash Flow Forecasts," *Journal of Accounting & Economics* (35: 2003), 73–100.

Gullapalli, D. "Free Cash Flow Gets Scrutiny," *Wall Street Journal* (November 18, 2004), C3.

Largay, J. A. III, and C. P. Stickney. "Cash Flows, Ratio Analysis and the W. T. Grant Company Bankruptcy," *Financial Analysts Journal* (July/August 1980), 51–54.

Livnat, Joshua, and Paul Zarowin. "The Incremental Informational Content of Cash-Flow Components," *Journal of Accounting and Economics* (May 1990), 25–46.

Lorek, Kenneth S., and G. Lee Willinger. "Multi-Step-Ahead Quarterly Cash-Flow Prediction Models," *Accounting Horizons* (March 2011), 71–86.

Nurnberg, Hugo. "Inconsistencies and Ambiguities in Cash Flow Statements Under FASB Statement No. 95," *Accounting Horizons* (June 1993), 60–75.

Perez, Evan. "Delta to Record $1.65 Billion in Noncash Charges for Quarter," *The Wall Street Journal* (July 14, 2004), A3.

Rapoport, Michael. "'Cash Flow' Isn't What It Used To Be," *The Wall Street Journal* (March 24, 2005), C3.

Rappaport, Alfred. "Show Me the Cash Flow," *Fortune* (September 16, 2002), 192, 194.

Rayburn, J. "The Association of Operating Cash Flow and Accruals with Security Returns," *Journal of Accounting Research* (Supplement 1986), 121–133.

Reichalstein, Stefan. "Providing Managerial Incentives: Cash Flows Versus Accrual Accounting," *Journal of Accounting Research* (Autumn 2000), 243–270.

Wasley, C. E., and J. S. Wu. "Why Do Managers Voluntarily Issue Cash Flow Forecasts?," *Journal of Accounting Research* (May 2006), 389–429.

Summary Analysis—Nike, Inc.

Beneish, Messod D. "The Dedication of Earnings Manipulation," *Financial Analysts Journal* (September/October 1999).

Kang, Stephanie. "Just Do It: Nike Gets Revelatory," *The Wall Street Journal* (April 13, 2005), B11.

Roth, Daniel. "Can Nike Still Do It Without Phil Knight?," *Fortune* (April 4, 2005), 59-64, 66, 68.

Tkacik, Maureen. "Protection Go?," *The Wall Street Journal* (January 10, 2003), B1.

Valokh, Eugene. "Nike and the Free-Speech Knot," *The Wall Street Journal* (June 30, 2003), A16.

11. Expanded Analysis

Altman, E. I. "Financial Ratios, Discriminant Analysis and the Prediction of Corporate Bankruptcy," *Journal of Finance* (September 1968), 589–609.

Altman, E. I., and M. Brenner. "Information Effects and Stock Market Response to Signs of Firm Deterioration," *Journal of Financial and Quantitative Analysis* (March 1981), 35–51.

Altman, E. I. *Corporate Financial Distress*, New York: John Wiley & Sons, 1993.

Arya, Anil, Jonathan C. Glover, and Shyam Sunder. "Are Unmanaged Earnings Always Better for Shareholders?," *Accounting Horizons* (Supplement 2003), 111–116.

Asquith, Paul, Michael B. Mikhail, and Andrea S. Au. "Information Content of Equity Analyst Reports," *Journal of Financial Economics* (75, 2005), 245–282.

Ballou, Brian, Norman H. Godwin, and Rebecca Toppe Shortridge. "Firm Value and Employee Attitudes on Workplace Quality," *Accounting Horizons* (December 2003), 329–341.

Barber, B., R. Lehavy, M. McNichols, and B. Trueman. "Can Investors Profit from the Prophets? Security Analyst Recommendations and Stock Returns," *The Journal of Finance* (56, 2001), 531–563.

Barker, Richard G. "Survey and Market-Based Evidence of Industry-Dependence in Analysts' Preferences Between the Dividend Yield and Price-Earnings Ratio Valuation Models," *Journal of Business Finance and Accounting* (April/May 1999), 393–418.

Barker, Richard G. "The Role of Dividends in Valuation Models Used by Analysts and Fund Managers," *The European Accounting Review* (8:2 1999), 195–218.

Barrett, A. "Slammed! Investors Are Telling Companies That Creative Accounting Will No Longer Fly," *Business Week* (March 4, 2002), 34.

Barwiv, Ran, Anurag Aggarwal, and Robert Leach. "Predicting Bankruptcy Resolution," *Journal of Business Finance & Accounting* (April/May 2002), 497–520.

Baver, Rob, and Robin Braun. "Misdeeds Matter: Long-Term Stock Price Performance After the Filing of Class-Action Lawsuits," *Financial Analysts Journal* (November/December 2010), 1–19.

Beasley, M. S. "An Empirical Analysis of the Relation Between the Board of Director Composition and Finance Statement Fraud," *The Accounting Review* (October 1996), 443–465.

Bell, T. B., and J. V. Carcello. "A Decision Aid for Assessing the Likelihood of Fraudulent Financial Reporting," *Auditing: A Journal of Practice & Theory* (Spring 1999), 169–184.

Beneish, Messod P. "The Detection of Earnings Manipulation," *Financial Analysts Journal* (September/October 1999), 24–36.

Bradshaw, M. T. "How Do Analysts Use Their Earnings Forecasts in Generating Stock Recommendations?," *The Accounting Review* (January 2004), 25–50.

Burgess, Deanna Qender. "Graphical Sleight of Hand," *Journal of Accountancy* (February 2002), 45-48, 51.

Burgstahler, D. C., and I. D. Dichev. "Earnings Adaptation and Equity Value," *Accounting Review* (2: 1997), 187–216.

Burkert, Rod P. "A Good Deal Depends on Preparation," *Journal of Accountancy* (November 2003), 47–52.

Casey, C. J., and N. J. Bartczak. "Using Operating Cash Flow Data to Predict Financial Distress: Some Extensions," *Journal of Accounting Research* (Spring 1985), 384–401.

Chandra, Uday, Bradley D. Childs, and Bturvg T. Ro. "The Association Between LIFO Reserve and Equity Risk: An Empirical Assessment," *Journal of Accounting Auditing & Finance* (Summer 2002), 185–208.

Chandra, Uday, and Byung T. Ro. "The Role of Revenue in Firm Valuations," *Accounting Horizons* (June 2008), 199–222.

Copeland, Tom, Tim Kaller, and Jack Murrin. "Valuation, Measuring, and Managing the Value of Companies, Third Edition," (New York: John Wiley & Sons, Inc. 2000), 1–494.

Dambolena, I. G., and S. J. Khorvry. "Ratio Stability and Corporate Failure," *Journal of Finance* (September 1980), 1017–1026.

Dechow, P. A., R. G. Sloan, and A. P. Sweeney. "Causes and Consequences of Earnings Manipulation: An Analysis of Firms Subject to Enforcement Actions by the SEC," *Contemporary Accounting Research* (Spring 1996), 1–36.

Demirakos, Efthimios G., Norman C. Strong, and Martin Walker. "What Valuation Models Do Analysts Use?," *Accounting Horizons* (December 2004), 221–240.

DiGabriele, James A. "The Moderating Effects of Acquisition Premiums in Private Corporations: An Empirical Investigation of Relative S Corporation and C Corporation Valuations," *Accounting Horizons* (December 2008), 415–424.

Dilla, William N., and Diane J. Janvrin. "Voluntary Disclosure in Annual Reports: The Association Between Magnitude and Direction of Change in Corporate Financial Performance and Graph Use," *Accounting Horizons* (June 2010), 257–278.

Dutta, Sunil, and Frank Gigler. "The Effect of Earnings Forecasts on Earnings Management," *Journal of Accounting Research* (June 2002), 631–656.

Frankel, R., M. Johnson, and K. Nelson. "Auditor Independence and Earnings Quality," *The Accounting Review* (Supplement 2002), 71–105.

Gombola, M. J., and J. E. Ketz. "Financial Ratio Patterns in Retail and Manufacturing Organizations," *Financial Management* (Summer 1983), 45–56.

Gramlich, Jeffrey D., and James E. Wheeler. "How Chevron, Texaco, and the Indonesian Government Structured Transactions to Avoid Billions in U.S. Income Taxes," *Accounting Horizons* (June 2003), 107–122.

Grent, C. Terry, Chaunrey M. Depree, Jr., and Gerry H. Grant. "Earnings Management and the Abuse of Materiality," *Journal of Accountancy* (September 2000), 41–44.

Harris, Larry. "The Increasing Need for Financial Analysis in Public Accounting Standards," *Financial Analysts Journal* (March/April 2011), 6–9.

Hodge, Frank D. "Investors' Perceptions of Earnings Quality, Auditor Independence, and the Usefulness of Audited

Financial Information," *Accounting Horizons* (Supplement 2003), 37–48.

Howell, Robert A. "Fixing Financial Reporting: Financial Statement Overhaul," *Financial Executive* (March/April 2002), 40–42.

Jaggi, B. "Which Is Better, D & B or Zeta in Forecasting Credit Risk?," *Journal of Business Forecasting* (Summer 1984), 13–16, 22.

Jones, Steward. "Does the Capitalization of Intangible Assets Increase the Predictability of Corporate Failure?," *Accounting Horizons* (March 2011), 41–70.

Kasznik, Ron, and Maureen F. McNichols. "Does Meeting Earnings Expectations Matter? Evidence from Analyst Forecast Revisions and Share Prices," *Journal of Accounting Research* (June 2002), 727–760.

Keune, Marsha B., and Karla M. Johnstone. "Staff Accounting Bulletin No. 108 Disclosures: Descriptive Evidence from the Revelation of Accounting Misstatements," *Accounting Horizons* (March 2009), 19–53.

Kirschenheiter, Michael, and Nahum D. Melumad. "Can 'Big Bath' and Earnings Smoothing Co-Exist as Equilibrium Financial Reporting Strategies?," *Journal of Accounting Research* (June 2002), 761–796.

Kohlbecck, Mark and Terry D. Warfield. "Unrecorded Intangible Assets: Abnormal Earnings and Valuation," *Accounting Horizons* (March 2007), 1–22.

Largay, James A. "Lessons from Enron," *Accounting Horizons* (June 2002), 153–156.

Lennox, C. S. "The Accuracy and Incremental Information Content of Audit Reports in Predicting Bankruptcy," *Journal of Business Finance & Accounting* (June/July 1999), 757–778.

Liv, Jing, Nissim Doren, and Thomas Jacob. "Equity Valuation Using Multiples," *Journal of Accounting Research* (March 2002), 135–172.

Lo, K., and T. Lys. "The Ohlson Model: Contribution to Valuation Theory, Limitations, and Empirical Applications," *Journal of Accounting, Auditing, and Finance* (13, 3: Summer 2000), 337–367.

Makeever, D. A. "Predicting Business Failures," *The Journal of Commercial Bank Lending* (January 1984), 14–18.

Marquardt, C., and C. Wiedman. "Earnings Management Through Transaction Structuring Contingent Convertible Debt and Diluted EPS," *Journal of Accounting Research* (May 2005), 205–244.

Mendenhall, Richard R. "How Naive Is the Market's Use of Firm-Specific Earnings Information?," *Journal of Accounting Research* (June 2002), 841–864.

Miller, Paul B. "Quality Financial Reporting," *Journal of Accountancy* (April 2002), 70–74.

Mills, J., L. Bible, and R. Mason. "Defining Free Cash Flow," *The CPA Journal* (January 2002), 37–41.

Moriarty, G., and P. Livingston. "Quantitative Measures of the Quality of Financial Reporting," *Financial Executive* (July 2001), 17.

Nelson, Mark W., John A. Elliott, and Robin L. Tarpley. "How Are Earnings Managed? Examples from Auditors," *Accounting Horizons* (Supplement 2003), 17–35.

Nichols, D. Craig, and James M. Wahlon. "How Do Earnings Numbers Relate to Stock Returns? A Review of Classic Accounting Research with Updated Evidence," *Accounting Horizons* (December 2004), 263–286.

Ohlson, J. A. "Earnings, Book Values, and Dividends in Equity Valuation," *Contemporary Accounting Research* (11 (2): 1995), 661–687.

Parsons, O. "Using Financial Statement Data to Identify Factors Associated with Fraudulent Financial Reporting," *Journal of Applied Business Research* (Summer 1995), 38–46.

Patell, J. M., and M. A. Wolfson. "The Intraday Speed of Adjustment of Stock Prices to Earnings and Dividend Announcements," *Journal of Financial Economics* (June 1984), 223–252.

Patrone, F. L., and D. duBois, "Financial Ratio Analysis in the Small Business," *Journal of Small Business Management* (January 1981), 35–40.

Peterson, M. "Putting Extra Fizz into Profits; Critics Say Coca-Cola Dumps Debt on Spinoff," *New York Times* (August 4, 1998), D1.

Plumlee, Marlene, and Teri Lombardi Yohn. "An Analysis of the Underlying Causes Attributed to Restatements," *Accounting Horizons* (March 2010), 41–64.

Rama, D. V., K. Raghunandan, and M. A. Gerger. "The association Between Audit Reports and Bankruptcies: Further Evidence," *Advances in Accounting* (1997 15), 1–15.

Rege, V. P. "Accounting Ratios to Locate Take-Over Targets," *Journal of Business Finance and Accounting* (Autumn 1984), 301–311.

Richardson, F. M., G. D. Kane, and P. Lobingier. "The Impact of Recession on the Prediction of Corporate Failure," *Journal of Business Finance & Accounting* (January/March 1998), 167, 186.

Schipper, Katherine, and Linda Vincent. "Earnings Quality," *Accounting Horizons* (Supplement 2003), 97–110.

Shelton, Sandra Waller, O. Ray Whittington, and David Landsittel. "Auditing Firms' Fraud Risk Assessment Practices," *Accounting Horizons* (March 2001), 19–33.

Simnett, Roger, Michael Nugent, and Anna L. Higgins. "Developing an International Assurance Standard on Greenhouse Gas Statements," *Accounting Horizons* (December 2009), 347–363.

Steinbart, Paul John. "The Auditor's Responsibility for the Accuracy of Graphs in Annual Reports: Some Evidence of the Need for Additional Guidance," *Accounting Horizons* (September 1989), 60–70.

Stober, T. L. "The Incremental Information Content of Financial Statement Disclosures: The Case of LIFO Liquidations," *Journal of Accounting Research* (Supplement 1986), 138–160.

Summers, S. L., and J. T. Sweeney. "Fraudulently Misstated Financial Statements and Insider Trading: An Empirical Analysis," *The Accounting Review* (January 1998), 131–146.

Trombetta, Marco. "Discussion of Implied Cost of Equity Capital in Earnings-Based Valuation: International Evidence," *Accounting and Business Research* (Volume 34, Number 4, 2004), 345–348.

Tse, S. "LIFO Liquidations," *Journal of Accounting Research* (Spring 1990), 229–238.

U.S. Government Accounting Office, "Financial Restatements: Update of Public Company Trends, Market Impacts, and

Regulatory Enforcement Activities," (July 2006), GAO-06-678, http://gao.gov/assets/260/250852.pdf.

Williams, Patricia A. "The Search for a Better Market Model Expectation of Earnings," *Journal of Accounting Literature* (14: 1995), 140–168.

Williamson, R. W. "Evidence on the Selective Reporting of Financial Ratios," *The Accounting Review* (April 1984), 296–299.

Wright, P., B. Dunford, and S. A. Snell. "Human Resources and the Resource-Based View of the Firm," *Journal of Management* (27: 2001), 701–721.

Xie, B., W. Davidson, and P. DaDalt. "Earnings Management and Corporate Governance: The Role of the Board and Audit Committee," *Journal of Corporate Finance* (9: 2003), 295–316.

York, Timothy. "Start a BV Engagement the Right Way," *Journal of Accountancy* (August 2003), 35–40.

12. Special Industries: Banks, Utilities, Oil and Gas, Transportation, Insurance, Real Estate Companies

Agnich, J. F. "How Utilities Account to the Regulators," *Management Accounting* (February 1981), 17–22.

Barniv, Ran. "Accounting Procedures, Market Data, Cash-Flow Figures, and Insolvency Classification: The Case of the Insurance Industry," *The Accounting Review* (July 1990), 578–604.

Begley, J., S. Chamberlain, and Y. La. "Modeling Goodwill for Banks: A Residual Income Approach with Empirical Tests," *Contemporary Accounting Research* (23: 2006), 31–68.

Christensen, Theodore E. "The Effects of Uncertainty on the Informativeness of Earnings: Evidence from the Insurance Industry in the Wake of Catastrophic Events," *Journal of Business Finance & Accounting* (January/March 2002), 223–256.

Gaver, J. J., and J. S. Paterson. "Managing Insurance Company Financial Statements to Meet Regulatory and Tax Reporting Goals," *Contemporary Accounting Research* (16 Summer 1999), 207–241.

Gore, R., and D. Stott. "Toward a More Informative Measure of Operating Performance in the REIT Industry: Net Income vs. Funds from Operations," *Accounting Horizons* (12: 1998), 323–339.

Hirst, E., P. Hopkins, and J. Wahlen. "Fair Values, Income Measurement, and Bank Analysts' Risk and Valuation Judgments," *The Accounting Review* (79: 2004), 453–472.

Ho, T., and A. Saunders. "A Catastrophe Model of Bank Failure," *The Journal of Finance* (December 1980), 1189–1207.

Kohlbec, M. "Investor Valuation and Measuring Bank Intangible Assets," *Journal of Accounting, Auditing, and Finance* (Winter 2004), 29–60.

Lindberg, Deborah L., and Deborah L. Seifert. "A New Paradigm of Reporting on the Horizon: International Financial Reporting Standards (IFRS) and Implications for the Insurance Industry," *Journal of Insurance Regulation* (Winter 2010), 229–252.

Owhoso, Vincent E., William F. Messer, Jr., and John G. Lynch, Jr. "Error Detection by Industry-Specialized Teams during Sequential Audit Review," *Journal of Accounting Research* (June 2002), 883–900.

Palmon, Dan, and Lee J. Zeidler. "Current Value Reporting of Real Estate Companies and a Possible Example of Market Inefficiency," *The Accounting Review* (July 1978), 776–790.

Ragharen, Kamala R. "Global Accounting Convergence and U.S. Financial Institutions," *Bank Accounting and Finance* (February 2009), 14–20.

Rose, P. L., and W. L. Scott. "Return-on-Equity Analysis of Eleven Largest U.S. Bank Failures," *Review of Business and Economic Research* (Winter 1980-81), 1–11.

Serwer, Andy. "Oh, the Games Insurance Companies Love to Play," *Fortune* (May 30, 2005), 53.

Shick, R. A., and L. F. Sherman. "Bank Stock Prices as an Early Warning System for Changes in Condition," *Journal of Bank Research* (Autumn 1980), 136–146.

Solomon, Deborah. "SEC Brings New Federal Oversight to Insurance Industry with Probes," *The Wall Street Journal* (April 1, 2005), 1, A4.

Wahlen, J. "The Nature of Information in Commercial Bank Loan Loss Disclosures," *The Accounting Review* (69 (3) 1994), 455–478.

13. Personal Financial Statements and Accounting for Governments and Not-for-Profit Organizations

Baber, William R., Andrea Alston Roberts, and Gnanakumar Visuana Dran. "Charitable Organizations' Strategies and Program-Spending Ratios," *Accounting Horizons* (December 2001), 329–343.

Barrett, W. "Look Before You Give," *Forbes* (December 27, 1999), 206–214.

Bernstein, David J. "Local Government Measurement Use in Focus on Performance and Results," *Evaluation and Program Planning, Vol. 24, No. 1* (January 2001), 95–101.

Biggs, Andrew G. "Proposed GASB Rules Show Why Only Market Valuation Fully Captures Public Pension Liabilities," *Financial Analysts Journal* (March/April 2011), 18–22.

Brevl, Jonathan D. "The Government Performance and Results Act – 10 Years Later," *Journal of Financial Management* (Spring 2003), 58–64.

Brown, Trevor L., and Matthew Potoski. "Managing Contract Performance: A Transaction Costs Approach," *Policy Analysis and Management* (Spring 2003), 275–298.

Brown, Victor H., and Susan E. Weiss. "Toward Better Not-for-Profit Accounting and Reporting," *Management Accounting* (July 1993), 48–52.

Chandra, Uday, Michael L. Ettrdge, and Mary S. Stone. "Enron-Era Disclosure of Off-Balance-Sheet Entities," *Accounting Horizons* (September 2006), 231–252.

Charnes, A., and W. Cooper. "Auditing and Accounting for Program Efficiency and Management Effectiveness in Not-for-Profit Entities," *Accounting Organizations and Society* 5 (1980), 87–108.

Chase, Bruce. "New Reporting Standards For Not-for-Profits," *Management Accounting* (October 1995), 34–37.

Chase, Bruce W., and Laura B. Triggs. "How to Implement GASB Statement No. 34," *Journal of Accountancy* (November 2001), 71–79.

Coggbum, Jerrell D., and Saundra Schrieder. "The Relationship Between State Government Performance and State Quality of Life," *International Journal of Public Administration*, Vol. 26, No. 12 (October 2003), 1337–1354.

Downs, G. W., and D. M. Rocke. "Municipal Budget Forecasting with Multivariate ARMA Models," *Journal of Forecasting* (October/December 1983), 377–387.

Eisenberg, Daniel. "Evaluating the Effectiveness of Policies Related to Drunk Driving," *Policy Analysis and Management* (Spring 2003), 249–274.

Fischer, Mary, Tresap Gordon, and Saleha B. Klumawala. "Tax-Exempt Organizations and Nonarticulation: Estimates Are No Substitute for Disclosure of Cash Provided by Operations," *Accounting Horizons* (June 2008), 133–158.

Freeman, Robert J., and Craig D. Shoulders. "GASB Statement 34: A Bold Step Forward," *The Government Accountants Journal* (Spring 2000), 8–17.

Gordon, Teresa P., Janet S. Greenlee, and Denise Nitterhouse. "Tax-Exempt Organization Financial Data: Availability and Limitations," *Accounting Horizons*, (June 1999), 113–128.

Holder, William W., Kenneth R. Schermann, and Ray Whittington. "Materiality Considerations," *Journal of Accountancy* (November 2003), 61–66.

Hu, Shih-Jen Kathy, and Linda Achey Kidwell, "A Survey of Management Techniques Implemented by Municipal Administrators," *The Government Accountants Journal* (Spring 2000), 46–52.

Iger, Venkataraman M., and Ann L. Watkins. "Adoption of Sarbanes-Oxley Measures by Nonprofit Organizations: An Empirical Study," *Accounting Horizons* (September 2008), 255–277.

Ives, Martin, "The Governmental Accounting Standards Board: Factors Influencing Its Operation and Initial Technical Agenda," *The Government Accountants Journal* (Spring 2000), 22–28.

Johnson, Laurence E., and David R. Bean. "GASB Statement No. 34: The Dawn of a New Governmental Financial Reporting Model," *The CPA Journal* (December 1999), 14–24.

Keeting, Elizabeth K. and Eric S. Berman. "Unfunded Public Employee Health Care Benefits and GASB No. 45," *Accounting Horizons* (September 2007), 245–263.

Kelly, Janet M., and David Swindell. "A Multiple Indicator Approach to Municipal Service Evaluation: Correlating Performance Measurement and Citizen Satisfaction Across Jurisdictions," *Public Administrative Review* (September/October 2002), 610–619.

Kinsman, Michael D., and Bruce Samuelson. "Personal Financial Statements: Valuation Challenges and Solutions," *Journal of Accountancy* (September 1987), 138–148.

Klasny, Edward M., and James M. Williams. "Government Reporting Faces an Overhaul," *Journal of Accountancy* (January 2000), 49–51.

Meeting, David T., Randall W. Luecke, and Edward J. Giniat. "Understanding and Implementing FASB 124," *Journal of Accountancy* (March 1996), 62–66.

Revell, Janice. "The Great State Health-Care Giveaway," *Fortune* (May 2, 2005), 43-44; 46.

Revenbark, William C., and Carla M. Pizzarella. "Auditing Performance Data in Local Government," *Public Performance and Management Review*, Vol. 25 (June 2002), 412–420.

Sacco, John. "GASB Statement 34, Part of Changing Political and Global Market Pressures," The *Government Accountants Journal* (Spring 2000), 20–21.

Statement of Position of the Accounting Standards Division 82-1, "Accounting and Financial Reporting for Personal Financial Statements." New York: American Institute of Certified Public Accountants, 1982.

Index